D1212935

International Dictionary of Anthropologists

Garland Reference Library of the Social Sciences (Vol. 638)

International Dictionary of Anthropologists

Compiled by   Library-Anthropology Resource Group (LARG)

Christopher Winters, *General Editor*

Editorial Board:
Michele Calhoun
Yvonne M. Damien
Lee S. Dutton
Francis X. Grollig, S.J.
David Lonergan
Thomas L. Mann
Hans E. Panofsky
Robert B. Marks Ridinger
Margo L. Smith
Sol Tax

Garland Publishing
New York & London
1991

Ref.
GN
20
.I5
1991

© 1991 Christopher Winters
All rights reserved

Library of Congress Cataloging-in-Publication Data
International dictionary of anthropologists / compiled by Library
-Anthropology Resource Group (LARG) ; general editor, Christopher
Winters ; editorial board : Michele Calhoun ...[et al.]
      p. cm. -- (Garland reference library of social science ; vol. 638)
    Includes index.
    ISBN 0-8240-5094-0
    1. Anthropology--Bio-bibliography--Dictionaries. I. Winters,
Christopher, 1944– . II. Calhoun, Michele. III. Library-
Anthropology Resource Group (Chicago, Ill.) IV. Series: Garland
reference library of social science ; v. 638.
GN20.I5 1991
016.301'03--dc20   91–4782
                                              CIP

Printed on acid-free, 250-year-life paper.
Manufactured in the United States of America.

contents

167627

preface

Modern anthropology has many different intellectual ancestors. Some of these ancestors were traditions which had relatively little to do with each other. Others might seem to the casual observer to have only a tenuous relationship to modern anthropology. Since full understanding of some of the *Dictionary*'s entries depends to some extent on understanding the history of anthropology, we present the following brief outline, hoping that it may be helpful to readers.

The term "anthropology" in much of Continental Europe has until recently referred to what is called "physical anthropology" or "biological anthropology" in the English-speaking world, i.e., the formal study of the human body with a view to understanding its evolution and its variants. In this sense, anthropology goes back in Europe at least to the 18th century. See, for example, the entries for Paul Broca, Petrus Camper and Jan Evangelista Purkyně. Although the emphasis has changed greatly over the decades, there is a direct line of descent from the work of these scholars to modern physical anthropology.

A quite different intellectual ancestor of modern anthropology is the study of European folk traditions, i.e., folklore, which, as an academic subject (albeit often a marginal one), can be traced back well into the 19th century. See, for example, the entries for Wilhelm Heinrich Riehl, Antonio Machado y Alvarez, Sergeï Vasil'evich Maksimov, Edit Fél, Kazimierz Moszyński and Giuseppe Cocchiara. Much of the work of these scholars has become essential reading to those with an interest in the anthropology of traditional Europe. For complicated reasons, folklore studies have never been as central to ethnological inquiry in the English-speaking world as in Continental Europe, although several British scholars, notably James G. Frazer, contributed much to the Continental folklore discourse.

Linguistics and archaeology are two additional disciplines that have played a major role in the history of anthropology. Most linguists and archaeologists would probably resist anthropology's claim that their disciplines form a part of anthropology, but there is no doubt that linguistic and archaeological studies have been closely linked to ethnographic study for centuries. Linguists have traditionally studied languages spoken by peoples of interest to anthropologists. Similarly, much of our knowledge of many cultures is based on archaeological remains. For examples of a 19th-century linguist and an early archaeologist working in areas of interest to anthropologists, see the entries for Franz Bopp and William Camden.

Ethnographic study of the people of what we now call the Third World—which became absolutely central to anthropology—goes back to the reports of explorers, merchants, missionaries and others traveling in foreign lands. Over the centuries thousands of such people, although they often did not know that they were doing so, contributed to the anthropological enterprise. For some (rather random) early examples of these figures, see the entries for Joseph-François Lafitau, Robert Knox and Alexander Mackenzie.

In the 19th century some explorers—natural historians—became more oriented to science. The natural historians' goal was the collection of specimens and data. They brought home (among other things) fossils, rocks, dried mounted insects and ethnographic facts. The variety did not seem as odd to them as it does to the modern scholar working within the confines of a single discipline. Elio Modigliani and Emília Snethlage are examples of such figures.

Contemporary anthropology, at least in the English-speaking world, often looks back on those who analyzed the facts presented by the explorers and natural historians as the first modern anthropologists. Thus there is a tendency to think of such 19th-century figures as Lewis Henry Morgan, Henry Sumner Maine and E.B. Tylor and several of their predecessors and contemporaries as the initiators of the modern discipline. Many of these men can fairly be called "evolutionists." That is, they tended to feel that man over time had evolved through a series of definable stages, e.g., from "barbarism" to "savagery" to "civilization" (many other schema were proposed).

In the United States, the mainstream continued in the 20th century with Franz Boas and the dozens of people trained or influenced by him (among them Alfred L. Kroeber, Ruth Benedict and Margaret Mead). The work of these scholars was rich and complex, but it is probably fair to say that much of its theoretical component was associated in some way with the concept "culture" and that much of its importance for the world at large lay in its deep and radical respect for all cultures, a tendency sometimes subsumed under the label "cultural relativism." The Boasians made a further major contribution to anthropology in the English-speaking world. It was they who insisted that physical anthropology, linguistics and archaeology belonged in the same discipline with ethnology (or cultural anthropology), and it was they who succeeded in attaching the term "anthropology" to this broad combination of fields.

In Britain, there was a rather different 20th-century mainstream which eventually centered on the work of those usually called structural functionalists or just functionalists (notably, A.R. Radcliffe-Brown and Bronislaw Malinowski). Like all other modern social scientists, they were reaching for greater significance by putting facts into an intellectual framework. Their particular aim was to determine the "function" of cultural elements rather than simply to describe them one by one. (One must add that their work was extraordinarily complicated and resists simple summary.)

In the years since Boas and Radcliffe-Brown, numerous scholars in the English-speaking world have developed other distinctive theoretical approaches to the subject. See, for example, the entries for Leslie A. White, George Peter Murdock, Karl Polanyi and Robert Redfield. Sometimes too there has been an interest in the practical uses of anthropology; this endeavor is often labeled "applied anthropology." See, for example, the entry for Allan R. Holmberg.

The standard histories of anthropology in English concentrate on the American and British traditions described in the previous paragraphs.[1] But anthropology was a going concern outside the English-speaking world as well, and, in many places, it took quite an independent course.

In Germany and in much of Continental Europe, the "Cultural-Historical School" or "Vienna School" dominated foreign ethnographic research from the late 19th century through World War II. Its more straightforward proponents aimed to identify culturally uniform geographical regions called "culture circles" (*Kulturkreisen*), to analyze cultural traits, or "culture layers" (*Kulturschichten*) in these areas and to study the diffusion of such traits from region to region. An underlying axiom was that the geographical distribution of culture traits was a key to their evolution. For the German and Austrian origins of the Cultural-Historical School, see, for example, the entries for Leo Frobenius, Fritz Graebner and Wilhelm Schmidt. For some Continental followers, see the entries for José Miguel de Barandiarán, Gerhard Lindblom and Stanisław Poniatowski.

---

[1]Examples: Robert H. Lowie, *The History of Ethnological Theory* (New York: 1937); E.E. Evans-Pritchard, *A History of Anthropological Thought* (New York: 1981); Marvin Harris, *The Rise of Anthropological Theory* (New York: 1968); J.O. Brew (editor), *One Hundred Years of Anthropology* (Cambridge, Mass.: 1968); John Joseph Honigmann, *Development of Anthropological Ideas* (Homewood, Ill.: 1976).

There were other schools in Europe as well. French ethnology developed rather separately from the German and British traditions. It is arguable in fact that, except for physical anthropology, there hardly was an "anthropology" in France at all until quite recently. Many French contributors to world anthropology were trained as sociologists; this was true, for example, of Marcel Mauss, Roger Bastide, Maurice Leenhardt and Claude Lévi-Strauss. Many other luminaries—Lucien Lévy-Bruhl, Michel Leiris and Georges Henri Rivière—came from other backgrounds altogether.

Russian *etnografiĩa* has a more distinct history, but, especially in the 20th century, it has been rather isolated from Western currents. Not only has its theoretical framework been Marxist but its objects of study—the peoples at the edges of the Russian Empire and the folk traditions of the Slavs—were quite different from the Third World peoples who were the chief concern of Western scholars. See, for example, the entries for M.G. Levin and S.A. Tokarev. Polish ethnology, with its focus on Polish folk customs, has in some respects resembled Soviet ethnology, although it has probably had closer ties to Western scholarship, often depending on foreigners for its theoretical frameworks.

Italian and Dutch anthropology have also tended to be subservient in theoretical matters to foreign traditions, but there have been dozens of important and original Italian and Dutch anthropologists and ethnographers. See, for example, the entries for Paolo Mantegazza and J.P.B. Josselin de Jong.

While anthropology has been predominantly an enterprise of the Western world, a great many scholars in Latin America, Asia and Africa have used anthropological ideas—although often calling them "sociological"—to study their own countries' cultures. See, for example, the entries for M.N. Srinivas, Kenji Kiyono, Raimundo Nina Rodrigues, Kofi Abrefa Busia and Miguel Acosta Saignes.

There have been numerous other somewhat independent anthropological traditions as well, and we have tried to include entries in this dictionary for figures representing as many as we could.

At the risk of simplifying excessively, it is possible to suggest that there have been two quite different models of the history of anthropology proposed in the scholarly literature. The first, which might be called the "center-periphery model," suggests that anthropology, resting on the work of a few forefathers, was almost entirely the creation of Americans and Britons or foreigners who passed through American and British universities. This is the model implicitly suggested by most of the standard English-language histories of the field.[2] The second, which might be called the "parallel-schools

[2]The sources given in footnote 1 suggest this model.

model," highlights more or less independent national schools.[3]

The *Dictionary*'s chief purpose is not to serve as a history of the discipline but rather to provide readily accessible concise biographical information about some major contributors to anthropology. But, if the *Dictionary* does have anything distinctive to contribute to anthropology's view of itself, it lies in its attempt to supplement and even build a bridge between these two simple models of the field. We have no fundamental quarrel with the excellent standard English-language histories of anthropology; but we *would* argue the incompleteness of their "center-periphery" view, in that they ignore or downgrade the alternate "centers" of the Cultural-Historical School and the European folklore movements as well as the various vital and distinctive national schools. The "parallel-schools" model has fewer pretensions to providing a definitive view of the field, but it is worth remembering that the vision of anthropology embedded in it is also, by definition, an incomplete one.

***

The editors of this volume have struggled greatly with the question of coverage. Generally, we have preferred to be inclusive. "Anthropology" is used in its North American (or Boasian) sense; it includes social and cultural anthropology, physical and biological anthropology, archaeology, folklore and some branches of linguistics. There are entries not only for academics but also for some of the travelers, missionaries, administrators, informants and others who clearly contributed to the anthropological enterprise.

We have gone to some lengths to assure broad *international* coverage, encouraging scholars from throughout the world to identify and write about the most important figures in their own countries. Our aim was to be able to present "native" views of anthropology from as many places as possible. We took a number of steps to further this goal. We contacted potential collaborators in most of the world's countries. We requested help from visitors to our respective institutions. One of our members presented a paper at

---

[3]Some major books reflecting this model are: S.A. Tokarev, *Istoriĭa russkoĭ ètnografii (dooktĭabr'skiĭ period)* (Moscow: 1966); Małgorzata Terlecka (editor), *Historia etnografii polskiej* (Wrocław: 1973); P. Clemente [et al.], *L'antropologia italiana: un secolo di storia* (Bari: 1985); Ole Høiris, *Antropologien i Danmark: museal etnografi og etnologi, 1860-1960* (Copenhagen: 1986); and Carlos García Mora (general coordinator), *La antropología en México: panorama historico* [15 vols.] (Mexico City: 1987-1988). There are also numerous studies of particular traditions within one or several countries. Two recent books about North American women anthropologists constitute a special case: Ute Gacs [et al.], *Women Anthropologists: a Biographical Dictionary* (New York: 1988); and Barbara Babcock and Nancy Parezo, *Daughters of the Desert: Women Anthropologists and the Native American Southwest, 1880-1980: an Illustrated Catalogue* (Albuquerque: 1988).

the meetings of the International Union of Anthropological and Ethnological Sciences in Zagreb. We are quite pleased that the result has been the publication of virtually the only biographical information in English about dozens of scholars in a great many countries.

We acknowledge one problem with this approach. Where we have found energetic local collaborators, coverage is excellent, but, where we have been unable to find local collaborators, it is not. For similar reasons, anthropology's subfields are covered unevenly. Because of the pattern of contributions, only a few of anthropology's forefathers are included, and we have done better by social and cultural anthropologists and ethnographers than by physical anthropologists, linguists, archaeologists and folklorists.

We *have* done some filling in ourselves—about fifteen percent of the entries have been written by members of LARG's editorial board. But we are painfully aware of missing names. It is arguable that the ideal dictionary of anthropologists would contain five or six times as many entries as does this one. However, it is difficult for us to imagine the staff it would take to compile such a work—or who could be convinced to publish it! And even a book on such a large scale would have missing names.

We *did* rigorously enforce one limitation on coverage. Only those born before 1920 were eligible for inclusion. We chose this cutoff since it seemed best to have entries only for those whose careers could be seen as whole. We acknowledge the arbitrariness of this date.

***

Each of the *Dictionary*'s 725 entries consists largely of a biographical essay. The entries also provide actuarial data and include lists of major works; most entries also list sources of additional information.

Some of the peculiarities of the entries have their roots in the instructions we gave our authors:

We strongly discouraged most collaborators from writing more than 500 words. We did not enforce this rule strictly, but the result is nonetheless that most entries are roughly the same length. There is therefore little correlation between the length of an entry and the importance of its subject.

We also discouraged our contributors from listing more than ten major works in their bibliographies. Consequently, prolific, or particularly important, authors are given rather short shrift. For the latter of course there are usually more extensive biographies and bibliographies already in print, to which we refer.

All citations are given in the original form. But for non-Western-European languages (except Russian) we have provided a translation of all titles, using square brackets, e.g.:

Türkiye Türk Toplumlarında Kültürel Antropolojik (Etnolojik) İncelemeler [*Ethnological Studies of Turkish Communities in Turkey*] (Ankara: 1972)

A different format is used for titles for which translations have been published, e.g.:

"Essai sur le don, forme et raison de l'échange dans les sociétés archaïques," *L'année sociologique*, 2nd sér., vol. 1 (1923-1924), pp. 30-186 [tr.: *The Gift* (New York: 1967)]

When possible, we have tried to indicate that a work is part of a monographic series (or constitutes a special issue of a journal) by the use of parentheses and an equals sign, e.g.:

Yana Texts (Berkeley: 1910) (= *University of California Publications in American Archaeology and Ethnology*, vol. 9, no. 1)

In the lists of major works. co-authored and edited works are indicated with a brief note *before* the citation, e.g.:

(editor) *Australian Aboriginal Anthropology* (Canberra: 1970)

(with Ralph Linton, Cora DuBois and James West) *The Psychological Frontiers of Society* (New York: 1945)

Uncertain parts of a few citations are bracketed, e.g.:

Phrayā ᶜAnumān Rātchathon tāmthatsanakhati khǫngkhonrūčhak [*Recollections of Phya Anuman Rajadhon by Those Who Knew Him*] ([Bangkok]: [198-])

Names of universities are generally given in English, but names of other institutions (e.g., museums) are usually given in their original form, unless the entry author preferred to use only an English-language form (this is often the case for the Dutch, Scandinavian, Eastern European and East Asian institutions). For non-English names, we provide an English translation, except in the case of a few well-known French names (e.g., Musée de l'Homme).

Entry subjects are usually identified by the names they used on most of their publications. But, when they tended to use initials (e.g., "Haddon, A.C."), current North American library practice is often followed; that is, a fuller form of the name is given in parentheses (thus, "Haddon, A.C. (Alfred Cort)"). We also provide notes about other variant name forms.

Hungarian and Japanese names are Westernized so that the family name comes last, but Chinese and Thai names are kept in their original order. Russian, Japanese, Arabic and Hebrew names and citations are Romanized according to the system used by the Library of Congress. But we avoid the politically controversial question of whether Wade-Giles or Pinyin is the better system for Chinese by letting contributors Romanize Chinese as they prefer. Similarly, we do only light standardization of the spelling of ethnic names; there are no doubt some inconsistencies.

We have wrestled at length with the question of whether to impose "politically correct" language on our contributors and have ended up limiting ourselves to gentle suggestions. We acknowledge the importance of language in defining reality, but we also point out the time- and culture-specific nature of politically correct labels. As long as African-Americans, for example, remain oppressed, it is likely that any term used to refer to them will, eventually, appear uncomfortable to some.

Editorial work has generally not affected content. We allowed authors to engage their subject as they wished, and not all entry-writers took the same approach. The style of many entries, for example, reflects a distinctive national tradition in the compilation of entries in biographical dictionaries. This is one of the reasons the Soviet and Polish entries are so straightforward, while some of the American and French entries are so analytic. Many of the authors even contradict each other. See, for example, the Margaret Mead and Derek Freeman entries, as well as those for Gunnar Landtman and Bronislaw Malinowski.

Finally, we acknowledge one peculiar consequence of our decision to include entries for the living, as long as they were born before 1920. Many of these scholars, we are pleased to say, remain intellectually active, and, inevitably, entries devoted to them have a different character from those for scholars who died long ago. Not only are these entries largely in the perfect rather than in the past tense; it has also been difficult for our authors to write as dispassionately.

LARG

This *Dictionary* was compiled under the aegis of LARG (the Library-Anthropology Resource Group), a Chicago-based group of anthropologists and librarians who have devoted themselves since 1971 to the production of useful reference materials in the field of anthropology. LARG was founded largely through the efforts of Sol Tax, Professor of Anthropology at the University of Chicago. He had some help from Jan Wepsiec, Bibliographer for the Social Sciences at the University of Chicago Library, and Fr. Francis X. Grollig, S.J., Professor of Anthropology at Loyola University of Chicago. LARG's existence has always been based on the idea that anthropologists and librarians might be able to cooperate fruitfully and contribute greatly to a field which is very poorly endowed with reference materials.

The *Dictionary* is LARG's fifth book.

Acknowledgments

Many individuals and institutions contributed to this project. The administration of the University of Chicago Library made available computer facilities and did not complain about the substantial telephone and postage costs incurred by its anthropology bibliographer. In addition, four Library staff members translated entries, and dozens of other staff members helped the project along in ways large and small; the total amount of knowledge possessed by staff members at a major research library is truly enormous. The Library's Slavic department, headed by June Pachuta Farris, was called on with particular frequency. The Field Museum of Natural History provided a room to meet in every month. The Field Museum of Natural History, Loyola University of Chicago, Northeastern Illinois University, Northern Illinois University, Northwestern University and the University of Chicago all allowed members of the Editorial Board time to work on this project. Margaret Joichi at Founders Memorial Library, Northern Illinois University, heroically input most of the entries. Sol Tax contributed some funding for clerical help. Chin See Ming of the Dept. of Anthropology, University of Chicago, worked long and hard checking citations. And William Kim provided a considerable amount of clerical help at the University of Chicago Library during the last stages of the project.

We are of course most in debt to the more than 300 people who wrote, or translated, entries. It is perhaps unfair to single out any, but we must mention that, in several countries, we had the special help of a collaborator who not only wrote entries himself or herself but who also took on the enormous work of gathering entries from several compatriots. Berthold Riese in Germany, Sandra Puccini in Italy, Fernando Estévez in Spain and V.V. Novotný in Czechoslovakia played this role. Mariza Corrêa in Brazil, Tamás Hofer in Hungary and the late Ronald Berndt in Australia undertook to send us long lists of names of those who should be included as well as of those whom we might ask to write entries. Paul Hockings did the same for India. Maria Niewadomska and Iwona Grzelakowska in Poland, A.M. Reshetov in the U.S.S.R. and Aygen Erdentuğ in Turkey single-handedly compiled large numbers of entries for contributors to anthropology from their countries. In the Netherlands we had two groups of collaborators. Jan J. de Wolf and S.R. Jaarsma wrote a dozen entries, and Pieter Hovens compiled several entries himself and gathered additional entries from colleagues. Among the other contributors of multiple entries, we would like to single out James R. Glenn who covered many of the major figures of the Bureau of American Ethnology.

A list of contributors—entry writers and translators—follows. Many of these contributors not only wrote entries but also provided other kinds of help, for which we are deeply grateful.

In addition, numerous people, who did not themselves write entries, offered advice. Some of these people do not really approve of this kind of project and are most certainly not responsible for the result. Among those who offered useful advice are: Michael Aung-Thwang, Robert J. Braidwood, Eliot D. Chapple, Lucas Chin, Dale Christofferson, Elizabeth Colson, James V. Di Crocco, W. Dupré, Robert Ehrich, Susan Tax Freeman, Paul Friedrich, Toy Goodman, Richard Gringeri, Karen Hartman, Gerald C. Hickey, Adam Kuper, Weston La Barre, the late Ruth Landes, I.M. Lewis, Nancy O. Lurie, Wyatt MacGaffey, Barbara Metzger, Mary Miller, Laurent Monnier, Claude-Hélène Perrot, Gregory M. Possehl, Mirko Ramovš, Berta Ribeiro, C. Savary, Mubin Sheppard, Kaisa Sinikara, Yoshihiko H. Sinoto, Pamela Smith, Eric Sunderland, Claude Tardits, Marina Aleksandrovna Tolmacheva, Gordon R. Willey, as well as editor Kennie Lyman and other staff members at Garland Publishing. This list is quite incomplete.

We also acknowledge, with gratitude, the *Encyclopedia Britannica*, which gave us permission to print parts of Sol Tax's entry on Franz Boas, and the University of New Mexico Press, which allowed us to print parts of Barbara Babcock and Nancy Parezo's entries for Natalie Curtis and Ruth Underhill, originally published in *Daughters of the Desert*.

CW

list of
contributors

Robert Ackerman
University of the Arts
Philadelphia, Pennsylvania 19102
USA

Encarnación Aguilar Criado
Dept. de Antropología Social y
   Sociología
Universidad de Sevilla
41004 Sevilla
Spain

Jan-Åke Alvarsson
Kulturantropologiska institutionen
Uppsala universitet
Trädgårdsgatan 18
752 20 Uppsala
Sweden

Veikko Anttonen
Dept. of Comparative Religion
University of Helsinki
00170 Helsinki
Finland

José Miguel Apaolaza Beraza
Dept. de Antropología Social
Universidad del País Vasco
20071 San Sebastian
Spain

George N. Appell
Dept. of Anthropology
Brandeis University
Waltham, Massachusetts 02154
USA

Antônio Augusto Arantes
Departamento de Ciências Sociais
Universidade Estadual de Campinas
13100 Campinas, São Paolo
Brazil

Mildred Archer
Hampstead
London
England

William Arens
Dept of Anthropology
State University of New York, Stony
    Brook
Stony Brook, New York 11794
USA

R. David Arkush
Dept. of History
University of Iowa
Iowa City, Iowa 52242
USA

Karel Arnaut
Seminarie voor Antropologie
Rijksuniversiteit-Gent
B-9000 Gent
Belgium

Mark Auslander
Dept. of Anthropology
University of Chicago
Chicago, Illinois 60637
USA

Jesús Azcona
Dept. de Antropología Social
Universidad del País Vasco
20071 San Sebastian
Spain

Thales de Azevedo
Salvador, Bahia
Brazil

Marietta L. Baba
Dept. of Anthropology
Wayne State University
Detroit, Michigan 48202
USA

Barbara A. Babcock
Dept. of English
University of Arizona
Tucson, Arizona 85721
USA

Peter Bakker
Institute of Linguistics
University of Amsterdam
1012 VT Amsterdam
Netherlands

John Barker
Dept. of Anthropology and Sociology
University of British Columbia
Vancouver, British Columbia V6T 2B2
Canada

Alan Barnard
Dept. of Social Anthropology
University of Edinburgh
Edinburgh EH8 9LL
Scotland

J.A. Barnes
Sociology
Research School of Social Sciences
The Australian National University
Canberra, ACT 2601
Australia

Richard A. Barrett
Dept. of Anthropology
University of New Mexico
Albuquerque, New Mexico 87131
USA

Ira Bashkow
Dept. of Anthropology
University of Chicago
Chicago, Illinois 60637
USA

Kathleen T. Baxter
National Anthropological Archives
National Museum of Natural History
Smithsonian Institution
Washington, D.C. 20560
USA

Jeremy Beckett
Dept. of Anthropology
University of Sydney
Sydney, New South Wales 2006
Australia

Paul F. Beelitz
Dept. of Anthropology
American Museum of Natural History
Central Park West and 79th St.
New York, New York 10024
USA

Thomas O. Beidelman
Dept. of Anthropology
New York University
New York, New York 10003
USA

Thomas Belmonte
Dept. of Anthropology and Sociology
Hofstra University
Hempstead, New York 11550
USA

J. Beneš
Dept. of Anthropology
Science Faculty
Masaryk University
Brno 600 00
Czechoslovakia

Linda A. Bennett
Dept. of Anthropology
Memphis State University
Memphis, Tennessee 38152
USA

Catherine H. Berndt
Dept. of Anthropology
University of Western Australia
Nedlands, Western Australia 6009
Australia

Ronald M. Berndt
Dept. of Anthropology
University of Western Australia
Nedlands, Western Australia 6009
Australia
(deceased)

Tat'iâna A. Bernshtam
Otdel etnografii vostochnoslaviânskikh
    narodov
Leningradskaiâ chast'
Institut ètnografii AN SSSR
199164 Leningrad
USSR

Gerald D. Berreman
Dept. of Anthropology
University of California, Berkeley
Berkeley, California 94720
USA

List of Contributors

Robert E. Bieder
National Museum of American History
Smithsonian Institution
Washington, D.C. 20560
USA
&
Angol Tanszék
Kossuth Lajos Tudományegyetem
4010 Debrecen 10
Hungary

Philip K. Bock
Dept. of Anthropology
University of New Mexico
Albuquerque, New Mexico 87131
USA

Jacques Bordaz
Dept. of Anthropology
University of Pennsylvania
Philadelphia, Pennsylvania 19104
USA

Lucy Jayne Botscharow
Dept. of Anthropology
Northeastern Illinois University
Chicago, Illinois 60625
USA

Gordon T. Bowles
Monterey, Massachusetts
USA

Emilie de Brigard
Dept. of Anthropology
Yale University
New Haven, Connecticut 06520
USA

William Bright
Dept. of Linguistics
University of Colorado
Boulder, Colorado 80309
USA

Elizabeth Briody
General Motors Research Laboratories
Warren, Michigan 48090
USA

Norman Britan
Dept. of Anthropology
Northeastern Illinois University
Chicago, Illinois 60625
USA

Jennifer S.H. Brown
Dept. of History
University of Winnipeg
Winnipeg, Manitoba R3B 2E9
Canada

Thomas Buckley
Dept. of Anthropology
University of Massachusetts, Boston
Boston, Massachusetts 02125
USA

Herman Burssens
Seminarie voor Afrikaanse
    Cultuurgeschiedenis
Seminar voor Etnische Kunst
Rijksuniversiteit-Gent
B-9000 Gent
Belgium

Abena P.A. Busia
Dept. of English
Rutgers, the State University of New
    Jersey
New Brunswick, New Jersey 09803
USA

Margaret M. Caffrey
Dept. of History
Memphis State University
Memphis, Tennessee 38152
USA

Michele Calhoun
Library
Field Museum of Natural History
Chicago, Illinois 60605
USA

Robert L. Carneiro
Dept. of Anthropology
American Museum of Natural History
New York, New York 10024
USA

W. Peter Carstens
Dept. of Anthropology
University of Toronto
Toronto, Ontario M5S 1A1
Canada

Douglas Caulkins
Dept. of Anthropology
Grinnell College
Grinnell, Iowa 50112
USA

K.C. Chang
Dept. of Anthropology
Harvard University
Cambridge, Massachusetts 02138
USA

Vilma Chiara
Teresina, Piauí
Brazil

Irvin L. Child
Dept. of Psychology
Yale University
New Haven, Connecticut 06520
USA

Catherine Clay
Dept. of History
Gettysburg College
Gettysburg, Pennsylvania 17325
USA

Kathryn M. Cleland
McCabe Library
Swarthmore College
Swarthmore, Pennsylvania 19081
USA

Carol J. Condie
Quivira Research Center
Albuquerque, New Mexico 87106
USA

T.S. Constandse-Westermann
AK Wageningen
Netherlands

Justine Cordwell
Chicago, Illinois
USA

Mariza Corrêa
Instituto de Filosofia e Ciências
 Humanas
Universidade Estadual de Campinas
13081 Campinas, São Paolo
Brazil

Osvaldo Rodrigues da Cunha
Museu Paraense Emílio Goeldi - CNPq
66 040 Belém, Pará
Brazil

George Dalton
Depts. of Economics and Anthropology
Northwestern University
Evanston, Illinois 60201
USA

List of Contributors

Yvonne M. Damien
Cudahy Library
Loyola University of Chicago
Chicago, Illinois 60626
USA

John Davis
All Souls College
Oxford University
Oxford OX1 4AL
England

Giorgio de Finis
Roma
Italy

Paola de Sanctis Ricciardone
Dipartimento di Studi
    Glottoantropologici
Università "La Sapienza"
00185 Roma
Italy

Jeffrey S. Dean
Laboratory of Tree-Ring Research
University of Arizona
Tucson, Arizona 85721
USA

Robert B. Dean
Chicago, Illinois
USA

Raymond J. DeMallie
Dept. of Anthropology
Indiana University
Bloomington, Indiana 47405
USA

René Devisch
Centrum voor Sociale en Culturele
    Antropologie
Katholieke Universiteit te Leuven
B-3000 Leuven
Belgium

Irving L. Diamond
Evanston, Illinois
USA

Margaret R. Dittemore
University Libraries
University of Pennsylvania
Philadelphia, Pennsylvania 19104
USA

Mary Douglas
Highgate
London
England

Emanuel Drechsel
Dept. of Linguistics
University of Hawaii at Manoa
Honolulu, Hawaii 96822
USA

Ruth Dunnell
Dept. of History
Kenyon College
Gambier, Ohio 43022
USA

Brian Durrans
Museum of Mankind
Burlington Gardens
London W1X 2EX
England

Lee S. Dutton
Donn V. Hart Southeast Asia Collection
Founders Memorial Library
Northern Illinois University
DeKalb, Illinois 60115
USA

Timothy Eastridge
Dept. of Foreign Languages
Northern Illinois University
DeKalb, Illinois 60115
USA

Irenäus Eibl-Eibesfeldt
Forschungsstelle für Humanethologie in
    der Max-Planck Gesellschaft
D-8138 Erling-Andechs
Germany

Melvin Ember
Human Relations Area Files, Inc.
New Haven, Connecticut 06520
USA

Aygen Erdentuğ
Edebiyat Fakültesi
Bilkent Üniversitesi
Bilkent 06533
Ankara
Turkey

Fernando Estévez
Laboratorio de Antropología Social
Universidad de La Laguna
38203 La Laguna, Tenerife
Spain

Nancy L. Evans
Kenosha Public Museum
Kenosha, Wisconsin 53140
USA

June Pachuta Farris
Joseph Regenstein Library
University of Chicago
Chicago, Illinois 60637
USA

William N. Fenton
Slingerlands, New York
USA

James W. Fernandez
Dept. of Anthropology
University of Chicago
Chicago, Illinois 60637
USA

J.V. Ferreira
Institute of Indian Culture
Bombay 400 093
India

Maurine S. Fletcher
Arlington, Texas
USA

Philippe Forêt
Committee on Geographical Studies
University of Chicago
Chicago, Illinois 60637
USA

Dominique Fournier
Maison des Sciences de l'Homme
75270 Paris Cedex 06
France

Mark Francillon
Dept. of Anthropology
University of Chicago
Chicago, Illinois 60637
USA

Barbara Frank
Institut für Völkerkunde und Afrikanistik
Ludwig-Maximilians-Universität
    München
Ludwigstrasse 27/I
D-8000 München 22
Germany

Ruth S. Freed
Dept. of Anthropology
American Museum of Natural History
New York, New York 10024
USA

Stanley A. Freed
Dept. of Anthropology
American Museum of Natural History
New York, New York 10024
USA

Morris Freilich
Dept. of Sociology and Anthropology
Northeastern University
Boston, Massachusetts 02115
USA

David H. French
Dept. of Anthropology
Reed College
Portland, Oregon 97202
USA

Stephen Fuchs, SVD
Institute of Indian Culture
Mahakali Road, Andheri East
Bombay 400 093
India

Jean-Claude Galey
Centre d'études de l'Inde et de l'Asie du
   Sud
Écoles des hautes études en sciences
   sociales
75279 Paris
France

Frederick C. Gamst
Dept. of Anthropology
University of Massachusetts, Boston
Boston, Massachusetts 02125
USA

Ernest Gellner
Dept. of Social Anthropology
University of Cambridge
Cambridge CB2 3RF
England

Thomas W. Gething
School of Hawaiian, Asian and Pacific
   Studies
University of Hawaii at Manoa
Honolulu, Hawaii 96822
USA

Eugene Giles
Dept. of Anthropology
University of Illinois
Urbana, Illinois 61801
USA

James R. Glenn
National Anthropological Archives
National Museum of Man
Smithsonian Institution
Washington, D.C. 20560
USA

Paolo Gnecco
Dept. of Anthropology
University of Chicago
Chicago, Illinois 60637
USA

Walter Goldschmidt
Dept. of Anthropology
University of California, Los Angeles
Los Angeles, California 90024
USA

Victor Golla
Center for Community Development
Humboldt State University
Arcata, California 95521
USA

Jack Golson
Dept. of Prehistory
Research School of Pacific Studies
Australian National University
Canberra, ACT 2601
Australia

Morris Goodman
Dept. of Linguistics
Northwestern University
Evanston, Illinois 60201
USA

Ian Graham
Peabody Museum of Archaeology and
    Ethnology
Harvard University
Cambridge, Massachusetts 02138
USA

Davydd J. Greenwood
Center for International Studies
Cornell University
Ithaca, New York 14853
USA

Francis X. Grollig, S.J.
Dept. of Sociology and Anthropology
Loyola University of Chicago
Chicago, Illinois 60626
USA

Iwona Grzelakowska
Polskie Towarzystwo Ludoznawcze
Ośrodek Dokumentacji i Informacji
    Etnograficznej
Katedra Etnografii
Uniwersyt Łódzki
90-243 Łódź
Poland

Massimo Guerra
Roma
Italy

Willem van Gulik
Dept. of Museum Affairs
Ministry of Welfare, Health and Culture
2280 RK Rijswijk-The Hague
Netherlands

John M. Gullick
Woodford Green
Essex
England

K. Hajniš
Dept. of Anthropology
Science Faculty
Charles University
120 00 Praha 2
Czechoslovakia

Tiny van Hal
AS Weesp
Netherlands

Thekla Hartmann
Museu de Arqueologia e Etnologia
Universidade de São Paulo
05508 São Paulo, São Paulo
Brazil

Emil W. Haury
Dept. of Anthropology
University of Arizona
Tucson, Arizona 85721
USA

Fred J. Hay
Tozzer Library
Harvard University
Cambridge, Massachusetts 02138
USA

Joseph Henninger
Anthropos-Institut
D-5205 St. Augustin 1
Germany

Regina Flannery Herzfeld
Dept. of Anthropology
Catholic University of America
Washington, D.C. 20064
USA

R.A. Hinde
MRC Unit on the Development and
    Integration of Behaviour
Cambridge University
Cambridge CB3 8AA
England

Curtis Hinsley
Dept. of History
Northern Arizona University
Flagstaff, Arizona 86011
USA

Paul Hockings
Dept. of Anthropology
University of Illinois at Chicago
Chicago, Illinois 60680
USA

E.A. Hoebel
Dept. of Anthropology
University of Minnesota
Minneapolis, Minnesota 55455
USA

Tamás Hofer
Hungarian Academy of Sciences
Ethnographical Institute
H-1250 Budapest I
Hungary

Anna Hohenwart-Gerlachstein
Commission on Urgent Anthropological
    Research
c/o Institut für Völkerkunde
Universitätsstraße 7
A-1010 Wien
Austria

William P. Hopkins
Cape Coral, Florida
USA

Pieter Hovens
Rijksmuseum voor Volkenkunde
2300 AE Leiden
Netherlands

Shu-min Huang
Dept. of Sociology and Anthropology
Iowa State University
Ames, Iowa 50011
USA

Jitka Hurych
Engineering and Sciences Division
Founders Library
Northern Illinois University
DeKalb, Illinois 60115
USA

Sharon Hutchinson
Dept. of Anthropology
Yale University
New Haven, Connecticut 06520
USA

John Hyslop
Dept. of Anthropology
American Museum of Natural History
New York, New York 10024
USA

Malgorzata Irek
Institut für Ethnologie
Freie Universität Berlin
1000 Berlin 33
Germany

S.R. Jaarsma
Vakgroep Culturele Antropologie
Faculteit der Sociale Wetenschappen
Rijksuniversiteit te Utrecht
3508 TC Utrecht
Netherlands

Jean-Pierre Jacob
Institut universitaire d'études du
    développement
CH-1211 Genève 21
Switzerland

Anita Jacobson-Widding
Kulturantropologiska institutionen
Uppsala universitet
Trädgårdsgatan 18
752 20 Uppsala
Sweden

Claude Jacques
École française d'extrême-orient
75116 Paris
France

Jean Jamin
Musée de l'Homme
Palais de Chaillot
75116 Paris
France

Juha Janhunen
Helsinki
Finland

Joel Janicki
Dept. of Foreign Languages
Northern Illinois University
DeKalb, Ilinois 60115
USA

Joseph G. Jorgensen
Program in Comparative Culture
School of Social Sciences
University of California, Irvine
Irvine, California 92717
USA

Hermann Jungraithmayr
Professur für Afrikanische
    Sprachwissenschaften
Johann Wolfgang Goethe-Universität
    Frankfurt am Main
D-6000 Frankfurt 90
Germany

Roland Kaehr
Musée d'ethnographie
CH-2006 Neuchâtel
Switzerland

Elisabeth Katschnig-Fasch
Institut für Völkerkunde
Universität in Graz
A-8010 Graz
Austria

Adria H. Katz
The University Museum
University of Pennsylvania
Philadelphia, Pennsylvania 19104
USA

Alice B. Kehoe
Dept. of Social and Cultural Sciences
Marquette University
Milwaukee, Wisconsin 53233
USA

M. Noordin Keling
Malaysian Branch of the Royal Asiatic
    Society
50470 Kuala Lumpur
Malaysia

James H. Kellar
Glenn A. Black Laboratory of
    Archaeology
Indiana University
Bloomington, Indiana 47405
USA

Jennifer O. Kelley
Dept. of Anthropology
Smithsonian Institution
Washington, D.C. 20560
USA

Robert V. Kemper
Dept. of Anthropology
Southern Methodist University
Dallas, Texas 75275
USA

Laurel Kendall
Dept. of Anthropology
American Museum of Natural History
Central Park West at 79th St.
New York, New York 10024
USA

Kenneth A.R. Kennedy
Section of Ecology and Systematics
Division of Biological Sciences
Cornell University
Ithaca, New York 14853
USA

Russell King
Dept. of Geography
University of Dublin
Dublin 2
Ireland

Victor T. King
Centre for South-East Asian Studies
University of Hull
Hull HU6 7RX
England

M. Dale Kinkade
Dept. of Linguistics
University of British Columbia
Vancouver, British Columbia V6T 1W5
Canada

Frieda Esau Klippenstein
Winnipeg, Manitoba
Canada

E. F. Konrad Koerner
Dept. of Linguistics
University of Ottawa
Ottawa, Ontario K1N 6N5
Canada

Dennis Kolinski
Illinois Humanities Council
Chicago, Illinois 60605
USA

Danielle de Lame
Section Anthropologie sociale et
    ethnohistoire
Musée Royal de l'Afrique Centrale
    (Koninklijk Museum voor Midden-
    Afrika)
B-1980 Tervuren
Belgium

Margaret Lantis
Dept. of Anthropology
University of Kentucky
Lexington, Kentucky 40506
USA

Rudolf Leger
Professur für Afrikanische
    Sprachwissenschaften
Johann Wolfgang Goethe-Universität
    Frankfurt am Main
D-6000 Frankfurt 90
Germany

André Leguebe
Anthropologie et Préhistoire
Institut royal des Sciences naturelles
B-1040 Bruxelles
Belgium

Corinne Leskovar
Chicago, Illinois
USA

Debra Lindsay
Winnipeg, Manitoba
Canada

Phyllis Liparini
Evanston, Illinois
USA

C. Scott Littleton
Dept. of Sociology and Anthropology
Occidental College
Los Angeles, California 90041
USA

David Lonergan
Founders Memorial Library
Northern Illinois University
DeKalb, Illinois 60115
USA

John A. Lucy
Dept. of Anthropology
University of Pennsylvania
Philadelphia, Pennsylvania 19104
USA

Carter Lupton
Anthropology Section
Milwaukee Public Museum
Milwaukee, Wisconsin 53233
USA

Maija M. Lutz
Tozzer Library
Harvard University
Cambridge, Massachusetts 02138
USA

Jeremy MacClancy
Institute of Social Anthropology
Oxford University
Oxford OX2 6PF
England

Martha Macintyre
Dept. of Sociology
LaTrobe University
Bundoora, Victoria 3083
Australia

T.N. Madan
Institute of Economic Growth
University Enclave
Delhi 110007
India

Thomas L. Mann
Northwestern University Library
Evanston, Illinois 60208
USA

William C. Manson
Dept. of Anthropology
Columbia University
New York, New York 10027
USA

Luise Margolies
EDIVA (Ediciones Venezolanas de
    Antropología)
Caracas 1010
Venezuela

Joan Mark
Peabody Museum of Archaeology and
    Ethnology
Harvard University
Cambridge, Massachusetts 02138
USA

List of Contributors

Piero Matthey
Facoltà di Lettere
Università di Torino
10124 Torino
Italy

Adrian Mayer
School of Oriental and African Studies
University of London
London WC1E 7HP
England

Lea S. McChesney
Peabody Museum of Archaeology and
    Ethnology
Harvard University
Cambridge, Massachusetts 02138
&
Dept. of Anthropology
New York University
New York, New York 10003
USA

Miriam Claude Meijer
Dept. of History
University of California, Los Angeles
Los Angeles, California 90024
USA

Roberto Melville
Centro de Investigaciones y Estudios
    Superiores en Antropología Social
Tlalpán 1400, D.F.
Mexico

Rhoda Métraux
Craftsbury, Vermont
USA

G. Miehe
Professur für Afrikanische
    Sprachwissenschaften
Johann Wolfgang Goethe-Universität
    Frankfurt am Main
D-6000 Frankfurt 90
Germany

Luis Millones
Seminario Interdisciplinario de Estudios
    Andinos
Lima 100
Peru

Mattison Mines
Dept. of Anthropology
University of California, Santa Barbara
Santa Barbara, California 93106
USA

Manuel Moreno
Dept. of Anthropology
Northeastern Illinois University
Chicago, Illinois 60625
USA

Liliana Mosca
Facoltà di Scienze Politiche
Università degli Studi di Napoli Federico
    II
80134 Napoli
Italy

Johannes Moser
Institut für Volkskunde
Universität in Graz
A-8010 Graz
Austria

D.J. Mulvaney
Dept. of History
The Australian National University
Canberra, ACT 2601
Australia

Robert F. Murphy
Dept. of Anthropology
Columbia University
New York, New York 10027
USA
(deceased)

Stephen O. Murray
El Instituto Obregón
San Francisco, California 94107
USA

Mamiko Nakamura
Joseph Regenstein Library
University of Chicago
Chicago, Illinois 69637
USA

Stanley M. Newman
Dept. of Anthropology
Northeastern Illinois University
Chicago, Illinois 60625
USA

Ralph W. Nicholas
Dept. of Anthropology
University of Chicago
Chicago, Illinois 60637
USA

M.E.R. Nicholson
Mill Valley, California
USA

Maria Niewiadomska
Polskie Towarzystwo Ludoznawcze
Ośrodek Dokumentacji i Informacji
   Etnograficznej
Katedra Etniografii
Uniwersyt Łódzki
90-243 Łódź
Poland

Chris Nissen
Dept. of Foreign Languages
Northern Illinois University
DeKalb, Ilinois 60115
USA

Marilyn Norcini
Arizona State Museum
University of Arizona
Tucson, Arizona 85721
USA

V.V. Novotný
Institute of Sports Medicine
First Medical Faculty
Charles University
120 00 Praha 2
Czechoslovakia

Ildiko D. Nowak
Joseph Regenstein Library
University of Chicago
Chicago, Illinois 60637
USA

James E. Officer
Dept. of Anthropology
University of Arizona
Tucson, Arizona 85721
USA

Eugene Ogan
Dept. of Anthropology
University of Minnesota
Minneapolis, Minnesota 55455
USA

Joyce Ogburn
Sterling Memorial Library
Yale University
New Haven, Connecticut 06520
USA

David G. Orr
National Park Service
Mid-Atlantic Regional Office
Philadelphia, Pennsylvania 19106
USA

Carmen Ortiz
Instituto de Filología
Consejo Superior de Investigaciones
    Científicas
Madrid 28014
Spain

Donald J. Ortner
Dept. of Anthropology
Smithsonian Institution
Washington, D.C. 20560
USA

Simon Ottenberg
Dept. of Anthropology
University of Washington
Seattle, Washington 98195
USA

Jan Ovesen
Kulturantropologiska institutionen
Uppsala universitet
Trädgårdsgatan 18
752 20 Uppsala
Sweden

M.O. Oyesola
Library
University of Lagos
Akoka
Lagos
Nigeria

Gianna Panofsky
Evanston, Illinois
USA

Hans E. Panofsky
Melville J. Herskovits Library of
    African Studies
Northwestern University
Evanston, Illinois 60208
USA

Merideth Paxton
Dept. of Art History
Tulane University
New Orleans, Louisiana 70118
USA

Nancy J. Parezo
Arizona State Museum
The University of Arizona
Tucson, Arizona 85721
USA

Douglas R. Parks
American Indian Studies Research
    Institute
Indiana University
Bloomington, Indiana 47405
USA

Raphael Patai
Forest Hills, New York
USA

Guy Patterson
Dept. of Geography
University of Dublin
Dublin 2
Ireland

Christopher S. Peebles
Glenn A. Black Laboratory of
    Archaeology
Indiana University
Bloomington, Indiana 47405
USA

W. Keith Percival
Dept. of Linguistics
University of Kansas
Lawrence, Kansas 66045
USA

João Baptista Borges Pereira
Departamento de Antropologia
Universidade de São Paulo
05508 São Paulo, São Paulo
Brazil

Nicolas Peterson
Dept. of Prehistory and Anthropology
The Australian National University
Canberra, ACT 2601
Australia

Donald Pierson
Harbor Oaks
Fruitland Park, Florida
USA

Stanisław Piłaszewicz
Dept. of African Languages and Cultures
Instytut Orientalistyczny
Uniwersyt Warszawski
00-325 Warszawa
Poland

Rik Pinxten
Seminarie voor Antropologie
Rijksuniversiteit-Gent
B-9000 Gent
Belgium

Gregory L. Possehl
The University Museum
University of Pennsylvania
Philadelphia, Pennsylvania 19104
USA

Marjory W. Power
Dept. of Anthropology
University of Vermont
Burlington, Vermont 05405
USA

Joan Prat
Dept. de Geografía, Historia y Filosofía
Universidad de Barcelona (Campus de
    Tarragona)
43005 Tarragona
Spain

Llorenç Prats
Estudi General de Lleida
Universidad de Barcelona
25080 Lleida
Spain

R.J. Preston
Dept. of Anthropology
McMaster University
Hamilton, Ontario L8S 4L9
Canada

Sally Price
Anse Chaudière
97217 Anses de l'Arlet
Martinique

M. Prokopec
Institute of Hygiene and Epidemiology
100 42 Praha 2
Czechoslovakia

Sandra Puccini
Dipartimento di Studi
    Glottoantropologici
Università "La Sapienza"
00185 Roma
Italy

Lothar Pützstück
Institut für Völkerkunde
Universität zu Köln
5000 Köln 41
Germany

Mojca Ravnik
Inštitut za Slovensko Narodopisje
Znanstvenoraziskovalni Center
Slovenske Akademije Znanosti in
    Umetnosti
61000 Ljubljana
Slovenia
Yugoslavia

A.M. Reshetov
Institut ėtnografii im. N.N. Miklukho-
    Maklaîâ
Leningradskoe otdelenie
199164 Leningrad
USSR

João Baptista Cintra Ribas
São Paulo, São Paulo
Brazil

Barnett Richling
Dept. of Anthropology
Mount Saint Vincent University
Halifax, Nova Scotia B3M 2J6
Canada

Robert B. Marks Ridinger
Founders Memorial Library
Northern Illinois University
DeKalb, Illinois 60115
USA

Berthold Riese
Berliner Gesellschaft für Anthropologie,
    Ethnologie und Urgeschichte
1000 Berlin 41
Germany

Frauke Johanna Riese
Museum für Völkerkunde
1000 Berlin 33
Germany

Louis Rosenfeld
Dept. of Pathology
New York University Medical Center
New York, New York 10016
USA

Anya Peterson Royce
Dept. of Anthropology
Indiana University
Bloomington, Indiana 47405
USA

Robert A. Rubinstein
Dept. of Anthropology
Northwestern University
Evanston, Illinois 60208
USA
&
Francis I. Proctor Foundation for
    Research in Ophthalmology
University of California
San Francisco, California 94143
USA

Joseph David Rudman
Library
John Marshall Law School
Chicago, Illinois 60604
USA

Mary Sacharoff-Fast Wolf
San Francisco, California
USA

Risto Sarho
Helsinki
Finland

Clifford A. Sather
Dept. of Anthropology
Research School of Pacific Studies
The Australian National University
Canberra, ACT 2601
Australia

George R. Saunders
Dept. of Anthropology and Sociology
Lawrence University
Appleton, Wisconsin 54912
USA

Egon Schaden
São Paulo, São Paulo
Brazil

Dorothea Schell
Volkskundliches Seminar
Universität Bonn
5300 Bonn 1
Germany

Nancy Scheper-Hughes
Dept. of Anthropology
University of California, Berkeley
Berkeley, California 94720
USA

Bernfried Schlerath
Seminar für Vergleichende und
    Indogermanische
    Sprachwissenschaften
Freie Universität Berlin
1000 Berlin 33
Germany

Lynne M. Schmeltz-Keil
Tozzer Library
Harvard University
Cambridge, Massachusetts 02138
USA

Éva Schmidt
Néprajzi Kutato Csoport
Magyar Tudományos Akadémia
H-1250 Budapest I
Hungary

Nancy J. Schmidt
Main Library
Indiana University
Bloomington, Indiana 47405
USA

Adelheid Schrutka-Rechtenstamm
Volkskundliches Seminar
Universität Bonn
5300 Bonn 1
Germany

William R. Seaburg
Dept. of Anthropology
University of Washington
Seattle, Washington 98195
USA

A.M. Shah
Dept. of Sociology
Delhi School of Economics
University of Delhi
Delhi 110007
India

Z. Siegelová
Dept. of Biology and Ecology
Science Faculty
J.A. Komenský University
Bratislava 842 15
Czechoslovakia

Michael Silverstein
Dept. of Anthropology
University of Chicago
Chicago, Illinois 60637
USA

Milton B. Singer
Dept. of Anthropology
University of Chicago
Chicago, Illinois 60637
USA

Craig A. Sirles
Dept. of English
DePaul University
Chicago, Illinois 60614
USA

Richard Slobodin
Dept. of Anthropology
McMaster University
Hamilton, Ontario L8S 4L9
Canada

Margo L. Smith
Northeastern Illinois University
Chicago, Illinois 60625
USA

Robert J. Smith
Dept. of Anthropology
Cornell University
Ithaca, New York 14853
USA

Bertil Söderberg
Järfälla
Sweden

Wilhelm G. Solheim II
Dept. of Anthropology
University of Hawaii at Manoa
Honolulu, Hawaii 96822
USA

Somchai Anuman Rajadhon
Bangkok
Thailand

M.P.K. Sorrenson
Dept. of History
University of Auckland
Auckland
New Zealand

Rosamond B. Spicer
Tucson, Arizona
USA

Justin Stagl
Institut für Soziologie
Universität München
8000 München 40
Germany

Timothy Stroup
Dept. of Art, Music and Philosophy
John Jay College of Criminal Justice
City University of New York
New York, New York 10019
USA

M.C. Subhadradis Diskul
SEAMEO Regional Centre for
    Archaeology and Fine Arts
Bangkok 10110
Thailand

Helen Sullivan
Slavic Library
University of Illinois Library
Urbana, Illinois 61801
USA

Sem C. Sutter
Joseph Regenstein Library
University of Chicago
Chicago, Illinois 60637
USA

Clara Lee Tanner
Dept. of Anthropology
University of Arizona
Tucson, Arizona 85721
USA

Helen Hornbeck Tanner
The Newberry Library
Chicago, Illinois 60610
USA

Sol Tax
Dept. of Anthropology
University of Chicago
Chicago, Illinois 60637
USA

Ignasi Terradas
Dept. de Historia Contemporánea
Universidad de Barcelona
08034 Barcelona
Spain

Donald J. Terras
Dept. of Anthropology
Northeastern Illinois University
Chicago, Illinois 60625
USA

B. Theunissen
Institute for the History of Science
State University of Utrecht
3512 LM Leiden
Netherlands

David H. Thomas
Dept. of Anthropology
American Museum of Natural History
New York, New York 10024
USA

Raymond H. Thompson
Arizona State Museum
The University of Arizona
Tucson, Arizona 85721
USA

Phillip V. Tobias
Dept. of Anatomy
Medical School
University of the Witwatersrand
Parktown
2193 Johannesburg
South Africa

Paul Tolstoy
Département d'anthropologie
Université de Montréal
Montréal, Québec H3C 3J7
Canada

Robert Tonkinson
Dept. of Anthropology
University of Western Australia
Nedlands
Perth, Western Australia 6009
Australia

Thomas R. Trautmann
Dept. of History
University of Michigan
Ann Arbor, Michigan 48109
USA

Bruce G. Trigger
Dept. of Anthropology
McGill University
Montréal, Québec H3A 2T7
Canada

Elfriede Üner
Institut für Soziologie
Universität München
8000 München 40
Germany

James Urry
Dept. of Anthropology
Victoria University of Wellington
Wellington
New Zealand

László Vajda
Institut für Völkerkunde
Universität München
8000 München 40
Germany

Lúcia Hussak von Valthem
Departamento de Ciências Humanas
Museu Paraense Emílio Goeldi - CNPq
66 040 Belém, Pará
Brazil

Geert Van Cleemput
Committee on the Ancient Mediterranean
  World
University of Chicago
Chicago, Illinois 60637
USA

James W. VanStone
Dept. of Anthropology
Field Museum of Natural History
Chicago, Illinois 60605
USA

Gianni Vanucci
Centre for Asian Studies Amsterdam
University of Amsterdam
1012 CE Amsterdam
Netherlands
&
Dipartimento di Filosofia e Scienze
  Sociali
Università degli Studi di Siena
53100 Siena
Italy

Gábor Vargyas
Hungarian Academy of Sciences
Ethnographical Institute
H-1250 Budapest I
Hungary

C.N. Venugopal
Centre for the Study of Social Systems
Jawaharlal Nehru University
New Delhi 110067
India

Dirk Verboven
Seminarie voor Antropologie
Rijksuniversiteit-Gent
B-9000 Gent
Belgium

Kincső Verebélyi
Folklore Tanszék
H-1364 Budapest V
Hungary

Johann Verhovsek
Institut für Volkskunde
Universität in Graz
A-8010 Graz
Austria

Honoré Vinck
Centre Aequatoria
Mbandaka
Zaïre

Charles Wagley
Dept. of Anthropology
University of Florida
Gainesville, Florida 32611
USA

S.L. Washburn
Dept. of Anthropology
University of California, Berkeley
Berkeley, California 94720
USA

Karen Ann Watson-Gegeo
Dept. of English as a Second Language
University of Hawai'i at Manoa
Honolulu, Hawai'i 96822
USA

Theodore Welch
Founders Memorial Library
Northern Illinois University
DeKalb, Illinois 60115
USA

Robert Welsch
Dept. of Anthropology
Field Museum of Natural History
Chicago, Illinois 60605
USA

Karl R. Wernhart
Institut für Völkerkunde
Universität Wien
A-1010 Wien
Austria

Swarna Wickremeratne
Cudahy Library
Loyola University of Chicago
Chicago, Illinois 60626
USA

Emilio Willems
Dept. of Anthropology
Vanderbilt University
Nashville, Tennessee 37235
USA

Laila Williamson
Dept. of Anthropology
American Museum of Natural History
New York, New York 10024
USA

K. Winkelmann
Professur für Afrikanische
    Sprachwissenschaften
Johann Wolfgang Goethe-Universität
    Frankfurt am Main
D-6000 Frankfurt 90
Germany

Christopher Winters
Joseph Regenstein Library
University of Chicago
Chicago, Illinois 60637
USA

Jan J. de Wolf
Vakgroep Culturele Antropologie
Faculteit der Sociale Wetenschappen
Rijksuniversiteit te Utrecht
3508 TC Utrecht
Netherlands

Richard Kent Wolf
Dept. of Musicology
University of Illinois at Champaign-
    Urbana
Urbana, Illinois 61801
USA

Nathalie F.S. Woodbury
American Anthropological Association
Washington, D.C. 20009
USA

Bin Yamaguchi
Dept. of Anthropology
National Science Museum
Shinjuku-Ku
Tōkyō 160
Japan

Michael W. Young
Dept. of Anthropology
Research School of Pacific Studies
The Australian National University
Canberra, ACT 2601
Australia

Mario D. Zamora
Dept. of Anthropology
College of William and Mary
Williamsburg, Virginia 23185
USA

Thomas de Zengotita
Rhinecliff, New York
USA

Rosemary Lévy Zumwalt
Dept. of Anthropology and Sociology
Davidson College
Davidson, North Carolina 28036
USA

International Dictionary of Anthropologists

a

Abbott, William Louis. Naturalist. Born in Philadelphia (Pennsylvania) 23 February 1860, died near North East (Maryland) 2 April 1936. Abbott received an M.D. from the University of Pennsylvania and also studied medicine in England, but he practiced for only a short time. Around 1880, largely using his own money, Abbott began a career as a collector of natural history specimens that carried him to the Greater Antilles, East Africa, Kashmir, Turkestan, Malaya and the East Indies. Later, between 1916 and 1923, he worked in Haiti and the Dominican Republic. Abbott is significant as a field naturalist primarily because of his vast collection of specimens. He donated more than 8,500 ethnological specimens to the Smithsonian alone, and other materials from his collections are in the Peabody Museum at Harvard University and in other museums. In addition, he collected archaeological and physical-anthropological specimens together with many anthropologically significant photographs. His collections, photographs, notes and correspondence were used by OTIS T. MASON and WALTER HOUGH, both of the Smithsonian Institution, for publications and exhibits for the United States National Museum.

In addition to his own work, Abbott sponsored the work of other collectors. Henry Cushier Raven was sent to the East Indies during 1912-1916 under Abbott's sponsorship, and HERBERT WILLIAM KRIEGER's work in the Antilles during 1928-1932 was largely financed by Abbott.

SOURCES: Abbott papers in the Smithsonian Archives and the Smithsonian Institution National Anthropological Archives; catalogs of specimens in the Smithsonian's Department of Anthropology; "William Louis Abbott," *Journal of Mammalogy*, vol. 17 (1936), p. 312; "Abbott, William Louis" in: *National Cyclopedia of American Biography* (New York [etc.]: 1892-), vol. 27, pp. 312-313;

1

Witmore Stone, "William Louis Abbott, M.D." in: T.S. Palmer [et al.], *Biographies of the Members of the American Ornithologists' Union, 1854-1954* (Washington: 1954), pp. 3-4.

James R. Glenn

Acosta Saignes, Miguel. Anthropologist, ethnohistorian, journalist, senator. Born in San Casimiro, Estado Aragua (Venezuela) 8 November 1908, died in Caracas (Venezuela) 10 February 1989. Acosta Saignes is best known to anthropologists for his contributions to Venezuelan ethnohistory and folklore, but his early training was in medicine and journalism. Expelled from Venezuela in 1937 because of his political participation in the "Generation of '28"—a group of student leaders opposed to the tyranny of the Juan Vicente Gómez regime—Acosta Saignes spent nine years in exile in Mexico. In 1939 he entered the Escuela Nacional de Antropología e Historia (National School of Anthropology and History) in Mexico City, graduating in 1945. He returned to Venezuela in 1946 as the first formally trained anthropologist in the country. He is generally considered to be the father of modern anthropology in Venezuela. He practiced a "holistic" anthropology, with broad interests in archaeology, ethnohistory and sociocultural studies.

Acosta Saignes's work was colored by his political views. He was a man obsessed with the injustices of his times: mistreatment of black workers on the cacao plantations of central Venezuela, long-term oppression of the peasants by a ruthless dictator, and expropriation of private land by the foreign petroleum companies. While in Mexico, Acosta Saignes was influenced both by revolutionary rhetoric and by the government's nationalization of the foreign oil companies. Exile strengthened the spirit of the young maverick, and his early polemical works were written abroad. *Latifundio* and *Petroleo en México y Venezuela* both focused on issues vital to the national economies of Venezuela and Mexico, that of "monoproduction" and its possible consequences. *Latifundio* was denounced in Venezuela as a Communist tract, and the prologue was published separately in an obscure Colombian magazine. Fifty years later, the book was reissued in Venezuela as a "classic." and was finally rejoined with the original prologue of Romulo Betancourt, founder of the Acción Democrática Party and ex-president of Venezuela.

Acosta Saignes carried out a prodigious amount of field work after his return to Venezuela. The country was poorly connected by dirt roads, yet he traveled from the Sierra de Perija along the Venezuelan-Colombia border to the Delta of the Orinoco. Some of these trips were undertaken in order to make practical recommendations to the Venezuelan government regarding indigenous groups. Acosta Saignes also carried out surface archaeological excavations in various parts of the country. The bulk of his work, however, was devoted to gathering information on the customs and practices of his fellow countrymen. He published hundreds of articles on the folklore and local traditions of Venezuela—on popular architecture, folk medicine, musical instruments, dances, ceremonies, folk religion, stories and tales, folk crafts and concepts of *indigenismo*. The regular appearance of his articles in the newly created *Archivos Venezolanos de Folklore* attests to the rhythm of his work. Today these articles constitute an invaluable resource because Acosta Saignes had the opportunity to document rural Venezuela before the vertiginous urbanization that took place in the early 1960s and that transformed Venezuela into an industrialized nation.

Acosta Saignes's field trips and his face-to-face contacts with informants were important methodological tools in his ethnohistorical research. His classic work, *Vida de los esclavos negros en Venezuela*, was based on archival research but was inspired by his boyhood contacts with the black population of Barlovento, the cacao region where he grew up. His research on the pre-Hispanic cultural areas of Venezuela was initially inspired by his familiarity with the extant ethnic groups. His approach to written sources was an active one. He treated documents like informants, asking them questions and refusing to accept the written word at face value. As a result he created crisp, clear evaluations of the historical chronicles of Venezuela. In the 1960s Acosta Saignes made several trips to western Africa and wrote numerous insightful articles on the African influence in Venezuela. Today, this compendium together with his earlier work on slavery constitute an important contribution to the general area of Afro-American studies.

Acosta Saignes believed that research was meaningless without diffusion of its results. In addition to his scholarly work, he published hundreds of newspaper articles as well as didactic booklets—small histories—for students and the general public. It was important to him to contribute introductory articles on anthropological themes to encyclopedias as well as to lecture to diverse audiences. He was a senator from 1964 to 1969 and was a highly visible figure.

Acosta Saignes was also instrumental in creating the Department of Anthropology at the Universidad Central de Venezuela (Central University of Venezuela). This department was shortly transformed into the Instituto de Antropología e Historia (Institute of Anthropology and History) and served as his home base for many years. He also taught in the Schools of Public Health and Journalism as well as in teachers' training colleges throughout the country. He was an exuberant lecturer and influenced a broad group of young professionals in addition to the small group of anthropologists he personally trained.

MAJOR WORKS: *Latifundio* (Mexico City: 1938); *Petroleo en México y Venezuela* (Mexico City: 1941); *Los Pochteca* (Mexico City: 1945); *Los Caribes de la Costa Venezolana* (Mexico City: 1946); *Esquema de las areas culturales de Venezuela* (Caracas: 1949); *Estudios de etnología de Venezuela* (Caracas: 1954); *La sociología del Cacique* (Caracas: 1958); *Observaciones sobre la familia extendida en Venezuela* (Caracas: 1961); *Breve historia del Instituto de Antropología e Historia* (Caracas: 1961); *Estudios de folklore venezolano* (Caracas: 1962); *Sobre los origenes del folklore en Venezuela* (Caracas: 1966); *La vivienda de los pobres* (Caracas: 1967); *Vida de los esclavos negros en Venezuela* (Caracas: 1967); *Los descendientes de africanos y la formación de la nacionalidad en Venezuela* (Caracas: 1966); *Bolivar: acción y utopia del hombre de las dificultades* (Havana: 1977) [won *premio extraordinario*, "Bolivar en Nuestra America"].

SOURCES: Miguel Acosta Saignes, *Breve historia del Instituto de Antropología e Historia* (Caracas: 1961); Luise Margolies and Maria Matilde Suarez, *Historia de la etnología contemporanea en Venezuela* (Caracas: 1978); Reinaldo C. Rojas and Abraham Toro R., *Miguel Acosta Saignes: recopilación bibliográfica y hemerográfica* (Valencia, Venezuela: 1984); *Life History* [taped interviews with Miguel Acosta Saignes, carried out by Luise Margolies in preparation for a book on the history of anthropology in Venezuela from July 1985 through September 1987].

Luise Margolies

Afanas'ev, A.N. (Aleksandr Nikolaevich). Historian, ethnographer, literary scholar, folklorist. Born in Boguchar, Voronezhskii Province (Russia) 11 July 1826, died in Petersburg (Russia) 23 October 1871. Afanas'ev was the first representative of the Russian school of mythology. An amateur scholar, Afanas'ev made use of folklore recorded by individual collectors. Between 1855 and 1866 he published (in eight volumes) the first collection of Russian tales. Afanas'ev sought similarities between Russian tales and beliefs and the folklore of all European peoples.

MAJOR WORKS: *Narodnye russkie skazki A.N. Afanas'eva* (introduction by ĬŪ.M. Sokolov) [3 vols.] (Moscow: 1936-1949); *Narodnye russkie skazki* (edited by V.ĬÀ. Propp) [3 vols.] (Moscow: 1957).

SOURCES: A.N. Pypin, *Istoriĭa russkoĭ étnografii*, vol. 2 (St. Petersburg: 1891), pp. 350-374; ĬŪ.M. Sokolov, "Zhizn' i nauchnaĭa deĭatel'nost' A.N. Afanas'eva" in: A.N. Afanas'ev, *Narodnye russkie skazki*, vol. 1 (Moscow: 1936); M.K. Azadovskiĭ, *Istoriĭa russkoĭ fol'kloristiki* (Moscow: 1958); É.V. Pomeranĭsev, "A.N. Afanas'ev i brat'ĭa Grimm," *Sovetskaĭa étnografiĭa*, no. 6 (1985), pp. 84-90. *Russkiĭ arkhiv* (1871), pp. 1948-1955 [contains complete list of the works of A.N. Afanas'ev].

A.M. Reshetov
[Translation from Russian: Thomas L. Mann]

Akiga (full name: Benjamin Akighirga Sai). Evangelist, author, newspaper editor, politician. Born in the area inhabited by the Shitire clan of the Tiv people in present-day Benue State (Nigeria) in the late 1890s, died May 1959. Akiga was the author of a substantial work on Tiv history and life.

After early contact with the Dutch Reformed Mission (starting in 1911) Akiga became an evangelist. In later years he was also editor of a monthly Tiv newspaper. From 1951 to 1956 he was a member of the Northern House of Assembly. Afterwards he was active in adult education with the Tiv Native Authority.

Akiga's book, an early piece of documentary literature from the "Middle Belt" region of Nigeria, was written in Tiv and intended essentially as a history of the Tiv people. About half of it has been translated into English and annotated by Rupert East (it was first published in 1939 under the title *Akiga's Story*). Whereas the original contains a wealth of information on persons and local events especially in the early colonial period, the English edition stresses the ethnographic aspects of the text, giving an exceptionally vivid picture of Tiv life. It is thus an important early source of information on the largest group of people of middle Nigeria. A short section on clan histories was later translated by Paul Bohannan. In addition to his major work, Akiga wrote an autobiography (primarily the narrative of his childhood) in Hausa; this was published in a German translation in 1938.

MAJOR WORKS: *Akiga's Story: the Tiv Tribe as Seen by One of Its Members* (translated and annotated by Rupert East) (London: 1939; reprinted with bibliography and new preface, London: 1965); "The 'descent' of the Tiv from Ibenda Hill" (translated and annotated by Paul Bohannan), *Africa*, vol. 24 (1954), pp. 295-310; "Benjamin Akiga aus Nordnigerien: Verfasser der Geschichte seines Volkes" in: Diedrich Westermann (editor), *Afrikaner erzählen ihr Leben* (Essen: 1938, 1943), pp. 319-338.

SOURCES: Rupert East: "Preface" and "Introduction" to: *Akiga's Story* (London: 1965), pp. vii-viii and 1-11; "Benjamin Akiga aus Nordnigerien: Verfasser der Geschichte seines Volkes" in: Diedrich Westermann (editor), *Afrikaner erzählen ihr Leben* (Essen: 1938, 1943), pp. 319-338.

Barbara Frank

Allen, Harrison. Anthropologist, comparative anatomist, physiologist. Born in Philadelphia (Pennsylvania) 17 April 1841, died in Philadelphia (Pennsylvania) 14 November 1897. Allen graduated with an M.D. from the University of Pennsylvania in 1861. His most influential teacher was JOSEPH LEIDY, who encouraged him to pursue scientific investigation. Allen was active in many scientific associations devoted to anatomy and natural science, maintaining the strongest relationship with the Academy of Natural Sciences of Philadelphia. He taught physiology and comparative anatomy at the University of Pennsylvania. Allen's first work was with bats, however, his primary interest was in human anatomy and physiology. In his studies of pathological conditions, Allen was not merely descriptive but was interested in physiological processes and their interactions with disease. Allen strongly advocated the inclusion of the study of morphology as a part of medical training (especially in his "Morphology as a factor in the study of disease") to enable the student to understand the interplay between physiology, morphology and pathology. Allen's work in human anatomy followed the research tradition of SAMUEL G. MORTON and James Aitken Meigs, which called for detailed measurements of skeletal features. To understand human variation and anatomy, he studied human skeletal material extensively. As part of his interest in anatomy, Allen sought to define the limits of human variation, especially as expressed in the skull. Allen based his evaluations of human fossil remains on their anatomical characteristics in comparison with modern humans. His research results convinced him that evolution, physiology, culture and pathology had more influence than race on the morphology of the skull. Unlike most anthropologists of his time, Allen preferred to study human variation across the species rather than confine his research to the anatomy of racial differences.

MAJOR WORKS: "The jaw of Moulin Quignon," *Dental Cosmos*, vol. 9 (1867), pp. 169-180; *Outlines of Comparative Anatomy and Medical Zoology* (Philadelphia: 1869); "Localization of disease action in the osseous system," *American Journal of the Medical Sciences*, vol. 16 (1870), pp. 401-409; *A System of Human Anatomy* (Philadelphia: 1884); "Clinical study of the skull," *Smithsonian Miscellaneous Collection*, vol. 34 (1890); "Morphology as a factor in the study of disease," *Transactions of the Congress of American Physicians and Surgeons* (May 1894), pp. 1-14; "Crania from the mounds of the St. John's River, Florida: a study made in connection with crania from other parts of North America," *Journal of the Academy of Natural Sciences of Philadelphia*, 2nd ser., vol. 10 (1896), pp. 367-448; "A study of Hawaiian skulls," *Transactions of the Wagner Free Institute of Science*, vol. 5 (1898), pp. xi-55.

SOURCES: Charles Bardeen, "Allen, Harrison" in: *American Medical Biographies* (Baltimore: 1920), pp. 15-17; Daniel G. Brinton, "Dr. Allen's contributions to anthropology," *Proceedings of the Academy of Natural Sciences of Philadelphia*, vol. 49 (1897), pp. 522-529; Edward J. Nolan, "Biographical notices of Harrison Allen and George Henry Horn," *Proceedings of the Academy of Natural Sciences of Philadelphia*, vol. 49 (1897), pp. 505-522; Bert G. Wilder, "Harrison, Allen," *Proceedings of the Association of American Anatomists* (December 1897), pp. 12-26.

Joyce L. Ogburn

Ancona, Alessandro D'. See: *D'Ancona, Alessandro.*

Angel, John Lawrence. Physical and forensic anthropologist. Born in London (England) 21 March 1915, died in Washington (D.C.) 3 November 1986. Angel received a Ph.D. from Harvard, where the influence of CLYDE KLUCKHOHN turned him from classical archaeology to physical anthropology. Angel's main objective was to explore the complex relationships between culture and biology in human groups through time. By comparing genetic variation in skeletal samples to archaeological knowledge, Angel attempted to test the hypothesis of his professor, E.A. HOOTON, that population mixture and the increase in the cultural and genetic variability that results is positively associated with biocultural adaptation. Angel called this "social biology." His first field trip in 1936 to Greece was also his honeymoon. By 1956, he had examined, measured and photographed more than one hundred adult skeletons from the Eastern Mediterranean, a model for the study of human microevolution, with a major focus on the role of health and disease as a significant factor. Angel's methodology was an outgrowth of the anthropometric tradition well established by the German and French Schools of physical anthropology (Rudolf Martin's *Lehrbuch*). Angel viewed the process of collecting data as a continuing series of approximations, i.e., he believed that future research would feed into the scientific process and might necessitate fundamental changes in one's conclusions. For this reason, he was not afraid to be creative in drawing conclusions based on his knowledge and data. By the time he joined the staff of the Natural History Museum at the Smithsonian Institution (1962), he had nineteen years of experience as professor of anatomy at Jefferson Medical College in Philadelphia and had acquired a vast knowledge as an anatomist.

Besides writing pioneering demographic studies of the Eastern Mediterranean, Angel was one of the nation's leading authorities on forensic anthropology. He commenced this work for the FBI and other law enforcement agencies when he came to the Smithsonian. Angel applied the same methodology of careful examination, measurement and photography, which was his trademark, to each case. In this way, he obtained a unique collection of anatomical information about American middle- and upper-class individuals, differing from that available in any current anatomy collection. In addition, he continued to work on historic sites such as Martin's Hundred, Cliffs Plantation, Catoctin Furnace and the First African Baptist Church in Philadelphia. He is known as one of the major forces in transforming the study of old bones into a study of past biology.

MAJOR WORKS: "Social biology of Greek culture growth," *American Anthropologist*, n.s., vol. 48 (1946), pp. 493-533; *Troy: the Human Remains* [Supplemental monograph to: C.W. Blegan (editor), *Troy Excavations Conducted by the University of Cincinnati, 1932-1938*] (Princeton: 1951); "Osteoporosis: Thalassemia?," *American Journal of Physical Anthropology*, n.s., vol. 22 (1964), pp. 369-373; "Human skeletal remains at Karatas" in: Machteld J. Mellink, "Excavations at Karatas-Semayuk in Lycia," vol. 70 (1966), vol. 72 (1968), vol. 74 (1970), vol. 77 (1973), vol. 80 (1976); "The basis of paleodemography," *American Journal of Physical Anthropology*, n.s., vol. 30 (1969), pp. 427-437; "Paleodemography and evolution," *American Journal of Physical Anthropology*, n.s., vol. 31 (1969), pp. 343-353; *The People of Lerna* (Princeton and Washington, D.C.: 1971); "Colonial to modern skeletal change in the U.S.A.," *American Journal of Physical Anthropology*, n.s., vol. 45 (1976), pp. 723-736; "Health as a crucial factor in the changes from hunting to developed farming in the Eastern Mediterranean" in: M. Cohen and G. Armelogos (editors), *Paleopathology at the Origins of Agriculture*, vol. 3 (Orlando: 1984), pp. 51-71; (co-editor with M.R. Zimmerman) *Dating and Age Determination of Biological Materials* (London: 1986).

SOURCES: *Harvard Alumni Bulletin* (18 February 1956), pp. 400-402; Michael Kernan, "Breathing life into dry bones," *Smithsonian*, vol. 7 (February 1977), pp. 116-124; "Angel brings bones to life," *Anthro Notes* [Smithsonian National Museum of Natural History newsletter for teachers], vol. 5 (1983); Blaine Harden, "The Smithsonian's Sherlock of bones," *The Washington Post* (13 March 1983) [in "Style" section]; W.G. Schulz, "Anthropologists take innovative measures of American health," *Smithsonian News Service* (February 1985); T. Lowe-Edwards, "Angel's world,"

G.W. Times [George Washington University], vol. 14 (Summer 1985), pp. 10-11; M. Yaşar İscan, "John Lawrence Angel, 1915-1986, a tribute and remembrance," *Journal of Forensic Sciences*, vol. 32 (1987), pp. 1484-1485; L.E. St. Hoyme, "J. Lawrence Angel, 1915-1986," *American Journal of Physical Anthropology*, vol. 75 (1988), pp. 291-301; D.J. Ortner and J.O. Kelley, "J. Lawrence Angel (1915-1986)," *American Anthropologist*, vol. 90 (1988), pp. 145-148; D.H. Ubelaker, "J. Lawrence Angel, 1915-1986," *American Antiquity*, vol. 54 (1989), pp. 5-8.

Jennifer O. Kelley and Donald J. Ortner

Antinori, Orazio. Naturalist, explorer. Born in Perugia (Italy) 23 October 1811, died at Let-Marefià (Ethiopia) 26 August 1882. Antinori studied natural sciences and pursued the activity of collecting and stuffing birds. He also participated in the uprisings of 1848 that preceded the unification of Italy. After visiting Greece and Istanbul, he organized an expedition to the Sudan at his own expense in 1859.

Antinori was the first Italian traveler to approach the exploration of Africa with a scientific method, a method that, conjoined with careful observation, allowed him to make precise and fascinating descriptions of the inhabitants. In 1861, upon his return from the Sudan, he sold his collection of birds to the Minister of Public Education, who placed it in the Zoological Museum of Turin. In 1867 he was one of the founders of the Società Geografica Italiana (Italian Geographical Society), which commissioned him in 1870 to guide an expedition to the region of Bogos (northern Ethiopia). During this trip he was witness to the treaty that established the Italian government's possession of the Bay of Assab (13 March 1870). In 1875 he worked in Tunisia, and in 1876, at the age of 66, he participated in an Italian Geographical Society expedition to the region of the large equatorial lakes in East Africa. A hunting accident forced him to withdraw from the expedition and left him convalescing in the village of Let-Marefià. When he recovered, he decided he would not return to Italy but instead would stay and convert the site into a scientific station with lodgings for all who passed through. Despite his advanced age he left Let-Marefià on occasion for brief excursions into the Shoa region (central Ethiopia). After his death his tomb was constructed according to Ethiopian custom, as he had requested: it consisted of a hut in the shade of a sycamore.

Antinori's writings contain a great deal of information on flora and fauna, local languages and the daily life of the people. His work, although lacking in studies of the rituals of the peoples he visited, is redeemed by the caliber of his observations; these are in most cases free from ethnocentrism and are characterized by the descriptive and classificatory interests typical of the positivist tradition.

MAJOR WORKS: *Catalogo descrittivo di una collezione di uccelli fatta da Orazio Antinori nell'Africa centrale nord dal maggio 1859 al luglio 1861* (Milan: 1864); "Note sul vitto e sul modo di preparare i cibi presso il popolo Scioa," *Bollettino della Società Geografica Italiana*, vol. 16 (1879), pp. 388-392; "Altre note sugli utensili scioani," *Bollettino della Società Geografica Italiana*, vol. 16 (1879), pp. 392-410; *Nel centro dell'Africa* (Rome: 1884); "Viaggio nei Bogos," *Bollettino della Società Geografica Italiana*, vol. 24 (1887), pp. 468-481, 511-550, 614-640, 668-694, 765-808; "Un viaggio nel Mar Rosso di Antinori, Issel e Beccari" in: Osio Egidio, *La spedizione inglese in Abissinia* (Rome: 1884), pp. 47-83.

SOURCES: R. Battaglia, "Antinori, Orazio" in: *Dizionario biografico degli Italiani* (Rome: 1960-), vol. 3, pp. 464-467; Elia Millosevich, *Le principali esplorazioni geografiche italiane nell'ultimo cinquantennio* (Milan: 1911); Silvio Zavatti, *Dizionario generale degli esploratori* (Milan: 1939).

Massimo Guerra
[Translation from Italian: Chris Nissen]

Anuchin, D.N. (Dmitrii Nikolaevich). Anthropologist, ethnographer, archaeologist, geographer. Born in St. Petersburg (Russia) 27 August (7 September) 1843, died in Moscow (Russian S.F.S.R.) 4 June 1923. Anuchin was a professor at Moscow University, an academician after 1896, the president of the Obshchestvo liûbiteleĭ estestvoznaniîâ, antropologii i ètnografii (Society of the Friends of Natural Science, Anthropology and Ethnography) and one of the founders of the journals *Ètnograficheskoe obozrenie* in 1889, *Zemlevedenie* in 1894, and *Russkiĭ antropologicheskiĭ zhurnal* in 1900. He was also the leader of the Moscow Anthropological-Ethnological School and the founder of the Antropologo-ètnicheskiĭ Muzeĭ (Anthropological-Ethnological Museum) of Moscow University.

His scholarly works were distinguished by the complex utilization of ethnographic, archaeological, physical-anthropological and geographic data. He tended toward a strict, consistent historicism. The range of his scholarly interests was exceptionally broad. He also occupied himself with the history of science. He was the author of more than 100 works.

MAJOR WORKS: "Materialy dlîâ antropologii Vostochnoĭ Azii. I. Plemîâ aĭnov," *Izvestiîâ imperatorskogo obshchestva liûbiteleĭ estestvoznaniîâ, antropologii, i ètnografii,* vol. 20 (1876), pp. 79-203; *O nekotorykh anomaliîâkh chelovecheskogo cherepa i preimushchestvenno ob ikh rasprostranenii po rasam* (Moscow: 1880); "Luk i strely: arkheologo-ètnograficheskiĭ ocherk" in: *Trudy u arkheologicheskogo s"ezda v Tiflise 1881* (Moscow: 1887); "Sani lad'îâ i koni kak prinadlezhnosti pokhoronnogo obrîâda: arkheologo-ètnograficheskiĭ ètîûd," *Drevnosti,* vol. 14 (1890), pp. 81-226; *O kul'ture kostromskikh kurganov i osobenno o nakhodimykh v nikh ukrasheniîâkh i religioznykh simvolakh* (Moscow: 1899); "K istorii iskusstva i verovaniĭ u Priural'skoĭ chudi: chudeskie izobrazheniîâ letîâshchikh ptifs i mificheskikh krylatykh sushchestv," *Materialy po arkheologii vostochnykh gubernĭĭ,* vol. 3 (1899), pp. 87-160; "O zadachakh i metodakh antropologii," *Russkiĭ antropologicheskiĭ zhurnal,* vol. 9, no. 1 (1902), pp. 62-88.

SOURCES: V.V. Bogdanov, "Dmitriĭ Nikolaevich Anuchin" in: *Sbornik v chest' semidesîâtiletiîâ professora Dmitriîâ Nikolaevicha Anuchina = Recueil d'articles scientifiques publiés en l'honneur du soixante-dixième anniversaire de la naissance du professeur Dmitri Nicolaïevitch Anoutchine = Festschrift für Professor Dmitrij Nikolajewitsch Anutschin zu seinem 70-ten Geburtstage* (Moscow: 1913), pp. vii-xliii [includes bibliography]; L.ÎA. Sternberg, "D.N. Anuchin kak ètnograf," *Ètnografiîâ,* no. 1-2 (1926), pp. 7-13; L.S. Berg, "D.N. Anuchin kak uchenyĭ," *Izvestiîâ Vsesoiûznogo geograficheskogo obshchestva,* vol. 80, no. 6 (1948), pp. 581-587; V.A. Esakov, *D.N. Anuchin i sozdanie russkoĭ universitetskoĭ geograficheskoĭ shkoly* (Moscow: 1955); M.G. Levin, *Ocherki po istorii antropologii v Rossii* (Moscow: 1960); G.V. Karpov, *Put' uchenogo* (Moscow: 1962).

A.M. Reshetov
[Translation from Russian: Thomas L. Mann]

Anuman Rajadhon, Phya ("Phya" is a title). Scholar, writer, ethnographer, philosopher, historian, government official. Born in Bangkok (Siam) 14 December 1888, died in Bangkok (Thailand) 1 July 1969. Phya Anuman Rajadhon distinguished himself in studies of many aspects of Thai culture including philosophy, religion, history, etymology, literature, arts, anthropology, archaeology, customs and traditions. He explored every aspect of Thai life with candor, keen interest and enthusiasm.

Phya Anuman was largely self-taught. He finished only Standard IV of a local school and never attended any university. As a young man he began a career in government service as a clerk in the Customs Department. He eventually became Deputy Governor-General of that department. He also served as Director-General of the Department of Fine Arts, president of the Siam Society, president of the Royal Institute and a member of the Senate.

Phya Anuman possessed an inquisitive mind and was extremely well read and perceptive. He deeply adored the "Land of the Thai," and called it "Sayam Mata Devi" ("Mother Goddess Thai"). To enable people—both Thai and foreigners—to know the country, he wrote on every aspect of Thai culture. H.R.H. Prince Wan Waithyakon Krom Muen Narathip Phongse Prabandh noted that he " ... always approaches the subject from a Thai point of view and tries to find a solution from a Thai point of view. Phya Anuman without neglecting etymology, would find out the meaning of the words in Thai by comparing [their] use in various contexts, various periods and various localities. The same applies to his knowledge of Thai culture. The traditional customs and ceremonies of Thailand have undergone rapid changes. Sometimes only the forms are still known—and that not too accurately—while the substance is only too hazy. We have to thank Phya Anuman for his analytical and interpretive descriptions of many of our traditional customs and ceremonies."

Systematically and consistently Phya Anuman established himself as an authority, through his research, on the meaning of words, their origins and their relationships to peoples and practices in various parts of the world. He was held in high esteem by scholars and experts in many fields. He became a part-time lecturer at several universities, devoting increased attention to this activity after his retirement from government service. He lectured on linguistics at Chulalongkorn University, comparative religion at Thammmasat University, and Thai customs and traditions at other educational institutions. His published works are widely known, both under the author's name "Anuman Rajadhon" and his pen name "Sathirakoses." During his career, Phya Anuman authored more than 200 books and articles chiefly in Thai. Major works were in the fields of ethnology, religion, Thai language, literature and history. One of his major works is *Kamanita*, first published in 1930. Phya Anuman wrote less frequently in English. Many of his English-language articles were collected and reprinted in 1968 in *Essays on Thai Folklore*. Several of Phya Anuman's writings have been translated from Thai into foreign languages. Phya Anuman completed an autobiography shortly before his death. He received the order of Chula Chomp Klan as a royal sign of appreciation for his contribution to Thai studies. The most exalted decoration he received was the highest class of the Order of the White Elephant. Among royal decorations bestowed upon him the one of which he was most proud was the "Dusdi Mala" medal, a rare decoration reserved only for exceptional accomplishments in the field of Thai studies. He was a recipient of honorary doctorate degrees from Chulalongkorn University and Silpakorn University. UNESCO also recognized Phya Anuman Rajadhon as a great scholar whose contributions to the literary world will always be remembered and appreciated.

With the death of Phya Anuman Rajadhon on 1 July 1969, the country lost not only an important man of letters but also a formidable link between the past and the present. The new generation, whether students, writers, scholars or government officials, regards Phya Anuman Rajadhon as their teacher—the lamp that guides their path to virtue.

MAJOR WORKS: *Kamanita* (Bangkok: 1930); *Praphēnī tāng tāng khǫngthai* [*Some Traditions of the Thai*] (Bangkok: 1959); *Fūn khwāmlang* [*Reflections on My Life*] (Bangkok: 1960); *Kānsuksā rūang praphēnīthai* [*Studies of Thai Customs*] (Bangkok: 1961); *Life and Ritual in Old Siam: Three Studies of Thai Life and Customs* (translated and edited by William J. Gedney) (New Haven: 1961); *Praphēnī thambun sūatmon līangphra* [*Traditions of Merit-making, Chanting and Offering Food to the Monks*] (Bangkok: 1962); *Chīwit khǫng chāonā* [*Life of the Farmer*] (Bangkok: 1963); *Rūang watthanatham* [*Stories about Thai Culture*] (Bangkok: 1963); *Essays on Thai Folklore* (Bangkok: 1968; 2nd ed., Bangkok: 1981; 3rd ed., Bangkok: 1988); *Kāntāengtūa khǫng chāothai* [*The Way Thai People Dress*] (Bangkok: 1969); *Some Traditions of the Thai and Other Translations of Phya Anuman Rajadhon's Articles on Thai Customs* (Bangkok: 1987); *Popular Buddhism in Siam and Other Essays in Thai Studies* (Bangkok: 1988).

SOURCES: Suthichai Yoon, "A great scholar passes on," *Bangkok Post* (2 July 1969), p. 4; *Phrayā ᶜAnumān Rātchathon tāmthatsanakhati khǫngkhonrūchak* [*Recollections of Phya Anuman Rajadhon by Those Who Knew Him*] ([Bangkok]: [198-]); *Phromdāen hāeng khwāmrū* [*A Place for Knowledge*] (Bangkok: 1989).

Somchai Anuman Rajadhon

Aranzadi, Telesforo. Naturalist, anthropologist. Born in Vergara, Guipúzcoa (Spain) 7 January 1860, died in Barcelona (Spain) 12 February 1945. Aranzadi received his doctorate in natural sciences from the University of Madrid in 1889. Like many Basques of that period Aranzadi studied and taught outside of the Basque Country, since this region had no university. However, Aranzadi differed from the majority of those of his countrymen who worked in scholarship, letters or the arts in that the greater part of his work focused on his own region. Aranzadi was a scientific illustrator for Madrid's Museo de Ciencias Naturales (Museum of Natural Sciences) and professor in Granada and Barcelona, but he spent almost every summer in the Basque Country investigating its paleoanthropology, flora and ethnography. Aranzadi exercised a strong influence on the direction that contemporary anthropological and ethnographical studies would take, above all through his pupil JOSÉ MIGUEL DE BARANDIARÁN.

From his earliest works, Aranzadi determined to demonstrate the unique characteristics of Basque culture and the Basque people, especially through craniology. In 1919 Aranzadi discovered the caves of Santimamiñe (Vizcaya). Aranzadi's discovery and exploration of the caves—and the publication of memoirs about them in 1925, 1931 and 1935—brought him international recognition. The first of these memoirs was written with José Miguel de Barandiarán, professor at Vitoria Seminary, and Enrique Eguren, professor at the University of Oviedo; the last two were written with Barandiarán alone. The majority of the archaeological exploration and research in the Basque Country between 1915 and 1930 was conducted by these three researchers. They were known as the "three musketeers" or the "three sad troglodytes."

During one of Aranzadi's last projects, the exploration of the Urtiaga cave in 1936 with Barandiarán, he discovered important evidence concerning the early life of the Basque people. The Spanish Civil War of 1936-1939, however, forced him to interrupt his research on the Basque Country, and this work was published in 1948 (in *Jakintza*, vol. 2, pp. 285-330), three years after his death.

In Aranzadi's ethnographic studies much attention is focused on the material culture of rural society. The majority of Aranzadi's works are consistent with the ideas of the major proponents of Basque nationalism founded by Sabino Arana (1865-1903) and with the assumptions of the Cultural-Historical School of FRITZ GRAEBNER and WILHELM SCHMIDT. For Aranzadi, race and culture were tightly bound together, culture being the spiritual manifestation of race.

MAJOR WORKS: *El pueblo euskalduna* (San Sebastián: 1889); "Consideraciones acerca de la raza vasca," *Euskal erria*, vol. 35 (1896), pp. 33-37, 65-72, 97-103, and 129-134; *Antropología y etnografía de País Vasco Navarro* (Barcelona: 1911); "Síntesis métrica de cráneos vascos," *Revista internacional de estudios vascos*, vol. 13 (1922), pp. 1-33 and 337-362; "Los vascos en la etnografía europa," *Revista internacional de estudios vascos*, vol. 17 (1926), pp. 269-280; "Restos humanos en las cavernas de Santimamiñe (Cortézubil), Arezti (Ereño) y Lumentxa (Lequeitio) en Vizcaya (Asociación Española para el Progreso de las Ciencias Naturales, Congreso de Barcelona)," *Ciencias Naturales*, vol. 6 (1929), pp. 71-99.

SOURCES: Angel Goicoetxea Marcaida, *Telesforo de Aranzadi: vida y obras* (San Sebastián: 1985); Jesús Azcona, "Notas para una historia de la antropología vasca: Telesforo de Aranzadi y José Miguel de Barandiarán," *Etnica* [Barcelona], no. 17 (1981), pp. 64-84; Julio Caro Baroja, "Elogio de D. Telesforo de Aranzadi (1860-1945)," *Revista de dialectología y tradiciones populares*, vol. 17 (1961), pp. 136-144.

Jesús Azcona
[Translation from Spanish: Margo L. Smith]

Archer, William George. Civil servant, art historian, ethnographer. Born in London (England) 11 February 1907, died in London (England) 6 March 1979. Archer's career falls into two phases: first in the Bihar cadre of the Indian Civil Service (1931-1948) and later as Keeper of the Indian Department of the Victoria and Albert Museum, London (1949-1974). It is mainly the first phase that relates to anthropology. Archer drew attention to the importance of a knowledge of village art and poetry in order truly to understand the people. Hence his research into Uraon and Santal poetry and various types of village and popular art such as the carvings of the Tiger God, Birnath, in Shahabad, the Madhubani paintings, which he discovered during the earthquake of 1934, Santal Jadupatua scrolls and Naga carving as well as Uraon and Santal poetry, material which was formerly almost unknown. Political and administrative pressures in India led to the suppression of his important three volume report on the Santals, which was not published until after Independence when K.S. Singh edited it as *Tribal Law and Justice*. Archer's papers including the *Report* are in the India Office Library, London (European Manuscripts Department).

MAJOR WORKS: *The Blue Grove: the Poetry of the Uraons* (London: 1940); *The Vertical Man: a Study in Primitive Indian Sculpture* (London: 1947); *Bazaar Paintings of Calcutta: the Style of Kalighat* (London: 1953); *The Loves of Krishna in Indian Painting and Poetry* (London: 1957); *India and Modern Art* (London: 1959); *Indian Painting in Bundi and Kotah* (London: 1959); *Kalighat Paintings: a Catalogue and Introduction* (London: 1971); *Indian Painting from the Punjab Hills: a Survey and History of Pahari Miniature Painting* [2 vols.] (London: 1973); *The Hill of Flutes: Life,*

Love and Poetry in Tribal India: a Portrait of the Santals (Pittsburgh: 1974); *Tribal Law and Justice: a Report on the Santal* (edited by K.S. Singh) (New Delhi: 1984).

Mildred Archer

Arensberg, Conrad M. (Conrad Maynadier). Anthropologist. Born in Pittsburgh (Pennsylvania) 12 September 1910. Arensberg received his A.B. degree in 1931 from Harvard College and his Ph.D. in anthropology in 1934 from Harvard University. His dissertation fieldwork led to a five-lecture series delivered at the Lowell Institute in Boston in 1936 and to his classic book on Irish rural life and community organization, *The Irish Countryman*. Following several reprintings, a second edition of the book was published in 1963 and reprinted in 1988 due to popular demand. It is a rare example of an enduring piece of scientific literature.

Professor Arensberg has provided important leadership in anthropology and the behavioral sciences. He served as president of the American Anthropological Association (1980-1981), president of the Society for Applied Anthropology (1945-1946), and editor of *Human Organization* (1946-1951).

He has spent much of his professional career affiliated with Columbia University (1970-present, Buttenwieser Professor of Human Relations; 1980-present, Professor Emeritus; 1953-1980, Professor of Anthropology; 1956-1959, Chairman; and 1946-1952, Associate Professor, Dept. of Sociology, Barnard College, Columbia University; 1946-1949, Chairman). Prior to 1946, Arensberg was Associate Professor and Chair, Department of Sociology and Anthropology, Brooklyn College (1941-1946); Assistant Professor, Dept. of Social Sciences and Economics, Massachusetts Institute of Technology (1938-1941); and Junior Fellow, Harvard University (1934-1938). Professor Arensberg has also held many key positions outside of academia including consultantships with UNESCO in Germany in the Survey of Social Science (1950), the Bureau of Indian Affairs of the U.S. Department of the Interior (1940-1942) and the U.S. Department of Agriculture (1938-1940).

Professor Arensberg has made several notable contributions to our understanding of culture and society. Beginning in the 1940s, he played a primary role in establishing and sustaining applied anthropology as a recognized area of anthropological inquiry and activity. He was highly instrumental in incorporating the study of European societies into the mainstream of anthropology through his pioneering work in Ireland beginning in the 1930s, his joint study with Solon T. Kimball in the late 1930s on *Family and Community in Ireland*, his professional work in Germany and his demonstration of the continuity of European community characteristics in American culture. Arensberg helped legitimize the study of modern, complex societies and stressed the importance and value of conducting research in organizational settings such as factories as a means to understand and find solutions to human problems. Through his extensive and effective collaborative work in the social and behavioral sciences—much of which was conducted cross-nationally—he has actively promoted inter-disciplinary collaboration. In his writings and teaching, Arensberg has had a clear impact on the development of interaction theory and the method of community study.

MAJOR WORKS: *The Irish Countryman* (New York and London: 1937; 2nd ed., New York: 1968); (with Solon T. Kimball) *Family and Community in Ireland* (Cambridge, Mass: 1940); "The community study method," *American Journal of Sociology*, vol. 40 (1954), pp. 109-124; "American communities," *American Anthropologist*, vol. 57 (1955), pp. 1143-1162; "Research relationships and cultural differences" in: Robert T. Livingston and Stanley H. Milberg (editors), *Human Relations in Industrial Research Management* (New York: 1957), pp. 287-295; "Anthropology as history" in: Karl Polanyi, Conrad M. Arensberg and Harry W. Pearson (editors), *Trade and Market in the Early Empires* (Glencoe, Ill.: 1957), pp. 97-113; "The American family in the perspective of other cultures" in: Eli Ginzberg (editor), *The Nation's Children* (New York: 1960), vol. 1, pp. 50-75; "The community as object and as sample," *American Anthropologist*, vol. 63 (1961), pp. 241-264; "The Old World peoples: the place of European cultures in world ethnography," *Anthropological Quarterly*, vol. 36 (1963), pp. 75-99; (with Solon T. Kimball) *Culture and Community* (New York: 1965); (with Solon T. Kimball) "Community study: retrospect and prospect," *American Journal of Sociology*, vol. 73 (1968), pp. 691-705; "The urban in crosscultural perspective" in: Elizabeth M. Eddy (editor), *Urban Anthropology* (Athens, Ga.: 1968) (= *Southern Anthropological Society, Proceedings*, no. 2), pp. 3-15; "Culture as behavior: structure and emergence," *Annual Review of Anthropology*, vol. 1 (1972), pp. 1-26; (with Alan Lomax) "A worldwide evolutionary classification of cultures by subsistence systems," *Current Anthropology*, vol. 18 (1977), pp. 659-708; "Theoretical contributions of industrial and development studies" in: Elizabeth M. Eddy and William L. Partridge (editors), *Applied Anthropology in America* (New York: 1978), pp. 49-78 [also: 2nd ed., New York: 1987, pp. 59-88]; "Cultural holism through interactional systems: presidential address for 1980," *American Anthropologist*, vol. 83 (1981), pp. 562-581; "Generalizing anthropology: the recovery of holism" in: E. Adamson Hoebel [et al.] (editors), *Crisis in Anthropology: View from Spring Hill, 1980* (New York: 1982), pp. 109-130.

SOURCE: Owen M. Lynch (editor), *Culture and Community in Europe: Essays in Honor of Conrad M. Arensberg* (Delhi: 1984).

Linda A. Bennett

Armstrong, Wallace Edwin. Anthropologist, economist. Born in England 24 February 1896, died in England 10 March 1980. Educated at Cambridge University, Armstrong lost a leg serving in the medical corps during World War I. He returned to Cambridge and was attracted into anthropology by A.C. HADDON and the writings of W.H.R. RIVERS. Armstrong carried out field research in the Suau District of Papua in 1920-1921 and, as an assistant anthropologist in government service, also worked among the inhabitants of Rossel (Yela) Island. These people, who speak a non-Austronesian language and have a fearsome history of cannibalism, had long fascinated anthropologists. Armstrong was attracted by the people's unique "monetary" system, and this became the main subject of his major ethnographic account of the islanders (*Rossel Island*). Armstrong's other writings and his unpublished lecture notes clearly reflect the influence of Rivers on his thought. Like Rivers, he combined an interest in psychology with the study of kinship terminology, social organization and diffusionism. When Armstrong returned from Papua in 1922 he succeeded Rivers in teaching social anthropology at Cambridge. But his position remained temporary, and when the anthropology department was reorganized in 1926 his contract was not renewed. He then took up the teaching of economics. In 1939 he was offered a post in economics at Southampton University where he eventually became Professor of Economic Theory until his retirement in 1961. He published little in anthropology and his economic writings were overshadowed by the rise of Keynesian theory. For the history of anthropology, Armstrong is interesting as the successor to Rivers at Cambridge and for his older, more broadly based vision of anthropology, which was replaced in the interwar period by the teaching and ideas of BRONISLAW MALINOWSKI and A.R. RADCLIFFE-BROWN, who were to dominate British anthropology for decades.

MAJOR WORK: *Rossel Island: an Ethnological Study* (Cambridge: 1928).

SOURCES: James Urry, "W.E. Armstrong and social anthropology at Cambridge, 1922-1926," *Man*, n.s., vol. 20 (1985), pp. 412-423; C.A. Gregory and James Urry, "Armstrong, Wallace Edwin" in: *The New Palgrave: a Dictionary of Economic Theory and Doctrine* (New York: 1987), vol. 1, pp. 114-115.

James Urry

Avebury, Lord. See: *Lubbock, John.*

Averkieva, (ĪŪ.P.) ĪŪliīā Pavlovna. Ethnographer. Born in Kareliīā (Russia) 24 July 1907, died in Moscow (Russian S.F.S.R.) 9 October 1980. After graduating from Leningrad University, Averkieva studied at Columbia University in New York, specializing in the ethnography of the Indians of North America. She worked in the Institut ètnografii (Institute of Ethnography) of the Soviet Academy of Sciences in Leningrad and Moscow and was the editor-in-chief of the journal *Sovetskaīā ètnografiīā*.

Averkieva devoted particular attention to theoretical problems of ethnography, primarily focusing on the process of transition from a primitive to a class society. She actively defended the concept of the phasic primacy of the matrilineal family and was interested in the problems of totemism and *potlatch*, as well as other theoretical areas in ethnography and allied scientific disciplines (e.g., the periodization of the history of primitive society, early forms of inheritance, and problems of war-time democracy). An important part of her research was devoted to the study of the state of contemporary ethnographic studies abroad, its schools and trends and the attitude of contemporary Western ethnography toward Marxism.

MAJOR WORKS: "K voprosu o totemizme u indeīĭsev severo-zapadnogo poberezh'īā Severnoī Ameriki," *Trudy Instituta ètnografii AN SSSR*, vol. 51 (1959), pp. 250-265; "K istorii metallurgii u indeīĭsev Severnoī Ameriki (obrabotka medi)," *Sovetskaīā ètnografiīā*, no. 2 (1959), pp. 61-79; "K istorii obshchestvennogo stroīā u indeīĭsev severo-zapadnogo poberezh'īā Severnoī Ameriki (rod i potlach u tlinkitiv, khaida i tĭimshiīān)," *Trudy Instituta ètnografii AN SSSR*, vol. 58 (1960), pp. 5-126; *Indeīskoe kochevoe obshchestvo KhUSh[XVIII]-XIX vv.* (Moscow: 1970); "O meste voennoī demokratii v istorii indeīĭsev Severnoī Ameriki," *Sovetskoe ètnografiīā*, no. 5 (1970), pp. 33-45; *Indeīĭsy Severnoī Ameriki: ot rodovogo obshchestva k klassovomu* (Moscow: 1974); "Polveka zhurnala sovetskikh ètnografov," *Voprosy istorii*, no. 3 (1977), pp. 40-52; *Istoriīā teoreticheskoī mysli v amerikanskoī ètnografii* (Moscow: 1979); "Istoriko-filosofskie vzglīādy Lesli A. Uaīta (1900-1975)" in: ĪŪ.V. Bromlei [et al.] (editors), *Ètnografiīā za rubezhom* (Moscow: 1979), pp. 48-69.

SOURCES: "Spisok rabot ĪŪ.P. Averkievoī," *Sovetskaīā ètnografiīā*, no. 6 (1977), pp. 137-138 [bibliography]; "ĪŪliīā Pavlovna Averkieva (nekrolog)," *Sovetskaīā ètnografiīā*, no. 6 (1980), pp. 181-183.

A.M. Reshetov
[Translation from Russian: Thomas L. Mann]

Aygen, Nermin. See: *Erdentuğ, Nermin.*

Azadovskiĭ, M.K. (Mark Konstantinovich). Folklorist, literary scholar, ethnographer. Born in Irkutsk (Russia) 5 (18) December 1888, died in Leningrad (Russian S.F.S.R.) 24 November 1954. He was a professor at Tomsk University, Irkutsk University and Leningrad University. During 1930-1949 he directed work on folklore in Leningrad at the Soviet Academy of Sciences

Azadovskiĭ's research is characterized by its careful methods of collection and notation and its detailed commentaries and descriptions of procedures. Azadovskiĭ gave special attention to the analysis of the processes that are active in contemporary folklore and the demonstration of the creative life of folklore even in modern times. He discovered and researched for the first time the rich ceremonial song-poems of various regions of Siberia. It was he who began systematic in-depth research on the folk poetry of the earliest Russian settlers in Siberia.

MAJOR WORKS: *Lenskie prichitaniĭa* (Chita: 1922); *Besedy sobirateliĭa: o sobiranii i zapisy-vanii pamĭatnikov ustnogo tvorchestva primenitel'no k Sibiri* (Irkutsk: 1924); (editor and compiler) *Vospominaniĭa Bestuzhevykh* (Moscow and Leningrad: 1931); *Russkaĭa skazka: izbrannye mastera, I-II* (Moscow and Leningrad: 1932); *Verkhnelenskie skazki* (Irkutsk: 1938); *Literatura i fol'klor: ocherki i étiudy* (Leningrad: 1938); *Skazki Mazaĭa* (Leningrad: 1940); *Ocherki literatury i kul'tury Sibiri* (Irkutsk: 1947); "Iz istorii razvitiĭa russkoĭ fol'kloristiki" in: P.G. Bogatyrev (editor), *Russkoe narodnoe poéticheskoe tvorchestvo* (Moscow: 1954), pp. 41-120, 135-140.

SOURCES: V.IŬ. Krupĭanskaĭa and È.V. Pomerantseva, "M.K. Azadovskiĭ (nekrolog)," *Sovetskaĭa étnografiĭa*, no. 2 (1955), pp. 149-151; "Spisok osnovnykh pechatnykh rabot M.K. Azadovskogo," *Sovetskaĭa étnografiĭa*, no. 2 (1955), pp. 151-152 [bibliography]; N.I. Gagen-Torn, "M.K. Azadovskiĭ," *Izvestiĭa Vsesoĭuznogo Geograficheskogo Obshchestva*, vol. 88, no. 1 (1956), pp. 93-94; È.B. Pomerantŝeva, "Azadovskiĭ, Mark Konstantinovich" in: *Kratkaĭa literaturnaĭa éntŝiklopediĭa*, vol. 1 (Moscow: 1962), p. 91; IÂ.R. Koshelev (editor), *Voprosy fol'klora* (Tomsk: 1965) [Festschrift for M.K. Azadovskiĭ].

A.M. Reshetov
[Translation from Russian: Thomas L. Mann]

Azevedo, Thales de. Anthropologist, historian. Born in Salvador, Bahia (Brazil) 26 August 1904, still living in Salvador. His primary and secondary education was in Jesuit schools. He received his M.D. degree in 1927 from the Faculty of Medicine of Bahia state. He practiced medicine for a short period in a small town of Bahia state but soon joined the state Department of Health. He served in various positions in this service until 1968. Early in his career he wrote several articles for medical journals incorporating anthropological concepts; some of these refuted racist ideas.

In 1942 Azevedo became professor of anthropology at the newly established Faculty of Philosophy (later Federal University of Bahia), a position from which he retired in 1969. During his tenure he founded the Seminar of Anthropology within the University as well as the Institute of Social Science. In 1950 he was appointed co-director (with CHARLES WAGLEY) of the Programa de Pesquisas Sociais do Estado da Bahia-Columbia University (Columbia University-Bahia Program of Social Research). As such, he super-vised the research of such anthropologists as Marvin Harris, Harry W. Hutchinson, Benjamin Zimmerman, Anthony Leeds, Conrad Kottak, Maxine Margolis and Josildete Gomes Consorte in their early research in Bahia state. In 1950 he participated in the UNESCO project on race relations with studies of the emerging elite of people of color in

Salvador. He was president of the Associação Brasileira de Antropologia (Brazilian Anthropology Association) in 1957. He was visiting professor at Columbia University during two periods as well as at the University of Wisconsin. He has lectured at several other American universities and at various centers in France.

He is best known for his use of history in his anthropological studies. He has done research and written on various cultural groups in the city of Salvador and on the contribution and interaction of Italian immigrants with the *gaucho* population of the state of Rio Grande do Sul, the southernmost state of Brazil. In addition to his anthropological interests, he is known as a lay Catholic leader and student of the Church in Brazil. He also writes a weekly column for *A Tarde*, the leading newspaper of Bahia state.

MAJOR WORKS: *Gauchos* (Bahia: 1945); *Povoamento da cidade do Salvador* (Bahia: 1949); *Les élites de couleur dans une ville bresilienne* (Paris: 1953) [tr.: *As elites de côr: um estudo de ascensão social* (Rio de Janeiro: 1955)]; *Ensaios de antropologia social* (Bahia: 1961); *Italianos e gauchos* (Porto Alegre: 1975); *Igreja e estado em tensão e crise* (São Paulo: 1978); *A religião civil brasileira* (Petrópolis: 1981); *As regras do namoro à antiga* (São Paulo: 1986); *A praia, espaço de socialidade* (Bahia: 1988).

Charles Wagley

b

Baal, Jan van. Anthropologist, colonial administrator. Born in Scheveningen
(Netherlands) 25 November 1909, now living at Doorn (Netherlands). Van Baal studied
Indologie, an academic course for colonial officials, from 1927 to 1932 at Leiden State
University. In 1934 he was awarded a doctorate for a thesis concerning the headhunting
complex of the Marind-anim of Southern Dutch New Guinea (*Godsdienst en samenleving
in Nederlandsch Zuid-Nieuw-Guinea*). That same year he officially entered the colonial
service. In 1936 he was appointed as assistant district commissioner (*adspirant controleur*)
at Merauke (Dutch New Guinea), where he served for two years. After returning to Java,
he rewrote his last "handing-over" report for publication ("De bevolking van Zuid-Nieuw-
Guinea onder Nederlandsch bestuur: 36 jaren").

Research on the island of Lombok (Indonesia) was cut short by the advent of the
Pacific War in 1942. Van Baal was detained by the Japanese. After the war he was first
sent to Sydney (Australia) and some months later to Holland for recuperative leave. There
he wrote his first work on the theory of religion (*Over wegen en drijfveren der religie*).

In 1951 he was once again posted to New Guinea, this time in order to set up a
Bureau of Native Affairs. He headed this Bureau for more than a year, then left New
Guinea for Holland, returning in April 1953 as Governor of Dutch New Guinea. He kept
this position for three years but in 1958 left the colonial administration for good.

In 1959 he began his academic career at the Department of Anthropology of the
Royal Tropical Institute in Amsterdam (Netherlands). In 1960 he was appointed to a part-
time professorship at the University of Utrecht and another, externally funded, part-time
professorship at the University of Amsterdam. During these years he wrote *Dema*, an extensive study of the culture of the Marind-anim. This work was based partly on his own

pre-war experiences at Merauke. Six years before his retirement in 1975 he was appointed to a full professorship in anthropology at Utrecht.

Van Baal's importance for the development of Dutch anthropology had three aspects. First, he had an enormous influence on the ethnographic description of Irian Jaya. This did not result from personal example as Van Baal did little fieldwork. However, due to his central position, first in the colonial administration and later in the academic world, he was able to instigate a great deal of research. This is probably the capacity in which he is best known. Second, beginning in the late 1940s and throughout his academic career, he wrote frequently on cultural change, often in the course of the advisory work on education in developing countries that he did for both UNESCO and the Dutch government. Finally, there is his theoretical work on religion as laid down in three major publications (*Over wegen en drijfveren der religie*, *Symbols for Communication*, and *Man's Quest for Partnership*). In his—often very personal—writings on religion van Baal treated religious beliefs as a fundamental part of the human condition. In this he is generally seen as an existentialist and phenomenologist, although he also made extensive, but not uncritical, use of insights derived from French structuralism.

MAJOR WORKS: *Godsdienst en samenleving in Nederlandsch Zuid-Nieuw-Guinea* (Amsterdam: 1934); "De bevolking van Zuid-Nieuw-Guinea onder Nederlandsch bestuur: 36 jaren," *Tijdschrift voor Indische taal-, land- en volkenkunde*, vol. 79 (1939), pp. 309-414; *Over wegen en drijfveren der religie: een godsdienst psychologische studie* (Amsterdam: 1947); "De Westerse beschaving als constante factor in het hedendaagse acculturatieproces," *Indonesië*, vol. 2 (1948), pp. 102-139; "Erring acculturation," *American Anthropologist*, vol. 62 (1960), pp. 108-121; *Dema: Description and Analysis of Marind-anim Culture (South New Guinea)* (The Hague: 1966); "The political impact of prophetic movements," *Internationales Jahrbuch für Religionssoziologie*, vol. 5 (1969), pp. 68-88; *Symbols for Communication: an Introduction to the Anthropological Study of Religion* (Assen: 1971); *Reciprocity and the Position of Women: Anthropological Papers* (Assen: 1975); *Man's Quest for Partnership* (Assen: 1981); (with W.E.A. van Beek) *Symbols for Communication: an Introduction to the Anthropological Study of Religion* (2nd revised ed., Assen: 1985).

SOURCES: J. van Baal, *Ontglipt verleden. Dl. I. Verhaal van mijn jaren in een wereld die voorbijging* (Franeker: 1986); J. van Baal, *Ontglipt verleden. Dl. II. Leven in verandering: 1947-1958* (Franeker: 1989); W.E.A. van Beek and J.H. Scherer, *Explorations in the Anthropology of Religion: Essays in Honour of Jan van Baal* (The Hague: 1975); F. Erdmann, *Symbolen en regels voor deelgenoten: religie en ethiek in de antropologische theorie van Jan van Baal* [unpublished M.A. thesis] (Amsterdam: 1988).

S.R. Jaarsma and J.J. de Wolf

Bachofen, Johann Jakob. Legal historian, antiquarian. Born in Basel (Switzerland) 22 December 1815, died in Basel (Switzerland) 25 November 1887. Bachofen belonged to an old and very wealthy family and could afford to be an eccentric. After studies in Berlin, Göttingen, Paris and Cambridge, he settled in Basel for the rest of his life. He was a confirmed reactionary. Despairing of his own times, he renounced a promising political career and only accepted honorary offices (Professor of Roman Law, Curator of the University, Judge at the Court of Appeal) in order to guard his independence. After a late marriage, Bachofen devoted himself wholly and doggedly to his scholarly work in the face of growing intellectual isolation. He gave up his legal studies, which had brought him early recognition and success, for studies on antiquity and mythology that were ignored or ridiculed. His tragedy was that he always claimed to be a strictly empirical historian, while he was actually a philosopher of history whose visionary power transcended the boundaries of scholarly method. He was deeply imbued by romanticism and by the mystical philosophies of antiquity, such as Pythagoreanism and gnosticism. Starting from an analysis of antique mortuary symbolism, Bachofen explored the mentality of archaic man and then went on to reconstruct his spiritual and social world with the help of analyses of myths and archaeological objects. Thus he arrived at an evolutionary theory of the prehistory of mankind. In *Versuch über die Gräbersymbolik der Alten* he identified three "ways of thought" that successively dominated three stages of religious and cultural development: a symbolical, a mythical and a logical stage. Similarly in his most famous book, *Das Mutterrecht*, he distinguished three stages of social development: "hetaerism," or primitive promiscuity connected with communism and hunting-gathering; "gynaecocracy," or matriarchy connected with marriage, property, agriculture and tribal organization; and "father right," or patriarchy connected with civilization and the state. Bachofen was arguably the first scholar to demonstrate that marriage, family and kinship took on quite different forms in different societies and were products of a social development. In his interpretation of symbolism and myth he was a precursor of structuralism. Both JOHN F. McLENNAN and LEWIS HENRY MORGAN, who later arrived independently at similar theories, generously recognized Bachofen as their precursor. Inspired by this, Bachofen turned in his last years from antiquarian studies to anthropology proper, especially to the study of kinship.

MAJOR WORKS: *Versuch über die Gräbersymbolik der Alten* (Basel: 1859); *Das Mutterrecht: eine Untersuchung über die Gynaikokratie der Alten Welt nach ihrer religiösen und rechtlichen Natur* (Stuttgart: 1861); *Die Unsterblichkeitslehre der orphischen Theologie auf den Grabdenkmälern des Altertums* (Basel: 1867); *Die Sage von Tanaquil: eine Untersuchung über den Orientalismus in Rom und Italien* (Heidelberg: 1870); *Antiquarische Briefe, vornehmlich zur Kenntnis der ältesten Verwandtschaftsbegriffe* (Strasbourg: 1880, 1886). The standard edition is *Gesammelte Werke* [10 vols.] (Karl Meuli, editor) (Basel: 1943-). For some translations, see *Myth, Religion and Mother Right: Selected Writings of J.J. Bachofen* (London and Princeton: 1967).

SOURCES: Johannes Dörmann, "War Johann Jakob Bachofen Evolutionist?" *Anthropos*, vol. 60 (1965), pp. 1-48; Thomas Gelzer, "Die Bachofen-Briefe," *Schweizerische Zeitschrift für Geschichte*, vol. 19 (1969), pp. 777-869; Lionel Gossman, *Orpheus Philologus: Bachofen versus Mommsen on the Study of Antiquity* (Philadelphia: 1983) (= *Transactions of the American Philosophical Society*, vol. 73, part 5); Andreas Cesana, *Johann Jakob Bachofens Geschichtsdeutung: eine Untersuchung ihrer geschichtsphilosophischen Voraussetzungen* (Basel: 1983); Hans-Juergen Hildebrandt, *Johann Jakob Bachofen: a Bibliography of the Primary and Secondary Literature, with an Appendix on the Present State of the Matriarchal Question* (Aachen: 1988); Justin Stagl, "Johann Jakob Bachofen's *Mother Right* and its consequences," *Philosophy of the Social Sciences*, vol. 19 (1989), pp. 183-200.

Justin Stagl

Baessler, Arthur. Traveler, collector. Born in Glauchau, Saxony (Germany) 6 May 1857, died in Eberswalde, Brandenburg (Germany) 31 March 1907. Born into a wealthy family, Baessler developed an early inclination toward traveling. His formal university education at Heidelberg, Munich and Berlin channeled his interests toward physical anthropology, archaeology and general ethnography, and, after receiving his Ph.D., he contacted leading anthropologists of his time, among others Rudolf Virchow (1821-1902) and ADOLF BASTIAN to obtain advice for his travel plans. Five extended voyages in 1887-

1889, 1891-1893, 1896-1898 and 1905 acquainted him thoroughly with India, Southeast Asia, Oceania, North America and Latin America. During his last trip, he suffered a stroke in Tahiti and only barely managed to travel back to Germany, never recovering from this fatal illness.

Baessler's extensive travels resulted in important anthropological collections, which he donated to museums and scholarly societies in Berlin, Dresden and Stuttgart. His cranial collection from caves in Southeast Asia and Polynesia and his archaeological collection of 11,500 items from the Central Andes of South America are outstanding and have served many scholarly purposes, especially since they were adequately studied and described in publications. Baessler was innovative in applying scientific methods (x-rays and chemical analysis) to the study of artifacts and human remains.

Baessler also had a great impact on German anthropology through his leading role in the Ethnologisches Hilfskommittee (Ethnologic Support Committee) and the founding of the Baessler Stiftung (Baessler Foundation) which he initially endowed with 100,000 RM for ethnographic research in Polynesia. He bequeathed an additional 1,250,000 RM to the Foundation for general ethnographic exploration and publication of such investigations. From this endowment the still existing journal *Baessler-Archiv* was established in 1907 and many young German scholars received grants-in-aid for fieldwork until 1920 when inflation wiped out the value of the endowment's capital.

MAJOR WORKS: *Südsee-Bilder* (Berlin: 1895); *Neue Südsee-Bilder* (Berlin: 1900) [contains the diary of his friend, the collector Wilhelm Joest]; *Altperuanische Kunst: Beiträge zur Archäologie des Inca-Reichs* [4 vols.] (Berlin and Leipzig: 1902-1903); *Peruanische Mumien: Untersuchungen mit X-Strahlen* (Berlin: 1904); *Altperuanische Metallgeräte* (Berlin: 1906); (with Felix von Luschan) *Sammlung Baessler: Schädel von polynesischen Inseln, gesammelt und nach den Fundorten beschrieben* (Berlin: 1907) (= *Veröffentlichungen aus dem Königlichen Museum für Völkerkunde*, no. 12).

SOURCES: "Dr. Arthur Bäslers Reisen und Sammlungen," *Globus*, vol. 75 (1899), pp. 28-29; A. Jacobi, [obituary], *Mitteilungen des Vereins für Erdkunde zu Dresden*, no. 5 (1907), pp. 3-9; Viktor Hantzsch, "Bäßler, Arthur," *Biographisches Jahrbuch und Deutscher Nekrolog*, vol. 12 (Berlin: 1909), pp. 155-158; "Sitzung vom 20. April 1907," *Zeitschrift für Ethnologie*, vol. 39 (1907), pp. 412-413.

Berthold Riese

Baldus, Herbert. Ethnologist. Born in Wiesbaden (Germany) 14 March 1899, died in São Paulo (Brazil) 24 October 1970. After graduating from the humanistic state school in Wiesbaden, Baldus was admitted to the Prussian corps of cadets in 1910, enlisting in the Army in 1915. After the war he was politically active in the Spartakist League while working as a literary writer. In 1920 he came to South America, living for a short time in Argentina and settling down in 1921 in São Paulo as a language teacher. In 1923 he led a cinematographic expedition to the Gran Chaco where he had his first contact with Indian populations. He then started his readings in ethnology and, after a visit to the coastal Guarani and a second trip into the Chaco region, returned in 1928 to Germany for systematic studies at the University of Berlin. In 1932 he received his Ph.D. degree with a dissertation on the Samuko language. In 1933 he returned to Brazil, undertaking successive stretches of fieldwork among Indians of Southern and Central Brazil (Kaingang, Guayaki, Chiripá, Terena, Karajá, Tapirapé). In 1939 Baldus became professor of Brazilian ethnology at the Escola de Sociologia e Política (School of Sociology and Politics) of São Paulo, and in 1946 he was appointed ethnologist at the Museu Paulista where he eventually was made the editor of the new series of the *Revista do Museu Paulista*. He became a naturalized Brazilian in 1941.

During the course of his studies in Berlin, Baldus attended all the lectures of RICHARD THURNWALD, his tutor, and studied South American ethnology with WALTER LEHMANN and KONRAD THEODOR PREUß. Philosophy and Spanish literature were constant interests throughout his university years.

With this training and his former field experience, Baldus's contribution to the establishment of scientific research patterns in Brazilian ethnology was fundamental, as anthropology and sociology had only been raised to the level of university studies in the 1930s. In his classes he stressed the need for the acquisition of consistent empirical data, suggesting themes for ethnographic investigation and the proper standards of fieldwork to a first generation of social scientists; much of his teaching was printed in *Sociologia*, the "didactic and scientific" journal through which the graduate students grew familiar with the theoretical currents that were shaping the social sciences abroad. In his own research he did not usually address larger theoretical issues, and he was not committed to any single methodology, although he initially focused on subjects favored by Thurnwald, approaching them from a socio-psychological angle. But in the course of his fieldwork he became increasingly interested in the problems and results of interethnic contacts: his 1937 essays set up acculturation studies as one of the focal points of theoretical interest for the next two decades. He introduced to Brazil the concepts of American applied anthropology and kept up a lifelong and vocal militancy on behalf of the native peoples in Brazil, arguing for an ethnological orientation in official Indian policy and favoring the anthropologist's involvement in the destinies of the peoples he studies.

With a thorough command of South American ethnographic literature, Baldus typically relied in his writings on the combined use of written sources and his own field data for comparative purposes. His lasting contribution to later generations of students was the *Bibliografia crítica da etnologia brasileira* in which, in a total of 2,834 entries, he appraised practically everything written from 1500 to 1968 about Brazilian Indians. Co-editor of *Sociologia* and *Sociologus* (Berlin), Baldus crowned his editorial activities by creating in 1947 the new series of *Revista do Museu Paulista* and publishing it up to its seventeenth volume (1967). Under his direction the *Revista* grew into a unique repertory of original fieldwork data on Indians in Brazil, a journal of international standing and a landmark in the development of anthropology in that country. In his writings Baldus maintained the vivid style of his early literary experiments: his complete war poems were published in 1916 by Ferger in Wiesbaden, and *Madame Lynch*, a novel about the American mistress of the Paraguayan dictator Solano Lopes, appeared in 1931 in Berlin.

MAJOR WORKS: *Indianerstudien im nordöstlichen Chaco: Forschungen zur Völkerpsychologie und Soziologie* (Leipzig: 1931); *Ensaios de etnologia brasileira* (São Paulo: 1937); *Dicionário de etnologia e sociologia* (São Paulo: 1939); *Bibliografia crítica da etnologia brasileira* [2 vols.] (São Paulo: 1954; Hannover: 1968) [there is also a vol. 3, compiled by Thekla Hartmann (Berlin: 1984)]; *Die Jaguarzwillinge: Mythen und Heilbringergeschichten, Ursprungssagen und Märchen brasilianischer Indianer* (Eisenach und Kassel: 1958); *Tapirapé, tribo tupi no Brasil central* (São Paulo: 1970).

SOURCES: Hans Becher, "Herbert Baldus 1899-1970," *Zeitschrift für Ethnologie*, vol. 95, no. 2 (1970), pp. 157-163 [tr.: "Herbert Baldus 1899-1970," *American Anthropologist*, vol. 74 (1972), pp. 1307-1312]; Egon Schaden, "Apresentação à 2a. edição" in: Herbert Baldus, *Ensaios de etnologia brasileira* (São Paulo: 1979); Egon Schaden, "Os estudos de aculturação na etnologia brasileira" in: *Aculturação indígena* (São Paulo: 1964), pp. 11-64; Herbert Baldus, "Lebenslauf" in: "Beiträge zur Sprachenkunde der Samuko-Gruppe," *Anthropos*, vol. 27 (1932), pp. 361-416.

Thekla Hartmann

Bandelier, Adolph (Adolphe Francis Alphonse Bandelier). Anthropologist, ethnohistorian, archaeologist. Born in Bern (Switzerland) 6 August 1840, died in Seville (Spain) 18 March 1914. Bandelier's research dealt primarily with ethnographic and documentary studies of Mexico, the American Southwest, and the Andes of Peru and Bolivia.

In 1848 Bandelier migrated with his family from Switzerland to Highland, Illinois. During 1865-1867 he studied geology at Bern University. He returned to Highland to work in a bank where his father was a partner. Bandelier disliked business and in the 1870s began documentary research on ancient Mexico, which culminated in monographs published between 1877 and 1879.

His fluency in several languages aided his ethnohistorical research. He was influenced by a close friendship with LEWIS HENRY MORGAN with whom he carried on a lengthy correspondence until the latter's death in 1881. Bandelier became a convert to Morgan's ideas on human evolution and one of Morgan's strongest defenders.

Between 1880 and 1892 Bandelier conducted research in the American Southwest (*Final Report of Investigations among the Indians of the Southwestern United States* and *Contributions to the History of the Southwestern Portion of the United States*). His detailed scholarship was instrumental in upsetting fanciful and fallacious traditions about the past of the Pueblo and other groups and in establishing a foundation for sound anthropological research.

Between 1892 and 1903 Bandelier lived in Peru and Bolivia. Large collections he acquired under the patronage of Henry Villard were transferred to the American Museum of Natural History in 1894. His association with the American Museum began at that time and lasted until 1906. In 1893, after the death of his first wife, Bandelier married Fanny Ritter in Lima. Of Swiss origin and an accomplished linguist like her husband, she became his invaluable assistant, particularly after he began to go blind in 1909.

Bandelier returned to the United States in 1903, beginning employment with the Hispanic Society in 1906. That society published his classic, *The Islands of Titicaca and Koati*. He spent his final years, 1911-1914, as a researcher for the Carnegie Institution doing archival work in Mexico and Spain.

Bandelier was the first American to do ethnohistorical research in a modern manner, cautiously relying on oral tradition and written documentation. He produced some 150 books and articles. His historical research has stood the test of time, somewhat overshadowing his archaeological and ethnographic endeavors. In his work, Bandelier proposed a still credible outline of the archaeology and early history of the Southwest. His research on the Titicaca islands was the first major ethnohistorical and interdisciplinary study carried out in the Andes.

MAJOR WORKS: "On the art of war and mode of warfare of the ancient Mexicans" in: *Tenth Report, Peabody Museum* (Cambridge, Mass.: 1877), pp. 95-161; "On the distribution and tenure of lands ... among the ancient Mexicans," *Eleventh Report, Peabody Museum* (Cambridge, Mass.: 1878), pp. 385-448; "On the social organization and mode of government of the ancient Mexicans," *Twelfth Report, Peabody Museum* (Cambridge, Mass.: 1978), pp. 557-699; *Final Report of Investigation among the Indians of the Southwestern United States, Carried on Mainly in the Years from 1880 to 1885* [2 vols.] (Cambridge, Mass.: 1890-1892) (= *Papers of the Archaeological Institute of America, American Series*, vols. 3-4); *Contributions to the History of the Southwestern Portion of the United States* (Cambridge, Mass.: 1890) (= *Papers of the Archaeological Institute of America, American Series*, vol. 5); *The Gilded Man (El Dorado) and Other Pictures of the Spanish Occupancy of America* (New York: 1893); *The Islands of Titicaca and Koati* (New York: 1910).

SOURCES: F.W. Hodge, "Adolph Francis Alphonse Bandelier" [with partial Bandelier bibliography], *American Anthropologist*, n.s., vol. 16 (1914), pp. 349-358; Leslie A. White, *Pioneers in American Anthropology: the Bandelier-Morgan Letters 1873-1883* (Albuquerque: 1940), pp. 1-108; Edgar F. Goad, "A study of the life of Adolph Francis Alphonse Bandelier, with an appraisal of his contribution to American anthropology and related sciences" [summary in the library of the American Museum of Natural History, New York, of Goad's unpublished dissertation, University of Southern California, 1940].

John Hyslop

Banks, Edward. Ethnographer, zoologist, curator. Born in Newport, Gwent (Wales) 1903, died in Minehead, Somerset (England) 19 December 1988. "Bill" Banks ("Tuan Bing" to local Malays and Iban) is best known to students of Southeast Asian ethnography as the longest-serving curator of the Sarawak Museum during the years before World War II. Although his scientific contributions were mainly in the field of natural history, especially ornithology, he also played an important role in building the Museum's collections as well as its strong tradition of field research and publishing and its international reputation as a center for Bornean archaeology, history and ethnography. His contribution should not be underestimated although much of his work was inconspicuous and created more opportunities for others than for himself.

Educated at Wrekin College and Queen's College, Oxford, Banks graduated in zoology in 1924 and immediately volunteered to fill the vacant curatorship at the Sarawak Museum in Kuching; there was no competition. He had little idea of what the work would be like and found little to guide him when he arrived in Kuching in early 1925.

The curator undertook a vast range of duties; he traveled widely, collecting specimens and publishing in the main fields of interest covered by the museum (natural history, ethnography, archaeology, history). He had to manage the staff and building, run the place as an information service, liaise with local informants, collectors and dignitaries, and assist visiting specialists from overseas, many of whom would proceed upcountry to carry out field research. Banks was, above all, enthusiastic about the curatorship: "one of the best jobs in the Far East," as he was later to call it.

With the help of his colleague, F.H. Pollard, Banks dealt with local organization and other practical aspects of the 1932 Oxford University Expedition to Sarawak, which he effectively led jointly with the late TOM HARRISSON, who would succeed him as curator. There were marked differences between the two men at that time—Banks being as responsible and unassuming as Harrisson was impatient and egotistical.

For Harrisson, the Expedition was a training exercise for which briskness and enthusiasm were paramount. In Banks' opinion, an expedition of undergraduates was inadequate to the great potential of scientific research in Sarawak, and he tried to reduce as far as possible the offenses to local custom that arose from expedition members' inexperience (for Harrisson's view, see *Borneo Jungle: an Account of the Oxford University Expedition of 1932* (London: 1938), which he edited, and especially his *World Within: a Borneo Story* (London: 1959)).

Like other Europeans in Sarawak, Banks was interned by the Japanese in Kuching from 1941 to 1945. He resigned as curator in 1946, and Harrisson became curator in 1947. In October 1947, Banks returned to Sarawak as Fisheries Research Officer "on agreement" and finally returned to England late in 1949, quickly taking up a two-year temporary appointment in the zoology department of the Natural History Museum at South Kensington. Thereafter, Banks made one last visit to Southeast Asia, a freelance ornithological trip to what was then British North Borneo. In the early 1960s he and his wife, Majorie, retired to Minehead, where she died a few years later. Banks then lived alone, maintaining a wide correspondence with friends and colleagues and later using audio tapes because of failing eyesight.

Banks' anthropological writings were opportunistic and informal and covered a wide field; in terms of detail and theoretical orientation they have been largely superseded by work based on more intensive research and more reliable paradigms. However, his recording of ethnographic facts and, in archaeology, his discovery of several significant Hindu remains constitute a permanent contribution to our knowledge of Bornean cultures, matching some of his best botanical and zoological work. Even when on other subjects, many of his papers also contain useful asides on ethnography and on the conditions in which he worked.

MAJOR WORKS: *Bornean Mammals* (Kuching: 1949); *A Naturalist in Sarawak* (Kuching: 1949); *The Green Desert* ([Minehead, Somerset: ca. 1969]); "Some Kalamantan vocabularies," *Sarawak Museum Journal,* vol. 4, part 3, no. 14 (1935), pp. 257-259; "Notes on birds in Sarawak, with a list of native names," *Sarawak Museum Journal,* vol. 4, part 3, no. 14 (1935), pp. 267-325; (with F.H. Pollard) "Teknonymy and other customs among the Kayans, Kenyahs, Kelamantans and others," *Sarawak Museum Journal,* vol. 4, part 4, no. 15 (1937), pp. 395-409; "Some megalithic remains from the Kelabit country in Sarawak with some notes on the Kelabits themselves," *Sarawak Museum Journal,* vol. 4, part 4, no. 15 (1937), pp. 411-437; "Native drink in Sarawak," *Sarawak Museum Journal,* vol. 4, part 4, no. 15 (1937), pp. 439-447; "Reminiscence of a curator," *Sarawak Museum Journal,* n.s., vol. 32, no. 53 (1983), pp. 59-60; "Dayaks and Nagas," *Sarawak Museum Journal,* n.s., vol. 32, no. 53 (1983), pp. 231-234; "Ancient times in Borneo," *Journal of the Malay Branch of the Royal Asiatic Society,* vol. 20, part 2, no. 143 (1947), pp. 26-34; Review of N.C. Scott's *A Dictionary of Sea Dayak* (1956), *Journal of the Malay Branch of the Royal Asiatic Society* vol. 33, part 1, no. 189 (1960), pp. 115-116; "A note on Iban omen birds," *Brunei Museum Journal,* vol. 5, no. 3 (1983), pp. 104-107. Banks was editor of the *Sarawak Museum Journal,* vols. 3 and 4 (1925-1937).

SOURCES: Charles Allen, *Tales from the South China Seas: Images of the British in South East Asia in the Twentieth Century* (London: 1983); E. Banks, "Reminiscence of a curator," *Sarawak Museum Journal,* n.s., vol. 32, no. 53 (1983), pp. 59-60; The Earl of Cranbrook and Charles M.U. Leh, "A history of zoology in Sarawak," *Sarawak Museum Journal,* n.s., vol. 32, no. 53 (1983), pp. 15-33; [obituary], *West Somerset Free Press* (30 December 1988); autobiographical audio cassette, dictated by E. Banks, in the Brunei Museum; personal communications from A.J.N. Richards, R. Nicholl, M.W.F. Tweedie, Madeline Daubeny, E. Banks.

Brian Durrans

Barandiarán, José Miguel de. Anthropologist, prehistorian. Born in Ataun, Guipúzcoa (Spain) 31 December 1889, now living in Ataun (Spain). Barandiarán is considered the patriarch of the study of Basque culture.

An uncloistered priest, Barandiarán became Rector of the Vitoria Seminary. From this position he both instituted and supported studies of the anthropology and prehistory of Basque culture. He carried out the first excavations in Euskal-Herria that were accomplished by means of the scientific method.

After his participation in courses and seminars taught by WILHELM SCHMIDT, Barandiarán accepted the position of *corresponsalía* (correspondent) of ethnology offered by Schmidt, the result of which was the publication of the first pages of *Euskal-Folklore*, which contained results of his first ethnographic survey in 1921. His work in paleontology was begun with Abbé HENRI BREUIL and Édouard Le Roy (1870-1954).

Exiled to France in 1937 because of the Spanish Civil War, Barandiarán returned to Spain in 1953 to accept the Manuel Larramendi chair at the University of Salamanca. (Larramendi had been an 18th-century scholar and defender of Euskara.)

Barandiarán is a member of the Real Academia de la Lengua Española (Royal Academy of the Spanish Language) and of Euskaltaindia (Academy of the Basque Language). He has received doctorates *honoris causa* from Madrid's Complutense University, the Deusto (of the Society of Jesus) and the Universidad del País Vasco (University of the Basque Country).

His work on the prehistory, culture and personality of the Basques, undertaken at first with Enrique Eguren and TELESFORO ARANZADI, was influenced by Schmidt and the Cultural-Historical School. This work has stamped and continued to mark in great measure the development of anthropological study on the Basques and on the Basque Country. A subtext of all his work—not surprising in a Catholic priest!—was a preoccupation with the social change resulting from industrialization, which, Barandiarán believed, was destroying the original rural society. For Barandiarán the "full person"—a realization of the ideal of the Basque and the Catholic—could develop only in the preindustrial Basque society.

Under Barandiarán's direction "Etniker" groups were organized whose goal was to assemble, according to previously developed questionnaires, ethnographic data about traits and cultural complexes on the verge of disappearing. The ultimate goal was the preparation of a Basque ethnographic atlas.

His works are collected in the *Obras completas*, which form part of *La gran enciclopedia vasca* and include materials in ethnography and paleontology. The works that had the greatest influence on the world of scholarship and the reading public include those on the paleontological study of the Basque people ("Contribución al estudio paleontológico del Pueblo Vasco"), Basque folklore (*Eusko-folklore*), ancient Basque religion ("La religion des anciennes basques") and prehistoric humanity in the Basque country (*El Hombre prehistórico*), as well as the Basque ethnographic atlas ("Bosquejo de un Atlas etnográfico"). Many additional articles were published separately and in different journals according to a preconceived plan. Assembled also in the *Obras completas*, they deal with Basque mythology, traditional life, tales and legends, traditional crafts and popular culture. In 1963 his pupils published a Festschrift in his honor entitled *Homenaje a José Miguel de Barandiarán*.

MAJOR WORKS: *Obras completas* (Bilbao: 1972-); "Contribución al estudio paleontológico del Pueblo Vasco: el magismo" [originally 1919] in: *Obras completas*, vol. 5, pp. 213-247; *Eusko-folklore: materiales y cuestionarios* [originally 1921] (= *Obras completas*, vol. 2); "La religion des anciennes basques" in: *Anuario de Eusko-Folklore* (Vitoria: 1922); *El hombre prehistórico en el País Vasco* (Buenos Aires: 1953); "Bosquejo de un Atlas etnográfico del Pueblo Vasco" [originally 1969] in: *Obras completas*, vol. 6, pp. 357-362.

SOURCES: Felipe de Barandiarán, *José Miguel de Barandiarán: patriarca de la cultura vasca* (San Sebastian: 1976); *Homenaje a Don José Miguel de Barandiarán* (Bilbao: 1964).

José Miguel Apaolaza Beraza
[Translation from Spanish: Margo L. Smith]

Barbeau, Marius (Charles Marius Barbeau). Anthropologist, folklorist, ethnomusicologist, *littérateur*. Born in Ste.-Marie-de-Beauce (Québec) 5 March 1883, died in Ottawa (Ontario) 27 February 1969. Reared in rural Québec (he once referred to it as being "stewed in folk lore"), Barbeau took a law degree at Université Laval, then studied as a Rhodes Scholar for three years at Oxford and in France, earning a B.Sc. and diploma in anthropology from Oxford in 1910. He thought of becoming an Egyptologist, but R.R. MARETT gave him a letter of recommendation for a position at the Geological Survey of Canada's new Division of Anthropology (now the Canadian Museum of Civilization), where he spent his career, continuing actively for some fifteen years past retirement. He was the founder of professional folklore study in Canada. He recorded many thousands of French-Canadian, Huron-Wyandot, Tsimshian and other songs and texts, organized and/or revived folklore societies in Québec and Ontario, and was a tireless lecturer. His urgent sense of mission led him to record the disappearing remnants of what he believed was a deep past: those of medieval France surviving in Québec, and those of Asian origin surviving in the mythology of the Tsimshian Indians. His views on origins are regarded by his successors as bold but doubtful hypotheses, and his works are not often cited in current academic discussions, but his collections laid the foundation for the development of professional institutions and museum galleries and increased popular awareness of the Native and French heritage of Canada. He published nearly 1,000 items.

MAJOR WORKS: "Growth and federation in the Tsimshian phratries" in: *Proceedings of the 19th International Congress of Americanists* (Washington: 1917), pp. 402-408; (with Edward Sapir) *Folk Songs of French Canada* (Ottawa: 1925); *The Downfall of Temlaham* (Toronto: 1928); *Québec, Where Ancient France Lingers* (Ottawa: 1936); *My Life in Recording Canadian-Indian Folk-Lore* [sound recording] (Cambridge, Mass.: 1957); *Medicine-Men on the North Pacific Coast* (Ottawa: 1958); *Indian Days on the Western Prairies* (Ottawa: 1960).

SOURCES: Nansi Swayze, *The Man Hunters* (Toronto: 1960); Luc Lacourciere, "The present state of French-Canadian folklore studies," *Journal of American Folklore*, vol. 74 (1961), pp. 374-378; Edith Fowke, "Marius Barbeau (1883-1969)," *Journal of American Folklore*, vol. 82 (1969), pp. 264-266; Israel J. Katz, "Marius Barbeau, 1883-1969," *Ethnomusicology*, vol. 16 (1970), pp. 129-142.

R.J. Preston

Bardavelidze, V.V. (Vera Vardenovna). Ethnographer, folklorist. Born in Tbilisi (Georgia, Russia) 17 November 1899, died in Tbilisi (Georgian S.S.R.) 23 November 1970. A doctor of historical sciences and a professor at Tbilisi University, Bardavelidze worked in the Institut istorii, arkheologii i ètnografii (Institute of History, Archaeology and Ethnography) of the Academy of Sciences of the Georgian S.S.R.

Bardavelidze wrote at length on the customs and culture of the Georgian people, above all on their communal organizations, patterns of land ownership and land use, calendar of national holidays, religion, ceremonial graphic arts, and so forth. Studying the stages of the ancient world-view of the Georgians and their ancestors, Bardavelidze singled out the primary deity with which the cult of the bull was connected. The important role of this animal in ancient Georgian ceremonies and customs enabled her to associate the old Georgian religion with the religious world of the civilized peoples of the ancient Near East and the Mediterranean.

Bardavelidze was also the compiler of major ethnographic collections for the museums of Tbilisi and Leningrad.

MAJOR WORKS: *Kalendar' svanskikh narodnykh prazdnikov. I. Novogodniĭ tsikl* [in Georgian] (Tbilisi: 1939); *Gruzinskiĭ narodnyĭ ornament* [in Georgian, Russian and French], vol. 1 (Tbilisi: 1939); "Glavnoe bozhestvo drevnegruzinskogo panteona Gmerti" in: G.S. Chitaĭa (editor), *Voprosy ètnografii Kavkaza* (Tbilisi: 1952), pp. 301-318; *Drevneĭshie religioznye verovaniĭa i obrĭadovoe graficheskoe iskusstvo gruzinskikh plemen* (Tbilisi: 1957); "Gruziny: obshchestvennyĭ byt: perezhitki ranneklassovykh otnosheniĭ: religiĭa i narodnye verovaniĭa," *Narody Kavkaza*, vol. 2 (Moscow: 1962), pp. 308-320.

SOURCE: "V.V. Bardavelidze," *Sovetskaĭa ètnografiĭa*, no. 2 (1971), pp. 179-181.

A.M. Reshetov
[Translation from Russian: Thomas L. Mann]

Barlow, Robert Hayward. Anthropologist, poet. Born in Leavenworth (Kansas) 18 May 1918, died in Azcapotzalco (Mexico) 2 January 1951. Robert Barlow was a prolific scholar and creative artist who abandoned several careers before settling on anthropology.

As a teenager in Florida, he wrote short stories of the *Weird Tales* sort, and corresponded with (and eventually befriended) the reclusive fantasy writer H.P. Lovecraft. At Lovecraft's death in 1937, the still-teenaged Barlow was his executor (a measure more of Lovecraft's small circle of acquaintance than of Barlow's maturity).

Barlow began his post-secondary education at the Kansas City Art Institute, where he studied with Thomas Hart Benton. He then enrolled at San Francisco Junior College, at which point he joined Lawrence Hart's Activist poetry group. He privately published two volumes of poetry, *Poems for a Competition* (1942) and *Views from a Hill* (1947); the former won the 26th annual Emily Chamberlain Cook poetry prize.

After a year at the School of Anthropology attached to Mexico's Instituto Nacional de Ciencias Biologicas (National Institute of Biological Sciences), Barlow studied anthropology and geography at the University of California, under ALFRED L. KROEBER and CARL SAUER. Obtaining his B.A. in 1942, Barlow continued working in anthropology at Berkeley as a research associate for a year and was then awarded a Rockefeller Foundation Fellowship in 1944. With this, and with his later Guggenheim Foundation

Fellowship (1946-1948), Barlow located and studied documentary sources on pre-Hispanic and colonial Mexico. He became fluent in both Spanish and Nahuatl; a measure of his mastery of both languages was his appointment in 1945 as head of the Nahuatl-speakers' literacy project for the state of Morelos. Barlow taught anthropology at the Universidad Nacional Autonoma (National Autonomous University) and Nahuatl at the Escuela Nacional de Antropología (National School of Anthropology) and was for the last two years of his life chairman of the anthropology department of Mexico City College. During this period he was also a research associate of the Carnegie Institute of Washington, studying Mayan languages and linguistics.

In 1943 Barlow founded *Tlalocan,* a journal that has long provided a home for articles on Mexican history and culture. Barlow himself published more than fifty articles in *Tlalocan,* but this represented only a small part of his output. He published more than ninety articles and translations in other journals as well, ranging in subject matter from archaeology to linguistics, ethnohistory to bibliography.

His amazing industry allowed Barlow to find and utilize a large number of documents pertaining to the Mexican past, and his depth of learning and sensitivity to cultural variation aided him in their interpretation. While he could fall victim to an *idée fixe* (for example, Barlow railed against the widely understood term "Aztec," demanding that it be replaced in scholarly usage by the obscure "Culhua México"), for the most part his contributions were sound. His work in the 1940s helped define the future direction of Mexican anthropology.

Barlow's productivity from 1943 to 1950 was staggering, but the major contributions of a mature scholar—the sustained efforts and magisterial syntheses—were never to come for Robert Barlow. Threatened with exposure as a homosexual, Barlow chose New Year's Day 1951 for his suicide. He took an overdose of seconal and left a note that read (characteristically, in Mayan) "Do not disturb me, I want to sleep a long time."

MAJOR WORKS: "The periods of tribute collection in Moctezuma's Empire," *Notes on Middle American Archaeology and Ethnology (Carnegie Institution),* no. 23 (1943); "La cronica X," *Revista Mexicana de Estudios Antropológicos,* vol. 7 (1945), pp. 65-87; "Conquistas de los antiguos Mexicanos," *Journal de la Société des Américanistes de Paris,* vol. 36 (1947), pp. 215-222; *The Extent of the Empire of the Culhua Mexica* (Berkeley: 1949); (with Byron McAfee) *Diccionario de elementos fonéticos en escritura jeroglífica (Codice Mendocino)* (Mexico City: 1949).

SOURCES: Charles E. Dibble, "Robert Hayward Barlow—1918-1951," *American Antiquity,* vol. 16 (1951), p. 347; Lawrence Hart, "A note on Robert Barlow," *Poetry,* vol. 78, pp. 115-119 (1951); Norman A. McQuown, "Robert Hamilton [sic] Barlow, 1918-1951," *American Anthropologist,* vol. 53 (1951), p. 543; H. Leon Abrams, Jr., *Robert Hayward Barlow: an Annotated Bibliography* (Greeley, Colorado: 1981).

David Lonergan

Barnett, Homer Garner. Anthropologist. Born in Bisbee (Arizona) 25 April 1906, died in Eugene (Oregon) 9 May 1985. Barnett was a long-time student of cultural change and acculturation and a pioneer of applied anthropology.

After taking a bachelor's degree in mathematics at Stanford in 1927, Barnett spent the next several years at a variety of jobs and traveling in Europe. In 1932 Barnett began graduate training in anthropology at Berkeley, a student of ALFRED L. KROEBER and

RONALD OLSON. Involved in "culture element distribution studies" in Oregon and British Columbia, Barnett retained a Pacific Coast orientation in fieldwork among the Yurok and in his doctoral dissertation, *The Nature and Function of the Potlatch.*

In 1939 Barnett joined the anthropology department at the University of Oregon, where he remained—apart from periods of government service—for the rest of his life. He became interested in the fledgling subdiscipline of applied anthropology and put his interest to active work during and after World War II. First as a staff member of the Bureau of American Ethnology during 1944-1946 and later as staff anthropologist for the Trust Territory of the Pacific (under the American Department of the Interior) in 1951-1953, Barnett was a specialist on change in Palau and neighboring islands. He also did independent fieldwork on Palau in 1947.

Throughout his career Barnett remained interested in two matters—the nature of cultural change and the potential of applied anthropology to improve the human condition. His approach was one of optimism.

In the early 1960s Barnett served as vice-president, then president, of the Society for Applied Anthropology, and in 1964-1965 he was a fellow at the Center for Advanced Study. He continued his research and writing on change into retirement, publishing his *Qualitative Science* at the age of 77.

MAJOR WORKS: *Palauan Society* (Eugene: 1949); *Innovation: the Basis of Cultural Change* (New York: 1953); *The Coast Salish of British Columbia* (Eugene: 1955); *Anthropology in Administration* (Evanston: 1956); *Indian Shakers* (Carbondale: 1957); *Being a Palauan* (New York: 1960); *The Nature and Function of the Potlatch* (Eugene: 1968); *Qualitative Science* (New York: 1983).

SOURCE: Theodore Stern, "Homer Garner Barnett (1906-1985)," *American Anthropologist,* vol. 89 (1987), pp. 701-703.

David Lonergan

Barrett, Samuel Alfred. Anthropologist, ethnologist, museologist. Born in Conway (Alaska) 12 November 1879, died in Santa Rosa (California) 9 March 1965. Barrett received his undergraduate and graduate education at the University of California, Berkeley, where he obtained a Ph.D. in anthropology in 1908. After graduation, he served as ethnologist of the George G. Heye Expedition for the year 1908-1909, engaging in ethnological and linguistic research among the Cayapa Indians of Ecuador. He held the position of curator of anthropology at the Milwaukee Public Museum from 1909 to 1920 when he became director of the museum, a post he occupied until 1940. During this same year, Barrett was called upon to direct the Exhibit of Aboriginal Cultures of the Western Hemisphere at the Golden Gate International Exposition in San Francisco. From 1943 to 1944, he served as associate director of the Army Specialized Training Program on the Berkeley campus of the University of California. Shortly thereafter, Barrett was appointed research associate of the Museum of Anthropology at Berkeley and from 1960 to 1965 served as director and principal investigator of American Indian Films.

From the standpoint of research, Samuel Barrett was most noted for his contributions to the ethnography of California. From 1903 to 1907 he undertook fieldwork among the Pomo, Miwok, Maidu, Yokuts, Yuki and Wintun for the Department of Anthropology at Berkeley. Barrett's appointment as curator of anthropology at the Milwaukee Public

Museum in 1909 gave him the opportunity to study other American Indians including the Chippewa and Menomini peoples of Northern Wisconsin and the Hopi of Arizona. He also contributed significantly to the archaeology of Wisconsin with his research of the Aztalan site located in Jefferson County, Wisconsin. Barrett's contributions to the field of museology are best viewed in his work in Wisconsin. The Barrett era at the Milwaukee Public Museum was characterized by the implementation of numerous projects along the lines of traditional anthropological research and those designed to improve the visual educational function of the museum. To this end, he utilized both still and motion picture film to supplement the verbal description of cultures. This was an important innovation that preceded its common use in ethnographic research by many years and served as an important adjunct to the education programs of the museum. Barrett was also a pioneer in the use of recreated cultural settings to convey information. This exhibit technique displayed groups of objects in context, allowing the visiting public glimpses into the life and culture of distant peoples. Barrett was also influential in initiating the Museum's *Bulletin* series as its primary source of publication.

Samuel Barrett and ALFRED L. KROEBER had been friends for many years and it was their collaboration that led to the establishment of American Indian Films. The primary goal of American Indian Films was the production of educational films; its secondary objective was the documentation of the remaining forms of traditional American Indian life. At the time of Barrett's death in 1965, there was motion picture documentation of fieldwork among twenty Indian groups. American Indian Films represents Barrett's final contribution to his discipline and probably his most significant contribution to the ethnography of North America.

MAJOR WORKS: *The Ethnogeography of the Pomo and Neighboring Indians.* (Berkeley: 1908); *Pomo Indian Basketry* (Berkeley: 1908); *The Cream Dance of the Chippewa and Menominee Indians of Northern Wisconsin* (Milwaukee: 1911); *The Wintun Hesi Ceremony* (Berkeley: 1919); *The Cayapa Indians of Ecuador* (New York: 1925); *Ancient Aztalan* (Milwaukee: 1933); *Pomo Myths* (Milwaukee: 1933); *Report of the Committee on Training for Museum Work, American Association of Museums* (Washington: 1926). FILMS: *The Sinew-Backed Bow and Its Arrows* (Berkeley: 1961); *Totem Pole* (Berkeley: 1963); *Calumet: the Pipe of Peace* (Berkeley: 1964).

SOURCES: David W. Peri and Robert W. Wharton, "Samuel Alfred Barrett, 1879-1965," *Kroeber Anthropological Society Papers*, vol. 33 (1965), pp. 3-35; Nancy O. Lurie, *A Special Style: the Milwaukee Public Museum, 1882-1982* (Milwaukee: 1983).

Donald J. Terras

Barrows, David Prescott. Educator, administrator, anthropologist, soldier. Born in Chicago (Illinois) 27 June 1873, died in Orinda (California) 5 September 1954. Barrows completed the B.A. degree at Pomona College (Claremont, California) in 1894. He was to spend nine summers doing field research among the Coahuilla and other tribal groups of southern California and Colorado. He completed the M.A. in political science at the University of California in 1895. His Ph.D. dissertation (1897) on Coahuilla ethnobotany was written at the University of Chicago under the direction of FREDERICK STARR. On the recommendation of a friend, Benjamin Ide Wheeler, Barrows was named in 1900 to the position of Superintendent of Schools for Manila (Philippine Islands). As chief of the Bureau of Non-Christian Tribes (1901-1903) Barrows traveled in remote regions of the islands, gathering ethnographic data and directing surveys of the Negritos, Ilongots and other minorities. Barrows' writings on Philippine ethnography include a major section of the 1903 *Census of the Philippine Islands* titled "Population." Barrows was responsible for planning the Philippine ethnographic exhibits for the 1904 Louisiana Purchase Centennial Exposition in St. Louis. From 1903 to 1909 Barrows occupied the Philippine government post of General Superintendent of Education. He pursued an innovative policy of "universal primary instruction" for young Filipinos. By 1906, Barrows' Jeffersonian educational policies were being increasingly opposed by advocates of utilitarian and industrial education. The history of this "Jeffersonian experiment" in Philippine education has been described by Glenn May in *Social Engineering in the Philippines*. Resigning his position as General Superintendent, Barrows returned to the United States in 1909 to become Professor of Education and, later, Dean of the Graduate School at the University of California. Barrows' subsequent career was varied and eventful. As President of the University of California (1919-1923), he presided over a period of growth at that institution. A volume of memoirs was completed prior to Barrows' death in 1954. Barrows' papers are at the Bancroft Library, University of California.

> MAJOR WORKS: *The Ethno-Botany of the Coahuillla Indians of Southern California* (Chicago: 1900); *A History of the Philippines* (Yonkers-on-Hudson: 1905); *Memoirs of David Prescott Barrows, 1873-1954* (Berkeley: [ca. 1954]); "David P. Barrows' notes on Philippine ethnology, edited by Edward Norbeck," *Journal of East Asiatic Studies*, vol. 5 (1956), pp. 228-254; "The Negrito and allied types in the Philippines," *American Anthropologist*, n.s., vol. 12 (1910), pp. 358-376; "Population" in: *Census of the Philippine Islands ... 1903*, vol. 1 (Washington: 1905), pp. 411-585.

> SOURCES: "Barrows, David Prescott" in: *National Cyclopedia of American Biography* (New York [etc.]: 1892-), vol. 52, p. 154; "David Barrows ...," *New York Times* (6 September 1954), p. 15; Lowell John Bean, "David Prescott Barrows: an ethnographic perspective" in: David P. Barrows, *The Ethno-Botany of the Coahuilla Indians of Southern California* (Banning, Calif.: 1967), pp. xi-xx; Kenton J. Clymer, "Humanitarian imperialism: David Prescott Barrows and the white man's burden in the Philippines," *Pacific Historical Review*, vol. 45 (1976), pp. 495-517; Glenn A. May, *Social Engineering in the Philippines: the Aims, Execution, and Impact of American Colonial Policy, 1900-1913* (Westport, Conn.: 1980), pp. 97-112.

Lee S. Dutton

Barth, Heinrich. Geographer, linguist, traveler. Born in Hamburg (Germany) 16 February 1821, died in Berlin (Germany) 25 November 1865. Barth was "one of the most significant scientific travelers of all time" (*Meyers-Konversations-Lexikon*). After attending the Johanneum in Hamburg, in 1839 Barth began to study geography, linguistics and archaeology in Berlin as a student of Carl Ritter (1779-1859). In 1840, he traveled to Italy and Sicily in order to become personally acquainted with historical sites. This fascination with antiquity may also be recognized in his dissertation, *Corinthiorum commercii et mercaturae historiae particula*, for which he was awarded a doctorate in 1844 at Berlin. After a brief stay in London, where he studied Arabic, Barth set out in 1845 on a three-year odyssey around the Mediterranean, traveling especially to the countries of North Africa and the Middle East. Upon returning to Berlin, he qualified as a university reader late in 1848.

At the urging of Chr. von Bunsen and A. Petermann, Barth, together with A. Overweg, joined the British expeditionary force to "Central Africa" in 1849 under the leadership of J. Richardson, whose objective was the abolition of the slave trade. On 24 March 1850, the expedition left Tripoli bound via Murzuk to Aïr, from which Barth made a sidetrip to Agadès. There he learned Tamasheq, the language of the Tuareg, and, most significantly, Hausa, which soon became his favorite tongue. In January of 1851, the travelers parted company, and Barth marched on via Katsina and Kano to Kuka (Kukawa), the capital of the state of Bornu. There, in early May 1851, he met with Overweg again. Richardson had died at Ungurutua on 4 March 1851. Barth assumed leadership of the expedition, investigated the shore of Lake Chad and initiated his fundamental studies on the language and history of the Kanuri. On 29 May 1851, he departed for Adamawa, where he came upon the upper Benue River on 18 June. He arrived back in Kuka on 22 July, from which he and Overweg made a three-month trip to Kanem in September. From November 1851 to January 1852, while traveling with a band of slave raiders, Barth visited the land of the Musgu and from March to August the territory of the Bagirmi. During these journeys Barth laid out geographical and cultural-historical notes and records as well as glossaries and vocabularies of the languages of the Teda (Tubu), Wandala, Bagirmi, Maba, Abu-Sarib and Logone. After the death of Overweg on 27 September 1852 at Maduari on Lake Chad, Barth set out in November on a journey to Timbuktu, which was to last two years. Traveling through Kano, Katsina and Sokoto, on 12 June 1853 he reached the Niger and on 7 September Timbuktu. Following a stay of eight months, despite great danger to his life, he succeeded in setting out on 18 May 1854 on his return journey to Kuka. On 1 December he encountered E. Vogel at Bundi; Vogel had been sent to his aid. In early May 1855, Barth departed Kuka, traveling via Bilma and Tripoli to Europe. Although he was received with great honors upon his arrival on 8 September, his contributions were not treated as having enduring value. ALEXANDER VON HUMBOLDT, for example, wrote (in *Briefwechsel mit Berghaus*) "It is a shame, an eternal shame, that Barth understands nothing of the most basic principle of geography, location. Through this deficiency the geography of Central Africa has suffered a great loss of exact data."

After returning to Berlin, Barth resumed his academic lecturing and in a very brief time completed his monumental five-volume account of his journey, *Reisen und Entdeckungen in Nord- und Zentralafrika in den Jahren 1849-1855*. The geographical societies of London and Paris awarded him their most distinguished gold medals and Oxford University granted him an honorary doctorate, and in 1863 he became Professor of Geography at Berlin. He established the K. Ritter Foundation and served as president of the Geographical Society of Berlin. Every year he undertook new journeys—in the autumn of 1858 to northern Turkey, in 1861 to Spain, in 1862 and 1865 back to Turkey and in 1864 to Italy. To comprehend and describe the "historical connection of humanity to the rich diversity of the surface of the earth" was Barth's chief goal, which he pursued via his exploratory travels. His survey of the routes of roads, river systems, fauna, flora, peoples and languages, carried out with painstaking care and persistence, shaped for the future an inexhaustible source of information on the history of Africa.

MAJOR WORKS: *Wanderungen durch die Küstenländer des Mittelmeeres, ausgeführt in den Jahren 1845, 1846 and 1847* (Berlin: 1849); *Reisen und Entdeckungen in Nord- und Zentralafrika in den Jahren 1849-1855* [5 vols.] (Gotha: 1857-1858; abridged ed. [2 vols.], Gotha: 1859-1860) [tr.: *Travels and Discoveries in North and Central Africa: being a Journal of an Expedition Undertaken under the Auspices of H.B.M.'s Government in the Years 1849-1855* [5 vols.] (New York and

London: 1857-1858); *Henri Barth chez les Touaregs de l'Aïr* (Niamey: 1972) (= *Études nigériennes*, no. 28)]; *Reise von Trapezunt durch die nördliche Hälfte Klein-Asiens nach Scutari im Herbst 1858* (Gotha: 1860); *Sammlung und Bearbeitung Central-Afrikanischer Vokabularien* (Gotha: 1862, 1863, 1866; 2nd ed. London: 1971); "Beschreibung einer Reise quer durch das Innere der Europäischen Türkei," *Zeitschrift für allgemeine Erdkunde in Berlin*, vol. 15 (1863), pp. 301-368 and vol. 16 (1864), pp. 117-208.

SOURCES: *Allgemeine Deutsche-Biographie*, vol. 2 (Berlin: 1875; 2nd ed., Berlin: 1967); P.A. Benton, *The Languages and Peoples of Bornu* [2 vols.] (London: 1912; 2nd ed., London: 1968); E.W. Bovill, "Henry Barth," *Journal of the Royal African Society*, 25/100 (1926), pp. 311-320; H. Schnee (editor), *Deutsches Kolonial-Lexikon*, vol. 1 (Leipzig: 1920); Herrmann Jungraithmayr and Rudolf Leger, "Barth, Heinrich B." in: H. Jungraithmayr and W.J.G. Möhlig (editors), *Lexikon der Afrikanistik* (Berlin: 1983), pp. 47-48; *Meyers Konversations-Lexikon* (3rd ed., Leipzig: 1874); R. Prietze, "Die sprachlichen Sammlungen Barth's, Nachtigal's und Rohlf's," *Zeitschrift für afrikanische und ozeanische Sprachen*, vol. 2 (1896), pp. 195-196; H. Schiffers, *Heinrich Barth: ein Forscher in Afrika: Leben, Werk, Leistung* (Wiesbaden: 1967).

Rudolf Leger
[Translation from German: Robert B. Marks Ridinger]

Bartlett, Harley Harris. Botanist, ethnographer. Born in Anaconda (Montana) 9 March 1886, died in Ann Arbor (Michigan) 21 February 1960. Bartlett received the A.B. degree in chemistry from Harvard University in 1908. Although most of his career would be devoted to the field of botany, he received little formal instruction in that discipline. A lifelong affiliation with the Faculty of Botany, University of Michigan, began in 1915. He served as director of the University of Michigan Botanical Gardens (1919-1956) and chair of the Department of Botany (1923-1947). Professor Bartlett's first Southeast Asian field experience was in 1918 when he worked in east Sumatra as a research botanist on behalf of the United States Rubber Company. Contacts with the Batak people of Asahan, eastern Sumatra, soon inspired an interest in Sumatran ethnography. Initial ethnographic writings include a study on the manufacture of sugar by the Batak and an article on Batak grave-posts ("The grave-post (Anisan) of the Batak of Asahan"). The American botanist became an enthusiastic collector of Batak bamboo manuscripts. Bartlett returned to Sumatra in 1927 and published a detailed study of Batak religion and magic, *The Labors of the Datoe*, in 1930-1931. Bartlett's ethnographic interests were broadened by subsequent visits to the Philippines and other tropical regions. During a year at the University of the Philippines (1934-1935) he expanded his collection of Philippine vernacular publications. A major bibliographic and documentation project on *Fire in Relation to Primitive Agriculture and Grazing in the Tropics* was only partially complete at the time of Bartlett's death in 1960. In 1973, many of his writings on the Batak were collected and reprinted in a retrospective volume, *The Labors of the Datoe and Other Essays*. In a review of this volume, Petrus Voorhoeve has emphasized the special value of Bartlett's pre-World War II work on the Batak, while noting that the post-war translations suffered as a result of the translator's long absence from Sumatra. A list of Bartlett's botanical, ethnographic and other publications is included in an article by Edward Voss. A very detailed source of autobiographical information is *The Harley Harris Bartlett Diaries (1926-1959)*. The Bartlett collection of Batak manuscripts has been described by Petrus Voorhoeve. Various Bartlett collections of botanical specimens, manuscripts, books, artifacts and photographs are now in several locations. Bartlett collections can be found at the University of Michigan (Ann

Arbor), at the Library of the American Philosophical Society (Philadelphia) and at the Logan Museum (Beloit, Wisconsin).

MAJOR WORKS: "The grave-post (Anisan) of the Batak of Asahan," *Michigan Academy of Science, Arts and Letters, Papers*, vol. 1 (1923), pp. 1-58; *The Labors of the Datoe* (Ann Arbor: 1930-1931) (= *Papers, Michigan Academy of Sciences, Arts and letters*, vol. 12, pp. 1-74; and vol. 14, pp. 1-34); *The Sacred Edifices of the Batak of Sumatra* (Ann Arbor: 1934) (= *Occasional Contributions from the Museum of Anthropology of the University of Michigan*, no. 4); *Fire in Relation to Primitive Agriculture and Grazing in the Tropics: Annotated Bibliography* [3 vols.] (Ann Arbor: 1955-1961); *The Labors of the Datoe and Other Essays on the Bataks of Asahan (North Sumatra)* (Ann Arbor: 1973) (= *Michigan Papers on South and Southeast Asia*, no. 5); *The Harley Harris Bartlett Diaries (1926-1959)* (Kenneth Lester Jones, editor) (Ann Arbor: 1975).

SOURCES: Edward G. Voss, "Harley Harris Bartlett," *Bulletin of the Torrey Botanical Club*, vol. 88, no. 1 (Jan. 1961), pp. 47-56; Petrus Voorhoeve, "H.H. Bartlett's batak manuscripts collection," *Indonesia Circle*, vol. 22 (June 1980), pp. 70-72; R.C. Ileto, "The Bartlett Collection and Philippine Studies in Australia" [unpublished, 7 leaves]; "Bartlett, Harley Harris" in: *American Men of Science: a Biographical Directory* (9th ed., Lancaster, Pa.: 1955), vol. 2 (*Biological Sciences*), p. 61.

Lee S. Dutton

Bascom, William R. Anthropologist, folklorist. Born in Princeton (Illinois) 23 May 1912, died in Berkeley (California) 11 September 1981. Bascom received his doctorate at Northwestern University in 1939 under MELVILLE J. HERSKOVITS and taught there with him until 1957, except during World War II. In 1957 he became Professor of Anthropology and Curator of the Robert H. Lowie Museum of Anthropology at the University of California, Berkeley, where he remained until he retired in 1979. He was a well known folklorist, contributing much to the analysis of African folklore, and he provided substantial evidence for the African provenience of African-American oral literature. He carried out extensive research over the years on the Yoruba of southwestern Nigeria, beginning in 1937. He was one of the first American anthropologists to work in Africa and also conducted research on the African-American connection with Africa among the Gulla of South Carolina in 1939 and in Cuba in the late 1940s. Following World War II he did fieldwork in Ponape in Micronesia. Bascom pioneered in the study of divination among the Yoruba and among African-Americans in the New World, showing historical connections and the possibilities of the close translation and analysis of diviners' texts. He was the first to call attention to the fact that Yoruba urban centers did not fit Western social science conceptions of the city, calling for a broadening of ideas on urbanism. He pioneered in the study of Yoruba cult groups, art and oral literature. A cultural rather than a social anthropologist, he is known for his careful delineation of basic concepts and terms and for his ethnographic excellence, rather than for grand theory. During his term as Director of the Robert H. Lowie Museum, extensive additions were made to its ethnographic collections.

MAJOR WORKS: *The Sociological Role of the Yoruba Cult Group* (Menasha, Wisconsin: 1944); *Drums of the Yoruba of Nigeria* [recording] (New York: 1953); (with Paul Gebauer) *Handbook of West African Art* (Milwaukee: 1953); (with Melville J. Herskovits) *Continuity and Change in African Cultures* (Chicago: 1959); *Ponape: a Pacific Economy in Transition* (Berkeley: 1965); *Ifa Divination: Communication Between Gods and Men in West Africa* (Bloomington: 1969); *The Yoruba of Southwestern Nigeria* (New York: 1969); *African Art in Cultural Perspective: an Introduction* (New York: 1973); *African Dilemma Tales* (The Hague: 1975); *Sixteen Cowries: Yoruba*

Divination from Africa to the New World (Bloomington: 1980); *Contributions to Folkloristics* (Meerut, India: 1981).

SOURCES: "The anthropology of William R. Bascom," and "Bibliography of William R. Bascom" in: Simon Ottenberg (editor), *African Religious Groups and Beliefs: Papers in Honor of William R. Bascom* (Meerut, India: 1982), pp. 3-18, 333-350; Daniel Crowley and Alan Dundas, "William Russell Bascom," *Journal of American Folklore*, vol. 95 (1982), pp. 465-467; William Bascom, "Perhaps too much to chew?" *Western Folklore*, vol. 40 (1981), pp. 285-293.

Simon Ottenberg

Basehart, Harry W. Anthropologist. Born in Zanesville (Ohio) 15 February 1910, died in Albuquerque (New Mexico) 27 December 1988. Basehart began formal study of anthropology in 1939 at the University of Chicago. Older than the average student, Basehart qualified for graduate study without an undergraduate degree by passing a series of examinations, an option then available at Chicago. He began fieldwork in 1941 among the Oneida Indians as an employee of the Works Progress Administration.

In 1942 Basehart was drafted into the Army and served more than four years as an intelligence officer. He spent part of the war in Africa, attached to the Office of Strategic Services. After the war, he returned to the University of Chicago and then moved to Harvard University where he took his master's and doctoral degrees in 1952 and 1953, respectively. His dissertation was on Iroquoian social organization; his interest in matriliny would manifest itself throughout his career.

Basehart taught at Goucher College and at Harvard before coming to the University of New Mexico in 1954, where he taught until his retirement in 1975. In Albuquerque Basehart rapidly became a favorite professor of the anthropology students and devoted much of his time to aiding and advising them.

In the late 1950s, Basehart directed a number of research projects on various Apache Indian reservations, largely with regard to land claims. He did a great deal of fieldwork himself, amassing information on land use patterns. By 1962 he and his colleague STANLEY NEWMAN had become the editors of the *Southwestern Journal of Anthropology*, a New Mexico-based journal. Basehart gave perhaps more time to the journal than was good for his career, for his own rate of publication suffered as he helped others improve their work. Basehart and Newman were co-editors until 1970 when Basehart became sole editor. He held that post until his retirement in 1975. In 1977, at his suggestion, its name was changed to the *Journal of Anthropological Research*; during 1981-1982 he was called back from retirement to serve as editor again. He remained on the editorial board for the rest of his life.

In 1963, at an age when many scholars have already begun to rest on their laurels, Basehart spent a year in Tanzania, doing fieldwork among the Matengo. Earlier he had participated in the DAVID M. SCHNEIDER/Kathleen Gough symposium on matrilineal kinship, presenting a paper on the Ashanti.

Basehart was chosen to head the anthropology department at the University of New Mexico in 1971 and served in that role for three years. He was also active in anthropological organizations, serving as treasurer of the American Ethnological Society, as a member of the editorial board of the *American Anthropologist* and in many other capacities.

Due to his late start in academe, his editorial and administrative duties, and his devotion to his students, Basehart's apparent mark upon the anthropological record is smaller than that of many of his contemporaries. However, in less evident ways, the activities that seem to have limited his written *oeuvre* allowed Basehart to make a mark on the quality of anthropological education and scholarship.

MAJOR WORKS: "Ashanti" in: David M. Schneider and Kathleen Gough (editors), *Matrilineal Kinship* (Berkeley: 1962), pp. 270-297; "Traditional history and political change among the Matengo," *Africa*, vol. 42 (1972), pp. 87-97; "Cultivation intensity, settlement patterns, and homestead forms among the Matengo of Tanzania," *Ethnology*, vol. 12 (1973), pp. 57-73; "Mescalero Apache subsistence patterns and socio-political organization" in: *Apache Indians*, vol. 12 (New York: 1974), pp. 9-178.

SOURCES: Stanley Newman, "Harry W. Basehart: an appreciation" in: Linda Cordell and Stephen Beckerman (editors), *The Versatility of Kinship* (New York: 1980), pp. xiii-xv; Claire R. Farrar, "Harry W. Basehart," *Anthropology Newsletter*, vol. 30, no. 3 (March 1989), p. 5.

David Lonergan

Bastian, Adolf. Ethnologist. Born in Bremen (Germany) 26 June 1826, died in Port of Spain (Trinidad) 2 February 1905. The son of a wealthy merchant family, Bastian began his academic training in the field of law at Heidelberg, followed by studies in medicine and the natural sciences at Berlin, Jena and Würzburg. After completing his professional training in the medical sciences at Charles University in Prague in 1850, he began the first of a series of lengthy voyages to far corners of the world as a ship's doctor. Between 1851 and 1860 his travels carried him to Peru, the West Indies, Mexico, China, the Malay Archipelago, Australia, China, India and Africa. Out of these experiences he drew much of the material that appeared in 1860 as *Der Mensch in der Geschichte*, which has been called "the first detailed description of exotic civilizations by one who had seen and heard for himself" (Goldenweiser, p. 476). Five more years of travel provided the core data for the six-volume work *Die Völker des östlichen Asiens: Studien und Reisen*, which describes the cultures of Burma, Thailand, Cambodia and Indonesia and which was followed in the later 1870s by *Die Culturländer des alten America*. It was these descriptive works that laid the foundations for many of Bastian's later theoretical proposals in the field of what would later become ethnology.

Noting similarities among the many cultures he had observed, he proposed a "psychic unity of mankind." The basic tenets of this view were set out in three separate publications, issued between 1881 and 1895, *Der Völkergedanke und seine Begründung auf Ethnologische Sammlungen*, *Zur Lehre von den geographischen Provinzen* and *Ethnische Elementargedanken in der Lehre vom Menschen*. Approaching the question of cultural similarities from the scientific and legal framework of thought that outlined uniform causes for disparate effects, Bastian proposed that the psychic unity of mankind took the form of a set of *Elementargedanken* (elementary ideas) that could be derived from the social institutions, aesthetics and religious concepts of a culture. These comprise a rather limited pool from which the *Völkergedanken* (folk ideas) emerge as expressions of the basic ideas, influenced by variations in physical environment and historical events.

Bastian was also the founder of the Königliche Museum für Völkerkunde (Royal Ethnographic Museum) in Berlin, an institution whose superb collections of ethnographic materials reflect his indefatigable career of travel, and together with Rudolf Virchow (1821-1902) was co-founder of the Berliner Gesellschaft für Anthropologie, Ethnologie und Urgeschichte (Berlin Society for Anthropology, Ethnology and Prehistory). The idea of the collective unconscious presented by Carl Jung derives directly from Bastian's work, and later anthropologists whose work showed the influence of Bastian's theories included FRANZ BOAS, A.R. RADCLIFFE-BROWN, BRONISLAW MALINOWSKI and A.C. HADDON.

MAJOR WORKS: *Ein Besuch in San Salvador, der Hauptstadt des Königreichs Congo: ein Beitrag zur Mythologie und Psychologie* (Bremen: 1859); *Der Mensch in der Geschichte: zur Begründung einer Psychologischen Weltanschauung* (Leipzig: 1860); *Die Völker des östlichen Asien: Studien und Reisen* [6 vols.: I. *Die Geschichte der Indochinesen*; II. *Reisen in Birma*; III. *Reisen in Siam*; IV. *Reise durch Kambodja*; V. *Reisen im indischen Archipel*; VI. *Reisen in China*] (Leipzig: 1866-1871); *Beiträge zur vergleichenden Psychologie: die Seele und ihre Erscheinungsweisen in der Ethnographie* (Berlin: 1868); *Das Beständige in den Menschenrassen und die Spielweite ihrer Veränderlichkeit: Prolegomena zu einer Ethnologie der Culturvölker* (Berlin: 1868); *Sprachvergleichende Studien, mit besonderer Berücksichtigung der indochinesischen Sprachen* (Leipzig: 1870); *Die Culturländer des alten America* [3 vols. in 4] (Berlin: 1878-1889); *Der Völkergedanke im Aufbau einer Wissenschaft vom Menschen: und seine Begründung auf ethnologische Sammlungen* (Berlin: 1881); *Allgemeine Grundzüge der Ethnologie* (Berlin: 1884); *Indonesien, oder, Die Inseln des Malayischen Archipel* [5 vols. in 1] (Berlin: 1884-1894); *Zur Lehre von den geographischen Provinzen* (Berlin: 1886); *Ethnische Elementargedanken in der Lehre vom Menschen* (Berlin: 1895); *Die Lehre vom Denken: zur Ergänzung der naturwissenschaftlichen Psychologie für Ueberleitung* [3 vols. in 2] (Berlin: 1902-1905).

SOURCES: Alexander Goldenweiser, "Bastian, Adolf" in: E.R.A. Seligman (editor), *Encyclopaedia of the Social Sciences* (New York: 1937), vol. 2, p. 476; Herbert Baldus, "Bastian, Adolf" in: David L. Sills (editor), *International Encyclopedia of the Social Sciences* (New York: 1968-1979), vol. 2, pp. 23-24; Hoffman Reynolds Hays, "Adolf Bastian" in: Hoffman Reynolds Hays, *Explorers of Man* (New York: 1971), pp. 63-103.

Robert B. Marks Ridinger

Bastide, Roger. Sociologist, ethnographer. Born in Nîmes (France) 1 April 1898, died in France 10 April 1974. Bastide was a major contributor to the study of Afro-Brazilian religion.

He came from a Protestant family and studied theology. Having published two works on the sociology of religion, Bastide went to Brazil in 1937 to lecture at the University of São Paulo. He stayed sixteen years, doing considerable field research; he also published a good deal, especially on popular religion but also on many other subjects. The years Bastide spent in Brazil were a period of great ferment in its cultural life, when Brazil's intellectuals were discovering their country and reforming its educational system. Bastide contributed in a major way to these activities. More than many scholars from Europe and North America in what we today call the Third World, he relied to a large extent on local scholarship as a source, e.g., the work of RAIMUNDO NINA RODRIGUES, ARTHUR RAMOS, Manuel Querino (1851-1923) and others; he was also familiar with the work of MELVILLE J. HERSKOVITS.

Bastide returned to France in 1954. It was here where he wrote and published his two major works on Brazilian religion, *Le candomblé* and *Les religions africaines au Brésil*. These works were not just about the popular religions of Afro-Brazilians but also dealt with such larger issues as the interpenetration of cultures. In later years Bastide also wrote on such subjects as race relations, the sociology of mental illness, the meaning of "structure" and applied anthropology. He taught at the École Pratique des Hautes Études, the Institut des Hautes Études d'Amérique Latine and at the University of Paris. During 1961-1962 he founded the Centre de Psychiatrie Sociale, which he directed until his death.

MAJOR WORKS: *Éléments de sociologie religieuse* (Paris: 1935); *Le candomblé de Bahia: rite Nagô* (Paris and The Hague: 1958) [tr.: *O candomblé da Bahia: rito Nagô* (São Paolo: 1958)]; *Les religions afro-brésiliennes: contribution à une sociologie des interpénétrations de civilisations* (Paris: 1960) [tr.: *The African Religions of Brazil* (Baltimore: 1978); *As religiões africanas no Brasil* [2 vols.] (São Paulo: 1971)]; *La sociologie des maladies mentales* (Paris: 1965) [tr.: *Sociologia das doenças mentais* (São Paulo: 1967)]; *Les Amériques noires* (Paris: 1967) [tr.: *African Civilizations in the New World* (London: 1971); *As Américas negras* (São Paulo: 1974)]; *Anthropologie appliquée* (Paris: 1971); *Estudos afro-brasileiros* (São Paulo: 1973); *Le sacré sauvage, et autres essais* (Paris: 1975).

SOURCES: Maria Isaura Pereira de Queiroz "Nostalgia do outro e do alhures: a obra sociológica de Roger Bastide" in: Maria Isaura Pereira de Queiroz (organizer), *Roger Bastide* (São Paulo: 1983), pp. 7-75 [contains bibliography of major works, pp. 71-72]; *L'autre et l'ailleurs: hommages à Roger Bastide* (Paris: 1976) [contains bibliography of major works, pp. 501-509, as well as several essays about Bastide]; Richard Price, "Foreword" to: Roger Bastide, *The African Religions of Brazil* (Baltimore: 1978), pp. vii-xii; Andrew P. Lyons, "Bastide, Roger" in: David L. Sills (editor), *International Encyclopedia of the Social Sciences* (New York: 1968-1979), vol. 18, pp. 40-42.

Bateson, Gregory. Anthropologist, natural historian, philosopher. Born in Grantchester (England) 9 May 1904, died in San Francisco (California) 4 July 1980. Bateson was the son of William Bateson, a pioneer in the study of genetics, and the grandson of William Henry Bateson, a vicar and the master of St. John's College, Cambridge. In 1917 Bateson entered Charterhouse School and in 1922 matriculated at St. John's College, where he studied natural history. He obtained his bachelor's degree in 1925.

After a brief trip to the Galapagos Islands, Bateson began studying anthropology under A.C. HADDON. Under parental pressure to become a biologist, Bateson had gradually become aware that his interests lay elsewhere; anthropology was for him a means to escape the dullness of taxonomy, which had been a major thrust of his education. Bateson earned a master's degree in anthropology in 1930 after two years of fieldwork in New Britain and New Guinea as an Anthony Wilkin Student of Cambridge University. He also briefly served as a lecturer in linguistics at the University of Sydney, under A.R. RADCLIFFE-BROWN, in 1928.

In 1931 Bateson was elected a fellow of St. John's College; he spent the next two years in New Guinea. There he met his future wife, anthropologist MARGARET MEAD, and carried out the research for which he is best known. His book about the Iatmul people, *Naven*, was issued in 1936. Bateson lectured at Columbia University and the University of Chicago during 1934 and spent the period 1936-1938 in Bali with Mead.

Upon his return to New York in the late 1930s (for Bateson made the United States his home from that point on, becoming a naturalized citizen in 1956), he involved himself in the growing study of cybernetics with researchers such as John Von Neumann and Norbert Wiener. This new field offered him a way of expressing his long-standing interest in the process of communication within and between individuals.

In 1941 Bateson worked as an analyst of German propaganda films at the Museum of Modern Art, in New York. From 1942 until 1945 he was attached to the Office of Strategic Services, lecturing at the Columbia University school of government and administration and later serving in China, Burma, Ceylon (Sri Lanka) and India in a staff role.

After the war, Bateson spent one year each at the New School for Social Research and Harvard University as a visiting professor of anthropology and then moved to the University of California at San Francisco for 1948-1949. There he began one of the major investigations of his career, into communication among schizophrenics and their families. In 1949 he became research associate at the Langley Porter Clinic and in 1951 staff ethnologist at the Veterans Administration hospital in Palo Alto, California (a position he held until 1962). From 1951 until his death he was a visiting professor of anthropology at Stanford University.

In 1963-1964 he was the associate director of the Communication Research Institute at St. Thomas, U.S. Virgin Islands, and from 1964 until 1972 he served as associate director for research of the Oceanic Institute at Waimanalo, Hawaii. During this period he was involved in the study of porpoise communication, a still-debated subject; relatively little resulted from this long study.

In 1972 Bateson became a faculty member at Kresge College of the University of California at Santa Cruz and in 1976 was appointed to the Board of Regents of the University of California by then-governor Jerry Brown. This necessitated giving up his relationship with Kresge College, and he became scholar-in-residence at Esalen Institute in Big Sur, California.

Bateson was not deeply involved in any one academic department or discipline and brought his particular perspective to bear on a number of fields. By the end of his life he had moved through zoology, anthropology, psychology and ethology into what some observers regard as ecological mysticism.

MAJOR WORKS: *Naven* (Cambridge: 1936); (with Margaret Mead) *Balinese Character: a Photographic Analysis* (New York: 1942); (with Jurgen Ruesch) *Communication: the Social Matrix of Psychiatry* (New York: 1950); *Steps to an Ecology of Mind* (San Francisco: 1972); *Mind and Nature: a Necessary Unity* (New York: 1979).

SOURCES: David Lipset, *Gregory Bateson: the Legacy of a Scientist* (Englewood Cliffs, N.J.: 1980); Les Ledbetter, "Gregory Bateson dies on Coast: anthropologist and philosopher," *The New York Times* (7 July 1980), p. D13; Robert I. Levy and Roy Rappaport, "Gregory Bateson, 1904-1980," *American Anthropologist*, vol. 84 (1982), pp. 379-394.

David Lonergan

Baudouin de Courtenay Ehrenkreutz-Jędrzejewiczowa, Cezaria.

Ethnologist, ethnographer, classical philosopher, linguist. Born in Dorpat [now Tartu] (Estonia, Russia) 2 August 1885, died in London (England) 28 February 1967. Baudouin de Courtenay Ehrenkreutz-Jędrzejewiczowa completed studies at the University of Petersburg where she received her degree in 1910. She obtained her doctorate in 1922 and conducted post-doctoral work in ethnology and ethnography, subjects of her lectures at the University of Vilnius (1927-1934) and the University of Warsaw (1935-1939). She occupied the chair of Polish ethnography at the University of Warsaw as a full professor. After World War II she served as rector at the Polish University Abroad in London, where she also lectured in the field of ethnography.

Baudouin de Courtenay's earliest studies were in classical philosophy and linguistics. Her ethnographic research concentrated on the cultural links between the Hellenic-Byzantine and Slavic worlds. Her work was primarily concerned with ritual. She was interested in the structural role of rituals and in their cultural function as folk art. She also displayed an interest in religion, studying folk Catholicism and devoting special attention to the analysis of the cult of saints.

MAJOR WORKS: *Święta Cecylia: przyczynek do genezy apokryfów* [*St. Cecilia: the Source of the Genesis of the Apocrypha*] (Lwów: 1922); *Ze studiów nad obrzędami weselnymi ludu polskiego. Cz. 1. Forma dramatyczna obrzędowości weselnej* [*Studies of the Wedding Customs of the Polish Peasant. Part 1. Dramatic Form of the Wedding Custom*] (Vilnius: 1923); "O potrzebach etnologii w Polsce" ["Concerning the needs of ethnology in Poland"], *Nauka Polska*, vol. 10 (1929), pp. 250-258; *Święty Jerzy: patronem Harcerstwa* [*St. George: Patron of Boy Scouts*] (Jerusalem: 1944); *Wskazówki dla zbierających przedmioty dla muzeów etnograficznych* [*Indexes for Collectors for Ethnographic Museums*] (Jerusalem: 1944); "Polskie obrzędy doroczne" ["Annual Polish customs"] in: Henryk Paskiewicz, *Polska i jej dorobek dziejowy* [*Poland and her Historical Heritage*] (London: 1956).

SOURCES: Lucjan Turkowski, "Prof. dr. Cezaria Baudouin de Courtenay Ehrenkreutz-Jędrzejowiczowa," *Lud*, vol. 52 (1968), pp. 357-360; Anna Zadrożyńska-Barącz, "Fenomenologiczna koncepcja historii i kultury" ["Phenomenological conception of history and culture"], *Etnografia Polska*, vol. 12 (1968), pp. 15-27.

Maria Niewiadomska and Iwona Grzelakowska
[Translation from Polish: Joel Janicki]

Baumann, Hermann. Ethnologist. Born in Freiburg im Breisgau (Germany) 9 February 1902, died in Munich (West Germany) 30 July 1972. A student of Ernst Grosse (1862-1927) and Eugen Fischer (1874-1967) in Freiburg and Bernhard Ankermann (1859-1943) in Berlin, Baumann began his academic career in 1921 at the Berliner Museum für Völkerkunde (Ethnographic Museum). From 1939 to 1945 he was professor of ethnology at the University of Vienna and from 1955 to 1967 at the University of Munich.

Baumann's chief area of scholarship was African ethnology. He undertook research trips to Angola in 1930, 1954 and 1972. He published comprehensive comparative studies of numerous ancient African cultural phenomena: creation myths and primordial myths, "bush souls," lords of the animals, conceptions of *mana*, sun myths, forms of division of labor between the sexes, agricultural implements, etc.

Baumann was a leading figure in the Cultural-Historical School of ethnology, which he modernized to a significant extent, for example, by complementing the evidence of ethnographic data with prehistoric, linguistic and anthropological material. Following the models of LEO FROBENIUS and Ankermann, he developed in 1934 and subsequently modified a comprehensive view of the historical division of African cultures (earlier called *Kulturkreise*—cultural circles—and *Kulturschichten*—cultural strata) or culture provinces (ethnographic provinces) ("Völker und Kulturen Afrikas," *Das doppelte Geschlecht* and *Die Völker Afrikas*). In the later, revised versions he abandoned his original assumption of the identity of cultures with certain races and language groups.

From the 1950s on Baumann no longer limited his comparative studies to Africa. Simultaneously with the global expansion of the scope of his research he achieved a radical revision of traditional ethnological conceptions of the position of "primitive cultures": he became a firm defender of the notion that cultures earlier assessed as "primitive" (not only in Africa, but in Oceania and North and South America) are in reality dependent on long-term influences of ancient high cultures.

MAJOR WORKS: *Lunda: Bei Bauern und Jägern in Inner-Angola* (Berlin: 1935); *Schöpfung und Urzeit des Menschen im Mythus der afrikanischen Völker* (Berlin: 1936; 2nd ed., Berlin: 1964); "Völker und Kulturen Afrikas" in: Hermann Baumann, Richard Thurnwald and Diederich Westermann, *Völkerkunde von Afrika* (Berlin and Essen: 1940), pp. 3-371 [tr.: *Les peuples et les civilisations d'Afrique* (Paris 1940)]; *Das doppelte Geschlecht, ethnologische Studien zur Bisexualität in Ritus und Mythus* (Berlin: 1955; 2nd ed., Berlin: 1980); *Die Völker Afrikas und ihre traditionellen Kulturen* [2 vols.] (Wiesbaden: 1975-1979)

SOURCES: Annemarie Laubscher, "Publikationsliste von Professor Dr. Hermann Baumann (Stand Juni 1967)," *Paideuma*, no. 13 (1967), pp. 5-10 [bibliography]; Helmut Straube, "Hermann Baumann," *Paideuma*, no. 18 (1972), pp. 1-15; Beatrix Heintze, "Hermann Baumann," *Baessler Archiv*, n.F., vol. 20 (1972), pp. 1-9.

László Vajda
[Translation from German: Sem C. Sutter]

Beaglehole, Ernest.

Beaglehole, Ernest. Psychologist, ethnologist. Born in Wellington (New Zealand) 1906, died in 1965. Beaglehole studied at Victoria University College of the University of New Zealand and at the London School of Economics where he received his doctorate based on research regarding the psychological basis of the acquisition of property. He went on to do field research among the Hopi through connections with Yale University, in Polynesia (especially on the culture of Pukapuka atoll) and Hawaii under the auspices of the Bishop Museum and the University of Hawaii, and among the Maori when he returned to Victoria University College.

His writings were well rounded analyses of the cultures he studied, but his emphasis was on the social psychology of the material cultures and economic activities. He studied how cultures dealt with their material world but also how they adapt to changes that result through contact with outside influences.

MAJOR WORKS: (with Pearl Beaglehole) *Ethnology of Pukapuka* (Honolulu: 1938) (= *Bernice P. Bishop Museum, Bulletin*, no. 150); *Property: a Study in Social Psychology* (London: 1932); (with Pearl Beaglehole) *Some Modern Maoris* (Wellington: 1946).

SOURCES: J.E. Ritchie, "Ernest Beaglehole," *Journal of the Polynesian Society*, vol. 75, no. 1 (March 1966), pp. 109-119; James E. Ritchie, "Ernest Beaglehole, 1906-1965," *American Anthropologist*, vol. 69 (1967), pp. 68-70.

Thomas L. Mann

Beals, Ralph L. (Ralph Leon).

Beals, Ralph L. (Ralph Leon). Anthropologist. Born in Pasadena (California) 19 July 1901, died in Los Angeles (California) 24 February 1985. Beals spent his whole life in California, his early youth in Pasadena and Oxnard and later in Berkeley, where he attended high school, graduated from the University of California (1926) and took his doctorate in anthropology (1930). He was the first anthropologist hired at the then new Los Angeles campus of the University of California (UCLA) (1936), established the Department of Anthropology and Sociology in 1941, serving as the first chair, and had a distinguished teaching career until his retirement in 1969. His textbook, *An Introduction to Anthropology* (with HARRY HOIJER), first published in 1953, was widely used and went to five editions. Beals gave the Faculty Research Lecture in 1953 and was awarded an honorary Doctorate of Law in 1970 by UCLA. Beals served on numerous committees of the

Academic Senate and was a major force in establishing the quality of the growing institution where he taught.

A trip to the largely unknown parts of western Mexico while he was still in high school quickened his interest in Latin America, and he devoted his life to research on Latin American cultures, starting with his doctoral dissertation, *The Comparative Ethnography of Northern Mexico*, and continuing with monographs on the Cahita, the Mixe, the Tarascan village of Cherán (all in western Mexico) and the village of Nayón in Ecuador. His last major work was a study of the markets of Oaxaca, and at the time of his death he was working on a history of Mexico from the viewpoint of the Indians, which he never completed. His chief theoretical interest was in the study of acculturation, and all of his works on Latin America bear the strong imprint of this orientation, which also reflects his lifelong concern with the welfare of the native peoples.

As a pioneer student of Latin American society, Beals was frequently called upon to serve in more public roles, starting in 1939 when he was technical adviser to the United States delegation of the first American Indianist Conference in Patzuaro and again for the 4th and 6th Mesas Redondas of the Pan-American Institute of History and Geography. In 1942 he took leave from UCLA to serve as Coordinator of Ethnic Studies for the Institute of Social Anthropology in Washington, D.C., and later made two extensive trips through Latin America and taught for one semester at the University of Buenos Aires. His services were recognized with an honorary professorship at the Faculty of Medicine at the University of Concepción in Chile. He also served as Honorary Patron for the Reorganization of the Ethnographic Section of the Museo Nacional de Antropología (National Museum of Anthropology) in Mexico City. Beals was active in the reorganization of the American Anthropological Association and served as its President in 1950. He also served as President of the Southwestern Anthropological Association (1958) and the Pacific Coast Council on Latin American Studies (1955-1956) and served on the executive committees of the Society for American Archaeology and Section H of the American Association for the Advancement of Science.

MAJOR WORKS: "Comparative ethnography of Northern Mexico," *Ibero-Americana*, vol. 2 (1932), pp. 93-226; *The Contemporary Culture of the Cahita Indians* (Washington: 1945) (= *U.S. Bureau of American Ethnology Bulletin*, no. 142); *Ethnology of the Western Mixe Indians* (Berkeley: 1945) (= *University of California Publications in American Archaeology and Ethnology*, vol. 42); *Cherán: a Sierra Tarascan Village* (Washington: 1946) (= *Smithsonian Institute of Social Anthropology Publications*, no. 2); "Urbanism, urbanization, and acculturation," *American Anthropologist*, vol. 53 (1951), pp. 1-10 [presidential address]; *Community in Transition: Nayón, Ecuador* (Los Angeles: 1966) (= *Latin American Studies Series*, vol. 2); *The Peasant Marketing System of Oaxaca, Mexico* (Berkeley: 1975); (with Harry Hoijer) *An Introduction to Anthropology* (New York: 1953; revised eds., 1959, 1965, 1971 and (with Alan R. Beals) New York: 1977).

SOURCES: "Ralph L. Beals, fifty years in anthropology," *Annual Reviews in Anthropology*, vol. 11 (1982), pp. 1-23; Diane L. Dillon (interviewer), "Anthropologist and educator" [unpublished manuscript, Oral History Program, University of California, Los Angeles]; Walter Goldschmidt, "Ralph Leon Beals (1901-1985)," *American Anthropologist*, vol. 88 (1986), pp. 947-953; Walter Goldschmidt and Harry Hoijer (editors), *The Social Anthropology of Latin America: Essays in Honor of Ralph L. Beals* (Los Angeles: 1970) (= *Latin American Studies Series*, vol. 14).

Walter Goldschmidt

Benedict, Laura Watson. Anthropologist. Born in Delhi (New York) 5 May 1861, died in Philadelphia (Pennsylvania) 13 December 1932. Benedict was one of the first women to aspire to a Ph.D. degree in anthropology and the first woman to earn the degree from Columbia University. She received a bachelor's degree from the University of Chicago in 1900 and in 1904 was awarded an M.A. degree from the same institution. She became interested in the Philippine Islands, probably influenced by the striking Philippine tribal exhibits at the 1904 Louisiana Purchase Centennial Exposition in St. Louis. Benedict was especially impressed by the material culture of the Bagobo, a non-Christian, non-Muslim group inhabiting the mountainous hinterlands of southeastern Mindanao. The Bagobo had not previously been the subject of professional anthropological investigation. Benedict undertook to live among this remote ethnic group, while assembling a collection of Bagobo handicrafts and artifacts and gathering data to support a Ph.D. dissertation to be submitted to the University of Chicago. During 1905 and 1906 she received systematic training in field study technique at the Field Museum and at major museums of Europe. In late 1906, she arrived in the Philippines, settling among Bagobo informants in the village of Santa Cruz, near the Gulf of Davao. She began the study of the Bagobo language while immersing herself in the life of the community. Benedict settled among a people noted for their pagan culture, a tradition of ritual human sacrifice and excellent handicrafts. Her field experiences brought anticipation and discovery, along with primitive living conditions, financial pressures, frequent isolation, and other obstacles and problems.

Benedict's planned three-year stay was apparently shortened due to hardship and exhaustion. By 1908 she had returned to Chicago. While she had anticipated that her extensive collection of Bagobo artifacts would be purchased by the Field Museum, it was not until January 1910, after numerous solicitations, that the Bagobo collection was finally sold to the American Museum of Natural History for $4000. Benedict's field studies in Mindanao ultimately formed the basis for a Ph.D. dissertation in anthropology; she received her degree from Columbia University in 1914. Benedict's hope to return to the Philippines was not to be realized. Nor did she achieve the professional employment to which she aspired, perhaps due to her mature age when she completed the Ph.D.

A pioneer in many respects, Benedict helped initiate the "participant-observer" style of field investigation before that concept had been elaborated. Her major work, *A Study of Bagobo Ceremonial, Magic and Myth*, the product of careful fieldwork in Davao, was published in 1916. This detailed study, along with her ethnographic collections, was her lasting contribution to Philippine studies and to her profession.

MAJOR WORKS: *A Study of Bagobo Ceremonial, Magic and Myth* (New York: 1916) (= *Annals of the New York Academy of Sciences*, no. 25); "Bagobo fine art collection," *American Museum Journal*, vol. 11 (1911), pp. 164-171; "Bagobo myths," *Journal of American Folk-Lore*, vol. 26 (Jan.-Mar. 1913), pp. 13-63.

SOURCES: Jay H. Bernstein, "The perils of Laura Watson Benedict: a forgotten pioneer in anthropology," *Philippine Quarterly of Culture and Society*, vol. 13, no. 3 (Sept. 1985), pp. [171]-197; "Coastal Bagobo" in: Frank M. Lebar (editor), *Ethnic Groups of Insular Southeast Asia* (New Haven: 1972-1975), vol. 2, pp. 58-61.

Lee S. Dutton

Benedict, Ruth (née Ruth Fulton). Cultural anthropologist, anthropological folklorist, and philosopher. Born in New York (New York) 4 June 1887, died in New York (New York) 17 September 1948. Benedict spent her first years on her maternal grandparents' farm in upstate New York, her father having died when she was eighteen months old. She then lived in St. Joseph, Missouri, and Owatonna, Minnesota, before her mother became a librarian in Buffalo, New York, when she was eleven. She attended Vassar, graduating in 1909, visited Europe, then spent one year as a social worker and three as a teacher before marrying Stanley Benedict, a biochemist, in 1914. In 1919 she returned to college to study with John Dewey at Columbia, then, when he went on sabbatical, she took anthropologist ELSIE CLEWS PARSONS' course in ethnology of the sexes at the New School for Social Research and discovered anthropology. Benedict went on to get her doctorate in anthropology at Columbia in 1923 under FRANZ BOAS. She remained at Columbia throughout her career, through the 1920s as a part-time teacher, then in the 1930s and 1940s as an assistant and associate professor, becoming the first woman to be promoted to full professor in the Faculty of Political Science in 1948. She did her field-work among the Serrano people of California and the Zuni, Cochiti and Pima in the Southwest with student training trips to the Mescalero Apache in Arizona and the Blackfoot and the Blood of the Northwest. Her best-known works are *Patterns of Culture, Race: Science and Politics* and *The Chrysanthemum and the Sword.*

Benedict's work was both influential in anthropology and had a great impact on American culture as a whole. *Patterns of Culture* helped shape the culture and personality movement within anthropology in the 1930s and got anthropologists interested in applying the idea of configurations to cultures with creative results. Outside anthropology *Patterns of Culture* was one of the most effective transmitters of anthropological ideas to the American public at large. Due in part to Benedict's book the anthropological idea of culture as learned behavior in all the various facets of life, from language to government, became part of the American vocabulary. Before she popularized it in this new way, the word "culture" meant to most Americans merely an interest in the fine arts, music and literature, not the web of context that defines human lives. She also popularized the concept of cultural relativity, the Boasian idea that each culture is neither higher nor lower in some evolutionary hierarchical scheme but instead is an alternative way of patterning life that must be judged on its own merits and not by American (or Western) culture-bound standards of right and wrong.

But in *Patterns of Culture* Benedict went beyond just being a transmitter of commonly held anthropological ideas. Her own unique contribution to the concept of culture was to compare it with the psychological concept of personality. She proposed that just as personality ordered individual development, causing acceptance of some behaviors and rejection of others, a mental pattern lay underneath cultures, a configuration of beliefs, values and expectations creating over time a world-view or ethos that accepted, rejected or changed culture traits with which it came in contact to fit the beliefs, standards and values it held most important. Her most famous examples of the underlying perspective of vision or world-view guiding cultures were the Apollonian perspective of the Zuni and the Dionysian perspective of the Plains and Pima Indians. The Zuni, she wrote, valued order, harmony, formality, communal over individual effort, and lack of excess. The Plains, Pima, and other Dionysian tribes sought excess through self-torture, use of drugs, and extreme acts of bravery to take them outside ordinary life. Benedict said that each of these groups unconsciously organized their culture in terms of these Apollonian and Dionysian world-views. In *Patterns* she also used the example of the Dobu of Melanesia and the Kwakiutl of the Pacific Northwest as peoples having underlying configurations that guided these cultures, but that Americans might view as paranoid or megalomaniac.

Benedict's work led anthropologists and those outside anthropology to explore cultural ideas, standards and expectations, to search for the ideal person of a culture and argue over the role of these ideals versus cultural reality. Although cultures are not seen as having only one theme threading them together now, Benedict's work was a crucial jumping off point for the development of later ideas such as that of multiple cultural themes. She also led people to question standards of normality, showing that what was normal and what was considered deviant differed from culture to culture, sometimes in opposition to Western expectations.

On a philosophical level Benedict was attempting to create for Americans a new configuration of underlying ideas that should govern American life. These included an overt and covert dismissal of 19th-century Victorian values as corrupt or outdated; an affirmation of the positive value of relativity as an orienting concept; the possibility of integrating purpose and chance, two seeming opposites, for, in cultures with underlying configurations, surface events happened by seeming chance or accident, yet were secretly coordinated by the values and beliefs that shaped the culture; the affirmation of a 20th-century urban-industrial definition of individualism in which self and society were not antagonists but able to compromise and work together; and the triumph of culture over biology as a causal factor in American life. As a corollary, her affirmation of the relativity of normality spoke against homophobia in America.

Benedict tried to influence American life in several other ways. In her book, *Race: Science and Politics*, she seems to have coined the word "racism," or at least popularized the concept in American society. She took the debate on racial ideas beyond the scientific and pseudo-scientific arguments of the 1930s, to study and analyze the non-rational side of the race issue, the ideas based on belief, not facts. She traced racism back to ethnocentrism, the desire of humans to be the center of the universe and superior to those around them, a desire and belief structure played out among native peoples as cultural superiority—my culture is better than yours, I am human, you are not—and in Western society through religious superiority and then through racial superiority. Benedict cited two primary codes of ethics—that toward one's in-group and that toward those outside the group—and the need to make everyone members of the in-group. She believed in the power of ideas and that the only way to uproot a value was to put in its place another value, giving a new direction to social activity. This was her purpose in writing about race, to try to root in people's minds the idea that all humans are a part of the same in-group and to eliminate out-groups altogether. She tried to reach people with this message through the use of ever more popular ways until her death in 1948, collaborating on a high school resource unit, a *Public Affairs Pamphlet* that became a movie and a comic book and later a children's book, *In Henry's Backyard*.

During World War II Benedict worked for the Office of War Information (OWI) in the federal government. Here she had her first taste of applying anthropological insights to policy decisions, as she wrote memos on how to understand and use cultural differences among enemies and allies to shorten the war. She considered her most successful memo to be "What should be done about the Emperor?," a short paper in which she recommended that the Japanese emperor not be deposed and his power as spiritual leader used to legitimate changes after the war.

After the war was over, she used her research on Japan for the OWI to write *The Chrysanthemum and the Sword*, her classic book on the Japanese that is still an important source of insight on this culture. The book was influential on American post-war understanding and treatment of the Japanese. After the war, understanding of and ability to work with cultural differences became for her the necessary preliminary condition for a working United Nations. This became the rationale behind her last great project, a study of "national character," in which she pioneered the anthropological study of contemporary, civilized cultures. She not only sought to understand differences, but in the project itself she created a model of how different groups could work together for positive results. She died before this project was finished and as a result the project did not have the broad impact it might have had if she had lived.

As an anthropological folklorist her most important works were *Tales of the Cochiti* and *Zuni Mythology*. In the former she suggested analogies between mythology and literature. In the latter she theorized that mythology acted as a compensation mechanism, an outlet in fantasy form for elements repressed in the culture. In both of these works she examined the role of the myth-teller as both potentially creative and mediated by the culture. She served as the editor of the *Journal of American Folk-Lore* from 1925 to 1940 and as editor of the American Folklore Society's *Memoir* series for this same period, concentrating on getting the raw material of folklore published before it vanished as native cultures were vanishing.

MAJOR WORKS: "Psychological types in the culture of the Southwest" in: *Proceedings of the Twenty-Third International Congress of Americanists, 1928* (New York: 1930), pp. 527-581; *Tales of the Cochiti* (New York: 1931); "Folklore" in: E.R.A. Seligman (editor), *Encyclopaedia of the Social Sciences* (New York: 1930-1935), vol. 6, pp. 288-293; "Configurations of culture in North America," *American Anthropologist*, n.s., vol. 34 (1932), pp. 1-27; "Magic" in: E.R.A. Seligman (editor), *Encyclopaedia of the Social Sciences* (New York: 1930-1935), vol. 10, pp. 39-44; "Myth" in: E.R.A. Seligman (editor), *Encyclopaedia of the Social Sciences* (New York: 1930-1935), vol. 11, pp. 178-181; "Anthropology and the abnormal," *Journal of General Psychology*, vol. 10 (1934), pp. 59-82; *Patterns of Culture* (Boston: 1934); *Zuni Mythology* (New York: 1935); "Continuities and discontinuities in cultural conditioning," *Psychiatry*, vol. 1 (1938), pp. 161-167; "Religion" in: Franz Boas (editor), *General Anthropology* (Boston: 1938), pp. 627-665; *Race: Science and Politics* (New York: 1940; rev. ed., New York: 1943); (with Gene Weltfish) *The Races of Mankind* (New York: 1943) (= *Public Affairs Pamphlet*, no. 85); *The Chrysanthemum and the Sword* (New York: 1946); "Anthropology and the humanities," *American Anthropologist*, vol. 50 (1948), pp. 585-593; (with Gene Weltfish) *In Henry's Backyard: the Races of Mankind* (New York: 1948).

SOURCES: Margaret M. Caffrey, *Ruth Benedict: Stranger in this Land* (Austin: 1989); Judith Schachter Modell, *Ruth Benedict: Patterns of a Life* (Philadelphia: 1983); Margaret Mead, *Ruth Benedict* (New York: 1974); Margaret Mead (editor), *An Anthropologist at Work: Writings of Ruth Benedict* (Boston: 1959); Viking Fund, *Ruth Fulton Benedict: a Memorial* (New York: 1949); Virginia Wolf Briscoe, "Ruth Benedict: anthropological folklorist," *Journal of American Folklore*, vol. 92 (1979), pp. 445-476; Margaret Mead, "Ruth Fulton Benedict, 1887-1948," *American Anthropologist*, vol. 51 (1949), pp. 457-463; Dorothy Lee, "Ruth Fulton Benedict (1887-1948)," *Journal of American Folk-Lore*, vol. 62 (1949), pp. 345-347.

Margaret M. Caffrey

Benet, Sula. Anthropologist, folklorist. Born in Warsaw (Poland) 24 September 1906, died in New York (New York) 12 November 1982. Benet earned a doctorate in ethnology in 1935 at the University of Warsaw, with a dissertation on hashish in the folk customs and beliefs of Poland. She came to the United States in 1936 and worked on Eastern European Studies with RUTH BENEDICT, taking her Ph.D. in anthropology in 1943 from Columbia University. From 1944 until her retirement in 1972 Benet was a member of the anthropology faculty at Hunter College, although she occasionally taught at Columbia, Fairleigh Dickinson University and elsewhere. After retirement she became a fellow of VERA RUBIN's Research Institute for the Study of Man.

Benet's major contribution to anthropology was a long-term study of longevity among the Abkhasian people of the Caucasus, made from 1970 on at the invitation of the Soviet Academy of Sciences. While accepting the beneficial aspects of Abkhasian diet, climate and other factors, Benet stressed the fact that the Abkhasians remained active members of their society in old age and that remaining active was an important influence on their longevity.

During World War II, Benet was a consultant to the United States Department of State on Eastern European affairs.

MAJOR WORKS: *Patterns of Thought and Behavior in the Culture of Poland* (New York: 1952); (translator and editor) *The Village of Viriatino* (New York: 1970); *Abkhasians: the Long-Living People of the Caucasus* (New York: 1974); *How to Live to Be 100* (New York: 1976).

SOURCES: "Benet, Sula," *Contemporary Authors*, vol. 89-92 (1980), pp. 53-54; and vol. 108 (1983), p. 52; Walter H. Waggoner, "Dr. Sula Benet, 76, a specialist in longevity and East Europe," *The New York Times* (13 November 1982), p. 16.

David Lonergan

Bennett, Wendell Clark. Anthropologist, archaeologist. Born in Marion (Indiana) 17 August 1905, died in Martha's Vineyard (Massachusetts) 6 September 1953. All of Bennett's higher education took place at the University of Chicago; he received his doctorate there in 1930.

His career included appointments as Assistant Curator at the American Museum of Natural History, Associate Professor at the University of Wisconsin and Yale University, and finally Professor at Yale University and Research Associate in the Yale Peabody Museum.

Bennett's first fieldwork, performed under the auspices of the Bernice P. Bishop Museum, was on the religions of the Hawaiian Islands and Polynesia. His geographic area of emphasis soon shifted to South America, especially Bolivia, Ecuador, Peru, Colombia and Venezuela, where he worked on the archaeological chronology of several parts of the Andean Region.

Bennett conducted his archaeological excavations as part of a team effort together with ethnologists, geographers and historians because of his belief that this cross-disciplinary cooperation would produce more meaningful reports. He also concentrated on relatively small areas of excavation in order to make it possible to do a thorough detailed analysis of the discoveries.

MAJOR WORKS: "Excavations in Bolivia," *American Museum of Natural History, Anthropological Papers*, vol. 35, pt. 4 (1936), pp. 327-507; "Excavations at La Mata, Maracay, Venezuela," *American Museum of Natural History, Anthropological Papers*, vol. 36, pt. 2 (1937), pp. 67-137; *Archaeology of the North Coast of Peru: an Account of Exploration and Excavation, Virú and Lambayeque Valleys* (New York: 1939) (= *American Museum of Natural History, Anthropological Papers*, vol. 37, pt. 1); *Archaeological Regions of Colombia: a Ceramic Survey* (New Haven: 1944) (= *Yale University Publications in Anthropology*, no. 30); *Excavations in the Cuenca Region, Ecuador* (New Haven: 1946) (= *Yale University Publications in Anthropology*, no. 35); "Foreword" to: Wendell C. Bennett (editor), *A Reappraisal of Peruvian Archaeology* (Menasha, Wisc.: 1948) (= *Society for American Archaeology, Memoirs*, no. 4), pp. v-vi; "The Peruvian co-tradition" in: Wendell C. Bennett (editor), *A Reappraisal of Peruvian Archaeology* (Menasha, Wisc.: 1948) (= *Society for American Archaeology, Memoirs*, no. 4), pp. 1-7; "A revised sequence for the South Titicaca Basin" in: Wendell C. Bennett (editor), *A Reappraisal of Peruvian Archaeology* (Menasha, Wisc.: 1948) (= *Society for American Archaeology, Memoirs*, no. 4), pp. 90-92; (with Junius Bird) *Andean Culture History* (New York: 1949) (= *American Museum of Natural History Handbook Series*, no. 15).

SOURCES: "Bennett, Wendell Clark" in: *International Directory of Anthropologists* (Washington: 1938), pp. 8-9; "Bennett, Wendell Clark" in: *International Directory of Anthropologists* (2nd ed., Washington: 1940), pp. 13-14; "Bennett, Wendell Clark" in: Melville J. Herskovits (editor), *International Directory of Anthropologists* (3rd ed., Washington: 1950), p. 14; "Notas y noticias," *Revista interamericana de bibliografía*, vol. 3 (September 1953), p. 356; G.H.S. Bushnell, "Obituary: Wendell Clark Bennett, 1905-1953," *Man*, vol. 53 (204) (September 1953), p. 133; "Department head at Yale drowned," *New York Times* (7 September 1953), p. 7; "Notes and news," *School and Society*, vol. 78 (19 September 1953), p. 94; Harry L. Shapiro, "Dr. Wendell C. Bennnett," *Nature*, vol. 172 (21 November 1953), pp. 936-937; Irving Rouse, "Wendell C. Bennett, 1905-1953," *American Antiquity*, vol. 19 (1954), pp. 265-270 [contains bibliography]; Alfred Kidder, "Wendell Clark Bennett, 1905-1953," *American Anthropologist*, vol. 56 (1954), pp. 269-273; Cornelius Osgood, "Wendell Clark Bennett, 1905-1953," *Science*, vol. 119 (14 May 1954), p. 674; "Bennett, Wendell C." in: Dwight B. Heath, *Historical Dictionary of Bolivia* (Metuchen, N.J.: 1972), p. 36.

Thomas L. Mann

Berens, William (Ojibwa name, Tab Ơsigizikweas, "Sailing Low in the Air after Thunder"). Chief of Berens River Indian Band, trader, fisherman, guide, informant. Born near Lake Winnipeg (Manitoba) 1865, died on Berens River (Manitoba) 23 August 1947. Berens, son of Jacob Berens, the first post-treaty chief at Berens River, and Mary McKay, of Algonquian and Scottish descent, is known to anthropologists principally through the publications of A. IRVING HALLOWELL on Saulteaux (Ojibwa) culture, psychology and religion. In July 1930, when Hallowell made his first trip up Lake Winnipeg to do fieldwork among the Swampy Cree, his ship stopped at Berens River. Chief Berens, who had a wide network of contacts around the lake, met the ship and entered into conversation with the newcomer, encouraging him to revisit Berens River on his way south. Hallowell accepted. The week he spent with Berens in August 1930 was seminal. For the next decade, his work centered upon Berens River and upon Chief Berens, who took him on several trips up the river, interpreted, introduced him to other informants, and generally facilitated the Ojibwa research that became the main focus of Hallowell's writing for the rest of his life.

Berens grew up among family members who included both converts to Methodism and practitioners of Midewiwin and shaking-tent ceremonies. He remembered the founding of the first Methodist mission at Berens River in 1874 and his father's role in the negotiating of Treaty No. 5 in 1875. He witnessed and participated in the rapid rise of commercial fishing on Lake Winnipeg in the 1880s, while also engaging in his people's much older occupation of trapping and trading for the Hudson's Bay Company. He guided novice surveyors and Indian agents to native communities in the region.

In Hallowell's frame of reference, Berens was an acculturated lakeside Ojibwa who effectively mediated the anthropologist's approach to the pagan, upriver people who were of most interest to him. Yet the myths, stories and reminiscences Hallowell collected from Berens in the years 1930-1940 are suggestive of the great extent to which the chief maintained Ojibwa values and outlooks in his own life, while functioning successfully in a rapidly changing social and economic world.

MAJOR WORK: *Reminiscences* (1940) [unpublished manuscript recorded by A.I. Hallowell, covering ca. 1865-1905].

SOURCES: Jennifer S.H. Brown, "A place in your mind for them all: Chief William Berens" in: James A. Clifton (editor), *Being and Becoming Indian: Biographic Studies of North American Frontiers* (Chicago: 1989), pp. 204-225; Jennifer S.H. Brown, "A. Irving Hallowell and William Berens revisited" in: William Cowan (editor), *Papers of the Eighteenth Algonquian Conference* (Ottawa: 1987), pp. 17-28; A.I. Hallowell papers [manuscript col. 26, American Philosophical Society, Philadelphia].

Jennifer S.H. Brown

Bergeyck, Jac. See: *Theuws, Jacques A.*

Bernal, Ignacio (Ignacio Bernal y García Pimentel). Archaeologist. Born in Paris (France) 13 February 1910. Bernal was an internationally known scholar who wrote prolifically on Mexican archaeology and ethnography and edited a bibliography with 13,390 entries on these subjects.

Bernal was the son of Rafael Bernal, a large landholder, and Rafaela García Pimentel Elguero. He studied at the Free School of Law, Mexico City, and received an M.A. from the National Institute of Anthropology in 1946 and a Ph.D. from the National Autonomous University of Mexico (UNAM) in 1949 as well as an LL.D. from the University of Mexico, 1949.

He was professor of archaeology at UNAM from 1948 and at Mexico City College from 1950 to 1962. He was director of anthropology at the University of the Americas from 1948 to 1959 and of the Escuela Nacional de Antropología y Historia (National School of Anthropology and History) from 1950. He has been a visiting professor at the Colegio de México, the University of Texas, the University of California, Harvard University, Cambridge University, the Sorbonne, the University of Madrid and the University of Rome.

He was a cultural attaché at the Mexican embassy in France (1955-1956); Mexico's permanent delegate to UNESCO (1955-1956); a member of the International Commission on Monuments (1956); the Director of Prehistoric Monuments, Secretary of Public Education (1956-1958); the president of the 35th International Congress of Americanists (1962); and a member of the National Academy of History (starting in 1962).

He served as co-director of the review, *Tlalcocán* (1962), director of the Proyecto Teotihuacán (1962-1964) and director of the Museo Nacional de Antropología (National Museum of Anthropology) (1962-1968).

Among honors received were those of the Order of Orange-Nassau, Netherlands (1964); the Légion d'Honneur, France (1964); and the Order of Merit, Italy (1964).

MAJOR WORKS: *La cerámica de Monte Alban III-A* (Mexico City: 1949); (with Alfonso Caso) *Urnas de Oaxaca* (Mexico City: 1952); *Guia de Oaxaca, Monte Alban y Mitla* (Mexico City: 1957); *Tenochtitlán en una isla* (Mexico City: 1959); *Bibliografía de arqueología e etnografía Mesoamerica y Norte de México, 1514-1930* (Mexico City: 1962) [among the 13,390 entries are 94 titles by Bernal]; *Mexican Wall Paintings* (Milan: 1963); (with Alfonso Caso and J. Acosta) *La cerámica de Monte Alban* (Mexico City: 1967); "Mexico-Tenochtitlán" in: Arnold Toynbee (editor), *Cities of Destiny* (London: 1967), pp. 194-209; *The Olmec World* (Berkeley: 1969).

SOURCES: "Bernal, Ignacio" in: *Directory of American Scholars*, vol. 1, *History* (8th ed., New York: 1982), p. 54; "Bernal y García Pimentel, Ignacio" in: *Enciclopedía de México* (Mexico City: 1978), vol. 2, p. 206 [lists 110 of Bernal's publications]; Bernal y García Pimentel, Ignacio" in: Lucien F. Lajoie (editor), *Who's Notable in Mexico* (Mexico City: 1972), p. 21; "Bernal, Ignacio Pimentel" in: *Who's Who in America* (45th ed., Wilmette, Ill.: 1988), vol. 1, p. 243; "Bernal y García Pimentel, Ignacio" in: Roderic Ai Camp, *Who's Who in Mexico Today* (Boulder: 1988), pp. 24-25; "Bernal, Ignacio" in: Sol Tax (editor), *Fifth International Directory of Anthropologists* (Chicago: 1975), p. 31; Jesús Silva Herzog, *Biografías de amigos y conocidos* (Mexico City: 1980), pp. 55-56; *Diccionario biográfico de México* (Monterrey: 1971), p. 71.

Francis X. Grollig, S.J.

Bernardi, Bernardo. Ethnologist. Born in Medicina, Province of Bologna (Italy) 7 December 1916. Bernardi graduated in 1946 with a thesis on the kinship system of the Kikuyu of Kenya and was subsequently sent to Kenya as a missionary. In 1952 he received a doctorate in African studies from the University of Cape Town, South Africa, under the guidance of ISAAC SCHAPERA.

During his missionary years, before he left the clergy, Bernardi embraced the Cultural-Historical School, but direct experience with social realities led him to a critical revision of his theoretical assumptions and he came to appreciate the heuristic value of the principles inherent in the structural-functional method.

During his stay among the Zezuru of Zimbabwe (1948) he sought a convergence of the historical and functionalist perspectives, after the example of Schapera's research among the Tswana of Botswana and also of E.E. EVANS-PRITCHARD and the circle of British social anthropologists. Bernardi's work among the Zezuru was reported in *The Social Structure of the Kraal among the Zezuru*, which has remained the basic reference work on this region, focusing on the structural changes undergone over four decades by a series of human settlements.

In the course of his later work among the Meru of Kenya (1956-1959), Bernardi uncovered a religious figure, the Mugwe, whose existence was kept secret by the Meru for fear of colonial interference. The publication of *The Mugwe: a Failing Prophet* aroused much interest, especially among scholars of symbolic anthropology, for the novelty of its ethnographic information and the quality of its documentation. The work also engendered debates and critical comments.

The theme of the age group system, already touched upon in his doctoral thesis, represents another important area of Bernardi's scholarship. He has produced comparative models to demonstrate the political value of such systems, which are typical of chiefless societies.

In 1970 Bernardi was appointed to the chair of cultural anthropology at the University of Bologna. In 1982 he accepted the chair of ethnology at the University "La Sapienza" of Rome.

MAJOR WORKS: *The Social Structure of the Kraal among the Zezuru* (Cape Town: 1950); "The age-system of the Nilo-Hamitic peoples," *Africa*, vol. 22 (1952), pp. 316-332; *Le religioni dei primitivi* (Milan: 1953); *The Mugwe: a Failing Prophet* (Oxford: 1959); *Uomo, cultura, società* (Milan: 1974); *The Concept and Dynamics of Culture* (Paris: 1977); *Africa meridionale* (Novara: 1977); *I sistemi delle classi d'età* (Turin: 1985) [tr: *Age Class Systems* (Cambridge: 1986)]; *Europa* (Novara: 1988).

SOURCES: Serge Tornay, "Vers une théorie des systèmes de classes d'âge," *Cahiers d'études africaines*, no. 110, vol. 28 (1988), pp. 281-291; A. Rosa Leone, "La chiesa, i cattolici e le scienze dell'uomo, 1860-1920" in: Pietro Clemente [et al.], *L'antropologia italiana: un secolo di storia* (Bari: 1985), pp. 51-96; Antonio Marazzi (editor), *Antropologia: tendenze contemporanee: scritti in onore di Bernardo Bernardi* (Milan: 1989).

Massimo Guerra
[Translation from Italian: Gianna Panofsky]

Berndt, Catherine Helen.

Berndt, Catherine Helen. Social anthropologist. Born in Auckland (New Zealand) 8 May 1918. Berndt went from New Zealand to study anthropology at the University of Sydney in 1940. There she met fellow student RONALD M. BERNDT and they married in 1941 before embarking on field research among Aborigines at Ooldea in South Australia. Her focus on Aboriginal women was to continue and intensify in subsequent research in a wide variety of Aboriginal communities, and she is now a leading world authority on this topic. This research period, spanning almost a half-century, was broken only by fieldwork in Papua New Guinea's eastern central Highlands (1951-1953) and a period as a postgraduate student at the London School of Economics and Political Science (1953-1955) where she obtained her doctorate.

Berndt's first detailed study of Aboriginal women's religious activity, *Women's Changing Ceremonies in Northern Australia*, was published in 1950 with an introduction by CLAUDE LÉVI-STRAUSS. For Berndt, the issue of Aboriginal male-female complementarity was a guiding principle with significant theoretical import, and she was able to argue successfully that for women—as for men—there was independence within a framework of interdependence. This approach has had far-reaching influence in the study of Aboriginal gender relations. In addition to its anthropological relevance, it has provided a framework for improved non-Aboriginal understanding of the status of Aboriginal women which, for more than a century, had been played down. Berndt has contributed much to the understanding of marriage, the family and socialization in both Aboriginal Australia and the Highlands of Papua New Guinea. Another major interest has been oral literature, as manifested through myth and stories. She has written widely on this topic and has been largely responsible for developing oral literature as a field of study in Australia. Berndt has maintained her concern with children's literature and with providing accurate and readable translations of traditional stories for use by Aboriginal and non-Aboriginal children alike.

In common with her husband, Berndt has long been vitally concerned with processes of social change. Her particular concern has been with the changing circumstances of women in the societies in which she has worked. The magnitude of these changes has persuaded her that a strong understanding of "traditional" societies and cultures is vitally necessary for adequate evaluation, theoretically, of the nature and trajectories of change. A painstaking and prodigious field researcher and a prolific writer of high-quality publications, Catherine Berndt has been partner to a unique professional collaboration. She and her husband thoroughly earned their reputation as the longest-serving and best-known scholars of Australian Aboriginal societies and cultures in the world.

MAJOR WORKS: *Women's Changing Ceremonies in Northern Australia* (Paris: 1950); "The quest for identity: the case of the Australian Aborigines," *Oceania*, vol. 32 (1961-1962), pp. 16-33; "Mateship or success: an assimilation dilemma," *Oceania*, vol. 33 (1962-1963), pp. 71-89; "Women and the 'secret life'" in: R.M. and C.H. Berndt (editors), *Aboriginal Man in Australia* (Sydney: 1965), pp. 238-282; "Digging sticks and spears, or, the two-sex model" in: F. Gale (editor), *Women's role in Aboriginal Society* (Canberra: 1970), pp. 39-48; (with Ronald M. Berndt) *The Barbarians: an Anthropological View* (London: 1971); "Oral literature" in: R.M. Berndt and E.S. Phillips (editors), *The Australian Aboriginal Heritage* (Sydney: 1973), pp. 72-90; (with Ronald M. Berndt) *Pioneers and Settlers: the Aboriginal Australians* (Melbourne: 1978); "Aboriginal children's literature" in: *Children's Literature: More than a Story* (Geelong: 1980), pp. 69-135; "Interpretations and 'facts' in Aboriginal Australia" in: F. Dahlberg (editor), *Woman the Gatherer* (New Haven: 1981), pp. 153-203; (with Ronald M. Berndt) *Aborigines in Australian Society* (Melbourne: 1985); "Blinded by the sound of weeping: reality and myth in Kaluli experience," *Semiotica*, vol. 61 (1986), pp. 347-367. See also R.M. Berndt entry for jointly authored material.

SOURCES: "Catherine Helen Berndt" in: Ute Gacs [et al.] (editors), *Women Anthropologists: a Biographical Dictionary* (New York: 1988), pp. 8-16; C. Lévi-Strauss, "Preface" to: C.H. Berndt, *Women's Changing Ceremonies in Northern Australia* (Paris: 1950), pp. 1-8; "The social position of women," *Australian Aboriginal Studies* (1963), pp. 319-334; "Berndt, Catherine Helen" in: *Who's Who in Australia* (Melbourne: 1988), p. 113; *Annals of the Association of Social Anthropologists of the Commonwealth and Directory of Members* (London: 1989); "The Berndts: a biographical sketch" in: Robert Tonkinson and Michael Howard (editors), *Going It Alone? Prospects for Aboriginal Autonomy: Essays in Honour of Ronald Berndt and Catherine Berndt* (Canberra: 1990), pp. 17-42; Ronald Berndt and Catherine Berndt, "The Berndts: a select bibliography" in: Robert Tonkinson and Michael Howard (editors), *Going It Alone? Prospects for Aboriginal Autonomy: Essays in Honour of Ronald Berndt and Catherine Berndt* (Canberra: 1990), pp. 45-63.

Robert Tonkinson

Berndt, Ronald M. Social anthropologist. Born in Adelaide (South Australia) 14 July 1916, died in Perth (Western Australia) 2 May 1990. Berndt began formal studies in social anthropology at the University of Sydney in 1940 and received his doctorate from the London School of Economics and Political Science in 1955. He pioneered research and teaching in Social Anthropology at the University of Western Australia (1956) and became Foundation Professor and Head when a separate Department of Anthropology was established in 1963. He became Emeritus Professor there in 1981. He and his wife CATHERINE H. BERNDT are the best known scholars of Australian Aboriginal societies in the world. Throughout Berndt's career his wife was always present, though each partner conducted field research predominantly with members of their own sex. In a career spanning almost a half-century, they worked in a greater number and variety of Aboriginal communities than any other anthropologists before or since. Their huge corpus of published work, based on in-depth and systematic fieldwork, is impressive testimony to the successful realization of their major professional goal: to reveal to a largely uninformed Australian public the complexities and genius of Aboriginal cultures. Their highly successful, comprehensive account, *The World of the First Australians* (first published in 1964 and still in print in revised versions) has played a significant role in heightening intellectual appreciation of Aboriginal social and cultural adaptations, past and present. One of Ronald Berndt's many signal contributions to the field of Aboriginal Studies has been in the study of religion, particularly myth, ritual and song-poetry. Several of his works on these topics carry significant theoretical implications; e.g., *Australian Aboriginal Religion* and his overview in *The Encyclopedia of Religion*. Berndt also wrote insightfully on law and order in both Aboriginal and Melanesian contexts. He and his wife carried out pioneering field research in the eastern central Highlands of Papua New Guinea (1951-1953), and his subsequent study, *Excess and Restraint*, aroused considerable controversy concerning the high levels of violence depicted. However, later research by other anthropologists in the same region has tended to confirm Berndt's major contentions. Another topic on which Berndt is a recognized world authority is Aboriginal art; he edited and wrote several major studies that have done much to stimulate interest in the analysis and aesthetic appreciation of Aboriginal art forms. Berndt was also a notable figure in attempts to bring to the public's attention and ameliorate the often deplorable conditions under which Aborigines exist. He was a strong proponent of applied anthropology, especially in relation to major issues such as Aboriginal land rights and the impact of resource development on Aborigines. He played a significant role in the development and expansion of the Australian Institute of Aboriginal Studies and advised countless official bodies concerned with the welfare of Aboriginal Australians. He and his wife have devoted their professional lives to the advancement of understanding and appreciation of Australian Aboriginal societies and cultures, and no scholars have done more for this admirable cause.

MAJOR WORKS: *Kunapipi* (Melbourne and New York: 1951); *Djanggawul* (London and Melbourne: 1952-1953); *An Adjustment Movement in Arnhem Land* (Paris: 1952); *Excess and Restraint: Social Control among a New Guinea Mountain People* (Chicago: 1962); (with C.H. Berndt) *The World of the First Australians* (Sydney and Chicago: 1964); (co-editor with C.H. Berndt) *Aboriginal Man in Australia: Essays in Honour of Professor A.P. Elkin* (Sydney: 1965); (editor) *Australian Aboriginal Anthropology* (Canberra: 1970); (with C.H. Berndt) *Man, Land and Myth in North Australia* (Sydney and East Lansing: 1970); *Australian Aboriginal Religion* (Leiden: 1974); *Love Songs of Arnhem Land* (Melbourne: 1976); (editor) *Aborigines and Change: Australia in the '70s* (Canberra: 1977); (editor) *Aboriginal Sites, Rights and Resource Development* (Perth: 1982); (with C.H. Berndt) *End of an Era: Aboriginal Labour in the Northern Territory* (Canberra: 1987); (with C.H. Berndt) *The Speaking Land: Myth and Story in Aboriginal Australia* (Ringwood: 1988); (co-editor with R. Tonkinson) *Social Anthropology and Australian Aboriginal Studies: a Contemporary Overview* (Canberra: 1988).

SOURCES: R.M. Berndt and R. Tonkinson (editors) *Social Anthropology and Australian Aboriginal Studies: a Contemporary Overview* (Canberra: 1988); *Annals of the Association of Social Anthropologists of the Commonwealth and Directory of Members* (London: 1989); "Berndt, Ronald Murray" in: *Who's Who in Australia* (1988), p. 113; "The Berndts: a biographical sketch" in: Robert Tonkinson and Michael Howard (editors), *Going It Alone? Prospects for Aboriginal Autonomy: Essays in Honour of Ronald Berndt and Catherine Berndt* (Canberra: 1990), pp. 17-42; Ronald Berndt and Catherine Berndt, "The Berndts: a select bibliography" in: Robert Tonkinson and Michael Howard (editors), *Going It Alone? Prospects for Aboriginal Autonomy: Essays in Honour of Ronald Berndt and Catherine Berndt* (Canberra: 1990), pp. 45-63.

Robert Tonkinson

Bernshtam, A.N. (Aleksandr Natanovich). Archaeologist, historian, ethnographer. Born in Dzhanka, Crimea (Russia) 1 October 1910, died in Leningrad (Russian S.F.S.R.) 10 December 1956. Bernshtam, one of the most prominent Soviet Orientalists, was an organizer of and participant in the first archaeological-ethnographic studies in the territory of Kazakhstan and Central Asia.

Bernshtam began his creative journey in the 1920s as a student of the Ethnography Section of the Geography Faculty at Leningrad University. After 1929 he was an active organizer of Soviet regional studies, working in the Leningrad and Central Biuro kraevedeniia (Bureau of Local Studies). From 1934 to 1956 he was the senior scientific associate of the Institut istorii material'noĭ kul'tury (Institute of the History of Material Culture). For many years he was also professor at the History Faculty of Leningrad University.

The first great work of Bernshtam, based on original material, was *Zhilishche Krymskogo predgor'ia*, a study of the Crimean Tatars, who had previously been neglected by scholars. But soon his interests returned completely to Central Asia. Starting in 1936, he led the Semirech'e Archaeological Expedition, during which he discovered numerous remains of the ethnic groups who had resided in the territory of southeastern Kazakhstan, Kirgizia and the Pamir Mountains. Bernshtam laid the basis of the study of the ancient history of the Kirghiz and the Kazakhs and did research on the nomadic tribes, their interrelationships, early forms of social structure, writing and culture. He wrote about 250 works in all, among which were twenty books, some scholarly and some aimed at a wide audience.

MAJOR WORKS: *Zhilishche Krymskogo predgor'ia* (Leningrad: 1931); *Kenkol'skiĭ mogil'nik* (Leningrad: 1940); *Pamiatniki stariny Talasskoĭ doliny* (Alma-Ata: 1941); *Istoriia kyrgyz i Kirgizstana s drevneĭshikh vremen do mongol'skogo zavoevaniia* [unpublished doctoral dissertation] (1942); *Kul'tura drevnego Kirgizstana* (Frunze: 1942); *Sotsial'no-ėkonomicheskiĭ stroĭ orkhonoeniseĭskikh tiurok VI-VIII vekov* (Moscow and Leningrad: 1946); *Uĭgurskaia ėpigrafika Semirech'ia* (Moscow and Leningrad: 1947, 1948); *Drevniaia Fergana* (Moskva: 1949); *Istoriia Kazakhskoĭ SSR s drevneĭshikh vremen do nashikh dneĭ* (Alma-Ata: 1949; Tashkent: 1951); *Arkhitekturnye pamiatniki Kirgizii* (Moscow and Leningrad: 1950); *Ocherk istorii gunnov* (Leningrad: 1951); (editor) N.IA. Bichurin (Iakinf), *Sobranie svedeniĭ o narodakh, obitavshikh v Sredneĭ Azii v drevnie vremena* (Moscow and Leningrad: 1950).

SOURCES: "Aleksandr Natanovich Bernshtam," *Sovetskaia arkheologiia*, no. 1 (1957), pp. 289-290; S. Tolstov, "Aleksandr Natanovich Bernshtam," *Sovetskaia ėtnografiia*, no. 1 (1957), pp. 178-183 [includes bibliography].

Tat'iana A. Bernshtam
[Translation from Russian: Thomas L. Mann]

Berry, Jack. Linguist, lexicographer, creolist, Africanist. Born in Leeds (England) 13 December 1918, died in Evanston (Illinois) 4 December 1980. Berry was considered an authority on West African languages, and he produced dictionaries and grammars of several Ghanaian and Sierra Leonean languages. In later years his scholarly attention focused increasingly on applied sociolinguistics, especially language planning and orthographic reform, and on English-based Caribbean pidgin and creole languages.

Berry's early training was in Classics (B.A., University of Leeds, 1939), and, following British Army service in the Gold Coast (now Ghana) during World War II, he studied comparative linguistics under J.R. FIRTH at the University of London, completing his dissertation, *Structural Affinities of the Volta River Languages*, in 1952. Berry joined the faculty of the School of Oriental and African Studies at London and was awarded its first Chair of West African Languages in 1960. In 1964 he founded Northwestern University's Department of Linguistics, and in 1972 he organized the Program of Oriental and African Languages at Northwestern.

Berry's descriptive work on Africa covered structural analyses of languages spoken in nine West African countries. He was the principal contributor on languages of the Gold Coast in the Ethnographic Survey of Africa (1950-1952), and he produced numerous articles and monographs on the phonology, morphosyntax and place names of many West African languages, along with dictionaries on Krio and Twi-Asante-Fante and textbooks on Ga and Akan. Berry supervised the "Madina Project" on language attitudes in Ghana, probably the first sociolinguistic survey of language users conducted in Africa. He also collected, translated and edited more than 140 traditional folktales from Nigeria and Ghana.

Berry is also well known for his work on orthographic reform and development. "The making of alphabets" was a seminal paper that substantially redefined the process of creating alphabets for uncodified languages. Here Berry urged designers of new writing systems to go beyond traditional linguistic and typographical concerns and to include pedagogical, psychological and social considerations in the planning process, thus making him one of the first scholars to regard alphabets as cultural as well as linguistic entities. A later work called "The making of alphabets revisited" assessed the state of orthographic planning research. Berry is also known for his 1965 "Introduction" to BRONISLAW MALINOWSKI's *The Language of Magic and Gardening*. In it Berry articulated a London School or "Firthian" view of semantics that affirmed the duality of meaning in language. Berry believed that meaning was analyzable not only as a context-free unit within the linguistic system but also as a context-bound or functional entity within larger contexts of situation and culture. This stance put Berry sharply at odds with both Malinowski's "speech only" view of language and Chomsky's syntax-based linguistic model.

Berry's scholarly contributions were bolstered by significant editorial work. He founded *The Journal of African Languages* and served as its first editor. He also edited or co-edited numerous other volumes, including the 1966 *Proceedings of the Conference on African Languages and Literatures*, *Linguistics in Sub-Saharan Africa* and *Sociolinguistics and Education in the Third World*.

MAJOR WORKS: *The Pronunciation of Ga* (Cambridge: 1951); *The Pronunciation of Ewe* (Cambridge: 1951); *African Languages and Dialects in Education* (Paris: 1953); "The making of alphabets" in: *Proceedings of the Eighth International Congress of Linguists* (Oslo: 1958), pp. 752-764; *An English-Twi-Asante-Fante Dictionary* (London: 1960); "Pidgins and creoles in Africa" in: *Colloque sur le multilinguisme = Symposium on Multilingualism* (Brazzaville: 1962), pp. 219-225; "Introduction" to: Bronislaw Malinowski, *Language of Magic and Gardening* [vol. 2 of: *Coral Gardens and Their Magic*] (Bloomington: 1965), pp. vii-xvii; *A Dictionary of Sierra Leone Krio* (Washington: 1967); "The Madina project, Ghana: language attitudes in Madina," *Research Review* [Institute of African Studies, University of Ghana], vol. 5, issue 2 (1969), pp. 61-79; *An Introductory Course in Ga* (Washington: 1969); *An Introduction to Akan* (Washington: 1975); (associate editor) *Linguistics in Sub-Saharan Africa* (The Hague: 1969) (= *Current Trends in Linguistics*, vol. 7); (editor) *Sociolinguistics and Education in the Third World* (The Hague: 1976) (= *International Journal of the Sociology of Language*, vol. 8).

Craig A. Sirles

Best, Elsdon. Ethnologist. Born at Tawa, near Wellington (New Zealand) 30 June 1856, died in Wellington (New Zealand) 9 September 1931. The first and in many ways the foremost New Zealand-born ethnologist, Best had no formal education beyond passing the Junior Civil Service Examination. Although briefly employed in the civil service, he opted for the open-air life of a frontiersman, served briefly in the New Zealand Armed Constabulary, spent several years wandering and working in the Pacific and the United States and, after his return to New Zealand, was employed on road works in the remote Uruwera ranges in the North Island, home of the Tuhoe Maori, in 1895. He spent the next fifteen years in the district recording the history and lore of the Tuhoe, one of the first ethnologists ever to engage in intensive fieldwork. Subsequently, Best was employed as ethnologist at the Dominion Museum in Wellington where he was able to write up and publish his Tuhoe material, as well as many other essays and monographs on Maori culture. Best was a founding member of the Polynesian Society, working closely with S. PERCY SMITH and succeeding him as editor of the *Journal of the Polynesian Society* in 1922. Altogether, Best published twenty-five books and monographs, more than fifty papers and many more newspaper articles. In his lifetime and for long afterward he was regarded as the doyen of Maori scholars. Some of his monographs and his general survey *The Maori As He Was* remain in print fifty years after first publication. Though some of his language now has an archaic flavor and his quest for an Indian (indeed, at times, a Middle Eastern) origin for the Maori and their customs is no longer accepted, in his day, Best was highly regarded by some of the founding fathers of British anthropology, including A.C. HADDON and G.H.L.F. Pitt-Rivers (1890-1966).

MAJOR WORKS: *The Land of Tara* (New Plymouth: 1919); *The Maori* [2 vols.] (Wellington: 1924); *The Maori As He Was* (Wellington: 1924); *Tuhoe: Children of the Mist* (New Plymouth, New Zealand: 1925) (= *Memoirs of the Polynesian Society*, vol. 6).

SOURCES: E.W.G. Craig, *Man of the Mist: a Biography of Elsdon Best* (Wellington: 1964); M.P.K. Sorrenson, *Maori Origins and Migrations* (Auckland: 1979); A.S. Bagnall, "Best, Elsdon (1856-1931)" in: *An Encyclopaedia of New Zealand* (Wellington: 1966), vol. 1, pp. 199-200; "The late Elsdon Best, F.N.Z. Inst.," *Journal of the Polynesian Society*, vol. 41 (1932), pp. 1-49 [contains bibliography].

M.P.K. Sorrenson

Beyer, H. Otley (Henry Otley). Anthropologist, archaeologist, prehistorian. Born in Edgewood (Iowa) 13 July 1883, died in Manila (Philippines) 31 December 1966. He received an A.B. degree from Iowa State College in 1904 and completed an A.M. degree (chemistry) at the University of Denver in 1905.

Beyer's lifelong involvement with the Philippines began in 1904 with a visit to the Louisiana Purchase Centennial Exposition in St. Louis. There Beyer met and was recruited by Albert Ernest Jenks, Chief of the Philippine Ethnological Survey. Beyer arrived in Manila in August 1905. Three eventful years were spent among the Ifugao in Banaue District of the Mountain Province as a supervising teacher. Returning to the United States, Beyer completed a year of graduate study in anthropology at Harvard University (1908-1909).

Beyer was an ethnologist at the Philippine Bureau of Science from 1909 to 1914. In 1912 he began assembling a set of cultural and historical documents that would be called the *Philippine Ethnographic Series.* Carbon copies of these papers were deposited at Harvard, at the University of the Philippines and in his personal collection. The founding member of the University of the Philippines anthropology department (1914), he was named chair in 1925.

Beyer's chief investigations, prior to 1921, were in Philippine ethnography. By 1926, when the Novaliches dam site was discovered, his interests had turned to archaeology and prehistory. A tireless collector, Beyer gathered extensive quantities of Philippine artifacts, stoneware, prehistoric tools, jewelry, Chinese ceramics and tektites at his Museum and Institute of Archaeology and Ethnology in Manila. Cataloging and documentation of the hundreds of thousands of items in the Beyer collections was a persistent problem that was never fully resolved. In addition, some portions of the collections were destroyed during the fighting at the end of World War II.

During the post-war years, Professor Beyer, who had become known as the "dean of Philippine anthropology," was often called on by traveling scholars and graduate students. He died in Manila at age 83, survived by his Ifugao wife, Lengngayu, and son, William. On 11 January 1967, burial ceremonies were performed at Banaue, Ifugao, according to Ifugao custom. Professor Beyer's contributions to Philippine anthropology, like his collections, were too varied and diverse to summarize readily. Philippine anthropologists are still exploring many of the problems that Beyer first addressed.

MAJOR WORKS: *Population of the Philippine Islands in 1916 = Población de las Islas Filipinas en 1916* (Manila: 1917); *Philippine Tektites: a Contribution to the Study of the Tektite Problem* ... (Quezon City: 1961-1962); "Origin myths among the mountain peoples of the Philippines," *Philippine Journal of Science,* vol. 8D, no. 2 (April 1913), pp. 85-[118]; "The non-Christian people of the Philippines" in: *Census of the Philippine Islands, 1918,* vol. 2 (Manila: 1921), pp. 907-957; "Outline review of Philippine archaeology by islands and provinces," *Philippine Journal of Science,* vol. 77, no. 3-4 (July-Aug. 1947), pp. 205-390; "Philippine and East Asian archaeology and its relation to the origin of the Pacific Islands population," *National Research Council of the Philippines Bulletin,* no. 29 (1948), pp. 1-130.

SOURCES: Rudolf Rahmann and Gertrudes R. Ang (editors), *Dr. H. Otley Beyer: Dean of Philippine Anthropology* (Cebu City: 1968); Mario D. Zamora (editor), *Studies in Philippine Anthropology in Honor of H. Otley Beyer* (Quezon City: 1967); Juan R. Francisco, "H. Otley Beyer's contribution to Indo-Philippine scholarship," *Bulletin of the American Historical Collection,* vol. 4, no. 2 (April 1976), pp. 25-42; Evett D. Hester, "Henry Otley Beyer," *Bulletin of the American Historical Collection,* vol. 8 no. 2 (April-June 1980), pp. 39-44; E. Arsenio Manuel, "The Beyer Collection of original sources in Philippine ethnography," *ASLP Bulletin (Association of Special Libraries of the Philippines),* vol. 4, no. 3-4 (September-December 1958), pp. 46-66; E. Arsenio Manuel, "H. Otley Beyer, 1883-1966, anthropologist" in: *Scientists in the Philippines* (Manila: 1975-1978), vol. 2, pp. 1-25; "Dr. Otley Beyer, anthropologist," *New York Times* (2 January 1967), p. 19; E. Arsenio Manuel, "The wake and last rites over H. Otley Beyer in Ifugaoland," *Philippine Studies,* vol. 23, no. 1-2 (1975), pp. 120-189.

Lee S. Dutton

Bichurin, N.ĪĀ. (Nikita ĪĀkovlevich) (religious name: Father Iakinf). Orientalist, ethnographer, historian. Born in Akulevo, Kazanskaĭâ Guberniĭâ (Russia) 1777, died in St. Petersburg (Russia) 11 May 1853. When Bichurin was twenty-two he took monastic vows and became known to scholars under his monastic name, Father Iakinf. He became a full corresponding member of the Academy of Sciences in 1828. From 1808 to 1821 he was in China. A brilliant connoisseur of the Chinese language, Bichurin became thoroughly familiar with Chinese historical writing and derived from it extraordinarily valuable information about the history and ethnography of the peoples of China, Tibet, Mongolia, Manchuria, Xinjiang and Southern Siberia, introducing this information to world scholarship. The materials he collected on the historical ethnography of the peoples of Eastern and Central Asia have retained their value to this day.

MAJOR WORKS: *Zapiski o Mongolii* [2 vols.] (St. Petersburg: 1828); *Opisanie Tibeta v nyneshnem ego sostoíanii* (St. Petersburg: 1828); *Opisanie Chzhungarii i Vostochnogo Turkestana v drevnem i nyneshnem sostoíanii* [2 vols.] (St. Petersburg: 1829); *Istoriía Tibeta i Khukhunora* [2 vols.] (St. Petersburg: 1833); *Kitaĭ, ego zhiteli, nravy, obychai, prosveshchenie v Kitae* (St. Petersburg: 1840); *Zemledelie v Kitae s 72 chertezhami raznykh zemledel'cheskikh orudiĭ* (St. Petersburg: 1844); *Kitaĭ v grazhdanskom i nravstvennom sostoíanii* [4 parts] (St. Petersburg: 1848); *Sobranie svedeniĭ o narodakh, obitavshikh v Sredneĭ Azii v drevnie vremena* [3 parts] (St. Petersburg: 1851; new ed., Moscow: 1950-1953).

SOURCES: S.A. Tokarev, *Istoriía russkoĭ étnografii (dooktíabr'skiĭ period)* (Moscow: 1966), pp. 152-162; P.E. Skachkov, *Ocherki istorii russkogo kitaevedeniía* (Moscow: 1977), pp. 90-120.

A.M. Reshetov
[Translation from Russian: CW]

Bidney, David. Philosopher, anthropologist. Born in the Ukraine (Russia) 25 September 1908, died in North York (Ontario) 8 January 1987. Bidney was raised in Toronto following his family's emigration from Russia. He earned his bachelor's and master's degrees (1928, 1929) in philosophy at the University of Toronto; his doctorate (1932) was from Yale, where he was a University Fellow. Bidney taught at Toronto from 1932 until 1934, whereupon he returned to Yale for two years as a postdoctoral fellow. After another two years of teaching, this time at Yeshiva University, he once again returned to Yale, to a prestigious Sterling Fellowship. He taught in the Yale Department of Philosophy from 1940 to 1942.

In all, Bidney spent nine years at Yale and came to know several members of the anthropology faculty there (presumably including the influential GEORGE PETER MURDOCK). He developed an interest in the philosophical underpinnings of anthropology and was able to study this topic when, from 1942 until 1950, he acted as both assistant to the director and research associate in the Wenner-Gren Foundation for Anthropological Research.

In 1950 Bidney moved to Indiana University. At first serving in both the anthropology and philosophy departments, he moved fully into anthropology by 1964. His last four years at Indiana, 1970-1974, included quarter-time service in the philosophy of education department.

Bidney was a memorable and exacting teacher and encouraged his students to bring a philosophical orientation to their anthropology. His own interests included morality and ethics of primitive societies and the development of a humanistic anthropology—an area in which he was a major innovator. He was the recipient of a Guggenheim Fellowship in 1950 and a Ford International Fellowship in 1964. Upon retirement, Bidney returned to the Toronto area where he grew up.

MAJOR WORKS: *The Psychology and Ethics of Spinoza* (New Haven: 1949); "The philosophical anthropology of Ernst Cassirer and its significance in relation to the history of anthropological thought" in: P.A. Schilpp (editor), *The Philosophy of Ernst Cassirer* (Evanston: 1949), pp. 465-544; *Theoretical Anthropology* (New York: 1953); "The concept of value in modern anthropology" in: A.L. Kroeber (editor), *Anthropology Today* (Chicago: 1953), pp. 682-699; "The philosophical pre-suppositions of cultural relativism and cultural absolutism" in: Leo R. Ward (editor), *Ethics and the Social Sciences* (South Bend: 1959), pp. 51-76; "Paul Radin and the problem of primitive monotheism" in: Stanley Diamond (editor), *Culture and History: Essays in Honor of Paul Radin* (New York: 1960), pp. 363-379; (editor) *The Concept of Freedom in Anthropology* (The Hague: 1963); "Cultural relativism" in: David L. Sills (editor), *International Encyclopedia of the Social Sciences* (New York: 1968-1979), vol. 3, pp. 543-547.

SOURCES: "Bidney, David," *Contemporary Authors*, vol. 9-12 (1974), p. 82; James H. Keller, "David Bidney" in: Bruce T. Grindal and Dennis M. Warren (editors), *Essays in Humanistic Anthropology* (Washington: 1979), pp. v-vii; "David Bidney," *Anthropology Newsletter*, vol. 28, no. 4 (April 1987), p. 4.

David Lonergan

Bird, Junius Bouton. Archaeologist, explorer, naturalist. Born in Rye (New York) 21 September 1907, died in New York (New York) 2 April 1982. Bird is well known primarily for his research on the early human populations of South America and for his investigation of prehistoric technologies, particularly textiles. His career as an archaeologist spanned a half-century at the American Museum of Natural History in New York City.

Early in life Bird sailed several times to the Arctic aboard the schooner Morrissey and became an accomplished sailor and outdoorsman. His first research dealt with East Greenland and Labrador. Thereafter Bird cast his sights toward South America where he would launch several major research projects. In 1936 and 1937, at Fell's Cave and other sites in Chilean Patagonia, Bird found human artifacts in clear association with extinct sloths and horses (*Travels and Archaeology in South Chile*), establishing the great antiquity of human population in South America. In 1941 Bird would create a long prehistoric sequence in northern Chile (*Excavations in Northern Chile*). In 1946 and 1947 Bird excavated a large mound in northern Peru (*The Preceramic Excavations at the Huaca Prieta, Chicama Valley, Peru*). This investigation defined the existence of preceramic cultures on the Peruvian coast and established the role of textiles as a major medium of cultural expression in ancient Andean culture. Bird carried out smaller investigations at numerous other sites in North and South America. In his final years he worked in Panama.

Bird was widely known as a careful and innovative fieldworker, introducing many new techniques of excavation and artifact analysis. He pioneered in dating with radiocarbon, in the analysis of botanical and faunal remains and in the conservation and study of textiles. He was an active member of the archaeological community and received many honors and awards including the Viking Fund Medal and the Order of the Sun of Peru. He served as president of the Society of American Archaeology and as chairman of the Anthropology Section of the New York Academy of Sciences. Wesleyan University granted him an honorary doctorate in 1958. Bird's numerous contributions to South American prehistory have provided a framework upon which the research of many other scholars was based.

MAJOR WORKS: "Antiquity and migrations of the early inhabitants of Patagonia," *Geographical Review*, vol. 28 (1933), pp. 250-275; *Excavations in Northern Chile* (New York: 1938) (= *Anthropological Papers of the American Museum of Natural History*, vol. 38); *Archaeology of the Hopedale Area, Labrador* (New York: 1945) (= *Anthropological Papers of the American Museum of Natural History*, vol. 39); "The Alacaluf" in: Julian H. Steward (editor), *Handbook of South American Indians*, vol. 1 (Washington: 1946), pp. 55-79; "America's oldest farmers," *Natural History*, vol. 57 (1948), pp. 32-35; (with W.C. Bennett) *Andean Culture History* (New York: 1949), "Art and life on old Peru," *Curator*, vol. 5 (1962), pp. 140-210; "The 'Copper Man': a prehistoric miner and his tools from Northern Chile" in: Elizabeth P. Benson (editor), *Pre-Columbian Metallurgy of South America* (Washington: 1979), pp. 105-132; (with J. Hyslop and M. Dimitrijevic Skinner) *The Preceramic Excavations at the Huaca Prieta, Chicama Valley, Peru* (New York: 1985) (= *Anthropological Papers of the American Museum of Natural History*, vol. 62); (with Margaret Bird) *Travels and Archaeology in South Chile* (Iowa City: 1988).

SOURCES: The Junius B. Bird archive at the Anthropology Department of the American Museum of Natural History, New York; Gordon R. Willey, "Junius Bouton Bird and American archaeology" in: Junius and Margaret Bird, *Travels and Archaeology in South Chile* (Iowa City: 1988), pp. xiii-xxxi; John Hyslop, "Portrait of an archaeologist," *Natural History* (February 1989), pp. 84-89.

John Hyslop

Birket-Smith, Kaj. Anthropologist, culture historian. Born in Copenhagen (Denmark) 20 January 1893, died in Alborg (Denmark) 28 October 1977. Birket-Smith is best known for his work among the Inuit (Eskimo) in Greenland and Alaska. After two shorter field trips to western Greenland in 1912 and 1918 he joined KNUD RASMUSSEN's Fifth Thule Expedition as ethnographer in 1921-1923; he concentrated on the study of the material culture of the Caribou Eskimos and suggested in his doctoral dissertation (*The Caribou Eskimos*) that the inland-dwelling, caribou-hunting Eskimos represented the most archaic, "Paleo-Eskimo" culture. In 1933 he returned to the Arctic to do a study of the little-known Chugach Eskimos on the Pacific coast.

Birket-Smith was keenly interested in cultural history and diffusion and derived his primary inspiration from the *Kulturkreis*-school of WILHELM SCHMIDT and his associates. He was correspondingly skeptical of Durkheimian sociology, but his only objection to British functionalism was its rejection of the importance of the historical dimension. His regional interests were not restricted to the Arctic; indeed, his learning and world-wide interests were impressive, and in the early 1950s he made field trips to the Philippines and Rennell Island in Melanesia.

Birket-Smith's academic career was centered at the Department of Ethnography of the Danish National Museum in Copenhagen, which he joined in 1929; he served as head curator from 1946 to 1963. He was awarded honorary doctorates at the Universities of Pennsylvania, Oslo (Norway), Basel (Switzerland), and Uppsala (Sweden). At his initiative, anthropology was established as an independent subject at the University of Copenhagen in 1945, and from his base at the Museum he trained the first generation of professional Danish anthropologists.

Birket-Smith also made his mark outside academia as author of several popular anthropological works, the best known being *Eskimoerne* and *Kulturens Veje*, both of which were translated into a number of European languages.

MAJOR WORKS: *Ethnography of the Egedesminde District with Aspects of the General Culture of West Greenland* (Copenhagen: 1924); *Eskimoerne* (Copenhagen: 1927; 2nd ed., Copenhagen: 1961) [tr.: *The Eskimos* (London: 1936; 2nd ed., London: 1959)]; *The Caribou Eskimos: Material and Social Life and Their Cultural Position* [2 vols.] (Copenhagen: 1929); *Knud Rasmussens Saga* (Copenhagen: 1936); *Kulturens Veje* [2 vols.] (Copenhagen: 1941-1942; 3rd ed. [3 vols.], Copenhagen: 1965-1967) [tr.: *The Paths of Culture: a General Ethnology* (Madison: 1965)]; *The Chugach Eskimo* (Copenhagen: 1953); *An Ethnological Sketch of Rennell Island, a Polynesian Outlier in Melanesia* (Copenhagen: 1956).

SOURCES: Helge Larsen, "Birket-Smith and the Arctic," *Folk*, vol. 5 (1963), pp. 1-10; Johannes Nicolaisen, "The anthropology of Birket-Smith," *Folk*, vol. 5 (1963), pp. 11-19; Kjeld Birket-Smith, "Kaj Birket-Smith: selected bibliography," *Folk*, vol. 5 (1963), pp. 21-31; Einar Storgaard, "Birket-Smith, Kaj" in: *Dansk Biografisk Leksikon* (Copenhagen: 1979), vol. 2, pp. 159-160; Johannes Nicolaisen, "Scandinavia: all approaches are fruitful" in: Stanley Diamond (editor), *Anthropology: Ancestors and Heirs* (The Hague: 1980), pp. 259-273.

Jan Ovesen

Biró, Lajos. Zoologist, ethnographer. Born in Tasnád, Zilah County, Transylvania (Hungary, now in Rumania) 29 August 1856, died in Budapest (Hungary) 2 September 1931. Biró was one of the founders of the New Guinea collection of the Néprajzi Múzeum (Ethnographical Museum), Budapest. Between 1 January 1896 and 27 December 1901 he spent six years in what was then German New Guinea gathering materials in natural history and ethnography for the Departments of Natural Sciences and Ethnography at the Nemzeti Múzeum (National Museum).

Biró's collection covered the entire colony although the most famous part came from Astrolabe Bay, the region of Madang, formerly Friedrich-Wilhelms-Hafen. In this area he confirmed the work of Sámuel Fenichel, another Hungarian ethnographic collector who had lived and died in the region several years earlier. Biró also spent longer periods of time in the Huon Gulf area (Tami Islands, Sattelberg, Jabim area), in New Ireland, on the Witu Islands, in the Aitape (formerly Berlin-Hafen) area, and also in the region of Potsdam-Hafen-Bogia.

Biró's collection was superior to those of his contemporaries in that all objects were accompanied by detailed explanations and descriptions, in many cases by veritable ethnographic monographs giving the local names of the objects in the collection, their mode of preparation and usage, as well as the names of the patterns on the objects and their symbolic interpretation. He also traced the various objects' points of origin, pattern of diffusion, and so on. He strove to gather complete sets for his collection and was thus able to illustrate the large number of variations in each type of object.

The first section of his collection, the result of his work in Berlin-Hafen and the first phase of his Astrolabe Bay research, was presented in the form of a descriptive catalog and published in the Ethnographical Museum series. The publication appeared in a bilingual edition (German and Hungarian) and was published while Biró was still living in New Guinea. The work brought him great professional acclaim and is considered a basic and authoritative reference work on the culture of the inhabitants of Western New Guinea. The second and larger collection, from Astrolabe Bay, the Huon Gulf, and other regions, has never been published.

Biró was one of the first pioneers of ethnography in the New Guinea Region. He spoke several native languages, spent lengthy periods—up to one year—in one or the other region, had several Papuan wives, and thus had intimate knowledge of the social and cultural life of the region. Nevertheless, he never published a comprehensive work on the natives of Papua New Guinea. His popular articles and books in Hungarian emphasized his scientific beliefs. For his time, his ideology was uncommonly humanitarian. His works demonstrate his deep regard for the Papuan peoples as warm human beings. As a collector he made a lasting contribution to the Budapest Ethnographical Museum by providing the basis for its world-renowned Astrolabe Bay and New Guinea collection.

After Biró's return to Hungary, he was named honorary custodian of the zoological department of the National Museum. He then reverted to his original professional field, the natural sciences. He continued collecting and analyzing his zoological materials until his death.

MAJOR WORKS: *Német-uj-Guineai (Berlinhafeni) néprajzi gyüjtéseinek leiró jegyzéke = Beschreibender Catalog der ethnographischen Sammlung Ludwig-Biró-s aus Deutsch-Neu-Guinea (Berlinhafen)* (Budapest: 1899) (= *A Magyar Nemzeti Múzeum Néprajzi Gyüjteményei [Hungarian National Museum Ethnographic Collection]*, vol. 1); *Német-uj-Guineai (Astrolabe-Öböl) néprajzi gyüjtéseinek leiró jegyzéke = Beschreibender Catalog der ethnographischen Sammlung Ludwig Biró's aus Deutsch-Neu-Guinea (Astrolabe-Bai)* (Budapest: 1901) (= *A Magyar Nemzeti Múzeum Néprajzi Gyüjteményei [Hungarian National Museum Ethnographic Collection]*, vol. 3); "Adalékok a Bismarck-szigetek lakóinak hajózásához és halászatához" ["Information on sailing (navigation) and fishing of the Bismarck Islands natives"], *Néprajzi Értesitő*, vol. 6 (1905), pp. 57-72; *Hét év Uj-Guineában: Levelek két világrészből [Seven Years in New Guinea: Letters from Two Continents]* (Budapest: 1923); *Új-guineai utzásom emlékei [Memoirs of my New Guinea Travels]* (Budapest: 1932).

SOURCES: Asztalos Sándor, *Biró Lajos: egy nagy magyar utazó [Biró Lajos: a great Hungarian traveler]* (Budapest: 1923); Benedek Zoltán, *A Szilágyságtól Uj-Guineáig: Biró Lajos természettudós életútja (1856-1931) [From Szilagyság to New Guinea: Biography of the Naturalist Lajos Biró (1856-1931)]* (Bucharest: 1979); Tibor Bodrogi, "Biró Lajos (1856-1931)" in: Lajos Biró, *Hat év Uj-Guineában [Six Years in New Guinea]* (Budapest: 1987), pp. 9-33; Gábor Vargyas, *Data on the Pictorial History of North-East Papua New Guinea* (Budapest: 1986) (= *Occasional Papers in Anthropology*, no. 1). SOURCES DEALING WITH THE LAJOS BIRÓ COLLECTION: Tibor Bodrogi, "Yabim drums in the Biró collection," *Folia Ethnographica*, vol. 1, no. 2-4 (1949), pp. 205-222; Tibor Bodrogi, "Some notes on the ethnography of New Guinea," *Acta Ethnographica*, vol. 3, no. 1-4 (1953), pp. 91-184; Tibor Bodrogi, "New Guinean style provinces: Astrolabe Bay" in: *Opuscula Ethnographica Memoria Ludovici Biró Sacra* (Budapest: 1959), pp. 39-99; Tibor Bodrogi, *Art in North-East New Guinea* (Budapest: 1959); Tibor Bodrogi, "Malangans in North New Ireland: Lajos Biró's unpublished notes," *Acta Ethnographica*, vol. 16 (1967), pp. 61-77; Tibor Bodrogi, "Zur Ethnographie der Vitu-(French)-Inseln," *Baessler-Archiv*, n.F., vol. 19 (1971), pp. 47-71.

Vargyas Gábor
[Translation from Hungarian: Ildiko D. Nowak]

Bittremieux, Leo. Priest in the missionary society of Scheut, linguist, ethnographer. Born in Sysseele (Belgium) 4 September 1880, died in Boma (Zaïre) 21 August 1946. Bittremieux was a self-taught linguist and ethnographer of the matrilineal Yombe, a western variation of the Kongo culture extending on both sides of the Zaïre river throughout Lower Zaïre, the south of the Republic of Congo, and north-western Angola. Bittremieux's *Mayombsch idioticon* is a very rich source of vocabulary, idiomatic expressions and ethnographic data. Drawing on his excellent command of the Yombe language, Bittremieux, in three publications (*Mayombsche namen*, *Woordkunst der Bayombe*, *Symbolisme in de negerkunst*), offered a representative sample of myths, tales, riddles, proverbs, praise names and songs. His insightful presentation of collective and domestic cults associated with uterine ancestors, ghosts and varieties of territorial and local spirits abounds in rituals, texts and set phrasings. The major *khimba* cult in Yombe society is akin to *kimpasi* and *khita* in the eastern Kongo land (*De geheime sekte der Bakhimba's, La société secrète des Bakhimba*). *Khimba* embraces the collective symbols of authority, adversity and protection. A variety of territorial spirits, anthropomorphic charms, offerings and ritual practices at certain river pools and caves enhance or renew the reproductive capacities in society and the soil. In this cult, the rainbow-serpent (*mbumba luangu*) is a potent cosmogonic metaphor associated with the fertility of land and people. Moreover, the *khimba* cult periodically sets the forms of solidarity and redistributes information between co-initiates and, hence, crosscuts the bounds of the corporate matrilineages.

As a pioneer Catholic missionary, Bittremieux blatantly rejected many ritual and reproduction-enhancing practices in Yombe culture as well as the kimbanguist messianic movement. Besides his many Yome-language booklets with Yombe lore, and the prayers and songs he composed himself, he edited the monthly periodical *Tsungi mona* and the almanac *Lutangu lu mvu*. In 1944, all his notes were lost when his mission station of Mbata-Mbenge burned down, three years before he died of the *kimputu* recurrent fever.

> MAJOR WORKS: *De geheime sekte der Bakhimba's* (Leuven: 1911) [revised and tr.: *La société secrète des Bakhimba* (Bruxelles: 1936)]; *Mayombsche namen* (Leuven: 1912; expanded ed., Leuven: 1934); *Mayombsch idioticon* [3 vols.] (vols. 1 and 2, Gent: 1923; vol. 3, Brussels: 1927); *Woordkunst der Bayombe* (Brussels: 1937); *Symbolisme in de negerkunst* (Brussels 1937).

> SOURCES: A. Doutreloux, *L'ombre des fétiches: société et culture Yombe* (Louvain: 1967); W. MacGaffey, *Religion and Society in Central Africa: the Bakongo of Lower Zaire* (Chicago: 1986).

René Devisch

Black, Glenn A. (Glenn Albert). Anthropologist, archaeologist. Born in Indianapolis (Indiana) 15 August 1900, died in Evansville (Indiana) 2 September 1964. Like many prehistoric archaeologists of his generation in the United States, Black was essentially self-taught and attracted to the field by his early collecting activities. He was director of archaeological research for the Indiana Historical Society (1931-1964) and a lecturer in anthropology at Indiana University (1944-1960). Black was awarded a Sc.D. by Wabash College in 1951.

His contributions were three-fold. (1) He played a significant role in professionalizing archaeology in the United States, particularly in the early history of the Society for American Archaeology, which he served in many capacities, including the presidency (1941-1942). (2) Reflecting a lifelong concern, he showed an interest in more precise field methods in, e.g. his textbook excavation of the Nowlin Mound in the mid-1930s; his critique of the Tepexpan Man (Mexico) excavation in 1949; and the first long-term testing of the potential of the proton magnetometer in a North American prehistoric site in the 1950s and 1960s. (3) In keeping with his position that the goal of archaeology was to write the ethnography of prehistoric life, he devoted twenty-seven years to research and excavation of a single large Mississippian site, Angel Mounds, located in the Ohio River Valley near Evansville (Indiana). Black's long-time partnership with ELI LILLY was responsible for founding an archaeological research program in Indiana, which continues.

MAJOR WORKS: (with Paul Weer) "A proposed terminology for shape classification of arti-
facts," *American Antiquity*, vol. 1 (1936), pp. 37-47; "Excavation of the Nowlin Mound," *Indiana
Historical Bulletin*, vol. 14 (1936), pp. 207-305; "'Tepaxpan Man,' a critique of method," *American
Antiquity*, vol. 14 (1949), pp. 344-346; *An Archaeological Consideration of the Walam Olum. Walam
Olum or Red Score, The Migration Legend of the Lenni Lenape or Delaware Indians* (Chicago and
Crawfordsville, Indiana: 1954), pp. 292-348; (with Richard B. Johnston) "A test of magnetometry as
an aid to archaeology," *American Antiquity*, vol. 28 (1963), pp. 199-205; *Angel Mounds: an
Archaeological, Historical, and Ethnological Study* (Chicago and Crawfordsville, Indiana: 1967).

SOURCES: James H. Keller, "Glenn A. Black, 1900-1964," *American Antiquity*, vol. 31
(1966), pp. 402-405; Lana Ruegamer, *A History of the Indiana Historical Society, 1830-1980*
(Indianapolis: 1980); James H. Madison, *Eli Lilly: Archaeologist* (Bloomington: 1988) (= *Glenn A.
Black Laboratory of Archaeology, Indiana University, Research Reports*, no. 8).

James H. Kellar

Blom, Frans (Frans Ferdinand Blom Peterson). Archaeologist, explorer. Born
in Copenhagen (Denmark) 9 August 1893, died in San Cristóbal de las Casas (Mexico) 23
June 1963. Blom was one of the great 20th-century scholars of Maya culture.

Blom learned English, French and German in his boyhood home, and this helped
prepare him for a life of travel and international research. He went to Mexico for the first
time in 1919 and began three years of work for the Compañia Petrolera El Aguila (Aguila
Oil Company), in the course of which he traveled widely. He visited, among other places,
the ruins at Palenque and became acquainted with the culture of the Indians.

Blom gradually drifted into professional archaeological work and, after acquiring
an M.A. from Harvard in 1924, joined the staff of the Middle American Research Institute
at Tulane University, where he was director between 1926 and 1941. During these years he
led several important scientific expeditions. In 1925, with Oliver LaFarge, he traveled
through Tabasco and Chiapas, making stops in La Venta, Comalcalco and Palenque, and
ended up in the Guatemalan highlands, visiting (among other places) Todos Santos,
Jacaltenango, Huehuetenango and Chiantla (this is the expedition described in *Tribes and
Temples*). In 1928 he traveled across the 2,500 heretofore unexplored kilometers between
Tapachula and Chichén Itzá, with stops at Tikal, Yaxchilán, Altar de Sacrificios and
Bacalar. In 1933 he visited Uxmal. He published many articles on Mexican Indian culture
during the the 1930s in both scholarly and popular journals. A difficult period in the early
1940s ended with his marriage to Gertrude Duby in 1943 (see GERTRUDE DUBY BLOM).

Blom returned to Mexico in the mid-1940s, exploring the territory of the
Lacondón Indians and eventually, in 1950, settling in San Cristóbal de la Casas, where he
and his wife turned their house, Na Bolom, into a center of linguistic and ethnological research and the best archaeological museum in Southwest Mexico. He became a Mexican
citizen in 1963. The last years of his life were spent writing about the Lacondón Indians
(e.g., in *La Selva Lacondona*) and acting as a powerful advocate for their rights and interests.

MAJOR WORKS: *Tribes and Temples* (New Orleans: 1927) [tr.: *Tribus y templos* (Mexico City:
1986)]; *La vida de los Mayas* (Mexico City: 1944) (= *Biblioteca enciclopédica popular*, vol. 25); *La
conquista de Yucatán* (1944) [tr.: *Conquest of the Yucatan* (Boston: 1936)]; (with Gertrude Duby) *La
Selva lacondona* (Mexico City: 1955).

SOURCES: Robert L. Brunhouse, *Frans Blom, Maya Explorer* (Albuquerque: 1976) [contains
bibliography, pp. 273-284]; Douglas S. Byers, "Frans Blom, 1893-1963," *American Antiquity*, vol.

31 (1966): pp. 406-407; "Frans Blom, archeologist, dies," *New York Times* (24 June 1963), p. 27; "Frans Blom, 69," *Time*, vol. 82 (5 July 1963), p. 72; Frank M. Dunbaugh, "Dr. Blom & the Lacondons," *Américas*, vol. 12 (1960), pp. 31-35; "Blom, Frans" in: *Enciclopedia de México* (Mexico City: 1978), vol. 2, p. 248.

Francis X. Grollig, S.J.

Blom, Gertrude Duby (née Gertrude Elizabeth Loertscher). Ethnographer, linguist, photographer. Born in the canton of Bern (Switzerland) 7 July 1901. At an early age Trudy Duby was introduced to socialist ideas by a neighbor, Herr Duby, general secretary of the trade union for Swiss railway workers, and became a close friend of his son to whom she was married for three years (1925-1928). She received a degree in horticulture from a Swiss school in Niederlintz and later completed two years of study at a school for social work in Zürich. As the European fascist movement emerged in the years following World War I, first in Italy and then in Germany, she became an active opponent of their activities. In 1924 she was arrested and jailed for a week in Italy for anti-fascist activities. Again in Paris, at the onset of World War II, she was arrested with other non-French anti-fascists and put in a detention camp. The Swiss government was able to obtain her release after five months internment.

In 1940 Duby came to Mexico as a journalist to study working conditions. It was at this time that she purchased her first camera and started taking the photographs for which she would eventually become famous. In 1943 she made her first trip to the Lacondón as part of the first government investigation of the living conditions of the Lacondón people to determine their need for governmental assistance. Since then she has made more than twelve trips of three- to seven-months duration to the Lacondón jungle and more than sixty trips lasting from five to twenty days. With her camera she has recorded the disintegration of Lacondón society from 1943 to the present. She has developed strong, lasting relationships with the Lacondón people as she fought unceasingly to save their traditional way of life as well as their jungle home. For twenty years (1943-1963) she worked closely with her husband, FRANS BLOM, whom she married in 1944, accompanying him on expeditions and collaborating with him in many other ways.

In 1950 the Bloms bought their home Na Bolom, in San Cristóbal, which ultimately became the Center for Scientific Studies in Chiapas. In 1975 Doña Blom established a tree nursery that now provides 25,000-30,000 native trees for planting in the Chiapas highlands each year. Her photo collection contains more than 20,000 black-and-white and color photos that document the cultural change of the Maya descendents of Chiapas, both in the highlands and in the jungle, and the destruction of the rain forest since 1943. Her photos have been displayed at a number of national and international exhibits including a three-year traveling exhibition in the United States in the 1980s.

MAJOR WORKS: *Los Lacondones* (Mexico City: 1944); *¿Hay razas inferiores?* (Mexico City: 1946); (with Frans Ferdinand Blom) *La Selva lacondona* (Mexico City: 1955); *Chiapas indígena* (Mexico City: 1961); *La familia de Na Bolom* (Monterey, Mexico: 1979). SELECTED PHOTOGRAPHY EXHIBITS: Musée d'Ethnographie, Geneva, Switzerland (1948); Ateneo de Mujeres, Havana, Cuba (1948); Geografisk Laboratorium, Copenhagen, Denmark (1948); Asociación Mexicana de Periodistas, Mexico City (1949); World Exhibition of Photography, Lucerne, Switzerland (1952); El Instituto Nacional de Bellas Artes, Mexico City (1961 and 1971); University of Arizona, Tucson (1978); International Center of Photography, New York (1984); Chicago Academy of Sciences, Chicago (1985).

Norman Britan

Bloomfield, Leonard. Linguist, comparative philologist. Born in Chicago (Illinois) 1 April 1887, died in New Haven (Connecticut) 18 April 1949. Bloomfield's interests in language ranged from the philosophical or metatheoretical underpinnings of linguistics to the practical teaching of foreign languages and of reading a first language, and included everything in between. He was one of the most noted linguists of the century, principally because he succeeded in articulating all of the generalizations in linguistics contributing to its emergence as a distinct discipline in the United States, from about 1925 to 1960, while quietly practicing specific description, comparison and reconstruction of superb quality in specific languages and families.

He was trained as a Germanic philologist with interests in the wider Indo-European family of languages and published modestly in this area. His decisive contributions are, by contrast, his general linguistic writings, his documentary, descriptive and comparative Algonquian materials (the most extensive published posthumously) and his descriptive and comparative Austronesian work.

Though he had published a somewhat derivative *Introduction to the Study of Language* in 1914, Bloomfield's mature doctrine emerged only later. It combined his own longing for positive scientific rigor with specific orientation to FERDINAND DE SAUSSURE (whose *Cours de linguistique générale* we know Bloomfield to have read in 1920) and with his experience of attempting (from field elicitation) to describe the Austronesian language Tagalog (1916-1917) and the Algonquian language Menomini (early 1920s). Its culmination was the book *Language* (1933), which set the tone for a generation or two of linguistic teaching through exegesis. Bloomfield's commitment was to scientific principles in the study of language that, once applicable in some specific field, must perforce be applicable everywhere. These were particularly important to his comparative Algonquian work, which demonstrated once and for all that the methods of historical linguistics—including predictive deduction—apply to unwritten languages just as much as to written ones we study from documentary records, a point at one time contested even among ranking scholars of Indo-European.

Bloomfield uncompromisingly promoted the disciplinary autonomy of linguistics, both in his metatheoretical writing and by his professional service. At the same time, as an intellectual matrix for that discipline, he articulated mechanist ("anti-mentalist"), behaviorist, operationalist and logical positivist beliefs. These deep commitments, some even at variance with his own actual practice in describing and doing the history of languages, constitute an intellectual style and program of a whole era of followers in disciplinary linguistics as well as in adjacent disciplines such as cultural anthropology and psychology. Hardened into a doctrine called "Bloomfieldianism" or "neo-Bloomfieldianism" by its opponents, it became the focus of sharp attacks by Noam Chomsky and his followers, who practice, ironically enough, a disciplinary approach much like Bloomfield's own actual one.

MAJOR WORKS: *An Introduction to the Study of Language* (New York: 1914); *Tagalog Texts with Grammatical Analysis* (Urbana: 1917); *First German Book* (Columbus, Ohio: 1923; 2nd ed., New York: 1928); "Notes on the Fox language," *International Journal of American Linguistics*, vol. 3 (1925), pp. 219-232; vol. 4 (1927), pp. 181-219; *Menomini Texts* (New York: 1928); *Sacred Stories of the Sweet Grass Cree* (Ottawa: 1930); *Language* (New York: 1933); *Plains Cree Texts* (New York: 1934); *Linguistic Aspects of Science* (Chicago: 1939) (= *International Encyclopaedia of Unified Science*, vol. 1, no. 4); *Colloquial Dutch* (New York: 1944); "Algonquian" in: Harry Hoijer [et al.], *Linguistic Structures of Native America* (New York: 1946) (= *Viking Fund Publications in Anthropology*, no. 6), pp. 85-129; *The Menomini Language* (Charles F. Hockett, editor) (New Haven: 1962); *A Leonard Bloomfield Anthology* (Charles F. Hockett, editor) (Bloomington: 1970).

SOURCES: Robert A. Hall, Jr. (editor), *Leonard Bloomfield: Appraisals of his Life and Work* (Amsterdam: 1987) (= *Historiographia Linguistica* vol. 14, no. 1/2); Robert A. Hall, Jr., *A Life for Language: a Biographical Memoir of Leonard Bloomfield* (Amsterdam: 1990); Henry M. Hoenigswald (editor), *The European Background of American Linguistics* (Dordrecht: 1979); Stephen R. Anderson, *Phonology in the Twentieth Century: Theories of Rules and Theories of Representations* (Chicago: 1985); Karl V. Teeter, "Leonard Bloomfield's linguistics," *Language Sciences*, no. 7 (October 1969), pp. 1-6; Bruce R. Stark, "The Bloomfieldian model," *Lingua*, vol. 30 (1972), pp. 385-421; Dell Hymes and John Fought, "American structuralism" in: Thomas A. Sebeok (editor), *Current Trends in Linguistics*, vol. 13 (1975), pp. 903-1176; Michael Silverstein, Review of: Charles F. Hockett, *The View from Language*, *International Journal of American Linguistics*, vol. 44 (1978), pp. 235-253.

Michael Silverstein

Blumentritt, Ferdinand. Ethnographer, geographer, educator. Born in Prague, Bohemia (Austria) 10 September 1853, died at Leitmeritz, Bohemia (Austria-Hungary) 20 September 1913. Blumentritt attended secondary school in Prague then studied geography and history at Charles University. At the age of twenty-four he became a professor of geography at the Atheneum of Leitmeritz. Blumentritt devoted much of his scholarly career to the study of Philippine ethnography and related topics. He authored more than 500 books, articles, maps and other publications, chiefly in German or Spanish. Noteworthy among these works is a pioneering survey of Philippine ethnic groups, *Versuch einer Ethnographie der Philippinen*. Also noteworthy is Blumentritt's *Diccionario mitológico de Filipinas*.

Like most of his European contemporaries, Blumentritt never visited the Philippines. His writings were based on a study of materials available in Europe, supplemented by correspondence with a network of colleagues and sources in Europe, the Philippines and elsewhere. Blumentritt is remembered by Filipinos today because of his close friendship and scholarly and political collaboration with the country's national hero, Dr. José Rizal (1861-1896). Details of this relationship have been preserved in *The Rizal-Blumentritt Correspondence*. Blumentritt received many awards during his lifetime. Following his death, the Philippine government published *Vida y obras de Ferdinand Blumentritt* in his honor.

MAJOR WORKS: *Versuch einer Ethnographie der Philippinen* (Gotha: 1882) [tr.: *An Attempt at Writing a Philippine Ethnography ... with an Appendix: The Spanish Maritime Discoveries in [the] Philippine Archipelago (with a map of the Philippines) ...* (Marawi City: 1980)]; *Die Chinesen auf der Philippinen* (Leitmeritz: 1879); *Diccionario mitológico de Filipinas* (2nd ed., Madrid: 1895) (= W.E. Retana, *Archivo del bibliófilo filipino* (Madrid: 1895-1905), vol. 2, pp. 335-454, 511); *Las razas del archipiélago filipino ...* I. *Vade-mecum etnográfico de Filipinas.* II. *Las razas indígenas de Filipinas* (Madrid: 1890).

SOURCES: Harry Sichrovsky, *Der Revolutionär von Leitmeritz: Ferdinand Blumentritt und der philippinische Freiheitskampf* (Vienna: 1983) (= *Berichte des Ludwig-Boltzmann-Instituts für China und Sudostasienforschung*, no. 19) [tr.: *Ferdinand Blumentritt: an Austrian Life for the Philippines* (Manila: 1987)]; *The Rizal-Blumentritt Correspondence* [2 parts] (Manila: 1961) (= *Publications of the Jose Rizal National Centennial Commission*, vol. 2); Philippine Islands. Legislature. Philippine Assembly, *Vida y obras de Ferdinand Blumentritt* (Manila: 1914); Daniel G. Brinton, "Professor Blumentritt's studies of the Philippines," *American Anthropologist*, n.s., vol. 1 (1899), pp. 122-125.

Lee S. Dutton

Boas, Franz. Born at Minden, Westphalia (Germany) 9 July 1858, died in New York (New York) 21 December 1942. One of the most influential U.S. anthropologists, Boas was a specialist in the cultures and languages of American Indians.

He studied physics and geography at Heidelberg and Bonn before receiving his Ph.D. from the University of Kiel (1881). His interest in primitive culture was aroused by observations of the Eskimos made during a scientific expedition to Baffin Island (1883-1884). In 1886 he made the first of many trips to the North Pacific Coast to study the Kwakiutl and other tribes of British Columbia, on which he later specialized. In 1887, having become a permanent resident of the United States, he joined the staff of *Science* as editor. He began his academic career as Instructor at Clark University in the following year. In 1896 he became Instructor and in 1899 Professor of Anthropology at Columbia University. During his long tenure at Columbia, where he remained for the rest of his life, Boas built up one of the foremost departments of anthropology in the United States and trained or influenced many notable ethnologists and linguists. He was largely responsible for encouraging women to enter the field of anthropology.

From 1901 to 1905 he was also curator of anthropology at the American Museum of Natural History; in that capacity he directed and edited reports of the Jesup North Pacific Expedition, the purpose of which was to investigate relationships between the aborigines of Siberia and North America.

Boas was an indefatigable fieldworker, collecting voluminous data on the languages, religion and material culture of North American tribes. His work was criticized for lacking integration, but his emphasis on facts rather than interpretation reflected a widespread reaction against the sweeping theories on cultural evolution in vogue during the 19th century. Boas also made important contributions to physical anthropology. After extensive metrical studies made on immigrants and their descendants, he demonstrated that head form is an adaptive trait, subject to environmental influences—a conclusion significant for racial studies and substantiated by later investigators.

Boas established the *International Journal of American Linguistics*, was one of the founders of the American Anthropological Association, president (in 1931) of the American Association for the Advancement of Science and a member of many other scientific societies in the U.S. and abroad.

Boas was a prolific although not always lucid writer.

MAJOR WORKS: *The Mind of Primitive Man* (New York: 1911; New York: 1938); *Primitive Art* (Cambridge, Mass.: 1927); *Anthropology and Modern Life* (New York: 1928); *Race, Language and Culture* (New York: 1940).

SOURCES: A.L. Kroeber, Ruth Benedict [et al.], *Frans Boas, 1858-1942* (Menasha, Wisconsin: 1943) (= *American Anthropological Association Memoir*, no. 61); Melville J. Herskovits,

Franz Boas (New York: 1953); George W. Stocking, Jr. (editor), *A Franz Boas Reader: the Shaping of American Anthropology, 1883-1911* (New York: 1974; rev. ed., Chicago: 1982).

Sol Tax

Boelaert, Edmond. Missionary, ethnologist. Born in Aaigem (Belgium) 1 December 1899, died at Ekeren (Belgium) 22 August 1966. Boelaert became a priest in the Congregation of the Missionaries of the Sacred Heart in 1924. He was active in the Belgian Congo from September 1930 to September 1954 as a teacher at the "junior seminary," as a "traveling father," and also as the person responsible for Catholic Action and for the printing office at Coquilhatville (now Mbandaka). Together with his colleague GUSTAAF HULSTAERT, he conceived the idea of starting the periodical *Aequatoria* in 1937. For many years this was the only scholarly journal published in the colony.

The great contribution of Edmond Boelaert lay mainly in his defending the rights of the native peoples against colonial conditions, especially the problems brought about by the uprooting of people through obligatory labor laws and industrialization, which caused several population groups to die out. Boelaert published about twenty pieces on depopulation. A second area of concern was the colonial legislation on the territorial rights of the natives (*L'état indépendant et les terres indigènes*).

Boelaert supported his actions with a thorough study of the Mongo people and their language. He published on the Mongo in diverse periodicals and newspapers. He was also a talented author of literature, writing plays and poems, and hence directed his attention to the spoken language of the Mongo people. His name will remain linked with the translation and publication of the national epic of the Mongo, *Nsong'a Lianja*. With Georges van der Kerken (*L'ethnie mongo*) he is responsible for the application of the ethnonym "Mongo" to the population groups of the Central Basin of what is now Zaïre ("De Nkundo-mongo: één volk, één taal"). He deserves special recognition for his "popular" works on the language, the history and the customs of the Mongo people. Many of these were written in Mongo and published in local journals (which for the most part he himself led) (1935-1960). His ten biographical studies of early colonial figures and a large number of unpublished studies about the history of Équateur province of the Belgian Congo (with emphasis on the abuses of the Léopoldian era) make him an obligatory author for colonial historiography.

MAJOR WORKS: "De Nkundo-mongo: één volk, één taal," *Aequatoria*, vol. 1 (1937-1938), fasc. 8, pp. 1-25; "La situation démographique des Nkundo-mongo," *Bulletin du Cepsi* (Elisabethville: 1946); *Nsong'a Lianja: l'épopée nationale des Nkundo* (Coquilhatville and Antwerp: 1949); "Charles Lemaire: premier commissaire de district de l'Équateur," *Bulletin de l'Institut Royal Colonial Belge*, vol. 24 (1953), pp. 506-535; *L'état indépendant et les terres indigènes* (Brussels: 1956); *Lianja-verhalen* [2 vols.] (Tervuren: 1957-1958); "Le Sanford Exploring Expedition," *Aequatoria*, vol. 22 (1959), pp. 121-131; "Vers un état mongo?," *Bulletin de l'Académie Royale des Sciences d'Outre-mer*, vol. 7 (1961), pp. 382-391.

SOURCES: M. Storme, "Edmond Boelaert," *Bulletin de l'Académie Royale des Sciences d'Outre-mer*, n.s., vol. 13 (1967), pp. 167-170; A. De Rop, "Bibliographie analytique," *Bulletin de l'Académie Royale des Sciences d'Outre-mer*, n.s., vol. 13 (1967), pp. 171-192; G. Hulstaert, "Edmond Eloi Boelaert," *Bibliographie Belge d'Outre-mer*, vol. 7, part A, col. 6-9; Georges van der

Kerken, *L'etnie mongo* (Brussels: 1944) (= *Mémoires de l'Institut Royal Colonial Belge, Section des Sciences Morales et Politiques*, vol. 13, fasc. 1-2).

Honoré Vinck
[Translation from Dutch: Geert Van Cleemput]

Bogatyrev, P.G. (Petr Grigor'evich). Ethnographer, folklorist, literary scholar, linguist. Born in Saratov (Russia) 29 January 1893, died in Moscow (Russian S.F.S.R.) 18 August 1971. From 1922 to 1940 Bogatyrev worked in Czechoslovakia, and after 1940 in the Soviet Union. A professor at Moscow University, he worked in the Institut ètnografii (Institute of Ethnography) and the Institut mirovoĭ literatury (Institute of World Literature) of the Soviet Academy of Sciences

Exploring both material and non-material culture, Bogatyrev consistently used a structural-functional method. He possessed great erudition, and, while studying the structure of rituals, beliefs and dress, he compared each phenomenon he discovered with a wide range of phenomena in the ethnography of other European peoples, closely examining their development. Examining the national theatre above all as a manifestation of art, he also revealed its connection with national ceremonies and customs and the multifunctional nature of national dramatic presentations. Bogatyrev was convinced that only the combination of research and fieldwork allows the researcher to penetrate with sufficient depth into the essence of the phenomenon of national creativity and culture. He was the author of more than 300 scholarly works.

MAJOR WORKS: *Cheshskiĭ kukol'nyĭ i russkiĭ narodnyĭ teatr* (Berlin and St. Petersburg: 1923); "Problemy izucheniĭa material'noĭ i dukhovnoĭ kul'tury naseleniĭa Karpat," *Sovetskaĭa ètnografiĭa*, no. 4 (1964), pp. 126-135; "Khudozhestvennye sredstva v ĭumoristicheskom ĭarmarochnom fol'klore (posviĭashcheno D.S. Likhachevu)" in: *Slaviĭanskie literatury* (Moscow: 1968) [4th International Conference of Slavists, Prague, 1968], pp. 294-336; *Voprosy teorii narodnogo iskusstva* (Moscow: 1971) .

SOURCES: N.N. Grafŝianskaĭa and È.V. Pomeranĭŝeva, "P.G. Bogatyrev (nekrolog)," *Sovetskaĭa ètnografiĭa*, no. 6 (1971), pp. 192-194; P.G. Bogatyrev, *Voprosy teorii narodnogo iskusstva* (Moscow: 1971), pp. 523-543 [contains list of works].

A.M. Reshetov
[Translation from Russian: Thomas L. Mann]

Boggiani, Guido. Painter, traveler, ethnologist. Born in Omegna (Italy) 25 September 1861, died in the interior of the Gran Chaco (Paraguay) August 1901. After studying design and painting at the Brera Academy of Milan, and after a successful personal show, Boggiani suddenly left for Argentina in 1887. Although without adequate scientific preparation or financial support, he made his way into the interior of Paraguay and the Mato Grosso where he remained for six years, painting, collecting specimens and (above all) gathering anthropological information on the Chamacoco people of the Paraguayan Gran Chaco and on the Caduveo of the Nabileque river of Brazil.

After his return to Italy, he rejoined the artistic and literary circles of Rome while he prepared his ethnographic material for publication. His monographs on the Chamacoco and the Caduveo as well as his vocabulary of the Guana language appeared in 1894 and 1895. The work on the Caduveo is his most important book and was published with the help of the Società Geografica Italiana (Italian Geographic Society) with an introduction by the ethnographer Angelo Colini (1857-1918). The volume is enriched by beautiful photographs and designs by Boggiani and has a text that is both rigorous and passionate, teeming with sensitive observations on the indigenous art forms.

Boggiani returned to Paraguay in 1896 to continue his geographic and ethnographic research, which resulted in new collections and new scientific works. In particular there were two geographical memoirs and his article on the Guaicurù.

His *Compendio de etnografía paraguayana moderna* appeared serially in the *Revista del Instituto Paraguayo*, which Boggiani founded in 1897 in Asunción. The work dealt with the inhabitants of the right bank of the Paraguay River.

In 1901 Boggiani tried again to penetrate the jungle of the Gran Chaco area to study the inhabitants of the left bank of the river but he was killed there for reasons that remain unknown.

The rich ethnological collections gathered by Boggiani were acquired by the Museo Preistorico-Etnografico (Prehistoric Ethnographic Museum) of Rome (then directed by LUIGI PIGORINI) and by the Museum für Völkerkunde (Ethnographic Museum) of Berlin.

The ethnographic work of Boggiani was warmly praised by CLAUDE LÉVI-STRAUSS (*Tristes tropiques*, p. 150).

MAJOR WORKS: "Notizie etnografiche sulla tribù dei Ciamacoco," *Atti della Società Romana di Antropologia*, vol. 1 (1894), pp. 9-125; "Vocabolario dell'idioma guanà," *Memorie dell'Accademia dei Lincei, Classe di Scienze Morali, Storiche e Filosofiche*, ser. 5, no. 3 (1895), pp. 59-80; *Viaggi di un artista nell'America meridionale: i Caduvei (Mbayà o Guaycurù)* (Roma: 1895); "Guaicurù: sul nome, posizione geografica e rapporti etnici e linguistici di alcune tribù antiche e moderne dell'America Meridionale," *Bollettino della Società Geografica Italiana*, ser. 3, vol. 8 (1898), pp. 244-294; *Etnografia del Alto Paraguay* (Buenos Aires: 1898) (= *Bollettino del Istituto Geografico Argentino*, no. 8); *Compendio de etnografía paraguayana moderna* (Asunción: 1900).

SOURCES: Enrico Hillyer Giglioli, "Guido Boggiani," *Bollettino dellà Società Geografica Italiana*, ser. 4, vol. 3 (1902), pp. 1039-1047; R. Giolli, "Per la psicologia di un esploratore: G. Boggiani tra i Caduvei," *Le vie d'Italia e dell'America*, vol. 31 (1925), pp. 1451-1460; Claude Lévi-Strauss, *Tristes tropiques* (Paris: 1955); Raffaele Pettazzoni, "G. Boggiani, pittore e americanista," *Nuova antologia* (16 December 1941), pp. 405-409; Pietro Scotti, "La collezione etnografica sudamericana di G. Boggiani," *Rivista di Biologia coloniale*, vol. 7 (1946), pp. 63-78; vol. 8 (1947), pp. 35-50; vol. 9 (1948), pp. 93-109; vol. 10 (1949/50), pp. 67-73; Pietro Scotti, *I contributi americanistici di G. Boggiani* (Genova: 1955); P. Scotti and N. Lehmen, "La collezione etnografica sudamericana di Boggiani al Museo Etnologico di Berlino," *Atti dell'Accademia Ligure di Scienze e Lettere*, vol. 28 (1971), pp. 121-141; Francesco Surdich, "Come viaggiava G. Boggiani," *Bollettino storico per la provincia di Novara*, vol. 80 (1989), pp. 69-96.

Sandra Puccini
[Translation from Italian: Gianna Panofsky]

Bogoras, Waldemar (Russian form of name: Vladimir Germanovich Bogoraz; born Nathan Mendeleevich). Anthropologist, revolutionary, novelist, poet. Born in the village of Ovruch (Ukraine, Russia) 1865, died en route from Leningrad to Rostov (Russian S.F.S.R.) 10 May 1936. Bogoras spent his childhood and youth in Taganrog (Ukraine) where he completed his education in the *lycée* before entering the University of St. Petersburg law school in 1880. In 1882, at the age of 17, he joined the revolutionary group Narodnaïa Volïa (Peoples' Will), and was soon arrested, imprisoned and exiled to Siberia. At this time he also changed his name from Nathan Mendeleevich to Waldemar Germanovich. However, he kept his original first name as his literary pseudonym, N.A. Tan, under which he wrote fiction and poetry.

During his years of exile in Siberia he began his studies of the tribal peoples of the Arctic. In 1895 he was asked to join the Sibirïakov expedition to Yakutia in northeastern Siberia, sponsored by the Russian Geographical Society. For the next two years, he traveled with the Chukchi and Lamut (Even) learning their language and culture. In 1898 the Academy of Sciences in St. Petersburg published his work on Chukchi mythology, shamanism and warfare. In 1900 Bogoras, together with his colleague and fellow revolutionary WALDEMAR JOCHELSON, was asked to participate in the Jesup North Pacific Expedition organized by FRANZ BOAS for the American Museum of Natural History in New York. Bogoras and his wife, Sofia Constantinovna, spent almost two years studying several Siberian tribes, primarily the Chukchi and the Eskimo. Enduring incredible hardships they collected priceless ethnographic data, linguistic notes, 150 texts, 5,000 ethnographic artifacts, skeletal material, plaster casts of faces, archaeological specimens, 95 phonographic records and somatological measurements of 860 individuals. Bogoras wrote several exhaustive monographs on his fieldwork for the Jesup Expedition. After the revolution of 1917, Bogoras became director of the Institute of the Peoples of the North, an agency concerned with the education and developmental work among the northern tribes of Siberia. He spent the rest of his life in the Soviet Union engaged in scientific and literary work.

MAJOR WORKS: "The Chukchee: material culture," *Memoirs of the American Museum of Natural History*, vol. 11 (1904), pp. 1-276 (= *The Jesup North Pacific Expedition*, vol. 7, pt. 1); "The Chukchee: religion," *Memoirs of the American Museum of Natural History*, vol. 11 (1907), pp. 277-536 (= *The Jesup North Pacific Expedition*, vol. 7, pt. 2); "The Chukchee: social organization," *Memoirs of the American Museum of Natural History*, vol. 11 (1909), pp. 537-733 (= *The Jesup North Pacific Expedition*, vol. 7, pt. 3); "Chukchee mythology," *Memoirs of the American Museum of Natural History*, vol. 12 (1910), pp. 1-197 (= *The Jesup North Pacific Expedition*, vol. 8, pt. 1); "The Eskimo of Siberia," *Memoirs of the American Museum of Natural History*, vol. 12 (1913), pp. 417-456 (= *The Jesup North Pacific Expedition*, vol. 8, pt. 3).

SOURCES: Franz Boas, "The Jesup North Pacific Expedition," *The American Museum Journal*, vol. 3, no. 5 (1903), pp. 72-119; Franz Boas, "Waldemar Bogoras," *American Anthropologist*, vol. 39 (1937), pp. 314-315; Stanley A. Freed, Ruth S. Freed and Laila Williamson, "Capitalist philanthropy and Russian revolutionaries: the Jesup North Pacific Expedition (1897-1902)," *American Anthropologist*, vol. 90 (1988), pp. 7-24; I.S. Gurvich and L.P. Kuzmina, "W.G. Bogoras et W.I. Jochelson: deux éminents représentants de l'ethnographie russe (1)," *Inter-Nord, Revue internationale d'études arctiques*, vol. 17 (1985), pp. 145-151; Lawrence Krader, "Bogoraz, Vladimir G., Sternberg, Lev. Y., and Jochelson, Vladimir" in: David L. Sills (editor), *International Encyclopedia of the Social Sciences* (New York: 1968-1979), vol. 2, pp. 116-119.

Stanley A. Freed, Ruth S. Freed and Laila Williamson

Bolk, Louis. Anatomist, physical anthropologist. Born in Overschie (Netherlands) 10 December 1866, died in Amsterdam (Netherlands) 17 June 1930. From 1888 to 1896 Bolk studied medicine at the University of Amsterdam, after which he accepted an assistantship at the Anatomical Laboratory. He received a professorship only two years later.

Bolk, considered to be the founder of modern physical anthropology in the Netherlands, had a broad set of interests and an extremely active professional life. His first research was in comparative anatomy: he studied the cerebellum of humans and mammals and human and mammal dentition. His later interest in evolutionary problems manifested itself in these early studies. In his later work Bolk would investigate the evolution of many characteristics of the human cranium. He also published on the evolution of human "racial" diversity. Parallel to these evolutionary studies he published on subjects pertaining to the human skeleton as well as on physiological and endocrinological themes. He was a co-founder of the Nederlandse Anatomendagen, and the establishment of the Anatomical Museum in Amsterdam was mainly his work.

His studies on the ontogenetic and phylogenetic development of man and the great apes resulted in his "retardation theory," in which he claimed that in human development many characteristics persist that are transitional in younger apes. He considered this phenomenon to be determined by the endocrine system. In Bolk's view, ontogenetic conservatism would enable man ultimately to reach a higher degree of development. This theory was never substantially undermined.

Bolk also worked on population studies. He investigated the geographical distribution of (among other phenomena) stature, pigmentation, and the cranial/cephalic index in the Netherlands, basing his conclusions on the investigation of more than 400,000 individuals. He also published on the etiology of red hair and on the age of menarche. His activities and efforts in the field of population studies resulted in the foundation of the Anthropological Committee of the Royal Netherlands Academy of Sciences over which Bolk presided. Most of his many articles were published in the proceedings of the academy (the Amsterdam titles).

MAJOR WORKS: *Is Red Hair a Nuance or a Variety?* (Amsterdam: 1907); *De bevolking van Nederland in hare antropologische samenstelling* (Utrecht: 1908); *On the Position and the Displacement of the Foramen Magnum in the Primates* (Amsterdam: 1909); "On the premature obliteration of sutures in the human skull," *Journal of Anatomy*, vol. 17 (1915), pp. 495-523; *On the Topographical Relations in Infantile and Adult Skulls in Man and Apes* (Amsterdam: 1919); *The Part Played by the Endocrine Glands in the Evolution of Man* (London: 1921); *On the Signification of the Supraorbital Ridges in the Primates* (Amsterdam: 1922); *On the Origin of Human Races* (Amsterdam: 1927).

SOURCES: C.U. Ariens Kappers, "In memoriam: L. Bolk," *Psychiatrische en Neurologische Bladen*, vol. 34 (1930), p. 393; A.J. van Bork-Feltkamp, *Anthropological Research in the Netherlands* (Amsterdam: 1938) (= *Verhandelingen der Koninklijke Nederlandsche Akademie van Wetenschappen. Afdeeling Natuurkunde*; 2nd section, vol. 37, no. 3); A.J.P. van den Broek, "In memoriam: Prof. Dr. Louis Bolk," *Nederlands Tijdschrift voor Geneeskunde*, vol. 74 (1930), pp. 307-308; T.S. Constandse-Westermann, *History of Physical Anthropology in the Netherlands* (Newcastle-upon-Tyne: 1983) (= *International Association of Human Biologists, Occasional Paper*, vol. 1, no. 3).

T.S. Constandse-Westermann

Boman, Eric. Archaeologist. Born in Falun (Sweden) 5 June 1867, died in Buenos Aires (Argentina) 29 November 1924. While a student of archaeology in 1889, Boman traveled to South America for the first time. There he carried out field research in the province of Catamarca.

During 1901-1902 he participated in ERLAND NORDENSKIÖLD's Swedish Chaco-Cordillera Expedition to Salta, Jujuy, Tarija and the Bolivian and Argentinian parts of the Gran Chaco. He joined the expedition on 8 May 1901 and stayed on until 16 February 1902 when he had to leave because of illness.

During 1903-1904 Boman excavated in a French project in Puna de Jujuy, the Mission Scientifique G. de Créqui-Montford et E. Sénéchal de la Grange. After this period he spent six years in Paris where he wrote up his material. In Paris, he published his major work on Andean archaeology, *Antiquités de la région andine de la république argentine et du désert d'Atacama*. Later, he returned to Argentina and in 1916 he became the director of the Museo Nacional de Historia Natural (National Museum of Natural History) in Buenos Aires.

Boman died in Argentina in 1924 and was buried at the Cementerio Alemán in Buenos Aires. More recently, his bones were moved to Tucumán where he has been honored by a special mausoleum. He is nowadays regarded as one of the "fathers of Argentinian archaeology" and has been characterized as having "a world-wide reputation as one of the most eminent experts in this subject" (Wassén, 1966/67, pp. 343-344).

MAJOR WORKS: "Arqueología del Chaco jujeño," *Historia*, vol. 1 (1903), pp. 42-56; "Migrations précolombiennes dans le Nord-Ouest de l'Argentine," *Journal de la Société des Américanistes de Paris*, n.s., vol. 2 (1905), pp. 92-108; *Antiquités de la région andine de la république argentine et du désert d'Atacama* [2 vols.] (Paris: 1908); *Alfarería de estilo draconiano de la región diaguita* (Buenos Aires: 1923); *Estudios arqueológicos riojanos* (Buenos Aires: 1927-1932).

SOURCES: Erland Nordenskiöld "Nécrologie de Eric Boman," *Journal de la Société des Américanistes de Paris*, vol. 17 (1925), pp. 317-318; S. Henry Wassén "Four Swedish anthropologists in Argentina in the first decades of the 20th century: bio-bibliographical notes," *Folk*, vol. 8-9 (1966/67), pp. 343-350.

Jan-Åke Alvarsson

Bopp, Franz. Comparative Indo-European linguist. Born in Mainz (Germany) 14 September 1791, died in Berlin (Germany) 23 October 1867. Bopp studied a short time in Aschaffenburg (Germany) with the philosopher and historian Karl Joseph Hieronymous Windischmann (1775-1839), who roused his interest in the Sanskrit language, which was then only known through the brief sketch in the book *Ueber die Sprache und Weisheit der Indier* (Heidelberg: 1808) by Friedrich Schlegel (1772-1829). From 1812 to 1816 Bopp lived in Paris; here he learned Sanskrit without a teacher with the help of the imperfect grammars of H. Colebrooke (1805) and W. Carey (1806), reading and translating the Sanskrit manuscripts in the Bibliothèque Nationale (Paris). Bopp was the first who through systematic and complete analysis of the grammatical elements of the Old Indo-European languages—Sanskrit, Greek, Latin, Gothic and Lithuanian—laid the base for the historical comprehension of Indo-European grammar. Thus he became the founder of comparative philology and Indo-European studies. In 1821 the University of Göttingen awarded him an honorary doctorate. In that same year Bopp was appointed professor of Oriental literature and general linguistics at the University of Berlin, where he lectured with extraordinary success until his retirement in 1864.

MAJOR WORKS: *Über das Conjugationssystem der Sanskritsprache in Vergleichung mit jenem der griechischen, lateinischen, persischen und germanischen Sprache* (Frankfurt am Main: 1816);

Ausführliches Lehrgebäude der Sanskrita-Sprache (Berlin: 1827); *Grammatica critica linguae sanscritae* (Berlin: 1829; 2nd ed., Berlin: 1833); *Glossarium Sanscritum* (Berlin: 1830; 2nd ed., Berlin: 1847); *Vergleichende Grammatik des Sanskrit, Zend, Griechischen, Lateinischen, Litthauischen, Gothischen und Deutschen* [6 vols.] (Berlin: 1833-1852; 2nd ed. [3 vols.], Berlin: 1857-1861; 3rd ed. [3 vols.], Berlin: 1868-1871) [tr.: *A Comparative Grammar of the Sanscrit, Zend, Greek, Latin, Lithuanian, Gothic, German, and Sclavonic Languages* (London: 1845-1854); *Grammaire comparée de langues indo-européennes ...* (Paris: 1866-1874)]; *Kritische Grammatik der Sanskrita-Sprache in kürzerer Fassung* (Berlin: 1834; 2nd ed., Berlin: 1854; 3rd ed., Berlin: 1863; 4th ed., Berlin: 1868); *Die celtischen Sprachen in ihrem Verhältnis zum Sanskrit, Zend, Griechischen, Lateinischen, Germanischen, Litthauischen und Slawischen* (Berlin: 1853); *Über die Sprache der alten Preussen in ihren verwandtschaftlichen Beziehungen* (Berlin: 1853); *Über das Albanesische in seinen verwandtschaftlichen Beziehungen* (Berlin: 1855).

SOURCES: T. Benfey, *Geschichte der Sprachwissenschaft und orientalischen Philologie in Deutschland seit dem Anfange des 19. Jahrhunderts* (Munich: 1869); Adalbert Kuhn, "Franz Bopp," *Unsere Zeit*, n.s, vol. 4, part 10 (1868); Salomon Lefmann, *Franz Bopp, sein Leben und seine Wissenschaft* [3 vols.] (Berlin: 1891-1897); August Leskien, "Bopp, Franz" in: *Allgemeine Deutsche Biographie*, vol. 3 (Leipzig: 1876), pp. 140-149; Russell Martineau, "Obituary of Franz Bopp," *Transactions of the Philological Society* (1867), pp. 305-314; Günter Neumann, *Indogermanische Sprachwissenschaft 1816 und 1966*, vol. 1, *Franz Bopp* (Innsbruck: 1967) (= *Innsbrucker Beiträge zur Kulturwissenschaft*, Sonderheft 24); Reinhard Sternemann, "Franz Bopp: Beitrag zur Entwicklung der vergleichenden Sprachwissenschaft," *Zeitschrift für Germanistik*, vol. 5 (1984), pp. 144-158; Reinhard Sternemann, *Franz Bopp und die vergleichende indoeuropäische Sprachwissenschaft* (Innsbruck: 1984) (= *Innsbrucker Beiträge zur Sprachwissenschaft*, no. 33); K.J. Windischmann, "Vorerinnerungen" in: Franz Bopp, *Über das Conjugationssystem* (Frankfurt am Main: 1816), pp. i-xxxxvi.

Bernfried Schlerath

Bowles, Gordon T. Born in Tōkyō (Japan) 25 June 1904, now living in Monterey (Massachusetts). Physical anthropologist, cultural anthropologist. Bowles has been one of the major American interpreters of East Asian anthropology, particularly that of Japan. His parents were missionaries in Japan, and he spent much of his childhood in that country. He did graduate work in anthropology at the University of Pennsylvania and at Harvard University, receiving a Ph.D. from the latter institution in 1935 for a dissertation on the peoples of the West China-East Tibet borderland. He has held numerous positions. He taught at the University of Hawaii for a period (1938-1942), spent several years (1942-1947) working for the U.S. government as an East Asia specialist, served as Professor and Visiting Professor of Anthropology at the University of Tōkyō (1951-1958) and has been a Professor of Anthropology at Syracuse University since 1962 (Emeritus since 1972).

His best known scholarly work is *The People of Asia*, that focuses on physical anthropology and which has become a standard text. It includes anthropomorphic data on more than eighty peoples much of which was collected by Bowles himself. Bowles has also written numerous more specialized materials on East Asian peoples. His 1932 work, *New Types of Old Americans at Harvard and Eastern Women's Colleges*, is a classic analysis of anthropomorphic changes in Americans.

With his knowledge of Japanese, Bowles has served as a major bridge between Western and Japanese anthropology. He introduced cultural anthropology to Tōkyō University and helped develop anthropology as a permanent department of that university.

During his years as emeritus professor he has maintained productive contacts with Japanese anthropology.

MAJOR WORKS: *New Types of Old Americans at Harvard and Eastern Women's Colleges* (Cambridge, Mass.: 1932); (co-editor with Earl W. Count) *Fact and Theory in Social Science* (Syracuse: 1964); *The People of Asia* (London and New York: 1977); "China, Mongolia, Korea" in: Ilse Schwidetzky (editor), *Rassengeschichte der Menschheit*, Lieferung 10 (1983), pp. 41-105.

SOURCE: *Gordon T. Bowles' Autobiographical Sketch* [manuscript] (1989).

Braidwood, Robert J. Anthropologist, archaeologist. Born in Detroit (Michigan) 29 July 1907. A leader in the field of Near Eastern prehistory, Braidwood is widely acclaimed for his investigations into the origins and early consequences of a food-producing way of life. In his research, he pioneered the assembling of problem-oriented interdisciplinary teams involving the natural sciences—now an accepted practice in archaeology.

Braidwood was educated at the University of Michigan and the University of Chicago, studying architecture, ancient history and anthropology. After completing his M.A. at Michigan in 1933, he joined the University of Chicago Oriental Institute's Syrian-Hittite Expedition on the Amouq Plain (now in Turkey) where he worked until 1938. He married his wife and lifelong collaborator, Linda, in 1937, and they returned to Chicago in 1938 to pursue their graduate degrees. Braidwood completed his Ph.D. in 1943 and began teaching in both the Oriental Institute and the Anthropology Department at Chicago where he remained until his retirement. As a teacher and mentor, he is held in high esteem by several generations of students.

Braidwood's scholarly concern with food-production developed when early teaching and research focused his attention on the lack of excavated sites concerning the shift from a hunting-and-gathering to a village-farming way of life. Drawing on the writings of H.J. Peake and H.J. Fleure as well as V. GORDON CHILDE, he set out to fill that gap. His pursuit was directed as well by the changing political realities of the Near East and the opportunities they offered for excavation.

The Oriental Institute's Iraq Jarmo Project launched in 1947 was the first field project specifically concerned with retrieving evidence of early food-production and solving the ecological problem of its origin and early consequences. Braidwood employed not only archaeologists but natural scientists to reconstruct the ancient environment. Radiocarbon dating, then in its infancy, was also introduced. The National Science Foundation invited him to apply for a grant and has continued to fund such interdisciplinary research.

The Project's findings challenged then-held beliefs, including Childe's "oasis theory." From the archaeological and paleo-environmental evidence, Braidwood formulated his own "nuclear" or "natural habitat zone theory" outlined in *Prehistoric Investigations in Iraqi Kurdistan*. Early domestication, he submitted, took place in the hilly flanks of JAMES HENRY BREASTED's "Fertile Crescent." This was an area in which wild but potentially domesticable plants and animals coexisted together with people who, as a result of familiarity and an appropriate level of cultural development, began to exploit them.

Braidwood's theory stimulated considerable discussion and debate, influencing the research aims and methods of several generations of scholars.

Braidwood has spent the last several decades exploring and refining this hypothesis. Political problems in Iraq ended work there in the late 1950s. The Prehistoric Project moved to the Iranian Zagros, uncovering occupation that dates back to the end of the Pleistocene and inspiring natural scientists to investigate climatic and vegetational history.

In the early 1960s, the Istanbul-Chicago Universities' Joint Prehistoric Project codirected by Braidwood and Professor Doctor HALET ÇAMBEL was formed. More than two decades (1963-1988) of very productive fieldwork in southeastern Turkey followed, reaffirming the value of team effort. Much information on early village farming life as well as the development of food-production was gathered, primarily through the excavation of Çayönü Tepesi. Questions concerning early metallurgy and the beginnings of architecture were also addressed.

In addition to his other responsibilities, Braidwood has been active in a number of professional societies and received numerous honorary degrees. In 1971 he was Distinguished Lecturer at the Annual Meetings of the American Anthropological Association. He received the Medal for Distinguished Archaeological Achievement from the Archaeological Institute of America in 1972. Braidwood has lectured and published widely, and his work has brought anthropology and prehistory to the attention not only of philologists and historians of the ancient Near East but to the attention of the wider public as well. Within the international scholarly community, his attempts to unravel one of history's major economic and social turning points are considered a milestone in the study of the human career.

MAJOR WORKS: *Prehistoric Men* (Chicago: 1948; plus seven succeeding editions, the most recent in 1975); *The Ancient Near East and the Foundations of Civilization* (Eugene: 1952); *Archaeologists and What They Do* (New York: 1960); (with L.S. Braidwood) *Excavations in the Plain of Antioch* (Chicago: 1960); (with Bruce Howe [et al.]) *Prehistoric Investigations in Iraqi Kurdistan* (Chicago: 1960); (editor with G.R. Willey and author) *Courses Toward Urban Life* (Chicago: 1962); (with Halet Çambel) *İstanbul ve Chicago Üniversiteleri Karma Projesi Güneydoğu Anadolu Tarihöncesi Araştırmaları*, I = *The Joint Istanbul-Chicago Universities' Prehistoric Research Project in Southeastern Anatolia*, I (İstanbul: 1980); (editor with L.S. Braidwood) *Prehistoric Village Archaeology in South-eastern Turkey: the Eighth Millenium B.C. Site at Çayönü* (Oxford: 1982); (editor with L.S. Braidwood [et al.]) *Prehistoric Archeology along the Zagros Flanks* (Chicago: 1983) (= *University of Chicago Oriental Institute Publications*, vol. 105).

SOURCES: R.J. Braidwood, "The Iraq Jarmo Project" in: G.R. Willey (editor), *Archaeological Researches in Retrospect* (Cambridge, Mass.: 1974), pp. 61-83; Charles L. Redman, *The Rise of Civilization* (San Francisco: 1978); R.J. Braidwood, "Archaeological retrospect 2," *Antiquity* vol. 55 (1981), pp. 19-26; T. Cuyler Young, P.E.L. Smith and Peder Mortensen (editors), *The Hilly Flanks and Beyond: Essays on the Prehistory of Southwestern Asia (Presented to Robert J. Braidwood)* (Chicago: 1983); personal communication from R.J. Braidwood.

Margaret R. Dittemore

Brauer, Erich. Ethnologist. Born in Berlin (Germany) 28 June 1895, died in Jerusalem (Palestine) 9 May 1942. Brauer studied ethnology in Berlin and Leipzig under FELIX VON LUSCHAN and Karl Weule (1864-1926), and was a follower of the *Kulturkreis* school of German and Austrian ethnology. His study, *Züge aus der Religion der Herero*, was received with considerable attention in ethnological and anthropological circles.

During 1925-1926 Brauer spent more than a year in Jerusalem studying the Yemenite Jews who had settled there. In 1934 his comprehensive monograph, *Ethnologie der jemenitischen Juden*, was published by Heidelberg University. In the same year Brauer returned to Jerusalem where he was to stay until his death. From 1936 to 1940 he was research fellow in Jewish ethnology at the Hebrew University of Jerusalem, where he laid the foundations of the ethnological collection of the university.

The central subject of Brauer's researches during the eight years he lived in Jerusalem was the ethnology of the Jews of Kurdistan. In 1937 and 1939 he published two papers in German based on his interviews of Kurdish Jewish immigrants, and in 1942 a paper of his on the Jews of Afghanistan was published in *Jewish Social Studies* in New York. When he died, he left behind a partially completed book-size manuscript in English on the ethnology of the Kurdish Jews; his sister, Mrs. Gerta Heller, who was his literary executor, asked RAPHAEL PATAI to complete it. Patai conducted interviews with Brauer's main informants, completed and edited the manuscript, translated it into Hebrew and published it in 1947 as one of the *Studies in Folklore and Ethnology* of the Palestine Institute of Folklore and Ethnology in Jerusalem.

Although his physical frailty (he was hunchbacked and very small of stature) prevented Brauer from doing fieldwork in the homelands of the Jewish communities he studied, he developed admirable techniques for obtaining complete and reliable information on many aspects of Jewish folk-life and folk-culture in Yemen and Kurdistan as remembered by immigrants from those countries whom he interviewed in Jerusalem. His lasting merit is to have been the first academically trained ethnologist to study contemporary Jewish communities.

MAJOR WORKS: *Züge aus der Religion der Herero: ein Beitrag zur Hamitenfrage* (Leipzig: 1925); *Ethnologie der jemenitischen Juden* (Heidelberg: 1934); "The Jews of Afghanistan: an anthropological report," *Jewish Social Studies*, vol. 4 (1942), pp. 121-138; *Yehude Kurdistan: Meḥḳar Etnologi = The Jews of Kurdistan* (Jerusalem: 1947) (= *Studies in Folklore and Ethnology*, vol. 2) [Hebrew text with English title page].

SOURCE: Raphael Patai, "Haḳdamah" to: Erich Brauer, *Yehude Kurdistan* (Jerusalem: 1947), pp. 9-14.

Raphael Patai

Breasted, James Henry. Egyptologist, historian. Born in Rockford (Illinois) 27 August 1865, died in New York (New York) 2 December 1935. After receiving his doctorate in Egyptology at Berlin in 1894, Breasted returned to America to develop a lifelong association with the University of Chicago and to become the founding father of American Egyptology. He was Assistant Director of the Haskell Oriental Museum from 1895 to 1901 and Director for the remainder of his life. Appointed Instructor in Egyptology in 1896, he was made full Professor of that subject in 1905, occupying the first chair of Egyptology in the United States. Thanks in part to his strong relationship with John D. Rockefeller, Jr., Breasted was able to develop the Haskell Museum into the Oriental Institute of the University of Chicago in 1919. Later, he founded its Egyptian field headquarters at Chicago House, Luxor. Under Breasted, the Oriental Institute undertook several projects throughout Egypt, including the Epigraphic Survey at Luxor, which was instituted in 1924 for the copying of monumental inscriptions and which still sets the standards in its field today. Breasted also selected young scholars to lead Oriental Institute expeditions to other areas of the Near East; some of the more notable excavations were conducted at Khorsabad (Iraq), Persepolis (Iran) and Megiddo (Palestine). In addition to the various field projects and their publication, the Oriental Institute under Breasted initiated purely philological efforts such as the Assyrian Dictionary Project.

Breasted's primary early emphasis was the recovery and publication of written historical documents, as best exemplified in his five volume *Ancient Records of Egypt*, which in turn formed the basis for his still classic *History of Egypt*. He also translated many important Egyptian medical papyri. Just as the mission of the Oriental Institute extended beyond Egypt to all parts of the ancient Near East, and beyond the rescue and recording of texts to include excavation and survey, so Breasted's interests also broadened in his later years. His view of the historical development of ancient civilizations and the modern trends in our own crystallized into a philosophy of moral evolution as detailed in *The Dawn of Conscience*. He cited family life as the means by which the "supreme values [of] the human soul" were manifest. This anti-Marxist belief, as he perceived it, would doubtless have been amplified had he lived to complete a projected multi-volume *History of Civilization*.

MAJOR WORKS: *A History of Egypt* (New York: 1905); *Ancient Records of Egypt* [5 vols.] (Chicago: 1906-1907); "The temples of Lower Nubia," *American Journal of Semitic Languages and Literatures*, vol. 23 (1906-1907), pp. 1-64; "The monuments of Sudanese Nubia," *American Journal of Semitic Languages and Literatures*, vol. 25 (1908-1909), pp. 1-110; *Development of Religion and Thought in Ancient Egypt* (New York: 1912); *Ancient Times* (Boston: 1916); *The Conquest of Civilization* (New York: 1926); *The Edwin Smith Surgical Papyrus* [2 vols.] (Chicago: 1930); *The Dawn of Conscience* (New York: 1933).

SOURCES: James H. Breasted, *The Oriental Institute* (Chicago: 1933); Charles Breasted, *Pioneer to the Past* (New York: 1943); John Wilson, "James Henry Breasted and the rescue of texts" in: John Wilson, *Signs and Wonders Upon Pharaoh* (Chicago: 1964), pp. 124-143; Warren R. Dawson and Eric P. Uphill, *Who Was Who in Egyptology* (London: 1972), pp. 38-39.

Carter Lupton

Brelich, Angelo. Historian of religions. Born in Budapest (Austria-Hungary) 20 June 1913, died in Rome (Italy) 1 October 1977. Brelich studied in Italy at the Università per Stranieri (University for Foreigners) at Perugia and in Hungary at the University of Pécs with András Alföldi (1895-1981) and Karl Kerényi (1897-1973); he received his degree from Pécs in 1937. In 1938 he established himself in Italy, and, after a brief period of work for the Superintendent of Antiquities of Ostia, he was asked to join the Department of the History of Religions as assistant to RAFFAELE PETTAZZONI who later designated Brelich as his successor. In 1958 he was appointed to the chair of history of religions in the Faculty of Letters and Philosophy at the University of Rome. (ERNESTO DE MARTINO had been among those who applied for this post.)

As scientific heir to Pettazzoni, Brelich can be considered the founder of the Roman school of historical-religious studies. Although Brelich's major studies dealt with mythology and classic religions, his use of historical comparisons often brought him near to the world of ethnology when he dealt with tribal religions and religion in prehistoric civilizations. Thus, he opened an anthropological dimension to the study of the history of religions. Brelich was very much in the Pettazzonian tradition when he widened the horizons of traditional historiography. He aimed at both historical rigor and comparison. The association of different cultures separated by time and space played a part in Brelich's historical analysis. This method was not adopted to show analogies and regularities, but rather to make evident the differences that must be considered to be true historical products.

Brelich's contribution to the conceptual redefinition of historical-religious terminology and his attention to questions of methodology will be long remembered. Among his numerous works, his *Introduzione alla storia delle religioni* has been the basic text for teaching the history of religion in Rome since 1966.

MAJOR WORKS: *Tre variazioni romane sul tema delle origini* (Rome: 1955); *Introduzione alla storia delle religioni* (Rome: 1966); *Paides e parthenoi* (Rome: 1969); "Symbol of a symbol" in: J.M. Kitagawa and Charles H. Long (editors), *Myths and Symbols: Studies in Honour of Mircea Eliade* (Chicago and London: 1969), pp. 195-207; "Prolégomènes à une histoire des religions" in: *Histoire des religions* (Paris: 1970-1976), vol. 1, pp. 2-59; "Perchè storicismo e quale storicismo (nei nostri studi)?" *Religioni e civiltà*, vol. 41 (= new ser., vol. 1) (1970-1972), pp. 7-28; *Grieken en Goden* (Bussum: 1975); "La metodologia della scuola di Roma" in: Bruno Gentile and Giuseppe Paioni (editors), *Il mito greco* (Rome: 1977), pp. 3-32; *Storia delle religioni: perchè?* (Naples: 1979).

SOURCES: Vittorio Lanternari, "L'apocalisse vissuta: Angelo Brelich" in: *Festa, carisma, apocalisse* (Palermo: 1983), pp. 281-288; Vittorio Lanternari, Marcello Massenzio and Daria Sabbatucci, "Introduzione" to: *Religione e civiltà: scritti in memoria di Angelo Brelich* (Bari: 1982), 1st 9 pp. (unnumbered) [contains bibliography]; Marcello Massenzio, "Per conoscere Angelo Brelich," *Culture*, no. 1 (1977-78), p. 111.

Giorgio de Finis
[Translation from Italian: Phyllis Liparini]

Breuil, Henri (Henri Edouard Prosper Breuil). Archaeologist, prehistorian. Born in Mortain, Normandy (France) 28 February 1877, died in l'Île-Adam (France) 14 August 1961. Often termed "the last representative of the heroic age of prehistory" (Broderick, p. 299), Breuil became interested in prehistoric cultures and, more specifically, prehistoric art during his time in training for the Catholic priesthood at the Issy-les-Moulineux seminary in the mid-1890s. Through a friendship with Geoffroy d'Ault du Mesnil, who had worked extensively in the gravel beds of the Somme Valley, Breuil became intrigued with the problems of working out a chronological sequence for the prehistoric cultures of Europe in the glacial and interglacial epochs. In 1897, he made his first tour of prehistoric sites in France, visiting Les Eyzies, Brassempouy and the Mas d'Azil in the foothills of the Pyrenees. Following his ordination in June 1900, he received a dispensation from his priestly duties from the Bishop of Soissons, which was to last a lifetime instead of the intended four years.

Breuil's first investigation of the Late Stone Age in Europe occurred as a result of his skill at draftsmanship, which he used in 1901 to copy the newly discovered paintings of Les Combarelles and the Font-de-Gaume caves in the Vézèré Valley. In 1902 he visited the cave of La Mouthe (where some of the earliest cave paintings in Europe had been noted in 1896 by Émile Rivière (1835-1922)) and Marsoulas, another recently discovered painting site in the Pyrenees. It was the quality of Breuil's drawings from these sites that led to an invitation from Émile Cartailhac for Breuil to visit the immense prehistoric art gallery painted in the cave of Altamira to copy its images. This was the beginning of a career specializing in prehistoric drawings and paintings and their explication. An appointment as a private instructor at the Catholic University of Fribourg in Switzerland in the fields of prehistory and ethnology in 1904 permitted him to sustain his interest in the paleolithic in Europe and to expand his involvement to working at the northern Spanish caves of El Castillo and Covalanas, as well as to continue explorations at Altamira. It was at the first that he became acquainted with Prince Albert of Monaco, who in 1910 hired Breuil for the staff of his Institute of Human Paleontology, newly founded in Paris. By 1912, Breuil had completed the paper "The subdivisions of the Upper Paleolithic and their significance," which was read at the Geneva Prehistoric Congress. It was the system of successive cultural periods, from Chatelperronian to Magdalenian, set forth in this text that was to become accepted as the framework for the interpretation of European prehistory.

Breuil also was involved in the debate over human origins, as evidenced by his travels to South Africa in 1929 and to China in 1931, the latter to visit the site of Choukoutien near Beijing. This interest led him to participate actively in some of the controversies surrounding the Neanderthal specimens that were being unearthed at such sites as Saccopastore (some of them by Breuil himself). The discovery of the cave of Lascaux in 1940 occupied him to some degree until 1941, when he accepted a professorship at the University of Lisbon, taking time to investigate raised beaches in portions of neighboring Morocco. A letter to C. Van Riet Lowe (1894-1956) led to an invitation from the University of Witwatersrand in Johannesburg in 1942 to serve as visiting lecturer and to participate in Lowe's work on the archaeological survey of South Africa. During the next three years he made twenty-four trips across southern Africa from Mozambique and Lesotho to the Cape Province, although he was not then able to reach the rock carvings in the Tsisab massif in Namibia, site of the famous "White Lady of the Brandberg." A brief interval of return to France and teaching in England was followed in 1947 by a trip to Nairobi for the Pan-African Congress on Prehistory, with a side trip to Olduvai Gorge. March 1948 was the beginning of his last major expedition to examine and record the rock art of southern Africa, which was to include two months in Namibia, resulting in an extraordinary set of copies of the Brandberg frescoes. The relationship between these artworks and the cave paintings and clay sculptures of western Europe, with which he was more familiar, was a question that was to occupy many of his later writings. With a continuing interest in all these areas, Breuil continued to write and publish on the role played by Upper Paleolithic art and imagery almost until his death, resulting in a mass of more than 800 articles, monographs and books. The synthesis Breuil built of the life and thought of paleolithic man—which was based on an understanding of both artistic images and cultural patterns—deeply colored the study of the later Stone Age as it exists today in much of the world.

MAJOR WORKS: "Les subdivisions du paléolithique supérieur et leur signification" in: *Proceedings of the Fourteenth International Congress of Anthropology and Prehistoric Archaeology* (Geneva: 1912), vol. 1, pp. 165-238; *Rock Paintings of Southern Andalusia: a Description of a Neolithic and Copper Age Art Group* (Oxford: 1929); *The Cave of Altamira at Santillana del Mar, Spain* (Madrid: 1935); *Four Hundred Centuries of Cave Art* (Montignac, France: 1952); *The White Lady of the Brandberg* (New York: 1955); *The Men of the Old Stone Age (Palaeolithic & Mesolithic)* (New York: 1965); *The Rock Paintings of Southern Africa* (London, Paris [etc.]: 1955-).

SOURCES: Alan Houghton Broderick, *Father of Prehistory: the Abbé Henri Breuil, His Life and Times* (New York: 1963); Francis Bordes, "Breuil, Henri" in: David L. Sills (editor), *International Encyclopedia of the Social Sciences* (New York: 1968-1979), vol. 2, pp. 150-153.

Robert B. Marks Ridinger

Brigham, William Tufts. Anthropologist, ethnologist, geologist, botanist. Born in Boston (Massachusetts) 24 May 1841, died 29 January 1926. Brigham graduated from Harvard College in 1862 and engaged in a variety of intellectual pursuits, both as field researcher and teacher. Brigham was active at various times from 1864 to 1887 in New England, Guatemala and Hawaii. In 1887 he settled in Hawaii and did research on the culture, biology and volcanology of the islands.

Charles R. Bishop asked Brigham to organize the artifacts of historical and ethnological importance that had been collected by Bernice Pauahi Bishop. Those materials became the initial holdings of the newly founded Bernice P. Bishop Museum in 1896. Brigham was the first curator and served as director from 1896 to 1918.

MAJOR WORKS: "Notes on the volcanoes of the Hawaiian Islands, with a history of their various eruptions," *Memoirs of the Boston Society of Natural History*, vol. 1, no. 3 (1868), pp. 341-472; "Notes on the eruption of the Hawaiian volcanoes, 1868" [Supplement to: "Notes on the volcanoes of the Hawaiian Islands"], *Memoirs of the Boston Society of Natural History*, vol. 1, no. 4 (1869), pp. 564-587; *Guatemala: the Land of the Quetzal: a Sketch* (New York: 1887); *Hawaiian Feather Work* (Honolulu: 1899-1918) (= *Bernice P. Bishop Museum, Memoirs*, vol. 1, no. 1; vol. 1, no. 5; vol. 7, no. 1); "Stone implements and stone work of the ancient Hawaiians," *Bernice P. Bishop Museum, Memoirs*, vol. 1, no. 4 (1902), pp. 5-100; "The ancient Hawaiian house," *Bernice P. Bishop Museum, Memoirs*, vol. 2, no. 3 (1908), pp. 185-378.

SOURCES: "Report of the Director for 1926, special topics," *Bernice P. Bishop Museum, Bulletin* (1927), pp. 24-25; Foster William Russell, *Mount Auburn Biographies* (Boston: 1953), p. 26; Roger R. Rose, "William T. Brigham and the founding of Bernice P. Bishop Museum" in: *A Museum to Instruct and Delight* (Honolulu: 1980), pp. 20-71.

Thomas L. Mann

Brinton, Daniel Garrison. Anthropologist, archaeologist, linguist, physician. Born in Thornbury (Pennsylvania) 13 May 1837, died in Atlantic City (New Jersey) 31 July 1899. Brinton, an M.D. by training, was an eclectic researcher who, during his lifetime, had much influence in national scientific circles. He is among the founders of the anthropology of American Indians.

After receiving his M.D. from Jefferson Medical College in 1860, he earned his living through the practice of medicine and publishing, while pursuing an interest in anthropology. In 1866 the University of Pennsylvania named Brinton Professor of Archaeology and Linguistics, the first such post in America, albeit an honorary one. He served as president of the American Association for the Advancement of Science in 1894.

As an anthropologist, Brinton defined races and types by a combination of cultural, linguistic, and physical characteristics, but was interested more in the mind than in the body and made his reputation through his studies of American Indian linguistics and culture. As part of this research, Brinton conducted comparative studies of religion, mythology, language and literature among "primitive" peoples.

Because of his adherence to the theory of psychic unity, he tended to stress the similarities among peoples instead of their differences. Similarities stemmed from the like mental capacities of all peoples, whereas variation resulted from more subtle differences in mental development. Like other anthropologists of his time, he viewed peoples through an evolutionary framework and developed a scheme of the stages of human cultural development based on mental development and progress. In his linguistic work, Brinton classified Indian languages, using a classification which differed from that of JOHN WESLEY POWELL. Brinton identified far fewer linguistic stocks than did Powell, but he also identified some that Powell missed. They also differed in their bases for classification; Brinton relied on grammar whereas Powell used lexicon. Brinton espoused the idea that American Indians were descended from European stock, not Asiatic, because he found no linguistic affinities with Asian languages.

Brinton also gathered a large amount of material on American Indian religion and mythology and published it as the *Library of Aboriginal American Literature*. In this work he presented for the first time many aboriginal texts with translations. In other work on American Indians, he countered the popular theory that the "Moundbuilders" were unrelated to modern Indian groups.

Brinton held a somewhat polygenic and neo-Lamarckian view of human evolution, attributing evolutionary change to a mixture of degeneration and modification due to environment.

Toward the end of his life Brinton addressed the American Association for the Advancement of Science as its outgoing president and expressed concern over the growth of American anthropology and its professionalization, advocating theoretical consensus-building and the development of a strong teaching program. In sum, Brinton's interests spanned the whole of the emerging field of anthropology, and he made numerous, though short-lived, contributions to its growth.

MAJOR WORKS: *Myths of the New World: a Treatise on the Symbolism and Mythology of the Red Race in America* (New York: 1868); *Library of Aboriginal American Literature* (Philadelphia: 1882-1887); *Essays of an Americanist* (Philadelphia: 1890); *Races and Peoples: Lectures in the Science of Ethnography* (New York: 1890); *The American Race: a Linguistic Classification and Ethnographic Description of the Native Tribes of North and South America* (New York: 1891); "The aims of anthropology," *Science*, vol. 1, n.s. (1895), pp. 241-252 [American Association for the Advancement of Science presidential address].

SOURCES: "The Brinton Memorial Meeting," *Proceedings of the American Philosophical Society, Memorial*, vol. 1 (1900), pp. 210-272; Truman Michelson, "Brinton, Daniel Garrison" in: *Dictionary of American Biography*, vol. 3 (New York: 1929), pp. 50-51; Clark Wissler, "Brinton, Daniel Garrison" in: E.R.A. Seligman (editor), *Encyclopedia of the Social Sciences* (New York: 1930-1935), vol. 2, pp. 4-5; Regna Diebold Darnell, "Daniel Brinton and the professionalization of American anthropology" in: John V. Murra (editor), *American Anthropology: the Early Years* (St. Paul: 1976), pp. 69-98; Regna Diebold Darnell, *Daniel Garrison Brinton: the Fearless Critic of Philadelphia* (Philadelphia: 1988).

Joyce L. Ogburn

Broca, Paul (Pierre-Paul Broca). Surgeon, anthropologist. Born at Sainte-Foy-la-Grande, Gironde (France) 28 June 1824, died in Paris (France) 8 or 9 July 1880. Broca's professional life was devoted to medicine both as a hospital surgeon and a professor of medicine at the University of Paris. In 1850 Broca was brought in to write a report on the human bones that had been recovered in the course of excavations begun in 1847 at the ancient church of the Celestins.

Between 1858 and 1863, Broca became interested in the phenomenon of hybridization, in particular in the genus *equus*, but also among dogs, wolves, rabbits and hares and crosses of the different species. The reactions provoked by his theory of polygenism led him to found the Société d'Anthropologie de Paris on 19 May 1859, an organization where all of the problems relating to human natural history could be discussed freely. Its communications were issued as its *Bulletins* and *Mémoires*.

Broca quickly understood the array of problems that anthropology had to consider, and it was this that gave his work such significant import. He precisely defined a methodology for the study of human groups, developed appropriate technical means for its application, ensured the collection of all equipment necessary for the performance of said observations and created the means for their dissemination. His methodology was based on the idea that it was essential to study a representative series of human groups, not to limit one's observations to limited data sets, and to use standardized defined measures that would then be processed by statistical techniques. Broca wrote instructions for and had constructed numerous anthropometric and osteometric measuring devices, chromatic gradations for eye, hair and skin pigmentation. He also published a collection of tables in order to facilitate the processing of anthropological data.

Beginning in 1869, probably as a result of his studies on human fossils, he became more directly interested in the position of man in nature, and he performed a series of studies on the order of primates, on the structure of the caudal vertebrae and on animal intelligence. He also began to address the problem of transformation through natural selection. Although involved with these issues, he did not consider the immutability of species as an acceptable doctrine, refusing to support the idea that only the mechanism of natural selection could explain the evolution of species.

The collections necessary for the realization of this work were assembled in the Laboratoire d'Anthropologie at the École Pratique des Hautes-Études which was founded in 1868. In 1872, he created the *Revue d'Anthropologie*, which was dedicated to the publication of the results of the work of the Laboratory, whose domain had been extended to include the areas of comparative anatomy and the study of the brain. This was done through the addition of collaborators including THÉODORE HAMY, Paul Topinard, Théophile Chudzinski and Gustave Kuhff.

In 1876 the dissemination of his methods in France and abroad was ensured by the foundation of the École d'Anthropologie (School of Anthropology).

MAJOR WORKS: *Mémoires d'anthropologie* [5 vols.] (Paris: 1871-1888) [contains Broca's principal anthropological writings]; "L'anthropologie: son but, son programme, ses divisions et ses méthodes" in: *Dictionnaire encyclopédique des sciences médicales* (Paris: 1866), vol. 5, pp. 275-300 [tr.: "Broca on anthropology," *Anthropological Review*, vol. 5 (1867), pp. 193-204; and vol. 6 (1868), pp. 35-52]; "L'ordre des primates: parallèle anatomique de l'homme et des singes," *Bulletin de la Société d'Anthropologie de Paris*, 2nd sér., vol. 4 (1869), pp. 228-401; "Sur le transformisme," *Bulletin de la Société d'Anthropologie de Paris*, 2nd sér., vol. 5 (1870), pp. 168-239; "Les sélections," *Revue d'Anthropologie*, vol. 1 (1872), pp. 683-770; "Antropologicheskie tablifsy," *Izvestiĭa Imperatorskogo Obshchestva lĭubiteleĭ estestvoznaniĭa antropologii i étnografii*, vol. 38, no. 1 (1879).

SOURCES: S. Pozzi, "Paul Broca," *Revue d'Anthropologie*, 2nd sér., vol. 2 (1880), pp. 577-600; S. Pozzi, "Paul Broca," *Revue scientifique*, 3rd sér., vol. 2 (1882), pp. 2-12; Paul Reclus, "Paul Broca," *Revue mensuelle de médecine et de chirurgie*, vol. 4 (1880), pp. 745-764; Francis Schiller, *Paul Broca: Founder of French Anthropology, Explorer of the Brain* (Berkeley and Los Angeles: 1979); Paul Topinard, *La Société, l'École, le Laboratoire et le Musée Broca* (Paris: 1890); D. Ferembach, *History of Human Biology in France. Part 1. The Early Years* (Newcastle-upon-Tyne: 1986) (= *Occasional papers, International Association of Human Biologists*, vol. 2, no. 1).

André Leguebe
[Translation from French: Timothy Eastridge and Robert B. Marks Ridinger]

Brucefoot, Robert. See: *Foote, Robert Bruce.*

Buck, Peter Henry. See: *Te Rangi Hiroa.*

Bunak, V.V. (Viktor Valer'ianovich). Physical anthropologist, ethnographer. Born in Moscow (Russia) 23 September 1891, died in Moscow (Russian S.F.S.R.) 11 April 1979. Bunak held a doctorate in biology. After graduating in 1912, he worked at Moscow University, eventually becoming head of the Department of Anthropology and director of the Anthropology Institute. From 1948 until his death he worked at the Institut ėtnografii (Institute of Ethnography) of the Soviet Academy of Sciences.

There was probably no area of anthropology in which Bunak was not involved and on which he did not leave a deep impression. Of particular note were his investigations in ethnic anthropology, the ethnogenesis of the peoples of the Soviet Union, the theoretical study of races, the principles of racial classification, the problems of "anthropogenesis," the evolution of the brain and the origin of speech and the intellect. Bunak personally led expeditions among Russians, Ukrainians, Belorussians, Mordvinians, Mari and the peoples of the Caucasus. He was also a founder of applied anthropology in the U.S.S.R.

MAJOR WORKS: *Metodika antropologicheskikh issledovaniĭ* (Moscow: 1925); *Rasa kak istoricheskoe poniatie* (Moscow: 1938); *Normal'nye konstitutsional'nye tipy v svete dannykh o korreliatsiiakh otdel'nykh priznakov* (Moscow: 1940); "Nachal'nye ėtapy razvitiia myshleniia i rechi po dannym antropologii," *Sovetskaia ėtnografiia*, no. 3 (1951), pp. 41-53; "Proiskhozhdenie rechi po dannym antropologii," *Trudy Instituta ėtnografii*, vol. 16 (1951), pp. 205-284; *Ėtnicheskie gruppy i antropologicheskie tipy, i ikh vzaimootnoshenie v protsesse formirovaniia* (Moscow: 1951); *Cherep cheloveka i stadii ego formirovaniia u iskopaemykh liudeĭ i sovremennykh ras* (Moscow: 1959) (= *Trudy Instituta ėtnografii*, vol. 49); *Proiskhozhdenie i ėtnicheskaia istoriia russkogo naroda* (Moscow: 1965); "Rech' i intellekt, stadii ikh razvitiia v antropogeneze," *Trudy Instituta ėtnografii*, vol. 92 (1966), pp. 497-555; "Ėtnicheskie obshchnosti i rasovye deleniia" in: I.M. Zolotareva (editor-in-chief), *Rasogeneticheskie protsessy v ėtnicheskoĭ istorii* (Moscow: 1974), pp. 3-10; *Rod homo: ego vozniknovenie i posleduiushchaia ėvoliutsiia* (Moscow: 1980).

SOURCES: "IUbileĭ professora V.V. Bunaka," *Sovetskaia ėtnografiia*, no. 1 (1962), pp. 105-106; M.I. Uryson, "V.V. Bunak: nekrolog," *Voprosy antropologii*, no. 62 (1979), pp. 150-153; V.V. Bunak (editor) *Antropologiia i genogeografiia: sbornik v chest' 80-letiia V.V. Bunaka* (Moscow: 1974); V.P. Alekseev, "V.V. Bunak: novator razrabotke teoreticheskikh osnov antropologicheskoĭ nauki," *Sovetskaia bibliografiia*, no. 4 (1982), pp. 88-92; H.V. Vallois, "Nécrologie: Victor Bounak," *L'Anthropologie*, vol. 83 (1979), pp. 672-673.

A.M. Reshetov
[Translation from Russian: Helen Sullivan]

Bunzel, Ruth Leah. Ethnologist. Born in New York (New York) 1898, died in New York (New York) 14 January 1990. Bunzel is remembered particularly for her pioneering studies of Zuni pottery-making and ceremonialism in the 1920s; however, her contributions went well beyond the initial area of her fieldwork. During 1930-1932, supported by a Guggenheim Fellowship, she studied in the towns of Chichicastenango in highland Guatemala and Chamula in Chiapas, Mexico, then went to Spain to perfect her Spanish and secure background for her Southwestern Indian studies. She was there when the Revolution began, and when World War II started she was in England where she worked for the Office of War Information. During 1946-1951 Bunzel participated in the Research in Contemporary Cultures Project directed by RUTH BENEDICT. There her interest in psychology found full play. She had participated in the seminars that ABRAM KARDINER initiated in 1936 at the New York Psychoanalytic Institute and brought to Columbia University the following year.

Bunzel, who graduated from Barnard College in 1918 with a degree in European history, followed ESTHER GOLDFRANK as secretary to FRANZ BOAS, with whom she had taken a course in college. In the summer of 1924 she went with Benedict to Zuni, encouraged by Boas to study the relationship of artist to craft rather than only serve as secretarial assistant to Benedict. This led to graduate study and in 1929 she received her Ph.D. with publication of *The Pueblo Potter.*

Ruth Bunzel taught off and on at Columbia from the 1930s as a lecturer. In 1954 she was appointed adjunct professor, retiring in 1972. A shy person, she preferred her research and writing to teaching but had a great deal to contribute in one-on-one and small-group discussions.

MAJOR WORKS: *The Pueblo Potter: a Study of Creative Imagination in Primitive Art* (New York: 1929); "Introduction to Zuni ceremonialism," *Annual Report, Bureau of American Ethnology,* no. 47 (1932), pp. 467-544; "Zuni origin myths," *Annual Report, Bureau of American Ethnology,* no. 47 (1932), pp. 545-609; "Zuni ritual poetry," *Annual Report, Bureau of American Ethnology,* no. 47 (1932), pp. 611-835; "Zuni katcinas," *Annual Report, Bureau of American Ethnology,* no. 47 (1932), pp. 837-1086; *Chichicastenango, a Guatemalan Village* (New York: 1952); "The role of alcoholism in two Central American cultures," *Psychiatry,* vol. 3 (1940), pp. 361-387.

SOURCES: "Ruth Bunzel, 1898-" in: Barbara A. Babcock and Nancy J. Parezo, *Daughters of the Desert* (Albuquerque: 1988), pp. 38-43; "Ruth Leah Bunzel" in: Ute Gacs [et al.] (editors), *Women Anthropologists: a Biographical Dictionary* (Westport, Conn.: 1988), pp. 29-36; F. Murphy, "Ruth Leah Bunzel," *Anthropology Newsletter,* vol. 31., no. 3 (March 1990), p. 5.

Nathalie F.S. Woodbury

Burlin, Natalie Curtis. See: *Curtis, Natalie.*

Burssens, Amaat F.S. Researcher in African languages and oral literature. Born in Dendermonde (Belgium) 1 September 1897, died in Ghent (Belgium) 20 October 1983. Burssens studied German philology at the University of Louvain and graduated in 1923 with a Ph.D. on a late Middle Dutch eschatological text on divine consideration (*Dat Boeck vander Voirsienichheit Godes*). During 1924-1925 he was sent to the Belgian Congo (now Zaïre) to study the languages spoken on the border of Lake Tanganyika. In 1926 he began to offer courses on Central African languages at the University of Ghent. He received tenure there in 1931, teaching both African languages and Dutch and German. In 1957-1958 the Eastern-African Institute at the University of Ghent was founded. Burssens contributed to its success until his retirement in 1967.

In 1934 he founded the Africanist journal, *Kongo-Overzee.* He edited the journal until 1960, publishing important material on linguistics and ethnography. In 1938, he expanded the journal with a series of books including the original text of PLACIDE TEMPELS' work on Bantu philosophy.

In 1927 he did linguistic research on Tshiluba (in Kasai Province) and Kiluba (in Katanga, now Shaba, Province) in the Belgian Congo. He was the first to point out that in both languages the musical accent has a semantic function, implying the theory of the reverse tone system. His book *Tonologische schets van het Tshiluba* resulted from his fundamental research on the genuine structure of that language and for many years was an example for other scholars in Bantu languages.

In 1944-1950 Burssens studied the Amashi language in Kivu and also did linguistic work in Ruanda-Urundi (now Rwanda and Burundi). In 1954-1955 he joined PAUL SCHEBESTA in a field trip to the Ituri Forest to study the languages and cultures of the Efe and Mbuti Pygmies and of some Bantu and non-Bantu peoples (Bira and Lesa). In 1959 he did research in northern Zaïre on Dho-Alur, a Nilotic language.

Burssens was a well known specialist on Central African oral literature and languages. He studied and described several of these languages extensively. Aside from those mentioned above, he also did work on Kikongo, Lingala and Swahili and, to a lesser extent, Basala, Mpasu, Tshiokwe and Mongo. Burssens was one of the pioneers in African linguistics, especially with his work on tone systems. He also did historical and comparative research. Moreover, he studied the impact of Africa on the Dutch (Flemish) language. Finally, apart from his scientific work, he also published semi-literary travel accounts, including hundreds of newspaper pieces. In his later life he wrote pure literature as well.

As professor, scientist, mentor and editor for twenty-five years of a well known journal, he gave new impulses to African studies and educated and guided scores of Africanists.

MAJOR WORKS: *Ein Vlaming op reis door Kongo* (Kortrijk: 1929); *Dat Boeck vander Voirsienichheit Godes* (Brussels: 1930); *Negerwoordkunst* (Antwerp: 1933; Amsterdam: 1935); *Tshiluba-teksten in Africa-spelling* (Antwerp: 1936); *Tonologische schets van het Tshiluba (Kasayi, Belgisch-Kongo)* (Antwerp: 1939); *Wako-Moyo: Zuidoost-Kongo in de lens* (Antwerp: 1943); *Manuel de Tshiluba* (Antwerp: 1946); *Introduction à l'étude des langues bantoues du Congo belge* (Antwerp: 1954); (with K. Jonckheere) *Kongo: het woord* (Antwerp: 1961); *Problemen en inventarisatie van de verbale structuren van het Dho alur* (Brussels: 1969); *De konnektieve konstruktie in het Swahili* (Antwerp: 1969); *De possessieve konstruktie in het Swahili* (Antwerp: 1971); *La notation des langues négro-africaines* (Brussels: 1972) (= *Académie Royale des Sciences d'Outre-mer, Classe des Sciences Morales et Politiques*, n.s., no. 41-42).

Herman Burssens

Burszta, Józef. Sociologist, historian, ethnographer. Born in Grodzisk Dolny, Galicia (Austria-Hungary, now in Poland) 17 April 1914, died in Poznań (Poland) 6 July 1987. Burszta studied in Warsaw and Poznań, obtaining his doctorate in 1947. He became Associate Professor in 1959 and full Professor in 1966. Between 1957 and 1984 he served as Director of the Department of Ethnography at the University of Poznań. He was editor of the edition of the complete works of OSKAR KOLBERG published between 1961 and 1987. He attached importance to organizational and scientific activities whose goal was the elevation of the status of Polish ethnography. For many years he was head of the Committee of Ethnological Studies of the Polish Academy of Sciences.

The major foci of Burszta's scientific studies were the sociology and social problems of the countryside. He was also interested in the economic and sociological history of the countryside. He used traditional ethnography's analysis of culture to research contemporary conditions. He was also concerned with the question of the mutual connections between folk culture and national culture, devoting much attention to the distinction between the concepts of *folklor* and *folkloryzm*. He investigated the processes of settlement and social and cultural integration, particularly in Western countries. He also took up the theoretical problems connected with regional ethnographic monographs. And he postulated the necessity of documentation of sources (historical and local) of the complex of culture known as folk (peasant).

MAJOR WORKS: *Wieś i karczma [Countryside and Inn]* (Warsaw: 1950); *Społeczeństwo i karczma [Society and the Inn]* (Warsaw: 1951); *Szkice z dziejów wsi [Sketches from the History of the Countryside]* (Warsaw: 1955); *Od osady słowiańskiej do wsi współczesnej [From Slavic Settlement to the Countryside of Modern Times]* (Wrocław: 1958); *Kultura ludowa Wielkopolski [Folk Culture of Wielkopolska]* [3 vols.] (Poznań: 1960-1967); (editor) *Kultura ludowa, kultura naradowa: szkice i rozprawy [Folk Culture, National Culture: Sketches]* (Warsaw: 1974); *Chłopskie źródła kultury [Peasant Sources of Culture]* (Warsaw: 1985).

SOURCES: *Encyklopedia Powszechna PWN*, vol. 1 (Warsaw: 1973); *Tradycja i przemiana [Tradition and Change]* (Poznań: 1978).

Maria Niewiadomska and Iwona Grzelakowska
[Translation from Polish: Joel Janicki]

Burton, Sir **Richard Francis.** Soldier, consul, linguist, anthropologist. Born either at Torquay or Barham House, Herefordshire (England) [accounts vary] 19 March 1821, died in Trieste (Austria-Hungary, now in Italy) 20 October 1890. Burton is today chiefly known for his attempt to discover the source of the River Nile, one of his greater failures, yet in his day he helped found British anthropology.

Burton's father, a retired army officer, could not long remain in one place, a trait shared by his son. Burton was privately educated in France and Italy and was a very difficult pupil. The elder Burton sent his son to Oxford (Trinity College) in 1840, with the unlikely goal of a career in the clergy. Burton lasted about a year at Oxford, at which point he engaged in behaviors sufficiently disrespectful of authority to guarantee his expulsion. He obtained a commission as an army officer and began a five-decade career of service to the British Empire.

During nineteen years in the Native Bombay Infantry, Burton spent relatively little time actually serving as an infantry officer. He qualified as an interpreter of Hindustani, Gujarathi, Marathi, Sindhi, Punjabi and Persian and studied many other languages as well. He took part in the Sind survey and subsequently obtained numerous lengthy leaves for purposes of exploration. He roamed India, Africa and North America writing voluminously of his travels. In 1853, in the guise of a Pathan, he made the pilgrimage to Mecca, adding to his already considerable fame. However, his disinterest in mundane military duties and his open fascination with the sexual mores of the Hindus and Moslems whom he had studied combined to block his career in the army. His truculent personality did not help matters.

When a restructuring of the Native Bombay Infantry provided the East India Company an excuse to let Burton go, he was able to obtain in 1861 the first of a series of consular posts. He was British consul successively at Fernando Po, Santos (Brazil), Damascus and Trieste, although he once again spent much of his time away from his duties, exploring—or merely touring the countryside.

Burton also occasionally visited Britain. In 1863 he was a founding member (and vice-president) of the Anthropological Society of London, which subsequently became the Royal Anthropological Institute of Great Britain and Ireland; he contributed prolifically to its journal, the *Anthropological Review*. He was also a member of the Royal Geographical Society, which had given him its gold medal in 1859 for explorations in East Africa. He published book after book, many on his travels, and others of translations of poetry and prose from several languages. (His own poetry was published under pseudonyms.) His most famous and successful work was a ten-volume translation of the *Thousand and One Nights*.

Burton remained as consul in Trieste from 1872 until his death in 1890. He was knighted at the age of 65 and died at 69, a few months short of his retirement.

As an anthropologist, Burton should be remembered more for the breadth and originality of his interests than for any particular contribution. Many of his works were purposefully disturbing to Victorians—to the end of his life, he enjoyed shocking the middle class from which he came—but this was to some extent an inevitable concomitant of his age's growing interest in non-Western cultures.

MAJOR WORKS: Burton produced more than forty volumes of original writings in his lifetime, along with many translations. Among these, perhaps the most significant are: *Personal Narrative of a Pilgrimage to El-Medinah and Meccah* [3 vols.] (London: 1855-1856); *First Footsteps in East Africa* (London: 1856); *The Lake Regions of Central Africa* [2 vols.] (London: 1860); *The City of the Saints and Across the Rocky Mountains* (London: 1861); *A Mission to Gelele, King of Dahomey* [2 vols.] (London: 1864); *Selected Papers on Anthropology, Travel and Exploration by Sir Richard Burton* (edited by N.M. Penzer) (London: 1924); (translator) *Camöens: His Life and his Lusiads* [2 vols.] (London: 1880).

SOURCES: Byron Farwell, *Burton* (New York: 1963); Fawn M. Brodie, *The Devil Drives* (London: 1967); "Burton, Sir Richard Francis" in: Leslie Stephan and Sidney Lee (editors), *Dictionary of National Biography* (Oxford: 1921-1922), vol. 22, pp. 349-356.

David Lonergan

Buschmann, Johann Carl Eduard von. Linguist. Born in Magdeburg/Sachsen (Germany) 14 February 1805, died in Berlin (Germany) 21 April 1880. Buschmann was educated by the leading philologists of his time, F.A. Wolf (1759-1824), FRANZ BOPP, A. Boeckh (1785-1867) and by the philosopher G.W.F. Hegel (1770-1831) from 1823-1826 at the Universities of Berlin and Göttingen. He then traveled to Mexico, returning to Germany in 1828. In 1832 he was appointed librarian at the Royal Public Library in Berlin, a position he kept for the rest of his life. He was posthumous editor of Moses Mendelssohn's (1729-1786) collected papers and of WILHELM VON

HUMBOLDT's studies of Malay and Polynesian languages; he also served as private secretary to ALEXANDER VON HUMBOLDT and was editor for him. After Alexander von Humboldt's death, Buschmann was in charge of the scholarly Humboldt estate which he was supposed to edit.

Buschmann's outstanding and lasting contribution to anthropology is his comparative grammatical and lexical work on Northern and Mesoamerican Indian languages, which he endeavored to classify genetically into large families. It is not clear, however, how much of Buschmann's initial interest in non-Indo-European languages and the linguistic theories published under his own name were inspired or based on earlier Humboldt works. The "Athapascan" (Athabaskan) and the "Uto-Aztecan" families were defined by him prior to 1860, a fact rarely acknowledged today.

MAJOR WORKS: (co-editor) *Moses Mendelssohn's Gesammelte Schriften* [7 vols.] (Leipzig: 1843-1845); *Aperçu de la langue des Îles Marquises et de la langue Taïtienne, précédé d'une introduction sur l'histoire et la géographie de l'Archipel des Marquises, accompagné d'un vocabulaire inédit de la langue taïtienne par Guil. de Humboldt* (Berlin: 1843); *Textes marquésans et taïtiens, publiés et analysés* (Berlin: 1843); *Über den Naturlaut* (Berlin: 1853); *Über die aztekischen Ortsnamen,* part 1 (Berlin: 1853); *Der athapaskische Sprachstamm: die Sprachen Kizh und Netela von Neu-Californien* (Berlin: 1855) (= *Abhandlungen der Preußischen Akademie der Wissenschaften, phil. hist. Klasse*); *Die Pimasprache und die Sprache der Koloschen* (Berlin: 1857) (= *Abhandlungen der königlich Preußischen Akademie der Wissenschaften zu Berlin aus dem Jahre 1856*); *Die Lautveränderungen aztekischer Wörter in den sonorischen Sprachen und die sonorische Endung ame* (Berlin: 1857) (= *Abhandlungen der königlichen Akademie der Wissenschaften zu Berlin aus dem Jahre 1856*); *Die Völker und Sprachen Neu-Mexikos und der Westseite des britischen Nordamerika* (Berlin: 1858) (= *Abhandlungen der königlich preußischen Akademie der Wissenschaften*); "Die Völker und Sprachen im Innern des britischen Nordamerikas," *Monatsberichte der königlichen Akademie der Wissenschaften zu Berlin, philologisch-historische Klasse* (1858), pp. 466-486; *Die Spuren der aztekischen Sprache im nördlichen Mexiko und höheren amerikanischen Norden* [3 parts: *Das Apache als eine athapaskische Sprache erwiesen; Die Verwandtschaftsverhältnisse der Athapaskischen Sprachen; Systematische Worttafel des athapaskischen Sprachstammes*] (Berlin: 1855-1862) (= *Abhandlungen der Berliner Akademie der Wissenschaften phil. hist. Klasse für die Jahre 1859-1863*); *Grammatik der sonorischen Sprachen, vorzüglich der Tarahumara, Tepeguana, Cora und Cahita* [3 parts: *Das Lautsystem; Der Artikel, das Substantivum und Adjectivum; Das Zahlwort*] (Berlin: 1864-1869) (= *Spuren der aztekischen Sprache,* Abteilung 9; also = *Abhandlungen der philologisch-historischen Klasse der preußischen Akademie der Wissenschaften zu Berlin*); "Die Wanderungen der amerikanischen Völker aus dem Norden," *Zeitschrift der Gesellschaft für Erdkunde,* vol. 1 (1866), pp. 487-498; *Die Ordinalzahlen der mexikanischen Sprache dargestellt* (Berlin: 1880) (= *Abhandlungen der königlichen Akademie der Wissenschaften zu Berlin aus dem Jahre 1879*); *Über die Verwandtschaft der Kinai-Idiome des russischen Nordamerikas mit dem großen athapaskischen Sprachstamme* (n.p.: n.d.).

SOURCES: Archives of the Akademie der Wissenschaften zu Berlin II; IIIa, vol. 4: Bl. 105, 106, 107, 149; vol. 6: Bl. 1, 2; *Gelehrtes Berlin im Jahre 1845* (Berlin: 1846), pp. 52-54; Daniel Garrison Brinton, *The American Race* (New York: 1891), passim; Wilhelm Pferdekamp, *Auf Humboldts Spuren: Deutsche im jungen Mexiko* (Stuttgart: 1959); *Alexander von Humboldt und seine Welt: 1769-1859* (Berlin: 1969), pp. 46-47; Ursula Thiemer-Sachse, "Sprachwissenschaftliche Beiträge zum deutschen Mexiko-Bild im 19. Jahrhundert," *Ethnographisch-Archäologische Zeitschrift,* vol. 21 (1980), pp. 117-136; *Gesamtverzeichnis des deutschsprachigen Schrifttums, 1700-1910* (Munich, New York and London: 1980), vol. 22.

Berthold Riese

Bushnell, David Ives, Jr. Anthropologist. Born in St. Louis (Missouri) 28 April 1875, died in Washington (D.C.) 4 June 1941. An intelligent, capable man of means,

Bushnell might be described as a dilettante or amateur, provided the terms are understood in their most positive sense. Certainly his background was more in keeping with scholars of the 19th rather than the 20th century. His formal training was limited to St. Louis schools, and his regular appointments were relatively brief. During 1901-1904 he was an archaeological assistant at the Peabody Museum of American Archaeology of Harvard University. Between 1912 and 1921 he worked with the Smithsonian Institution's Bureau of American Ethnology (BAE) as an editor. His Smithsonian affiliation had started in 1907, however, when he became a collaborator (i.e., research associate) of the BAE, and he continued in that role after 1921.

As a researcher, Bushnell pursued diverse studies in archaeology, ethnology and history, concentrating in the latter on early Virginia. His anthropological activities began in the course of pleasure trips during 1899-1900, when he collected material on Chippewa Indians and participated in an archaeological survey at Mille Lac in Minnesota. Following study of museum collections and archaeology in Europe, he continued ethnological field investigations with a visit to remnant Choctaw groups in Louisiana during 1908-1909 and 1917-1918. He also carried out archaeological investigations at Cahokia in 1904, along the Cape Fear River in 1914, at mounds on the Pinellas Peninsula in Florida in 1925 and in several regions of Virginia over an extended period of time.

While affiliated with the BAE, Bushnell worked on the *Handbook of American Indians North of Mexico* (*Bureau of American Ethnology Bulletin*, no. 30) and undertook revision of Cyrus Thomas's *Catalogue of Prehistoric Works East of the Rocky Mountains* (*Bureau of American Ethnology Bulletin*, no. 12). Although Bushnell's work for the latter project was never published, his material was utilized in other publications.

Bushnell was a collector of note, assembling many pieces of art depicting American Indians and publishing noteworthy articles on several of the artists represented among them. The collection was formerly in the Peabody Museum at Harvard University.

MAJOR WORKS: *Choctaw of Bayou Lacomb* (Washington: 1909) (= *Bureau of American Ethnology Bulletin*, no. 48); *Native Villages and Village Sites East of the Mississippi* (Washington: 1919) (= *Bureau of American Ethnology Bulletin*, no. 69); *Native Cemeteries and Form of Burial East of the Mississippi* (Washington: 1920) (= *Bureau of American Ethnology Bulletin*, no. 71); *Villages of the Algonquian, Siouan, and Caddoan Tribes West of the Mississippi* (Washington: 1922) (= *Bureau of American Ethnology Bulletin*, no. 77); *Burials of the Algonquian, Siouan, and Caddoan Tribes West of the Mississippi* (Washington: 1927) (= *Bureau of American Ethnology Bulletin,*, 83).

SOURCES: John R. Swanton, "David I. Bushnell, Jr.," *American Anthropologist*, n.s., vol. 44 (1942), pp. 104-110; miscellaneous manuscripts, photographic copies of the Bushnell American Indian art collection, and vertical file in the Smithsonian Institution National Anthropological Archives; "Bushnell, David Ives, Jr.," *Washington Post* (6 June 1941), p. 33.

James R. Glenn

Bushotter, George. Informant, storyteller. Born in Dakota Territory 1864, died in Hedgesville (West Virginia) 2 February 1892. Through his writings in the Lakota (Western Sioux) language, Bushotter recorded one of the most significant sources representing traditional Lakota culture from an insider's point of view.

Bushotter was a Sioux Indian from the Lower Brule Reservation (now in South Dakota). His English name was originally George Bush and his Lakota name was Oteri ("Trouble"); the surname Bushotter resulted from conflation of the two names.

Born into 19th-century Sioux society, Bushotter received boarding school education at Hampton Institute, Virginia. In 1887, seeking employment, he approached JAMES OWEN DORSEY of the Smithsonian Institution's Bureau of American Ethnology, who recommended that he be hired as a consultant on the Lakota language. During ten months he wrote 258 stories in Lakota, totalling more than 3,000 handwritten pages, and worked with Dorsey to translate them word-by-word into English. They include a long autobiography, myths and legends, games, social customs and ceremonies. Although Dorsey published some in translation, and included many of them in his "A study of Siouan cults," Bushotter's writings have not yet been published in full.

MAJOR WORKS: *Lakota Texts* [unpublished manuscript, National Anthropological Archives, Smithsonian Institution, 1887]; J. Owen Dorsey, "A study of Siouan cults," *Annual Report of the Bureau of American Ethnology*, vol. 11 (1894), pp. 351-544.

SOURCES: Raymond J. DeMallie, "George Bushotter: the first Lakota ethnographer" in: Margot Liberty (editor), *American Indian Intellectuals* (St. Paul: 1978) (= *1976 Proceedings of the American Ethnological Society*), pp. 91-102; Raymond J. DeMallie, "A partial bibliography of archival manuscript material relating to the Dakota" [including an inventory of Bushotter's writings] in: Ethel Nurge (editor), *The Modern Sioux: Social Systems and Reservation Culture* (Lincoln: 1970), pp. 316-324.

Raymond J. DeMallie

Busia, Kofi Abrefa. Educator, sociologist, anthropologist, politician, Prime Minister of Ghana, 1969-1972. Born in Wenchi (Gold Coast, now Ghana) 11 July 1913, died in Oxford (England) 28 August 1978. Although a great deal more attention has been paid to Busia's political career, he had an equally prominent career as an academic and teacher. For him, the two activities were intertwined. In his role as an activist-scholar, Busia should be seen within a Ghanaian tradition that includes such thinkers as Casely Hayford (1866-1930) and J.B. Danquah (1895-1965). His first political appointment as District Commissioner and his first academic appointment, as lecturer and later the first professor of sociology in the newly established University College, were both in his native Ghana. Subsequently, his academic career as a sociologist of the culture of Africa, pursued while in political exile, led him to professorships and chairs at institutions around the world including the Institute of Social Studies in the Hague, inaugural professorships at the Afrika-Studiecentrum at the University of Leiden and the Colegio de México in Mexico City, and lastly as a Fellow of St. Antony's College in Oxford.

Busia is best known for his landmark study, *The Position of the Chief in the Modern Political System of Ashanti*. Following on the work of ROBERT RATTRAY, this book is a revision of his Oxford doctoral dissertation undertaken under the tutelage of A.R. RADCLIFFE-BROWN and MEYER FORTES. A study of the influence of contemporary social changes on Asante political institutions, this work, along with his earlier *Social Survey of Sekondi-Takoradi* are considered among the more authoritative works on social change in Ghana.

The quest for an understanding of the dynamics of social change can perhaps be seen as a key uniting all of Busia's seemingly disparate corpus of published works ranging from parliamentary speeches to cultural and sociological studies. Busia grounded his empirical studies on social interaction, whether localized or continental, and on a systematic understanding of the religious and ethical foundations of human societies. True to his African traditions, he saw the mythical and the mundane as mutually co-existing and co-dependent. The detail of information in his two Ghanaian studies reveals Busia's skills as a sympathetic ethnographic participant observer as well as his equally keen understanding of urban anthropology.

For Busia, human societies were collective embodiments of living active people in appointed or chosen cultural groups, operating within their specific moral universes. This approach was as true of his African studies as of his study of church life, undertaken for the World Council of Churches, *Urban Churches in Britain.* A study of the interrelatedness of church life with social and public life, this publication established Busia as the first African to undertake such a sociological study of the British. In his three later works contemplating the continent of Africa undergoing rapid social transformation, Busia considered traditional ideologies and practices and the institutions they supported, to two interdependent ends. He sought to understand the influence of native institutions and systems of thought on the modern nation state and to reflect on their continuing role in a healthy democratic environment (*Africa in Search of Democracy*). Whether discussing purposeful educational planning for modern Africa (*A Purposeful Education for Africa*) or delineating the manifold challenges of culture, colonial history and emancipation, or a common humanity and morality (*The Challenge of Africa*), the questions always asked were: what sort of human being? what sort of society? what moral universe?

MAJOR WORKS: *A Social Survey of Sekondi-Takoradi* (London: 1950); *The Position of the Chief in the Modern Political System of Ashanti* (Oxford: 1950); *The Challenge of Africa* (New York: 1962); *A Purposeful Education for Africa* (The Hague: 1964); *Urban Churches in Britain* (London: 1966); *Africa in Search of Democracy* (London: 1967); *Ghana's Struggle for Democracy and Freedom: Speeches, 1957-1969* (compiled by H.K. Akyeampong) (Accra: n.d.).

SOURCES: "A political giant passes," *The Legon Observer,* vol. 10, no. 2 (15-28 September 1978), pp. 25-27 [editorial]; Max Assimeng, "The sociology of Kofi Busia," *The Legon Observer,* vol. 10, no. 2 (15-28 September 1978), pp. 31-33; "Busia, Dr Kofi Abrefa" in: *Who Was Who, 1971-1980* (London: 1981), p. 116.

Abena P.A. Busia

Butinov, N.A. (Nikolaĭ Aleksandrovich). Ethnographer. Born in Petrograd (Russia) 19 December 1914. Butinov is a doctor of historical sciences and a professor. He directed the Section on the Ethnography of the Peoples of Australia, Oceania, the Philippines and Indonesia of the Leningrad branch of the Institut ètnografii (Institute of Ethnography) of the Soviet Academy of Sciences. He is a major specialist on the ethnography of Australia and Oceania and the theoretical problems of ethnography. The main areas of the Butinov's scholarly work are: problems of pre-literate, pre-class societies; communal-tribal structures; the development of the conception of exogamy; tribal community; the form of the family; precolonial social structures among the Papuans of New Guinea and the peoples of Oceania; the contemporary processes occurring in the young governments of

Melanesia; the main schools in foreign ethnography (the school of cultural circles, the functional school, American economic anthropology, structuralism); and the publications of N.N. MIKLUKHO-MAKLAĬ.

MAJOR WORKS: "Problema ėkzogamii (po avstraliĭskim materialam)," *Trudy Instituta ėtnografii AN SSSR*, vol. 14 (1951), pp. 3-27; "O pervobytnoĭ lingvisticheskoĭ nepreryvnosti," *Sovetskaĭā ėtnografiĭā*, no. 2 (1951), pp. 179-181; (with ĬŪ.V. Knorozovym), "Predvaritel'noe soobshchenie ob izuchenii pis'mennosti ostrova Paskhi," *Sovetskaĭā ėtnografiĭā*, no. 4 (1956), pp. 77-91; "Maori (istoriko-ėtnograficheskiĭ ocherk)," *Trudy Instituta ėtnografii AN SSSR*, vol. 38 (1957), pp. 87-173; "Ieroglificheskie teksty ostrova Paskhi," *Vestnik istorii mirovoĭ kul'tury*, no. 3 (1959), pp. 69-80; "Razdelenie truda v pervobytnom obshchestve," *Trudy Instituta ėtnografii AN SSSR*, vol. 54 (1960), pp. 109-150; *Papuasy Novoĭ Gvinei* (Moscow: 1968); *N.N. Miklukho-Maklaĭ: velikiĭ russkiĭ uchenyĭ i gumanist* (Leningrad: 1971); *Put' k beregy Maklaĭā* (Khabarovsk: 1974); "O spet̄sifike proizvodstvennykh otnosheniĭ obshchenno-rodovoĭ format̄sii," *Sovetskaĭā ėtnografiĭā*, no. 3 (1977), pp. 47-58; *Polineziĭt̄sy ostrovov Tuvalu* (Moscow: 1982); "Levi-Stross, ėtnograf i filosof" in: Claude Lévi-Strauss ["K. Levi-Stross" in Romanized Cyrillic], *Kul'turnaĭā antropologiĭā* (Moscow: 1983), pp. 422-466.

SOURCES: S.M. Miliband, "Butinov, Nikolaĭ Aleksandrovich" in: *Biobibliograficheskiĭ slovar' sovetskikh vostokovedov* (Moscow: 1975), p. 100; "Spisok osnovnykh rabot N.A. Butinova," *Sovetskaĭā ėtnografiĭā*, no. 1 (1985), pp. 130-132 [bibliography].

A.M. Reshetov
[Translation from Russian: Thomas L. Mann]

Bystroń, Jan Stanisław. Ethnographer, folklorist, sociologist, cultural historian. Born in Kraków, Galicia (Austria-Hungary, now in Poland) 20 October 1892, died in Warsaw (Poland) 18 November 1964. Bystroń's intensive scientific activity occurred in the years between 1914 and 1945. He studied in Kraków and Paris. In 1925 he obtained a full professorship. He was the organizer of the Departments of Ethnography and Ethnology at the Universities of Poznań, Kraków and Warsaw. In his methodology Bystroń combined the genetic and sociological approach with the synchronic and diachronic point of view. He investigated folk culture as a collection of material transmitted orally. He researched and systematized knowledge concerning the culture of various social groups living in specific territorial and temporal zones, and he created functional models of historical, social and cultural reality. As a folklorist he was engaged in the study of Polish folk songs, proverbs and tales.

MAJOR WORKS: *Zwyczaje żniwiarskie w Polsce* [*Harvesting Customs in Poland*] (Kraków: 1916); *Wstęp do ludoznawstwa polskiego* [*Introduction to Polish Folk Studies*] (Lwów: 1926); *Warszawa* [*Warsaw*] (Warsaw: 1928); *Dzieje obyczajów, wiek XVI-XVIII* [*History of Customs, 16th-18th Centuries*] (Warsaw: 1932); *Megalomania narodowa* [*National Megalomania*] (Warsaw: 1935); *Kultura ludowa* [*Folk Culture*] (Warsaw: 1936); *Komizm* (Lwów: 1939); *Etnografia polski* [*Polish Ethnography*] (Warsaw: 1947); *Tematy, które mi odradzano* [*Elusive Topics*] (Warsaw: 1980).

SOURCES: Józef Chałasinski, "Jan Stanisław Bystroń," *Przegląd Socjologiczny*, vol. 28 (1976), pp. 205-216; Małgorzata Terlecka (editor), *Historia etnografii polskiej* [*History of Polish Ethnography*] (Wrocław: 1973); Anna Kutrzeba-Pojnarowa, *Kultura ludowa i jej badacze* [*Folk Culture and its Researchers*] (Warsaw: 1977).

Maria Niewiadomska and Iwona Grzelakowska
[Translation from Polish: Joel Janicki]

C

Çambel, Halet. Archaeologist, educator. Born in Berlin (Germany) 1916. A scholar of ancient Anatolia, Çambel has contributed both her own research and her commitment to unraveling the region's past through advancing its study by others.

The daughter of a distinguished Turkish statesman, Çambel lived and was educated both in Turkey and abroad. She completed her *licence-ès-lettres* at the Sorbonne in 1938 and began a doctorate at the École Pratique des Hautes Études (Institut Catholique) and the École du Louvre. With World War II, she returned to Turkey, completing her Ph.D. at Istanbul University under Helmuth Theodor Bossert (1889-1961), a philologist and archaeologist, in 1944. She remained to teach and became a full professor in 1960. In 1964 she founded the Prehistory Institute at the University, which she chaired until her retirement in 1988. As a teacher and mentor, she is held in high esteem by several generations of students, a number of whom are now teaching in the Institute.

Çambel's experience in Anatolian archaeology covers most time periods and many different problems; however, her long-term concerns have been with the pre- and early history of Southeastern Anatolia. Her work at Karatepe and nearby Domuztepe (excavated by U. Bahadır Alkım) began in 1947 under the direction of Bossert and spans over four decades. From the time of the discovery by Bossert of a bilingual inscription permitting decipherment of Hittite hieroglyphs, much important information about life in the Neo-Hittite states, including their relations beyond Anatolia, has been recovered. Çambel's renovation of the site has also resulted in an especially fine open-air museum.

Also in southeastern Turkey, Çambel established and co-directed the Istanbul-Chicago Universities' Joint Prehistoric Project. Begun with ROBERT J. BRAIDWOOD in 1963, it resulted in two-and-one-half decades (1963-1988) of very productive fieldwork, primarily at Çayönü Tepesi, concerning the origins of food production. Much information on early village farming was gathered.

Under the direction of the Turkish General Directorate of Antiquities and Museums, Çambel had an important part in organizing the international archaeological rescue efforts from the 1960s into the 1980s that preceded completion of both the Keban and Lower Euphrates Dams. She is a member of numerous scientific societies, including the Union Internationale des Sciences Préhistoriques et Protohistoriques (since 1954), the Deutsches Archaeologisches Institut (since 1964) and the American Philosophical Society (since 1979). Within the international world of Near Eastern prehistorians, she is a dynamic, influential and respected member.

MAJOR WORKS: (with H.Th. Bossert, U.B. Alkım, N. Ongunsu and İ. Süzen) *Karatepe Kazıları = Die Ausgrabungen auf dem Karatepe* (Ankara: 1950); (editor, with K. Bittel) *Boğazköy* (İstanbul: 1951); "The Southeast Anatolian Prehistoric Project and its significance for culture history," *Belleten*, vol. 38 (1974), pp. 361-377; (with Robert J. Braidwood) *İstanbul ve Chicago Üniversiteleri Karma Projesi Güneydoğu Anadolu Tarihöncesi Araştırmaları*, I = *The Joint Istanbul-Chicago Universities' Prehistoric Research Project in Southeastern Anatolia*, I (İstanbul: 1980).

SOURCES: *American Journal of Archaeology* (1949-present); *Anatolian Studies* (1951-present); R.J. and L.S. Braidwood (editors), *Prehistoric Village Archaeology in South-eastern Turkey: the Eighth Millenium B.C. Site of Çayönü* (Oxford: 1982); personal communication from H. Çambel.

Margaret R. Dittemore

Camden, William. Antiquarian, schoolmaster. Born in London (England) 2 May 1551, died in Chiselhurst (England) 9 November 1623. He was educated at Christ's Hospital and, though the son of a poor painter, went on to St. Paul's School, then Pembroke College, Oxford, where he was befriended by Richard and George Carew, both antiquarians. He finally got a B.A. at Christchurch College after sixteen years of study and was later given an honorary M.A. at Oxford. Leaving there in 1571, he traveled in England eventually becoming a teacher at Westminster School, London. He was its headmaster between 1593 and 1603. Camden spent all his vacations examining ruined monuments and ferreting out historical manuscripts. He was widely known in Europe for his scholarship, and it was probably the great geographer Ortelius who persuaded him to pull his vast knowledge together into a book. He never married and stopped teaching in 1603 so as to be able to devote himself to writing and to his public duties as Clarenceux King of Arms. The Camden Professorship was established at Oxford during his lifetime and the Camden Society named after him in 1838. Though he traveled throughout England and Wales in the search for manuscripts and antiquities, he never went overseas. He is buried in Westminster Abbey. When his *Britannia* first appeared in 1586, it covered every part of the British Isles, including even the off-shore islands. A history of each county from the earliest times was provided, complete with some folklore and observations on the antiquities and rarer flora. The book has forty-eight detailed maps showing towns, villages, hills, roads and mansions, along with many other illustrations. His drawing of Stonehenge is the first accurate document for the site; some of the antiquities depicted no longer exist. One of Camden's chief problems in writing a history for his time was that there was then no concept of prehistory. He recorded the first coal fossils but called them "mock plants." Many of the great earthworks and stone structures that he recorded (and which today are known to belong to the Bronze or Iron Ages) he attributed to Romans or to Danes. Much of his historical data came from privately owned manuscripts, and he was critical in his use of them. He was particularly dismissive of the ancient legends of the Irish. The sixth, greatly enlarged edition of *Britannia* came out in 1607, and after his death there were numerous further editions in English and Latin, most of them usefully expanded by their several editors (e.g., 1695). In order to complete his work, Camden had learnt not only Latin and Greek but also Anglo-Saxon and Gaelic. In his later years he was constantly trying to improve his book, and his final revision appeared in 1625.

MAJOR WORKS: *Camden's Britannia, Newly Translated into English: with Large Additions and Improvements* (edited by Edmund Gibson) (London: 1695; Latin original, 1586); *Annales ... Regnante Elizabetha ... ad annum 1589* (London: 1615-1627); and other minor works.

SOURCES: "Life of Mr. Camden" in: *Camden's Britannia, Newly Translated into English: with Large Additions and Improvements* (edited by Edmund Gibson) (London: 1695) [11 unnumbered pp.]; "Camden, William" in: *Dictionary of National Biography*, vol. 3 (Oxford: 1921), pp. 729-737; "Camden, William" in: *Encyclopaedia Britannica* (Cambridge: 1910), vol. 5, p. 101.

Paul Hockings

Camper, Petrus. Physician, surgeon, obstetrician, comparative anatomist, zoologist, palaeontologist, physical anthropologist, artist, educator. Born in Leiden (Netherlands) 11 May 1722, died in The Hague (Netherlands) 7 April 1789. Camper earned a Ph.D. and an M.D. from the University of Leiden. He taught various subjects at the Universities of Franeker, Amsterdam and Groningen. During his lifetime Camper became famous for his skills as an anatomist and as an artist. Today he is remembered as the first to discover a precisely measurable characteristic for distinguishing the varieties of the human species, the "facial angle," which he derived empirically.

As a result of his observation of skulls arrested in various stages of life, Camper began to speculate on the laws behind the amazing diversity of skull shapes in nature. After sawing several skulls perpendicularly down the middle, he observed that a general regularity was maintained by the brain cavity's oval form, but the key to pluriformity rested in the extension of the jaw. Although the principle was not new, Camper's originality lay in reducing the variety of shapes to a single factor that could be quantified.

Camper transferred the forms of craniums onto paper in the architect's manner and traced a line from the front of the incisor teeth to the prominent part of the forehead. This *linea facialis*, or facial line, intersected with the horizontal line, drawn from the nosebase to the earhole, at an angle which provided a specific numerical degree. Camper illustrated the results of his measurements by a famous series of profiled heads. The last head showed an angle of one hundred degrees for the ideal Greek statue profile, then, moving from right to left, the heads displayed angles that descended in quantity of degrees from the Roman statue (90°-85°), to the European human head (80°), to the Kalmuck (70°), to the Angolan (70°), to the orangutan (58°), to the tailed monkey (42°) and theoretically (as Camper's text outlines) through the vertebrates to a bird's bill or fish.

19th-century anthropologists interpreted Camper's spectrum of skulls to mean that, the further a human race departed from the ideal form represented by Classical statuary, the lower it must rank on the scale of humanity. They invented instruments for measuring the facial angle directly on subjects and used the facial angle as an indication in craniometry of intelligence. Thus Camper has been accused by many of introducing a measure that placed the African between the European and the ape. This opinion of Camper's work is now being revised, however. Several of Camper's works which have not been translated into English and his unpublished papers clearly indicate that Camper had no racist intentions. On the contrary, Camper was more liberal than most of his contemporaries. In his "Redevoering over den oorsprong en de kleur der zwarten," Camper demonstrated by dissection that, while skin color frequently varied, the composition of skin was the same in all human beings. He reduced skin color to a characteristic of minor importance. He also defended the blacks, who were thought ugly by most Europeans, when he proved in his lecture, "Over het gedaante schoon," that aesthetic judgments were relative. Camper's considerable abilities as an artist and draftsman (he was an outstanding scientific illustrator) helped him to understand the nature of aesthetic preference and prejudice. It was his contention that unfamiliarity with blacks made whites at the time regard them as ugly.

Camper also disproved through comparative anatomy the then-current theories regarding the abilities of apes to speak and to walk upright. He was the first to find evidence that distinguished the orangutan from the chimpanzee. Late in his life, the increasing discoveries of animal fossils convinced him that they were created and became extinct prior to the creation of Adam and Eve.

MAJOR WORKS: "Redevoering over den oorsprong en de kleur der zwarten," *De Rhapsodist*, vol. 2 (1772), pp. 373-394; "Account of the organs of speech of the orang outang," *Philosophical Transactions*, vol. 69 (1779), pp. 139-159; "Conjectures relative to the petrifactions found in St. Peter's Mountain, near Maestricht," *Philosophical Transactions*, vol. 76 (1786), pp. 443-456; *Natuurkundige verhandelingen over den orang outang en eenige andere aap-soorten, over den rhinoceros met den dubbelen horen en over het rendier* (Amsterdam: 1782); *Verhandeling van Petrus Camper, over het natuurlijk verschil der wezenstrekken in menschen van onderscheiden landaart en ouderdom; over het schoon in antyke beelden en gesneedene steenen: Gevolgd door een voorstel van eene nieuwe manier om hoofden van allerleye menschen met zekerheid te tekenen* (Utrecht: 1791); *Redenvoeringen van wylen Petrus Camper, over de wyze, om de onderscheidene hartstogten op onze wezens te verbeelden; over de verbaazende overeenkomst tusschen de viervoetige dieren, de vogelen, de visschen en den mensch; en over het gedaante schoon* (Utrecht: 1792) [tr.: *The Works of the late Professor Camper, on the Connexion between the Science of Anatomy and the Arts of Drawing, Painting, Statuary, etc. in Two Books containing a Treatise on the Natural Difference of Features in Persons of Different Countries and Periods of Life; and on Beauty, as Exhibited in Ancient Sculpture; with a New Method of Sketching Heads, National Features, and Portraits of Individuals, with Accuracy, etc.* (London: 1794) [the last essay of *Redenvoeringen ...*, "Over het gedaante schoon," was not translated by Thomas Cogan]].

SOURCES: Jacob van Sluis (translator and editor), *Petrus Camper, "Oratio de mundo optimo" en "Prolegomena in philosophia"* (Leeuwarden: 1988); Antonie M. Luijendijk-Elshout, "Petrus Camper als antropoloog" in: J. Schuller tot Peursum-Meijer and W.R.H. Koops (editors), *Petrus Camper (1722-1788): Onderzoeker van Nature* (Groningen: 1989), pp. 65-68; Robert Paul Willem Visser, *The Zoological Work of Petrus Camper, 1722-1789* (Amsterdam: 1985); Anonymous, "Biographical sketch of Camper," *Edinburgh Medical and Surgical Journal*, vol. 7 (1807), pp. 257-262; Claude Blanckaert, "'Les vicissitudes de l'angle facial' et les débuts de la craniométrie (1765-1875)," *Revue de Synthèse*, vol. 3-4 (1987), pp. 417-453; A.J. van Bork-Feltkamp, "Anthropological research in the Netherlands, a historical survey," *Verhandelingen der Koninklijke Nederlandsche Akademie van Wetenschappen, afd. Natuurkunde*, 2 sectie, vol. 37 (1938), pp. 1-166; J.D. Cunningham, "Anthropology in the 18th century," *Journal of the Royal Anthropological Institute*, vol. 38 (1908), pp. 10-35; *Dictionary of Scientific Biography*, vol. 3 (1971), pp. 37-38; Stephen Jay Gould, "Petrus Camper's angle: the grandfather of scientific racism has gotten a bum rap," *Natural History*, vol. 96 (1987), pp. 12-16; G. Schamelhout, "Petrus Camper (1722-1789): zijn verdiensten als geneeskundige, natuuronderzoeker en anthropoloog," *Verhandelingen van de Koninklijke Vlaamsche Academie voor Geneeskunde van Belgie*, vol. 5 (1943), pp. 41-86; J.E. Schulte, "Petrus Camper en de studie der menschenrassen," *Geneeskundige Gids*, vol. 17 (1939), pp. 441-449; Paul Topinard, "Étude sur Pierre Camper et sur l'angle facial dit de Camper," *Revue d'anthropologie*, vol. 3 (1874), pp. 193-222; Robert Visser, "Die Rezeption der Anthropologie Petrus Campers (1770-1850)" in: Gunter Mann, Jost Benedum and Werner F. Kümmel (editors), *Die Natur des Menschen: Probleme der physischen Anthropologie und Rassenkunde (1750-1850)* (Stuttgart: 1990) (= *Soemmerring-Forschungen*, vol. 6), pp. 325-335.

Miriam Claude Meijer

Caro Baroja, Julio. Anthropologist, historian, linguist, essayist. Born in Madrid (Spain) 13 November 1914. Caro Baroja received his doctorate in anthropology at the University of Madrid. Except for a brief period managing the Museo del Pueblo Español (Museum of the Spanish People) and teaching at the Universidad del País Vasco (University of the Basque Country), he has pursued a life of independent scholarship. He was named to the Real Academia de la Historia (Royal Academy of History) in 1963 and to the Real Academia Española de la Lengua (Royal Spanish Academy of Language) in 1986. He has also received a number of prestigious Spanish prizes for his writings and scholarships.

His work, a unique blend of anthropology, history, classical and literary studies, provides one of the most sustained examples of an anthropology of large-scale, literate societies. He has published, as of this writing, forty-eight books, twenty collections of essays, and hundreds of articles and essays. His ethnographic work includes monographic studies of social structure, culture, and folklore in the Basque Country, the rest of Spain, and North Africa, as well as a number of synthetic studies of the ethnology of Spain. Perhaps the most outstanding feature of Caro Baroja's work is his ability to weave together historical sources, the study of material culture and anthropological concepts into a coherent whole. His historical works include a huge corpus of anthropological and historical studies of ethnogenesis and ethnic conflict in Spain and a variety of studies of urban and rural "built environments." His essays are often philosophical or political and are widely noted for their erudition and critical spirit.

MAJOR WORKS: *Los pueblos de España* (Barcelona: 1946; 2nd ed., Madrid: 1976; 3rd ed., Madrid: 1981); *Los vascos* (San Sebastian: 1949; 2nd ed., Madrid: 1958; 3rd ed., Madrid: 1971); *Los moriscos del Reino de Granada* (Madrid: 1957; 2nd ed., Madrid: 1976); *Razas, pueblos, y linajes* (Madrid: 1957); *Los judíos en la España moderna y contemporánea* (Madrid: 1962; 2nd ed. Madrid: 1978); *El Carnaval* (Madrid: 1965); *Vidas mágicas e inquisición* (Madrid: 1967); *El señor inquisidor y otras vidas por oficio* (Madrid: 1968); *La hora navarra del XVIII* (Pamplona: 1969; 3rd ed., Pamplona: 1985); *Los Baroja* (Madrid: 1972; 2nd ed., Madrid: 1978); *Las formas complejas de la vida religiosa* (Madrid: 1978; 2nd ed., Madrid: 1985); *La aurora del pensamiento antropológico* (Madrid: 1983); *Historia de la fisionomía* (Madrid: 1988).

SOURCES: *Julio Caro Baroja-ri Omenaldia* [*Homage to Julio Caro Baroja*] (San Sebastián: 1986) (= *Revista de Estudios Vascos*, vol. 31, año 34, no. 2) [contains bibliography, complete to 1986]; Antonio Carreira [et al.] (editors), *Homenaje a Julio Caro Baroja* (Madrid: 1978); Julio Caro Baroja and Emilio Temprano, *Disquisiciones antropológicas* (Madrid: 1985); Davydd J. Greenwood, "Julio Caro Baroja: sus obras e ideas" in: *Julio Caro-Baroja-ri Omenaldia* [see above], pp. 227-245; Davydd J. Greenwood, "Community-region-government: an interpretation of anthropology and history" in: *Homenaje a Julio Caro Baroja* [see above], pp. 511-532.

Davydd J. Greenwood

Casagrande, Joseph Bartholomew. Anthropologist, linguist, administrator. Born in Cincinnati (Ohio) 14 February 1915, died in Las Vegas (Nevada) 2 June 1982. Casagrande grew up in Chicago and Milwaukee and made his first acquaintance with anthropology when he was "mesmerized" by RALPH LINTON in an introductory class at the University of Wisconsin. He also studied with ALEXANDER A. GOLDENWEISER and CHARLOTTE GOWER CHAPMAN (then Charlotte Gower) during his years as an undergraduate at Wisconsin. He rejoined Linton in 1940 at Columbia University which he entered as a graduate student of anthropology. His graduate training was interrupted by World War II (he served in North Africa and Italy). Upon his return to Columbia, he worked as CHARLES WAGLEY's assistant while completing his dissertation on Commanche ethnolinguistics (Ph.D., 1949).

Though remembered as an excellent teacher (Queens College, University of Rochester, American University and the University of Illinois), Casagrande was most effective as an administrator. He organized the 29th International Congress of Americanists (1949), served on the staff of the Social Science Research Council (1950-1960), was Secretary of the Anthropological Society of Washington (1954-1957), President of the American Ethnological Society (1963-1964), President of the American Anthropological Association (1972-1973) and the first Chair of the Department of Anthropology at the University of Illinois.

Casagrande's two major fieldwork experiences were in the U.S. Southwest and in Ecuador. He coordinated the Southwest Project in Comparative Psycholinguistics, an SSRC project that used a team of seventeen linguists, anthropologists and psychologists in a study of six ethnic groups (Zuni, Hopi, Hopi-Tewa, Navajo, Hispanic and Tewa). The purpose of the project was to test various aspects of the "linguistic relativity hypothesis" associated with EDWARD SAPIR and BENJAMIN LEE WHORF.

From 1962 until his death (at a Las Vegas blackjack table), Casagrande was involved in ethnographic fieldwork in Ecuador. This included his work for the Columbia-Cornell-Harvard-Illinois Summer Field Training Program in Social Anthropology and his own frequent field trips to South America. His best-known publication resulting from this research is the frequently reprinted "Strategies for survival: the Indians of Highland Ecuador."

Casagrande was above all else a champion of humanist anthropology and is best known for his compilation of twenty personal portraits by anthropologists of their chief informants. This work, *In the Company of Man*, has become a perennial classic of the discipline and included Casagrande's remarkable portrait of John Mink, a Wisconsin Ojibwa shaman.

MAJOR WORKS: "Commanche baby language," *International Journal of American Linguistics*, vol. 14 (1948), pp. 11-14; "Commanche linguistic acculturation" [in 3 parts], *International Journal of American Linguistics*, vol. 20 (1954), pp. 140-151 and 217-237; and vol. 21 (1955), pp. 8-25; (with John B. Carroll) "The function of language classifications in behavior" in: Eleanor E. Maccoby [et al.] (editors), *Readings in Social Psychology* (New York: 1958), pp. 18-31; "Some observations on the study of intermediate societies" in: Verne F. Ray (editor), *Intermediate Societies: Social Mobility and Communication* (Seattle: 1959), pp. 1-10; *In the Company of Man: Twenty Portraits by Anthropologists* (New York: 1960); "The relations of anthropology with the social sciences" in: David G. Mandelbaum [et al.] (editors), *The Teaching of Anthropology* (Washington: 1963), pp. 462-474; "Language universals in anthropological perspective" in: Joseph H. Greenberg (editor), *Universals of Language* (Cambridge, Mass.: 1963), pp. 220-235; (with Stephen I. Thompson and

Philip D. Young) "Colonization as a research frontier: the Ecuadorian case" in: Robert A. Manners (editor), *Process and Pattern in Culture: Essays in Honor of Julian H. Steward* (Chicago: 1964), pp. 281-325; "Strategies for survival: the Indians of Highland Eduador" in: Dwight B. Heath (editor), *Contemporary Cultures and Societies of Latin America* (Prospect Heights, Ill.: 1988), pp. 93-107.

SOURCES: "Casagrande, Joseph B." in: Melville J. Herskovits (editor), *International Directory of Anthropologists* (Washington: 1950), p. 28; "Casagrande, Joseph Bartholomew" in: Sol Tax (editor), *Fifth International Directory of Anthropologists* (Chicago: 1975), p. 61; Stephen I. Thompson, "Joseph Bartholomew Casagrande (1915-1982)," *American Anthropologist*, vol. 87 (1985), pp. 883-888.

Fred J. Hay

Caso, Alfonso (Alfonso Caso Andrade). Archaeologist, historian, social anthropologist. Born in Mexico City (Mexico) 1 February 1896, died in Mexico City (Mexico) 30 November 1970. Following initial training in law and philosophy at the National University of Mexico, in the mid-1920s a visit to the archaeological site of Xochicalco in the state of Morelos aroused an interest in archaeology and ethnology. His early training in anthropology took place through course work offered by the National Museum under the direction of Hermann Beyer. By 1930 Caso was recognized as an authority in his new fields with his appointments in ethnology and archaeology at the National University and National Museum respectively. In 1931 excavation was begun at the Zapotec site of Monte Alban near the city of Oaxaca, which remained a focus of action and study until 1943. A spectacular tomb laden with exquisite goldwork is perhaps the most generally known of the finds. As early as 1928 Caso had already begun his lifelong research on the calendrical systems of Oaxaca and Central Mexico and the numerous codices of the Zapotec and Mixteca nations. His training in ethnology led to a concern for the contemporary Indian cultures of Mexico, an interest that was to be expressed by the creation in 1949 of the Instituto Nacional Indigenista (National Indianist Institute) under his direction. The purpose of the coordinating centers set up by the Institute was to foster the development of the various groups through joint participation of community leaders and also to permit traditional cultural values to be preserved. While these centers were successfully established in eight Mexican states, that for the Tzeltal and Tzotzil of Chiapas in San Cristóbal de las Casas was viewed as a model in the field of applied anthropology. His appointment in the late 1940s as Minister of the Public and Historical Properties resulted in both legal measures and practical steps to promote the conservation of the pre-Columbian and colonial sites and buildings of Mexico. Of his many publications, perhaps best known are *Urnas de Oaxaca*, *La cerámica de Monte Alban* and *El tesoro de Monte Alban*, based on some twenty years of excavation results, and the posthumous *Reyes y reinos de la Mixteca*. Caso's work provided a framework for the training of a generation of Mexican anthropologists and archaeologists and established the study of pre-Hispanic codices as a field of science in Mexico.

MAJOR WORKS: *Las exploraciones en Monte Alban temporada 1934-1935* (Mexico City: 1935); *Exploraciones en Mitla, 1934-1935* (Mexico City: 1936); *The Religion of the Aztecs* (Mexico City: 1937); *Urnas de Oaxaca* (Mexico City: 1952); *El pueblo del sol* (Mexico City: 1953) [tr.: *The Aztecs: People of the Sun* (Norman: 1958)]; *La cerámica de Monte Alban* (Mexico City: 1967); *Los calendarios prehispánicos* (Mexico City: 1967); *El tesoro de Monte Alban* (Mexico City: 1969); *La comunidad indígena* (Mexico City: 1971); *Trabajos ineditos del Dr. Alfonso Caso y del Prof.*

Federico Gomez Orozco en la B.N.A.H. (Biblioteca Nacional de Antropologia e Historia) (Mexico City: 1979); *Reyes y reinos de la Mixteca* [2 vols.] (Mexico City: 1972-1979).

SOURCES: Ignacio Bernal, "Alfonso Caso Andrade, 1896-1970," *American Antiquity*, vol. 36 (1971), pp. 449-450; Miguel Leon-Portilla, "Alfonso Caso, 1896-1970," *American Anthropologist*, vol. 75 (1973), pp. 877-885; Luis Calderon Vega, *Los siete sabios de Mexico* (Mexico City: 1972), pp. 31-50; *Homenaje al Dr. Alfonso Caso* (Mexico City: 1951).

Robert B. Marks Ridinger

Castrén, Matthias Alexander (Matias Aleksanteri Castrén). Linguist, ethnologist, orientalist. Born in Tervola (Finland, then in Russia) 2 December 1813, died in Helsinki (Finland, then in Russia) 7 May 1852. With a background in classical and Oriental studies at Helsinki University, Castrén was selected by the Finnish academician in St. Petersburg, Anders Johan Sjögren, to carry out the linguistic and ethnological part of an extensive research program organized by the Russian Imperial Academy of Sciences. The program was planned to yield fresh information about the aboriginal peoples and languages of Arctic Russia and Siberia and came to require of Castrén more than seven years (1841-1849) of solitary fieldwork under harsh conditions. Living during the period of the national awakening of the Finnish-speaking part of the population of Finland and an ethnic Finn himself, Castrén initially aimed at discovering the "origin" of the Finnish language. This goal he did, indeed, achieve, in that he gathered a huge corpus of grammatical and lexical material on three previously little-known Finno-Ugric and five Samoyedic languages and thus laid a scientific basis for the understanding of the Uralic language family.

However, in spite of this contribution to Uralic studies, Castrén should definitely not be regarded only as a Finno-Ugrist or Uralist. Rather, he should, in the first place, be recognized as an early forerunner of linguistic anthropology in Russia and Siberia. Castrén had an exceptional talent for studying unknown and unwritten languages directly from the speakers. He completed the descriptions of twelve Arctic and Siberian languages and of an even greater number of local dialects with amazing speed and accuracy. Moreover, he did not confine his work to the Uralic family, but also covered a number of non-Uralic languages representing the Turkic, Tungusic, Mongolic and Yeniseic families. For instance, in clear contrast to the earlier philological tradition of Mongolic studies, Castrén approached the Mongolic Buryat language as a living idiom and prepared the first description of spoken Mongolic. Another idiom, the Yeniseic Kott language, was recorded by Castrén only a few years before its extinction, a circumstance that renders his description an invaluable source for Yeniseic comparative studies. In all of his linguistic descriptions, Castrén exhibited an understanding of the structural and functional aspects of language that was unparalleled in his time.

Although language studies were the focus of his fieldwork, Castrén also systematically recorded information on all other aspects of the native communities in which he stayed: their folklore, religion, ethnography, ethnic history and physical anthropology. His observations on Siberian shamanism are particularly valuable. Thus, Castrén's approach was that of a multidisciplinary modern anthropologist. Because of his concentration on Siberia, he can also be regarded as the founder of modern Siberian anthropology and as one of the pioneers of Siberian studies in general.

During his fieldwork, Castrén became seriously ill with tuberculosis. Having returned to Finland, he was appointed the first professor of Finnish at Helsinki University (1851), but, weakened by the illness, he died the following year, leaving part of his field notes unedited. The editing work was, however, rapidly and professionally completed by Castrén's contemporary and colleague in St. Petersburg, Anton Schiefner (1817-1879).

MAJOR WORKS: *Nordische Reisen und Forschungen* (edited by Anton Schiefner) [12 vols.: (1) *Reiseerinnerungen aus den Jahren 1838-1844* (1853); (2) *Reiseberichte und Briefe aus den Jahren 1845-1849* (1856); (3) *Vorlesungen über die finnische Mythologie* (1853); (4) *Ethnologische Vorlesungen über altaischen Völker nebst samojedischen Märchen und tatarischen Heldensagen* (1857); (5) *Kleinere Schriften* (1862); (6) *Versuch einer ostjakischen Sprachlehre nebst kurzem Wörterverzeichniss* (1858); (7) *Grammatik der samojedischen Sprachen* (1854); (8) *Wörterverzeichnisse aus den samojedischen Sprachen* (1855); (9) *Grundzüge einer tungusischen Sprachlehre nebst kurzem Wörterverzeichniss* (1856); (10) *Versuch einer burjätischen Sprachlehre nebst kurzem Wörterverzeichniss* (1857); (11) *Versuch einer koibalischen und karagassischen Sprachlehre nebst Wörterverzeichnissen aus den tatarischen Mundarten des Minussinschen Kreises* (1857); (12) *Versuch einer jenissei-ostjakischen und kottischen Sprachlehre nebst Wörterverzeichnissen aus den genannten Sprachen* (1858)] (St. Petersburg: 1853-1862).

SOURCES: *Pamîati M.A. Kastrena* (Leningrad: 1927); B. Estlander, *Matthias Alexander Castrén: hans resor och forskningar* (Helsingfors: 1928); Pentti Aalto, *Oriental Studies in Finland, 1828-1918* (Helsinki: 1971); Mikko Korhonen, *Finno-Ugrian Language Studies in Finland, 1828-1918* (Helsinki: 1986).

Juha Janhunen

Catherwood, Frederick. Lithographer. Born in London (England) 27 February 1799, died in a shipwreck off the coast of Newfoundland September 1854. Catherwood produced the first generally accurate lithographs of numerous ruins in the Middle East and Meso-America. His lithographs of Maya ruins, produced to illustrate the books of JOHN LLOYD STEPHENS, were particularly important.

Catherwood underwent a rigorous apprenticeship in architectural drawing in London. Among his tutors was J.M.W. Turner; among his models were the drawings of Piranesi. Induced by his friend John Severn to visit Rome, in 1821 Catherwood began to experience at first hand the archaeological vistas that had earlier been so enticing in the work of Piranesi. From Rome, Catherwood moved on to Greece and Egypt. In 1824 Catherwood and two associates systematically mapped ruins in the Upper Nile area, and in 1828 he accepted Robert L. Hay's invitation to join the first major scholarly investigation of the region since the Napoleonic campaign. Catherwood drew the first accurate copies of some of the Egyptian monuments.

Catherwood met Stephens in London in 1835, where the two began planning an expedition to the Maya ruins of Mexico, Guatemala and Honduras, which were still little known. Their first expedition took place during 1839-1840. Stephens' resulting book, *Incidents of Travel in Central America, Chiapas and Yucatán*, was illustrated by Catherwood. His drawings represented a major advance in the objective recording of the ruins.

A second expedition resulted in *Incidents of Travel in Yucatán*. In this book, numerous sites, including some rarely visited even in the 20th century, were presented, and illustration and description of the ruins occupied an even greater proportion of the publication. *Views of the Ancient Monuments of Central America, Chiapas and Yucatán*, published in 1844 by Catherwood alone, was a suite of color lithographs that summarized the observations made during the two trips with Stephens.

Working at first with the *camera lucida*, then with the newly invented daguerreotype, Catherwood used technology as a tool to support an artistic vision that had its roots in classical drawing and was comparable in some respects to that of the 19th-century naturalists such as John James Audubon. His drawings, while not completely accurate, were generally much more so than any that had come before and vividly supported Stephens' contention that the Maya monuments were indigenous and not offshoots of Mediterranean culture.

MAJOR WORKS: (illustrator) *Incidents of Travel in Central America, Chiapas and Yucatán* [2 vols.] (New York: 1841); (illustrator) *Incidents of Travel in Yucatán* [2 vols.] (New York: 1843); *Ancient Monuments of Central America, Chiapas and Yucatán* (New York: 1844).

SOURCES: Merideth Paxton, "Frederick Catherwood and the Maya: reorientation of nineteenth-century perceptions" in: Peter Briggs (editor), *The Maya Image in the Western World: a Catalog to an Exhibition at the University of New Mexico* (Albuquerque: 1986); Victor W. von Hagen, *Frederick Catherwood, Archt.* (New York: 1950); Victor W. von Hagen, *Search for the Maya: the Story of Stephens and Catherwood* (Westmead: 1973).

Merideth Paxton

Catlin, George. Artist, attorney, amateur ethnologist. Born in Wilkes-Barre (Pennsylvania) 27 July 1796, died in Jersey City (New Jersey) 23 December 1872. The son of a farmer and former attorney, Catlin studied law in Connecticut and practiced in Pennsylvania before abandoning that career to become a painter of miniature portraits in Philadelphia. He was largely self-taught as an artist and by 1821 had seen his work exhibited in the Pennsylvania Academy of Art; three years later he was elected a fellow of that organization. Shortly after, Catlin encountered a group of western Indians in Philadelphia on their return from a visit to Washington, D.C., and he decided to travel west himself to paint unsubjugated Indians while there was still time.

Catlin set out to transform his painting style, abandoning miniatures for large canvases and learning to paint in rapid strokes. He became a protégé of New York's governor DeWitt Clinton and made a new reputation for himself as a painter of large portraits and sweeping scenes. In 1830, Catlin journeyed to St. Louis and made himself known to General William Clark, the Superintendent of Indian Affairs. Accompanying Clark on his travels, Catlin painted members of many different tribes.

The next year Catlin accompanied an Indian agent going further west and painted Oto, Pawnee, Missouri and Omaha peoples. In 1832 he was able to land a place on the maiden voyage of trader Louis Choteau's paddlewheel steamer, the Yellowstone, on its trip upstream on the Missouri. He painted many Indians, including members of the Ponca, Sioux (Dakota), Blackfoot, Crow, Assiniboin, Plains Cree, Mandan, Hidatsa and Plains Ojibwa tribes. Catlin traveled alone with Blackfoot warriors, and spent the winter of 1832-1833 in a Mandan village. Obsessed by his worry that the Indians would be subjugated or exterminated, he worked at a feverish pace to record their lifeways in words and pictures.

Upon his return to the east, Catlin raised money by exhibiting more than 100 of his paintings in Pittsburgh. In 1834 he was back in the west, accompanying the First Dragoon Regiment in an overland trip to meet the Comanche. Catlin painted many

Comanches and en route also documented on canvas the deplorable conditions of reservation life for the transplanted Creek, Choctaw, and Cherokee peoples.

From 1836 to 1846, Catlin simultaneously exhibited his paintings and collections of Indian artifacts and attempted to sell them to the American government. These efforts were foiled by Congress, perhaps because of Catlin's outspoken criticisms of Indian Affairs policy.

In 1836 Catlin had his last adventure in the United States, locating the quarry from which the red pipestone used by Plains Indians was mined and convincing the Sioux to let him visit it. He was the first non-Indian to see it, and in honor of his achievement the pipestone was later named catlinite.

Bankrupt and hopeless in 1846, after ten years of showing his works in America and Europe, Catlin gave up his children to his late wife's brother. He supported himself by painting, was befriended by ALEXANDER VON HUMBOLDT, and in 1853 set out again to explore and paint. This time he went to South America, to paint the native peoples of Venezuela, Peru and the Guianas. He later sailed from California to Siberia, stopping along the way to paint Chinook, Nootka, Haida, Aleut and many other Indian tribes.

Catlin lived on until 1872, in worsening health but able to support himself writing books on his experiences. Well after his death his works ended up where he had always claimed that they belonged; hundreds of Catlin paintings now hang in the Smithsonian Institution, the Newberry Library, the American Museum of Natural History and many other important collections. In many cases, they represent the only picture available of individuals, rituals, and personal decorations from a vanished era.

MAJOR WORKS: Aside from his hundreds of paintings, Catlin produced a number of books. Many were forgettable, but a few stand out: *Letters and Notes on the Manners, Customs, and Condition of the North American Indians* [2 vols.] (London: 1841); *North American Indian Portfolio* (London: 1844); *Life Amongst the Indians* (London: 1861); *O-kee-pa: a Religious Ritual* (London: 1867).

SOURCES: Robert Plate, *Palette and Tomahawk* (New York: 1962); Harold McCracken, *George Catlin and the Old Frontier* (New York: 1959).

David Lonergan

Chapman, Charlotte Gower (née Charlotte Day Gower). Anthropologist. Born in Kankakee (Illinois) 5 May 1902, died in Washington (D.C.) 1982. Chapman is best known as the author of the earliest study of a pre-literate European peasant society, her work on the Sicilian village of Milocca being second in age on a world scale to ROBERT REDFIELD'S study of Tepoztlán (1930). However, Chapman's book, now regarded as a minor classic, was not published until 1971 because the original manuscript was lost; only in 1966 was a brittle, yellowed carbon discovered in the files of the University of Chicago.

Chapman took her B.A. in psychology at Smith College in 1922, intending a medical career. After a year as Assistant in Psychology at Smith and another year as Instructor in Education at the University of Texas, she moved in 1924 to the Department of Sociology and Anthropology at the University of Chicago where (under her maiden name of Charlotte Day Gower) she completed her M.A. (1926) and Ph.D. (1928) dissertations. In her M.A. thesis, *Origin and Spread of Antillean Culture*, she developed some of her earlier interests in archaeology and physical anthropology. But she also had a facility for languages and dialects, and she used this to help her in her fieldwork in Chicago's "Little Sicily" where she collected information for her doctoral thesis, *The Supernatural Patron in Sicilian Life*. Her post-doctoral work in Sicily was a natural extension from this, aided by a Social Science Research Council Fellowship that enabled her to spend eighteen months in Milocca (now called Milena) during 1928-1929.

She returned to a post in the anthropology department at the University of Wisconsin, Madison, but after 1938 her career shifted overseas, first to the University of Lingnan in China where she taught sociology for four years and then into the U.S. Marine Corps, Women's Section, where she was a training officer working mainly in the Far East. Between 1948 and 1965 she was an analyst for the U.S. Central Intelligence Agency.

After its belated publication in 1971, *Milocca* (virtually the only published output of Chapman) was received enthusiastically as a beautifully written and exquisitely detailed account of Sicilian peasant life and social systems during the Italian Fascist era. Although Chapman was not free from the compromise of relying on the help of Fascist officials during her fieldwork, and although the book is notably silent on certain issues such as emigration and the Mafia, it stands as a unique account of rural life at a critical juncture in Sicily's modern history.

MAJOR WORK: *Milocca: a Sicilian Village* (New York: 1971).

Russell King and Guy Patterson

Chapple, Eliot Dismore. Anthropologist, biologist, consultant. Born in Salem (Massachusetts) 29 April 1909, now living in Sarasota (Florida). Chapple has made a major contribution to the study of human interaction in organizational settings.

Chapple's formal education occurred largely at Harvard University. With a long interest in natural history and museums, he concentrated in anthropology, beginning fieldwork in his senior year (1930) in Newburyport (Massachusetts) ("Yankee City"). He became Research Assistant in Industrial Research at the Business School and field director of the Newburyport study (1931-1935). His Ph.D. dissertation (1933), *The Theory of Associations*, was based on this fieldwork. In 1935 he became Instructor at the Business School and Tutor in the Department of Anthropology (where he stayed until 1939). He was also a Research Associate at the Medical School (1940-1945). Chapple also held several later positions in academia, for example at Columbia University (1959-1960) and Cornell University (1966-1969). However, because his methods and interests crossed disciplinary lines, Chapple encountered both funding difficulties and a lack of widespread acceptance of his work by those engaged in traditional anthropological research. Most of his employment has been outside academic anthropology, often in consulting positions. Chapple was one of the first in the field of anthropology to earn a living working for large corporations.

Much of Chapple's work has been devoted to analyzing the behavior of people in work situations. Many of his explanations of behavior are biologically grounded. Since 1940 the predominant thrust of his research has been to identify the numerous basic personality and temperament characteristics elicited by introducing programmed patterns of interactional asynchrony (stress) in small amounts and determining the degree of vulnerability a person evidenced. This work has had substantial practical application. Chapple has also done research and published in numerous other fields.

In 1941 Chapple played a major role in founding the Society for Applied Anthropology and was the editor of *Applied Anthropology* (now titled *Human Organization*) (1941-1945 and 1950-1954).

MAJOR WORKS: (with Conrad M. Arensberg) "Measuring human relations: an introduction to the study of the interaction of individuals," *Genetic Psychology Monographs*, vol. 22 (1940), pp. 3-147; (with Carleton S. Coon) *Principles of Anthropology* (New York: 1942; 2nd revised ed., Huntington, N.Y.: 1978); "The interaction chronograph: its evolution and present application," *Personnel*, vol. 25 (1949), pp. 295-307; (with Leonard R. Sayles) *The Measure of Management: Designing Organizations for Human Effectiveness* (New York: 1961; Ann Arbor: 1989); *Culture and Biological Man: Explorations in Behavioral Anthropology* (New York: 1970; 2nd revised ed., retitled *Biological Foundations of Individuality and Culture*, Huntington, N.Y.: 1980); *Rehabilitation: Dynamic of Change: an Anthropological View* (Ithaca: 1970; 2nd ed., Huntington, N.Y.: 1979); "Towards a mathematical model of interaction: some preliminary considerations" in: Paul Kay (editor), *Explorations in Mathematical Anthropology* (Cambridge, Mass.: 1971), pp. 141-178; *Adolescent Sociopaths* (Arlington, Va.: 1977); "The unbounded reaches of anthropology as a research science, and some working hypotheses," *American Anthropologist*, vol. 82 (1980), pp. 741-758; (with Martha Davis) "Expressive movement and performance: towards a unifying theory of music and dance, and their tributary forms," *Drama Review*, vol. 32, no. 4 (1988), pp. 53-79.

Elizabeth K. Briody and CW

Charnay, Desiré. Photographer. Born in Fleure-sur-l'Arbresle, Rhône (France) 2 May 1828, died in Paris (France) 24 October 1915. Following an education at the Lyceé Charlemagne in Paris and subsequent travels to England and Germany, Charnay accepted a teaching position in New Orleans, Louisiana, in 1850.

In 1857, inspired by the travel accounts and line drawings of JOHN LLOYD STEPHENS and FREDERICK CATHERWOOD, Charnay led his first expedition to Mexico with the intention of visiting and photographing major sites. Due to numerous delays occasioned by a civil war, this initial effort lasted three years and was not completed until 1860. This was the first of three such explorations, with later visits during 1880-1882 and 1886.

Photographic plates of the main architectural complexes at Mitla, Palenque, Izamal, Chichen Itzá and Uxmal were published in *Cités et ruines américaines* in 1863. These plates were among the first substantial applications of photography to archaeological fieldwork and occasioned great excitement when they appeared.

Between 1863 and 1879 Charnay also contributed to the documentation of physical anthropology through further photographic documentation (chiefly of racial and physical types) in Madagascar, Java and Australia. However, his central interest remained with the ancient civilizations of Mexico. The two later expeditions included excavations at Teotihuacán, Kabah, Tula, Comalcalco and Palenque.

The 1880-1882 expedition is noteworthy for Charnay's ascension of Popocatépetl and Ixtaccihuatl and his discovery of wheeled toy dogs in a cemetery on Ixtaccihuatl, a claim flatly disbelieved during Charnay's lifetime. His later books of travel and photographic plates, including the limited-edition *Atlas fotográfico mexicano*, served to popularize the idea of ancient Mesoamerican civilization as a distinctive entity as well as to present documentary material on Charnay's own theories of its origin. Charnay's further contributions to Mexican archaeology include the discovery of the site of Tula and of the first of the famous "Atlantean" columnar figures as well as the first attempt to dredge the Sacred Cenote at Chichen Itzá. The final expedition of 1886 took him to the sites of Izamal (where a comparative set of images was made of the pyramid), Techoch, Ekbalam and the island of Jaina.

While Charnay's images were little regarded by serious scholars in his own era, their importance as records of a transitional period in the archaeology of central Mexico, Guatemala and the Yucatán Peninsula is becoming increasingly apparent.

MAJOR WORKS: *Atlas fotográfico mexicano* (Mexico City: 1860); *Cités et ruines américaines: Mitla, Palenque, Izamal, Chichen-Itzá, Uxmal* (Paris: 1863); *Le Mexique* (Paris: 1863); "Mémoires, notices de la civilisation nahua," *Bulletin de la Société de Géographie*, 7th ser., vol. 1 (1881), pp. 269-386; *La civilisation tolteque* (Paris: 1885); *Les anciennes villes du nouveau monde: voyages d'exploration au Mexique et dans l'Amérique centrale, 1857-1882* (Paris: 1885) [tr.: *The Ancient Cities of the New World: Being Voyages and Explorations in Mexico and Central America from 1857-1882* (London: 1885)].

SOURCES: Keith F. Davis, *Désiré Charnay, Expeditionary Photographer* (Albuquerque: 1981); "Désiré Charnay" in: *Appletons' Cyclopedia of American Biography* (New York: 1897-1901), vol. 7, p. 57.

Robert B. Marks Ridinger

Cheboksarov, N.N. (Nikolaĭ Nikolaevich). Ethnographer, physical anthropologist. Born in Simbirsk (Russia) 6 May 1907, died in Moscow (Russian S.F.S.R.) 1 February 1980. Cheboksarov's range of scientific interests was unusually broad. He worked on the ethnography of the peoples of the Northern Europe and Central Asia, of the Baltic and Western Europe, of East, Southeast and South Asia; the problems of Finno-Ugric; and the question of race. In ethnic anthropology, Cheboksarov was most noted for his elaboration of a scheme of classification of the human races. In the area of ethnography, Cheboksarov studied the problems of the economic-cultural classifications of peoples, theories of ethnicity, types of ethnic communities and national development. Cheboksarov was a great scholar of economics and of the material cultures of the peoples of the world. Together with M.G. LEVIN, S.P. TOLSTOV and S.A. TOKAREV, Cheboksarov developed the study of economic-cultural types and the field of ethnohistory.

He was a doctor of historical sciences and a professor. At various times, he held the chair of ethnography at Moscow University and worked in the sections on Europe and the foreign parts of Asia, Australia and Oceania of the Institut ėtnografii (Institute of Ethnography) of the Soviet Academy of Sciences.

MAJOR WORKS: (with M.G. Levin) "Khozíaĭstvenno-kul'turnye tipy i istoriko-ėtnograficheskie oblasti (k postanovke voprosa)," *Sovetskaía ėtnografiía*, no. 4 (1955), pp. 3-17; (with M.V. Vitov and K.ÍŪ. Mark) *Ėtnicheskaía antropologiía Vostochnoĭ Pribaltiki* (Moscow: 1959); (with Lin' ÍAokhua) "Khozíaĭstvenno-kul'turnye tipy Kitaía," *Trudy Instituta ėtnografii AN SSSR*, vol. 73 (1971), pp. 5-46; (with I.A. Cheboksarova) *Narody, rasy, kul'tury* (Moscow: 1971; 2nd ed., Moscow: 1985); (with S.A. Arutíunov) "Protoindiĭskaía fsivilizafsiía i sovremennye dravidy" in: *Soobshcheniía ob issledovanii protoindiĭskikh tekstov. I. Protoindica* (Moscow: 1972), pp. 153-164; (with M.V. Kríukov and M.V. Sofronov) *Drevnye kitaĭfsy: problemy ėtnogeneza* (Moscow: 1978); (with A.M. Reshetov), "Antropologiía i ėtnografiía o proiskhozhdenii kitaĭfsev," *Rasy i narody*, vol. 3 (1973), pp. 89-114; "Raboty po ėtnicheskoĭ antropologii Indii v 1964 i 1966 gg." in: M.G. Abdushelishvili and K.Ch. Malkhotra (editors), *Novye dannye k antropologii Severnoĭ Indii* (Moscow: 1980), pp. 183-217; (with I.A. Cheboksarova), "Formirovanie antropologicheskogo sostava naseleniía Kitaía" in: M.V. Kríukov (editor), *Ėtnicheskaía istoriía narodov Vostochnoĭ i ÍUgovostochnoĭ Azii v drevnosti i v srednie veka* (Moscow: 1981), pp. 162-201; *Ėtnicheskaía antropologiía Kitaía: rasovaía morfologiía sovremennogo naseleniía* (Moscow: 1982); (with M.V. Sofronov) *Drevnie kitaĭtsy v ėpokhu ṫsentralizovannykh imperiĭ* (Moscow: 1983).

SOURCES: V.L. Alekseev and G.G. Stratanovich, "N.N. Cheboksarov," *Sovetskaía ėtnografiía*, no. 3 (1967), pp. 125-126; G.G. Stratanovich, "Predislovie" to: G.F. Stratonovich (editor), *Problemy ėtnografii i ėtnicheskoĭ istorii narodov Vostochnoĭ i ĬUgovostochnoĭ Azii* (Moscow: 1968), pp. 5-10; "Spisok osnovnykh rabot N.N. Cheboksarova," *Sovetskaía ėtnografiía*, no. 6 (1977), pp. 139-142 [bibliography]; B.V. Andrianov, A.A. Zubov, and M.V. Krī͡ukov, "N.N. Cheboksarov (1907-1980)," *Sovetskaía ėtnografiía*, no. 4 (1980), pp. 185-188; I.A. Cheboksarova, "Zhizn' i deía͡tel'nost' N.N. Cheboksarova" in: M.V. Krī͡ukov and A.I. Kuznet͡sov (editors), *Istoricheskaía dinamika rasovoĭ i ėtnicheskoĭ diferent͡siat͡sii naseleniía Azii* (Moscow: 1987), pp. 4-13.

A.M. Reshetov
[Translation from Russian: Thomas L. Mann]

Chernet͡sov, V.N. (Valeriĭ Nikolaevich).

Anthropologist, archaeologist, linguist. Born in Moscow (Russia) 17 March 1905, died in Moscow (Russian S.F.S.R.) 29 March 1970. Chernet͡sov was a pioneer in the investigation of North-West Siberia in the Soviet period. In the 1930s he was adopted into the *por* moiety of the Vogul (Mansi) people; his fieldwork among these people enabled him to publish fundamental works on their social organization, religion and folklore. From 1940 on he worked as an archaeologist and became the author of the most accepted theory of his time on the early ethnohistory of Finno-Ugric peoples.

MAJOR WORKS: *Vogul'skie skazki* (Leningrad: 1935); "Fratrial'noe ustroĭstvo obsko-ī͡ugorskogo obshchestva," *Sovetskaía ėtnografiía*, vol. 2 (1939), pp. 20-43; "Bärenfest bei den Obugriern," *Acta Ethnographica* [Budapest], vol. 23 (1974), pp. 285-319; *Naskal'nye izobrazheniía Urala* [2 vols.] (Moscow: 1964-1971).

SOURCES: A.P. Smirnov, "V.N. Chernetsov," *Sovietskaía arkheologiía*, no. 1 (1971), pp. 309-310; Veres Péter, "V.N. Csernyecov," *Ethnographia*, vol. 83 (1972), pp. 99-103 [with bibliography]; A.K. Omel'chuk, *Ryt͡sary Severa* (Sverdlovsk: 1982).

Éva Schmidt

Chętnik, Adam.

Ethnographer, musicologist. Born in Nowogród k/Łomża (Poland) 20 December 1880, died in Warsaw (Poland) 29 May 1967. Chętnik participated in political activity in the Mazury (1914-1919) and Kurpie (1922-1927) regions. He studied at the University of Warsaw and attended underground courses during World War II. He obtained his doctorate in 1946. In that same year he was designated Associate Professor at the University of Poznań.

Chętnik was a regionalist, an outstanding specialist on the culture of Kurpie. From private sources he built the Muzeum Kurpiowsko-Nadnarwiańskie (Kurpian-Nadnarwian Museum) (1919-1927) and served as director of its operations. In the years 1933-1939 and 1945-1950 he served as director of the Station of Scientific Research of Middle Narwia in Nowogród, which provided assistance to Polish and foreign researchers. After World War II he continued to be interested in museology and Kurpian culture. He reorganized the Muzeum Okręgowe (District Museum) in Łomża among others. He created the section of Northern Mazovian and Kurpian Culture at the Muzeum Kultur Ludowych (Museum of Folk Cultures) in Młociny near Warsaw, and between 1951 and 1958 he was the curator of the Division of National Amberwork in the Muzeum Ziemi (Museum of the Earth) in Warsaw.

MAJOR WORKS: *Puszcza Kurpiowska* [*The Kurpian Forest*] (Warsaw: 1913); *Chata kurpi-owska* [*The Kurpian Hut*] (Warsaw: 1915); *O Kurpiach* [*On the Kurpians*] (Warsaw: 1919); *Kurpie* [*Kurpians*] (Kraków: 1924); *Z kurpiowskich borów w narzeczu kurpiowskim* [*With Kurpians in the Kurpian Dialect*] (Lwów: 1931); *Spław na Narwi: tratwy, oryle i orylka: studium etnograficzne* [*Floating on the Narew: Rafts: Ethnographic Studies*] (Warsaw: 1935); *Pożywienie Kurpiów* [*The Diet of the Kurpians*] (Kraków: 1936); *Przemysł i sztuka bursztyniarska nad Narwią* [*Production and Amber Artwork on the Narew*] (Kraków and Poznań: 1952); *Strój kurpiowski Puszczy Zielonej* [*Kurpian Costumes of Puszcza Zielona*] (Wrocław: 1961); *Życie puszczańskie Kurpiów* [*Life in the Kurpian Wilderness*] (Warsaw: 1971); *Z Puszczy Zielonej* [*From Puszcza Zielona*] (Warsaw: 1978).

SOURCES: Anna Kutrzeba-Pojnarowa, *Kultura ludowa i jej badacze* [*Folk Culture and its Researchers*] (Warsaw: 1977); Hanna Muszyńska-Hoffmanowa, *Saga rodu Chętników* [*Saga of the Chętnik Clan*] (Olsztyn: 1982); Henryk Syska, *Adam Chętnik* (Warsaw: 1969).

Maria Niewiadomska and Iwona Grzelakowska
[*Translation from Polish: Joel Janicki*]

Chicherov, V.I. (Vladimir Ivanovich). Folklorist, ethnographer, literary scholar. Born in Vladimirskaĭa oblast' (Russia) 29 May (11 June) 1907, died in Moscow (Russian S.F.S.R.) 11 May 1957. Chicherov was a doctor of historical sciences and a professor. He gave a course on folklore at the Department of Ethnography at Moscow University, and he directed the section of Slavic-Russian ethnography and folklore in the Institut ėtnografii (Institute of Ethnography) of the Soviet Academy of Sciences (1949-1953). He also created and headed the section of the section on folk literature of the Institut mirovoĭ literatury (Institute of World Literature) of the Soviet Academy of Sciences (1953-1957).

A prominent specialist on epics, V.I. Chicherov examined the process of the national epic's development and attempted to clarify the distinctive features of its contents and form in various historical periods. He made an important contribution to the study of the Russian national annual cycle, in which he saw not only a reflection of ancient religious rituals but also a synthesizing of the centuries-old practical experience of the folk-farmer, that is, the combining of the annual rituals with agriculture.

MAJOR WORKS: "Tvorchestvo narodov SSSR," *Sovetskaĭa ėtnografiĭa*, no. 1 (1938), pp. 210-222; "Tradiĭsiĭa i avtorskoe nachalo v fol'klore," *Sovetskaĭa ėtnografiĭa*, no. 2 (1946), pp. 29-40; (editor and compiler) *Onezhskie byliny* (Moscow: 1948); "Russkie koliadki i ikh tipy," *Sovetskaĭa ėtnografiĭa*, no. 2 (1948), pp. 105-129; "Materialy k istorii sovetskogo fol'klora," *Sovetskaĭa ėtnografiĭa*, no. 4 (1949), pp. 20-41; *Russkoe narodno-poėticheskoe tvorchestvo v Tatarskoĭ ASSR* (Kazan': 1955); (compiler and editor) *Istoricheskie pesni* (Leningrad: 1956); *Zimniĭ period russkogo zemledel'cheskogo kalendarĭa XVI-XIX vv.: ocherki po istorii narodnykh verovaniĭ* (Moscow: 1957) (= *Trudy Instituta ėtnografii AN SSSR*, vol. 40); *Voprosy teorii i istorii narodnogo tvorchestva* (Moscow: 1959).

SOURCES: V. Sokolova, "V.I. Chicherov (nekrolog)," *Sovetskaĭa ėtnografiĭa*, no. 3 (1957), pp. 187-188; "Spisok rabot B.I. Chicherova," *Sovetskaĭa ėtnografiĭa*, no. 3 (1957), pp. 188-189 [bibliography]; *Kratkaĭa literaturnaĭa ėnĭsiklopediĭa*, vol. 8 (Moscow: 1975), pp. 533-534.

A.M. Reshetov
[*Translation from Russian: Thomas L. Mann*]

Chil y Naranjo, Gregorio. Anthropologist, historian, physician. Born in Telde, Grand Canary, Canary Islands (Spain) 13 March 1831, died in Las Palmas, Grand Canary, Canary Islands (Spain) 4 July 1901. Chil y Naranjo received his doctorate in medicine from the Faculty of Medicine of the University of Paris, but his intellectual interest soon turned toward history and anthropology. In these two disciplines, he carried out numerous investigations that permitted him to develop the most complete 19th-century synthesis of the history and anthropology of the Canary Islands.

As a student of PAUL BROCA, Chil y Naranjo was well acquainted with the new trends in contemporary French physical anthropology and applied its methodology and techniques to the study of the original inhabitants of the Canary Islands, generically known as the "Guanches." In this area, he paid special attention to the study of craniology and racial typology and developed the first systematic work on the paleopathology of the early inhabitants of the islands. In particular, he investigated the relationship between the Canary aborigines and Cro-Magnon man, a topic that had interested Broca, THÉODORE HAMY, ARMAND DE QUATREFAGES and, later, René Verneau (1852-1938). Chil y Naranjo's principal work, *Estudios históricos, climatológicos y patológicos de las Islas Canarias*, is a literature review and historical interpretation combined with anthropology and medical geography in a monumental attempt to synthesize the history of the Canary Islands.

Chil y Naranjo, a decided advocate of the new movements in science against the obscurantism of the Church, developed a powerful defense of the scientific method using the evolutionary theories of Charles Darwin and Ernst Haeckel, the geology of Charles Lyell and the anthropology of Broca, especially as those theories applied to the fields of anthropology and prehistory. But, after the publication of the *Estudios*, Chil y Naranjo was accused of atheism and materialism and excommunicated from the Catholic Church in spite of support from many Canarian and French intellectuals.

Chil y Naranjo was also interested in the conservation and organization of aboriginal human and cultural remains. He founded the Museo Canario (Museum of the Canaries), the most important center of Canarian research of its age, and was its director and principal driving force.

MAJOR WORKS: *Estudios históricos, climatológicos y patológicos de las Islas Canarias* [3 vols.] (Las Palmas: 1876-1891); "Mémoire sur l'origine des guanches ou habitants primitifs des Îles Canaries" in: *Congrès International des Sciences Anthropologiques, Paris, 1878* (Paris: 1880), pp. 167-220; "Antropología," *El Museo Canario*, vol. 1 (1880); "Anatomía patológica de los aborígenes canários," *El Museo Canario*, vol. 8 (1900).

SOURCES: Baltasar Champsaur, *Transformismo* (Las Palmas: 1928); Juan Bosch Millares, *Don Gregorio Chil y Naranjo: su vida y su obra* (Las Palmas: 1971); Thomas F. Glick "Spain" in: Thomas F. Glick (editor), *Comparative Reception of Darwinism* (Austin: 1972), pp. 307-345; Fernando Estévez, *Indigenismo, raza y evolución: el pensamiento antropológico canario, 1750-1900* (Tenerife: 1987).

Fernando Estévez
[Translation from Spanish: Robert B. Marks Ridinger]

Childe, V. Gordon (Vere Gordon). Archaeologist, prehistorian. Born in North Sydney (New South Wales) 14 April 1892, died at Govett's Leap (New South

Wales) 19 October 1957. Childe is widely recognized as the leading archaeological theoretician of the first half of the 20th century.

Childe studied classics at Sydney University and classical archaeology at Oxford. In 1916 he returned from Oxford to Australia to oppose conscription and became involved in Labour Party politics. Between 1919 and 1921 he was private secretary to John Storey, premier of New South Wales. After the fall of the Labour government, he wrote *How Labour Governs*, still widely regarded as the most authoritative source on the history of the Australian Labour movement prior to 1921. Then, lacking employment and disillusioned with Australian politics, he returned to the study of archaeology.

Childe's ability to read most European languages and his unrivaled knowledge of archaeological collections throughout Europe soon made him one of the continent's leading prehistorians. He was Abercromby Professor of Prehistory at the University of Edinburgh from 1927 to 1946 and Director of the Institute of Archaeology at the University of London from 1946 until he retired in 1956. In addition to his theoretical writings and his major works of synthesis, Childe carried out a large number of archaeological excavations in Scotland, the most important at the Neolithic settlement of Skara Brae.

Childe played a leading role in the culture-historical and functionalist movements that successively transformed European archaeology. He pioneered the culture-historical approach in *The Dawn of European Civilization*, which for the first time synthesized the archaeological evidence for Neolithic and Bronze Age Europe in terms of the histories of specific peoples rather than simply as evidence of general cultural evolution. He combined the concept of the archaeological culture refined by Gustaf Kossinna (1858-1931) with the diffusionism of Oscar Montelius (1843-1921), who believed that technological skills had spread to Europe from their place of origin in southwestern Asia; however, like his Oxford mentors, Arthur Evans (1851-1941) and John L. Myers (1869-1954), Childe stressed the creativity with which Europeans had used this knowledge. This approach encouraged archaeologists to interpret geographical variations in the archaeological record that evolutionary archaeologists had generally ignored as ethnic differences. Childe's culture-historical approach dominated European archaeology until the radiocarbon revolution undermined Montelius' chronology in the 1960s.

For the rest of his life Childe sought to devise ways to interpret the archaeological record in behavioral terms. Beginning in the late 1920s he studied the impact of the development of agriculture and bronze-working on southwestern Asia and Europe. He excelled all contemporary archaeologists in the consistency with which he applied an economic approach to the study of prehistory and in the scope of his formulations. Instead of attributing cultural change to technological innovation, he sought to understand technological progress within the context of economic and political patterns. Although often misrepresented, especially in the United States, as a unilinear evolutionist, he saw cultural development as occurring in a multilinear fashion.

In 1935 Childe visited the Soviet Union and was impressed by the manner in which Soviet archaeologists were attempting to account for change in terms of contradictions between the forces and relations of production. This had led them to pay special attention to how ordinary people had lived in prehistoric times. While Childe disapproved of certain aspects of Soviet archaeology, hereafter he tried to understand the role that social, political and economic institutions had played in bringing about or preventing change. His two most widely read books, *Man Makes Himself* and *What Happened in History*, were primarily studies of how entrenched elites and inflexible belief systems can halt economic and social progress, but only at the cost of making it harder for such societies to compete with their more progressive neighbors.

After World War II, disillusionment with the quality of archaeological research in the Soviet Union led Childe to acquire a more profound understanding of Marxism as an analytical tool and to apply it to the interpretation of archaeological data. He became a significant Marxist thinker who rejected determinism as a basis for understanding human history and whose ideas had much in common with those later expressed by Western European Marxists, such as Jean-Paul Sartre. Most of his writings of the post-war period have only been appreciated by a substantial number of archaeologists since the 1970s. In his final works he stressed that social and political organization provided the framework within which archaeological data could most productively be understood.

Troubled by failing health and growing fear that incipient senility was preventing him from making progress in developing new procedures for inferring prehistoric social organization from archaeological data, Childe committed suicide in the course of a visit to Australia.

MAJOR WORKS: *How Labour Governs: a Study of Workers' Representation in Australia* (London: 1923); *The Dawn of European Civilization* (London: 1925); *The Most Ancient East* (London: 1928); *The Danube in Prehistory* (Oxford: 1929); *The Bronze Age* (Cambridge: 1930); *Skara Brae: a Pictish Village in Orkney* (London: 1931); *New Light on the Most Ancient East* (London: 1934); *Man Makes Himself* (London: 1936); *What Happened in History* (Harmondsworth: 1942); *Scotland Before the Scots* (London: 1946); *History* (London: 1947); *Social Evolution* (New York: 1951); *Piecing Together the Past: the Interpretation of Archaeological Data* (London: 1956); *Society and Knowledge: the Growth of Human Traditions* (New York: 1956); *The Prehistory of European Society* (Harmondsworth: 1958).

SOURCES: Sally Green, *Prehistorian: a Biography of V. Gordon Childe* (Bradford-on-Avon: 1981); Barbara McNairn, *Method and Theory of V. Gordon Childe* (Edinburgh: 1980); Bruce G. Trigger, *Gordon Childe: Revolutions in Archaeology* (London: 1980); Jim Allen, "Aspects of Vere Gordon Childe," *Labour History*, no. 12 (1967), pp. 52-59; V. Gordon Childe, "Retrospect," *Antiquity*, vol. 32 (1958), pp. 69-74; V. Gordon Childe, "Valediction," *Bulletin of the Institute of Archaeology, University of London*, vol. 1 (1958), pp. 1-8; Glyn Daniel, "Editorial," *Antiquity*, vol. 54 (1980), pp. 1-3; Peter Gathercole, "Patterns in prehistory: an examination of the later thinking of V. Gordon Childe," *World Archaeology*, vol. 3 (1971), pp. 225-232; Stuart Piggott, "Vere Gordon Childe, 1892-1957," *Proceedings of the British Academy*, vol. 44 (1958), pp. 305-312; A. Ravetz, "Notes on the work of V. Gordon Childe," *The New Reasoner*, vol. 10 (1959), pp. 55-66; Bruce G. Trigger, *A History of Archaeological Thought* (Cambridge: 1989), pp. 167-174, 254-263.

Bruce G. Trigger

Chistov, K.V. (Kirill Vasil'evich). Folklorist, ethnographer. Born in Petrograd (Russian S.F.S.R.) 20 November 1919. Chistov worked in Petrozavodsk, then from 1961 in the Leningrad department of the Institut ètnografii (Institute of Ethnography) of the Soviet Academy of Sciences as head of the section of ethnography of East Slavic peoples (1961-1990). He became chief editor of the journal *Sovetskaīa ètnografiīa* in 1980 and an associate member of the Soviet Academy of Sciences in 1981.

Chistov's major scholarly interests are concentrated in the study of the ethnography and folklore of the Eastern Slavs, including the problems of the ethnography of the

Russian North and Slavic cultural links in history. He placed great importance on the study of the works of individual folk-story-tellers and the folk-story-teller "school." Chistov often and productively occupied himself with the study of contemporary ethnic processes, the problems of general ethnography and folklore studies, contemporary linguistics and theories of folklore, the history of science and museum management. He is the author of approximately 400 scholarly works.

MAJOR WORKS: *Narodnaîa poètessa I.A. Fedosova* (Moscow: 1955); *Russkie narodnye sofsial'no-utopicheskie legendy XVII-XIX vv.* (Leningrad: 1967); *Russkie skaziteli Karelii: ocherki i vospominaniîa* (Petrozavodsk: 1980); (with B.E. Chistova and I.A. Fedosova) *Izbrannoe* (Petrozavodsk: 1981); "Prichitaniîa u slaviânskikh i finno-ugorskikh narodov (nekotorye itogi i problemy)" in: V.K. Sokolova (editor), *Obriâdy i obriâdovyĭ fol'klor* (Moscow: 1982), pp. 101-114; "Variativnost' i poètika fol'klornogo teksta" in: L.A. Astafeva [et al.] (editors), *Istoriîa, kul'tura, ètnografiîa i fol'klor slaviânskikh narodov* (Moscow: 1983), pp. 143-169; "Iz istorii sovetskoĭ ètnografii 30-80-kh godov XX veka: k 50-letiîu Instituta ètnografii AN SSSR," *Sovetskaîa ètnografiîa*, no. 3 (1983), pp. 3-18; (with B.E. Chistova) *Russkaîa narodnaîa poèziîa: obriâdovaîa poèziîa* (Leningrad: 1984); *Narodnye tradifsii i fol'klor: ocherki teorii* (Leningrad: 1986); *I.A. Fedosova: istoriko-kul'turnyĭ ocherk* (Petrozavodsk: 1988); (general editor) *Ètnografiîa vostochnykh slavian: ocherki tradifsionnoĭ kul'tury* (Moscow: 1987); "Nafsional'nye problemy v Leningrade i Leningradskoĭ oblasti," *Sovetskaîa ètnografiîa*, no. 3 (1989), pp. 3-12.

SOURCES: "Spisok osnovnykh rabot K.V. Chistova," *Sovetskaîa ètnografiîa*, no. 1 (1980), pp. 186-189; and no. 6 (1989), pp. 126-128.

A.M. Reshetov
[Translation from Russian: Thomas L. Mann]

Chitaîa, G.S. (Georgiĭ Spiridonovich). Ethnographer. Born in Poti (Georgia, Russia) 10 November 1890, died in Tbilisi (Georgian S.S.R.) 21 August 1986. Chitaîa was the founder of Soviet Georgian ethnography. He was an academician of the Academy of Sciences of the Georgian S.S.R. He worked in the Museĭ Gruzii (Georgian Museum) (he directed the department of ethnography), at Tbilisi University (he created a chairmanship and directed it until 1973), in the Institut istorii, arkheologii i ètnografii im. I.A. Dzhavakhishvili (Dzhavakhishvili Institute of History, Archaeology and Ethnography) of the Academy of Sciences of the Georgian S.S.R. (he headed the section for the ethnography of Georgia and the Caucasus), and he established the Museĭ narodnogo byta pod otkrytym nebom (Open-Air Museum of Folk Life) in Tbilisi.

Chitaîa fruitfully studied such pivotal subjects as the traditional forms of material and non-material culture, rural culture, social relationships and ideology. He was important for the study of ethnographic parallels in the pattern of Georgian-Caucasian cultural-historical interrelationships. He used ethnographic methods to explore actively the culture and customs of peasants and workers. Among his scholarly interests was the question of method in ethnographic fieldwork and museum management.

MAJOR WORKS: "Rachinskoe pakhotnoe orudie" [in Georgian], *Izvestiîa Instituta îazyka, istorii i material'noĭ kul'tury*, vol. 1 (Tbilisi: 1937), pp. 247-294; (with V.V. Bardavelidze), *Gruzinskiĭ narodnyĭ ornament: Khevsurskiĭ ornament* [in Georgian] (Tbilisi: 1939); "O zadachakh kavkazskoĭ sovetskoĭ ètnografii," *Trudy Instituta istorii AN GruzSSR*, vol. 1 (1955), pp. 375-385; "Prinfsipy i metod polevoĭ ètnograficheskoĭ raboty," *Sovetskaîa ètnografiîa*, no. 4 (1957), pp. 24-30; "Gruzinskiĭ ètnograficheskiĭ atlas (fsel', prinfsipy, metody)" [in Georgian], *Vestnik Otdeleniîa obshchestvennykh nauk AN GruzSSR*, no. 1 (1960), pp. 207-216; "Narodnye èkonomicheskie predaniîa," *Trudy Instituta istorii AN GruzSSR*, vol. 1 (1955), pp. 387-394; *Pakhotnye orudiîa i sistemy zemledeliîa v*

Gruzii (Moscow: 1960); "Osnovnye prinčsipy ustroĭstva muzeĭa pod otkrytym nebom v g. Tbilisi" [in Georgian], *Dzeglis megobari*, no. 25 (1971), pp. 40-51.

SOURCES: "Spisok osnovnykh rabot G.S. Chitaĭa," *Sovetskaĭa ėtnografiĭa*, no. 2 (1982), pp. 108-110 [bibliography]; A.I. Robakidze, "G.S. Chitaĭa," *Sovetskaĭa ėtnografiĭa*, no. 2 (1987), pp. 171-173.

A.M. Reshetov
[Translation from Russian: Thomas L. Mann]

Chodakowski, Zorian Dołęga. See: Czarnocki, Adam.

Ciszewski, Stanisław.
Ethnologist, philologist, historian. Born in Krążek near Olkusz (Poland) 18 December 1865, died in Warsaw (Poland) 27 May 1930. Ciszewski studied in Prague, Zagreb, Berlin and Leipzig, where in 1897 he obtained his doctorate. As a student of ADOLF BASTIAN, FELIX VON LUSCHAN, FRIEDRICH RATZEL and others, Ciszewski received excellent preparation for work in ethnography, ethnology and related fields. In 1920 he was appointed to the first chair of ethnology in Poland at the University of Lwów; however, after a year of teaching, he resigned. During World War I he resided in Warsaw and devoted himself exclusively to scholarly work.

Ciszewski was interested above all in aspects of social life. He was an inductive worker. By focusing first on the details and by collecting as many facts as possible, he would arrive at a general law governing a given cultural phenomenon. He adhered to the precepts of evolutionism. His particular contribution lay in his helping to develop Polish historical ethnography.

MAJOR WORKS: *Krakowiacy [Krakovians]* (Kraków: 1894); *Wróżda i pojednanie [Hostility and Reconciliation]* (Warsaw: 1900); *Ognisko: studium etnologiczne [The Hearth: an Ethnological Study]* (Kraków: 1903); *Kuwada* (Kraków: 1905); *Sól [Salt]* (Warsaw: 1922); *Ród [The Clan]* (Warsaw: 1936).

SOURCES: Adam Fischer, "Stanisław Ciszewski," *Lud*, vol. 29 (1930), pp. 174-176; Małgorzata Terlecka (editor), *Historia etnografii polskiej [History of Polish Ethnography]* (Wrocław: 1973); Ludwik Zembrzuski, "Ciszewski, Stanisław Bronisław" in: *Polski słownik biograficzny [Polish Biographical Dictionary]*, vol. 4 (Warsaw: 1938), pp. 85-87.

Maria Niewiadomska and Iwona Grzelakowska
[Translation from Polish: Joel Janicki]

Cocchiara, Giuseppe.
Folklorist, ethnologist. Born in Messina (Italy) 5 March 1904, died in Palermo (Italy) 24 January 1965. After taking a degree in jurisprudence at the University of Palermo in 1927, Cocchiara resided in Great Britain from 1930 to 1932 and undertook ethnological and folkloristic studies under BRONISLAW MALINOWSKI in London and R.R. MARETT at Oxford. In 1934 he was called upon to collaborate with the Museo Etnografico Siciliano "G. Pitrè" (G. Pitrè Sicilian Ethnographic Museum) in Palermo. He became the museum's director by 1935. He was a docent of the history of popular traditions and ethnology at the University of Palermo, and in 1950 he founded the journal, *Annali del Museo Pitré*. In 1959 the University of Athens conferred upon him the degree of *honoris causa* in letters.

In the first phase of his activities Cocchiara was particularly influenced by the evolutionary theories of E.B. TYLOR and George Laurence Gomme (1853-1916): by interpreting folkloristic data as remnants and traces that allow a reconstruction of the past, he maintained that it was necessary to regard folklore studies, long considered a branch of philology and literature in Italy, as belonging to the domain of ethnology (*Il linguaggio del gesto, La leggenda di Re Lear, The Lore of the Folk Song*).

After World War II, under the influence of the works of Benedetto Croce, ERNESTO DE MARTINO and RAFFAELE PETTAZZONI, he adopted the historical concepts of the Italian ethnological tradition, which derived ultimately from the thought of G.B. Vico. Abandoning his evolutionary position, he refused to conceive of primitive thought as having existed at an historically determinable moment in time, interpreting it instead as an essential element of human experience that can be evaluated through its manifestations in the cultural activities of human beings throughout history (*Il mito del buon selvaggio, L'eterno selvaggio*). Cocchiara's best-known work is probably his *Storia del folklore in Europa*, in which he examined the different schools of folklore studies according to the philosophical concepts that produced them. He treated the history of social anthropology as a part of the general history of ideas. Cocchiara contributed to the diffusion of the concepts of British evolutionism in Italy, maintaining the tradition of Marett (*Introduzione allo studio dell'Uomo*), and JAMES G. FRAZER (*Introduzione all'antropologia sociale, Il ramo d'oro*). His last works (*Storia del folklore in Europa, L'eterno selvaggio*) have provoked considerable interest among Soviet Marxist anthropologists.

MAJOR WORKS: *Il linguaggio del gesto* (Turin: 1932); *La leggenda di Re Lear* (Turin: 1932); *The Lore of the Folk Song* (Oxford: 1932); *Genesi di leggende* (Palermo: 1940); *Il diavolo nella tradizione populare italiana* (Palermo: 1945); *Pitré, la Sicilia e il folklore* (Messina: 1951); *Storia del folklore in Europa* (Turin: 1952) [tr.: *History of Folklore in Europe* (Philadelphia: 1980)]; *Il paese di Cuccagna e altri studi di folklore* (Turin: 1956); *Popolo e letteratura in Italia* (Turin: 1959); *L'eterno selvaggio* (Milan: 1961); *Il mondo alla rovescia* (Turin: 1963); *Le origini della poesia popolare* (Turin: 1966); (editor) R.R. Marett, *Introduzione allo studio dell'Uomo* (Palermo: 1944); (editor and translator) J.G. Frazer, *Introduzione all'antropologia sociale* (Palermo: 1945); "Prefazione" to: J.G. Frazer, *Il ramo d'oro* [translation of *The Golden Bough*] (Turin: 1950), p. 11.

SOURCES: B. Bonomo and A. Buttitta, "L'opera di Giuseppe Cocchiara" in: G. Grana (editor), *Letteratura italiana: i critici* (Milan: 1969), pp. 2807-2824; A.M. Cirese, *Cultura egemonica e culture subalterne* (Palermo: 1979); P. Clemente [et al.], *L'antropologia italiana: un secolo di storia* (Bari: 1985).

Gianni Vannucci
[Translation from Italian: Chris Nissen]

Codrington, Robert Henry. Clergyman, schoolmaster, linguist, ethnologist. Born in Wroughton (England) 15 September 1830, died in Chichester (England) 10 or 11 September 1922. Educated at Wadham College, Oxford (B.A. 1852), Codrington was ordained as an Anglican priest in 1855 and elected a fellow of his college the same year. He was a curate at Oxford until 1860, when he was sent to a diocese in New Zealand. In 1867 he was assigned to the remote mission station on Norfolk Island, where he served as headmaster of St. Barnabas' School until 1887 (and again in 1892-1893). This school, which educated the children of influential families from many parts of Melanesia, allowed Codrington to learn dozens of Melanesian languages from his students. He eventually wrote grammars and vocabularies of thirty-four languages and translated the *Bible* into Motu, the chief language of the school.

Codrington also recorded what his students told him of their homes, in order to refute the wide-spread inaccuracies of European travelers' tales. His writings were quickly recognized as important sources of data on Melanesia; his description of *mana*—an impersonal or neutral supernatural power—especially excited the imaginations of ethnological theorists in Great Britain.

In 1885 Codrington was awarded an honorary doctorate in divinity from Oxford. Two years later he resigned his Wadham College fellowship, left the island mission, and became a vicar in the British diocese of Chichester. (He had refused appointment as Bishop of Melanesia, preferring that the post go to a younger, healthier man, new to the region.) Codrington was a lecturer at Chichester Theological College for twenty-five years, retiring at age eighty. His wide circle of friends included William Wordsworth, Lewis Carroll and Hans Christian Andersen. He died the week of his ninety-second birthday.

MAJOR WORKS: *The Melanesian Languages* (Oxford: 1885); *The Melanesians: Studies in their Anthropology and Folk-Lore* (Oxford: 1891); "Religious beliefs and practices in Melanesia," *Journal of the Royal Anthropological Institute*, vol. 10 (1880-1881), pp. 261-316.

SOURCES: David Hilliard, *God's Gentlemen* (St. Lucia, Australia: 1978); David L. Hilliard, "Codrington, Robert Henry" in: Robert D. Craig and Frank P. King (editors), *Historical Dictionary of Oceania* (Westport, Conn.: 1981), p. 55; Frederic Harrison, "Apostle of Melanesia," *The Times* [London] (15 September 1922), p. 13.

David Lonergan

Coedès, George. Epigraphist and historian of Southeast Asia, particularly of Cambodia. Born in Paris (France) 10 August 1886, died in Paris (France) 10 October 1969. While still in his first year of university studies in 1904, Coedès, who had learned Sanskrit during his secondary-school studies, published his first Sanskrit inscription from Cambodia in the *Bulletin de l'École Française d'Extrême-Orient* (*BEFEO*). His passionate interest in the history of Southeast Asia continued throughout his entire life. As a member of the École française d'Extrême-Orient in 1911, after having already written approximately fifteen articles on the epigraphy and archaeology of Cambodia and Champa, he went to Indochina. He resided for a while in Hanoi (the city in which the École was based) but spent most of his time in Cambodia, at Phnom Penh and Siem Reap near the monuments of Angkor. He became interested not only in inscriptions (almost all of which were from Cambodia) and in Khmer art, but also in Cambodian manuscripts. In 1918 he left for Bangkok to become curator of the National Library of Siam, a position he held until 1929. During this time, he published numerous Siamese inscriptions in two volumes as well as the study which firmly established the date of the Bayon of Angkor. Coedès was also Secretary General of the Royal Institute of Siam during his last two years in Bangkok. In 1929 he returned to Hanoi to become director of the École française, a position he held until his retirement in 1947. During his retirement in Paris, he continued to write actively, publishing major works until shortly before his death. He was elected a member of the Académie des Inscriptions et Belles Lettres in 1958.

Although Coedès was not the founder of the modern Western study of Khmer history, which was recreated by French researchers at the end of the last century, he contributed more than any other European to its development. No one can claim to study this history without beginning with the work of Coedès. With great modesty, however, he continually invited his students to push further on, even at the risk of upsetting some of his hypotheses.

Coedès is considered to be the master of the epigraphy of the land of the Khmer, which is almost the exclusive written source of information on this subject. One finds his ideas in his synthetic works and especially in a great many articles (the École Française d'Extrême Orient has gathered in three volumes his articles that were previously published in *BEFEO*, but only the first has appeared). Moreover, he enabled others to make decisive progress in the knowledge of the history of Southeast Asia, particularly of the Scrivijaya empire.

> MAJOR WORKS: "Études cambodgiennes," I to XL, in: *Bulletin de l'École Française d'Extrême-Orient* (1911-1956) [republished in: G. Coedès, *Articles sur le pays khmer* (Paris: 1989)]; *Les inscriptions du Cambodge* [8 vols.] (Hanoi: 1937 and 1943; Paris: 1951, 1952, 1953, 1954, 1964 and 1966); *Histoire ancienne des états hindouisés d'Indochine et d'Indonesie* (3rd ed., revised, Paris: 1964) [tr.: *The Indianized States of Southeast Asia* (Honolulu: 1968)]; *Pour mieux connaître Angkor* (Hanoi: 1943; Paris: 1947) [tr.: *Angkor: an Introduction* (Hong Kong: 1963)]; *Les peuples de la péninsule indochinoise: histoire, civilisations* (Paris: 1962) [tr.: *The Making of Southeast Asia* (Berkeley and Los Angeles: 1966)].

> SOURCE: Jean Filliozat, "Notice sur la vie et les travaux de M. George Coedès," *Bulletin de l'École Française d'Extrême-Orient*, vol. 57 (1970), pp. 1-24.

Claude Jacques
[Translation from French: Timothy Eastridge]

Colbacchini, Antonio. Missionary, ethnologist. Born in Bassano del Grappa (Italy) 19 February 1881, died in Castel di Godego (Italy) 12 March 1960. Colbacchini, first schooled by the Salesians, joined Father Balzola's expedition to Brazil at the age of eighteen. For two years he worked in Cuiabá, the capital of the state of Mato Grosso, but after becoming ill with beriberi he was sent back to Italy where he completed his theological studies and entered the priesthood. He rejoined the Brazilian mission in 1903 and contributed to the preparations for missionary work among the remote Bororo. In the following years he was among the founders of the Salesian Missions network in the Mato Grosso. He directed the centers of Coxipó (1905-1906), Barreiro (1908-1920), Rio das Mortes (1920-1921), Santa Rita (1934-1935) and Xavantina (1950-1953). During his stay in Brazil Colbacchini received the "Cruzeiro do Sul," the highest national honor. In 1959, gravely ill with rheumatic fever, Colbacchini returned to Italy where he died the following year.

Colbacchini's missionary zeal was coupled with his geographic research and his scholarly studies of peoples he encountered in the course of his missionary activities. His major work, *I Bororos orientali*, made possible the compilation of the *Enciclopedia Bororos*, which was used by CLAUDE LÉVI-STRAUSS in his *Structures élémentaires de la parenté*. The vast collection of ethnographic data in Colbacchini's *I Bororos orientali* is complemented by his systematic treatment of that population's lifestyle. Colbacchini observed all elements of the Bororo's social life while maintaining a scientific detachment free from subjective and moral involvement even with respect to religious practices. He was particularly interested in studying and collecting the products of oral tradition, especially songs, legends and myths dealing with Bororo cosmology, knowledge and beliefs. In the linguistic area his efforts resulted in the compilation of a grammar and a dictionary.

His less extensive but not less interesting work on the Xavantes, whom he visited in 1949, was published in a series of articles in *Bollettino Salesiano*.

MAJOR WORKS: *I Bororos orientali (Orarimugudoge) del Matto Grosso (Brasile)* (Turin: 1925); *Grammatica dei Bororos-Orarimugudoge del Matto Grosso (Brasile)* (Turin: 1926); *A tribu dos Bororos* (Rio de Janeiro: 1919).

SOURCES: C. Albisetti and A. Venturelli, *Enciclopedia Bororo* (Campo Grande-Mato Grosso: 1962); Claude Lévi-Strauss, *Les structures élémentaires de la parenté* (Paris: 1947); *Bollettino Salesiano* (Turin: 1877-); *Dizionario biografico dei Salesiani* (Turin: 1969); *Bibliografia generale delle Missioni Salesiane* (Rome: 1975).

Massimo Guerra
[Translation from Italian: Gianna Panofsky]

Cole, Fay-Cooper. Anthropologist, archaeologist. Born in Plainwell (Michigan) 8 August 1881, died in Santa Barbara (California) 3 September 1961. Cole is considered to be one of the founders of modern archaeology. After graduation from Northwestern University in 1903, he did post-graduate work at the University of Chicago. Cole joined the then Field Columbian Museum in 1904 as an ethnologist under the direction of GEORGE A. DORSEY and was assigned to field research in the Philippines. In order to prepare for this fieldwork, Dorsey sent him to Columbia University for graduate work under FRANZ BOAS and then to Berlin for training with FELIX VON LUSCHAN. He spent the years 1906-1908 studying the Tinguian people of Luzon. This study resulted in the publication of his first major work, *A Study of Tinguian Folklore*, which served as his doctoral dissertation from Columbia University in 1914 and was later published in an expanded version as "Traditions of the Tinguian." A second expedition to Mindanao in 1910-1912 resulted in the work, "The wild tribes of the Davao District, Mindanao."

Upon returning from his last major expedition to Indonesia in 1922-1923, he accepted an offer from the University of Chicago to develop a program in anthropology. Cole's zeal for his subject and personal experience combined to attract so much interest in anthropology that a separate department was established in 1929 with Cole as chairman. His main interest was in developing a broad research-oriented program with training in all fields of anthropology, and he succeeded in bringing both EDWARD SAPIR and A.R. RADCLIFFE-BROWN to the university.

At this time, Cole's own research interests turned to the archaeology of Illinois and the Midwest. His introduction of dendrochronology and other field techniques into the Mississippi Valley helped to develop a heretofore nonexistent interest in the prehistory of the Midwest. The close proximity to this geographic area afforded a large number of students excellent fieldwork experience. His dedication to the extensive training of these students was demonstrated by the publication of the presentation volume, *Archeology of the Eastern United States* (edited by JAMES B. GRIFFIN) in 1952; this volume was organized and prepared in Cole's honor by former students of the Department of Anthropology.

Cole's interest in and enthusiasm for archaeology remained with him to the end of his life. Even after retirement in 1947, he continued to teach, lecture, publish and maintain involvement in professional organizations and activities. Earlier he had been one of the founders of the Society for American Archeology; president of the American Anthropological Association for two terms (1933-1935); active member in both the Social Science Research Council (1925-1930) and the National Research Council (1927-1930); and chief of the social science division of the Century of Progress (1933).

MAJOR WORKS: (with Berthold Laufer) "Chinese pottery in the Philippines," *Field Museum of Natural History Publication*, no. 162 (1912), pp. 1-47 (= *Anthropological Series*, vol. 12, no. 1); "The wild tribes of Davao District, Mindanao," *Field Museum of Natural History Publication*, no. 170 (1913), pp. 19-203 (= *Anthropological Series*, vol. 14, no. 2); "Traditions of the Tinguian: a study in Philippine folk-lore," *Field Museum of Natural History Publication*, no. 180 (1915), pp. 3-226 (= *Anthropological Series*, vol. 14, no. 1); "The Tinguian: social, religious, and economic life of a Philippine tribe," *Field Museum of Natural History Publication*, no. 209 (1922), pp. 231-493 (= *Anthropological Series*, vol. 14, no. 2); *The Long Road from Savagery to Civilization* (Baltimore: 1933); (with Mabel Cook Cole) *The Story of Man* (Chicago: 1937); *The Peoples of Malaysia* (New York: 1945); (with Robert Bell [et al.]) *Kincaid: a Prehistoric Illinois Metropolis* (Chicago: 1951); "The Bukidnon of Mindanao," *Chicago Natural History Museum*, pp. 5-140 (= *Fieldiana: Anthropology*, vol. 46).

SOURCES: "Fay-Cooper Cole," *The Living Museum*, vol. 23 (1961), p. 43; Fred Eggan, "Fay-Cooper Cole, architect of anthropology," *Science*, vol. 135 (1962), pp. 412-413; Jesse D. Jennings, "Fay-Cooper Cole, 1881-1961" *American Antiquity*, vol. 27 (1962), pp. 573-575; Fred Eggan, "Fay-Cooper Cole, 1881-1961," *American Anthropologist*, vol. 65 (1963), pp. 641-648; "Cole, Fay-Cooper" in: *The New Encyclopaedia Britannica* (Chicago: 1986), vol. 3, p. 444.

Michele Calhoun

Collier, Donald. Archaeologist, ethnologist, museologist. Born in Sparkill (New York) 1 May 1911. Collier received a Ph.D. in anthropology from the University of Chicago in 1954 and spent most of his career at the Field Museum of Natural History, Chicago, where he was Curator of Middle American Archaeology and Ethnology from 1941 to 1976 and then Curator Emeritus. He served as Chief Curator of the department from 1964 to 1970 and was a lecturer in anthropology at the University of Chicago from 1950 to 1970.

Collier is known primarily for his contributions to Ecuadoran and Andean archaeology, particularly his delineation of late prehistoric pottery sequences in southern Ecuador and the Virú Valley of Peru where he carried out fieldwork between 1937 and 1956. At the Field Museum Collier was responsible for the installation of permanent exhibition halls on the archaeology of Mesoamerica and Central America and on the Indians of South America, as well as for several important temporary exhibitions of American Indian art and culture. Between 1945 and 1965 Collier participated in the organization and teaching of one of the earliest museology courses in cooperation with the Department of Anthropology, University of Chicago. He was president of the Central States Anthropological Society during 1953-1954, and a founding trustee of the Council on Museum Anthropology.

MAJOR WORKS: (with Alfred E. Hudson and Arlo Ford) *Archaeology of the Upper Columbia Region* (Seattle: 1942) (= *University of Washington Publications in Anthropology*, vol. 9, no. 1); (with John V. Murra) *Survey and Excavations in Southern Ecuador* (Chicago: 1943) (= *Field Museum of Natural History, Anthropological Series*, vol. 35); (with Paul S. Martin and George I. Quimby) *Indians before Columbus* (Chicago: 1947); (with Harry Tschopik, Jr.) "The role of museums in American anthropology," *American Anthropologist*, vol. 56 (1954), pp. 768-779; *Cultural*

Chronology and Change as Reflected in the Ceramics of the Virú Valley, Peru (Chicago: 1955) (= *Fieldiana: Anthropology*, vol. 43); *Indian Art of the Americas* (Chicago: 1959); (with Donald W. Lathrop and Helen Chandra) *Ancient Ecuador: Culture, Clay and Creativity* (Chicago: 1975).

James W. VanStone

Collins, Henry B. Anthropologist, museum curator. Born in Geneva (Alabama) 9 April 1899, died in Campbelltown (Pennsylvania) 21 October 1987. Collins was trained at Millsaps College (Mississippi) (B.A., 1922; Sc.D., 1940) and at George Washington University (M.A., 1925). He was on NEIL M. JUDD's Pueblo Bonito expeditions of 1922-1924 and worked for the Mississippi Department of Archives and History in 1923. Appointed an aid in the Smithsonian's Division of Ethnology in 1924, he rose to become associate curator in 1938. Between 1939 and 1963, he was a senior scientist with the Bureau of American Ethnology (BAE) and its acting director during 1963-1965. When the BAE was merged into the Smithsonian Office of Anthropology in 1965, Collins again became a senior scientist. He retired in 1967 but remained active at the Smithsonian until 1986.

Originally trained in geology, Collins was introduced to anthropology during his work with Judd. His independent fieldwork during the 1920s mainly concerned the culture, history and relationship among the peoples of his native South. He worked at village and mound sites in eastern and southern Mississippi, carried out archaeological reconnaissance and excavations in southern Louisiana and explored areas of southwestern Florida, becoming especially concerned there with problems concerning the Calusa.

Collins is best known, however, for his endeavors in Arctic archaeology, where he become involved in the puzzles of Eskimo history, including its Asian affinities, western rather than eastern origins, culture sequences, and influences on non-Eskimo cultures. For his report on St. Lawrence Island, Collins won the gold medal of the Royal Danish Academy of Sciences and Letters. During 1948-1952, his work expanded eastward to Baffin, Cornwallis and Southampton Islands. He was particularly concerned with the origins of the Dorset culture and Thule migrations. In his work, Collins "introduced Arctic archeology as a modern science" and "resolved or framed [its] overriding issues of the twentieth century" (Fitzhugh).

Collins was also active with anthropological organizations. He served the International Congresses of Ethnological and Anthropological Sciences as vice-president in Copenhagen in 1938, member of the permanent council in 1952, and president at Moscow in 1965. For the International Congress of Americanists at Copenhagen in 1956, he was an honorary vice-president. A founding member of the Arctic Institute of North America, Collins was on the board of governors for several terms, and in 1946, he became chairman of the directing committee of *Arctic Bibliography*. He was president of the Anthropological Society of Washington in 1938-1939 and vice-president of the Society for American Archaeology in 1942 and 1952. For the Ethnogeographic Board, a World War II agency, he was assistant director during 1943-1944 and director during 1944-1946.

MAJOR WORKS: *Archeology of St. Lawrence Island, Alaska* (Washington: 1937) (= *Smithsonian Miscellaneous Collections*, vol. 96); *Outline of Eskimo Prehistory* (Washington: 1940) (= *Smithsonian Miscellaneous Collections*, vol. 100); (with A.H. Clark and E.H. Walker) *The Aleutian Islands: Their People and Natural History* (Washington: 1946) (= *Smithsonian Institution*

War Background Studies, no. 21); (editor) *Science in Alaska: Selected Papers of the Alaskan Science Conference* ([Washington?]: 1952) (= *Arctic Institute of North America Special Publication*, no. 1).

SOURCES: William W. Fitzhugh, "Henry Bascom Collins," *Anthropology Newsletter*, vol. 29, no. 1 (January 1988), p. 20; "Henry Bascom Collins" in: Wilcomb Washburn (editor), *History of Indian-White Relations* (Washington: 1988) (= William C. Sturtevant (general editor), *Handbook of North American Indians*, vol. 4), p. 633; Collins papers and vertical file in the Smithsonian Institution National Anthropological Archives; Nigel Elmore, *Register to the Papers of Henry Bascom Collins* (1981).

James R. Glenn

Colson, Elizabeth Florence. Anthropologist. Born in Hewitt (Minnesota) 15 June 1917. Colson is a distinguished anthropologist who has made contributions to both theoretical and applied anthropology. Best known for her long-term research among the Gwembe Tonga of Zambia, she also has done fieldwork in Australia and among the Makah and Pomo in North America. She has made major contributions to the study of kinship, marriage, divorce, politics, law, development and culture change.

Colson received her B.A. from the University of Minnesota (1938), where she studied with Wilson Wallis, with whom she later collaborated on research, and her M.A. (1941) and Ph.D. (1945) from Radcliffe College. Her dissertation, *The Makah Indians*, which is still in print, was her first research on culture change. Instead of focusing on "traditional" cultures of the past, as did many of her contemporaries, Colson focused on the realities of contemporary culture. Her research among the Gwembe Tonga began in 1946, when she was affiliated with the Rhodes-Livingstone Institute in Northern Rhodesia (now Zambia) and began collaboration with Max Gluckman. It has continued into the 1980s in collaboration with Thayer Scudder as the Gwembe were relocated when Lake Kariba was created. Many important articles and books describe this research including *Marriage and Family Among the Plateau Tonga of Northern Rhodesia*, *Social Organization of the Gwembe Tonga*, *The Plateau Tonga of Northern Rhodesia*, *The Social Consequences of Resettlement* and *For Prayer and Profit*.

From 1948 to 1951 Colson was Director of the Rhodes-Livingstone Institute; subsequently she taught at Manchester University (1951-1953), Goucher College (1954-1955), Boston University (1955-1959), Brandeis University (1959-1963), Northwestern University (1963-1964) and University of California, Berkeley (1964-1987), where she became Emeritus Professor in 1987. Colson was active in academic life and became an advocate for academic freedom at Brandeis and the elimination of sex discrimination at Berkeley. In 1977 Colson was elected to the National Academy of Sciences, an honor bestowed on few women anthropologists. Other honors include fellowships from the Center for Advanced Study in Behavioral Sciences (Stanford, California), the California Institute of Technology and the American Association of University Women; honorary membership in the Royal Anthropological Institute, London; and honorary degrees from Brown University and the University of Rochester, where she gave the Lewis Henry Morgan Lecture, "Tradition and contract: the problem of order," in 1973. Colson continues to be active in retirement conducting research, participating in professional meetings, lecturing and consulting with students and colleagues on fieldwork and shared concerns in anthropology.

MAJOR WORKS: *Life Among the Cattle-Owning Plateau Tonga* (Livingstone: 1949); (editor with Max Gluckman) *Seven Tribes of British Central Africa* (Manchester: 1951); *The Makah Indians* (Minneapolis: 1953; Westport, Conn.: 1974); *Autobiographies of Three Pomo Women* (Madison: 1956); *Marriage and Family Among the Plateau Tonga of Northern Rhodesia* (Manchester: 1958); *Social Organization of the Gwembe Tonga* (Manchester: 1960); *The Plateau Tonga of Northern Rhodesia* (Manchester: 1962); *The Social Consequences of Resettlement* (Manchester: 1971); *Tradition and Contract* (Chicago: 1974); (editor with George M. Foster [et al.]) *Long-term Field Research in Social Anthropology* (New York: 1978); (with Thayer Scudder) *Secondary Education and the Formation of an Elite* (New York: 1980); (editor with Scott M. Morgan) *People in Upheaval* (New York: 1987); (with Thayer Scudder) *For Prayer and Profit* (Stanford: 1988).

SOURCES: Elizabeth Colson and Thayer Scudder, "Long-term research in Gwembe Valley, Zambia" in: George M. Foster [et al.] (editors), *Long-term Field Research in Social Anthropology* (New York: 1979), pp. 227-254; Jack Glazier [et al.] (editors), *Opportunity, Constraint and Change: Essays in Honor of Elizabeth Colson* (Berkeley: 1984); "Colson, Elizabeth" in: *Who's Who in America, 1988-89* (Chicago: 1988), p. 608.

Nancy J. Schmidt

Comas, Juan (Juan Comas Camps). Biologist, anthropologist. Born in Alayor, Mallorca (Spain) 1900, died in Mexico 1978. Comas began his academic activities as a teacher and educator, collaborating in the educational reform in Spain that was directed by the Institución Libre de Enseñanza (Free Teaching Institute). Exiled by the Franco government in 1939, he continued his pedagogical work and his anthropological research in Mexico. He completed his doctoral thesis under the direction of Eugène Pittard in Geneva; its subject was metopism, the persistance into adulthood of the medio-frontal suture in the human skull. In 1944 he was one of the founders of the Escuela Nacional de Antropología e Historia (National School of Anthropology and History) in Mexico City; he also became head of the anthropology section of the National University of Mexico.

Comas undertook exhaustive research on the bibliography and history of anthropology. He was director of the *Boletín Bibliográfico de Antropología Americana* between 1945 and 1955. Among his bibliographical reference works and books on the history of anthropology, the most outstanding are those dedicated to physical anthropology and to the congresses of anthropological sciences and of Americanists. Always interested in the teaching of anthropology, he also translated many books. Nevertheless, it is above all his *Manual de antropología física* that best reflects his educational biases. The *Manual* covers different themes from paleontology to the history of physical anthropology, the chapters on biological types and osteology being especially outstanding. Comas's most notable research was carried out in the field of anthropometry, but he openly criticized the anthropometric indices and measurements used to establish racial histories, coming to doubt their utility in resolving problems of human biological variability. He belonged to the International Committee for Standardizing Anthropological Measurements, and, as a strong critic of racism, he also played a role on several United Nations and UNESCO commissions on racial discrimination.

His opposition to racism was energetically combined with his work in the Mexican Indian movement. Comas contributed to numerous research projects and collaborated actively with the Interamerican Indian Institute in initiatives aimed at improving the social situation of Indian populations.

MAJOR WORKS: *La antropología física en México y Centroamérica* (Mexico City: 1943); *Bibliografía morfológica humana de América del Sur* (Mexico City: 1948); *Ensayos sobre indigenismo* (Mexico City: 1953); *Síntesis histórica e índice general bibliográfico de los XXX Congresos Internacionales de Americanistas, 1875-1952* (Mexico City: 1954); *Historia y bibliografía de los Congresos Internacionales de Ciencias Antropológicas, 1865-1954* (Mexico City: 1956); *Manual de antropología física* (Mexico City: 1957) [tr.: *Manual of Physical Anthropology* (Springfield, Ill.: 1960)]; "'Scientific' racism again?" *Current Anthropology*, vol. 2 (1961), pp. 303-340; *Historia sumaria de la Asociación Americana de Antropólogos Físicos, 1928-1968* (Mexico City: 1969); *Cien años de Congresos Internacionales de Americanistas* (Mexico City: 1974); *Antropología de los pueblos iberoamericanos* (Barcelona: 1974).

SOURCES: *Curriculum vitae de Juan Comas* (Mexico City: 1972); Fermín del Pino, "En memoria de Juan Comas Camps (1900-1978)," *Revista de Indias*, vol. 38 (1978), pp. 855-867 [contains bibliography]; Carlos García Mora (coordinator), *La antropología en México: panorama histórico* [3 vols.] (Mexico City: 1987-1988); Luis A. Vargas, "La antropología física" in: Jorge Carpizo, *Las humanidades en México* (Mexico City: 1978), pp. 645-666; María Villanueva, "La antropología física de los antropólogos físicos en México" in: *Estudios de antropología física: Primer Coloquio Juan Comas, 1980* (Mexico City: 1982), pp. 75-124.

Fernando Estévez
[Translation from Spanish: Margo L. Smith]

Coon, Carleton Stevens. Anthropologist. Born in Wakefield (Massachusetts) 23 June 1904, died in West Gloucester (Massachusetts) 3 June 1981. Coon was a general anthropologist who made major contributions in archaeology, physical anthropology and ethnology and who was able to convey the results of his remarkable range of scholarship to both anthropologists and the general public in readable, authoritative accounts as well as in museum exhibits and on television talk shows.

Trained at Harvard University (B.A., 1925; Ph.D., 1928), he was a member of the Harvard University anthropology faculty from 1927 to 1948, except for 1942 to 1945 when he was on leave to serve the Department of State and U.S. Army during World War II, for which he received the Legion of Merit. From 1948 until his retirement in 1963 he was curator at the University of Pennsylvania Museum and a member of the anthropology faculty. During these years he brought anthropology to the public by installing a Hall of Man at the University Museum and appearing regularly on the television program, *What in the World?*, which received the Peabody Award in 1952.

Coon was an inveterate fieldworker in archaeology and ethnology throughout his professional career and after his retirement, going to Morocco (1924-1928, 1939, 1947, 1965), Albania (1929-1930), Ethiopia and Arabia (1933-1934), Iran (1949, 1951), Afghanistan and Syria (1954-1955), Tierra del Fuego (1959), Sierra Leone (1965) and Chad and Libya (1966-1967). He received many academic honors including the Viking Medal in Physical Anthropology in 1951 and election to the National Academy of Sciences in 1955. Early in his career he wrote a classical textbook, *Principles of Anthropology*; ethnology, *Tribes of the Rif*; fiction based on his fieldwork, *Flesh of the Wild Ox*; and an account of the problems of fieldwork, *Measuring Ethiopia and Flight into Arabia*, showing himself a master of both scholarly and popular genres. His archaeological fieldwork led to major discoveries that contributed to his theories of evolution, which were developed in a series of books including *The Races of Europe, Races ... a Study of the Problem of Race Formation in Man, The Origin of the Races, The Living Races of Man* and *Racial*

Aptitudes. These works were soundly based on scientific data, imaginative and controversial. Coon presented both data from his archaeological excavations and conveyed the excitement of fieldwork to general readers in such works as *The Story of Man* and *Seven Caves*. He planned to write an autobiographical trilogy, but completed only two volumes, *A North African Story* and *Adventures and Discoveries*, which provide insights into the intellectual development of this eclectic and unusually productive scholar.

MAJOR WORKS: *Tribes of the Rif* (Cambridge, Mass: 1931); *Flesh of the Wild Ox* (New York: 1932); *The Riffian* (Boston: 1933); *Measuring Ethiopia and Flight into Arabia* (Boston: 1935); (with Carl C. Seltzer) *The Racial Characteristics of Syrians and Armenians* (Cambridge, Mass.: 1936); *The Races of Europe* (New York: 1939); (with Eliot D. Chapple) *Principles of Anthropology* (New York: 1942); *A Reader in General Anthropology* (New York: 1948); *Cave Explorations in Iran, 1949* (Philadelphia, 1951); *The Mountain Giants* (Cambridge, Mass: 1950); (with Stanley M. Garn and Charles C. Thomas) *Races ... a Study of the Problems of Race Formation in Man* (Springfield, Ill.: 1950); *Caravan: the Story of the Middle East* (New York: 1951; revised ed., New York: 1958); *The Story of Man* (New York: 1954); published as *The History of Man from the First Human to Primitive Culture and Beyond* (London: 1955; revised ed., New York: 1962); *The Origin of Races* (New York: 1962); (editor with Edward E. Hunt) *Anthropology A to Z* (New York: 1963); (with Edward E. Hunt) *The Living Races of Man* (New York: 1965); (with Harvey M. Bricker, Frederick Johnson and C.C. Lamberg-Karlovsky) *Yengema Cave Report* (Philadelphia: 1968); *The Hunting Peoples* (Boston: 1971); *A North African Story* (Ipswich, Mass.: 1980); *Adventures and Discoveries* (Englewood Cliffs, N.J.: 1981); *Racial Aptitudes* (Chicago: 1982).

SOURCES: Carleton S. Coon, *Adventures and Discoveries* (Englewood Cliffs, N.J.: 1981); Carleton S. Coon, *A North African Story* (Ipswich, Mass.: 1980); Robert H. Dyson, "Carleton S. Coon," *Expedition*, vol. 23, 4 (1981), p. 3; Edward E. Hunt, "Carleton Stevens Coon, 1904-1981," *American Journal of Physical Anthropology*, vol. 58 (1982), pp. 239-241; *Current Biography Yearbook* (1955), pp. 136-138.

Nancy J. Schmidt

Cooper, John Montgomery. Anthropologist, ethnographer, priest. Born in Rockville (Maryland) 28 October 1881, died in Washington (D.C.) 22 May 1949. Cooper received a Ph.D. from the American College, Rome (Italy) in 1902 and the degree Doctor of Sacred Theology in 1905, the year in which he was ordained. He spent most of his life teaching at the Catholic University of America (Washington, D.C.), becoming a full professor in 1928. He became chairman of the Department of Anthropology when it was established in 1934, a position he held until his death. From 1917 to 1925 Cooper's attention turned to subjects broadly sociological in nature. His writings primarily concerned group work, social hygiene and related topics. His last contribution in applied sociology was his book *Children's Institutions*. Although he made original contributions to several fields of anthropology, such as linguistics, and to the psychiatric approach to certain ethnographic phenomena, Cooper was primarily an ethnologist. His vacation trips to northern Canada led to an interest in American Indians, which was encouraged by JOHN REED SWANTON and FREDERICK WEBB HODGE, ethnologists at the Smithsonian Institution. His first notable contribution to ethnology, which preceded his sociological work, was his *Analytical and Critical Bibliography of the Tribes of Tierra del Fuego*. His recurrent visits to the Algonquian-speaking Indians of northeastern Canada and the Great Plains resulted in many papers on various aspects of their cultures. His last full-length monograph, the second part of *The Gros Ventres of Montana*, was published posthumously. As a theorist Cooper was particularly intrigued with questions of distribution and historical reconstruction. His 1942 paper on the areal and temporal distribution of culture in South America inspired the overall arrangement of the *Handbook of South American Indians*, edited by JULIAN H. STEWARD. To this large compendium he contributed ten articles. In his *Temporal Sequence and the Marginal Cultures* he presented evidence for the hypothesis that the non-literate peoples of the ethnographic present represent "tarriers" with relatively unchanged cultures from prehistoric times, and he worked out several canons to be applied in historical reconstruction. Cooper was aware that the applicability of his canons was distinctly limited. "As is obvious they cannot yield a total all-embracing reconstruction of prehistoric culture ..." (*Temporal Sequence and the Marginal Cultures*, p. 66). Lowie, in his 1949 obituary (p. 291), stated that Cooper's essay "Andamanese-Semang-Eta cultural relations," "which presents a powerful argument for the pristine unity of the Asiatic Pygmies, [was possibly] the most superb example of what sound judgement coupled with control of the material can accomplish." Cooper's interpretative paper, "The relations between religion and morality," was selected for inclusion in *The Golden Age of American Anthropology*.

In addition to his purely academic activities Cooper initiated and edited several valuable publications, including the periodical *Primitive Man* (title changed to *Anthropological Quarterly* in 1953). He never shirked professional responsibility and participated actively in numerous organizations.

MAJOR WORKS: *Analytical and Critical Bibliography of the Tribes of Tierra del Fuego and Adjacent Territory* (Washington: 1917); *Children's Institutions: a Study of Programs and Policies in Catholic Children's Institutions in the United States* (Philadelphia: 1931); "The relations between religion and morality in primitive culture" in: Margaret Mead and Ruth Bunzel (editors), *The Golden Age of American Anthropology* (New York: 1960), pp. 560-572; "Mental disease situation in certain cultures: a new field for research," *Journal of Abnormal and Social Psychology*, vol. 24 (1934), pp. 10-17; "Andamanese-Semang-Eta cultural relations," *Primitive Man*, vol. 13 (1940), pp. 29-47; *Temporal Sequence and the Marginal Cultures* (Washington: 1941); "Areal and temporal aspects of aboriginal South American culture," *Primitive Man*, vol. 15 (1942), pp. 1-38; "Tête-de-Boule Cree," *International Journal of American Linguistics*, vol. 11 (1945), pp. 36-44; *The Gros Ventres of Montana. Part 2. Religion and Ritual* (Regina Flannery, editor) (Washington: 1957).

SOURCES: Regina Flannery and M. Elizabeth Chambers, "John M. Cooper's investigation of James Bay family hunting grounds, 1927-1934," *Anthropologica*, n.s., vol. 28 (1986), pp. 108-144; Paul H. Furfey, "John Montgomery Cooper, 1881-1949," *Primitive Man*, vol. 23 (1950), pp. 49-65; Robert H. Lowie, "John Montgomery Cooper, 1881-1949," *Boletín bibliográfico de antropología americana*, vol. 12, pt. 2 (1949), pp. 289-292; Alfred Métraux, "The contribution of the Rev. Father Cooper to southern American ethnography," *Primitive Man*, vol. 23 (1950), pp. 39-48; Julian H. Steward (editor), *Handbook of South American Indians* [7 vols.] (New York: 1946-1959); Leopold H. Tibesar, "Doctor Cooper initiates the Catholic Anthropological Conference," *Primitive Man*, vol. 23 (1950), pp. 35-38; "Bibliography of John Montgomery Cooper," *Primitive Man*, vol. 23 (1950), pp. 66-84.

Regina F. Herzfeld

Cotter, John Lambert. Anthropologist, educator, archaeologist, government administrator. Born in Denver (Colorado) 6 December 1911. Cotter received his A.B. degree in anthropology in 1934 from the University of Denver and his M.A. in 1935. His early work dealt with major prehistoric American sites, e.g., the Lindenmeier site in western Colorado where he served as crewman and at the Clovis Type site where he served as chief of party and on which the two parts of "The occurrence of flints and extinct animals in pluvial deposits near Clovis, New Mexico" are based. After supervising the state archaeological survey in Kentucky (1938-1940), Cotter joined the National Park Service and became the site manager and archaeologist at Tuzigoot National Monument in Arizona. After service in World War II, Cotter continued his National Park Service career at several sites on the Natchez Trace Parkway. However, it was his work at Jamestown, Colonial National Historical Park, from 1953 to 1957, that stimulated a whole new generation of historical archaeologists and helped spur interest in the 17th- and 18th-century Virginia Tidewater.

Cotter's report (*Archaeological Excavations at Jamestown*) not only detailed the new excavations but summarized much of the work that had come before. Ably assisted by Ed Jelks, Joel Shiner, and others, Cotter proceeded from the earlier work of J.C. Harrington. Cotter's report served as the thesis for his Ph.D. at the University of Pennsylvania and for his course in historical archaeology at the University of Pennsylvania, the first such course taught in the United States (1960). Cotter's work in historical archaeology was to help bring the new discipline, historical archaeology, firmly into the anthropological "camp" from both a theoretical and methodological perspective. Additionally, Cotter emphasized a broad, holistic approach to the study of historical archaeology. As an educator, Cotter's teaching inspired more than a dozen Ph.D. dissertations and more than two dozen master's theses. In the 1950s, 1960s and 1970s, Cotter served as an eloquent spokesman for the new discipline of historical archaeology. Cotter was the co-founder, first president and first editor of the Society for Historical Archaeology, now the major organization in America for study in this field. His broad-based approach to cultural history, his enthusiasm for new fields, such as industrial archaeology, and his flexible stance for both historical archaeology and the study of American material culture define his major contributions to anthropology. In 1984 the Society for Historical Archaeology awarded him the J.C. Harrington medal for outstanding contributions to the field.

MAJOR WORKS: "The occurrence of flints and extinct animals in pluvial deposits near Clovis, New Mexico, part 4," *Proceedings of the Academy of Natural Sciences of Philadelphia*, vol. 84 (1932), pp. 1-16; "The occurrence of flints and extinct animals in pluvial deposits near Clovis, New Mexico, part 6," *Proceedings of the Academy of Natural Sciences of Philadelphia*, vol. 90 (1938), pp. 113-117; (with John M. Corbett) *Archaeology of the Bynum Mounds, Mississippi* (Washington: 1951); *Archaeological Excavations at Jamestown, Virginia* (Washington: 1958); *Above Ground Archaeology* (Washington: 1974); *The Walnut Street Prison Workshop* (Philadelphia: 1988); (with D. Roberts and M. Parrington) *An Archaeological History of Philadelphia* (in press).

SOURCE: David G. Orr [unsigned], "John L. Cotter, J.C. Harrington Medal in Historical Archaeology," *Historical Archaeology*, vol. 18, no. 2 (1984), pp. 1-3.

David G. Orr

Crawley, Ernest (Alfred Ernest Crawley). Educator, sportsman, journalist, amateur ethnologist. Born in Great Britain 1869; died in Kensington (England) 21 October 1924. Crawley obtained a first-class degree in classics at Cambridge in 1890 and was an instructor of classics at several British schools. In 1906 he became headmaster of Derby School but resigned the appointment and left teaching entirely in 1908. For the rest of his life, Crawley devoted his efforts to writing; for several years he was a frequent contributor on sports topics to the *The Times* of London.

His father, the Reverend Samuel Crawley, was one of the chief British proponents of lawn tennis, and the Crawley family produced several well known sportsmen. Ernest Crawley was a leading British tennis player in the 1890s, while one of his brothers was an Olympic gold-medal winner. Crawley also excelled at golf, figure-skating and shooting, and published three successful books on sports between 1913 and 1922.

It was as a comparative ethnologist that Crawley made his lasting contribution, however. His chief interest was in the rituals of primitive marriage, which he approached from a psychological viewpoint. In *The Mystic Rose*, which has gone through a number of revisions and reprintings, he argued that primitive beliefs in the inferiority and polluting ability of women led to protective rituals in the form of marriages, designed to lessen the potential danger to men. His books are thickly documented with the ethnological data of his day. It is not so much for his conclusions as for his willingness to adopt an innovative psychological stance that Crawley should be remembered.

MAJOR WORKS: *The Mystic Rose: a Study of Primitive Marriage* (London: 1902); *The Tree of Life: a Study of Religion* (London: 1905); *The Idea of the Soul* (London: 1909); *Studies of Savages and Sex* (edited by Theodore Besterman) (London: 1929).

SOURCES: Theodore Besterman, "Crawley, Alfred Ernest" in: E.R.A. Seligman (editor), *Encyclopaedia of the Social Sciences* (New York: 1931), vol. 4, pp. 544-545; "Death of A.E. Crawley," *The Times* [London] (25 October 1924), p. 14.

David Lonergan

Crazzolara, Pasquale. Missionary, linguist, ethnologist. Born in San Cassiano Val Badia (Italy) 12 April 1884, died at San Cassiano Val Badia (Italy) 25 March 1976. At the age of fourteen he began studies at the Istituto Comboniano di Milland, where he was ordained a priest in 1907. The following year he left for Khartoum and in 1910 he began his long sojourn (sixty-three years) on the African continent.

Crazzolara worked among the Shilluk and Nuer peoples of the Sudan, among the Lango and the Karimojong in Uganda and the Lwoo (Luo) in Kenya. In 1975 he moved permanently back to Italy.

In the years 1926 and 1927 he was called back to Europe and had the opportunity to meet E.E. EVANS-PRITCHARD; his meeting with the British anthropologist gained him a scholarship to the University of London, where he improved his knowledge of the Acholi language. He was also in Vienna, where he took a course at the school run by Father WILHELM SCHMIDT.

Crazzolara's linguistic interests are revealed in important articles (for the most part in the journals *Africa* and *Anthropos*) and in published monographs, most notably a Nuer grammar and an Acholi dictionary.

As an ethnologist he published some short but significant studies on the initiation ceremonies of the Nuer (the Gar) and on the role of the Zebu in their culture ("Die Gar-Zeremonie bei den Nuer" and "Die Bedeutung des Rindes bei den Nuer"); he also published a collection of Nuer and Dinka legends concerning the presence of Pygmies along the Baḥr al-ᶜArab and an extensive study of the Shilluk people ("Beiträge zur Kenntnis der Religion und Zauberei bei den Schilluk").

Crazzolara's principal work is his three-volume monograph on the Lwoo (Luo) people; this aroused great interest among Africanists, as it contained large amounts of data and fundamental information useful to students of the Nilotic peoples. In 1953 he published the first comprehensive monograph on the Nuer religion, which was reviewed by Evans-Pritchard in glowing terms. In fact, the British anthropologist made extensive use of Crazzolara's studies in his own celebrated analysis of the Nuer religion.

For his efforts in the field of linguistic and anthropological research, Crazzolara received in 1963 the M.B.E. medal (Member of the Order of the British Empire) and two years later the medal of the Royal African Society of London.

MAJOR WORKS: "Die Gar-Zeremonie bei den Nuer," *Africa*, vol. 7 (1932), pp. 28-29; "Beiträge zur Kenntnis der Religion und Zauberei bei den Schilluk," *Anthropos*, vol. 27 (1932), pp. 188-211 and 881-897; "Die Bedeutung des Rindes bei den Nuer," *Africa*, vol. 9 (1934), pp. 300-320; *A Study of the Acooli Langauage* (London: 1938); *The Lwoo. I. Migrations* (Verona: 1950); *The Lwoo. II. Clans* (Verona: 1951); *Outlines of a Nuer Grammar* (Vienna: 1953); *Zur Gesellschaft und Religion der Nuer* (Vienna: 1953); *The Lwoo. III. Traditions* (Verona: 1954); *Study of the Logbara (Ma'di) Language* (London: 1960).

SOURCES: Leone A. Rosa. "La Chiesa, i cattolici e le scienze dell'uomo: 1860-1960" in: Pietro Clemente [et al.], *L'antropologia italiana: un secolo di storia* (Bari: 1985), pp. 51-96; "Comboniani," *Nigrizia*, no. 2 (1967), p. 36; "68 anni d'Africa," *Nigrizia*, no. 9 (1976), p. 7; E.E. Evans-Pritchard, Review of: *Zur Gesellschaft und Religion der Nuer*, *Anthropos*, vol. 50 (1955), pp. 476-477.

Massimo Guerra
[Translation from Italian: Chris Nissen]

Cummings, Byron.

Cummings, Byron. Anthropologist, archaeologist, humanitarian, classicist, museologist. Born in Westerville (New York) 20 September 1860, died in Tucson (Arizona) 21 May 1954. Educated in the classical languages and culture, he enriched his archaeological background through advanced studies at the University of Berlin.

First at Rutgers, later at the University of Utah, Salt Lake City, and still later at the University of Arizona, Tucson, Cummings pursued the classical traditions, continuing to teach Latin and Greek culture. At the University of Utah he was head of the Department of Ancient Languages and Literature and later the Dean of the College of Arts and Sciences. From the University of Utah, he made his first trip on horseback, alone, and, as a pioneer to Southwestern archaeological sites, gave courses at the university level on this subject. Cummings' archaeological investigations in Utah and Arizona continued to the end of his career. Cummings also excavated the famous site of Cuicuilco, Mexico, and was the first to recognize Pleistocene man in southern Arizona.

Not only did Cummings encourage men going into the field in the late 19th and early 20th centuries but he became the teacher of and inspiration to many of the leading archaeologists and museologists of the later 20th century. At the University of Arizona, Tucson, Cummings built up and was director (1915-1938) of the Arizona State Museum, which now houses one of the most comprehensive collections on Southwestern archaeology and ethnology in the nation, and he established and directed the Department of Archaeology. His interest in the dissemination of knowledge led him to aid in the establishment of the Arizona Archaeological and Historical Society in Tucson, and in 1935 he sponsored *The Kiva*, a quarterly publication of the society.

In addition to excavating, teaching, and writing, Cummings was also interested in academia and the community in Tucson. At the University of Arizona he was Dean of Men; Dean of the College of Letters, Arts, and Sciences; and several times President of the University. In the community, he served on the boards of various groups. He was classed as "a leader among educators in the west."

"In the classroom and in the field, the Dean was ever an inspiration to his students. His singleness of purpose, his deep honesty in his approach to knowledge, his philosophy of life, could not and did not fail to reach all who heard him—Dr. Cummings' activity as a professor—had a deeper expression than the mere imparting of knowledge. It included a distinctive human element" (Tanner, 1954).

MAJOR WORKS: *Ancient Inhabitants of the San Juan Valley* (Salt Lake City: 1910); *Cuicuilco and the Archaic Culture of Mexico* (Tucson: 1933); *Kinishba: a Prehistoric Pueblo of the Great Pueblo Period* (Tucson: 1940); *First Inhabitants of Arizona and the Southwest* (Tucson: 1953); *Indians I Have Known* (Tucson: 1952); "Kivas of the San Juan Drainage," *American Anthropologist*, vol. 17 (1915), pp. 272-282; "Primitive man in America," *The Kiva*, vol. 1, no. 1 (1935), pp. 2-3; "Apache puberty ceremony," *The Kiva*, vol. 5, no. 1 (1939), pp. 1-4; "Segazlin Mesa ruins," *The Kiva*, vol. 7, no. 1 (1941), pp. 1-4.

SOURCES: Clara Lee Tanner, "Byron Cummings, 1860-1954," *The Kiva*, vol. 20, no. 1 (October 1954), pp. 1-20; Eric K. Reed and Dale D. King (editors), *For the Dean* (Tucson: 1950).

Clara Lee Tanner

Curtis, Edward Sheriff. Photographer, author. Born in Madison (Wisconsin) 19 February 1868, died in in Los Angeles (California) 19 October 1952. Curtis began his life's work of photographing and recording American Indians and their cultures after becoming a professional photographer in Seattle, Washington, in 1891. He took his first photographs of Puget Sound's Coast Salish Indians in the mid-1890s and joined the Washington (D.C.) Academy of Science's Harriman Alaska Expedition of 1899 as chief photographer. As a result of this work he became acquainted with such nationally known outdoorsmen as John Muir, Gifford Pinchot, George Bird Grinnell and Theodore Roosevelt.

Curtis, having seen what was happening to the Indians of Alaska and Washington, determined to make a photographic record of the tribes of the western United States while their cultures were still extant. He traveled widely in the west from 1900 until 1927, spending up to half of each year on Indian reservations, making thousands of photographs and numerous documentary motion pictures. Talks and slide shows based on his work were very successful, and Curtis wrote several books and articles illustrated by his own photographs.

The financier J.P. Morgan underwrote the publication of Curtis's masterpiece, the twenty-volume set entitled *The North American Indian*.

In later life Curtis operated two photographic studios, one in Seattle and the other in Los Angeles.

MAJOR WORKS: *Indian Days of the Long Ago* (Yonkers-on-Hudson: 1914); *In the Land of the Head-Hunters* (Yonkers-on-Hudson: 1915); *The North American Indian* [20 vols.] (vols. 1-5, Cambridge, Mass.: 1907-1911; vols. 6-20, Norwood, Conn.: 1911-1930).

SOURCES: Bill Holm and George I. Quimby, *Edward S. Curtis in the Land of the War Canoes* (Seattle: 1980); Turner Brown and Elaine Partnow, *Macmillan Biographical Encyclopedia of Photographic Artists and Innovators* (New York: 1983).

David Lonergan

Curtis, Natalie (married name: Natalie Curtis Burlin). Born in New York (New York) 26 April 1875, died in Paris (France) 23 October 1921. Curtis planned a career as a concert pianist and pursued her musical education in both America and Europe. While visiting her brother in Arizona after her return to America, she became interested in Indian music, and in 1900 she began the "self-appointed task of reverently recording" native songs. As she later recalled, "the voice sang on and I turned to seek it" ("Two Pueblo Indian grinding songs"). She was, however, advised to keep her work secret since native songs and languages were forbidden in government schools. Aided by family friendship, Curtis took her plea for Native American "cultural and spiritual" rights to President Theodore Roosevelt, whom she persuaded not only to lift the assimilationist ban prohibiting Indian music and language but also to enact policy to preserve and encourage Indian music, art and poetry.

Curtis's sensitive and forward-looking scholarship was epitomized in *The Indians' Book* in which both title and prefatory note announce that "The Indians are the authors of this volume." This collection of 200 songs from eighteen tribes was so successful that Curtis received an urgent request to similarly record African-American music, which occupied the next decade of her life. Here, as with Native American music, she was indefatigable not only in meticulously recording "the spiritual life of a race" but in lecturing and writing to white America about the indigenous cultural heritage that it was ignoring if not destroying. When she was struck by a car in Paris in 1921, she had just delivered an address before the International Congress on the History of Art. At the time of her death she was planning to return to the study of Indian music and looking forward to a revision of *The Indians' Book.*

MAJOR WORKS: *Songs of Ancient America* (New York: 1905); *The Indians' Book* (New York: 1907); *Hampton Negro Folk Songs* (New York: 1918); *Songs and Tales from the Dark Continent* (New York: 1920); "Two Pueblo Indian grinding songs," *The Southern Worker*, vol. 33, no. 5 (1904), pp. 284-293.

SOURCE: Barbara A. Babcock and Nancy J. Parezo, *Daughters of the Desert: Women Anthropologists and the Native American Southwest, 1880-1980: an Illustrated Catalogue* (Albuquerque: 1988), pp. 94-97, 230-231.

Barbara A. Babcock and Nancy J. Parezo

Cushing, Frank Hamilton. Anthropologist. Born in Northeast (Pennsylvania) 22 July 1857, died in Washington (D.C.) 10 April 1900. Cushing was a colorful and controversial figure in the history of American anthropology. He presents a contrast between unquestioned brilliance and equally clear lack of real achievement, compared with what he might have accomplished.

Cushing's parents enforced little in the way of schooling, and Cushing as a youth spent much of his time wandering in nearby woods, searching for Indian artifacts or learning how to fabricate replicas of them. At eighteen he briefly attended Cornell University but was hired away as an assistant in ethnology at the Smithsonian Institution.

The following year Cushing was made the curator of ethnology; at about this time he became the protégé of JOHN WESLEY POWELL, head of the Bureau of American Ethnology. In 1879 Cushing was part of a National Museum-sponsored collecting expedition to the American southwest. He visited Zuni, one of the Pueblo Indian villages, and determined to stay longer than the three months allotted to him by the expedition. Cushing forced himself on the people of Zuni, eventually staying for more than two and a half years in his first visit, and became accepted as a member of the group. In 1881 he was initiated into the lowest rank of the Priests of the Bow. His compulsion to learn everything about the Zuni was both more expensive and more ambitious than what was desired by the Smithsonian Institution; Cushing was transferred to Powell's Bureau of Ethnology, a wise move for all concerned.

At Zuni, Cushing was developing a new research method for anthropologists. Himself untutored in ethnology and self-taught as a fieldworker, Cushing simply attempted to live as a Zuni. What is now called "participant observation" is often ascribed to BRONISLAW MALINOWSKI, yet Cushing—over thirty years earlier—spent long periods in Zuni, learned the language well, and even became a participant in rituals. He also served as an advocate for Zuni interests, helping to block a land-grab scheme put into motion by powerful Easterners. Perhaps as a result, he was recalled to Washington in 1884 during his second period of residence at Zuni.

Powell hoped for extensive reports from Cushing, but the latter apparently succumbed to some unnamed illness under stress and did not comply. While Cushing did in fact write a good deal about Zuni over the years, his contemporaries lamented how much was left undone at his death, twenty-one years after he first visited the village.

It has been suggested that Cushing at some point decided that he could no longer betray the confidences of his Zuni friends and informants. However, when one examines his life's work, it is clear that he never finished any of the projects on which he labored, nor ever adequately wrote up his findings.

Cushing, attempting to discuss the nature of social and religious life at Zuni, began in the late 1880s to use the word "culture" in a new way. Previously it had referred to civilizations or societies as entities. Cushing used "culture" to mean an integrated and internally consistent social and material whole. The new meaning of the term was largely accepted by the mid-1890s.

By 1886 Cushing had persuaded MARY HEMENWAY, an elderly widow from Massachusetts, to finance what was eventually called the Hemenway Southwestern Archaeological Expedition. It was another innovation, the first major expedition to work in the American Southwest; the group of eight included Cushing, his wife and her sister, ADOLPH BANDELIER, HERMAN F.C. TEN KATE and FREDERICK WEBB HODGE. The expedition had barely started before Cushing confided to the press that the Zuni were the descendants of the central Mexican Toltec; this did wonders for the project's publicity but disturbed many archaeologists. Cushing was not an effective leader, and the other men in the group soon persuaded him to visit California for reasons of health. The expedition continued seasonally until 1894, but Cushing had the leadership taken from him in 1889.

He suffered a collapse after his removal from the project and was for a long time unproductive and morose. He eventually returned to an earlier interest of his, the making of stone (and now copper) implements.

In 1895 Cushing became involved in the archaeology of the Florida Keys. Once again he found a wealthy benefactor, this time the wife of publisher William Randolph Hearst. Phoebe Hearst financed an expedition with Cushing in charge, which during a three-month season in 1895 found many interesting and unique objects. At least one of the finds appears to have been a forgery, made by Cushing himself; it was subsequently alleged that he faked at least one item during his Southwestern stint as well. Cushing did not admit guilt in either case.

When Cushing died he was only forty-two; with him died an unequaled knowledge of the Zuni in the late 19th century, a knowledge only partially entered into the ethnographic record.

MAJOR WORKS: "The Zuni social, mythic, and religious systems," *Popular Science Monthly*, vol. 21 (June 1882), pp. 186-192; "A study of Pueblo pottery as illustrative of Zuni culture-growth," *Annual Report of the Bureau of Ethnology*, vol. 4 (1886), pp. 467-521; "Zuni fetiches," *Annual Report of the Bureau of Ethnology*, vol. 2 (1883), pp. 9-45; "Manual concepts: a study of the influence of hand-usage on culture-growth," *American Anthropologist*, vol. 5 (1892), pp. 389-317; "Outline of Zuni creation myths," *Annual Report of the Bureau of Ethnology*, vol. 13 (1896), pp. 321-447; *Zuni Folk Tales* (New York: 1901); *Zuni Breadstuff* (New York: 1920); *Zuni: Selected Writings of Frank Hamilton Cushing* (edited by Jesse Green) (Lincoln: 1979); *The Mythic World of the Zuni* (edited by Barton Wright) (Albuquerque: 1988).

SOURCES: Joan Mark, *4 Anthropologists: an American Science in its Early Years* (New York: 1980); "Cushing, Frank Hamilton" in: *National Cyclopaedia of American Biography*, vol. 11 (New York: 1909), pp. 26-27; Walter Hough, "Cushing, Frank Hamilton" in: *Dictionary of American Biography*, vol. 4 (New York: 1930), p. 630.

David Lonergan

Czarnocki, Adam (used the pseudonym Zorian Dołęga Chodakowski). Amateur researcher, pioneer of Polish and Slavic folk studies. Born in Podhajna near Nieswież (Polish Republic, now in the U.S.S.R.) 24 December 1784, died in Petrovskoe in the Province of Tver (Russia) 17 November 1825. While serving a term in the Tsar's army in Siberia (1808-1811), he collected material relating to the local ethnography and topographic names. Starting in 1812 he traveled under his assumed name across Southern Ruthenia and Galicia. In the years 1820-1821 he set off on a journey across European Russia.

Czarnocki collected songs as well as ethnographic, historical, archaeological and geographical material. He believed strongly in learning from the personal inspection of folk culture. In his investigations of ancient Slavic artifacts, he sought out information on the culture of the past, emphasizing the idea of Slavic unity in prehistoric times and attempting to determine the specific characteristics of national cultures. Czarnocki also formulated the tasks and aims for future folkloric investigations. He considered the folk as a carrier of national elements of culture. In his personal archives he left in manuscript a collection of Ruthenian and Polish songs, material for a historical and geographical dictionary with a map of castle ruins and a treatise on ancient roads.

MAJOR WORKS: "O Słowiańszczyźnie przed chrześcijaństwem" ["On Slavic culture before Christianity"], *Ćwiczenia Naukowe*, vol. 2, no. 5 (1818), pp. 3-27; "Puti soobshcheniĭa v drevneĭ Rossii" ["Crossroads in ancient Russia"], *Russkiĭ istoricheskiĭ sbornik*, vol. 1 (1837), pp. 1-50; "Donesenie o pervykh uspekhakh v Rossii Zorĭana Doluga-Chodakovskago" ["Reports on the initial successes in Russia of Zorian Dołęga Chodakowski"], *Russkiĭ istoricheskiĭ sbornik*, vol. 8 (1844), pp. 1-378.

SOURCES: Adam Fischer, "Zorian Dołęga Chodakowski," *Lud*, vol. 36 (1945), pp. 89-106; Julian Maślanka, *Chodakowski Zorian Dołęga: jego miejsce w kulturze polskiej i wpływ na polskie piśmiennictwo romantyczne* [*Chodakowski Zorian Dołęga: His Place in Polish Culture and his Influence on Polish Romantic Literature*] (Wrocław: 1965); Ryszard Walicki, "Wacław Maciejowski i Chodakowski Zorian Dołęga: studium z dziejów słowianofilstwa polskiego" ["Wacław Maciejowski and Chodakowski Zorian Dołęga: a study of the history of Polish Slavophilism"], *Archiwum Historii Filozofii i Myśli Społecznej*, vol. 13 (1967), pp. 271-301.

Maria Niewiadomska and Iwona Grzelakowska
[Translation from Polish: Joel Janicki]

Czarnowski, Stefan Zygmunt. Sociologist, specialist in the Celts, historian of religion. Born in Kroczew (Poland) 1 September 1879, died in Warsaw (Poland) 29 December 1937. Czarnowski studied in Leipzig and Berlin and in Paris at the École Pratique des Hautes Études under the direction of Henri Hubert (1872-1927) and MARCEL MAUSS. In 1930 he was awarded the Chair of the History of Culture at Warsaw University (which was expanded in 1933 to include sociology).

Czarnowski accepted and propagated Émile Durkheim's sociological ideas. As a researcher and teacher he was especially engaged in the problems of the sociology of religion. He introduced a wide range of historical material for examination and was able to proceed from a concrete analysis of facts to a precise general theory. His works on the Celts as well as his *Kultura,* in addition to their rich bibliographies, contain a theory recognized as fundamental for investigative studies concerning the ethnography of Europe. He introduced the preliminary principal of the "complete local society." He analyzed the mechanism of cultural change under conditions of contact between two cultures. Under the influence of Durkheim he arrived at the research postulate of social relations as objects. By means of Marx's model he adapted in his investigations of culture an experiential method in which experiment is replaced by a comparative method. His social and political interests and his approach to scientific work as a fundamental category of objective social relations and their superstructure led him to investigations of the culture of the working class. Czarnowski also formulated criteria for distinguishing cultural factors, perceiving culture as a unity of objectified elements of the output of society, common to a number of groups and due to its objectivity capable of expanding spatially.

MAJOR WORKS: *Le culte des héros et ses conditions sociales: Saint Patrick, l'héros national de l'Irlande* (Paris: 1919); *Idee kierownicze ludzkości* [*Leading Ideas of Humanity*] (Warsaw: 1928); "Podłoże ruchu chłopskiego: uwagi socjologiczne" ["Foundations of the peasant movement: a sociological approach"], *Zagadnienia Pracy Kulturalnej*, vol. 2 (1935), pp. 1-24; *Kultura* [*Culture*] (Warsaw: 1938); *Społeczeństwo—kultura: prace z socjologii i historii kultury* [*Society—Culture: Studies in the Sociology and History of Culture*] (Warsaw: 1939).

SOURCES: Stefan Czarnowski, *Wybór pism socjologicznych* [*Selection of Sociological Writings*] (Warsaw: 1982); Stanisław Kot, "Czarnowski, Stefan Zygmunt" in: *Polski słownik biograficzny* [*Polish Biographical Dictionary*], vol. 4 (Warsaw: 1938), pp. 238-240.

Maria Niewiadomska and Iwona Grzelakowska
[*Translation from Polish: Joel Janicki*]

Czekanowski, Jan. Anthropologist, ethnologist. Born in Głuchów (Poland) 6 October 1882, died in Szczecin (Poland) 20 July 1965. Czekanowski studied in Zürich, obtaining his doctorate in 1906. While working in the Museum für Völkerkunde (Ethnographic Museum) in Berlin he participated in an expedition to the regions between the Upper Nile and the Congo rivers (1907-1909). From 1913 he was associated with the University of Lwów (1913-1941), the Catholic University of Lublin (1944-1949) and the University of Poznań (1946-1960).

Czekanowski was particularly interested in African and Slavic studies and in methodology. Under the influence of the Vienna branch of the Cultural-Historical School he introduced "historico-migratory" theory into Poland. He was an adherent of the cartographic method and a pioneer in the use of the quantitative method in ethnology, believing that an index of correlations of phenomena would establish their relative chronology on broad reaches of territory. In the field of Slavistics he held the position that one can arrive at the synthetic understanding of the ethnogenesis of the Slavs through investigation of physical-anthropological, archaeological, linguistic and ethnological data. In the field of African studies he investigated the functioning of pastoral states and their ethnic relations.

MAJOR WORKS: *Forschungen im Nil-Kongo-Zwischengebeit* [5 vols.] (Leipzig: 1911-1927); *Zarys metod statystycznych w zastosowaniach do antropologii* [*Outline of Statistical Methods for Antropology*] (Warsaw: 1913); *Wstęp do historii Słowian: perspektywy antropologiczne, etnograficzne, prehistoryczne i językoznawcze* [*Introduction to the History of the Slavs: Anthropological, Ethnographic, Prehistoric and Linguistic Perspectives*] (Lwów: 1927); *Polska–Słowiańszczyzna: perspektywy antropologiczne* [*Poland–Slavdom: Anthropological Perspectives*] (Warsaw: 1948); "Badania antropologiczne w międzyrzeczu Nilu i Kongo: crania africana" ["Anthropological investigations in the territories between the Nile and Congo: crania africana"], *Przegląd Antropologiczny*, vol. 17 (1951), pp. 34-188; *W głąb lasów Aruwimi* [*In the Depths of the Aruwimi Forests*] (Wrocław: 1958); "Założenia teoretyczne antropologii polskiej a obserwowane fakty" ["Theoretical foundations of Polish anthropology and observed facts"], *Materiały i Prace Antropologiczne*, vol. 63 (1962), pp. 1-40.

SOURCES: Małgorzata Terlecka (editor), *Historia etnografii polskiej* [*History of Polish Ethnography*] (Wrocław: 1973); *Księga pamiątkowa dla uczczenia 60 lat pracy naukowej Jana Czekanowskiego* [*Commemorative Volume in Honor of 60 years of the Scientific Work of Jan Czekanowski*] (Wrocław: 1964).

Maria Niewiadomska and Iwona Grzelakowska
[*Translation from Polish: Joel Janicki*]

Czermak, Wilhelm. Egyptologist, Africanist. Born in Vienna (Austria) 10 September 1889, died in Vienna (Austria) 13 March 1953. After attending gymnasia in Prague and Vienna, Czermak began his studies of Egyptology and African languages with H. Junker in Vienna in 1907. He also studied Semitic languages under D.H. Müller and M. Bittner. In 1911, he was awarded his doctorate for a work in Arabic linguistics, and between 1912 and 1914 he served as an assistant at the ongoing excavations of the Giza pyramids being conducted by the Academy of Sciences and on several expeditions investigating the dialects of Nubia. During the war he was a reconnaissance officer in the northern Syrian city of Aleppo. He obtained his *Habilitation* in 1919 in Hamito-Semitic and African languages at Vienna, where in 1925 he became *außerordentlicher Professor* in African studies and, in 1931, full professor (*Ordinarius*) in the field of Egyptology and African studies as Junker's successor. In 1935, at the invitation of the Geographical Society in Cairo, he delivered lectures in the Arabic language, of which he had a solid command. In 1939 he became a corresponding member of the Vienna Academy of Sciences and was made a regular member in 1945. At the beginning of 1952 he was elected rector of the University of Vienna.

Psycholinguistics and the philosophy of language were particularly important for Czermak; thus, in African studies he was above all interested in "local representations" and their significance for the grammatical structure of language. The search for deeper connections and for the meanings that lay behind surface linguistic manifestations is also quite evident in Czermak's works in Egyptology. Investigation of the Egyptian supernatural world with its images of life after death was of great concern to him. Thus the Vienna Commission for Research on the Egyptian Book of the Dead—whose most accurate interpreter he was considered to be—was organized at his instigation. In all of Czermak's works one recognizes both a strict logic of pure scientific deduction and also a great capacity for empathy with the spiritual life of non-European cultures.

MAJOR WORKS: "Ein Beitrag zur ägyptischen Beduinenpoesie," *Wiener Zeitschrift für die Kunde des Morgenlandes*, vol. 26 (1912), pp. 253-262; *Kordofannubische Studien* (Vienna: 1919) (= *Sitzungsberichte der Wiener Akademie der Wissenschaften*. vol. 177, Abhandlung 1); *Zur Sprache der Ewe-Neger: ein Beitrag zur Seelenkunde* (Innsbruck: 1924) (= *Supplementa Africana*, Folge 1); "Die Lokalvorstellung und ihre Bedeutung für den grammatischen Aufbau afrikanischer Sprachen" in: Franz Boas [et al.] (editors), *Festschrift Meinhof* (Hamburg: 1927), pp. 204-222; "Rhythmus und Umbildung im Ägyptisch-Koptischen," *Zeitschrift für Ägyptische Sprache und Altertumskunde*, vol. 63 (1928), pp. 78-89; *Die Laute der ägyptischen Sprache* [2 vols.] (Vienna: 1931-1934); "Sprachgeist und tieferer Wortsinn in Afrika," *Anzeiger der philosophisch-historischen Klasse der Österreichischen Akademie der Wissenschaften*, no. 51/3 (1951), pp. 17-29.

SOURCES: W.R. Dawson and E.P. Uphill, *Who Was Who in Egyptology* (London: 1972); Hermann Jungraithmayr and Rudolf Leger, "Czermak, Wilhelm" in: H. Jungraithmayr and W.J.G. Möhlig (editors), *Lexikon der Afrikanistik* (Berlin: 1983), pp. 66-67; A. Klingenheben and J. Lukas, "Zum Tode von Wilhelm Czermak," *Afrika und Übersee*, vol. 37 (1952-1953), p. 97; R. Meister, "Wilhelm Czermak +," *Forschungen und Fortschritte*, vol. 27 (1953), pp. 120-121; H. Mitscha-Märheim "Wilhelm Czermak +," *Mitteilungen der Anthropologischen Gesellschaft in Wien*, vol. 83 (1954), pp. 61-63; G. Thausing, "Wilhelm Czermak +, 13. März 1953," *Wiener Zeitschrift für die Kunde des Morgenlandes*, vol. 52 (1953), pp. 1-6.

Herrmann Jungraithmayr and Rudolf Leger
[Translation from German: Robert B. Marks Ridinger]

d

Dal', V.I. (Vladimir Ivanovich). Ethnographer, folklorist, lexicographer, writer. Born in Lugansk (Ukraine) 10 (22) November 1801, died in Moscow (Russia) 22 September (4 October) 1872. Dal' was a prominent collector of folklore and materials on folklife. His major work, *Tolkovyĭ slovar' zhivogo velikorusskogo ĭazyka*, preserves his scientific knowledge and has warranted numerous editions since its original publication. The lexical and folkloristic material in Dal''s work is closely connected with ethnography. Dal' also published the collection *Poslovitsy russkogo naroda*, the ethnographic essays *Bolgarka, Ural'skiĭ kazakh* and other works. As a Slavophile Dal' defended the distinctiveness of Russian folklore.

Dal' was awarded the Lomonosov Prize of the Academy of Sciences and was elected an honorary member of the St. Petersburg Academy of Sciences.

MAJOR WORKS: *Polnoe sobranie sochineniĭ* [10 vols.] (St. Petersburg: 1897-1898); *Tolkovyĭ slovar' zhivogo velikorusskogo ĭazyka* [4 vols.] (St. Petersburg and Moscow: 1880; 2nd ed., Moscow: 1882; reprinted, Moscow: 1978); *Poslovitsy russkogo naroda* (Moscow: 1984).

SOURCES: A.N. Pypin, *Istoriĭa russkoĭ étnografii*, vol. 1 (St. Petersburg: 1890); S.A. Tokarev, *Istoriĭa russkoĭ étnografii: dooktĭabr'skiĭ period* (Moscow: 1966), pp. 233-238.

A.M. Reshetov
[Translation from Russian: Thomas L. Mann]

D'Albertis, Luigi Maria. Explorer, zoologist, ethnographer. Born in Voltri (Italy) 21 November 1841, died in Sassari (Italy) 1901. D'Albertis's early interest in natural sciences was stimulated by the French missionary and naturalist Armand David (1826-

1900), who was his teacher in secondary school and who eventually would make important contributions to the geographical and zoological knowledge of northern Tibet. Father David also introduced D'Albertis to GIACOMO DORIA. By making use of the materials kept in the Museo Civico di Storia Naturale (Civic Museum of Natural History) in Genoa, D'Albertis rounded out his studies of zoology and ethno-anthropology as an autodidact. While at this museum, he met Odoardo Beccari with whom he made his first voyage, in 1871, to New Guinea; in time three other excursions were to follow: in 1875 to the island of Roro (Yule) and in 1876 and 1877 along the Fly, the main river of New Guinea. All of these voyages were undertaken with the minimal financial support of the Museum in Genoa, and in all of them D'Albertis traveled alone, accompanied by a few Malay servants.

During his numerous long stays in New Guinea he made substantial zoological and ethnographical collections (the former for the Museum in Genoa, the latter for the museum of anthropology in Florence). Moreover, he compiled accurate anthropological observations. Upon his return to Italy he wrote an account of his journeys, which was published in 1880 by Sampson Low and Co. in both London and Turin.

Solitary, romantic, courageous and impulsive, D'Albertis cut the ideal figure of a 19th-century explorer. His book, presented in the form of a diary, contains many often ingenuous reflections on the artificiality of civilization and the "natural" freedom of primitive life; it is also well stocked with ethnographical observations, as well as physical and racial descriptions of the natives, which are among the very first scientific observations made on the Papuans of New Guinea.

MAJOR WORKS: "Un mese tra i Papuani del Monte Arfak," *Bollettino della Società Geografica Italiana*, vol. 10 (1873), pp. 71-87; "Escursione a Mou: note etnografiche" [letter to Cesare Correnti], *Cosmos*, vol. 3 (1875/76), pp. 364-379; *Alla Nuova Guinea: cio che ho veduto e cio che ho fatto* (Turin: 1880) [tr.: *New Guinea: What I Did and What I Saw* (London: 1880)].

SOURCES: M. Ghiglione, *Luigi Maria D'Albertis e il suo contributo alla conoscenza dell'etnografia papuana* (Genoa: 1941); U. Santini, *L.M. D'Albertis e l'esplorazione della Nuova Guinea* (Rome, Florence and Padua: 1937); P. Scotti, *Contributi di L.M. D'Albertis alla etnologia della Nuova Guinea* (Florence: 1941); Sandra Puccini, "La comunicazione etnografica: incontri con l'altro nei resoconti di viaggio dell'Ottocento," *Problemi del Socialismo*, no. 1 (1988), pp. 184-207.

Sandra Puccini
[Translation from Italian: Chris Nissen]

Dall, William H. (William Healey). Naturalist. Born in Boston (Massachusetts) 21 August 1845, died in Washington (D.C.) 27 March 1927. Dall was educated at private schools in West Newton and Boston in Massachusetts. He studied medicine at Harvard but did not graduate. For the sake of experience, he also spent a brief period working under Louis Agassiz (1807-1873) at the Museum of Comparative Zoology at Harvard University; and later, while employed by the Illinois Central Railway in Chicago, he worked under similar arrangements at the Academy of Science museum under ROBERT KENNICOTT and at the Smithsonian Institution in Washington, D.C., under Spencer F. Baird (1823-1887).

Determined to devote himself to scientific work, Dall traveled repeatedly to Alaska between 1865 and 1899. Through exploration sponsored by the Western Union

Telegraph, the United States Coast and Geodetic Survey, the United States Geological Survey, the Smithsonian Institution, and E.H. Harriman, Dall developed into one of the foremost scientists concerned with Alaska, his work helping to bring the potential of that land to official and public attention. His interests were far-reaching and included many areas of natural science. In anthropology, he attempted to name and provide data about the tribes of Alaska and the Yukon. His work included synonymies and population figures. In addition, he made a large collection of Eskimo and Athabaskan artifacts and recorded some linguistic data. Dall also carried out archaeological investigations on the Aleutians. It has been pointed out that his "were the earliest excavations in Alaska to take careful note of location and relationships among artifacts and to note and record evidence of stratification" (Dekin).

MAJOR WORKS: *Alaska and Its Resource* (Boston: 1870); "On the distribution of the natives tribes of Alaska and the adjacent territory," *American Association for the Advancement of Science, Proceedings*, vol. 18 (1870), pp. 263-273; "Tribes of the extreme Northwest," *Contributions to North American Ethnology*, vol. 1 (1877), 1-156; "Native tribes of Alaska," *American Association for the Advancement of Science, Proceedings*, vol. 34 (1885), pp. 3-19.

SOURCES: Paul Bartsch [et al.], *A Bibliography and Short Biographical Sketch of William Healey Dall* (Washington: 1946) (= *Smithsonian Miscellaneous Collections*, vol. 104); Marcus Benjamin, "William Healey Dall" in: Allen Johnson and Dumas Malone, *Dictionary of American Biography*, vol. 5 (1930), pp. 35-36; Albert A. Dekin, Jr., "The Arctic" in: James E. Fitting (editor), *The Development of North American Archaeology* (University Park, Pennsylvania: 1973), pp. 15-48; Edward A. Herron, "William Healey Dall: Alaska pioneer," *Natural History*, vol. 57 (1948), pp. 176-179; C. Hart Merriam, "William Healey Dall," *Science*, vol. 65 (1927), pp. 345-347.

James R. Glenn

Damrong Rajanubhab, Prince (originally: Prince Disvarakumarn). Administrator, archaeologist, historian. Born in the Grand Palace in Bangkok (Thailand) 21 June 1862, died in Bangkok (Thailand) 1 December 1943. Prince Damrong was the son of King Mongkut (Rama IV, reigned 1851-1868) and Chao Chom Marnda Chum. After his education in Thai, Pali and English, in 1880 Prince Damrong was placed in charge of the Royal Pages; in 1885 he was appointed full commander of the corps and also became head of the incipient Royal Survey Department. In 1888 he became a deputy commander in the army's Military Operations Department. By 1889 (when he was transferred to take charge of educational affairs), he had attained the rank of major general.

In 1890, Prince Damrong became Minister of Public Instruction, and while holding this office he served as a special ambassador to the courts of Europe in 1891 and 1892. During this period, King Chulalongkorn (Rama V, reigned 1868-1910), his elder half-brother, was gradually restructuring the traditional Thai system of administration. In 1892, when the modern system of functional ministries was officially proclaimed, Prince Damrong was appointed Minister of the Interior.

For the next twenty-three years Prince Damrong headed only one ministry. He began with a ministerial post that had authority over only the up-country towns and dependency states away from the sea-coast, but it rapidly evolved into a true Interior Ministry. His tenure was a remarkable burst of creativity, as he completely restructured the traditional system of provincial administration, consolidated hundreds of governorships into the modern system of about seventy departments, organized a civil-service school to train the incipient centralized bureaucracy and helped to find new methods of harnessing the kingdom's resources (notably provincial taxation, forests and mines) for the benefit of the national treasury. In 1895 all powers over the peninsular territories were transferred to Prince Damrong's ministry, thereby bringing responsibility for provincial affairs throughout the country under the venue of a single ministry for the first time.

After leaving the cabinet in the reign of King Vajiravudh (Rama VI, reigned 1910-1925), Prince Damrong served from 1915 to 1932 as Chairman of the Capital Library (the present-day National Library), where he produced several books on the history, archaeology, literature and traditions of Thailand, which are still used as textbooks or reference documents. This literary work continued until his death. In April 1926, King Prajadhipok (Rama VII, reigned 1925-1935) founded the Royal Academy and appointed Prince Damrong chairman. Under his guidance the National Museum came into being. In November 1926 he was appointed to the newly established Supreme Council of State, holding the position until the Council was abolished in July 1932 after the change from the absolute monarchy into the constitutional one.

In November 1933 Prince Damrong moved to Penang and took up residence the following month in Cinnamon Hall, a spacious home originally owned by a member of the royal family of Kedah. Prince Damrong lived at Cinnamon Hall until October 1942, when he returned to his family home, Voradis Palace in Bangkok, during World War II, where he died, aged eighty-one.

MAJOR WORKS: "The foundation of Ayuthia," *Journal of the Siam Society*, vol. 1 (1904), pp. 7-10; "Historical sketch of Lophburi," *Journal of the Siam Society*, vol. 5, no. 3 (1908), pp. 5-6; "The story of the records of Siamese history," *Journal of the Siam Society*, vol. 11, no. 2 (1914), pp. 1-20; *Phrarātchaphongsāwadāan Krung Rattanakōsin ratchakān thī 2* [*The Reign of King Rama II of Bangkok*] (Krungthep: 1916); "Siamese history prior to the founding of Ayuddhyā, translated from the Siamese by J. Crosby," *Journal of the Siam Society*, vol. 13, no. 2 (1919), pp. 1-66; "The Golden Pavilion at Wat Sai ... translated from the Siamese by B.O. Cartwright," *Journal of the Siam Society*, vol. 14, no. 2 (1921), pp. 1-6; "The introduction of Western culture in Siam," *Journal of the Siam Society*, vol. 20, no. 2 (1926), pp. 89-100; "Wat Benchamabopit and its collection of images of the Buddha," *Journal of the Siam Society*, vol. 22, no. 1 (1928), pp. 19-28; *Thai rop Phamā* [*The Wars between the Thai and the Burmese*] (Krungthep: 1951); "Angkor from a Siamese point of view," *Journal of the Siam Society*, vol. 19, no. 3 (1952), pp. 141-152; *Monuments of the Buddha in Siam* (2nd rev. ed., Bangkok: 1973) (= *Siam Society Monograph*, no. 2).

SOURCES: A.B. Griswold, "Thoughts on a centenary," *Journal of the Siam Society*, vol. 52, part 1 (1964), pp. 21-[55]; Benjamin Batson, "Sources in Thai history: the papers of Prince Damrong," *Journal of the Siam Society*, vol. 63, part 2 (1975), pp. 334-342.

M.C. Subhadradis Diskul

D'Ancona, Alessandro. Historian of Italian literature, philologist. Born in Pisa (Italy) 1835, died in Florence (Italy) 1914. D'Ancona taught Italian literature at the University of Pisa. He was among the first to apply the philological and comparative criteria characteristic of a positivistic scientific approach to the study of popular poetry. It must be added that in his works there were still many romantic notions, such as the idea that popular poetry is a collective and anonymous expression of the "folk"—who are gifted with poetic skills not found among the contemporary masses.

One of his principal fields of study was the history of Italian theatre (*Le origini del teatro in Italia*). He was especially interested in the continuous interchange over time between popular and literary drama. He also wrote on the origin of Italian theatre, attributing it to the first forms of Christian liturgical representation, from which dramatic *laude* (hymns of praise), *devozioni* (devotions) and miracle-plays progressively developed.

D'Ancona also concerned himself with popular Italian poetry and—in close contact with the ideas of COSTANTINO NIGRA—proposed a theory of the origin of lyrical one-stanza poems (e.g., *stornelli, strambotti, rispetti*, etc.), suggesting that they could be traced back to a type of Sicilian tetrastich (quatrain) that had diffused with numerous variations throughout Italy. The theory of the "Sicilian monogenesis" of the tetrastic (which was based particularly on meter) did not inspire unanimous agreement on the part of the scholars of the epoch. However, D'Ancona anticipated subsequent scholarly thought in his work on the modes of propagation of the poetic compositions which he situated (among other places) in the diffusion of leaflets containing the transcriptions of the oral versions.

The last work published by D'Ancona was a collection of brief essays (*Viaggiatori e avventurieri*), which remained incomplete but would have constituted the beginning of a substantial collection of the accounts of foreign travelers in Italy and Italian travelers in Europe from the middle of the 16th through the 17th century and whose ultimate goal was to deepen our understanding of the circulation of culture.

MAJOR WORKS: *Le origini del teatro in Italia* (Rome: 1877); *La poesia popolare italiana* (Florence: 1878); *Studi di critica e storia letteraria* (Bologna: 1880); *Studi sulla letteratura italiana dei primi secoli* (Ancona: 1884); *Viaggiatori e avventurieri* (Florence: 1912).

SOURCES: A.M. Cirese, *Cultura egemonica e culture subalterne* (Palermo: 1980); G. Cocchiara, *Storia del folklore in Italia* (Palermo: 1981).

Gianni Vanucci
[Translation from Italian: CW and Paolo Gnecco]

Dart, Raymond A. Anthropologist, anatomist. Born in Toowong, Brisbane (Queensland) 4 February 1893, died in Sandton, near Johannesburg (South Africa) 22 November 1988. He graduated in science from the University of Queensland (Brisbane) and in medicine from the University of Sydney. His early career was marked by war service in France and England (1918-1919), teaching duties as a Demonstrator and then Senior Demonstrator in Anatomy under Sir GRAFTON ELLIOT SMITH at University College, London, and a year as one of the first two foreign fellows of the Rockefeller Foundation in the United States, spent mainly in the Anatomy Department of Washington University, St. Louis, Missouri, under Robert J. Terry. In January 1923 Dart succeeded E.P. Stibbe as Professor of Anatomy at the newly established University of the Witwatersrand, Johannesburg. For thirty-six years he filled the Chair of Anatomy; for eighteen of those years he was Dean of the School of Medicine. Some years after his retirement in 1958, he was appointed United Steelworkers of America Professor of Anthropology in the Avery Postgraduate Institute of the Institutes for the Achievement of Human Potential, Philadelphia (1966-1986), spending half of each year in Philadelphia and half in Johannesburg until he was ninety-three.

Dart's name will be forever associated with the discovery of the Taung skull, the first of Africa's early hominids to be found, and with his prescient recognition of its significance. The skull was recovered from a limestone deposit at the Buxton Limeworks, near Taung (then called Taungs) in the northern Cape Province in November 1924. It reached him in Johannesburg on 28 November 1924. Once he had chipped it out of the encompassing matrix, Dart recognized that the skull showed signs of having been carried erect on the spine, its canine teeth were small like those of hominids, its brain-size was small like those of apes, though Dart detected signs that the form of the brain was human-like in several respects. Then he made a great intellectual leap: he interpreted this curious blend of traits as evidence of the former presence in Africa of an anthropoid that had moved substantially in a human direction. He made this claim in a historic article published in *Nature* on 7 February 1925. He named the species represented by the Taung skull *Australopithecus africanus*. Furthermore, he reminded his colleagues that in 1871 Charles Darwin had predicted that such ancestral forms were more likely to be found in Africa than anywhere else.

Dart's claims were received with surprise, derision and hostility. Objections were based on the geographical locality of the find, the nature of the creature's anatomy, its infantile age at death, its incompatibility with the ill-starred Piltdown bones—even the Greco-Latin name Dart had given the species! For twenty-five years the place of *Australopithecus* was in dispute. Not until many more specimens were found in the Transvaal and carefully compared with the skeletons of modern apes was it realized that Dart had been right; moreover, it came to be accepted that they should be classified in the Hominidae (the family of man).

Dart was thoroughly vindicated and in 1984 a prominent scientific periodical included the Taung child and what Dart made of it as one of twenty scientific discoveries that had shaped the life of man in the 20th century. Perhaps the most significant feature of Dart's breakthrough lay in his willingness to overlook the small brain-size of *Australopithecus*. Brain-size alone, he declared in a 1956 paper, was not the acid test; the form of the brain was more important. Dart had shown that the principle of mosaic evolution had applied to these early claimants to human ancestry, that is, that some parts of the body had hominized in advance of other parts. He had shown, too, that the particular pattern of mosaicism in *Australopithecus* was totally at variance with that prognosticated by Dart's old mentor, Elliot Smith, who had held that brain enlargement must have been in the vanguard of evolution: instead, in *Australopithecus* absolute brain enlargement was hardly evident, whereas dental and postural hominization were!

Another revolutionary idea flowed from Dart's fertile brain in the 1950s. He proposed that before the Stone Age, there had been a Bone Age—an era in which *Australopithecus* had used as implements the bones, teeth and horns of his prey animals. Dart's Osteodontokeratic Culture was based on this concept. His novel hypothesis arose from his study of thousands of fossilized, broken bones of antelopes in the *Australopithecus*-bearing cave of Makapansgat in the northern Transvaal. This notion of Dart has been largely rejected as evidence has accumulated that big cats, hyenas and porcupines were probably the bone breakers and accumulators. But Dart's hypothesis had a remarkable spin-off. When he first proposed his bone tool theory in 1955, scarcely anything was known of what other animals, or agencies like sun and water, did to bones after death. To disprove Dart's proposal, a host of new studies were made on what happens to bones after death. A new scientific discipline came into being, called taphonomy (*taphos*, Greek, a grave). Dart's ideas were a major catalyst in the birth of this new field.

Thus, it may be claimed of Dart that he effected a revolution in knowledge about man's place in nature and that he triggered the foundation of a new scientific discipline. To few men of the 20th century has it been given so greatly to expand the frontiers of humanity's understanding of its own origins.

MAJOR WORKS: "Australopithecus Africanus: the man-ape of South Africa," *Nature*, vol. 115 (1925), pp. 195-199; "Cultural status of the South African man-apes," *Annual Report of the Board of Regents of the Smithsonian Institution* (1955), pp. 317-318; *The Osteodontokeratic Culture of Australopithecus Prometheus* (Pretoria: 1957) (= *Transvaal Museum Memoirs*, no. 10); (with Dennis Craig) *Adventures with the Missing Link* (New York and London: 1959).

SOURCES: Robert Broom, *Finding the Missing Link* (London: 1950); Raymond A. Dart with Dennis Craig, *Adventures with the Missing Link* (New York and London: 1959); Phillip V. Tobias, "Homage to Emeritus Professor Raymond Arthur Dart on his 75th birthday, 4 February 1968," *South African Journal of Science*, vol. 64 (1968), pp. 41-140 [contains list of works to 1967]; R.A. Dart, "Recollections of a reluctant anthropologist," *Journal of Human Evolution*, vol. 2, no. 6 (1973), pp. 417-422; Frances Wheelhouse, *Raymond Arthur Dart: a Pictorial Profile* (Sydney: 1983); Phillip V. Tobias, *Dart, Taung and the "Missing Link"* (Johannesburg: 1984).

Phillip V. Tobias

De Gubernatis, Angelo.   India specialist, folklorist, mythologist, man of letters. Born in Turin (Italy) 7 April 1840, died in Rome (Italy) 26 February 1913. After graduation (Turin, 1861), De Gubernatis went to Berlin to study with Albert Weber and FRANZ BOPP. In 1863, when he was barely twenty-three, he was offered the chair of Sanskrit and comparative glottology at the University of Florence. In 1890 he went to Rome to teach Italian literature. His many works in comparative mythology became so well known internationally that they were published in England and France before being published in Italy.

Following the theories of Max Müller (1823-1900), De Gubernatis did research on the nuptial, birth and burial customs among Indoeuropean peoples, thus (along with GIUSEPPE PITRÈ) interrupting the exclusive focus on music and poetry that had characterized Italian folklore scholarship up to the middle of the 19th century.

In 1885 he went to India and the following year, with the rare manuscripts and ethnographic material collected on his trip, he established the Museo Indiano (Indian Museum) of Florence and the Società Asiatica Italiana (Italian Asian Society).

De Gubernatis was a very productive and eclectic scholar. His interests included Italian literature and history. He was a man of letters, a dramatist, a biographer and a founder and director of important scholarly journals. In 1893 he founded the Società Nazionale per le Tradizioni Popolari (National Society for Popular Traditions) and its *Rivista*. In spite of the fact that the society was short-lived (it folded in 1895) its orientation was remarkable: De Gubernatis believed that the task of folklore studies was the study of the culture of subordinate classes and of the clashes of different peoples. In this he followed in the path of the philosopher Carlo Cattaneo (1801-1869) and of GIOVENALE VEGEZZI RUSCALLA and anticipated some of the positions of LAMBERTO LORIA.

De Gubernatis was active in the Società Italiana di Antropologia ed Etnologia (Italian Anthropological and Ethnological Society) founded by PAOLO MANTEGAZZA. He was also a sustaining member of the Società di Etnografia Italiana (Italian Society of

Ethnography) founded by Loria whose main theoretical underpinnings had been anticipated by his own Società per le Tradizioni Popolari.

MAJOR WORKS: *Storia comparata degli usi nuziali in Italia e presso gli altri popoli indoeuropei* (Milan: 1869); *Zoological Mythology* (London: 1872) [tr.: *Mythologie zoologiques, ou les légendes animales* [2 vols.] (Paris: 1874)]; *Storia popolare degli usi funebri indoeuropei* (Milan: 1873) [2nd ed., *Storia comparata degli usi funebri in Italia e presso gli altri popoli indoeuropei* (Milan: 1878)]; *Max Müller e la mitologia comparata* (Florence: 1875); *Storia comparata degli usi natalizi in Italia e presso gli altri popoli indoeuropei* (Milan: 1878); *La mythologie des plantes, ou légendes du Règne végétal* (2 vols.) (Paris: 1878-1882); *Mitologia comparata* (Milan: 1889); *Peregrinazioni indiane* [3 vols.] (Florence: 1886-1887); "Le sommosse popolari ed il folklore," *Rivista delle Tradizioni Popolari Italiane*, vol. 1 (1893), pp. 171-172; "La storia nell'etnografia," *Atti del Primo congresso di etnografia italiana* (Perugia: 1912), pp. 65-70.

SOURCES: Giuseppe Cocchiara, *Storia degli studi delle tradizioni popolari in Italia* (Palermo: 1947); Alberto Mario Cirese, *Cultura egemonica e culture subalterne* (Palermo: 1971); Alberto Mario Cirese, *Intellettuali, folklore, istinto di classe: note su Verga, Deledda, Scotellaro, Gramsci* (Turin: 1976); Rosi Susanna, "Gli studi di orientalistica a Firenze nella seconda metà dell'Ottocento" in: U. Marazzi (editor), *La conoscenza dell'Asia e dell'Africa in Italia nei secoli XVIII e XIX* (Naples: 1984), vol. 1, tomo 1, pp. 103-120; V. Grossato, "L'interpretazione naturalista dei miti e dei simboli negli scritti indologici di A. De Gubernatis" in: U. Marazzi (editor), *La conoscenza dell'Asia e dell'Africa in Italia nei secoli XVIII e XIX* (Naples: 1984), vol. 2, tomo 1, pp. 417-434.

Sandra Puccini
[Translation from Italian: Gianna Panofsky]

De Martino, Ernesto. Historian of religions, anthropologist, folklorist. Born in Naples (Italy) 1 December 1908, died in Rome (Italy) 6 May 1965. De Martino has been referred to as the father of modern Italian anthropology (Filippini, 1984), and he has certainly been one of the most significant and influential figures in contemporary Italian folklore studies and anthropology.

De Martino's intellectual career spanned a dramatic period in Italian political history, beginning in the fascist era (though De Martino himself early took an active anti-fascist posture) and carrying through World War II and into the socialist movements of the post-war period. His work demonstrates an original blend of the major intellectual trends of these times and reflects his activist engagement with a complex and tumultuous political milieu.

De Martino was brought up as a Protestant in Catholic Italy, an experience that may have contributed to his lifelong interest in popular religion. As a student at the University of Naples, he pursued classical studies, working under historian Adolfo Omodeo (1889-1946) and in 1932 received his degree (*laurea*) in letters. Subsequently, he came under the influence of historian and philosopher Benedetto Croce (1866-1952) and of RAFFAELE PETTAZZONI, a historian of religions with some interest in ethnology. De Martino's best known work of this period, *Naturalismo e storicismo nell'etnologia*, is essentially a Crocean critique of the dominant ethnological approaches to religion, particularly of LUCIEN LÉVY-BRUHL and Émile Durkheim, for their lack of historical perspective.

At about the time of the publication of *Naturalismo e storicismo nell'etnologia*, however, De Martino became a founding member of the first anti-fascist committee in Bari, and, as he became more politically engaged, his theoretical approach became both deeper and more eclectic. De Martino entered the Socialist Party after the war and in 1950 became a member of the Italian Communist Party. He worked actively in political and union organizing for several years, work that also brought him into regular contact with peasants and laborers in the south of Italy, who became the subjects of most of his later work. This period also saw the first publication of the work of Antonio Gramsci, the brilliant and original Italian Marxist, and many of De Martino's post-war concerns parallel Gramsci's focus on the cultural and ideological aspects of class stratification, though popular religion, magic and folk metaphysics remain for De Martino the central topics of investigation.

In 1949 De Martino published a very controversial article entitled "Intorno a una storia del mondo popolare subalterno," in which he proposed that the historical investigation of popular religion and ideology could contribute to class consciousness and genuine popular liberation. Marxist categories and ideological premises are evident in much of his later work, though sometimes only in subtle ways, and he also dealt extensively with existential crises, illness and death, and dissociative states, topics usually ignored in Marxist analyses.

De Martino's field studies in Lucania and the Salentine Peninsula, conducted primarily between 1949 and 1959, stand as classics in Italian anthropology. *Morte e pianto rituale nel mondo antico* concerns funeral rituals and laments in the Mediterranean, presenting primary data from the 1950s as well as analysis of funeral rites throughout the ancient Mediterranean. *Sud e magia* focuses on popular religious practice in southern Italy. *La terra del rimorso* reports the results of a team study of the Tarantist possession cult in Apulia. From 1953 to 1958 De Martino taught at the University of Rome and from 1959 until his death was on the faculty of the University of Cagliari in Sardinia.

MAJOR WORKS: *Naturalismo e storicismo nell'etnologia* (Bari: 1941); *Il mondo magico: prolegomeni a una storia del magismo* (Turin: 1948); "Intorno a una storia del mondo popolare subalterno," *Società*, vol. 5 (1949), pp. 411-435; *Morte e pianto rituale nel mondo antico: dal lamento pagano al pianto di Maria* (Turin: 1958); *Sud e magia* (Milan: 1959); *La terra del rimorso: contributo a una storia religiosa del Sud* (Milan: 1961); *Furore simbolo valore* (Milan: 1962); *Mondo popolare magia in Lucania* (edited and with preface by Rocco Brienza) (Rome: 1975); *La fine del mondo: contributo all'analisi delle apocalissi culturali* (edited by Clara Gallini) (Turin: 1977).

SOURCES: A.M. Cirese, "Gli studi demologici come contributo alla storia della cultura," *Lares*, vol. 22 (1956), pp. 66-75; Pietro Clemente, Maria Luisa Meoni, and Massimo Squillacciotti, *Aspetti del dibattito sul folklore in Italia nel primo decennio del secondo dopoguerra: materiali e prime valutazioni* (Siena: 1974); P. Clemente [et al.], *L'antropologia italiana: un secolo di storia* (Rome: 1985), pp. 3-50, 205-229; Enrico Filippini, "Perchè Giove sorrise," *La Repubblica* (26 June 1984); Giuseppe Galasso, *Croce, Gramsci e altri storici* (Milan: 1969), pp. 373-471; Clara Gallini, "Le scienze umane nella rivista *Società*," *Uomo e cultura*, vol. 29-32 (1982-1983), pp. 95-107; Clara Gallini, "Note su De Martino e l'etnocentrismo critico," *Problemi del socialismo*, vol. 15 (1979), pp. 211-222; Mario Gandini, "Ernesto De Martino: nota bio-bibliografica," *Uomo e cultura*, vol. 5 (1972), pp. 223-268; Vittoria Lanternari, "Ernesto De Martino, etnologo meridionalista: vent'anni dopo," *L'Uomo*, vol. 1 (1977), pp. 29-56; L.M. Lombardi Satriani, "La ricerca demartiniana" in: *Il silenzio, la memoria e lo sguardo* (Palermo: 1979), pp. 240-254; George R. Saunders, "Contemporary Italian cultural anthropology," *Annual Review of Anthropology*, vol. 13 (1984), pp. 447-466; Tullio Tentori, *Per una storia del bisogno antropologico* (Rome: 1983); Clara Gallini, *Ernesto de Martino: la ricerca e i suoi percorsi* (Brescia: 1986) (= *La ricerca folklorica*, no. 13).

George R. Saunders

De Puydt, Marcel. Prehistorian, lawyer. Born in Antwerp (Belgium) 20 February 1855, died in Antwerp (Belgium) 22 January 1940. With doctorates in law and in political and administrative sciences from the University of Liège, he served as director of the legal department of the City of Liège.

Between 1881 and 1913 he carried out an extremely large number of excavations in the region around Liège and in Hesbaye and is considered to be the father of that region's prehistory. Among his notable accomplishments are the discovery of the Neolithic deposits at Sainte-Gertrude (in Limbourg in the Netherlands) and numerous pit dwellings (*fonds de cabanes)* at the Omalian site of Rullen (Fouron-Saint-Pierre). The results of his excavations may be seen in the Musée Curtius in Liège.

In his youth, he availed himself of the chance to make a journey to the cavern of Spy: in 1885 he started excavations there with MAX LOHEST that led to the discovery of an important Mousterian site containing two Neanderthal skeletons.

MAJOR WORKS: "La station et l'atelier préhistoriques de Sainte-Gertrude (Pays-Bas)," *Matériaux pour l'histoire primitive et naturelle de l'homme*, 3rd sér., vol. 2 (1885), pp. 449-452; "Atelier néolithique de Rullen et découvertes faites sur le territoire de Fouron-Saint-Pierre," *Bulletin de l'Institut archéologique liégeois*, vol. 43 (1913), pp. 191-253; "L'homme contemporain du mammouth à Spy, province de Namur," *Annales de la Fédération archéologique et historique de Belgique* (1885), pp. 207-235; "Fonds de cabanes de la Hesbaye: compte-rendu de fouilles exécutées à Omal en 1900-1901," *Mémoires de la Société d'Anthropologie de Bruxelles*, vol. 21, no. 1 (1903); "Grotte de Spy: souvenir du premier Congrès de Namur," *Annales de la Fédération archéologique et historique de Belgique* (1938), pp. 147-152.

SOURCE: Jean Servais, "Marcel De Puydt, 1855-1940 (notice biographique)," *Bulletin de l'Institut archéologique liégeois*, vol. 64 (1940), pp. 119-135.

André Leguebe
[Translation from French: Timothy Eastridge and Robert B. Marks Ridinger]

Debefs, G.F. (Georgiĭ Franfševich). Physical anthropologist, archaeologist, ethnographer. Born in Tomsk (Russia) 7 December 1905, died in Moscow (Russian S.F.S.R.) 19 January 1969. Debefs became a doctor of biological sciences in 1941 and a professor in 1944. He investigated an exceptionally wide geographic area of the country, including in fact almost all the peoples of the Soviet Union. It is largely because of the work of Debefs that the anthropological structure of the peoples of the U.S.S.R. is adequately understood. In the course of many years, beginning in 1964, he worked in Afghanistan, inspecting all the ethnographic groups of that country (eighty-six groups). A characteristic trait of the anthropological work of Debefs is the great care he took in processing materials, which for the most part he carried out himself. Debefs played a distinguished role in the working out of the principles of the use of materials as historical sources for the analysis of intricately complex problems of ethnogenesis and various phases of ethnic history. He is renowned for his classification of the races of mankind. Debefs showed great erudition in the problems of archaeology and ethnography. The breadth of his scientific outlook is one of his characteristic traits as a scholar, and it won him exceptional respect among colleagues.

MAJOR WORKS: *O polozhenii paleoliticheskogo rebenka iz peshchery Teshik-Tash v sisteme iskopaemykh form cheloveka* (Moscow: 1947); *Paleoantropologiïa SSSR* (Moscow and Leningrad: 1948) (= *Trudy Instituta étnografii AN SSSR*, vol. 4); *Antropologicheskie issledovaniïa v Kamchatkoĭ oblasti* (Moscow: 1951) (= *Trudy Instituta étnografii AN SSSR*, vol. 17); (with M.G. Levin and T.A. Trofimova), "Antropologicheskiĭ material kak istochnik izucheniĭa voprosov étnogeneza," *Sovetskaĭa étnografiĭa*, no. 1 (1952), pp. 22-35; *O nekotorykh napravleniĭakh izmenenii v stroenii cheloveka sovremennogo vida* (Moscow: 1960); (with V.P. Alekseev), *Kraniometriĭa: metodika antropologich-eskikh issledovanii* (Moscow: 1964); "Antropologicheskie issledovaniĭa v Afganistane," *Sovetskaĭa étnografiĭa*, no. 4 (1967), pp. 75-93; *Problems of Physical Anthroplogy in Arctic Regions* (Copenhagen: 1960) (= *Acta Arctica*, vol. 12).

SOURCES: I.I. Gokhman, "G.F. Debetš," *Sovetskaĭa étnografiĭa*, no. 2 (1966), pp. 136-139; "G.F. Debetš (nekrolog)," *Sovetskaĭa étnografiĭa*, no. 1 (1969), pp. 184-189; H.V. Vallois, "Debetz, G., nécrologie," *L'Anthropologie*, vol. 73, no. 3/4 (1969), pp. 313-314; O.G. Gerassimenko, "F. Debetz (1905-1969)," *American Journal of Physical Anthropology*, vol. 37 (1972), pp. 1-2; I.M. Zolotareva, "Osnovnye étapy izucheniĭa antropologii Sibiri v trudakh G.F. Debetša," *Rasy i narody*, no. 2 (1972), pp. 31-41.

A.M. Reshetov
[*Translation from Russian: Thomas L. Mann*]

Dempwolff, Otto (Otto Heinrich August Louis Dempwolff). Physician, linguist. Born in Pillau (East Prussia) 25 May 1871, died in Hamburg (Germany) 27 November 1938. Following completion of coursework at the Gymnasium in Memel, Dempwolff studied at the Universities of Königsberg, Marburg, Leipzig, Berlin and Tübingen between 1888 and 1893, when he received his certification as a physician. His first position following his graduation was as a ship's doctor, and he was attached to the New Guinea Company as a physician from 1895 to 1897. From 1898 to 1911, he served as a public health officer for the imperial defense forces in many locations, among them New Guinea and German Southwest Africa (now Namibia), rising to a final rank of chief of the medical service of German East Africa (now Tanzania). In his leisure time time Dempwolff devoted himself to studies in linguistics, receiving the title of professor in 1918. He obtained his *Habilitation* in 1920 in African and South Pacific languages at the University of Hamburg (where he was an unofficial *außerordentlicher Professor*) and in 1931 the University of Kiel awarded him the degree of Doctor of Philosophy, *honoris causa*.

Dempwolff became acquainted with CARL MEINHOF very early in his studies and utilized his basic methodological principals. He not only applied the reconstructed Ur-Bantu, which Meinhof had developed in his own researches into the Bantu languages (which until that time had hardly been known to science), but also as a model for his *Vergleichende Lautlehre des austronesischen Wortschatzes*. In the field of African studies Dempwolff focused chiefly on East and Southwest Africa, compiling linguistic materials from the so-called "undrained" region of Tanzania and reconstructed a great number of eastern Bantu roots. In addition to continuing study on the Nama language, he produced the first monograph on Sandawe. Despite this, his main area of research lay in Indonesian and Austronesian languages such as Ngadju (Dajak), Graged and Malay. For these language groups Dempwolff not only provided fundamental reconstructions but also a substantial quantity of phonological and grammatical descriptions.

MAJOR WORKS: "Beiträge zur Kenntnis der Sprachen von Deutsch-Neuguinea," *Mitteilungen des Seminars für Orientalische Sprachen*, vol. 8 (1905), pp. 182-254; "Sagen und Märchen der Bilibili," *Baessler Archiv*, vol. 5 (1911), pp. 63-102; "Beiträge zur Kenntnis der Sprachen in Deutsch-Ostafrika," *Zeitschrift für Kolonialsprachen*, vol. 2 (1911-1912), pp. 81-107 and 257-260; vol. 3 (1912-1913), pp. 61-81; vol. 5 (1914-1915), pp. 26-44, 113-136, 227-253, and 270-298; vol.

6 (1915-1916), pp. 1-27 and 102-123; vol. 7 (1916-1917), pp. 102-123, 134-160, 167-192 and 309-325; *Beiträge zur Volksbeschreibung der Hehe* (Leipzig and Berlin: 1913); *Die Sandawe: Linguistisches und ethnographisches Material aus Deutsch-Ostafrika* (Hamburg: 1916); "Einige Probleme der vergleichenden Erforschung der Südsee-Sprachen," *Anthropos*, vol. 26 (1931), pp. 157-170; *Grammar of the Graged Language* (Narer, Karkar Island: no date); *Vergleichende Lautlehre des austronesischen Wortschatzes* [3 vols.] (Berlin: 1934-1938); "Einführung in die Sprache der Nama-Hottentotten," *Zeitschrift für Eingeborenen-Sprachen*, vol. 25 (1924-1925), pp. 30-66, 89-134 and 188-229; *Einführung in die malaiische Sprache* (Berlin: 1941) (= *Zeitschrift für Eingeborenen-Sprachen*, Beiheft 22).

SOURCES: R. Blust, "Dempwolff's contributions to Austronesian linguistics," *Afrika und Übersee*, vol. 71 (1988), pp. 167-176; E. Dammann, "Otto Dempwolffs bantuistische Arbeiten," *Zeitschrift für Phonetik, Sprachwissenschaft und Kommunikationsforschung*, vol. 16 (1963), pp. 13-18; E. Dammann, "Zur Erinnerung an Otto Dempwolff," *Africana Marburgensia*, vol. 4, no. 2 (1971), pp. 71-77; E. Dammann, "Otto Dempwolff," *Afrika und Übersee*, vol. 71 (1988), pp. 161-166; Ernst Dammann, "Dempwolff, Otto Heinrich August Louis" in: H. Jungraithmayr and W.J.G. Möhlig (editors), *Lexikon der Afrikanistik* (Berlin: 1983), pp. 71-72; P. de V. Pienaar, "Otto Dempwolff," *Bantu Studies*, vol. 13 (1939), p. 164.

Rudolf Leger
[Translation from German: Robert B. Marks Ridinger]

Dillmann, August (Christian Friedrich August Dillmann). Theologist, Orientalist. Born in Illingen/Württemberg (Germany) 25 April 1823, died in Berlin (Germany) 4 July 1894. Dillmann was the founder of modern Ethiopian studies in Germany. After his academic training in Stuttgart and Schöntal, Dillmann studied theology, philology and philosophy with H. Ewald and F. Chr. Baur (among others) in Tübingen between 1840 and 1844. In the fall of 1845 he assumed the post of vicar in Sersheim. In 1846 he obtained a doctorate and afterward went for two years to Paris, London and Oxford in order to devote himself to the study of Ethiopian manuscripts. In 1851 he obtained his *Habilitation* in the Faculty of Theology at Tübingen, where he was named *außerordentlicher Professor* in 1853. In 1854 he was invited to the University of Kiel. There, he was *Extraordinarius*—and from 1859 *Ordinarius—Professor* in the theology faculty, at which he gave lectures on Semitic languages and Sanskrit. In 1864 Dillmann was invited as an *Ordinarius Professor* to the University of Giessen and in 1869 to the theology faculty at the University of Berlin where he was active until 1894. In 1877 he became a member of the Academy of Sciences in Berlin.

Besides questions of exegesis of the Old Testament, Dillmann's scholarly interests lay mainly in Ethiopian philology. His philological preoccupation with apocryphal Old Testament books in Ethiopian (Ge'ez) led to precise grammatical, lexical and literary descriptions of this language, which have come to be accepted as standard works in modern Ethiopian studies. In addition, Dillmann was concerned with Ethiopian history and culture. For many years he worked on a complete edition of the Ethiopian Old Testament, of which he himself was able to complete the first, second and fifth volumes. Dillmann was not able to carry through to the end his plan for a history of Ethiopia. Nevertheless, many preliminary sketches appeared that even today supply important insights in this area.

MAJOR WORKS: *Biblia Veteris Testamenti Aethiopica, in quinque tomos distributa, ad librorum manuscriptorum fidem editit et apparatu critico instruxit* [5 vols.] (Leipzig: 1853-1894); *Grammatik der äthiopischen Sprache* (Leipzig: 1857; edited by C. Bezold, Leipzig: 1899; reprinted,

Graz: 1959); *Lexicon linguae Aethiopicae cum indice Latino* (Leipzig: 1865; New York: 1955); *Chrestomatia Aethiopica* (Leipzig: 1866; Darmstadt: 1967).

SOURCES: Rud. Kittek, "Dillman, Christian Friedrich August" in: *Allgemeine Deutsche Biographie*, vol. 47 (Berlin: 1903; reprinted, Berlin: 1971), pp. 699-702; W.W. v. Baudissin, *August Dillmann* (Leipzig: 1895); Ludwig Gerhardt, "Dillmann, Christian Friedrich August" in: H. Jungraithmayr and W.J.G. Möhlig (editors), *Lexikon der Afrikanistik* (Berlin: 1983), p. 75; R. Paret and A. Schall (editors), *Ein Jahrhundert Orientalistik: Lebensbilder aus der Feder von Enno Littmann* (Wiesbaden: 1955); H. Haering and O. Hohenstatt (editors), *Schwäbische Lebensbilder*, vol. 1 (Stuttgart: 1940).

Rudolf Leger
[*Translation from German: Robert B. Dean*]

Dixon, Roland B. *(Roland Burrage).* Anthropologist, natural historian.

Born in Worcester (Massachusetts) 6 November 1875, died in Harvard (Massachusetts) 19 December 1934. Dixon was regarded by fellow Boasians as exceptionally erudite and almost inhumanly impersonal.

Appointed an assistant in the Peabody Museum after graduating from Harvard in 1897, he became a member of the Jesup North Pacific Expedition in 1898 (doing fieldwork in British Columbia and Alaska), and of the Huntington Expedition in California in 1899. His 1900 doctoral dissertation dealt with the language of the Maidu Indians of California. He published a monograph on the Maidu and another on the Shasta and later collaborated with ALFRED L. KROEBER in typologies of California indigenous languages. Dixon also organized the statistical presentation of results on the Amerindian population from the 1910 U.S. census.

While advancing through the ranks of the Harvard faculty and the Peabody Museum, Dixon traveled extensively in Asia and the Pacific. During 1918-1919 he participated in a U.S. congressional inquiry on political conditions in Central Asia and in the U.S. delegation to the Paris Peace Conference, which produced the Treaty of Versailles, ending World War I.

Following his California fieldwork, Dixon focused on studies of geographical distributions. He published a survey of Oceanic mythology in 1916. For *The Racial History of Mankind* he cross-classified three physical measurements for all the peoples of the world about whom he could find data, computed the proportions of each of the eight resulting combinations in various populations and tried to fit the results to facts of history and geography. As Kroeber put it, "Dixon's reliance on the objectivity of his method induced him to follow it even when it led to fantastic results, evidently due to factors which he had omitted from consideration; and the use of his wide range of knowledge to prop some of his less probable findings, only made matters worse."

Along with JOHN REED SWANTON, EDWARD SAPIR and CLARK WISSLER, but in opposition to ROBERT H. LOWIE and others of FRANZ BOAS's later students, Dixon maintained what Kroeber characterized as "a sane and constructive interest in tribal and ethnic migrations" and cultural distributions. In his magnum opus, *The Building of Cultures*, he refined the age and area method by distinguishing components of culture traits more finely than was usual in such work and exhaustively analyzed similarities in material objects to understand the early movements of peoples over the world and to propound a theory of the diffusion of cultural traits.

MAJOR WORKS: "The Northern Maidu," *Bulletin of the American Museum of Natural History*, no. 17 (1905), pp. 119-346; "Maidu," *Handbook of American Indian Languages*, no. 1 (1911), pp. 679-734; (with John Swanton) "Primitive American history," *American Anthropologist*, n.s., vol. 16 (1914), pp. 376-412; *Oceanic Mythology* (Boston: 1916); (with A.L. Kroeber) "Linguistic families in California," *University of California Publications in American Archaeology and Ethnology*, no. 16 (1919), pp. 47-118; *The Racial History of Mankind* (New York: 1923); *The Building of Cultures* (New York: 1928).

SOURCES: Alfred M. Tozzer and Alfred L. Kroeber, "Roland Burrage Dixon," *American Anthropologist*, vol. 38 (1936), pp. 291-300; Stephen O. Murray, "Historical inferences from ethnohistorical data: Boasian perspectives," *Journal of the History of the Behavioral Sciences*, vol. 19 (1983), pp. 335-340.

Stephen O. Murray

Dobrowolski, Kazimierz. Historian, sociologist, ethnographer. Born in Nowy Sącz, Galicia (Austria-Hungary, now in Poland) 20 December 1894, died in Kraków (Poland) 26 March 1987. Dobrowolski studied history (especially social and cultural history), ethnology, sociology and economic history in Kraków, Paris, Vienna and London. He obtained his doctorate (in philosophy) in 1919 and post-doctoral degree (in the history of Polish culture) in 1932. In 1935 he became an associate professor of sociology and ethnology at Jagiellonian University. He became a full professor in 1946.

Dobrowolski aimed for the historicization of ethnography, the investigation of ethnographic facts in their historical context. He conducted research on Old Polish thought and scientific culture and on the history of settlement and the character of the economy of the Carpathian regions. He stressed the origin and causes of the ethnographic variation of the Carpathian cultures. He also outlined a program of ethnographic studies. After World War II, in addition to doing research on the structure of life within the new boundaries of Poland, Dobrowolski devoted himself to investigations of the theory of social and cultural change; he was one of the creators of the theory of cultural transformation. In addition, he was interested in research methodolgy.

MAJOR WORKS: *Dzieje kultu św. Floriana w Polsce do połowy XVI w.* [*History of the Cult of St. Florian in Poland up to the mid-16th Century*] (Warsaw: 1923); *Wróżda i pojednanie w sądownictwie polskich wsi beskidowych XVI i XVII wieku* [*Hostility and Reconciliation in the Neighboring Lands of the Countryside of the Polish Beskid Mountains in the XVI and XVII Centuries*] (Lwów: 1924); *Najstarsze osadnictwo Podhala* [*Earliest Settlements of Podhale*] (Lwów: 1935); *Dwa studia nad powstaniem kultury ludowej w Karpatach Zachodnich* [*Two Studies of the Emergence of Folk Culture in the Western Carpathian Mountains*] (Kraków: 1938); *Zagadnienie metodologii nauki w Polsce epoki Odrodzenia* [*Problem of the Methodology of Science in Poland during the Renaissance*] (Warsaw: 1953); "Chłopska kultura tradycyjna" ["Traditional peasant culture"], *Etnografia Polska*, vol. 1 (1958), pp. 19-52; "Studia nad teorią kultury ludowej" ["Studies on the theory of folk culture"], *Etnografia Polska*, vol. 4 (1961), pp. 15-92; "Trzy studia z teorii kultury ludowej" ["Three studies on the theory of folk culture"], *Etnografia Polska*, vol. 8 (1964), pp. 11-74; *Studia nad życiem społecznym i kulturą* [*Studies on Social Life and Culture*] (Wrocław: 1966); *Studia z pogranicza historii i socjologii* [*Studies on the Borderland of History and Sociology*] (Wrocław: 1967); *Teoria procesów żywiołowych w zarysie* [*The Theory of Elemental Processes in Outline*] (Wrocław: 1973).

SOURCES: Anna Kutrzeba-Pojnarowa, *Kultura ludowa i jej badacze* [*Folk Culture and its Researchers*] (Warsaw: 1977); Władysław Kwaśniewicz, "Kazimierz Dobrowolski," *Lud*, vol. 53 (1969), pp. 9-29; Władysław Kwaśniewicz, "Metoda integralna Kazimierza Dobrowolskiego" ["The integrative method of Kazimierz Dobrowolski"], *Etnografia Polska*, vol. 13 (1969), pp. 41-57; *Studia* z zakresu socjologii, etnografii i historii ofiarowane Kazimierzowi Dobrowolskiemu [*Studies from the Sphere of Sociology, Ethnography and History in Honor of Kazimierz Dobrowolski*] (Kraków: 1972).

Maria Niewiadomska and Iwona Grzelakowska
[Translation from Polish: Joel Janicki]

Dolgikh, B.O. (Boris Osipovich). Ethnographer, historian, folklorist. Born in Riga (Latvia) 18 April 1904, died in Moscow (Russian S.F.S.R.) 31 December 1971. Dolgikh was a doctor of historical sciences and a professor. At first he did practical work. Between 1937 and 1944 he was research assistant of the Krasnoĭarskiĭ kraevyĭ muzeĭ (Krasnoĭarskiĭ Kraĭ Museum). After 1944 he was in Moscow at the Institut ėtnografii (Institute of Ethnography) of the Soviet Academy of Sciences.

In Dolgikh's works the results of his field research and archival investigations were completely merged. His scholarly interests included the study of the ethnic history and social organization of the peoples of Siberia and also the history of their material and non-material culture. He developed a new method for the use of archival materials as sources for determining the population and settlement patterns of various groups, tribes and peoples. He did research on both the history of the peoples of Siberia and the theoretical problems of ethnography, using folklore broadly as a historical source.

MAJOR WORKS: *Keti* (Irkutsk: 1934); *Legendy i skazki nganasanov* (Krasnoĭarsk: 1938); *Rodoplemennoĭ sostav narodov Sibiri v XVII v.* (Moscow: 1956); *Rodovoĭ i plemennoĭ sostav narodov Sibiri v XVII v.* (Moscow: 1960) (= *Trudy Instituta ėtnografii AN SSSR*, vol. 55); *Mifologicheskie skazki i istoricheskie predaniĭa ėnĭsev* (Moscow: 1961) (= *Trudy Instituta ėtnografii AN SSSR*, vol. 16); *Bytovye rasskazy ėnĭsev* (Moscow: 1962) (= *Trudy Instituta ėtnografii AN SSSR*, vol. 25); *Rod, fratriĭa, plemĭa u narodov Severnoĭ Sibiri* (Moscow: 1964); *Ocherki po ėtnicheskoĭ istorii nenĭsev i ėnĭsev* (Moscow: 1970); "K voprosu o sootnoshenii bol'shoĭ i maloĭ sem'i u narodov Severa v proshlom" in: I.S. Gurvich (editor), *Soĭsial'naĭa organizaĭsiĭa i kul'tura narodov Severa: posvĭashchaeĭsĭa pamĭati Borisa Osipovicha Dolgikh* (Moscow: 1974), pp. 21-57.

SOURCES: "B.O. Dolgikh," *Sovetskaĭa ėtnografiĭa*, no. 2 (1972), pp. 176-179; "B.O. Bolgikh" in: I.S. Gurvich (editor), *Soĭsial'naĭa organizaĭsiĭa i kul'tura narodov Severa: posvĭashchaeĭsĭa pamĭati Borisa Osipovicha Dolgikh* (Moscow: 1974), pp. 4-20.

A.M. Reshetov
[Translation from Russian: Thomas L. Mann]

Dolores, Juan. Teamster, anthropological consultant. Born (according to his family reckoning) in northwest Mexico on or near 24 June 1880, died in Vamori (Arizona) 19 July 1948. A member of the Papago Indian tribe, Dolores spent his early childhood in Mexico and the southwestern United States and was educated in government schools. He graduated from Hampton Institute in December 1901. As a result of his background and education, Dolores was tri-lingual; he spoke Papago, Spanish and English.

From around 1909 on, he was a linguistic informant for ALFRED L. KROEBER at the University of California, interspersing paid linguistic work with the more remunerative horse-team handling that was his profession. During 1918 and 1919 Dolores collected Papago texts in Arizona as a research fellow of Kroeber's anthropology department.

Between 1912 and 1936 he spent long periods of time as an employee of the University of California's Museum of Anthropology, during which time he accomplished considerable work on Papago linguistics. In 1936 Dolores took part in a Works Progress

Administration project under W. LLOYD WARNER at the University of Chicago, while from 1937 until shortly before his death he was a museum preparator at the Museum of Anthropology in San Francisco.

The best-known account of Dolores is to be found in Theodora Kroeber's *Ishi in Two Worlds* (Berkeley: 1962), for Dolores was one of the Yahi Indian's friends and guides during the short period that Ishi lived in the Museum of Anthropology.

MAJOR WORKS: "Papago verb stems," *University of California Publications in American Archaeology and Ethnology*, vol. 10 (1913), pp. 241-263; "Papago noun stems," *University of California Publications in American Archaeology and Ethnology*, vol. 20 (1923), pp. 19-31; "Papago nicknames" in: Robert H. Lowie (editor), *Essays in Anthropology Presented to A.L. Kroeber* (Berkeley: 1936), pp. 45-47; (with L.M. O'Neale) "Notes on Papago color designations," *American Anthropologist*, vol. 45 (1943), pp. 387-397.

SOURCE: A.L. Kroeber, "Juan Dolores, 1880-1948," *American Anthropologist*, vol. 51 (1949), pp. 96-97.

David Lonergan

Doria, Giacomo. Naturalist, geographer, traveler. Born in La Spezia (Italy) 1 November 1840, died in Genoa (Italy) 19 September 1913. From a rich aristocratic family, Doria was a pupil of the paleontologist Giovanni Cappellini. In 1861 he founded the journal *L'Archivio per la Zoologia, l'Anatomia e la Fisiologia* together with the zoologists Filippo De Filippi (1814-1867) and Michele Lessona (1823-1894). In the same year the three naturalists left for Persia, attached to the Italian diplomatic mission to the Shah. Doria stayed in Persia for a year and put together a notable zoological collection. Between 1865 and 1866 he visited Borneo with the botanist Odoardo Beccari (1843-1920). Upon his return to Italy he founded the Museo Civico di Storia Naturale (Civic Museum of Natural History) in Genoa (1867) and, three years later, started the museum's *Annali*. All of Doria's collections ended up in the museum (including those acquired in later voyages to Abyssinia and Tunisia) as did those of some of the other major Italian explorer-naturalists of the time, including ORAZIO ANTINORI, Odoardo Beccari, Enrico D'Albertis, LEONARDO FEA, ELIO MODIGLIANI and LAMBERTO LORIA.

In the history of Italian ethnology and anthropology, Doria is not remembered for the richness of his scientific production but instead for his institutional work and for his role in organizing and funding most of the Italian explorers of the second half of the 19th century. Doria sent travelers to the least known regions of the globe and had them collect cultural artifacts. He was particularly concerned with scientific and methodological preparation, and he financed expeditions that would make his museum a focal point for scholars.

In 1867, along with Cristoforo Negri, Cesare Correnti, Orazio Antinori and others, Doria founded the Società Geografica Italiana (Italian Geographical Society) of which he was president from 1891 to 1900 and which supported (among others) the voyages of LUIGI ROBECCHI BRICCHETTI in Somalia, GUIDO BOGGIANI in the Chaco, and Leonardo Fea in Southwest Africa.

MAJOR WORKS: "I naturalisti italiani alla Nuova Guinea e specialmente delle loro scoperte zoologiche," *Bollettino della Società Geografica Italiana*, vol. 12 (1878), pp. 154-169; "L. Fea nel Tenasserim," *Bollettino della Società Geografica Italiana*, vol. 20 (1888), pp. 627-689; "L. Loria alla Nuova Guinea," *Bollettino della Società Geografica Italiana*, vol. 24 (1890), pp. 479-494, 559-586.

SOURCES: O. Antinori, O. Beccari and A. Issel, "Relazione sommaria del viaggio nel Mar Rosso," *Bollettino della Società Geografica Italiana* (1870), pp. 43-60; O. Beccari, "Cenno di un viaggio a Borneo," *Bollettino della Società Geografica Italiana* (August 1868), pp. 193-214; M. Carazzi, *La Società Geografica Italiana e l'esplorazione coloniale in Africa, 1867-1900* (Florence: 1972); F. De Filippi, *Note di un viaggio in Persia nel 1862* (Milan: 1865).

Sandra Puccini
[Translation from Italian: CW]

Dorsey, George A. (George Amos). Anthropologist, journalist. Born in Hebron (Ohio) 6 February 1868, died in New York (New York) 29 March 1931. Dorsey was awarded an A.B. (1888) and an L.L.D. (1909) from Denison College and an A.B. (1900) from Harvard University. He also received the first Ph.D. in anthropology awarded in the United States, from Harvard University in 1894. As one of the promising students of FREDERIC WARD PUTNAM, who had been appointed Chief of the Department of Ethnology of the 1893 World's Columbian Exposition, he was selected to do fieldwork in South America and to make anthropological investigations and collections for the Exposition. This work took him to Peru, Ecuador, Chile and Bolivia during 1891-1892 and was followed in 1893 by Putnam's making him Superintendant of Archaeology at the Exposition's Department of Anthropology. During 1895-1896 he was Instructor of Anthropology at Harvard and in 1896 became Assistant Curator in charge of physical anthropology at the newly organized Field Columbian Museum in Chicago.

The source of most of the museum's original collections was the World's Columbian Exposition, and there was a need for organization of these collections, creation of guidelines for their future development and agreement on the basic philosophy the institution was to follow. W.H. Holmes, who had been made the first Curator of Anthropology by the museum's board of trustees, resigned in 1898 to go to the Smithsonian Institution. Dorsey, at the age of twenty-nine, was made Curator, a position he held until 1915. At the Board's direction, he immediately set about amassing a large collection, one seeking to represent all parts of the world and highlighting the Northwest Coast. His own whirlwind collecting trips were augmented by those of staff members who were sent both to record cultures and to purchase artifacts. He also hired on-site agents to acquire artifacts. During this time Dorsey published many articles, particularly on the Plains Indians, including "The Cheyenne" and "The Mishongnovi ceremonies of the Snake and the Antelope fraternities." He was Professor of Comparative Anatomy, Northwestern University Dental School (1898-1915), and Assistant, later Associate, Professor of Anthropology, University of Chicago (1905-1915). On a leave of absence from the museum (1909-1912), he was foreign correspondent for the *Chicago Tribune*, writing articles on such diverse topics as China during the Boxer Rebellion and European immigration into the United States. His resignation from the museum in 1915 was followed by the publication in 1917 of *Young Low*, a novel with autobiographical overtones. During World War I, Dorsey served as Assistant Naval Attaché in Madrid and Lisbon. After the war he continued his writing career as a correspondent of the *London News* and became a lecturer on anthropology in the New School of Social Research in New York. He also published popular works that aimed at explaining science to the public at large, the most successful of which was *Why We Behave Like Human Beings*.

MAJOR WORKS: "The Oraibi soyal ceremony," *Field Columbian Museum Publication*, no. 55 (1901), pp. 1-59 (= *Anthropological Series*, vol. 3, no. 1); "The Mishongnovi ceremonies of the Snake and Antelope fraternities," *Field Columbian Museum Publication*, no. 66 (1902), pp. 159-261 (= *Anthropological Series*, vol. 3, no. 3); "The Arapaho sun dance: the ceremony of the offerings lodge," *Field Columbian Museum Publication*, no. 75 (1903), pp. 1-228 (= *Anthropological Series*, vol. 4); (with Alfred L. Kroeber) "Traditions of the Arapaho," *Field Columbian Museum Publication*, no. 81 (1903), pp. 1-475 (= *Anthropological Series*, vol. 5); "Traditions of the Arikara," *Carnegie Institution of Washington Publication*, no. 17 (1904), pp. 1-202; "Traditions of the Osage," *Field Columbian Museum Publication*, no. 88 (1904), pp. 1-60 (= *Anthropological Series*, vol. 7, no. 1); "The mythology of the Wichita," *Carnegie Institution of Washington Publications*, no. 21 (1904), pp. 1-351; "The Cheyenne," *Field Columbian Museum Publications*, nos. 99 and 103 (1905), pp. 1-55 and 57-186 (= *Anthropological Series*, vol. 9, nos. 1-2); "The Ponca sun dance," *Field Columbian Museum Publication*, no. 102 (1905), pp. 61-88 (= *Anthropological Series*, vol. 7, no. 2); "The Pawnee: mythology (part 1)," *Carnegie Institution of Washington Publications*, no. 59 (1906), pp. 1-546; (with James R. Murie; prepared for publication by Alexander Spoehr) "Notes on Skidi Pawnee Society," *Field Museum of Natural History Publication*, no. 479 (1940), pp. 67-119 (= *Anthropological Series*, vol. 27, no. 2).

SOURCES: Fay-Cooper Cole, "George A. Dorsey," *American Anthropologist*, n.s., vol. 33 (1931), pp. 413-414; Fay-Cooper Cole, "Eminent personalities of the half century," *American Anthropologist*, vol. 54 (1952), pp. 162-163; *Who's Who in America*, vol. 16 (1930-1931), p. 703; *Annual Report of the Director to the Board of Trustees, Field Columbian Museum*, vols. 1-5 (1896-1915); Douglas Cole, *Captured Heritage: the Scramble for Northwest Coast Artifacts* (Seattle: 1985), pp. 150-308; Curtis M. Hinsley, Jr., *Savages and Scientists: the Smithsonian Institution and the Development of American Anthropology, 1846-1910* (Washington: 1981), pp. 250, 271-273.

Michele Calhoun

Dorsey, James Owen. Ethnologist, linguist, Episcopal minister. Born in Baltimore (Maryland) 31 October 1848, died in Washington (D.C.) 4 February 1895. Dorsey was trained at the Theological Seminary of Virginia and ordained in 1871. As an anthropologist, he was primarily an ethnological and linguistic fieldworker, a recorder of much data. His gift for learning languages is demonstrated by his learning Hebrew at age ten. His mature research was on the Siouan-speaking tribes of the northern plains, the study of which he began as a missionary to the Ponca (1871-1873). After illness forced Dorsey to return east, he came under the influence of Joseph Henry, Secretary of the Smithsonian Institution, and, later, JOHN WESLEY POWELL, the director of the Geological and Geographical Survey of the Rocky Mountain Regions and founder in 1879 of the Smithsonian's Bureau of American Ethnology (BAE). After further illness forced him to leave the ministry as a vocation, Dorsey joined the Powell Survey as an ethnologist and continued that service at the BAE until his death. Most of his work concentrated on the Omaha, Kansa, Osage, Quapaw, Iowa, Oto, Winnebago and Dakota. FRANZ BOAS maintained that Dorsey's faithful recording of texts of the Ponca and Omaha, although somewhat limited in scope, represented a model of anthropological work soundly based on philological endeavor.

For the BAE's project to classify American languages, Dorsey worked on the Siouan, Athabaskan and Caddoan languages. He was also sent to the field and thus collected data, primarily linguistic but in some cases also ethnographic, on the Arikara,

Pawnee, Caddo, Kichai, Wichita, Tutelo, Applegate, Galice, Chastacosta, Mikonotunne, Chetco, Smith River, Upper Coquille, Yaquina, Alsea, Siuslaw, Lower Umpqua, Lower Coquille, Takelma, Klickitat, Shasta and Biloxi.

MAJOR WORKS: "Omaha sociology," *Annual Report of the Bureau of American Ethnology*, vol. 3 (1884), pp. 205-370; "Osage traditions," *Annual Report of the Bureau of American Ethnology*, vol. 6 (1888), pp. 373-397; *The Chegiha Language* (Washington: 1890) (= *Contributions to North American Ethnology*, vol. 6); "A study of Siouan cults," *Annual Report of the Bureau of American Ethnology*, vol. 11 (1894), pp. 351-544; "Siouan sociology: a posthumous paper," *Annual Report of the Bureau of American Ethnology*, vol. 15 (1897), pp. 205-244.

SOURCES: Franz Boas, "Some philological aspects of anthropological research," *Science*, vol. 23 (1906), pp. 641-645; Raymond J. DeMallie, "James Owen Dorsey" in: Wilcomb Washburn (editor), *History of Indian-White Relations* (Washington: 1988) (= William C. Sturtevant (general editor), *Handbook of North American Indians*, vol. 4), p. 640; Dorsey manuscripts and vertical file in the Smithsonian Institution National Anthropological Archives; J.N.B. Hewitt, "James Owen Dorsey," *American Anthropologist*, vol. 8 (1895), pp. 180-183; Curtis Hinsley, *Savages and Scientists* (Washington: 1981); Walter Hough, "James Owen Dorsey" in: Allen Johnson and Dumas Malone, *Dictionary of American Biography*, vol. 5 (1930), pp. 384-385; "James Owen Dorsey," *Annual Report of the Bureau of American Ethnology*, vol. 16 (1897), pp. lxxxii-lxxxiv.

James R. Glenn

Dorson, Richard M. Folklorist, historian. Born in New York (New York) 12 March 1916, died in Bloomington (Indiana) 11 September 1981. Dorson was educated in American history at Harvard University, receiving his bachelor's, master's and doctor's degrees in 1933, 1940 and 1943, respectively. The topics chosen for his thesis and dissertation were what might be termed folk-literature studies, and starting in 1942 Dorson experimented with fieldwork in folklore. During 1943-1944 he was an instructor of history at Harvard. He then moved to Michigan State University, where he spent thirteen years in the history department.

Dorson's serious fieldwork began in Michigan and resulted in several books and articles on folktales and folk traditions. With little cooperation from the university, he began to offer courses in folklore and was active in the American Folklore Society. He also attended Stith Thompson's Folklore Institute of America summer sessions at Indiana University on several occasions.

When Dorson returned from a Fulbright year in Japan (1956-1957), it was to Indiana, where he replaced the retiring Thompson, and at last he found himself in a folklore department. In Bloomington Dorson chaired the department, which he built into one of the most prestigious folklore programs extant, and edited first the *Journal of American Folklore* (1957-1962) and then the *Journal of the Folklore Institute* (from 1962). Perhaps his most significant contribution was his work with graduate students; he chaired more than eighty doctoral dissertation committees and influenced several decades of folklore scholars.

It is difficult to overestimate Dorson's importance in the development of folklore as a legitimate field of inquiry in the United States. He was a scholar of renown, a spokesman for folklore to academe as well as to the public and a tireless worker in the American Folklore Society (of which he was president from 1966 to 1968).

MAJOR WORKS: *Bloodstoppers and Bearwalkers: Folk Traditions of the Upper Peninsula* (Cambridge, Mass.: 1952); *Negro Folktales in Michigan* (Cambridge, Mass.: 1956); *American Folklore* (Chicago: 1959); *The British Folklorists: a History* (London: 1968); *American Folklore and the Historian* (Chicago: 1971); *America in Legend* (New York: 1973); *Folklore and Fakelore* (Cambridge, Mass.: 1976).

SOURCE: Jan Harold Brunvand, "Richard M. Dorson (1916-1981)," *Journal of American Folklore*, vol. 95 (1982), pp. 347-353.

David Lonergan

Douglass, A.E. (Andrew Ellicott). Astronomer, dendrochronologist, physicist, university administrator, public servant. Born in Windsor (Vermont) 5 July 1867, died in Tucson (Arizona) 20 March 1962. Douglass received a B.A. degree from Trinity College (Connecticut) in 1889 and shortly thereafter joined the Harvard College Observatory to begin a long and illustrious career devoted primarily to astronomy. His interests were not limited by disciplinary constraints, however. In addition to his accomplishments in astronomy, he originated a new science; pioneered the scientific study of cycles; designed and built several unique scientific instruments; made important contributions to physics, geography, geology, and archaeology; and served as a probate judge, a college dean and a university president. He was involved in the establishment and operation of three astronomical observatories—the Harvard College Observatory at Arequipa, Peru; the Lowell Observatory in Flagstaff, Arizona; and the Steward Observatory at the University of Arizona in Tucson—and the preeminent dendrochronological facility in the world, the Laboratory of Tree-Ring Research at the University of Arizona. He also was instrumental in founding the Tree-Ring Society and its periodical, the *Tree-Ring Bulletin*, the principal journal of world dendrochronology.

Although he was born in New England, his name is indelibly associated with the state of Arizona and three of its major educational and scientific institutions: the Lowell Observatory (1894-1901), Northern Arizona Normal School (now Northern Arizona University) (1905-1906) and The University of Arizona (1906-1958). Around 1900, his interest in the effects of sunspots on terrestrial weather led him to investigate the annual growth layers of Southwestern conifers as proxy climate records. Subsequently, he developed the study of tree rings into the science of dendrochronology, aspects of which have become integral components of modern archaeology. Apart from varve dating, dendrochronology was the first of many independent chronometric techniques to be used in archaeology during the 20th century. Douglass constructed the original long tree-ring sequences that underly Southwestern archaeological chronology, derived absolute tree-ring dates for numerous sites in the region and helped formulate the principals that guide the evaluation of tree-ring dates from archaeological contexts. His success in the Southwest stimulated the expansion of archaeological tree-ring dating into other regions, notably the Arctic, the British Isles, central Europe, and the Mediterranean Basin. Douglass also pioneered the use of dendroclimatic reconstructions in the archaeological study of human behavioral adaptation to environmental variability. Although his ideas about the effects of "drought" on prehistoric Southwestern populations have been superseded by more sophisticated conceptions of culture-environment relationships, his early work established a firm conceptual and methodological foundation for subsequent research.

MAJOR WORKS: "Weather cycles in the growth of big trees," *Monthly Weather Review*, no. 37 (1909), pp. 225-237; "A method of estimating rainfall by the growth of trees," *Carnegie Institution of Washington, Publication*, no. 192 (1914), pp. 101-122; *Climatic Cycles and Tree*

Growth [3 vols.] (Washington: 1919, 1928, 1936) (= *Carnegie Institution of Washington, Publication*, no. 289); "Dating our prehistoric ruins," *Natural History*, vol. 21 (1921), pp. 27-30; "The secret of the Southwest solved by talkative tree rings," *National Geographic Magazine*, vol. 56 (1929), pp. 736-770; "Evidences of cycles in tree ring records," *Proceedings of the National Academy of Sciences*, vol. 19 (1933), pp. 350-360; *Dating Pueblo Bonito and other Ruins of the Southwest* (Washington: 1935) (= *National Geographic Society, Contributed Technical Papers, Pueblo Bonito Series*, no. 1); *Tree Rings and Chronology* (Tucson: 1937) (= *University of Arizona Bulletin*, vol. 8, no. 4; = *Physical Science Bulletin*, no. 1); *Precision of Ring Dating in Tree-Ring Chronologies* (Tucson: 1946) (= *University of Arizona Bulletin*, vol. 8, no. 3).

SOURCES: George Ernest Webb, *Tree Rings and Telescopes: the Scientific Career of A.E. Douglass* (Tucson: 1983); "Andrew Ellicott Douglass, 1867-1962," *Tree-Ring Bulletin*, vol. 24, nos. 3-4 (1962), pp. 2-10; Emil W. Haury, "HH-39: recollections of a dramatic moment in Southwestern archaeology," *Tree-Ring Bulletin*, vol. 24, nos. 3-4 (1962), pp. 11-14.

Jeffrey S. Dean

Dozier, Edward P. Cultural anthropologist, linguist. Born in Santa Clara Pueblo (New Mexico) 23 April 1916, died in Tucson (Arizona) 2 May 1971. Dozier was arguably the first Native American to receive his master's degree (University of New Mexico, 1949) and his doctorate (University of California, Los Angeles, 1952) in anthropology. Raised as a Tewa in Santa Clara Pueblo, Dozier attended a Bureau of Indian Affairs grade school and a predominately Hispanic Roman Catholic high school. In this multicultural environment he learned several languages—Tewa, Spanish and English. Dozier served as a cultural bridge between the social and linguistic knowledge of Southwestern Indian cultures and the scholarly pursuits of anthropologists in several American universities during his twenty-year career as an academic anthropologist. He taught at the University of Oregon (1951-1952), Northwestern University (1953-1958) and the University of Arizona (1960-1971).

More than seventy articles and three major ethnographies (*The Tewa of Arizona, Hano* and *The Pueblo Indians of North America*) written by Dozier were oriented toward a functional and social-organizational interpretation of culture. His first ethnography on the "Hopi-Tewa" was conducted as dissertation research with an insider's (Tewa) advantage that provided Dozier with privileged access to ethnographic sources. In general, his professional publications dealt with issues of acculturation, social organization and later with ethnohistory.

Dozier's most significant contribution to the university curriculum was the establishment of the American Indian Studies program at The University of Arizona. Conceptualized as an interdisciplinary program in Indian Studies for Indian and non-Indian graduate students, this optional minor included coursework in anthropology, art, education, English, history, law, linguistics and sociology. A Ford Foundation grant originally funded the program in 1971, the year of Dozier's death. The American Indian Studies program remains a vital area of concentration for both undergraduate and graduate students today.

Throughout his career, Dozier was a scholar devoted to improving cross-cultural understanding. He served as a board member for the Association on American Indian Affairs (1957-1971) and testified at congressional hearings on the condition of Indians.

MAJOR WORKS: "Resistance to acculturation and assimilation in an Indian pueblo," *American Anthropologist*, vol. 53 (1951), pp. 56-66; *The Tewa of Arizona* (Berkeley: 1954) (= *University of California Publications in American Archaeology and Ethnology*, vol. 44, part 3); "Two examples of linguistic acculturation: the Yaqui of Arizona and the Tewa of New Mexico," *Language*, vol. 32 (1956), pp. 146-157; "The Rio Grande Pueblos" in: Edward Spicer (editor), *Perspectives in American Indian Culture Change* (Chicago: 1961), pp. 94-186; *Hano: a Tewa Village in Arizona* (New York: 1966); *Mountain Arbiters: the Changing Life of a Philippine Hill People* (Tucson: 1966); *The Kalinga of Northern Luzon, Philippines* (New York: 1967); "Linguistic acculturation studies in the Southwest" in: Dell Hymes (editor), *Studies in Southwestern Ethnolinguistics* (The Hague: 1967), pp. 389-402 (= *Studies in General Anthropology*, no. 3); *The Pueblo Indians of North America* (New York: 1970).

SOURCES: Edward P. Dozier papers, Arizona State Museum Archives, University of Arizona; Fred Eggan and Keith Basso, "Edward P. Dozier, 1916-1971," *American Anthropologist*, vol. 74 (1972), pp. 740-746; E. Haury, B. Fontana and T. Weaver, "Edward P. Dozier," *Indian Programs Newsletter, University of Arizona*, vol. 2, no. 3 (1972), pp. 6-8; Marilyn Norcini, *The Education of a Native American Anthropologist: Edward P. Dozier (1916-1971)* [unpublished master's thesis, University of Arizona] (Tucson: 1988).

Marilyn Norcini

Drake, St. Clair (John Gibbs St. Clair Drake). Anthropologist. Born in Suffolk (Virginia) 2 January 1911, died in Palo Alto (California) 20 June 1990. Drake was one of the most influential of all scholars of African-American life.

He was educated at Hampton Institute in Virginia, Pendle Hill (a Quaker school near Philadelphia) and the University of Chicago, from which he received a Ph.D. in anthropology in 1954. At Chicago, he was particularly influenced by W. LLOYD WARNER and ROBERT REDFIELD, as well as by Allison Davis and A.R. RADCLIFFE-BROWN.

Black Metropolis, a study of the Chicago South Side ghetto of "Bronzeville," written with Horace Cayton, is a classic statement on the problems of African-Americans living in urban areas. Drake also published the results of his research in Africa and in Britain.

Drake taught at Roosevelt University from 1946 until 1969. In 1969 he started the Black Studies program at Stanford University.

He was frequently a political activist, often working on behalf of African-Americans.

MAJOR WORKS: (with Horace R. Cayton) *Black Metropolis: a Study of Negro Life in a Northern City* (New York: 1945; revised ed., New York: 1970); *Race Relations in a Time of Rapid Social Change: Report of a Survey* (New York: 1966); *Black Folk Here and There: an Essay in History and Anthropology* (Los Angeles: 1987).

SOURCES: George Clement Bond, "A social portrait of John Gibbs St. Clair Drake," *American Ethnologist*, vol. 15 (1988), pp. 762-781; "St. Clair Drake, pioneer in study of Black Americans, dies at 79," *The New York Times* (21 June 1990), p. B7.

Driberg, Jack Herbert. Anthropologist, classical scholar, poet. Born in Assam (India) 2 April 1888, died in London (England) 5 February 1946. Driberg studied the classics at Lancing College and Hertford College, Oxford, before joining the colonial service. He served in the British colonial administration in Uganda (1912-1921), where he lived among the Lango, Lugbwara and Acholi. In 1921 he was transferred to the Sudan.

Before retiring from the colonial service in 1925 he had also spent time in Kenya, Ethiopia, Congo (Zaïre) and Morocco.

An exceptional linguist who spoke eleven languages, Driberg readily learned the languages of the people among whom he served in Africa and, unlike most colonial administrators of his time, fully participated in the people's lives and gained their confidence. He published his anthropological classic, *The Lango*, as well as several ethnographic articles in anthropological journals, before receiving formal training in anthropology.

After his retirement from colonial service Driberg studied anthropology with BRONISLAW MALINOWSKI and C.G. SELIGMAN at the London School of Economics, where he also lectured in anthropology (1927-1929). From 1931 to 1942 he taught in the Department of Archaeology and Anthropology at Cambridge University where he was highly regarded as an eclectic and successful teacher and made a major contribution to building the department. In 1942 he joined the British Ministry of Information, where he served until his death.

Driberg was best known as an ethnologist of the East African peoples among whom he lived. *The Lango* was an outstanding ethnography based on unusually thorough research for the time in which it was written. Driberg also published numerous ethnographic articles in anthropological journals after his formal training in anthropology. He brought anthropology to the public in descriptive works such as *The Savage as He Really Is* and *At Home with the Savage*, the short stories in *People of the Small Arrow*, which depicted the humanity of individual Africans, and in the translation of Didinga and Lango poems in *Initiation*, a unique presentation of African oral literature for the period.

MAJOR WORKS: *Poems* (London: 1908); *The Lango* (London: 1923); *The Savage as He Really Is* (London: 1929); *The East African Problem* (London: 1930); *People of the Small Arrow* (London: 1930); *At Home with the Savage* (London: 1932); *Initiation* (Waltham St. Lawrence: 1932); *Engato the Lion Cub* (New York: 1934).

SOURCES: Critic, "A London diary," *New Statesman and Nation* (16 Feb. 1946), p. 117; E.E. Evans-Pritchard, "Jack Herbert Driberg, 1888-1946," *Man*, vol. 47, no. 4 (1947), pp. 11-13; E.B. Haddon, "Mr. J.H. Driberg," *Nature*, vol. 157 (2 March 1946), pp. 257-258; P.P. Howell, "Jack Herbert Driberg," *Sudan Notes and Records*, vol. 28 (1947), pp. 197-198.

Nancy J. Schmidt

Driver, Harold E. Anthropologist. Born in Berkeley (California) 17 November 1907. Driver received bachelor's (1930) and doctoral (1936) degrees in anthropology from the University of California, Berkeley. He was the recipient of the American Anthropological Association's Distinguished Service Award in 1987.

As an undergraduate student Driver became impressed with the possibility of developing a formal comparative science of cultural anthropology. His interests in formal comparative studies in ethnology were renewed during a seminar directed by ALFRED KROEBER in Driver's first graduate year. Driver completed his Ph.D. degree during the depths of the Great Depression. He was awarded a post-doctoral research year but was unable to secure a professorship at its conclusion. Driver gave up the hope of a career in anthropology and went to work in the trucking industry, the business in which his family had been engaged and he had been reared.

In 1948, after ten years outside of anthropology, Driver returned to Berkeley as an unpaid research associate and later secured a grant to begin a massive comparative study of North American Indian cultures. The following year he assumed a visiting lectureship at Indiana University where he went on to gain a full professorship, retiring in 1974. From his return to research in 1948 to his retirement in 1974, Driver focused his research energies on formal comparative studies, principally on American Indian ethnology. His several unique contributions to comparative ethnology are theoretical and methodological. He recognized that, for any and all societies in a comparative study, some features can be independently invented, some borrowed and some inherited.

Driver argued that valid explanations require the ethnologist to discriminate among the "causes" of all features under investigation in any comparative study. Whereas evolutionists sought to resolve the problem by eliminating societies known to be historically related from their studies, in *his* samples Driver included societies that were known to be related. This allowed him to control for interdependence. He developed ways to distinguish independent from interdependent correlations. As a graduate student, Driver was equally wary of Kroeber's historical explanations of the meanings of similarities among cultures (i.e., that almost all similarities were the result of borrowing or inheritance), the evolutionary explanations offered by Albert Keller and GEORGE PETER MURDOCK (who believed that almost all similarities were the result of independent invention), and functional explanations offered by a host of British social anthropologists (because they were *ad hoc* and *ex post facto*).

In his major studies of girls' puberty rites, developmental kinship cycles and kin avoidances, Driver developed increasingly powerful methodologies to integrate historical, evolutionary and functional theories by means of multivariate techniques. In an especially important exchange with anthropologists over the causes of in-law avoidance customs ("Geographical-historical vs. psycho-functional explanations of kin avoidances"), he computed some partial correlations for a sample of 280 North American Indian societies that showed the best prediction of the presence of parent-in-law/children-in-law avoidances are made from knowledge of the culture area in which a society was located, the second best from knowledge of the language family to which the society belonged and only the third best from the commonly accepted social factors used to predict avoidances. This is the reverse of what his non-comparativist opponents claimed, believing as they did in "psychofunctional" explanations. Driver also was the first scholar to create culture-area taxonomies by correlational methods. His major comparative work on the 280 Indian societies of North America has never been superseded. Driver conducted fieldwork among many American Indian societies in California and among the Chichimeca-Jonaz in northeastern Mexico.

MAJOR WORKS: *The Reliability of Culture Element Data* (Berkeley: 1938) (= *University of California Anthropological Records*, vol. 1); *Girls' Puberty Rites in Western North America* (Berkeley: 1941) (= *University of California Anthropological Records*, vol. 6); *An Integration of Functional, Evolutionary, and Historical Theory by Means of Correlations* (Baltimore: 1956) (= *International Journal of American Linguistics Memoir*, no. 12); (with Wm. C. Massey) *Comparative Studies of North American Indians* (Philadelphia: 1957) (= *Transactions of the American Philosophical Society*, n.s. vol. 47, no. 2); *Indians of North America* (Chicago: 1961; rev. ed., Chicago: 1969); *The Contributions of A.L. Kroeber to Culture Area Theory and Practice* (Baltimore: 1962) (= *International Journal of American Linguistics Memoir*, no. 18); "Geographical-historical vs.

psycho-functional explanations of kin avoidances" *Current Anthropology*, vol. 7 (1966), pp. 131-182; (with James L. Coffin) *Classification and Development of North American Indian Cultures: a Statistical Analysis of the Driver-Massey Sample* (Philadelphia: 1975) (= *Transactions of the American Philosophical Society*, n.s., vol. 65, no. 3).

SOURCES: Joseph G. Jorgensen, "Biographical sketch and bibliography of Harold E. Driver" in: Joseph G. Jorgensen (editor), *Comparative Studies by Harold E. Driver and Essays in His Honor* (New Haven: 1974), pp. 1-8; Douglas R. White, "Process, statistics and anthropological theory: an appreciation of Harold E. Driver," *Reviews in Anthropology*, vol. 2 (1975), pp. 295-314.

Joseph G. Jorgensen

Drucker, Philip. Anthropologist, archaeologist, naval officer. Born in Chicago (Illinois) 13 January 1911, died in Lexington (Kentucky) 28 February 1982. Drucker received Bachelor of Arts and Doctor of Philosophy degrees in anthropology from the University of California, Berkeley. In the first twenty years of his career, periods of ethnographic or archaeological field research were interrupted by two tours of duty in the U.S. Navy, one of them as Staff Anthropologist in the U.S.-administered Trust Territory, Micronesia. Drucker's early studies of Northwest Coast Indian cultures, for which he received his first and probably most enduring recognition, were part of a University of California Pacific Coast ethnographic survey to which he contributed other reports. His archaeological work in Mexico, the second major career interest, was done for the Bureau of American Ethnology, Smithsonian Institution. During the period 1955-1967, Drucker was a rancher in Vera Cruz, Mexico. From that experience came a vivid and accurately descriptive book, *Tropical Frontier*, published under the name Paul Record. After his return to the U.S., Drucker taught at four universities, principally at the University of Kentucky, where a fourth region of work developed: research basic to applied anthropology projects in rural Kentucky. Although Drucker is not usually considered an applied anthropologist, this was actually his third arena of such work, after the Northwest Coast and Micronesia.

Drucker's work was characterized by its variety and comprehensiveness geographically, culturally, historically, and technically. In his fifty publications, he not only systematized large quantities of data, for example in his work on Olmec (Mexico) ceramics; he also characterized and ventured explanatory theories of the prehistoric and historic developments that he had recorded. His concern with cultural adaptation by living people appears in his writing on Northwest Coast community organization in Alaska and British Columbia and on Mexican swidden agriculture. Regarding both material and expressive aspects of culture, he provided useful works on Olmec architecture, art and iconography and Kwakiutl (British Columbia) ceremony. Besides detailed reports for specialists, he wrote two books on Northwest Coast Indians for school and general use. From the 1930s to the 1980s, Drucker related ethnography and archaeology to each other, as an early practitioner of ethno-archaeology.

MAJOR WORKS: *The Northern and Central Nootkan Tribes* (Washington: 1951); *La Venta, Tabasco: a Study of Olmec Ceramics and Art* (Washington: 1952); *The Native Brotherhoods: Modern Intertribal Organizations on the Northwest Coast* (Washington: 1958); (with R.F. Heizer and R.J. Squier) *Excavations at La Venta, Tabasco, 1955* (Washington: 1959); (with R.F. Heizer) *To Make My Name Good: a Reappraisal of the Southern Kwakiutl Potlatch* (Berkeley: 1967); *Tropical Frontier* (New York: 1969).

SOURCES: Homer G. Barnett, *Anthropology in Administration* (New York: 1956), pp. 98-101; Margaret Lantis, "Philip Drucker, 1911-1982," *American Anthropologist*, vol. 85 (1983), pp. 897-902; *The Excavations at La Venta* [film] (Berkeley: 1963).

Margaret Lantis

DuBois, Cora. Anthropologist. Born in Brooklyn (New York) 26 October 1903, died in Cambridge (Massachusetts) 7 April 1991. As a cultural anthropologist DuBois made important contributions to culture and personality studies, the study of change in complex societies, and interdisciplinary, international team research. Trained at Barnard (B.A., 1927), Columbia (M.A., 1928) and the University of California at Berkeley (Ph.D., 1932), where she was influenced by ROBERT H. LOWIE, DuBois did her first fieldwork, salvage ethnography, among the Wintu of California in 1929.

During 1938-1939 she did pioneering fieldwork among the Alor, in which she used psychological projective tests and collected autobiographies and children's drawings as supplements to ethnography. *The People of Alor* had an impact on both theory and methodology in psychological anthropology. From 1961 to 1972 DuBois directed interdisciplinary research conducted by American and Indian anthropology students on culture change in Bhubaneswar, Orissa, India, in which she provided the students with social science training while they were engaged in research. Although she chose not to publish the results of this research, her research material is available for others to use at the Regenstein Library at the University of Chicago.

DuBois taught anthropology at Hunter College (1936) and Sarah Lawrence College (1939-1942). From 1942 to 1954 she was engaged in applied anthropology for the World Health Organization, the U.S. State Department and the International Institute of Education, which took her to Switzerland, India, Ceylon (Sri Lanka) and Southeast Asia; this period also provided an opportunity to apply anthropological principles to understanding American culture. From 1954 until her retirement in 1969, DuBois was affiliated with the Harvard University Departments of Anthropology and Social Relations, as holder of the Radcliffe College Zemurray Professorship. DuBois served as President of the American Anthropological Association (1968-1969) and of the Association of Asian Studies (1969-1970). For her applied anthropology she received the U.S. Army Exceptional Civilian Award (1945) and the Order of the Crown of Thailand Peace Medal (1949). Among her other honors are the American Association of University Women Achievement Award (1961) and honorary degrees from Harvard University and Mills, Mount Holyoke, Wheaton and Wilson Colleges. Throughout her career DuBois was interested in individuals and cultural values and questioned the validity of anthropology as a science. She considered anthropology to be "philosophical humanism ... an attempt to understand."

MAJOR WORKS: *Wintu Ethnography* (Berkeley: 1935) (= *University of California Publications in American Archaeology and Ethnography*, vol. 36, no. 1); *The People of Alor* (Minneapolis: 1944; reissued with new chapter, Cambridge, Mass: 1960); "The Alorese" in: Abram Kardiner (editor), *The Psychological Frontiers of Society* (New York: 1945), pp. 101-258; "The dominant value profile of American culture," *American Anthropologist*, vol. 57 (1955), pp. 1232-1239; "Some notions on learning intercultural understanding" in: George D. Spindler (editor), *Education and Anthropology* (Stanford: 1955), pp. 89-105; *Foreign Students and Higher Education in the United States* (Washington: 1956); "The cultural interplay between East and West" in: Cora DuBois [et al.], *The*

East and West Must Meet, a Symposium (East Lansing: 1959), pp. 1-20; "Studies in an Indian town" in: Peggy Golde (editor), *Women in the Field* (Chicago: 1970), pp. 221-236; "Some anthropological hindsights," *Annual Review of Anthropology*, vol. 9 (1980), pp. 1-13; (editor) *Lowie's Selected Papers in Anthropology* (Berkeley: 1960).

SOURCES: Cora DuBois, "Some anthropological hindsights," *Annual Review of Anthropology*, vol. 9 (1980), pp. 1-13; Cora DuBois, "Studies in an Indian town" in: Peggy Golde (editor), *Women in the Field* (Chicago: 1970), pp. 221-236; Susan Seymour, "Cora DuBois" in: Ute Gacs [et al.] (editors), *Women Anthropologists: a Biographical Dictionary* (New York: 1988), pp. 72-79.

Nancy J. Schmidt

Dubois, Eugène (Marie Eugène François Thomas Dubois). Anthropologist, anatomist, paleontologist. Born in Eijsden (Netherlands) 28 January 1858, died in Haelen (Netherlands) 16 December 1940. Dubois earned world-wide fame through his discovery of *Pithecanthropus erectus* (now *Homo erectus*), the "upright, walking, ape-man of Java."

Dubois was educated as an anatomist at Amsterdam University. Later on in his career, in 1899, he became professor of crystallography, mineralogy, geology and paleontology at the same university. Meanwhile, he had followed his predilection for paleoanthropological research and embarked on a search for man's primitive ancestors in the Netherlands East Indies. Supported by the Dutch colonial government, Dubois worked in Sumatra and Java from 1888 until 1895. The famous remains of *Pithecanthropus* (a skullcap, a thigh bone and a few molars) and a wealth of other vertebrate fossils were discovered near the village of Trinil, Java, during the years 1891-1893. For Dubois, these remains provided conclusive proof of man's descent from more primitive primates. *Pithecanthropus*, in his view, was the missing link between ape and man. After his return to Europe, Dubois spent several years trying to convince the world of the importance of his find. Although no consensus of opinion was reached on its exact nature, most researchers agreed that *Pithecanthropus* did indeed represent a link in the chain that connects man with his primitive ancestors. Thus, Dubois' fossils were the first hominid remains to be accepted as material proof for human evolution. His find also inspired researchers to an evolutionary interpretation of Neanderthal remains, which had been known since 1856 but until then had been ascribed to a primitive, yet fully human, race. Dubois' pioneering efforts thus helped give shape to the rising science of paleoanthropology.

After 1900 Dubois withdrew from the debate on *Pithecanthropus* and devoted himself to various anatomical, paleontological and geological studies. Among the most important of these was an investigation of cephalization (i.e., the mathematical relation between brain size and body size) in vertebrates, including the hominids. Although Dubois' results have become obsolete, his investigation must be seen as a pioneering attempt to establish allometric relations. His cephalization studies convinced Dubois that evolution in vertebrates proceeded in jumps. The distance between the apes and human beings, he believed, had been covered in two jumps: one from the apes to *Pithecanthropus* and one from *Pithecanthropus* to man. Against the background of this rather idiosyncratic theory it is perhaps understandable that Dubois never accepted the new *Pithecanthropus* finds that were made in Java in the 1930s by G.H.R. von Koenigswald (1902-1982). For von Koenigswald concluded—correctly—from his investigation of the new evidence that

Pithecanthropus was much closer to *Homo sapiens* than Dubois, on the basis of his cephalization studies, was prepared to allow.

MAJOR WORKS: "Over de wenschelijkheid van een onderzoek naar de diluviale fauna van Ned. Indië, in het bijzonder van Sumatra," *Natuurkundig Tijdschrift voor Nederlandsch-Indië*, vol. 48 (1889), pp. 148-165; *Pithecanthropus erectus, eine menschenähnliche Uebergangsform aus Java* (Batavia: 1894); "The proto-Australian fossil man of Wadjak, Java," *Proceedings of the Section of Sciences of the Koninklijke Akademie van Wetenschappen*, vol. 23 (1921), pp. 1013-1051; "On the principal characters of the cranium and the brain, the mandible and the teeth of *Pithecanthropus erectus*," *Proceedings of the Section of Sciences of the Koninklijke Akademie van Wetenschappen*, vol. 27 (1924), pp. 265-278 and 459-464; "On the principal characters of the femur of *Pithecanthropus erectus*," *Proceedings of the Section of Sciences of the Koninklijke Akademie van Wetenschappen*, vol. 29 (1926), pp. 730-743; "Die phylogenetische Grosshirnzunahme autonome Vervollkommnung der animalen Funktionen," *Biologia Generalis*, vol. 6 (1930), pp. 247-292; "The distinct organization of *Pithecanthropus* of which the femur bears evidence, now confirmed from other individuals of the described species," *Proceedings of the Section of Sciences of the Koninklijke Akademie van Wetenschappen*, vol. 35 (1932), pp. 716-722; "On the gibbon-like appearance of the *Pithecanthropus erectus*," *Proceedings of the Section of Sciences of the Koninklijke Akademie van Wetenschappen*, vol. 38 (1935), pp. 578-585; "The fossil remains discovered in Java by Dr. G.H.R. von Koenigswald and attributed by him to *Pithecanthropus erectus*, in reality remains of *Homo wadjakensis* (syn. *Homo soloensis*)," *Proceedings of the Section of Sciences of the Koninklijke Akademie van Wetenschappen*, vol. 43 (1940), pp. 494-496, 842-851 and 1268-1275.

SOURCES: B. Theunissen, *Eugène Dubois and the Ape-Man from Java: the History of the First Missing Link and its Discoverer* (Dordrecht, Boston and London: 1988); L.D. Brongersma, "De verzameling van Indische fossielen (Collectie Dubois)," *De Indische Gids*, vol. 63 (1941), pp. 97-116.

B. Theunissen

Dubois, Jean-Antoine. Roman Catholic Abbé with the Missions-étrangères de Paris. Born in Saint-Remèze, Ardèche (France) 10 January 1766, died in Paris (France) 17 February 1848. As a boy he attended school at Bourg-Saint-Andéol and then the seminary of his mission in Paris, completing his training there in 1792. Though he was to write an early French version of the *Panchatantra* or *Indian Book of Fables*, he is still remembered and widely read for his one massive masterpiece, *Hindu Manners, Customs and Ceremonies*, the fruit of his missionary wanderings in South India during the years 1793-1823. He acquired an excellent command of English, Latin, Greek, Tamil and Kannada as well as some acquaintance with Telugu, Sanskrit and Persian, or so his book implies. He seems to have had no training in anything like proto-ethnology—first taught in Paris by PAUL BROCA in 1859—but he was thoroughly familiar with Montesquieu's *Spirit of the Laws* (1748). Most probably he also knew J.N. Demeunier's *Customs and Manners of Different Peoples* (1776), since Demeunier covers precisely the same categories that are in Dubois' major work. Further influences on Dubois are suggested in Hockings (1977).

Dubois was a royalist, generally pro-British, and devoted to the physical welfare of the people, both Hindu and Christian, who lived in his sphere of influence. He conducted his inquiries in Tamil and Kannada dressed as a Hindu holy man. The breadth of his anthropological interests is staggering for such an early writer: culture and personality, comparative religion, primitive economics, linguistics, prehistory, in addition to his central interest in ethnography. He advances no particular theory of society but remains strongly empirical throughout the 722 pages of his book.

But was it his? Sylvia Murr (1977; 1987) has adduced much compelling evidence to suggest the Abbé Dubois was one of the most effective plagiarists in the history of anthropology. While the actual manuscript still exists at the India Office Library in London and would appear to be in his hand, Dr. Murr has demonstrated (to general surprise) that the great bulk of the book is taken from two earlier French writers, Fr. G.-L. Coeurdoux, S.J., and Nicolas-Jacques Desvaulx (1745-1825), whose manuscript *Moeurs et Coutumes des Indiens*, written about 1776, also rests in the India Office Library. The fact that Dubois was paid a handsome sum by the Madras Government for his manuscript does not make this discovery any more palatable.

MAJOR WORKS: *Letters on the State of Christianity in India, in which the Conversion of the Hindoos is Considered as Impracticable* (London: 1823); *Hindu Manners, Customs and Ceremonies* (Oxford, etc.: 1817, 1897, etc.) [there are several editions in various languages].

SOURCES: Paul Hockings, "The Abbé Dubois, an early French ethnographer," *Contributions to Indian Sociology*, n.s., vol. 11 (1977), pp. 329-343; Albin Mazon, *Un Missionaire vivarois aux Indes (L'Abbé Dubois, de Saint-Remèze)* (Privas: 1899); Sylvia Murr, "Nicolas Jacques Desvaulx (1745-1823), véritable auteur des *Moeurs, Institutions et Cérémonies des Peuples de l'Inde* de l'Abbé Dubois," *Puruṣārtha*, vol. 3 (1977), pp. 245-258; Sylvia Murr, *L'Inde philosophique entre Bossuet et Voltaire*. Vol 1. '*Moeurs et Coutumes des Indiens*' *de G.L. Coeurdoux, s.j., et N.J. Desvaulx* (Paris: 1987).

Paul Hockings

Dumézil, Georges. Comparative mythologist, Indo-European philologist. Born in Paris (France) 4 March 1898, died in Paris (France) 11 October 1986. Dumézil attended the Lycée Louis-le-Grand and later the École Normale Supérieure. He received a doctorate from the University of Paris in 1924. Although he contributed significantly to a variety of subjects of interest to anthropologists, from Caucasian folklore to Quéchua linguistics, his chief contribution to scholarship was the development of what has come to be called "the new comparative mythology."

Drawing on the Durkheimian postulate that belief systems are necessarily grounded in social facts, as well as on the theories and methods of Indo-European philology, Dumézil was able to rescue comparative mythology from the relative oblivion into which it had sunk in the early decades of this century by synthesizing a comprehensive model of the common Indo-European ideology—that is, the cognitive structure in terms of which the ancient Indo-European speakers ordered their social and supernatural universes. This model, which forms the core of the "new comparative mythology," is predicated on three fundamental principles: (1) the maintenance of juridical and sacerdotal sovereignty; (2) the exercise of physical prowess; and (3) the promotion of physical well-being, fertility, wealth, etc. Each principle forms the basis of what Dumézil called a *fonction* (function)—a complex whole that includes both the ideological principle itself and its numerous social and mythological manifestations. At least some evidence for the presence of this tripartite ideology can be found in almost every ancient Indo-European speaking tradition, from India to Iceland. Moreover, it is manifested not only in the structure of myth and social organization, but also in triads of epic heroes, threefold categories of diseases, and even tripartite conceptions of physical space.

At first glance, the foregoing thesis might seem similar to that espoused by CLAUDE LÉVI-STRAUSS, who has indeed described Dumézil as a pioneer structuralist. However, the two French scholars differ profoundly when it comes to their basic assumptions. Unlike Lévi-Strauss, Dumézil did not claim to have discovered a set of universal structural principles that govern the way human beings everywhere look at the world. On the contrary, the tripartite ideology is, by definition, uniquely Indo-European, and is therefore bounded in time and space.

Dumézil's theories and methods have not always met with universal approval, and some critics have suggested that on occasion he was wont to impose the tripartite model on data that are amenable to other interpretations. However, the great bulk of his work has stood the test of time and is today widely considered to be the most important contribution yet made to our understanding of the ancient Indo-European *Weltanschauung*.

From 1948 to his retirement in 1968, Dumézil was Professeur de la Civilisation Indo-Européenne at the Collège de France (Paris). In 1978 he was elected to the Académie Française.

MAJOR WORKS: *Jupiter, Mars, Quirinus: Essai sur la conception indo-européenne de la société et sur les origines de Rome* (Paris: 1941); *Mitra-Varuna*, 2nd ed. (Paris: 1948) [tr.: *Mitra-Varuna* (New York: 1988)]; *Les dieux des Indo-Européens* (Paris: 1952); *L'idéologie tripartie des Indo-Européens* (Brussels: 1958); *Les dieux des Germains* (Paris: 1959) [tr.: *Gods of the Ancient Northmen* (Berkeley: 1973)]; *La religion romaine archaïque* (Paris: 1966) [tr.: *Archaic Roman Religion* (Chicago: 1970)]; *Mythe et épopée. I. L'Idéologie des trois fonctions dans les épopées des peuples indo-européens* (Paris: 1968); *Heur et malheur du guerrière* (Paris: 1969) [tr.: *The Destiny of the Warrior* (Chicago: 1970)]; *Du mythe au roman* (Paris: 1970) [tr.: *From Myth to Fiction* (Chicago: 1973)]; *Mythe et épopée. II. Types épiques indo-européens: un héros, un sorcier, un roi* (Paris: 1971) [3rd part tr.: *The Destiny of a King* (Chicago: 1973), 1st part tr.: *The Stakes of the Warrior* (Berkeley: 1983), 2nd part tr.: *The Plight of a Sorcerer* (Berkeley: 1986)]; *Mythe et épopée III. Histoires romaines* (Paris: 1973) [2nd part tr.: *Camillus: a Study of Indo-European Religion as History* (Berkeley: 1980)]; *Les dieux souverains des Indo-Européens* (Paris: 1977).

SOURCES: Georges Dumézil, *Entretiens avec Didier Erebon* (Paris: 1987); Lucien Gerschel, "Georges Dumézil's comparative studies in tales and traditions," *Midwest Folklore*, vol. 7 (1957), pp. 141-147; C. Scott Littleton, "Dumézil, Georges" in: David L. Sills (editor), *International Encyclopedia of the Social Sciences* (New York: 1968-1979), vol. 18, pp. 159-162; Claude Lévi-Strauss, "Social structure" in: A.L. Kroeber (editor), *Anthropology Today* (Chicago: 1953), pp. 524-553 (see especially p. 535); C. Scott Littleton, *The New Comparative Mythology: an Anthropological Assessment of the Theories of Georges Dumézil* (3rd ed., Berkeley: 1982); C. Scott Littleton, "'Je ne suis pas ... structuraliste': some fundamental differences between Dumézil and Lévi-Strauss," *Journal of Asian Studies*, vol. 34 (1974), pp. 151-158; Jean-Claude Rivière (editor), *Georges Dumézil á la découverte des Indo-Européens* (Paris: 1979); P. Smith and D. Sperber, "Mythologiques de Georges Dumézil," *Annales économies, sociétés, civilisations*, vol. 26 (1971), pp. 559-586; Udo Strutynski, "Introduction" to: Georges Dumézil, *Camillus: a Study of Indo-European Religion as Roman History* (Berkeley: 1980), pp. 1-39.

C. Scott Littleton

Dumont, Louis. Anthropologist, Indianist, comparative sociologist. Born in Salonika [now Thessaloniki] (Turkey, now Greece) 1911. Dumont is Directeur d'études at the École des Hautes Études en Sciences Sociales, Paris. He is best known for his landmark study of the Indian caste system (*Homo Hierarchicus*), his conceptual views on hierarchy, and his innovative analysis of the western ideology of egalitarianism through its national variants (*Homo Aequalis*). A specialist in kinship models, he designed an original theory of the role of marriage alliance (*Introduction à deux théories d'anthropologie sociale*; *Dravidien et Kariera*; *Affinity as a Value*). A student of MARCEL MAUSS and of Louis Renou, he became closely associated with E.E. EVANS-PRITCHARD during his lectureship at Oxford (1951-1955), developing a methodological synthesis between the French tradition of Durkheimian sociology and British structuralism.

In his early works, emerging out of prolonged fieldwork, Dumont became well known as a talented ethnographer. His analysis of a festival in Provence, centered on the cult of Sainte Marthe in relation to a dragon (*La Tarasque*), demonstrated the importance of regional configurations within Mediterranean Christianity, while his comprehensive description of an Indian caste and village life in South India (*Une souscaste de l'Inde du sud*) was intended as a first step in the application of social anthropology to the understanding of complex societies and great civilizations. In the 1960s, Dumont played a crucial role in remodeling the area of Indian studies in France, through the *Contributions to Indian Sociology* (1957-1966), a journal he jointly edited with D.F. Pocock and as the director of the Centre d'études indiennes (Center of Indian Studies). At the confluence of Indology and sociology (*Une souscaste de l'Inde du sud, La civilisation indienne et nous*), his project took shape against the then-dominant trends of Orientalist philology.

While his works on caste and on kinship are widely recognized and considered landmarks for every student of South Asia, the hierarchical model he derived from the ritual opposition between the pure and the impure and the disjunction he established between status and power have raised many debates and still challenge most theories on social stratification. Over the last twenty years Dumont's interests in hierarchy have shifted to new directions, reversing the holistic approach he had applied to traditional societies to a comparative study of the history of Western ideas and social theory. In his work, the emergence of the individual during the first centuries of the Christian Church is seen against the background of the Hindu renouncer, while in his study the historical and ideological separation of the political and of the economic domains from the religious universe is considered part of a process leading toward egalitarianism. In his comparative studies, Dumont daringly combines cultural relativism, multiple acculturations and universalistic assumptions to establish the growth and identity of nationalist values that allow him to produce extended discussions of the political economy of British liberalism; the literary, philosophical and aesthetic thought of German idealism; and the political cleavages of French society since the Third Republic.

Among the first to have proposed a comparative approach toward an anthropology of modernity, Dumont also proposed a radical interpretation of racism, totalitarianism and religious fundamentalism, which he considered the results of dangerous drives present within individualism, a dialectical outcome of universalist ideas on identity and sameness confusing discrimination and difference but remaining intensified expressions of ideological values that have also produced democracy. One can also argue that Dumont's commitment to systems theory, formal logic and thought processes he approaches under a conceptual framework of hierarchy—conceived after Saint Augustine, A.M. HOCART, GEORGES DUMÉZIL and Talcott Parsons, as the relationship of the encompassing and the encompassed—may foster innovative views that lead toward an anthropology of cognition.

Dumont holds honorary degrees from the University of Chicago and the University of Lausanne. He is a member of the British Academy and of the American

Academy for the Arts and Sciences, and he has been awarded the Académie Française Prize (1984) and the Tocqueville Prize (1987).

MAJOR WORKS: *La Tarasque* (Paris: 1951; new ed., Paris: 1987); *Une souscaste de l'Inde du sud* (Paris: 1957) [tr.: *A South Indian Subcaste* (Delhi: 1986)]; *Hierarchy and Marriage Alliance in South India* (London: 1957); *La civilisation indienne et nous* (Paris: 1964; new ed., Paris: 1975); *Homo Hierarchicus: essai sur le système des castes* (Paris: 1967; new ed., *Homo Hierarchicus: le système des castes et ses implications*, Paris: 1979) [tr.: *Homo Hierarchicus* (Chicago: 1970, 1980)]; *Introduction à deux théories d'anthropologie sociale* (Paris: 1971); *Dravidien et Kariera: l'alliance de mariage dans l'Inde du Sud et en Australie* (Paris: 1975); *Homo Aequalis: I* (Paris: 1977) [tr.: *From Mandeville to Marx: the Genesis and Triumph of Economic Ideology* (Chicago: 1977)]; *Affinity as a Value: Marriage Alliance in South India, with Comparative Essays on Australia* (Chicago: 1983); *Essais sur l'individualisme: une perspective anthropologique sur l'idéologie moderne* (Paris: 1983) [tr.: *Essays on Individualism: Modern Ideology in Anthropological Perspective* (Chicago: 1986)].

SOURCES: Personal contact; T.N. Madan (editor), *Way of Life: King, Householder, Renouncer: Essays in Honour of Louis Dumont* (Delhi: 1982; new ed., New Delhi: 1988); J.C. Galey (editor), *Différences, valeurs, hiérarchie* (Paris: 1984); G. Berthoud and G. Busino, *L'exploration de la modernité* (Geneva: 1984); V. Descombes, *Philosophie par gros temps* (Paris: 1989); *Dictionnaire de l'ethnologie et de l'anthropologie* (Paris: 1991).

Jean-Claude Galey

Dunham, Katherine. Anthropologist, dancer, choreographer, dance ethnologist. Born in Glen Ellyn (Illinois) 22 June 1912. Dunham's importance to anthropology stems from her dual perspective as a dancer and as an anthropologist. She developed the two careers simultaneously through her studies in anthropology at the University of Chicago and her study of ballet and modern dance with Ludmilla Speranzeva, Ruth Page and Mark Turbyfill.

Influenced first by ROBERT REDFIELD and later by MELVILLE HERSKOVITS, Dunham went to the West Indies in 1935 on a Rosenwald fellowship to do research on dance. During that year, she worked in Jamaica, Trinidad, Martinique and Haiti. Her analysis of dance in its cultural context, *Dances of Haiti*, was one of the earliest serious works in the anthropology of dance.

Dunham's influence extends far beyond the usual academic sphere. Her conviction that African-American dance was a cultural tradition in its own right led her to present that tradition in performance. She established the Negro Dance Group in Chicago and from 1937 to the mid-1960s, the company had regular seasons in New York, toured widely throughout Latin America, Europe, the United States, and the Far East and performed in a number of films and musicals. Dunham brought her anthropological expertise to bear on the choreography of the repertoire. It was a considerable change from the commonly held public stereotypes of Black performance. Audiences were more accustomed to seeing Blacks in vaudeville routines reminiscent of minstrel shows or as tap dancers. Dunham's presentation of West Indian, African, and African-American dances forced a reexamination of the role of African-American performers and their cultural heritage.

In her writings, her choreography, and her development of a technique, Dunham argued for a sociological rather than a racial interpretation of African-American dance traditions. While she herself used the term "primitive" in reference to those traditions, it is clear that she did not adhere to any evolutionary explanation. She was acutely aware of the impact of industrialization and all the baggage of the western technological world on the dances of third-world peoples.

Dunham has sometimes been criticized for her theatricality, for not presenting authentic dance choreography. Like any good artist, Dunham was concerned with presenting universal themes and situations. She took her subject matter from the African-American tradition but did not attempt to reproduce every step and every gesture. In her best works, she succeeds in giving us the essence of these various African-American traditions.

Driven by the need to foster an appreciation of the cultural heritage of black Americans, Dunham established a cultural arts program in East St. Louis. Talented youngsters received training at her Performing Arts Training Center. The Katherine Dunham Museum, with its collections of African and West Indian art, was opened in that same community in 1978. In recognition of her work, Dunham was given the Albert Schweitzer Music Award in 1979. In 1983, she was honored by the American Anthropological Association with its Distinguished Service Award.

MAJOR WORKS: "Form and function of primitive dance" *Educational Dance*, vol. 4, no. 4 (October 1941), pp. 2-4; "The Negro dance" in: Sterling Brown, A. Davis, and U. Lee (editors), *The Negro Caravan* (New York: 1941), pp. 990-1000; "Ethnic dancing," *Dance Magazine* (September 1946), pp. 22-35; *Katherine Dunham's Journey to Accompong* (New York: 1946); "The dances of Haiti," *Acta Anthropologica*, vol. 2, no. 4 (1947), pp. 1-60; *A Touch of Innocence* (New York: 1959); *Island Possessed* (New York: 1969).

SOURCES: Joyce Aschenbrenner, *Katherine Dunham: Reflections on the Social and Political Contexts of Afro-American Dance* (New York: 1981) (= *Dance Research Annual*, no. 12); Anatole Chujoy and P.W. Manchester, *The Dance Encyclopedia* (New York: 1967), pp. 318-319; Barbara Naomi Cohen-Stratyner, *Biographical Dictionary of Dance* (New York: 1982), pp. 284-285; Lynne Fauley Emery, *Black Dance in the United States from 1619 to 1970* (Palo Alto: 1972).

Anya Peterson Royce

Dupont, Edouard François. Geologist, paleontologist. Born in Dinant, Namur (Belgium) 30 January 1841, died in Cannes (France) 31 March 1911. A doctor of natural sciences, he was instructed in geology by J.B. d'Omalius d'Halloy. He was director of the Musée d'Histoire Naturelle (Natural History Museum) in Brussels from 1868 to 1909.

In May 1864 his project for the excavation of the caves in the province of Namur received the approval of the Ministry of the Interior. He began his excavations with the caves of the Furfooz massif, notably the Trou du Frontal (celebrated for the discovery of two crania) and the Trou de la Naulette, where the discovery of a mandible excited much interest by virtue of the archaic characteristics exhibited.

Dupont assembled a large collection of paleontological and lithic materials that he used to establish the existence of three different ages he termed the age of the elephant, the age of the reindeer and the age of polished stone. By the beginning of 1867, twenty-seven caves in the valley of the Lesse had been studied. Dupont also explored the caves of Chaleux and Montaigle, the Trou Magrite at Pont-à-Lesse and the cave of Goyet (where he discovered two *bâtons de commandements*). In 1872 he explored the caves of Engis and in 1877 and 1892 several Neolithic ossuaries at Hatière and Waulsort.

MAJOR WORKS: "Étude sur l'ethnographie de l'âge du renne dans les cavernes de la vallée de la Lesse," *Mémoires couronnés de l'Académie royale de Belgique*, vol. 19 (1867), pp. 1-76; "Sur la succession des temps quaternaires d'après les modifications observées dans la taille du silex," *Bulletin de l'Académie royale de Belgique*, 2nd sér., vol. 25 (1868), pp. 38-41; *Les temps préhistoriques en Belgique* (Brussels: 1872); "Théorie des âges de la pierre en Belgique," *Bulletin de la Société d'Anthropologie de Paris*, 2nd sér., vol. 9 (1874), pp. 728-761; "Quelques mots sur l'évolution," *Bulletin de l'Académie royale de Belgique*, 3rd sér., vol. 35 (1898), pp. 601-636.

SOURCES: F. Twiesselmann, "Notice sur l'oeuvre archéologique d'Edouard-François Dupont" in: *Études d'histoire et d'archéologie namuroises dédiées à Ferdinand Courtoy* (Namur: 1952), pp. 17-30 [contains bibliography]; Fr. Stockmans, "Notice sur Edouard Dupont," *Annuaire de l'Académie royale de Belgique*, vol. 131 (1965), pp. 1-57 [contains bibliography].

André Leguebe
[Translation from French: Timothy Eastridge and Robert B. Marks Ridinger]

Durham, Mary Edith. Traveler, ethnographer. Born in London (England) 8 December 1863, died in London (England) 15 November 1944. Durham was first trained as an artist, held a few exhibitions of drawings and paintings and illustrated several books. From 1900 onward she traveled extensively through the Balkans, especially in Montenegro and Albania, where she studied the manners and customs of the different peoples.

In her first book, *Through the Lands of the Serb*, Durham is primarily a skillful and humorous narrator, although the first deliberate investigations can already be seen. *The Burden of the Balkans* and *High Albania* show her growing interest in Albania and provide us with a mine of highly interesting ethnological information about tribal life in the area, against the background of recent and earlier history. Her later books and articles focus more and more on political issues. In these Durham identifed herself with the national struggle of the Albanians.

During her travels Durham collected information on the organization of tribal systems; on the different laws and ideas of justice; on tattooing and the symbols tattooed; on social relationships and blood customs; on customs concerning birth, marriage, and death; on magic and medicine; and on Balkan taboos. She compiled all this information in her last book, *Some Tribal Origins: Laws and Customs of the Balkans*. Besides writing, Durham collected many garments and other material objects and labeled them with information on their historical and regional context. She also made many sketches, water colors and photographs, which she used to illustrate her books.

Durham's ethnographic work has been recognized by Balkan anthropologists, especially for the data she was in a position to collect and for her insights on the region during a turbulent historical period. However, her firm political stance made her many enemies too. She was condemned for her unbending one-sidedness in defending the rights of the Albanians against the Great Serbian Idea and against the imperialistic ideas of the Great Powers. On the other hand she won the confidence of the Albanians and became something of a living legend.

She was made a Fellow of the Royal Anthropological Institute.

MAJOR WORKS: *Through the Lands of the Serb* (London: 1904); *The Burden of the Balkans* (London: 1905); *High Albania* (London: 1909); *The Struggle for Scutari* (London: 1914); *Twenty Years of Balkan Tangle* (London: 1920); *Some Tribal Origins: Laws and Customs of the Balkans* (London: 1928); *The Durham Collection of Garments and Embroideries from Albania and Yugoslavia* (by Laura E. Start, with notes by M. Edith Durham) (Halifax: 1939).

SOURCES: King Zog of Albania, "Miss Edith Durham," *The Times* (21 November 1944), p. 6; John L. Myres, H.J. Braunholtz, Beatrice Blackwood, "Mary Edith Durham: 8 Dec., 1863-15 Nov., 1944," *Man*, vol. 45 (1945), nos. 12, 13, 14, pp. 21-23; John Hodgson, "Introduction" to: M.E. Durham, *High Albania* (London: 1985), p. ix-xvi; Kudret Isai, "Edith Durham, an outstanding friend of the Albanian people," *New Albania* (1988), no. 5; Shaqir Shaqiri, "Edith Durham et les albanais" in: *Les lettres albanaises* (1982), pp. 188-199; Dea Birkett, *Spinsters Abroad* (Oxford: 1989); John Hodgson, "Edith Durham, traveller and publicist" in: Antonia Young and John Allcock, *Black Lambs and Grey Falcons* (Bradford: forthcoming); Tiny van Hal, *Reiziger of Etnograaf, de betekenis van Mary Edith Durham's werk voor de antropologie* [unpublished M.A. thesis] (Amsterdam: forthcoming).

Tiny van Hal

Dynowski, Witold. Ethnologist. Born in Harbin (Manchuria under Russian occupation, now in China) 23 August 1903, died in Warsaw (Poland) 31 July 1986. Dynowski began studying law at the University of Warsaw in 1922. In 1924 he transferred to the University of Vilnius where he changed his field of studies to philosophy and ethnography. Under the guidance of CEZARIA BAUDOUIN DE COURTENAY-EHRENKREUTZ-JĘDRZEJOWICZOWEJ, he obtained a master's degree (1929) and doctorate (1937). In 1935 he moved to Warsaw where he was employed as an adjunct in the Department of Polish Ethnography. After World War II he played an active role in the renewed activity of the Department. In 1947 he was appointed as assistant professor and in 1949 he became the director of the Department and Institute of Ethnography. He later became an associate and then a full professor. In 1973 he retired, but still remained active in research. Dynowski was actively engaged in the creation of the Institute of the History of Material Culture of the Polish Academy of Sciences (1953), and for many years he was the Director of the Department of Polish and General Ethnography at the above Institute. He was also the founder and editor-in-chief of *Etnografia Polska*.

Dynowski's research was concerned with the dynamics of cultural change in light of the slow rhythm of transformations isolated geographically, historically or socially, hence his interest in the culture of Kurpie, Podlasie and, outside of Poland, Australia and Mongolia. He also organized ethnographic expeditions to Bulgaria and Mongolia.

MAJOR WORKS: *Barwne kufry chłopskie z Wileńszczyzny i Polesia* [*Painted Peasant Boxes from the Vilnius Region and Polesie*] (Vilnius: 1934); *Sztuka ludowa Wileńszczyzny i Nowogródczyzny*] [*Folk Art of the Vilnius and Nowogrod Regions*] (Vilnius: 1935); "Dawne i nowe w kulturze chłopskiej na Mazowszu" ["Old and new in the peasant culture of Mazovia"] in: *Rok ziemi Mazowieckiej* [*The Year of the Mazovian Land*] (Warsaw: 1972); *Współczesna Mongolia* [*Modern Mongolia*] (Wrocław: 1968).

SOURCES: Zofia Sokolewicz, "Jubileusz 75-lecia urodzin i 55-lecia pracy naukowej prof. dra Witolda Dynowskiego" ["75th anniversary of the birth and 55 years of scientific work of Professor Witold Dynowski"], *Roczniki Uniwersytetu Warszawskiego* [*Yearbook of the University of Warsaw*], vol. 18 (1978), pp. 152-156; Zofia Sokolewicz, "Witold Dynowski," *Etnografia Polska*, vol. 31 (1987), pp. 12-17.

Maria Niewiadomska and Iwona Grzelakowska
[Translation from Polish: Joel Janicki]

e

Eells, Myron. Missionary, clergyman. Born in Walker's Prairie (Washington) 7 October 1843, died in Twana (Washington) 4 January 1907. Eells was born at a Congregationalist mission in eastern Washington Territory, the son of two committed missionaries. After the Whitman Massacre of 1848 put a temporary halt to missionary activity in the region, the Eells family settled in Oregon's Willamette Valley, where Eells' father was a farmer, preacher, and instructor at the local college. Eells graduated from Pacific University in 1866, and attended Hartford Theological Seminary two years later. He was ordained in 1871 and spent the next three years as the Congregationalist minister in Boise City, Idaho. By 1874 he resigned to become a missionary, in the family tradition. His older brother Edwin was the U.S. Indian Agent for the Skokomish Indian Reservation, on Hood Canal, Washington, and Eells served as missionary there (for the American Mission Association) from 1874 until his death. In time, as the population of settlers in the area grew, he also became the Congregationalist minister for several local churches.

Were it not for two facts, Eells would likely have been quick to fade from the written record: he had more than average influence and authority as a missionary (due to his association with his powerful and forceful older brother), and he was a very prolific writer. Eells was an indefatigable student of Coast Salish languages and lifeways, and wrote dozens of articles on these subjects for the Smithsonian Institution and for popular and mission-oriented periodicals. (He also wrote a great deal on the mission movement, Marcus Whitman, and related topics.)

In 1893, four years after Washington became a state, Eells was chosen as the state's Superintendent of Ethnological Exhibits at the Columbian Exposition in Chicago.

Eells' work on the Coast Salish was never disinterested; he continually sought to convert them to Christianity and to maintain them as converts. A knowledge of languages and cultures clearly would aid that process, so he developed an impressive knowledge by dint of rigorous study. His written record of the Puget Sound and Olympic Peninsula peoples was a fortunate by-product of his missionary activities.

MAJOR WORKS: *The Indians of Puget Sound: the Notebooks of Myron Eells* (edited by George Pierre Castile) (Seattle: 1985); "The Twana language of Washington Territory," *American Antiquarian and Oriental Journal*, vol. 3 (1881), pp. 296-303; "Indians of Puget Sound," *American Antiquarian and Oriental Journal*, vol. 10 (1888), pp. 174-178; "The Twana, Chemakum and Klallam Indians of Washington Territory," *Smithsonian Institution, Annual Report* (1889), pp. 605-681; "The religion of the Indians of Puget Sound," *American Antiquarian and Oriental Journal*, vol. 12 (1890), pp. 160-165; "Indians of Puget Sound," *American Antiquarian and Oriental Journal* (1890), vol. 12, pp. 160-165; "Shaking religions," *The American Missionary*, vol. 46 (1892), pp. 157-158; "The Chinook Jargon," *American Anthropologist*, vol. 7 (1894), pp. 300-12.

SOURCES: "Eells, Myron" in: *Who Was Who in America*, vol. 1 (Chicago: 1968), p. 362; Robert H. Ruby and John A. Brown, *Myron Eells and the Puget Sound Indians* (Seattle: 1976).

David Lonergan

Eggan, Fred. Anthropologist. Born in Seattle (Washington) 12 September 1906, died in Santa Fe (New Mexico) 7 May 1991. The hallmark of Eggan's distinctive contribution was the reconciliation of American historical ethnology with the structural-functional approach of British social anthropology.

Although he began graduate work in psychology at the University of Chicago, Eggan soon decided to study archaeology and ethnology under FAY-COOPER COLE (see "The ethnological cultures and their archeological backgrounds"). When British social anthropologist A.R. RADCLIFFE-BROWN joined the faculty in 1931, Eggan became his research assistant and was assigned the task of summarizing the data on American Indian social systems. Although most anthropologists considered the American and British approaches to be competing, Eggan brought them together in his ethnographic studies, eventually articulating the synthesis in his presidential address to the American Anthropological Association, "Social anthropology and the method of controlled comparison." He taught anthropology at the University of Chicago from 1935 to 1974.

Eggan focused much of his career on the study of North American Indians. Based on field work with the Hopi, Choctaw, Cheyenne and Arapaho, he interpreted patterns of differences in the kinship and social systems of the Western Pueblos, as well as those of Indian groups in the Southeast and on the Plains, as representing change through time and reflecting the influence of ecology. Eggan's students, beginning with Alexander Spoehr, tested the method of controlled comparison in many ethnographic contexts, most notably in native North America. Through his teaching and writings, Eggan vitalized the study of American Indian kinship and social systems, conceptually one of the weakest areas of the Boasian ethnological approach.

In addition to his American Indian field work, under Cole's sponsorship Eggan also studied culture change among the Tinguian in the northern Philippines, using the concept of "cultural drift" (analogized from EDWARD SAPIR's "linguistic drift") to explain variation among geographically contiguous tribes as representing a series of changes with definite direction, intrinsic to the cultures rather than simply reflecting outside influences (see "Some aspects of culture change in the Northern Philippines" and "Cultural drift and social change"). In 1953, when the University of Chicago founded a Philippines Study Center, Eggan served as its director, training students in ethnography and in applied anthropology designed to help prepare the country for independence.

Eggan's writings are characterized by elegant syntheses of complex social and cultural data brought into focus around the underlying structures of social life. His writings reflect a talent for generalization and for the clear articulation of research problems. "Social anthropology: methods and results" is a masterful summary of work on North American Indian social systems, and Eggan's Lewis Henry Morgan lectures delivered at the University of Rochester (published as *The American Indian*) constitute the most thorough and readable synthesis of American Indian kinship and social organization in the literature and serve as a model comparative study.

MAJOR WORKS: (editor) *Social Anthropology of North American Tribes* (Chicago: 1937; enlarged ed., Chicago: 1955); "Some aspects of culture change in the Northern Philippines," *American Anthropologist*, vol. 43 (1941), pp. 11-18; *Social Organization of the Western Pueblos* (Chicago: 1950); "The ethnological cultures and their archeological backgrounds" in: James B. Griffin (editor), *Archaeology of Eastern United States* (Chicago: 1952), pp. 35-45 [reprinted in: *Essays in Social Anthropology and Ethnology* [see below], pp. 157-189]; "Social anthropology and the method of controlled comparison," *American Anthropologist*, vol. 56 (1954), pp. 743-763 [reprinted in: *Essays in Social Anthropology and Ethnology* [see below], pp. 191-217]; "Social anthropology: methods and results" in: *Social Anthropology of North American Tribes* (Chicago: 1955), pp. 485-551; "Cultural drift and social change," *Current Anthropology*, vol. 4 (1963), pp. 347-355 [reprinted in: *Essays in Social Anthropology and Ethnology* [see below], pp. 253-274]; *The American Indian: Perspectives for the Study of Social Change* (Chicago: 1966); *Essays in Social Anthropology and Ethnology* (Chicago: 1975).

SOURCES: Raymond D. Fogelson, "Eggan, Fred" in: David L. Sills (editor), *International Encyclopedia of the Social Sciences* (New York: 1968-1979), vol. 18, pp. 163-166; Fred Eggan, "Among the anthropologists," *Annual Review of Anthropology*, vol. 3 (1974), pp. 1-19; Ernest L. Schusky, "Fred Eggan: anthropologist full circle," *American Ethnologist*, vol. 16 (1989), pp. 142-157.

Raymond J. DeMallie

Eiseley, Loren C. Anthropologist, writer. Born in Lincoln (Nebraska) 3 September 1907, died in Philadelphia (Pennsylvania) 9 July 1977. Eiseley was educated in anthropology and English literature at the University of Nebraska, where he was one of the founders of the *Prairie Schooner*, a literary magazine that is still in production. He earned his B.A. in anthropology in 1933 and started graduate work at the University of Pennsylvania that year. There he became a protégé of the Americanist FRANK G. SPECK. Eiseley taught at the University of Kansas from 1937 to 1944 and was chair of sociology and anthropology at Oberlin College until 1947, when he returned to Pennsylvania as professor and chair of anthropology. He remained the chair until 1959, when he became the provost of the university, and upon stepping down from that position in 1961 he was named the Benjamin Franklin and University Professor of Anthropology and History of Science.

As a youth Eiseley was interested in paleontology and natural history, and his approach to anthropology retained that orientation. He specialized in early man in the New

World, particularly in paleo-Indian hunting. Eiseley wrote relatively little in anthropology, and was from early on in his career more a critic or commentator than an original thinker. Beginning with *The Immense Journey* and *Darwin's Century*, however, Eiseley found his forte: he wrote numerous prize-winning volumes combining natural science, a poetical prose style and concerns for the future of the environment and the human species. As a naturalist-cum-philosopher Eiseley attained world-wide fame, and his already small output in anthropology dwindled. At his death, none of the major American journals of anthropology published an obituary.

Eiseley was vice-president of the American Anthropological Association (1948-1949), the American Association for the Advancement of Science (1969) and the Philadelphia Anthropological Society (1947) as well as president of the latter in 1948 and of the American Institute of Human Paleontology in 1949-1952.

MAJOR WORKS: (with Frank G. Speck) "Significance of hunting territory systems of the Algonkian in social theory," *American Anthropologist*, vol. 41 (1939), pp. 269-280; "Pollen analysis and its bearing upon American prehistory," *American Antiquity*, vol. 5 (1939), pp. 115-139; "Archaeological observations on the problem of post-glacial extinction," *American Antiquity*, vol. 8 (1943), pp. 209-217; "The fire-drive and the extinction of the terminal Pleistocene fauna," *American Anthropologist*, vol. 48 (1946), pp. 54-59; "Early man in South and East Africa," *American Anthropologist*, vol. 50 (1948), pp. 11-17; *The Immense Journey* (New York: 1957); *Darwin's Century* (New York: 1958); *Francis Bacon and the Modern Dilemma* (Lincoln: 1963).

SOURCES: Loren C. Eiseley, *All the Strange Hours* (New York: 1975); "Eiseley, Loren Corey 1907-1977," *Contemporary Authors*, new revision series, vol. 6 (1982), pp. 158-159.

David Lonergan

Ekholm, Gordon F. Anthropologist, archaeologist. Born in St. Paul (Minnesota) 25 November 1909, died in Tarrytown (New York) 17 December 1987. Ekholm was one of the world's foremost authorities on the archaeology of pre-Columbian Mesoamerica. He is perhaps best known for his pioneering work from 1937 to 1942 in northwestern and northeastern Mexico, where he outlined the cultural sequences that are fundamental to our present understanding of events in those regions. Notable also was his long-term interest in the controversial problem of pre-Columbian trans-Pacific contacts between Mesoamerica and eastern Asia. As curator of pre-Columbian collections at the American Museum of Natural History in New York, he contributed in a major way to the appreciation of Middle American art by nonspecialists, particularly through his two revisions of its permanent Hall of Mexico and Central America, of which the second was completed to critical acclaim in 1970. As an outgrowth of his curatorial concerns, he became a leading expert on forgeries in pre-Columbian art.

In his research, Gordon Ekholm was above all a realist who eschewed grand theoretical schemes and doctrinaire programs in favor of meticulous attention to evidence and careful inference. His sequence-building work in Mexico and his later syntheses, both of his own work and of that of others ("Regional sequences"), stand therefore as permanent contributions that later work has built upon and enlarged but not substantially revised. Ekholm's daring and originality are evident in his pursuit of the problem of Asian-American parallels. For a time, he worked virtually alone in this area among American archaeologists, though he shared his interest with some foreign scholars, among them

ROBERT VON HEINE-GELDERN. While he was solidly grounded in the formal attributes of objects, which he liked to examine and compare, his advocacy of the significance of contacts between Asia and Mesoamerica reflected a sober assessment of the limitations of the archaeological record, a true-to-life vision of the societies involved (particularly that of Mesoamerica) and a recognition of the importance of interaction between societies in understanding cultural change. These positions were unpopular among many of Ekholm's contemporaries, who placed greater trust in the evidence (both negative and positive) of the archaeological record, were more schematic in their models of past societies and tended to be geographically more parochial. New World archaeology has since shown some signs of returning to Ekholm's positions.

MAJOR WORKS: "Excavations at Guasave, Sinaloa, Mexico," *Anthropological Papers, American Museum of Natural History*, vol. 38, pt. 2 (1942), pp. 23-139; "Excavations at Tampico and Panuco in the Huasteca, Mexico," *Anthropological Papers, American Museum of Natural History*, vol. 38, pt. 5 (1944), pp. 321-509; "Ceramic stratigraphy at Acapulco, Guerrero" in: *El Norte de Mexico y el Sur de Estados Unidos* (Mexico City: 1944), pp. 276-283; "The probable use of Mexican stone yokes," *American Anthropologist*, vol. 48 (1946), pp. 593-596; "A possible focus of Asiatic influence in the late classic cultures of Mesoamerica" in: Marian W. Smith (editor), *Asia and North America, Transpacific Contacts* (Salt Lake City: 1953) (= *Memoirs of the Society for American Archaeology*, no. 9), pp. 72-89; "Regional sequences in Mesoamerica and their relationships" in: *Middle American Anthropology, Special Symposium of the American Anthropological Association* (Washington: 1958) (= *Social Science Monographs, Pan American Union*, no. 5), pp. 15-25; "Transpacific contacts" in: Jesse D. Jennings and Edward Norbeck (editors), *Prehistoric Man in the New World* (Chicago: 1964), pp. 489-510; "The problem of fakes in pre-Columbian art," *Curator*, vol. 7, no. 1 (1964), pp. 19-32; (editor, with Gordon R. Willey) *Handbook of Middle American Indians*, vol. 4 (Austin: 1966).

SOURCE: Peter B. Flint, "Dr. Gordon Ekholm, 78, a curator at the Museum of Natural History," *New York Times* (12 December 1987), p. 34.

Paul Tolstoy

Elkin, A.P. (Adolphus Peter). Social anthropologist, doyen of Australian anthropology. Born in West Maitland (New South Wales) 27 March 1891, died in Sydney (New South Wales) 9 July 1979. Elkin was educated at the University of Sydney (first-class honours degree, 1915) and ordained as a deacon (1915) then as a priest (1916) in the Anglican Church; he gained his M.A. degree in philosophy with a thesis entitled *The Religion of the Australian Aborigines* (1922) and his Ph.D. at the University of London (1927) with *Myth and Ritual of the Australian Aborigines*. He was Rector of Morpeth from 1929 to 1937. With support from A.R. RADCLIFFE-BROWN he became Professor of Anthropology at the University of Sydney (1933), retiring as Emeritus in 1956. For twelve of these 23 years, his was the only department that taught anthropology in Australia. Elkin's initial research (1927) was in the Kimberleys of northwest Western Australia, followed up by a detailed survey of social organization in South Australia and for various periods (1946-1952) in Arnhem Land. He had an active interest in Papua New Guinea and worked briefly in the Western Highlands. His theoretical orientation was influenced by Durkheim and W.H.R. RIVERS, but also by Radcliffe-Brown.

His major field was Aboriginal Australia. The publication of *The Australian Aborigines* provided him with an unassailable position in this respect. So did *Aboriginal Men of High Degree*. His approach was primarily empirical or, as he preferred to call it, philosophical. Prior to the establishment of academic anthropology in Australia (1926), the Aboriginal field had been bedeviled by unsystematic enquiry and archaic theoretical speculation. He wanted to remedy that situation and provide a firm basis on which anthropological research could proceed. Over and above that issue was his preoccupation with human welfare. Throughout his career he was concerned about rapidly changing social conditions and their implications for people caught within a maze of contradictory values and attitudes. Between 1944 and 1946 he published three significant booklets on the recognition of Australian Aboriginal rights. With his seminal *American Anthropologist* paper on "Reaction and interaction ..." these constituted the basis for contemporary developments in Australian Aboriginal policy. He had a similar concern for the problems of rehabilitation and reconstruction in the immediate post-war period in Papua New Guinea, publishing two important books (*Wanted: a Charter for the Native People of the South-West Pacific* and *Social Anthropology in Melanesia*) on this general topic.

Elkin was general editor of the journal *Oceania* from 1933 to 1979. It was inevitable that with his concern with changing social contexts he should also write generally on Australian society. In fact, it was Elkin who encouraged the development of formal sociology in Australia. For him anthropology was not merely an academic subject but a way of life.

MAJOR WORKS: *Studies in Australian Totemism* (Sydney: 1933) (= *Oceania Monographs*, no. 2); *The Australian Aborigines: How to Understand Them* (Sydney: 1938); *Society, the Individual and Change* (Sydney: 1941); *Wanted: a Charter for the Native People of the South-West Pacific* (Sydney: 1943); *Citizenship for the Aborigines* (Sydney: 1944); *Aboriginal Men of High Degree* (Sydney: 1946); *Man, Society and Change* (Sydney: 1946); (with W.E. Harney) *Songs of the Songmen* (Melbourne: 1949); "Reaction and interaction: a food gathering people and European settlement in Australia," *American Anthropologist*, vol. 53 (1951), pp. 164-186; *Social Anthropology in Melanesia* (London: 1953); (editor) *Marriage and the Family in Australia* (Sydney: 1957); "Elements of Australian Aboriginal philosophy," *Oceania*, vol. 40 (1969), pp. 85-98; (with T.A. Jones) *Arnhem Land Music* (Sydney: 1958) (= *Oceania Monographs*, no. 9, pp. 1-242).

SOURCES: R.M. Berndt, "Professor A.P. Elkin—an appreciation," *Mankind*, vol. 5 (1956), pp. 89-101; R.M. and C.H. Berndt (editors), *Aboriginal Man in Australia: Essays in Honour of Emeritus Professor A.P. Elkin* (Sydney: 1965); R.M. and C.H. Berndt, "Adolphus Peter Elkin, 1891-1979," *Oceania*, vol. 50 (1979), pp. 81-87; "A.P. Elkin," *Australian Institute of Aboriginal Studies Newsletter*, no. 11 (1979), pp. 6-8; *Who's Who in Australia, 1974* (Melbourne: 1974), p. 338; Association of Social Anthropologists of the Commonwealth, *List of Members* (London: 1961); T. Wise, *The Self-made Anthropologist* (Sydney: 1985) [note: the latter is a highly negative, biased and inaccurate biography of A.P. Elkin].

Ronald M. and Catherine H. Berndt

Elwin, Verrier. Government anthropologist, folklorist. Born in Sierra Leone (then part of British West Africa) 1902, died in New Delhi (India) 22 February 1964. A self-taught but greatly respected student of India's tribal peoples, Elwin was both a chronicler and a protector of the Gonds and other tribes.

Elwin took a bachelor's degree in English at Oxford, then was ordained an Anglican minister, becoming chaplain of Merton College in 1927. Within a year, however, he traveled to Poona, India, to join an Anglican Franciscan missionary society. Before long he abandoned the Anglican faith and became a follower of Mohandas K. (Mahatma) Gandhi. Convinced by 1932 that the tribal peoples of India were the most in need of help and advocacy, Elwin and his friend Shamrao Hivale spent the next several years setting up schools, welfare centers and medical clinics in central India. Elwin wrote and lectured widely to raise funds for these establishments.

During his years with Gandhi, Elwin had agitated for Indian independence; on a visit to Britain in 1930, he was prohibited from returning to India until he agreed to stay out of the independence struggle. Unable to participate in this arena, he turned his considerable energies to improving conditions for the tribes. He lived with various central Indian tribes from 1932 to 1946 and from 1949 to 1953; at other times he was often among them.

Elwin became a naturalized citizen of India in 1954. He was at various times social worker, anthropologist to the government of Orissa, deputy director of India's anthropological survey and advisor for tribal affairs in the northeastern frontier area. He co-edited *Man in India* from 1943 to 1948 and wrote prolifically both for that journal and in monographs. His many books helped to publicize the plight of India's tribes and sought to make the tribesmen and their lifeways comprehensible to the outside world.

Given an honorary D.Sc. by Oxford and seven major British and Indian anthropological and humanitarian awards, Elwin was both a productive scholar and a very influential civil servant. Advocacy of the tribes' welfare was the keystone of his life in India; his participation in government and his ethnographic writings were only by-products of his primary task and interest.

MAJOR WORKS: *The Tribal World of Verrier Elwin* (New York: 1964); *The Baiga* (London: 1939); *The Religion of an Indian Tribe* (Bombay: 1955); *The Muria and their Ghotul* (Bombay: 1947); *Nagaland* (Shillong: 1961); *Maria Murder and Suicide* (Bombay: 1950).

SOURCES: Christoph von Fürer-Haimendorf, "Verrier Elwin: 1902-1964," *Man*, vol. 64 (1964), pp. 114-115; David Mandelbaum, "Verrier Elwin, 1902-1964," *American Anthropologist*, vol. 67 (1965), pp. 448-452; "Verrier Elwin, student of India," *New York Times* (24 February 1964), p. 25.

David Lonergan

Embree, John Fee. Anthropologist. Born in New Haven (Connecticut) 26 August 1908, died in Hamden (Connecticut) 22 December 1950. Embree was first exposed to Asian societies as a teenager when with his parents he traveled in China and Japan. He earned his bachelor's degree in English literature from the University of Hawaii, but his M.A. (from the University of Toronto) and his Ph.D. (from the University of Chicago) were in anthropology. Embree's doctoral research, directed by A.R. RADCLIFFE-BROWN, was conducted in a Japanese farming village and was the first thorough study of such a village by a western ethnologist. The resulting monograph, *Suye Mura*, is recognized as an anthropological classic.

Between 1937, when he received his doctorate, and 1941, when the United States entered Worl War II, Embree taught at Hawaii and then Toronto. Embree's knowledge of Japanese culture brought him into positions of importance during the war; he was a consultant to the Office of Strategic Services, as well as to the War Relocation Authority, which administered wartime forced "relocation camps" for Americans of Japanese descent. In 1943 Embree became head of Japanese studies at the Civil Affairs Training School of the University of Chicago. He also served in other consultative positions in the last months of the war and then taught once again at the University of Hawaii until 1947. He then returned to government service, becoming a Cultural Attaché to American embassies in Bangkok and Saigon for more than a year.

In 1948 Embree joined the faculty of Southeast Asia Studies at Yale. At the time of his death he had recently been appointed the head of that program and also named a consultant to the newly formed United Nations.

He was a pioneer applied anthropologist and opposed the notion of anthropology-at-a-distance; Embree reviewed RUTH BENEDICT's *The Chrysanthemum and the Sword* no less than three times—negatively. In addition to research-based scholarly papers, Embree produced many popular articles and Asian Studies bibliographies. He also wrote a number of pieces on applied anthropology and military government and was at the time of his death a regional vice-president of the Society for Applied Anthropology.

MAJOR WORKS: *Suye Mura* (Chicago: 1937); "New local and kin groups among the Japanese farmers of Kona, Hawaii," *American Anthropologist,* n.s., vol. 41 (1939), pp. 400-407; *Acculturation among the Japanese of Kona, Hawaii* (Menasha: 1941) (= *Memoirs of the American Anthropological Association,* no. 59); "Community analysis—an example of anthropology in government," *American Anthropologist,* vol. 46 (1944), pp. 277-291; *The Japanese Nation: a Social Survey* (New York: 1945); "American military government" in: Meyer Fortes (editor), *Social Structure: Studies Presented to A.R. Radcliffe-Brown* (Oxford: 1949), pp. 207-225; "Thailand—a loosely structured social system," *American Anthropologist,* vol. 52 (1950), pp. 181-193; (with William Thomas, Jr.) *Ethnic Groups of Northern Southeast Asia* (New Haven: 1950).

SOURCES: Fred Eggan, "John Fee Embree, 1908-1950," *American Anthropologist,* vol. 53 (1951), pp. 376-382; Alexander Spoehr, "John Fee Embree, 1908-1950," *Human Organization,* vol. 10 (1951), pp. 33-34.

David Lonergan

Emeneau, Murray Barnson. Anthropologist, linguist, Indologist. Born in Lunenburg (Nova Scotia) 28 February 1904. Although Emeneau's doctoral degree from Yale University (1931) was in classics and Sanskrit, his postdoctoral studies with EDWARD SAPIR involved him in what was to become known as linguistic anthropology. Following three years of fieldwork with the Toda and other Dravidian peoples of South India (1935-1938), he became one of the most eminent participants in the Sapirian tradition—working not only in ethnography, descriptive linguistics and historical linguistics, but also doing pioneering research in ethnosemantics, sociolinguistics and oral literature. As Professor of Sanskrit and General Linguistics at the University of California, Berkeley, he was founder-chairman of the Department of Linguistics at that institution in 1953 and became Emeritus Professor in 1971.

Emeneau has been famous for the breadth of his interests. He is one of the few Indologists who has received the highest recognition in both Sanskritic and Dravidian studies; and within Indology, he has consistently pursued a vision of the integrated study of culture, language and verbal art. (As he has written, his background led him to take a holistic view of India in which everything was of interest and was, so far as it was possible, fitted into the one large picture.) During World War II, under military auspices, he taught Vietnamese and wrote a grammar of that language. Finally, continuing an interest in the American Indian languages, which he had studied with Sapir, he was principally responsible for initiating the Survey of California Indian Languages at Berkeley and for inspiring several academic generations of fieldworkers in the area of Native American linguistics.

Emeneau is especially well known for his research on the concept of the *Sprachbund* or "linguistic area": a geographical region in which a number of languages (not necessarily having any common origin) have, through borrowing of linguistic traits, come to share distinctive patterns. Emeneau's demonstration of the phenomenon in South Asia—as he has said, "This was essentially an injection of ethnological thinking into diachronic linguistics"—has provided a model for studies in other parts of the world and has strongly influenced conceptions of historical relationship among languages.

MAJOR WORKS: *Kota Texts I-IV* (Berkeley: 1944-1946); *Studies in Vietnamese (Annamese) Grammar* (Berkeley: 1951); *Kolami, a Dravidian Language* (Berkeley: 1955); (with T. Burrow) *A Dravidian Etymological Dictionary* (Oxford: 1961; revised ed., Oxford: 1984); *Brahui and Dravidian Comparative Grammar* (Berkeley: 1962); *India and Historical Grammar* (Annamalainagar: 1965); *Dravidian Linguistics, Ethnography, and Folktales: Collected Papers* (Annamalainagar: 1967); *Toda Songs* (Oxford: 1971); *Ritual Structure and Language Structure of the Todas* (Philadelphia: 1974); *Language and Linguistic Area* (Stanford: 1980); *Toda Grammar and Texts* (Philadelphia: 1984); *Sanskrit Studies of M.B. Emeneau: Selected Papers* (Berkeley: 1988).

William Bright

Emory, Kenneth Pike. Anthropologist, ethnologist. Born in Fitchburg (Massachusetts) 23 November 1897. Emory received his bachelor's degree at Dartmouth College in 1920, his master's degree at Harvard University in 1923 and his doctoral degree at Yale University in 1947.

From the very beginning, Emory's anthropological field experience was in Polynesia, from the Hawaiian Islands southward. He spent much of his time on such field expeditions, even after his appointment in 1926 as anthropologist on the staff of the Bernice P. Bishop Museum.

During World War II Emory provided instruction to U.S. personnel who were preparing for military operations in the Pacific region. By drawing on his knowledge of the island environments and the cultural adaptations of the native peoples, he provided guidance on how to survive on local resources.

He has been a prolific writer, with more than 150 publications reporting on his fieldwork in Polynesia since the beginning of his association with the Bishop Museum in 1920. His outstanding knowledge of the languages and cultures of Polynesia has made him the Museum's senior anthropologist and brought him many honors and awards for his contributions to the understanding of that region.

MAJOR WORKS: *The Island of Lanai: a Survey of Native Culture* (Honolulu: 1924) (= *Bernice P. Bishop Museum, Bulletin*, no. 12); *Archaeology of Hihoa and Necker* (Honolulu: 1928) (= *Tanager Expedition Publication*, no. 5; *Bernice P. Bishop Museum, Bulletin*, no. 53); *Stone Remains in the Society Islands* (Honolulu: 1933) (= *Bernice P. Bishop Museum, Bulletin*, no. 116); *South Sea Lore* (Honolulu: 1943) (= *Bernice P. Bishop Museum, Special Publication*, no. 36); *Kapingamarangi: Social and Religious Life of a Polynesian Atoll* (Honolulu: 1965) (= *Bernice P. Bishop Museum, Bulletin*, no. 228); *Material Culture in the Tuamotuan Archipelago* (Honolulu: 1975) (= *Bernice P. Bishop Museum, Pacific Anthropological Records*, no. 22).

SOURCES: "Who's who in Bishop Museum, Kenneth P. Emory," *Ka 'Elele*, no. 17 (1 May 1965), pp. 4-5; "Emory, Kenneth P." in: *Who's Who in Oceania, 1980-81* (Laie, Hawaii: 1980), p.

52; "Kenneth P. Emory receives a tribute for his accomplishments," *Honolulu Star-Bulletin* (22 November 1984), p. A-6.

Thomas L. Mann

Erdentuğ, Nermin (née Nermin Aygen). Physical anthropologist, ethnologist, social anthropologist. Born on Malta Island 25 December 1917. Erdentuğ received her degree in physical anthropology from the Faculty of Languages, History and Geography (D.T.C.F.) in Ankara, Turkey. After 1944 she became increasingly interested in ethnology, achieving later academic titles as the first Turkish professional ethnologist. She founded the Chairs of Ethnology (1961) and Social Anthropology (1982) at Ankara University, teaching there until her retirement (1986). She has been instrumental in encouraging the inclusion of social anthropology at the Schools of Medicine, Nursing, Social Work and Education in Turkey.

The important contribution in Erdentuğ's early work was the identification of the blood groups of the modern Turkish people. Her increasing interest in cultural anthropology led to a period of study at British and American universities, converting her to the British structural-functionalist school. She became the Turkish pioneer in the use of professional fieldwork techniques with the publication of the first book-length ethnographies of two isolated rural communities, Hal and Sün (Elazığ, Turkey) in Turkey's underdeveloped eastern hinterland. Her later work has been more of the introductory kind, disclosing the scope and subject matter of the science of culture to Turkish readers. In the face of the magnitude of resistance to change in rural Turkey, Erdentuğ's research during the 1960s focused on the informal powers behind the issues encountered during the implementation of technical aid programs in education, social work and health services. Her extensive research on the latter subjects in the villages of Ankara (*Ankara İli Köylerinde Sosyal Hizmetler ve Sosyal Antropoloji*) was a particularly important contribution. Erdentuğ showed the significance of the findings of medical, developmental and educational anthropology in the training of personnel for technical aid programs in Turkey. She also pointed out that the reforms of Atatürk were, from an anthropological perspective, examples of state-forced culture borrowings from the West, serving the ambition of creating a new Western-oriented Turkish culture.

MAJOR WORKS: *Türklerin Kan Grupları ve Kan Gruplarının Antropolojik Karakterle İlgisi Üzerine Bir Araştırma* [*Research on the Blood Groups of the Turks and the Relation of the Blood Groups to Anthropological Characteristics*] (Ankara: 1946); *Hal Köyü'nün Etnolojik Tetkiki* [*An Ethnological Study of Hal*] (Ankara: 1956, 1968, 1975, 1983); *Sün Köyü'nün Etnolojik Tetkiki* [*An Ethnological Study of Sün*] (Ankara: 1959, 1971); *A Study of the Social Structure of a Turkish Village* (Ankara: 1959); *Ankara İli Köylerinde Sosyal Hizmetler ve Sosyal Antropoloji Bakımından Bir Araştırma* [*Research in Social Anthropology and Social Work in the Villages of Ankara*] (Ankara: 1966); "Kıbrıs ve Türkiye Türk toplumlarının kültür birliği" ["The cultural uniformity of the Turkish communities of Turkey and Cyprus"], *A.Ü.D.T.C.F. Dergisi*, vol. 25, nos. 1-2 (1967), pp. 1-10; "A comparative ethnological study of the rural societies of Turkey, İran and Pakistan," *Antropoloji*, no. 3 (1967), pp. 7-10; *Türkiye Türk Toplumlarında Kültürel Antropolojik (Etnolojik) İncelemeler* [*Ethnological Studies of Turkish Communities in Turkey*] (Ankara: 1972); "Türk köylerinde öğretmen-imam ve muhtar ilişkilerinin eğitim açısından değerlendirilmesi" ["Education and the teacher-imam-headman triangle in Turkish villages"], *A.Ü. Eğitim Fakültesi Dergisi*, vol. 7, nos. 1-4 (1974), pp. 211-236; "Culture dynamics and Atatürk" in: *Prof. Dr. Ahmet Şükrü Esmer'e Armağan* [*Festschrift for Prof. Dr. Ahmet Şükrü*] (Ankara: 1981), pp. 65-74.

SOURCES: P.J. Magnarella and O. Türkdoğan, "The development of Turkish social anthropology," *Current Anthropology*, vol. 17 (1976), pp. 263-274; Aygen Erdentuğ, "A.Ü.D.T.C.F. antropoloji bibliyografyası (1935-1983)" ["Bibliography of anthropology, D.T.C.F., Ankara University (1935-1983)"], *Antropoloji*, no. 12 (1985), pp. 464-470; "Erdentuğ, Zubeyde Nermin" in: *Günümüz Türkiyesi'nde Kim Kimdir? [Who's Who in Contemporary Turkey?]* (İstanbul: 1988).

Aygen Erdentuğ

Esteva Fabregat, Claudio. Anthropologist. Born in Marseille (France) 11 November 1918. Esteva Fabregat lived in Barcelona until the age of 20. Exiled in 1939, he was trained at the Escuela Nacional de Antropología e Historia (ENAH, the National School of Anthropology and History) in Mexico, receiving his master's degree in anthropology (specializing in ethnology). In 1956 he returned to Madrid and earned his doctorate on the history of America. He devoted himself to the teaching of cultural anthropology on a university level. It was to a large extent Esteva Fabregat who introduced the field to Spain. In 1965 he founded the Escuela de Estudios Antropológicos (School of Anthropological Studies) in Madrid. In 1968 he moved to Barcelona where, in 1970, he was appointed to the first chair in cultural anthropology at a Spanish university. In 1971 he founded the first Spanish specialized professional journal in anthropology, *Ethnica: revista de antropología cultural*; he was the director of this journal until it ceased publication in 1984.

During his professional career Esteva undertook field research in Mexico (San Nicolás Totolapán); Equatorial Guinea (among the Fang); the Spanish provinces of Zamora, Huesca and Barcelona; Chinchero, Peru; and also New Mexico and Arizona (among the Hispanic communities).

During his Mexican period, Esteva Fabregat was interested in the problems of ethnicity, *mestizaje* (ethnic mixing), and acculturation among indigenous groups. Likewise, influenced by the cultural psychoanalytic approach of Erich Fromm, with whom he collaborated, he underwent psychoanalysis and oriented himself toward the study of questions of culture and personality, national character, cultural determinism and the analysis of values.

His interest in industrial anthropology was stimulated by his arrival in Spain. His work on urban anthropology dates from his stay in Barcelona from the 1970s. In several publications he has analyzed phenomena related to immigration, acculturation of immigrants, bilingualism and biculturalism, ethnicity and interethnic relationships. Simultaneously, Esteva continued to publish on Latin American indigenous cultures.

Esteva Fabregat has always supported the concept of cultural anthropology as a holistic discipline (as opposed to the narrower definition of British social anthropology) as several works in anthropological theory demonstrate.

As of 1989, Esteva Fabregat is professor emeritus at the University of Barcelona and distinguished member of Spanish, European and American scientific organizations.

MAJOR WORKS: *Función y funcionalismo en las ciencias sociales* (Madrid: 1965); *Antropología y filosofía* (Barcelona: 1972); *Antropología industrial* (Barcelona: 1973); *Cultura y personalidad* (Barcelona: 1973); *Razas humanas y racismo* (Barcelona: 1975); *Cultura, sociedad y personalidad* (Barcelona: 1978); *Estado, etnicidad y biculturalismo* (Barcelona: 1984); *El mestizaje en Iberoamérica* (Madrid: 1988).

SOURCES: Angel Aguirre Baztan, "Claudio Esteva Fabregat y la etnología" in: *La antropología cultural en España* (Barcelona: 1986), pp. 397-455; Claudio Esteva Fabregat, *Autobiografía intelectual de Claudio Esteva Fabregat* (Barcelona: 1982) (= *Anthropos: boletín de información y documentación*, no. 10); P. Hernández, "Entrevista amb Claudi Esteva," *Ciència*, no. 16 (1982), pp. 44-51; "Curriculum vitae de Claudio Esteva Fabregat (vida académica y publicaciones, 1947-1989)" [unpublished].

Joan Prat
[Translation from Spanish: Margo L. Smith]

Evans, I.H.N. (Ivor Hugh Norman). Ethnologist, civil servant. Born in Cambridge (England) 6 October 1886, died in Labuan (British North Borneo, now in Malaysia) 3 May 1957. Evans was admitted to Clare College, Cambridge University, in 1906 and completed the B.A. degree in 1909. He first came to British North Borneo in 1910 as a junior civil service employee of the North Borneo Chartered Company. As a Chartered Company cadet, Evans was responsible for administration of Tempassuk Subdistrict. His impressions of the peoples of North Borneo were published in a popular narrative, *Among Primitive Peoples in Borneo.* This account of the Dusuns, Malays, Chinese and other North Bornean peoples was based on observations in 1910 and 1911, although it was not published until 1922. In 1911 Evans returned to England, and in April 1912 his career took a decisive turn when he was appointed as an ethnographer and assistant curator at the Perak Museum (Taiping, Federated Malay States). As editor of the *Journal of the Federated Malay States Museum* he became further involved in the progress of archaeological studies in Malaya. In 1917 Evans began the exploration of archaeological sites in Perak and Pahang including Lenggong, Batu Kurau and Kuala Selinsing. In May 1919 Evans completed the M.A. degree at Cambridge University. Named Ethnographer, Federated Malay States Museums in 1926 Evans occupied this position until 1932 when (due to the economic "slump") he was offered and accepted early retirement. Many of Evans' writings were collected in book form in 1927 when *Papers on the Ethnology and Archaeology of the Malay Peninsula* was published. After 1932 Evans spent five years in retirement at Oulton Broad, Suffolk (England). During this time he completed one of his more important works, *The Negritos of Malaya.* This monograph relied in part on previous work by W.W. SKEAT, C.O. Blagden (1864-1949) and PAUL SCHEBESTA. In 1938 he sold his house at Oulton Broad and returned to Kota Belud in British North Borneo. There he began collecting data for a book on the religion of the Tempasuk Dusuns. In May 1942 he was interned by the Japanese, first at Jesselton (North Borneo) and later at Kuching (Sarawak). After the war Evans learned that his Dusun manuscript (which had been stored in Labuan) and various other records and artifacts had been lost or destroyed. Resuming work on the Dusun monograph, he reconstructed data and added new information. *The Religion of the Tempasuk Dusuns of North Borneo* was published in 1953. In the course of his career, Evans produced ethnographic studies of peninsular (e.g., Negrito) as well as Bornean (e.g., Dusun) peoples. He also prepared the way for the new field of Malayan/Malaysian archaeology. In the Federation, Evans first described the Haobinhian Culture, cave and megalithic sites and a prehistoric site at Kuala Selinsing. Evans' typescript autobiography is at the Cambridge University Museum of Archaeology and

Anthropology. Also at this location are other Evans papers and his extensive collection of artifacts.

MAJOR WORKS: *Among Primitive Peoples in Borneo* (London: 1922; Singapore: 1990); *Studies in Religion, Folk-lore, & Custom in British North Borneo and the Malay Peninsula* (Cambridge: 1923); *Papers on the Ethnology & Archaeology of the Malay Peninsula* (Cambridge: 1927); *The Negritos of Malaya* (Cambridge: 1937); *The Religion of the Tempasuk Dusuns of North Borneo* (Cambridge: 1953).

SOURCES: M.W.F. Tweedie, "Ivor Hugh Norman Evans, M.A.," *Journal of the Malayan Branch, Royal Asiatic Society*, vol. 33 (May 1960), pp. 109-110; Wilhelm G. Solheim II, Floyd Wheeler and Jane Allen-Wheeler, "Archaeology in Malaysia, Brunei and Singapore" in: John A. Lent and Kent Mulliner (editors), *Malaysian Studies: Archaeology, Historiography, Geography, and Bibliography* (DeKalb: 1985) (= *Northern Illinois University Center for Southeast Asian Studies Monograph Series on Southeast Asia*, occasional paper no. 11), pp. 1-86 (especially pp. 1-2); B.A.V. Peacock, "The later prehistory of the Malay Peninsula" in: *Early South East Asia: Essays in Archaeology, History and Historical Geography* (New York: 1979), pp. 199-214; I.H.N. Evans, "Preface" in: I.H.N. Evans, *The Religion of the Tempasuk Dusuns of North Borneo* (Cambridge: 1953), pp. xv-xviii; letter from David W. Phillipson, Curator, Cambridge University Museum of Archaeology and Anthropology; letter from S.C. Johnston, Archivist, Clare College, Cambridge University; Brian Durrans, "Introduction" to: Ivor H.N. Evans, *Among Primitive Peoples in Borneo* (Singapore: 1990), pp. v-xvi.

Lee S. Dutton

Evans-Pritchard, Sir *E.E. (Edward Evan).* Social anthropologist. Born in Crowborough, Sussex (England) 21 September 1902, died in Oxford (England) 11 September 1973. As an undergraduate Evans-Pritchard studied history at Oxford and as a graduate student did anthropology at the University of London where he worked under C.G. SELIGMAN and BRONISLAW MALINOWSKI.

Evans-Pritchard is the most important social anthropologist of post-World-War-II Britain on account both of his numerous influential writings and the many students he produced while Professor of Anthropology at the University of Oxford. Evans-Pritchard's researches span many ethnic groups but mainly are remembered for analyses of the Nuer, Azande, Anuak and Shilluk of the southern Sudan, and the Sanusi religious brotherhood among the Arabs of Libya, North Africa. His brilliant 1937 study of witchcraft among the Azande is the first account of an African people published by a professionally trained anthropologist; it remains the single most important empirical work in the sociological analysis of the thinking of preliterate peoples. Building on and yet criticizing E.B. TYLOR, JAMES G. FRAZER, LUCIEN LÉVY-BRUHL and Vilfredo Pareto, it complexly underscores two seemingly contradictory truths: that all systems of thought (preliterate and literate alike) exhibit self-justifying, circular logic while also containing important, nonrational inconsistencies. It is recognized as the first great defense of the thinking of preliterate peoples as being coherent and logical, but it is less often also recognized as a subtle undercutting of all systems of thought as being inevitably caught up in illogicality as much as in logic and in supporting the self-interested and at times cynical actions of "believers."

Evans-Pritchard's great trilogy on the Nuer is equally influential, both within anthropology and in other disciplines in social studies. The first volume established contemporary, sophisticated anthropological analysis of politics in stateless societies. The last presented the first account of the religious beliefs of a preliterate society as serious theology and morality. The second provided one of the richest accounts of normative rules and practices of kinship and domestic life since HENRY SUMNER MAINE. Evans-Pritchard's study of the Sanusi initiated modern anthropological study of Near Eastern peoples and popular Islam.

With his important studies of kingship among the Anuak and Shilluk and his writings on Nuer conflict and feud, Evans-Pritchard deeply influenced political theory. His introduction to *African Political Systems*, co-authored with MEYER FORTES, shaped Africanist thinking for decades, for better or worse. Important essays by Evans-Pritchard revitalized anthropological interest in oral literature, the dance, ethno-history, and divine kingship.

The common theme through most of these profoundly original and significant works involves the problems posed by the translation of alien systems of thought into Western terms. His works stress the problems of how societies are ordered and persist on account of normative beliefs and values, despite the onslaughts of misfortune and conflict—and at times even because of them. Although he criticized the French sociological school toward the end of his career, his works are deeply influenced by Émile Durkheim, MARCEL MAUSS, Henri Hubert and ROBERT HERTZ. Of course, both he and his French predecessors were in turn influenced by W. ROBERTSON SMITH whose impact on Evans-Pritchard is particularly prominent in *The Nuer*. Except for his writings on the Sanusi, Evans-Pritchard pays scant attention to social change or any Marxist or Weberian theories of domination or social action. Unfortunately, his works are also flawed by a neglect of women as significant social protagonists (see Gough, Hutchinson, cited below).

Evans-Pritchard rejected scientific claims for social anthropology, instead equating it with comparative history. More than any other anthropologist in Britain, he is responsible for reintroducing historical thinking (in the sense advocated by Collingwood) back into anthropology after the attacks history suffered at the hands of Malinowski and A.R. RADCLIFFE-BROWN.

His later works display this historical concern, though his Nuer works suffer from ahistoricism. At the close of his career, Evans-Pritchard was converted to Roman Catholicism and increasingly, though unsuccessfully, sought to resolve contradictions between anthropology's analytical claims and religious demands and explanations. Some consider that his conversion accounts for a falling off in Evans-Pritchard's analytical acuity.

It would be difficult to overstate the immense direct and indirect impact that Evans-Pritchard's works have had on the study of African societies in particular and the study of non-Western systems of thought in general. To this day, no useful anthropological studies of systems of belief, witchcraft, religion, politics, oral literature or popular Islam can afford to ignore him.

MAJOR WORKS: *Witchcraft, Oracles and Magic among the Azande* (Oxford: 1937); *The Political System of the Anuak* (London: 1940); *The Nuer* (Oxford: 1940); (with Meyer Fortes) "Introduction" to: *African Political Systems* (edited by E.E. Evans-Pritchard and M. Fortes) (London: 1940), pp. 15-23; *The Sanusi of Cyrenaica* (Oxford: 1949); *Social Anthropology* (London: 1951); *Kinship and Marriage among the Nuer* (Oxford: 1951); *Nuer Religion* (Oxford: 1956); *Essays in Social Anthropology* (London: 1962) [contains key essays on Shilluk and Azande]; *Theories of Primitive Religion* (Oxford: 1965); *The Position of Woman in Primitive Societies and Other Essays* (London: 1965) [contains famous essays on obscenity, sanza, dance, Nuer, Dinka and Azande]; *The*

Azande: History and Political Institutions (Oxford: 1971); *Man and Woman among the Azande* (London: 1974).

SOURCES: John Barnes, "Edward Evan Evans-Pritchard," *Proceedings of the British Academy*, vol. 73 (1987), pp. 447-490 [the best over-all review]; T.O. Beidelman (editor), *A Bibliography of the Writings of E.E. Evans-Pritchard* (London: 1974); "Sir Edward Evan Evans-Pritchard," *Anthropos*, vol. 69 (1974), pp. 553-587; Mary Douglas, *Evans-Pritchard* (London: 1980) [unreliable on Evans-Pritchard's intellectual roots]; Louis Dumont, "Preface by Louis Dumont to the French Edition of *The Nuer*" in: J.H.M. Beattie and R.G. Lienhardt (editors), *Studies in Social Anthropology: Essays in Memory of E.E. Evans Pritchard* (Oxford: 1975), pp. 328-342 [highly idiosyncratic view]; Clifford Geertz, "Slide show, Evans-Pritchard's African transparencies," *Raritan* vol. 3 (1983), pp. 62-80; Kathleen Gough, "Nuer kinship: a re-examination" in: T.O. Beidelman (editor), *The Translation of Culture* (London: 1971), pp. 79-121; Sharon Hutchinson, "Relations between the sexes among the Nuer," *Africa*, vol. 50 (1980), pp. 371-388; Douglas Johnson, "Evans-Pritchard, the Nuer, and the Sudan Political Service," *African Affairs*, vol. 71 (1982), pp. 231-246; Ivan Karp and K. Maynard, "Reading the Nuer," *Current Anthropology*, vol. 24 (1983), pp. 481-492 [best reanalysis of *The Nuer*]; R.G. Lienhardt, "E-P: a personal view," *Man*, vol. 9 (1974), pp. 299-304; Robin Maugham, *Nomad* (New York: 1948), pp. 39-49, 66-67 [striking personal vignettes]; Audrey Richards, "A problem of anthropological approach," *Bantu Studies*, vol. 15 (1941), pp. 45-52; Peter Winch, "Understanding a primitive society," *American Philosophical Quarterly*, vol. 1 (1964), pp. 307-324 [a wrong-headed but famous reanalysis of Zande witchcraft].

T.O. Beidelman

Fahrenfort, J.J. (Johannes Jacobus). Ethnologist, geographer. Born in Amsterdam (Netherlands) 8 July 1885, died in Amsterdam (Netherlands) 25 May 1975. Fahrenfort did not start his academic career until he was thirty-six years old. He was educated as a primary school teacher and later he acquired secondary school teaching certificates in history and geography. When in 1921 geography was recognized as an honors degree subject, it became possible for Fahrenfort, without a grammar school education, to register as a student. Thus he could pursue his studies at the University of Amsterdam, and under the guidance of S.R. STEINMETZ he took a degree in geography.

In 1927 Fahrenfort presented his Ph.D. thesis in which he criticized Father WILHELM SCHMIDT's theory of the monotheistic origins of religion. He objected especially to what he called "prejudiced ethnography," referring to anthropological expeditions that had been sent out to prove Schmidt's thesis and had no difficulty in doing so. It involved Fahrenfort in an acrimonious debate with Schmidt. Fahrenfort gave a similar critical treatment to the Marxist idea of primitive communism and LUCIEN LÉVY-BRUHL's prelogical mentality.

When Steinmetz retired in 1934, his chair, covering human geography (interpreted as sociography) and ethnology, was divided. Unfortunately no money was available for a professorship in ethnology, only for a part-time readership, to which Fahrenfort was appointed. It was not until after the war that a proper chair was established for him, which he held until his retirement in 1955. Fahrenfort never did any fieldwork, probably because of a lack of financial resources. (Before the 1950s academic anthropological research was not supported by public funds in Holland.)

Fahrenfort was convinced of the essential mental similarity of all members of the human race and held moderate evolutionary views. These views may well explain his special interest in economic anthropology. Like Steinmetz he insisted on careful comparison of similar phenomena in different cultures before generalizations could be made. However, Fahrenfort's ideas on the relation between theory and observation were rather more sophisticated than those of Steinmetz, who believed that the truth would emerge inductively from uninterpreted empirical facts.

MAJOR WORKS: *Het hoogste wezen der primitieven: studie over het "oermonotheisme" bij enkele der laagste volken* (Groningen: 1927); *Wie der Urmonotheismus am Leben erhalten wird* (Groningen 1930); *Dynamisme en logies denken bij natuurvolken* (Groningen: 1933); "De tegenwoordige stand van de evolutiegedachte in de ethnologie," *Synthese*, vol. 3 (1938), pp. 341-357; *Het socialisme in oude tijden* (Amsterdam: 1945); "De verwerving van distinctie door wegschenken en verkwisting," *Sociologisch Jaarboek*, vol. 6 (1952), pp. 84-105.

SOURCES: J. Brummelkamp, "Prof. Dr. J.J. Fahrenfort: de man en zijn werk" in: J. Brummelkamp [et al.] (editors), *De wereld der mensen* (Groningen: 1955), pp. 1-12; A.H. Sijmons and D.G. Jongmans, "Prof. Dr. J.J. Fahrenfort als academisch docent" in: J. Brummelkamp [et al.] (editors), *De wereld der mensen* (Groningen: 1955), pp. 13-21; W.F. Heinemeyer, "In memoriam prof. dr. J.J. Fahrenfort," *Geografisch Tijdschrift*, vol. 9 (1975), pp. 341-343; A.F.J. Kobben, "J.J. Fahrenfort (1885-1975): portret van een schoolmeester in de gunstige zin van het woord," *Antropologische Verkenningen*, vol. 7, nos. 1/2 (1988), pp. 75-94.

S.R. Jaarsma and J.J. de Wolf

Fea, Leonardo. Naturalist, traveler. Born in Turin (Italy) 1852, died in Turin (Italy) 1903. A scholar of zoology, Fea participated in numerous expeditions in the course of which he compiled a vast collection of zoological specimens and a considerable quantity of historical, geographical and ethnographical notes.

He left in 1885 for the Burmese Peninsula—the goal of numerous Italian travelers after the treaty of friendship and commerce between Italy and Burma that followed the official mission of Captain Carlo Alberto Racchia in 1869—and stayed there four years (until 1889) completing expeditions to Tenasserim and Pegu. From the trip the Italian naturalist brought back 80,000 zoological specimens, among which were 8,400 species of which 2,000 were new to science. This largely entomological collection was given by Fea to the Museo Civico di Storia Naturale (Civic Museum of Natural History) in Genoa, which was founded and directed by GIACOMO DORIA who had contributed, both financially and in his capacity as president of the Società Geografica Italiana (Italian Geographic Society), to Fea's explorations. The ethnographic materials were donated to the Museo Preistorico (Prehistoric Museum) in Rome, directed by LUIGI PIGORINI. In 1896, six years after his return, Fea published his only book, *Quattro anni fra i Birmani e le tribù limitrofe*, a report of his travels rich in observations on the traditions and customs of the Burmese people, although zoological and biological descriptions dominate here as in Fea's later works. Among the principal ethnic groups treated by Fea were the Kachin, the Shan, the "Ghecù," the Padaung and the Karen.

In 1898 Fea explored the fauna of the Cabo Verde archipelago and in 1890 he visited Portuguese Guinea (Guinea-Bissau), publishing his observations in the form of correspondence in the *Bollettino della Società Geografica Italiana*.

MAJOR WORKS: *Quattro anni fra i Birmani e le tribù limitrofe* (Milan: 1896); "Dalle Isole del Capo Verde," *Bollettino della Società Geografica Italiana*, ser. 3, vol. 11 (1898), pp. 358-368, 537-552; and ser. 3, vol. 12 (1899), pp. 7-26, 163-174, 302-312; "Dalla Guinea portoghese," *Bollettino della Società Geografica Italiana*, ser. 4, vol. 1 (1900), pp. 436-457.

SOURCES: R. Carmignani, *La Birmania* (Rome: 1950); R. Carmignani, "Le fonti storiche in lingua italiana per una storia generale della Birmania," *Barnabiti Studi*, no. 2 (1985), pp. 57-85.

Giorgio de Finis
[Translation from Italian: CW]

Fei Hsiao-T'ung (Fei Xiaotong). Anthropologist, sociologist, political and social commentator. Born in Wujiang, Jiangsu Province (China) 2 November 1910. Fei was educated in Western-oriented and missionary-founded schools in China, including the elite Yenching (B.A., 1933) and Tsinghua (M.A., 1935) Universities in Beijing and then at the London School of Economics (Ph.D., 1938) where he was BRONISLAW MALINOWSKI's last student. His belief that anthropological methods were needed to study the Chinese peasantry is perhaps a measure of the gulf that had grown between intellectuals and peasants in 20th-century China. Fei's fieldwork was all in China; after a brief and disastrous experience (his first wife was killed in an accident) among Yao aborigines in the mountains of Guangxi province in 1935 came two valuable village studies of different parts of China: of the lower Yangtze village of Kaixiangong in his native area in 1936 (reported on in *Peasant Life in China*; brief revisits in the 1950s and 1980s are described in *Chinese Village Close-up*) and in Yunnan in the southwest during the war with Japan (described in English in *Earthbound China*). His concern was reformist, focusing on economic aspects; he advocated the promotion of widespread rural light industry as the only way out of poverty for China (developments of the 1980s have not discredited this approach). Other influential articles were about the "social erosion" of leadership talent from Chinese villages and the history of the "gentry" class in China (see *China's Gentry* for some translations).

A gifted and fluent essayist, Fei became widely popular in the 1940s for his prolific magazine and newspaper articles on a range of social and political topics, from China's family system and historical social structure to international politics and his visits to the United States and England; these articles (and also translations he made) introduced much information about the West and modern social science concepts to a broad Chinese audience. Never a Communist or even a Marxist, he was nonetheless a patriot repelled by Chiang Kai-shek's inept, corrupt and oppressive regime and he came to look favorably on the Communists. But the Communists did not trust such intellectuals, and Fei's career was abruptly cut short by the 1949 revolution. He was assigned to national-minorities work and wrote occasional bland pieces on that and in support of various government policies in the early 1950s. Then, at the time of the "Hundred Flowers" in 1957 he spoke out in favor of greater autonomy for intellectuals and was consequently branded a "bourgeois rightist" and subjected to a nationwide propaganda campaign, the burden of which was that Chinese intellectuals were too divorced from the masses to be relied on to support socialism. For the next two decades Fei was consigned to oblivion and untold suffering—twenty completely lost years. Only since Mao's death and the great changes of the late 1970s has he reemerged and even, in spite of advanced years, gradually attained prominence, traveling abroad frequently, struggling to get sociology reestablished and to train students, and writing on the growth of small cities in present-day China, the development of Inner Mongolia, and the village of Kaixiangong again, on which he has data stretching over fifty years. As of the late 1980s, he was a professor of sociology at Beijing University and vice-president of the National People's Congress standing committee.

MAJOR WORKS: "Ch'in-ying hun-su chih yen-chiu" ["The marriage custom of going to meet the bride"], *She-hui hsüeh-chieh*, vol. 8 (1934), pp. 155-186; *Peasant Life in China* (London: 1939); (with Chang Tzu-i*) Earthbound China* (Chicago: 1945); *Ch'u-fang Mei-kuo [First visit to America]* (Chongqing: 1945); "Peasantry and gentry," *American Journal of Sociology*, vol. 52 (1946), pp. 1-17; *Min-chu hsien-fa jen-ch'üan [Democracy, Constitutions, Human Rights]* (Shanghai: 1946); *Sheng-yü chih-tu [The Institution of the Family]* (Shanghai: 1947); (with P'an Kuang-tan) "City and village: the inequality of opportunity" [tr. of 1947 orig.] in: J.M. Menzel (editor), *The Chinese Civil Service* (Boston: 1963), pp. 9-21; *Hsiang-t'u Chung-kuo [Rural China]* (Shanghai: 1948); *Hsiang-t'u ch'ung-chien [Rural Reconstruction]* (Shanghai: 1948); *Wo che-i nien [This Year for Me]* (Beijing: 1950); *China's Gentry* (Chicago: 1953); *Toward a People's Anthropology* (Beijing: 1981); *Chinese Village Close-up* (Beijing: 1983); *Ts'ung-shih she-hui hsueh wu-shih nien [Fifty Years as a Sociologist]* (Tianjin: 1983); *Tsa-hsieh chia/i/ping/ting chi [Miscellaneous Writings]* [4 vols.] (Tianjing: 1982-1986); *Small Towns in China* (Beijing: 1986).

SOURCES: R. David Arkush, *Fei Xiaotong and Sociology in Revolutionary China* (Cambridge, Mass.: 1981); Burton Pasternak, "A conversation with Fei Xiaotung," *Current Anthropology*, vol. 29 (1988), pp. 637-662.

David Arkush

Fél, Edit. Ethnographer, anthropologist. Born in Kiskőrös (Hungary) 14 September 1910, died in Budapest (Hungary) 28 June 1988. Fél received her training in the Hungarian school of European "national" ethnography. The discipline was regarded as part of the humanities, concerned with the description and historical interpretation of traditional elements of national peasant culture. Fél, during her long professional career, appreciated and utilized the knowledge of and special sensitivity to cultural detail created in national ethnography, but she set herself the task of broadening the scope of ethnographic research by introducing new approaches, methods and concepts from other social sciences. She initiated ethnographic research in Hungary on peasant social institutions, the extended family, more or less corporate lineages, kinship, neighborhood and so forth, and she had a pioneering role in the introduction and development of the community study method.

Her three volumes on the village of Átány are especially renowned and are considered by anthropologists and historians alike as one of the richest and most profound documentary studies on Central European village life in the era before industrialization and the socialist transformation.

In her early work, Fél analyzed the cultural continuities and processes of adaptation in a German village in Hungary (*Harta néprajza*) and described the contemporary stratification and social differentiation in a Hungarian village (*Kocs 1936-ban*). Edit Fél worked at the Budapest Ethnographic Museum for thirty-six years, did extensive collecting for the museum, and arranged significant exhibitions at home and abroad. In the interpretation of peasant artifacts she tried to reveal the social and cultural context in which these objects were made and used. In her research on folk costumes she studied the expression of social status, interpersonal relations, everyday and ceremonial circumstances and the manifestation of individual taste. She viewed folk art as an expression of the peasants' awareness of their social status and of their pride and pointed to the connection between the flourishing of folk art in the 19th century and the relative prosperity of the peasants, freed from feudal bondage, in the early stage of capitalist transformation in East Central Europe (*Magyar népművészet*).

Fél's distinctive approach—which made use of both the ethnographer's traditional skills and anthropological models in order to record the details of peasant life and to grasp the peasants' mentality, their interpersonal ties and their way of life as a process—was carried out in full in her studies of the village of Átány. Together with her disciple and colleague, Tamás Hofer, she wrote three books on Átány. The first volume (*Proper Peasants*) deals with the village's social institutions and its system of interpersonal relationships. The second volume (*Bäuerliche Denkweise*) analyzes the conceptual system by which peasants perceive their farming and housekeeping resources and possibilities and that influences their day-to-day decisions. The third volume (*Geräte der Átányer Bauern*) describes the agricultural implements of diverse peasant farms and examines what kind of knowledge, experience, values, feelings, social constraints and obligations of the peasants' work ethic are connected to them.

Fél's efforts to deepen the understanding of the peasants' general lot and to show peasant culture as a human life style led her to narrow the focus of her investigations from a community to a single individual. In her last work (*Margit Gari ...*) she presented the life history of a very poor, deeply religious peasant woman and her world and her encounters with historical events, including world wars and revolutions.

In the decades when Fél's books on peasant communities and life stories were published, the Hungarian peasantry suffered under inhuman political pressure. Her writings, published abroad, were planned as memorials for a vanishing life style.

MAJOR WORKS: *Harta néprajza* [*Ethnography of Harta*] (Budapest: 1935); *Kocs 1936-ban: néprajzi monográfia* [*Kocs in 1936: an Ethnographic Monograph*] (Budapest: 1941); *A nagycsalád és jogszokásai a komárommegyei Martoson* [*The Extended Family and its Legal Customs in Martos, Komárom County*] (Budapest: 1944); (with Tamás Hofer) *Proper Peasants: Traditional Life in a Hungarian Village* (Chicago: 1969) (= *Viking Fund Publications in Anthropology*, no. 46); (with Tamás Hofer) *Bäuerliche Denkweise in Wirtschaft und Haushalt: eine ethnographische Untersuchung über das ungarische Dorf Átány* (Göttingen: 1972) (= *Veröffentlichungen des Instituts für Mitteleuropäische Volksforschung an der Philipps-Universität Marburg-Lahn*, vol. 7); (with Tamás Hofer) *Geräte der Átányer Bauern* (Copenhagen and Budapest: 1974); (with Tamás Hofer) *Magyar népművészet* (Budapest: 1975) [tr.: *Hungarian Folk Art* (Oxford: 1979)]; *Margit Gari: le vinaigre et le fiel: la vie d'une paysanne hongroise* (Paris: 1983).

SOURCES: Magda S. Gémes, "Fél Edit irodalmi munkássága" ["Edit Fél's literary works"], *Néptajzi Értesítő*, vol. 42 (1960), pp. 17-29; Klára K.-Csilléry, "Edit Fél: 70 Jahre," *Österreichische Zeitschrift für Volkskunde*, vol. 84 (1981), pp. 45-48; Tamás Hofer, "Néhány vonás Fél Edit tudományos pályaképéhez" ["A few lines on Edit Fél's scientific career"], *Ethnographia*, vol. 101 (1990).

Tamás Hofer
[*Translation from Hungarian: Ildiko D. Nowak*]

Ferreira Penna, Domingos Soares.

Geographer, ethnologist, archaeologist, journalist, historiographer. Born in Oliveira, near Mariana, Minas Gerais (Brazil) 6 June 1818, died in Belém, Pará (Brazil) 6 January 1888. Ferreira Penna did not take any advanced academic courses but he received a good humanistic education at the Mariana

Seminary. From his youth he nourished the ideals of liberty and democracy under a republican regime. He was a politician in Minas, Rio de Janeiro and Pará. His intelligence, strong will and incorruptible character led him into public service. Invited to serve in the government, he moved to Belém, Pará to fill the role of secretary from 1858 to 1868. Here he lived thirty years, developing his public roles of professor, explorer and naturalist. It was while traveling through several regions of Amazônia that Ferreira Penna came to be interested in the Indian problem and in the archaeology of the region to which he dedicated the best years of his life and the largest share of his intellectual energy.

Ferreira Penna was a pioneer together with Canadian geologist and ethnologist Charles Frederick Hartt (1840-1878) in archaeological research in Amazônia, especially on Marajó (Camutins and Pacoval), along the Mazagão and Maracá Rivers (now in the state of Amapá), on the lower Tocantins and in coastal Pará. He was the first to study the Sambaqui Indians of this region and did surveys of the prehistoric rock inscriptions in some areas, principally the Xingu River. In his explorations, he contacted several indigenous groups along the Negro, Madeira, Tapajós, Tocantins and Capim Rivers and also observed acculturated or "semi-civilized" indigenous groups. Ferreira Penna was a vehement defender of the rights of Indians and of the preservation of Amazonian archaeological sites, causes that he led in 1882. He was, in general, a combative conservationist, defending both the natural ecology and the popular culture of this region.

In 1866 he brought together a group of intellectuals from Belém society and founded the Museu Paraense (Pará Museum) (later the Museu Paraense Emílio Goeldi), the goal of which was Amazonian research in the fields of natural history, ethnology, geography and history and which acquired collections for study and display. Until the arrival of EMÍLIO GOELDI in 1894, the best geographical and archaeological works published on this region were those of Ferreira Penna, a pioneer Amazonologist.

MAJOR WORKS: *A região occidental da Província do Pará* (Belém: 1869); *A ilha de Marajó* (Belém: 1875); *Breve notícia sobre os Sambaquis do Pará* (Rio de Janeiro: 1878); *Apontamentos sobre os ceramios do Pará* (Rio de Janeiro: 1879); *Algumas palavras da língua dos Aruans* (Rio de Janeiro: 1881); *Índios de Marajó* (Rio de Janeiro: 1885); *Índios e Jesuítas* (Belem: 1888); *Colonização e catequese no Solimões* (Belém: 1888).

SOURCES: José Veríssimo, "D.S. Ferreira Penna: notícia biographica," *Boletim do Museu Paraense*, vol. 1 (1894), pp. 57-73; Osvaldo Cunha, "Domingos Soares Ferreira Penna: uma analise de sua vida e sua obra" in: *Obras completas de Domingos Soares Ferreira Penna*, vol. 1 (Belém: 1973), pp. 11-41.

Osvaldo Rodrigues da Cunha
[Translation from Spanish: Margo L. Smith]

Fetter, Vojtěch. Physical anthropologist. Born in Kutná Hora (Czechoslovakia) 7 April 1905, died in Prague (Czechoslovakia) 26 September 1971. Fetter was a professor of anthropology at the Faculty of Natural Sciences of Charles University in Prague; he was also assistant to JINDŘICH MATIEGKA and an associate dean at the same university.

He graduated from a gymnasium in Prague and, following graduation from the Faculty of Natural Sciences of Charles University in 1930, worked at the Institute of Anthropology. During the war, when the University was closed, he taught at a gymnasium in Prague and after the reopening of institutions of higher education in 1945, served as an assistant to Jiří Malý and lectured on the biology of the child in pedagogical departments in České Budějovice (Southern Bohemia) and in Olomouc (Moravia), where a department of anthropology had been established. In 1950, after Malý's death, he became head of the Institute of Anthropology in Prague, where in 1954 he was promoted to associate professor and in 1963 became full professor.

Fetter worked in all areas of physical anthropology. Among his main contributions were nationwide scientific investigations of youth development in Czechslovakia and the physical characteristics of adult populations (including young people working in the coal mines and steel mills of Ostrava, forest workers, the inhabitants of Domažlice and participants of nationwide sporting events such as the Spartakiad). He successfully applied methods and findings from physical anthropology to forensic medicine, criminology and clinical medicine. His works on the prevention and control of obesity in children and on the diagnosis of craniostenosis in children were especially valuable.

He surrounded himself with a great many fellow researchers and students and established a modern school of anthropology. He was an author of numerous textbooks and a leading author of the first university textbook in anthropology to be used in Czechoslovakia (*Antropologie*). He founded the professional organization of the anthropologists of Czechoslovakia by establishing an anthropology division of the Society of the National Museum in 1955 (together with M. Prokopec and J. Suchý) and became the first president of the Czechoslovakian Anthropological Society (a part of the Czechoslovak Academy of Science), which he helped to establish. In 1956, with a trip to Poland, he began the first official post-war scientific cooperation with anthropologists from other countries.

MAJOR WORKS: "Tělesně vlastnosti mládeže z Ase a okolí po světové válce" ["Physical characteristics of adolescents from Ash and vicinity after the World War"], *Anthropologie*, vol. 11 (1933), pp. 279-287; "Lebky a kosti z t. zv. 'Francouzského hřbitova' z Mikulova na Moravě" ["Skulls and bones from the so called French cemetery at Mikulov in Moravia"), *Anthropologie*, vol. 6 (1928), pp. 255-267; "Anthropologické vyšetření ostatků slavného českého houslisty Ferdinanda Lauba" ["Anthropologic examination of remains of a famous Czech violinist Ferdinand Laub"], *Zprávy anthropologické společnosti*, vol. 4, no. 3-4 (1952), pp. 33-41; (with J. Dittrich) "Kefalometrie jako diagnostická pomůcka při léčení patologických lebečních deformit" ["Cephalommetry as a diagnostic aid in treatment of pathological deformities of a skull"], *Acta Universitatis Carolinae. Biologica* (1958), pp. 109-119; *Etnická antropologie, vysokoškolské skriptum* [*Ethnic Anthropology, University Textbook*] (Prague: 1962); "Vývojová akcelerace u mládeže podle antropometrických výzkumů z let 1951 a 1961" ["Developmental acceleration of adolescents according to anthropometric research between 1951 and 1961"], *Čseskoslovenské. pediatrie*, vol. 18, no. 8 (1963), pp. 673-677; *Antropologie* (Prague: 1967).

SOURCES: J. Suchý, "Professor Dr. Vojtěch Fetter (1905-1971)," *Zprávy Československé společnosti anthropologické při ČSAV*, vol. 24, no. 1-2 (1971), pp. 2-3; Hanulík Matěj, "Prof. RNDr. Vojtěch Fetter, jeho život a dílo" ["Prof. RNDr. Vojtěch Fetter. his life and works"], *Zprávy Československé společnosti antropologické při ČSAV*, vol. 24, no. 3 (1971), pp. 40-41.

M. Prokopec
[Translation from Czech: Jitka Hurych]

Firth, J.R. (John Rupert). Linguist. Born in Keighley, Yorkshire (England) 17 June 1890, died in Lindfield, Sussex (England) 14 December 1960. Recognized as the father of the "London School of Linguistics," which placed the study of meaning at the heart of linguistic science, Firth served as teacher or guiding influence for many of

Britain's leading linguists during the middle part of the 20th century. Educated at the University of Leeds (M.A. in history, 1913), Firth began a career as teacher of language and linguistics in the Indian Education Service in 1915 and later served as Professor of English at the University of the Punjab at Lahore and Senior Lecturer in Phonetics at University College, London, before joining the faculty of the London School of Economics. In 1944 he became Britain's first Professor of General Linguistics at the University of London, a position he held until his retirement in 1956.

One hallmark of Firthian linguistics was the place of "prosody" in phonological analyses of language. Prosodies were bundles of sound units and sound-clustering rules that came together to form syllables and words. Firth believed that prosodic features provided a more universal and psychologically valid basis for representing sound phenomena than did the more conventional notion of phoneme, which he regarded as too closely rooted in languages that used alphabetic writing systems. He thought, too, that the focus of phonetics should be on speech sounds found within meaningful utterances rather than on discrete acoustic signals in isolation, and he emphasized the link between phonetic data and meaning.

Firth's treatment of syntax, which later came to be known as "systemic grammar," differed radically from the approach taken by LEONARD BLOOMFIELD and other American descriptivists. To Bloomfield, the study of syntax comprised phonological and morphological but not semantic considerations; to Firth, syntax could be analyzed only in terms of meaning. Firth viewed grammars as containing linearly arranged chains of syntagms, or operative syntactic units. Each syntagm theoretically represented a set of semantic choices available to the speaker, and the grammaticality of the chain was partially a product of communicative function and of expected or probable occurrence. This notion of function-based grammar has remained a centerpiece of British linguistics for most of the last half century.

Firth is best known, and perhaps most criticized, for his views on linguistic meaning. He is generally credited with developing the notion "semantic collocation," the tendency of words to acquire specific meanings when paired or collocated with other lexical items. Like his colleague BRONISLAW MALINOWSKI at the London School of Economics, Firth believed that the meaning of a word or sentence was the totality of its effects on the social situation when the act of speech occurred. Thus, meaning of speech is indicated by the social action that arises or results from the utterance. This position on meaning is generally accepted by London School linguists. But Firth actually took a more extreme view and argued that utterances could be judged meaningful only within appropriately ascribed contexts of situation. This stance rendered as meaningless any sensible sounding sentence that could be formulated but for which no probable context could be imagined, a position that most linguists find untenable.

Critics and supporters alike have noted Firth's abstruse, sometimes impenetrable style of writing and the disjointed, uncohesive nature of his scholarship. He never authored a major book, and his 1937 monograph, *The Tongues of Men*, a sociologically based treatise on language written for general audiences, remains his best known work. Nonetheless, the tradition and influence of Firth and Firthian linguistics continues to be seen in the writings of later generations of British linguists.

MAJOR WORKS: *Speech* (London: 1930); "The technique of semantics" in: *Transactions of the Philological Society* (London: 1935), pp. 36-72 [reprinted in: J.R. Firth, *Papers in Linguistics, 1934-1951* (London: 1957), pp. 7-33]; "The use and distribution of certain English sounds: phonetics from a functional point of view" in: *English Studies*, vol. 17 (1935), pp. 2-12 [reprinted in: *Papers in Linguistics, 1934-1951*, pp. 34-46]; *The Tongues of Men* (London: 1937); "The English school of phonetics" in: *Transactions of the Philological Society* (London: 1946), pp. 92-132 [reprinted in: *Papers in Linguistics, 1934-1951*, pp. 92-120]; "Sound and prosodies" in: *Transactions of the Philological Society* (London: 1948), pp. 127-152 [reprinted in: *Papers in Linguistics, 1934-1951*, pp. 121-138]; "Modes of meaning" in: *Essays and Studies of the English Association* (London: 1951), pp. 118-149 [reprinted in: *Papers in Linguistics, 1934-1951*, pp. 190-215]; "General linguistics and descriptive grammar," *Transactions of the Philological Society* (London: 1951), pp. 69-87 [reprinted in: *Papers in Linguistics, 1934-1951*, pp. 216-228]; "Linguistic analysis as a study of meaning" in: F.R. Palmer (editor), *Selected Papers of J.R. Firth, 1952-1959* (Bloomington: 1968), pp. 12-26; "Ethnographic analysis and language with reference to Malinowski's views" in: Raymond W. Firth (editor), *Man and Culture: an Evaluation of the Work of Bronislaw Malinowski* (London: 1957), pp. 93-118 [reprinted in: *Selected Papers of J.R. Firth, 1952-1959*, pp. 137-167]; "A synopsis of linguistic theory, 1930-1955" in: *Studies in Linguistic Analysis* (Oxford: 1957) [special volume of: *Transactions of the Philological Society*], pp. 1-31 [reprinted in: *Selected Papers of J.R. Firth, 1952-1959*, pp. 168-205].

SOURCES: John Lyons, "Firth's theory of meaning" in: C.E. Bazell [et al.] (editors), *In Memory of J.R. Firth* (London: 1966), pp. 288-302; T.F. Mitchell, *Principles of Firthian Linguistics* (London: 1975); Geoffrey Sampson, *Schools of Linguistics* (Stanford: 1980).

Craig A. Sirles

Firth, Sir **Raymond William.** Social anthropologist, economic anthropologist. Born in Auckland (New Zealand) 25 March 1901. Best known in anthropology for his work on social organization, kinship, Polynesian economics and Tikopia ethnography, Firth completed a master's degree in economics (1922) and a diploma in social science (1923) at the University of Auckland. In 1924 he went to the London School of Economics intending to focus his doctoral work on economics, as no anthropological positions were then available anywhere in New Zealand. However, given the opportunity to study with BRONISLAW MALINOWSKI, Firth turned his attention to anthropology and completed a doctoral dissertation on Maori economics in 1927 (published as *Primitive Economics of the New Zealand Maori*). Firth conducted extensive fieldwork in Tikopia (Solomon Islands). He also worked in Malaysia and London and spent lesser periods in New Guinea and West Africa. His work on Tikopia is the most comprehensive in Polynesian ethnography and has made Tikopia one of the best known cultures in the ethnographic record. From 1930 to 1932 he taught anthropology at the University of Sydney and the following year returned to the London School of Economics where he was Professor of Anthropology from 1944 until his retirement in 1968.

Firth's most significant contribution to anthropology is his development of a theoretical framework emphasizing choice, decision, organization and process in social and institutional behavior (the most complete theoretical discussions of which are in *Elements of Social Organization* and *Essays on Social Organization and Values*). His major works span virtually all areas of sociocultural anthropology—economics, kinship, marriage, rank and authority, art, music, symbols and ritual, religion, myth, social change and language. Regarded as one of the two founders of the formal paradigm in economic anthropology, Firth's emphasis on choice, institution and organization in economic activities strongly affected the work of Michael Polanyi and theorists associated with decision analysis and the institutional paradigm. Firth was the first anthropologist to question prevailing typologies and evolutionary assumptions in economics, using field data to demonstrate the interrelationships among social institutions and the limitations and utility of conventional economic concepts. Although critical of Marx's work, Firth has also recognized Marx's basic contributions to economics and has been supportive of Marxist approaches in anthropology.

The distinction between social structure and social organization proposed by Firth in 1951 is a fundamental theoretical and methodological contribution to social anthropology and to the functional and structural-functional positions with which he is associated. He defined social structure as the principles on which the form of social relations depend. Social organization refers to directional activity, to the working out of social relations in everyday life. Firth's distinction has frequently been misunderstood as idealized social structure contrasted with empirical social organization, but he argued instead that structure refers to persistence and order and organization to adaptation, decision-making and choice among alternatives. The distinction was an important step toward overcoming the static limitations of structural-functional (e.g., A.R. RADCLIFFE-BROWN) and functionalist (e.g., Malinowski) theories, which could account for neither social change nor individual behavior. Moreover, the distinction provided theoretical grounding for moving ethnographic research methods from an almost exclusive focus on people's statements of expected behavior to observations of their actual behavior, as Malinowski had argued earlier. *We, the Tikopia*, in which Firth demonstrated the importance of detailed accounts of daily behavior in Tikopia families to understanding kinship patterns, was the first comprehensive model for modern ethnographic research methods.

Over the years Firth has maintained contact with Tikopia with whom he has worked, and his good relations with the Tikopia have benefitted other anthropologists working in the Solomons. *We, the Tikopia* has been read by several generations of Tikopia.

Together with LUCY MAIR and ISAAC SCHAPERA, Firth, by dint of his intellectual leadership and his commitment to teaching, has been credited with creating an important school of anthropology at the London School of Economics. He trained many anthropologists, including Maurice Freedman, EDMUND LEACH, Sutti Ortiz, Joseph Loudon, Adrian Mayer, Joan Metge, William Shack, Michael Swift, Marjorie Topley and Burton Benedict. After his retirement in 1968, Firth toured the United States and Canada on a series of visiting professorships through 1974, during which he played an important role in synthesizing ideas from British and American schools of anthropology for American students. His contributions to anthropology have been recognized by two Festschrifts, one from his British students in 1967 (*Social Organization: Essays Presented to Raymond Firth*) and one by his North American students in 1978 (*Adaptation and Symbolism: Essays on Social Organization*). He was knighted on 25 July 1973, and he has been Life-President of the Association of Social Anthropologists of the Commonwealth since 1975.

MAJOR WORKS: *Primitive Economics of the New Zealand Maori* (London: 1929); *We, the Tikopia: a Sociological Study of Kinship in Primitive Polynesia* (London: 1936); *Art and Life in New Guinea* (London: 1936); *Human Types: an Introduction to Anthropology* (Edinburgh: 1938); *Primitive Polynesian Economy* (London: 1939); *The Work of the Gods in Tikopia* (London: 1940); *Malay Fishermen, Their Peasant Economy* (London: 1946); *Elements of Social Organization* (London: 1951); (editor) *Studies of Kinship in London* (London: 1956); (editor) *Man and Culture: an Evaluation of the Work of Bronislaw Malinowski* (London: 1957); *Social Change in Tikopia: Re-study* of a Polynesian Community after a Generation (London: 1959); *History and Traditions of Tikopia* (Wellington: 1961); *Essays on Social Organization and Values* (London: 1964); (with Basil S. Yamey) *Capital, Savings, and Credit in Peasant Societies* (London: 1964); (editor) *Themes in Economic Anthropology* (London: 1967); *Tikopia Ritual and Belief* (Boston: 1967); (with W.H.R. Rivers and David M. Schneider) *Kinship and Social Organization* (London: 1968); *Rank and Religion in Tikopia: a Study in Polynesian Paganism and Conversion to Christianity* (London: 1970); (with Jane Hubert and Anthony Forge) *Families and their Relatives: Kinship in a Middle-Class Sector of London: an Anthropological Study* (New York: 1970); *Symbols: Private and Public* (New York: 1973); *Tikopia-English Dictionary* [*Taranga fakatikopia ma taranga fakainglisi*] (Auckland: 1985); (with Mervyn McLean) *Tikopia Songs: Poetic and Musical Art of a Polynesian People of the Solomon Islands* (Cambridge: 1990) [plus a separately issued audiocassette of recorded songs].

SOURCES: Maurice Freedman, "Preface" in: Maurice Freedman (editor), *Social Organization: Essays Presented to Raymond Firth* (Chicago: 1967), pp. vii-ix; Cyril S. Belshaw, "Theoretical problems in economic anthropology" in: Maurice Freedman (editor), *Social Organization: Essays Presented to Raymond Firth* (Chicago: 1967), pp. 25-42; Rhoda H. Halperin, *Economics across Cultures: towards a Comparative Science of the Economy* (New York: 1988); Sutti Ortiz, "What is decision analysis about? The problems of formal representations" in: Sutti Ortiz (editor), *Economic Anthropology: Topics and Theories* (New York: 1983), pp. 249-297; Karen Ann Watson-Gegeo, "Introduction" to: Karen Ann Watson-Gegeo and S. Lee Seaton (editors), *Adaptation and Symbolism: Essays on Social Organization, Presented to Sir Raymond Firth by his Students in the United States and Canada, 1968-1974* (Honolulu: 1978), pp. ix-xix.

Karen Ann Watson-Gegeo

Fischer, Adam. Ethnologist. Born in Przemyśl, Galicia (Austria-Hungary, now in Poland) 7 June 1889, died in Lwów (General Province, now in the U.S.S.R.) 22 December 1943. Fischer studied at the University of Lwów, obtaining his doctorate in Romance philology in 1912. Under the influence of Porębowicz he became interested in folklore. He became affiliated with the Polish Society of Folk Studies and was the secretary of the Society from 1910 to 1939 as well as the editor of *Lud* (1914-1939) and the publisher of the series *Prace Etnologiczne* (from 1934). In the years 1914-1924 he worked at the Ossolinski Publishing House. His contacts with A. Brückner, FELIX VON LUSCHAN and JAN CZEKANOWSKI deepened his interest in ethnology. He became assistant professor in 1921. In 1924 he was named professor at the University of Lwów and was entrusted with the position of director of the Institute of Ethnology.

Fischer developed a program of systematic investigations of the ethnography of Poland's neighbors. He was an adherent of the diffusionism of the Viennese School. In his numerous studies he analyzed the distribution of cultural artifacts in order to create models of the course of historical processes. He left a legacy of many publications in the sphere of folklore and folklore studies.

MAJOR WORKS: *Znaczenie etnologii dla innych nauk* [*The Significance of Ethnology for Other Sciences*] (Lwów: 1922); *Lud polski: podręcznik etnografii Polski* [*The Polish Folk: a Handbook of Polish Ethnography*] (Lwów: 1926); *Diabeł w wierzeniach ludu polskiego* [*The Devil in the Beliefs of the Polish Peasant*] (Lwów: 1928); *Rusini: zarys etnografii Rusi* [*The Ruthenians: Outline of Ruthenian Ethnography*] (Lwów: 1929); *Rośliny w wierzeniach i zwyczajach ludu polskiego* [*Plants in the Beliefs and Customs of the Polish Folk*] (Lwów: 1929); *Etnografia słowiańska* [*Slavic Ethnography*] [3 parts: *Połabianie* [*Polabian*], *Łużyczanie* [*Lusatian*], *Polacy* [*Poles*] (Lwów and Warsaw: 1932-1934); *Kaszubi na tle etnografii Polski* [*Kaszubians on the Background of Polish Ethnography*] (Torun: 1934); *Pierwiastki wierzeniowe w polskim zdobnictwie ludowym* [*Elements of Faith in Polish Folk Art*] (Lwów: 1937); *Drzewa w wierzeniach i obrzędach ludu polskiego* [*Trees in the Beliefs and Rituals of the Polish Folk] (Lwów: 1939); *Zarys etnografii Polski południowo-wschodniej [Outline of the Ethnography of Southeast Poland]* (Lwów: 1939).

SOURCES: Józef Gajek, "S.p. Professor Adam Fischer," *Lud*, vol. 36 (1939-1945), pp. 6-18; Józef Gajek, "Fischer, Adam" in: *Polski słownik biograficzny [Polish Biographical Dictionary]*, vol. 7 (Kraków: 1948-1958), pp. 48-49.

Maria Niewiadomska and Iwona Grzelakowska
[Translation from Polish: Joel Janicki]

Fischer, Henri Théodore. Cultural anthropologist. Born in Poerwakarta (Dutch East Indies) 6 April 1901, died in Utrecht (Netherlands) 27 September 1976. Fischer was one of the first students to register for an honors degree in geography at Utrecht when this subject was introduced at university level in the Netherlands in 1921. At that time the degree course included a good deal of ethnography and ethnology, which were taught at Utrecht by J.H.F. KOHLBRUGGE. Kohlbrugge had acquired much practical knowledge about life in rural Java during his years as a medical officer and had done some research in physical anthropology. Although Fischer completed his Ph.D. thesis under Kohlbrugge's supervision in 1929, his choice of topic—the sacred marriage of heaven and earth—showed the influence of the history of religion, which was an important and well established discipline in the Netherlands in those years, rather than reflecting the main interests of Kohlbrugge.

In 1925 a number of large business firms with interests in the Dutch East Indies proposed an alternative degree course for the education of colonial civil servants at the University of Utrecht, as the existing course at Leiden was considered to be too liberal by conservative colonialists. The initiative was welcomed by the government and the course was established. Fischer was elected to become lecturer in Indonesian ethnology for this course and undertook a trip to the Dutch East Indies in preparation for this task. His topic of study was the role of Christian missions in areas outside Java and, more specifically, the relationship between colonial administrators and missionaries.

In 1936 Fischer succeeded Kohlbrugge as professor of anthropology and held this chair until his retirement in 1970. Fischer made important contributions to the study of kinship and marriage in Indonesia and to kinship theory in general. He was skeptical of the attempts of many Leiden anthropologists to reconstruct archaic social relationships on the basis of the study of contemporary Indonesian myths and was a consistent critic of speculations that, in his opinion, were not based on empirically established facts. Fischer encouraged academic research in Western New Guinea during the period 1949-1962 when this region remained separated from independent Indonesia under Dutch control. This resulted in several theses by his students.

MAJOR WORKS: *Het heilig huwelik van hemel en aarde* (Utrecht: 1929); *Zending en volksleven in Nederlands-Indie* (Zwolle: 1932); "De aanverwantschap bij enige volken van de Nederlands-Indische Archipel," *Mensch en Maatschappij*, vol. 11 (1935), pp. 285-297 and 365-378; "Polyandry," *Internationales Archiv für Ethnographie*, vol. 46 (1952), pp. 106-115; "Some notes on kinship systems and relationship terms of Sumba, Manggarai and South Timor," *Internationales Archiv für Ethnographie*, vol. 48 (1957), pp. 1-31; "The cognates in the Minangkabau kinship structure," *Oceania*, vol. 35 (1964-1965), pp. 96-110; "Toba Batak kinship terms," *Oceania*, vol. 36 (1965-1966), pp. 253-263.

SOURCES: J.H. Scherer and J.J. de Wolf, "Henri Théodore Fischer, 1901-1976," *Bijdragen tot de Taal-, Land- en Volkenkunde*, vol. 133 (1977), pp. 1-10; J.J. de Wolf, "J.H.F. Kohlbrugge en H.Th. Fischer en de beoefening van de culturele antropologie aan de Rijksuniversiteit te Utrecht," *Antropologische Verkenningen*, vol. 7, no. 1/2 (1988), pp. 95-117.

S.R. Jaarsma and J.J. de Wolf

Fison, Lorimer. Missionary, anthropologist, journalist. Born in Barningham (England) 9 November 1832, died in Melbourne (Victoria) 29 December 1907. Fison played a significant role in sustaining the study of kinship and social organization in the manner of LEWIS HENRY MORGAN through the last quarter of the 19th century. His accounts of Aboriginal Australia in particular provided paradigms of the maximally "primitive" forms of society for subsequent speculation in the evolutionary vein—in the later work of Morgan himself, then in that of JAMES G. FRAZER, Charles Stanisland Wake, E.B. TYLOR, Josef Kohler and Émile Durkheim.

A Wesleyan missionary in Fiji from 1864 to 1871 and again from 1875 to 1884, Fison received one of Morgan's kin terminology questionnaires in 1869. This questionnaire aroused his interest in anthropology, and he became a zealous disciple of Morgan, maintaining a voluminous correspondence with him until Morgan's death in 1881. In Australia from 1871 to 1875, Fison made inquiries into Aboriginal social organization but did so by correspondence with European settlers rather than by personal investigation. Fison's early accounts of the Australian class systems—interpreted as involving just the kind of "group marriage" Morgan's theory required, but evidence for which had theretofore been very thin—were given a prominent position in the revised evolutionary scheme of Morgan's *Ancient Society*. Fison's full exposition of these types of organization was then presented in *Kamilaroi and Kurnai*, written with A.W. Howitt, with whom Fison collaborated in Australian studies from 1873.

Fison was in epistolary contact with Tylor from 1879 until at least 1895. This correspondence provided an important source of theoretical direction for Fison, especially after Morgan's death. A shift in Fison's orientation, from the strictly social structural approach of Morgan toward the inclusive Tylorian conception of culture, is evident in the early 1880s, especially in a series of papers on diverse Fijian topics appearing in the *Journal of the Anthropological Institute*. And yet the influence was reciprocal, for Tylor's later studies of social organization drew on Fison's recension of Morgan.

Although Fison did not publish much in anthropology after he returned to Australia in the mid-1880s and became editor of a Wesleyan newspaper, he remained an important figure: as an adviser to many younger workers in Australia and the Pacific—to BALDWIN SPENCER and F.J. Gillen, most significantly—and as a crucial link, by way of his continuing correspondence with Tylor and Frazer, between local and metropolitan anthropology.

Fison is also of interest in connection with the question of the relationship between anthropology and colonialism. During his second tour of Fiji he set forth a conception of the Fijian social order as based on a clan system of the usual Morganian type. Originally intended specifically as a critique of the entrenchment of chiefly privilege in the policies of then-governor Sir Arthur Gordon, this conception—since much criticized—became for some time the underpinning of colonial land policy in Fiji.

MAJOR WORKS: "The classificatory system of kinship," *Transactions of the Royal Society of Victoria*, o.s., vol. 10 (1874), pp. 154-179; (with A.W. Howitt) *Kamilaroi and Kurnai* (Melbourne: 1880); "Notes on Fijian burial customs," *Journal of the Anthropological Institute*, vol. 10 (1881), pp. 137-149; "Land tenure in Fiji," *Journal of the Anthropological Institute*, vol. 10 (1881), pp. 332-352; (with A.W. Howitt) "From Mother-right to Father-right," *Journal of the Anthropological Institute*, vol. 12 (1883), pp. 30-46; "The classificatory system of relationship," *Journal of the Anthropological Institute*, vol. 24 (1895), pp. 360-371; *Tales from Old Fiji* (London: 1904); "Selections from the letters of Lorimer Fison and A.W. Howitt to Lewis Henry Morgan" (edited by Bernhard Stern), *American Anthropologist*, vol. 32 (1930), pp. 257-279, 419-453.

SOURCES: Peter France, *The Charter of the Land* (Melbourne: 1969), pp. 102-128; J.G. Frazer, "Fison and Howitt," *Folklore*, vol. 20 (1909), pp. 144-80; Adam Kuper, *The Invention of Primitive Society* (London: 1988), pp. 92-100; Carl Resek, *Lewis Henry Morgan* (Chicago: 1960), pp. 126-30; A.R. Tippett, "Lorimer Fison: his place in the history of the Church in the Pacific," *Church History* [Sydney], vol. 3 (1983), pp. 1-30, 122-148; A.R. Tippett, "Lorimer Fison: inventory of material known to exist," *Church History* [Sydney], vol. 3 (1983), pp. 149-181.

Mark Francillon

Fletcher, Alice Cunningham. Anthropologist, political activist, reformer of Indian policy. Born in Cuba 15 March 1838, died in Washington (D.C.) 6 April 1923. Of New England parentage, Fletcher was a member of the first generation of professional anthropologists in the United States. A pioneering fieldworker, Fletcher is known for her studies of Indian music and Plains Indians religious ceremonies and for two monographs that are among the classics in ethnography: *The Hako: a Pawnee Ceremony*, and *The Omaha Tribe*, the latter written in conjunction with FRANCIS LAFLESCHE, the young Omaha Indian whom she informally adopted as her son. Fletcher also worked actively to reform U.S. Indian policy. An opponent of the "agency system" in which Native Americans were considered wards of the U.S. government and confined to reservations under the control of a federal agent, she was one of the principal architects of the Dawes Act of 1887, the goal of which was to break up reservations and improve the lot of Indians by giving them education, citizenship and private ownership of homesteads of land. The failure of that policy has cast a shadow on Fletcher's reputation. By 1898 she herself knew that it had been a mistake, although she never acknowledged this publicly. Instead she threw herself into her ethnographic work, producing the detailed and careful monographs that are increasingly recognized as of enduring value.

In 1890 Fletcher was awarded a lifetime fellowship founded for her at the Peabody Museum of American Archaeology and Ethnology at Harvard University by Mary C. Thaw. By virtue of the Thaw Fellowship, Fletcher became the first woman to have a paid professional position at Harvard. She continued, however, to live in Washington, D.C., where in her later years she was informally associated with the Bureau of American Ethnology (BAE). She wrote more than thirty entries for the *Handbook of the North American Indians* published by the BAE. Fletcher held many national offices in anthropology. She was an early proponent of the preservation of archaeological monuments in the United States and a major force behind the founding of the School of American Archaeology (later School of American Research) in Santa Fe, New Mexico.

MAJOR WORKS: "Five Indian ceremonies," *16th Annual Report, Peabody Museum of American Archaeology and Ethnology* (Washington: 1884), pp. 260-888; *Indian Education and Civilization* (Washington: 1888); "A Study of Omaha Indian music," *Archaeological and*

Ethnological Papers, Peabody Museum of American Archaeology and Ethnology, vol. 1 (1893), pp. 237-287; (with James R. Murie) *The Hako: a Pawnee Ceremony* (Washington: 1904) (= *22nd Annual Report of the Bureau of American Ethnology, 1900-1901*, part 2); (with Francis La Flesche) *The Omaha Tribe* (Washington: 1911) (= *27th Annual Report of the Bureau of American Ethnology, 1905-1906*, pp. 15-659).

SOURCES: Joan Mark, *A Stranger in Her Native Land: Alice Fletcher and the American Indians* (Lincoln, Nebraska: 1989); Frederick E. Hoxie and Joan Mark (editors), E. Jane Gay, *With the Nez Perces: Alice Fletcher in the Field, 1889-92* (Lincoln, Nebraska: 1981); Joan Mark, *4 Anthropologists: an American Science in Its Early Years* (New York: 1980); Nancy O. Lurie, "Women in early American anthropology" in: June Helm (editor) *Pioneers of American Anthropology* (Seattle: 1966), pp. 29-83; Walter Hough, "Alice Cunningham Fletcher," *American Anthropologist*, n.s., vol. 25 (1923), pp. 254-257; Thurman Wilkins, "Alice Cunningham Fletcher" in: Edward T. James and Janet W. James (editors), *Notable American Women* (Cambridge, Mass.: 1971), pp. 1, 630-633; Andrea S. Temkin, "Alice Cunningham Fletcher" in: Ute Gacs [et al.] (editors), *Women Anthropologists: a Biographical Dictionary* (New York: 1988), pp. 95-101; Joan Mark, "Alice C. Fletcher" in: Alden Whitman (editor), *Great American Reformers* (New York: 1985), pp. 294-295; Joan Mark, "The American Indian as anthropologist: Francis La Flesche," *Isis*, vol. 73 (1982), pp. 497-510.

Joan Mark

Folkmar, Daniel (born Daniel Fulcomer). Anthropologist, statistician, government employee. Born in Roxbury (Wisconsin) 28 October 1861, died in Washington (D.C.) 21 July 1932. Folkmar was trained at Clark College in Iowa and at several American and European universities. He received a certificate from the École d'Anthropologie in Paris and doctorates in social sciences from the Université nouvelle in Brussels (1899) and the University of Paris (1900). The primary focus of his study was physical anthropology, but he held a view of anthropology that stressed its great breadth and unity.

Folkmar was a teacher at and the president of Indiana Normal College (1890-1892) and West Michigan College (1892-1893), and he was on the staff of Milwaukee State Normal School and the Université nouvelle in Brussels. As a teacher, he professed several disciplines, including psychology, political science, and sociology as well as anthropology. He joined the U.S. civil service, becoming an anthropologist with the Philippines ethnological survey and provincial lieutenant governor of the troublesome Bontoc-Lepanto region during 1903-1907. He later served in various capacities with the U.S. Immigration Commission, Census Bureau, and the War Department.

Influenced by European positivism, Folkmar was a champion of applied anthropology, placing it at the apex of his theoretical framework. In his government career, he worked on several notable projects. For the Immigration Commission, he carried out a special project during 1908-1909, compiling descriptions of the nationalities that had formed the American population. During 1910-1914, as a special agent of the Census Bureau, he carried out studies of the national origins of the American population. As a statistician with the War Department during World War I, he was placed in charge of the anthropological measurement of soldiers in 1919.

MAJOR WORKS: *Leçons d'anthropologie philosophique: ses applications à la morale positive* (Paris: 1900); *Album of Philippine Types* (Manila: 1904); *Dictionary of Races or Peoples* (Washington: 1911) (= *Reports of the Immigration Commission*, Sen. Doc. 662, 61st Cong., 2nd Sess.).

SOURCES: "Folkmar, Daniel" in: *Who Was Who* (Chicago: 1942), vol. 1, pp. 409-410; [Obituary], *Washington Star* (22 July 1932); untitled manuscript of experiences in the Philippines in the Smithsonian Institution National Anthropological Archives.

James R. Glenn

Foote, Robert Bruce (sometimes called Robert Brucefoot). Geologist, prehistorian, India Civil Service officer. Born in Cheltenham (England) 22 September 1834, died in Madras (India) 29 December 1912. Called the "father of Indian prehistory," Foote discovered and recognized a Paleolithic stone tool in India on 30 May 1863 in a Pleistocene gravel pit at Palavaram near Madras, thereby establishing for the first time the presence of early man in southern Asia with a technological lithic tradition similar to the handaxe-cleaver Acheulian industries from Europe and western Asia. With William King, a fellow officer of the Geological Survey of India, Foote collected additional handaxes and cleavers at Attirampakkam later that same year, returning to Pallavaram in 1864 when he found some stone tools *in situ* in a lateritic gravel bed. These discoveries were brought to the attention of British archaeologists in London in 1865, and in 1868 Foote presented a paper to the International Congress of Prehistoric Archaeology at Norwich. There he first announced his theory that the manufacturers of the quartzite implements were not Aryans but the ancient ancestors of the tribal peoples surviving today in remote jungle and hill regions of India. Foote argued that these first human inhabitants of the Indian subcontinent had migrated from some single center of human origins situated between India and Europe. He maintained that India lacked a Copper Age, a hiatus separated Paleolithic from Neolithic cultures and the Neolithic and Iron Age overlapped. He did not recognize a Mesolithic cultural period, although he discovered microlithic tools at one of the teri sites at Sawyerpuram, a locality later prehistorians recognized as belonging to the Indian Mesolithic. Some of Foote's artifact collections were displayed at the Vienna International Expedition of 1873.

Foote's most outstanding contributions to Indian prehistory include his correct identification of the South Indian ashmounds as Neolithic rather than natural formations; his studies of Neolithic sites in the Bellary-Anantapur and Kurnool regions; the excavations at the Billa Surgam caves in collaboration with his son, Lt. Henry Foote; and his attention to the geological contexts of prehistoric sites throughout southern India as well as in Maharashtra and Gujarat. In geological circles, Foote is highly regarded for his research on the crystalline rocks of peninsular India, recognition and separation of the Dharwar system from the crystalline complex, establishment of the division of Archaen rocks into distinct systems and extensive surveys of Pleistocene deposits, which led to his discovery of mammal fossils including the new species *Rhinoceros deccanensis*.

Foote joined the Geological Survey of India in 1858 and retired as a Senior Superintendent in 1891. After retirement, Foote served for three years as a geologist for the Baroda State, publishing a study of the geology and mineral resources of this part of Gujarat. In Mysore State he organized a State Geological Survey. At his residence at Yearend in the Shevaroy Hills of Salem District, Foote conducted independent research in prehistory and geology until 1904 when he resettled in Madras in order to prepare the catalogue of his extensive collection of artifacts for the Madras Museum where a special hall had been built for its reception. Ill health and failing eyesight retarded his progress on this project, and the two volumes of his *Catalogue* were published posthumously.

MAJOR WORKS: "On the occurrence of stone implements in lateritic formations in various parts of the Madras and North Arcot Districts" *Madras Journal of Literature and Science*, part 2 (1866), pp. 1-35; "On quartzite implements of palaeolithic types from the laterite formation of the east coast of southern India" in: *Transactions of the Third Session of the International Congress of Prehistoric Archaeology, Norwich and London* (London: 1868), pp. 224-239; "On the geology of parts of the Madras and North Arcot Districts lying north of the Palar River," *Memoirs of the Geological Survey of India*, vol. 10 (1873), pp. 1-132; "The geological features of the south Mahratta country and adjacent districts," *Memoirs of the Geological Survey of India*, vol. 12 (1876), pp. 1-268; "On the geological structure of the eastern coast from Latitude 15 (degrees) northward to Masulipatam, *Memoirs of the Geological Survey of India*, vol. 16 (1880), pp. 1-107; "Notes on the results of Mr. H.B. Foote's further excavations in the Billa Surgam caves," *Records of the Geological Survey of India*, vol. 18 (1885), pp. 227-235; "Notes on some recent Neolithic and Palaeolithic finds in South India," *Journal of the Asiatic Society of Bengal*, vol. 56 (1887), pp. 259-282; "Geology of Bellary District, Madras Presidency," *Memoirs of the Geological Survey of India*, vol. 25 (1895), pp. 1-218; *The Foote Collection of Indian Prehistoric and Protohistoric Antiquities: Catalogue Raisonné* (Madras: 1914); *The Foote Collection of Indian Prehistoric and Protohistoric Antiquities: Notes on Their Ages and Distribution* (Madras: 1916).

SOURCES: "Robert Bruce Foote" in: D. Sen and A.K. Ghosh (editors), *Studies in Prehistory: Robert Bruce Foote Memorial Volume* (Calcutta: 1966), pp. v-vi; Dilip K. Chakrabarti, *A History of Indian Archaeology from the Beginning to 1947* (New Delhi: 1988), pp. 193-200; H.H. Hayden, "Robert Bruce Foote" in: "General report of the Geological Survey of India for the year 1912," *Records of the Geological Survey of India*, vol. 43 (1913), pp. 7-8; R.D. Oldham, "Anniversary address of the President (Aubrey Strahan)," *Quarterly Journal of the Geological Society of London*, vol. 69 (1913), pp. livvvvv-lxxiii, esp. pp. lxv-lxvi.

Kenneth A.R. Kennedy

Ford, Clellan Stearns. Anthropologist. Born in Worcester (Massachusetts) 27 July 1909, died in New Haven (Connecticut) 4 November 1972. Ford's undergraduate education was in the field of chemistry, but in 1935 he took his Ph.D. in sociology at Yale University. His topic for doctoral research was an anthropological one, the comparative study of primitive technology.

After a year of fieldwork in Fiji, as a research fellow of Honolulu's Bernice P. Bishop Museum, Ford joined Yale's Institute of Human Relations. There he worked with JOHN W.M. WHITING and GEORGE PETER MURDOCK, and in 1937 helped found the Cross-Cultural Survey. In 1940 Ford was made a member of the anthropology faculty at Yale.

During World War II, Ford served briefly in civilian capacities, then was commissioned a lieutenant in the U.S. Naval Reserve. With his long-time mentor Murdock, Ford was assigned the task of preparing military government handbooks on a number of Pacific Island groups, including the Ryūkyūs.

Back at Yale, Ford was appointed the director of the Cross-Cultural Survey, which soon became the Human Relations Area Files (HRAF). Its size and scope expanded considerably under Ford's leadership.

Aside from his year in Fiji, Ford's only fieldwork was among Kwakiutl Indians in British Columbia. This resulted in the classic biography of a Kwakiutl chief, *Smoke from Their Fires*. A great deal of Ford's attention was devoted to HRAF, and his major contribution to anthropology utilized both the cross-cultural method and HRAF's immense collection of data. Begun before the war, but published in 1945 or later, Ford's studies of human sexual behavior were fact-based, nonsensationalized, and widely read. (*Patterns of Sexual Behavior* was translated into at least six major European languages.) Ford contrasted human reproduction with that of other mammals and compared a wide variety of different human societies. In all, he published three monographs and five articles on the subjects of sex and reproduction.

MAJOR WORKS: (with George P. Murdock [et al.]) *Outline of Cultural Materials* (New Haven: 1938); "The role of a Fijian chief," *American Sociological Review*, vol. 3 (1939), pp. 514-550; *Smoke from Their Fires* (New Haven: 1941); *A Comparative Study of Human Reproduction* (New Haven: 1945) (= *Yale University Publications in Anthropology*, vol. 32); (with Frank A. Beach) *Patterns of Sexual Behavior* (New York: 1951); "Sex offenses: an anthropological perspective," *Law and Contemporary Problems*, vol. 25 (1960), pp. 226-243; *Field Guide to the Study of Human Reproduction* (New Haven: 1964).

SOURCE: George P. Murdock, "Clellan Stearns Ford, 1909-1972," *American Anthropologist*, vol. 76 (1974), pp. 83-85.

David Lonergan

Ford, James Alfred. Archaeologist, museum curator. Born in Water Valley (Mississippi) 12 February 1911, died in Gainesville (Florida) 25 February 1968. Ford was trained at Louisiana State University (A.B., 1936), the University of Michigan (M.A., 1938) and Columbia University (Ph.D., 1949). Early in his career, he was connected with the Smithsonian Institution as a field assistant and with the Louisiana Geological Survey as an archaeologist. He was curator of archaeology at the American Museum of Natural History (1947-1964) and at the Florida State Museum (1964-1968). During the latter period, he was also professor of anthropology at the University of Florida.

Ford made several significant contributions to archaeology. In his first area of concentration, he carried out much fieldwork in the southeastern United States, establishing the Lower Mississippi Valley as a distinct archaeological province. He was also a major figure in providing the outlines of culture sequences for the Southeast in particular and for the eastern United States in general. His work included excavations under HENRY B. COLLINS at the Deasonville site in Mississippi (1929), surveys along the Mississippi-Louisiana boundary (1933), excavations at the Marksville site in Louisiana with FRANK M. SETZLER (1933) and at Ocmulgee National Monument for Arthur Randolph Kelly (1933-1934), excavations in Avoyelles Parish (Louisiana) (1938-1940), a survey along the Lower Mississippi Valley in Arkansas and Mississippi in search of the origins of Middle Mississippi culture together with JAMES B. GRIFFIN and Philip Phillips (1939-1940), excavations at the Jaketown site in Mississippi with William G. Haag and Phillips Ford (1951), and excavations at Poverty Point in Louisiana with C.H. Webb and R. Stuart Nietzel (1952-1955). He also carried out excavations at the Menard site in Arkansas (1958) and at a burial mound near Helena, Arkansas (1960-1961).

In his second area of concentration, Ford did fieldwork in Alaska; and, although acting in a secondary role, he shared in work concerned with the origins and development of Eskimo culture. His Alaskan work was largely under Henry B. Collins, whom he served as assistant on St. Lawrence Island in 1930 and at the Birnirk site in 1931. With an assignment from Collins, he carried out a survey of the Point Barrow region and wintered at

Barrow during 1931-1932, living among the Eskimos and conducting physical anthropological studies as well as the archaeological work. In 1936, again for Collins, he carried out a survey along the coast of Alaska between Cape Prince of Wales and Point Barrow. During World War II, Ford was a senior design specialist with a unit of the U.S. Army Office of the Quartermaster General, which was engaged in designing and testing military clothing and equipment. Some of this work involved travel to Alaska. In 1953 he returned to Point Barrow to continue his earlier archaeological work.

In his third area of concentration, Ford carried out fieldwork in Latin America—Mexico, Colombia and Peru—and contributed to an understanding of culture sequences in those countries. The work began during 1941-1942 when he participated in WENDELL CLARK BENNETT's archaeological survey of the Cauca Valley in Colombia, a project of the Institute of Andean Research. In 1946 he participated in the institute's Virú Valley project, working specifically on chronology in conjunction with GORDON RANDOLPH WILLEY's study of settlement patterns and land use. He was again in Peru during 1958-1959 and 1963, carrying out surveys and excavations in the Chira, Piura and Lambayeque Valleys. During 1963-1966, he worked with Alfonso Medellín Zenil and Matthew Wallrath in a survey of the Veracruz coast of Mexico.

Ford contributed significantly to archaeological methodology, the institutional growth of archaeology and broad theoretical constructs. It was he who, working in the southeastern United States, introduced pottery seriation in establishing historical sequences and insisted on historically useful typologies. With James B. Griffin, he organized the first Southeastern Archaeological Conference in 1938, and he served as president of the Society for American Archaeology during 1963-1964. Late in his life, he brought together his interests in the southeastern United States and Latin America in a theory concerning the relationships of formative sites in those regions and neighboring areas. Although archaeologists have generally been critical of Ford's broad synthesis, several prominent scholars, rather than rejecting it outright, have expressed the thought that the work was not so much in error as it was premature considering how relatively little data there was to support it.

MAJOR WORKS: *Analysis of Indian Village Site Collection from Louisiana and Mississippi* (New Orleans: 1936) (= *Louisiana Department of Conservation Anthropological Study*, no. 2); "A chronological method applicable to the Southeast," *American Antiquity*, vol. 3 (1938), pp. 260-264; (with Gordon R. Willey) *Crooks Site: a Marksville Period Burial Mound in La Salle Parish, Louisiana* (New Orleans: 1940) (= *Louisiana Department of Conservation Anthropological Study*, no. 3); (with Gordon R. Willey) "An interpretation of the prehistory of the Eastern United States," *American Anthropology*, n.s., vol. 43 (1941), pp. 325-363; (with George Quimby) *The Tchefuncte Culture: an Early Occupation of the Lower Mississippi Valley* (Menasha, Wisc.: 1945) (= *Memoirs of the Society of American Archaeology*, no. 2); *Cultural Dating of Prehistoric Sites in the Virú Valley, Peru* (New York: 1949) (= *Anthropological Papers of the American Museum of Natural History*, vol. 43); *Greenhouse: a Troyville-Coles Creek Period Site in Avoyelles Parish, Louisiana* (New York: 1951) (= *Anthropological Papers of the American Museum of Natural History*, vol. 44); (with Clarence H. Webb) *Poverty Point: a Late Archaic Site in Louisiana* (New York: 1956) (= *Anthropological Papers of the American Museum of Natural History*, vol. 46); *Menard Site: a Quapaw Village of Osotouy on the Arkansas River* (New York: 1961) (= *Anthropological Papers of the American Museum of Natural History*, vol. 48); *A Quantitative Method for Deriving Cultural Chronology* (Washington: 1962) (= *Pan American Union, Department of Social Affairs, Technical Manual*, no. 1); *A Comparative of Formative Cultures in the Americas: Diffusion or the Psychic Unity of Man* (Washington: 1969) (= *Smithsonian Contributions to Anthropology*, vol. 11).

SOURCES: Ian W. Brown, "James Alfred Ford: the man and his works," *Southeastern Archaeological Conference, Special Publication*, no. 4 (1978), pp. 1-40; Clifford Evans, "James Alfred Ford, 1911-1968," *American Anthropologist*, vol. 70 (1968), pp. 1161-1167; Ford papers and vertical file in the Smithsonian Institution National Anthropological Archives; William G. Haag, "James Alfred Ford, 1911-1968," *The Florida Anthropologist*, vol. 21 (1968), pp. 31-33; Betty J. Meggers, "James A. Ford, 1911-1968," *Etnía*, no. 6 (July-December 1968), pp. 3-5; David Hurst Thomas, "James A. Ford (1911-1968)" in: *Archaeology* (New York: 1979), pp. 39-42; Clarence Webb, "James Alfred Ford, 1911-1968," *Texas Archaeological Society, Bulletin*, vol. 38 (1968), pp. 135-146; Gordon R. Willey, "James Alfred Ford, 1911-1968," *American Antiquity*, vol. 34 (1969), pp. 62-71 [with bibliography compiled by Stephen Williams]; "James Alfred Ford (1911-1968)" in: Gordon R. Willey, *Portraits in American Archaeology* (Albuquerque: 1988), pp. 169-216.

James R. Glenn

Forde, Daryll (Cyril Daryll Forde). Anthropologist. Born in Tottenham, Middlesex (England) 16 March 1902, died in London (England) 3 May 1973. Forde exerted a profound influence on social anthropology and especially on African studies. He always tried to maintain the links between physical anthropology, archaeology and the cultural and sociological studies of man. His early training in geography gave him the bias toward ecological analysis that became the hallmark of his thought, making him a pioneer in that field.

His first degree was in geography at University College, London, where he later wrote his doctoral thesis on prehistoric archaeology and, from 1923 to 1928, held the post of Lecturer in Geography. He received his doctorate in 1928. For the next two years he was a Commonwealth Fellow at the University of California, and, in 1930, he was appointed to the Gregynog chair of geography and anthropology at the University of Wales, the youngest full professor in the United Kingdom. His early publications stress the balance between human geography and archaeology. *Ancient Mariners* was followed by articles on megaliths and prehistoric metallurgy and reports on excavations in England, Scotland, Wales and Brittany.

Forde worked in Arizona and New Mexico between 1928 and 1929 and returned to New Mexico later in 1929. His 1934 publication, *Habitat, Economy and Society*, which instantly became a classic, pays special attention to the interaction of technology with environment. His 1935 field trip to southeastern Nigeria started the intensive fieldwork among the Yakö of the Cross River that he followed up with another expedition in 1939. This fieldwork led him away from archaeology to a concern with contemporary and historical Africa.

In 1944 Forde was appointed administrative director of the International African Institute. A year later he returned to University College London to a newly founded chair of anthropology. The first of these appointments led to the most comprehensive program of publishing and organizing research that any one British anthropologist has ever achieved. The other involved the teaching and reflection by which he worked out his own intellectual position.

His publications on the Yakö came out in specialized articles, starting with "Land and labour on the Cross River," that were published in one volume, *Yakö Studies*, in which he described a complex system of double unilineal inheritance and an oligarchical system of government in which various ties of cult and descent affiliation cut across each other. His writing was distinguished by careful measurement, an eye for internal adaptations and a fervent belief that anthropological analysis could not be made in a vacuum, but must include the effects of environmental and external political pressures. "The cultural map of West Africa" is a superb example of his wide synoptic view, mastery of detail and controlled argument.

His work can be seen as contrapuntal to the structural functionalism of his day. At many points ahead of his contemporaries and at others correcting their bias, the more they left reality for the sake of elegant abstract models, the more he doubted their fundamental assumptions and questioned their data base.

His major concern was that anthropology keep its broad perspective, remain concerned with biological and historical evolution and focus on adaptive processes.

When Forde was appointed as director of the International African Institute in 1944 and editor of the quarterly journal *Africa*, his task was to build up an international fellowship of Africanist scholars with linguistic and ethnographic skills. *Africa* published articles in French and English, and its circulation grew to 2,300 by 1970. At the same time other vehicles of African scholarship also grew. *African Abstracts*, founded to keep track of new information, contained more than one thousand abstracts in its 1969 volume. In the same period the Ethnographic Survey of Africa published eighty-two monographs, eight handbooks of African languages and ten monographs on African languages. From 1959 to 1970, with the support of the Ford Foundation, he organized international seminars in Africa and published an important series of books on issues of common African interest.

African anthropology held a dominant place in British and world anthropology through its volume and its theoretical initiatives, both nourished by Forde's energy, entrepreneurial talents and scholarship.

MAJOR WORKS: *Ancient Mariners: the Story of Ships and Sea Routes* (London: 1927); *Habitat, Economy and Society: a Geographical Introduction to Ethnology* (London: 1934; 12th ed., London: 1967); "Land and labour on the Cross River: the economic organization of a Yakö Village, Nigeria," *Man*, vol. 36 (1936), p. 97; *Marriage and the Family among the Yakö in South-eastern Nigeria* (London: 1941); (with Richenda Scott) *The Native Economies of Nigeria* (London: 1946); "The anthropological approach in the social sciences," *Advancement of Science*, vol. 4 (1947), pp. 213-224 [Forde's presidential address to the Association for the Advancement of Science]; *The Ibo and Ibibio-speaking Peoples of Southeastern Nigeria* (Oxford: 1950); "Integrative aspects of Yakö first fruits rituals," *Journal of the Royal Anthropological Institute of Great Britain and Ireland*, vol. 79 (1951), pp. 1-10 [Forde's 1949 presidential address to the Royal Anthropological Institute]; "The cultural map of West Africa," *Transactions of the New York Academy of Sciences*, ser. 2, vol. 15 (1953), pp. 206-219 [also in: Simon and Phoebe Ottenberg (editors), *Cultures and Societies of Africa* (New York: 1960), pp. 116-130]; *The Context of Belief: a Consideration of Fetishism Among the Yakö* (Liverpool: 1958) [Frazer Lecture]; "Spirits, witches and sorcerers in the supernatural economy of the Yakö," *Journal of the Royal Anthropological Institute of Great Britain and Ireland*, vol. 88, part 2 (1958), pp. 165-178; "Death and succession: an analysis of Yakö mortuary ceremonial" in: Max Gluckman (editor), *Essays on the Ritual of Social Relations* (Manchester: 1960), pp. 89-123; [Simon lecture]; *Yakö Studies* (Oxford: 1964); "Anthropology and the development of African Studies," *Africa*, vol. 37 (1967), pp. 389-406 [tenth Lugard memorial lecture]; (co-edited with Phyllis Kaberry) *West African Kingdoms in the Nineteenth Century* (Oxford: 1967).

Mary Douglas

Förstemann, Ernst Wilhelm. Librarian, Germanist, Mayanist. Born in Danzig (Germany) 18 September 1822, died in Berlin (Germany) 4 November 1906. He studied Germanic languages and linguistics at Halle and Berlin and graduated from the University of Halle in 1844 with a dissertation on the comparative linguistics of Greek and Latin. After serving in a teaching position at Danzig (1844-1851) and as a teacher and librarian at Wernigerode (1851-1865) (during which time, in addition to his professional duties, he also did basic work on German proper names and place names), Förstemann became head librarian and reorganizer of the Königliche Öffentliche Bibliothek (Royal Public Library) in Dresden, a post he held from 1865 to 1887. The honorary titles of "Hofrat" and, later, "Geheimer Hofrat" were awarded to him in 1872 and 1884 respectively in recognition of his service.

In Dresden, Förstemann became acquainted with the Mayan codex that was preserved in the Royal Library. In addition to performing his official activities as librarian, Förstemann produced numerous pioneering works on the decipherment of Mayan writing, working first with the Dresden Codex, subsequently extending his researches to the two well known manuscripts of the Paris and Madrid codices and finally to inscriptions on stone. In 1880 Förstemann was the first to produce a photomechanical edition of the Dresden Codex, which until that time had only been published in an inaccessible edition by Lord Kingsborough. For the next fourteen years, nearly every year saw the appearance of a new study by Förstemann on Mayan writing. He succeeded in deciphering the complicated system of the Maya calendar, identifying the hieroglyphs for the months, the numbers zero and twenty, and the 260-day cycle. Förstemann recognized that the Maya calendar was founded on a vigesimal system, which was used to the sixth place with a few exceptions. He deciphered the astronomical tables for the calculation of the cycles of the planet Venus in the Dresden Codex and possibly also recognized the significance of the lunar eclipse tables in the same document. Förstemann determined that the Maya "Long Count" started from the base date of 4 Ahau 8 Cumku. He was able to use his insights from the manuscripts to make substantial contributions to the decipherment of the stone inscriptions as well. Among these were the identification of the variant forms of signs for the five periods of time of the Long Count and Initial Series on several monuments at Copán. It is possible that Förstemann also was the first to recognize the system of numbers relating to distances, and it was definitely he who identified the nature of the Lunar Series as a complement to the Initial Series.

MAJOR WORKS: *Die Maya-Handschrift der Königlichen Öffentlichen Bibliothek zu Dresden* (Leipzig: 1880); *Erläuterung zur Mayahandschrift der Königlichen Öffentlichen Bibliothek zu Dresden* (Dresden: 1886); *Zur Entzifferung der Mayahandschriften* [6 parts] (Dresden: 1887-1897); "Zur Maya-Chronologie," *Zeitschrift für Ethnologie*, vol. 23 (1891), pp. 142-155; "Die Zeitperioden der Mayas," *Globus*, vol. 63 (1893), pp. 30-32; *Commentar zur Mayahandschrift der Königlichen Öffentlichen Bibliothek zu Dresden* (Dresden: 1901) [tr.: *Commentary on the Maya manuscript in the Royal Public Library of Dresden* (Cambridge, Mass.: 1906) (= *Papers of the Peabody Museum of American Archaeology and Ethnography, Harvard University*, vol. 4, no. 2)]; "Eine historische Maya-Inschrift," *Globus*, vol. 81 (1902), pp. 150-153; [English translations of several papers], *Bureau of American Ethnology, Bulletin*, no. 28 (1904), pp. 393-590.

SOURCES: Walter Lehmann, "Geh. Hofrat Prof. Dr. Ernst Förstemann," *Globus*, vol. 90, no. 22 (1906), pp. 341-342; Ernst Friedrich Förstemann, "Ernst Wilhelm Förstemann" in: Ernst Wilhelm Förstemann, *Altdeutsches Namenbuch* (edited by Hermann Jellinghaus) (3rd ed., Bonn: 1913), vol. 2, pp. 3-21; John Eric S. Thompson, *Maya Hieroglyphic Writing* (Norman: 1960), pp. 29-30; Alfred M. Tozzer, "Ernst Förstemann," *American Anthropologist*, n.s., vol. 9 (1907), pp. 153-159.

Frauke Johanna Riese

[Translation from German: Robert B. Marks Ridinger]

Fortes, Meyer. Social anthropologist. Born in Britstown, Cape Province (South Africa) 25 April 1906, died in Cambridge (England) 27 January 1983. Fortes is best known for his work on kinship, particularly in preindustrial societies. He wrote extensively on comparative religion and ideas of personhood. *African Political Systems*, which he co-edited with E.E. EVANS-PRITCHARD, dominated the fieldwork and analysis of British social anthropologists for a generation.

His early training was in psychology, but his anthropological interests were also heavily influenced by his early life in a poor immigrant Jewish family in South Africa, with its institutionalized racial discrimination and economic inequalities. After working for a few years in London as a clinical psychologist, he came under the influence of BRONISLAW MALINOWSKI and C.G. SELIGMAN at the London School of Economics and was recruited in 1933 to carry out psychological and anthropological fieldwork in West Africa. He went on to teach at Accra (Ghana) and Oxford and in 1950 moved to Cambridge as Professor of Social Anthropology. He wrote about humanity as a whole in the light of psychoanalysis but retained his professional focus of interest in West Africa, making many field trips to the Tallensi people of Ghana until prevented in 1973 by ill-health.

Fortes saw empirical observation and analysis as necessarily interlinked if social anthropology was to be scientific. His writings are laden with theoretical assertions but these are closely bound up with ethnographic data, so that his complete theoretical schema has to be inferred piecemeal by the reader. Perhaps for this reason his direct influence, apart from *African Political Systems* and his explicitly comparative work on religions in West Africa, *Oedipus and Job*, was greatest on his close colleagues and the many students he trained as anthropologists. He became the defender of A.R. RADCLIFFE-BROWN's reputation and stressed the corporateness of agnatic lineage segments. He argued strongly for the "irreducible facts of parenthood, siblingship and marriage" but was criticized for his views on kinship by EDMUND LEACH and Rodney Needham.

MAJOR WORKS: (co-editor with E.E. Evans-Pritchard) *African Political Systems* (London: 1940); *The Dynamics of Clanship* (London: 1945); *The Web of Kinship* (London: 1949); *Oedipus and Job in West African Religion* (Cambridge: 1959); *Kinship and the Social Order* (Chicago: 1969); *Time and Social Structure and Other Essays* (London: 1970); *Rules and the Emergence of Society* (London: 1983); *Religion, Morality and the Person* (Cambridge: 1987).

SOURCES: Louis Dumont, "Meyer Fortes" in: *Introduction à deux théories d'anthropologie sociale* (Paris: 1971), pp. 75-81; Meyer Fortes, "An anthropologist's apprenticeship," *Annual Review of Anthropology*, vol. 7 (1978), pp. 1-30; J.A. Barnes, "Irreducible principles" in: J.A. Barnes, *Three Styles in the Study of Kinship* (London and Berkeley: 1971), pp. 179-264; J.A. Barnes, "Fortes, Meyer" in: David L. Sills (editor), *International Encyclopedia of the Social Sciences* (New York: 1968-1979), vol. 18, pp. 195-197; Jack Goody, "Introduction" to: Jack Goody (editor), *The Character of Kinship* (Cambridge: 1973), pp. ix-xii; Susan Drucker-Brown [et al.] (editors), "In memory of Meyer Fortes," *Cambridge Anthropology*, vol. 8 (special edition) (1983), pp. 1-70; Gilbert Lewis, "Meyer Fortes, 1906-1983," *Jewish Journal of Sociology*, vol. 25 (1983), pp. 47-52;

Fortes, Meyer

Susan Drucker-Brown, "Notes towards a biography of Meyer Fortes," *American Ethnologist*, vol. 16 (1989), pp. 375-385.

J.A. Barnes

Foster, George McClelland. Anthropologist. Born in Sioux Falls (South Dakota) 9 October 1913. Foster received a Ph.D. from the University of California at Berkeley in 1941 and taught there as a professor from 1953 until his retirement in 1979. He remained at Berkeley as Professor Emeritus into the 1990s.

His dissertation research (1940-1941) among the Sierra Popoluca of Veracruz (Mexico) focused on their economy, a theme to which he would return in many of his later studies in peasant communities. Subsequently, after a brief sojourn teaching at the University of California, Los Angeles and Syracuse University, Foster was appointed as the representative of the Smithsonian Institution's Institute of Social Anthropology to the National School of Anthropology and History in Mexico City. This gave him the opportunity to carry out fieldwork during 1944-1946 in Tzintzuntzan, Michoacán (Mexico), which later proved to be the basis of a major long-term field research project.

In the early 1950s he carried out a systematic comparison of Spanish peasant culture and Latin American peasant life. The resulting study of acculturation emphasized the linkages between 16th-century Spanish culture traits and 20th-century culture patterns in Latin America within a framework that Foster characterized in terms of "conquest culture" and "cultural crystallization."

In 1958 he returned to the peasant community of Tzintzuntzan (Mexico) where he initiated an innovative long-term community study of economic, demographic and social and cultural change. From 1958 to 1990 Foster visited Tzintzuntzan at least once each year. This research resulted in numerous important contributions to the understanding of peasant life, especially in his classic monographs and articles about the "dyadic contract," "the image of limited good" and "hot-cold" theories of illness. In all of these works, Foster developed useful (although sometimes controversial) models to account for the problems facing villagers whose worldviews emphasized balance, harmony and reciprocity in the face of a national and international system undergoing rapid and permanent change.

Foster was a leader in the development of the field of applied anthropology in the United States and in Latin America, and he also carried out important applied research and training assignments in South Asia, Southeast Asia and East Africa. His publications on traditional cultures and the impact of technological change and on the general characteristics of applied anthropology are among the most widely read in the field.

In the later decades of his career, Foster devoted most of his research to the growing field of medical anthropology and public health. He co-authored the first comprehensive text on the biocultural and sociocultural dimensions of health and illness, and he focused his long-term field research in Tzintzuntzan on problems of health, illness and aging.

In nearly 300 publications, including more than 20 books and monographs, his influence on the development of anthropology and the social sciences around the world has been extraordinary. For his work, he was honored with election to the National Academy of Sciences, he received the Distinguished Service Award of the American Anthropological

Association (which he also served as President) and he was awarded the Malinowski Award by the Society for Applied Anthropology.

MAJOR WORKS: *A Primitive Mexican Economy* (New York: 1942); *Empire's Children: the People of Tzintzuntzan* (Washington, D.C.: 1948); *Culture and Conquest: America's Spanish Heritage* (New York: 1960); "The dyadic contract: a model for social structure of a Mexican peasant village," *American Anthropologist*, vol. 63 (1961), pp. 1173-1192; *Traditional Cultures and the Impact of Technological Change* (New York: 1962; 2nd ed., *Traditional Societies and Technological Change*, New York: 1973); "Peasant society and the image of limited good," *American Anthropologist*, vol. 67 (1965), pp. 293-315; *Tzintzuntzan: Mexican Peasants in a Changing World* (Boston: 1967; 2nd ed., New York: 1979; 3rd ed., Prospect Heights, Ill.: 1988); (co-editor, with Jack M. Potter and May N. Diaz) *Peasant Society: a Reader* (Boston: 1967); *Applied Anthropology* (Boston: 1969); (co-editor, with Robert V. Kemper) *Anthropologists in Cities* (Boston: 1974); (co-author, with Barbara G. Anderson) *Medical Anthropology* (New York: 1978); (co-editor, with Elizabeth Colson, Thayer Scudder and Robert V. Kemper) *Long-Term Field Research in Social Anthropology* (New York: 1979).

SOURCES: Margaret Clark, Robert V. Kemper and Cynthia Nelson (editors), *From Tzintzuntzan to the "Image of Limited Good": Essays in Honor of George M. Foster* (Berkeley: 1979) (= *Kroeber Anthropological Society Papers*, nos. 55/56).

Robert V. Kemper

Foster, Mary LeCron. Linguistic anthropologist. Born in Des Moines (Iowa) 1 February 1914. Foster received a bachelor's degree in anthropology from Northwestern University in 1936 and a doctoral degree in linguistics from the University of California, Berkeley, in 1965. She was for many years Assistant Professor of Anthropology at California State University at Hayward. Her contributions to anthropology include expanding the methodology of structural and symbolic analyses in anthropology and linguistics and, in recent years, initiating peace, conflict and conflict-resolution studies in anthropology. Her early work includes two grammars of Indian languages in Mexico. She then turned to an examination of the role of structure and symbol in culture. Her work on these issues includes both synchronic studies (e.g., *Symbol as Sense*, "Tzintzuntzan marriage" and "Structural hierarchy and social good in Tzintzuntzan") and diachronic studies (e.g., "The growth of symbolism in culture," "Culture as metaphor" and "Reconstruction of the evolution of language"). In these works, she has been concerned with the symbolic structure of ritual and with the evolution of symbolism, the latter using the comparative method of linguistic investigation.

Since 1981, much of Foster's work has been concerned with peace studies. She was a member of the organizing board of the Commission on the Study of Peace for the International Union of Anthropological and Ethnological Sciences and continues to serve on that board. From 1983 to 1986 she was a member of the Committee on Science, Arms Control and National Security for the American Association for the Advancement of Science. She has organized or participated in numerous symposia on this subject and has jointly edited two volumes on peace and war (*Peace and War: Cross-Cultural Perspectives* and *The Social Dynamics of Peace and Conflict: Culture in International Security*). In these studies, as in her previous work, she has concentrated on the symbolic dimensions of peace and conflict. In 1987 she received the Outstanding Achievement Award from the Society of Women Geographers.

MAJOR WORKS: (with George Foster) *Sierra Popoluca Speech* (Washington: 1948); *The Tarascan Language* (Berkeley: 1969); (with Stanley H. Brandes) *Symbol as Sense: New Approaches to the Analysis of Meaning* (New York: 1980); (with Robert Rubinstein) *Peace and War: Cross-Cultural Perspectives* (New Brunswick, N.J.: 1986); (with Robert Rubinstein) *The Social Dynamics of Peace and Conflict: Culture in International Security* (Boulder: 1988); "The symbolic structure of primordial language" in: S.L. Washburn and E.R. McCown (editors), *Human Evolution: Bio-social Perspectives* (Menlo Park: 1978), pp. 77-121; "Culture as metaphor: a new look at language and culture in the Pleistocene," *Kroeber Anthropological Society Papers*, vol. 59-60 (1979), pp. 1-12; "The growth of symbolism in culture" in: Mary L. Foster and Stanley Brandes (editors), *Symbol as Sense: New Approaches to the Analysis of Meaning* (New York: 1980), pp. 371-397; "Meaning as metaphor," *Quaderni di Semantica*, vol. 3 (1982), pp. 95-102 and 313-321; "Tzintzuntzan marriage: an analysis of concordant structure" in: Jarich Oosten and Arie de Ruyter (editors), *The Future of Structuralism* (Göttingen: 1983), pp. 127-152; "Structural hierarchy and social good in Tzintzuntzan," *International Journal of Psychology*, vol. 20 (1986), pp. 617-635; (co-edited with Lucy Jayne Botscharow) *The Life of Symbols* (Boulder: 1990); "Reconstruction of the evolution of language" in: Andrew Locke and Charles Peters (editors), *Handbook of Symbolic Evolution* (Oxford: in press).

Lucy Jayne Botscharow

Fraipont, Charles-Marie-Julien-Joseph de. Paleontologist, paleoanthropologist. Born in Chênée, Liège (Belgium) 21 March 1883, died in Brussels (Belgium) 15 April 1946. Son of JULIEN FRAIPONT. Originally a mining engineer with a degree from the University of Liège, he received a doctorate in paleontological sciences in 1913. Keeper of the paleontological collections, he became professor of paleontology in 1919.

Founder of the École libre d'Anthropologie de Liège in 1919, he contributed to the creation of a doctoral program in anthropological sciences at the University of Liège in 1928. He was the director of the *Revue anthropologique* (Paris) from 1921 to 1930 and a member of the international committee for the standardization of the technique of physical anthropology.

His research in physical anthropology was dedicated to the morphology of the talus, the bend of the femur, and the relationships between the facial and the cranial parts of the skull. His study of the Neanderthal child skull discovered by PHILIPPE SCHMERLING in 1829 was a key work, comparable to the description of the La Quina skull by Henri Martin. His interest in the question of evolution and his explanation of the distribution of species by ologenism aroused the attention of biogeographers.

His election as senator in 1936 marked, essentially, the end of his academic life.

MAJOR WORKS: "L'astragale chez l'homme moustérien de Spy," *Bulletin de la Société d'Anthropologie de Bruxelles*, vol. 31 (1912), pp. 195-212; "Sur l'importance des caractères de l'astragale chez l'homme fossile," *Bulletin de la Société d'Anthropologie de Bruxelles*, vol. 32 (1913), pp. 145-208; "Contribution à l'étude de la station verticale: la courbure fémorale," *Revue anthropologique*, vol. 35 (1925), pp. 329-340; *L'évolution cérébrale des primates, en particulier des hominiens* (Paris: 1931) (= *Archives de l'Institut de Paléontologie humaine*, Mémoire, no. 8); (with S. Leclercq) *L'évolution: adaptations et mutations, berceaux et migrations* (Paris: 1932); *Adaptations et mutations: position du problème* (Paris: 1932); *Les hommes d'Engis* (Paris: 1936) (= *Archives de l'Institut de Paléontologie humaine*, Mémoire, no. 16).

SOURCES: Léon Halkin, *L'Université de Liège de 1867 à 1935* (Liège: 1936), vol. 2, pp. 303-310 [contains bibliography]; G. Ubaghs, "Charles de Fraipont" in: Robert Demoulin, *L'Université de Liège de 1936 à 1966* (Liège: 1967), vol. 2, pp. 413-417.

André Leguebe

Fraipont, Julien (Jean Joseph Julien Fraipont). Anthropologist, paleontologist, zoologist. Born in Liège (Belgium) 17 August 1857, died in Liège (Belgium) 22 March 1910. He was a student of Edouard Van Beneden and professor of paleontology at the University of Liège. His work concerned the morphology and classification of the family *Archiannelidae*, in particular the fossils from the carboniferous limestone of the Upper Devonian period. He is best known for his anatomical studies of the skeletons discovered at Spy in 1886 by MAX LOHEST and MARCEL DE PUYDT. In fact, these were the first two relatively complete Neanderthal skeletons to be found in a clearly defined faunal, lithic and stratigraphic context. In the publication devoted to this study done in collaboration with Lohest, he gave extremely precise measurements and descriptions, isolating clearly the essential morphological features of this stage of human development. Through comparison of the two skulls from Spy with those from the Neanderthal site at Canstatt, Fraipont established the existence of a Neanderthal race which was clearly distinguished from Cro-Magnon, Neolithic and modern man. Comparison of the skeletons with those of the anthropoid apes led Fraipont to hypothesize a very remote phylogenetic origin for man from either the Dryopithecines or a third anthropoid still unknown.

MAJOR WORKS: (with M. Lohest) "La race humaine de Néanderthal ou de Canstadt en Belgique," *Bulletin de l'Académie Royale de Belgique*, 3rd sér., vol. 12 (1886), pp. 741-784; "La race humaine de Neanderthal ou de Canstadt en Belgique," *Archives de Biologie*, vol. 7 (1887), pp. 587-757; *Les cavernes et leurs habitants* (Paris: 1896).

SOURCES: P. Fourmarier, "Notice biographique sur Julien Fraipont," *Annales de la Société géologique de Belgique*, vol. 41 (1919), pp. B337-350; Max Lohest, Ch. Julin and A. Rutot, "Notice sur Julien Fraipont," *Annuaire de l'Académie royale de Belgique*, vol. 91 (1925), pp. 131-197.

André Leguebe
[Translation from French: Timothy Eastridge and Robert B. Marks Ridinger]

Frankowski, Eugeniusz. Archaeologist, anthropologist, ethnographer. Born in Siedlce (Poland) 21 November 1884, died in Poznań (Poland) 8 February 1962. Frankowski studied at Jagiellonian University, obtaining his doctorate in 1921, and was appointed assistant professor in 1922. Later, he occupied the chair of ethnography and ethnology at the University of Poznań. At the same time (during 1921-1939) he directed the Muzeum Etnograficzne (Ethnographic Museum) in Warsaw.

In the field of museology Frankowski created a new exhibition technique. During 1910-1914 he conducted anthropological and ethnographic investigations on the Lachy Sądeckie and in Polesia. During 1914-1920 and 1927-1939 he investigated archaisms of European culture on the Iberian Peninsula with particular attention paid to Basque culture. In his research he utilized the principles of evolutionism as well as a method related to the approach of the Cultural-Historical School. In the field of Polish ethnography he worked on folk art and material culture. In his studies on art he served as the originator of the "Emotional School." He also proposed criteria for identifying folk style (harmony of form with actual technique and material).

MAJOR WORKS: "La lucha entre el hombre y los espiritus malos por la posesión de la tierra y su usufructo," *Boletín de la Real Sociedad Española de Historia Natural*, vol. 16 (1916), pp. 408-425; "Los signos quemados y esquilados sobre los animales de tiro de la Península Ibérica," *Memorias de la Real Sociedad Española de Historia Natural*, vol. 10, no. 5 (1916), pp. 267-309;

Sztuka ludu polskiego [*Art of the Polish Folk*] (Warsaw: 1928); *Wycinanki ludu polskiego* [*Paper Cutouts of the Polish Folk*] (Warsaw: 1928); *Sochy, radła, płużyce i pługi w Polsce* [*The History of the Plow in Poland*] (Poznań: 1929); "Zagadnienie metodologii badań nad sztuką ludową" ["The problem of research methodology of folk art"], *Materiały do studiów i Dyskusji z Zakresu Teorii i Historii Sztuki*, vol. 5 (1951), pp. 369-383; "Złotogłowie kaszubskie" ["Kaszubian goldenheads"], *Polska Sztuka Ludowa*, vol. 8, no. 3 (1954), pp. 148-161.

SOURCE: Anna Kutrzeba-Pojnarowa, "Wspomnienie o profesorze Eugeniuszu Frankowskim" ["Recollections of Professor Eugeniusz Frankowski"], *Etnografia Polska*, vol. 7 (1963), pp. 425-439.

Maria Niewiadomska and Iwona Grzelakowska
[Translation from Polish: Joel Janicki]

Frazer, Sir *James George.* Anthropologist, historian of religion, classical scholar. Born in Glasgow (Scotland) 1 January 1854, died in Cambridge (England) 7 May 1941. After a B.A. from Glasgow in 1874 Frazer took a second B.A. from Trinity College, Cambridge, in 1878. In 1879 he won a classical fellowship to Trinity that, renewed twice, became tenable for life in 1895. Except for 1907-1908, which he spent as professor of social anthropology in the University of Liverpool, Frazer remained at Trinity from 1879 to 1914. He never taught and was essentially a professional man of letters, living mainly off his book royalties. By the 1920s, his panoramic vision and highly colored style had virtually single-handedly created a reading public for anthropology in Britain, and a number of his books were best sellers. A shy man, he took no part in the professionalization of anthropology in Britain; he did, however, have one important protégé, BRONISLAW MALINOWSKI. Ironically, one of the effects of Malinowskian structural-functional, fieldwork-centered ethnography was the near total eclipse of Frazer as an "armchair anthropologist."

During 1884-1885, the Scottish biblical scholar WILLIAM ROBERTSON SMITH opened Frazer's eyes to the possibilities of anthropology. Smith, editor of the ninth edition of the *Encyclopaedia Britannica*, assigned Frazer the articles on "taboo" and "totemism"; these led directly to the first edition of his best-known work, *The Golden Bough*. In it he adopted the rationalist, comparativist, evolutionary framework to which he remained faithful lifelong. The book's nominal subject is the explication of an obscure ritual of priestly combat that took place at Nemi, near Rome, in ancient times. Frazer, however, asserted that the beliefs and behavior of classical antiquity could be fully understood only in the light of, and in comparison with, those of "savages" and "primitives," which they closely resembled.

Frazer was always primarily interested in epistemology, in tracing the stages in the evolution of the mind. He argued that the world-view of the primitives had survived and could be discerned in the myths and rituals of their direct descendants, the contemporary European peasantry (the influence of Mannhardt is strong here). Moderns could educe that world-view with the aid of a few simple "laws" of mental functioning of an associationist kind. To understand the priesthood at Nemi, Frazer was led to analyze the origins of the state in the person of the priest-king, the ideas involved in taboo and totemism, and ritual human sacrifice (here one notes the influence of Robertson Smith). In the second edition of *The Golden Bough*, emboldened by new data on the Australian Aborigines from BALDWIN SPENCER and F.J. Gillen, Frazer asserted that the human mind evolved through three distinct stages, characterized in its relation to the natural world by magic, religion and positive science.

Although privately Frazer held Voltairean opinions about religion, publicly his position was that of the dispassionate scientist, following the data wherever they might lead. His not-so-very-hidden agenda was to use a seemingly scientific method to hammer the last nail into the coffin of religion, thereby completing the job begun by Darwin. Although his style had many admirers, and everyone was in awe of his erudition, his work was sharply criticized as naively rationalistic by his peers virtually from the outset. Nevertheless, it was immensely popular among the "advanced" sections of the public, especially after World War I, because it seemed to demonstrate scientifically that religion was a relic, now happily obsolete, of an earlier stage of mental evolution. His main influence has not been in anthropology as such, where he is generally regarded as antediluvian, but in the history of religion and in classics, where his work continues to be well regarded. He was widely read by artists and intellectuals in the first half of the century, and his ideas about the "primitive" substrate of modern culture constitute a significant element in the cultural history of our time.

MAJOR WORKS: *The Golden Bough* (1st ed. [2 vols.], London: 1890; 2nd ed. [3 vols.], London: 1900; 3rd ed. [12 vols.], London: 1911-1915; abridged ed., London: 1922); *Pausanias's Description of Greece* [6 vols.] (London: 1898); *Totemism and Exogamy* [4 vols.] (London: 1910); *Folk-Lore in the Old Testament* [3 vols.] (London: 1918); *Apollodorus, The Library* [2 vols.] (London: 1921); *The Gorgon's Head* (London: 1927); *Publii Ovidii Nasonis Fastorum Libri Sex* [5 vols.] (London: 1929) [Ovid, Fasti]; *Garnered Sheaves* (London: 1931).

SOURCES: Robert Ackerman, *J.G. Frazer: His Life and Work* (Cambridge: 1987); Theodore Besterman, *A Bibliography of Sir James George Frazer, O.M.* (London: 1934); R.A. Downie, *Frazer and The Golden Bough* (London: 1970); I.C. Jarvie, *The Revolution in Anthropology* (London: 1964); Bronislaw Malinowski, "Sir James George Frazer: a biographical appreciation" in: *A Scientific Theory of Culture and Other Essays* (New York: 1970; orig. pub., Chapel Hill: 1944), pp. 177-221; Robert Ackerman, "Frazer on myth and ritual," *Journal of the History of Ideas*, vol. 36 (1975), pp. 115-134; Robert Ackerman, "J.G. Frazer revisited," *American Scholar*, vol. 47 (1978), pp. 232-236; Edmund Leach, "Golden Bough or Gilded Twig?" *Daedalus*, vol. 90 (1961), pp. 371-399.

Robert Ackerman

Freeman, J. Derek. Anthropologist, behavioral scientist. Born in Wellington (New Zealand) 16 August 1916. He is known for his meticulous and thorough ethnographic research and reporting; his devotion to the search for the truth; and his concern since 1961 with the development of a holistic approach to anthropological and human problems, an approach both scientific and humanistic whose goal is to improve the human condition. He has been Senior Fellow (1955-1957), Professorial Fellow (1957-1982), Professor of Anthropology (1972-1982) and Professor Emeritus (1982-) at the Research School of Pacific Studies, the Australian National University. He is a titled Samoan chief, Logona-i-taga (1943). He has done fieldwork in: Samoa (1940-1943, 1946, 1965-1968, 1981); among the Iban (Sarawak) (1949-1951, 1957-1958, 1976); and the Worora Tribe (Northwest Australia) (1974). He studied with Ernest Beaglehole, H.D. Skinner, S.F. NADEL, RAYMOND FIRTH, Audrey Richards and MEYER FORTES, under whom he wrote his Ph.D. dissertation on the Iban of Borneo at the University of Cambridge. He studied at the London Institute of Psychoanalysis (1963-1964) and underwent analysis. He married

Monica Maitland (1948) who participated in his Iban and Samoan researches. He is a practicing Buddhist.

Freeman has made lasting contributions to a wide range of anthropological fields: social organization and kinship, swidden farming systems, human ethology, psychoanalytic anthropology, evolutionary anthropology and choice behavior. His criticism that sociobiology when applied to human populations is irremediably deficient unless part of a holistic approach derives from his work on the human capacity for choice. He is known for his exceptionally thorough study of Iban swidden agriculture and his ground-breaking work on cognatic social organization. The latter arose from his Iban research; in it he pioneered in the use of quantitative data, and it has been an exemplar for others working in Borneo.

Freeman is also known for his criticism of cultural relativism and his contributions to psychoanalytic anthropology, which includes his critique of *Totem and Taboo*; he argued in this that Freud was a Lamarckian determinist. His best known work is probably his criticism of MARGARET MEAD'S study of Samoan adolescent behavior and her conclusion that this behavior cannot be explained other than in terms of "the social environment." This is arguably the first major Popperian refutation in anthropology. On the basis of his extensive Samoan fieldwork, information collected from court archives and observations by other investigators, Freeman succeeded in convincing a large proportion of the anthropology profession that Mead's conclusions were in error and argued that the doctrine of cultural relativism, on which Mead based her conclusions, is inadequate to explain human behavior, as it fails to incorporate biological variables and choice in a holistic approach. This precipitated a major paradigmatic controversy in American anthropology over the issue of cultural determinism. Freeman, after replying to his critics, claimed closure of the controversy on theoretical and empirical grounds in October 1987, but it has continued. In 1988 a documentary film reviewing the controversy (*Margaret Mead and Samoa*) contained a report of a statement by Mead in 1964 that Freeman had proven her wrong and an interview with Mead's principal informant, who testified under oath that she and a friend had lied to Mead about sexual behavior. Freeman (in "Fa'apua'a Fa'amū and Margaret Mead") provides a brief account of the life of this informant and her relations with Mead and is currently preparing a monograph analyzing the controversy and its role in the history of anthropology.

MAJOR WORKS: *Iban Agriculture: a Report on the Shifting Cultivation of Hill Rice by the Iban of Sarawak* (London: 1955); "The family system of the Iban of Borneo" in: Jack Goody (editor), *The Developmental Cycle in Domestic Groups* (Cambridge: 1957) (= *Cambridge Papers in Social Anthropology*, no. 1), pp. 15-52; "On the concept of the kindred," *Journal of the Royal Anthropological Institute*, vol. 91 (1961), pp. 192-220 [the Curl Bequest Prize Essay]; "Anthropology, psychiatry and the doctrine of cultural relativism" *Man*, vol. 65 (1965), pp. 65-67; "Totem and Taboo: a reappraisal," *The Psychoanalytic Study of Society*, vol. 4 (1967), pp. 315-344; *Report of the Iban* [new edition] (London: 1970) (= *LSE Monograph on Social Anthropology*, no. 41); "Kinship, attachment behaviour and the primary bond" in: Jack Goody (editor), *The Character of Kinship* (Cambridge: 1974), pp. 109-119; "Severed heads that germinate" in: R.H. Hook (editor), *Fantasy and Symbol: Studies in Anthropological Interpretation* (London: 1979), pp. 233-246; *Some Reflections on the Nature of Iban Society* (Canberra: 1981) (= *Occasional Paper of the Department of Anthropology, Research School of Pacific Studies, The Australian National University*); "The anthropology of choice," *Canberra Anthropology*. vol. 4 (1981), pp. 82-100; *Margaret Mead and Samoa: the Making and Unmaking of an Anthropological Myth* (Cambridge: 1983); "Inductivism and the test of truth: a rejoinder to Lowell D. Holmes and others" in: G. Acciaioli (editor), *Fact and Context in*

Ethnography: the Samoa Controversy (Canberra: 1983) (= *Canberra Anthropology*, vol. 6), pp. 101-192; "Fa'apua'a Fa'amū and Margaret Mead," *American Anthropologist*, vol. 91 (1989), 1017-1022.

SOURCES: "Selected bibliography" in: G.N. Appell and T.N. Madan (editors), *Choice and Morality in Anthropological Perspective: Essays in Honor of Derek Freeman* (Albany: 1988), pp. 27-30; G.N. Appell and T.N. Madan, "Derek Freeman: notes toward an intellectual biography" in: G.N. Appell and T.N. Madan (editors), *Choice and Morality in Anthropological Perspective: Essays in Honor of Derek Freeman* (Albany: 1988), pp. 3-25; Frank Heimans, *Margaret Mead and Samoa* [film] (Sydney: 1988).

George N. Appell

Frikel, Protásio (Gunther Protasius Frikel). Philosopher, theologian, anthropologist. Born in Breslau (Germany) (now Wrocław, Poland) 24 March 1912, died in Belém, Pará (Brazil) 27 September 1974. Frikel went to Brazil as a result of his religious vocation, joining the Franciscan Order. He completed courses of study in philosophy in Pernambuco and in theology in Salvador between 1931 and 1937. While a student, he became interested in the religious cults of Bahian *candomblé* and eventually wrote one of the first anthropological investigations of this topic, the 1941 article "Die Seelenlehre der Gege und Nago." In 1938 his missionary work took him to the Munduruku of the Cururu River, Pará, where he was drawn definitively to the anthropological study of indigenous groups.

At the end of the 1940s, he urged, as a man of religion, the re-establishment of contact with the Tiriyó Indians of Brazilian Guiana. At that time he began a series of trips that lasted until the 1960s along the Maicurú, Curuá, Cuminá, Erepecuru and Eastern Paru Rivers. He contacted the Kaxuyana, Parukotó, Kayana, Wayana, Apalai and Tiriyó Indians and founded the Tiriós Mission. In 1957 he joined the Museu Paraense Emílio Goeldi (Emílio Goeldi Pará Museum) in Belém, dedicating himself to research. Unable to reconcile his missionary obligations with scientific investigation, he left the Franciscan Order and got married. He died in Belém, wasted away by malaria, which he contracted on his last trips to the Cururu River.

Frikel's most important works resulted from his research among Carib-speaking Indians. Particularly noteworthy among his numerous writings about the Tiriyó is the monograph, *Os Tiriyó: seu sistema adaptativo*, in which he synthesized his ideas and research methods.

Frikel can be described as a field anthropologist and as an efficient collector of empirical data. Leaning on the old masters of anthropology as well as on the first students of the Carib (Walter E. Roth and W. Ahlbrinck), Frikel conducted detailed surveys of the material cultures of different indigenous groups and also began the formation of extensive collections of ethnographic artifacts, the majority of which are deposited at the Goeldi Museum. At the same time, he always tried to uncover the past technology of the groups he studied, to follow its trajectory to and to detect its remnants in the present. His preoccupation with detailed ethnography makes his works indispensable references for students of Carib ethnology and material culture.

MAJOR WORKS: "Tradições histórico-lendárias dos Kachuyana e Kayana," *Revista do Museu Paulista*, vol. 9 (1955), pp. 203-233; "Classificação lingüístico-etnológica das tribos indígenas do Pará setentrional e zonas adjacentes," *Revista de Antropologia*, vol. 6 (1958), pp. 113-189; "A agricultura dos índios Munduruku," *Boletim do Museu Goeldi*, no. 4 (1959); "Fases culturais e aculturação intertribal no Tumucumaque," *Boletim do Museu Goeldi*, no. 16 (1961); *Os Xikrin: equipamentos e tecnicas de subsistência* (Belém: 1968) (= *Publicações Avulsas do Museu Goeldi*, no. 7); *Os Kaxuyana: notas etno-históricas* (Belém: 1970) (= *Publicações Avulsas do Museu Goeldi*, no. 14); (with Paulo Cavalcante) *A Farmacopéia Tiriyó* (Belém: 1973) (= *Publicações Avulsas do Museu Goeldi*, no. 24); *Os Tiriyó: seu sistema adaptivo* (Hannover: 1973).

SOURCE: Eduardo Galvão, "Gunther Protasius Frikel: 1912-1974," *Revista de Antropologia*, vol. 21 (1978), pp. 224-225.

Lúcia Hussak van Velthem
[Translation from Portuguese: Margo L. Smith]

Frobenius, Leo. Ethnologist, Africanist, cultural theorist. Born in Berlin (Germany) 29 June 1873, died in Biganzolo (Italy) 9 August 1938. Frobenius was an autodidact without academic training. In 1893 he began a collection of all available publications, pictures and documents related to Africa that eventually became the vast Afrika-Archiv, today in the Frobenius-Institut, Frankfurt am Main, Germany. The Forschungsinstitut für Kulturmorphologie (Research Institute for Cultural Morphology) that he founded in 1920 was also originally his private undertaking, financed by donors as well as the income from his own books and lectures. This was likewise true for most of the twelve research expeditions in various parts of Africa (some of several years' duration) that he led between 1904 and 1935. Only toward the end of his life did he hold official positions as *Honorarprofessor* at the University of Frankfurt (1932) and as director of the Frankfurt Museum für Völkerkunde (Ethnographic Museum) (1934).

Frobenius was a pioneer of cultural-historical ethnology. He originated the concept of the *Kulturkreis* that was later used in a modified sense by FRITZ GRAEBNER, Bernhard Ankermann (1859-1943) WILHELM SCHMIDT and others. His contributions to ethnological research on Africa culminated in the perception of a rich African intellectual tradition, incontrovertibly proven by his scrupulously documented accounts of numerous illuminating cultural complexes: the discovery of ancient Ife art (Nigeria); the interpretation of the ruins of Great Zimbabwe (in present-day Zimbabwe) as an African creation; photographing more than 5,000 rock paintings; and recording an unsurpassed number of orally transmitted myths, epic texts and stories.

In contrast to his inductive comparative ethnological works, as a cultural theoretician Frobenius employed intuitive methods and apparently irrational opinions: "cultural morphology" and the theory of *paideuma*, or "soul of the culture," a variant of the romantic idea of *Volksgeist*. In the development of cultures he contrasted a creative, predominantly emotionally conditioned early phase, *Ergriffenheit* (emotional involvement), with a primarily rational, decadent late phase, *Anwendung* (application), and a transitional phase, *Ausdruck* (expression). The intellectual kinship to the cultural pessimism of Oswald Spengler is clear. Nonetheless, Frobenius rejected a racist interpretation as well as any prognostication of the future.

MAJOR WORKS: *Der westafrikanische Kulturkreis* (Gotha: 1897); *Der Ursprung der afrikanischen Kulturen* (Leipzig: 1898); *Und Afrika sprach* [2 vols.] (Berlin: 1912-1913) [tr.: *The Voice of Africa* (London: 1913)]; *Paideuma, Umrisse einer Kultur- und Seelenlehre* (Munich: 1921); *Atlantis, Volksmärchen und Volksdichtung Afrikas* [12 vols.] (Jena: 1921-1928); (with Ludwig von Wilm) *Atlas Africanus* (Munich: 1922-1933); *Das unbekannte Afrika* (Munich: 1923); (with Hugo Obermaier) *Hadschra Maktuba, Urzeitliche Felsbilder Kleinafrikas* (Munich: 1925); *Erlebte Erdteile* [7 vols.]

(Frankfurt a. M.: 1925-1929); *Erythräa, Länder und Zeiten des heiligen Königsmordes* (Berlin and Zürich: 1931); *Madsimu Dsangara, Südafrikanische Felsbildchronik* [2 vols.] (Berlin and Zürich: 1931); *Kulturgeschichte Afrikas* (Zürich: 1933); *Ekade Ektab: die Felsbilder Fezzans* (Leipzig: 1927); (with Douglas C. Fox) *Prehistoric Rock Pictures in Europe and Africa* (New York: 1937); (with Douglas C. Fox) *African Genesis* (New York: 1937); *Ethnographische Notizen aus den Jahren 1905 und 1906* (edited by Hildegard Klein) [3 vols.] (Wiesbaden: 1985-1988); *Notes sur l'ethnographie du Nord-Cameroun* (edited by Eike Haberland) (Wiesbaden: 1987).

SOURCES: *Leo Frobenius: ein Lebenswerk aus der Zeit der Kulturenwende, dargestellt von seinen Freunden und Schülern* (Leipzig: 1933); Helmut Petri, "Leo Frobenius und die kulturhistorische Ethnologie," *Saeculum*, vol. 4 (1953), pp. 45-60; Helmut Straube, "Frobenius, Leo" in: David L.. Sills (editor), *International Encyclopedia of the Social Sciences* (New York: 1968-1979), vol. 8, pp. 17-21; J.M. Ita, "Frobenius in West African history," *Journal of African History*, vol. 13 (1972), pp. 673-688; Eike Haberland (editor), *Leo Frobenius 1873/1973: une anthologie: avec une préface de Léopold Sédar Senghor* (Wiesbaden: 1973); László Vajda, "Leo Frobenius heute," *Zeitschrift für Ethnologie*, vol. 98 (1973), pp. 19-29; Jürgen Christoph Winter, "Frobenius, Leo Viktor" in: H. Jungraithmayr and W.J.G. Möhlig (editors), *Lexikon der Afrikanistik* (Berlin: 1983), pp. 86-87.

László Vajda
[Translation from German: Sem C. Sutter]

Fuchs, Stephen. Roman Catholic priest (Society of the Divine Word), historical ethnologist, Indianist. Born in Bruck a/d Mur (Austria) 30 April 1908. Fuchs studied under WILHELM SCHMIDT and WILHELM KOPPERS and took his Ph.D. in 1950 at the University of Vienna writing a dissertation on his ethnographic-ethnological research in India. He is widely recognized for his descriptive ethnographies on the Nimar Balahis (an untouchable weaving caste in India), on the Gonds and Baigas (central Indian tribes) and on the Korkus (westernmost of the Munda-speaking tribes).

He established a branch of the Anthropos Institute in Bandra (Bombay) in 1950, which was later transferred to Andheri (Bombay) and renamed the Institute of Indian Culture. He has been its director since its inception. The prime interest of the institute is research on the tribes and castes of India and on Indian religion and culture.

Among the many subjects of Fuchs' writing are messianic movements in India; he detected forty-six that until then had been unknown. More generally, Fuchs writes about man, culture and religious origins. He has more than 200 articles and papers to his credit.

MAJOR WORKS: *The Children of Hari* (Vienna: 1950); *The Gond and Bhumia of Eastern Mandla* (Bombay: 1960, 1968); *Rebellious Prophets: a Study of the Messianic Movements in Indian Religions* (Bombay: 1965); *Aboriginal Tribes of India* (Delhi: 1974); *At the Bottom of Indian Society* (Delhi: 1981); *The Korkus of the Vindhya Hills* (Delhi: 1988).

SOURCE: Mahipal Bhuriya and S.M. Michael (editors), *Anthropology as a Historical Science: Essays in Honour of Stephen Fuchs* (Indore: 1984).

J.V. Ferreira

Fürer-Haimendorf, Christoph von. Anthropologist, adviser-administrator. Born in Vienna (Austria) 27 July 1909. Fürer-Haimendorf is best known for his many books on tribal societies in India and Nepal and for his contribution as an adviser on the administration of these peoples. Trained in the Vienna school, Fürer-Haimendorf's first work was on the history and development of cultures from prehistoric times. But his first fieldwork, in northeast India, followed a period of study under BRONISLAW MALINOWSKI and was broadly functionalist in approach. This was followed by a ten-year stay in central India when Fürer-Haimendorf also acted as adviser to the government of India in the Northeast Frontier Agency and to the Nizam of Hyderabad; the fruits of this stay are *The Chenchus*, *The Reddis* and *The Raj Gonds*. In 1953 Nepal was opened to field research. Fürer-Haimendorf was first in the field and for the next twenty-five years carried out a large number of studies there, mainly of peoples of the high Himalayas (e.g., *The Apa Tanis* and *The Sherpas of Nepal*). More recently, he has returned to restudy each of his main areas of research (e.g., *The Gonds of Andhra Pradesh* and *A Himalayan Tribe*).

Fürer-Haimendorf's prolific output has three main strands. The first is monographic. His publications provide detailed and comprehensive accounts of institutions, practices and beliefs. The second is comparative. That the comparison is almost entirely anchored to those societies personally studied is made possible by the unrivaled range of Fürer-Haimendorf's fieldwork. This applies equally to limited comparisons, e.g., the trading networks of high-altitude Himalayan communities (*Himalayan Traders*), as it does to Fürer-Haimendorf's broadest work, *Morals and Merit*, in which he seeks to identify the elements of trans-cultural morality. Any lack of a strong theoretical framework is compensated for by his own knowledge of the cultures involved. The third strand is that of applied anthropology and concerns the weakening of tribal institutions under the intrusion of a dominant non-tribal population. During the 1940s, in his official role as adviser in northeast and central India, Fürer-Haimendorf formulated (and in some cases was able to implement) policies by which the tribespeople could retain cultural and economic resources and compete successfully under the new conditions. His writings of a generation later (*A Himalayan Tribe* and *Tribes of India*) show how successful had been the adaptation in the former area and how unsuccessful in the latter.

Fürer-Haimendorf's main interest has been the manifold variation of cultures, from which stems the duty of the anthropologist to record these while the opportunity still exists, to document the changes they undergo and to use this knowledge to add to the welfare of the peoples studied.

MAJOR WORKS: *The Chenchus* (London: 1943); *The Reddis of the Bison Hills* (London: 1945); *The Raj Gonds of Adilabad* (London: 1948); *The Apa Tanis and Their Neighbours* (London: 1962); *The Sherpas of Nepal* (London: 1964); *Morals and Merit* (London: 1967); *Himalayan Traders* (London: 1975); *The Gonds of Andhra Pradesh* (New Delhi: 1979); *A Himalayan Tribe: from Cattle to Cash* (Berkeley: 1980); *Tribes of India: the Struggle for Survival* (Berkeley: 1982).

Adrian C. Mayer

Furness, William Henry, 3rd. Physician, traveler, amateur ethnographer. Born in Wallingford (Pennsylvania) 18 August 1866, died in Wallingford (Pennsylvania) 11 August 1920. Furness graduated from Harvard in 1888 and received an M.D. from the University of Pennsylvania in 1891. Between 1895 and 1903 Furness, along with Hiram M. Hiller and Alfred C. Harrison, Jr., traveled extensively in Asia and the Pacific, making ethnographic and zoological collections for the University of Pennsylvania. Furness described the material culture and customs of the various peoples he visited, in papers for learned societies and in two books, *The Home-Life of Borneo Head-Hunters* and *The Island of Stone Money*. From 1903 to 1905 he was associated with the Free Museum of Science and Art (now The University Museum, University of Pennsylvania) as Curator of General Ethnology and Secretary of the Board of Managers. In later years he devoted himself to the project of teaching primates to speak.

Furness's first trips, during 1895-1896 and 1897, were to Sarawak where he was guided and assisted by CHARLES HOSE. Subsequent expeditions to Assam, Sumatra and the Caroline Islands were undertaken with the object of tracing the origins of Bornean culture and peoples. Furness's work with chimpanzees and orangutans was designed to test whether these apes, when properly raised and trained, might attain a level of reasoning approaching that of the Punan, whom he regarded as Borneo's most primitive inhabitants.

MAJOR WORKS: "Glimpses of Borneo," *Proceedings of the American Philosophical Society*, vol. 2, no. 153 (1896), pp. 309-320; *Folk-lore in Borneo* (Wallingford: 1899); "Life in the Luchu Islands," *Bulletin of the Museum of Science and Art, University of Pennsylvania*, vol. 2, no. 1 (1899), pp. 1-28; *The Home-Life of Borneo Head-Hunters* (Philadelphia: 1902; reprinted, New York: 1979); (with H.M. Hiller) *Notes of a Trip to the Veddahs of Ceylon* (London: 1902); "The ethnography of the Nagas of Eastern Assam," *Journal of the Anthropological Institute of Great Britain and Ireland*, vol. 32 (1902), pp. 445-466; "The stone money of Uap, Western Caroline Islands," *Transactions, Department of Archaeology, Free Museum of Science and Art*, vol. 1, no. 1 (1904), pp. 51-60; *The Island of Stone Money, Uap of the Carolines* (Philadelphia: 1910); "Observations on the mentality of chimpanzees and orang-utans," *Proceedings of the American Philosophical Society*, vol. 55, no. 3 (1916), pp. 281-290.

Adria H. Katz

g

Gabus, Jean. Ethnologist, museologist. Born in Le Locle (Switzerland) 16 October 1908. Gabus studied at Neuchâtel and Fribourg, notably with the prehistorian, Hugo Obermaier. He received his *doctorat ès lettres* (Ph.D.) under Father WILHELM SCHMIDT, director of the Anthropos Institute. He was Director of the Musée d'Ethnographie in Neuchâtel (1945-1978) and of the Institut d'Ethnologie of the University of Neuchâtel (1949-1974).

Jean Gabus participated in numerous surveys and missions, first among the Skolt and Finnish Lapps (1937), then among the Caribou Eskimos northwest of Hudson Bay (1938-1939) before concentrating on Africa and especially on the Sahara.

While head of the Musée d'Ethnographie, in 1955 he launched a new conception of museography, the *"musée spectacle."* Aiming to bring museums closer to daily life, he mounted twenty-five major exhibitions. In 1965 two issues of the journal *Museum* described his ideas.

Besides the thirteen multidisciplinary ethnographic missions to the Sahara and the Sahel, which he organized between 1942 and 1976 and which led to the three-volume *Au Sahara*, he also participated in diverse "museographic" missions, largely as a UNESCO expert. He worked on the reorganization of the National Museum of Kabul, in Afghanistan (1957-1960); he helped start the pilot training center of museum specialists of West and East Africa at Jos (Nigeria); he helped to inventory the treasures of the chiefdoms of the Bamum, the Bamiléké and the Northern territories in Cameroon; and, in Dahomey (now Bénin), he aided in the study of the protection and management of the royal palaces of Abomey (1963, 1964, 1965). He was asked to produce the *Art Nègre* exhibition at the World Festival of Negro Arts and to create the Musée Dynamique in Dakar (1963-1966).

He was invited as a consultant to Côte d'Ivoire (1967), Vanuatu (1971), Brazil (1972-1973) and Thailand (1973). He was also the leading organizer of the exhibition sponsored by Pro Helvetia at the Musée Dynamique at Dakar, *La Suisse présente la Suisse* (1971). Finally, he was asked to participate in a project for the Musée des Civilisations Nègres (Museum of Black Civilizations) in Dakar with the Mexican architect Pedro Ramirez Vazquez (1974).

MAJOR WORKS: *Vie et coutumes des Esquimaux Caribous* (Lausanne: 1944) [tr.: *A Karibu-eszkimók* (Gondolak: 1970)]; *L'homme primitif devant la mort* (Neuchâtel: 1952); *Au Sahara: les hommes et leurs outils* (Neuchâtel: 1954) [tr.: *Völker der Wüste* (Olten: 1957)]; *Au Sahara: art et symboles* (Neuchâtel: 1958) [tr.: *Kunst der Wüste II: Formen, Zeichen und Ornamente im Kunsthandwerk der Saharavölker* (Olten: 1959)]; *Parures et bijoux dans le monde* (Neuchâtel: 1962); *Art nègre: recherche de ses fonctions et dimensions* (Neuchâtel: 1967); *L'objet témoin: les références d'une civilisation par l'objet* (Neuchâtel: 1975); *Oualata et Gueïmaré des Nemadi* (Neuchâtel: 1977); *Au Sahara: bijoux et techniques* (Neuchâtel: 1982).

SOURCES: Romulus Vulcanescu, "Gabus, Jean" in: *Dictionar de etnologie* (Bucharest: 1979), pp. 338-339; "Aesthetic principles and general planning of educational exhibitions = Principes esthétiques et préparation des expositions didactiques," *Museum*, vol. 18 (1965), pp. 1-59, 65-97.

Roland Kaehr
[Translation from French: CW]

Gallatin, Albert (Abraham Alfonse Albert Gallatin).

Legislator, Secretary of the Treasury, diplomat, banker, ethnologist. Born in Geneva (Switzerland) 29 January 1761, died in New York (New York) 12 August 1849. Upon the completion of his course of study in classical and modern languages, geography and mathematics at the Geneva Academy, Gallatin left Geneva in 1789 for America. A youthful romantic, he moved to the Pennsylvania frontier and it was there in 1790 that he began a government career that included positions as state legislator; Congressman; Secretary of the Treasury; and diplomat in Russia, France and England. During his years in France as minister, Gallatin established a friendship with ALEXANDER and WILHELM VON HUMBOLDT and shared with them an interest in philology. Alexander, who in 1823 was preparing a work on American Indian languages, urged Gallatin to contribute an essay. When he retired from public service in 1827, Gallatin moved to New York City. There he again engaged in the study of American Indian languages begun in 1823. In his publication, *A Table of Indian Languages in the United States* in 1826, Gallatin provided the first tribal language map and was the first to attempt to designate language groups by the comparative method. This publication was followed in 1836 by "A synopsis of the Indian tribes ... in North America," a greatly extended version of the unpublished essay he wrote for Humboldt's volume. In 1843 Gallatin proved a vital force in the founding of the American Ethnological Society (AES) and served as its first president. He published his "Notes on the semi-civilized nations of Mexico, Yucatan and Central America" in the first volume of *AES Transactions* and his "Introduction to Hale's *Indians of North-West America*, and vocabularies of North America" in the second volume.

Although criticized by some for his stand on monogenism, Gallatin did not depart from this position nor from his Enlightenment optimism with respect to progress, environmentalism, and the "evolutionary" nature of American Indian society.

MAJOR WORKS: *A Table of Indian Languages of the United States, East of the Stoney Mountains, Arranged According to Languages and Dialects* (N.p.: 1826); "A synopsis of the Indian tribes ... in North America," *Archaeologia Americana: Transactions and Collections of the American Antiquarian Society*, vol. 2 (1836), pp. 1-422; "Notes on the semi-civilized nations of Mexico, Yucatan, and Central America," *Transactions of the American Ethnological Society*, vol. 1 (1845), pp. 1-352; "'Introduction' to Hale's *Indians of North-west America*, and vocabularies of North America," *Transactions of the American Ethnological Society*, vol. 2 (1848), pp. xxiii-clxxxviii.

SOURCES: Henry Adams, *The Life of Albert Gallatin* (Philadelphia: 1880); Robert E. Bieder and Thomas G. Tax, "From ethnologists to anthropologists: a brief history of the American Ethnological Society" in: John V. Murra (editor), *American Anthropology: the Early Years* (St. Paul: 1976) (= *1974 Proceedings of the American Ethnological Society*), pp. 11-22; Robert E. Bieder, "Albert Gallatin and the survival of Enlightenment thought in nineteenth-century American anthropology" in: Timothy H.H. Thoresen (editor), *Toward a Science of Man: Essays in the History of Anthropology* (The Hague: 1975), pp. 91-98; Robert E. Bieder, *Science Encounters the Indian, 1820-1880: the Early Years of American Ethnology* (Norman: 1986), pp. 16-54; Albert Gallatin, *Selected Writings of Albert Gallatin* (edited by E. James Ferguson) (Indianapolis: 1967); Albert Gallatin, *The Writings of Albert Gallatin* [3 vols.] (edited by Henry Adams) (Philadelphia: 1879); James Gallatin, *The Diary of James Gallatin, Secretary to Albert Gallatin, A Great Peace Maker 1813-1827* (edited by Count Gallatin) (New York: 1916); "Gallatin, Abraham Alfonse Albert" in: *Dictionary of American Biography* (New York: 1960), pp. 103-109.

Robert E. Bieder

Gamio, Manuel. Anthropologist. Born in Mexico City (Mexico) 2 March 1883, died in Mexico City (Mexico) 16 July 1960. In a period of great political change, Gamio contributed to making anthropology a means of studying the many regions of Mexico and its inhabitants. His scholarly activity was oriented to changing the conditions of life of the indigenous groups and to designing "indigenist" policies on the American continent.

His interest in anthropology arose as a result of his living with day laborers on a relative's rubber plantation where he learned the Náhuatl language. In 1909, on the recommendation of ZELIA NUTTALL, he was awarded a scholarship to study anthropology at Columbia University under the direction of FRANZ BOAS. On his return to Mexico during the turbulent period of the Revolution, Gamio published *Forjando patria* and transformed the office responsible for archaeological monuments to an office of anthropology oriented to the study of past and present Mexican cultures—and to the formulation of means to achieve cultural development. He proposed an interdisciplinary and regional approach to the study of the Mexican Republic. He presented the summary and conclusions of *La población del valle de Teotihuacán* as his doctoral thesis at Columbia. In 1925 he denounced the high-level corruption in the office of the Secretary of Public Education and left the country, interrupting his regional research. At this point, the U.S. Social Science Research Council entrusted him with a study of Mexican migration in the United States.

Returning to Mexico in 1930, he held many positions in the government from which he conducted sociologically oriented studies. He found that a combination of scholarly activity and public duty would permit him to develop his own conception of the science of anthropology and apply it to the development of the Indian population. This blend was pulled together in the directorship of the Interamerican Indian Institute, a position he held from 1942 until his death.

MAJOR WORKS: *Forjando patria* (Mexico City: 1916); *La población del valle de Teotihuacán* (Mexico City: 1922; Mexico City: 1985); *Mexican Immigration to the United States: a Study of Human Migration and Adjustment* (Chicago: 1930); *The Mexican Immigrant: His Life-Story* (Chicago: 1931) [tr.: *El inmigrante mexicano* (Mexico City: 1969)]; "Exploración económico-cultural en la región oncocercosa de Chiapas, México," *América Indígena*, vol. 6 (1946), pp. 199-246; *Consideraciones sobre el problema indígena* (Mexico City: 1948).

SOURCES: Angeles González Gamio, *Manuel Gamio: una lucha sin final* (Mexico City: 1987); Juan Comas, "Outstanding Latin American social scientists: Manuel Gamio" in: *Social Sciences in Mexico and South and Central America*, vol. 1 (1948), pp. 75-82; *Estudios antropológicos publicados en homenaje al doctor Manuel Gamio* (Mexico City: 1956); Gonzalo Aguirre Beltrán, *Lenguas vernáculas: su uso y desuso* (Mexico City: 1983); Eduardo Matos Moctezuma, *Manuel Gamio: arqueología e indigenismo* (Mexico City: 1973); Manuel Gamio, *La población del valle de Teotihuacán* (Mexico City: 1985).

Roberto Melville
[Translation from Spanish: Margo L. Smith]

Garcilaso de la Vega. Inca chronicler, writer, ethnographer, historian. Born in Cuzco (Peru) 12 April 1539, died in Córdoba (Spain) 23 April 1616. Garcilaso de la Vega was the son of the Spanish Captain Sebastian Garcilaso de la Vega Vargas and the Inca princess Isabel Chimpu Ocllo. Because he belonged to the first generation of Peruvian *mestizos* and because of his noble rank, he was permitted to enjoy a privileged education in the midst of the turbulence of the years that followed the conquest.

In his twenty-first year, Garcilaso de la Vega traveled to Spain where he fought against the Moors under Don Juan of Austria, reaching the rank of captain. For much of this time he also attempted to gain recognition for the services of his father. His limited success in both enterprises fed his nostalgia for his maternal ancestors and gave force to the idealized image of the Incas that he perpetuated with his pen. His books synthesize the memories of his childhood and adolescence, and they serve as an exceptional testament to this period of Inca decline.

Garcilaso de la Vega acquired a permanent interest in Peru, gathering documents in his library and holding broad-ranging conversations with those who came from America to his home in Montilla. His decision to publish late in life appears to have permitted his manipulation of the Spanish language to mature in such a way as to make his arguments more convincing. In his work, he combined the official tradition of the Incas (to which he had access through his maternal relatives) and his personal testimony on the organizational period of the Viceroyalty of Peru. Both historiographical lines were imbued with the passions of the moment, giving his work something of the flavor of the conflict that must have profoundly affected him. This does not alter the seriousness with which he treated his information. He always clearly stated whether his information came from direct experience or originated second hand, identifying his sources with a care exemplary for his time. Garcilaso's writing is marked by the humanistic culture which he had worked hard to acquire. As a result, we have more than a chronicle; we have the work of a modern historian, endowed with a respectable critical apparatus and the capacity to convince.

Garcilaso died without seeing the publication of the second part of the *Comentarios Reales*, which would later become known as the *Historia General*. One should note the caution of the author in that, by calling them "commentaries," he was reducing the value and importance of his writings. Nevertheless, his book, "inspired by a natural love of country," assumed a position from the beginning as an expression of Peruvian national feeling.

> MAJOR WORKS: *La traduzión del Indio de los tres Diálogos de León Hebreo* (Madrid: 1590); *La Florida del Ynca, Historia del Adelantado Hernando de Soto ...* (Lisbon: 1605) [tr: *The Florida of the Inca: a History of the Adelantado Hernando de Soto ...* (Austin: 1951)]; *Primera parte de los Comentarios Reales que traten del origen de los Yncas ...* (Lisbon: 1609) [tr.: *The Royal Commentaries of Peru* (London: 1688); *The Royal Commentaries of the Incas* (Austin: 1966)]; *Historia General del Peru trata del descubrimiento ...* (Cordoba: 1617); *Relación de la descendencia del famoso Garci Perez de Vargas ...* (Lima: 1929).

> SOURCES: Raúl Porras Barrenechea, *Los cronistas del Perú* (Lima: 1986); Aurelio Miró Quesada, *El Inca Garcilaso* (Lima: 1945); José Durand, *El Inca Garcilaso, clásico de America* (Mexico City: 1976); José de la Riva Aguero, *Del Inca Garcilaso a Eguren* (Lima: 1962); Susana Jákfalvi-Leiva, *Traducción, escritura y violencia colonizadora: un estudio de la obra del Inca Garcilaso* (Syracuse, N.Y.: 1984); Luis A. Arocena, *El Inca Garcilaso y el humanismo renacentista* (Buenos Aires: 1949); Carlos Daniel Valcarcel, *Garcilazo Inka: ensayo sico-histórico* (Lima: 1939); Raquel Chang Rodriguez, *Violencia y subversión en la prosa colonial hispanoamericana, siglos XVI y XVII* (Madrid and Potomac, Maryland: 1982); J.B. Avalle-Arce, *El Inca Garcilaso en sus "Comentarios"* (Madrid: 1964); Max Hernández y Fernando Saba, "Garcilaso Inca de la Vega, historia de un patronimico" in: *Perú: identidad nacional* (Lima: 1979), pp. 109-122.

Luis Millones
[Translation from Spanish: Robert B. Marks Ridinger]

Gardner, Burleigh B.

Gardner, Burleigh B. Sociocultural anthropologist, consumer research company executive. Born in Galveston (Texas) 4 December 1902. Gardner received his M.A. in anthropology from the University of Texas (1930) and his Ph.D. in social anthropology from Harvard University (1936), held a position at the Business School of the University of Chicago (1943-1946) and was president and then chairman of Social Research, Inc., in Chicago (1946 to present). He has been one of the leading practitioners, in both the academic and the business worlds, of the "human-relations school" of social science. His *Human Relations in Industry* depicts businesses as social systems within the wider systems of community and society. This book is a major treatise of the school that was developed by social anthropologists, among others, beginning with the "primeval" studies in industrial social science at Western Electric's Hawthorne plant. As the Western Electric study turned more toward a clinical psychology, Gardner directed research in employee relations and personnel counseling at Hawthorne from 1937 to 1942. His discussions in *Human Relations in Industry* of organizational problems and of extra-company influences on employee attitudes are shaped in considerable part by his Hawthorne experiences. The human-relations school has been criticized for (1) being management-oriented, (2) deemphasizing (with its functionalist-equilibrium approach) the natural significance in business of the use of power and the conflicts of factions and (3) neglecting the influence of extra-organizational political and economic pressures. The latter two criticisms are to some extent answered by Gardner's work. While at the University of Chicago, Gardner was secretary of the seminal Committee on Human Relations in Industry, which brought about innovations in personnel matters in some of the country's leading firms. At Social Research, Gardner applied social science to the solution of business problems and to consumer research. His fieldwork during the early 1930s in Natchez, under the tutelage of mentor W. LLOYD

WARNER, resulted in *Deep South: a Social Anthropological Study of Caste and Class*. This book bridges two of the directions taken in the early ethnology of the contemporary United States, that of the American community study and the investigation of social stratification in a democratic society.

> MAJOR WORKS: *Deep South: a Social Anthropological Study of Caste and Class* (Chicago: 1941); "The man in the middle: position and problems of the foreman," *Applied Anthropology* vol. 4, no. 2 (1945) [entire issue]; *Human Relations in Industry* (4th ed., Homewood, Ill.: 1965); *A Conceptual Framework for Advertising* (Chicago: 1982).

> SOURCES: Eliot D. Chapple, "Applied anthropology in industry" in: A.L. Kroeber (editor), *Anthropology Today* (Chicago: 1953), pp. 819-831; B.B. Gardner, "The anthropologist in business and industry," *Anthropological Quarterly*, vol. 50, no. 4 (1977), pp. 171-173; B.B. Gardner, "Doing business with management" in: E.M. Eddy and W.L. Partridge (editors), *Applied Anthropology in America* (New York: 1978), pp. 245-260.

Frederick C. Gamst

Gaudet, Charles Philip. Trader, collector. Born in Montréal (Québec) 1 May 1827, died in Winnipeg (Manitoba) 22 September 1917. The Smithsonian Institution received forty-nine specimens of Inuit material culture from Gaudet while he was stationed at Fort Good Hope, a Hudson's Bay Company post situated on the Mackenzie River immediately south of the Arctic Circle. The specimens he sent south between 1865 and 1867 formed only a small segment of one of North America's early anthropological collections, but they were important acquisitions because they depicted the dress and technology of one of the most isolated and distant North American native populations and because, as part of the Mackenzie River Collection, they were the first examples of indigenous Arctic culture registered in a North American museum.

> SOURCES: *Annual Report of the Smithsonian Institution* (Washington: 1860-1871); accession records, Anthropology Department, Smithsonian Institution; collected notes, lists and catalogue on birds, Gaudet papers, Smithsonian Institution Archives; Alexander Preble papers, Smithsonian Institution Archives; J.L. Gaudet, "Chief trader Charles Philip Gaudet," *The Beaver* (September 1935), p. 45.

Debra Lindsay

Geddes, William Robert. Anthropologist, ethnographic film-maker. Born in New Plymouth (New Zealand) 29 April 1916, died in Sydney (New South Wales) 27 April 1989. His early training was in psychology, which he taught in New Zealand (1945) and London (1948) before making his definitive entry into social anthropology with fieldwork in Sarawak (1949-1951). Earlier anthropological experience, obtained as a soldier in Fiji and the Solomon Islands during the Pacific War, served as the basis for his Ph.D. at the London School of Economics (*Cultural Change in Fiji*, 1948). He thus joined a remarkable group of New Zealanders who became social anthropologists before the subject was formally taught at any New Zealand university.

During his years in the brand-new Department of Anthropology at the University of Auckland (1951-1957) and as chair of the long-established department at the University of Sydney (1958-1981), he did fieldwork in the Pacific Islands, Sarawak, China and Thailand. He was interested in the values that give meaning to life in small-scale societies and the structures that serve them and, following from this, the interactions of both values and structures with the modernizing forces of the outside world. He came to see the ultimate value of the anthropological endeavor as documenting, explaining and making known the variety and worth of the human experience represented by minority cultures increasingly under threat. There is no better exemplification of his stance than his contribution to the 1975 exchange in *Current Anthropology* occasioned by Frederick Barth's attack on Colin Turnbull's *The Mountain People*. He found the ideal means for his purposes in ethnographic films. Those he made have become both a record for the subject people of their disappearing ways of life and a rich medium of instruction and the basis for television versions reaching a world-wide audience.

With his convictions, it was a short step to involvement in practical affairs. He was a leading figure in the formation and activities of the Foundation for Aboriginal Affairs, an organization set up in 1964 to provide services to Aboriginal migrants to Sydney in the years before Aborigines were recognized as Australian citizens, and with which many Aborigines now publicly prominent were associated. In consequence of his research with hill tribes in northern Thailand (1957-1959, 1962), he advised on the establishment (in Chiangmai in 1965) of a Tribal Research Centre to facilitate the delivery of services in education, welfare and economic improvement. He was a member of two United Nations missions on the economic and social needs of the opium-producing tribes of the area (1967) and on the replacement of poppy-growing (1970). In the context of the developing debate on social responsibility in anthropological research, the Vietnam War brought anthropological activities in Thailand under scrutiny. The Tribal Research Centre came under suspicion and Geddes personally under attack.

After his retirement in 1981, he was active in the affairs of the Academy of the Social Sciences in Australia, with a concern to consolidate links with Australia's Asian neighbors through the Association of Asian Social Science Research Councils.

MAJOR WORKS: *Deuba: a Study of a Fijian Village* (Wellington: 1945); *Land Dayaks of Sarawak* (London: 1954); *Nine Dayak Nights* (London: 1956); "Fijian social structure in a period of transition" in: J. Derek Freeman and William R. Geddes (editors), *Anthropology in the South Seas: Essays Presented to H.D. Skinner* (New Plymouth: 1959), pp. 201-220; "Maori and Aborigine: a comparison of attitudes and policies," *The Australian Journal of Science*, vol. 24 (1961-1962), pp. 217-225; *Peasant Life in Communist China* (Princeton: 1963); "The Tribal Research Centre, Thailand: an account of plans and activities" in: Peter Kundstadter (editor), *Southeast Asian Tribes, Minorities, and Nations*, vol. 2 (Princeton: 1967), pp. 553-581; (with John F.V. Phillips and Frederick T. Merrill) *Report of the United Nations Survey Team on the Economic and Social Needs of the Opium-Producing Areas in Thailand* (Bangkok: 1967); *Migrants of the Mountains: the Cultural Ecology of the Blue Miao (Hmong Njua) of Thailand* (Oxford: 1976); "Research and the Tribal Research Centre" in: John McKinnon and Wanat Bhruksasri (editors), *Highlanders of Thailand* (Kuala Lumpur: 1983), pp. 3-12; (editor and contributor) *Asian Perspectives in Social Science* (Seoul: 1985). FILMS: *The Land Dayaks of Borneo: the Village of Mentu Tapuh in Sarawak* (Sydney: 1963); *Miao Year* (Sydney: 1968); *Vatulele: Island in Fiji* (Sydney: ca. 1977; shortened version, *Island of the Red Prawns*, Sydney: ca. 1977); *The Ritual of the Field* [Sarawak] (Kuching and Sydney: 1980; shortened version, *The Soul of the Rice*, Kuching and Sydney: 1980); *Brides of the Gods* (Clareville [Sydney]: 1985); *The Sacred Cow of India* (Sydney: 1987; modified version, with new title, forthcoming).

SOURCES: Jack Golson, "William Robert Geddes, 1916-1989," *Journal of the Polynesian Society*, vol. 98 (1989), pp. 369-370; Jack Golson, "Emeritus Professor William Robert Geddes, 1916-1989," *Borneo Research Bulletin*, vol. 21 (1989), pp. 80-83; Charles Perkins, *A Bastard like Me* (Sydney: 1975), pp. 99-106; Peter Read, *Cockatoo and Crow: a Biography of Charles Perkins*

(Ringwood: 1990), chapter 4; "Australian academics in Thailand: Geddes-Roberts exchange plus reprint, SEATO reports, Hinton, reading list etc.," *Retrieval: Newsletter of Current Events* [Kingsford, N.S.W.], vol. 1, no. 3 (July/August 1971); "Court rules anthropologist defamed by media reports of involvement in Thai research center," *Anthropology Newsletter*, vol. 17, no. 2 (1976), p. 3; George N. Appell, *Ethical Dilemmas in Anthropological Enquiry: a Case Book* (Waltham: 1978), p. 278; James N. Hill, "The Committee on Ethics: past, present and future" in: Joan Cassell and Sue-Ellen Jacobs (editors), *Handbook on Ethical Issues in Anthropology* (Washington: 1987), pp. 11-19.

Jack Golson

Gennep, Arnold van. Anthropologist, folklorist. Born in Ludwigsburg (Germany) 23 April 1873, died in Épernay (France) 7 May 1957. Van Gennep received his doctorate from the École des Hautes Études. He held the chair of ethnography at the University of Neuchâtel (1912-1915). The rest of his life he spent in private scholarship, supporting himself through translations and free-lance writing.

Van Gennep is primarily known for *Les rites de passage* in which he examined the ceremonial sequence accompanying a change of status for an individual or a group or for the annual cycle. Every rite of passage, according to his theory, followed a three-fold pattern—that of the rites of separation, transition and incorporation. Though van Gennep was involved in folklore studies throughout his life, many of his early publications were concerned with ethnography. In *Tabou et totémisme à Madagascar*, he examined taboo as the fundamental element of individual and social life. He considered as part of taboo all manner of proscriptive beliefs in religious practices, oral narratives, folk medicine, folk botany, political organization and family structure. In *Mythes et légendes d'Australie*, van Gennep critically reviewed theories of Australian totemism, particularly those of ANDREW LANG and Émile Durkheim; he also posited his own theory that totemism was a system of classification. In *L'état actuel du problème totemique*, he discussed totemism as a means of assuring social cohesion and continuity through time. He intensified his criticism of Durkheim, accusing him of careless generalization, imprudent use of evolutionary theory, and denial of the import of individual creativity. Van Gennep conducted brief fieldwork in Algeria (1911-1912) and extensive fieldwork throughout France, especially in the *départements* of Savoie, Dauphiné, Bourgogne, Flandres and Hainaut Français. His research in French folklore was directed toward providing rigorous documentation of traditional practices and establishing folklore as a recognized discipline in France. While he published seven volumes of folklore collections of the French *départements*, his major work in folklore was the nine-part *Manuel de folklore français contemporain*, which was to serve as a resource for both the lay public and the scholar. In all his work, van Gennep drew together the two fields of folklore and anthropology, which in Europe were viewed as separate disciplines. He brought to his work in anthropology a knowledge of folklore, and, above all, he sought to make folklore a thorough account of a living people, an ethnography.

MAJOR WORKS: *Tabou et totémisme à Madagascar* (Paris: 1904); *Mythes et légendes d'Australie* (Paris: 1906); *Religions, moeurs et légendes* [5 vols.] (Paris: 1908-1914); *Les rites de passage* (Paris: 1909) [tr.: *The Rites of Passage* (Chicago: 1960)]; *Les demi-savants* (Paris: 1911) [tr.: *The Semi-Scholars* (London: 1967)]; *En Algérie* (Paris: 1914); *L'état actuel du problème totemique* (Paris: 1920); *Manuel de folklore français contemporain* [9 vols.] (Paris: 1943-1958).

SOURCES: Nicole Belmont, *Arnold van Gennep, le créateur de l'ethnographie française* (Paris: 1974) [tr.: *Arnold van Gennep, the Creator of French Ethnography* (Chicago: 1979)]; Rosemary Lévy Zumwalt, *The Enigma of Arnold van Gennep (1873-1957): Master of French Folklore and Hermit of Bourg-la-Reine* (Helsinki: 1988) (= *Folklore Fellows Communications*, no. 241); Nicole Belmont, "Ethnologie et histoire dans l'oeuvre d'Arnold van Gennep," *Ethnologie française*, vol. 5 (1975), pp. 184-188; Rodney Needham, "Introduction" to: Arnold van Gennep, *The Semi Scholars* (London: 1967), pp. ix-xx; Ketty van Gennep, "Introduction" to: *Bibliographie des oeuvres d'Arnold van Gennep* (Paris: 1964), pp. 3-12; Rosemary Zumwalt, "Arnold van Gennep: the Hermit of Bourg-la-Reine," *American Anthropologist*, vol. 84 (1982), pp. 299-313.

Rosemary Lévy Zumwalt

Geramb, Viktor. Cultural historian, folklorist. Born in Deutschlandsberg (Austria) 24 March 1884, died in Graz (Austria) 8 January 1958. In his early years Geramb achieved recognition above all for his research into the cultural history and distribution of farmhouses. His chief interests lay in the study of the material world and the folklore of particular subjects, in which he gave special emphasis to the etymological relationship between words and objects.

In 1907 Geramb completed his studies at the University of Graz with a specialization in history and shortly thereafter built up a museum of folklore in Graz, which he directed until 1949. In 1924 he obtained his *Habilitation* in the field of Germanic folklore with the work "Die Kulturgeschichte der Rauchstuben." His appointment as *außerordentlicher Professor* followed in 1931 as, one year later, did the establishment of an academic chair in folklore. Graz thus became the first university in the German-speaking world where one could study folklore as a principal subject.

Geramb's methodology was always marked by extensive collecting and observation of the cultural artifacts of the rural population. In his later years he published numerous works on folksongs, fairy tales and proverbs, customs and practices, popular arts and national costumes. He felt especially dependent on the historical method and promoted the renewal and reintroduction of older forms into contemporary life. His spiritual model was the German cultural historian WILHELM HEINRICH RIEHL; he described himself as Riehl's student. Just as Riehl did, Geramb rambled through the field, systematically noting observable data and placing them in order from an historical point of view.

MAJOR WORKS: "Das Bauernhaus in Steiermark," *Zeitschrift des Historischen Vereines für Steiermark*, vol. 9 (1911), pp. 188-264; *Deutsches Brauchtum in Österreich* (Graz: 1924); "Die Kulturgeschichte der Rauchstuben," *Wörter und Sachen*, vol. 9 (1924), 1-67; "Zur Frage nach den Grenzen, Aufgaben und Methoden der deutschen Volkskunde," *Zeitschrift des Vereins für Volkskunde*, vol. 37/38 (1927/1928), pp. 163-181; *Kinder- und Hausmärchen aus Steiermark* (Graz: 1941); *Wilhelm Heinrich Riehl: Leben und Werk* (Salzburg: 1954).

SOURCES: Hans Koren, *Viktor von Geramb* (Graz: 1974) (= *Zeitschrift des Historischen Verines für Steiermark*, Sonderband 5); Viktor Geramb, [Autobiography] in: Nikolaus Grass (editor), *Österreichische Geschichtswissenschaft der Gegenwart in Selbstdarstellung*, vol. 2 (Innsbruck: 1951), pp. 78-92; Maria Kundegraber, "Viktor von Geramb" in: *Blätter für Heimatkunde*, vol. 58 (1984), pp. 3-15; Helmut Eberhart, "Die Entwicklung des Faches Volkskunde an der Karl-Franzens-Universität Graz" in: Wolfgang Brückner (editor), *Volkskunde als akademische Disziplin* (Vienna: 1983) (= *Sitzungsberichte der Österreichischen Akademie der Wissenschafen, Philosophisch-Historische Klasse*, vol. 414), pp. 35-50.

Johann Verhovsek
[Translation from German: Robert B. Marks Ridinger]

Ghurye, Govind Sadashiv. Anthropologist, sociologist, Indologist. Born in Malvan village, western Maharashtra (India) 12 December 1893, died in Bombay (India) 28 December 1983. Ghurye taught sociology in Bombay University from 1924 to 1959; he retired as Emeritus Professor. In his long academic career he trained a large number of post-graduate and research students in sociology. His early works on caste and kinship were the products of his anthropological training received at Cambridge University (1929-1932). He emphasized the integrative and accommodative roles of caste and kingroups in Indian society. During this period and also later he wrote on a variety of themes related to Indian society such as religious phenomena, rural-urban networks, family and marriage, social customs and usages. As an Indologist he wrote on Indo-European kinship, Indian art and architecture and Vedic heritage. In his Indological studies, he highlighted the roles of values and ideals in the evolution of Indian society.

Although Ghurye wrote his research papers and books in a descriptive style, his writings were not devoid of theory. He studied the intergroup relations such as caste-tribe or Hindu-Muslim interactions from the perspective of normative Hinduism. According to him, the various tribes in India, especially those of the south-central region, were to be regarded as "backward Hindus." In other words, these groups had lost their place in Hindu society presumably due to their moral lapses such as drinking liquor, indulgence in free sex, etc. In the amelioration of tribes in India, the moral dimension must be borne in mind by the policy makers of free India.

Ghurye regarded the Hindus and Muslims as disparate groups that could not build up effective and long-lasting rapproachements. The Muslim rulers of India (11th to 17th century A.D.) destroyed temples and forcibly converted many Hindus to Islam. In contrast to the tolerant spirit of Hinduism, Islam in India held fast to a dogmatic theology. Ghurye, in these studies, failed to recognize two points. First, the tribes have often been compelled by the dominant castes to accept Hindu hegemony. Second, Sufism and Bhaktism (devotionalism) were products of Hindu-Muslim interactions, especially in northern India. Together they lessened caste rigidities and religious bigotry. They also gave rise to literary and other types of creative output.

Ghurye made an outstanding contribution to the study of Indian religions. He wrote a book on the Indian Sadhus (ascetics). Although the Indian ascetics had renounced the world, they contributed to the good of society. Most of them were organized into religious orders that not only guided the society but created new values for it. The Jaina, Buddhist and Hindu ascetics were activistic in spite of a contemplative bent of mind. The revitalization of Indian religions by these ascetic orders lent dynamism to society. Ghurye also wrote a book on the evolution of Indian "gods." The major deities of India were not merely the relics of an "animistic" past. Their rise symbolized the integration of ethnic and regional identities into a common religious framework.

As a citizen of modern India, Ghurye subscribed to a liberal creed, derived from Western education. He was dismayed by the spread of aggressive, competitive caste consciousness in free India. He felt that the caste patriotism was damaging the national unity. He was also disturbed by the tribal dissidence in India's northeast, which undermined political stability. He believed that India's progress should be in tune with the cultural heritage of India that could help in checking the centrifugal tendencies.

MAJOR WORKS: *Family and Kin in Indo-European Cultures* (Bombay: 1961); *Anatomy of a Rururban Community* (Bombay: 1962); *Anthropo-sociological Papers* (Bombay: 1963); *Scheduled Tribes* (Bombay: 1963); *Indian Sadhus* (Bombay: 1964); *Rajput Architecture* (Bombay: 1968); *Gods and Men* (Bombay: 1968); *Caste and Race in India* (5th ed., Bombay: 1969); *Whither India* (Bombay: 1977).

SOURCES: G.S. Ghurye, *I and Other Explorations* (Bombay: 1977); A.K. Saran, "India" in: J.S. Roucek (editor), *Contemporary Sociology* (New York: 1959), pp. 1013-1033; C.N. Venugopal, "G.S. Ghurye's ideology of normative Hinduism," *Contributions to Indian Sociology*, vol. 20, no. 2 (1986), pp. 305-314.

C.N. Venugopal

Gifford, Edward Winslow. Anthropologist, museologist. Born in Oakland (California) 14 August 1887, died in Chico (California) 16 May 1959. Gifford was a productive scholar who contributed in many areas of anthropology.

In 1903 Gifford served as a student zoological researcher on the California Academy of Sciences' expedition to Revillagigedo Island, Mexico; the following year he was hired as an assistant in the Academy's department of ornithology, where he stayed until 1912. During the years 1905-1906 he participated in the Academy's expedition to the Galapagos Islands.

In 1912 Gifford was made an assistant curator at the University of California's Museum of Anthropology. He was promoted to associate curator in 1915, curator in 1925 and museum director in 1947. By 1920 he was appointed a lecturer in the Berkeley Department of Anthropology; promotions to associate professor and professor came in 1938 and 1945, respectively. His achievements in this double career are even greater in light of his never having attended college.

Gifford's early work in anthropology was primarily in California, emphasizing archaeology. Physical anthropology and ethnology joined the list of his interests as he ranged farther and farther from the San Francisco area. Gifford served as a staff member of Honolulu's Bernice P. Bishop Museum (1920-1921), spending nine months in Tonga as a part of the Bayard Dominick Expedition. This research resulted in two monographs; in all, Gifford published more than one hundred articles and monographs on a wide array of topics.

During the 1940s and 1950s he engaged in archaeological research in Nayarit and Sonora states, Mexico, and in Fiji, New Caledonia and Yap, in Oceania.

Gifford was not only an active fieldworker but also a pioneer in archaeological sampling and typological studies of artifacts. He left his mark most firmly on Californian prehistory and ethnology, where he accomplished an impressive amount of the basic work. He also was a significant influence on several decades of Berkeley's anthropology graduate students.

MAJOR WORKS: "Composition of California shellmounds," *University of California Publications in American Archaeology and Ethnology*, vol. 12, no. 1 (1916), pp. 1-29; "Miwok myths," *University of California Publications in American Archaeology and Ethnology*, vol. 12, no. 8 (1917), pp. 283-338; "Clans and moieties in Southern California," *University of California Publications in American Archaeology and Ethnology*, vol. 14, no. 2 (1918), pp. 155-219; "Clear Lake Pomo society," *University of California Publications in American Archaeology and Ethnology*, vol. 18, no. 2 (1926), pp. 287-390; "Californian anthropometry," *University of California Publications in American Archaeology and Ethnology*, vol. 22, no. 2 (1926), pp. 217-390; (with W.

Egbert Schenck) *Archaeology of the Southern San Joaquin Valley, California* (Berkeley: 1926) (= *University of California Publications in American Archaeology and Ethnology*, vol. 23, no. 1); "Pottery-making in the Southwest," *University of California Publications in American Archaeology and Ethnology*, vol. 23, no. 8 (1928), pp. 353-373; *Tongan Society* (Honolulu: 1929); "Californian bone artifacts," *University of California Anthropological Records*, vol. 3, no. 2 (1940), pp. 153-237; "Surface archaeology of Ixtlan del Rio, Nayarit," *University of California Publications in American Archaeology and Ethnology*, vol. 43, no. 2 (1950), pp. 183-302; "Archaeological excavations in Fiji," *University of California Anthropological Records*, vol. 13, no. 3 (1951), pp. 189-288; (with Dick Shutler, Jr.) *Archaeological excavations in New Caledonia* (Berkeley: 1956) (= *University of California Anthropological Records*, vol. 18, no. 1).

SOURCES: Robert F. Heizer, "Edward Winslow Gifford, 1887-1959," *American Antiquity*, vol. 25 (1959), pp. 257-259; George M. Foster, "Edward Winslow Gifford, 1887-1959," *American Anthropologist*, vol. 62 (1960), pp. 327-329.

David Lonergan

Giglioli, Enrico Hillyer. Zoologist, ethnologist, traveler. Born in London (England) 23 June 1845, died in Florence (Italy) 16 December 1909. His mother was English and his father Italian. He attended the London School of Mines, was a pupil of Lyell, Owen and Huxley, participated in the lively debate concerning Darwin's work, and established strong relations with the English scientific community, which he maintained throughout his life. In 1863 he received a degree in natural sciences from the University of Pisa. Two years later he joined Filippo De Filippi, professor of zoology at the University of Turin and one of Italy's earliest Darwinists, as assistant on the first voyage around the world sponsored by the Italian government. Giglioli traveled for three years on the ship Magenta visiting Brazil, Uruguay, Malaysia, Indochina, Japan, China and Patagonia.

Once home, Giglioli dedicated himself to reorganizing the impressive zoological and ethno-anthropological collections gathered during this circumnavigation. In 1869 he began teaching zoology and comparative veterbrate anatomy at the University of Florence and was instrumental in the founding of the Società di Antropologia (Anthropological Society) of PAOLO MANTEGAZZA where, due to Giglioli's travel experience and international contacts, he always played a leading role.

In 1874 and 1875 his monograph on the Tasmanians and his volume dedicated to the voyage of the Magenta were published. In the second volume, the historical and geographic description of places was accompanied by a full and detailed account of the peoples visited. The text immediately became an obligatory landmark for all Italian ethno-anthropologists of the time and remained so for decades.

During the next few years, Giglioli directed his ethnographic energies toward analyzing cultural material but never completely abandoned the field of zoology to which he still made important contributions. From 1872 on, he began the collection and the analogical and comparative study of the stone tools of modern day "primitives" as sources for the reconstruction of the material techniques and ways of life of the Stone Age. Giglioli's notable collection contained thousands of items and after his death became part of the Museo Preistorico-etnografico (Prehistoric Ethnographic Museum) of Rome.

Along with this major focus of his research, Giglioli also made other anthropological contributions (studies on the Negrito, a group of Negroid peoples of small stature found in Oceania and the southeastern part of Asia, and the classifications of the human races), contributed to the field of museum classification (attributing the 18th-century ethnographic collection discovered in Florence's Museo di Antropologia (Anthropology Museum) to Cook), participated in the development of travel guides in 1873, 1881 and 1883 and frequently contributed to international journals such as *Nature, Man, The Ibis* and *International Archiv für Ethnographie.*

MAJOR WORKS: *I Tasmaniani: cenni storici ed etnologici di un popolo estinto* (Milan: 1874); *Viaggio intorno al globo della r. pirocorvetta italiana "Magenta" negli anni 1865-66-67-68* (Milan: 1875); "Studi sulla razza Negrita," *Archivio per l'Antropologia e la Etnologia,* vol. 6 (1876), pp. 293-335; "Prodromo di una proposta di classificazione della specie umana, con una ipotesi sulla origine delle razze umane," *Archivio per l'Antropologia e la Etnologia,* vol. 8 (1878), pp. 536-539; "Appunti intorno a una collezione etnografica fatta durante il terzo viaggio di Cook e conservata sin dalla fine del secolo scorso nel Regio Museo di Fisica e Storia Naturale di Firenze," *Archivio per l'Antropologia e la Etnologia,* vol. 23 (1893), pp. 173-244; "Appunti intorno a una collezione etnografica fatta durante il terzo viaggio di Cook e conservata sin dalla fine del secolo scorso nel R. Museo di Fisica e Storia Naturale di Firenze: Isole Sandwich o Hawai," *Archivio per l'Antropologia e la Etnologia,* vol. 25 (1895), pp. 57-144; "Materiali per lo studio della 'Età della pietra' dai tempi preistorici all'epoca attuale: origine e sviluppo della mia collezione," *Archivio per l'Antropologia e la Etnologia,* vol. 31 (1901), pp. 19-264; (with Paolo Mantegazza and Charles Letourneau) "Istruzioni per lo studio della psicologia comparata delle razze umane," *Archivio per l'Antropologia e la Etnologia,* vol. 3 (1873), pp. 316-321; (with Arturo Zannetti) "Antropologia ed etnologia" in: Arturo Issel (editor), *Istruzioni scientifiche per i viaggiatori* (Rome: 1881), pp. 115-159; (with Paolo Mantegazza, A. von Fricken and S. Sommier) "Istruzioni etnologiche per il viaggio dalla Lapponia al Caucaso dei Soci Loria e Michela," *Archivio per l'Antropologia e la Etnologia,* vol. 13 (1883), pp. 109-114.

SOURCES: Decio Vinciguerra, "E.H. Giglioli," *Annali del Museo Civico di Genova,* vol. 4 (25 February 1910), pp. 479-493; Joseph Whitaker, "Bibliographical notice of the late professor E.H. Giglioli," *The Ibis* (July 1910), pp. 7-12; Costanza Casella Giglioli, *La collezione etnografica del prof. E.H. Giglioli: opera compilata sui manoscritti di E.H. Giglioli dalla sua vedova* [2 vols.] (Florence: 1911-1912); Enrico Balducci, "E.H. Giglioli," *Annali di Agricoltura* (1912), pp. 7-40; Franceso Ammannati and Silvio Calzolari, *Un viaggio ai confini del mondo (1865-1868): la crociera della pirocorvetta "Magenta" dai documenti dell'Istituto Geografico Militare* (Florence: 1985).

Sandra Puccini
[Translation from Italian: Phyllis Liparini]

Gladwin, Harold Sterling. Stockbroker, archaeologist. Born in Gramercy Park, New York (New York) 21 December 1883, died in Santa Barbara (California) 28 May 1983. He received his formal education in England where he attended a prep school at Temple Grove from 1890 to 1894 and Wellington College in Berkshire from 1894 to 1901. After returning to the United States in 1901 Gladwin entered the business field, holding a seat on the New York Stock Exchange from 1908 to 1922.

Although successful in business, he failed to find in it the challenges and satisfactions demanded by an active and inquisitive mind. When he retired in 1922 he moved to Santa Barbara, California, where he became associated with the Santa Barbara Museum of Natural History. Here he began intensive studies on mutations of certain species of *Lepidoptera.* At about the same time he developed an interest in the prehistory of California, which soon crowded out his earlier preoccupation with natural history. This interest eventually widened to include the archaeology of the Americas, especially as related to theories of migrations from Asia.

In 1924 Gladwin turned his attention to Arizona. As a friend of A.V. KIDDER and a research fellow in archaeology of the Southwest Museum, Los Angeles, he conducted excavations in the ruins known as Casa Grande in Arizona, making the first systematic studies of occupational refuse in order to develop a chronology at this famous monument. Out of this study came the identification of the prehistoric Hohokam culture and the revival of interest in the archaeology of southern Arizona, which had been quiescent since the work of FRANK HAMILTON CUSHING and Jesse Walter Fewkes before and at the turn of the century.

In 1928 Gladwin and Winifred MacCurdy, who later married Gladwin, established the Gila Pueblo Archaeological Foundation located three miles south of Globe, Arizona. This laboratory was to serve as a base and nerve center for research in Southwestern prehistory. Under Gladwin's direction, Gila Pueblo expanded in less than ten years from an idea to a large and well equipped physical plant with a staff of from five to eight people. He not only promoted aggressive investigation of ruins in the Southwest but also assembled representative archaeological material from the western United States and northern Mexico, which has not been duplicated in scope anywhere. Gila Pueblo came to be the mecca for the student and professional alike. In January of 1951, Gila Pueblo was given to The University of Arizona and its collections were transferred to the Arizona State Museum where they now reside.

Although Gila Pueblo as a new research laboratory started modestly, it was not long before its influence was felt in professional circles through the medium of its publications. Gladwin launched the *Medallion Papers* as the outlet for Gila Pueblo's research endeavors. Between 1928 and 1950 there appeared thirty-nine papers and monographs prepared by thirteen authors. Twenty-three of these papers were written by Gladwin in whole or in part.

In the field of publication, Gladwin is most widely known for his provocative, witty book *Men Out of Asia*, issued by Whittlesey House in 1947 as second prize winner in that year's contest of popular science writing. In 1957 he wrote and published a synthesis of Southwestern prehistory called *A History of the Ancient Southwest*, a type of writing for which he had a special and unique gift.

To Gladwin must be attributed the creation of a number of new methods in the field of pure archaeology and in disciplines related thereto. He initiated a method of archaeological surveying for collecting data extensively yet economically. Out of this grew records of 10,000 ruins and habitation sites in the western United States from Santa Barbara to the Mississippi River, and from Montana to Zacatecas, Mexico, which were the basis for formulating problems and guiding research. He developed a system of laboratory analysis and arrangement of cultural material that was appreciated by all who saw it. Perhaps his contributions of greatest importance have been in the area of cultural reconstruction. In this connection he recognized that time was the basic quantity; consequently any system for measuring it, as dendrochronology, commanded his searching attention.

American archaeology has benefited enormously from Gladwin's encouragement and support of research—directly, as in the case of the development of Gila Pueblo, and indirectly, by stimulating studies in which he challenged what he considered to be anthropological heresies. Even his severest critics would agree that his untrammeled thinking has been a wholesome solvent for the reexamination of professional dogma.

MAJOR WORKS: (with Winifred Gladwin) *A Method for Designation of Cultures and Their Variations* (Globe, Arizona: 1934) (= *Medallion Paper*, no. 15); (with Emil W. Haury, E.B. Sayles, and Nora Gladwin) *Excavations at Snaketown: Material Culture* (Globe, Arizona: 1937) (= *Medallion Paper*, no. 25); *Excavations at Snaketown, II: Comparisons and Theories* (Globe, Arizona: 1937) (= *Medallion Paper*, no. 26); *A Review and Analysis of the Flagstaff Culture* (Globe, Arizona: 1943) (= *Medallion Paper*, no. 31); *Men Out of Asia* (New York: 1947); *A History of the Ancient Southwest* (Portland, Maine: 1957).

SOURCE: Personal contact with Gladwin as a former employee and Assistant Director of Gila Pueblo.

Emil W. Haury

Gładysz, Mieczysław. Ethnographer. Born in Dąbrowa Górnicza (Poland) 9 August 1903, died in Kraków (Poland) 12 October 1984. Gładysz studied Polish philology (1922-1927) and ethnography (1930-1935) at Jagiellonian University, obtaining his doctorate in 1947. In 1954 he was named associate professor. During 1927-1960 he was affiliated with several museums in Silesia. Simultaneously with his work in museology, he headed the Department of Ethnography at the Institute of the History of Material Culture of the Polish Academy of Sciences in Kraków (1954-1960). In 1960 he became the director of the Department of Slavic Ethnography of Jagiellonian University.

Gładysz conducted his research primarily in Silesia. Some of his best-known studies dealt with the metal and wood decorative art of the Silesian mountain folk. After World War II he organized monographic team research in Upper Silesia and the Opole Silesia area. In 1959 under the auspices of the International Commission for Research in Folk Culture in the Carpathians he undertook an investigation of Carpathian folk culture. His interests in Slavic Studies were reflected in the international publishing house "Etnografia narodów słowiańskich" which he founded. He was also an outstanding teacher.

MAJOR WORKS: *Góralskie zdobnictwo drzewne na Śląsku* [*Wooden Ornamental Art of the Mountain Folk of Silesia*] (Kraków: 1935); *Zdobnictwo metalowe na Śląsku* [*Metallic Ornamental Art in Silesia*] (Kraków: 1938); "Zagadnienia śląskiej kultury ludowej" ["Problems of Silesian folk culture"] in: *Oblicze ziem odzyskanych: Dolny Śląsk* [*The Face of Recovered Lands: Lower Silesia*], vol. 2 (Wrocław: 1948), pp. 453-497; "Prace nad etnograficzną monografią Górnego Śląska" ["Studies in the ethnographic monograph of Upper Silesia"], *Etnografia Polska*, vol. 1 (1958), pp. 85-108; "Kultura ludu śląskiego" ["Silesian folk culture"] in: *Górny Śląsk* [*Upper Silesia*], vol. 1 (Poznań: 1959), pp. 453-523; "Zarys planu działalności i organizacji MKKKB" ["Outline of the plan of action and organization of MKKKB"], *Etnografia Polska*, vol. 6 (1962), pp. 15-40; *Bibliografia etnografii Śląska w zarysie* [*Bibliography of Ethnography of Silesia in Outline*] (Katowice: 1966); "Z zagadnień procesów kulturowych pogranicza etnicznego" ["On problems of cultural and ethnic processes"], *Zeszyty Naukowe UJ: Prace Etnograficzne*, vol. 6 (1972), pp. 7-41.

SOURCES: Jan Bujak, Teresa Dobrowolska, "Działalność naukowa i osiągnięcia prof. dr. Mieczysława Gładysza" ["Scientific activity and achievements of Professor Mieczysław Gładysz"], *Etnografia Polska*, vol. 25, no. 2 (1981), pp. 11-25; Zofia Szromba-Rysowa, "Mieczysław Gładysz," *Etnografia Polska*, vol. 30, no. 1 (1986), pp. 220-222.

Maria Niewiadomska and Iwona Grzelakowska
[*Translation from Polish: Joel Janicki*]

Glob, Peter Vilhelm. Archaeologist. Born in Kalundborg (Denmark) 20 February 1911, died in Ebeltoft (Denmark) 20 July 1985. Glob specialized in Danish prehistoric archaeology and in the archaeology of the Persian Gulf. Both as curator at the Danish National Museum (1937-1949) and professor of archaeology at Aarhus University (1949-1960) he conducted numerous excavations in various parts of Denmark, many of them as "urgent archaeology tasks" as a consequence of the Natural Preservation Act of 1937. He published his results in both scholarly and popular writings; his book (*Mosefolket*) on iron-age bodies preserved in bogs reached a particularly wide audience. In the early 1950s a colleague told him about the island of Bahrain where there were 100,000 burial mounds but no archaeologists. The traditional opinion was that Bahrain had been uninhabited in prehistory but had served as a gigantic necropolis, but during his first expedition in 1953 Glob found evidence of settlements and located Bahrain's former capital. During 1953-1956 he made repeated expeditions to the Gulf states and convinced the authorities of the value and urgency of archaeological research in times of rapid modernization; it was partly thanks to his persuasive presence that the National Museum of Bahrain was established.

MAJOR WORKS: *Danske Oldtidsminder* (Copenhagen: 1942; 2nd edition, Copenhagen: 1967) [tr.: *Denmark: an Archaeological History from the Stone Age to the Vikings* (Ithaca: 1971)]; *Studier over den jyske Enkeltgravskultur* (Copenhagen: 1945); *Ard og plov i Nordens oldtid* (Copenhagen: 1951); *Mosefolket: Jernalderens mennesker bevaret i 2000 år* (Copenhagen: 1965) [tr.: *The Bog People: Iron-age Man Preserved* (London: 1969)]; *Al-Bahrain, De danske ekspeditioner til oldtidens Dilmun* (Copenhagen: 1968); *Helleristninger i Danmark* (Copenhagen: 1969); *Højfolket: Bronzealderens mennesker bevaret i 3000 år* (Copenhagen: 1970) [tr.: *The Mound People: Danish Bronze-age Man Preserved* (London: 1974)].

SOURCES: Poul Kjærum, "Glob, Peter Vilhelm" in: *Dansk Biografisk Leksikon* (Copenhagen: 1980), vol. 5, pp. 218-219; Olaf Olsen, "Peter Vilhelm Glob," Det Kongelige Danske Videnskabernes Selskab, *Oversigt over Selskabets Virksomhed = Annual Report, 1985-1986* (Copenhagen: 1987), pp. 236-250.

Jan Ovesen

Gloger, Zygmunt. Ethnographer, folklorist, excursionist. Born in Tybory-Kamianka [Kamionka] (Poland) 3 November 1845, died in Warsaw (Poland) 15 August 1910. Gloger studied history at Jagiellonian University. He was a landowner (from 1870), a social activist, a careful observer and recorder of the disappearing traditional folk and gentry culture, and the author of a collection of materials that served as the basis for the reconstruction of many aspects of that culture. He treated ethnography as a historical science. He led excursions on the northeastern lands of Mazovia and in particular Kurpie.

MAJOR WORKS: *Obchody weselne* [*Wedding Customs*] (Kraków: 1869); *Pieśni ludu* [*Folk Songs*] (Kraków: 1892); *Encyklopedia staropolska ilustrowana* [*Illustrated Encyclopedia of Old Poland*] [4 vols.] (Warsaw: 1900-1903); *Rok polski w życiu, tradycji i pieśni* [*The Polish Year in Life, Tradition and Song*] (Warsaw: 1900).

SOURCES: Teresa Komorowska, *Gloger: opowieść biograficzna* [*Gloger: Biographical Narrative*] (Warsaw: 1985); "Wincenty Pol i Zygmunt Gloger (z historii polskiej szkoły etnograficznej II połowy XIX w.)" ["Wincenty Pol and Zygmunt Gloger (from the history of the Polish school of ethnography of the second half of the 19th century)"], *Łódzkie Studia Etnograficzne*, vol. 9 (1967), pp. 99-106; Krystyna Kawerska (editor), *Zygmunt Gloger: badacz przeszłości ziemi ojczystej* [*Zygmunt Gloger: Investigator of the Homeland's Past*] (Warsaw: 1979).

Maria Niewiadomska and Iwona Grzelakowska
[*Translation from Polish: Joel Janicki*]

Glueck, Nelson. Biblical archaeologist, college president, rabbi. Born in Cincinnati (Ohio) 4 June 1900, died in Cincinnati (Ohio) 12 February 1971. Glueck was a highly visible figure in Palestinian archaeology for almost four decades. He is perhaps best known to archaeologists for the scope and scale of his field surveys in Transjordan (1932-1947) and in the Negev of Israel (1952-1964) and for his comprehensive volume on the Nabataean civilization, *Deities and Dolphins*. After earning degrees at Hebrew Union College and the University of Cincinnati, Glueck received a Ph.D. in Biblical studies at the University of Jena (Germany) in 1927. He was trained in archaeology by W.F. Albright at the American School of Oriental Research in Jerusalem. Early in his career he excavated two sites—Khirbet el-Tannur, a Nabataean temple, and Tell el-Kheleifeh, a Solomonic fortress on the Gulf of Aqaba—but he perceived his mission to be that of a surface explorer. With the aid of Albright's Palestinian ceramic typology as a chronological tool, and relying on the Bible for its "historical memories and descriptions," Glueck was the first person to conduct systematic investigations in Transjordan and the Negev desert. In all, he described and mapped more than 1,500 sites representing Neolithic through Byzantine occupations. His publications, including books written in popularized form (e.g., *Rivers in the Desert*), reflect his interests in cultural ecology and settlement patterns. As a measure of Glueck's influence on Biblical archaeology, the occupational sequence that he proposed for Transjordan's Bronze and Iron Ages, including the Kingdoms of Ammon, Moab and Edom, is still in use as a data base by scholars active in the field. Throughout his life, Glueck was affiliated with Hebrew Union College (after 1950, Hebrew Union College-Jewish Institute of Religion); as he moved through the ranks, he divided his time between the Holy Land and Cincinnati. He was promoted to Professor of Bible and Biblical Archaeology in 1936 and served as President from 1947 to 1971.

MAJOR WORKS: *The Other Side of the Jordan* (New Haven: 1940; revised ed., Warsaw: 1970); *The River Jordan* (Philadelphia: 1946; revised ed., New York: 1968); *Rivers in the Desert: a History of the Negev* (New York: 1959; revised ed., New York: 1968); *Deities and Dolphins: the Story of the Nabataeans* (New York: 1965).

SOURCES: G. Ernest Wright, "The phenomenon of American archaeology in the Near East" in: James A. Sanders (editor), *Near Eastern Archaeology in the Twentieth Century: Essays in Honor of Nelson Glueck* (New York: 1970), pp. 3-40; W.F. Albright, "The phenomenon of Israeli archaeology" in: James A. Sanders (editor), *Near Eastern Archaeology in the Twentieth Century: Essays in Honor of Nelson Glueck* (New York: 1970), pp. 57-63; G. Ernest Wright, "The achievement of Nelson Glueck" in: G. Ernest Wright and David Noel Freedman (editors), *The Biblical Archaeologist Reader* (New York: 1961), vol. 1, pp. 11-13; James A. Sauer, "Ammon, Moab and Edom" in: Janet Amitai (editor), *Biblical Archaeology Today: Proceedings of the International Congress on Biblical Archaeology* (Jerusalem: 1985), pp. 206-214; "Archaeology: the shards of history," *Time*, vol. 82 (13 December 1963), pp. 50-60; "Glueck, Nelson" in: Charles Moritz (editor), *Current Biography Yearbook* (New York: 1969), vol. 30, pp. 164-167; "Glueck, Nelson" in: Cecil Roth (editor), *Encyclopedia Judaica* (Jerusalem: 1971), vol. 7, p. 627.

Marjory W. Power

Goddard, Pliny Earle. Linguist, anthropologist. Born in Lewiston (Maine) 24 August 1869, died in New York (New York) 12 July 1928. Goddard was the foremost Athabaskanist of his generation, and between 1910 and 1928, the year of his death, he was a major figure in American Indian linguistics and anthropology generally.

Of Quaker background, Goddard attended Earlham College in Richmond, Indiana (A.B., 1892; M.A., 1896), where he studied classical languages. Between 1892 and 1896 he taught in secondary schools in Indiana and Kansas. In 1897 he went as an interdenominational missionary to the Hupa Indians of northwestern California, where he became deeply interested in the traditional culture and language of this Athabaskan group. Goddard enrolled as a postgraduate student at the University of California in 1900 and the following year joined the newly formed Department of Anthropology as Instructor. His doctoral dissertation (1904) was a grammar of Hupa, and the degree was the first ever granted by a United States university in the field of linguistics. By 1906 he was an assistant professor and had responsibility for most of the undergraduate instruction offered by the department. Between 1900 and 1909 Goddard carried out extensive linguistic research on Hupa and other Athabaskan languages in California; his preferred technique of working from texts rather than wordlists was in advance of his time, and his documentation of such now-extinct languages as Wailaki and Kato continues to be of interest to scholars.

In 1909 Goddard left California for the American Museum of Natural History in New York, where became Curator of Ethnology in 1914. In this position he exerted wide influence, primarily as a writer on general ethnological topics and as the editor of the *American Anthropologist* (1915-1920). He continued his Athabaskan linguistic research with visits to the Southwest and to Canada, as well as several return trips to California, but he found his linguistic work increasingly overshadowed by that of EDWARD SAPIR, who had turned to Athabaskan field research in 1921 after proposing the controversial "Na-Dene" relationship among Athabaskan, Tlingit and Haida. During this time Goddard formed a close intellectual alliance with FRANZ BOAS and became a forceful proponent of Boas's views in anthropology and linguistics, in particular of Boas's conservative view of linguistic relationship. With Boas, Goddard co-founded and edited the *International Journal of American Linguistics*, since 1917 the principal organ of American Indian linguistic scholarship.

MAJOR WORKS: *Life and Culture of the Hupa* (Berkeley: 1903) (= *University of California Publications in American Archaeology and Ethnology*, vol. 1, no. 1); *Hupa Texts* (Berkeley: 1904) (= *University of California Publications in American Archaeology and Ethnology*, vol. 1, no. 2); *The Morphology of the Hupa Language* (Berkeley: 1905) (= *University of California Publications in American Archaeology and Ethnology*, vol. 3); *Kato Texts* (Berkeley: 1909) (= *University of California Publications in American Archaeology and Ethnology*, vol. 5, no. 3); *Jicarilla Apache Texts* (New York: 1911) (= *Anthropological Papers of the American Museum of Natural History*, vol. 8); *Elements of the Kato Language* (Berkeley: 1912); *Indians of the Southwest* (New York: 1913; and subsequent editions); "The present condition of our knowledge of North American Languages," *American Anthropologist*, vol. 16 (1914), pp. 555-592); *Notes on the Chilula Indians of Northwestern California and Chilula Texts* (Berkeley: 1914) (= *University of California Publications in American Archaeology and Ethnology*, vol. 10, no. 6); *The Beaver Indians, Beaver Texts, and The Beaver Dialect* (New York: 1916-1917) (= *Anthropological Papers of the American Museum of Natural History*, vol. 10, parts 4, 5, 6); *San Carlos Apache Texts* (New York: 1919) (= *Anthropological Papers of the American Museum of Natural History*, vol. 14, part 3); *White Mountain Apache Texts* (New York: 1920) (= *Anthropological Papers of the American Museum of Natural History*, vol. 14, part 4); *Indians of the Northwest Coast* (New York: 1924; and subsequent editions).

SOURCES: Franz Boas, "Pliny Earle Goddard," *Science*, vol. 68, no. 1755 (17 August 1928), pp. 149-150; A.L. Kroeber, "Pliny Earle Goddard," *American Anthropologist*, vol. 31 (1929), pp. 1-3; Franz Boas, "Pliny Earle Goddard," *International Journal of American Linguistics*, vol. 6 (1930), pp. 1-2; A.L. Kroeber, "Goddard's California Athabascan texts," *International Journal of American Linguistics*, vol. 33 (1967), pp. 269-275; Michael Krauss, "Edward Sapir and Athabaskan linguistics" in: William Cowan, Michael K. Foster and Konrad Koerner (editors), *New Perspectives in Language, Culture, and Personality: Proceedings of the Edward Sapir Centenary Conference (Ottawa), 1-3 Oct. 1984* (Amsterdam and Philadelphia: 1986), pp. 147-190 (esp. pp. 149-156, 158-162).

Victor Golla

Goeldi, Emílio Augusto. Zoologist, ethnologist, archaeologist. Born in Ennetbuhl, Canton of St. Gall, District of Upper Toggenburg (Switzerland) 28 August 1859, died in Bern (Switzerland) 5 July 1917. Goeldi was essentially a zoologist, but he became quite well known for his research on the Indians and on the archaeology of Amazônia. His scientific training, strongest in the area of natural history, began in Switzerland. In 1880 he did work at the Dorhn Institute of Marine Research at the University of Naples, and in 1882 he went to finish his studies at the Universities of Jena and Leipzig, Germany, where he was assistant to the celebrated evolutionary zoologist Ernst Haeckel (1834-1919). He graduated in 1883. Goeldi was most influenced by the natural philosophy of the European biological scientists of the time, as well as by his mentor Haeckel. In 1885, Emperor Pedro II of Brazil hired Goeldi to work in the National Museum where he remained until 1890. Married, he went to Terezópolis, the mountain city above Rio de Janeiro, to undertake zoological and meteorological research. At this point in his life he was not yet interested in ethnographic and archaeological studies. He acquired these interests when he established himself in Belém, Pará, where he was hired as director and reorganizer of the Museu Paraense (Pará Museum) by Governor Lauro Sodré in 1894.

Here, together with his duties in administration, exploration and zoological and meteorological studies, Goeldi began the archaeological and ethnographic work that would make him famous over the next twelve years. From the beginning, Goeldi sketched his ideas concerning the problem of the Amazonian Indian, especially as regards the "primitive" people who had lived in that region in past epochs. Goeldi not only enriched our knowledge of Amazonian archaeology but also stimulated an enormous amount of further research. He organized important ethnographic collections from several tribes (some of which today are extinct or acculturated) and assembled valuable ceramic pieces from several sites in the region. The research of Goeldi and of his assistants was decisive in the 1895-1896 discovery of burial caves on the Cunani River and of the cemetary sites on Pará Island and on the Mazagão, Maracá and Anauerapucu Rivers, along the contested Franco-Brazilian frontier, now the state of Amapá, Brazil. Their work in this period (1895-1900) led to the first and most important contributions to Amazonian archaeology published by the Pará Museum and was responsible for the fact that today the Pará Museum possesses the best collections from Cunani and Maracá.

Goeldi left the directorship of the Pará Museum on 22 March 1907 when he returned to Switzerland where he was made professor at the University of Bern.

MAJOR WORKS (IN ETHNOLOGY AND ARCHAEOLOGY): *Ensaio sobre o Dr. Alexandre Rodrigues Ferreira, mormente em relação ás suas viagens na Amazônia e sua importáncia como naturalista* (Belém: 1895); *O Estado actual dos conhecimentos sobre os Índios do Brasil, especialmente sobre os Índios da foz do Amazonas no passado e no presente* (Belém: 1896); *Ein Naturforscher fahrt nach dem Litoral des südlichen Guyana zwischen Oyapock und Amazonenstrom* (St. Gallen: 1897); *Excavações archaeologicas em 1895 executadas pelo Museu Paraense no littoral da Guyana Brazileira entre o Oyapock e Amazonas. I. As cavernas funerárias artificiaes de Índios hoje extinctos no Rio Cunany (Goanany) e sua cerámica* (Belém: 1900; 2nd. ed., Belém: 1904); *Altindianische Begräbnishöhlen im südlichen Guyana und in denselben vorgefundene kunstvolle Topfereiprodukte* (Zürich: 1900); *Altindianische Thon und Stein: Idole aus Amazonas-Region* (Stuttgart: 1904).

SOURCES: Theophil Studer, "Professor Dr. Emil August Goeldi (1859-1917), *Verhandlungen der Schweizerische Naturforschenden Gesellschaft,* vol. 99 (1918), pp. 36-59; R. Hubert Laeng, "Emil August Goeldi," *Mitteilungen der Naturforschenden Gesellschaft in Bern,* vol. 30 (1973), pp. 27-29; Osvaldo R. da Cunha, "Emílio Augusto Goeldi," *Ciência e Cultura,* vol. 35, no. 12 (1983), pp. 1965-1972.

Osvaldo Rodrigues da Cunha
[Translation from Portuguese: Margo L. Smith]

Goldenweiser, Alexander A. Anthropologist, sociologist, social philosopher, cultural psychologist. Born in Kiev (Ukraine, Russia) 29 January 1880, died in Portland (Oregon) 6 July 1940. He was the oldest son of a prominent lawyer whose home was a center of liberal, critical-minded, intellectual conversations. The Ukrainian locale meant little to his family, which was Germanic, Jewish (secularly oriented), Russian, and cosmopolitan. Goldenweiser remained urbane throughout his life. He was educated in Kiev, at Harvard and (especially) at Columbia, where he received an anthropology Ph.D. in 1910. He was one of FRANZ BOAS's most promising students.

Goldenweiser's field research was limited to a total of ten months during 1911 and the next few years. He worked with Ontario Iroquois and published abbreviated, but useful, reports. All, or almost all, of his notes have survived and are available for further utilization at the National Museum of Civilization, Ottawa, and at the American Philosophical Society; included are copies of notes that he had never delivered to Ottawa and that his widow gave instead to Reed College (see Dobbin, 1986).

Early in this century, Boas and his students lived in a world of dogmas outside and inside anthropology, e.g., racism, geographic determinism and simplistic unilinear cultural evolution. Goldenweiser was among those who vigorously criticized these positions. A more subtle problem was the widespread practice of assuming that phenomena that had acquired the same name were the same "thing." In one sense of the term, Boasians were "nominalists" as well as skeptics: names are human inventions, and their referents vary. Goldenweiser's "Totemism ..." demonstrated that the practices that had been called "totemic" were indeed similar but significantly diverse. He continued to use the term "totemism," but he had convinced others that it had been reified and was not an entity; discussion of it waned. Goldenweiser also helped to refute the German-Austrian-British doctrines of extreme diffusionism—e.g., "all civilization started in Egypt." His *Early Civilization ...* was widely used as a textbook, but his later *Anthropology ...* did not become as well known.

The topics of a few of Goldenweiser's numerous articles illustrate the diversity of his interests: causality, education, Freud, morality, immigration, and history. His discussions of "the individual" may have correlated with his (quiet) anarchist beliefs. He had a variety of teaching appointments, but he never held a tenured academic position. His early teaching was at Columbia and the New School for Social Research. Subsequently, he worked in various ways, for example as an editor and an author in the creation of the *Encyclopaedia of the Social Sciences.* During most of his final years he taught at Reed

College and simultaneously at the Portland Extension Center (University of Oregon), where he was Professor of Thought and Culture. His lectures were often brilliant, but he could be irresponsible about standard academic practices. Anti-Semitism may also have limited his employment opportunities.

Goldenweiser's writings are not widely known today, but some are still worth reading. Others were important in their day because his critical-mindedness was needed, as such writings always will be.

MAJOR WORKS: "Totemism, an analytical study," *Journal of American Folk-Lore*, vol. 23 (1910), pp. 179-293; "The principle of limited possibilities in the development of culture," *The Journal of American Folk-Lore*, vol. 26 (1913), pp. 259-290; *Early Civilization: an Introduction to Anthropology* (New York, London, etc.: 1922); *Robots or Gods: an Essay on Craft and Mind* (New York: 1931); *History, Psychology, and Culture* (New York: 1933); *Anthropology: an Introduction to Primitive Culture* (New York: 1937).

SOURCES: Ruth Benedict, "Alexander A. Goldenweiser (1880-1940)," *American Sociological Review*, vol. 5 (1940), p. 782; George Riely Dobbin, *Digging for Goldie: Alexander Goldenweiser's Contributions and His Iroquois Notes* [unpublished Reed College B.A. thesis] (Portland: 1986); David H. French, "Goldenweiser, Alexander A." in: David L. Sills (editor), *International Encyclopedia of the Social Sciences* (New York: 1968-1979), vol. 6, pp. 196-197; Wilson D. Wallis, "Alexander A. Goldenweiser," n.s., *American Anthropologist*, vol. 43 (1941), pp. 250-255; Leslie A. White, "Goldenweiser, Alexander Alexandrovich" in: *Dictionary of American Biography: Supplement Two* (New York: 1958), vol. 22, pp. 244-245.

David H. French

Goldfrank, Esther Schiff. Ethnologist. Born in New York (New York) 5 May 1896. Goldfrank came to anthropology as FRANZ BOAS's secretary, after graduating from Barnard College in 1918, and persuaded him in 1921 to let her join him in fieldwork at Laguna and Cochiti Pueblos, New Mexico. This experience was followed by graduate courses at Columbia University, interrupted by marriage to Walter Goldfrank. In 1924 she spent one month at Isleta Pueblo. In 1935, after the death of her husband, she resumed taking courses at Columbia, although not for a degree. After a study of New York City adolescents for the General Education Board of the Rockefeller Foundation and participation in ABRAM KARDINER's and RALPH LINTON's culture-and-personality seminars at Columbia, she went in 1939 with a group of Columbia students, under RUTH BENEDICT's direction, to study the Blood Indians in Alberta. With both her Pueblo material and Blood kinship study she questioned some of Benedict's interpretations, notably the Apollonian view of Pueblo culture.

She married Sinologist Karl Wittfogel in 1940 and was stimulated to consider the implications of irrigation in the native Southwest. She continued to publish articles from both her Southwestern and Blood research and also participated in the Columbia University Chinese History Project. In 1962 she assembled and edited a volume about a group of Isleta paintings that had been secured by ELSIE CLEWS PARSONS. This was followed by *The Artist of "Isleta Paintings" in Pueblo Society*, letters from the artist to Parsons, assembled and correlated with the paintings by Goldfrank.

Goldfrank was closely associated with the American Ethnological Society, serving as secretary-treasurer from 1945 until elected president in 1948. From 1952 to 1956 she was editor of its monograph series. Aspects of anthropology from the 1920s into the 1970s as well as details of Goldfrank's career are delightfully recounted in *Notes on an Undirected Life: As One Anthropologist Tells It.*

MAJOR WORKS: *The Social and Ceremonial Organization of Cochiti* (Menasha, Wisc.: 1927) (= *American Anthropological Association, Memoir,* no. 33); "Irrigation agriculture and Navaho community leadership: case material on environment and culture," *American Anthropologist,* vol. 47 (1945), pp. 262-277; *Changing Configurations in the Social Organization of a Blackfoot Tribe during the Reserve Period* (New York: 1945) (= *American Ethnological Society Monograph,* no. 8); (editor) *Isleta Paintings* (Washington: 1962) (= *Bureau of American Ethnology Bulletin,* no. 181); *The Artist of "Isleta Paintings" in Pueblo Society* (Washington: 1967) (= *Smithsonian Contributions to Anthropology,* no. 5).

SOURCES: Esther S. Goldfrank, *Notes on an Undirected Life: As One Anthropologist Tells It* (Flushing, N.Y.: 1977) (= *Queens College Publications in Anthropology,* no. 3); "Esther Goldfrank, 1896-" in: Barbara A. Babcock and Nancy J. Parezo, *Daughters of the Desert* (Albuquerque: 1988), pp. 32-37; Gloria Levitas, "Esther Schiff Goldfrank" in: Ute Gacs [et al.] (editors), *Women Anthropologists: a Biographical Dictionary* (New York: 1988), pp. 120-126.

Nathalie F.S. Woodbury

Goldstein, Marcus S. Physical anthropologist, public health analyst. Born in Philadelphia (Pennsylvania) 22 August 1906. Goldstein received his B.A. and M.A. in anthropology from George Washington University, Washington, D.C., under the tutelage of Professor Truman Michelson, and his Ph.D. from Columbia University, where he was FRANZ BOAS's student. Research and fieldwork during the Great Depression were done in several settings, as a student-aide to ALEŠ HRDLIČKA at the U.S. National Museum, under HARRY L. SHAPIRO at the Laboratory of Anthropology and with Comanche Indians. His research has generally been problem oriented. He has done work on dental anthropology (with Eskimos and Indians in the United States), skeletal anthropology (in Israel and among Indians in Texas), child growth and development, paleopathology, health care in the United States, anthropomorphic and demographic effects of migration and environmental changes and ways of using anthropology to attain sympathetic understanding and tolerance between peoples. His specific research interests have included child growth in relation to dental occlusion-malocclusion, Mexican immigrants in Texas and their American-born and -raised offspring, and parents and children in Mexico. During World War II he worked in the U.S. Office of Strategic Services and in 1946 he joined the U.S. Public Health Service as an analyst. He remained in the health field (working at the Division of Public Health Methods, National Institutes of Mental Health, Administration on Aging and the Office of Research and Statistics in the Social Security Administration) until he retired in 1971.

Following his retirement Goldstein and his wife immigrated to Israel where he was offered an Associate Professorship in the Department of Anatomy and Anthropology, Tel Aviv University, a position he still holds. Goldstein was instrumental in organizing the Israel Anthropological Association and was its first President. In 1987 he was honored by the Association with a "Distinguished Service Award" acknowledging his pioneering efforts in establishing the Association and for his continuing contributions in advancing the discipline of anthropology in Israel. Goldstein's contributions have earned him recognition as "one of the forefathers of dental anthropology." A diary of his early field experiences with Mexicans both in the United States and Mexico has been "worked up" with relevant commentary and submitted for publication.

MAJOR WORKS: "Recent trends in physical anthropology," *American Journal of Physical Anthropology*, vol. 26 (1940), pp. 191-209; "The museum as a potential force for social enlightenment," *Science*, vol. 92 (1940), pp. 192-197; *Demographic and Bodily Changes in Descendants of Mexican Immigrants: with Comparable Data on Parents and Children in Mexico* (Austin: 1943); "Franz Boas' contributions to physical anthropology," *American Journal of Physical Anthropology*, n.s., vol. 6 (1948), pp. 143-162; "Longevity and health status of whites and nonwhites in the United States," *Journal of the American Medical Association*, vol. 46 (1954), pp. 83-104; "Theory of survival of the unfit," *Journal of the American Medical Association*, vol. 47 (1955), pp. 223-226; "Anthropological research, action, and education in modern nations, with special reference to the United States," *Current Anthropology*, vol. 9 (1968), pp. 247-269; (with B. Arensburg and H. Nathan) "Skeletal remains of Jews from Hellenistic and Roman periods in Israel," *Bulletins et Mémoires de la Société d'Anthropologie de Paris*, sér. 13, vol. 8 (1981), pp. 11-24; (with E. Kobyliansky) "Anthropomorphic traits, balanced selection and fertility," *Human Biology*, vol. 56 (1984), pp. 35-46.

Stanley M. Newman

Gower, Charlotte Day. See: *Chapman, Charlotte Gower.*

Graebner, Fritz. Ethnologist. Born in Berlin (Germany) 4 March 1877, died in Berlin (Germany) 13 July 1934. It was by chance that Graebner, a history student, came to the Royal Museum for Ethnography in Berlin in February 1899 as a *Wissenschaftlicher Hilfsarbeiter* (research assistant). After graduation in 1910, collaboration with his museum colleague Bernhard Ankermann (1859-1943) stimulated his interest in ethnographic problems. To both belongs the credit of having on 17 November 1904 at the Berliner Gesellschaft für Anthropologie, Ethnologie und Urgeschichte (Berlin Society for Anthropology, Ethnology and Prehistory) founded *Kulturkreislehre* (the study of culture circles) as a part of "cultural-historical ethnology." This they did with lectures on *Kulturkreise* (culture circles) and *Kulturschichten* (culture strata) in Oceania and Africa. They were stimulated by the works of the researcher-traveler LEO FROBENIUS and the geographer FRIEDRICH RATZEL. With *Kulturkreislehre*, they were turning away from the then-dominant biological-evolutionary concepts.

In 1907 Graebner became an assistant at the Rautenstrauch-Joest-Museum in Cologne, which had opened in 1906. While the Museum's director, Willy Foy (1873-1929), was burdened with administrative matters, Graebner could devote himself to the investigation of the museum's collections as well as undertake further theoretical researches. The result was his major work, *Die Methode der Ethnologie*, whose goal was the creation of epistemologically solid, nonspeculative, practical and useful methods for "cultural-historical" research. Graebner exerted lasting influence on ethnology in central and northern Europe, above all on the Vienna School of *Kulturkreislehre*. Quite new for ethnology in Graebner's historical approach was his insistence on a methodic critique of sources and his insistence on the importance of cultural-historical connections for the interpretation of data as well as for the understanding of development sequences. As his regional area of interest Graebner chose the South Pacific and attempted to comprehend it "culturally-historically" through works on different *Kulturkreise* (e.g., "Kulturkreise und Kulturschichten in Ozeanien," "Die melanesische Bogenkultur und ihre Verwandten"). Together with Foy he founded the museum publication, *Ethnologica*.

In the summer of 1914, while Graebner was trying to leave Australia after a scientific convention, he was arrested and interned five years for smuggling documents. After his return to Germany in 1919 he resumed his position as *Privatdozent* (unsalaried lecturer) at the University of Bonn, where he had earned his *Habilitation* in 1911. He was named *Außerordentlicher Professor* there in 1921. In 1923 Graebner became acting director of the Cologne Museum, succeeding Foy who had become ill. Graebner became director on 1 June 1925. In 1926 the University of Cologne named him *Honorarprofessor*, but because of a mental illness he could not take up teaching. Two years later he was prematurely pensioned because of this illness and returned to his home city of Berlin.

Graebner represented a widespread type of "museum man" of his time, who, without ever having engaged in fieldwork himself, possessed an enormously broad knowledge about virtually all foreign cultures, which he acquired largely through intimate acquaintance with collections. His studies on Oceania still merit attention today. The cultural-historical theories he put forward stimulated and enormously influenced researchers in central Europe and Scandinavia until the middle of the 20th century, even though today they have generally come to be seen as reductionist.

MAJOR WORKS: *Böhmische Politik vom Tode Ottokars II. bis zum Aussterben der Piremysliden*. I. Teil. *Rudolf von Habsburg gegen Otto von Brandenburg* [Ph.D. Dissertation] (Berlin: 1901); "Kulturkreise und Kulturschichten in Ozeanien," *Zeitschrift für Ethnologie*, vol. 37 (1905), pp. 28-53; "Die melanesische Bogenkultur und ihre Verwandten," *Anthropos*, vol. 4 (1909), pp. 726-780 and 998-1032; "Völkerkunde der Santa Cruz Inseln," *Ethnologica*, vol. 1 (1909), pp. 71-184; *Die Methode der Ethnologie* (Heidelberg: 1911); "Amerika und die Südseekulturen," *Ethnologica*, vol. 2 (1913), pp. 43-66; "Thor und Maui," *Anthropos*, vol. 14/15 (1919/1920), pp. 1099-1119; "Alt- und neuweltliche Kalender," *Zeitschrift für Ethnologie*, vol. 52/53 (1920/1921), pp. 6-37; "Ethnologie" in: G. Schwalbe [et al.] (editors), *Die Kulturen der Gegenwart* 3. Teil, 5. Abteilung. *Anthropologie* (Leipzig and Berlin: 1923), pp. 435-587; *Das Weltbild der Primitiven* (München: 1924).

SOURCES: Graebner file in the University Archives in Bonn; Archives of the Rautenstrauch-Joest Museums für Völkerkunde in the Historisches Archiv der Stadt Köln; Joseph Henninger, "Fritz Graebner und die kulturhistorische Methode der Ethnologie," *Ethnologica*, n.F., vol. 8 (1979), pp. 7-51; Paul Leser, "Fritz Graebner, 4 März 1877 bis 13 Juli 1934," *Ethnologischer Anzeiger*, vol. 3, pt. 2 (1932/1935), pp. 294-301; Paul Leser, "Fritz Graebner: eine Würdigung," *Anthropos*, vol. 72 (1977), pp. 1-55; Julius Lips, "Fritz Graebner, March 4, 1877 to July 13, 1934," *American Anthropologist*, n.s., vol. 37 (1935), pp. 320-326; Wilhelm Schmidt, "Fritz Graebner," *Anthropos*, vol. 30 (1935), pp. 203-214.

Lothar Pützstück
[Translation from German: Robert B. Dean]

Greenberg, Joseph Harold. Linguist, anthropologist, Africanist. Born in Brooklyn (New York) 28 May 1915. Greenberg attended FRANZ BOAS's classes as an undergraduate at Columbia University and went on to earn a doctorate in anthropology (1940) at Northwestern University under MELVILLE J. HERSKOVITS. He also spent a year (1937-1938) studying linguistics at Yale, to which he returned for a semester in 1945. While there he studied with such scholars as LEONARD BLOOMFIELD and BENJAMIN LEE WHORF. His dissertation was based on ethnological field research among the Hausa of Nigeria. In 1946 he began his teaching career at the University of Minnesota, joined the anthropology department of Columbia University in 1948 and moved to Stanford University in 1962, where he remained until his retirement in 1985.

Although early in his career he published an ethnographic monograph, *The Influence of Islam on a Sudanese Religion*, a revised version of his dissertation, virtually all his major subsequent research and writing has been in linguistics, concentrated primarily in two areas, the genetic classification of languages (including the theory and methodology on which it is based) and language typology and universals (diachronic as well as synchronic). In 1948 he began work on the genetic classification of African languages. A series of seven journal articles (1949-1950) plus additional material was published as a separate volume in 1955, *Studies in African Linguistic Classification*. A revised and substantially consolidated classification appeared in *The Languages of Africa*, which grouped all the indigenous languages of the continent into four macro-families. Despite some initial resistance, Greenberg's classification, at least in its general outlines, soon won over most Africanists (linguists as well as others), though significant revision of the subgrouping within the macro-families has taken place and a number of controversies and uncertainties still remain.

Because of his success in classifying African languages, Greenberg has since the 1960s applied his methods (in particular mass comparison) to other areas of the world whose language classification had proved recalcitrant, notably the South Pacific and the Americas. He published *The Indo-Pacific Hypothesis* in 1971, dealing with the former, and *Language in the Americas* in 1987, which offered a radical reclassification of all indigenous languages of the Western Hemisphere. The latter, though by no means without influential supporters, has aroused much controversy, and it remains to be seen whether it eventually receives the same degree of general acceptance as his African classification.

Greenberg has also made a lasting contribution to the study of linguistic typology and universals. In 1954 he published "A quantitative approach to the morphological typology of language" and in 1957 "Order of affixing: a study in general linguistics" (in *Essays in Linguistics*), in which he argued for typological comparison of languages and the investigation of language universals. In 1961 he participated in a Conference on Language Universals and two years later edited *Universals of Language*, consisting of papers presented there, including his own "Some universals of grammar with particular reference to the order of meaningful elements," which had considerable influence on the subsequent study of syntactic universals. In 1978 he edited a four-volume anthology, *Universals of Human Language*, to which he contributed the introduction plus several additional articles.

Among Greenberg's many honors and distinctions are the Haile Selassie I Prize for African Research (1967) and the presidencies of the African Studies Association (1964-1965) and the Linguistic Society of America (1976).

MAJOR WORKS: *The Influence of Islam on a Sudanese Religion* (New York: 1946); "A quantitative approach to the morphological typology of language" in: R.F. Spencer (editor), *Method and Perspective in Anthropology: Papers in honor of Wilson D. Wallis* (Minneapolis: 1954), pp. 192-220; *Studies in African Linguistic Classification* (New Haven: 1955); *Essays in Linguistics* (Chicago: 1957); (editor) *Universals of Language* (Cambridge, Mass.: 1963); *The Languages of Africa* (Bloomington: 1963); *Language, Culture and Communication* (edited by Anwar S. Dil) (Stanford: 1971); "The Indo-Pacific hypothesis," *Current Trends in Linguistics*, vol. 8 (1971), pp. 807-871; (editor) *Universals of Human Language* [4 vols.] (Stanford: 1978); *Language in the Americas*

(Stanford: 1987); *On Language: Selected Writings of Joseph H. Greenberg* (edited by Keith Denning and Suzanne Kemmer) (Stanford: 1990).

SOURCE: Anwar S. Dil, "Introduction" to: Joseph Greenberg, *Language, Culture and Communication* (edited by Anwar S. Dil) (Stanford: 1971), pp. xi-xiv.

Morris Goodman

Griaule, Marcel. Ethnologist. Born in Aisy-sur-Armençon (France) 16 May 1898, died 23 February 1956. Griaule was one of the most famous of French ethnographers. His work on the Dogon is particularly renowned.

Conversations with the Ethiopian, Agagnaou Enguédo, in the mid-1920s are said to have stimulated him and decided his career. He attended the École Nationale des Langues Orientales Vivantes, which awarded him a degree in Abyssinian studies in 1927. The next year he led an expedition to Ethiopia in the course of which much research was accomplished and many important manuscripts and objects collected.

Griaule was associated with the famous Mission Dakar-Djibouti that surveyed fifteen African countries between 1931 and 1933. This enormously productive expedition resulted in a massive amount of important research, including Griaule's *doctorat ès lettres* at the University of Paris, *Masques dogons*.

Griaule also organized additional expeditions—the Mission Sahara-Soudan (1935), the Mission Sahara-Cameroun (1936-1937), and the Mission Niger-lac Iro (1938-1939). Numerous publications came out of these expeditions, by Griaule himself and also by associates.

Increasingly, Griaule's own work came to concentrate on the Dogon of Mali, and especially on the Dogon living in the village of Bandiagara. His most famous work is probably *Dieu d'eau*, which consists of a series of interviews with the Dogon "sage," Ogotemmêli. The work, written in a popular style, demonstrated the richness and complexity of Dogon religious thought. Implicitly the work contradicted all simple schema concerning the nature of "primitive religion," and for many *Dieu d'eau* was thus a revelation.

In recent years, however, there has been much comment on the essentially *colonial* nature of much of Griaule's work, and its reliability has been called into question.

MAJOR WORKS: *Masques dogons* [originally his thesis, University of Paris] (Paris: 1938) (= *Travaux et mémoires de l'Institut d'Ethnologie de l'Université de Paris*, vol. 33); *Les flambeurs d'hommes* (Paris: 1934) [tr.: *Abyssinian Journey* (London: 1935); *Burners of men* (Philadelphia: 1935); *Die lebende Fackel: Menschen und Geister in Abessinien* (Berlin: 1936); *Torce d'uomini in Etiopia* (Milan: 1936)]; *Les Saô légendaires* (Paris: 1943); *Dieu d'eau: entretiens avec Ogotemmêli* (Paris: 1948) [tr.: *Conversations with Ogotemmêli: an Introduction to Dogon Religious Ideas* (London: 1965)]; (with Germaine Dieterlen) *Le renard pâle* (Paris: 1965).

SOURCES: *Ethnologiques: hommages à Marcel Griaule* (Paris: 1987) [contains bibliography, pp. xxix-xxxvi]; Jean-Paul Lebeuf, "Marcel Griaule," *Revue de Paris*, vol. 63 (May 1956), pp. 131-136; P. Champion, "Marcel Graiule," *Journal de la Société des Africanistes*, vol. 36 (1956), pp. 267-190 [includes bibliography]; James Clifford, "Power and dialogue in ethnography: Marcel Griaule's initiation" in: George W. Stocking, Jr. (editor), *Observers Observed: Essays on Ethnographic Fieldwork* (Madison: 1983) (= *History of Anthropology*, vol. 1), pp. 121-156; Walter E.A. van Beek, "Dogon restudied: a field evaluation of the work of Marcel Griaule," *Current Anthropology*, vol. 32 (1991), pp. 139-167.

Griffin, James Bennett. Anthropologist, archaeologist, curator, scholar. Born in Atchinson (Kansas) 12 January 1905. Griffin received the Ph.B. and M.A. from the University of Chicago in 1927 and 1930, respectively; he received the Ph.D. from the University of Michigan in 1936. He spent the whole of his professional life associated with the University of Michigan Museum of Anthropology and the Department of Anthropology at that institution. He was Director of the Museum of Anthropology from 1946 to 1975, Professor of Anthropology from 1949 to 1976 and Chairman of the Department of Anthropology from 1972 to 1975 and became Curator Emeritus and Professor Emeritus in 1976. Since 1984 he has been a Research Associate of the National Museum of Natural History, Smithsonian Institution. During his tenure, and in large measure due to his leadership, the Museum of Anthropology became one of the outstanding centers of archaeological research in the world. Despite his association with many of the individuals who were counted as founders of what came to be called the "new" archaeology, he was an implacable foe of this movement and a trenchant critic of much of the research done under its banner.

Griffin has been a pivotal figure in the development of eastern North American archaeology and prehistory. Over the last sixty years he has developed an encyclopedic knowledge of the archaeology of one-half a continent. The great breadth of this knowledge is seen in his summary works on the region: "Cultural change and continuity in Eastern United States archaeology," *Archaeology of Eastern United States* and "Eastern North American archaeology: a summary." His knowledge of the southwest United States and Mesoamerica allowed for fruitful comparisons to be made and connections to be traced with prehistoric developments in the Southeast; his interest in Siberia likewise yielded insights about the archaeological sequences in Alaska. He has been a pioneer in the application of techniques from the physical and biological sciences to the solution of archaeological problems. He and Professor H.R. Crane, a physicist, established one of the first radiocarbon laboratories, the University of Michigan Radiocarbon Laboratory, in 1949; he and Professor A.A. Gordus, a chemist, developed techniques for trace elemental analyses of obsidian, cherts and other raw materials in the 1960s. During the 1960s and into the early 1970s he directed research programs in the Mid-Continent and Great Lakes regions that deployed geological and ecological methods in the service of archaeological research. Several generations of graduate students profited from this interdisciplinary collaboration and developed their dissertation topics from this research. His association with European colleagues and his membership on the Permanent Council and Executive Committee of the International Union of Prehistoric and Protohistoric Sciences opened additional research opportunities for himself and for students in Europe and the Soviet Union. Professor Griffin was a founder of the Society for American Archaeology. He served in every Society office, except Treasurer and Editor, including that of President (1951), and he received the highest awards the Society offers, The Fryxell Award (1980) and the Distinguished Service Award (1984). Among his other awards are the Distinguished Service Award and the Russel Lectureship from the University of Michigan. He received the Viking Medal in Archaeology in 1957. Indiana University bestowed the Sc.D. degree (*honoris causa*) on him in 1971. He was elected a member of the National Academy of Sciences in 1968.

MAJOR WORKS: *The Fort Ancient Aspect: Its Cultural and Chronological Position in Mississippi Valley Archaeology* (Ann Arbor: 1943); "Culture change and continuity in Eastern United States archaeology," *Papers of the Robert S. Peabody Foundation for Archaeology*, vol. 3 (1946), pp. 37-96; (with Philip Phillips and James A. Ford) *Archaeological Survey in the Lower Mississippi Alluvial Valley, 1940-1947* (Cambridge, Mass.: 1951) (= *Papers of the Peabody Museum of American Archaeology and Ethnology*, no. 25); (editor and contributor) *Archaeology of Eastern United States* (Chicago: 1952); "Some prehistoric connections between Siberia and America," *Science*, vol. 131 (1960), pp. 801-812; "Late Quaternary prehistory in the Northeastern woodlands" in: H.E. Wright, Jr. and David G. Frey (editors), *The Quaternary of the United States* (Princeton: 1965), pp. 655-669; "Hopewell and the dark black glass," *Michigan Archaeologist*, vol. 11 (1965), pp. 115-155; "Mesoamerican and the Eastern United States in prehistoric times" in: Robert Wauchope (editor), *Handbook of Middle American Indians*, vol. 4 (Austin: 1967), pp. 111-131; "Eastern North American archaeology: a summary," *Science*, vol. 156 (1967), pp. 175-191; "Late prehistory of the Ohio Valley," William C. Sturtevant (editor), *Handbook of North American Indians*, vol. 15 (1978), pp. 547-559; "Changing concepts of the prehistoric Mississippian cultures of the Eastern United States" in: R. Reid Badger and Lawrence A. Clayton (editors), *Alabama and the Borderlands* (Tuscaloosa: 1985), pp. 40-63.

SOURCES: James B. Griffin, "A commentary on some archaeological activities in the Mid-Continent, 1925-1975," *Mid-Continental Journal of Archaeology*, vol. 1 (1976), pp. 5-38; "An individual's participation in American archaeology," *Annual Review of Anthropology*, vol. 14 (1985), pp. 1-23; "The formation of the Society for American Archaeology," *American Antiquity*, vol. 50 (1985), pp. 261-271; George I. Quimby and Charles E. Cleland, "James Bennett Griffin: appreciation and reminiscences" in: Charles Cleland (editor), *Culture Change and Continuity: Essays in Honor of James Bennett Griffin* (New York: 1976), pp. xxi-xxxvii; Volney H. Jones, "James Bennett Griffin, archaeologist" in: Charles E. Cleland (editor), *Culture Change and Continuity: Essays in Honor of James Bennett Griffin* (New York: 1976), pp. xxxix-lxxvii; "James B. Griffin: 1957 Viking Fund Medalist in Archaeology," *American Antiquity*, vol. 23 (1958), p. 419; "Griffin, James Bennett" in: *Who's Who in America* (44th ed., Chicago: 1986-1987), vol. 1, p. 1114.

Christopher Peebles

Grottanelli, Vinigi Lorenzo.

Grottanelli, Vinigi Lorenzo. Ethnologist. Born in Avigliana, Province of Turin (Italy) 3 August 1912. Grottanelli graduated in economics from the University of Turin in 1933. His thesis on the human geography of the lower region of the Scebeli made possible his first stay in Equatorial Africa.

In 1935 he earned a degree in jurisprudence and from the year 1936 he devoted himself to ethnological studies and carried out numerous research projects in Africa. In 1937, when he was barely twenty-four, he was called to serve as Assistant Professor at the University of Rome, Department of Political Science.

As an anthropo-geographer, Grottanelli participated in the study mission to the basin of Lake Tana (Ethiopia) that was funded by the Reale Accademia d'Italia (Italian Royal Academy), of which he was an officer from 1936 to 1942. The academy also sponsored his research on the Mao and the Koma of southern and western Ethiopia.

In 1945 Grottanelli became inspector and then superintendent of the Museo Nazionale Preistorico Etnografico Luigi Pigorini (Luigi Pigorini National Museum of Prehistory and Ethnography). In 1947 he began teaching at the Propaganda Fide Pontifical Urbaniana University of Rome. In 1967 he became Professor of Ethnology at the University of Rome, Department of Philosophy and Letters. From 1957 to 1981 he was the director of the Ethnological Institute of the University of Rome, which continues to be the main Italian center for ethnological studies.

Grottanelli is to be considered an Africanist in the tradition of his teacher, Carlo Conti-Rossini. His theoretical positions can be traced to the Viennese school of which he is the most distinguished Italian disciple. Of the Cultural-Historical School Grottanelli accepted the anti-evolutionist thrust as well as the interest in the study of cultural diffusion and the practice of fieldwork. From the point of view of disciplinary organization he endorsed the separation between physical anthropology (a biological science) and ethnology (a philosophical science), while rejecting the thesis of primordial monotheism and of cultural stagnation proposed by WILHELM SCHMIDT.

In his writings on African and Oceanic peoples, Grottanelli explored the religious, artistic and ergological aspects of culture and focused especially on cultural dynamics and the methods of fieldwork.

Grottanelli wrote several celebrated works of cultural synthesis, for example, *Etnologica: l'uomo e la civiltá*. He also directed the sections on ethnology, anthropology, and prehistory of the *Dizionario enciclopedico italiano* and the *Enciclopedia universale dell'arte*.

In addition, Grottanelli conducted research in southern Somalia and Kenya (1951-1952) and some twelve study missions to Ghana (Nzima region) under the sponsorship of the Ministry of Foreign Affairs, the National Research Center and the University of Rome. He also undertook study trips to the Ivory Coast, Asia and the Americas and initiated and directed the Italian ethnological missions to Ghana and Mexico.

MAJOR WORKS: *Missione etnografica nel Vollega Occidentale: i Mao* (Rome: 1940); *Pescatori dell'Oceano Indiano* (Rome: 1955); (editor) *Etnologica: l'uomo e la civiltà* (Milan: 1965-1966); *Gerarchie etniche e conflitto culturale: saggi di etnologia nordest-africana* (Milan: 1976); (editor) *Una società guineana: gli Nzema* [2 vols.] (Turin: 1977-1978); *Storia universale dell'arte: Australia, Oceania, Africa nera* (Turin: 1987); *The Python Killer: Stories of Nzema Life* (Chicago: 1988).

SOURCES: B. Bernardi, *Uomo, cultura, società* (8th ed., Milan: 1985); A.R. Leone, "La chiesa, i cattolici e le scienze dell'uomo, 1860-1960" in: Pietro Clemente [et al.], *L'antropologia italiana: un secolo di storia* (Bari: 1985), pp. 53-96; E. Haberland (editor), [Festschrift for Vinigi Grottanelli], *Paideuma*, vol. 24 (1978).

Giorgio de Finis
[Translation from Italian: Gianna Panofsky]

Guáman Poma de Ayala, Felipe. Chronicler, ethnographer, folklorist, draftsman. Born in Huamanga (Peru) in 1534 or 1535, presumably died in Lima (Peru) 1615. The little that we know of his life comes from a 1,179-page letter written in his old age and addressed to the King of Spain. This illustrated manuscript was discovered in 1908 in the Royal Collection of the Library of Copenhagen. Since that time several other documents have been found that contain notes about the author, but these have not added much to the information about him.

From the text it can be deduced that Guáman Poma de Ayala was a *curaca* or native chief of lesser rank in a provincial zone. His Spanish, although precarious in its written form, must have been sufficiently fluent to allow him to serve as an intermediary between the local Spanish authorities and the native population of which he proclaimed himself defender. He was employed as a *lengua* (translator) on numerous occasions. In his letter he related how he accompanied Cristóbal de Albornoz, the *extirpador de idolatrías*, who had been commissioned to persecute natives who had deserted the Christian faith in the Bishopric of Huamanga. He retained this mediating position until his death, always fighting for a fair administration of justice and attempting to construct a society where Spaniards and natives would find convivial harmony and mutual respect.

Guáman Poma de Ayala's letter is the fruit of the constant and exhausting interaction of the two societies, united and divided by the system of exploitation. Guáman Poma de Ayala expresses this in an exceptional manner in both his text (written in Spanish and Quechua) and his drawings. The text and imagery deal above all with the direct and pithy expression of the problems of domination. In its form, it constitutes a valuable record of the Andean mentality in this difficult period of its history. As is expressed by the title of the work, the *Nueva Corónica* claimed to be a new kind of history of the Andes, from the creation of the world until shortly before the author's death. But it was intended as well to offer advice to the Spanish sovereign on the *"Buen Gobierno"* of his overseas subjects. With these interests in mind, Guáman Poma de Ayala gathered the oral traditions of his region and cast them as occurring to humanity in general, inserting the Incas and their predecessors in the Biblical narrative, which he reinterpreted completely. On each page of his account, there appeared a drawing that the Spanish text (or the phonetic rendering of Quechua) would comment on or explain. Especially when he describes the contemporary epoch, Guáman Poma de Ayala testifies to the daily features of colonial provincial life, denouncing abuses and proposing solutions.

This gigantic mental construction of the universe "as it should be" raises his work to a level of rarefied abstraction. He was one of the first American thinkers of continental significance.

MAJOR WORKS: *Nueva Corónica y Buen Gobierno* (Paris: 1936) [facsimile edition]; *El Primer Nueva Corónica y Buen Gobierno* (Mexico City: 1980) [critical edition by John Victor Murra and Rolena Adorno] [tr.: *Letter to a King: a Peruvian Chief's Account of Life under the Incas and under Spanish Rule* (New York: 1978)].

SOURCES: José Varallanos, *Guáman Poma de Ayala* (Lima: 1979); Raúl Porras Barrenechea, *El cronista indio Felipe Huaman Poma de Ayala* (Lima: 1948); Rolena Adorno, *Guáman Poma: Writing and Resistance in Colonial Peru* (Austin: 1986); Rolena Adorno (editor), *From Oral to Written Expression: Native Andean Chronicles of the Early Colonial Periods* (Syracuse: 1982); Mercedes López-Baralt, "La persistencia de las estructuras simbólicas andinas en los dibujos de Guáman Poma de Ayala," *Journal of Latin American Lore*, vol. 5 (1979), pp. 83-116; Raquel Chang-Rodriguez, *La apropiación del signo* (Tempe, Arizona: 1988); Emilio Mendizábal Losack, "Don Phelipe Guáman Poma de Ayala, Señor y Príncipe, último quellqacamayoc," *Revista del Museo Nacional*, vol. 30 (1961), pp. 228-330; Lorenzo López y Sebastián, "La iconografía imaginaria de las ciudades andinas en la Nueva Corónica y Buen Gobierno de Felipe Guáman" in: Francisco de Solano y Fermín del Pino (editors), *Homenaje a Gonzalo Fernández de Oviedo, Cronista de Indias, América y la España del siglo XVI* (Madrid: 1983), pp. 213-230; César Guardia Mayorga, *Vida y pasión de Waman Poma de Ayala* (Lima: 1980); Franklin Pease, "Prólogo" to: Felipe Guáman Poma de Ayala, *Nueva Corónica y Buen Gobierno* (Caracas: 1980), pp. ix-lxxiii.

Luis Millones
[Translation from Spanish: Robert B. Marks Ridinger]

Gunther, Erna. Anthropologist, museum director. Born in Brooklyn (New York) 9 November 1896, died in Seattle (Washington) 25 August 1982. Gunther attended

Barnard College, graduating with a B.A. in English in 1919. Her M.A. from Columbia (1920), however, was in anthropology; like many of her contemporaries in the discipline, she changed interests after taking a course from FRANZ BOAS. (Like a surprising number of his favorite students, she was a child of immigrants and spoke fluent German.) In 1921 she married fellow Boasian LESLIE SPIER and moved with him to the University of Washington. Her Coast Salish studies began shortly after their arrival in Seattle and were influenced by Boas's giving her the Puget Sound research notes of his late student HERMAN HAEBERLIN.

Employed periodically as an instructor by the University of Washington from 1923 on, Gunther could not obtain a permanent position there until after her 1930 divorce from Spier. He left the university and she became both chair of the two-person department and director of the Washington State Museum (also located on campus). Her Ph.D. from Columbia had been awarded in 1928 at the publication of her diffusionist dissertation on the first-salmon ceremony in North America.

Gunther engaged in field trips to the Olympic Peninsula's Klallam and Makah reservations from 1924 until about 1935. Increasingly, however, her duties as chair and director absorbed her time, and her research and publication efforts lessened. Gunther raised awareness of (and funds for) her twin charges by giving numerous talks to the public, appearing on radio programs and eventually hosting her own television shows.

Her interests within anthropology became more focused over time; American Indians gave way to Northwest Coast Indians, and all other interests paled before native fine arts. First as a museum curator, organizing exhibits, but subsequently in her research activities as well, Gunther studied the material forms, the cultural contexts, and the aesthetic significance of Northwest Coast art. The 1950s saw her produce a number of museum catalogs on Northwest exhibits, while during the following decade she published several articles on the artistic traditions of various Northwest peoples. Later still came statements on the place of fine arts in primitive cultures.

Other major contributions to the anthropology of the Northwest Coast were her translations (from the German) of Aurel Krause's book on the Tlingit (Seattle: 1956), and Adrian Jacobson's account of his Alaskan expedition (Chicago: 1977).

From early on, Gunther campaigned against widespread (and widely accepted) racism toward Washington's Indian peoples. This did not endear her to some members of the state legislature, the powers of which included setting the university's budget. Thus, she likewise became unpopular with certain elements of the university administration. Her habit of speaking out and frequently being interviewed, which had done so much good for the museum under her directorship, worked against her personally when she allowed political issues to surface. It is possible that the anthropology department and the museum suffered, in a budgetary sense, due to dislike for Gunther. She was forced from the department chair in 1955 and lost the museum directorship in 1962. Especially in the case of the directorship, there seems to have been little justification for this move, for she faced mandatory retirement in only four more years. Gunther had held the two posts 25 and 32 years, respectively, during periods of considerable growth and achievement.

In 1966 she resigned, rather than retire, and accepted the post of chair in the University of Alaska at Fairbanks' anthropology department. Within three years she was back in Seattle, retired at last and continuing her advocacy for Northwest Coast Indians and their arts.

MAJOR WORKS: *Klallam Ethnography* (Seattle: 1927); *A Further Analysis of the First Salmon Ceremony* (Seattle: 1928); (with H. Haeberlin) *The Indians of Puget Sound* (Seattle: 1930); *Ethnobotany of Western Washington* (Seattle: 1945); "The Shaker religion of the Northwest" in: Marian W. Smith (editor), *The Indians of the Urban Northwest* (New York: 1949), pp. 37-76; "Art in the life of primitive peoples" in: James A. Clifton (editor), *Introduction to Cultural Anthropology* (Boston: 1968), pp. 77-114; "Northwest Coast Indian art" in: Charlotte M. Otten (editor) *Anthropology and Art* (Garden City: 1971), pp. 318-340; *Indian Life on the Northwest Coast of North America as Seen by the Early Explorers and Fur Traders During the Last Decades of the Eighteenth Century* (Chicago: 1977).

SOURCES: Viola E. Garfield and Pamela T. Amoss, "Erna Gunther (1896-1982)," *American Anthropologist*, vol. 86 (1984), pp. 394-399; Lenore Ziontz, "Erna Gunther and social activism: profit and loss for a state museum," *Curator*, vol. 29 (1986), pp. 307-315; Pamela T. Amoss, "Erna Gunther" in: Ute Gacs [et al.] (editors), *Women Anthropologists: a Biographical Dictionary* (New York: 1988), pp. 133-139.

David Lonergan

Györffy, István. Born in Karcag (Hungary) 11 February 1884, died in Budapest (Hungary) 3 October 1939. Györffy was one of Hungary's outstanding scholars of national ethnography and is still its best known and most popular representative. Györffy was mainly interested in the history and origins of Hungarian peasant culture. Most of his predecessors and contemporaries were seeking answers to historical questions through comparison and analysis of the geographical distribution of "cultural elements" and by arranging individual cultural traits into "historical layers." In contrast, Györffy, in an innovative way, turned to archival sources, old maps, and travelers' accounts and tried to reconstruct the everyday life of former generations. Cultural change was for him a concrete historical process. By combining the results of his fieldwork with historical research, he painted a vivid picture of 18th- and 19th-century ranching and herding on the Hungarian Great Plain (the Alföld), of farming techniques and the organization of work in the agro-towns and of buildings and communal organization in the agrarian settlements.

Györffy himself was born in an agricultural town in the Alföld, into a family of craftsmen and farmers, and in his works he drew on his childhood experiences. He studied both geography and history. In his historical works he refuted the romantic notion that there were direct connections among the peasants' life style, artistic expressions around the turn of the century and the culture of the pre-conquest (pre-896) Hungarian nomads. Instead, he stressed the importance of new developments brought about during the early modern age, such as the evolvement of large-scale ranching on the Alföld in the 16th and 17th centuries. To clarify some nomadic traits in the herdsmen's way of life, he did fieldwork in Anatolia to study vestiges of nomadism. His research on folk art and folk costume showed a connection among 19th-century modernization, *embourgeoisement* and the development of colorful art forms among Hungarian peasants. His book on the ornamental *szűr*, a coat made of coarse woolen cloth and richly decorated with appliqué-work and embroidery, demonstrated that its characteristic decoration developed in the early- and mid-19th century.

Györffy founded the Department of Ethnography at the University of Budapest and trained many excellent students.

In the 1930s Hungarian researchers compiled a four-volume handbook categorizing, by subject, available information on the peasants' cultural life prior to the time of the Industrial Revolution. Györffy co-edited the first two volumes, which dealt with material aspects, and authored the chapters on farming and dress.

MAJOR WORKS: *Nagykunsági krónika* [*Nagykunság Chronicle*] (Karcag: 1922); *Magyar népi himzések I.A cifraszűr* [*Hungarian Folk Embroidery: the Ornamental Szűr*] (Budapest: 1930); "Gazdálkodás" ["Farming"] in: *A magyarság néprajza* [*Ethnography of the Hungarian People*], vol. 2 (Budapest: 1934), pp. 15-273; *Magyar nép–magyar föld: összegyűjtött tanulmányok* [*The Hungarian People–Hungarian Land: Collected Works*] (Budapest: 1942); *Magyar falu–magyar ház: összegyűjtött tanulmányok* [*The Hungarian Village–the Hungarian House: Collected Works*] (Budapest: 1943); *Matyó népviselet* [*Costumes of the Matyó Region*] (edited by Edit Fél) (Budapest: 1956).

SOURCES: Attila Selmeczi-Kovács, *Györffy István* (Budapest: 1981); Tibor Bellon (editor), *A Magyar nép tudósa* [*Scholar of the Hungarian People*] (Karcag: 1979); Tibor Bellon and László Szabó (editors), *Györffy István: az Alföld kutatója* [*István Györffy: the Researcher of the Hungarian Great Plains*] (Karcag and Szolnok: 1988).

Tamás Hofer
[Translation from Hungarian: Ildiko D. Nowak]

h

Haas, Mary R. Anthropologist, linguist, Americanist. Born in Richmond (Indiana) 23 January 1910. Haas did her graduate studies in anthropological linguistics under the direction of EDWARD SAPIR, receiving her doctorate at Yale in 1935. Her first fieldwork—carried out with her fellow student and first husband, MORRIS SWADESH—was with the Nitinat of British Columbia. For her doctoral research, however, she went to Louisiana to work with the lone surviving speaker of Tunica; her grammar of that language is a classic, and she subsequently published a dictionary and text collection as well. Her work on Tunica launched her career as the principal authority on languages of the native southeastern United States, including Natchez and several members of the Muskogean family. In 1958 Haas published the first conclusive evidence for a relationship of the Wiyot and Yurok languages, in northwestern California, to the Algonquian family; and her other works have ranged over a broad variety of North American linguistic families.

Between 1940 and 1948, in response to the national need for expertise on languages of the Far East, Haas carried out work on Thai and was eventually appointed Lecturer in Thai at Berkeley. Many classroom materials were prepared during this period in collaboration with her second husband, Heng R. Subhanka. From 1948 onward Haas held a regular appointment at Berkeley, continuing work on Thai (and Burmese) but also returning increasingly to her interests in general and American Indian linguistics. In 1953 she was instrumental in founding the Survey of California Indian Languages at Berkeley, and was program coordinator of that project until her retirement. This program sent several academic generations of linguists into the field; salvaged much priceless linguistic and cultural data; and produced whole shelves of grammars, dictionaries and text collections. From 1957 until Haas's retirement in 1977, she was Professor of Linguistics, serving for several years as department chair. In a period when few women achieved such academic honors, she was also President of the Linguistic Society of America in 1963.

Haas has been recognized as a leader in anthropological linguistics not only because of her work on American Indian languages but also because of her pioneering research in ethnolinguistic and sociolinguistic topics, including men's and women's speech, word taboos, word games, kinship vocabulary and language contact. She has shown how a reconstructed proto-language can be, in her words, "a glorious artifact, ... far more precious than anything an archaeologist can ever hope to unearth." Her later work has also focused on questions of ancient diffusion among languages, opening the possibility of reconstructing details of contact among the diverse prehistoric languages and cultures of Native America.

MAJOR WORKS: *Tunica* (New York: 1941); (with H.R. Subhanka) *Spoken Thai I-II* (New York: 1946-1948); *Tunica Texts* (Berkeley: 1950); *Tunica Dictionary* (Berkeley: 1953); *Thai Reader* (Washington: 1954); *Thai Vocabulary* (Washington: 1955); *The Thai System of Writing* (Washington: 1956); (with G.V. Grekoff [et al.]) *Thai-English Student's Dictionary* (Stanford: 1964); *The Prehistory of Languages* (The Hague: 1969); *Language, Culture, and History* (Stanford: 1978).

SOURCE: William Shipley, "Introduction" to: William Shipley (editor), *In Honor of Mary Haas* (Berlin: 1988), pp. vii-x.

William Bright

Haddon, A.C. (Alfred Cort). Zoologist, anthropologist. Born in London (England) 24 May 1855, died in Cambridge (England) 20 April 1940. Haddon is regarded as the father of anthropology at the University of Cambridge.

The son of a London printer, Haddon worked in the family business until he was twenty years old. His interest in natural history, and reputed inability as a businessman, led to his attending Cambridge. He took an honours degree in natural history in 1878; after a brief period as curator of the Zoological Museum at Cambridge, he was in 1880 named professor of zoology at Dublin's Royal College of Science.

Initially interested in marine biology, Haddon gradually involved himself in anthropology. During an 1888-1889 field trip to the Torres Straits, between New Guinea and Australia, Haddon was exposed to native cultures that he came to fear would change beyond recognition before they could be recorded. Upon his return to Great Britain, he presented several papers on the peoples of the Torres Straits, attracting the attention of Sir JAMES G. FRAZER. By 1894 Haddon was hired as a part-time lecturer in physical anthropology at Cambridge, holding that position as well as his chair at Dublin. He took a Sc.D. at Cambridge in 1897.

For several years after his marine biology field trip, Haddon worked to organize and finance a major anthropological expedition to the Torres Straits, which he eventually led during 1898-1899. It was the first multidisciplinary expedition of its kind and was a milestone in the history of anthropology. Among his six co-workers were W.H.R. RIVERS and C.G. SELIGMAN; the six-volume report of the expedition, which covered the Straits and areas of neighboring New Guinea, included ethnological, psychological, linguistic, medical and physiological data as well as accounts of decorative arts and religion.

Haddon was made a lecturer in anthropology by 1900 and was elected a fellow of Christ's College (his old school) in 1901. The added income allowed him to resign the zoology chair in Dublin. In 1904 he was given a readership, but the Cambridge professorship in anthropology for which Haddon so strongly argued was not established until 1933, after his retirement. He was made a Fellow of the Royal Society in 1899 and was repeatedly honored by his discipline, serving as president of the Royal Anthropological Institute from 1902 to 1904 and as president of the anthropology section of the British Association for the Advancement of Science in 1902 and 1905. The Royal Anthropological Institute awarded Haddon its Huxley Medal in 1920 and its Rivers Memorial Medal in 1924.

At Cambridge, Haddon was a major force in the development of an anthropological curriculum and was also an important figure in the Museum of Archaeology and Ethnology. His own chief interests were in physical anthropology and the decorative arts, two areas that are highly amenable to museum research and display.

Haddon was an educational and welfare worker with the British Army in World War I and retired from active teaching at Cambridge in 1925. He remained a productive writer and museum administrator until his death.

MAJOR WORKS: *Introduction to the Study of Embryology* (London: 1887); *Decorative Arts of British New Guinea* (Dublin: 1894); *Evolution in Art* (London: 1895); *The Study of Man* (London: 1898); *Head-hunters: Black, White, and Brown* (London: 1901); (editor and major author) *Reports of the Cambridge Anthropological Expedition to Torres Straits* [6 vols.] (Cambridge: 1901-1935); *Races of Man and their Distribution* (London: 1905); *History of Anthropology* (London: 1910); *Wanderings of Peoples* (Cambridge: 1911); (with James Hornell) *Canoes of Oceania* [3 vols.] (Honolulu: 1936-1938).

SOURCES: A.H. Quiggin, "Haddon, Alfred Cort" in: David L. Sills (editor), *International Encyclopedia of the Social Sciences* (New York: 1968-1979), vol. 6, pp. 303-304; H.J. Fleure, "Haddon, Alfred Cort" in: *Dictionary of National Biography*, 5th supplement (Oxford: 1949), pp. 382-384; A.H. Quiggin and E.S. Fegan, "Alfred Cort Haddon, 1855-1940," *Man*, vol. 40 (1940), pp. 97-100.

David Lonergan

Haeberlin, Herman. Anthropologist. Born in Akron (Ohio) 11 September 1891, died in Cambridge (Massachusetts) 12 February 1918. Haeberlin was a student of FRANZ BOAS and, in his short career as an anthropologist, he made contributions in ethnology, linguistics and archaeology.

Haeberlin studied anthropology at the Universities of Leipzig and Berlin, his family having returned to Germany while he was still a boy. In 1913 he met Boas during the latter's visit to Berlin, and in 1914 Haeberlin enrolled in doctoral studies under Boas at Columbia University. He obtained his Ph.D. in anthropology, and from 1916 until his death was a research fellow at Columbia.

Haeberlin interpreted culture as both a historical and a psychological phenomenon and defended this approach in a 1915 response to ALFRED L. KROEBER's "Professions" in the *American Anthropologist*. He was particularly interested in questions of aesthetics, and did considerable museum research on the material cultures of the Pueblo and Northwest Coast Indians. His fieldwork consisted of a brief archaeological project in Puerto Rico, and a longer period of research among the Coast Salish Indians of Puget Sound.

Had he lived longer, Haeberlin would likely have taken a place of honor among the Boasians of his generation. With wide-ranging interests and a thorough grounding in anthropology, he had at age twenty-six already made a good start.

MAJOR WORKS: "The idea of fertilization in the culture of the Pueblo Indians," *Memoirs of the American Anthropological Association*, vol. 3 (1916), pp. 1-55; "The theoretical foundation of Wundt's folk psychology," *The Psychological Review*, vol. 23 (1916), pp. 279-302; "Sbetetda'q, a shamanistic performance of the Coast Salish," *American Anthropologist*, n.s., vol. 20 (1918), pp. 249-257; "Types of reduplication in the Salish dialects," *International Journal of American Linguistics*, vol. 1 (1918), pp. 154-174; "Principles of esthetic form in the art of the North Pacific Coast," *American Anthropologist*, n.s., vol. 20 (1918), pp. 258-264; *Indians of Puget Sound* (Seattle: 1930) (= *University of Washington Publications in Anthropology*, vol. 4) [a posthumous collaboration with Erna Gunther].

SOURCE: Franz Boas, "In memoriam: Herman Karl Haeberlin," *American Anthropologist*, n.s., vol. 21 (1919), pp. 71-74.

David Lonergan

Hale, Horatio Emmons. Philologist, ethnologist, attorney. Born in Newport (New Hampshire) 3 May 1817, died in Clinton (Ontario) 28 December 1896. Son of Sarah Josepha Buell Hale (1790-1879), journalist and editor of *Godey's Lady's Book* and feminist. Hale early manifested an interest in Indians and a talent for languages, entered Harvard at age sixteen and studied Oriental languages and literature. During his freshman year he made his first field study of an unknown language, recording from Indians encamped nearby a vocabulary of an Algonquian dialect of Maine that he demonstrated to be a Micmac variant. His first publication *Remarks on the Language of the St. John's or Wlastukweek Indians ...* is now quite rare.

After graduation with the Harvard class of 1837, he was appointed philologist of the U.S. South Seas Exploring Expedition. During this voyage (1838-1842), Hale collected vocabularies and sketched grammars of Oceanic dialects. He confirmed the affinity of Malayan and Polynesian languages and advanced a theory based on phonetic shifts to establish the eastward migration of Polynesian peoples. Nor did he neglect Aboriginal languages of Australia.

Put ashore in Oregon territory he worked his way homeward mapping the ethnography and linguistic diversity of native peoples from California to British Columbia. This accomplishment attracted the admiration of Americanists from ALBERT GALLATIN to FRANZ BOAS.

Returning to Philadelphia, he wrote *Ethnography and Philology*, the first scientific report of the expedition to be published. After several *Wanderjahren* in Europe, in 1853 he studied law, a family tradition, married, tried Chicago, and settled in Clinton, Ontario, as administrator of the estate of his wife's father. Conveyancing was not a lucrative practice.

At age fifty an original interest in linguistics and ethnological research was rekindled by the presence nearby at Brantford, Ontario, of speakers of Iroquoian languages. And there was a language called Tutelo of unknown affiliation.

In his forty-one contributions to science, which Boas wrote would "rank among the best work done in America," Hale made two important discoveries. He demonstrated the relationship of Tutelo, once spoken in Virginia, to the Siouan linguistic stock and reported his finding to the American Philosophical Society, to which he was elected in 1872.

The second discovery was finding Mohawk and Onondaga versions of the ritual texts of the Iroquois ceremony for mourning and installing League chiefs, of which he traced the Mohawk text to an 18th-century native source. Hale translated and edited these texts for publication as *The Iroquois Book of Rites*. This "Iroquois Veda," as he styled it, was a major contribution to Iroquois studies, it was read widely and it sparked much later research.

Hale and a committee of chiefs worked on the history of their confederacy, he recorded the mnemonic belts of *wampum* and their symbolism and in 1871 persuaded the chiefs to sit for their portrait with the wampum records, distributing copies to JOHN WESLEY POWELL, William Martin Beauchamp, LEWIS HENRY MORGAN and E.B. TYLOR in Oxford. Hale and Morgan were contemporaries and correspondents.

Having resumed linguistic work, Hale concentrated on the Iroquoian family. He concluded that Mohawk was the senior language of the Five Nations, that Huron more nearly resembled proto-Iroquoian and he identified Cherokee as Iroquoian. He worked out tribal movements, anticipated glottochronology and approached a theory of phonemes in a study of intermediates in Mohawk. In 1886 he advanced one of the more sensible theories of languages and their diversity in a study of children's private tongues. He dispelled then current notions of primitivism by demonstrating that native speakers were powerful classifiers.

He planned and directed a program to investigate and publish reports on the Northwestern tribes of Canada as Secretary of a Committee of the British Association for the Advancement of Science (1884). As its research director he edited seven reports and launched Boas on his long career of fieldwork on the Northwest Coast. Boas later wrote a tribute to his mentor.

He was elected Vice-President, Section H of American Association for the Advancement of Science (1888); Fellow of the Royal Society of Canada (1889); President, American Folklore Society (1893); and Vice-President, Anthropology Section, British Association for the Advancement of Science (1897), an honor he declined in failing health. His manuscripts and field notes were lost in a fire that destroyed his Clinton study. He was buried in Clinton, and a memorial plaque was erected in 1963 in the yard of St. Paul's Anglican Church.

MAJOR WORKS: *Remarks on the Language of the St. John's or Wlastukweek Indians, with a Penobscot Vocabulary* (Boston: 1834), pp. 1-8; *Ethnography and Philology* (Philadelphia, 1846; reprinted, Ridgewood, N.J.: 1968) (= *U.S. Exploring Expedition, 1838-1842*, vol. 6); *The Iroquois Book of Rites* (Philadelphia: 1883; reprinted, Toronto: 1963); "The Tutelo tribe and language," *Proceedings of the American Philosophical Society*, vol. 21 (1884), pp. 1-47.

SOURCES: Paul S. Boyer, "Sarah Josepha Hale (1788-1879)," *Notable American Women*, vol. 2, pp. 110-114; *Memorials of the Class of 1837, Harvard University* (Cambridge, Mass.: 1887); *Proceedings and Transactions of the Royal Society of Canada* (Ottawa: 1894); Franz Boas, "Horatio Hale," *The Month in Literature, Art and Life*, vol. 1, no. 3 (March 1897), pp. 262-263; William N. Fenton, "Horatio Hale (1817-1896)" in: Horatio Hale, *Iroquois Book of Rites* (2nd ed., New York: 1963), pp. vii-xxvii; Albert Gallatin, "Hale's Indians of North-west America, and vocabularies," *Transactions of the American Ethnological Society*, vol. 2 (1848), pp. 1-130; Jacob W. Gruber, "Horatio Hale and the development of American anthropology," *Proceedings of the American Philosophical Society*, vol. 111 (1967), pp. 5-37; Adrienne L. Kaeppler, "Anthropology and the U.S. Exploring Expedition" in: Herman J. Viola and Carolyn Margolis (editors), *Magnificent Voyagers ... 1838-1842* (Washington: 1985), pp. 119-147; William Stanton, *The Great United States Exploring Expedition of 1838-1842* (Berkeley: 1975).

William N. Fenton

Hall, Edward T. (Edward Twitchell). Anthropologist, educator, author, consultant. Born in Webster Groves (Missouri) 16 May 1914. Hall received a Ph.D. from Columbia University in 1942 and held teaching positions at the University of Denver (1946-1948), Bennington College (1948-1951), Foreign Service Institute (1950-1955), Washington School of Psychiatry (1952-1956, 1960-1963), Harvard Graduate School of Business Administration (1962), Illinois Institute of Technology (1963-1967) and Northwestern University (1967-1977). Hall also has served as a consultant to multinational corporations, departments of the U.S. government and private foundations.

Hall is best known for his work in the fields of intercultural communication and international relations, which began in the early 1950s (1950-1955) when he served as director of the U.S. State Department's "Point Four" training program for technicians assigned to overseas duty. Hall attributed difficulties experienced by technicians working overseas to failures in cross-cultural communication, and he believed that such failures were serious impediments to social well-being, economic growth, and world peace. From the 1950s, Hall devoted his life to understanding communication systems. Although his work is often theoretical, his objectives are mainly pragmatic.

In his first book, *The Silent Language*, Hall set forth a theory of culture as communication. Hall's thesis in this book is that culture is not a monolithic entity, but a network of biologically based "primary message systems" that humans extend and enhance through social communication. At the heart of Hall's theory is a distinction between levels of cultural experience (a concept that extends CLYDE KLUCKHOHN's distinction between explicit and implicit culture). The three levels—formal, informal and technical—are characterized by explicit, implicit and expert knowledge, respectively. Experience at each level is learned, shared and communicated differently, and different cultures apportion experience to each of these levels in different ways.

Beginning with his early work and continuing throughout his life, Hall has viewed communication as a complex system involving much more than language. He is most interested in the nonverbal and contextual aspects of communication, and he believes that many failures in international relations are due to ignorance of culturally bound contextual variables. For Hall, two of the most important contextual dimensions of communication are space and time, and much of his work over the past twenty-five years explicates the role of space and time as key factors in intercultural communication. In *The Hidden Dimension*, Hall defined "proxemics" as the study of the human use of space within the context of culture. His most important work in the field of proxemics concerns cross-cultural differences in the perception and use of personal and organizational space. His study of time as a contextual variable in communication systems has yielded several important and original concepts including monochronic and polychronic time (i.e., time experienced as linear and segmented versus time experienced as cyclical and nonsegmented), high-context and low-context cultures (i.e., cultures in which most of the information content of communication is embedded in contextual variables versus cultures in which most of the information is explicit and carried in language), and action chains (a concept borrowed from ethology that refers to an interlocking sequence of stimulus and response behaviors involving two or more persons and oriented toward some outcome that cannot be interrupted without jeopardizing the outcome). These concepts were presented in *Beyond Culture* and *The Dance of Life*.

In recent years, Hall and his partner Mildred Reed Hall have written a series of books applying Hall's theoretical work on intercultural communication to the field of international business. In these works, Hall and his partner enable businesspeople in the United States, France, Germany, and Japan to translate and interpret communication processes and events across one another's cultural boundaries. Hall's books have been translated into sixteen languages, and his work is often cited in social science and business textbooks.

Although Hall's major works are aimed generally at the educated public, his early writings were criticized nevertheless by academic colleagues, primarily on methodological grounds. Recently, as the importance of Hall's contributions to intercultural relations have become more evident, he has been defended by many anthropologists as one of the most original thinkers in 20th-century American anthropology and one of the great pioneers of anthropological practice in the business community. His work has been recognized by the Université Catholique de Louvain with the award of a *Doctor Honoris Causa* and by the American Anthropological Association with the first Edward J. Lehman Award for contributions to business, both in 1987.

MAJOR WORKS: *The Silent Language* (Garden City: 1959); *The Hidden Dimension* (Garden City: 1966); *Handbook for Proxemic Research* (Washington: 1974); (with Mildred Reed Hall) *The Fourth Dimension in Architecture: the Impact of Building on Man's Behavior* (Santa Fe: 1975); *Beyond Culture* (Garden City: 1976); *The Dance of Life: the Other Dimension of Time* (Garden City: 1983); (with Mildred Reed Hall) *Hidden Differences: Studies in International Communication* (Hamburg: 1983); (with Mildred Reed Hall) *Getting Over Frictions: Japanese-American Business* (Tōkyō: 1987); (with Mildred Reed Hall) *Hidden Differences: Doing Business with the Japanese* (Garden City: 1987).

SOURCES: Gary Blonston, "The translator," *Science*, vol. 6 (July/August 1985), pp. 79-85; "Edward Twitchell Hall, Jr.," *Contemporary Authors*, vol. 65-68 (1977), p. 270; Kenneth Friedman, "Learning the Arab's silent language," *Psychology Today*, vol. 13 (August 1979), pp. 45-54; Elizabeth Hall, "How cultures collide," *Psychology Today*, vol. 10 (July 1976), pp. 66-75; Michael Kolbenschlag, "Edward T. Hall: proxemics in the global village," *Human Behavior*, vol. 4 (December 1975), pp. 56-61; Carol Tarvis, "Edward T. Hall: a social scientist with a gift for solving human problems," *Geo* (March 1983), pp. 11-16.

Marietta L. Baba

Hallowell, Alfred Irving. Anthropologist. Born in Philadelphia (Pennsylvania) 28 December 1892, died in Wayne (Pennsylvania) 10 October 1974. Hallowell graduated from the Wharton School of Finance and Commerce of the University of Pennsylvania in 1914 with training mainly in commerce, economics and sociology and began a career as a social worker. Introduced to anthropology by FRANK G. SPECK, he shifted directions and began graduate studies in that field, completing his Ph.D. in 1924. Speck and FRANZ BOAS (whose Columbia University seminars Hallowell attended for a semester) gave Hallowell a deep appreciation of anthropology as a holistic discipline, while ALEXANDER A. GOLDENWEISER introduced him to Freud and psychoanalytic theory. His interests and talents eventually ranged across many subfields of anthropology, from material culture, folklore, myth and religion, kinship and social structure, ecology, personality and acculturation, to ethnohistory and the history of anthropology. Yet his diverse researches and writings had some strong unifying themes.

Regionally, he focused, like Speck, on Algonquian peoples: he did fieldwork with the St. Francis Abenaki at Odanak, Québec, in the 1920s and then in the 1930s, among the Cree and Ojibwa of Manitoba, with briefer visits to other related groups. His most enduring fieldwork ties were with the Berens River Ojibwa east of Lake Winnipeg, with whom he spent a succession of summers between 1930 and 1940 in fruitful collaboration with the band chief, WILLIAM BERENS. The study of social and historical change and its implications for culture and personality became a major area of interest; Hallowell's comparisons of Berens River communities from the river's isolated headwaters down to its mouth, and his explorations of the uses of projective tests (Rorschach and TAT) to measure personality differences among more and less acculturated Ojibwa dominated much of his writing from the mid-1930s on.

Perhaps most influential among anthropologists were Hallowell's analyses of the dynamic relationships between the self and its culturally constituted behavioral environment and of the cultural variability of concepts of the "person." Pursuing the implications of his finding that Ojibwa "persons" included other-than-human beings, Hallowell also critically elucidated some unanalyzed culturally constituted categories in anthropology, pointing out that "a thoroughgoing 'objective' approach to the study of cultures cannot be achieved solely by projecting upon those cultures categorical abstractions derived from Western thought" ("Ojibwa ontology, behavior and world view" [1960] in: *Contributions to Anthropology*, p. 359). In subsequent publications, Hallowell carried this perspective over to his studies of the history of his own discipline, as in his 1965 essay on "The history of anthropology as an anthropological problem" (*Contributions to Anthropology*, pp. 21-35).

Hallowell's teaching career centered on the University of Pennsylvania until he retired in 1962; he then served as visiting professor at several other institutions. His contributions were acknowledged with numerous honors and offices including the Viking Medal in anthropology, presidency of the American Anthropological Association, the American Folklore Society and the Society for Projective Techniques. He was a fellow of the National Academy of Sciences and of the American Philosophical Society, where his papers are now housed, and a board member of the Social Science Research Council and the American Council of Learned Societies, among others. He profoundly influenced a generation of scholars who have gone on to testify to his versatility through the diversity of their own careers—a point illustrated best perhaps, in the Festschrift volume, *Context and Meaning in Anthropology*, organized on the occasion of his retirement.

MAJOR WORKS: "Bear ceremonialism in the Northern Hemisphere," *American Anthropologist*, vol. 28 (1926), pp. 1-175; *The Role of Conjuring in Saulteaux Society* (Philadelphia: 1942); *Culture and Experience* (Philadelphia: 1955); "The beginnings of anthropology in America" in: Frederica de Laguna (editor), *Selected Papers from the American Anthropologist, 1888-1920* (Evanston: 1960), pp. 1-90; *Contributions to Anthropology: Selected Papers of A. Irving Hallowell* (Chicago: 1976).

SOURCES: Raymond D. Fogelson and Melford E. Spiro, Introduction to: Melford E. Spiro (editor), *Context and Meaning in Cultural Anthropology* (New York: 1965), pp. xv-xxii; "Bibliography of A. Irving Hallowell" in: Melford E. Spiro (editor), *Context and Meaning in Cultural Anthropology* (New York: 1965), pp. 417-425; R.D. Fogelson, George W. Stocking, Jr. [et al.], Introductions to sections of: *Contributions to Anthropology: Selected Papers of A. Irving Hallowell* (Chicago: 1976); "Supplementary bibliography of works by A. Irving Hallowell" in: *Contributions to Anthropology: Selected Papers of A. Irving Hallowell* (Chicago: 1976), pp. 531-534;

Melford E. Spiro, "A. Irving Hallowell, 1892-1974," *American Anthropologist*, vol. 78 (1976), pp. 608-611.

Jennifer S.H. Brown

Hamy, Théodore (Jules Ernest Théodore Hamy). Born in Boulogne-sur-Mer, Pas-de-Calais (France) 22 June 1842, died in Paris (France) 18 November 1908. A doctor of medicine, in 1868 Hamy became PAUL BROCA's assistant at the École des Hautes Etudes and presented a course at the Sorbonne broadly devoted to the comparative anatomy of the human races, tertiary man in the Americas and the theory of multiple centers of creation. Following an 1868 voyage to Egypt on the occasion of the opening of the Suez Canal, he published a revised translation of Charles Lyell's work, *The Geological Evidences of the Antiquity of Man*, to which he added his appropriate *Précis de paléontologie humaine*. Joining the Muséum d'Histoire Naturelle (Natural History Museum) as a naturalist's aide and assistant to the chair of anthropology, he undertook the publication of *Crania ethnica*, which appeared in sections in 1873 and as a complete volume in 1882. This work collected thirty-eight cranial and forty facial measurements from a significant group of skulls of different human populations. From a descriptive point of view, this effort constitutes the apex in the development of the field of craniometry.

After 1877 the direction of Hamy's activities was modified. The organization of exhibits of an ethnographic nature in the Palais de l'Industrie during the Universal Exposition established the need to create a permanent museum devoted to ethnography. A decision to appropriate the Palais du Trocadéro was made in 1879 and Hamy was named as chief conservator in charge of organizing the collections. In the same general line, in 1882 he founded the *Revue d'Ethnographie*, which was merged into *L'Anthropologie* in 1890. In 1892, Hamy succeeded Quatrefages as professor of anthropology at the Muséum National d'Histoire Naturelle.

In consequence, his researches derived a definite order from the historical ethnographic sources and the archives of the Museum d'Histoire Naturelle. He showed a special interest in the Société des Américanistes and published many contributions in the area of New World archaeology in the *Journal des Américanistes*, which had been founded in 1895.

MAJOR WORKS: *Précis de paléontologie humaine* (Paris: 1870); *Origines du Musée d'Ethnographie: histoire et documents* (Paris: 1889); *Crania ethnica: les crânes des races humaines* (Paris: 1882); *Questionnaire de sociologie* (Paris: 1888); *Anthropologie du Mexique: mission scientifique au Mexique et dans l'Amérique centrale* (Paris: 1891).

SOURCES: Henri Cordier, "Le docteur E.T. Hamy," *La Géographie* (1909), pp. 1-14; Henri Cordier, "Liste des ouvrages et mémoires publiés de 1866 à 1908 par le docteur Ernest-T. Hamy," *Nouvelles Archives du Museum d'Histoire naturelle, Paris*, 5th sér, vol. 1, no. 2 (1909), pp. xi-c; Théodore Reinach, *Notice sur la vie et les travaux de M. Ernest Hamy* (Paris: 1910); R. Verneau, "Le professeur E.-T. Hamy et ses prédécesseurs au Jardin des Plantes," *L'Anthropologie*, vol. 21 (1910), pp. 257-279; D. Ferembach, *History of Biological Anthropology in France (Part 2)* (Newcastle-upon-Tyne: 1987) (= *Occasional Papers, International Association of Human Biologists*, vol. 2, no. 2).

André Leguebe
[Translation from French: Timothy Eastridge and Robert B. Marks Ridinger]

Handy, Edward Smith Craighill. Ethnologist. Born 1892, died in Fairfax (Virginia) 26 December 1980. Handy received his Ph.D. from Harvard University in 1920 and immediately joined the staff of the Bernice P. Bishop Museum (Honolulu) and maintained that affiliation until his retirement.

Working most often with his wife, WILLOWDEAN CHATTERSON HANDY, he did much fieldwork to gather information about the plants grown by the native Hawaiians and about the culture and traditions of the people themselves. They also did ethnographic studies in the Marquesas, the Society Islands and elsewhere in the South Pacific region. Edward Handy traced the origins of the peoples of the South Pacific and the cultural interchanges of India and Southeast Asia with Polynesia.

MAJOR WORKS: *The Native Culture in the Marquesas* (Honolulu: 1923) (= *Bayard Dominick Expedition, Publication* no. 9; *Bernice P. Bishop Museum, Bulletin*, no. 9); "History and culture in the Society Islands," *Bernice P. Bishop Museum, Bulletin*, no. 79 (1930), pp. 1-110; "Problems of Polynesian origins," *Bernice P. Bishop Museum, Occasional Papers*, vol. 2, no. 8 (1930), pp. 1-27; *The Hawaiian Planter: His Plants, Methods and Areas of Cultivation* (Honolulu: 1940) (= *Bernice P. Bishop Museum, Bulletin*, no. 161.

SOURCES: "Who's who in Bishop Museum: Dr. and Mrs. E.S.C. Handy," *Ka 'Elele*, no. 13 (1 January 1965), p. 3; Katharine Luomala, "Deaths: Edward Smith Craighill Handy," *Anthropology Newsletter*, vol. 22, no. 5 (May 1981), p. 3.

Thomas L. Mann

Handy, Willowdean Chatterson. Ethnologist. Born in Louisville (Kentucky) 1889, died in Honolulu (Hawaii) 5 November 1965. Handy did her fieldwork while married to EDWARD S.C. HANDY. She worked with him to gather information about the plants grown by the native Hawaiians and about the culture and traditions of the people themselves. The two were also part of a Bishop Museum expedition to the Marquesas and Society Islands during 1920-1921, where she did fieldwork on tattooing and artistic traditions.

MAJOR WORKS: *Tattooing in the Marquesas* (Honolulu: 1922) (= *Bernice P. Bishop Museum, Bulletin*, no. 1); *L'art des Îles Marquises* (Paris: 1938); *Forever the Land of Men* (New York: 1965).

SOURCES: "Who's who in Bishop Museum: Dr. and Mrs. E.S.C. Handy," *Ka 'Elele*, no. 13 (1 January 1965), p. 3; "Mrs. Handy dies: South Seas expert," *Honolulu Advertiser* (6 November 1985); [Obituary], *Honolulu Star-Bulletin* (5 November 1965), p. 5.

Thomas L. Mann

Hansen, Henny Harald. Anthropologist. Born in Copenhagen (Denmark) 18 April 1900. Hansen was the first woman to become a fully trained anthropologist in Denmark in 1951, but by 1944 she was already associated with the Department of Ethnography at the National Museum of Denmark, where she was responsible for the department's large collection of costumes, in particular the costumes brought back by HENNING HASLUND-CHRISTENSEN from the Central Asian Expeditions in the 1930s. Hansen specialized in the study of Middle Eastern Muslim societies and did fieldwork in Yugoslavia (1952 and 1963), Iraq (1957), Bahrain (1960), Iran (1963), Turkey (1963) and Egypt (1966-1967). She was a pioneer of what was later to become anthropological women's studies in the Islamic world. As a fully participating observer she had the opportunity to see the veil from the inside, and, on the basis of her experiences as a woman in a number of Muslim societies, she has challenged the received opinion about the oppression of Muslim women and has argued that the veil serves the important function of protecting the women's social and personal integrity.

Apart from her scholarly work, for which she was awarded an honorary doctorate at the University of Copenhagen in 1979, she has written a number of popular books and articles about costumes from all over the world and about Muslim women.

MAJOR WORKS: *Mongol Costumes* (Copenhagen: 1960); *Klaededraktens kavalkade* (Copenhagen: 1954) [tr.: *Costume Cavalcade* (London and New York: 1956)]; *Allah's døtre: Blandt muhammedanske kvinder i Kurdistan* (Copenhagen: 1958) [tr.: *Daughters of Allah: among Muslim Women in Kurdistan* (London: 1960)]; *The Kurdish Woman's Life: Field Research in a Muslim Society, Iraq* (Copenhagen: 1961); *Investigations in a Shi'a Village in Bahrain* (Copenhagen: 1968); "Cliterodectomy: female circumcision in Egypt," *Folk*, vol. 14-15 (1973), pp. 15-27.

SOURCES: Lise Rishøj Pedersen, "Henny Harald Hansen," *Folk*, vol. 21-22 (1979-1980), pp. 5-10; Annie Hagen Eriksen, "Henny Harald Hansen: selected bibliography," *Folk*, vol. 21-22 (1979-1980), pp. 11-15; Lise Rishøj Pedersen, "Hansen, Henny Harald" in: *Dansk Biografisk Leksikon* (Copenhagen: 1980), vol. 5, pp. 622-623.

Jan Ovesen

Hardisty, William Lucas. Trader. Born ca. 1822 in Québec, died 16 January 1881 at Lachine (Québec). Hardisty was the chief trader in charge of the Mackenzie River District (Northwest Territories) for the Hudson's Bay Company. He was stationed at Fort Simpson on the Mackenzie River for seventeen years, and he was both a participant in and an observer of native life. Hardisty had first-hand experience with native culture through his mother, a woman of northern Algonquian ancestry, but his article on the Loucheux Indians also reflects the methodological reorientation associated with the first stage in the development of the social sciences. Hardisty's paper is one of the earliest accounts of the Loucheux Indians and, although it contains much personal prejudice, it follows the model for ethnological data collection outlined in the Smithsonian Institution's "Instructions for research relative to the ethnology and philology of America" (*Smithsonian Annual Report* (1863), pp. 2-47). His account, unlike those kept previously by missionaries, colonial administrators and fur traders, specifically recorded the information that "scientific ethnologists" considered necessary and relevant to a comprehensive description of "primitive man."

MAJOR WORK: "The Loucheux Indians," *Annual Report of the Smithsonian Institution* (1866), pp. 311-320.

SOURCES: Hudson's Bay Company correspondence collection, Smithsonian Institution Archives; Jennifer S.H. Brown, "William Lucas Hardisty" in: *Dictionary of Canadian Biography* (Toronto: 1966-), vol. 11, pp. 384-385.

Debra Lindsay

Haring, Douglas Gilbert. Anthropologist, sociologist, theologian. Born in Watkins Glen (New York) 6 August 1894, died in Syracuse (New York) 24 August 1970. With a B.S. in chemistry from Colgate in 1914, Haring turned to theology and in 1917 joined the mission field in Japan. After studying the Japanese language and culture and teaching underprivileged boys for three years, Haring became convinced of the need for further training. He received an M.A. in sociology from Columbia and a B.D. from Colgate-Rochester Divinity School and returned to Japan just after the great earthquake in 1923. After two years of teaching history at Tōkyō Gakuin he left the mission field, however, and became a columnist for the *Buffalo Evening News*. He also authored his first major publication, *The Land of Gods and Earthquakes*. Still not satisfied with his training, the turning point in his career came after he turned to anthropology for a year of intensive study under FRANZ BOAS, LESLIE SPIER and RUTH BENEDICT. He became aware of the scope of the discipline that incorporated all aspects of his previous studies and experiences and felt prepared to accept a teaching post in the Maxwell School of Syracuse University, a post he held from 1928 until retirement in 1962.

Haring is best known for his action-system theory in the study of human societies, but his World War II service as a teacher in the Civil Affairs Training School at Harvard and his term as advisor to the Civil Government in Okinawa provided numerous opportunities to apply his knowledge and skills to the goals of the Occupation. Although most widely known for his interpretations of Japanese culture before and after World War II, his most significant anthropological contributions were *Order and Possibility in Social Life*, co-authored with Johnson and his multi-authored compilation textbook, *Personal Character and Cultural Milieu*.

In studying human societies, Haring's action-system theory stresses facts and patterns of behavior rather than the classification of interpretations. Social behavior is limited by what individuals or groups are biologically capable of doing, and differences thus provide an endless variety in human relationships. The organic and the behavioral are viewed as reciprocals. Furthermore, the larger the society and the culture area, "the more readily are further inventions achieved." Throughout his teaching career, Haring remained close to his professional colleagues, notably MARGARET MEAD and Benedict, the latter a schoolmate from high school days; and while Benedict was helpful in shaping his professional career, it was Haring who helped her in drafting *The Chrysanthemum and the Sword*.

MAJOR WORKS: *The Land of Gods and Earthquakes* (New York: 1929); (with M.E. Johnson) *Order and Possibility in Social Life* (New York: 1940); *Blood on the Rising Sun* (Philadelphia: 1943); (editor and contributor) *Japan's Prospect* (Cambridge: 1946); (compiler and contributor) *Personal Character and Cultural Milieu* (Ann Arbor: 1948; 2nd ed., Syracuse: 1949; 3rd rev. ed., Syracuse: 1956).

SOURCES: Paul Meadows, "The action-system theory of social behavior" in: Earl W. Count and Gordon T. Bowles, *Fact and Theory in Social Science* (Syracuse: 1964), pp. 9-23; Douglas G. Haring, "Anthropology: one point of view" in: Douglas G. Haring, *Personal Character and Cultural Milieu* (3rd rev. ed., Syracuse: 1956), pp. 4-31; "Haring, Prof. Douglas G(ilbert)" in: Jaques Cattell (editor), *Directory of American Scholars* (Lancaster, Pa.: 1961), p. 384.

Gordon T. Bowles

Harrington, John Peabody. Anthropologist, linguist. Born in Waltham (Massachusetts) 29 April 1884, died in San Diego (California) 21 October 1961. Harrington was educated at Stanford University (B.A., 1905) and the Universities of California, Leipzig and Berlin. He received an honorary Sc.D. from the University of Southern California in 1934.

Harrington became interested in American Indian languages under the influence of ALFRED L. KROEBER and PLINY E. GODDARD during an undergraduate summer session at the University of California; and, early in his career while teaching in high school, he devoted spare time to fieldwork among the Chumash, Yuma and Mojave. During 1909-1915, he served as ethnologist at the School of American Archaeology of the Archaeological Institute of America at Santa Fe and studied the languages of Picuris, Jemez and Zuni. In 1915, he joined the staff of the Smithsonian Institution's Bureau of American Ethnology and continued there until he retired in 1954.

Throughout his life, Harrington continued his interest in California Indians, and he amassed a large quantity of notes, much of them on the Chumash and Costanoan groups. His study of Southwestern languages was almost as long-lived as his California work, and his interest in the relationship between Navajo and Northern Athabaskan languages eventually directed his fieldwork to the Northwest Coast and Alaska where, in addition to Indian languages, he recorded Aleut. He investigated Latin American languages, working largely with travelers to North America. In addition, Harrington studied Plains Indian languages, especially Cheyenne and Kiowa, and he had some knowledge of many other languages of the American Indian as well as several of Europe and Asia.

Harrington is credited with having discovered the relationship between Tanoan and Kiowa. He also contributed to the growth of the concept of Hokan languages. He was among the first ethnologists to realize the significance of the American Indians' knowledge of the world around them and to collect material on subjects like ethnoastronomy, ethnobotany and ethnogeography.

Harrington's greatest legacy, however, is his trove of notes, an amazingly large and rich body of documents concerning more than ninety languages. Harrington almost obsessively sought out last survivors of many languages in order to record them both in script and in sound recordings. The value of his linguistic data lies partly in its very rich and diverse nature and partly in its accuracy. It has been claimed by users of his material that Harrington heard phonetics more accurately than any other 20th-century student of American Indians.

Intensely competitive with other fieldworkers and suspicious and intolerant of interference from officialdom, Harrington demonstrated tendencies toward secretiveness, reclusiveness, and obsessiveness in his work habits. At the same time, he was capable of inspiring friendship and loyalty to his cause of recording American Indian languages and cultures, and several people have described him as being capable of great charm. That many found Harrington humorously eccentric—often endearingly and sometimes outrageously so—is demonstrated through a large body of anecdotes that has survived him.

MAJOR WORKS: (with Junius Henderson) *Ethnozoology of the Tewa Indians* (Washington: 1914) (= *Bureau of American Ethnology Bulletin*, no. 56); (with Wilfred Robbins and Barbara Freire-Marreco) *Ethnobotany of the Tewa Indians* (Washington: 1916) (= *Bureau of American Ethnology Bulletin*, no. 55); "Ethnogeography of the Tewa Indians," *Annual Report of the Bureau of American Ethnology*, vol. 29 (1916), pp. 29-618; "Exploration of Burton Mound at Santa Barbara, California," *Annual Report of the Bureau of American Ethnology*, vol. 44 (1928), pp. 23-168; (with Helen H. Roberts) "Picuris children's stories with texts and songs," *Annual Report of the Bureau of American Ethnology*, vol. 43 (1928), pp. 289-447; *Vocabulary of the Kiowa Language* (Washington: 1928) (= *Bureau of American Ethnology Bulletin*, no. 84); *Karuk Indian Myths* (Washington: 1932) (= *Bureau of American Ethnology Bulletin*, no. 107); *Tobacco among the Karuk Indians of California*

(Washington: 1932) (= *Bureau of American Ethnology Bulletin*, no. 94); (editor) Geronimo Boscana, *Chinigchinich* (Santa Ana, Calif.: 1933).

SOURCES: Catherine A. Callaghan, "John P. Harrington: California's great linguist," *Journal of California Anthropology*, vol. 2 (1975), pp. 183-187; Harrington papers in the Smithsonian Institution National Anthropological Archives; Mark R. Harrington, "John P. Harrington," *Masterkey*, vol. 36 (1962), p. 68; Kathryn A. Klar, "John P. Harrington: accounts of his work compiled from the Annual Reports of the Bureau of American Ethnology, 1914-1954" [on file in the Smithsonian Institution National Anthropological Archives]; Carobeth Laird, *Encounter with an Angry God: Recollections of My Life with John Peabody Harrington* (Banning, Calif.: 1976); Elaine L. Mills, *The Papers of John Peabody Harrington in the Smithsonian Institution, 1907-1957* [7 vols.] (Millwood, N.Y.: 1981-1988); Mathew W. Stirling, "John Peabody Harrington, 1884-1961," *American Anthropology*, vol. 65 (1963), pp. 1270-1381 [with bibliography by Karlena Glemser]; Jane McClaren Walsh, *John Peabody Harrington: the Man and His California Indian Fieldnotes* (Ramona, Calif.: 1976).

James R. Glenn

Harrisson, Tom. Ethnologist, archaeologist, ornithologist, explorer, conservationist, museum curator, editor. Born in England 26 September 1911, died near Bangkok (Thailand) 21 January 1976. Harrisson meant different things to different people and it is difficult to say what his major contribution was. Perhaps his major achievement was putting Sarawak before the world as a place where anthropology and archaeology were still exciting and major new discoveries could still be made.

A graduate of Harrow and a student for a time at Pembroke College, Cambridge, Harrisson's academic training was in biology with ornithology his primary interest. He early developed his taste for studying people by taking part in an Oxford University Expedition to Arctic Lapland, leading an Oxford Expedition to interior Sarawak in 1932, and then spending two years in the New Hebrides, Melanesia, one year of which he spent living with mountain tribes on Malekula. At age twenty-six he published his first book, *Savage Civilization*, a popular ethnography about his experiences in Malekula. Returning to England in 1936, Harrisson, with Charles Madge, founded Mass Observation, a form of public opinion research and a very successful enterprise. Toward the end of World War II, Harrisson was parachuted into interior Sarawak to organize guerrillas among the local people. His experience there with the Kelabit and other ethnic groups was recalled in his best known book *World Within*, published in 1959. After the war he was appointed Curator of the Sarawak Museum and Government Ethnologist in Sarawak.

In his new position Harrisson reorganized the Sarawak Museum, restarted the *Sarawak Museum Journal* and encouraged both local and foreign scientists to do research on all phases of Sarawak life including its botany and zoology. Through exchanges for the *Journal* he built up an unusually good scientific library at the Museum. Much of the publication resulting from the research Harrisson encouraged was published in the *Journal*, which became very popular as a result of its lively style. He published prolifically on many Sarawak subjects, both in the *Journal* and in other publications. He became interested in the prehistory of Sarawak, teaching himself somewhat dated archaeological methods, and organized a well publicized series of excavations on the Niah Caves, developing a research program that involved specialists in many different fields. Much of the fame of the Great Cave of Niah came with dating of archaeological levels back to around 40,000 B.C. and recovery of a controversial—for its dating to ca. 40,000 B.P.—skull cap of a young boy which, for many years, was the earliest dated *Homo sapiens* in the world. He spread the fame of Sarawak, and the Niah Caves, through a series of documentary films jointly produced with Hugh Gibb. The first of these, *Birds Nest Soup*, won the Eurovision Grand Prix for documentary television films at the Cannes Film Festival. This series of six television films titled *The Borneo Story* was shown around the world (but not in the United States). Even after retiring and leaving Sarawak Harrisson continued writing and publishing articles on his previous research there.

In 1946 he was made a member of the British Distinguished Service Order (DSO). In 1959 he became an Officer of the Order of the British Empire (OBE).

MAJOR WORKS: *Savage Civilization* (London: 1937); "The Great Cave of Niah: a preliminary report on Bornean prehistory," *Man*, vol. 57 (1957), pp. 161-166; "The caves of Niah: a history of prehistory," *Sarawak Museum Journal*, n.s., vol. 8 (1958), pp. 549-595; *World Within: a Borneo Story* (London: 1959); "New archaeological and ethnological results from Niah Caves, Sarawak," *Man*, vol. 59 (1959), pp. 1-8; "Borneo death," *Bijdragen tot de Taal-, Land- en Volkenkunde*, vol. 118 (1962), pp. 1-41; "Borneo writing," *Bijdragen tot de Taal-, Land- en Volkenkunde*, vol. 121 (1965), pp. 1-57; (with Stanley J. O'Connor, Jr.) *Excavations of the Pre-historic Iron Industry in West Borneo* [2 vols.: I. *Raw Materials and Industrial Waste*; II. *Associated Artifacts and Ideas*] (Ithaca: 1969); "The prehistory of Borneo," *Asian Perspectives*, vol. 13 (1970), pp. 17-45; *The Malays of South-West Sarawak before Malaysia* (London: 1970); (with Barbara Harrisson) *The Prehistory of Sabah* (Kota Kinabalu, Malaysia: 1970) (= *The Sabah Society Journal, Monograph*, no. 4); (with Barbara Harrisson) "Kota Batu in Brunei (introductory report)," *Sarawak Museum Journal*, n.s., vol. 7 (1956), pp. 283-319.

SOURCES: "A selected bibliography: Tom Harrisson," *Borneo Research Bulletin*, vol. 8 (1976), pp. 122-128; Barbara Harrisson, "Tom Harrisson: living and working in Borneo," *Borneo Research Bulletin*, vol. 8 (1976), pp. 25-30; Barbara Harrisson, "Tom Harrisson's unpublished legacy on Niah," *Journal of the Malaysian Branch of the Royal Asiatic Society*," vol. 50 (1977), pp. 41-51; Barbara Harrisson, "Tom Harrisson and the uplands: a summary of his unpublished ethnographic papers," *Asian Perspectives*, vol. 20 (1977), pp. 1-7; Alastair Lamb, "Tom Harrisson and Indian influence in early Southeast Asia," *Journal of the Malaysian Branch of the Royal Asiatic Society*, vol. 50 (1977), pp. 8-13; "Exploring life under cannibals and bombers," *The Times* [London] (21 January 1976), p. 18 [republished in: "Obituary Tom Harrisson, 'Exploring life under cannibals and bombers,' *London Times* (21 Jan. 1976)," *Borneo Research Bulletin*, vol. 8 (1976), pp. 22-25]; Jonathan H. Kress, "Tom Harrisson, North Borneo, and Palawan: a preliminary assessment," *Asian Perspectives*, vol. 20 (1977), pp. 75-86; Stanley J. O'Connor, Jr., "Tom Harrisson and the literature of place," *Borneo Research Bulletin*, vol. 8 (1976), pp. 77-80; Stanley J. O'Connor, Jr., "Tom Harrisson and the ancient iron industry of the Sarawak River delta" *Journal of the Malaysian Branch of the Royal Asiatic Society*, vol. 50 (1977), pp. 4-7; Benedict Sandin, "Tom Harrisson," *Borneo Research Bulletin*, vol. 8 (1976), pp. 61-62; Benedict Sandin, "Tom, as I knew him," *Journal of the Malaysian Branch of the Royal Asiatic Society*, vol. 49 (1976), pp. 147-148; Richard Shutler, Jr., "Tom Harrisson's contribution through radiocarbon dating to the understanding of the prehistory of Southeast Asia," *Asian Perspectives*, vol. 20 (1977), pp. 8-12; Wilhelm G. Solheim II, "Tom Harrisson and Borneo archaeology," *Borneo Research Bulletin*, vol. 9 (1977), pp. 3-7; Wilhelm G. Solheim II, "The Niah research program," *Journal of the Malaysian Branch of the Royal Asiatic Society*, vol. 50 (1977), pp. 28-40; Wilhelm G. Solheim II and Barbara Jensen, "Tom Harrisson—bibliography of publications concerning Southeast Asian prehistory," *Asian Perspectives*, vol. 20 (1977), pp. 13-20.

Wilhelm G. Solheim II

Hart, Donn Vorhis. Anthropologist, administrator. Born in Anaheim (California) 15 February 1918, died in DeKalb (Illinois) 10 July 1983. Donn Hart completed the A.B. degree at the University of California (Berkeley) in 1941. He received an

M.A. from Harvard University in 1942 and a Ph.D. in anthropology from Syracuse University in 1954. What was to become a lifelong interest in the Philippines was aroused in 1946 while he was employed at the UNESCO Secretariat in London and Paris. That same year, Hart co-authored, with Howard E. Wilson, a social science text on the Philippines for use in American high schools. Fieldwork for a dissertation in anthropology was carried out at Barrio Caticugan in the southernmost part of Negros Island in the Philippines. His dissertation was completed in 1954.

Hart was with the Department of Anthropology, Syracuse University, from 1958 to 1971. He became director of the Center for Southeast Asian Studies at Northern Illinois University in 1971, remaining in that position until 1981. A prolific author, he wrote on many aspects of Philippine (especially Visayan) culture. His interests included folklore, popular culture, kinship, ethnomedicine and Filipino-Americans. Northern Illinois University's important Southeast Asia library was named for him in 1985.

MAJOR WORKS: *Barrio Caticugan: a Visayan Filipino Community* [unpublished PhD. dissertation] (Syracuse: 1954); *The Philippine Plaza Complex: a Focal Point in Culture Change* (New Haven: 1955) (= *Yale University, Graduate School, Southeast Asia Studies, Cultural Report Series*, no. 3); *The Cebuan Filipino Dwelling in Caticugan: Its Construction and Cultural Aspects* (New Haven: 1959) (= *Yale University, Graduate School, Southeast Asia Studies, Cultural Report Series*, no. 7); *Riddles in Philippine Folklore: an Anthropological Analysis* (Syracuse: 1964); *Compadrinazgo: Ritual Kinship in the Philippines* (DeKalb: 1977).

SOURCES: Morton J. Netzorg, "The works of Donn V. Hart: an annotated bibliography," *Kinaadman*, vol. 7, no. 2 (1985), pp. 215-296; "Donn Vorhis Hart: biodata, *Kinaadman*, vol. 7, no. 2 (1985), pp. 206-208; "Curriculum vitae of Donn V. Hart," *Crossroads: an Interdisciplinary Journal of Southeast Asian Studies*, vol. 1, no. 2 (June 1983), pp. 3-16; "Hart, Donn V." in: Robert O. Tilman (project director), *International Biographical Directory of Southeast Asia Specialists, 1969* (Athens: 1969), pp. 88-89. Field notes from Barrio Caticugan and other papers are in the Northern Illinois University Libraries.

Lee S. Dutton

Harva, Uno (Uno Holmberg until 1927). Historian of religions, ethnographer, folklorist, sociologist. Born in Ypäjä (Finland, then in Russia) 1882, died in Turku (Finland) 13 August 1949. Harva became an internationally well known scholar through his numerous books on the religious traditions of Finno-Ugric and Middle Asian peoples. He studied theology first then he served as an Evangelic-Lutheran priest for one year but resigned in order to specialize on the comparative study of the "folk religions" of agrarian and hunting societies. Under the tutelage of EDWARD WESTERMARCK at the University of Helsinki, Harva was instructed in theories of religious evolution and methods of ethnographic fieldwork prevalent in British anthropology in the 1900s. He studied the Udmurt (Votyak), Mari (Cheremiss), Ket (Eniseï-Ostiaks) and Evenk (Tungus) in Russia and Siberia in 1911, 1913 and 1917. He held a professorship in sociology at the University of Turku from 1926 to 1949.

Harva started his scholarly activity as a Wundtian folk psychologist, a Westermarckian evolutionist and a geo-historicalist of the Finnish school of folkloristics. In the 1920s he adopted a rationalist strain of thought in the manner of Carl Wilhelm von Sydow in Swedish scholarship and, moreover, became a Ratzelian diffusionist and an adherent of the *"Kulturkreise"* approach in European ethnology.

Harva was very nationalistic (Finland was a Grand Duchy of Russia until 1917). His main concern was to learn through comparative analysis of popular culture "the origin and development" of indigenous Finnish religious and societal elements, i.e., cultural traits that the Finns share with eastern "kinfolk." Harva theorized that the religious past of the Finns could still be glimpsed not only among the Finns in the Baltic Sea area, but also among "the Volga Finns" and Ugrians of the River Ob in Siberia. As an analyst of shamanism and myth traditions, Harva pioneered the line of inquiry for which Mircea Eliade became famous. In his works *Der Baum des Lebens, Finno-Ugric, Siberian* and *Die Religiösen Vorstellungen der Altaischen Völker*, Harva revealed the mythic structure of ancient cosmology. He showed morphologically related themes in mythic narratives of shamanic hunters, cattle-breeding agriculturalists, and nomadic pastoralists. These included conceptions of the shaman's tree and ascent to the sky and center-of-the-world (*axis mundi*) symbolism. Harva's achievements as a student of myth and shamanism have been highly esteemed not only by Eliade, but also by (among others) BRONISLAW MALINOWSKI and WESTON LA BARRE.

MAJOR WORKS: *Die Wassergottheiten der Finnisch-ugrischen Völker* (Helsinki: 1913) (= *Mémoires de la Société finno-ougrienne*, no. 32); *Der Baum des Lebens* (Helsinki: 1922) (= *Annales Academiae Scientiarum Fennicae*, series B, vol. 16, no. 3); "Über die Jagdriten der Nördlichen Völker Asiens und Europas," *Journal de la Société finno-ougrienne*, vol. 41 (1925-1926), pp. 1-53; *Die Religion der Tscheremissen* (Helsinki: 1926) (= *FF Communications*, vol. 61); *Finno-Ugric, Siberian* (Boston: 1927) (= *The Mythology of All Races* (Boston: 1916-1964), vol. 4); *Die Religiösen Vorstellungen der Altaischen Völker* (Helsinki: 1938) (= *FF Communications*, vol. 125); *Die Religiösen Vorstellungen der Mordwinen* (Helsinki: 1952) (= *FF Communications*, vol. 142).

SOURCES: Veikko Anttonen, *Uno Harva ja suomalainen uskontotiede* [*Uno Harva and the Science of Religion in Finland*] (Helsinki: 1987); Veikko Anttonen, "Uno (Holmberg-) Harva as field-ethnographer" in: Mihály Hoppál and Juha Pentikäinen (editors), *Uralic Mytholgy and Folklore* (Budapest: 1989) (= *Ethnologica Uralica*, vol. 17), pp. 33-48; Lauri Honko, "Uno Harva," *Arv: Tidskrift för Nordisk Folkminnesforskning*, vol. 25-26 (1969-1970), pp. 57-66; Weston La Barre, *The Ghost Dance* (New York: 1978); Bronislaw Malinowski, *Sex, Culture and Myth* (New York: 1962).

Veikko Anttonen

Hasebe, Kotondo. Physical anthropologist. Born in Tōkyō (Japan) 10 June 1882, died in Tōkyō (Japan) 3 December 1969. Hasebe graduated from the Faculty of Medicine at the University of Tōkyō in 1906. He pursued a career in human anatomy and in 1913 received the degree of Doctor of Medicine with his study on the Japanese spine. He served as professor of anatomy at Kyōto University, Niigata University and Tōhoku University. From 1921 to 1922 he studied anthropology under Rudolf Martin in Germany. He did bio-anthropological research in Micronesia from 1927 to 1929. In 1938 he held the chair of anthropology at the University of Tōkyō and in 1939 he founded the anthropology sequence at the Faculty of Science at the University of Tōkyō and established a base for the development of biological anthropology in Japan.

Hasebe had a great influence on academia through his original "transformation" theory on the origin of the modern Japanese. He argued that the drastic changes in the physical characteristics of the Japanese between the Jōmon and Yayoi periods were not due to the genetic influence of immigrants from the continent. Instead, they occurred as a result of an evolutionary process stimulated by changes in the environment and by the shift in the predominant livelihood from hunting and gathering to agriculture. His study included not only osteology and somatology but also prehistory and ethnology.

In his later years he studied the origin of Japanese domestic animals based on bones found in archaeological excavations.

MAJOR WORKS: "Die Wirbelsäule der Japaner," *Zeitschrift für Morphologie und Anthropologie*, vol. 15 (1913), pp. 259-380; *Shizen Jinruigaku Gairon* [*Introduction to Physical Anthropology*] (Tōkyō: 1927); *Senshigaku Kenkyū* [*Study of Prehistory*] (Tōkyō: 1927); *Nihon Minzoku no Seiritsu* [*Formation of the Japanese People*] (Tōkyō: 1949); *Nihonjin no Sosen* [*Japanese Ancestry*] (Tōkyō: 1951).

SOURCES: Teruya Esaka (editor), *Hasebe Kotondo Shū* [*Hasebe Kotondo Collection*] (Tōkyō: 1975); Hisashi Suzuki, "Ko Hasebe Kotondo Sensei" ["Memoirs of the late Prof. Kotondo Hasebe"], *Kaibōgaku Zasshi* [*Acta Anatomica Nipponica*], vol. 46 (1971), pp. 369-370.

Bin Yamaguchi
[*Translation from Japanese: Mamiko Nakamura*]

Haslund-Christensen, Henning.

Haslund-Christensen, Henning. Ethnographer, traveler. Born in Copenhagen (Denmark) 31 August 1896, died in Kabul (Afghanistan) 13 September 1948. As an infantry lieutenant Haslund participated in the setting up of an experimental farm and fur trade station on the Zobel Plain in northern Outer Mongolia (1923-1926). During this time he learned the Mongolian language and collected folklore material. When the farm closed down, Haslund traveled (1927-1930) through what had now become the People's Republic of Mongolia as caravan leader for SVEN HEDIN. In 1936 he set out for the First Danish Expedition to Central Asia, where he collected ethnographic material in Manchuria for the Danish National Museum. In 1938 he embarked on the Second Danish Expedition to Central Asia, this time focusing on the collection of ethnographic, archaeological and linguistic material from Inner Mongolia. During World War II Haslund planned the Third Danish Expedition to Central Asia, which was aimed at an ethnographic coverage of the area from Afghan Pamir to Manchuria. The members of the expedition started work in Afghanistan in early 1948, and when Haslund died, several members continued, more or less individually, in Afghanistan, Chitral and Sikkim.

Haslund's greatest strength was as a practical organizer and ardent collector of costumes, ornaments and other artifacts as well as of folklore and music. Thanks to his efforts, the Ethnographic Department of the Danish National Museum can boast of a unique Central Asian collection. Haslund had no academic training, but he reached a wide audience in Denmark and Sweden through his popular books and radio programs.

MAJOR WORKS: *Jabonah* (Copenhagen: 1932); *Zajagan* (Copenhagen: 1935); *Asiatiske Strejftog* (Copenhagen: 1945).

SOURCES: Lennart Edelberg and Klaus Ferdinand, "Arselan: et udblik over dansk forskning i Centralasien," *Naturens verden* (September 1958), pp. 257-289; Lennart Edelberg, "Haslund-Christensen, Henning" in: *Dansk Biografisk Leksikon* (Copenhagen: 1980), vol. 6, pp. 63-65.

Jan Ovesen

Haury, Emil Walter.

Haury, Emil Walter. Anthropologist, archaeologist, educator, museum administrator. Born in Newton (Kansas) 2 May 1904. Haury was the leading figure in southwestern U.S. archaeology for more than fifty years during the mid-20th century. One of the few scholars to work in the three major prehistoric culture zones, he contributed to the study of the Anasazi culture of the northern plateaus. He and HAROLD GLADWIN defined the Hohokam culture of the southern deserts and he quickly became the leading authority on the Hohokam. He introduced the concept of the Mogollon culture for the intervening mountainous region. His excavations at Ventana Cave and in several elephant kill sites made him a key figure in Early Man research.

Haury studied under BYRON CUMMINGS and A.E. DOUGLASS at the University of Arizona and ROLAND B. DIXON at Harvard. He learned the basics of tree-ring research while working for Douglass early in his career. He and Lyndon Hargrave discovered Beam HH-39 at the Show Low Ruin that enabled Douglass to link his historic and prehistoric tree-ring chronologies. He was also influenced by Gladwin, for whom he worked at the Gila Pueblo Archaeological Foundation in Globe, Arizona, and by ALFRED V. KIDDER, whose role as "dean of southwestern archaeology" he assumed early in his career. Head of the Department of Anthropology and Director of the Arizona State Museum at the University of Arizona for a quarter of a century, Haury brought both institutions to national and international prominence. A superb field archaeologist, he emphasized field training and made the University of Arizona Archaeological Field School the model for such training during the post-World War II period. His ideas about Southwestern archaeology have worn well in large measure because he always documented his views with solid field evidence. A striking example was his synthesis of early agricultural developments in the Southwest in the *Courses Toward Urban Life* volume edited by Braidwood and Willey.

MAJOR WORKS: *The Canyon Creek Ruin and the Cliff Dwellings of the Sierra Ancha* (Globe, Arizona: 1934) (= *Medallion Paper*, no. 14); *The Mogollon Culture of Southwestern New Mexico* (Globe, Arizona: 1936) (= *Medallion Paper*, no. 20); (with Harold S. Gladwin, E.B. Sayles and Nora Gladwin) *Excavations at Snaketown: Material Culture* (Globe, Arizona: 1937 (= *Medallion Paper*, no. 25); 2nd ed., Tucson: 1965; 3rd ed., Tucson: 1975; *Excavation of Los Muertos and Neighboring Ruins in the Salt River Valley, Southern Arizona* (Cambridge, Mass.: 1945) (= *Papers of the Peabody Museum, Harvard University*, vol. 24, no. 1); *The Stratigraphy and Archaeology of Ventana Cave, Arizona* (Tucson and Albuquerque: 1950; 2nd ed., Tucson: 1975); *The Hohokam: Desert Farmers and Craftsmen: Excavations at Snaketown, 1964-1965* (Tucson: 1976); *Mogollon Culture in the Forestdale Valley, East Central Arizona* (Tucson: 1985); *Emil W. Haury's Prehistory of the American Southwest* (edited by J.J. Reid and D.E. Doyel) (Tucson: 1986) [reprint of major papers]; "Gila Pueblo Archaeological Foundation: a history and some personal notes," *Kiva*, vol. 54, no. 1 (1988), pp. 1-96; *Point of Pines, Arizona: a History of the University of Arizona Archaeological Field School* (Tucson: 1989) (= *Anthropological Papers of the University of Arizona*, no. 50); "The greater American Southwest" in: Robert Braidwood and Gordon R. Willey (editors), *Courses Toward Urban Life: Archeological Considerations of Some Cultural Alternates* (Chicago: 1962), pp. 106-131.

SOURCES: J. Jefferson Reid, "Emil Walter Haury: the archaeologist as humanist and scientist" in: J.J. Reid and D.E. Doyel (editors), *Emil W. Haury's Prehistory of the American Southwest* (Tucson: 1986), pp. 3-17; Watson Smith, "Emil Haury's Southwest: a Pisgah view," *Journal of the Southwest*, vol. 29 (1987), pp. 102-120; Peter L. Steere, "Annotated bibliography of the works of Dr. Emil W. Haury," *Bulletin of Bibliography*, vol. 46 (1989), pp. 173-194; Arizona State Museum Archives, University of Arizona, Tucson.

Raymond H. Thompson

Hearne, Samuel. Explorer, fur trader, naturalist, writer. Born in London (England) 1745, died in London (England) November 1792. Hearne joined the Hudson's

Bay Company (HBC) in 1766 and served as a seaman in the trade with the Inuit north of Churchill (Manitoba). Largely because of his notable skill and interest in learning the languages and ways of the native peoples, Hearne was chosen for exploration expeditions and fur-trade pursuits on the barrens, along the northern coast and in the interior. Hearne is remembered as the first European to trek successfully over the barren lands from Churchill to the mouth of the Coppermine River (Northwest Territories). This accomplishment, which followed two unsuccessful attempts, was largely the result of Hearne defying the HBC governor at Churchill by selecting his own guide, Matonabbee, a skillful leader of great prestige among the Chipewyan and the Athabasca Cree. On 30 June 1772, after eighteen months of remarkable adventures and hardships, they returned to Churchill. Hearne concluded that there was no northwest passage via Hudson Bay, and for more than a century his journals and maps contributed the only available information on much of Canada's northland. The journals also contain Hearne's great ethnographic contribution: his intimate, meticulously recorded observations on the life style, customs, beliefs and social structure of the Chipewyan in the early stage of contact. Hearne made anthropological generalizations supported by vivid first-hand accounts of individuals and events. His manuscript was of great interest to scientists and naturalists of his day. After ill health prompted him to retire from the fur trade in 1787, Hearne spent his time speaking about his adventures as an explorer/trader and revising the manuscript. A separate chapter on Matonabbee reveals a relationship of mutual respect. *A Journey* was published in London three years after Hearne's death and was soon translated into German (1797), Dutch (1798), Swedish (1798), French (1799), and Danish (1802).

MAJOR WORKS: *A Journey from Prince of Wale's Fort, in Hudson's Bay, to the Northern Ocean ... in the Years 1769, 1770, 1771 & 1772* (London: 1795); *Journals of Samuel Hearne and Philip Turnor between the Years 1774 and 1792* (J.B. Tyrrell, editor) (Toronto: 1911); Hudson's Bay Company Archives.

SOURCES: J.B. Tyrrell, "Editor's introduction" to: Samuel Hearne, *A Journey from Prince of Wale's Fort* (Toronto: 1911) (= *Publications of the Champlain Society*, vol. 6), pp. 1-23; R. Glover, "Editor's introduction" to: Samuel Hearne, *A Journey from Prince of Wales's Fort in Hudson Bay to the Northern Ocean* (Toronto: 1958), pp. vii-xliii; Gordon Speck, *Samuel Hearne and the Northwest Passage* (Caldwell, Idaho: 1963); Edwin Ernest Rich, "Samuel Hearne: the coppermine and the Cumberland house" in: *History of the Hudson's Bay Company, 1670-1870* (Toronto: 1960), vol. 2, pp. 44-65; C.S. Mackinnon, "Hearne, Samuel" in: *Dictionary of Canadian Biography*, vol. 4 (Toronto: 1979), pp. 339-342.

Frieda Esau Klippenstein

Hedin, Sven. Explorer, ethnographer. Born in Stockholm (Sweden) 19 February 1865, died in Stockholm (Sweden) 26 November 1952. Even as a young man Sven Hedin was fascinated by traveling. He made his first long voyage to the Caucasus, Persia and Mesopotamia in 1885 when he was only twenty years old. Five years later, in 1890, he acted as an interpreter for the Swedish-Norwegian expedition to Nāser od-Dīn, the shah of Iran. This was the beginning of a long series of expeditions into the interior of Asia. In 1891 he traveled to Khorāsān in northeastern Persia and Russian Turkestan. In 1893 he embarked on a five-year-long expedition across the continent, traveling to Peking by way of the Urals, the Pamir Range and Lake Lop of western China. In 1899 he started the second phase of the expedition, following the Tarim River through western China into the Gobi desert, where he stayed for extensive exploration and mapping until 1902. Only three years later he embarked on a new expedition, this time to explore the Trans-Himalaya mountain range of Tibet and to map this part of the country. This expedition lasted from 1905 to 1908.

Sven Hedin was much appreciated in the whole of northern Europe and created much enthusiasm whenever he returned from his expeditions. He was especially honored in Germany, a country he had known since he was young. During World War I, he maintained strong relations with his German connections, a fact that cost him much prestige in Asia. Nevertheless, he initiated and directed the important Sino-Swedish expedition of 1927-1933. This expedition located 327 archaeological sites between Manchuria and Sinkiang in western China. During this trip, Sven Hedin probably made his most important archaeological and ethnographic contributions ever, shedding light on historic foraging cultures of this region.

MAJOR WORKS: *En färd genom Asien, 1893-97* [2 vols.] (Stockholm: 1898) [tr.: *Through Asia* (London: 1898)]; *Southern Tibet* [13 vols.] (Stockholm: 1917-1922); *My Life as an Explorer* (New York: 1925); *Sidenvägen: en bilfärd genom Centralasien* (Stockholm: 1936) [tr.: *The Silk Road* (London: 1938)].

SOURCES: "Hedin, Sven Anders" in: *The New Encyclopaedia Britannica* (Chicago: 1986), vol. 5, p. 796; Sigvald Linné, "Sven Hedin and the Ethnographical Museum of Stockholm," *Ethnos*, vol. 30 (1965), pp. 25-38; Gösta Montell, "Sven Hedin, the explorer," *Geografiska Annaler*, vol. 36 (1954), pp. 1-8 [republished in: *Ethnos*, vol. 30 (1965), pp. 7-24].

Jan-Åke Alvarsson

Heine-Geldern, Freiherr *Robert von.* Ethnographer. Born in Grub (Austria) 16 July 1885, died in Vienna (Austria) 25 May 1968. Following his graduation from secondary education in 1903, Heine-Geldern pursued higher studies at the Universities of Munich and Vienna. The disciplines he studied were philosophy, art history and anthropology—in anthropology specializing in ethnology, prehistory and archaeology. His first visit to Southeast Asia, a region that would occupy much of his scientific career, occurred in 1910, when he worked along the common border of India and Burma researching the hill tribes. He completed doctoral work at the University of Vienna in 1914. After World War I, in 1919, he began volunteer work at the Ethnographic Department of the (Naturhistorisches Museum) Museum of Natural History in Vienna, an institution with which he would be associated until 1927. He qualified as a docent in ethnology at Vienna in 1927 with a specialization in India and Southeast Asia and in 1931 was awarded the rank of professor. In 1938 he was invited to give a series of lectures in the United States, where he remained after the *Anschluss* until 1950. During his twelve years' residence, he served as a research associate in the Department of Anthropology at the American Museum of Natural History in New York City and was active in many organizations seeking to aid Austria. When he returned to Vienna in 1950, he accepted a position as professor at the Institut für Völkerkunde (Institute of Ethnology), where he lectured on the problems of cultural diffusion (including possible trans-Pacific contacts), cultural contacts between the Old and New Worlds and megalithic cultures and their background.

From 1950 until his death in 1968 Heine-Geldern was extremely active on the international anthropological scene. His involvement began in 1952 at the Fourth

International Congress of Anthropological and Ethnological Sciences in Vienna, where he urged cooperation for the rescue of peoples and cultures that were threatened with extinction and advocated the possible role of UNESCO. Four years later, at the Fifth International Congress in Chicago, the International Committee on Urgent Anthropological and Ethnological Research was created at his initiative and an annual bulletin started. Through participation in such bodies as the International Congress of Americanists, the Pacific Science Congress and the International Congress in Iranian Art and Archaeology (whose meeting he attended in Persia a few weeks before his death), he continued to champion research in his areas of interest and to call for attention to the issues of cultural survival.

MAJOR WORKS: *Die Bergstämme des nordöstlichen Birma* [Ph.D. dissertation] (Vienna: 1914) [republished in: *Robert Heine-Geldern: Gesammelte Schriften* (Vienna: 1970) (= *Acta Ethnologica et Linguistica*, no. 35, *Series Generalis*, no. 4), pp. 17-273]; "Südostasien" in: Georg Buschan [et al.], *Illustrierte Völkerkunde* (Stuttgart: 1923), vol. 2, pp. 689-768; "Ein Beitrag zur Chronologie des Neolithikums in Südost-Asien" in: Wilhelm Koppers (editor), *Festschrift: publication d'hommage offerte au P.W. Schmidt* (Vienna: 1928), pp. 809-843; "Urheimat und früheste Wanderungen der Austronesier," *Anthropos*, vol. 27 (1932), pp. 543-619; "The archaeology and art of Sumatra" published in the same volume as the much longer: Edwin M. Loeb, *Sumatra: Its History and People* (Vienna: 1935) (= *Wiener Beiträge zur Kulturgeschichte und Linguistik*, vol. 3), pp. 305-350; "Significant parallels in the symbolic arts of Southern Asia and Middle America" in: Sol Tax (editor), *The Civilizations of Ancient America* (Chicago: 1951) (= *Proceedings of the 29th International Congress of Americanists*, vol. 1), pp. 299-309; "Das Problem vorkolumbischer Beziehungen zwischen Alter und Neuer Welt und seine Bedeutung für die allgemeine Kulturgeschichte," *Anzeiger der Philosophisch-historischen Klasse der Österreichischen Akademie der Wissenschaften*, vol. 24 (1954), pp. 343-357; "Das Megalithproblem" in: *Beiträge Österreichs zur Erforschung der Vergangenheit und Kulturgeschichte der Menschheit: Bericht über das erste Österreichische Symposium auf Burg Wartenstein* (Horn: 1959), pp. 162-182; "Some tribal art styles of Southeast Asia: an experiment in art history" in: Douglas Fraser (editor), *Many Faces of Primitive Art: a Critical Anthology* (Englewood Cliffs, N.J.: 1966), pp. 165-221; "Transozeanische Kultureinflusse im alten Amerika: der gegenwärtige Stand der Forschung," *Zeitschrift für Ethnologie*, vol. 93 (1968), pp. 1-22; *Gesammelte Schriften* (edited by Engelbert Stiglmayr, co-edited by Anna Hohenwart-Gerlachstein) [7 vols. to date] (Vienna: 1976-) (= *Acta Ethnologica et Linguistica*, no. 35, *Series Generalis*, no. 4; *Acta Ethnologica et Linguistica*, no. 48, *Series Generalis*, no. 7; *Acta Ethnologica et Linguistica*, no. 51, *Series Generalis*, no. 8; *Acta Ethnologica et Linguistica*, no. 52, *Series Generalis*, no. 9; *Acta Ethnologica et Linguistica*, no. 55, *Series Generalis*, no. 11; *Acta Ethnologica et Linguistica*, no. 57, *Series Generalis*, no. 12; *Acta Ethnologica et Linguistica*, no. 60, *Series Generalis*, no. 13).

SOURCES: "Nachrufe" and "Bibliographie" in: Robert Heine-Geldern, *Gesammelte Schriften* (edited by Engelbert Stiglmayr and co-edited by Anna Hohenwart-Gerlachstein) (Vienna: 1976) (= *Acta Ethnologica et Linguistica*, no. 35, *Series Generalis*, no. 4), vol. 1, pp. ix-xlvi and 3-11 respectively; plus material in later volumes of this series of complete works [see above for citations].

Anna Hohenwart-Gerlachstein

Held, Gerrit Jan. Ethnologist, linguist. Born in Kampen (Netherlands) 1 July 1906, died in Djakarta (Indonesia) 28 September 1955. Held studied Indologie, an academic course for colonial officials, at Leiden State University from 1926 until 1931. In 1935 he was awarded a doctorate *cum laude* for his thesis on the *Mahabharata* (*The Mahabharata: an Ethnological Study*). This work, which confirmed MARCEL MAUSS's postulate that the main theme of this epic is an extensive *potlatch*-ritual, was later used by CLAUDE LÉVI-STRAUSS in his structural analysis of Indian kinship (*Les structures élémentaires de la parenté*, 1949).

Held did not join the colonial administration until 1940. From 1935 until 1940 he worked as linguist and anthropologist for the Dutch Bible Society, mainly in Dutch New Guinea, but also on Bali, Celebes and Java. In New Guinea he did extensive research among the Waropen (*Geelvink Bay*). Two studies were published as a direct result of his fieldwork, one a grammar of the Waropen language (*Grammatica van het Waropensch*), the other a dictionary (*Woordenlijst van het Waropensch*). After World War II Held published several articles and three more books based on his work in New Guinea. His *De Papoea: Cultuurimprovisator* is of special interest, as it is one of the very few comparative evaluations of the ethnography of both eastern and western New Guinea.

In 1941 Held began teaching anthropology at the University of Indonesia (Djakarta), and in 1946 he was officially appointed to the chair in anthropology. In this position—and from 1948 on also in the position of Director of the Institute for Linguistic and Cultural Research—he worked intensively to expand the role of the social sciences in Indonesia and to eliminate prejudices against ethnographic studies both among his Indonesian students and the Dutch colonial administration.

In 1951 he was invited to be a visiting professor at Yale University and a research associate at the Human Relations Area Files (HRAF). Held, who as a student of J.P.B. DE JOSSELIN DE JONG was a structuralist, mainly limited himself to lecturing, as he could not agree with the cross-cultural survey method used by the HRAF. In 1952 he returned to the University of Indonesia. During the next two years he worked on a research project at Bima (Sumbawa). The results of this project were never published due to his sudden demise in 1955, shortly before he was to return to the Netherlands to take up a post at the Royal Tropical Institute (Amsterdam).

Held was, as most of the Leiden anthropologists of his generation, a structuralist, developing and refining the ideas of the *Année*-school of Émile Durkheim and Mauss. He was decidedly opposed to the applied use of anthropology if this meant compromising the scientific rigor of ethnographic research. He made this clear both in his confrontations with mission and administration during his stay in New Guinea and later in his academic career.

MAJOR WORKS: *The Mahabharata: an Ethnological Study* (Amsterdam and London: 1935); *Grammatica van het Waropensch* (Batavia: 1942); *Woordenlijst van het Waropensch* (Batavia: 1942); *Papoea's van Waropen* (Leiden: 1947) [tr.: *The Papuans of Waropen* (The Hague: 1957)]; *Magie, hekserij en toverij* (Groningen and Djakarta: 1950); *De Papoea: Cultuurimprovisator* (The Hague and Bandung: 1951); "Applied anthropology in government: the Netherlands" in: A.L. Kroeber (editor), *Anthropology Today* (Chicago: 1953), pp. 866-879; *Waropense teksten* (The Hague: 1956).

SOURCES: J.P.B. de Josselin de Jong, "Herdenking van Gerrit Jan Held (1 juli 1906—28 september 1955)," *Jaarboek Koninklijke Akademie van Wetenschappen* (1955-1956), pp. 239-252; J.P.B. de Josselin de Jong, "Herdenking van Gerrit Jan Held (1 juli 1906—28 september 1955)," *Bijdragen tot de Taal-, Land- en Volkenkunde*, vol. 112 (1956), pp. 343-353; R. Needham, "Gerrit Jan Held, 1906-1955," *Man*, vol. 55 (1955), pp. 153-154.

S.R. Jaarsma and J.J. de Wolf

Hemenway, Mary (née Mary Porter Tileston). Philanthropist. Born in New York (New York) 20 December 1820, died in Boston (Massachusetts) 6 March 1894. Hemenway is known to anthropologists for her sponsorship of the Hemenway Southwestern Archaeological Expedition (1886-1894), which was directed in two phases by

FRANK HAMILTON CUSHING and Jesse Walter Fewkes (1850-1930). Undertaken before the full institutionalization of anthropology as an academic discipline, the expedition helped establish the southwestern United States as a culture area. It was the most complex of Hemenway's diverse but related endeavors, based in Boston yet national in scope, that comprised a thirty-year career. Although her own work was never published, Hemenway provided for the publication of books and journals related to her philanthropic works.

Hemenway was eldest daughter of a wealthy and socially prominent New England family. Her father had interests in shipping, banking and insurance; she was educated in New York private schools and socialized conservatively. Her interest in art, music and literature was lifelong; history, biography and sermons were also important intellectual pursuits. Unitarianism guided her actions in adult life and provided a theoretical framework for the formation of the Hemenway Expedition. In 1840, she married Edward Augustus Holyoke Hemenway (1805-1876), a distant cousin fifteen years her senior who was a shipping merchant like her father. Augustus Hemenway established his business headquarters in Boston, and it was there that the Hemenways spent their married life and raised five children. Wealth and the social milieu of prominent elites were both the instrument and avenue for Mary Hemenway's personal and public concerns.

She began her career at middle age, although she had earlier provided art training for talented youth. Entering public life after the Civil War, she was concerned that public institutions provide a moral education, instilling patriotism and democratic values, and teach practical skills. She was also deeply involved with the formation of a national identity and ideology. Her concerns matured with her successive endeavors and addressed social issues stemming from reconstruction, immigration, urbanism, and industrialization. Notable among them were: sponsoring sewing, cooking and gymnastics instruction for young girls in Boston public schools (1865, 1885, 1888), programs that remain integrated in the national public school curriculum; providing the major financial contribution to preserve the Old South Meeting House as a local symbol of the young nation (1877), with education programs in American history before it was a popular subject; and sponsoring the Hemenway Expedition (1886), which was a synthesis of her interests in art, history, and public education.

The Expedition broke new ground with its comprehensive approach to investigating living and ancient Pueblo cultures as America's indigenous civilization. Mary Hemenway apparently intended to found a museum of Pueblo culture as a means to foster education in American history. Her museum was never established; collections and records were dispersed among several institutions. The Expedition has principally been assessed as a scientific enterprise in terms of the subsequent development of the discipline rather than on its own terms as a humanistic enterprise of the period. Yet the work of the Expedition continues to stimulate research and to shed light on individuals like Mary Hemenway who were instrumental in the professionalization of anthropology.

SOURCES: Charles G. Ames, "A memorial tribute," *Boston Gazette* (18 March 1894); Frank H. Cushing, "Preliminary notes on the origin, working hypothesis, and primary researches on the Hemenway Southwestern Archaeological Expedition" in: *Congrès International des Américanistes, Compte-rendu da la septième session, Berlin 1888* (Berlin: 1890), pp. 151-194; Emil W. Haury, *The Excavation of Los Muertos and Neighboring Ruins in the Salt River Valley, Southern Arizona* (Cambridge, Mass.: 1945) (= *Papers of the Peabody Museum*, vol. 24, no. 1); Frederick W. Hodge, "Foreword" in: Emil W. Haury, *The Excavation of Los Muertos ...* (Cambridge, Mass.: 1945) (=

Papers of the Peabody Museum, vol. 24, no. 1), pp. vii-ix; Phyllis Keller, "Mary Porter Tileston Hemenway" in: E.T. James, J.W. James and P.S. Boyer (editors), *Notable American Women, 1607-1950*, vol. 2 (Cambridge, Mass.: 1971), pp. 179-181; Mary W. Tileston, *A Memorial of the Life and Benefactions of Mary Hemenway, 1820-1894* (Boston: 1927); Edwin L. Wade and Lea S. McChesney, *America's Great Lost Expedition: The Thomas Keam Collection of Hopi Pottery from the Second Hemenway Expedition, 1890-1894* (Phoenix: 1980); Nathalie F.S. Woodbury, "Women's money and the 'study of man': The Hemenway Expeditions, part I," *Anthropology Newsletter*, vol. 29, no. 3 (March 1988), p. 19; *Boston Advertiser* (7 March 1894); "Mrs. Mary Hemenway" and "A great and noble woman," *Boston Herald* (7 March 1894); "Mrs. Mary Hemenway dead" and "Mrs. Hemenway," *Boston Transcript* (6 March 1894); "How Mrs. Hemenway worked," *Boston Transcript* (10 March 1894); "In memory of Mrs. Hemenway," *Boston Transcript* ((9 May 1894); Curtis M. Hinsley and Lea S. McChesney, "Anthropology as cultural exchange: the shared vision of Mary Hemenway and Frank Cushing" [unpublished paper presented at the joint meetings of the American Ethnological Society and the Southwestern Anthropological Association, Monterey, 1984]; Lea S. McChesney, "Appropriation for cultural reproduction: the vision of Mary Hemenway" [unpublished paper presented at the 87th Annual Meetings of the American Anthropological Association, Phoenix, 1988]. Important sources of archival information include the Old South Meeting House, Boston; Peabody Museum Archives, Harvard University; Phillips Library, Peabody Museum, Salem (these include Hemenway family papers); Southwest Museum, Los Angeles.

Lea S. McChesney

Henshaw, Henry Wetherbee.

Naturalist, ethnologist, government official, photographer. Born in Cambridge (Massachusetts) 3 March 1850, died in Washington (D.C.) 1 August 1930. Henshaw was educated in the Cambridge public schools, briefly attended Columbian College (now George Washington University) and read medicine informally with Henry Crecy Yarrow. Mainly, however, he was a self-trained naturalist. During 1869-1871 he was on bird-collecting expeditions in the South and during 1872-1879 he was a naturalist with the U.S. Geographic Surveys West of the One Hundredth Meridian (Wheeler Survey). With the latter assignment, his duties included anthropological work in California and in the Southwest in collaboration with Yarrow and Paul Schumacher.

When JOHN WESLEY POWELL established the Bureau of American Ethnology (BAE) in 1879, he selected Henshaw as his chief lieutenant; it was Henshaw to whom he entrusted administration of the BAE. Henshaw continued in that capacity until 1893 when poor health caused his resignation and removal to Hawaii, where he devoted himself to natural history and photography. He returned to the mainland in 1904 and joined the staff of the U.S. Bureau of Biological Survey. He served as the Biological Survey's assistant chief during 1905-1910 and its chief during 1910-1916.

Henshaw was of a retiring nature, functioning best as a second to a stronger person and often making major contributions to works published under the name of others. Thus, some of his outstanding contributions in anthropology have been obscured. He was, for example, the supervisor of the BAE's Indian work during the tenth United States census. His work on American Indian tribal nomenclature was eventually redirected toward the preparation of an Indian encyclopedia, work that eventually led to FREDERICK WEBB HODGE's *Handbook of American Indians North of Mexico* (1907, 1910) (= *Bureau of American Ethnology Bulletin*, no. 30). He also contributed to the BAE's classificatory work that was eventually reported in Powell's "Indian linguistic families of America north of Mexico" in the *Annual Report of the Bureau of American Ethnology*, vol. 7 (1891). In spite of Powell's authorship, Henshaw was a key figure in the execution of this landmark work, marking it with biologically derived rules of nomenclature. In addition, he carried out fieldwork in the West Coast and Plateau areas. Resulting from the latter is an appreciable amount of photographic and linguistic material concerning the Cayuse, Chumash, Costanoan, Diegueno, Esselen (a moribund language that Henshaw is credited with having saved from oblivion), Gabrieleno, Cahuilla, Miwok, Nez Perce, Paipai, Panamint, Pomo, Salinan, San Antonio, San Miguel, Serrano, Washo and Yokuts.

Henshaw was the first editor of the *American Anthropologist*, serving between 1889 and 1893.

MAJOR WORKS: "Animal carvings from the mounds of the Mississippi Valley," *Annual Report of the Bureau of American Ethnology*, vol. 2 (1883), pp. 117-166; "Who are the American Indians?" *American Anthropologist*, vol. 2 (1889), pp. 198-214; "A new linguistic family in California," *American Anthropologist*, vol. 3 (1890), pp. 45-49; *Tribes of North America, with Synonymy: Skittagetan Family* (Washington: 1890) (= *Smithsonian Miscellaneous Collections*, no. 5); *Chumash Place Names Lists* (edited by Robert F. Heizer; also includes material by A.L. Kroeber and C.H. Merriam) (Berkeley: 1975).

SOURCES: Henry Wetherbee Henshaw, "Autobiographical notes," *The Condor*, vol. 21 (1919), pp. 102-107, 165-171, 177-181, 217-222; vol. 22 (1920), pp. 3-10, 55-60, 95-101; Robert F. Heizer, "California Indian linguistic records: the Mission Indian Vocabularies of H.W. Henshaw," *University of California Anthropological Records*, Vol. 15 (1955), pp. 85-89; Henshaw manuscripts in the Smithsonian Institution National Anthropological Archives; F.W. Hodge and C. Hart Merriam, "Henry Wetherbee Henshaw," *American Anthropologist*, n.s., vol. 33 (1931), pp. 98-105; Jenks Cameron, *The Bureau of Biological Survey* (Baltimore: 1929); William A. Jones, "A naturalist's vision: the landscape photography of Henry Wetherbey [sic] Henshaw," *History of Photography*, vol. 8 (1984), pp. 169-174; A.L. Kroeber, "Powell and Henshaw: an episode in the history of ethnolinguistics," *Anthropological Linguistics*, vol. 2 (1960), pp. 1-5; E.W. Nelson, "Henry Wetherbee Henshaw—naturalist, 1850-1839," *The Auk*, vol. 49 (1932), pp. 399-427; T.S. Palmer, *Biographies of Members of the American Ornithologists' Union* (Washington: 1954), pp. 264-266; Frederic Ward Putnam, assisted by H.W. Henshaw [et al.], *Reports upon Archaeological and Ethnological Collections from Vicinity of Santa Barbara, California, and from Ruined Pueblos of Arizona and New Mexico and Certain Interior Tribes* (Washington: 1879); William C. Sturtevant, "Authorship of the Powell linguistic classification," *International Journal of Linguistics*, vol. 25 (1959), pp. 196-199; "Dr. H.W. Henshaw dies at age 80," *Washington Star* (2 August 1930), p. A5.

James R. Glenn

Herder, Johann Gottfried. Philosopher of history and language, translator, pastor, folklorist, critic. Born in Mohrungen (East Prussia) 25 August 1744, died in Weimar (Germany) 18 December 1803. A student of Kant and Hamann, teacher, friend and colleague to Goethe, Herder was a leader of the German movement away from the rational abstractions of the Enlightenment to the aesthetic participations of Romanticism. Determined to establish German language and culture on the European stage, Herder gradually extended his sympathy and scholarship to cultures more disparaged than his own, to the Middle Ages, to Hebrew and Arabic, and to folk and tribal traditions. At the same time, in his philosophical reflections on language and history, Herder pursued unity in the diversity he cherished. He proposed a common origin for humanity and a common end in a global yet pluralist civilization. That twofold extension of his thought underlies Herder's reputation among historians of anthropology as the virtual author of the comparative method and the modern critique of ethnocentrism. In the judgment of his biographer,

"Herder's ideal philosopher is the cultural anthropologist" (Clark, p. 322) and his life's work was an effort to realize that ideal.

In the *Ideen* and elsewhere, Herder pursued his grand synthesis of language, thought, sensation, body structure, custom and environment. In *Volkslieder*, in his Biblical hermeneutics, in critical essays and translations, he insisted on grounding all synthesis in irreducible historical particulars. Herder's dialectic depended on a reconception of God—the divine Maker as the Artist of world history rather than the Engineer of physics. Seen in the context of his project and his time, Herder's celebration of the German *Volksgeist* takes on a significance precisely opposed to widespread but superficial readings of him as a progenitor of fascism. The divine *poiesis* of world history constituted an evolving hierarchy of nested holisms in which each individual creature, species, society and *Volksgeist* realized its unique pattern even as the ultimate significance of all particulars derived from their participation in the pattern of the whole—itself conceived as the ultimate particular, the universal *Geist*. Human understanding, at all levels, had to be interpretive rather than explanatory, a participatory reconstruction of the organic unfolding of the patterns from their *Ur*-forms (original forms). Herder's epistemology and ontology might themselves be described as the *Ur*-form of 19th-century historical consciousness, the single most important influence on German historical linguistics and the anthropological concept of culture.

MAJOR WORKS: *Abhandlung über den Ursprung der Sprache* (Berlin: 1772) [tr.: *Treatise upon the Origin of Language* (London: 1827)]; *Volksleider* (Leipzig: 1778-1779); *Vom Geist der Ebräischen Poesie* (Dessau: 1782-1783) [tr.: *The Spirit of Hebrew Poetry* (London: 1833)]; *Ideen zur Philosophie der Geschichte der Menschheit* (Karlsruhe: 1784-1791) [tr.: *Outlines of a Philosophy of the History of Man* (London: 1800)]; *Gott: einige Gesprache* (Gotha: 1787) [tr.: *God: some Conversations* (New York: 1940)]. For the authoritative edition of the original works see: *Herders Sammtliche Werke* (Berlin: 1887-1913).

SOURCES: Rudolf Haym, *Herder nach seinem Leben und seinen Werken dargestellt* [2 vols.] (Berlin: 1880-1885); R.T. Clark, *Herder: His Life and Thought* (Berkeley: 1955); Isaiah Berlin, *Vica and Herder: Two Studies in the History of Ideas* (London: 1976); Edward Sapir, "Herder's 'Ursprung der Sprache,'" *Modern Philology*, vol. 5 (1907), pp. 109-142; Christian Growe, *Herder's Kulturanthropologie* (Bonn: 1977); Robert S. Mayo, *Herder and the Beginning of Comparative Literature* (Chapel Hill: 1969); G. Wells, *Herder and After: a Study in the Development of Sociology* (The Hague: 1959); T. de Zengotita, "Speakers of being: romantic refusion and cultural anthropology" in: George W. Stocking, Jr. (editor), *Romantic Motives: Essays on the Anthropological Sensibility* (Madison: 1989) (= *History of Anthropology*, vol. 6), pp. 74-123.

Thomas de Zengotita

Herskovits, Melville J. (Melville Jean). Anthropologist, Africanist, Caribbeanist. Born in Bellefontein (Ohio) 10 September 1895, died in Evanston (Illinois) 25 February 1963. Herkovits was a wide ranging anthropologist who, like his mentor FRANZ BOAS, contributed to many subfields of his discipline and did important ethnographic work in Africa, in North and South America and in the Caribbean. He also contributed in a major way as a statesman of anthropology to public debates on such issues as racism and the place of area and cross-cultural studies in education and American life. He founded the first African Studies Program in the United States at Northwestern University where he spent most of his career. He also founded and was first President of the African Studies Association of the United States. The focus of his theoretical interest was cultural dynamics and acculturation, and he developed enduring theoretical concepts in several areas including the study of culture areas, culture focus, syncretism, enculturation and historical ethnography. He also made a major contribution to the doctrine of "cultural relativism," which he more than any anthropologist of his generation helped to define and promulgate.

Herskovits' early work, in the 1920s, was in physical anthropology, and he made pioneering studies of the physical type—and variation from type—of the American "Negro." His interest in the Negro soon led him and his wife Frances (with whom he frequently collaborated) to field study that resulted in four ethnographies about the Caribbean area and Africa. It was in this early field study in Africa that he collected material for his massive historical ethnography, *Dahomey: an Ancient West African Kingdom*. The ethnographic projects of the 1930s and early 1940s were accompanied by more theoretical works on "primitive" economics and on acculturation. One of his best known and most widely read (and frequently republished) volumes of the period concerned the African antecedents and persisting influences of things African in New World Negro culture (*The Myth of the Negro Past*).

Herskovits' magnum opus was perhaps *Man and His Works*, which provided a theoretical overview both of his own broad interests and of the entire discipline (the subtitle, *The Science of Cultural Anthropology*, is misleading). The book was subsequently issued in an abridged version as *Cultural Anthropology*.

In the 1950s and early 1960s Herskovits turned his attention mainly to Africa and to the Program of African Studies at Northwestern University. He returned to Africa numerous times both as a scholar and as a statesman while a steady stream of Africans and Africanists made the African Studies Program at Northwestern one of the liveliest centers in the country for the study of that continent. The wisdom accumulated in the main preoccupation of this decade was brought together in *The Human Factor in Changing Africa*.

Herskovits wrote so much (nearly 500 items) and had such broad-ranging and eclectic interests that it would be difficult to render summary judgement. Though he did much quantitative work and considered himself, preeminently, a scientist, the humanist emphasis in his career was, perhaps, predominant. He was ever ready to defend individual realities and relativity against scientific reductionism and to defend human creativity against the flattening effect of scientific generalization, prediction and the laws of large numbers. He had enduring interests and published much, for example, in music and the oral, visual and plastic arts. Above all he argued for the humanizing effect in public and international affairs of a thoroughgoing anthropological, that is to say, cross-cultural perspective.

MAJOR WORKS: *The American Negro: a Study in Racial Crossing* (New York: 1928); (with Frances S. Herskovits) *An Outline of Dahomean Religious Belief* (Menasha, Wisc. 1933) (= *American Anthropological Association, Memoir*, no. 41); (with Frances S. Herskovits) *Rebel Destiny: among the Bush Negros of Dutch Guiana* (New York: 1934); (with Frances S. Herskovits) *Suriname Folk-lore* (New York: 1936); *Life in a Haitian Valley* (New York: 1937); *Dahomey: an Ancient West African Kingdom* [2 vols.] (New York: 1938); *Acculturation: the Study of Culture Contact* (New York: 1938); *The Economic Life of Primitive People* (New York: 1940); *The Myth of the Negro Past* (New York: 1942); (with Frances S. Herskovits) *Trinidad Village* (New York: 1946); *Man and His Works: the Science of Cultural Anthropology* (New York: 1948); *Economic Anthropology: a Study of Comparative Economics* (2nd revised ed., New York: 1952); *Cultural Anthropology* (New York: 1955) [abridgment of: *Man and His Works*]; (with Frances S. Herskovits) *Dahomean Narrative: a*

Cross Cultural Analysis (Evanston: 1958); (edited with W.R. Bascom) *Continuity and Change in African Culture* (Chicago: 1959); *The Human Factor in Changing Africa* (New York: 1962); (with M.H. Segall and D.T. Campbell) *The Influence of Culture on Visual Perception* (Indianapolis: 1966); *Cultural Relativism: Perspectives in Cultural Pluralism* (edited by Frances S. Herskovits) (New York: 1972).

SOURCES: James W. Fernandez, "Tolerance in a repugnant world: the cultural relativism of Melville J. Herskovits," *Ethos*, vol. 18 (1990), pp. 140-164; Alan P. Merriam, "Melville Jean Herskovits," *American Anthropologist*, vol. 66 (1964), pp. 75-109; George E. Simpson, *Melville J. Herskovits* (New York: 1973); James H. Vaughan, Jr., "Herskovits, Melville Jean" in: David L. Sills (editor), *International Encyclopedia of the Social Sciences* (New York: 1968-1979), vol. 6, pp. 353-354.

James W. Fernandez

Hertz, Robert. Philosopher, sociologist, ethnographer. Born in Saint-Cloud (France) 22 June 1881, died in Marchéville (France) 13 April 1915, a war casualty. Although incomplete and composed essentially of articles and notes collected by MARCEL MAUSS in 1928, the work of Hertz was to exert an important influence on the development of theoretical ethnology by pointing out the role of symbols in the structuring of social life.

A former student of the École Normale Supérieure and a disciple of Émile Durkheim with an *agrégation* in philosophy, Hertz contributed to *L'Année sociologique* starting in 1905. In 1905 and 1906, having received a scholarship, he conducted research in London, where he discovered materials in the works on ethnography in the library of the British Museum that were to play an essential role in his later research in ethnology and in religious sociology. His life as a scholar and a citizen resembled the life of Mauss, who, as Raymond Aron said so well, recommended that the sociologist "not avoid, in spite of all the dangers, objects of study that divide parties and incite passions." A socialist like quite a few of his former classmates of the École Normale, and like Mauss himself, Hertz founded in 1908 a small study group that published a series of pamphlets titled *Les Cahiers du socialiste*.

Taking up PAUL BROCA's celebrated statement that "We are right-handed because we are left-brained," in 1905 Hertz wondered about the reason for the paradoxical conversion of this fact of nature into a cultural ideal: every society seems to believe that right-handedness is the indication as well as the symbol of the proper image of things and of signs, the corollary being that every society subjects the left hand to a sort of mutilation. Hertz sought to discover the meaning and the function of the preeminence of the right hand of human societies in the opposition that all religious thought introduces between the sacred and the profane, and within the sacred itself, between the right side (pure, auspicious, defined) and left side (impure, inauspicious, vague). He had already recognized the dualism that characterizes all symbolic thought. For this reason, Hertz can be considered as one of the first anthropologists to have demonstrated that abstract intellectual concepts are in fact categories that precede every individual experience and are connected to the structure of social thought itself.

Extending and even radicalizing the thought of Durkheim, who had already found symbolism to be one of the conditions of the intelligibility of social phenomena, Hertz first started the reversal that structural anthropology was later to emphasize: the appearance of language makes social life at once possible and necessary. In an earlier study, he had inaugurated this approach and had shown the importance of the function of symbols in the comprehension of the ritual "double or second funerals" practiced by a considerable number of societies that, by offering a final burial to a corpse, permit the soul or spirit to enter the world of the dead and acquire the status of ancestor. His incomplete thesis (of which only the introduction remains), is devoted to "sin and atonement in primitive societies." This thesis was to envision the dynamic of oppositions and their transformations and to analyze the means by which a society restores things that ought to have been separated symbolically but are confounded by error and infractions.

The reflections of Hertz on sin, religious polarity and the collective concept of death, as well as his application in 1912 of the ethnographical approach to the study of a religious cult (the cult of Saint Besse in the Aoste valley) were taken up notably by the founders of the Collège de Sociologie in 1937—Roger Caillois, Georges Bataille and MICHEL LEIRIS—in order to explore the dark side of human nature and to clarify the dialectic of attraction and repulsion that is at the foundation of religious thought, i.e., according to Georges Bataille, at the center of social life.

MAJOR WORKS: *Sociologie religieuse et folklore* (Paris: 1928); *Le péché et l'expiation dans les sociétés primitives* (Paris: 1988).

SOURCES: Raymond Aron, *De la condition historique du sociologue* (Paris: 1971); Marc Augé, *Le Dieu objet* (Paris: 1988); Isac Chiva, "Entre livre et musée: émergence d'une ethnologie de la France" in: Isac Chiva and Utz Jeggle, *Ethnologies en miroir* (Paris: 1987), pp. 9-33; Louis Dumont, *Essais sur l'individualisme* (Paris: 1983); Émile Durkheim, "Notice biographique sur Robert Hertz," *Annuaire de l'Association des anciens élèves de l'École normale* (1916), pp. 116-120; Denis Hollier (editor), *Le Collège de sociologie* (Paris: 1979); Claude Lévi-Strauss, *La pensée sauvage* (Paris: 1962); Marcel Mauss, "In memoriam: l'oeuvre inédite de Durkheim et de ses collaborateurs" in: *Oeuvres*, vol. 3 (Paris: 1969), pp. 473-567; Rodney Needham, *Right and Left: Essays on Dual Symbolic Classification* (Chicago: 1973).

Jean Jamin
[Translation from French: Timothy Eastridge]

Hertzberg, Hans T.E. Physical-and-human-factors anthropologist, engineering anthropologist. Born in San Antonio (Texas) 18 September 1905. Hertzberg graduated from the Army Air Corps Flying School at Kelley Field, Texas (1929), completed graduate work in anthropology at the University of Texas (1931-1933), and received an M.A. in anthropology from Harvard University (1942) where he worked with E.A. HOOTON. After World War II, his career was spent in the applied anthropology of human factors and aerospace medicine with the U.S. Air Force. He was among the pioneers in applying anthropometric data on human size, mobility and strength to the design of clothing, protective equipment and the worksite to further safety, efficiency and comfort. He regarded structure, mechanical function and size variability of the human body to be the central elements in man-machine design, in both civil and military applications.

Hertzberg was the senior physical anthropologist for the Air Force from 1946 through 1972 and a member of the Society of Automotive Engineers' Committee on Human Factors and the National Research Council's Committee on Physical Anthropology. He assisted with projects ranging from those involving the P-80, to the B-36, to NASA's Mercury capsule, to suited human propulsion in space, to prone-position operations by aircrew members. He established the criteria underlying an entire family of anthropomorphic dummies that were used in crash research by the U.S. Bureau of Standards and Department of Transportation. His extensive applied research resulted in more than seventy published articles, chapters, and technical reports. Influential among these is his monograph, *Anthropometry of Flying Personnel ...*, which for decades has been used not only by manufacturers of civil and military aircraft but also by clothiers, including national retail chains. His pioneering cross-societal study, *Anthropometric Survey of Turkey, Greece, and Italy*, was favorably reviewed. His "Engineering anthropology" is still the basic text on this subject.

MAJOR WORKS: "Post-war anthropometry in the Air Force," *American Journal of Physical Anthropology*, vol. 6 (1948), pp. 363-371; *Anthropometry of Flying Personnel—1950* (Wright-Paterson Air Force Base: 1954) (= *WADC Technical Report*, 52-231); "Dynamic anthropometry of working positions," *Human Factors*, vol. 2 (1960), pp. 147-155; *Anthropometric Survey of Turkey, Greece, and Italy* (New York: 1963); "Conference on standardization of anthropometric techniques and terminology," *American Journal of Physical Anthropology*, vol. 28 (1968), pp. 1-16; "Engineering anthropology" in: P. Van Cott and R.G. Kincade (editors), *Human Engineering Guide to Equipment Design* (2nd ed., Washington: 1972), pp. 467-632; "Engineering anthropology: past, present, and potential" in: Walter Goldschmidt (editor), *The Uses of Anthropology* (Washington: 1979), pp. 184-204.

SOURCES: "Anthropology and high technology: an engineering anthropologist's perspective," *Anthropology Newsletter*, vol. 21, no. 1 (1980), p. 6; Frederick C. Gamst, "The diesel-electric locomotive as a work environment," *Rice University Studies*, vol. 61, no. 2 (1975), pp. 37-39, 76.

Frederick C. Gamst

Heyerdahl, Thor. Explorer, adventurer, anthropologist. Born in Larvik (Norway) 6 October 1914. Heyerdahl was educated in Norway through the B.A. level. He was engaged in graduate studies in the United States and Canada when World War II put an end to these formal programs of study. After serving with the Norwegian military forces in exile during the war, he led the Kon Tiki expedition across the Pacific. The aim of this adventure was to demonstrate the possibility of an alternate method of migration to the New World and from there to the Pacific. This was followed by the first serious archaeological work on Easter Island since the turn of the century. Later journeys of the reed ship Ra were undertaken in order to prove the possibility of connection between North Africa and the Middle East with the Mesoamerican heartland of the New World.

Heyerdahl is associated with a revival of the diffusionist theory that was so popular early in the 20th century. He argued that early man tended to use the oceans rather than the more difficult overland routes for communication and trade. He did not see the oceans as uncrossable barriers but tended rather to view them as conduits for intercontinental connections.

The imagination and the excitement that Heyerdahl has managed to convey to the general public have not usually been shared by members of the academic community. Perhaps a reassessment is in order, looking at what Heyerdahl has said rather than what he is thought to have said.

MAJOR WORKS: *Kon-Tiki: across the Pacific by Raft* (New York: 1950); *Aku-Aku: the Secret of Easter Island* (London: 1958); *The Ra Expeditions* (New York: 1971); *American Indians in the Pacific: the Theory Behind the Kon-Tiki Expedition* (New York: 1951); *Fatu-Hiva: Back to Nature* (New York: 1975); *Early Man and the Ocean: a Search for the Beginnings of Navigation and*

Seaborne Civilizations (New York: 1979); *Tigris Expedition: In Search of Our Beginnings* (New York: 1981); *The Maldive Mystery* (London: 1986).

SOURCES: Arnold Jacoby, *Senior Kon-Tiki: the Biography of Thor Heyerdahl* (New York: 1967); "Portrait," *Illustrated London News*, vol. 227 (6 August 1955), p. 233; "Talk with the author," *Newsweek*, vol. 42, no. 10 (8 September 1958), p. 99; "Mr. Heyerdahl," *New York Times Book Review* (27 November 1960), p. 8; J. Lear, "Thor Heyerdahl's next voyage," *The Saturday Review*, vol. 52 (3 May 1969), p. 49-56; "Heyerdahl," *Current Biography* (1972), pp. 218-221; "Thor Heyerdahl speaks his mind," *Scandinavian Review*, vol. 68 (June 1980), pp. 31-41.

William P. Hopkins

Hilger, Sister *Inez* (M. Inez Hilger). Benedictine nun, anthropologist, sociologist, teacher, nurse. Born in Roscoe (Minnesota) 16 October 1891, died in St. Joseph (Minnesota) 18 May 1977. Hilger was trained in history, literature, sociology and anthropology at the University of Minnesota and the Catholic University of America (Ph.D., 1939). Her primary institutional affiliation was with the College of St. Benedict in St. Joseph, Minnesota. After training as a nurse and teacher, she joined its staff while it was still a high school. A plan to convert the school into a college led her into graduate work and eventually into anthropology. She was the first woman fully admitted to the Catholic University of America. In 1955 she became a research associate of the Bureau of American Ethnology. Hilger's fieldwork began during the 1930s with concern for the social problems of Chippewa Indians of Minnesota; but, influenced by Rhoda Métraux and MARGARET MEAD, she eventually developed a special interest in the life of children. She pursued such studies among the Chippewa (1932-1966), Arapaho (1935-1942), Araucanian (1946-1947, 1951-1952) and Ainu and Japanese (1962-1963). For the Human Relations Area Files, she prepared a field guide for the study of childlife. In addition, she carried out miscellaneous ethnological studies among several Plains, southwestern, southeastern and Latin American tribes. At the end of her life, Hilger was working among the Blackfeet collecting what she called "grandmother tales." Her work was basically descriptive.

MAJOR WORKS: *A Social Study of One Hundred Fifty Chippewa Indian Families on the White Earth Reservation of Minnesota* (Washington: 1939); *Chippewa Child Life and Its Cultural Background* (Washington: 1951) (= *Bureau of American Ethnology Bulletin*, no. 146); *Arapaho Child Life and Its Cultural Background* (Washington: 1952) (= *Bureau of American Ethnology Bulletin*, no. 148); *Araucanian Child Life and Its Cultural Background* (Washington: 1957) (= *Smithsonian Miscellaneous Collections*, vol. 155); *Field Guide to the Ethnological Study of Child Life* (New Haven: 1960) (= *Human Relations Area Files Behavior Science Field Guides*, vol. 1); (with Margaret Mondloch) *Huenun Ñamku: an Araucanian Indian of the Andes Remembers the Past* (Norman: 1966); *Together with the Ainu: a Vanishing People* (Norman: 1971).

SOURCES: Hilger papers and vertical file in the Smithsonian Institution National Anthropological Archives; Robert F. Spencer, "Sister M. Inez Hilger, O.S.B., 1891-1977," *American Anthropologist*, vol. 80 (1978), pp. 650-653.

James R. Glenn

Hill-Tout, Charles. Anthropologist, schoolteacher. Born in Bridgwater (England) 28 September 1858, died in Vancouver (British Columbia) 30 June 1944. Hill-Tout was an amateur ethnologist in western Canada at a time when there were few trained anthropologists in the whole nation; his efforts at ethnography recorded much that otherwise would have been lost.

Born Charles Tout, he adopted his mother's maiden name as a surname only after his arrival in British Columbia at the age of 32. Educated to be an Anglican clergyman, Hill-Tout decided against taking holy orders when his interest in the writings of Darwin and Huxley created difficulties with his instructors. In 1884 Hill-Tout emigrated to Canada, teaching in and directing several boys' schools in Toronto and, after 1890, in Vancouver. He purchased a farm near Vancouver in 1896 and left teaching for full-time farming in 1899.

Hill-Tout had been interested in anthropology before his arrival in British Columbia, but only after relocating in the growing city of Vancouver did he have the opportunity to do significant primary research. He involved himself in archaeological surveys and in ethnography among the nearby Coast and Interior Salish peoples; though untutored in anthropology, Hill-Tout attempted to remedy this by reading widely and by communicating with academics and specialists in the field.

When FRANZ BOAS visited Vancouver in 1897, Hill-Tout greeted him enthusiastically. He aided Boas and his assistant Harlan Smith in their research in British Columbia, but no close ties could be forged. Boas was a champion of a trained, rational, fact-based approach to ethnology, while Hill-Tout laced his works with speculations concerning the origins of ceremonies, terms, even of peoples. This approach was clearly antithetical to Boas's vision of anthropology as a science.

Hill-Tout's speculations did not prevent him from producing a great deal of worthwhile ethnographic and linguistic writing, however. From his earliest days in Canada, Hill-Tout had been a member of one or another scientific institute, and by 1896 he had come to the attention of the British Association for the Advancement of Science. When that group created a Committee for an Ethnological Survey of Canada, Hill-Tout was made a member. He was also made a fellow of the American Ethnological Society in 1908, vice-president of the Canadian branch of the Archaeological Institute of America (1911), and vice president (1921) and president (1922) of the anthropological section of the Royal Society of Canada. He continued to write prolifically into old age and produced a number of popularizing articles on anthropology for newspapers as far from Vancouver as London, England. One of Hill-Tout's most appreciated activities was giving talks on new anthropological discoveries to a public avid for an entertaining form of education.

Hill-Tout was nominated for an honorary doctorate from the University of British Columbia in 1935, but the university administration did not choose to so honor him. His habit of going by the title of "professor" when his highest actual academic rank was that of headmaster may have alienated the local university faculty, while his speculative approach to anthropology also did him no good in academic circles. To the people of Vancouver, however, he remained an important citizen and one strongly identified with the anthropology of their province.

MAJOR WORKS: *The Salish People* [4 vols.] (Vancouver: 1978); "Some features of the language and culture of the Salish," *American Anthropologist*, vol. 7 (1905), pp. 674-687; *The Native Races of the British Empire. British North America*. Vol. 1. *The Far West, the Home of the Salish and Dene* (London: 1907); "Report on the ethnology of the Okanaken of British Columbia, an interior division of the Salish stock," *Journal of the Royal Anthropological Institute*, vol. 41 (1911), pp. 130-161 .

SOURCES: Ralph Maud, "Introduction[s]" to: Charles Hill-Tout, *The Salish People* (Vancouver: 1978), vol. 1, pp. 11-19; vol. 2, pp. 11-17; vol. 3, pp. 11-19; vol. 4, pp. 17-32; Ralph Maud, "Bio-bibliography of Charles Hill-Tout" in: Charles Hill-Tout, *The Salish People* (Vancouver: 1978), vol. 4, pp. 17-32.

David Lonergan

Hirschberg, Walter. Cultural anthropologist, ethnologist, ethnohistorian. Born in Neugradinska (Austria-Hungary, now Yugoslavia) 17 December 1904. Hirschberg studied ethnology (*Völkerkunde*) and anthropology at the University of Vienna. He received his Ph.D. in 1928. For a time he was Librarian at the Anthropos Institute in St. Gabriel and Curator at the Museum für Völkerkunde (Ethnographic Museum) in Vienna (heading the Africa section). He did field studies in Kamerun (Cameroon) and Sierra Leone. From 1962 to 1975 he was full professor of ethnology, holding the Chair of Ethnology II at the University of Vienna. He was the founder of ethnohistorical research in Vienna.

Hirschberg's major contribution to Viennese ethnology has been the establishment of "ethnohistorical research" as the adequate application of historical methods within ethnology. The beginnings of this approach dates back to the 1930s, when it emerged as a result of the opposition to the Vienna School of Historical Ethnology (*Wiener Schule der Ethnologie*, "*Kulturkreislehre*") as represented by Professor Father WILHELM SCHMIDT and Professor Father WILHELM KOPPERS. In contrast to their evolutionary approach, Hirschberg introduced the empirical historical method into ethnology in Vienna. Under his direction this new academic research program called "ethnohistory" mainly focuses on the reconstruction of the cultural history of African societies from the period of early contacts with Europeans up until the 19th century.

Apart from numerous articles dealing with problems of ethnology and ethnohistory in Black Africa, Hirschberg published sixteen books referring to general problems in ethnology (e.g., *Wörterbuch der Völkerkunde*; *Technologie und Ergologie in der Völkerkunde*) and culture history of Africa (e.g., *Die Kulturen Afrikas*).

As president of the Anthropologische Gesellschaft in Wien (Anthropological Society of Vienna) from 1964 to 1985, and as chairman of the Gesellschaft der Freunde der Forschungsgemeinde Wilhelminenberg (Society of the Friends of the Wilhelminenberg Research Community), Hirschberg pursued a holistic approach to the study of man, confronting cultural evidence with the findings of the new discipline of "human ethology" and aiming to arrive at a broader understanding of human nature.

MAJOR WORKS: *Völkerkunde* (Vienna, Leipzig and Olten: 1936); *Schwarzafrika* (Graz: 1962) (= *Monumenta Ethnographica: frühe völkerkundliche Bilddokumente*, vol. 1); *Die Kunstlerstrasse: auf Studienreise durch Kamerun* (Vienna: 1962); *Völkerkunde Afrikas* (Mannheim: 1965); (editor) *Wörterbuch der Völkerkunde* (Stuttgart: 1965); *Technologie und Ergologie in der Völkerkunde* (Mannheim: 1966); *Religionsethnologie und ethnohistorische Religionsforschung: eine Gegenüberstellung* (Vienna: 1972) (= *Wiener Ethnohistorische Blatter*, Beiheft 1); *Die Kulturen Afrikas: Handbuch der Kulturgeschichte* (Frankfurt am Main: 1974); *Frosch und Kröte in Mythos und Brauch* (Vienna: 1988); (editor) *Neues Wörterbuch der Völkerkunde* (Berlin: 1988).

SOURCES: Karl R. Wernhart, "Walter Hirschberg 80 Jahre, oder 'zum Kanon der Fächer der Anthropologie,'" *Mitteilungen der Anthropologischen Gesellschaft in Wien*, vol. 114 (1984), pp. 1-11; Karl R. Wernhart, "Walter Hirschbergs Weg zum Frosch—oder der Kulturanthropologe am Schnittpunkt der Disziplinen" in: Walter Hirschberg, *Frosch und Kröte in Mythos und Brauch* (Vienna: 1988), pp. 9-20.

Karl R. Wernhart

Hocart, A.M. (Arthur Maurice). Anthropologist. Born in Etterbeck, near Brussels (Belgium) 26 April 1883, died 1939. Hocart is known both for his work on Fiji and for his insights into the workings of early society, which have inspired and foreshadowed much recent work in anthropology, particularly that focusing on symbols.

His first trip to the Pacific occurred when, after an Oxford education in classics, he participated in a research expedition to the Solomon Islands with W.H.R. RIVERS during 1908-1909. He was headmaster of a school in Fiji from 1909 to 1912, and it was during this period that he acquired his considerable knowledge of Fijian culture and developed many of his ideas. He held many different positions over the next years of his life, mostly of short duration: he was lecturer at Oxford (1915), soldier (1915-1919), archaeological commissioner in Ceylon (1921-1929), honorary lecturer at University College, London, and librarian at the Council of the Royal Anthropological Institute (early 1930s), and professor of sociology at the Fuad I University in Cairo (from 1935 until his death). The latter was his only stable academic position.

His work made only a modest impression on academic anthropology during his lifetime, as it contributed little to the functionalist thought dominant at the time. Its goal was in many ways far more ambitious: to "'reconstruct the history of thought' and the 'development of human institutions'" (Needham, "Hocart, A.M.," p. 306). Much of it is frankly speculative; little of it is completely straightforward. But, thanks in part to the efforts of several enthusiasts—notably LORD RAGLAN and Rodney Needham—and in part due to its intrinsic interest—it has played a major role in the thinking of many scholars over the last twenty years.

MAJOR WORKS: *Kingship* (London: 1927); *The Progress of Man: a Short Survey of His Evolution, His Customs, and His Works* (London: 1933) [tr.: *Les progrès de l'homme* (Paris: 1935)]; *Kings and Councillors: an Essay in the Comparative Anatomy of Human Society* (Cairo: 1936; revised ed., Chicago: 1970); *Caste: a Comparative Study* (London: 1950) [tr.: *les castes* (Paris: 1938 [sic])]; *The Life-giving Myth, and Other Essays* (edited by Lord Raglan) (London: 1952; new ed., London: 1973); *The Northern States of Fiji* (edited by Lord Raglan) (London: 1952) (= *Occasional Publication of the Royal Anthropological Institute of Great Britain and Ireland*, no. 11); *Social Origins* (edited by Lord Raglan) (London: 1954).

SOURCES: E.E. Evans-Pritchard, "Arthur Maurice Hocart, 1884 [sic]-March 1939," *Man*, vol. 39 (1939), p. 131; Rodney Needham, *A Bibliography of Arthur Maurice Hocart (1883-1939)* (Oxford: 1967); Rodney Needham, "Hocart, A.M." in: David L. Sills (editor), *International Encyclopedia of the Social Sciences* (New York: 1968-1979), vol. 18, pp. 305-307; E.E. Evans-Pritchard, "Foreword" to: A.M. Hocart, *Kings and Councillors* (Chicago: 1970), pp. ix-xi; Rodney Needham, "Editor's introduction" to: A.M. Hocart, *Kings and Councillors* (Chicago: 1970), pp. xiii-xcix.

Hodge, Frederick Webb. Anthropologist, historian, museum director. Born in Plymouth (England) 28 October 1864, died in Santa Fe (New Mexico) 28 September

1956. Hodge was a prolific scholar and a major influence on the development of anthropology in the United States.

Hodge's family moved to Washington, D.C., when he was a small child, and he attended Columbian University (now George Washington University) there. Hodge was employed as secretary to the U.S. Geological Survey and the Bureau of American Ethnology (BAE) for several years, leaving that position to serve as secretary to the Hemenway Southwestern Archaeological Expedition, from 1886 until 1889. During his time in the Southwest, Hodge learned archaeological techniques and became extremely knowledgeable about American Indian cultures, while associating with scholars such as FRANK HAMILTON CUSHING and ADOLPH BANDELIER.

When he returned to the BAE in 1889, Hodge was employed as archaeologist, ethnologist, editor, and librarian. He was deeply involved in many facets of the BAE's activities and was increasingly recognized as a specialist in the history and archaeology of the Southwest.

From 1901 until 1905, Hodge was an executive assistant in the Smithsonian Institution, responsible for its extensive publication exchange program. In 1905 he returned to the BAE and edited the important two-volume work *Handbook of American Indians North of Mexico*. He also edited the multi-volume study of the American Indian by EDWARD SHERIFF CURTIS from 1907 to 1911. In 1910 Hodge was appointed Ethnologist-in-Charge of the Bureau, where he stayed until 1917. From 1918 to 1932 he was director of the Museum of the American Indian and editor of its publications as well as one of the leading field archaeologists.

In 1932 Hodge was persuaded to move to Los Angeles and assume the directorship of the Southwest Museum, a post he retained from the age of sixty-seven to the age of ninety. There he was editor of its publication, *The Masterkey*, for twenty-four years and engaged in a great deal of writing and editorial work on Spanish explorations of the Southwest. (His anthropological and historical fieldwork in that area took place at intervals from 1886 until 1947.) Hodge retired in 1956, following a sabbatical year, and moved to Santa Fe at the age of 91. He died one month short of his ninety-second birthday.

Although he was a prolific writer, with more than 300 items published, Hodge's most important contributions to anthropology were as an organizer and editor. As a member of the Anthropological Society of Washington, he edited its *American Anthropologist* (old series) from 1899 until 1902. After he helped found the American Anthropological Association (AAA) in 1902, Hodge once again edited, single-handedly, the *American Anthropologist* (new series), this time from 1902 until 1910 and from 1912 to 1914. He undertook a great deal of committee work in the fledgling AAA and was its president from 1915 to 1917. During subsequent periods he was a representative to the National Research Council and a trustee of the School of American Research.

Hodge was the recipient of a number of honorary doctorates and was a fellow of the American Association for the Advancement of Science, the American Geographical Society, the Royal Anthropological Institute, the American Folklore Society, the New York Academy of Sciences and many other learned associations.

MAJOR WORKS: (editor) *Handbook of American Indians North of Mexico* (Washington: 1907-1910) (= *Bureau of American Ethnology Bulletin*, no. 30); (with George Heye and George Pepper) *The Nagoochee Mound in Georgia* (New York: 1918) (= *Museum of the American Indian,*

Contributions, vol. 4, no. 3); *Hawikuh Bonework* (New York: 1920) (= *Museum of the American Indian, Indian Notes and Monographs*, vol. 3, no. 3); *The Age of the Zuni Pueblo of Kechipauan* (New York: 1920) (= *Museum of the American Indian, Indian Notes and Monographs*, vol. 3, no. 2); *Turquoise Work of Hawikuh, New Mexico* (New York: 1921) (= *Museum of the American Indian, Leaflet*, no. 2); *Circular Kivas Near Hawikuh, New Mexico* (New York: 1923) (= *Museum of the American Indian, Contributions*, vol. 7, no. 1); *History of Hawikuh, New Mexico, One of the So-Called Cities of Cibola* (Los Angeles: 1937) (= *The Southwest Museum, Frederick Webb Hodge Anniversary Publication Fund*, vol. 1).

SOURCES: Neil M. Judd [et al.], "Frederick Webb Hodge, 1864-1956," *American Antiquity*, vol. 22 (1957), pp. 401-404; Fay-Cooper Cole, "Frederick Webb Hodge, 1864-1956," *American Anthropologist*, vol. 59 (1957), pp. 517-520; Arthur J.O. Anderson, "Frederick Webb Hodge, 1864-1956," *Hispanic American Historical Review*, vol. 38 (1958), pp. 263-267.

David Lonergan

Hodgkin, Thomas. Anatomist, ethnologist, philanthropist. Born in Pentonville (England) 17 August 1798, died in Jaffa (Syria) 4 April 1866. As a Quaker, Hodgkin was barred from education at Oxford or Cambridge, as were all religious nonconformists, and was educated privately. After a two-year apprenticeship to a pharmaceutical chemist he entered Guy's Hospital in September 1819 as a physician's pupil. In October 1820 he enrolled in Edinburgh University as a medical student for two sessions, 1820-1821 and 1822-1823. During the 1821-1822 session he studied in Paris and learned the use of the stethoscope from its inventor, Laennec. Hodgkin graduated from Edinburgh with an M.D. in August 1823 and in the fall of 1825 joined Guy's Hospital Medical School as its first demonstrator (lecturer) in morbid anatomy and curator of the museum.

Hodgkin is known primarily as the eponym for the unusual disease of enlarged lymph nodes associated with an enlarged spleen, a syndrome that he described in 1832. Denied promotion to assistant physician, he resigned in September 1837. His rejection was mainly due to his outspoken sympathy for the North American Indian. This led to a conflict with the hospital's treasurer, who was also an official in the Hudson's Bay Company's fur trade. Hodgkin's interest in uncivilized and oppressed peoples developed at an early age as a result of the activities of Quakers to "civilize" American Indians. He opposed slavery and the slave trade and supported efforts to colonize freed slaves in Africa. Hodgkin was a founder of the Aborigines' Protection Society (1837) and, as secretary, wrote letters and petitions to colonial governors and foreign secretaries expressing the society's concerns about exploitation and threat of extinction facing the natives of the territories being overrun by European settlers and commercial enterprises. The Aborigines' Protection Society intended to be an ethnological society and political pressure group but emphasized its political role. It wanted basic legal and political rights for natives in their contacts with British settlers—not to stop colonization, only to change its character—and to correct false allegations that the aborigines were naturally inferior. Hodgkin frequently urged that capable aboriginal youths who had some knowledge and exhibited ability in missionary or other native schools be brought to England to be studied as well as to be educated.

In 1844 Hodgkin helped found the Ethnological Society of London to study races threatened with extinction. Political objectives were to be left to the Aborigines' Protection Society. For Hodgkin, ethnology combined his humanitarian interests in primitive peoples with an organized scientific approach to collection of data about them. He prepared standardized guidelines for explorers and travelers to gather information about the cultures and physical and social structures of distant peoples and races. Hodgkin advocated the study and preservation of native African culture and languages. In 1858, as honorary secretary of the Royal Geographical Society of London, he recommended an African location to an American group inquiring about settlement sites for freed slaves. At home, Hodgkin addressed the problems of the socially and economically disadvantaged in pamphlets on medical care, public health, housing and sanitation. He consistently maintained that the basic problems of the poor were not medical but socioeconomic and could best be relieved by useful employment instead of charity.

Hodgkin was a monogenist and believed in the unity of the human species and that observable differences in the races were superficial. He looked for similarities in the languages spoken among physically different groups as evidence that would tie all mankind into a single family tree and urged the study and preservation of non-European languages as a means of revealing man's physical history. Hodgkin was not disturbed by the idea of evolution or the discoveries of geology and believed that religion had nothing to fear from scientific investigations. He was a religious man and tried to reconcile the opposing views of science and religion within a religious framework. He used comparative anatomy to explain the structural similarities in all vertebrate animals as well as in lower forms of life and referred to a sublime unity of plan pervading the whole animal kingdom. Hodgkin believed that creation of distinct species had occurred at different times and locations and he presumed that new species were coming into existence in his own time.

MAJOR WORKS: "On some morbid appearances of the absorbent glands and spleen," *Medico-Chirurgical Transactions*, vol. 17 (1832), pp. 68-114; *A Letter from Dr. Hodgkins* [sic] *to Hannah Kilham on the State of the Colony of Sierra Leone: Being remarks on the Report of the Commissioners Relative to the State of the Liberated Africans in that Colony and Suggestions for the General Improvement of Their Condition* (Lindfield: 1827); *On Negro Emancipation and American Colonization* (London: 1832); *An Inquiry into the Merits of the American Colonization Society: and A Reply to the Charges Brought Against It: with an Account of the British African Colonization Society* (London: 1833); *On the British African Colonization Society: to Which Are Added Some Particulars Respecting the American Colonization Society; and a Letter from Jeremiah Hubbard, Addressed to a Friend in England, on the Same Subject* (London: 1834); "On the importance of studying and preserving the languages spoken by uncivilized nations, with the view of elucidating the physical history of Man," *London and Edinburgh Philosophical Magazine and Journal of Science*, vol. 7 (1835), pp. 27-36, 94-106; "On the practicability of civilizing aboriginal populations," *Monthly Chronicle*, vol. 4 (1839), pp. 309-321; "Varieties of human race: queries respecting the human race, to be addressed to travellers and others: drawn up by a Committee of the British Association for the Advancement of Science, appointed in 1839," *Report of the British Association for the Advancement of Science*, vol. 10 (1840), pp. 447-458; vol. 11 (1841), pp. 332-339; "On the progress of ethnology," *Edinburgh New Philosophical Journal*, vol. 36 (1844), pp. 118-136; "On the dog, as the companion of man in his geographical distribution," *Zoologist*, vol. 3 (1845), pp. 1097-1105; "On the ancient inhabitants of the Canary Islands," *Edinburgh New Philosophical Journal*, vol. 39 (1845), pp. 372-386; "A manual of ethnological inquiry; being a series of questions concerning the human race, prepared by a sub-committee of the British Association for the Advancement of Science, appointed in 1851 (consisting of Dr. Hodgkin and Richard Cull, Esq.), and adapted for the use of travellers and others in studying the varieties of man," *Report of the British Association for the Advancement of Science*, vol. 22 (1852), pp. 243-252; "A proposal to form a new Indian settlement," *The Aborigines' Friend, and Colonial Intelligencer*, n.s., vol. 2 (1859), pp. 96-98; *Narrative of a Journey to Morocco, in 1863 and 1864, with Geological Annotations* (London: 1866).

SOURCES: Michael Rose, *Curator of the Dead: Thomas Hodgkin (1798-1866)* (London: 1981); "Hodgkin, Thomas, M.D." in: *Dictionary of National Biography*, vol. 9 (London: 1921-1922), pp.

957-958; "Obituary: Thomas Hodgkin, M.D.," *Lancet*, vol. 1 (1866), pp. 445-446; "The late Thomas Hodgkin, M.D.," *British Medical Journal*, vol. 1 (1866), p. 447; "Obituary: Dr. Thomas Hodgkin," *Medical Times and Gazette* (14 April 1866), p. 403; "The late Dr. Hodgkin," *The Aborigines' Friend, and Colonial Intelligencer*, n.s., vol. 2 (1866), pp. 519-522; "On inquiries into the races of man," *Report of the British Association for the Advancement of Science*, vol. 11 (1841), pp. 52-55; Samuel Wilks, "An account of some unpublished papers of the late Dr. Hodgkin," *Guy's Hospital Reports*, vol. 23 (1878), pp. 55-127; Samuel Wilks, "A short account of the life and works of Thomas Hodgkin, M.D.," *Guy's Hospital Gazette*, vol. 23 (1909), pp. 528-532; Edward H. Kass and Anne H. Bartlett, "Thomas Hodgkin, M.D. (1798-1866): an annotated bibliography," *Bulletin of the History of Medicine*, vol. 43 (1969), pp. 138-175; Louis Rosenfeld, "Thomas Hodgkin (1798-1866): morbid anatomist and social activist," *Bulletin of the New York Academy of Medicine*, vol. 62 (1986), pp. 193-205.

Louis Rosenfeld

Hoebel, E. Adamson *(Edward Adamson)*. Anthropologist, legal ethnographer. Born in Madison (Wisconsin) 16 November 1906. Hoebel received a Ph.D. from Columbia University where he began his teaching career, which continued primarily at the Universities of Utah and Minnesota. Hoebel had a seminal international and interdisciplinary influence on the mid-20th-century study of non-Western law. Beginning as a legal ethnographer of the Comanche and the Cheyenne, he developed a broadly comparative view of social control as an integral part of each society (in, e.g., *The Law of Primitive Man*). Hoebel did not accept BRONISLAW MALINOWSKI's interpretation of all social control as law, but concentrated only on those customs enforced by physical coercion on the part of a society's authorized agents. He used "jural postulates," or basic underlying principles, as his cross-cultural analytical approach. He explored the increasing complexity of legal systems concomitant with technological specialization and social stratification without expounding any unilinear theory. Hoebel served to expand the boundaries of both anthropology and law through his collaboration with lawyer Karl Llewellyn (*The Cheyenne Way*) and with legal scholar Harold Berman in leading the first (1956) Social Science Research Council Institute on law and social science. He shared his descriptive talents and provocative ideas over the years and around the world through a beginning anthropology textbook, his teaching at Oxford University and the Catholic University of Nijmegen and his interaction with fellow scholars at the Center for Advanced Study in the Behavioral Sciences and the Center for Cultural and Technical Interchange between East and West.

MAJOR WORKS: (with Karl Llewellyn) *The Cheyenne Way: Conflict and Case Law in Primitive Jurisprudence* (Norman: 1941); *Man in the Primitive World* (New York: 1949; revised 2nd ed., 1958); (with Earnest Wallace) *The Comanches: Lords of the South Plains* (Norman: 1953); *The Law of Primitive Man: a Study on Comparative Legal Dynamics* (Cambridge, Mass.: 1954); *The Cheyennes: Indians of the Great Plains* (New York: 1961; revised 2nd ed., New York: 1978); (with K. Petersen) *A Cheyenne Sketchbook* (Norman: 1964); *Anthropology: the Study of Man* (New York: 1966); *The Plains Indians: a Critical Biography* (Bloomington: 1978); (with Thomas Weaver) *Anthropology: The Human Experience* (New York: 1979).

SOURCES: Richard D. Schwartz, "To Ad Hoebel—with thanks," *Law and Society Review*, vol. 7 (1973), pp. 531-532; "Hoebel, Edward Adamson, 1906-," *Contemporary Authors*, new revision series, vol. 1 (1981), p. 273.

M.E.R. Nicholsen

Hoernlé, Agnes Winifred (née Agnes Tucker). Social anthropologist, social reformer. Born in Kimberly (Cape of Good Hope) 6 December 1885, died in Johannesburg (South Africa) 17 March 1960. Hoernlé ranked among the most distinguished teachers of social anthropology in her day. At the University of the Witwatersrand she gave Max Gluckman, Eileen and J.D. Krige, HILDA KUPER, Ellen Hellmann and others their basic training. Her research and scholarly writing focused on both the Nama Khoi (Hottentots) and the Southeast Bantu-speaking peoples. Her influence on ISAAC SCHAPERA's ethnographic compilations was considerable.

Hoernlé was trained in anthropology at Cambridge (1908-1910) working closely with A.C. HADDON, W.H.R. RIVERS and C.S. Myers. In 1911 she went to Leipzig and Bonn to pursue her interest in psychology, familiarizing herself also with the German school of historical anthropology. Later she attended the Sorbonne to read sociology under Durkheim.

On her return to Southern Africa in 1912 she made the first of three research expeditions among the Nama and became the first trained woman social anthropologist to carry out fieldwork in the strict sense of the term.

Hoernlé and A.R. RADCLIFFE-BROWN became close friends and colleagues while the latter held his professorship at the University of Cape Town (1921-1926). Like Radcliffe-Brown she believed in the possibility of establishing a natural science of society, but her ideas were always flexible and designed to accommodate human variability. Her paradigm for the discipline in 1933 was presented in "New aims and methods in social anthropology" in which she proposed working toward a synthesis of both functionalist and historical methods.

Her marriage in 1914 to R.F. Alfred Hoernlé, a professor of philosophy with deep interests in race relations, fostered her advocacy of applied anthropology; and in later life she devoted her energy to the practical issues of public life in South Africa, notably penal reform and the improvement of black education.

MAJOR WORKS: "Certain rites of transition and the conception of !nau among the Hottentots," *Harvard African Studies*, vol. 2 (1918), pp. 65-82; "The expression of the social value of water among the Naman of South-West Africa," *South African Journal of Science*, vol. 20 (1923), pp. 514-526; "The social organization of the Nama Hottentots of Southwest Africa," *American Anthropologist*, n.s., vol. 27 (1925), pp. 1-24; "New aims and methods in social anthropology," *South African Journal of Science*, vol. 30 (1933), pp. 74-92; "Social organization" and "Magic and medicine" in: Isaac Schapera (editor), *The Bantu-speaking Tribes of South Africa* (London: 1937), pp. 67-94 and 221-245; *Penal Reform and Race Relations* (Johannesburg: 1945) [Hoernlé Memorial Lecture, South African Institute of Race Relations].

SOURCES: Peter Carstens (editor), *The Social Organization of the Nama and Other Essays by Winifred Hoernlé* (Johannesburg: 1985); Peter Carstens, Gerald Klinghardt, and Martin West (editors), *Trails in the Thirstland: the Anthropological Field Diaries of Winifred Hoernlé* (Cape Town: 1987); Max Gluckman and Isaac Schapera, "Dr. Winifred Hoernlé: an appreciation," *Africa*, vol. 30 (1960), pp. 262-263; E. Jensen Krige, "Agnes Winifred Hoernlé: an appreciation," *African Studies*, vol. 19 (1960), pp. 138-144.

Peter Carstens

Hoffmann-Krayer, Eduard. Folklorist, Germanist. Born in Basel (Switzerland) 5 December 1864, died in Basel (Switzerland) 28 November 1936.

Hoffmann-Krayer provided a significant impetus to the development of folklore as a science in the German-speaking world through his theoretical contributions and through his organizational activity.

Hoffmann-Krayer studied philology in Basel (with Behagel), Freiburg, Leipzig and Berlin. He graduated in Basel in 1890 and gained his *Habilitation* one year later in Zürich. In 1900 he was appointed *Extraordinariat* (associate professor) at the University of Basel, where in 1909 he also became Professor of German Language and Literature.

Together with E.A. Stückelberg he founded the Schweizer Gesellschaft für Volkskunde (Swiss Folklore Society) in 1896. The following year he founded the *Schweizer Archiv für Volkskunde*, one of the first scholarly folklore journals. In 1906 he and John Meier established the Schweizer Volksliedarchiv (Swiss Folksong Archive) and encouraged through the publication *Wörter und Sachen* the emergence of the Schweizer Museum für Volkskunde (Swiss Folklore Museum).

Hoffmann-Krayer viewed the task of folklore as the systematic description and recording of the developmental history of popular notions. His theses on *"vulgus in populo,"* on the "generally stable" spiritual condition and on the individual driving forces (*Triebkräften*) with which folklore was to be concerned led to animated theoretical and methodological discussions with A. Strack and H. Naumann around the turn of the century and in the 1930s.

MAJOR WORKS: *Die Volkskunde als Wissenschaft* (Zürich: 1902); *Kleine Schriften zur Volkskunde* (edited by Paul Geiger) (Basel: 1946); (editor) *Volkskundliche Bibliographie* (Strasbourg: 1919-1930); (co-editor with Hanns Bächtold-Stäubli) *Handwörterbuch des deutschen Aberglaubens* (Berlin and Leipzig: 1927-1942).

SOURCES: Paul Geiger, "Eduard Hoffmann-Krayer, 1864-1936" in: Paul Geiger (editor), *Kleine Schriften zur Volkskunde* (Basel: 1946), pp. 1-18; Hanns Bächtold-Staubli, "Eduard Hoffmann-Krayer: Erinnerungen an meinen Lehrer und Freund," *Schweizer Archiv für Volkskunde*, vol. 35 (1936), pp. 1-15; John Meier, "Worte des Gedenkens an Eduard Hoffmann-Krayer," *Schweizer Volkskunde*, vol. 27 (1937), pp. 47-49.

Adelheid Schrutka-Rechtenstamm
[Translation from German: Robert B. Dean]

Hoijer, Harry. Anthropologist, linguist, Americanist. Born in Chicago (Illinois) 6 September 1904, died in Santa Monica (California) 4 March 1976. Hoijer received his doctorate at the University of Chicago in 1931, under the direction of EDWARD SAPIR; his dissertation was a grammar of Tonkawa, an American Indian language then remembered by a few surviving speakers in Oklahoma. Subsequently Hoijer became Sapir's principal co-worker in research on the Athabaskan family of languages, including the Chiricahua and Mescalero Apache languages of New Mexico, as well as Navajo. By the end of Hoijer's life, he had published a grammar, dictionary and text collection not only for Tonkawa but also for Navajo (using data collected by Sapir), and he was internationally acknowledged as the dean of Athabaskan linguistics.

In 1940 Hoijer accepted an appointment in the Department of Anthropology and Sociology at the University of California, Los Angeles. In his early years there, he and his colleague RALPH L. BEALS prepared the first version of the "Beals and Hoijer" textbook, *An Introduction to Anthropology*, which remained a standard text for some two decades.

Hoijer spent the rest of his academic career at UCLA, serving two terms as department chair. He was President of the American Anthropological Association in 1958 and of the Linguistic Society of America in 1959.

Hoijer held a position of seniority and leadership among the scholars who continued the Sapirian tradition of linguistic anthropology, particularly as applied to North American Indian languages. He considered language to lie within the larger framework of culture, and therefore regarded himself primarily as an anthropologist whose major research interest was in language—and in its role with respect to other aspects of human life. His teacher, Sapir, had been particularly interested in the interdependence of language with the rest of culture and with psychological patterns of cognition and perception; later, another student of Sapir's, BENJAMIN L. WHORF, developed this into the "Sapir-Whorf hypothesis." After the early deaths of both Sapir and Whorf, it was Hoijer who became the leader of further research in the field. In 1953 he organized and chaired a landmark conference on the topic, at Chicago, and edited the proceedings.

MAJOR WORKS: *Tonkawa, an Indian Language of Texas* (New York: 1933); *Chiricahua and Mescalero Apache Texts* (Chicago: 1938); (with Edward Sapir) *Navaho Texts* (Iowa City: 1942); *Navaho Phonology* (Albuquerque: 1945); (editor) *Linguistic Structures of Native America* (New York: 1946); *An Analytical Dictionary of the Tonkawa Language* (Berkeley: 1949); (with Ralph L. Beals) *An Introduction to Anthropology* (New York: 1953; revised eds., New York: 1959; New York: 1965; New York: 1971); (editor) *Language in Culture: Proceedings of a Conference on the Interrelations of Language and Other Aspects of Culture* (Chicago: 1954); (editor) *Studies in the Athapaskan Languages* (Berkeley: 1963); (with Edward Sapir) *The Phonology and Morphology of the Navaho Language* (Berkeley: 1967); *Tonkawa Texts* (Berkeley: 1972); *A Navajo Lexicon* (Berkeley: 1974).

SOURCES: Ralph Beals, "Harry Hoijer," *American Anthropologist*, vol. 79 (1977), pp. 105-110; Victoria Fromkin, "Harry Hoijer," *Language*, vol. 53 (1977), pp. 169-173.

William Bright

Holmberg, Allan R. Anthropologist. Born in Renville (Minnesota) 15 October 1909, died in Ithaca (New York) 13 October 1966. Holmberg came from a liberal family of Swedish origin. He did undergraduate work at the University of Minnesota and graduate work at the University of Chicago under FAY-COOPER COLE and ROBERT REDFIELD and at Yale University under BRONISLAW MALINOWSKI, GEORGE PETER MURDOCK, EDWARD SAPIR and ALFRED MÉTRAUX. He did his doctoral research on the Siriono Indians of Bolivia. In 1948 he accepted a position at Cornell University, where he remained until his untimely death.

Holmberg is best known for his research and development approach to the study of change. His work in the Peruvian *hacienda* called Vicos (1952-1957) was a landmark in this kind of applied anthropology, which became known as "participant intervention." Holmberg recognized the limitations of this approach when he said " ... I have not suggested that this approach be applied to the exclusion of others. My greatest doubts about it, on the basis of my experience at Vicos, stem from the unlikelihood of mobilizing sufficient funds and personnel to do a research and development job well" (paper given at the meeting of the American Anthropological Association, Chicago, 1957).

MAJOR WORKS: *Nomads of the Long Bow: the Siriono of Eastern Bolivia* (Washington: 1950) (= *Smithsonian Institution, Institute of Social Anthropology, Publication*, no. 10); "Lizard hunters of the North Coast of Peru," *Chicago Fieldiana*, vol. 36, no. 98 (26 November 1957), pp. 203-241;

"Changing community attitudes and values in Peru: a case study in guided change" in: Richard N. Adams [et al.], *Social Change in Latin America To-day: Its Implication for United States Policy* (New York: 1960), pp. 63-107; "Changing values and institutions in Vicos in the context of national development" in: James A. Clifton (editor), *Applied Anthropology* (Boston: 1970), pp. 4-105; "The research and development approach to the study of change," *Human Organization*, vol. 17 (1958), pp. 12-16.

SOURCES: Alfred E. Kahn, Morris E. Opler and Lauriston Sharp, "Allan Richard Holmberg, October 15, 1909-October 13, 1966," *Necrology of the Faculty, Cornell University* (1956-1957), pp. 30-34; "Allan Holberg of Cornell dies," *The New York Times* (14 October 1966), p. 40; Henry F. Dobyns, Paul L. Doughty and Harold Lasswell (editors), *Peasants, Power and Applied Social Change: Vicos as a Model* (Beverly Hills: 1971) [bibliography, pp. 215-227]; John van Willigan, *Applied Anthropology, an Introduction* (South Hadley, Mass.: 1986), pp. 79-91. The Vicos Papers are in the Department of Manuscripts and University Archives, Cornell University Library.

Hans E. Panofsky

Holmberg, Uno. See: *Harva, Uno.*

Holmes, William Henry.

Holmes, William Henry. Anthropologist, archaeologist, geologist, artist. Born on a farm in Jefferson County (Ohio) 1 December 1846, died in Red Oak (Michigan) 20 April 1933. Holmes played a major role in the world of Washington anthropology in the last decades of the 19th and first decades of the 20th century. He also made significant contributions to the archaeological study of North American Indians.

Holmes drifted into anthropology in a rather roundabout way. His first professional experience was as an artist; he worked for the Smithsonian Institution (with, among others, WILLIAM H. DALL and Spencer F. Baird) and for the Hayden's Geological and Geographical Survey of the Territories. The geological sketches he made for the latter expedition led him to geology, and he served for a time as a geologist with the U.S. Geological Survey under JOHN WESLEY POWELL. While working for Powell, Holmes did some archaeological work, and in 1882 he was appointed Honorary Curator of Aboriginal American Ceramics at the National Museum. While making an archaeological study in Mexico City in 1884, he engaged in what is arguably the first sophisticated use of stratigraphy in the New World. In succeeding years he participated actively in many of the major archaeological discussions of the day, making contributions to the study of the Mound Builders, and to the question of whether or not paleolithic man had existed in the New World (Holmes argued that he had not).

In 1897 Holmes was appointed head of the Department of Anthropology at the National Museum. The Loubat Prize in 1898 confirmed his position in American anthropology, and he was appointed Powell's successor at the Bureau of American Ethnology (BAE) in 1903. One of the major products of the BAE during the years Holmes was its head was the *Handbook of American Indians*, edited by FREDERICK WEBB HODGE. In 1909 Holmes returned to being head curator at the National Museum.

Holmes was a major force behind the American Anthropological Association's censure of FRANZ BOAS in 1919. This action was the result of many factors, chiefly perhaps Boas's pacifism during World War I and his attack on anthropologists who had helped the war effort. It also seems to have been the culmination of long-standing tensions between Boas's internationally oriented, intellectually sophisticated, New York-based anthropology and the U.S.-oriented, somewhat atheoretical anthropology of Washington. One reason for these tensions may have been that fact that so many of Boas's collaborators were Jewish; virtually all the Washington anthropologists were white Anglo-Saxon Protestants.

Holmes' last position was as head of the National Gallery of Art, an office he assumed in 1920.

MAJOR WORKS: "Natural history of flaked stone implements" in: *Memoirs of the International Congress of Anthropology* (Chicago: 1894), pp. 120-139; "Stone implements of the Potomac-Chesapeake Tidewater province," *Annual Report of the Bureau of American Ethnology*, vol. 15 (1897), pp. 13-152; *Aboriginal Pottery of the Eastern United States* (Washington: 1903) (= *Annual Report of the Bureau of American Ethnology*, vol. 20); *Handbook of Aboriginal American Antiquities*, part 1 (Washington: 1919) (= *Bureau of American Ethnology Bulletin*, no. 60).

SOURCE: Joan Mark, "William Henry Holmes" in: *4 Anthropologists: an American Science in its Early Years* (New York: 1980), pp. 131-171.

Honigmann, John Joseph. Anthropologist. Born in the Bronx (New York) 7 June 1914, died in Chapel Hill (North Carolina) 4 August 1977. Honigmann was trained at Brooklyn College (B.A., 1941) and Yale University (Ph.D., 1947). After brief teaching appointments elsewhere, he joined the faculty of the University of North Carolina in 1951 and spent the rest of his career there.

As a field anthropologist, Honigmann devoted most of his investigations to Subarctic and Arctic peoples, including Eskimos and Athabaskan and Algonquian Indians. He demonstrated a thorough interest in their ethnography; and, sensitive to the times in which he worked, he also recorded the problems they encountered and changes they underwent as they came increasingly into contact with the modern world.

Honigmann was regularly in the field. Beginning in 1943, he carried out ethnographic study of the Fort Nelson Slave in Canada. During 1944-1945 he was with the Kaska in British Columbia. During 1947-1948 he worked at Attawapiskat on James Bay and during 1949-1950 at Great Whale River on Hudson Bay. In 1963 he worked at Frobisher Bay and in 1967 at Inuvik. From this broad experience in Canada, he prepared several general works on the native people of that country. In addition to his American studies, Honigmann studied town life in Pakistan during 1952 and 1957-1958, and he worked in an Austrian village during several summers of the 1960s and 1970s.

Honigmann was also a specialist in personality, acculturation and social problems, and he prepared a number of general works concerning the history, theory and methods of these subjects and on anthropology in general.

MAJOR WORKS: *Ethnography and Acculturation of the Fort Nelson Slave* (New Haven: 1946) (= *Yale University Publications in Anthropology*, no. 33); *Culture and Ethos of Kaska Society* (New Haven: 1949) (= *Yale University Publications in Anthropology*, no. 40); *The Kaska Indians: an Ethnographic Reconstruction* (New Haven: 1954) (= *Yale University Publications in Anthropology*, no. 51); *Culture and Personality* (New York: 1954); "The Attawapiskat Swampy Cree: an ethnographic reconstruction," *Anthropological Papers of the University of Alaska*, vol. 5 (1956), pp. 23-82; *Three Pakistan Villages* (Chapel Hill: 1958); *The World of Man* (New York: 1959); *Personality in Culture* (New York: 1967); (with Irma Honigmann) *Arctic Townsmen* (Ottawa: 1970); *Handbook of Social and Cultural Anthropology* (Chicago: 1973); *The Development of Anthropological Ideas* (Homewood, Ill.: 1976).

SOURCES: John Gulick [et al.], "John Joseph Honigmann, 1914-1977," *American Anthropologist*, vol. 80 (1978), pp. 630-639; Honigmann papers in the Smithsonian Institution

National Anthropological Archives; Irma Honigmann, "John Joseph Honigmann," *Anthropology and Humanism Quarterly*, vol. 7 (1982), pp. 10-14; Gilbert Kushner, "A personal appreciation," *Anthropology and Humanism Quarterly*, vol. 7 (1982), pp. 52-54; Ann McElroy, "Selected bibliography of writings by John J. Honigmann," *Anthropology and Humanism Quarterly*, vol. 7 (1982), pp. 54-58; Arthur J. Rubel, "Some personal recollections of John J. Honigmann as a teacher," *Anthropology and Humanism Quarterly*, vol. 7 (1982), pp. 8-10; George D. Spindler, "John Honigmann: the man and his works," *Journal of Psychological Anthropology*, vol. 1 (1978), pp. 441-445.

James R. Glenn

Hooton, E.A. (Earnest Albert). Physical anthropologist. Born in Clemensville (Wisconsin) 20 November 1887, died in Cambridge (Massachusetts) 3 May 1954. Hooton's academic training was in the classics at Lawrence College, Appleton, Wisconsin (B.A., 1907) and the University of Wisconsin, Madison (Ph.D., 1911). As a Rhodes Scholar in University College, Oxford, Hooton's interest in Roman religion and archaeology led him further into the study of the peoples of antiquity. He received a diploma in anthropology in 1912 and the B.Litt. in 1913. After a summer human anatomy course back at Wisconsin in 1913, he began a teaching career at Harvard University that lasted until his death.

Although Hooton excavated human skeletal material in England in 1912 and published *The Ancient Inhabitants of the Canary Islands* based on fieldwork there in 1915 and laboratory analysis at Harvard, his subsequent research rarely led him away from Cambridge. The diversity of that research, however, and Hooton's accommodation of his graduate students' interests, defined the range of physical anthropology in the United States well into the 1950s.

Hooton's research career roughly divides into three sequential foci. His interest in the skeletal biology of prehistoric populations emerged at Oxford and perhaps culminated with his monumental study, *The Indians of Pecos Pueblo*, in 1930. Hooton's efforts to assess racial history from skeletal remains foreshadowed both in scope and in data analysis the research of physical anthropologists, such as his student and Harvard successor W.W. HOWELLS a generation later.

Hooton traced his interest in the relationship between criminal activity and physical characteristics to two years' employment in the state penitentiary at Waupun, Wisconsin, during his college days. In the 1930s he organized a ten-state study of the anthropological characteristics of prisoners that resulted in a massive treatise associating the physical characteristics of men and their crimes, *The American Criminal*, as well as a flurry of popular articles and reportage. Ultimately, however, Hooton came to believe that he had convinced virtually no one but himself of the connection.

In the 1940s and 1950s Hooton's main interest shifted to constitutional studies, or the anthropology of the individual. Initially stimulated by W.H. Sheldon, Hooton eventually applied a modified, pragmatic version of Sheldonian somatotyping to large samples of military personnel, the results of which are essentially available only in government reports. Hooton again was convinced of a relationship between body form and behavior and the relevance of constitutional anthropology to medicine.

Integral to all three of these research programs was Hooton's development of the Statistical Laboratory at Harvard's Peabody Museum. Supported initially by IBM and the

Rockefeller Institute, later essentially on a pay-as-you-go basis, Hooton promoted and maintained the most sophisticated "data-crunching" operation that anthropologists had until the 1950s. Ancillary to this was Hooton's pioneering effort in applied physical anthropology during World War II in, for example, the design of gas masks and airplane turrets. After the war, he arranged a contract, perhaps the first between academic anthropology and private enterprise, for an anthropometric survey of thousands of railway passengers to guide a furniture manufacturer in the radical redesign of coach seats.

An interest in living primates, fed by an early visit to a primate collection in Cuba and later a tour of the Yale primate facility in Florida, led Hooton to articulate in many ways "the importance of primate studies in anthropology," the title of his last scientific paper, published in *Human Biology* in 1954. Most important in this effort, however, was his book *Man's Poor Relations*, an entertaining and accurate summary of what was known of primate anatomy and behavior by 1942. He did not live to see the virtually ubiquitous insertion of primatology into American physical anthropology programs spearheaded in the late 1950s by his student S.L. Washburn.

No anthropologist other than MARGARET MEAD has managed to be in the public eye as much as Hooton. He appears always to have been available for a pungent quote and sometimes would use unconventional ideas—military conscription only for men over 45, a woman for president—to gain public attention for his anthropological viewpoints. In turn, this led to widespread reporting of all his presentations, such as his keynote address to the NAACP in 1944, even when they lacked attention-grabbing gimmicks. There is no question that the visibility such reportage gained him, along with the widespread professional and popular success of his survey of physical anthropology, *Up from the Ape*, which became a widely used text, made him a magnet for aspiring students of physical anthropology.

Hooton's greatest contribution to American physical anthropology may have been the training of its academic practitioners. Until after World War II there was essentially no place for graduate work in physical anthropology other than Harvard, consequently most senior physical anthropology positions have been held by his students. Acerbic and witty to the public, but helpful and kindly to his students (afternoon tea with the Hootons was a Harvard anthropology tradition for decades), Hooton encouraged his students to undertake independent, even conflicting, research. His success, measured by their success, was enormous.

MAJOR WORKS: *The Ancient Inhabitants of the Canary Islands* (Cambridge, Mass.: 1925); "The asymmetric character of human evolution," *American Journal of Physical Anthropology*, vol. 8 (1925), pp. 125-141; *The Indians of Pecos Pueblo* (New Haven, Conn.: 1930); *Up from the Ape* (New York: 1931; rev. ed., New York: 1946); *Apes, Men, and Morons* (New York: 1937); *The American Criminal: an Anthropological Study* (Cambridge, Mass.: 1939); *Twilight of Man* (New York: 1939); *Man's Poor Relations* (Garden City, N.Y.: 1942); *Young Man You Are Normal* (New York: 1945); (with C.W. Dupertuis) *The Physical Anthropology of Ireland* (Cambridge, Mass.: 1955).

SOURCES: W.W. Howells, "Memoriam—Earnest Albert Hooton," *American Journal of Physical Anthropology*, vol. 12 (1954), pp. 445-454; H.L. Shapiro "Earnest A. Hooton, 1887-1954—in memoriam cum amore," *American Journal of Physical Anthropology*, vol. 56 (1981), pp. 431-434.

Eugene Giles

Hose, Charles. Ethnographer, natural historian, collector, administrator, photographer, explorer. Born in Willian, Hertfordshire (England) 12 October 1863, died in Purley, Surrey (England) 14 November 1929. Hose is best known for his standard ethnography *The Pagan Tribes of Borneo*, based on his work as an administrative officer in Sarawak under Rajah Charles Brooke from 1884 to 1907. He was well acquainted with the major indigenous cultures, all of which were represented in Sarawak's 4th division where he was mainly based, and offered an evolutionary synthesis which, if misleading in some respects, usefully stimulated further work. During his lifetime, the anthropological reputation of his writing was marred by his fondness for anecdote, self-reference and speculative theory, although in retrospect, it also reflects the positivism of pre-functionalist anthropology. In his schematic overview of Bornean ethnography, evolutionary/diffusionist theory was combined with administrative convenience. Hose's approach led to *Pagan Tribes* becoming required reading for Sarawak's officer cadets and to greater popularization of the subject in *Natural Man*. Although *Pagan Tribes* became a standard work, it did not win full acclaim among specialists because the evolutionary/diffusionist paradigm was then faltering and it was widely felt that Hose would have served Bornean anthropology better by recording his observations more systematically and in greater detail, especially among the Kenyah and Kayan whom he knew best.

A.C. HADDON, whom Hose persuaded to visit Sarawak with the rest of the returning Cambridge Torres Straits Expedition for six months in 1898-1899, respected much of Hose's work while criticizing aspects of it. Hose's various visitors in Marudi, or further upriver, witnessed their host's close relationship with local peoples. Out of his administrative experience in the special conditions of Sarawak, Hose developed principles of liberal, indirect colonial rule that he set out with remarkable clarity in an appendix to *Fifty Years of Romance and Research*; comparable ideas were expressed in several other papers.

Hose was a pioneer not only in Bornean ethnography but also in a form of applied anthropology. His encouragement of boat racing to replace traditional warfare on the Baram was inspired by the Oxford and Cambridge Boat Race; this, and his manipulation of traditional oracles to suit administrative ends, are well documented in several of his books. Even more innovative was his use of wood carvings, which were closely associated with head-hunting, in new settings designed to help promote peace between conflicting groups.

MAJOR WORKS: (with William McDougall) *The Pagan Tribes of Borneo* [2 vols.] (London: 1912); *Natural Man: a Record from Borneo* (London: 1926); *Fifty Years of Romance and Research; or, a Jungle-Wallah at Large* (London: 1927); *The Field-Book of a Jungle-Wallah* (London: 1929); (with W. McDougall) "The relations between man and animals in Sarawak," *Journal of the Anthropological Institute of Great Britain and Ireland*, vol. 31 (1901), pp. 173-213; "A journey up the Baram River to Mount Dulit and the Highlands of Borneo," *Geographical Journal*, vol. 1 (1893), pp. 193-208; "Among the Madangs: a visit to the Madang country in unexplored Borneo" in: *Travel and Exploration*, vol. 3 (London: 1900), pp. 73-82; "In the heart of Borneo, with a complete survey of the district, covering 12,000 square miles, read at the Royal Geographical Society," *Geographical Journal*, vol. 16 (1900), pp. 39-62; "The constitutional development of Sarawak," *Asiatic Review*, vol. 25 (1929), pp. 481-491; (with R. Shelford) "Materials for a study of tatu in Borneo," *Journal of the Anthropological Institute of Great Britain and Ireland*, vol. 36 (1906), pp. 60-91; *Map of Sarawak* [4 sheets] (London: 1924) [survey of the whole country at a scale of 1:500,000, showing the distribution of the tribes]; "Sarawak: an independent state within the Empire" in: Paul H. Kratoska (editor), *Honourable Intentions: Talks on the British Empire in South-East Asia, delivered at the Royal Colonial Institute, 1874-1928* (Singapore: 1983), pp. 366-381 [lecture delivered on 27 February 1923].

SOURCES: G.N. Appell, "The journal of James Austin Wilder during his visit to Sarawak in 1896," *Sarawak Museum Journal*, vol. 16, no. 32-33 (1968), pp. 407-434 and vol. 17, no. 34-35 (1969), pp. 315-335; H. Balfour, "Hose, Charles (1863-1929)" in: *Dictionary of National Biography, 1922-1930* (London: 1937), pp. 431-433; Otto C. Doering III, "Government in Sarawak under Charles Brooke," *Journal of the Malaysian Branch of the Royal Asiatic Society*, vol. 39, part 2 (1966), pp. 95-107; Brian Durrans, "Introduction" to reissue of: Charles Hose, *Natural Man* (Kuala Lumpur: 1988); personal communication with Violet Fairbairn (née Hose); Alfred C. Haddon, *Head-Hunters Black, White, and Brown* (London: 1932); Charles Hose, *Fifty Years of Romance and Research ...* (London: 1929); *The Contributions to Science of Charles Hose, Hon. Sc.D. (Cantab.) (1887-1926)* (Cambridge: 1926); A.C. Haddon, "Dr. Charles Hose," *Nature*, vol. 124 (1929), p. 845; C.H. Blagden, "Dr. Charles Hose," *Man*, vol. 30, no. 35 (March 1930), p. 49; audio cassette recording of Ernest Hose in conversation with John Cordeaux (Head of Programmes, Radio Sarawak, 1959-1961) recorded at E.H.'s home in Royden, Diss, Norfolk, on August 25, 1962 (courtesy of John Cordeaux); William McDougall, "A savage peace-conference," *The Eagle: a Magazine Supported by Members of St. John's College* [Cambridge], vol. 21 (1900), pp. 70-82; Robert Pringle, *Rajahs and Rebels: the Ibans of Sarawak under Brooke Rule, 1841-1941* (London: 1970); *Sarawak Civil List* (Kuching: 1930), pp. 17-18.

Brian Durrans

Hough, Walter. Anthropologist, museum curator, administrator. Born in Morgantown (West Virginia) 23 April 1859, died in Washington (D.C.) 20 September 1935. Hough was trained in chemistry and geology at West Virginia University (Ph.D., 1894). His anthropological training came largely through his work under OTIS TUFTON MASON at the Smithsonian Institution, and many of his interests paralleled those of Mason. This influence began in 1886 after Hough's appointment as a copyist in the Smithsonian's Division of Ethnology. He became a museum aid in 1887, an assistant curator in 1894, and curator of ethnology in 1911. He was acting head curator of the Department of Anthropology during 1908-1910 and 1920-1923. He was head curator from 1923 to 1935.

Early in his career, Hough's work largely consisted of cataloging ethnological specimens and preparing exhibits. Developing from such efforts, much of his later scientific work was primarily descriptive and often oriented toward material culture. It has been said that his few interpretive efforts aimed to demonstrate the generally progressive nature of man's inventive activities (Judd). He was also interested in the relationship of culture and environment.

Hough was involved in rather wide ranging studies that reflected the variety of objects in the Smithsonian's ethnological collections. These included such diverse subjects as dolls, weapons, musical instruments and Chinese punishments. The work for which he was best known, however, involved man's use of fire and the related subjects of illumination and cooking methods. In addition to such cross-cultural studies, he also published articles on features of Oceanic, Asian, African, and American Indian culture.

Hough also carried out archaeological and ethnological fieldwork, mainly in Arizona and New Mexico. During 1896-1897, with Jesse Walter Fewkes, he was involved in surveys of ruins on the Little Colorado River and in eastern Arizona especially along the Gila River. Between 1901 and 1905, with financial support from Peter Goddard Gates, he continued archaeological surveys and carried on ethnological research in the Pueblos of New Mexico and Arizona. During this period, he also carried out ethnological work among the Apache, Navajo and Hopi and additional archaeological surveys in New Mexico and

Arizona, especially in the Holbrook region. In 1899, with J.N. Rose, Hough collected ethnobotanical specimens in northern Mexico.

Hough was president of the American Anthropological Association in 1924.

MAJOR WORKS: *Antiquities of the Upper Gila and Salt River Valleys in Arizona and New Mexico* (Washington: 1907) (= *Bureau of American Ethnology Bulletin*, no. 35); "Collection of heating and lighting utensils in the United States National Museum," *Bulletin of the United Stated National Museum*, no. 141 (1928), pp. 1-113; "Fire making apparatus in the United States National Museum," *Proceedings of the United States National Museum*, vol. 73 (1928), pp. 1-72.

SOURCES: Hough papers and vertical file in the Smithsonian Institution National Anthropological Archives; Neil M. Judd, "Walter Hough," *Science*, vol. 82 (6 December 1935), pp. 541-542; Neil M. Judd, "Walter Hough: an appreciation," *American Anthropologist*, vol. 38 (1936), pp. 471-481.

James R. Glenn

Howell, P.P. (Paul Philip). Administrator, diplomat, anthropologist. Born in London (England) 13 February 1917. Howell, an administrator with a background in academic anthropology, has had a strong interest in the potential use of anthropology in applied development projects, and he has led several key multidisciplinary research studies of the potential impact of projects along the Nile on the peoples of this region.

Howell received an M.A. from Trinity College, Cambridge, and a D.Phil. from Christ Church, Oxford. While pursuing a highly varied career in the Sudan Political Service (1938-1955), he came in contact with E.E. EVANS-PRITCHARD who encouraged him to make a comparative study of Nilotic (Dinka, Nuer, Shilluk) customary law and to investigate the way that chiefs' courts were being established by the British colonial administration as a new vehicle for settling disputes in the region. This study culminated in the publication of *A Manual of Nuer Law*, which carefully traced transformations in the Nuer customary law wrought by the colonial administration, highlighting the impact of Western legal concepts in this process. This study was followed up by other essays on the Nuer. During the same period Howell continued studies of Shilluk social and political organization in relation to land use. He went on to study the institution of the *reth* (spiritual and political head) of the Shilluk. As the District Commissioner of Western Kordofan (1944-1948) Howell also carried out research on the Ngok Dinka of this region.

In 1948 he became chairman of a multidisciplinary team investigating the hydrological and ecological effects of the proposed Equatorial Nile Project—of which the Jonglei Canal Project was an important part—on the economy of the Nilotic peoples. This study was one of the very first coordinated environmental studies using a multidisciplinary approach.

Howell went on to head the Southern Development Investigation Team (1953-1955), whose goal was the formulation of an integrated policy of development in the Southern Sudan. This project was cut short by the process of independence in 1955.

Howell carried out subsequent work in Uganda between 1956 and 1961, e.g, as head of the East African Nile Waters Coordination Committee. He worked as head of the Middle East Development Division of the British Foreign Office between 1961 and 1969 and between 1969 and 1983 as Director of Development Studies at Cambridge University where he established the first courses in development studies.

His recent work on the Jonglei Canal project is the culmination of his long interest in development along the Upper Nile.

MAJOR WORKS: *A Manual of Nuer Law* (Oxford: 1954); "The Shilluk settlement," *Sudan Notes and Records*, vol. 26 (1945), pp. 95-103; "A note on elephants and elephant hunting among the Nuer," *Sudan Notes and Records*, vol. 26 (1945), pp. 95-103; "The Zeraf Hills," *Sudan Notes and Records*, vol. 26 (1945), pp. 319-328; "The death of a *reth* of the Shilluk and the installation of his successor," *Sudan Notes and Records*, vol. 27 (1946), pp. 4-85; "The Ngok Dinka of Western Kordofan," *Sudan Notes and Records*, vol. 32 (1951), pp. 239-293; "Observations on the Shilluk of the Upper Nile," *Africa*, vol. 22 (1952), pp. 97-119; "The Equatorial Nile Project and its effects on the Sudan," *Geographical Journal*, vol. 149 (1953), pp. 33-48; "Some observations on divorce among the Nuer," *Journal of the Royal Anthropological Institute*, vol. 83 (1953), pp. 136-146; "Some observations on 'earthly spirits' among the Nuer," *Man*, n.s., vol. 3 (1953), pp. 85-88; (with other members of the Jonglei Investigation Team) *The Equatorial Nile Project and its Effects on the Anglo-Egyptian Sudan* [6 vols.] (Khartoum: 1954); (with other members of the Southern Development Investigation Team) *Natural Resources and Development Potential in the Southern Provinces of the Sudan* (Khartoum: 1955); (co-edited with M. Lock and S. Cobb) *The Jonglei Canal: Impact and Opportunity* (Cambridge: 1988).

Sharon Hutchinson

Howells, W.W. (William White).

Howells, W.W. (William White). Physical anthropologist. Born in New York (New York) 27 November 1908. Howells received both his S.B. (1930) and his Ph.D. (1934) degrees in anthropology from Harvard University under E.A. HOOTON. Howells first joined the anthropology staff at the American Museum of Natural History in New York City, but accepted a professorial appointment in 1939 at the University of Wisconsin, Madison. During World War II Howells served in the U.S. Office of Naval Intelligence and then returned to Wisconsin. Following Hooton's death in 1954 he was named professor of anthropology at Harvard University, the position from which he retired in 1974.

Howells' ongoing methodological contribution to physical anthropology is his innovative application of multivariate statistical techniques to a variety of problems. In one major research program he examined metric data personally collected from seventeen skeletal collections representing major population groups worldwide. These data, analyzed by multivariate discriminant function means, provided the basis for his epochal monograph, *Cranial Variation in Man*, in which he was able to demonstrate convincingly that such variation is, despite its previous inept or pernicious use, a feasible database for assessing relationships among human populations.

Although Howells has participated only marginally in original reporting on fossil remains, he has produced over the years a series of papers, book chapters and books evaluating the paleoanthropological record in an unusually perceptive, even-handed fashion. Of his generation, perhaps only S.L. Washburn has made a comparable contribution to our understanding, as contrasted with description, of human ancestry.

Beginning with his doctoral dissertation on the anthropometry of Australian Aboriginal peoples, Howells has maintained an areal focus in Oceania. He has visited many of the island groups and was involved in the development as well as the fieldwork of Harvard's Solomon Islands Project (1966-1972), a long-term study of health, human biology and culture change. He synthesized both his own research and a wide variety of anthropological data (linguistic, archaeological and cultural as well as physical) in *The*

Pacific Islanders. In that volume he ultimately recognizes the movement from Asia into Oceania of two "fundamental and ancient" population complexes: that of Old Melanesia moving into Australia and the area of modern Melanesia (and extending into the Philippines) and one he terms Proto-Mongoloid, subsequently moving into the island groups.

During his teaching years, Howells' writing intercalated papers reporting his anthropological research with books designed for a more general audience that were simultaneously usable as texts. The latter included *Mankind So Far*, later replaced by *Mankind in the Making* (a similar but new book by, as Howells put it, a "revised author"), *The Heathens*, and *Back of History*. The enormous success of these books, representing, respectively, surveys of physical anthropology, "primitive" religion and archaeology has made Howells the most widely translated of physical anthropologists.

MAJOR WORKS: *Mankind So Far* (New York: 1944); *The Heathens* (New York: 1948); *Back of History: the Story of Our Own Origins* (New York: 1954); *Mankind in the Making: the Story of Human Evolution* (New York: 1959; rev. ed., Garden City, N.Y.: 1967); *Cranial Variation in Man* (Cambridge, Mass.: 1973); *Evolution of the Genus* Homo (Reading, Mass.: 1973); *The Pacific Islanders* (London: 1973); "Explaining modern man: evolutionists versus migrationists," *Journal of Human Evolution*, vol. 5 (1976), pp. 477-495; "*Homo erectus*—who, when and where: a summary," *Yearbook of Physical Anthropology*, vol. 23 (1980), pp. 1-23; (co-editor with G.N. van Vark) *Multivariate Statistical Methods in Physical Anthropology: a Review of Recent Advances and Current Developments* (Dordrecht: 1984).

SOURCES: Eugene Giles and J.S. Friedlaender (editors), *The Measures of Man: Methodologies of Biological Anthropology* (Cambridge, Mass.: 1976); Eugene Giles, "Howells, William W." in: David L. Sills (editor), *International Encyclopedia of the Social Sciences* (New York: 1968-1979), vol. 18, pp. 328-330; J.S. Friedlaender (editor) *The Solomon Islands Project: a Long-Term Study of Health, Human Biology, and Culture Change* (Oxford: 1987).

Eugene Giles

Hoyos Sáinz, Luis de. Physical anthropologist, ethnologist, folklorist, archaeologist. Born in Madrid (Spain) 21 June 1868, died in Madrid (Spain) 4 December 1951. After acquiring a broad education as a naturalist, Hoyos continued specialized studies in Paris between 1891 and 1893. After a first stage of his career dedicated almost exclusively to craniology (influenced by the methods and criteria of the French school founded by PAUL BROCA), he turned toward a more biological perspective in his physical anthropology. It was Hoyos who introduced to Spain the anthropological value of blood groups. At the same time he took up studies of ethnology and folklore. In spite of the fact that his teaching career developed in the field of physiology, he created a school focused entirely on folklore and ethnographic research. Among the students who received their first initiation to anthropology from him is JUAN COMAS. Hoyos was also founder of the Museo del Pueblo Español (Museum of the Spanish People) in 1934; he directed it until 1938.

Together with the concept of anthropology as a natural science, what stands out as a characteristic of Hoyos is a global vision of the discipline and, along with it, his intense dedication as much to physical anthropology as to ethnology. Furthermore, he extended anthropological analysis not only to living but also to prehistoric peoples. No less characteristic is his exclusive attention to the study of his own cultural group, exceptions being some general works, for example, the *Lecciones de Antropología* and his interest in

American anthropology. The largest body of the work written by Hoyos was directed by the fundamental idea that it is necessary to develop an anthropological knowledge of the different racial and cultural groups that have inhabited the Iberian Peninsula. To realize this, together with his colleagues, he first undertook the enormous task of compiling information; only then did he reflect in his works on the *Crania Hispanica*. In addition, he focused on ethnographies in which the urgency of rescuing more or less archaic and differentiated traits before their certain disappearance served to support the priority given to the accumulation of data. A later step was the application of some criteria, which were above all anthropological, but also geographical and historical, to a series of specially selected traits or subjects in order to obtain a geographical distribution of the existing cultural differences. His ultimate goal was to isolate the particular or, at times, original character of the culture of these regions.

Even though the work of Hoyos became more complex with time, he always maintained the same basic ideas as a guide. Besides his specific contribution to research one must also cite the prestige and credit that his presence at international professional conferences and associations brought to Spanish anthropology.

MAJOR WORKS: (with Telesforo de Aranzadi) "Un avance a la antropología de España," *Anales de la Sociedad Española de Historia Natural*, vol. 21 (1892), pp. 31-101; (with Telesforo de Aranzadi) *Lecciones de Antropología* [4 vols.] (Madrid: 1899-1900); "Caractères généraux de la 'Crania Hispanica'," *XIVe Congrès International d'Anthropologie et d'Archéologie Préhistoriques* (Geneva: 1914), vol. 2, pp. 446-464; *La antropología: métodos y problemas* (Madrid: 1917); (with Telesforo de Aranzadi) *Etnografía: sus bases, métodos y aplicaciones a España* (Madrid: 1917); "Etnografía española: cuestionario y bases para el estudio de los trajes regionales," *Actas y Memorias de la Sociedad Española de Antropología, Etnografía y Prehistoria*, vol. 1 (1922), pp. 91-129; "Cráneos normales y deformados de los Andes," *Actas y Memorias de la Sociedad Española de Antropología, Etnografía y Prehistoria*, vol. 2 (1923), pp. 151-184; vol. 3 (1924), pp. 3-37 and 185-230; *Raciología prehistórica española* (Madrid: 1943); "Los métodos de investigación en el folklore," *Revista de Dialectología y Tradiciones Populares*, vol. 1 (1945), pp. 455-490; *Distribución geográfica de los grupos sanguíneos en España: ensayo de seroantropología* (Madrid: 1947); (with Nieves de Hoyos) *Manual de folklore: la vida popular tradicional* (Madrid: 1947); *Investigaciones de antropología prehistórica de España* [2 vols.] (Madrid: 1953).

SOURCES: Carmen Ortiz, *Luis de Hoyos Sáinz y la antropología española* (Madrid: 1987); Julio Caro Baroja, "Don Luis de Hoyos Sáinz (1868-1951)," *Publicaciones del Instituto de Etnografía y Folklore Hoyos Sáinz*, vol. 3 (1971), pp. 7-18; José M. Calvo, "D. Luis de Hoyos Sáinz en Toledo (1898-1909)," *Toledo*, vol. 15, no. 53 (1981), pp. 1-12; Nieves de Hoyos Sancho, "Nuestros antecesores: Telesforo de Aranzadi y Luis de Hoyos Sáinz," *Etnología y Tradiciones Populares*, vol. 1 (1969), pp. 59-65; Juan Comas, "Luis de Hoyos Sáinz (1868-1951), *Boletín Bibliográfico de Antropología Americana*, vol. 14 (1952), pp. 1-10; Henri Vallois, "Luis de Hoyos Sáinz," *L'Anthropologie*, vol. 56 (1952), pp. 165-166; Barbara Aitken, "Obituaries: Luis de Hoyos Sáinz, 1868-1951," *Man*, vol. 53 (1953), p. 40.

Carmen Ortiz
[Translation from Spanish: Margo L. Smith]

Hrdlička, Aleš. Physical anthropologist. Born in Humpolec (110 kilometers southeast of Prague) (Czechoslovakia) 30 March 1869, died in Washington (D.C.) 5 September 1943. Hrdlička was Curator of the Anthropological Division of the Smithsonian Institution in Washington, D.C. He was born into a family of a master joiner, the eldest of five children. At the age of 13, he and his parents and brothers and sisters emigrated to

New York where at first he worked in a tobacco shop. At the age of 19, after a serious illness, with the advice and help of his attending doctor, he began his medical studies, and in 1892 he was graduated from the Eclectic Medical College in New York and in 1893 from the New York Homeopathic College, passing his medical examininations in Baltimore in 1894.

Originally a practicing physician, he later became a researcher at the state mental institution in Middletown, New York, and also worked at the state pathological institute in Middletown.

Before coming to the State Pathological Institute, he went to Paris to study a then-new branch of science—anthropology—under the guidance of Professor Manouvrier at the École d'Anthropologie and other institutions. After his return, he built an anthropology laboratory and intensively collected anthropometric data with the goal of determining norms of body characteristics of the American population. During the summers of 1898-1902, he took part in several expeditions to study the Indians of the American Southwest and Mexico, for the most part under the auspices of the American Museum of Natural Science.

From 1903 on, he worked at the Smithsonian Institution's Department of Anthropology in Washington, D.C., where, over the course of forty years, he gradually built the most complete collection of human skeletal materials of all races. In connection with the theory of the Asiatic origins of American Indians, which he advocated, he disproved the antiquity of skeletons discovered in North and South America thati were considered to be evidence of the development of man on these continents. He personally visited the sites of the discoveries that provided this evidence of the development of man, no matter where in the world they happened to be, and described these findings in the book *Skeletal Remains of Early Man*. In support of the theory about the first American inhabitants coming from Asia, during the years 1926-1938, Hrdlička undertook ten expeditions to Alaska, to Kodiak Island and the Aleutian Islands. The archaeological riches and anthropological material from this area supplemented a 1939 study of materials from Asia deposited in Soviet museums.

Hrdlička founded an anthropological journal, *The American Journal of Physical Anthropology* (1918), as well as the American Association of Physical Anthropologists. He instituted an endowment attached to Charles University and the Czech Academy of Arts and Sciences for the support of an independent journal and the development of anthropology in Czechoslovakia, the fund to be used for the building of a Museum of Man in Prague (under the auspices of Charles University) and for the support of a school in his native town of Humpolec.

Hrdlička was a member of the American Academy of Sciences and was honored by its members.

In 1927 Hrdlička received the Huxley Memorial Medal form the Royal British Anthropological Institute for his lecture "The Neanderthal phase in the development of mankind." Charles University in Prague and the Purkyně University in Brno presented him with honorary doctorates.

MAJOR WORKS: *Early Man in South America* (Washington: 1912) (= *Smithsonian Institution, Bureau of American Ethnology Bulletin*, no. 52); *Physical Anthropology: Its Scope and Aims* (Philadelphia: 1919); *Anthropometry* (Philadelphia: 1920); *The Old Americans* (Baltimore: 1925);

"The Neanderthal phase of man," *Journal of the Royal Anthropological Institute*, vol. 58 (1927), pp. 249-274; *The Skeletal Remains of Early Man* (Washington: 1930) (= *Smithsonian Miscellaneous Collections*, vol. 83); "Catalogue of human crania in the United States Museum collections," *Proceedings, U.S. National Museum*, vol. 63 (1924), article 12, pp. 1-51; vol. 69 (1926), article 5, pp. 1-127; vol. 71 (1928), article 24, pp. 1-140; vol. 78 (1930), article 2, pp. 1-95; vol. 87 (1940), pp. 315-364; vol. 91 (1942), pp. 189-429; vol. 93 (1944), pp. 1-177; and *American Anthropologist*, n.s., vol. 27 (1925), pp. 239-340; *Children Who Run on All Fours* (New York: 1931); "The coming of man from Asia in the light of recent discoveries," *Proceedings of the American Philosophical Society*, vol. 81 (1935), pp. 393-402; *Alaska Diary* (Lancaster, Pa.: 1943); *Anthropology of Kodiak Island* (Philadelphia: 1944).

SOURCE: Jindřich Matiegka, "Dr. Aleš Hrdlička: životopisný nástin" ["Dr. Aleš Hrdlička: biographical sketch"], *Antropologie*, vol. 7 (1929), pp. 6-61; Vladimír V. Novotný (editor), *Anthropological Congress of Aleš Hrdlička* (Prague: 1982); T.D, Stewart, "The life and writings of Dr. Aleš Hrdlička," *American Journal of Physical Anthropology*, vol. 26 (1940), pp. 3-40 [contains bibliography]; Adolph H. Schultz, "Biographical memoir of Aleš Hrdlička, 1869-1943," *National Academy of Sciences, Biographical Memoirs*, vol. 23 (1943), pp. 305-338.

M. Prokopec
[Translation from Czech: June Pachuta Farris]

Huard, Pierre-Alphonse. Military physician, professor of surgery, physical anthropologist, ethnologist. Born in Bastia, Corsica (France) 16 October 1901, died in Paris (France) 28 April 1983. Huard attended secondary school in Montpelier and Nantes and in 1920 enrolled at the École de Santé Navale (Bordeaux) where he studied anatomy and surgery. At Bordeaux Huard was awarded the title Prosecteur d'Anatomie in 1925. Between 1925 and 1927 Huard was assigned to the French colonial army as a field surgeon, seeing service in Syria and Lebanon. From 1927 to 1933 he taught military surgery at Marseilles.

In 1933 Huard was assigned to duty in Hanoi, Indochina. He remained there for most of the ensuing twenty-two years, serving as professor and, later, dean at the Hanoi University Medical School. His activities included surgery, teaching, research and administration. It was during this period that he became a fluent speaker of Vietnamese, acquired a comprehensive knowledge of Vietnamese life and wrote his book-length synthesis of information on Vietnamese culture, *Connaissance du Viêt-Nam*. During the first Indochina war, he served as President of the Red Cross and as an advocate for the humane treatment of prisoners of war. In 1954 Huard negotiated the evacuation of 858 wounded French and Vietnamese prisoners on the battlefield at Dien Bien Phu.

Returning to France in 1955, he joined the School of Medicine of Rennes (1955-1963) and later (1966-1973) the School of Medicine of Paris. After 1954, his research interests turned increasingly to the medical systems of East Asia. A detailed work on Chinese medicine, *La médecine chinoise au cours des siècles*, was completed in 1959. A major history of Japanese medical systems, *La médecine japonaise des origines à nos jours* was published in 1974. His books and articles often explored the relationship of medical systems, culture and the natural sciences. Many of his writings reflect a historical perspective. He was one of the most energetic of Western interpreters of Asian (especially Sino-Vietnamese, Chinese and Japanese) medical systems. His publications on Western medical topics are also numerous. Huard was an admirer of PAUL BROCA, noted surgeon, craniologist and the founder of French physical anthropology, as well as a disciple of the physical anthropologist Henri Victor Vallois (1889-). During his long scholarly career, Huard authored or co-authored some thirty-five books as well as several hundred articles and other publications. He remained active to the end. He was fatally injured in a traffic mishap on 28 April 1983 while crossing the Rue Saint-Jacques, a load of books in hand. Huard served as president of the Société d'Anthropologie de Paris (1960) and was honored by election to the Académie Nationale de Médecine (1981).

MAJOR WORKS: *Connaissance du Viêt-Nam* (Hanoi: 1954); (with Ming Wong) *La médecine chinoise au cours des siècles* (Paris: 1959); (with Zensetsou Ohya and Ming Wong) *La médecine japonaise des origines à nos jours* (Paris: 1974); (with Ming Wong) *Soins et techniques du corps en Chine, au Japon et en Inde* (Paris: 1971); (with Jean Bossy and Guy Mazars) *Les médecines de l'Asie* (Paris: 1978); (with A. Bigot) *Les caractéristiques anthropobiologiques des indochinois* (Hanoi: 1938) (= *Travaux de l'Institut anatomique de l'École supérieure de médecine de l'Indochine (section anthropologique)*, vol. 4); (with Maurice Durand) "Lan-Ong et la médecine sino-vietnamienne," *Bulletin de la Société des études indochinoises*, n.s., vol. 28 (1953), pp. 221-294; "Paul Broca (1824-1880)," *Revue d'histoire des sciences et de leurs applications*, vol. 14 (1961), pp. 47-86; "La médecine khmere populaire," *Concours Medical*, vol. 85, no. 20 (18 May 1963), pp. 3169-3275; and vol. 85, no. 21 (25 May 1963), pp. 3437-3444.

SOURCES: "Huard (Pierre)" in: *Who's Who in France*, 16th éd. (1983-1984) (Paris: 1982), p. 724; Bernard B. Fall, *Hell in a Very Small Place* (Philadelphia: 1976), pp. 426-427; George Sarton, "The history of medicine in Vietnam: Pierre Huard," *Bulletin of the History of Medicine*, vol. 28 (1954), pp. 566-571; *International Biographical Directory of Southeast Asia Specialists, 1969* (Athens: 1969), p. 101; Lucien Brumpt, "Éloge de Pierre Huard (1901-1983)," *Bulletin de l'Académie Nationale de Médecine*, vol. 168 (Jan.-Feb. 1984), pp. 181-187; Georges Olivier and Claude Chippaux, "Pierre Huard (1901-1983)," *Bulletins et Mémoires de la Société d'Anthropologie de Paris*, 13th sér., vol. 10 (1983), pp. 155-157.

Lee S. Dutton

Hulstaert, Gustaaf. Missionary, ethnologist, linguist. Born in Melsele (Belgium) 5 July 1900, died in Bamanya (Zaïre) 12 February 1990. He became a priest in the Congregation of the Missionaries of the Sacred Heart in 1924 and was active in the Belgian Congo (later Zaïre) from 1925 until his death. He performed the functions of headmaster (Boteka), inspector for the diocesan school system and religious superior (1936-1946). These positions gave him the opportunity to traverse the central basin of Zaïre where the Mongo people live. During his many trips he acquired an encyclopedic knowledge of this region's language, people and nature. In 1931 he started to publish. In 1937, together with his colleague EDMOND BOELAERT, he founded the periodical *Aequatoria*.

From 1950 he occupied himself exclusively with scholarly research. He directed his attention mainly to linguistics (Lomongo) and to a lesser degree toward ethnology (the Mongo and related peoples). He managed to publish in almost all the genres of spoken literature. At his urging, and with the cooperation of a few colleagues and natives, a complete terminology was created for the courses of primary and secondary education. His *Dictionnaire* and *Grammaire* of Lomongo rank among the most complete and comprehensive in the field of Bantu studies. In the 1960s and 1970s he translated liturgical texts as well as the whole Bible.

His stance on the problems of colonial policy (language in education, depopulation, territorial rights) brought him into conflict with the highest Church authorities of the colony (Mgr. Dellepiane, apostolic nuncio), and publication of the periodical *Aequatoria* was suspended for a brief period in 1945.

Hulstaert's carefully preserved correspondence (from 1936) with leading personalities of the colonial period (PLACIDE TEMPELS, Alexis Kagame, Émile Possoz, Jean Sohier, JOSEPH VAN WING) gives an extraordinary image of the development of colonial thinking. The developments after independence in 1960, during which the French language and imitation of Western habits spread, caused him much disillusionment.

The Centre Aequatoria at Bamanya (Mbandaka) continues to operate in his spirit in part on the basis of the documentation gathered by him.

MAJOR WORKS: *Le mariage des Nkundo* (Brussels: 1938); *Praktische Grammatica van het Lonkundo* (Antwerp: 1938); "Coutumes funéraires des Nkundo," *Anthropos*, vol. 32 (1937), pp. 502-527 and 729-742; *Les sanctions coutumières contre l'adultère chez les nkundo* (Brussels: 1938); *Dictionnaire français-lomongo* (Tervuren: 1952); *Carte linguistique du Congo belge* (Brussels: 1950); *Dictionnaire lomongo-français* (Tervuren: 1957); *Proverbes mongo* (Tervuren: 1958); *Grammaire du lomongo* [3 vols.] (Tervuren: 1961-1966); *Notes de botanique mongo* (Brussels: 1966); *Poèmes mongo anciens* (Tervuren: 1978).

SOURCES: *Annales Aequatoria* (1980), pp. 3-57; A. De Rop, *Bibliographie analytique de G. Hulstaert* (Borgerhout: 1972); A. De Rop, "À l'occasion du 70ème anniversaire de G. Hulstaert," *Africa-Tervuren*, vol. 16 (1970), pp. 107-112.

Honoré Vinck
[Translation from Dutch: Geert Van Cleemput]

Humboldt, Baron *Alexander von.* Naturalist, explorer. Born in Berlin (Germany) 19 September 1769, died in Berlin (Germany) 6 May 1859. Humboldt was educated partly through private lessons, partly at academic institutions, in economics, natural sciences and mining. His first employment (1792) was as inspector of mines in Prussia.

Long-standing plans for explorations in non-European countries finally materialized with a trip to the Caribbean, South, Middle and North America from 1799-1804. Its main purpose was to make geographical and botanical studies. However, Humboldt also studied Indian populations and antiquities (especially in Mexico) and published his findings in expensively printed and lavishly illustrated sets of volumes in Paris. After his return to Berlin he was instrumental in establishing sciences and learning in Prussia (Academy of Sciences, University of Berlin, order "Pour le Mérite") together with his brother WILHELM VON HUMBOLDT and others.

A second major trip to Russia in 1829 was not as remarkable in its scientific results as his American exploration. Except for repeated diplomatic services for the Prussian king, Humboldt occupied the rest of his life with fostering follow-up field research by young scholars and discussing all matters of scientific research in private meetings at his Berlin home and in written correspondence with leading scientists of Europe and the Americas. Although he never held a formal academic position, his lectures for the royal court and the Berlin public (the *Kosmos Vorlesungen*) were well received and influential. His collection of artifacts and pictorial manuscripts from Mexico, and his pertinent publications have laid the foundation of anthropological research in Berlin, for which he and the geographer Carl Ritter (1779-1859) inaugurated plans for the Ethnographic Museum, which was actually founded ten years after Humboldt's and Ritter's deaths.

MAJOR WORKS (OF ANTHROPOLOGICAL OR BIOGRAPHICAL IMPORT): *Voyage de Humboldt et Bonpland. Première Partie. Relation historique: Voyage aux régions équinoxiales du Nouveau Continent, fait en 1799, 1800, 1801, 1802, 1803 et 1804* [3 vols.] (Paris: 1814-1825); *Alexander von Humboldt in Kolumbien: Auswahl aus seinen Tagebüchern* (Bogotá: 1982); *Alexander von Humboldt: Lateinamerika am Vorabend der Unabhängigkeitsrevolution* (Berlin [East]: 1982) (= *Beiträge zur Alexander-von-Humboldt-Forschung*, vol. 5); *Alexander von Humboldt: Reise auf dem Río Magdalena, durch die Anden und in Mexiko. Teil I: Texte; Teil II: Kommentare* (Berlin [East]: 1986-1989) (= *Beiträge zur Alexander-von-Humboldt-Forschung*, vols. 8 and 9); "Über die Urvölker von Amerika und die Denkmäler, welche von ihnen übriggeblieben sind," *Neue Berlinische Monatshefte*, vol. 15 (1806), pp. 177-208; *Vue des cordillières et monumens* [sic] *des peuples indigènes de l'Amérique* (Paris: 1810) [major publication on history and archaeology of American Indians; German edition (1810)]; *Essai politique sur le royaume de la Nouvelle Espagne* [2 vols. and atlas] (Paris: 1811); *Évaluation numérique de la population du Nouveau Continent, considérée sur les rapports de la différence des cultes, des races et des idiomes* (Paris: 1825); *Essai politique sur l'île de Cuba, avec une carte et un supplément* [2 vols.] (Paris: 1826); "Über den neuesten Zustand des Freistaates von Central-Amerika oder Guatemala," *Hertha*, 6 (1826), pp. 131-161; "Über die bei den verschiedenen Völkern üblichen Systeme von Zahlzeichen und über den Ursprung des Stellenwertes in den indischen Zahlen," *Journal für eine reine und angewandte Mathematik*, vol. 4 (1829), pp. 205-231; "Über den Namen und die ältesten Karten von Amerika (Auszug)," *Annalen der Erd-, Völker-und Staatenkunde*, 3rd ser., vol. 1 (1835), pp. 209-212.

SOURCES: Ilse Jahn and Fritz G. Lange (editors) *Die Jugendbriefe Alexander von Humboldts 1787-1799* (Berlin [East]: 1973) (= *Beiträge zur Alexander-von-Humboldt-Forschung*, vol. 2); Kurt-R. Biermann (editor), *Briefwechsel zwischen Alexander von Humboldt und Carl Friedrich Gauß* (Berlin [East]: 1977) (= *Beiträge zur Alexander-von-Humboldt-Forschung*, vol. 4); Kurt-R. Biermann (editor), *Briefwechsel zwischen Alexander von Humboldt und Heinrich Christian Schumacher* (Berlin [East]: 1979) (= *Beiträge zur Alexander-von-Humboldt-Forschung*, vol. 6); Alexander von Humboldt, *Antrittsrede in der Königlich-preußischen Akademie der Wissenschaften zu Berlin am 21. November 1805* [privately printed] ([1805]); Alexander von Humboldt, "Autobiographische Skizze," *Die Gegenwart*, 8 (1853), pp. 749-762; Karl Bruhns, *Alexander von Humboldt* [3 vols.] (Leipzig: 1872); Hanno Beck, *Alexander von Humboldt* [2 vols.] (Wiesbaden: 1959-1961); Adolf Meyer-Abich, *Alexander von Humboldt* (Reinbek: 1967); *Alexander von Humboldt und seine Welt 1769-1859* (Berlin: 1969) [exhibition catalogue]; Kurt R. Biermann, *Alexander von Humboldt* (Leipzig: 1980) (= *Biographien hervorragender Naturwissenschaftler, Techniker und Mediziner*, vol. 47); Kurt Schleucher, *Alexander von Humboldt* (Berlin: 1987); Alfred Gebauer, *Alexander von Humboldt: Sein Lebensbild: ein großer Sohn Berlins* (Berlin: 1987); Berthold Riese, *Indianische Handschriften und Berliner Forscher* (Berlin 1988), pp. 21-22.

Berthold Riese

Humboldt, Karl Wilhelm von. Statesman, classical scholar, man of letters (in the literal as well as extended sense), libertarian-humanist political philosopher, educational reformer, anthropologist, linguist. Born in Potsdam (Germany) 22 June 1767, died in Tegel, near Berlin (Germany) 8 April 1835.

Older brother of the illustrious naturalist, geographer and explorer ALEXANDER VON HUMBOLDT and often known as the "other" Humboldt, Wilhelm attained achievements as impressive as Alexander's. Still commanding the full range of human knowledge of their times, the two brothers were perhaps the last true polymaths, complementing each other in their areas of interest and with the older of the two embodying the humanities. Hans Hartmann observed poignantly that Alexander was interested in the language of nature and Wilhelm in the nature of language.

Early in his life and as a private scholar, Humboldt became concerned with religion, personal liberty, *Bildung* (education, including cultivation of one's character and intellect), the political issues of the day (such as the French Revolution and the emancipation of Jews), aesthetics, the Classics and literature. He was a master of letter-writing as a literary form and became the third member of the scholarly triangle including the poets Johann Wolfgang Goethe and Friedrich Schiller. Humboldt also made a political career in various functions of the Prussian government. Apart from serving as envoy to Rome, Vienna and London, he reformed Prussia's educational system and founded the University of Berlin, a model for modern higher education in Europe and America. Moreover, he played a significant role in Prussia's resistance to Napoleon and participated in the discussion of a federal constitution for Germany. Whereas Humboldt came to figure as a kind of Thomas Jefferson for Germans, the increasingly authoritarian state of Prussia dismissed him in 1819 into premature retirement, which he primarily devoted to scholarly pursuits.

Among Humboldt's varied concerns was a strong interest in comparative anthropology, although it is evident only from fragments of his early writings. While reflecting a philosophical inclination in his search for a moral order and the ideal human, Humboldt addressed with sympathy questions of human diversity and cultural relativity, hence integrating ideas from both the Enlightenment and the Romantic period. Much of his thinking drew on his direct ethnographic observations made under fieldwork-like conditions and on an explicitly historical perspective. During his travels through France and Spain in search of the "national character" of modern civilizations, Humboldt had already paid close attention to "primitive" Basque language and culture. As Prussian resident at the Vatican, he had also drawn on its rich documentary collections as well as the resources of his younger brother and such contacts as the Jesuit Lorenzo Hervás y Panduro and had developed a special fascination for American Indian languages, which remained a major, lasting interest. Humboldt extended his studies to ancient Egyptian, Sanskrit, Chinese, Japanese, Southeast Asian and Pacific languages.

Relying on his own polyglot experiences, Humboldt maintained a broad empirical basis for his research that few, if any, contemporaries could match and that Humboldt scholars have overlooked in their frequently exclusive focus on his philosophy. In Humboldt's mind, philosophy and philology actually were not separate disciplines, but integrated the *a priori* and the empirical into a "cosmographic" scholarly endeavor, including still other fields of study such as history. His comparative anthropology eventually found its crowning realization in his broadly defined approach to the study of languages, which he viewed as part of their encompassing cultures. In a continuing dialogue with himself, Humboldt addressed the following major themes: language as the medium and mediator of thought and understanding (their dynamic interaction becoming most evident in conversation and dialogue-like letter-writing); linguistic relativity (without precluding universals in language and thought, translation from one language to another, knowledge or science); language as a system or "organism" (understood not as a biologism, but solely as a metaphor); a relativistic conception of its *innere Form* (comparable to the modern anthropological-linguistic notion of "emic" in its broadest terms); grammatical processes such as isolation, agglutination, incorporation and inflection (without the rigid classificatory-typological or even cryptoracist implications so often ascribed to Humboldt); and linguistic creativity (not to be misinterpreted in the narrow Chomskyan sense). In spite of apparent and real contradictions, these themes were interrelated for Humboldt, who thus set the stage for modern linguistics.

Among other pursuits, he secured a faculty position for FRANZ BOPP at the University of Berlin, in effect institutionalizing comparative-historical linguistics, and influenced the linguist Heymann Steinthal, the psychologist WILHELM WUNDT and his *Völkerpsychologie*, and the so-called neo-Humboldtians of a century later. Yet, by providing a broad comparative perspective and a holistic model of language, Humboldt also had a great impact on the burgeoning of American linguistics and anthropology, which were struggling with the analysis and classification of American Indian languages. His ideas found their ways into the thought of Peter S. Du Ponceau, John Pickering, Albert S. Gatschet, DANIEL GARRISON BRINTON, even FRANZ BOAS, and—perhaps most significantly—EDWARD SAPIR.

MAJOR WORKS: *Über die Kawi-Sprache auf der Insel Java, nebst einer Einleitung über die Verschiedenheit des menschlichen Sprachbaues und ihren Einfluss auf die geistige Entwickelung des Menschengeschlechts* [3 vols.] (Berlin: 1836-1839) [tr. of introduction: *Linguistic Variability and Intellectual Development: Introduction to the Kawi Work* (Coral Gables, Florida: 1971); *On Language: the Diversity of Human Language Structure and Its Influence on the Mental Development of Mankind* (Cambridge: 1988)]; *Wilhelm von Humboldt: Gesammelte Werke* [7 vols.] (Berlin: 1841-1852); "On the verb in American languages: translated from the unpublished original by Daniel G. Brinton," *Proceedings of the American Philosophical Society*, vol. 22 (1885), pp. 332-352; *Wilhelm von Humboldts Gesammelte Schriften* [17 vols.] (Berlin: 1903-1936) [tr. of excerpts: *Humanist Without Portfolio: an Anthology of the Writings of Wilhelm von Humboldt* (Detroit: 1963)].

SOURCES: Paul R. Sweet, *Wilhelm von Humboldt: a Biography* [2 vols.] (Columbus, Ohio: 1978-1980); Robert Leroux, *L'anthropologie comparée de Guillaume de Humboldt* (Paris: 1958); Helmut Gipper, "Wilhelm von Humboldt als Begründer moderner Sprachforschung," *Wirkendes Wort*, vol. 15 (1965), pp. 1-19; Martin L. Manchester, *The Philosophical Foundations of Humboldt's Linguistic Doctrine* (Amsterdam: 1985); Daniel G. Brinton, "The philosophic grammar of American languages, as set forth by Wilhelm von Humboldt, with the translation of an unpublished memoir by him on the American verb," *Proceedings of the American Philosophical Society*, vol. 22 (1885), pp. 306-352; Hans Hartmann, "Wilhelm und Alexander von Humboldt, Natur- und Geisteswissenschaft heute" in: Herbert Kessler and Walter Thoms (editors), *Die Brüder Humboldt heute* (Mannheim: 1968) (= *Abhandlungen der Humboldt-Gesellschaft für Wissenschaft, Kunst und Bildung*, vol. 2), pp. 11-40; John Viertel, "The concept of 'diversity' in Humboldt's thought," *Lingua e stile*, vol. 8 (1973), pp. 83-105; Roger L. Brown, *Wilhelm von Humboldt's Conception of Linguistic Relativity* (The Hague: 1967); W. Keith Percival, "Humboldt's description of the Javanese verb" in: Dell Hymes (editor), *Studies in the History of Linguistics* (Bloomington: 1974), pp. 380-389; Eugenio Coseriu, "Über die Sprachtypologie Wilhelm von Humboldts: ein Beitrag zur Kritik der sprachwissenschaftlichen Überlieferung" in: *Beiträge zur vergleichenden Literaturgeschichte: Festschrift für Kurt Wais zum 65. Geburtstag* (Tübingen: 1972), pp. 107-135; E.F.K. Koerner, "The Humboldtian trend in linguistics" in: *Studies in Descriptive and Historical Linguistics: Festschrift for Winfred P. Lehmann* (Amsterdam: 1977), pp. 145-158; Kurt Müller-Vollmer, "Wilhelm von Humboldt und der Anfang der amerikanischen Sprachwissenschaft: die Briefe an John Pickering" in: Klaus Hammacher (editor), *Universalismus und Wissenschaft im Werk und Wirken der Brüder Humboldt* (Frankfurt: 1976), pp. 259-334; Harold Basilius, "Neo-Humboldtian ethnolinguistics," *Word*, vol. 8 (1952), pp. 95-105; Emanuel J. Drechsel, "Wilhelm von Humboldt and Edward Sapir: analogies and homologies in their linguistic thoughts" in: William Shipley (editor), *In Honor of Mary Haas: from the Haas Festival Conference on Native American Linguistics* (Berlin: 1988), pp. 225-264.

Emanuel J. Drechsel

Hunt, George. Interpreter, fieldworker, ethnologist. Born at Fort Rupert (British Columbia) 1854, died at Fort Rupert (British Columbia) 5 September 1933. Hunt was best known for his role as field researcher and local expert in Kwakiutl culture for FRANZ BOAS, but he had also acted as interpreter for the Indian Reserve Commission surveys of British Columbia in 1879 and for Johan Adrian Jacobsen's expedition of 1881-1883. Hunt met Boas in 1886 and by 1887 was employed by him as interpreter for the American Museum of Natural History's Jesup North Pacific Expedition.

Hunt's background uniquely qualified him for this position. The son of Robert Hunt, a Scot in the employ of the Hudson's Bay Company, and Mary Ebbetts, a Tlingit from southeast Alaska, Hunt was raised among the Kwakiutls of Fort Rupert. He was literate, could speak English, Tlingit and Kwakiutl, and was accustomed to dealing with members of several cultures. His earlier guiding and interpreting experiences, during which he capitalized on his linguistic abilities, prepared him for his life's work with and for Boas. Going far beyond mere interpreting, Hunt investigated many aspects of Kwakiutl culture under Boas's direction and communicated his findings by mail to Boas in New York.

Boas never became fluent in the Kwakiutl language and depended on Hunt to record and translate Kwakiutl texts for him. While Hunt is listed as the co-author of a few of Boas's publications on the Kwakiutl, his input was critical to the body of Boas's Kwakiutl works. The working relationship with Boas continued for much of Hunt's adult life, with Hunt using his knowledge of Indian lifeways to earn income as a fieldworker and his income as an informant to become a man of substance among the Kwakiutl. He managed to use each of his roles—as researcher for outside interests and as local leader—to improve his situation in the other. Though unrelated to the people of Fort Rupert, he eventually won the right to *potlatch* and to occupy a chief's seat.

MAJOR WORKS: (with Franz Boas) *Kwakiutl Texts* (New York: 1905) (= *American Museum of Natural History, Memoirs*, vol. 5); (with Franz Boas) *Kwakiutl Texts—Second Series* (New York: 1906); "The rival chief: a Kwakiutl story" in: *Boas Anniversary Volume* (New York: 1906) (= *American Museum of Natural History, Memoirs*, vol. 14), pp. 108-136.

SOURCES: Frederick J. Dockstader, *Great North American Indians* (New York: 1977); Jeanne Cannizzo, "George Hunt and the invention of Kwakiutl culture," *Canadian Review of Sociology and Anthropology*, vol. 20 (1983), pp. 44-58.

David Lonergan

Hurston, Zora Neale. Folklorist, writer, anthropologist. Born in Eatonville (Florida) 7 January 1901, died in Fort Pierce (Florida) 28 January 1960. Hurston was one of the first black anthropologists in the United States, as well as one of the first anthropologists to study African-American culture and to use ethnographic data extensively in writing fiction. She studied anthropology with FRANZ BOAS, RUTH BENEDICT and GLADYS REICHARD at Barnard College, where she received a B.A. in 1928, and began her fieldwork collecting folklore in Florida in 1927 with a fellowship Boas obtained for her. The remainder of her life involved fieldwork focusing on folklore and religion in the United States and the Caribbean, writing in numerous genres based on both fieldwork and personal experiences and personally coming to terms with being a highly imaginative black woman in America. She was active during the Harlem Renaissance but in later years expressed views that were considered reactionary by civil rights activists and incendiary by publishers. Because all of her writing was creative (her folklore reflects the experience of performance; her essays, fiction and drama incorporate ethnographic data in a variety of narrative styles), her work as an anthropologist was not appreciated in her lifetime. Although she was well known as a writer and lecturer, Hurston was plagued by financial problems throughout her life and died in poverty and obscurity.

In the 1970s and 1980s her work was rediscovered and given more extensive attention by African-American scholars, literary critics and anthropologists than it had ever received in her lifetime. Most of her books have been reprinted, including her autobiography, *Dust Tracks on a Road* and her creative writing, *Mules and Men*; *Their Eyes Were Watching God*; *Tell My Horse*; *Moses: Man of the Mountain*; and *Seraph on the Suwanee*. Her essays, stories and drama have been anthologized and some of her unpublished manuscripts published.

MAJOR WORKS: *Jonah's Gourd Vine* (Philadelphia: 1934); *Mules and Men* (Philadelphia: 1935); *Their Eyes Were Watching God* (Philadelphia: 1937); *Tell My Horse* (Philadelphia: 1938); *Moses: Man of the Mountain* (Philadelphia: 1939); *Dust Tracks on a Road* (Philadelphia: 1942); *Seraph on the Suwanee* (New York: 1948); *I Love Myself When I Am Laughing: a Zora Neale Hurston Reader* (edited by Alice Walker) (Old Westbury, N.Y.: 1979); *The Sanctified Church* (Berkeley: 1983); *Spunk: the Selected Short Stories of Zora Neale Hurston* (Berkeley: 1985).

SOURCES: Harold Bloom (editor), *Zora Neale Hurston* (New York: 1986); Nina Thanz Borremans and Dwight Lee Schmidt, "Zora Neale Hurston: a seraph in anthropology," *Florida Journal of Anthropology*, vol. 4 (1979), pp. 4-10; Hugh M. Gloster, "Zora Neale Hurston: novelist and folklorist," *Phylon*, vol. 4 (1943), pp. 153-159; Robert E. Hemenway, *Zora Neale Hurston: a Literary Biography* (Urbana: 1977); Marion Kilson, "The transformation of Eatonville's ethnographer," *Phylon*, vol. 33 (1972), pp. 112-119; Gwendolen Mikell, "Zora Neale Hurston" in: Ute Gacs [et al.] (editors), *Women Anthropologists: a Biographical Dictionary* (New York: 1988), pp. 160-166.

Nancy J. Schmidt

Hüsnü, Seniha. See: *Tunakan, Seniha.*

—

i

Iakinf, Father. See: *Bichurin, N.ĪA. (Nikita ĪAkovlevich)*.

Innokentiĭ. See: *Veniaminov (Popov), I.E. (Ivan Evseevich)*.

Izikowitz, Karl Gustav. Anthropologist. Born in Jönköping (Sweden) 26 November 1903, died in Göteborg (Sweden) 1984. Izikowitz was the son of a Jewish merchant in southern Sweden and developed an interest in ethnography at an early stage. He obtained his M.A. (*fil. lic.*) in 1931 and, only four years later, he was awarded his doctorate in Göteborg, under the supervision of ERLAND NORDENSKIÖLD. A year later, in 1936, he was appointed docent of general and comparative ethnography at the University of Göteborg.

Izikowitz remained faithful to the city of his mentor, Göteborg, all his life. He started his career as a professional museum curator at the Göteborg Museum in 1944 and became its director in 1953, a position he held until his retirement in 1970. In 1955 he was also appointed professor of anthropology at the University of Göteborg.

Under the influence of Nordenskiöld, Izikowitz wrote his thesis on the distribution of musical instruments of the South American Indians, a work that fit well with the diffusionist and Americanist interests of his professor. Although this thesis has been considered a major work on South American ethnography, Izikowitz is better known for his works on the Indo-Chinese people Lamet (especially *Lamet, Hill Peasants in French Indo-China*).

While Izikowitz in his initial field trip first went to Mexico, he continued from there to Asia. For almost a year, he stayed with the Lamet in a cultural area (Laos) that at the time was virtually unknown to anthropology.

World War II put an end to Izikowitz' Lamet studies and after the war he moved on to the Gabada of India. Again, he took special care in learning the language and the customs of the group he studied.

Izikowitz introduced "social anthropology" to Göteborg, and, as the altered name (from the former "ethnography") suggests, he was quite oriented to present-day issues, socio-economic organization and the study of sociology. He also brought new ideas from French anthropology and applied them to what he taught.

MAJOR WORKS: *Musical and Other Instruments of the South American Indians* (Göteborg: 1935) (= *Göteborgs kungl. vetenskaps- och vittterhets-samhälle. Handlingar,* 5:e följden, ser. A, vol. 5, no. 7); *Över Dimmornas Berg* (Stockholm: 1944) [travel book]; *Lamet, Hill Peasants in French Indo-China* (Göteborg: 1951).

Jan-Åke Alvarsson

J

Jacobs, Melville. Anthropologist, folklorist, linguist. Born in New York (New York) 3 July 1902, died in Seattle (Washington) 31 July 1971. Jacobs is best known for his pioneering research on Northwest Coast American Indian languages and folklore. Jacobs' Ph.D. dissertation, written under FRANZ BOAS's direction at Columbia University (1924-1927), was a grammar of Sahaptin (*A Sketch of Northern Sahaptin Grammar*). His subsequent contributions to North American Indian linguistics include a structural sketch of Chinook Jargon and a delineation of the areal spread of sound features in the languages of the peoples of the Northwest. Extensive linguistic fieldwork notwithstanding, Jacobs thought of himself primarily as a cultural anthropologist.

Jacobs was a professor of anthropology at the University of Washington from 1928 to 1971. During his early years at Washington, he engaged in intensive field research in cultural anthropology, folklore, music and linguistics, primarily among western Oregon American Indian groups. From 1926 to 1939 he collected large quantities of lexical, grammatical and textual materials as well as audio recordings from speakers of Sahaptin, Molale, Kalapuya (Tualatin, Santiam, and Yonkalla), Clackamas Chinook, Coos (Hanis and Miluk), Tillamook, Alsea, Upper Umpqua, Galice and Chinook Jargon. Often working with the last speakers of these indigenous languages, Jacobs conducted much of his fieldwork by means of phonetically recorded texts with translations. Such texts provided at the same time valuable linguistic, folkloric, and ethnographic data.

During the 1930s and 1940s Jacobs' theoretical interests were concerned with correlating types of historical processes of change in cultures with types of socioeconomic systems. In the 1950s his interests turned to the psychological analysis of cultures, especially as reflected in folklore. Utilizing a psychodynamic model, Jacobs interpreted the expressive content of folktales as the "projection" onto myth and tale "screens" of stressful events and social relationships, which were apparently not satisfactorily resolved by other cultural means. Jacobs eschewed the traditional folklore concepts of plot, tale-type and motif; in their stead he borrowed from Western drama such terms as play, act and scene to describe the structure of non-Western folktales (e.g., *The Content and Style of an Oral Literature*). Jacobs stressed the need for anthropological folklorists to relate the folklore of a culture to its system of social relationships, value ideals and world views.

MAJOR WORKS: *Northwest Sahaptin Texts*, 1 (Seattle: 1929) (= *University of Washington Publications in Anthropology*, vol. 2, no. 6); *A Sketch of Northern Sahaptin Grammar* (Seattle: 1931) (= *University of Washington Publications in Anthropology*, vol. 4, no. 2); *Northwest Sahaptin Texts* [2 vols.] (New York: 1934-1937) (= *Columbia University Contributions to Anthropology*, vol. 19, parts 1-2); *Coos Narrative and Ethnologic Texts* (Seattle: 1939) (= *University of Washington Publications in Anthropology*, vol. 8, no. 1); *Coos Myth Texts* (Seattle: 1940) (= *University of Washington Publications in Anthropology*, vol. 8, no. 2); *Kalapuya Texts* (Seattle: 1945) (= *University of Washington Publications in Anthropology*, vol. 11); *Clackamas Chinook Texts*, part 1 (Bloomington: 1958) (= *Publications of the Indiana University Research Center in Anthropology, Folklore, and Linguistics*, no. 8); *Clackamas Chinook Texts, Part 2* (Bloomington: 1959) (= *Publications of the Indiana University Research Center in Anthropology, Folklore, and Linguistics*, no. 11); *The Content and Style of an Oral Literature* (Chicago: 1959); *The People are Coming Soon* (Seattle: 1960); *Pattern in Cultural Anthropology* (Homewood, Ill.: 1964).

SOURCES: Laurence C. Thompson, "The Northwest" in: Thomas A. Sebeok (editor), *Current Trends in Linguistics*, vol. 10 (The Hague: 1973), pp. 979-1045; Laurence C. Thompson, "Melville Jacobs, 1902-1971," *American Anthropologist*, vol. 80 (1978), pp. 640-646; William R. Seaburg, "Bibliography of Melville Jacobs," *American Anthropologist*, vol. 80 (1978), pp. 646-649; William R. Seaburg, *Guide to Pacific Northwest Native American Materials in the Melville Jacobs Collection and in Other Archival Collections in the University of Washington Libraries* (Seattle: 1982).

William R. Seaburg

Jenness, Diamond. Anthropologist, classicist. Born in Wellington (New Zealand) 10 February 1886, died in Ottawa (Ontario) 29 November 1969. After receiving degrees in classics at the University of Wellington and at Oxford, Jenness took up studies in anthropology under R.R. MARETT. As an Oxford Scholar, he completed a year of ethnographic research (1911-1912) in the D'Entrecasteaux Archipelago of Papua New Guinea in cooperation with his brother-in-law, Rev. A. Ballantyne, a missionary in the region. At the invitation of EDWARD SAPIR, Jenness joined the Canadian Arctic Expedition in 1913, which was led by the noted explorer-anthropologist VILHJALMUR STEFANSSON. Following the accidental death of Henri Beuchat, the expedition's other anthropologist, during their first Arctic season, Jenness assumed responsibility for ethnographic, linguistic, archaeological and physical anthropological investigations of Alaskan Yuit and Canadian Inuit. His extensive observations of the people of the Coronation Gulf area resulted in a number of publications, including the classic ethnographic account, *Life of the Copper Eskimos*.

Following service in France during the last years of World War I, Jenness returned to Ottawa, married Frances Eileen Bleakney and joined the staff of the Anthropological Division, National Museum of Canada, as Associate Ethnologist. He remained at the Museum until the end of World War II, succeeding Sapir as Division Head in 1926. During these years he made field trips among western (Carrier, Salish, Sarcee and

Sekani) and eastern (Ojibwa) tribes, made archaeological investigations in northwestern Alaska and Newfoundland and was the first anthropologist to recognize and name two prehistoric Eskimo cultural traditions: "Dorset" in the eastern Arctic and "Old Bering Sea" in Alaska. In 1932 he published *The Indians of Canada*, still a standard sourcebook on the ethnology of aboriginal peoples in Canada. On loan to the Geographical Bureau for intelligence work during World War II, Jenness's return to civilian life coincided with retirement from the Museum in 1946. A continuing interest in Greek studies led to the research for *The Economics of Cyprus*.

In his last years, back in Ottawa, he again addressed himself to the problems of northern natives, producing a five-volume comparative study of *Eskimo Administration* in Alaska, Canada, Labrador and Greenland.

Jenness held no academic appointments. However, during his long career he made numerous substantive contributions to anthropology, supported the work of many scholars through the offices of the National Museum, served as president of the American Anthropological Association (1939-1940) and the Society for American Archaeology (1936-1937) and as vice-president of the American Association for the Advancement of Science (1938) and was an advocate for aboriginal peoples faced with rapid modernization. Canada recognized the breadth of his contributions to the discipline and to national interests by appointing him a Companion of the Order of Canada in 1969.

MAJOR WORKS: (with Rev. A. Ballantyne) *The Northern D'Entrecasteaux* (Oxford: 1920); *The Life of the Copper Eskimos* (Ottawa: 1923); "A new Eskimo culture in Hudson Bay," *Geographical Review*, vol. 15 (1925), pp. 428-437; *The People of the Twilight* (New York: 1928); *The Indians of Canada* (Ottawa: 1932; 7th ed., Toronto: 1977); *Dawn in Arctic Alaska* (Minneapolis: 1957); *The Economics of Cyprus* (Montréal: 1962); *Eskimo Administration* [5 vols.] (Montréal: 1962-1968).

SOURCES: Henry B. Collins and William E. Taylor, Jr., "Diamond Jenness (1886-1969)," *Arctic*, vol. 23 (1970), pp. 71-81; Frederica De Laguna, "Diamond Jenness, C.C., 1886-1969," *American Anthropologist*, vol. 73 (1971), pp. 248-254; Nansi Swayze, *Canadian Portraits: Jenness, Barbeau, Wintemberg* (Toronto: 1960), pp. 39-97.

Barnett Richling

Jennings, Jesse David. Anthropologist. Born in Oklahoma City (Oklahoma) 7 July 1909. Jennings received a Ph.D. from the University of Chicago in 1943. After a ten-year career (1937-1947) with the National Park Service (except for service as an officer in the U.S. Navy during World War II), he joined the anthropology faculty at the University of Utah, where he remained from 1948 until retirement in 1986.

He has been Editor, *American Antiquity* (1950-1954); President, Society for American Archaeology (1959-1960); Vice-President (1961) and Chair (1971), Section H, American Association for the Advancement of Science; Viking Fund Medalist in Archaeology (1958); elected to the National Academy of Sciences; and a recipient of a University of Utah Distinguished Professorship in Anthropology.

Jennings' work in numerous areas of the continental United States, Central America and the South Pacific has contributed to his prowess as a synthesizer, and he has authored or edited several comprehensive volumes, particularly on the prehistory of North and South America. Perhaps his most important contribution has been the concept of the

"Desert Culture" (or "Desert Archaic"). In the western desert's multitudes of site types, located in diverse environmental situations and bearing disparate arrays of artifacts that seemed to represent numerous subsistence strategies, Jennings saw a prehistoric analogy to JULIAN H. STEWARD's ethnographic analysis of the Western Shoshones as generalists. He saw the Desert Archaic as constituting the base from which later specialized cultures formed. Critics who have taken issue with Jennings' jacks-of-all-desert-trades notion point to various lacustrine adaptations of the western Great Basin by specialized and sedentary groups who focused almost exclusively on fish, waterbirds, animals and plants of marshes, lakes and rivers. Defenders of the Desert-Culture concept argue that (1) information on the total subsistence patterns of apparently specialized lacustral archaeological cultures is lacking and (2) pockets of specialized resource exploitation fit easily into the Desert-Archaic model.

MAJOR WORKS: (with A.V. Kidder and E.M. Shook) *Excavations at Kaminal Juyu, Guatemala* (Washington: 1956) (= *Carnegie Institution of Washington Publications*, no. 561); *Plainsmen of the Past* (Omaha: 1948); "Prehistory of the Lower Mississippi Valley" in: J.B. Griffin (editor), *Archaeology of Eastern United States* (Chicago: 1952), pp. 256-271; *Danger Cave* (Salt Lake City: 1957) (= *University of Utah Anthropological Papers*, no. 27; and: *Memoirs of the Society for American Archaeology*, no. 14); "Prehistory of the Desert West" in: Jesse D. Jennings and Edward Norbeck (editors), *Prehistoric Man in the New World* (Chicago: 1964), pp. 149-174; "Perspective and later specializations" [prehistory] in: Robert F. Spencer, Jesse D. Jennings [et al.], *The Native Americans* (New York: 1965; 2nd ed., New York: 1977), pp. 1-99; *Glen Canyon: a Summary* (Salt Lake City: 1966) (= *University of Utah Anthropological Papers*, no. 81; also = *Glen Canyon Series*, no. 31); *Prehistory of North America* (New York: 1968; 2nd ed. New York: 1974); (with Richard Holmer and Gregory Jackmond), "Samoan village patterns: four examples," *Journal of the Polynesian Society*, vol. 91 (1982), pp. 81-102; "Prehistory: introduction" in: William C. Sturtevant (editor), *Handbook of North American Indians*, vol. 11 [*The Great Basin*] (Washington: 1986), pp. 113-119 .

SOURCE: C. Melvin Aikens, "Jesse D. Jennings, archeologist" in: Carol J. Condie and Don D. Fowler (editors), *Anthropology of the Desert West: Essays in Honor of Jesse D. Jennings* (Salt Lake City: 1986), pp. 1-5 .

Carol J. Condie

Jensen, Adolf Ellegard. Anthropologist, historian of religions. Born in Kiel (Germany) 1 January 1899, died in Mammolsheim (West Germany) 20 May 1965. Jensen was educated at the Universities of Bonn and Kiel, earning the *doctorandus* degree (more an honors B.A. than a Ph.D.) in philosophy in 1922. In 1923 he was hired by LEO FROBENIUS as a research assistant in the Forschungsinstitut für Kulturmorphologie (Research Institute for Cultural Morphology). Two years later the institute was moved from Munich to Frankfurt, and Jensen remained in that city for the rest of his academic career. After Frobenius's death in 1938, Jensen became the director of the institute; that same year he was appointed director of the city's ethnological museum. In 1946 he was given the professorial chair of the University of Frankfurt's Department of Ethnology.

Influenced by his mentor Frobenius, Jensen specialized in the analysis of myths in their relation to earlier phases of cultural development. He believed that myths, while often apparently arbitrary or confused with regard to the contemporary cultures that know and repeat them, made perfect sense to the archaic cultures that formed them and enacted them in cultic ritual. Jensen formulated his theory of *dema* myths after fieldwork on the South

Pacific island of Ceram in 1937; he held that these myths, of a deity or semi-deity whose body became the source of vegetable foodstuffs when torn apart and buried, were ubiquitous in groups dependent upon root and tuber vegetables.

Jensen led ethnological and folkloristic expeditions to South Africa in 1928-1930, to Libya in 1932 and to Ethiopia in 1934-1935, 1950-1951 and 1954-1955. He was a prolific writer and theorist.

MAJOR WORKS: (with H. Niggemeyer) *Hainuwele* (Frankfurt: 1939); *Im Lande des Gada* (Stuttgart: 1936); *Die drei Ströme* (Leipzig: 1948); *Altvölker Süd-Äthiopiens* (Stuttgart: 1959); *Mythos und Kult bei Naturvölkern* (Wiesbaden: 1951) [tr: *Myth and Cult among Primitive Peoples* (2nd ed., Chicago, 1969)].

SOURCE: Otto Zerries, "Jensen, Adolf E." in: Mircea Eliade (editor), *The Encyclopedia of Religion* (New York: 1987), vol. 7, pp. 567-568.

David Lonergan

Jochelson, Waldemar (Russian form of name: Vladimir Il'ich Iokhelson). Anthropologist, revolutionary. Born in Vilnius (Lithuania, then in Russia) 14 June 1855, died in New York (New York) 1 November 1937. Jochelson engaged in revolutionary activities in his youth and had to flee Russia in 1875 to avoid arrest. In 1884, trying to enter Russia under an assumed name, he was recognized and arrested. After three years in solitary confinement he was exiled to northeastern Siberia for ten years. He spent his time in ethnological and linguistic studies of the native tribes, writing articles for various Russian scientific societies. His articles led to an invitation to head the Yakut division of the 1895-1897 Sibiriâkov expedition sponsored by the Russian Geographical Society. He studied the culture and languages of the Yakut, Yukaghir and Lamut (Even).

In 1900, together with his colleague and fellow revolutionary, WALDEMAR BOGORAS, Jochelson joined the Jesup North Pacific Expedition organized by FRANZ BOAS for the American Museum of Natural History. Jochelson and his wife, Dina Brodsky, took long and extremely hazardous trips to study the Koryak and the Yukaghir. Among the materials they collected were 3,000 ethnographic artifacts, measurements of 900 individuals, 41 casts of faces, 1,200 photographs, phonographic cylinders, skulls, archaeological materials, and zoological specimens. Jochelson wrote five massive monographs on the Koryak and Yukaghir as well as a useful handbook, *Peoples of Asiatic Russia*.

During 1909-1911 Jochelson led the Aleut-Kamchatka Expedition of the Russian Geographical Society. From 1912 to 1922 he was division curator of the Museum of Anthropology and Ethnography in St. Petersburg/Leningrad and a collaborator of the Asiatic Museum of the Academy of Sciences of the same city. From 1922 until his death, Jochelson lived in the United States, where he was associated with the American Museum of Natural History and the Carnegie Institution of Washington.

MAJOR WORKS: "Religion and myths of the Koryak," *Memoirs of the American Museum of Natural History*, vol. 10 (1905), pp. 1-382 (= *The Jesup North Pacific Expedition*, vol. 6, pt. 1); "Material culture and social organization of the Koryak," *Memoirs of the American Museum of Natural History*, vol. 10 (1908), pp. 383-811 (= *The Jesup North Pacific Expedition*, vol. 6, pt. 2); "The Yukaghir and the Yukaghirized Tungus: social organization," *Memoirs of the American Museum of Natural History*, vol. 13 (1910), pp. 1-133 (= *The Jesup North Pacific Expedition*, vol. 9, pt. 1); "The Yukaghir and the Yukaghirized Tungus: religion and folklore," *Memoirs of the American Museum of Natural History*, vol. 13 (1924), pp. 135-342 (= *The Jesup North Pacific Expedition*, vol.

9, pt. 2); "The Yukaghir and the Yukaghirized Tungus: material culture," *Memoirs of the American Museum of Natural History*, vol. 13 (1926), pp. 343-454 (= *The Jesup North Pacific Expedition*, vol. 9, pt. 3); *Peoples of Asiatic Russia* (New York: 1928).

SOURCES: "Dr. Waldemar Jochelson," *American Anthropologist*, n.s, vol. 32 (1930), pp. 375-377; "Recent deaths," *American Anthropologist*, n.s, vol. 40 (1938), p. 345; Franz Boas, "The Jesup North Pacific Expedition," *The American Museum Journal*, vol. 3, no. 5 (1903), pp. 72-119; Stanley A. Freed, Ruth S. Freed and Laila Williamson, "Capitalist philanthropy and Russian revolutionaries: the Jesup North Pacific Expedition (1897-1902)," *American Anthropologist*, vol. 90 (1988), pp. 7-24; I.S. Gurvich and L.P. Kuzmina, "W.G. Bogoras et W.I. Jochelson: deux éminents représentants de l'ethnographie russe (1)," *Inter-Nord: Revue Internationale d'Études Arctiques*, vol. 17 (1985), pp. 145-151; Lawrence Krader, "Bogoraz, Vladimir G., Sternberg, Lev Y., and Jochelson, Vladimir" in: David L. Sills (editor) *International Encyclopedia of the Social Sciences* (New York: 1968-1979), vol. 2, pp. 116-119.

Stanley A. Freed, Ruth S. Freed and Laila Williamson

Jones, Joseph. Physician, teacher, archaeologist. Born in Liberty County (Georgia) 6 September 1833, died in New Orleans (Louisiana) 17 February 1896. Jones graduated from Princeton (1853) before attending medical school at the University of Pennsylvania, from which he received his M.D. in 1855. Jones is most remembered for serving as a surgeon for the Confederate Army at Andersonville during the Civil War, an experience that greatly expanded his understanding of infectious diseases. After the war Jones spent time studying disease processes and made some of the first observations of pathogenic microorganisms under the microscope. He also served as a consultant in forensic medicine. His work during the war and afterward afforded him ample opportunity to observe and autopsy patients with diseases such as syphilis. Indeed, Jones became an acknowledged expert on diseases endemic to the South.

While practicing medicine in Tennessee between 1866 and 1868, Jones excavated aboriginal artifacts. He fully described the earthworks, burial sites, and skeletal material he found. His meticulous investigation of these remains, coupled with his medical expertise, enabled him to make diagnoses of the diseases of the early inhabitants of Tennessee. His examination of the skeletal remains demonstrated lesions typical of syphilis. Because of this Jones is credited with being the first to detect the presence of syphilis in pre-Columbian Indian skeletal remains in 1876, although Rudolf Virchow (1821-1902) disputed his claims in 1898. Jones's work on the archaeological remains in Tennessee was a pioneering effort in American paleopathology and mortuary studies.

MAJOR WORKS: "The aboriginal mound builders of Tennessee," *American Naturalist*, vol. 3 (1869), pp. 57-73; *Explorations of the Aboriginal Remains of Tennessee* (Washington: 1876) (= *Smithsonian Contributions to Knowledge*, vol. 22); *Medical and Surgical Memoirs: Containing Investigations on the Geographical Distribution, Causes, Nature, Relation and Treatment of Various Diseases* (New Orleans: 1876-1890).

SOURCES: Stanhope Bayne-Jones, "Joseph Jones (1833-1896)," *Bulletin of the Tulane University Medical Faculty*, vol. 16 (1958), pp. 223-230; James O. Breeden, *Joseph Jones, M.D.: Scientist of the Old South* (Lexington: 1975); Saul Jarcho, "The development and present condition of human palaeopathology in the United States" in: Saul Jarcho (editor), *Human Palaeopathology* (New Haven: 1966), pp. 3-42.

Joyce L. Ogburn

Jones, William. Anthropologist. Born on the Sauk and Fox Reservation (Oklahoma) 28 March 1871, died in Luzon (Philippines) April 1909. Jones's father was the son of a Fox Indian mother and a father of Welsh descent. His mother was an English girl who died when Jones was one year old. He was given by his father to his Indian grandmother to be raised and lived with her until the age of nine when she died.

Jones attended Hampton Institute (1889-1892), Phillips Andover (1892-1896), and Harvard University (1896-1900). He went on to Columbia University, where he received an M.A. in 1901 and a Ph.D. in 1904. Jones had originally intended to go to medical school, but in March 1897 he met FREDERIC WARD PUTNAM, Peabody Professor of American Anthropology and Ethnology at Harvard, and changed his field from medicine to Indian research. He spent the next four summers in the field recording the stories, customs and languages of the Fox and Sauk Indians. At Columbia his chief instructor was FRANZ BOAS, then also the Curator of Anthropology at the American Museum of Natural History. In 1901 he was appointed University Fellow under Boas, a position he held for two years. Boas sent him west where he did further fieldwork with the Sauk and Fox Indians. In 1903 the American Museum sent him to the Great Lakes region of Canada. His thesis, *Some Principles of Algonquian Word-Formation*, was published in *American Anthropologist* in 1904.

Jones wanted to begin his permanent work by going to Labrador and working with the Naskapi Indians, but there were no positions open for such research. The Carnegie Institution gave him a grant to finish work on the Ojibwa papers he had started after his 1903 fieldwork. In 1906 GEORGE A. DORSEY of the Field Museum of Natural History offered him his choice of three expeditions—to Africa, the South Sea Islands, and the Philippines. He accepted the expedition to the Philippines. In August of 1907 he sailed for Luzon. He started his work with the Ilongots in the area south of Echague on the Cagayan River. He worked in this area for approximately fourteen months, recording the ethnology of the peoples he lived with and making collections of artifacts to be sent back to the Field Museum. Jones was embarking on his final river voyage back to Manila in early April 1909 when he was murdered by the Ilongots.

MAJOR WORKS: "Episodes in the culture-hero myth of the Sauks and Foxes," *Journal of American Folk-Lore*, vol. 14 (1901), pp. 225-239; *Some Principles of Algonquian Word-Formation* [Ph.D. dissertation] (Lancaster, Pa.: 1904) (= *American Anthropologist*, n.s., vol. 6, no. 3 [supplement]); *Fox Texts* (Leiden: 1907) (= *Publications of the American Ethnological Society*, vol. 1); "Notes on the Fox Indians," *Journal of American Folk-Lore*, vol. 24 (1911), pp. 209-237; "Algonquian (Fox)" (revised by Truman Michelson) in: Franz Boas, *Handbook of American Indian Languages* (Washington: 1911) (= *Bureau of American Ethnology Bulletin*, vol. 40, part 1), pp. 735-873; "The Algonkin Mantou," *Journal of American Folk-Lore*, vol. 18 (1915), pp. 183-190; *Kickapoo Tales* (collected by William Jones, translated by Truman Michelson) (Leiden: 1915) (= *Publications of the American Ethnological Society*, vol. 9); "Ojibwa Tales from the North Shore of Lake Superior," *Journal of American Folk-Lore*, vol. 29 (1916), pp. 368-391; *Ojibwa Texts* (collected by William Jones, edited by Truman Michelson) [2 parts] (Leiden: 1917-1919) (= *Publications of the American Ethnological Society*, vol. 7); *Ethnography of the Fox Indians* (edited by Margaret Welpley Fisher) (Washington: 1939) (= *Bureau of American Ethnology Bulletin*, no. 125).

SOURCES: *The Diary of William Jones, 1907-1909: Robert F. Cummings Philippine Expedition* [unpublished, at Field Museum]; Henry Milner Rideout, *William Jones: Indian, Cowboy, American Scholar, and Anthropologist in the Field* (New York: 1912); Barbara Stoner, "Why was William Jones killed?," *Field Museum of Natural History Bulletin*, vol. 42, no. 8 (September 1971), pp. 10-13; *Annual Report of the Director of the Board of Trustees for the Year 1909, Field Museum of*

Natural History, vol. 3, no. 4 (1910), p. 332; William Jones, *Ethnography of the Fox Indians* (edited by Margaret Welpley Fisher) (Washington: 1939) (= *Bureau of American Ethnology Bulletin*, no. 125).

Michele Calhoun

Josselin de Jong, J.P.B. de (Jan Petrus Benjamin de). Ethnologist, linguist. Born in Leiden (Netherlands) 13 March 1886, died in Zeist (Netherlands) 15 November 1964. De Josselin de Jong was one of the most influential Dutch ethnologists of this century. He studied Dutch language and literature with linguist C.C. UHLENBECK, whom he joined for fieldwork among the Blackfoot and Ojibwa Indians in 1910 and 1911. On finishing his studies in 1910, he was appointed as conservator to the National Ethnographic Museum in Leiden, a post he held until 1935. In 1913 he was awarded a doctorate for a linguistic thesis that combined theoretical insights both from linguistics and ethnology (*De waarderingsonderscheiding van 'levend' en 'levenloos' in het Indo-germaansch vergeleken met hetzelfde verschijnsel in enkele Algonkin-talen: een ethnopsychologische studie*). This combination would remain a hallmark of his work; in his view the study of language was the single most reliable way to penetrate beneath the surface of a society's way of life. In 1922 he was appointed to an externally funded part-time professorship in general ethnology at Leiden University. Between 1922 and 1928 he gradually began developing a structuralist view of society, partly resulting from the training by his mentor Uhlenbeck, partly influenced by W.H. RASSERS; one result was "The Natchez social system." A Rockefeller Fellowship enabled him to engage in fieldwork in Eastern Indonesia from November 1932 until March 1934. In 1935 he was appointed to a regular professorship in ethnology, a post he would retain—with a break during World War II—until 1956.

De Josselin de Jong's publications are few, mostly articles. He had a strong personality but was not a brilliant lecturer. Especially in his lectures he was a staunch critic of the extremes of colonialism. This did not emanate from a political standpoint, but from a sound respect for humanity and a pessimistic view of his own materialistic society. Though closely linked to Leiden structuralism, de Josselin de Jong himself never did champion any explicit theory. Most characteristic were the high scientific standards that he set not only for himself but also for his pupils. This led to a range of excellent dissertations written under his supervision. In the post-war period almost all Dutch chairs in anthropology and sociology of non-Western peoples were at one time or another occupied by one of his pupils.

In his inaugural lecture in 1935 (*De Maleische archipel als ethnologisch studieveld*) he formulated the main points of what was to become a research program for Leiden anthropology: the notions of the ethnological field of study, double unilinear descent systems, the relation between myth and culture, and the problems of change in Hindu-Javanese culture and Indonesian Islam. This structural approach toward comparison of cultural phenomena led to an immediate response when CLAUDE LÉVI-STRAUSS' *Structures élémentaires de la parenté* appeared in 1949. De Josselin de Jong was practically the first to acknowledge the importance of this work and review it critically in a series of lectures, later published as *Lévi-Strauss' Theory on Kinship and Marriage*. In his article "Ethnolinguïstiek," de Josselin de Jong anticipated Lévi-Strauss's panchronic search for structural universals present in all cultural systems.

MAJOR WORKS: *De waarderingsonderscheiding van 'levend' en 'levenloos' in het Indo-germaansch vergeleken met hetzelfde verschijnsel in enkele Algonkintalen: een ethnopsychologische studie* (Leiden: 1913); "A new ethnological method," *Internationales Archiv für Ethnographie*, vol. 24 (1918), pp. 158-168; "De Couvade," *Meededelingen der Koninklijke Akademie van Wetenschappen, afdeeling Letterkunde*, vol. 54, series B, pp. 53-84 (1922); *Cultuurtypen en cultuurphasen* (Leiden: 1922); "The Natchez social system" in: *Proceedings of the 23rd International Congress of Americanists* (New York: 1928), pp. 553-562; "De oorsprong van den goddelijken bedrieger," *Meededelingen der Koninklijke Akademie van Wetenschappen, afdeeling Letterkunde*, vol. 68, series B, pp. 1-30 (1929); *De Maleische Archipel als ethnologisch studieveld* (Leiden: 1935) [tr.: "The Malay Archipelago as a field of ethnological study" in: P.E. de Josselin de Jong (editor), *Structural Anthropology in the Netherlands* (The Hague: 1977), pp. 164-182]; *Customary Law: a Confusing Fiction* (Amsterdam: 1948); "Ethnolinguïstiek," *Bijdragen tot de Taal-, Land- en Volkenkunde*, vol. 107 (1951), pp. 161-178; *Lévi-Strauss' Theory on Kinship and Marriage* (Leiden: 1952).

SOURCES: J. van Baal, "Jan Petrus Benjamin de Josselin de Jong, 13 maart 1886—15 november 1964," *Bijdragen tot de Taal-, Land- en Volkenkunde*, vol. 121 (1965), pp. 293-302; J.J. Fox (editor), *The Flow of Life* (Harvard: 1980); S.R. Jaarsma, *Structuur :: Realiteit. Kernelementen van de Leidse antropologie in theorie en praktijk tussen de jaren twintig en vijftig* (Leiden: 1984); P.E. de Josselin de Jong, "Jan Petrus Benjamin de Josselin de Jong, 13 march 1886—15 november 1964," *Lingua*, vol. 13 (1965), pp. 223-229; F.B.J. Kuiper, "Jan Petrus Benjamin de Josselin de Jong (13 maart 1886—15 november 1964)," *Jaarboek der Koninklijke Nederlandse Akademie van Wetenschappen* (1965/1966), pp. 397-403; G.W. Locher, "J.P.B. de Josselin de Jong (in memoriam)," *Mens en Maatschappij*, vol. 40 (1965), pp. 36-47.

S.R. Jaarsma and J.J. de Wolf

Judd, Neil Merton. Archaeologist, museum curator. Born in Cedar Rapids (Nebraska) 27 October 1887, died in Washington (D.C.) 19 December 1976. While he was a student at the University of Utah, Judd was introduced to archaeology by BYRON CUMMINGS. His first explorations were as a member of Cummings' expeditions to Arizona and Utah in 1907 and 1908. In 1909 he was a member of the Cummings-William Boone Douglass expedition to Rainbow Natural Bridge. Judd continued his studies at the University of Utah (B.A., 1911) and at George Washington University (M.A., 1913).

In 1911 Judd became an aid with the Division of Archeology in the Smithsonian Institution's United States National Museum, and he remained employed at the museum until he retired in 1949, rising to the position of curator of archaeology. He was a member of the Archaeological Institute of America's Fourth Quirigua [Guatemala] Expedition in 1914 and later supervised the construction of a model of the ruins for the Pacific-California International Exposition in San Diego. In 1915 he investigated "Spanish Diggings" flint quarries in Wyoming.

Judd is best known for his fieldwork in the Southwest. He undertook partial restoration of Betatakin in 1917 and worked on excavations at Paragonah, Utah, in 1918. Between 1920 and 1927 he carried out major excavations at Pueblo Bonito and other sites of Chaco Canyon, New Mexico. In connection with the latter work, he was also involved in the Beam Expeditions to locate timber useful in dating his archaeological finds. In 1930 he directed an aerial reconnaissance of ancient canals in the Salt and Gila river valleys in Arizona.

Judd's work has been described as the "first systematic archaeological work in the Intermontane West" (Rohn). For it, he received the Franklin L. Burr Award of the National Geographic Society in 1953 and 1962 and the Society of American Archaeology's

Alfred Vincent Kidder Award in 1965. He was president of the Society for American Archaeology in 1939 and of the American Anthropological Association in 1945.

MAJOR WORKS: *Archeological Observations North of the Rio Colorado* (Washington: 1926) (= *Bureau of American Ethnology Bulletin*, no. 82); *The Material Culture of Pueblo Bonito* (Washington: 1954) (= *Smithsonian Miscellaneous Collections*, vol. 125); *The Architecture of Pueblo Bonito* (Washington: 1964) (= *Smithsonian Miscellaneous Collections*, vol. 147); *The Bureau of American Ethnology: a Partial History* (Norman: 1967); *Men Met Along the Trail: Adventures in Archeology* (Norman: 1968).

SOURCES: J.O. Brew, "Neil Merton Judd, 1887-1976," *American Anthropologist*, vol. 80 (1978), pp. 352-354; James R. Glenn, *Register to the Papers of Neil Merton Judd* ([Washington?]: 1982); Judd papers in the Smithsonian Institution National Anthropological Archives; Waldo R. Wedel, "Neil Merton Judd, 1887-1967," *American Antiquity*, vol. 43 (1978), pp. 399-404; Arthur H. Rohn, "The Southwest and Intermontane West" in: James E. Fitting (editor), *The Development of North American Archaeology* (University Park, Penn.: 1973), pp. 185-211.

James R. Glenn

Junod, Henri-Alexandre. Missionary, anthropologist, naturalist. Born in Chézard-Saint-Martin, Canton of Neuchâtel (Switzerland) 1863, died in Geneva (Switzerland) 1934. After studying at the School of Protestant Theology of Neuchâtel, Junod worked for long periods of time as a missionary between 1880 and 1920 in Mozambique and South Africa. He wrote several books based on his systematic research on the Bantu. The most well known is *The Life of a South African Tribe*, which was first published in 1912-1923 before appearing in a revised and expanded second edition in 1927. Although Junod was influenced by his missionary zeal and by the evolutionism of JAMES G. FRAZER, a genuine interest in the society he studied is apparent in his ethnographic descriptions, which are without a doubt the best part of his anthropological work. Describing *The Life of a South African Tribe*, BRONISLAW MALINOWSKI said that it is "the only entirely satisfying synthesis that embraces every aspect of tribal life." Junod has inspired or stimulated the thought of such authors as LUCIEN LÉVY-BRUHL (*La mentalité primitive*, 1922), A.R. RADCLIFFE-BROWN (*The Mother's Brother in South Africa*, 1924), Radcliffe-Brown and DARYLL FORDE (*African Systems of Kinship and Marriage*, 1950), ROBERT H. LOWIE (*Primitive Society*, 1947), CLAUDE LÉVI-STRAUSS (*Les structures élémentaires de la parenté*, 1947) and MEYER FORTES (*Rules and Emergence of Society*, 1983).

In his role as a missionary, Junod never acted in a short-sighted manner. Although he believed that colonization was necessary and criticized aspects of native customs that he considered harmful (dowries, polygamy, sorcery), he never ceased denouncing the evils that resulted from Westernization (notably alcoholism). He fought to defend the use of vernacular languages in the elementary schools of Mozambique and South Africa. After returning to Switzerland, Junod became president of the Bureau International pour la Défense des Indigènes de Genève in 1925.

MAJOR WORKS: *Les chants et les contes des Ba-Ronga de la baie de Delagoa* (Lausanne: 1897); *Les Ba-Ronga: étude ethnographique sur les indigènes de la baie de Delagoa* (Neuchâtel: 1898); *Nouveaux contes ronga* (Neuchâtel: 1898); *The Life of a South African Tribe* [2 vols.] (Neuchâtel: 1912-1913; revised and expanded ed., London: 1927) [tr.: *Moeurs et coutumes des Bantous: la vie d'une tribu sud-africaine* [2 vols.] (Paris: 1936); *Usos e costumes dos Bantos: a vida de uma tribo sud-africana* (Lourenço Marques: 1944)].

SOURCES: Henri-Philippe Junod, *Henri-Alexandre Junod: missionnaire et savant (1863-1934)* (Lausanne: 1934); Henri-Philippe Junod, "Henri-Alexandre Junod (1863-1934): bibliographie de ses ouvrages," *Genève-Afrique*, vol. 4 (1965), pp. 271-277; Gérald Berthoud, "Entre l'anthropologue et le missionnaire: la contribution d'Henri-Alexandre Junod (1863-1934)" in: Musée d'ethnographie de Genève, *Le visage multiplié du monde: quatre siècles d'ethnographie à Genève* (Geneva: 1985), pp. 59-74.

Jean-Pierre Jacob
[Translation from French: Timothy Eastridge]

k

Kaberry, Phyllis Mary. Social anthropologist. Born in California 17 September 1910, died in London (England) 30 October 1977. Kaberry studied anthropology at the University of Sydney where she attained her master's degree. Her first field research (1934-1936) was carried out in the Kimberleys, northwest Western Australia, and some of the results were later written up for her Ph.D. degree under BRONISLAW MALINOWSKI at the London School of Economics (University of London). During 1939-1940 she worked among the Abelam of the Sepik district, Papua New Guinea, focusing on law and political organization. Returning to England, she joined DARYLL FORDE's Department at University College, London, where she remained lecturing and writing until her official retirement in 1977.

It was inevitable, because of British interests during this period, that Kaberry should spend most of her professional career as an Africanist. However, in general and specific terms, Kaberry was especially notable for her pioneering anthropological research on women in their social contexts. Her first volume, *Aboriginal Woman: Sacred and Profane*, took up a number of issues made popular in Émile Durkheim's *Elementary Forms*. Her book is recognized as a classic study of a subject that had up to that time been virtually neglected. Her interests clustered around relations between men and women, especially in the religious sphere, and she was not concerned with isolating women as an entity for study. Her theoretical contentions did not go unchallenged at the time. However, she was responsible, in Australia as elsewhere, for the emergence of the systematic study of gender relations.

Her African research made a considerable impact on anthropologists and administrators in the post-World-War-II period, mainly because of its concern with applied anthropology when issues of decolonization were being raised. Her book, *Women of the Grassfields*, was an important signpost in that direction, focusing on rural development and the everyday work of women. As a measure of the esteem in which she was held in Bamenda (West Cameroon), she was proclaimed a Queen Mother by the Fon of Nso.

Throughout her career she was interested not only in the theoretical implications of her research but also in the personal lives of people. Her writing and her conversations affirmed the importance of women, equally with men, and their personal welfare.

MAJOR WORKS: *Aboriginal Woman: Sacred and Profane* (London: 1939); "Law and political organization in the Abelam tribe, New Guinea," *Oceania*, vol. 12 (1941-1942), pp. 79-95, 209-225, and 331-343; (editor) Bronislaw Malinowski, *The Dynamics of Culture Change* (New Haven: 1945); *Women of the Grassfields* (London: 1951); "Malinowski's contribution to field-work methods and the writing of ethnography" in: Raymond Firth (editor), *Man and Culture* (London and New York: 1957), pp. 71-91; (co-editor with Darryl Forde) *West African Kingdoms in the 19th Century* (Oxford: 1967); (co-editor with Mary Douglas) *Man in Africa* (London: 1969).

SOURCES: P. Burnham, M. Rowlands and E.M. Chilver, "Dr. P.M. Kaberry," *Times* [London] (18 November 1977), p. 17; A.P. Elkin, "Phyllis M. Kaberry," *Oceania*, vol. 48 (1978), pp. 301-302; Raymond Firth, "Phyllis Kaberry," *Africa*, vol. 48 (1978), pp. 296-297; M. Reay, "The social position of women" in: H. Sheils (editor), *Australian Aboriginal Studies* (Melbourne and Oxford: 1963), pp. 319-334; C.H. Berndt, "Phyllis Mary Kaberry" in: Ute Gacs [et al.] (editors), *Women Anthropologists: a Biographical Dictionary* (New York: 1988), pp. 167-174; *Association of Social Anthropologists of the Commonwealth Register of Members* (London: 1974), pp. 106-107.

Catherine H. Berndt

Kamma, F.C. (Freerk Christiaans). Protestant missionary, ethnologist.

Born in Wierum (Netherlands) 16 February 1906, died in Leiden (Netherlands) 24 September 1987. Kamma was trained as a missionary at the Protestant Missionary College at Oegstgeest (Netherlands) from 1925 to 1931. This training was focused on the Dutch East Indies. Apart from theology the courses included Javanese, Malay, and knowledge of Islam. Kamma's generation was for the first time also trained in native law (*adatrecht*), ethnology and the ethnography of Indonesia. These new courses were given by staffmembers of the nearby Leiden University.

In 1931 Kamma was appointed to a post in Dutch New Guinea by the Utrecht Missionary Society. He arrived in New Guinea in 1931 and was posted to Genjem (Nimboran area). In 1933 he was posted to Sorong where he began working in the Bird's Head area. On furlough in Holland in 1938 he published his first articles. These were, by and large, descriptions of missionary activities in New Guinea but contained much ethnographic detail. Returning to New Guinea in December 1939, he was detained by the Japanese in 1942. His stay in detention camps during the war practically ruined his health. Repatriated in 1946 he was found to be not fit enough to return to New Guinea and was given a teaching post at the Missionary College at Oegstgeest. At the same time he began studying ethnology in Leiden under J.P.B. DE JOSSELIN DE JONG. Meanwhile, he actively published on several subjects: the ethnography of the Biak and Numfoor areas of New Guinea and the Biak-related groups in the Bird's Head area, culture contact (especially between Protestant missions and the Papuan population, but also predating European contact) and acculturation. In 1954 he was awarded his doctorate for a thesis based on an ethnological analysis of the occurrences of messianic cults (the Koreri movement) among the

Biak-related peoples of northwest New Guinea (*De Messiaanse Koreri-bewegingen in het Biaks-Noemfoorse cultuurgebied*). In 1955 he returned to New Guinea, mainly working in Hollandia, but also conducting research among the Papuans of the Bird's Head area. After the transfer of New Guinea to Indonesia, Kamma went back to Holland, where he remained active in an advisory position. After his retirement in 1971 he wrote one more major work. This was a description of the Protestant missionary process in Dutch New Guinea, which he himself characterized as "a socio-missiological approach to the problem of communication between East and West" (*Dit wonderlijke werk*). This work, though not ethnographic, is typical of Kamma's major preoccupation with the problem of acculturation.

Cultural change is a recurring theme in Kamma's publications. Though influenced by his work as a missionary, his ethnographic work always shows him to have an open mind and balanced opinion on this subject. In his thesis on messianic cults he not only reviews a multitude of descriptions of these phenomena but also critically comments on a number of current explanations for them. While Kamma is mainly known for his vast knowledge and personal experience of the Papuans of the northwestern parts of Dutch New Guinea, his work often shows that he was well aware of theoretical developments in anthropology.

MAJOR WORKS: "De verhouding tussen Tidore en de Papoese eilanden in legende en historie," *Indonesië*, vol. 1 (1947), pp. 361-370 and 536-559; vol. 2 (1948), pp. 177-188 and 256-275; "Messianic movements in Western New Guinea," *International Review of Missions*, vol. 41 (1952), pp. 148-160; *Kruis en korwar: een honderdjarig waagstuk op Nieuw Guinea* (The Hague: 1953); "Zending" in: W.C. Klein (editor), *Nieuw-Guinea: de ontwikkeling op economisch, sociaal en cultureel gebied, in Nederlands en Australisch Nieuw-Guinea* (The Hague: 1953-1954), vol. 1, pp. 82-159; *De messiaanse Koreri-bewegingen in het Biaks-Noemfoorse cultuur-gebied* (The Hague: 1954) [tr.: *Messianic Movements in the Biak-Numfor Culture Area* (The Hague: 1972)]; "Sociale problematiek in Nieuw-Guinea," *De Heerbaan*, vol. 12 (1959), pp. 45-60; "Spontane acculturatie op Nieuw-Guinea," *De Heerbaan*, vol. 14 (1961), pp. 4-30; "A spontaneous 'capitalistic' revolution in the western Vogelkop of West Irian" in: *Anniversary Contributions to Anthropology: Twelve Essays, Published on the Occasion of the 40th Anniversary of the Leiden Ethnological Society W.D.O.* (Leiden: 1970), pp. 132-142; *Dit wonderlijke werk: het probleem van de communicatie tussen Oost en West gebaseerd op de ervaringen in het zendingswerk op Nieuw-Guinea (Irian Jaya), 1855-72: een sociomissiologische benadering* (Oegstgeest: 1977).

SOURCES: S. Kooijman, "In memoriam F.C. Kamma (16 februari 1906—24 september 1987), *Bijdragen tot de Taal-, Land- en Volkenkunde*, vol. 144 (1988), pp. 411-418. Further material for this description was taken from a curriculum vitae of F.C. Kamma and a list of his publications compiled by Mrs. M.R. Kamma-van Dijk.

S.R. Jaarsma and J.J. de Wolf

Kanaseki, Takeo. Anthropologist. Born in Kotohira (Japan) 18 February 1897, died in Nara (Japan) 27 February 1983. Kanaseki graduated from the Faculty of Medicine at Kyōto University in 1923 and studied anthropology at the Department of Anatomy. He received his doctorate in medicine in 1930 with his dissertation *Ryūkyūjin no Jinruigakuteki Kenkyū* [*Anthropological Study of the People of Ryūkyū*]. In 1936 he became a professor of anatomy at Taipei University and did research mainly on the body types and skeletal structures of the Taiwanese mountain people. In 1949 he came back to Japan, and the next year he became professor of anatomy at Kyūshū University. Until 1960 he actively worked with colleagues on somatological and osteological research, mainly in Kyūshū and in the Ryūkyū Islands.

His work is collected in the *Jinruigaku Kenkyū* [*Quarterly Journal of Anthropology*] [7 vols.] (1954-1960), a journal that he edited. More than 270 articles on physical anthropology were written under his direction, including the works on Taipei.

From 1953 to 1957 Kanaseki excavated the Yayoi-Period sites in Doigahama (Yamaguchi Prefecture). For the first time he proved, by the study of human bones from these sites, that during the Yayoi Period continental, oval-faced people who were taller than the people in the Jōmon Period crossed over to Japan from the Korean Peninsula. Through this study it gradually became clear that the Yayoi people played a major role in forming the genetic stock of the modern Japanese.

In his late years Kanaseki studied folklore and archaeology, mainly in the Ryūkyū Islands, and started the diverse and unique Kanaseki School.

MAJOR WORKS: *Nihonjin no Jinshugaku* [*Japanese Ethnology*] (Tōkyō: 1931); *Mokuba to Sekigyū* [*Wooden Horses and Stone Cows*] (Tōkyō: 1976); *Nihon Minzoku no Kigen* [*The Origin of the Japanese People*] (Tōkyō: 1976); *Keishitsu Jinruishi* [*Characters of Human Races*] (Tōkyō: 1978); *Ryūkyū Minzokushi* [*Ryūkyū Folklore*] (Tōkyō: 1978).

SOURCES: Takahiko Ogata, "Kanaseki Takeo Sensei o shinonde" ["The late Professor Takeo Kanaseki"], *Journal of the Anthropological Society of Nippon*, vol. 91 (1983), pp. 429-433.

Bin Yamaguchi
[*Translation from Japanese: Mamiko Nakamura*]

Kansu, Şevket Aziz. Medical doctor, physical anthropologist, prehistorian. Born in Edirne (Turkey) 6 May 1903, died in Ankara (Turkey) 10 April 1983. Kansu had an advantageous start in his career, his pioneer work coinciding with an interest in the cultural origins, historical development, and anthropometric characteristics of the Turks, thus securing him the full support of Atatürk, the founder of modern Turkey. He was a forerunner throughout his professional life. He was the first Turkish professional anthropologist to become *Ordinarius Professor*. He initiated instruction in physical-biological anthropology and ethnology, under the influence of the French School, at the Turkish Anthropological Institute at İstanbul, a pioneer institution first established in 1925 at the Faculty of Medicine and then transferred, on Atatürk's orders, to Ankara in 1934, to the Faculty of Languages, History and Geography (D.T.C.F.). Kansu, the author of the first-generation textbooks in anthropology in Turkey, was, for years, the only instructor in the anthropology undergraduate program at this institution. He continued occupying the Chair at the Department of Anthropology and teaching there until retirement in 1973, serving a term as the Dean and another as the first President (Recteur) of Ankara University when the Faculty was annexed in 1946. He had been the pioneer anthropologist member of the Turkish Historical Association in its initial stages. He later became president of this association between 1962 and 1972. Kansu was also the first Turkish member of a number of European associations of anthropology and the Permanent Council of the IUAES.

After a period as assistant in internal medicine at the Faculty of Medicine in İstanbul, he was sent to France to continue his studies under Professor G. Papillaut and received the degree *diplôme des sciences anthropologiques* in 1929. His early work was on the anthropometry of contemporary Turks, the major undertaking under his supervision being the cephalic measurements of 64,000 Turkish men and women, completed in four months. He also initiated anthropometric studies, developed by his first-generation students, of Turkish children. He was successful in clarifying the place of the Anatolian Turks among the races of the world; Caucasian, they were mainly Alpine with the Dinaric and Mediterranean as secondary subgroups. The collaboration with N.H. von der Osten at a site he discovered at Eti Yokuşu (Ankara) resulted in a middle Paleolithic (Mousterian) station; Kansu was a pioneer in this field in Turkey. He later focused on the ancient inhabitants of Anatolia, found at the excavations at Alacahöyük (Ankara), Arslantepe (Malatya), Kumtepe (Çanakkale), Ahlatlıbel (Ankara), Kusura (Afyon), Tilkitepe (Van), Yazılıkaya (Kars), Karaoğlan (Eskişehir), Tuzla (İstanbul) and Küçükçekmece (İstanbul). At some of these sites he also distinguished various Paleolithic tools. His invaluable contributions on the racial structure of these ancient peoples, ranging from the Calcholithic to the Bronze Age, clarified their place in the racial history of Anatolia and Thrace, earning him international recognition.

MAJOR WORKS: "Anadolu ve Rumeli Türklerinin antropometrik tetkikleri: birinci muhtıra: boy ve gövde nispetleri" ["The anthropometric study of the Turks of Thrace and Anatolia: first report: height and body indexes"], *Türk Antropoloji Mecmuası*, no. 11 (1931), pp. 3-19; "Anadolu ve Rumeli Türklerinin antropometrik tetkikleri: ikinci muhtıra: etraf va baş nispetleri" ["The anthropometric study of the Turks of Thrace and Anatolia: second report: cephalic and bodily extremities indexes"], *Türk Antropoloji Mecmuası*, no. 12 (1931), pp. 97-110; "Craniologie de l'Anatolie," *L'Anthropologie*, vol. 45, no. 1-2 (1935), pp. 105-107; "Kız ve erkek çocukları üzerinde antropometrik araştırmalar" ["Anthrometric research on Turkish male and female children"], *Ülkü*, vol. 12, no. 71 (1939), pp. 398-402; "Anadolu'nun ırk tarihi üzerine antropolojik bir tetkik" ["An anthropological study of the racial history of Anatolia"], *Belleten*, vol. 9, no. 9 (1939), pp. 127-162; *Türk Tarih Kurumu Tarafından Yapılan Eti Yokuşu Hafriyatı Raporu (1937)* [*The Report of the Excavation at Eti Yokuşu (1937) under the Auspices of the Turkish Historical Association*] (Ankara: 1940); "Anadolu'da Mezolitik kültür buluntuları" ["Mesolithic culture findings in Anatolia"], *A.Ü.D.T.C.F. Dergisi*, vol. 2, no. 3 (1944), pp. 673-682; (with Seniha Tunakan) "Alacahöyük (1943-45) kazılarında çıkarılan Kalkolitik, Bakır ve Tunç çağlarına ait halkın antropolojisi" ["The anthropology of the remains of the peoples of the Chalcolithic, Copper and Bronze Ages found in the 1943-45 excavations at Alacahöyük"], *Belleten*, vol. 10, no. 40 (1946), pp. 539-555; (with Seniha Tunakan) "Karaoğlan höyüğünde çıkarılan Eti, Frig, ve Klasik devir iskeletlerinin antropolojik incelenmesi" ["An anthropological study of the Hittite, Phrygian, and Classic Period skeletons found in the tumulus at Karaoğlan"], *Belleten*, vol. 12, no. 48 (1948), pp. 759-774; "Marmara Bölgesi ve Trakya'da prehistorik iskan tarihi bakımından araştırmalar (1950-1962)" ["Researches at the prehistoric settlements in Thrace and the Marmara Region"], *Belleten*, vol. 27, no. 108 (1963), pp. 205-214.

SOURCES: Ş.A. Kansu, *Türk Antropoloji Enstitüsü Tarihçesi* [*The History of the Turkish Anthropological Institute*] (İstanbul: 1940); P.J. Magnarella and O. Türkdoğan, "The development of Turkish social anthropology," *Current Anthropology*, vol. 17 (1976), pp. 263-274; Nermin Erdentuğ, "Hocamız Kansu'nun anısına" ["In memoriam Kansu"], *Antropoloji*, no. 12 (1985), pp. 1-4; *Meydan-Larousse*, vol. 6 (1976), p. 874; *Türk ve Dünya Ünlüleri Ansiklopedisi* [*Encyclopedia of Turkish and World Celebrities*], vol. 6 (1983), p. 3121; Aygen Erdentuğ, "A.Ü.D.T.C.F. antropoloji bibliyografyası (1935-1983)" ["Bibliography of anthropology, D.T.C.F., Ankara University (1935-1983)"], *Antropoloji*, no. 12 (1985), pp. 473-482.

Aygen Erdentuğ

Kardiner, Abram. Psychoanalyst, psychiatrist, psychocultural theorist. Born in New York (New York) 17 August 1891, died in Easton (Connecticut) 20 July 1981.

Kardiner was awarded his M.D. in psychiatry from Cornell University medical school and subsequently received a didactic analysis under Sigmund Freud in Vienna. His research in the 1920s focused on the etiology of the "war neuroses" and resulted in important theoretical insights on the adaptive maneuvers of the ego in response to traumatic stress. As an early contributor to ego psychology, Kardiner was also a major influence on the emergence of the "culture and personality" field in anthropology. Like the "neo-Freudian" psychoanalysts Karen Horney and Harry Stack Sullivan, he emphasized the importance of social factors in personality formation. Collaborating with leading anthropologists RALPH LINTON and CORA DUBOIS in the 1930s and 1940s, Kardiner investigated the impact of varying cultural practices on the genesis of ego structure. In his interdisciplinary seminars at the New York Psychoanalytic Institute and Columbia University, Kardiner developed a psychocultural model for tracing the relationship between child-rearing dynamics (as patterned by family and economic organization) and the integrative formation of "basic personality structure" in different societies. In his psychodynamic theory of "basic personality," he also demonstrated how the formative experiences of early parent-child relations are expressively refashioned in the "projective systems" of religion, supernaturalism, and folklore. Kardiner's innovative research design, in which the ethnographic presentations by DuBois and others were complemented by the "blind" analysis of life histories and projective tests (such as the Rorschach) by participating psychiatrists, set a methodological precedent for subsequent collaborations between anthropologists and psychiatrists investigating the cultural context of personality adaptation. His detractors pointed to problematic inferences in his psychoanalytic interpretations, the inadequacy of ethnographic data employed, and the questionable uniformity of "basic personality" in complex societies. Nonetheless, Kardiner's work is increasingly recognized as a pivotal influence on the post-war development of psychological anthropology and cross-cultural studies of socialization and personality.

MAJOR WORKS: *The Individual and His Society* (New York: 1939); *The Traumatic Neuroses of War* (Washington: 1941); (with Ralph Linton, Cora DuBois, and James West) *The Psychological Frontiers of Society* (New York: 1945); (with Lionel Ovesey) *The Mark of Oppression* (New York: 1951); (with Edward Preble) *They Studied Man* (Cleveland: 1961); *My Analysis With Freud* (New York: 1977).

SOURCES: William C. Manson, *The Psychodynamics of Culture: Abram Kardiner and Neo-Freudian Anthropology* (New York: 1988); Mikel Dufrenne, *La personnalité de base* (Paris: 1966); *The Reminiscences of Abram Kardiner* (New York: 1965) [in the Columbia University Oral History Collection]; William C. Manson, "Abram Kardiner and the Neo-Freudian alternative in culture and personality" in: George W. Stocking, Jr. (editor), *Malinowski, Rivers, Benedict and Others* (Madison: 1986) (= *History of Anthropology*, vol. 4), pp. 72-94; Helen C. Meyers, "Abram Kardiner: a tribute to his life and work," *Association of Psychoanalytic Medicine Bulletin*, vol. 19 (1980), pp. 50-52.

William C. Manson

Karłowicz, Jan Aleksander Ludwik. Ethnographer, linguist, musician. Born in Subortowicze (Lithuania, then in Russia) 28 May 1836, died in Warsaw (Poland) 14 June 1903. Karłowicz studied history in Moscow, Paris, Heidelberg and Berlin, obtaining his doctorate in 1866. In the 1860s he became interested in linguistics and folk studies. An outstanding folklorist, in 1887 he joined the editorial board of *Wisła,* a position he held until 1899.

Karłowicz was the first Polish scholar to undertake methodical research on legends, fairy tales and songs. A supporter of evolutionism, he applied historical methods to ethnology. He worked out a morphological typology of cultural elements, especially in the sphere of folk literature. On the basis of the analysis of forms, motifs, plots and their spatial location he sought out their genesis and the paths of their migration. In material culture and, particularly, folk architecture, he attempted to find convincing proofs of the autochthony of the Slavs. He was also interested in the mythology and beliefs of the folk. His latter years were devoted to studies undertaken for the dictionary of the Polish language (the so-called *Warsaw Dictionary*). His linguistic works included material in the fields of onomastics and etymology.

MAJOR WORKS: *Poradnik dla zbierających rzeczy ludowe* [*Handbook for Collecting Folk Artifacts*] (Vilnius: 1871); "Słoworód ludowy" ["Folk etymology"], *Dwutygodnik Naukowy*, vol. 2 (1878); "Imiona niektórych plemion i ziem dawnej Polski" ["Names of certain tribes and lands of Old Poland"], *Pamiętnik Fizjograficzny*, vol. 2 (1882), pp. 497-516; "Chata polska" ["The Polish villager's hut"], *Pamiętnik Fizjograficzny*, vol. 4 (1884), pp. 383-411; "Systematyka pieśni ludu polskiego" ["Systematization of the songs of the Polish peasant"], *Wisła*, vol. 3 (1889), pp. 253, 531; vol. 4 (1890), pp. 156, 393; vol. 9 (1895), pp. 522, 645; *Słownik gwar polskich* [*Dictionary of Polish Dialects*] [6 vols.] (Kraków: 1900-1911); *Lud: rys ludoznawstwa polskiego* [*The Folk: Description of Polish Folk Studies*] (Lwów: 1904).

SOURCES: Olga Gajkowa and Stanisław Urbańczyk, "Karłowicz, Jan Aleksander Ludwik" in: *Polski słownik biograficzny* [*Polish Biographical Dictionary*], vol. 12 (Wrocław: 1966-1967), pp. 53-57; Julian Krzyżanowksi, "Karłowicz, Jan" in: Julian Krzyżanowksi (editor), *Słownik folkloru polskiego* [*Dictionary of Polish Folklore*] (Warsaw: 1965), p. 164.

Maria Niewiadomska and Iwona Grzelakowska
[*Translation from Polish: Joel Janicki*]

Karve, Irawati. Cultural anthropologist, sociologist, physical anthropologist, Sanskritist, Marathi writer-essayist. Born in Myingyan (Burma, now Myanmar) 15 December 1905, died in Poona (India) 11 August 1970. Karve's degrees include a B.A. in philosophy, Fergussen College (Poona, 1926); an M.A. in sociology, University of Bombay (1928); and a D.Phil. in anthropology, University of Berlin (1930). She was Registrar, S.N.D.T. Indian Women's University (Poona and Bombay), and post-graduate teacher, University of Bombay (1931-1936). Appointed to the first Readership in Sociology (then housed in the Department of History) in Deccan College Postgraduate and Research Institute, Poona (1939), she later became first Professor and Head of the Department of Sociology and Anthropology there, a post she continued to occupy until her death.

Karve was Guest Lecturer, School of Oriental and African Studies, University of London (1951-1952), and Distinguished Visiting Scholar, Department of Anthropology, University of California, Berkeley (1959-1960). She won the Sahitya Akadami Award for her contributions to Marathi literature, specifically for *Yuganta*, on the Hindu epic poem *Mahabharata* (1968).

Karve is internationally known for her many anthropological works on Indian society and culture, the most prominent of which are *Kinship Organization in India* and *Hindu Society: an Interpretation*. The former, indispensable to students of Indian society, draws on a lifetime of first-hand research throughout India as well as in its classical texts, which was facilitated by her knowledge of several languages and her scholarship in Sanskrit. Its major contribution is the definition and analysis of five major "zones" of kinship organization and language in India and the distinctive regions within each. For each she discusses variations in kinship terminology and behavior; rules of descent, marriage and family organization; and, in the revised editions, "ownership of property, succession and inheritance." All of these topics were addressed comparatively and historically and with respect to their functioning in contemporary India. The second of the books is a brief, almost impressionistic, but broadly informed and highly original account of the origin and development of the caste system, based on extensive field research and intensive examination of classic texts. She argues that castes (*jati*) are kin-based groups derived from the unstratified, multi-ethnic (tribal) population of pre-Aryan South Asia, upon which the Aryan *varna* (sometimes called "caste category") system, with its hierarchical structure, was later superimposed with the result that every ethnic group within a region came to be ranked relative to every other; hence, India's caste system as we know it.

Karve's books and some 100 articles drew heavily upon her Maharashtrian, and especially her own Chitpavan Brahman caste, experience. These works extended beyond cultural-anthropological analyses of caste, stratification, kinship and family to include writings cited in the three volumes edited by M.N. SRINIVAS [et al.], *A Survey of Research in Sociology and Social Anthropology*, under such topics as urban studies, social change, community development, sociology of law, sociology of religion, tribal ethnography, folklore, applied anthropology/education and research methodology. In addition Karve did significant research and publication in physical anthropology beginning with her dissertation in Berlin on *Normal Asymmetry of the Human Skull* (cf., R.K. Gulati, cited below). Her interest in caste colored her work in physical anthropology, as the titles of her articles make clear. She sought to determine the degree to which castes could be demonstrated—as she believed they could—to be genetically distinct breeding isolates. She also published several articles on language and at least one on archaeological research, thereby exemplifying her commitment to the four-field approach to anthropology so esteemed in America but relatively unfamiliar in much of the rest of the world at that time.

These anthropological contributions, combined with her literary, philosophical and applied ones, made her a major figure not only in Indian anthropology but also in international scholarship and letters.

MAJOR WORKS: *Kinship Organization in India* (Poona: 1953; 2nd ed., revised, Bombay: 1965; 3rd ed., revised, Bombay: 1968); "What is caste?" *The Economic Weekly*, "(I) Caste as extended kin," vol. 10 (1958), pp. 125-138; "(II) Caste and occupation," vol. 10 (1958), pp. 401-407; "(III) Caste as a status group," vol. 10 (1959), pp. 881-888; "(IV) Caste society and Vedantic thought," vol. 11 (1959), pp. 49-63; *Hindu Society: an Interpretation* (Poona: 1961); "A family through six generations" in: Bala Ratnam (editor), *Anthropology on the March* (Madras: 1963), pp. 241-267; *Indian Women in 1965* (New Delhi: 1966); *Yuganta: the End of an Epoch* (Poona: 1969).

SOURCES: W. Norman Brown, *Introduction to Hindu Society: an Interpretation* (Poona: 1961), pp. v-vii; R.K. Gulati, "Review of Karve's contribution to Indian physical anthropology," *Bulletin of the Deccan College Research Institute*, vols. 31-32 (1973) [Karve memorial volume], pp. 273-277; N.G. Kalelkar, "Iravati Karve" [sic], *Bulletin of the Deccan College Research Institute*, vols. 31-32 (1973) [Karve memorial volume], pp. 1-4; "Karve, Irawati (Karmarkar), 1905-1970," *Contemporary Authors*, permanent series, vol. 1 (1975), p. 337; K.C. Malhotra, "Bibliography of Professor Irawati Karve's works," *Bulletin of the Deccan College Research Institute*, vols. 31-32 (1973) [Karve memorial volume], pp. i-viii; A.M. Shah, "Annotated bibliography, Irawati Karve" in: *The Household*

Dimension of the Family in India (New Delhi: 1973), pp. 218-220; M.N. Srinivas, M.S.A. Rao, and A.M. Shah (editors), *A Survey of Research in Sociology and Social Anthropology* [3 vols.] (New Delhi and Bombay: 1972-1974).

Gerald D. Berreman

Kate, Herman F.C. ten.

Kate, Herman F.C. ten. Anthropologist, physician. Born in Amsterdam (Netherlands) 7 February 1858, died in Carthage (Tunisia) 4 February 1931. Ten Kate is known for his archaeological, physical-anthropological and ethnological studies of American Indians, Indonesian peoples and Japanese, as well as for his contributions to applied and partisan anthropology. He was also among the first to study the imagery of non-Western peoples in art and literature.

Ten Kate studied medicine, geography, ethnology and non-Western languages at Leiden University (1877-1879), where he was influenced by the humanistic ideas of ethnologist P.J. VETH. Subsequent studies at the École d'Anthropologie in Paris (1879-1880) under PAUL BROCA, Paul Topinard and ARMAND DE QUATREFAGES strengthened his knowledge of physical anthropology and his strongly empirical research attitude. In Berlin, ADOLF BASTIAN reinforced his realization of the rapid destruction of aboriginal cultural traditions outside Europe. At the University of Heidelberg ten Kate received a Ph.D. in zoology (1882). Later he completed his medical studies at French and German institutions.

Ten Kate conducted fieldwork in Corsica, the United States, Mexico, Lapland, Surinam, Venezuela, the Caribbean, Canada, Algeria, Indonesia, Australia, the Tonga and Society Islands, Argentina, Paraguay, Japan and Tunisia. He was a member of the Hemenway Southwestern Archaeological Expedition under FRANK HAMILTON CUSHING in the American Southwest (1887-1888) and of the Calchaqui Expedition under Francisco Moreno in northwestern Argentina (1893). For a number of years he was the curator of physical anthropology at the Museo de la Plata, Argentina. His fieldwork was financed by his own modest capital, Prince Roland Bonaparte, Dutch and French scientific societies and the Dutch government. For more than fifteen years he lived in Japan as a practicing physician. He rejected a professorship in Indonesian ethnology at the University of Utrecht in 1911.

MAJOR WORKS: *Reizen en onderzoekingen in Noord Amerika* (Leiden: 1885); *Verslag eener reis in de Timorgroep en Polynesie* (Leiden: 1894); *Anthropologie des anciens habitants de la région calchaqui* (La Plata: 1896); "Mélanges anthropologiques" [7 articles], *L'Anthropologie* (1913-1917); *Psychologie en ethnologie in de koloniale politiek* (Amsterdam: 1916); *Over land en zee* (Zutphen: 1925).

SOURCES: J. Heyink and F.W. Hodge, "Herman Frederik Carel ten Kate," *American Anthropologist*, n.s., vol. 33 (1931), pp. 415-418; Paul Rivet, "Herman Frederik Carel ten Kate," *Journal de la Société des Américanistes*, vol. 23 (1931), pp. 236-242; Pieter Hovens, *Herman F.C. ten Kate (1858-1931) en de antropologie der Noord Amerikaanse Indianen* (Meppel: 1989).

Pieter Hovens

Kennicott, Robert.

Kennicott, Robert. Naturalist, explorer. Born in New Orleans (Louisiana) 13 November 1835, died in Nulato (Alaska) 13 May 1866. Kennicott received informal training as a naturalist from America's leading scientists. His interest lay in reptilian studies but he embraced all facets of zoological studies, and he added anthropological collecting to his field activities. He collected for Northwestern University, the Illinois Central Railroad and the Illinois Agricultural Society before taking up explorations on behalf of the Smithsonian Institution.

In 1859 Kennicott traveled to the sub-Arctic and spent two and a half years in the area around the Hudson's Bay Company post on the Yukon River. He was the Smithsonian's representative in the field, and he implemented the Institution's collecting policies. The Smithsonian had, beginning in 1850, begun rationalizing collecting processes, and Kennicott taught northern traders and trappers the skills necessary for collecting and preserving natural history specimens. Kennicott also sent the Smithsonian several examples of Kutchin material culture, as well as specimens of Inuit dress and technology.

Although Kennicott never published any ethnographic essays, he was responsible for sending 179 anthropological specimens from the Inuit, Slave, Dogrib, Yellowknife, Hare, Kutchin and Fort Liard Indians. Kennicott's career as a naturalist and explorer was curtailed prematurely when he died at Nulato, while representing the Smithsonian on the Western Union Telegraph Company expedition that had been sent north to determine the feasibility of communications with Europe, overland via the northwest.

SOURCES: Accession records, Anthropology Department, Smithsonian Institution; Robert Kennicott papers (1863, 1865), Smithsonian Institution Archives; collected notes, lists and catalogues on birds, Kennicott papers, Smithsonian Institution Archives; Spencer F. Baird papers, 1833-1889, incoming correspondence, Smithsonian Institution Archives; James Alton James, *The First Scientific Exploration of Russian America and the Purchase of Alaska* (Chicago: 1942); Grace Lee Nute, "Kennicott of the North," *The Beaver* (September 1943), pp. 28-32; Donald Zochert, "Notes on a young naturalist," *Audubon* (March 1980), pp. 34-47.

Debra Lindsay

Kenyatta, Jomo. First president of Kenya, anthropologist. Born in Kamau wa Ngengi near Fort Hall [now Murang'a] (Kenya) ca. 1894, died in Nairobi (Kenya) 3 August 1978. The child of a Kikuyu farmer, Kenyatta attended a Church of Scotland mission school at Fort Hall. In 1920 he took the name Johnstone Kamau, and in 1921 he was employed as a water inspector in Nairobi. It was at this time that he was given the nickname Kenyatta, taken from a Kikuyu word for a style of beaded belt that Kenyatta was noted for wearing.

Kenyatta became the general secretary of the Kikuyu Central Association in 1928 and, as such, testified before the British Parliament on the subject of Kikuyu land grievances in that same year. He returned to Britain in 1931 and lived there for sixteen years. With the assistance of BRONISLAW MALINOWSKI, he obtained a scholarship from the University of London in 1936 and, under Malinowski's tutelage, wrote *Facing Mount Kenya*, which was published in 1938. Kenyatta never received a bachelor's degree, but he was given a master's degree as a result of writing this book.

Facing Mount Kenya was the first major study of an African culture by a participant in that culture. It is part ethnography and part polemic. As ethnography, it remains the standard work on the Kikuyu. As polemic, it stressed the drastic changes in Kikuyu culture brought about by colonialism. With the publication of this book, Kenyatta took the name "Jomo," neither a Kikuyu word nor name, in order to augment the romanticism of a book written by a "native." In the same way, Kenyatta was photographed for the book jacket wearing a borrowed monkey skin (never a part of traditional Kikuyu clothing) and holding a spear.

With Kwame Nkrumah and W.E.B. DuBois, Kenyatta organized the Fifth Pan-African Congress in Manchester in 1945. This congress marked the first attempt to unite the indigenous leaders of British colonies. Kenyatta returned home in 1946 and became president of the pan-tribal Kenya African Union. The KAU was banned after the outbreak of the insurgency known as Mau-Mau, the original impetus for which was the return of lost land to the Kikuyu but which eventually came to demand extension of the franchise to all residents of the colony. Kenyatta was arrested by the British in 1953 and sentenced to seven years in prison. He was detained another two years and freed in 1961. He was elected president of Kenya after successfully negotiating for independence in 1963. He remained president until his death in 1978. As a founding father of his country, as a symbol of independence from colonialism and, as leader of one of the more stable and open of African nations during his rule, Kenyatta made a contribution to world affairs that is perhaps more significant than his contribution to anthropology. Nevertheless, his role as author of the first indigenous ethnography, although not as dramatic as his other accomplishments, is not insignificant.

MAJOR WORKS: *Facing Mount Kenya* (London: 1936); *My People of Kenya* (London: 1942).

SOURCES: Dennis Wepman, *Jomo Kenyatta* (New York: 1985); Bethwell A. Ogot, *Historical Dictionary of Kenya* (Metuchen, N.J.: 1981), pp. 98-99; Robert W. Wulff, "The Hon. Mzee Jomo Kenyatta," *Practicing Anthropologist*, vol. 1, no. 1 (October 1978), p. 10.

Lucy Jayne Botscharow

The **Kharuzins.** Russian ethnographers. Brothers and sisters, they accomplished a great deal in the development of ethnographic education and research in Russia. They were followers of the evolutionary school in ethnography. Each of the Kharuzins had his preferred theme in the study of the ethnography of the peoples of Russia. A brief article about each follows.

SOURCES: S.A. Tokarev, *Istoriia russkoĭ etnografii: dooktiabr'skiĭ period* (Moscow: 1966); R.S. Lipeš, "Kharuziny" in: *Sovetskaia istoricheskaia entsiklopediia*, vol. 15 (Moscow: 1974), pp. 537-538.

Kharuzin, M.N. (Mikhaĭl Nikolaevich). Ethnographer. Born in Moscow (Russia) 4 (16) June 1860, died 25 September (7 October) 1888. M.N. Kharuzin died at age twenty-eight from tuberculosis, but succeeded in making substantial contributions to the study of common law and led a series of field trips.

MAJOR WORKS: *Ocherk iuridicheskogo byta narodnosteĭ Sarapul'skogo uezda, Viatskoĭ gubernii* (Moscow: 1883); *Svedeniia o kazatskikh obshchinakh na Donu*, issue 1 (Moscow: 1885); *Programma dlia sobiraniia svedeniĭ ob iuridicheskikh obychaiakh* (Moscow: 1887).

Kharuzin, N.N. (Nikolaĭ Nikolaevich). Ethnographer. Born in Moscow (Russia) 1865, died in Moscow (Russia) 25 March (7 April) 1900. In 1898 N.N. Kharuzin was the first in Russia to present a course of ethnography at Moscow University and Lazarevskiĭ Institute of Eastern Languages. He was one of the founders of the journal *Etnograficheskoe obozrenie*. He led field research among various peoples of Russia. His major works were devoted to common law, the development of kinship and family, religious beliefs and the history of dwellings.

MAJOR WORKS: *Russkie lopari: ocherki proshlogo i sovremennogo byta* (Moscow: 1890); *Istoriīa razvitiīa zhilishcha u kochevykh i polukochevykh tīurkskikh i mongol'skikh narodnosteĭ Rossii* (Moscow: 1896); *Iz materialov, sobrannykh sredi krest'īan Pudozhskogo uezda Oloneīskoĭ gubernii* (Moscow: 1889); *Ėtnografiīa: (kurs lekīsiĭ)* [4 vols.] (St. Petersburg: 1901-1905).

Kharuzina, V.N. (Vera Nikolaevna).
Ethnographer, folklorist, museologist. Born in Moscow (Russia) 17 (29) September 1866, died in Moscow (Russian S.F.S.R.) 17 May 1931. V.N. Kharuzina was the first female professor of ethnography in Russia. She performed intensive educational work, including some at Moscow University. She made ethnographic field trips with her brother N.N. KHARUZIN. Her scholarly interests were focused above all on the study of beliefs, religion and folk creativity. Like N.N. Kharuzin, she made wide use of the methods of related sciences—philology, history, geography and others. She was a major popularizer of science.

MAJOR WORKS: *Na Severe: putevye vospominaniīa* (Moscow: 1890); *Skazki russkikh inorodīsev* (Moscow: 1898); *Materialy dlīa bibliografii ėtnograficheskoĭ literatury* (St. Petersburg: 1904); "Ob uchastii deteĭ v religiozno-obrīadovoĭ zhizni," *Ėtnograficheskoe obozrenie*, no. 1-2 (1911), pp. 1-78; "Igrushki u malokul'turnykh narodov'" in: *Igrushka: ee istoriīa i znachenie* (Moscow: 1912), pp. 85-139; *Ėtnografiīa: (kurs lekīsiĭ)* [2 vols.] (Moscow: 1909-1914); "Primitivnye formy dramaticheskogo iskusstva," *Ėtnografiīa*, no. 1 (1927), pp. 57-85; no. 2 (1927), pp. 283-300; no. 1 (1928), pp. 22-43; no. 2 (1928), pp. 3-31; *Vvedenie v ėtnografiīu i klassifikaīsiīa narodov zemnogo shara* (Moscow: 1941).

SOURCES: E.N. Ėleonskaīa, "V.N. Kharuzina (1866-1931)," *Sovetskaīa ėtnografiīa*, no. 1-2 (1931), pp. 153-155; D.K. Zelenin, "V.N. Kharuzina," *Lud Słowiański*, vol. 2, no. 2 (1931), pp. 275-281.

Kharuzin, A.N. (Alekseĭ Nikolaevich).
Ethnographer, archaeologist, anthropologist, museum worker. Born in Moscow (Russia) 29 February (12 March) 1864, died in Moscow (Russian S.F.S.R.) 1933. A.N. Kharuzin carried out a series of ethnographic expeditions among the Russians, the Kazakhs and the peoples of the Caucasus as well as to the Baltic region. A series of works were devoted to the study of dwellings; he also wrote monographic studies of the Kazakhs (Kirgizia).

MAJOR WORKS: *Bosniīa-Gerīsegovina* (Moscow: 1901); "Materialy dlīa istorii razvitiīa slavianskikh zhilishch: zhilishche slovinīsa Verkhneĭ Kraĭny," *Zhivaīa starina*, no. 3-4 (1902), pp. 259-357; *Kirgizy Bukeevskoĭ ordy*, no. 1-2 (Moscow: 1889-1891); "K voprosu o proiskhozhdenii kirgizskogo naroda," *Ėtnograficheskoe obozrenie*, vol. 7, no. 3 (1895), pp. 49-92; *Slavianskoe zhilishche v Severo-Zapadnom krae* (Vil'no [Vilnius]: 1907);

A.M. Reshetov
[Translation from Russian: Thomas L. Mann]

Khlebnikov, K.T. (Kirill Timofeevich).
Ethnographer, historian, compiler of ethnographic and other materials. Born in Kungur, Urals (Russia) 18 March 1784, died in St. Petersburg (Russia) 14 August 1838. Khlebnikov was a corresponding member of the St. Petersburg Academy of Sciences (1837). For thirty-five years, he was in service in the Rossiĭsko-Amerikanskaīa Kompaniīa (Russian-American Company). As an eyewitness he gathered a considerable amount of data about the life of the population of Russian America during the first decade of the 19th century.

MAJOR WORKS: *Pervonachal'nye poseleniia russkikh v Amerike*, vol. 4 (Raduga: 1833); *Colonial Russian America; Kirill T. Khlebnikov's Reports, 1817-1832* (edited by B. Dmytryshyn and E.A.P. Crownhart-Vaughan) (Portland: 1976); *Russkaia Amerika v neopublikovannykh zapisakh K.T. Khlebnikova* (compiled by R.G. Liapunova and S.G. Fedorova) (Leningrad: 1979); *The Khlebnikov Archive: Unpublished Journal (1800-1837) and Travel Notes (1820, 1822 and 1824)* (Fairbanks: 1990).

SOURCES: N. Polevoĭ, "K.T. Khlebnikov," *Syn otechestva*, vol. 4 (1838), *otdel* [part] 6 [*Izvestiia i smes'*], pp. 1-7; V.V. Lukin, "Novye publikafsii raboty K.T. Khlebnikova," *Sovetskaia ėtnografiia*, no. 2 (1982), pp. 163-165.

A.M. Reshetov
[Translation from Russian: Thomas L. Mann]

Kidder, Alfred V. (Alfred Vincent). Archaeologist. Born in Marquette (Michigan) 29 October 1885, died in Cambridge (Massachusetts) 11 June 1963. One of the first to be professionally trained in the field of archaeology in the United States, Kidder grew up in a household where copies of the annual reports of the Smithsonian Institution and JOHN LLOYD STEPHENS' *Incidents of Travel in Yucatán* were available in his father's library. After completing his secondary education, he enrolled at Harvard in 1904 with the intention of pursuing a career in medicine. ROLAND B. DIXON's course on the American Indian, which he took in his sophomore year, awakened an interest in anthropology that would prove lifelong. Following further coursework with ALFRED M. TOZZER, he had his first experience in fieldwork through participation in a summer of surveying and mapping in the McElmo Canyon region of southwest Colorado under the aegis of Edgar Hewett of the Archaeological Institute of America in 1907. In company with SYLVANUS GRISWOLD MORLEY, Kidder helped create detailed maps of the Four Corners region and its ruins, with the rest of the summer devoted to assisting Hewett at ongoing work at Mesa Verde and Puye, New Mexico. In 1908, following graduation, Kidder returned to the Southwest to work with BYRON CUMMINGS. That winter Kidder traveled to Greece and Rome, where he became aware of the field methods being employed by George Reisner, with whom he studied in 1909. Reisner's approach to field archaeological excavation stressed exact recording of materials and stratigraphic theory. Kidder brought these ideas back to America (Wauchope, p. 151).

Following further fieldwork in Utah, Newfoundland and Labrador, Kidder worked in the Kayenta district of northern Arizona in 1914. The resulting publication, *Archaeological Explorations in Northeastern Arizona*, addressed the relationship of the "Basket Maker" culture to the Cliff Dweller ruins. Kidder's first lengthy work of significance for the archaeology of the Southwest, *Pottery of the Pajarito Plateau*, appeared in 1917. Derived from a chapter of his doctoral thesis, it emphasized stratigraphic and typological techniques as well as "hypotheses regarding the sociocultural significance of ancient pottery" (Wauchope, p. 152). These approaches were to be tested in Pecos Pueblo in eastern New Mexico, the site of an in-depth exploration that was to last some fifteen years beginning in 1915. Out of this and other fieldwork came the practical knowledge of the cultures of the region, that appeared in print in 1924 as *Introduction to the Study of Southwestern Archaeology*, one of the most influential works in the spreading of the stratigraphic, controlled approach to American archaeology. Another emphasis of Kidder's work, which also appeared in the work at Pecos, was his interest in ethnohistory.

In 1929, Kidder was approached by the Carnegie Institution of Washington (at the instigation of Morley) to direct their ongoing program of archaeological research in the Yucatán, Guatemala and Honduras. Continuing a tradition begun with the first Pecos Conference in 1927, Kidder called a meeting at Chichén Itzá in 1929 to plan the future of Maya study, emphasizing the application of stratigraphic methods and the creation of a body of information on Maya life, both historical and contemporary. The massive involvement with the publication of excavation results that had begun in the Southwest continued with the appearance in 1932 of *The Artifacts of Pecos* and the initiation of excavations at Kaminaljuyu, Guatemala, in 1935. The site report on this major Maya complex of tombs and pyramids paralleled the publication of the results of the Pecos project and served to emphasize the approach Kidder had tried to inculcate at the Chichén conference; it included recommendations for tackling specific types of excavation problems.

Concerned with the relationship of history to archaeology, Kidder continued to study artifacts recovered by subsequent Carnegie expeditions to the Maya highlands but also found time to pose, in "Looking backward," "broad cultural questions that archaeology could illuminate" (Wauchope, p. 163). Following his retirement in 1950, an award was created in his name by the American Anthropological Association. His influence on American archaeology can be seen in the adoption of his recommendations on excavation, analysis and prompt description and publication, his view on the value of ethnohistorical research for archaeological fieldwork and the application of models of regional synthesis to the plotting of past cultures in both the U.S. Southwest and Mesoamerica. In addition to the aforementioned, Kidder also served as mentor to several generations of students, many of whom were later to make significant contributions to archaeology and the field of anthropology as a whole.

MAJOR WORKS: *Pottery of the Pajarito Plateau and Some Adjacent Regions of New Mexico* (Lancaster, Pa.: 1915); (with Samuel J. Guernsey) *Archaeological Explorations in Northeastern Arizona* (Washington: 1919); *An Introduction to the Study of Southwestern Archaeology* (New Haven: 1924; rev. ed., New Haven: 1962); *Artifacts of Pecos* (New Haven: 1923) (= *Papers of the Phillips Academy Southwestern Expedition*, no. 6); *Excavations at Kaminaljuyu, Guatemala* (Washington: 1946) (= *Carnegie Institution of Washington, Publication*, no. 561); *Artifacts of Uaxactun* (Washington: 1947) (= *Carnegie Institution of Washington, Publication*, no. 576); *Excavations at Nebaj, Guatemala* (Washington: 1951) (*Carnegie Institution of Washington, Publication*, no. 594); *Pecos, New Mexico: Archaeological Notes* (Andover: 1958) (= *Papers of the Robert S. Peabody Foundation for Archaeology*, no. 5); "Looking backward," *Proceedings of the American Philosophical Society*, vol. 83 (1940), pp. 527-537.

SOURCES: Robert E. Greengo, "Alfred Vincent Kidder, 1885-1963," *American Anthropologist*, vol. 70 (1968), pp. 320-325; Robert Wauchope, "Alfred Vincent Kidder, 1885-1963," *American Antiquity*, vol. 31 (1965), pp. 149-171; Richard B. Woodbury, *Alfred V. Kidder* (New York: 1973).

Robert B. Marks Ridinger

Kirchhoff, Paul. Ethnologist, Americanist. Born in Hörste, Westphalia (Germany) 17 August 1900, died in Mexico City (Mexico) 12 September 1972. Kirchhoff studied Protestant theology and comparative religion in Berlin and Freiburg, and psychology and ethnology in Leipzig, where he also developed an interest in the native cultures of the Americas. In 1927 he completed his studies with a dissertation on the kinship organizations of the South American Indian groups. In his dissertation, Kirchhoff developed typologies of kinship terminologies; they preceded those of GEORGE PETER MURDOCK and were developed at the same time as those of ROBERT H. LOWIE. Until 1929 he served as a staff member of the Berlin Museum für Völkerkunde (Ethnographic Museum). Later, he collaborated on different international research projects overseas. In 1939 Kirchhoff was deprived of his German citizenship; he became a Mexican citizen in 1941. In Mexico he was employed at first by the Museo Nacional de Antropología (National Anthropological Museum). In 1955 he was one of the co-founders of the Escuela Nacional de Antropología e Historia (National School of Anthropology and History), which became the leading training center for ethnologists in Mexico. Kirchhoff was engaged there until 1965 and at the same time held a professorial chair in the graduate division of anthropology at the Universidad Nacional Autónoma de México (National Autonomous University of Mexico). As a visiting lecturer, Kirchhoff taught in 1960 and 1967 at the Universities of Bonn, Heidelberg and Frankfurt. Kirchhoff's efforts to create scientific cooperation between Germany and Mexico culminated in 1963 in the interdisciplinary Puebla-Tlaxcala Project, which lasted for more than twenty years.

Of the great number and diversity of Kirchhoff's researches, those on the Indians of North and South America and his archaeological and ethno-historical work on the little-considered northern and northwestern regions of Mexico must be emphasized. His most significant contribution to research on the Americas is the cultural-geographic concept of "Mesoamerica." This term encompassed the Indian civilizations of the Central American land bridge, i.e., the central and southern portion of Mexico, Guatemala, El Salvador, Belize, the northwestern section of Honduras and the northern Pacific coast of Nicaragua. Kirchhoff defined this region as a culture area based on common cultural characteristics such as ball courts, hieroglyphic writing and stepped pyramids.

MAJOR WORKS: "Die Verwandtschaftsorganisationen der Urwaldstämme Südamerikas," *Zeitschrift für Ethnologie*, vol. 63 (1931), pp. 85-193; "Verwandtschaftsbezeichnungen und Verwandtenheirat," *Zeitschrift für Ethnologie*, vol. 64 (1932), pp. 41-71; "Kinship organisation: a study of terminology," *Africa: Journal of the International Institute of African Languages and Cultures*, vol. 5 (1932), pp. 184-191; "Versuch einer Gliederung der Südgruppe des Athapaskischen" in: *Verhandlungen des XXIV. Internationalen Amerikanistenkongresses Hamburg 1930* (Hamburg: 1934), pp. 258-263; "Mesoamérica: sus límites geográficos, composición étnica y carácteres culturales," *Acta Americana*, vol. 1, no.1 (1943), pp 92-107 [tr.: "Meso-America: its geographic limits, ethnic composition and cultural characteristics" in: Sol Tax (editor), *Heritage of Conquest: the Ethnology of Middle America* (Glencoe: 1952), pp. 17-30]; "Das Toltekenreich und sein Untergang," *Saeculum*, vol. 12 (1961), pp. 248-265; (with Lina Odena Güemes and Luis Reyes García) *Historia Tolteca-Chichimeca* (Mexico City: 1976); "The Warrau," "The Caribbean Lowland tribes," "Patángoro and Amani," "The northeastern extension of Andean Culture," "The Guayupe and Sae," "The Otomac," "Food-gathering tribes of the Venezuelan Llanos," "The tribes north of the Orinoco River" and "The social and political organization of the Andean peoples" in: Julian H. Steward (editor), *Handbook of South American Indians*, vols. 3, 4, 5 (Washington: 1948-1949).

SOURCE: Gerdt Kutscher, "Paul Kirchhoff (1900-1972)," *Indiana*, vol. 2 (1974), pp. 239-255.

Frauke Johanna Riese
[Translation from German: Robert B. Marks Ridinger]

Kisliākov, N.A. (Nikolaĭ Andreevich). Ethnographer, Orientalist, folklorist, linguist. Born in St. Petersburg (Russia) 11 December 1901, died in Leningrad

(Russian S.F.S.R.) 8 October 1973. Kislîakov's scientific work began in Tadzhikistan, and after that he worked in Leningrad in the Institut ètnografii (Institute of Ethnography) of the Soviet Academy of Sciences Kislîakov was a doctor of historical sciences and a renowned specialist on the ethnography of the Tadzhiks. An important part of his research was devoted to the theoretical problems of social relations: the remnants of ancestral social order; the history of the family; marriage; wedding ceremonies; dowry; bride-money; rules of inheritance; patriarchal-feudal relationships among nomads, seminomads, and settled peoples; and the ethnography of contemporary times. In his work on these subjects, Kislîakov always attempted to trace historical evolution. He was also an experienced museum worker.

MAJOR WORKS: "Opisanie govora tadzhikov Vakhio-Bolo," *Trudy Tadzhikistanskoĭ bazy AN SSSR*, vol. 3 (Moscow and Leningrad: 1936), pp. 29-57; *Sledy pervobytnogo kommunizma u gornykh tadzhikov Vakhio-Bolo* (Moscow and Leningrad: 1936) (= *Trudy Instituta antropologii, ètnografii i arkheologii AN SSSR*, vol. 10, Ètnograficheskaîâ serîâ, no. 2); *Ocherki po istorii Karategina: k istorii Tadzhikistana* (Dushanbe and Leningrad: 1941); *Sem'îâ i brak u tadzhikov* (Moscow: 1959) (= *Trudy Instituta ètnografii AN SSSR*, vol. 44); *Patriarkhal'no-feodal'nye otnoshenîâ sredi osedlogo sel'skogo naselenîâ Bukharskogo khanstva konîsa XIX–nachala XX v.* (Moscow: 1962) (= *Trudy Instituta ètnografii AN SSSR*, vol. 74); *Ocherki po istorii sem'i i braka u narodov Sredneĭ Azii i Kazakhstana* (Leningrad: 1969); "Alovkhona—dom ognîâ u gornykh tadzhikov," *Problemy afrikanistiki (k 70-letîîû D.A. Ol'derogge)* (Moscow: 1973), pp. 88-94; "O sushchnosti i ponîâtîîâ patronimîîâ," *Strany i narody Vostoka*, no. 18 (1976), pp. 269-280; *Nasledovanie i razdel imushchestva narodov Sredneĭ Azii i Kazakhstana (XIX–nachalo XX v.)* (Leningrad: 1977).

SOURCES: "N.A. Kislîakov," *Sovetskaîâ ètnografîîâ*, no. 3 (1974), pp. 186-189; B.V. Lunin, "Kislîakov Nikolaĭ Andreevich," *Biobibliograficheskie ocherki o deîâtelîâkh obshchestvennykh nauk Uzbekistana*, vol. 2 (Tashkent: 1977), pp. 387-390; *Ètnografîîâ v Tadzhikistane: sbornik stateĭ* (Dushanbe: 1989).

A.M. Reshetov
[Translation from Russian: Thomas L. Mann]

Kîûner, N.V. (Nikolaĭ Vasil'evich). Ethnographer, geographer, historian, Orientalist. Born in Tbilisi (Georgia) 15 (25) September 1877, died in Leningrad (Russian S.F.S.R.) 5 April 1955. Kîûner was a professor of the Eastern Institute and the Far Eastern University in the city of Vladivostok, professor at Leningrad University (1925-1955) and a fellow at and director of the Section on Eastern and Southeastern Asia of the Institut ètnografii (Institute of Ethnography) of the Soviet Academy of Sciences (1934-1955). He was a major specialist on China, Korea, Mongolia and Japan. Knowledge of both Eastern and Western languages enabled him to make a major contribution to the expansion of the corpus of authoritative ethnographic sources: he compiled both translations of and commentaries on the sources. He was the author of more than 400 works. Kîûner's enormous scholarly archive is preserved in the Institute of Ethnography of the Soviet Academy of Sciences in Leningrad.

MAJOR WORKS: *Geograficheskoe opisanie Tibeta* (Vladivostok: 1907) (= *Izvestîîâ Vostochnogo Instituta*, vol. 21); *Ètnograficheskoe opisanie Tibeta* (Vladivostok: 1908) (= *Izvestîîâ Vostochnogo Instituta*, vol. 26, no. 1); *Lekîsii po istorii razvitîîâ glavneĭshikh osnov kitaĭskoĭ i material'noĭ i dukhovnoĭ kul'tury* (Vladivostok: 1921); *Geografîîâ Îâponii* (Moscow: 1927); *Ocherki noveĭsheĭ politicheskoĭ istorii Kitaîâ* (Khabarovsk and Vladivostok: 1927); "Kollektivnye okhoty u formozskikh plemen (u plemeni ataîîâl)," *Sovetskaîâ ètnografîîâ*, no. 2-3 (1937), pp. 100-110; "Rabota N.Îâ. Bichurina (Iakinfa) nad kitaĭskimi istochnikami dlîâ 'Sobranîîâ svedeniĭ'" in: N.Îâ.

Bichurin, *Sobranie svedeniĭ o narodakh, obitavshikh v Sredneĭ Azii v drevnie vremena*, vol. 1 (Moscow and Leningrad: 1950), pp. 6-36; (with E.T. Dubrovina), "Drevniĭ koreĭskiĭ farfor iz kollekt͡siĭ Muze͡ia antropologii i ėtnografii," *Sbornik Muze͡ia antropologii i ėtnografii*, vol. 15 (1953), pp. 332-356; *Kitaĭskie izvesti͡ia o narodakh iuzhnoĭ Sibiri, T͡Sentral'noĭ Azii i Dal'nego Vostoka* (Moscow: 1961).

SOURCES: "N.V. Ki͡uner (nekrolog)," *Sovetska͡ia ėtnografi͡ia*, no. 3 (1955), pp. 171-172; L.V. Zenina, "Istoriko-bibliograficheskie materialy N.V. Ki͡unera" in: A.D. Norichev and L.A. Bereznyĭ (editors), *Voprosy istorii stran Azii* (Leningrad: 1965), pp. 78-94; A.M. Reshetov, "N.V. Ki͡uner: vyda͡iushchiĭs͡ia russkiĭ i sovetskiĭ vostokoved (k 100-leti͡iu so dn͡ia rozhdeni͡ia)," *Izvesti͡ia Sibirskogo otdeleni͡ia AN SSSR. Seri͡ia obshchestvennykh nauk*, no. 1, issue 1 (1978), pp. 103-108.

A.M. Reshetov
[Translation from Russian: Thomas L. Mann]

Kiyono, Kenji. Physical anthropologist. Born in Okayama (Japan) 14 August 1885, died in Tōkyō (Japan) 27 December 1955. Kiyono graduated from the Faculty of Medicine at Kyōto University in 1909. From 1912 to 1914 he pursued the study of pathology at Freiburg University with Ludwig Aschoff and became a professor at his alma mater in 1921. Although he taught microbiology and pathology, he also began excavations and studies of prehistoric skeletons and became completely absorbed in the study of Japanese origins as revealed in ancient bone materials, observing and recording more than 1,500 human skeletal remains from the Jōmon and Ancient-Tombs Periods. By 1940 he and his students had compiled the *Kiyono Kenkyūshitsu Jinruigaku Rombushu* [*Compilation of the Kiyono Research Laboratory Anthropological Treatises*] in ten volumes. This formidable work remains a preeminent resource, offering the most complete physical anthropological data on prehistoric Japan.

Through measurement of bones and statistical manipulation Kiyono sought to understand the gaps between population groups and criticized YOSHIKIYO KOGANEI's and others' theories that the prehistoric inhabitants of Japan during the Jōmon Period were the Ainu. Kiyono felt that both Ainu and Japanese were descended from the proto-Japanese people of the Jōmon Period and asserted that the modern Japanese were formed from a mixing of the people of the Jōmon Period with outsiders from mainland Asia during the Yayoi and subsequent Kofun Periods. In Northern Japan, influences from northeastern Asia blended with the Jōmon populations to create the Ainu, who developed along different lines. His thinking concerning the first ancestors of modern Japanese formed the gist of his work and has resulted in a wide following among contemporary scholars.

MAJOR WORKS: *Nihongenjin no Kenkyū* [*Study of the Proto-Japanese People*] (Tōkyō: 1925); *Nihon Sekki Jidaijin no Kenkyū* [*Study of Japan's Stone Age People*] (Tōkyō: 1928); *Kodai Jinkotsu no Kenkyū ni Motozuku Nihon Jinshū Ron* [*Study of Ancient Bones as a Basis for a Theory of the Japanese Race*] (Tōkyō: 1949).

SOURCE: Teruya Esaka (editor), *Kiyono Kenji Shū* [*Collected Works of Kenji Kiyono*] (Tōkyō: 1982).

Bin Yamaguchi
[Translation from Japanese: Theodore Welch]

Klingenheben, Hermann August. Africanist, Semitist. Born in Barmen (Germany) 11 May 1886, died in Hamburg (Germany) 26 January 1967. Starting in 1905

Klingenheben studied first theology, then Semitic languages as a student of the Orientalists F. Praetorius and C. Brockelmann at the Universities of Tübingen, Marburg and Halle. In 1911 he took a position as *Wissenschaftlicher Hilfsarbeiter* (research assistant) at the Hamburg Seminar for Colonial Languages and in 1914 accompanied CARL MEINHOF to the Anglo-Egyptian Sudan as assistant and translator. As a soldier, he served on the eastern front until 1914, and from 1917 to 1919 as a Turkish *Oberleutnant* (lieutenant) in Mesopotamia and the Near East. In 1920 he was graduated from the University of Leipzig where he had studied with H. Stumme and wrote a dissertation on phonetic aspects of the Hausa dialect of Katagum. He obtained his *Habilitation* in 1924 in African and Semitic linguistics at the University of Hamburg, and in 1926 and 1927 he continued his studies of Berber in Spanish Morocco and the Vai language and writing system in Liberia. In 1930 he accepted an appointment as *Extraordinarius* professor at the University of Leipzig, coming to Hamburg in 1936 as *Ordinarius* (full) professor and director of the Seminars for African Languages, taking the position formerly held by Meinhof. In 1938 Klingenheben journeyed to Tripoli to work on studies in Berber, Amharic, Tigrinya and Hausa. He undertook a more extensive research trip in 1951, traveling to Liberia and northern Nigeria. While there he occupied himself chiefly with Vai, Hausa and Fulfulde. After being named Emeritus Professor in 1954 he made two major research trips—to Ethiopia in 1954 and to Liberia in 1962.

Shifting his attention from the study of Semitic languages, Klingenheben turned to the languages spoken along the northern boundary of Black Africa. Thus, in addition to Hausa (where his description of a rule for the final syllables has found its way into African studies under the term "Klingenheben's Law"), he worked intensively with the Nubians, the Amhara, the Oromo and the Somali. He also did research for almost forty years on the Vai language and writing, even serving as a consultant to the government of Liberia in 1962. Despite this, Klingenheben's greatest achievement lies in the analysis of the language of the Fulani, Fulfulde. On the grounds of his precise observation of sounds as well as his adequate description and grasp of the principles of the grammatical system of the language, he may be seen as the founder of Fulfulde studies. In a scientific historical sense, he contributed decisively to the reexamination of the "Hamitic" thesis regarding Fulfulde advanced by Meinhof. His decades-long work on Vai and Amharic remained unfinished. Klingenheben, who was equally conversant with Turkish, Fulfulde, Vai, Amharic and Arabic, helped make the study of African languages accepted as a distinct academic discipline.

MAJOR WORKS: "Die Präfixklassen des Ful," *Zeitschrift für Eingeborenen-Sprachen*, vol. 14 (1923-1924), pp. 189-222 and 290-315; "Die Permutation des Biafada und des Ful," *Zeitschrift für Eingeborenen-Sprachen*, vol. 15 (1924-1925), pp. 180-213 and 266-272; *Die Laute des Ful* (Hamburg: 1927) (= *Zeitschrift für Eingeborenen-Sprachen*, Beiheft 9); "Die Silbenauslautgesetze des Hausa," *Zeitschrift für Eingeborenen-Sprachen*, vol. 18 (1927-1928), pp. 272-297; "Die Tempora Westafrikas und die semitischen Tempora," *Zeitschrift für Eingeborenen-Sprachen*, vol. 19 (1928-1929), pp. 241-268; "Ablaut in Afrika," *Zeitschrift für Eingeborenen-Sprachen*, vol. 21 (1930-1931), pp. 81-98; "Der Bau der Sprache der Vai in Westafrika," *Nachrichten von der Gesellschaft der Wissenschaften zu Göttingen* (1933), pp. 307-404; *Die Suffixklassen des Ful* (Hamburg: 1941) (= *Zeitschrift für Eingeborenen-Sprachen*, Beiheft 23); "Die Präfix- und die Suffixkonjugationen des Hamitosemitischen," *Mitteilungen des Instituts für Orientforschung*, vol. 4 (1956), pp. 211-277; *Die Sprache der Ful* (Hamburg: 1963); *Deutsch-Amharischer Sprachführer* (Wiesbaden: 1966).

SOURCES: B.W. Andrzejewski, "Professor Dr. August Klingenheben," *Journal of African Languages*, vol. 6 (1966-1967), p. 189; E. Dammmann, E. Kähler-Meyer and J. Lukas, "August Klingenheben," *Afrika und Übersee*, vol. 50 (1967), pp. 241-243; Hermann Jungraithmayr, "Klingenheben, August" in: *Neue Deutsche Biographie* (Berlin: 1980), vol. 12, p. 80; Hermann Jungraithmayr, "Klingenheben, Hermann August" in: H. Jungraithmayr and W.J.G. Möhlig (editors), *Lexikon der Afrikanistik* (Berlin: 1983), pp. 130-131; Johannes Lukas, "Vorwort" to: Johannes Lukas (editor), *Neue Afrikanistische Studien (August Klingenheben zum 80. Geburtstag gewidmet)* (Hamburg: 1966) (= *Hamburger Beiträge zur Afrika-Kunde*, vol. 6), pp. 5-6.

Rudolf Leger
[Translation from German: Robert B. Marks Ridinger]

Kluckhohn, Clyde Kay Maben. Anthropologist, scholar, administrator. Born in Le Mars (Iowa) 11 January 1905, died in Santa Fe (New Mexico) 29 July 1960. Kluckhohn is often remembered as one of the last true generalists in American anthropology; he made significant contributions in both socio-cultural and physical anthropology, as well as in archaeology and linguistics. He is also remembered as an expert on the Navajo, a brilliant cultural theorist, an astute administrator (he was an organizer of Harvard's Department of Social Relations and head of its Russian Research Center), a pioneer in the study of psychological anthropology (Kluckhohn was psychoanalyzed in Vienna in 1931-1932, and his continued interest in individual psychology influenced both his ethnography and his theoretical interests, especially his work on values), the author of *Mirror for Man*, perhaps the best book on anthropology written for the general public, and a scholar of unusually broad interests and erudition.

Majoring in the classics, Kluckhohn received the A.B. degree in 1928 from the University of Wisconsin. He studied at the University of Vienna during 1931-1932 and attended Oxford University as a Rhodes Scholar (and student of R.R. MARETT) in 1932. In 1932 Kluckhohn married Florence Rockwood, sociologist and frequent collaborator, and began a two-year stint as Assistant Professor of Anthropology at the University of New Mexico. In 1936 Kluckhohn received the Ph.D. in anthropology from Harvard University where he studied with ALFRED M. TOZZER, E.A. HOOTON and ROLAND B. DIXON. He subsequently joined the faculty at Harvard and there he remained (except for the World War II years when he served as a government consultant) for the rest of his career. In 1947 Kluckhohn served as President of the American Anthropological Association.

Kluckhohn's first introduction to the Navajo was in 1923, at age seventeen, when he was recuperating from rheumatic fever at the Vogt family ranch in New Mexico. His research among the Navajo continued until his premature death and resulted in a number of publications in Navajo ethnography. This body of literature on the Navajo has earned Kluckhohn the reputation as one of anthropology's most accomplished ethnographers.

Neither dogmatic nor rigid in his theoretical formulations, Kluckhohn instead chose an eclectic, dynamic approach that focused on the tensions between cultural relativism and cultural universals, between the individual and the collective and between "explicit" and "implicit" culture. Kluckhohn's work on the concept of culture and in the field of values drew heavily on his diverse knowledge of the social sciences, natural sciences, arts and humanities. In his mature work, Kluckhohn reintroduced the seminal ideas of FRANZ BOAS and his students to the mainstream of contemporary social thought.

MAJOR WORKS: *Navaho Witchcraft* (Cambridge, Mass.: 1944); (with W.H. Kelly) "The concept of culture" in: Ralph Linton (editor), *The Science of Man in the World Crisis* (New York: 1945), pp. 78-106; (with Dorothea Leighton) *The Navaho* (Cambridge, Mass.: 1946); (with Dorothea Leighton) *Children of the People* (Cambridge, Mass.: 1947); *Mirror for Man* (New York: 1949); (with A.L. Kroeber) *Culture: a Critical Review of Concepts and Definitions* (Cambridge, Mass.: 1952); "Universal categories of culture" in: A.L. Kroeber (editor), *Anthropology Today* (Chicago: 1953), pp. 507-523; (with Raymond A. Bauer and Alex Inkeles) *How the Soviet System Works* (Cambridge, Mass.: 1956); "Toward a comparison of value emphases in different cultures" in: Leonard D. White (editor), *The State of the Social Sciences* (Chicago: 1956), pp. 116-132; "Recurrent themes in myths and mythmaking," *Daedalus*, vol. 88 (1959), pp. 268-279; *Anthropology and the Classics* (Providence, R.I.: 1961); *Culture and Behavior: Collected Essays of Clyde Kluckhohn* (Glencoe, Ill.: 1961).

SOURCES: Walter W. Taylor, John L. Fischer and Evon Z. Vogt (editors), *Culture and Life: Essays in Memory of Clyde Kluckhohn* (Carbondale, Ill.: 1973); Harry M. Davis, "An interview with Clyde Kluckhohn," *New York Times Book Review* (27 March 1949), p. 25; Melville J. Herskovits, "Clyde Kay Maben Kluckhohn, January 11, 1905-July 28, 1960," *National Academy of Sciences, Biographical Memoirs*, vol. 37 (1964), pp. 129-159; Alex Inkeles, "Clyde Kay Maben Kluckhohn, 1905-1960," *American Journal of Sociology*, vol. 66 (1961), pp. 617-618; George Peter Murdock, "Clyde Kluckhohn (1905-1960)," *Behavioral Science*, vol. 6 (1961), pp. 1-4; Talcott Parsons and Evon Z. Vogt, "Clyde Kay Kluckhohn, 1905-1960," *American Anthropologist*, vol. 64 (1962), pp. 140-148; Evon Z. Vogt, "Kluckhohn, Clyde" in: David L. Sills (editor), *International Encyclopedia of the Social Sciences* (New York: 1968-1979), vol. 8, pp. 419-421; Lucy Wales (compiler), "A bibliography of the publications of Clyde Kluckhohn," *American Anthropologist*, vol. 64 (1962), pp. 148-161; Richard B. Woodbury, "Clyde Kay Maben Kluckhohn, 1905-1960," *American Antiquity*, vol. 26 (1961), pp. 407-409.

Fred J. Hay

Knez, Eugene Irving (born Eugene Irving Knezevitch). Ethnologist, museum curator. Born in Clinton (Indiana) 12 May 1916. Knez was trained at the University of New Mexico (B.A., 1941) and Syracuse University (Ph.D., 1959). In service with the U.S. Army during 1945-1946, he was military chief of the Bureau of Culture in the Korean Department of Education. In that position, he was responsible for an early attempt to establish a national theatre, the successful reestablishment of the National Museum of Korea with Korean personnel instead of Japanese, the founding of the National Museum of Anthropology (now the Museum of Korean Folklore) and the preservation of Korean historical monuments. Later he served in various American cultural and informational positions in both Korea and Japan.

In 1959 following several positions as a teacher and museum curator in the United States, including one at the Peabody Museum at Yale University, Knez joined the staff of the Smithsonian's Department of Anthropology as its first Asian specialist in ethnology, and he continued in that position until he retired in 1978. During his tenure, the exhibits in the National Museum of Natural History were undergoing modernization, and Knez's chief contribution lay in his work with the exhibits and in the many additions he gained for the Asian collections.

In his early work, Knez assisted the National Museum of Korea in excavations at Kyongju and on Cheju Island. Later, he became interested in modern Korean village life, including its material culture. That interest continued into his Smithsonian career. As a Smithsonian curator emeritus, Knez lives in Honolulu and has been involved in studies of Tibetans who settled in India following the occupation of their country by the Chinese.

MAJOR WORKS: *Sam Jong Dong: a South Korean Village* [unpublished Ph.D. dissertation, University of Syracuse] (Syracuse: 1959); (with Chang-su Swanson) *A Selected and Annotated Bibliography of Korean Anthropology* ([Seoul?]: 1968).

SOURCES: "Eugene I. Knez: a friend of Korea," *Kae Chok Ja* [*Pioneer Magazine*] (summer 1977), pp. 3 and 9; Knez papers in the Smithsonian Institution National Anthropological Archives; personal interviews with Knez, 1978.

James R. Glenn

Knox, Robert. Ship's captain with the East India Company. Born in London (England) 8 February 1641, died in London (England) 19 June 1720. After attending boarding school at Roehampton, Knox at age nineteen sailed with his father, Captain Robert Knox, Sr., to India; but, while renovating the ship on the coast of Ceylon after a storm, they and others were taken captive by soldiers of the King of Kandy. Although his father soon died of malaria, Knox and fifteen other sailors were billeted in different villages by King Rajasingha II, a peculiar man who maintained "a sort of menagerie of European captives," more than 500 of them. These were not hostages, as the king would not release any of them for ransom; he simply liked having them around. During his life there Knox stayed in several scattered villages, and, while his food was provided, he had to work to earn his other needs. Over the years he knitted, raised cattle, engaged in mixed farming, and finally became quite rich lending out grain at 50% per annum interest. He remained a Puritan and a misogynist and, unlike most of the other captives, never married a local woman. After many years Knox was allowed to move around the country as a peddler, and this gave him the opportunity to escape in 1679, after twenty years of captivity (another sailor escaped after forty-nine years).

Returning to England at the age of forty, Knox took a course in navigation and then became a captain for the East India Company. In all he completed seven voyages to the Orient; in the process he established settlements at Tristan de Cunha and St. Helena and received a royal commission to "wage war" against the Moghul emperor Aurangzeb. He retired in 1701, famous because of his one book, *An Historical Relation of the Island Ceylon, in the East-Indies*, written in 1679. It was the first book on Ceylon to appear in English (in 1681), and several translations soon followed. It inspired Defoe's novel *Robinson Crusoe* (1719) and provided the commentary for Basil Wright's classic documentary film *Song of Ceylon* (1934). The 304 pages of the book are an early ethnography based entirely on Knox's own observations, to which is added an account of his adventures. In 1911 a manuscript autobiography, written in 1696, was discovered in the Bodleian Library, Oxford.

MAJOR WORK: *An Historical Relation of the Island Ceylon, in the East Indies* (London: 1681, etc.; numerous editions in several languages; best critical edition, edited by S.D. Saparamadu, published as *The Ceylon Historical Journal*, vol. 6 [Colombo: 1958]).

SOURCES: S.D. Saparamadu, "Introduction," *Ceylon Historical Journal*, vol. 6 (1958); Gordon Goodwin, "Knox, Robert" in: *Dictionary of National Biography* (London: 1917-), vol. 11, pp. 330-331; H.G. Rawlinson, "The adventures of Robert Knox, 1640-1720" in: H.G. Rawlinson, *Indian Historical Studies* (London: 1913), pp. 145-168. Further sources are given by S.D. Saparamadu [see above].

Paul Hockings

Koganei, Yoshikiyo. Physical anthropologist. Born in Nagaoka (Japan) 17 January 1859, died in Tōkyō (Japan) 16 October 1944. Koganei graduated from the Faculty of Medicine at the University of Tōkyō in 1880. While in school he studied under the German professor Erwin Baelz. From 1881 to 1885 he lived in Germany and did research under W. von Waldeyer on the histology of the retina and the iris. After returning to Japan, he became professor of anatomy at the University of Tōkyō and taught histology.

As a scholar, Koganei devoted his life to research on anthropology and became a pioneer in physical anthropology in Japan. In 1888 and 1889, he made two research trips to Hokkaidō. He measured and surveyed the Ainu and collected 166 skulls and 92 skeletons. He wrote a paper on this research in German which was long considered the most comprehensive article on the physical anthropology of the Ainu.

Based on the results of his research on the Ainu, Koganei then studied human skeletal remains from the Jōmon Period. He criticized the theory of SHŌGORO TSUBOI, that the Jōmon people were Korobokkuru, the legendary aboriginals of Hokkaidō, and put forward the idea that they were Ainu. He criticized the theory that the Ainu belonged to the Mongoloid racial family and considered them a *"Rasseninsel"* (a "racial island"), belonging to no larger racial group. His theories have often been the object of criticism, but today they are being reevaluated.

MAJOR WORKS: "Beiträge zur physischen Anthropologie der Aino," *Mitteilungen der Medizinischen Fakultät der Kaiserlichen Universität zu Tōkyō,* vol. 2 (1893-1894), pp. 1-249, 251-402; "Über die Urbewohner von Japan," *Mitteilungen der Deutschen Gesellschaft für Natur-und Völkerkunde Ostasiens,* vol. 9 (1903), pp. 297-329; *Jinruigaku Kenkyū [Research on Anthropology]* (Tōkyō: 1926); "Zur Frage der Abstammung der Aino und ihre Verwandschaft mit anderen Völkern," *Anthropologischer Anzeiger,* vol. 4 (1927), pp. 201-207; *Jinruigaku Kenkyū Zokuhen [Research in Anthropology, Second Series]* (Tōkyō: 1958).

SOURCES: Yasuo Yokoo, "Koganei Yoshikiyo Sensei nenpu" ["Chronology of Dr. Yoshikiyo Koganei"], *Kaibōgaku Zasshi [Acta Anatomica Nipponica],* vol. 33 (1958), pp. 471-477; Hisashi Suzuki, "Koganei Yoshikiyo Sensei to Erwin von Baelz Hakushi" ["Yoshikiyo Koganei and Erwin von Baelz"], *Journal of the Anthropological Society of Nippon,* vol. 82 (1974), pp. 1-9 [with English summary].

Bin Yamaguchi
[Translation from Japanese: Mamiko Nakamura]

Kohlbrugge, J.H.F. Ethnologist, physical anthropologist, physician. Born in Wertherbruch (Germany), 28 March 1865, died in Zeist (Netherlands), 24 August 1941. Kohlbrugge studied medicine at the Universities of Utrecht, Freiburg im Breisgau, Naples, Paris and Vienna. In 1892 he was employed by the Colonial Medical Service in the Dutch East Indies. For twelve years he worked on the island of Java, practicing medicine, studying tropical diseases and putting together a sizeable skeletal collection. At the University of Utrecht he taught climatology and tropical medicine and commenced scientific work on comparative anatomy and human evolution. In 1913 he was appointed professor of ethnology at this institution. From 1921 to 1928 he also taught sociology.

Kohlbrugge was a strong believer in morphological skeletal change and propagated the ideas of FRANZ BOAS in the Netherlands. He rejected many key elements of evolutionary theory. He published on human evolution as well as on tropical medicine and the history of physical anthropology. As professor of ethnology he wrote several textbooks. He developed a special interest in megalithic monuments and tried to trace their origin and diffusion. His general ethnological approach can be termed as interdisciplinary as he equally valued the contributions of ethnolinguistics, physical anthropology, sociology, psychology and the comparative study of law and religion. His studies on tribal religions focus on the analysis of cognitive processes. He stressed the importance of ethnopsychology as a basis for the formulation of colonial policy and advocated adaptation of the educational and legal system in the Dutch East Indies on the basis of this knowledge. He also spoke against the exploitation of native peoples by white commercial interests, especially the sugar industry in Indonesia, and was an advocate of penal reform.

MAJOR WORKS: *Die morphologische Abstammung des Menschen* (Stuttgart: 1908); *Historisch-kritische Studien über Goethe als Naturforscher* (Würzburg: 1913); *Het zieleleven van den misdadiger* (Groningen: 1922); *Practische sociologie* [6 vols.] (Groningen: 1925-1931); *Tier- und Menschenantlitz als Abwehrzauber* (Bonn: 1926); *De inlandsche beweging en de onrust in Indie* (Utrecht: 1927); *Systematisch en beschrijvend leerboek der volkenkunde* (Groningen: 1930) *s'Menschen religie* [2 vols.] (Groningen: 1932-1933).

SOURCES: G.A. Lindeboom, *Dutch Medical Biography: a Biographical Dictionary of Dutch Physicians and Surgeons, 1475-1975* (Amsterdam: 1984); J. de Wolf, "J. Kohlbrugge en H.Th. Fischer en de beoefening van de culturele antropologie aan de Rijksuniversiteit te Utrecht," *Antropologische Verkenningen*, vol. 7, nos. 1-2 (1988), pp. 95-117.

Pieter Hovens

Kökten, İsmail Kılıç. Anthropologist, prehistorian. Born in Ünye (Ordu, Turkey) 18 September 1904, died in Ankara (Turkey) 25 July 1974. Kökten received his degree from the Anthropological Institute of the Faculty of Languages, History and Geography (D.T.C.F.), Ankara University, where he also achieved later professional titles and spent his life teaching. He was the founder (1960) and chairman of the Department of Prehistory at this institution until his death. He was a well known member of various national and international professional associations besides being a fellow of the German Archaeological Institute.

In the field he collaborated with Franz Hančar and Eugène Pittard (1951), HENRI BREUIL, and Raymond Vaufrey and F. Keller (1956) of the German-Austrian school. His prehistoric investigations at innumerable caves and sites have been cornerstones in the development of the map of prehistoric settlements of Anatolia. His excavation at Karain (Antalya) was a landmark in the prehistoric studies of Anatolia, revealing a stratigraphy of settlements from the Pleistocene to the Bronze Age, aside from the remains of Pleistocene fauna and Neanderthal man, earning him international recognition. His other noteworthy discoveries have been the Paleolithic artifacts at the excavations at Küçükçekmece/Yarımburgaz (İstanbul), mural art caves at Yazılıkaya (Kars), and various Paleolithic remains at Tekeköy (Samsun), the Kars Plateau, and the area now under the waters of the Keban Dam Lake in eastern Anatolia, besides some Chalcolithic and Early Bronze Age remains in the tumulus of Dündartepe (Samsun).

MAJOR WORKS: "Orta, doğu ve kuzey Anadolu'da yapılan tarihöncesi araştırmaları" ["Prehistoric researches in Central, Eastern and Northern Anatolia"], *Belleten*, vol. 8, no. 32 (1944), pp. 659-680; "1940 ve 1941 yıllarında Türk Tarih Kurumu adına yapılan Samsun bölgesi kazıları hakkında ilk kısa rapor" ["Preliminary report on the excavations in the region of Samsun in 1940-1941 under the auspices of the Turkish Historical Association"], *Belleten*, vol. 2, no. 35 (1945), pp.

362-400; "Anadolu prehistorik yerleşme yerleri ve 1944-1948 yılında yapılan tarihöncesi araştırmaları" ["The prehistoric settlements of Anatolia and the prehistoric researches of 1944-1948"], *V. Türk Tarih Kurumu Kongresi* [*Proceedings of the Fifth Congress of the Turkish Historical Association*] (Ankara: 1948), pp. 195-289; "Türkiye'deki Karain mağarasında yapılan prehistorya araştırmalarına toplu bir bakış" ["A review of the prehistoric research at Karain, Turkey"], *Belleten*, vol. 19, no. 75 (1955), pp. 271-293; "Karain'in Türkiye prehistoryasındaki yeri" ["Karain and the prehistory of Turkey"], *Türk Coğrafya Dergisi*, vol. 18-19, no. 22-23 (1964), pp. 17-27; *Karain Kılavuzu* [*A Guide to Karain*] (Ankara: 1967); "Yazılıkaya ve Kurbanağa mağarasında (Kars-Çamuşlu) yeni bulunan diptarihle ilgili resimler" ["The recently discovered prehistoric mural paintings in the caves of Yazılıkaya and Kurbanağa (Kars)"], *Kars Eli*, no. 69 (1970), pp. 2-3 and 14-16; *Keban Baraj Gölü Alanında Taş Devri Araştırmaları* [*Stone-Age Explorations in the Keban Dam Lake Area*] (= *A Series of Publications by the Middle East Technical University, Ankara*, nos. 2, 3, 4, 5) (Ankara: 1969-1976).

SOURCES: "İ. Kılıç Kökten," *Antropoloji*, no. 8 (1978), pp. 1-5; Ş.A. Kansu, "Kılıç Kökten için" ["For K. Kökten"], *Antropoloji*, no. 8 (1978), pp. 699-701; *Meydan-Larousse*, vol. 7 (1976), p. 531; "Kökten, İsmail Kılıç" in: *Türk ve Dünya Ünlüleri Ansiklopedisi* [*Encyclopedia of Turkish and World Celebrities*], vol. 6 (1983), p. 3323; Aygen Erdentuğ, "A.Ü.D.T.C.F. antropoloji bibliyografyası (1935-1983)" ["Bibliography of anthropology, D.T.C.F., Ankara University (1935-1983)"], *Antropoloji*, no. 12 (1985), pp. 473-482.

Aygen Erdentuğ

Kolberg, Henryk Oskar. Ethnographer, composer. Born in Przysucha (Duchy of Warsaw, now in Poland) 22 February 1814, died in Kraków, Galicia (Austria-Hungary, now in Poland) 3 June 1890. Kolberg studied musical theory and composition in Berlin and at the same time participated in bookkeeping courses at the Academy of Trade. In 1836 he passed the composition and musical examinations under Józef Elsner (1769-1854). He worked as a private teacher of music and (from 1841) as an accountant as well. In 1861 he resigned from business practice and made his living from piano lessons and occasional literary studies, contributing substiantially to Orgelbrand's encyclopedia.

Kolberg's research activity began during the crest of interest in folk culture during the period of romanticism. From 1839 he began collecting folk songs and melodies in the field. From age forty-four, he devoted himself exclusively to research on folk culture throughout the Polish ethnic region as well as in neighboring areas. His investigations embraced the areas of Mazovia, Wielkopolska, Małopolska, Silesia, Pomerania, Podolia, Volhynia, Ruthenia, Pokucia and Lithuania. He also reached Lusatia as well as the lands of the Czechs, Slovaks and Southern Slavs. His final ethnographic journey took place in 1885 to Sanok region and Przemyśl. At first, starting in 1871, he published *Pieśni ludu polskiego* at his own expense. Later, the Scientific Society of Kraków provided him with material support for work in the field and printing operations. He gathered a collection of approximately 25,000 Polish and Slavic songs and dances with melodies, more than 2,000 fables and other folk tales, approximately 18,000 proverbs and riddles and other material as well. His research was based on the idea that folk songs and their variants were an expression of the ethnographic differentiation of the country. His interest in ethnographic differences was what led him (from 1865) to broaden the sphere of collection to all fields of folk culture. His works consist of actual field material, material of field correspondents, and ethnographic bibliographies. In Poland he was the creator of the model of the ethnographic-folkloristic monograph on the particular region.

On 13 July 1960 the Government of Poland began the publication of an edition of his complete works, including his articles in *Lud* and *Obrazy etnograficzne* and his numerous manuscripts.

MAJOR WORKS: *Pieśni ludu polskiego* [*Songs of the Polish People*], vol. 1 (Warsaw: 1957); "Pieśni czeskie i słowackie" ["Czech and Slovakian songs"], *Dzwon literacki*, vol. 4 (1846), pp. 272-284; *Pieśni ludu weselne* [*Folk Wedding Songs*] (Warsaw: 1847-1849); *Lud: jego zwyczaje, sposób życia, mowa, podania, przysłowia, obrzędy, gusła, zabawy, pieśni, muzyka i tańce* [*The Folk: Its Customs, Lifestyle, Speech, Legends, Proverbs, Rituals, Instruments, Games, Songs, Music and Dances*], vols. 2-23 (Warsaw and Kraków: 1867-1890); *Obrazy etnograficzne* [*Ethnographic Portraits*], vols. 24-36 (Kraków: 1882-1907); *Dzieła Wszystkie Oskara Kolberga* [*Complete Works of Oskar Kolberg*], vols. 1-67 (Poznań: 1961-1986).

SOURCES: Józef Gajek, "Oskar Kolberg jako etnograf" ["Oskar Kolberg as ethnographer"], *Lud*, vol. 2 (1955), pp. 35-48; Ryszard Górski, *Oskar Kolberg: zarys życia i działalności* [*Oskar Kolberg: Outline of his Life and Activity*] (Warsaw: 1970); Maria Turczynowiczowa, "Kolberg, Henryk Oskar" in: *Polski słownik biograficzny* [*Polish Biographical Dictionary*], vol. 13 (Wrocław: 1968), pp. 300-304.

Maria Niewiadomska and Iwona Grzelakowska
[*Translation from Polish: Joel Janicki*]

Koppers, Wilhelm. Roman Catholic priest, anthropologist, Indologist. Born in Menzelen (Germany) 8 February 1886, died in Vienna (Austria) 23 January 1961. Koppers is best known as joint author with Father WILHELM SCHMIDT of *Völker und Kulturen*, the basic work of the *Kulturkreislehre* (the study of "culture circles"), published in 1924. At first strongly committed to Schmidt's cultural-historical system, Koppers gradually became aware that human ingenuity is too individualistic to be pressed into a rigid system of culture-circles as Schmidt had conceived them. But Koppers did not live to build up an alternative system, if this were at all possible. So far the German anthropologists have not been able to create a new system to replace the cultural-historical system.

From 1913 to 1931 Koppers cooperated very actively with Schmidt's journal *Anthropos* and was its main editor from 1923 to 1931. But by 1924 he had become associated with the Department of Anthropology, University of Vienna, where he became assistant professor in 1928 and professor in 1935. As an uncompromising critic of the ideology of national socialism, in 1938 he was deprived of his professorship but used the leisure time forced on him for fieldwork among the Bhils of Central India. (He had earlier, in 1922, done some fieldwork in Tierra del Fuego among the Yamanas.) After his return from India in 1940 Koppers stayed at Fribourg in Switzerland where the Anthropos Institute had found refuge. Until 1945 he worked out the material collected in India and published a monograph on the Bhils and a number of papers on various topics, mainly connected with Indian anthropology. When World War II came to an end, Koppers hastened back to Vienna where he was reinstalled as professor and head of the Institut für Völkerkunde (Institute for Ethnology). In 1957 he retired, and in 1961 he died of a sudden heart attack.

After 1928 Koppers gradually shifted his activity from the Anthropos Center to the Institut für Völkerkunde at the University of Vienna. Under his devoted guidance the institute developed into an important study center that attracted many students from all European countries and even from overseas. Koppers guided 117 students to their doctorate; among them were anthropologists CLYDE KLUCKHOHN, HELMUT PETRI and Masao Oka.

Koppers published more than 200 books and papers on anthropology. Though initially Koppers wrote his books and papers, such as his thesis, *Anfänge des menschlichen Gemeinschaftslebens*, within the framework of the Cultural-Historical School of Vienna, later some of his specialized studies were of a more neutral character. His publications *Die Religion der Indogermanen*, *Pferdeopfer und Pferdekult der Indogermanen* and *Der Urmensch und Sein Weltbild* belong to this type.

While Koppers was for the first twenty years of his scientific careeer actively connected with the editing of *Anthropos*, he later made himself independent and after 1930 edited *Wiener Beiträge zur Kulturgeschichte und Linguistik* and after 1950 *Acta Ethnologica et Linguistica*. Koppers was also a member of several anthropological and sociological associations whose meetings he regularly attended and at which he frequently gave well prepared lectures. Maintaining all his life a strict intellectual integrity, Koppers had a broad vision and a generous tolerance for the opinions of others. His quiet and dignified bearing earned him the respect of his colleagues, while his generosity and personal interest in his students made him popular among them. Koppers was, in the succinct opinion of one of his students, not only "a competent professor, but also a perfect Christian gentleman."

MAJOR WORKS: *Anfänge des menschlichen Gemeinschaftslebens* (Mönchen-Gladbach: 1921); *Die Religion der Indogermanen* (St. Gabriel, Mödling bei Wien: 1929); *Pferdeopfer und Pferdekult der Indogermanen* (Vienna: 1936); *Der Urmensch und Sein Weltbild* (Vienna: 1949) (= *Wiener Beiträge zur Kulturgeschichte und Linguistik*, vol. 4).

SOURCES: A. Burgmann, "Professor Dr. Wilhelm Koppers SVD," *Anthropos*, vol. 56 (1961), pp. 721-736; C. von Fürer-Haimendorf, "Wilhelm Koppers, 1886-1961," *Man*, vol. 61 (1961), p. 140; J. Henninger, "Wilhelm Koppers SVD," *Mitteilungen der Anthropologischen Gesellschaft in Wien*, vol. 91 (1961), pp. 1-14; L. Luzbetak, "Father Wilhelm Koppers, SVD (1886-1961)," *Anthropological Quarterly*, vol. 34 (1961), p. 164.

Stephen Fuchs

Kotnik, France. Linguist, literary historian, folklorist/ethnologist. Born in Dobrije pri Guštanju (Slovenia) 20 November 1882, died in Celje (Slovenia) 6 February 1955. Kotnik studied linguistics at the University of Graz; he graduated in 1908. His research concerned material, social and religious culture; in it he combined his basic knowledge of Slovenian culture and literary history with ethnology. Most important was his research on the writers, poets, singers, and musicians of the peasant class. Kotnik was the author of the first review of the development of Slovenian ethnology.

MAJOR WORKS: *Slovenske starosvetnosti* (Ljubljana: 1943); "Pregled slovenskega narodopisja," *Narodopisje Slovencev*, vol. 1 (1944), pp. 21-52; "Naši bukovniki, ljudski pesniki in pevci," *Narodopisje Slovencev*, vol. 2 (1952), pp. 86-102; "Verske ljudske igre," *Narodopisje Slovencev*, vol. 2 (1952), pp. 103-121; "Iz ljudske medicine," *Narodopisje Slovencev*, vol. 2 (1952), pp. 122-133.

SOURCES: Vilko Novak, "Etnografsko delo Franceta Kotnika," *Slovenski etnograf*, vol. 5 (1952), pp. 179-194; Vilko Novak, *Raziskovalci slovenskega življenja* (Ljubljana: 1986).

Mojca Ravnik

[*Translation from Slovene: Corrine Leskovar*]

Kotula, Franciszek. Ethnographer, regionalist. Born in Głogów Małopolski, Galicia (Austria-Hungary, now in Poland) in 1900, died in Rzeszów (Poland) 22 April 1983. Kotula graduated from Teachers' College. At first he worked as a teacher in the countryside; later he moved to Rzeszów.

From his early years Kotula demonstrated an interest in the region and a passion for collecting. In 1935 he became the curator of the museum established by the Regional Society of the District of Rzeszów. He gathered and appraised collections, not interrupting his work even during World War II. After the war, as director of the museum, he expanded his role as a researcher, penetrating to the Sandomierz Woods, the outskirts of Rzeszów and Podgórze. He was interested in all the "signs of the past" and aimed at a comprehensive history of the region and its material culture. In the 1960s he became interested in verbal folklore as a collection of "archetypes."

Kotula's activity in museology was only one of the symptoms of his passion as a collector-researcher. His private collections included huge archives of printed material, manuscripts and notes from his own investigations. He left behind more than seven hundred publications. He is considered to be the most outstanding regionalist of his time.

MAJOR WORKS: *Strój rzeszowski* [*Costumes of Rzeszów*] (Lublin: 1951); *Strój łańcucki* [*Costumes of Łańcut*] (Wrocław: 1955); *Materiały do dziejów garncarstwa z terenu województwa rzeszowskiego* [*Material for the History of Pottery from the Area of the Province of Rzeszów*] (Rzeszów: 1956); *Z Sandomierskiej Puszczy: gawędy kulturowo-obyczajowe* [*From the Sandomierz Woods: Tales of Folk Customs*] (Kraków: 1962); *Folklor słowny osobliwy* [*Peculiarities of Verbal Folklore*] (Lublin: 1969); *Hej, leluja* [*Hey, Lily*] (Warsaw: 1970); *W starym domu Czarnej Madonny* [*In the Old House of the Black Madonna*] (Kraków: 1970); *Po Rzeszowskim Podgórzu błądząc* [*Wandering About the Rzeszówian Hillsides*] (Kraków: 1974); *Opowieści ziemi z dorzecza Górnej Wisłoki i Wisłoka zebrane przez zauroczonego łazęgę* [*Tales of the Land between the Upper Wisłoka and the Wisłok Collected by an Enchanted Gadabout*] (Rzeszów: 1975); *Znaki przeszłości* [*Signs of the Past*] (Warsaw: 1976); *Muzykanty* [*Folk Musicians*] (Warsaw: 1979); *Miasteczko: na przykładzie Głogowa Małopolskiego i jego sąsiadów* [*The Small Town: the Example of Głogów Małopolski and its Neighbors*] (Rzeszów: 1981); *Chłopi bronili się sami: reportaż historyczny* [*The Peasants Defended Themselves: Historical Journalism*] (Rzeszów: 1982); *U źródeł* [*At the Sources*] (Rzeszów: 1983).

SOURCES: Józef Burszta, "Pamięci Rzeszowskiego Kolberga: Franciszek Kotula" ["Recollections of the Kolberg of Rzeszów, Franciszek Kotula"], *Lud*, vol. 67 (1983), pp. 431-433; Franciszek Kotula, "Z doświadczeń, prac i przemyśleń regionalisty" ["From experiences, studies and the thoughts of a regionalist"], *Lud*, vol. 57 (1973), pp. 263-300; *Prace i materiały z badań etnograficznych* [*Studies and Materials from Ethnographic Researches*] (Rzeszów: 1979).

Maria Niewiadomska and Iwona Grzelakowska

[*Translation from Polish: Joel Janicki*]

Kretzenbacher, Leopold. Folklorist. Born in Leibnitz (Austria) 13 November 1912. Kretzenbacher obtained his university degree in 1936 with a project on folk drama and began working at the Steirisches Volkskundemuseum (Styrian Folklore Museum) in

Graz in 1938. In 1939 he obtained his *Habilitation* with an investigation into Germanic myths in the epic folk poetry of Slovenia. He became a *Dozent* in 1941 and in 1943 *außerordentlicher Professor* of German folklore at the University of Graz and visiting professor of Germanistics at Zagreb. Following his release from wartime detention in 1945, he returned to his work at the Styrian Folklore Museum and served as an instructor at the University of Graz until 1961, when he was offered an academic chair at Christian Albrecht University in Kiel. In 1966 he accepted a position at the University of Munich where he remained until his rise to *emeritus* in 1978.

Kretzenbacher's conception of the comparative study of folklore should be seen as his chief accomplishment. With it he linked numerous phenomena spread over a large part of the Western world using varied methodological strategies. At the beginning of his scientific career he concerned himself principally with religious folk dramas. In due course he delineated southeastern Europe as a field of investigation and laid the groundwork for his main scientific effort in comparative folklore research. At first his publications covered the analysis of popular traditions rooted in legends and the area of religious folk culture. During his tenure in Kiel he expanded his frame of reference through investigative trips to Scandinavia and Holland and while at Munich directed his attention again to southeastern Europe. Many motifs from this region entered into works such as *Kynokephale Dämonen südosteuropäischer Volksdichtung*. For Kretzenbacher, research on legends remained a central theme, although in his overall corpus of scholarly work one also finds essays on aspects of folk law and Baroque culture. In his analyses (in which social, spatial and historical conditions were all significant) it was primarily in those regions where different culture areas intersected (such as the Balkans, where Eastern Orthodox, Catholic, Protestant and Islamic traditions were intermingled) that he made cultural diversity and its significance in the life of the common people comprehensible.

MAJOR WORKS: *Lebendiges Volksschauspiel in Steiermark* (Vienna: 1951) (= *Österreichische Volkskultur: Forschungen zur Volkskunde*, no. 6); *Santa Lucia und die Lutzelfrau: Volksglaube und Hochreligion im Spannungsfeld Mittel- und Südosteuropas* (Munich: 1959) (= *Südosteuropäische Arbeiten*, no. 53); *Heimat im Volksbarock: Kulturhistorische Wanderungen in den Südostalpenländern* (Klagenfurt: 1961) (= *Buchreihe des Landesmuseums für Karnten*, no. 8) [tr.: *Minshū barokku to kyōdo* (Nagoya: 1988)]; *Ringreiten, Rolandspiel und Kufenstechen: Sportliches Reiterbrauchtum von heute als Erbe aus abendländischer Kulturgeschichte* (Klagenfurt: 1966) (= *Buchreihe des Landesmuseums für Kärnten*, no. 20); *Kynokephale Dämonen südosteuropäischer Volksdichtung: Vergleichende Studien zu Mythen, Sagen, Maskenbräuchen um Kynokephaloi, Werwölfe und südslawische Pesoglavci* (Munich: 1968) (= *Beiträge zur Kenntnis Südosteuropas und des Nahen Orients*, no. 5); *Kettenkirchen in Bayern und in Österreich: Vergleichend-volkskundliche Studien zur Devotionalform der "cinctura" an Sakralobjekten als kultisches Hegen und magisches Binden* (Munich: 1973) (= *Abhandlungen der Bayerischen Akademie der Wissenschaften, Philosophisch-historsiche Klasse*, n.F. 76); *Legende und Sozialgeschehen zwischen Mittelalter und Barock* (Vienna: 1977) (= *Sitzungsberichte der Österreichischen Akademie der Wissenschaften, philosophisch-historische Klasse*, vol. 318); *Das verletzte Kultbild: Voraussetzungen, Zeitschichten und Aussagewandel eines abendländischen Legendentypus* (Munich: 1977) (= *Sitzungsberichte der Bayerischen Akademie der Wissenschaften, philosophisch-historische Klasse*, Jahrgang 1977, Heft 1).

SOURCES: Helge Gerndt and Georg R. Schroubek, *Vergleichende Volkskunde: Bibliographie Leopold Kretzenbacher* (Munich and Würzburg: 1977); Elfriede Grabner, "Leopold Kretzenbacher zum 75. Geburtstag," *Südostdeutsches Archiv*, vol. 30/31 (1987/1988), pp. 193-196; Helge Gerndt, "Zur Bedeutung des Vergleichs in der volkskundlichen Methodik," *Zeitschrift für Volkskunde*, vol. 68 (1972), pp. 179-195; Eva Heller, "Volkskundler in und aus Bayern heute," *Ethnologia Bavarica*,

Heft 14 (1985), pp. 28-29; Gerda Mohler, *Vergleichende Volkskunde: Bibliographie Leopold Kretzenbacher II* (Munich: 1989).

Johannes Moser
[Translation from German: Robert B. Marks Ridinger]

Krickeberg, Walter. Anthropologist, museologist. Born in Schwiebus (Germany) 27 June 1885, died in Berlin (Germany) 15 July 1962. Krickeberg started his academic career in Berlin as student of American anthropology under EDUARD SELER. In 1906 Krickeberg began working as *wissenschaftlicher Hilfsarbeiter* (research assistant) at the Museum für Völkerkunde (Ethnographic Museum), which remained his lifelong institutional affiliation. Due to World War I he received his Ph.D. somewhat belatedly, in 1922; his important dissertation on the Totonac was not published until 1925. This was the first synthetic monograph of archaeology, history and ethnology in Mesoamerican research and has served as a model for later authors. Krickeberg, unlike most of his museum colleagues in the American section (KONRAD THEODOR PREUß, WALTER LEHMANN, KARL VON DEN STEINEN), was not a distinguished fieldworker (he made only two sightseeing trips to Mexico in 1939-1940 and 1958-1959). Instead he was the leading German writer of well informed overviews and synthetic monographs on the American Indian during the first half of the 20th century. His first works were two popular books on myths and legends and general surveys of American Indian cultures for the handbooks of Georg Buschan (1863-1942) and Hugo Bernatzik (1897-1953). One of the best monographs of an American culture area is his *Altmexikanische Kulturen*. Between 1949 and 1969 he co-authored a survey of American Indian religions and prepared a survey on rock art, which was never completed. These publications are all characterized by his vast knowledge of basic facts and his diligent perusal of current research as well as his outstanding ability to work out general characteristics and historical trends for ethnic groups and entire culture areas. Krickeberg adhered to the Cultural-Historical School of ethnology more on the lines of ALFRED L. KROEBER and ROBERT H. LOWIE than to the German *Kulturkreislehre*. In contrast to the American Cultural-Historical School, however, Krickeberg, like ROBERT VON HEINE-GELDERN and GORDON F. EKHOLM was favorably inclined to the notion of trans-Pacific cultural diffusion.

During the period of the Nazi regime Krickeberg misused his institutional power against colleagues (there was controversy over the *Lehrbuch für Völkerkunde*) and against employees of the museum of which he was director. Nevertheless he was acquitted of all charges by the U.S. military government and was reinstalled as director of the Berlin Ethnographic Museum and as honorary professor until his retirement in 1954.

MAJOR WORKS: *Die Totonaken: ein Beitrag zur historischen Ethnographie Mittelamerikas* [Ph.D. dissertation] (Berlin: 1919-1925) (= *Baessler Archiv*, vols. 7 and 9) [tr.: *Los Totonaca: contribución a la etnografía histórica de la America Central* (Mexico City: 1933)]; *Indianermärchen aus Nordamerika* (Jena: 1924; plus many later editions); *Märchen der Azteken und Inkaperuaner, Maya und Muisca* (Jena: 1928; plus various later editions); "Das mittelamerikanische Ballspiel und seine religiöse Symbolik," *Paideuma*, vol. 3 (1948), pp. 118-190; *Felsplastik und Felsbilder bei den Kulturvölkern Altamerikas, mit besonderer Berücksichtigung Mexicos* [2 vols., vol. 2 posthumously edited] (Berlin: 1949-1969); *Altmexikanische Kulturen* (Berlin: 1956; 2nd ed., Berlin: 1966 with an additional chapter by Gerdt Kutscher; various reprints); (with H. Trimborn) *Die Religionen des alten Amerika* (Stuttgart: 1961) (= *Religionen der Menscheit*, vol. 7).

SOURCES: H. Trimborn, "Walter Krickeberg (27 Juni 1885 + 15 Juli 1962)," *Baessler Archiv*, n.F., vol. 11 (1963), pp. 1-8; H. Trimborn, "Walter Krickeberg, 27.6.1885 + 15.7.1962," *Ethnos* 28 (1964), pp. 252-254; K. Hissink, "Walter Krickeberg," *Paideuma*, vol. 9 (1963), pp. 79-81; Egon Erwin Kisch, *Entdeckungen in Mexiko* (Mexico City: 1945).

Berthold Riese

Krieger, Herbert William. Anthropologist, museum curator. Born in Burlington (Iowa) 8 December 1889, died in Arlington (Virginia) 1 July 1970. Krieger was educated in social science and politics at Wartburg College (B.A., 1907) and at the University of Iowa (M.A., 1908). He studied anthropology at the University of Minnesota during 1922-1924. Krieger was a teacher in the United States and the Philippines between 1908 and 1924. In the latter year, he was appointed a museum aid in the Department of Anthropology of the Smithsonian Institution's United States National Museum. He continued at the museum until he retired in 1959, having become curator of ethnology in 1925.

Much of Krieger's work involved museum administration and studies of artifacts in the Smithsonian's ethnological collections. His fieldwork was largely archaeological and at first involved investigations into the feasibility of restoring the Alaskan village of Old Kasaan, reconnaissance along the Columbia and Yukon Rivers and salvage work near Bonneville, Oregon. His major work, carried out during 1928-1937 and 1947-1952, consisted of investigations into sites visited by Columbus and efforts to plot regions previously occupied by the Arawak, Carib and other tribes of the Greater Antilles, the Bahamas and the Virgin Islands. During World War II, Kreiger was affiliated with the Ethnogeographic Board, where he prepared works on Oceania, the Philippines and Japan, which were based on library research.

MAJOR WORKS: *The Collection of Primitive Weapons and Armor of the Philippine Islands in the United States National Museum* (Washington: 1926) (= *United States National Museum Bulletin*, no. 137); *Material Culture of the People of Southeastern Panama Based on Specimens in the United States National Museum* (Washington: 1926) (= *United States National Museum Bulletin*, no. 134); "American Indian costumes in the United States National Museum," *Annual Report of the Smithsonian Institution* (1928), pp. 623-661; *Archeological and Historical Investigations in Samaná, Dominican Republic* (Washington: 1929) (= *United States National Museum Bulletin*, no. 147); *Aboriginal Indian Pottery of the Dominican Republic* (Washington: 1931) (= *United States National Museum Bulletin*, no. 158); *Peoples of the Philippines* (Washington: 1942) (= *Smithsonian War Background Studies*, no. 4); *Island Peoples of the Western Pacific, Micronesia and Melanesia* (Washington: 1943) (= *Smithsonian War Background Studies*, no. 16).

SOURCES: "Herbert W. Krieger, 80, curator at Smithsonian," *Washington Post* (3 July 1970), p. B8; Krieger papers and vertical file and records of the Department of Anthropology in the Smithsonian Institution National Anthropological Archives.

James R. Glenn

Kroeber, Alfred L. (Alfred Louis). Anthropologist, natural historian, humanist. Born in Hoboken (New Jersey) 11 June 1876, died in Paris (France) 5 October 1960. In 1901 Kroeber completed the first Ph.D. in anthropology to be awarded by Columbia University where he had studied under FRANZ BOAS. In that same year he was hired by FREDERIC WARD PUTNAM as an instructor in the fledgling Department of Anthropology at the University of California. He took charge of the Berkeley department after 1909, sharing this responsibility with Robert H. Lowie from 1922 until Kroeber's retirement in 1946. He remained an active contributor to anthropology until his death, fourteen years later, teaching at Harvard, Columbia, Brandeis and Yale Universities during these years.

Kroeber's scholarly interests included history and literature and he practiced as a psychoanalyst between 1918 and 1923. Yet above all he was, as Ralph Leon Beals has noted, "an anthropologist's anthropologist," and his lifelong concern was with "civilization" and its history. He contributed significantly to all four fields within anthropology. His work in any of three of these—e.g., ethnology, linguistics, archaeology—alone would have secured his place in the history of the discipline, and he published important articles on physical anthropology as well.

Kroeber considered himself primarily an ethnologist. His most extensive ethnographic work was in North America, where he did fieldwork among the Arapahoe, the Zuni and, especially, in native Californian cultures, most notably Mohave and Yurok. A variety of descriptive ethnographies and monographs resulted as well as important ethnological hypotheses and methods. Kroeber published pivotal articles on many ethnological topics (his work on kinship has had especially long-lasting influence) and was an innovator in historical approaches and statistical methods. His contribution to culture-area theory remains basic, and his investigations of the areal distribution of cultural elements, though less successful and enduring, contributed importantly to the emergence of quantitative and linguistics-based methods in ethnology.

His commitment to an historical perspective is evident in his linguistics as well as in his ethnology. Kroeber was largely concerned with historical relationships within and between languages, especially—but not exclusively—in native North America. His studies of the Hokan, Penutian and Athabaskan languages in California were fundamental. He brought statistical methods to bear on problems in historical linguistics, as on ethnological problems, contributing to the development of glottochronology and lexicostatistics. While primarily concerned with historical linguistics, Kroeber was also among the first to study speech varieties, such as Zuni children's speech and Yurok ritual speech.

In archaeology, Kroeber's focus was, predictably, on time depth, and he made important early contributions to the development of seriation techniques through the study of Zuni pottery shards. His extensive work in Mexican and, especially, Peruvian archaeology remains fundamental to continuing study. In physical anthropology, he was a perceptive critic and interpreter of others' work and was among the first to recognize the potential importance of blood-group typing.

While Kroeber considered himself "by nature a worker with concrete data," he was a central figure in the development of general theory in cultural anthropology. His theory of culture, first detailed in "The superorganic" and reiterated in "So-called social science," dominated anthropological discourse and debate on the culture concept for several decades. Kroeber held that "the immediate causes of cultural phenomena are other cultural phenomena" and viewed other explanations—functional, structural or psychological—as reductionistic. His objective, whether in ethnology, archaeology or linguistics, was to integrate separate phenomena into larger descriptive wholes, "patterns," "complexes" or "configurations," that in turn were analytically combined to form "types" whose constitution and comparative relationships revealed the histories of their growth. While his classificatory and typological emphases owed much to his early study of biology, Kroeber held that pattern recognition was a deductive and subjective act, more closely related to the study of literature. He did not view anthropology as a science but saw his discipline as a branch of natural history and himself as a humanist whose chief aim it was to reconstruct the history of civilization through the "descriptive integration" of its concrete phenomena, or "content." He ultimately came into conflict with his mentor, Boas, who Kroeber felt was more concerned with causal processes and general explanation, and hence with science, than with concrete phenomena and an understanding of their histories. However, the classificatory and typological "schemes" that resulted from Kroeber's "humanistic statistics" have seemed overly "particularistic" to his own critics, who have also questioned the progressivism of Kroeber's historiography. Again, although Kroeber's theory of cultural growth stressed the periodic emergence of individual geniuses, for him the actions of these and all individuals were culturally determined. He discounted the importance of individual experience and, especially, variation, ending in determinism, for which he has been frequently taken to task. Finally, the "superorganic" nature of culture, as Kroeber conceived of it, has been attacked as metaphysical reification from the time that Kroeber first proposed it.

Despite all such criticisms, Kroeber's contribution to the establishment and development of anthropology as an academic discipline in the United States is beyond dispute. From the time of Boas's death in 1942 until the end of Kroeber's own long and productive life, Kroeber was, to quote his biographers, "the dean" of American anthropology and its "living embodiment."

MAJOR WORKS: [A.L. Kroeber published well over 500 separate works during his lifetime; any selection must be somewhat arbitrary. The following list of major publications is largely Kroeber's own.] *The Arapaho* (New York: 1902-1907) (= *Bulletin of the American Museum of Natural History*, vol. 18); *The Yokuts Language of South Central California* (Berkeley: 1907) (= *University of California Publications in American Archaeology and Ethnology*, vol. 2, no. 5); *Zuni Kin and Clan* (New York: 1917) (= *Anthropological Papers of the American Museum of Natural History*, vol. 18, part 2); "The superorganic," *American Anthropologist,* n.s., vol. 19 (1917), pp. 163-213 [republished in: *The Nature of Culture* (Chicago: 1952), pp. 22-51]; *The Peoples of the Philippines* (New York: 1919) (= *American Museum of Natural History Handbook Series*, no. 8); *Anthropology* (New York: 1923; later ed., New York: 1948); *Handbook of the Indians of California* (Washington: 1925) (= *Bureau of American Ethnology Bulletin*, no. 78); "So-called social science," *Journal of Social Philosophy*, vol. 1 (1936), pp. 317-340 [republished in: *The Nature of Culture* (Chicago: 1952), pp. 66-78]; *Cultural and Natural Areas of Native North America* (Berkeley: 1939) (= *University of California Publications in American Archaeology and Ethnology*, vol. 38); *Configurations of Culture Growth* (Berkeley and Los Angeles: 1944); *Peruvian Archaeology* (New York: 1944) (= *Viking Fund Publications in Anthropology*, no. 4); *The Nature of Culture* (Chicago: 1952); *Style and Civilizations* (Ithaca: 1957); *An Anthropologist Looks at History* (edited by Theodora Kroeber) (Berkeley and Los Angeles: 1963); *Yurok Myths* (Berkeley and Los Angeles: 1976).

SOURCES: Theodora Kroeber, *Alfred Kroeber: a Personal Configuration* (Berkeley and Los Angeles: 1970); Julian H. Steward, *Alfred Kroeber* (New York: 1973); Dell Hymes, "Alfred Louis Kroeber," *Language*, vol. 27 (1961), pp. 1-28; Harold E. Driver, "The contribution of A.L. Kroeber to culture area theory and practice," *Indiana University Publications in Anthropology and Linguistics*, memoir 18 (1962), pp. 1-28 (= supplement to: *International Journal of American Linguistics*, vol. 28, no. 2); John Howland Rowe, "Alfred Louis Kroeber, 1876-1960," *American Antiquity* vol. 27 (1962), pp. 395-415; Julian Steward, "Alfred Louis Kroeber, 1876-1960," *American Anthropologist* vol. 63 (1961), pp. 1038-1060; Eric R. Wolf, "Alfred L. Kroeber" in: Sydel Silverman (editor), *Totems and Teachers: Perspectives on the History of Anthropology* (New York: 1981), pp. 34-65; Ann J. Gibson and John H. Rowe, "A bibliography of the publications of Alfred Louis Kroeber,"

American Anthropologist vol. 63 (1961), pp. 1060-1087; Ralph Beals, "Kroeber, Alfred L." in: David L. Sills (editor), *International Encyclopedia of the Social Sciences* (New York: 1968-1979), vol. 8, pp. 454-463.

Thomas Buckley

Kruyt, A.C. (Albertus Christiaan). Protestant missionary, ethnographer, ethnologist. Born in Soerabaja (Dutch East Indies, now Indonesia) 10 October 1869, died in The Hague (Netherlands) 19 January 1949. Kruyt combined his work as a missionary with ethnographic research of high quality. His scientific work was highly regarded by professional anthropologists, at least among those who could read Dutch (e.g., MARCEL MAUSS and JAMES G. FRAZER) and may be compared with that of HENRI-ALEXANDRE JUNOD, MAURICE LEENHARDT and Bruno Gutmann (1876-1966), who were his contemporaries.

Kruyt was the son of a Dutch Protestant missionary who worked on Java. (Two of his older brothers also became missionaries, as did his own son.) Kruyt went to Holland to attend school and was admitted to the missionary training college at Rotterdam in 1884. His interest in ethnology was stimulated by the vice-principal, Roskes, who was well informed about recent developments in this field through his brother-in-law, G.A. WILKEN, professor of ethnology at Leiden. The Nederlandsch Zendeling Genootschap (Dutch Missionary Association) wanted him to start work among the Toradja of central Sulawesi at the invitation of the Dutch administration, which had, however, not yet established its own rule in this region. After a few prolonged visits to the area Kruyt finally settled down at Poso in 1892. In 1895 he was joined here by the linguist Nikolaus Adriani (1865-1926), who was seconded by the Dutch Bible Society. The two worked together until Adriani's death in 1926. Kruyt himself left Poso for the Netherlands in 1932. He had the satisfaction of seeing the Protestant church well established among the Toradja though he had had to wait until 1909 for the first baptisms to occur. Serious interest in conversion on the part of the Toradja coincided with and was partly caused by the consolidation of colonial rule and the prohibition of such customs as head hunting.

Kruyt's missionary work was based on a solid knowledge of the local culture and language. His powers of patient observation and thorough description resulted in a flood of ethnographic publications, not only on the Toradja but also on other Indonesian peoples among whom he did comparative research (especially on the islands of Sumba, Timor, Roti and Mentawei). One of Kruyt's preoccupations was the nature of religious beliefs. At first he paid much attention to animistic explanations. He supplemented and criticized Wilken's ideas, without rejecting the importance of the belief in souls altogether. Later on he adopted more completely the dynamistic perspective of KONRAD THEODOR PREUß as put forward in the latter's articles on "Der Ursprung der Religion und der Kunst" in *Globus*, vol. 86 (1904) and vol. 87 (1905). Kruyt was also fascinated by the megalithic speculations of W.J. Perry (1889-1940) and tried to explain many aspects of Toradja culture in terms of immigration and conquest. But on the whole he was careful not to let such hypotheses unduly influence his descriptions.

MAJOR WORKS: "Het koppensnellen der Toradja's van Midden Celebes en zijne beteekenis," *Verslagen en Mededeelingen der Koninklijke Academie van Wetenschappen*, 4e reeks, vol. 3 (1899), pp. 147-229; "De Rijstmoeder in de Indische Archipel," *Verslagen en Mededeelingen der Koninklijke*

Academie van Wetenschappen, 4e reeks, vol. 5 (1903), pp. 361-411; *Het Animisme van den Indischen Archipel* (The Hague: 1906); (with N. Adriani) *De Bare'e sprekende Toradja's van Midden Celebes* [3 vols.] (Batavia: 1910-1912; 2nd revised ed., Amsterdam: 1950-1951); "Measa, een bijdrage tot het dynamisme der Bare'e sprekende Toradja's en enkele omwonende volken," *Bijdragen van het Koninklijk Instituut voor Taal-, Land- en Volkenkunde van Nederlandsch Indie*, vol. 74 (1918), pp. 233-266; vol. 75 (1919), pp. 36-133; vol. 76 (1920), pp. 1-116; "Koopen in midden Celebes," *Verslagen en Mededeelingen der Koninklijke Academie van Wetenschappen*, vol. 56, Serie B, no. 5 (1923), pp. 149-178; "Les statues en pierre de la région centrale de Celebes," *Revue anthropologique*, vol. 33 (1923), pp. 271-278; *Van Heiden tot Christen* (Oegstgeest: 1925); *De West-Toradja's op Midden Celebes* [4 vols.] (Amsterdam: 1937).

SOURCES: K.J. Brouwer, *Dr. A.C. Kruyt: Dienaar der Toradja's* (The Hague: 1951); I.H. Enklaar, "Kruyt, Albertus Christiaan" in: D. Nauta [et al.] (editors), *Biografisch Woordenboek voor de Geschiedenis van het Nederlandse Protestantisme* (Kampen: 1978), vol. 1, pp. 111-113; W.H. Rassers, "Herdenking van Albertus Christiaan Kruyt," *Jaarboek der Koninklijke Nederlandsche Akademie van Wetenschappen* (1948-1949), pp. 161-170; H.Th. Fischer, "In memoriam dr. Alb. C. Kruyt," *Indonesië*, vol. 2 (1948-1949), pp. 481-485; C.W.Th. van Boetzelaer van Asperen en Dubbeldam, "Albertus Christiaan Kruyt," *Bijdragen tot de Taal-, Land- en Volkenkunde*, vol. 105 (1949), pp. 143-146.

S.R. Jaarsma and J.J. de Wolf

Krzywicki, Ludwik (Ludwik Joachim Franciszek Krzywicki). Sociologist. Born in Płock (Poland) 21 August 1859, died in Warsaw (Poland) 10 June 1941. Krzywicki studied in Warsaw, Kraków, Leipzig (socio-economic studies), Paris (anthropology, ethnology and archaeology) and Lwów. He was awarded his Ph.D. in 1906. After Poland obtained independence he worked in the Main Statistical Bureau, at the Polish Free University, the Main School for Trade and the University of Warsaw (administering the Department of the History of Social Systems in the years 1921-1936). After 1921 he directed the studies of the Institute of Social Economics.

Krzywicki's scholarly work was never completely separate from his journalistic and popular writings. A sower of socialistic ideas on Polish soil, he took an active role in the workers' movement. He was one of the most outstanding theoreticians on the agricultural question. He also compiled methodological directives pertaining to historical materialism, linking elements of historical thought to the theory of evolution. He undertook studies from the perspective of the theory of social development. He investigated the mechanisms of the development of the classless society of the clan. He took up the problems of the relation of ideas to the economic system in which they evolve. Basing his historical materialism on data from various epochs in Europe, he stressed the importance of the dissemination of ideas. The complexity and variety of cultural phenomena inclined him to research that often crossed disciplinary boundaries. In ethnography Krzywicki was engaged in problems of methodology, formulating theoretical statements and popularizing foreign and domestic achievements in the field.

Krzywicki underscored the need for judicious and conscientious investigative studies. In his works he described the significance of research on folk legends and tales in which he saw traces of ancient customs. He was also interested in ethnic groupings of Polish lands (the history of settlement, the extent of the occurrence of dialects, economic relations, costumes and rituals).

MAJOR WORKS: *Kurpie* [*Kurpie*] (Warsaw: 1892); *Ludy: zarys antropologii etnicznej* [*Folk: Outline of Ethnic Anthropology*] (Warsaw: 1893); *Żmudź starożytna* [*Ancient Samogitia*] (Warsaw: 1906); *Ustroje społeczno-gospodarcze w okresie dzikości i barbarzyństwa* [*Socio-Economic Systems in Primitive and Barbarous Times*] (Warsaw: 1914); *Primitive Society and its Vital Statistics* (Warsaw and London: 1934); *Studia socjologiczne* [*Sociological Studies*] (Warsaw: 1951).

SOURCES: Małgorzata Terlecka (editor), *Historia etnografii polskiej* [*History of Polish Ethnography*] (Wrocław: 1973); Henryka Hołda-Róziewicz, *Ludwik Krzywicki jako teoretyk społeczeństw pierwotnych* [*Ludwik Krzywicki as Theoretician of Primitive Societies*] (Wrocław: 1976); Tadeusz Kowalik and Henryka Hołda-Róziewicz, *Ludwik Krzywicki* (Warsaw: 1976); Tadeusz Kowalik, "Krzywicki, Ludwik Joachim Franciszek" in: *Polski słownik biograficzny* [*Polish Biographical Dictionary*], vol. 15 (Wrocław: 1970), pp. 572-578.

Maria Niewiadomska and Iwona Grzelakowska
[Translation from Polish: Joel Janicki]

Kuftin, B.A. (Boris Alekseevich). Ethnographer, physical anthropologist, archaeologist.

Born in Samara (Russia) 21 April 1892, died in Moscow (Russian S.F.S.R.) 2 August 1953. Kuftin was a professor at Moscow University and an academician of the Academy of Sciences of the Georgian S.S.R. (from 1946).

Kuftin carried out a series of ethnographic expeditions in various regions of the central section of Russia, in the Baĭkal region, on the Amur, in Kazakhstan and in the Crimea. He made a great contribution to the study of the material culture of the peoples of the U.S.S.R. and of their ethnogenesis. After 1933, working in the Gosudarstvennyĭ Muzeĭ Gruzii (Georgian State Museum), he devoted special attention to archaeological research. Primarily based on his own material, he proved the Caucasian roots of Georgian culture. Broad historical-cultural generalizations are characteristic of the work of Kuftin.

MAJOR WORKS: "Kalendar' i pervobytnaĭa astronomiĭa kirgiz-kazakhskogo naroda," *Ėtnograficheskoe obozrenie*, vols. 111-112 (1916-1918), pp. 123-150; *Zhilishche krymskikh tatar v sviĭazi s istorieĭ zaseleniĭa poluostrova* (Moscow: 1925); *Material'naĭa kul'tura russkoĭ meshchery*, part 1 (Moscow: 1926); *Kratkiĭ ocherk severnogo buddizma i lamaizma b sviĭazi s istorieĭ ucheniĭa* (Moscow: 1927); *Arkheologicheskie raskopki v Trialeti: opyt periodizaĭsii pamiĭatnikov*, vol. 1 (Tbilisi: 1941); "K voprosu o drevneĭshikh kornĭakh gruzinskoĭ kul'tury na Kavkaze po dannym arkheologii," *Vestnik Gosudarstvennogo Muzeĭa Gruzii* [Tbilisi], vol. 12-B (1944), pp. 291-397; *Materialy k arkheologii Kolkhidy*, vol. 1-2 (Tbilisi: 1949-1950).

SOURCE: G. Debeĭs, "Pamĭati B.A. Kuftina," *Sovetskaĭa ėtnografiĭa*, no. 1, pp. 166-168 [contains bibliography].

A.M. Reshetov
[Translation from Russian: Thomas L. Mann]

Kuper, Hilda Beemer. Anthropologist.

Born in Bulawayo (Rhodesia, now Zimbabwe) 23 August 1911. Kuper studied anthropology with WINIFRED HOERNLÉ and ISAAC SCHAPERA at the University of the Witwatersrand, where she obtained a B.A. in 1930 and an M.A. in 1934. While an undergraduate she began research on Indians in the Johannesburg slums. Later as a research assistant for the South African Institute of Race Relations she studied the socioeconomic effects of liquor laws on women. This early research reflected her lifelong concern with racism in South Africa. She received her Ph.D. in anthropology in 1942 from the London School of Economics where she served as a research assistant to BRONISLAW MALINOWSKI and was influenced by psychology and

Marxism. Her dissertation research in Swaziland, funded by the International African Institute, was the beginning of a lifetime of research for which she received the Rivers Memorial Medal. She considered stratification, rank, power and interracial relations the most useful concepts to understand Swazi society, which was a departure from the prevailing functional social anthropological theories of the time. Her dissertation was published in two volumes: *The Uniform of Colour* and *An African Aristocracy*. Upon her arrival in Swaziland in 1934, Kuper met King Sobhuza and resided with the Queen Mother during her initial fieldwork, personal contacts that were maintained over the next forty years and led to her being appointed Sobhuza's official biographer in 1972.

Kuper taught at the University of Witwatersrand (1940-1945); the University of Natal (1959-1962); and the University of California, Los Angeles (1963-1978). She received numerous postdoctoral fellowships including: Simon Senior Research Fellowship, Manchester, England (1958-1959); National Science Foundation (1966-1968); Guggenheim (1969-1970); Ford Foundation (1972-1975); and Center for Advanced Studies in Behavioral Sciences, Palo Alto (1976-1977). Kuper emphasized humanism in anthropology, for from her first research she realized that anthropological data could not be objective. She published short stories based on her fieldwork and thoughtful articles on apartheid in South African periodicals. Kuper considered her play, *A Witch in My Heart*, the best ethnography she ever wrote. *Sobhuza II* was the culmination of a lifetime of research among the Swazi in which she combined history, interviews and ethnography to show the role of King Sobhuza in his social and cultural milieu.

MAJOR WORKS: *The Uniform of Colour* (Johannesburg: 1947); *An African Aristocracy* (London: 1947); *The Swazi* (London: 1952) *The Shona* (London: 1955); *Indian People of Natal* (Natal: 1960); *Inhliziyo Ngumthakathi* (Pietermaritzburg: 1962); *The Swazi: a South African Kingdom* (New York: 1963); *Bite of Hunger: a Novel of Africa* (New York: 1965); *A Witch in My Heart: a Play Set in Swaziland in the 1930s* (London: 1970); "Bird of the storm" in: Meyer Fortes and Sheila Patterson (editors), *Studies in African Social Anthropology* (New York: 1975), pp. 221-227; *Sobhuza II: Ngwenyama and King of Swaziland* (New York: 1978); *Biography as Interpretation* (Bloomington: 1981); (editor) *African Law: Adaptation and Development* (Los Angeles: 1965); (editor) *Urbanization and Migration in West Africa* (Los Angeles: 1965).

SOURCES: Hilda Kuper, "Function, history, biography" in: George S. Stocking, Jr. (editor), *Functionalism Historicized* (Madison: 1984) (= *History of Anthropology*, vol. 2), pp. 192-213; L.L. Langness and Gelya Frank, *Lives: an Anthropological Approach to Biography* (Novato: 1981), pp. 143-154; Katy Moran, "Hilda Beemer Kuper" in: Ute Gacs [et al.] (editors), *Women Anthropologists: a Biographical Dictionary* (New York: 1988), pp. 194-201.

Nancy J. Schmidt

Kuret, Niko. Romance-language specialist, folklorist/ethnologist, translator. Born in Trieste (Austria-Hungary, now Italy) 24 April 1906. Kuret studied Romance languages in Ljubljana. At first he translated, directed and wrote plays for the theater. From this base he went into research and the theoretical study of the contemporary and folk theatre and liturgical plays. The result of his research can be found in his fundamental work on folk theater, plays, masques and masquerades among Slovenians. Kuret's research is based on precise fieldwork, knowledge of the literature and wide-ranging comparison with the culture of other nationalities.

Kuret also devoted much energy to research on the customs of the yearly cycle. Also important was his contribution to the development of visual documentation. It was under his direction that the section on folk customs at the Institute for Slovene Ethnography at the Slovenian Academy of Science and Art in Ljubljana used film as a means of documenting ethnological research.

MAJOR WORKS: *Ziljsko štehvanje in njegov evropski okvir* (Ljubljana: 1963); *Praznično leto Slovencev* [4 vols.] (Celje: 1965-1971; later ed., Ljubljana: 1989); *Jaslice na Slovenskem* (Ljubljana: 1981); *Maske slovenskih pokrajin* (Ljubljana: 1984).

SOURCES: Vilko Novak, "Etnološko delo Nika Kureta," *Traditiones*, nos. 5-6 (1979), pp. 11-17; Helena Ložar-Podlogar, "Bibliografija etnoloških objav Nika Kureta," *Traditiones*, nos. 5-6 (1979), pp. 18-30.

Mojca Ravnik
[Translation from Slovene: Corrine Leskovar]

l

La Barre, Weston. Anthropologist. Born in Uniontown (Pennsylvania) 13 December 1911, now living in North Carolina. La Barre has made major contributions to psychoanalytic anthropology.

He was educated at Princeton (A.B., summa cum laude, 1933) and Yale (Ph.D. with Honors, 1937). A research internship at the Menninger Clinic followed a Social Science Research Council Post-Doctoral Research Training Fellowship. La Barre's first field trip was to the Kiowa with a Santa Fe Laboratory of Anthropology group; his second, to study peyotism in fifteen Plains Indian societies, was jointly financed by the American Museum of Natural History and the Yale Institute of Human Relations. At Yale his principal influences were EDWARD SAPIR, LESLIE SPIER and John Dollard. La Barre's doctoral dissertation on *The Peyote Cult* has been published thirteen times by five publishers (these figures include a Spanish edition). As Sterling Fellow of Yale he studied the Aymara and the Uru of the Lake Titicaca plateau. As a Guggenheim Fellow he wrote on the Orient. La Barre was the first incumbent of the Géza Róheim Memorial Award in 1958. As a National Science Foundation fellow, and again jointly with the Viking Fund, he lived several years in London, Rome and Paris (where CLAUDE LÉVI-STRAUSS was his official sponsor) and wrote *The Ghost Dance*. As a Visiting Scholar at the Rockefeller Villa Serbelloni, Bellagio, Lake Como, he wrote *Muelos: a Stone Age Superstition About Sexuality*. With others of the committee on adolescence of the Group for the Advancement of Psychiatry, where he was invited consultant twenty-one times, he wrote *Normal Adolescence, Its Dynamics and Impact*. *They Shall Take Up Serpents* was a psychiatric study of the Southern snakehandling cult. La Barre edited some hundred volumes of older classics in the reprint series *Landmarks in Anthropology* and has published several hundred articles in seven European languages.

La Barre has taught at Rutgers and Duke University, where he was the James B. Duke Professor of Anthropology for many years. He has also taught in summer school at New York University, the Universities of Wisconsin, Northwestern and Minnesota and at the University of North Carolina Medical School in Chapel Hill.

La Barre's approach to anthropology is holistic and he considers ethnography, linguistics, physical anthropology, archaeology, prehistory and psychology all required in the proper study of mankind. In *The Human Animal* he proposed that, although biological race has nothing to do with specific cultural traits, nevertheless generic or species-specific human biology must account for the human potential for culture and language, particularly handedness and the neotenous human brain. A similarly holistic view is propounded in La Barre's principal work, *The Ghost Dance: Origins of Religion*.

La Barre characterizes himself as "a psychiatrically oriented anthropologist with a firm foundation in human biology."

MAJOR WORKS: *The Peyote Cult* (New Haven: 1938); *The Aymara Indians of the Lake Titicaca Plateau, Bolivia* (Menasha, Wisc.: 1948) (= *Memoirs of the American Anthropological Association*, no. 68); *The Human Animal* (Chicago: 1954); *They Shall Take Up Serpents* (Minneapolis: 1962); *The Ghost Dance: Origins of Religion* (Garden City, N.Y.: 1970); *Muelos: a Stone Age Superstition about Sexuality* (New York: 1984); (as a member of the Group for the Advancement of Psychiatry) *Normal Adolescence, Its Dynamics and Impact* (New York: 1968); (editor) *Landmarks in Anthropology* [reprint series] (New York: 1968-1971); *Shadow of Childhood: Neoteny and the Biology of Religion* (Norman: 1991); *Culture in Context: the Selected Writings of Weston La Barre* (Durham, N.C.: 1980).

SOURCES: Howard F. Stein, "Towards a psychoanalytic bioanthropology: a retrospective study of the contributions of Weston La Barre," *Journal of Social and Biological Structures*, vol. 6 (1983), pp. 249-264; George A. De Vos (editor), *Special Issue of the Journal of Psychoanalytic Anthropology Dedicated to Psychoanalytic Anthropologist Weston La Barre* (New York: 1986) (= *Journal of Psychoanalytic Anthropology*, vol. 9, no. 3); Benjamin Kilbourne, "Weston La Barre: a tribute," *Journal of Psychoanalytic Anthropology*, vol. 9 (1983), pp. 193-198.

Lafitau, Joseph-François. Priest, Jesuit missionary. Born in Bordeaux (France) May 1681, died in Bordeaux (France) July 1746. Brother of Pierre-François (1685-1764), Bishop of Sisteron (France). The Lafitau family were wine merchants and bankers. Lafitau received a typical Jesuit education, finished his novitiate in 1698, studied philosophy and rhetoric at Pau, and then taught at a series of Jesuit colleges, culminating at the Collège Louis-le-Grand, completing the course in theology in 1711. He read widely in classical and modern languages on the customs and languages of ancient peoples and on the New World; his reading provided background for his studies of the customs of the Iroquois.

In 1711 he was granted permission to join the mission in New France and was ordained a priest. He arrived in Québec in 1712, was assigned to Sault-Saint-Louis (Caughnawaga) (opposite Montréal) and remained nearly six years. He studied the Iroquoian language with Julian Garnier, S.J., veteran of fifty years in the Iroquois missions. Meanwhile he pronounced his vows on 25 August 1716 at Montréal. He commenced to gather information on cultural topics from native informants, he read the *Relations* of his predecessors and mined his knowledge of antiquity for leads. His scientific approach combined theory with verification. He was an excellent observer. Lafitau was the first to employ botanical plates in the field to elicit information from native informants. His discovery of a native New World species of ginseng, previously reported from China as an aphrodisiac, created a furor in Europe and nearly eradicated the species in the Saint Lawrence Valley. His ability to combine observation with theoretical inference can also be seen in his observations on the longhouse and residence, the village council as the module of Iroquois government, and the ecological basis of material culture, and in the fact that he discovered classificatory kinship a century before LEWIS HENRY MORGAN.

Recalled to France in 1717 to present at court a memorial opposing the brandy trade, he was retained as procurator of the missions in 1722. He shared this duty with another Jesuit, thus Lafitau was free to write. He returned to Canada during 1727-1728 as superior of the mission.

Lafitau is of especial interest to anthropologists. He departed from other grand comparators in insisting on describing cultures in their own terms. He was largely ignored by the great minds of the Enlightenment. Voltaire ridiculed him. But he was read by the Scottish moral philosophers and a host of later intellectual historians. In his own day Lafitau was a man of the past; but he was a voyager in the mainstream of empirical ethnography. Modern French savants have reclaimed him.

MAJOR WORKS: *Mémoire ... concernant la precieuse plante du ginseng* (Paris: 1718); *Moeurs des sauvages ameriquains, comparées aus moeurs des premiers temps ...* [2 vols.] (Paris: 1724) [tr.: *Customs of the American Indians Compared with the Customs of the Primitive Times* (edited by William N. Fenton and Elizabeth L. Moore) [2 vols.] (Toronto: 1974-1977)]; *Histoire des découvertes et conquestes des Portugais dans le Nouveau Monde ...* [2 vols.] (Paris: 1733).

SOURCES: William N. Fenton and Elizabeth L. Moore (translators and editors), Joseph-François Lafitau, *Customs of the American Indians Compared with the Customs of the Primitive Times* [2 vols.] (Toronto: 1974-1977); William N. Fenton, "Lafitau, Joseph-François" in: *Dictionary of Canadian Biography* (Toronto: 1966-), vol. 3, pp. 334-338; Michèle Duchet, "Discours ethnologique et discours historique: le texte de Lafitau," *Studies on Voltaire and the XVIIIth Century*, vols. 151-155 (1976), pp. 607-623; Edna Hindie Lemay, "Introduction, choix de texte et notes" in: Joseph-François Lafitau, *Moeurs des sauvages américains: comparées aux moeurs des premiers temps* [2 vols.] (Paris: 1983), pp. 5-38.

William N. Fenton

LaFlesche, Francis.

LaFlesche, Francis. Ethnologist. Born on the Omaha Reservation (Nebraska) 1857, died near Macy (Nebraska) 5 September 1932. LaFlesche was formally trained at a Presbyterian mission school, and he took a degree in law at National University in 1892. He was awarded an honorary LL.D. by the University of Nebraska in 1926. LaFlesche was a member of a prominent and progressive Omaha Indian family. Joseph LaFlesche, his father, was a chief of his tribe; and two of his sisters—Susette, an educator and lecturer, and Susan, a physician—enjoyed some renown as accomplished women and champions of Indian rights. Francis LaFlesche toured the East with a Ponca chief in 1879 and, afterwards, became employed as a clerk with the Bureau of Indian Affairs. During 1910-1929 he was an ethnologist with the Bureau of American Ethnology (BAE).

In 1881 LaFlesche was introduced to anthropology as an informant and assistant to ALICE CUNNINGHAM FLETCHER, with whom he formed a very close personal and professional relationship. While the intense personal relationship lasted until Fletcher's death—Fletcher legally adopting LaFlesche in 1891—LaFlesche grew professionally independent following his appointment to the BAE. At first he had focused on anthropological studies of his own tribe, but in time he came to concentrate on the Osage, particularly on their ceremonies and music. In addition to his publications, he left a large body of notes and sound recordings.

MAJOR WORKS: (with Alice C. Fletcher) "The Omaha tribe," *Annual Report of the Bureau of American Ethnology*, vol. 27 (1911), pp. 17-654; "The Osage tribe: rite of the chiefs: sayings of the ancient men," *Annual Report of the Bureau of American Ethnology*, vol. 36 (1921), pp. 37-604; "The Osage tribe: the rite of vigil," *Annual Report of the Bureau of American Ethnology*, vol. 39 (1925), pp. 31-630; "The Osage tribe: rite of the Wa-xo'-be," *Annual Report of the Bureau of American Ethnology*, vol. 45 (1930), pp. 523-833; *A Dictionary of the Osage Language* (Washington: 1932) (= *Bureau of American Ethnology Bulletin*, no. 109).

SOURCES: Hartley B. Alexander, "Francis LaFlesche," *American Anthropologist*, vol. 35 (Washington: 1933), pp. 328-331; Michael Coleman, "The mission education of Francis LaFlesche," *American Studies in Scandinavia*, vol. 18 (1986), pp. 67-82; Alice C. Fletcher, "Francis LaFlesche" in: *Handbook of American Indians North of Mexico* (Washington: 1907) (= *Bureau of American Ethnology Bulletin*, no. 30), vol. 1, pp. 751-752; Fletcher and LaFlesche papers and LaFlesche manuscripts in the Smithsonian Institution National Anthropological Archives; Margot Liberty, "Francis LaFlesche: the Osage Odyssey" in: Margot Liberty, *American Indian Intellectuals* (editor) (St. Paul: 1978) (= *1976 Proceedings of the American Ethnological Society*), pp. 44-59; Margot Liberty, "Native American informants: the contribution of Francis LaFlesche" in: John V. Murra, *American Anthropology: the Early Years* (St. Paul: 1976), pp. 99-110; Joan Mark, "Francis LaFlesche: the American Indian as anthropologist," *Isis*, vol. 73 (1982), pp. 497-510; Ronald Walcott, "Francis LaFlesche: American Indian scholar," *Folklife Center News*, vol. 4 (1981), pp. 1, 10-11; Ronald Walcott, "Francis LaFlesche: the first professional American Indian ethnomusicologist" [unpublished paper in the Smithsonian Institution National Anthropological Archives] (1980).

James R. Glenn

Lagercrantz, Sture. Ethnologist. Born in Sweden 13 June 1910. Lagercrantz, who was the student of GERHARD K. LINDBLOM, received his Ph.D. in Stockholm in 1938. In 1944 he started teaching general and comparative ethnography at Uppsala University; he was Professor at Uppsala from 1962 to 1976.

His teaching and writing mainly concerned the ethnology of the African continent. Like his teacher Lindblom, Lagercrantz was an adherent of the Cultural-Historical School of ethnology, in its German-Austrian version.

His main interests are material culture and the distribution of customs related to twinship and anomalous births. In the realm of hunting methods, his scholarship encompassed not only Africa but the entire Eurasian continent. One of his important contributions to African ethnography is the editing and posthumous publication of KARL EDVARD LAMAN's manuscripts on the Kongo. Lagercrantz was also the editor of the series *Studia Ethnographica Upsaliensia.*

MAJOR WORKS: *Über willkommene und unwillkommene Zwillinge in Afrika* (Göteborg: 1941) (= *Etnografiska Studier*, vol. 12/13, pp. 5-292); *Contribution to the Ethnography of Africa* (Uppsala: 1950) (= *Studia Ethnographica Upsaliensia*, no. 1); *African Methods of Fire-Making* (Uppsala: 1954) (= *Studia Ethnographica Upsaliensia*, no. 10); (with B. Anell) *Geophagical Customs* (Uppsala: 1958) (= *Studia Ethnographica Upsaliensia*, no. 17); *The Petrified Ones* (Uppsala: 1973) (= *Occasional Papers*, no. 1).

Anita Jacobson-Widding

Laman, Karl Edvard. Missionary, linguist, ethnographer, natural scientist. Born in Norrbärke, St. Kopparberg (Sweden) 18 March 1867, died in Stjärnorp (Sweden) 27 June 1944. Following his secondary education at Västerås, he began preparing to become a gardener. But, after a few years of study at the missionary training school at Kristinehamn, he went to the Congo (modern Zaïre) in 1891 in the service of the Svenska Missionsförbundet (Swedish Missionary Society). Prior to his departure for the Congo he prepared himself by studying Congolese languages. He wrote early articles for the newly founded publication *Minsamu Miayenge* [*The Commandment of Peace*] and created handbooks and manuals for the schools. His first major work was an edition of the *New Testament* and a translation of the *Old Testament* printed in London in 1905.

MAJOR WORKS: (with J.W. Håkanson and R. Walfridsson) *Lörobok i kongospråket (Kikongo)* (Stockholm: 1912) [tr.: *Grammar of the Congo Language (Kikongo)* (New York: 1912)]; (with W. Heinitz) *The Musical Accent or Intonation in the Kongo Language, with Graphic Schemes and Tables of Notes* (Stockholm: 1922); *Svensk kikongo ordbok* (Stockholm: 1931); *Dictionnaire Kikongo-Français, avec une étude phonétique décrivant les dialectes les plus importants de la langue dite kikongo* (Brussels: 1936); *The Kongo*, vol. 1 (Uppsala: 1953) (= *Studia Upsaliensia*, vol. 4); *The Kongo*, vol. 2 Uppsala: 1953) (= *Studia Upsaliensia*, vol. 8); *The Kongo*, vol. 3 (Uppsala: 1953) (= *Studia Upsaliensia*, vol. 12); *The Kongo*, vol. 4 (Uppsala: 1953) (= *Studia Upsaliensia*, vol. 16).

SOURCES: Bertil Söderberg and Ragnar Widman, *Publications en Kikongo: bibliographie relative aux contributions suédoises entre 1885 et 1970* (Uppsala and Stockholm: 1978); Bertil Söderberg, "Karl Edvard Lamans litterära verk, en analytisk bibliografi," *Svensk missionstidskrift* (1981), pp. 73-95; Bertil Söderberg, *Karl Edvard Laman: missionär-språkforskare-etnograf* (Stockholm: 1985); Wyatt MacGaffey, "Report on the Laman archive" [stencil] (Haverford College, Penn.: 1984).

Bertil Söderberg
[*Translation from Swedish: Robert B. Marks Ridinger*]

Lambrecht, Francis Hubert. Missionary, anthropologist, linguist, administrator. Born in Kortrijk (Belgium) 6 March 1895, died in Baguio (Philippines) 29 October 1978. Lambrecht spent most of his career in the Mountain Province of northern Luzon, where he was a missionary to the Ifugao.

As a youth in Belgium, he attended St. Amand's College and Roeselare Seminary. In 1914 he entered the Congregation of the Immaculate Heart of Mary (CICM) at Scheut. Lambrecht was ordained in 1923 and arrived in the Philippines on 9 October 1924. He was first assigned to Kiangan (Ifugao) where he began the study of Philippine languages and cultures. His first paper (co-authored with Jerome Moerman) was on Kiangan tales and songs. During ensuing decades, he was to produce numerous studies of Ifugao culture. As a missionary as well as an anthropologist, he took a special interest in the religion and ritual of the mountain peoples of Ifugao. His major publication of this period was *Mayawyaw Ritual*, which was published in seven parts between 1932 and 1957. Transcriptions and translations of the Ifugao epics (*hu'dhud*) were published between 1957 and 1967. Studies of the Kalinga epics (*ullalim*) were published in 1970 and 1974. Lambrecht's linguistic investigations led to the publication in 1978 of an *Ifugaw-English Dictionary*. Selections from his many writings were collected and reprinted in a commemorative issue of the *Journal of Northern Luzon* in 1981.

Lambrecht's contributions reflect an intensive interest in the Ifugao, extending over a period of several decades. His detailed studies of Ifugao language, epics and rituals provide exceptional documentation of a complex Southeast Asian culture.

MAJOR WORKS: (with Fr. Francisco Billiet) *Studies on Kalinga Ullalim and Ifugaw Orthography* (Baguio City: 1970); (with Fr. Francisco Billiet) *The Kalinga Ullalim II* (Baguio City: 1974); *Ifugaw-English Dictionary* (Baguio City: 1978); *Mayawyaw Ritual* [parts 1-5] (Washington: 1932-1941) (= *Publications of the Catholic Anthropological Conference*, vol. 4, nos. 1-5); *Mayawyaw Ritual* [parts 6-7] (Manila: 1955-1957) (= *University of Manila Journal of East Asiatic Studies*, vol. 4, no. 4 (October 1955), pp. 1-155; vol. 6, no. 1 (January 1957), pp. 1-28).

SOURCES: Bonifacio V. Ramos, "Father Francis Hubert Lambrecht, CICM (1895-1978): a bio-bibliography," *Journal of Northern Luzon*, vol. 11, nos. 1-2 (July 1980-January 1981), pp. 1-24; John Van Bauwel, "In memorium: Father Francis Hubert Lambrecht, CICM (1895-1978)," *Journal of Northern Luzon*, vol. 8, nos. 1-2 (July 1977-January 1978), pp. 1-8.

Lee S. Dutton

Landtman, Gunnar. Anthropologist, sociologist. Born in Helsinki (Finland) 6 May 1878, died in Helsinki (Finland) 30 October 1940. Landtman was one of the students of EDWARD WESTERMARCK who began the practice of anthropological research in Finland in its modern sense: the systematic comparison of cultures based on fieldwork among non-European peoples. In Landtman's eyes, sociology and social anthropology were synonymous: sociology encompassed social science in all of its ramifications. The roots of the approach to sociology that Landtman represented lay in British anthropology. Landtman studied for some time in England, where he was a student of A.C. HADDON, and where he wrote his dissertation, *The Origin of Priesthood*, and his study, *The Primary Cause of Social Inequality*. The origin of social differentiation was in fact the problematic with which Landtman's original studies were to be concerned later on when he taught at the University of Helsinki.

Among anthropologists, Landtman is known primarily for his fieldwork (1910-1912) among the Kiwai Papuans of New Guinea. The aggregation of a large quantity of notes and artifacts typified his fieldwork in New Guinea. Landtman organized two separate collections of the artifacts he had gathered: the main collection for the National Museum of Finland (described in *Ethnographic Collection from the Kiwai District of British New Guinea*) and a corresponding collection for Cambridge University in England (University Museum of Archaeology and Anthropology). The objects of Landtman's research and collecting activities in New Guinea were not limited to material culture; he also collected a sizable quantity of Kiwai Papuan folk tales. Fifteen years were to pass, however, before Landtman published the scientific results of his fieldwork among the Kiwai Papuans in *The Kiwai Papuans of British New Guinea*. This delay was due in part to World War I, which prevented Landtman from getting to London to organize his materials for publication. However, during this interval, he published several briefer studies about the Kiwai Papuans and the comprehensive collection of folk tales, *The Folk-Lore of Kiwai Papuans*. Landtman's study, *The Kiwai Papuans of British New Guinea*, received widespread recognition following its publication and was considered to be among the classics of anthropology. Landtman was among the first practitioners of Haddon's "intensive study of limited areas" method. The modern fieldwork tradition is generally associated with BRONISLAW

MALINOWSKI, but it is noteworthy that Landtman completed his fieldwork in New Guinea two years before Malinowksi left his armchair in the British Museum for the Trobriand Islands where he engaged in a type of fieldwork very much like that of Landtman earlier in New Guinea.

Landtman was primarily a social researcher, an ethnoanthropologist, who exhaustively gathered and preserved facts and presented them in a purely descriptive manner. This approach accorded with Landtman's concept of sociology, the aims of which he considered to be the explanation and presentation of relevant facts.

MAJOR WORKS: *The Origin of Priesthood* (Ekenaes, Finland: 1905); *The Primary Cause of Social Inequality* (Helsingfors: 1909) (= *Öfversigt af Finska Vetenskaps-Societetens Förhandlingar*, vol. 51, afd. B, no. 2); *The Folk-Tales of the Kiwai Papuans* (Helsingfors: 1917) (= *Acta Societatis Scientiarum Fennicae*, vol. 47); *The Kiwai Papuans of British New Guinea* (London: 1927); *Ethnographical Collection from the Kiwai District of British New Guinea* (Helsingfors: 1933); *The Origin of the Inequality of the Social Classes* (Chicago and London: 1938).

SOURCES: Rolf Lagerborg, "Gunnar Landtman," *Societatis scientarum fennica årsbok-vuosikirja*, vol. 21C, no. 1 (1942); Ragnar Numelin, "Gunnar Landtman," *Historiska och litteraturhistoriska studier*, vol. 40 (1965), pp. 5-44.

Risto Sarho
[Translation from Finnish: Joseph David Rudman]

Lang, Andrew. Folklorist, ethnologist, poet. Born in Selkirk (Scotland) 31 March 1844, died in Banchory (Scotland) 20 July 1912. Lang was educated at St. Andrews University and Oxford and was elected a fellow of Merton College at Oxford in 1868. His early interest was in the classics and he went on to translate a number of works from Greek. By 1872 he had published the first of several volumes of verse. In 1875 he married, gave up his fellowship at Merton and became a professional writer. He was very successful at his new calling, publishing articles in many of the leading magazines of the day. He also wrote dozens of books, ranging from novels and biographies to treatments of folklore, mythology and religion.

In an early article, Lang demolished Max Müller's contention that myths are "a disease of language"—something no longer understood because of linguistic change—by demonstrating that similar myths were found in cultures separated by both space and language. Lang argued that myths reflect how people think and are in some sense a form of history. He also took JAMES G. FRAZER and E.B. TYLOR to task for simplistic evolutionary approaches to complicated primitive cultures. Lang concluded that the commonly encountered primitive belief in a benevolent creator-god (a forerunner of theories of primitive monotheism) overturned evolutionist thought on religion. Technology might proceed in a predictable progressive fashion, but religion could not be so easily explained.

Lang's earlier books on myth and religion were more influential than his later ones, but he continued to publish prodigiously as long as he lived. In many ways a better critic than an original thinker, Lang performed a service for ethnology and the history of religions by examining current theories in light of common sense and the ethnographic record. In another area he did not fare so well. Lang was susceptible to claims of psychic phenomena and wrote many articles and two major books on the subject. In 1911 he was president of the Society for Psychical Research, forfeiting much of the respect and prestige his earlier work had earned him among scholars.

MAJOR WORKS: *Custom and Myth* (London: 1884); *Myth, Ritual and Religion* (London: 1887); *Modern Mythology* (London: 1897); *The Making of Religion* (London: 1898); *Magic and Religion* (London: 1901); *Social Origins* (London: 1903); *The Secret of the Totem* (London: 1905); *The World of Homer* (London: 1910).

SOURCES: Benjamin C. Ray, "Lang, Andrew" in: Mircea Eliade (editor), *The Encyclopedia of Religion* (New York: 1987), vol. 8, pp. 438-439; "Lang, Andrew" in: *The Dictionary of National Biography*, 3rd supplement (Oxford: 1927), pp. 319-323; Jacob W. Gruber, "Lang, Andrew" in: David L. Sills (editor), *International Encyclopedia of the Social Sciences* (New York: 1968-1979), vol. 8, pp. 580-581.

David Lonergan

Langsdorff, Georg Heinrich (Russian form of name: G.I. (Grigoriĭ Ivanovich) Langsdorf). Traveler, ethnographer. Born in southwestern Germany 6 (18) April 1774, died in Freiburg (Germany) 17 (29) June 1852. A German by birth, Langsdorff spent a large part of his life in Russian service. In 1803 he was chosen to be a corresponding member of the St. Petersburg Academy of Sciences. Between 1803 and 1808 he took part in the circumnavigation of the world on the ship under the leadership of Ivan Fedorovich Kruzenshtern (1770-1846) and ĬUriĭ Fedorovich Lisĭanskiĭ (1773-1837). In 1812, having been elected as an extraordinary academician of the St. Petersburg Academy of Sciences, he was immediately appointed as Russian General Consul in Brazil. He headed an expedition to that country during 1821-1829, the archives of which were long mislaid but rediscovered in Leningrad in about 1930. They consist of 4,000 pages of manuscripts and about 600 sketches, plans and maps. These unique ethnographic materials have been of exceptional importance to scholarship.

MAJOR WORKS: "Opisanie uzorov, navodimykh zhitelĭami ostrova Vashingtona na ikh tele," *Tekhnologicheskiĭ zhurnal*, vol. 7 no. 2 (1810), pp. 114-117, 103-112 [sic]; *Bemerkungen auf einer Reise um die Welt im Jahren 1803 bis 1807*, vol. 1 (Frankfurt-am-Main: 1812) [tr.: *Voyages and Travels in Various Parts of the World during the Years 1803, 1804, 1805, 1806 and 1807* [2 vols.] (London: 1813-1814)]; *Materialy èkspedifsii akademika Grigoriĭa Ivanovicha Langsdorfa v Braziliĭu v 1812-1829 gg.: nauchnoe opisanie* (Leningrad: 1873).

SOURCES: S.A. Tokarev, *Istoriĭa russkoĭ ètnografii (dooktĭabr'skiĭ period)* (Moscow: 1966), p. 156; B.N. Komissarov, *Grigoriĭ Ivanovich Langsdorf* (Leningrad: 1975).

A.M. Reshetov
[Translation from Russian: Thomas L. Mann]

Lanternari, Vittorio. Ethnologist. Born in Ancona (Italy) 11 November 1918. With ERNESTO DE MARTINO and ANGELO BRELICH, Lanternari is among the major representatives of the Italian historical school of religious studies. His most salient contributions have been oriented toward the development of a secular historiography of religion and are characterized by a unique integration of the anthropological and the religious-historical perspectives.

While his early training had been in the agricultural sciences (University of Bologna), the end of racial discrimination in the post-war period allowed Lanternari to resume his humanistic studies at the University of Rome, which he pursued under the guidance of RAFFAELE PETTAZZONI. In 1946 Lanternari presented his thesis on the history of religions. In 1951 he was appointed assistant professor at the the University of Rome; he taught history of religions and ethnology as *libero docente* at the University of Bari from 1959 to 1968; and has been professor at the University of Rome since 1972.

In one of his earlier works (*La grande festa*) Lanternari conducted an historical-comparative analysis of New Year's festivities, in which religious phenomena were studied in light of their respective systems of socioeconomic production. His approach inaugurated a materialist ethnology of religion in Italy, seeking as it did to draw the symbolic and the technical-economic dimensions of sociocultural life into a single framework. Lanternari's analyses of religious phenomena in primitive cultures show a concern for critical confrontation with the categories of Western civilization; indeed, the attempt to broaden the historical-religious "object" is to be found throughout his work. His discussion of emergent religious liberation movements (*Movimenti religiosi*, translated into six European languages and Japanese) and his treatment of the larger issues of Third World modernization and attendant processes of cultural transformation (*Occidente e Terzo Mondo*) constitute landmarks in Italian ethnological studies and contributed significantly to the intellectual debates of the 1960s.

Focusing his research on religious phenomena and the relations between peasant economies and social structures, In 1971 Lanternari conducted fieldwork in Ghana (especially among the Nzima) as a member of VINIGI GROTTANELLI's ethnographic expedition. He went back to Ghana in 1974 and 1977, and the results of his research there appear in *Dei, profeti e contadini*.

MAJOR WORKS: *La grande festa: vita rituale e sistemi di produzione nelle società tradizionali* (Milan: 1959); *Movimenti religiosi di libertà e di salvezza dei popoli oppressi* (Milan: 1960; revised ed., Milan: 1977) [tr.: *Les mouvements religieux de liberté et de salut des peuples opprimés* (Paris: 1983)]; *Miti e leggende: Oceania* (Turin: 1963); *Occidente e Terzo Mondo: incontri di civiltà e religioni differenti* (Bari: 1967); *Antropologia e Imperialismo, e altri saggi* (Turin: 1974); *Crisi e ricerca d'identità* (Naples: 1977); *L'incivilimento dei barbari* (Bari: 1983); *Festa, carisma, apocalipse* (Palermo: 1983); *Identità e differenza: percorsi storico-antropologici* (Naples: 1986); *Dei, profeti, contadini: incontri nel Ghana* (Naples: 1988).

SOURCES: [various authors] Reviews of *The Religions of the Oppressed*, *Current Anthropology*, vol. 6 (1965), pp. 447-465; P. Cherchi, "Introduzione a V. Lanternari" in: Vittorio Lanternari, *Preistoria e folklore* (Sassari: 1984), pp. 7-74; P. Cherchi, "Etnos e apocalisse in due recenti libri di Vittorio Lanternari," *Studi Bresciani*, no. 1 (1986), pp. 63-75; J. Henninger, "Primitialopfer und Neujahrfest: Vittorio Lanternari: Publikationen über Primitialopfer und Neujahrfest: Wertung von Vittorio Lanternari Ergebnissen" in: *Antropica: Gedenkschrift zum 100. Geburtstag von W. Schmidt* (St. Agustin: 1968), pp. 153-189; E. Hobsbawm, Review of *Movimenti religiosi di libertà e di salvezza dei popoli oppressi*, *Times Literary Supplement* (29 September 1961), p. 649; M. Massenzio, "Mito e dinamica storica: il caso dei 'Cargo-Cults'," *MondOperaio* (January 1990), pp. 147-150; M. Nowaczyk, "Rozmawia z prof. Vittorio Lanternarim o nowych kultach religijnych," *Argumenty* [Warsaw] (4 March 1984); P.G. Solinas, "Idealismo, Marxismo, Strutturalismo" in: Pietro Clemente [et al.], *L'antropologia italiana: un secolo di storia* (Bari: 1985), pp. 241-244; I. Tanoni, "L'etnoantropologia religiosa di Vittorio Lanternari," *Il Tetto*, no. 152/3 (1989), pp. 261-280.

Giorgio de Finis
[Translation from Italian: Paolo Gnecco]

Larco Hoyle, Rafael. Businessperson, planter, archaeological writer, museum director, collector/connoisseur of prehistoric Peruvian artifacts. Born in Hacienda Chiclín, Virú Valley (Peru) 18 May 1901, died in Lima (Peru) 23 October 1966. Larco is famous in Peru for donating his vast artifact collections to the Lima museum he founded in memory of his father, Rafael Larco Herrera. He is remembered by Peruvianist archaeologists for his excavations, his knowledge of north coast prehistory and his theory of the coastal origins of prehistoric Andean civilization.

Born to prosperous *hacienda* owners, Larco was educated to head the family agricultural and business interests, which focused on sugar cane production. He attended Colegio Nuestra Señora de Guadalupe and Barranco English Institute in Trujillo before leaving to complete high school in the United States, at Tome High School in Maryland. He studied agriculture at Cornell University, then engineering at New York University. Larco was interested in the technology related to mechanizing the sugar cane industry and traveled to cane-producing areas (Cuba, Puerto Rico and Hawaii) as well as to Europe before returning to Peru in 1923 to manage *Haciendas* Chiclín and Salamanca. He became Mayor of Trujillo in 1938.

Not long after Larco's return from studies abroad, his father gave him 600 prehistoric artifacts. He was active in archaeological fieldwork by the early 1930s. Although he was not a professionally trained archaeologist, Larco kept detailed records of his own excavations in the manner of professional archaeologists. In this he was exceptional, and he was accepted as a colleague by many practicing archaeologists of his day. Larco worked extensively in several coastal valleys before other Peruvians or many North Americans excavated there. MAX UHLE's excavations at Moche were the first documented for the entire north coastal region, while WENDELL CLARK BENNETT's north coast excavations for the American Museum of Natural History in 1936 were the first in the region by a North American.

As Larco's collection grew he developed sensitivity to style change and supporting evidence for it. The stylistic sequence he developed from excavating Mochica (Moche) gravelots remains the basis for Virú-Chicama Early Intermediate Period pottery chronology. He knew his collection (more than 40,000 items at his death) well and developed personal interpretations of Mochica (Moche) iconography (*Los Mochicas I* and *II*, *Chécan*). He proposed coastal origins for complex Andean societies following finds of Chavínoid artifacts in Cupisnique Quebrada. Peruvian scholarship of that day was focused on the question of autochthonous or diffused sources of cultural development. Despite having detailed field notes, Larco rarely documented his published interpretations in terms of stratigraphy or associations from field data. His records are generally unavailable to scholars.

Larco's artifact collection from his purchases and excavations was kept in a museum at Chiclín, which he directed and where he offered hospitality to North American archaeologists. He hosted the Chiclín Conference for members of the Virú Valley Project in 1946, at which he and the team members evaluated the state of the art of prehistoric Andean cultural chronology. He published several chronologies, including revisions and refinements of his original works (*Las épocas peruanas*). There was a hiatus in his writing due to his business interests until he moved to Lima around 1960. It was there that he wrote his most comprehensive work (*Perú*) and founded the Museo Larco Herrera in Pueblo Libre, which houses the vast Chiclín collections.

MAJOR WORKS: *Los Mochicas I* (Lima: 1938); *Los Mochicas II* (Lima: 1939); *Los Cupisniques: trabajo presentado al Congreso Internacional de Americanistas de Lima, XXVII sesión* (Lima: 1941); *La cultura Virú* (Buenos Aires: 1945). "La cultura Salinar," *Revista Geográfica Americana*, vol. 23, no. 141 (1945), pp. 327-336; "A culture sequence for the North Coast of Peru" in: Julian H. Steward (editor), *Handbook of South American Indians*, vol. 2 (Washington: 1946), pp. 149-175; *Cronología arqueológica del Norte del Perú* (Buenos Aires: 1948); *La cultura Santa* (Lima:1960); *Las épocas peruanas* (Lima: 1963); *La cerámica de Vicús* (Lima: 1965); *Chécan: Essay on Erotic elements in Peruvian Art* (Geneva: 1965); *Archaeología mundi: Perú* (Geneva: 1966); *La cerámica de Vicús y sus nexos con las demás culturas* (Lima: 1967).

SOURCES: "Larco Hoyle, Rafael" in: *Who's Who in Latin America* (3rd ed., Stanford: 1946-1951), part 3, p. 177; Gordon R. Willey, "The Chiclín Conference for Peruvian Archaeology, 1946" in: "Notes and news," *American Antiquity*, vol. 12 (1946), pp. 132-134; Clifford Evans, "Rafael Larco Hoyle, 1901-1966," *American Antiquity*, vol. 33 (1968), pp. 233-236.

Kathryn M. Cleland

Laufer, Berthold. Anthropologist, curator, philologist, Sinologist. Born in Cologne (Germany) 11 October 1874, died in Chicago (Illinois) 13 September 1934. Berthold Laufer is remembered as a savant of Asian languages and antiquities and as the collector of extensive Asian collections for the American Museum of Natural History and the Field Museum of Natural History. Laufer led Museum expeditions to Sakhalin Island and the Amur River region of Siberia (1898-1899), to China (1901-1904, 1908-1910, 1923) and to Tibet (1908-1910). He authored more than 200 works on ethnology, archaeology, philology, art and the histories of domestic animals and cultivated plants.

His work on such wide-ranging and occasionally esoteric topics as Han dynasty pottery, the diffusion of maize and tobacco from the New World, the decorative art of the Amur tribes, loan words in Tibetan and the Chinese pigeon whistle reveals the range of interests that Laufer deemed appropriate to a comprehensive anthropology of China and the peoples on China's rim.

Originally trained at the University of Leipzig as a textual scholar of Oriental languages, Laufer added the practical experience of exacting fieldwork in Siberia during the Jesup North Pacific Expedition before leading an expedition to China in 1901. In China, as in Siberia, Laufer embarked on the holistic anthropological enterprise envisaged by his mentor FRANZ BOAS; he was to be ethnologist, archaeologist, physical anthropologist, ethnomusicologist and collector. Nevertheless, an expedition to study the history and culture of a literate and technologically sophisticated people represented a major departure for American anthropology, theretofore restricted to the study of small, organizationally simple societies and oral traditions.

Laufer's early immersion in the Boasian enterprise would be reflected in the omnivorous research and collecting of his subsequent career as the Field Museum's Curator of Anthropology. Nevertheless, although he periodically affirmed the value of field observations and informants' explanations, his studies were grounded in historical texts and in the exacting examination of museum collections. The anthropology of China would develop in another direction, as an enterprise that emphasized village studies in the tradition of rural sociology. Decades would pass before anthropologists of China evolved a fruitful collaboration with social historians and other textual scholars, bridging the disciplinary contradictions that Laufer embraced in a single career.

MAJOR WORKS: *The Decorative Art of the Amur Tribes* (New York: 1902); "A plea for the study of the history of medicine and natural sciences," *Science*, vol. 25 (1906), pp. 889-895; *Chinese Pottery of the Han Dynasty* (New York: 1909); *Jade: A Study in Chinese Archaeology and Religion* (Chicago: 1912); *Descriptive Account of the Collection of Chinese, Tibetan, Mongol and Japanese Books in the Newberry Library* (Chicago: 1913); *Chinese Clay Figures*, Part 1, *Prolegomena on Chinese Defensive Armor* (Chicago: 1914); *The Diamond: A Study in Chinese and Hellenistic Folklore* (Chicago: 1915); *Sino-Iranica: Chinese Contributions to the History of Civilization in Ancient Iran, with Special Reference to the History of Cultivated Plants and Products* (Chicago: 1919); "The American plant migration," *Scientific Monthly*, vol. 28 (1929), pp. 239-251; *China and the Discovery of America* (New York: 1931).

SOURCES: Franz Boas, "The Jesup North Pacific Expedition," *The American Museum Journal*, vol. 3, no. 5 (1903), pp. 69-119; Correspondence of the Jesup and Schiff Expeditions, Department of Anthropology Archive, American Museum of Natural History; Stanley A. Freed, Ruth S. Freed and Laila Williamson, "Capitalist philanthropy and Russian revolutionaries: the Jesup North Pacific Expedition (1897-1902)," *American Anthropologist*, vol. 90 (1988), pp. 7-24; Walter Hough, "Berthold Laufer: an appreciation," *The Scientific Monthly*, vol. 39 (1934), pp. 478-480; K.S. Latourette, "Berthold Laufer, 1874-1934," *National Academy of Sciences, Biographical Memoirs*, vol. 18 (1936), pp. 43-68.

Laurel Kendall

Layard, John. Anthropologist, Jungian analyst. Born in London (England) 28 November 1891, died in Oxford (England) 26 November 1972. After reading modern languages at Cambridge, Layard studied anthropology under W.H.R. RIVERS. One of the earliest intensive fieldworkers, he lived for a year from 1914-1915 on the islet of Atchin, Malakula Island, Vanuatu (then the New Hebrides). Mentally ill for many years, he became a patient, and later disciple, of Carl Jung in the 1930s. His main contribution to anthropology is his ethnography, *Stone Men of Malekula*. Layard's intellectual approach is distinctive for its marriage of Riversian diffusionism and Jungian psychology. According to Layard's "structural Jungianism," social function is to be interpreted in terms of Jungian archetypes. For an individual the supreme value is the achievement of "wholeness," a sort of rebirth in which opposites are reconciled and after which the newly integrated person can be at peace with the world. Layard, transposing Jungianism from the level of the individual to that of society, saw kinship as "an externalized form" of the self. Similarly, the passage of a Malakulan male through the sequence of initiation and other ceremonies to final rest, on death, in a nearby volcano was a Melanesian version of the striving toward wholeness.

Layard's original and imaginative interpretations failed to influence his contemporaries who promoted functionalism and its variants against diffusionism. They also wished to exclude psychological explanations, which were regarded as too speculative for the strongly empiricist version of British anthropology that was then emerging. Since Layard himself never held an academic post, he had no students to further his work and thus his unique, if somewhat eccentric, contribution to the history of British anthropology has not been given the attention it deserves.

MAJOR WORK: *Stone Men of Malekula* (London: 1942).

SOURCES: Ian Langham, *The Building of British Social Anthropology: W.H.R. Rivers and his Cambridge Disciples in the Development of Kinship Studies, 1898-1931* (Dordrecht: 1981); Jeremy MacClancy, "Unconventional character and disciplinary convention: John Layard, Jungian and anthropologist" in: George S. Stocking, Jr. (editor), *Malinowski, Rivers, Benedict and Others: Essays on Culture and Personality* (Madison: 1986) (= *History of Anthropology*, vol. 4), pp. 50-71.

Jeremy MacClancy

Leach, Edmund Ronald. Anthropologist. Born in Sidmouth (England) 7 November 1910, died in Cambridge (England) 6 January 1989. Educated at Marlborough and Clare College, Cambridge, Leach graduated with a B.A. in Mathematics: Mechanical Sciences in 1932. He worked as a Commercial Assistant for a British company in China, traveling widely. In 1936 he went to Botel Tobago as a member of an ethnographic expedition and when he returned to England began postgraduate studies at the London School of Economics, attending BRONISLAW MALINOWSKI's seminars. His research among the Kachin of Burma was interrupted by the outbreak of World War II. From 1939 to 1946 he was a member of the Burma Army, attaining the rank of Major. He completed his doctoral thesis, *Cultural Change with Special Reference to the Hill Tribes of Burma and Assam*, in 1947 under the supervision of RAYMOND FIRTH and was appointed as a lecturer in social anthropology at the London School of Economics in the same year.

In 1953 Leach took up a lectureship at Cambridge University and was Professor of Social Anthropology there (1972-1978). He was Provost of King's College, Cambridge (1966-1978); President of the Royal Anthropological Institute (1971-1975); a fellow of the British Academy (from 1972); and was knighted (1975).

Leach's most influential ethnographic works all focused on Asia and were based on fieldwork in Burma, Sarawak and North Borneo (Sabah) and Ceylon (Sri Lanka). His first major book, *Political Systems of Highland Burma*, challenged prevailing theories of social structure and cultural change, positing instead a view of culture that involved contradictory and competing ideologies within an unstable political environment. In *Pul Eliya: a Village in Ceylon* he directed his critical attention to theories of kinship as ideal systems, arguing that kinship relationships were actually ways of representing economic and political interests.

Leach introduced structuralist theory to the English-speaking world of anthropology and to a wider audience through his critical writings on CLAUDE LÉVI-STRAUSS and numerous essays on religion, culture and language. His influence was not confined to the academy. His 1967 Reith Lectures for the British Broadcasting Corporation, *A Runaway World?*, established him as a provocative critic of British society and culture. His writings on Biblical interpretation and European cultural traditions reflect the breadth of his scholarship and his view of anthropology as a discipline concerned with human universals. Intellectually he was a self-styled maverick, distancing himself from any "school" or tradition, while acknowledging his debt to mentors as diverse as Malinowski, Firth, Roman Jakobson and Giambattisto Vico.

MAJOR WORKS: *Political Systems of Highland Burma: a Study of Kachin Social Structure* (London: 1954); *Pul Eliya: a Village in Ceylon* (Cambridge: 1961); *Rethinking Anthropology* (London: 1961); *A Runaway World?* [The Reith Lectures, 1967] (London: 1968); *Lévi-Strauss* (London: 1970); *Genesis as Myth and Other Essays* (London: 1970); *L'unité de l'homme et autres essais* (Paris: 1980); *Social Anthropology* (London: 1982); (with D.A. Aycock) *Structuralist Interpretations of Biblical Myth* (London: 1983).

SOURCES: Adam Kuper, *Anthropology and Anthropologists: the Modern British School* (London: 1983); Edmund R. Leach, "Glimpses of the unmentionable in the history of British social anthropology," *Annual Review of Anthropology*, vol. 13 (1984), pp. 1-23; Adam Kuper, "An interview with Edmund Leach," *Current Anthropology*, vol. 27 (1986), pp. 375-382; *Edmund Leach: a Bibliography* (London: 1990) (= *Occasional Paper, The Royal Anthropological Institute*, no. 42); Martha Macintyre, videotaped interview with Edmund Leach, Departmental Archives, Research School of Pacific Studies, Canberra.

Martha Macintyre

Leakey, L.S.B. (Louis Seymour Bazett). Archaeologist, prehistorian, paleoanthropologist, paleontologist, ethnographer, natural historian. Born at Kabete near Nairobi (Kenya) 7 August 1903, died in London (England) 1 October 1972. Leakey's lifetime of only sixty-nine years embraced almost half a century of contributions to archaeology, paleontology and anthropology. It is probably true to claim that no other single person did more to unravel the story of the human past in Africa than Dr. Leakey.

Leakey was born to missionary parents and much of his schooling was informal. After World War I, he received formal schooling at Weymouth College in England and gained entry into St. John's College, Cambridge University in 1922. In 1924, following a rugby injury, Leakey took a year's leave and joined W.E. Cutler's expedition to collect dinosaurs in Tanganyika Territory. On his return to Cambridge, he completed his degree, taking "firsts" in languages as well as in archaeology and anthropology, and completed his Tripos in 1926. He led four major East African archaeological research expeditions between 1926 and 1935. These field researches laid a firm foundation for his life's work, in which he was to reveal the prehistory of a vast area on the eastern flank of Africa.

Brought up in Kikuyu territory, he spoke the language fluently and made a detailed study of the people and their customs. His 1,000-page report on the Kikuyu, undertaken for the Rhodes Trustees between 1937 and 1939, was prepared for publication posthumously by his second wife, MARY D. LEAKEY, and appeared as a three-volume work in 1977. He published a number of other works on the living peoples of East Africa, especially the Kikuyu, to whose welfare he was devoted. However, his greatest contributions were made in the study of Africa's past and the emergence of the *Hominidae* (the zoological family of man).

In an area whose prehistory was largely unknown until Leakey's work began, he did much to clarify the archaeological sequence through excavations in the basins of Lake Nakuru and Lake Naivasha, at Gamble's Cave, Njoro, Kariandusi, Olorgesaillie and other sites in Kenya, Tanzania and northeastern Angola. His evaluation and systematization of this archaeological record and of the fabricators of the stone tools formed the subject of a series of works such as *The Stone Age Cultures of Kenya Colony, Adam's Ancestors, The Stone Age Races of Kenya, Stone Age Africa* and *The Progress and Evolution of Man in Africa*. His discoveries included the fossil human remains of Kanam and Kanjera on the northern shore of the Gulf of Kavirondo, off Lake Victoria, as well as more recent human remains from Bromhead's Site, Njoro River Cave, Naivasha Cave, Hyrax Hill, and very ancient fossils of *Hominoidea* especially from Rusinga Island in the Gulf of Kavirondo. Later, from Fort Ternan, Kenya, he added early hominoid remains, which he assigned to *Kenyapithecus wickeri* and *Kenyapithecus africanus*. Some of these remains were later shown to be closely related to two other ancient hominoid genera, *Ramapithecus* and *Dryopithecus*.

To the archaeological archive of East Africa, Leakey made valuable contributions. He related the East African sequence partly to the southern African sequence established by A.J.H. Goodwin and C. Van Riet Lowe, and partly to the European sequence. He was an experimental archaeologist and developed proficiency in making stone tools from the same geological materials as had been employed by fossil man. He set human evolution in East Africa against a background of a series of pluvial and interpluvial periods for which he believed he had found evidence, though his supposed climatic sequence has not stood the test of time.

Leakey seemed determined to find a direct line, with minimal change, between early hominid remains that he and his collaborators discovered in East Africa and modern humans. His Kanam jaw, found in 1932, he claimed to be a very ancient member of *Homo sapiens*, or of a form of man (*Homo kanamensis*) closely allied to sapient man. Later, he believed that *Homo habilis*, found by various members of his family at Olduvai Gorge, was a yet older direct ancestor, while *H. habilis* in turn, Leakey believed, could be traced back to his *Kenyapithecus* from Fort Ternan. Thus, he relegated the South African australopithecines and also *Homo erectus* to the status of side-branches in hominid phylogeny. In these respects, some of Leakey's views have been contradicted by the interpretations of other paleoanthropologists.

Louis Leakey's name, and that of his wife Mary, are indelibly associated with their discoveries at the famous site of Olduvai Gorge on the Serengeti Plain of northern Tanzania. Before World War I, when Tanganyika was still German East Africa, H. Reck had found fossilized bones there, as well as a human skeleton which Reck believed to belong to the Middle Pleistocene, but which was later shown to be a relatively recent burial. After the war, Reck ceded scientific "ownership" of Olduvai to Leakey, who was responsible for finding the first stone tools in the Gorge. There began a lengthy series of excavations in the Gorge by Louis and Mary Leakey, their sons and other helpers. When Mary discovered the well preserved cranium of Olduvai hominid 5 in July 1959, Louis erected a new genus and species, *Zinjanthropus boisei*, to accommodate the large-toothed australopithecine specimen ("*Zinj*" is an old word for East Africa; "*anthropus*" means "man"; while Charles Boise financed Leakey's excavations). In 1967 P.V. Tobias sank the genus *Zinjanthropus* and reassigned the specimen to the species *Australopithecus boisei*. At first, when the bones of no other hominid were known from Olduvai (save for the recent human skeleton of Olduvai hominid 1), Louis attributed authorship of the Oldowan tools to this new species. Subsequently, however, a more hominized species was found to be represented in the same beds of the Olduvai Formation, namely the one to which Leakey, Tobias and Napier in 1964 gave the name *of Homo habilis*. When it was demonstrated that that creature had a cranial capacity much greater than those of the australopithecines, and after Mary had shown the strong likelihood that *H. habilis* was the Olduvai tool-maker, Louis abandoned the idea that "Zinj" was the main tool-maker of Olduvai in favor of the claims of *H. habilis*.

The Leakeys' finds at Olduvai, and the dating of "Zinj" and *H. habilis* to 1.8-1.6 million years before the present, generated a world-wide spate of interest and a fillip was given to African paleoanthropology and archaeology. Leakey entered into the promotional aspects of his work with tremendous energy and enthusiasm. Within the National Museum (formerly the Coryndon Museum) in Nairobi, he established the Centre for Prehistory and Palaeontology, which for some years after his death was called the International Louis Leakey Memorial Institute for African Prehistory, powerfully promoted by Richard Leakey, the second son of Louis and Mary. There, in Nairobi, Louis and then Richard built up one of the world's leading centers for the study of hominid evolution and countless scholars were attracted to study there. Leakey's reputation and charismatic personality led directly to the establishment of the L.S.B. Leakey Foundation for Research Related to Human Origins, Behavior and Survival, at Pasadena (California) and of the L.S.B. Leakey Trust in London (England). These bodies have stimulated and subsidized numerous researches on prehistory, paleoanthropology and primatology in Africa and elsewhere. Through his impact on other scholars and philanthropists, Leakey was an unexampled catalyst of researches in paleoanthropology and related disciplines.

> MAJOR WORKS: *The Stone Age Cultures of Kenya Colony* (Cambridge: 1931); *Adam's Ancestors* (London: 1934); *The Stone Age Races of Kenya* (London: 1935); *Stone Age Africa: an Outline of Prehistory in Africa* (London: 1936); *Kenya: Contrasts and Problems* (Cambridge, Mass.: 1936); *Olduvai Gorge: a Report on the Evolution of the Hand-axe Culture in Beds I-IV* (Cambridge: 1951); *Mau Mau and the Kikuyu* (London: 1952); *Some East African Pleistocene Suidae* (London: 1958); *The Progress and Evolution of Man in Africa* (London and New York: 1961); *Olduvai Gorge, 1951-1961.* Vol. I. *A Preliminary Report on the Geology and Fauna* (Cambridge: 1965); *The Southern Kikuyu before 1903* [3 vols.] (London, New York and San Francisco: 1977).

> SOURCES: L.S.B. Leakey, *White African* (London: 1937); J.D. Clark, *Louis Seymour Bazett Leakey, 1903-1972* (London: 1973) (= *Proceedings of the British Academy*, vol. 59); P.V. Tobias, "Louis Seymour Bazett Leakey, 1903-1972," *South African Archaeological Bulletin*, vol. 28 (1973), pp. 3-7; L.S.B. Leakey, *By the Evidence* (New York and London: 1974); S. Cole, *Leakey's Luck: the Life of Louis Leakey, 1903-72* (London: 1975); S.C. Coryndon, "A bibliography of the written works of Louis Seymour Bazett Leakey" in: G.L. Isaac and E.R. McCown (editors), *Human Origins: Louis Leakey and the East African Evidence* (Menlo Park: 1976), pp. 542-564; P.V. Tobias, "White African: an appreciation and some personal memories of Louis Leakey" in: G.L. Isaac and E.R. McCown (editors), *Human Origins: Louis Leakey and the East African Evidence* (Menlo Park, Calif.: 1976), pp. 55-74; Mary Leakey, *Disclosing the Past* (London: 1984).

Phillip V. Tobias

Leakey, Mary D. (née Mary Douglas Nicol). Archaeologist. Born in London (England) 6 February 1913. Leakey's education was informal; it occurred at the hands of a series of tutors and through attendance at lectures in geology at University College, London, and archaeology at the London Museum in Lancaster House. Thus, she entered into the field of archaeology without having been an undergraduate or post-graduate student in the customary sense. Like her father, Erskine Edward Nicol, Mary was a talented artist, and her skill in drawing stone tools brought her to the attention of Dorothy Liddell, whom Leakey assisted in Liddell's excavation at Hembury in Devon, and of Gertrude Caton-Thompson, who invited Leakey to draw the stone tools from her excavations at Fayūm in Egypt for her book, *The Desert Fayoum*. Caton-Thompson introduced Mary Nicol to L.S.B. LEAKEY, when the latter lectured to the Royal Anthropological Institute on his work in East Africa, and he invited her to help illustrate his famous early work, *Adam's Ancestors*. It was 1933 and she was twenty years old. She participated in several more excavations in England, including one at Swanscombe with Louis Leakey and another at

Jaywick near Clacton, with Kenneth Oakley. Her work in Africa started in 1935 and in the following year she became the the the second Mrs. L.S.B. Leakey. Thus started their remarkable husband-and-wife partnership in East African prehistory, which was to continue for more than thirty years.

Among Mary Leakey's significant discoveries was that of the skull of Proconsul, an extinct Miocene ape, which she found on Rusinga Island in the Gulf of Kavirondo, Lake Victoria, on 2 October 1948. Another of her contributions was based on the study of the rock paintings at Kondoa-Irangi in Tanzania during 1951: this culminated in her book, *Africa's Vanishing Art: the Rock Paintings of Tanzania*. Many "digs" in caves and open sites in various parts of East Africa, especially Kenya, followed, but pride of place must be accorded her work at Olduvai Gorge in northern Tanzania.

After many earlier visits to this famous site on the Serengeti Plain, Leakey discovered the cranium of *Zinjanthropus boisei* (later redesignated *Australopithecus boisei*) on 17 July 1959. It was almost a quarter of a century since her first visit to the site. She and Louis had uncovered numerous fossilized animal bones and stone tools. Save for a few rather indeterminate fragments, the skeletal remains of the early hominid or hominids of Olduvai had eluded them. Hence, her find was of high importance. It provided the first convincing evidence of the presence in East Africa of a representative of the australopithecines, previously known only from South Africa. Moreover, it was the first hominid find of high antiquity to be securely dated by the then newly established potassium-argon dating technique: it turned out to be about 1.75 million years old. This discovery aroused intense excitement and led to a flurry of new researches in East Africa by visiting scholars and much new enthusiasm, especially in the United States, for the study of human evolution.

Leakey avoided the attendant publicity and embarked on a program of meticulous excavations in the Olduvai Gorge. During the next two decades and more, she laid bare the archaeological sequence in the well stratified deposits and brought to light numerous fossils of vertebrates, including a number of hominid remains. She revealed that the stone tools of the so-called Oldowan Culture were almost certainly made not by *Australopithecus boisei* but by another species of hominid which L.S.B. Leakey, P.V. Tobias and J. Napier in 1964 called *Homo habilis* (the name having been suggested by RAYMOND A. DART). A popular account of her work at Olduvai is given in her book *Olduvai Gorge: My Search for Early Man*, while a technical report on the Oldowan stone tools appeared as volume 3 in the *Olduvai Gorge* series published by Cambridge University Press. Her volume 5 in that series will deal with the Acheulean stone tools of Olduvai.

A few years after her husband's death, Leakey moved her seat of operations to Laetoli, southeast of Olduvai. There she began a new series of major discoveries by herself and her collaborators. From 1974 to 1981, numbers of new mammalian species were uncovered from the fossil record in the Laetolil Formation. Among these were hominid remains dated to about 3.7 million years ago, that is, some 2 million years older than the Olduvai australopithecine. The Laetoli hominid is different from both *A. boisei* and *H. habilis*. D. Johanson and T.D. White have assigned it to a proposed new species that they called *Australopithecus afarensis*. In the 1976 season, a remarkable array of fossil animal footprints were found, including four that appeared to be hominid. This was followed during 1978 by the uncovering of two long trails of fossil hominid footprints, these being dated to about 3.5 million years. They provided the first direct evidence of their kind, confirming what had previously been inferred from skeletal remains, namely that the small-brained early hominids of the genus *Australopithecus* were bipedal creatures.

By her painstaking researches in deposits ranging from the Miocene to the Holocene Iron Age, Leakey has made significant contributions to the practice of field archaeology, including her pioneering work on "living floors" and on field museums, where implements and fossils were left *in situ*, partially exposed. Her patience and keen powers of observation have been rewarded by the discovery of many crucial finds bearing on the early evolution of the hominids and on their cultural life and development.

MAJOR WORKS: *Excavations in Beds I and II, 1960-1963* (Cambridge: 1971) (= *Olduvai Gorge*, vol. 3); *Olduvai Gorge: My Search for Early Man* (London: 1979); *Africa's Vanishing Art: the Rock Paintings of Tanzania* (London and New York: 1983); *Disclosing the Past: an Autobiography* (London: 1984).

SOURCES: M.D. Leakey, *Excavations in Beds I and II, 1960-1963* (Cambridge: 1971) (= *Olduvai Gorge*, vol. 3); L.S.B. Leakey, *By the Evidence* (New York and London: 1974); S. Cole, *Leakey's Luck: the Life of Louis Leakey, 1903-72* (London: 1975); M.D. Leakey, *Olduvai Gorge: My Search for Early Man* (London: 1979); M.D. Leakey, *Africa's Vanishing Art* (London and New York: 1983); M.D. Leakey, *Disclosing the Past: an Autobiography* (London: 1984); "Leakey, Mary Douglas" in: *International Who's Who*, vol. 50 (London: 1986-1987), p. 920.

Phillip V. Tobias

Lebedeva, N.A. (Natalïïa Ivanovna). Ethnographer. Born in Rïazan' (Russia) 19 July 1894, died in Rïazan' (Russian S.F.S.R.) 19 May 1978. Lebedeva's major works were devoted to the problems of the evolution of the material culture of the East Slavic peoples in connection with their ethnic history. She made major contributions to the study of the spinning, weaving, special design features and typology of the dress of the Russians, Ukrainians and Belorussians and also of their dwellings and work buildings. She was in the forefront of the development of the typology of material culture phenomena and the method of their study. Lebedeva was also a great museologist, working in museums of Moscow and Rïazan'.

MAJOR WORKS: *Narodnyi byt v verkhov'ïakh Desny i v verkhov'ïakh Oki (énologicheskaïa ékspedïtsïïa v Brïanskoï i Kaluzhskoï gubernïïakh v 1925-1926 gg.)* (Moscow: 1927); *Zhilishche i khozïaïstvennye postroïki Belorusskoï SSR* (Moscow: 1929); "Priadenie i tkachestvo vostochnykh slavian v XIX—nachale XX v.," "Vostochnoslavïanskiï étnograficheskiï sbornik: ocherki narodnoï material'noï kul'tury russkikh, ukraïntsev i belorusov v XIX—nachale XX v.," *Trudy Instituta étnografii AN SSSR*, vol. 31 (Moscow: 1956), pp. 461-540; (with G.S. Maslova), "Russkaïa krest'ïanskaïa odezhda XIX—nachala XX v." in: P.I. Kushner (editor), *Russkie: istoriko-étnograficheskiï atlas* (Moscow: 1967), pp. 193-267.

SOURCE: G.S. Maslova and M.N. Morozova, "Vydaïushchiïsïa sovetskiï étnograf N.I. Lebedeva," *Sovetskaïa étnografïïa*, no. 6 (1979), pp. 90-94.

A.M. Reshetov
[Translation from Russian: Thomas L. Mann]

Leenhardt, Maurice. Sociologist, ethnologist, missionary. Born in Montauban (France) 4 March 1878, died in Paris (France) 26 January 1954. Leenhardt was arguably the most distinguished French scholar of the Pacific. He was also one of the most capable fieldworkers in the history of French ethnology.

Leenhardt came from a bourgeois Protestant family (his father was a well known geologist). He became a pastor in 1901 and almost immediately set off to work as a missionary in New Caledonia where he stayed for most of the period from 1902 to 1926. In his work as a missionary he often sided with the "Canaque" natives in their disputes with the colonial administration. During his missionary years he contributed some ethnographic studies to scholarly journals, but his most elaborate work occurred only after his return to France, where he studied for a period at the École Pratique des Hautes Études with MARCEL MAUSS to whose chair of primitive religion he eventually succeeded (the next occupant of the chair was CLAUDE LÉVI-STRAUSS). Leenhardt's teaching years were interrupted by further fieldwork.

It has been argued that it was as a fieldworker that Leenhardt most distinguished himself. His studies vividly portray the culture of the New Caledonians and of other Melanesians, often concentrating on their religious life and myths. According to Crapanzano, Leenhardt was sometimes reacting to LUCIEN LÉVY-BRUHL's too simple notion of the mental life of "primitive" peoples and may have contributed to Lévy-Bruhl's repudiation of some of his own early work.

Leenhardt also played a major role as an organizer. He was the major instigator of the Oceania Department at the Musée de l'Homme. He founded the Société d'Études Mélanesiennes (Society of Melanesian Studies). And he helped to organize the Société des Océanistes (Society of Oceania Specialists), serving as its first president.

MAJOR WORKS: *Vocabulaire et grammaire de la langue houaïlou* (Paris: 1935) (= *Travaux et mémoires de l'Institut d'ethnologie*, vol. 10); *Gens la Grande Terre: Nouvelle-Calédonie* (Paris: 1937; rev. ed, Paris: 1953); *Langues et dialectes de l'Austro-Mélanesie* (Paris: 1946) (= *Travaux et mémoires de l'Institut d'ethnologie*, vol. 46); *Do Kamo: la personne et la mythe dans le monde mélanesien* (Paris: 1947) [tr.: *Do Kamo: Person and Myth in the Melanesian World* (Chicago: 1979)]; *Arts de l'Océanie* (Paris: 1948) [tr.: *Arts of the Oceanic Peoples* (London: 1950)].

SOURCES: James Clifford, *Person and Myth: Maurice Leenhardt in the Melanesian World* (Berkeley and Los Angeles: 1982) [contains bibliography, pp. 257-264]; "Hommage à Maurice Leenhardt," *Journal de la Société des Océanistes*, vol. 10, no. 10 (1954), pp. 5-158 [contains bibliography, pp. 73-76]; Vincent Crapanzano, "Introduction" to: *De Kamo* (Chicago: 1979), pp. vii-xxix.

Lehmann, Walter. Americanist. Born in Berlin (Germany) 16 September 1878, died in Berlin (Germany) 7 February 1939. After receiving an M.D., Lehmann joined the Museum für Völkerkunde (Berlin Ethnographic Museum) in 1903 as *Volontär* in the American Department; he also pursued Americanistics at the university under the tutorship of EDUARD SELER. He was sent to Central America by the Museum, where he undertook a linguistic survey between 1907 and 1909. Upon his return he was appointed curator at the Ethnographic Museum in Munich and received a Ph.D. in 1913 and a *Habilitation* in 1915 from the University of Munich, both on the basis of studies of Central American Indian languages and linguistics (*Vokabular der Rama-Sprache ...* and "Über die Stellung und Verwandtschaft der Subtiaba-Sprache ..."). In 1920 Lehmann returned to the Berlin Museum as head of a recently created *Forschungs- und Lehrinstitut* (research and teaching institute) and, later, was also appointed director of the American, Oceanic and African

Collections, which gave him the power to overrule decisions of the departmental curators. On his second and third field trips to Latin America (1925-1926 and 1929-1930) he continued his linguistic survey and extended it to Andean South America. He also collected portable artifacts from excavations and dealers, copied ancient American stone sculpture and mural paintings and acquired manuscripts and rare books. It was his untiring spirit as a collector that finally resulted in the most comprehensive and valuable private-document and book collection on Indian America assembled during the 20th century in Germany. This collection is completely preserved at the Iberoamerikanisches Institut (Iberoamerican Institute) in Berlin. After his last field trip Lehmann was active as a university teacher and as an organizer of two great exhibits on American and Oceanic art in Berlin. In 1934 he had to relinquish all posts under Nazi reorganization laws ("to simplify the adminstration") but was permitted to continue his personal research at the Iberoamerikanisches Institut, then headed by General Faupel. There he inaugurated a series of documentary publications (*Quellenwerke zur alten Geschichte Amerikas*) that contain his editions and translations of Nahuatl sources. To date thirteen book-size monographs have been published in this series, four of which contain material translated by Lehmann but mostly edited posthumously by Gerdt Kutscher (1913-1979).

Lehmann's research on Central American languages and linguistic classification was the first successful effort to study this important intermediate region. His classification of language groups and his analysis of these languages' external genetic relationships to Mesoamerican and South American language families still stand. Lehmann himself, however, considered the disentangling of Central Mexican cultural chronology the most challenging problem. By taking the written indigenous sources as historical documents and by analyzing their chronologies, he made important progress in defining the Toltecs as a historical tribe of the Late Classic and Early Postclassic times. After his death, archaeology did much to refine his work on the so-called *Toltekenfrage* (Toltec question).

Lehmann was also very successful as a popularizer of American Indian art through two widely read books (*Altmexikanische Kunstgechichte* and *Kunstgeschichte des alten Peru*) and the aforementioned exhibition. His influence might well have reached the contemporary art scene. Lehmann's importance for modern research lies mainly in his editorial endeavors. In Germany his impact is most felt through his library and his collections, around which an Anthropological Research Department at the Iberoamerikanisches Institut was built.

MAJOR WORKS: "Les peintures Mixtéco-Zapotèques et quelques documents apparentés," *Journal de la Société des Américanistes de Paris*, n.s., vol. 2 (1905), pp. 241-280 [incomplete tr.: *Pinturas mixteco "zapotecas" y algunos documentos emparentados con ellas* (Mexico City: 1945, 1948 and 1950)]; "Ergebnisse und Aufgaben der mexikanistischen Forschung," *Archiv für Anthropologie*, n.F., vol. 6 (1907), pp. 113-168 and plates VIII-IX [tr.: *Methods and Results in Mexican Research* (Paris: 1909)]; *Vokabular der Rama-Sprache nebst einem grammatischen Abriss* [Ph.D. dissertation] (Munich: 1914) (= *Abhandlungen der Bayrischen Akademie der Wissenschaften, philosophisch-philologische und historische Klasse*, vol. 28, no. 2); "Über die Stellung und Verwandtschaft der Subtiaba-Sprache der Pazifischen Küste Nicaraguas und über die Sprache von Tapachula in Südchiapas" [Habilitationsschrift], *Zeitschrift für Ethnologie*, vol. 47 (1915), pp. 1-34; *Zentral-Amerika*. I. Teil [only part published]. *Die Sprachen Zentral-Amerikas in ihren Beziehungen zueinander sowie zu Süd-Amerika und Mexiko* [2 vols.] (Berlin: 1920); *Altmexikanische Kunstgeschichte* (Berlin: 1921; 2nd ed., Berlin: 1922) [tr.: *The History of Ancient Mexican Art: an Essay in Outline* (New York: 1922) (= *Orbis Pictus, the Universal Library of Art*, vol. 8); *L'art an-*

cien du Mexique (Paris: 1922)]; (with Heinrich Ubbelohde-Doering) *Kunstgeschichte des alten Peru* (Berlin 1924) [tr.: *The Art of Old Peru* (London: 1924); *Historia del arte antiguo del Perú* (Berlin and Lima: 1926)]; *Die Geschichte der Königreiche von Colhuacan und Mexico* (Berlin: 1938; reprinted with additional materials, Stuttgart: 1974) (= *Quellenwerke zur alten Geschichte Amerikas, aufgezeichnet in den Sprachen der Eingeborenen*, no. 1); (translator and editor with Gerdt Kutscher and Günter Vollmer) *Geschichte der Azteken: Codex Aubin und verwandte Dokumente* (Berlin: 1981) (= *Quellenwerke zur alten Geschichte Amerikas, aufgezeichnet in den Sprachen der Eingeborenen*, no. 13).

SOURCES: Walter Lehmann archives at the Iberoamerikanisches Institut, Preußischer Kulturbesitz, Berlin (West); Gerdt Kutscher, "Zum Gedächtnis von Walter Lehmann," *Archiv für Anthropologie*, n.F. vol. 25 (1939), pp. 140-149; *Gedenkschrift Walter Lehmann* [3 parts] (Berlin: 1981-1983) (= *Indiana*, vols. 6-8) [vols. 6 and 7 contain short biographies and portraits; vol. 8, pp. 311-341, contains a lengthy biography and updated bibliography of Lehmann by Berthold Riese]; Berthold Riese, "Lehmann, Walter" in: *Neue Deutsche Biographie*, vol. 14 (Munich: 1984), pp. 95-96; Berthold Riese, *Indianische Handschriften und Berliner Forscher* (Berlin: 1988), pp. 34-38; Michael Dürr, "Unveröffentlichtes Sprachmaterial aus dem Nachlaß Walter Lehmanns," *Indiana*, vol. 12 (1990).

Berthold Riese

Lehmann-Nitsche, Robert. Physician, physical anthropologist, ethnologist. Born in Radowitz, Posen (Germany) 9 November 1872, died in Berlin (Germany) 9 April 1938. He studied anthropology and medicine at Freiburg im Breisgau, Berlin and Munich. He earned doctorates of philosophy and medicine at Munich in 1894 and 1897, respectively. In 1898 he was awarded the Goddard Prize by the French Anthropological Society for his dissertation on the long bones found in the southern Bavarian line graves (*Reihengräber*). His later studies on the fossil men of the *pampas* would be awarded the Broca Prize from the University of Paris in 1910. In 1897 Francisco Moreno, the founder of the Museo de la Plata (La Plata Museum), sent for Lehmann-Nitsche to serve as director of the anthropology department and curator of ethnography and archaeology at the museum in Buenos Aires. By 1905 he had also become employed at the University of Buenos Aires, and in 1906 he received the first professorial chair in physical anthropology set up in South America at La Plata University, remaining in Argentina until his retirement in 1929.

At the beginning of his scientific career his major areas of specialization were physical anthropology, medicine and prehistory, but he became increasingly interested in many other fields, including the material culture of the original inhabitants of Argentina, folklore, Indian languages, mythology, astronomy, paleontology, ethnography, archaeology, ethnozoology and ethnobotany. His 375 publications illustrate this breadth of interest in an impressive manner. Lehmann-Nitsche was also interested in the popular circulation of his ideas and contributed much to the exchange of information between Argentinian and German researchers. He gathered materials for his publications not only from literary sources but also from his own journeys in Argentina. These travels were directed toward the development of his area of chief interest, the ethnography and folklore, in particular the myths and legends, of the Indians of Argentina. In 1900 he undertook his first trip into southern Argentina as far as Patagonia and Tierra del Fuego, regions whose geology, language, customs and manners had hardly been investigated. In 1906 he journeyed into northern Argentina to the Chaco as far as Jujuy, collecting myths and legends in the native languages, some of which could be traced back to the 16th century. The majority of his material was published, with extensive annotations and bibliographies, while a portion remains in the Iberoamerikanisches Institut (Iberoamerican Institute) in Berlin awaiting scientific interpretation. An example of the latter is the three-volume manuscript of *Textos Araucanos*. The Iberoamerikanisches Institut also possesses his *Biblioteca Criolla*, a collection of popular articles and pamphlets on the Argentine Gauchos.

> MAJOR WORKS: *Über die langen Knochen der südbayrischen Reihengräberbevölkerung* (Munich: 1895); *Beiträge zur prähistorischen Chirurgie nach Funden aus deutscher Vorzeit* (Buenos Aires: 1898); "Über den fossilen Menschen der Pampaformation," *Correspondenz-Blatt der Deutschen Gesellschaft für Anthropologie, Ethnologie und Urgeschichte*, no. 10 (1900), pp. 107-109 [tr.: "L'Homme fossile de la formation pampéenne (communication préliminaire)," *Congrès international d'Anthropologie et d'Archéologie Préhistorique, Compte rendue de la douzième session* (Paris: 1900) and *L'Anthropologie*, vol. 12 (1901), pp. 160-165]; "Nouvelles recherches sur la formation pampéenne et l'homme fossile de la République Argentine," *Revista del Museo de la Plata*, vol. 14 (2nd ser., vol. 1) (1907); "Folklore argentino I-VII," *Biblioteca Centenaria de la Universidad Nacional de La Plata* (Buenos Aires: 1911), *Boletín de la Academia Nacional de Ciencias*, vol. 20-23 (1914-1919), *Revista de la Universidad de Buenos Aires*, seccion 6, vol. 3, no. 6 (1928); "Mitología sudamericana I-XXI," *Revista del Museo de La Plata* (1919-1938); *Texte aus den La Plata-Gebieten in volkstümlichem Spanisch und Rotwelsch* (Leipzig: 1923) [this appeared under the pseudonym Victor Borde] [tr.: *Textos eróticos del Río de la Plata: ensayo lingüístico sobre textos sicalípticos* (Buenos Aires: 1981)].

> SOURCES: "Robert Lehmann-Nitsche," *Boletín Bibliográfico de Antropología Americana*, vol. 3 (1939), pp. 89-95; José Torre Revello, "Contribución a la biobibliografía de Robert Lehmann-Nitsche," *Boletín del Instituto de Investigaciones Históricas, Facultad de Filosofía y Letras*, vol. 29, nos. 101-104 (July 1944-June 1945, published in 1947), pp. 724-805; Heinrich Snethlage, "Schrifttum Lehmann-Nitsche's," *Ethnologischer Anzeiger*, vol. 4 (1939), pp. 250-260; Heinrich Snethlage, "Robert Lehmann-Nitsche zum Gedächtnis," *Archiv für Anthropologie*, no. 24 (1938), pp. 275-278; Julian Cáceres Freyre, *Robert Lehmann-Nitsche* (Santa Fé: 1970); E.M.S. Danero, "Roberto Lehmann-Nitsche y su obra," *Humboldt*, no. 67 (1978), pp. 60-70.

Frauke Johanna Riese
[Translation from German: Robert B. Marks Ridinger]

Lehmer, Donald J. (Donald Jayne).

Archaeologist. Born in Omaha (Nebraska) 9 October 1918, died in Omaha (Nebraska) 5 June 1975. Lehmer was educated at the University of Arizona (B.A., 1940), the University of Chicago (M.A., 1948) and Harvard University (Ph.D., 1952). He was on the staff of the Museum of New Mexico from 1940 to 1942, serving the last year of the appointment as assistant curator for branch museums. During 1950-1951 he was an archaeologist with Smithsonian Institution River Basin Surveys. In 1952 he was field director of the University of Nebraska field school in Harlan County, Nebraska; in 1953, he was an archaeologist with the El Paso Natural Gas Company Pipeline Project. Lehmer served as visiting professor at the University of Washington during 1953-1954 and as lecturer with the Strategic Air Command Headquarters and the University of Omaha during 1955-1960. In 1961 he became a professor at Dana College in Blair, Nebraska and continued in that position until his death. Between many of these appointments, he worked in various management positions with archaeological field projects.

Lehmer's early career was spent in the southwestern United States. During 1938-1939 he was an excavation supervisor on the La Junta de los Rios Expedition, a Work Projects Administration project jointly conducted by the Museum of New Mexico and Sul

Ross College. During 1940-1941 he served as director of the Mesilla Valley Expedition in Dona Ana County, New Mexico, which was sponsored by the Museum of New Mexico and Arizona State Museum. In 1948 he became director of the Mexican (Sonora) Archeological Expedition jointly sponsored by the Field Museum of Natural History, the University of Chicago and the University of Arizona.

During 1950-1951 Lehmer's work with the River Basin Survey (RBS) brought him to the archaeology of the Missouri Basin, the work for which he would be best remembered. With the exception of a detail to Oklahoma, where he undertook excavation of the Cookson site of Tenkiller Reservoir, most of his fieldwork with the RBS was devoted to excavations of the Dodd and Philips Ranch sites in the Oahe Reservoir of South Dakota.

After this, most of Lehmer's endeavors were concentrated on the archaeology of the middle Missouri and studies of the Hidatsa and Mandan Indians. Among other activities, he served the Smithsonian under contract to prepare reports for the Buffalo Pasture site and the Leavitte site in the Oahe Reservoir, Nightwalker's Butte site and Rock Village site in the Garrison Reservoir of North Dakota and the Fire Heart Creek site in North Dakota. In the mid 1960s he was engaged by the National Park Service to prepare a report on the progress of salvage archaeological work in the middle Missouri.

From his position at Dana College, Lehmer served as a research archaeologist at the State Historical Society of North Dakota, visiting professor of anthropology at the University of Minnesota and member of the planning committee of the Smithsonian's *Handbook of North American Indians* for the volume concerning the Plains region. For several years, he was also on the board of directors of the *Plains Anthropologist*.

MAJOR WORKS: "The Jornada Branch of the Mogollon," *University of Arizona Bulletin*, vol. 19 (1948), pp. 1-99; *Archeological Investigations in the Oahe Dam Area, South Dakota, 1950-1951* (Washington: 1954) (= *Bureau of American Ethnology Bulletin*, no. 158); *The Fire Heart Creek Site* (Lincoln, Nebr.: 1966) (= *River Basin Surveys Publications in Salvage Archeology*, 1); (with David T. Jones) *Arikara Archeology: the Bad River Phase* (Lincoln, Nebr.: 1968) (= *River Basin Surveys Publications in Salvage Archeology*, 7); *Introduction to Middle Missouri Archeology* (Washington: 1971) (= *National Park Service Anthropological Papers*, no. 1).

SOURCES: W. Raymond Wood, "Donald Jayne Lehmer, 1918-1975," *American Antiquity*, vol. 41 (1976), pp. 178-180; Lehmer papers in the Smithsonian Institution National Anthropological Archives.

James R. Glenn

Leidy, Joseph. Anatomist, anthropologist, physician, geologist, paleontologist, teacher. Born in Philadelphia (Pennsylvania) 9 September 1823, died in Philadelphia (Pennsylvania) 30 April 1891. Leidy, one of the premier American scientists of the 19th century, conducted research in vertebrate and invertebrate anatomy, paleontology, geology, mineralogy, botany, zoology and anthropology. He has been called the founder of parasitology and vertebrate paleontology in the United States. He received an M.D. from the University of Pennsylvania in 1844 and in 1847 began teaching there. Leidy belonged to numerous scientific associations and was among the first elected members of the National Academy of Sciences. During his years at the University of Pennsylvania he instructed JOSEPH JONES, physician and archaeologist, HARRISON ALLEN, anatomist and anthropologist, and Edward Drinker Cope, paleontologist.

Leidy was a great surveyor of nature, discovering numerous species and gathering an immense array of data on the natural world. Osborn (1913) called him an accumulator of facts for Darwin and one of the first to accept Darwin's theories. Leidy is among those named as a precursor to Darwin, for in his 1853 work, *A Flora and Fauna within Living Animals*, Leidy claimed that spontaneous generation was not responsible for the origin of new life and that slight modifications in the environment could produce the variation found among life forms. In paleontology he made many contributions, including proving that the horse was indigenous to America.

Leidy's expertise in anatomy and geology allowed him to make informed judgments on fossil human remains. Leidy contributed a letter on human paleontology to Nott and Gliddon's *Indigenous Races of the Earth* in which he warned against relying on fossilization of bone as an indicator of antiquity. He discussed the supposed antiquity of some U.S. finds in "Notice of some fossil human bones," concluding on the basis of their similarity to modern humans, the general appearance of the material and the circumstances surrounding their discovery that they were not of great antiquity. Leidy's published contributions to anthropology are small; however, he was a recognized expert in evaluating the early finds of fossil humans and was instrumental in defining the morphological and geological criteria by which they were judged.

MAJOR WORKS: *A Flora and Fauna within Living Animals* (Washington: 1853) (= *Smithsonian Contributions to Knowledge*, vol. 5); "Lecture on the peculiarities of the Negro," *Medical Surgical Reporter*, vol. 10 (1853), p. 228; "On human paleontology" in: Josiah Clark Nott and George R. Gliddon, *Indigenous Races of the Earth* (Philadelphia: 1857), pp. xxi-xix; *An Elementary Treatise of Human Anatomy* (Philadelphia: 1861); "Notice of some human fossil bones," *Transactions of the Wagner Free Institute of Science*, vol. 2 (1889), pp. 9-12.

SOURCES: Henry Chapman, "Memoir of Joseph Leidy, M.D., LL.D.," *Proceedings of the Academy of Natural Sciences of Philadelphia*, vol. 43 (1891), pp. 342-388; Charles S. Minot, "A tribute to Joseph Leidy," *Science*, vol. 37 (1913), pp. 809-814; Edward Morse, "Joseph Leidy's influence on science," *Scientific Monthly*, vol. 18 (1924), pp. 422-427; Henry Fairfield Osborn, "Biographical memoir of Joseph Leidy 1823-1891," *Biographical Memoirs of the Academy of Natural Sciences*, vol. 7 (1913), pp. 339-396; Charles A. Pfender, "Leidy, Joseph" in: Howard A. Kelly and Walter L. Burrage (editors), *American Medical Biographies* (Baltimore: 1920), pp. 692-696; W.S.W. Ruschenberger, "A sketch of the life of Joseph Leidy," *Proceedings of the American Philosophical Society*, vol. 30 (1892), pp. 135-184.

Joyce L. Ogburn

Leighton, Dorothea C. (née Dorothea Cross). Social psychiatrist. Born in Lunenburg (Massachusetts) 2 September 1908, died in Fresno (California) 15 August 1989. Leighton was educated in chemistry and biology at Bryn Mawr College (B.A., 1930) and in medicine at the Johns Hopkins University (M.D., 1936). She married Alexander H. Leighton in 1937. After working closely together for several decades, they were divorced in 1965. Dorothea Leighton had teaching appointments at Cornell University during 1949-1952 as a professor of child development and family relations and at the University of North Carolina during 1964-1974 as a professor of mental health. She also taught at the University of California at San Francisco in 1977 and at Berkeley during 1981-1982.

Stimulated during their psychiatric residencies to work with people of other cultures, Dorothea and Alexander Leighton carried out fieldwork among the Navajo and the

Inuit in 1940, concentrating on life histories of their subjects. Out of the work with the Navajo, Dorothea Leighton, assisted by her husband, wrote a book on Navajo culture that was intended for the use of Bureau of Indian Affairs medical personnel. Some consider it the first book in medical anthropology.

During 1942-1945 Leighton returned to the field as a special physician for Indian Personality and Education Research, a joint applied anthropology project of the Bureau of Indian Affairs and the University of Chicago. The project's purpose was to study the development of personality and the effects of government policy among five Indian tribes. Involved were medical and social workers as well as anthropologists. Leighton's duties mainly involved psychological studies of Navajo and Zuni children and the preparation of publications on those tribes.

Much of the remainder of Leighton's fieldwork was devoted to studies in psychiatric epidemiology in Nova Scotia and Nigeria. As a teacher, however, she offered courses in medical anthropology, and she played an instrumental role in founding the Society for Medical Anthropology in 1971 and served as its first president.

MAJOR WORKS: (with Alexander H. Leighton) *The Navaho Door: an Introduction to Navaho Life* (Cambridge, Mass.: 1944); (with Alexander H. Leighton) *Gregorio: the Hand-Trembler* (Cambridge, Mass.: 1949); (with Clyde Kluckhohn) *The Navaho* (Cambridge, Mass.: 1946); (with Clyde Kluckhohn) *Children of the People: the Navaho Individual and His Development* (Cambridge, Mass.: 1947); (with Alexander H. Leighton [et al.]) *Psychiatric Disorder Among the Yoruba* (Ithaca, N.Y.: 1963); *The Character of Danger: Psychiatric Symptoms in Selected Communities* (New York: 1963); (with John Adair) *People of the Middle Place* (New York: 1966); (with Alexander H. Leighton) *Eskimo Recollections of Their Life Experiences* (Moscow, Idaho: 1984) (= *Northwest Anthropological Research Notes*, vol. 17, no. 1/2).

SOURCES: Joyce Griffen, "Dorothea Cross Leighton" in: Ute Gacs [et. al.] (editors), *Women Anthropologists: a Biographical Dictionary* (New York: 1988), pp. 231-237; "Dorothea C. Leighton," *Anthropology Newsletter*, vol. 30, no. 7 (October 1989), p. 4; Leighton papers relating to the Indian personality and education research in the National Anthropological Archives.

James R. Glenn

Leiris, Michel. Poet, writer, ethnologist. Born in Paris (France) 20 April 1901, died in Saint-Hilaire (France) 29 September 1990. More than most participants in the academic world, Michel Leiris eludes pigeonholing in terms of traditional categories of intellectual activity. With one foot in anthropology (beginning as a student of MARCEL MAUSS at the Institut d'Ethnologie) and the other in literature, his life also centered on close personal relations with a diverse network of creative artists and thinkers, from Picasso to Sartre. His interest in poetry and theater inspired aspects of his anthropological work in the realms of language and performance (for example, *La langue secrète des Dogons de Sanga, La possession et ses aspects théâtraux chez les Ethiopiens de Gondar* and his introduction to ALFRED MÉTRAUX's *Le vaudou haïtien*). His role as diarist during France's famous 1931-1933 ethnographic expedition across Africa (the Mission Dakar-Djibouti, under the direction of MARCEL GRIAULE) prepared the way for his later autobiographical writing (most notably *L'âge d'homme, Biffures, Fourbis, Fibrilles* and *Frêle bruit*). In a similarly cross-pollinating vein, his involvement with 20th-century artists at a time when "primitivism" was becoming a vibrant inspirational force allowed him to play a unique role in mediating between the perceptions of non-Western cultures espoused by anthropologists and artists.

A political concern with colonialism and an aesthetic attraction to the exotic merged, for Leiris, during his participation in the early years of the surrealist movement (which he described as "a rebellion against Western civilization, plain and simple"). This experience fed directly into his relationships with non-European intellectuals such as the Martiniquan poet Aimé Césaire and the Cuban artist Wifredo Lam. It also opened the door to his reflections on systems of thought located beyond the boundaries of Western rationalism and contributed to his fascination with the "clash" of cultures (jazz epitomizing for him exoticism in the context of industrialism, and Caribbean societies representing collages composed of fragments brought from Africa and Europe against a background of the Americas). As James Clifford has remarked, the particular combination of ethnography and surrealism that Leiris, among others, espoused, "delight[ed] in cultural impurities and disturbing syncretisms."

Leiris's preoccupation with the subtle, complex, elusive interplay between objectivity and subjectivity and his precocious acknowledgment of the inescapable presence of the anthropologist in anthropological observation always led him to play in original and creative ways with the traditional boundaries of genres. The negotiation of his simultaneous roles as author and subject in *L'Afrique fantôme*, for example, produced neither the scientific treatise nor the autobiographical travelogue that one might have expected to emerge from the pen of an officially designated expedition chronicler, but rather a voluminous collection of diversities that range over details of his dreams, descriptions of collecting strategies, reports on his bodily functions, potential "prefaces" for the book that might have been written, reflections on colonialism and racism, the outline for a novel, erotic fantasies, ethnographic field notes, verbal snapshots of African scenery, methodological commentary and much more.

MAJOR WORKS: *L'Afrique fantôme* (Paris: 1934); *L'âge d'homme* (Paris: 1939) [tr.: *Manhood* (New York: 1968)]; *La langue secrète des Dogons de Sanga (Soudan français)* (Paris: 1948); *La règle du jeu: I. Biffures* (Paris: 1948); *II. Fourbis* (Paris: 1955); *III. Fibrilles* (Paris: 1966); *IV. Frêle bruit* (Paris: 1976); *Contacts de civilisations en Martinique et Guadeloupe* (Paris: 1955); *La possession et ses aspects théâtraux chez les Ethiopiens de Gondar* (Paris: 1958); (with Jacqueline Delange) *Afrique noire: la création plastique* (Paris: 1967) [tr.: *African Art* (London: 1968)]; *Cinq études d'ethnologie* (Paris: 1969).

SOURCES: Denis Hollier (editor), *Le Collège de Sociologie (1937-1939)* (Paris: 1979); Maurice Nadeau, *The History of Surrealism* (New York: 1965); James Clifford, "On ethnographic surrealism" in: James Clifford, *The Predicament of Culture* (Cambridge, Mass.: 1988), pp. 117-151; James Clifford (editor), "New translations of Michel Leiris," *Sulfur: a Literary Tri-Quarterly of the Whole Art*, no. 15 (1986), pp. 4-125; Jean Jamin, "Les métamorphoses de *L'Afrique fantôme*," *Critique*, vol. 38, no. 418 (1981), pp. 200-212; Sally Price and Jean Jamin, "A conversation with Michel Leiris," *Current Anthropology*, vol. 29 (1988), pp. 157-174; Susan Sontag, "Michel Leiris's *Manhood*" in: Susan Sontag, *Against Interpretation* (New York: 1966), pp. 61-68.

Sally Price

Lessa, William Armand. Anthropologist. Born in Newark (New Jersey) 3 March 1908. Lessa was trained at Harvard University (A.B. in chemistry, 1928) and the

University of Chicago (Ph.D., 1947). In 1947 Lessa began teaching at the University of California at Los Angeles, and that has remained his major institutional affiliation.

Lessa's first scientific work was in physical anthropology as an assistant to E.A. HOOTON. In 1929 he began work under HARRY L. SHAPIRO at the Constitution Clinic at Columbia Presbyterian Hospital in New York and also assisted Shapiro in other scientific work. Beginning graduate studies at the University of Chicago in 1938, Lessa broadened his interest to all areas of anthropology. His master's thesis was a generally unfavorable review of constitutional studies. His doctoral dissertation was an anthropological report based on his experience as an officer with the U.S. Army military government in Italy during World War II.

In 1947, under the sponsorship of the U.S. Office of Naval Research, Lessa began studies in Micronesia, where he concentrated on the Caroline Islands, especially Ulithi Atoll, and his concern with that area occupied much of the rest of his career. His aim was to carry out a thorough ethnographic study of Ulithi, and his efforts led him into social anthropology, folklore, physical anthropology, ethnohistory and the study of "somatomancy." He also carried out an ethnobotanical study of the Carolines and a study of Ulithi's reaction to a devastating typhoon.

MAJOR PUBLICATIONS: *Landmarks in the Science of Human Types* ([Brooklyn]: 1942); *An Appraisal of Constitutional Typologies* (Menasha, Wisc.: 1942) (= *Memoir Series of the American Anthropological Association*, no. 42); *The Ethnography of Ulithi Atoll* (Los Angeles: 1950) (= *Coordinated Investigation of Micronesian Anthropology Report*, no. 28); (with Marvin Spiegelman) *Ulithian Personality* (Berkeley: 1954) (= *University of California Publications in Culture and Society*, vol. 2, no. 5); (with Evon Z. Vogt) *Reader in Comparative Religion: an Anthropological Approach* (Evanston: 1958); *Tales from Ulithi Atoll* (Berkeley: 1961) (= *University of California Publications in Folklore Studies*, no. 13); *Ulithi: a Micronesian Design for Living* (New York: 1966); *Chinese Body Divination* (Los Angeles: 1968); *Drake's Island of Thieves: Ethnological Sleuthing* (Honolulu: 1975); *More Tales from Ulithi Atoll* (Berkeley: 1980) (= *University of California Publications in Folklore and Mythology Studies*, no. 32); *Spearhead Governatore: Remembrances of the Campaign in Italy* (Malibu: 1985).

SOURCES: Cynthia R. Fadool, "Lessa, William A(rmand)," *Contemporary Authors*, vol. 61-64 (1976), p. 326; Lessa papers in the Smithsonian Institution National Anthropological Archives, including notes provided by Lessa.

James R. Glenn

Lesser, Alexander. Anthropologist. Born in New York (New York) 1902, died in East Meadow (New York) 1982. Lesser did his undergraduate work at Columbia in the 1920s where he came under the influence of John Dewey and FRANZ BOAS. Deeply impressed with Boas's project of remaking American anthropology into an empirical science that was at once comparative, historical, anti-evolutionist and non-racist, Lesser decided to become an anthropologist. His early work, including his dissertation, was focused on the study of Native American (Plains) cultures. His dissertation was an overview and theoretical reconsideration of the extant data on Siouan kinship, but his first major ethnological contribution was his detailed study of the Pawnee Ghost Dance Hand Game. This work provided the ethnographic foundation and exemplar of the critique of functionalism that Lesser subsequently mounted (nominally against A.R. RADCLIFFE-BROWN) in the 1930s and for which he is still renowned. Lesser argued for the historicity that saturates all culture and exposed the futility of comprehending the manifold and oft-hidden past causes (or rather conditioners) of events by recourse to a hypothesized network of merely synchronic relations. Later papers on evolution and on the concept of the social field were attempts to reconcile the Boasian theme of the autonomy of the "local" with the discovery of evolutionary convergences in the development of culture.

Throughout the 1950s Lesser was the director of the Association of American Indian Affairs. Returning to the academy in 1960, he brought his decade of experience as an advocate of Native American rights to fruition in what is probably his most famous paper, "The right not to assimilate." Here, he explored the underlying causes of the Native American will to cultural survival and analyzed the unconscious sources of the dominant society's hostility and resistance to pluralism as a working principle of democratic society. Finally, toward the end of his career, Lesser, in his capacity as both a first-hand witness and a theoretician, wrote a series of papers dealing with the enduring impact of his mentor, Franz Boas, on the scientific goals as well as the political and moral mandates (and contradictions) of 20th-century anthropology.

MAJOR WORKS: *The Pawnee Ghost Dance Hand Game* (New York: 1933; Madison: 1978); "The right not to assimilate" in: Morton H. Fried (editor), *Readings in Anthropology* (New York: 1968), pp. 583-593 [originally: "Education and the future of tribalism in the United States: the case of the American Indian," *Social Service Review*, vol. 35 (1961), pp. 135-143]; *History, Evolution and the Concept of Culture: Selected Papers by Alexander Lesser* (Cambridge: 1985).

SOURCES: Thomas Belmonte, "Alexander Lesser, 1902-1982," *American Anthropologist*, vol. 87 (1985), pp. 637-644; Douglas Parks, "Alexander Lesser, 1902-1982," *Plains Anthropologist*, vol. 30 (1985), pp. 65-71; Sydney Mintz, Introduction and commentaries in: Alexander Lesser, *History, Evolution and the Concept of Culture: Selected Papers by Alexander Lesser* (edited by Sidney W. Mintz) (Cambridge: 1985); Joan Vincent, "Ahead of his time? production and reception in the work of Alexander Lesser," *American Ethnologist*, vol. 15 (1988), pp. 743-751.

Thomas Belmonte

Lévi-Strauss, Claude. Ethnologist, anthropologist, philosopher. Born in Brussels (Belgium) 28 November 1908. Lévi-Strauss is generally considered one of the most important figures in contemporary anthropology. He is the major theorist of structuralism in anthropology, and his graceful writings on many other subjects have made him one of the best-known intellectuals of his time.

He attended the University of Paris, which awarded him an *agrégation* in philosophy in 1931. Then, he worked as a teacher in a *lycée* for two years.

Lévi-Strauss's interest in ethnology was aroused during a five-year period (1934-1939) spent largely in Brazil. He taught sociology at the University of São Paulo during part of the first three years; he also engaged in fieldwork among Brazilian Indians. He did further fieldwork in 1938-1939. Lévi-Strauss's experiences in Brazil are described informally in *Tristes tropiques*, one of anthropology's only best-sellers. They also colored all of his formal academic writing.

He spent part of the World War II years in New York, teaching at the New School for Social Research. During this period he made personal contact with many of the major figures in anthropology in the English-speaking world. He stayed in the United States for some period after the war as cultural attaché.

After his return to France Lévi-Strauss held posts at the Musée de l'Homme and at the École Pratiques des Hautes Études. He was appointed to the Chair of Social Anthropology of the Collège de France in 1959.

Les structures élémentaires de la parenté, the first large-scale application of structuralist ideas to the study of kinship, was published in 1949 and has came to be considered one of the landmarks of contemporary anthropology.

Later writings—for example, *La pensée sauvage* and *Mythologiques*—treated such subjects as myths from a structuralist point of view.

Structuralism as practiced by Lévi-Strauss derived in part from the work of FERDINAND DE SAUSSURE and Roman Jakobson in linguistics. The goal of structuralism was to elucidate the patterns underlying surface phenomena. For Lévi-Strauss these structures have often involved binary oppositions. Followers argue that such patterns are in some sense a clue to the nature of man. Detractors have sometimes wondered whether a method that works well in helping one to understand the phonetic structure of human speech was altogether appropriate in analyzing more complicated phenomena like myths. Other critics have dwelled on the lack of clarity in some of Lévi-Strauss's prose.

Lévi-Strauss's *oeuvre* has fostered a major academic cottage industry. A bibliography published in 1977 (*Claude Lévi-Strauss and His Critics*) listed nearly fifty books and more than one thousand articles about his work. Since 1977, hundreds of additional items have been published. No other anthropologist has inspired this quantity of literature about his work.

MAJOR WORKS: *Les structures élémentaires de la parenté* (Paris: 1949; 2nd ed., Paris: 1967) [tr.: *The Elementary Structures of Kinship* (Boston: 1969)]; *Races et histoires* (Paris: 1952); *Tristes tropiques* (Paris: 1955) [tr.: *Tristes tropiques* (New York: 1961) [London ed. called: *World on the Wane*]]; *Antropologie structurale* (Paris: 1958) [tr.: *Structural Anthropology* (New York: 1968)]; *Le totemisme aujourd'hui* (Paris: 1962) [tr.: *Totemism* (Boston: 1963)]; *La pensée sauvage* (Paris: 1962) [tr.: *The Savage Mind* (Chicago: 1966)]; *Mythologiques* [4 vols.: *Le cru et le cuit*; *Du miel aux cendres*; *L'origine des manières de table*; *L'homme nu*] (Paris: 1964-1971) [tr.: *The Raw and the Cooked* (New York: 1969); *From Honey to Ashes* (London: 1973); *The Origin of Table Manners* (New York: 1978); *The Naked Man* (New York: 1981)]; *La potière jalouse* (Paris: 1985); *Le regard éloigné* (Paris: 1988).

SOURCES: François H. Lapointe and Claire C. Lapointe, *Claude Lévi-Strauss and His Critics: an International Bibliography of Criticism (1950-1976), Followed by a Bibliography of the Writings of Claude Lévi-Strauss* (New York: 1977) [the title is accurate; contains exhaustive bibliographies]; Edmund Leach, *Lévi-Strauss* (London: 1970); E. Nelson Hayes and Tanya Hayes (editors), *Claude Lévi-Strauss: the Anthropologist as Hero* (Cambridge, Mass.: 1970); Ino Rossi (editor), *The Unconscious in Culture: the Structuralism of Claude Lévi-Strauss in Perspective* (New York: 1974); Jean Pouillon and Pierre Maranda (editors), *Échanges et communications: mélanges offerts à Claude Lévi-Strauss à l'occasion de son 60ème anniversaire* [2 vols.] (The Hague: 1970) (= *Studies in General Anthropology*, vol. 5); James A. Boon, *From Symbolism to Structuralism: Lévi-Strauss in Literary Tradition* (New York: 1972).

Levin, M.G. (Maksim Grigor'evich).

Physical anthropologist, ethnographer, archaeologist, geographer. Born in Slonim (Belorussia) 29 October 1904, died in Moscow (Russian S.F.S.R.) 18 April 1963. Levin was a doctor of historical sciences and a professor. He worked in Moscow in the T͡Sentral'nyi muzeĭ narodovedeniiâ (Central Museum of Ethnology), then in the Institut ètnografii (Institute of Ethnography) of the Soviet Academy of Sciences as deputy director (from 1944) and as director of the anthropology section (from 1949).

The major areas of Levin's scholarly interests were the physical anthropology and ethnography of the peoples of Siberia, the problems of general ethnography and physical anthropology and the history of science. Levin was also a prominent organizer of scholarly projects. As an author and editor he published such major works as *Proiskhozhdenie cheloveka i drevnee rasselenie chelovechestva*, *Narody Sibiri* and *Istoriko-ètnograficheskiĭ atlas Sibiri*.

MAJOR WORKS "Kraniologicheskiĭ tip ul'cheĭ," *Antropologicheskiĭ zhurnal*, no. 1 (1937), pp. 82-90; "Problema pigmeev v antropologii i ètnografii," *Sovetskaĭa ètnografiĭa*, no. 2 (1946), pp. 17-28; "O proiskhozhdenii i tipakh uprĭazhnogo sobakovodstva," *Sovetskaĭa ètnografiĭa*, no. 2 (1946), pp. 75-108; (with G.M. Vasilevich), "Tipy olenevodstva i ikh proiskhozhdenie," *Sovetskaĭa ètnografiĭa*, no. 1 (1951), pp. 63-87; (editor) *Istoriko-ètnograficheskiĭ atlas Sibiri* (Moscow and Leningrad: 1961) (= *Trudy Instituta ètnografii AN SSSR*, vol. 16); "K probleme istoricheskogo sootnosheniĭa khozĭaĭstvenno-kul'turnykh tipov Sredneĭ Azii," *Kratkie soobshcheniĭa Instituta ètnografii*, no. 2 (1947), pp. 84-86; (with N.N. Cheboksarov) "Khozĭaĭstvenno-kul'turnye tipy i istoriko-ètnograficheskie oblasti," *Sovetskaĭa ètnografiĭa*, no. 4 (1955), pp. 3-17; (with ĬA.ĬA. Roginskiĭ) *Osnovy antropologii* (Moscow: 1955); *Antropologicheskie tipy Sibiri i ikh genezis* (Moscow: 1955); (co-editor with L.P. Potapov) *Narody Sibiri* (Moscow: 1956); *Ètnicheskaĭa antropologiĭa i problemy ètnogeneza narodov Dal'nego Vostoka* (Moscow: 1958) (= *Trudy Instituta ètnografii*, vol. 36); *Ocherki po istorii antropologii v Rossii* (Moscow: 1960); "Ètnograficheskie i antropologicheskie materialy kak istoricheskiĭ istochnik (k metodologii izucheniĭa istorii bespis'mennykh narodov)," *Sovetskaĭa ètnografiĭa*, no. 1 (1961), pp. 20-28; (co-editor with L.P. Potapov) *Proiskhozhdenie cheloveka i drevnee rasselenie chelovechestva* (Moscow: 1961); (with S.I. Bruk and V.I. Kozlov) "O predmete i zadachakh ètnogeografii," *Sovetskaĭa ètnografiĭa*, no. 1 (1963), pp. 11-25; *Ètnicheskaĭa antropologiĭa ĬAponii* (Moscow: 1971).

SOURCES: "Pamiati M.G. Levina," *Sovetskaĭa ètnografiĭa*, no. 4 (1963), pp. 3-9; ĬA.V. Chesnov, "O sofsial'no-èkonomicheskikh i prirodnykh usloviĭakh vozniknoveniĭa khozĭaĭstvenno-kul'turnykh tipov (v sviĭazi s rabotami M.G. Levina)," *Sovetskaĭa ètnografiĭa*, no. 6 (1970), pp. 15-26; V.P. Alekseev, "M.G. Levin: antropolog, ètnograf i organizator nauki (k 80-letiĭu so dnĭa rozhdeniĭa)," *Sovetskaĭa ètnografiĭa*, no. 6 (1984), pp. 65-76.

A.M. Reshetov
[Translation from Russian: Thomas L. Mann]

Lévy-Bruhl, Lucien. Anthropologist, philosopher, sociologist. Born in Paris (France) 10 April 1857, died in Paris (France) 13 March 1939. Lévy-Bruhl is best known to anthopologists for his writing on "primitive mentality." His early training, however, was in philosophy, and in his long academic career at the Sorbonne and elsewhere he served largely as a professor of philosophy. His first scholarly works also focused on philosophy. He was apparently led to his interest in "primitive man" by the question of the extent to which Western philosophical ideas are universal.

In Lévy-Bruhl's earlier works on the subject (e.g., *Les fonctions mentales dans les sociétés primitives* and *La mentalité primitive*), he argued that primitive man's reasoning processes are quite different from those of modern man. In particular, primitive reason is "prelogical": governed largely by mysticism and subject to the "law of participation" according to which a being can at the same time be both itself and something else. In response to criticism, he conceded in later works (e.g., *Les carnets de Lévy-Bruhl*) that the fundamental structure of the human mind is the same everywhere but still argued that mysticism plays a more important role in the mental life of primitive man than in that of modern man.

Lévy-Bruhl's ideas were disseminated widely during his lifetime, in part through his voluminous writing, in part as a result of lecture tours undertaken in his later years under the aegis of the Alliance Française. His work has been the object of a great deal of comment. Many observers have argued that his model of "primitive man" is too simple. Committed cultural relativists have been uncomfortable with the extent to which he seemed to suggest a gulf between "primitive" and modern man. However, his work is often considered important in that it forced anthropologists to consider clearly the extent to which "primitive man" exists at all. Defenders have argued that he was one of the first social scientists to study seriously the thought processes of non-Western man and as such that he was a forerunner both of cognitive and of symbolic anthropology.

MAJOR WORKS: *La philosophie d'Auguste Comte* (Paris: 1900) [tr.: *The Philosophy of Auguste Comte* (New York: 1903)]; *La morale et la science des moeurs* (Paris: 1903) [tr.: *Ethics and Moral Science* (London: 1905)]; *Les fonctions mentales dans les sociétés primitives* (Paris: 1910) [tr.: *How Natives Think* (London: 1926)]; *La mentalité primitive* (Paris: 1922) [tr.: *Primitive Mentality* (New York: 1923)]; *L'âme primitive* (Paris: 1923) [tr.: *The "Soul" of the Primitive* (New York: 1928)]; *Le surnaturel et la nature dans la mentalité primitive* (Paris: 1931) [tr.: *Primitives and the Supernatural* (New York: 1935)]; *La mythologie primitive* (Paris: 1935) [tr.: *Primitive Mythology* (St. Lucia: 1983)]; *L'expérience mystique et les symboles chez les primitifs* (Paris: 1938); *Les carnets de Lévy-Bruhl* (Paris: 1949) [tr.: *The Notebooks on Primitive Mentality* (New York: 1975)].

SOURCES: Jean Cazeneuve, *Lucien Lévy-Bruhl: sa vie, son oeuvre, avec un exposé de sa philosophie* (Paris: 1963) [tr.: *Lucien Lévy-Bruhl* (Oxford: 1972)]; Rodney Needham, *Belief, Language and Experience* (Chicago: 1972); Jean Cazeneuve, "Lévy-Bruhl, Lucien" in: David L. Sills (editor), *International Encyclopedia of the Social Sciences* (New York: 1968-1979), vol. 9, pp. 263-266; C. Scott Littleton, "Lucien Lévy-Bruhl and the concept of cognitive relativity" in: Lucien Lévy-Bruhl, *How Natives Think* (Princeton: 1985), pp. v-lviii; Frederica de Laguna, "Lévy-Bruhl's contribution to the study of primitive mentality," *Philosophical Review*, vol. 49 (1940), pp. 552-566; Paul Émile Duroux, "Lucien Lévy-Brühl" in: *Dictionnaire des anthropologistes* (Paris: 1975), pp. 192-193.

Lewis, Albert Buell. Anthropologist. Born in Clifton (Ohio) 21 June 1867, died in Chicago (Illinois) 10 October 1940. Best known for his studies of Melanesian material culture, Lewis spent nearly four years in Melanesia from 1909 to 1913 as leader of the Joseph N. Field South Pacific Expedition, which he undertook on behalf of Field Museum of Natural History where he was assistant curator of African and Melanesian ethnology. During this expedition he visited all of the colonial territories of Melanesia—Fiji, New Caledonia, the New Hebrides, the Solomon Islands, German New Guinea, Papua and Dutch New Guinea—and made a collection of more than 14,000 objects and took nearly 2,000 photographs of village life.

Lewis was the first American anthropologist to conduct systematic, long-term field research in Melanesia, and his collection remains the largest and best documented assemblage of Melanesian material ever collected in the field. Through his field notes, his photographs and his collection, Lewis attempted to document the cultural diversity of Melanesian communities and the movement of local handicrafts through trade. His field notes and other documentation are unrivaled in their attention to details of trade. His monograph, *The Ethnology of Melanesia*, is the first English-language publication to deal with the varied cultures of the whole of Melanesia as parts of a common ethnographic region.

Lewis began his career in the biological sciences, attending Wooster College from 1890 to 1893 and completing his A.B. in biology at the University of Chicago in 1894. For three years he held fellowships at the University of Chicago in biology, histology and bacteriology before accepting a position as a fellow, and later lecturer, in zoology at the University of Nebraska from 1897 to 1902. At the age of thirty-five, Lewis returned to graduate school at Columbia University where he studied anthropology under FRANZ BOAS, becoming Boas's third Ph.D. student in 1906. His dissertation, *Tribes of the Columbia Valley and the Coast of Washington and Oregon*, was a regional comparison of material culture, customs and practices that attempted to identify the influences of the various cultural groups on one another. The zoologist's attention to local variation, the Boasian attention to detail and his early interest in the influence of one culture on another were important influences that shaped his later Melanesian research and writings.

During the summer of 1906 Lewis assisted William C. Mills in the excavation of Siep Mound near Bainbridge, Ohio. The following winter he joined the staff of the Department of Anthropology at Field Museum as an assistant. He was promoted to assistant curator in 1908 and curator in 1937. After his return from Melanesia in 1913, Lewis spent the rest of his career cataloging collections and preparing exhibits at Field Museum that would illustrate patterns of cultural diversity in Melanesia. Most of his publications were aimed at popular audiences and attempted to illustrate and interpret Melanesian life and its regional variations to the public.

MAJOR WORKS: "Tribes of the Columbia Valley and the coast of Washington and Oregon" [Ph.D. thesis], *Memoirs of the American Anthropological Association*, vol. 1 (1906), pp. 147-209; *Block Prints from India for Textiles* (Chicago: 1924) (= *Field Museum of Natural History, Anthropology Design Series*, no. 1); *Javanese Batik Designs from Metal Stamps* (Chicago: 1924) (= *Field Museum of Natural History, Anthropology Design Series*, no. 2); *Decorative Art of New Guinea: Incised Designs* (Chicago: 1925) (= *Field Museum of Natural History, Anthropology Design Series*, no. 4); *Melanesian Shell Money in Field Museum Collections* (Chicago: 1929) (= *Field Museum of Natural History Publication*, no. 268; *Anthropological Series*, vol. 19, no. 1); "Tobacco In New Guinea," *American Anthropologist*, vol. 33 (1931), pp. 134-138; *Carved and Painted Designs from New Guinea* (Chicago: 1931) (= *Field Museum of Natural History, Anthropology Design Series*, no. 5); *Ethnology of Melanesia* (Chicago: 1932) (= *Field Museum of Natural History, Department of Anthropology, Guide*, part 5); "New Britain notebook," *Field Museum of Natural History Bulletin*, vol. 59, no. 8 (September 1988), pp. 16-23.

SOURCES: Joseph N. Field South Pacific Expedition, *Field Diaries, 1909-1913* [not published, at Field Museum]; unpublished correspondence and files of the Department of Anthropology, Field Museum of Natural History; Franz Boas Professional Correspondence, deposited with the American Philosophical Society, Philadelphia; Archives of the College of Wooster, Wooster, Ohio; W.D. Hambly, "Albert Buell Lewis," *American Anthropologist*, vol. 43 (1941), pp. 256-257; W.D. Hambly, "In memoriam Albert Buell Lewis, June 21, 1867—October 11, 1940," *Field Museum News*, vol. 11, no. 11 (November 1940), p. 6; John H. Miller, "Woosterians who are achieving: Albert B. Lewis, '93," *Wooster Alumni Bulletin* (1925); Susan B. Parker, "New Guinea adventure: sketch of a working anthropologist," *Field Museum of Natural History Bulletin* vol. 49, no. 5 (May 1978), pp. 4-9; Robert L. Welsch, "The A.B. Lewis Collection from Melanesia—75 years later," *Field Museum of Natural History Bulletin*, vol. 59, no. 8 (September 1988), pp. 10-15; *Book of Chicagoans* (Chicago: 1917), p. 413; "Albert Buell Lewis, anthropologist, 73," *The New York Times* (11 October 1940), p. 21; *Who's Who in America*, vols. 8-21 (1914-1941).

Robert L. Welsch

Lewis, Oscar. Anthropologist. Born in New York (New York) 25 December 1914, died in New York (New York) 14 December 1970. Lewis was the son of Polish immigrant parents; his original name was Yehezkiel Lefkowitz, though he was called Oscar from childhood. (His surname he changed while in graduate school.) Lewis's father was a rabbi and cantor in Liberty, New York, where the family ran a small hotel.

Entering the City College of New York in 1930 at the age of fifteen, Lewis majored in history. He received his B.A. in 1936. He began graduate work in history that fall at Columbia Teachers College but was soon dissatisfied with his situation. An interview with RUTH BENEDICT convinced him to study anthropology instead, and Lewis quickly changed departments. He earned his doctorate in 1940, with a library-researched dissertation on the Blackfoot Indians.

After taking his degree, Lewis taught night school courses at Brooklyn College and drove a cab to eke out a living. In 1942 he moved to Yale University, where he worked for the Human Relations Area Files on Latin America, a culture area to which he had previously devoted little attention. It would be the major focus of his career from that point forward, however. In 1943 Lewis was hired by the Justice Department for the Special War Policies Unit, while later that year he was sent to Mexico City as liaison between the U.S. Office of Indian Affairs and the Interamerican Indian Institute.

In Mexico Lewis undertook a restudy of Tepoztlán, a village described during the 1920s by anthropologist ROBERT REDFIELD. Lewis's findings diverged considerably from Redfield's, to some extent due to the passage of time, but also to the very different viewpoints possessed by the two researchers. However, Lewis and Redfield remained on good terms throughout their lives, and Lewis's book, *Life in a Mexican Village: Tepoztlán Restudied*, was dedicated to Redfield.

In 1944 Lewis was transferred to the Department of Agriculture as a social scientist for the Bureau of Agricultural Economics. He supervised large numbers of field researchers in the study of various rural American communities. In 1946 he carried out a study of Bell County, Texas, which resulted in *On the Edge of the Black Waxy*.

In the autumn of 1946 Lewis was appointed associate professor of anthropology at Washington University in St. Louis. Two years later he moved to the University of Illinois at Urbana, where he was a major force in shaping the anthropology department. Lewis remained on the Illinois faculty for the rest of his life, spending nearly half of his time doing fieldwork in such places as Mexico, Puerto Rico, Spain, India, Cuba and New York City.

The Ford Foundation hired Lewis in 1952 to evaluate the progress of rural reconstruction projects in north India. He refused to limit his participation to dry statistical analyses and engaged in community studies resulting in his book *Village Life in Northern India*. Lewis became seriously ill in the field in 1953, undergoing hospitalization in Rome and in New York, and did not return to India to finish his projected two-year stay.

A follow-up of his research in Tepoztlán, the study of villagers who had relocated in Mexico City, led Lewis to considerable fame and to a long-lasting controversy. Beginning with *Five Families*, Lewis chronicled what he termed the "culture of poverty," a wide-spread lifestyle predicated on, and in adaptation to, enduring poverty. Having known poverty himself, and politically committed since his youth, Lewis saw his work among the poor of Latin America as both anthropology and advocacy. Critics of the "culture of poverty" theory have claimed, among other things, that it blames poverty on the poor; Lewis's apparent intention was instead to demonstrate that the psychological and cultural effects of a poverty-stricken life in capitalistic countries often can be more difficult to escape than the economic condition itself.

Lewis's fame came not only from the subject matter of his later works but from his methods. Employing graduate students and other assistants, Lewis recorded the daily lives of people from a variety of Latin American cultures. His books provided a rich documentation of individual lives, rather than the impersonal summary of "cultures" and "lifeways" still so common in the literature. Lewis has been criticized for his emphasis on the very poor, an emphasis easy to understand if one perceives his purposes; he has also been criticized for a tendency toward insufficient acknowledgement of the efforts of co-workers.

The critical and financial success of *Five Families* and subsequent books brought Lewis serious attention, more as an author than as an anthropologist, and he rarely published in scholarly journals in the latter half of his career. At the time of his death, Lewis was involved in a study of Cuban workers; a three-volume account was published posthumously.

MAJOR WORKS: *The Effects of White Contact upon Blackfoot Culture* (Seattle: 1942); *On the Edge of the Black Waxy* (St. Louis: 1948); *Life in a Mexican Village: Tepoztlán Restudied* (Urbana: 1951); "Controls and experiments in anthropological field work" in: A.L. Kroeber (editor), *Anthropology Today* (Chicago: 1953), pp. 352-375; "Medicine and politics in a Mexican village" in: Benjamin Paul (editor), *Health, Culture and Community* (New York: 1955), pp. 403-435; *Village Life in Northern India* (Urbana: 1958); *Five Families: Mexican Case Studies in the Culture of Poverty* (New York: 1959); *The Children of Sanchez: Autobiography of a Mexican Family* (New York: 1961); *Pedro Martinez: a Mexican Peasant and His Family* (New York: 1964); *La Vida: a Puerto Rican Family in the Culture of Poverty--San Juan and New York* (New York: 1966); (with Ruth M. Lewis and Susan M. Rigdon) *Living the Revolution: An Oral History of Contemporary Cuba* [3 vols.] (Urbana: 1977-1978).

SOURCES: Alden Whitman, "Oscar Lewis, author and anthropologist, dead," *The New York Times* (18 December 1970), p. 42; Douglas Butterworth, "Oscar Lewis, 1914-1970," *American Anthropologist*, vol. 74 (1972), pp. 747-757; Susan M. Rigdon, *The Culture Facade: Art, Science and Politics in the Work of Oscar Lewis* (Urbana: 1988); Sol Tax, "Lewis, Oscar" in: David L. Sills, *International Encyclopedia of the Social Sciences* (New York: 1968-1979), vol. 18, pp. 446-450.

David Lonergan

Li Fang-Kuei. Linguist, anthropologist. Born in Canton (China) 20 August 1902, died in Oakland (California) 21 August 1987. Educated in Peking at the Tsinghua Junior College, Li completed his baccalaureate at the University of Michigan (Ann Arbor) in 1926 and his graduate degrees at the University of Chicago where he studied under LEONARD BLOOMFIELD, Peter Buck (see TE RANGI HIROA) and EDWARD SAPIR. His M.A. was awarded in 1927 and the Ph.D. in 1928. He was recognized for his significant scholarly achievements by his alma mater, the University of Michigan, with an honorary doctorate in 1972.

The early portion of Li's career was devoted to American Indian languages, chiefly the Athabaskan family, and he served as an editor of the *International Journal of American Linguistics* for many years. His descriptive and historical-comparative work, as well as his insights into American Indian ethnology, are highly regarded by scholars of Amerindian peoples. Returning to China in 1929 Li turned his substantial intellectual skills to Asian languages, beginning with a period of fieldwork on Chinese dialects. In addition to his Chinese analyses, Li studied and wrote extensively on Tibetan and also on Miao-Yao and, most significantly for the scholarly community, on the Tai family. In 1946 he returned to the United States, teaching first at Harvard and Yale, then moving westward to the University of Washington (Seattle) in 1949 and the University of Hawaii (Honolulu) in 1969. Honored in Hong Kong, Taipei and Bangkok, Li drew the acclaim of both colleagues and students for his thorough and detailed explications and his penetrating and creative insights into synchronic and diachronic questions. Because of his pioneering work and the genius of his analyses, Li is universally regarded as the founder of the field of Tai linguistics. It was his study of phonological features (in terms of distribution and in terms of variation) and lexical items that led him to classify the Tai languages in three subgroups: Southwestern, Central and Northern, thus defining the field. The compendium, *A Handbook of Comparative Tai*, is no less than a classic.

MAJOR WORKS: *Mattole, an Athabaskan Language* (Chicago: 1930); "A list of Chipewyan stems," *International Journal of American Linguistics*, vol. 7 (1932), pp. 122-151; "Archaic Chinese -iwang, -iwak and -iwag," *Bulletin of the Institute of History and Philology, Academica Sinica*, vol. 5 (1935), pp. 65-74; "Languages and dialects," *The Chinese Year Book* (1936-1937), pp. 121-128; "The hypothesis of a pre-glottalized series of consonants in primitive Tai," *Bulletin of the Institute of History and Philology, Academica Sinica*, vol. 11 (1943), pp. 177-188; "Some Old Chinese loan words in the Tai languages," *Harvard-Yenching Journal of Asiatic Studies*, vol. 8 (1945), pp. 333-342; "Notes on the Mak Language," *Bulletin of the Institute of History and Philology, Academica Sinica*, vol. 19 (1948), pp. 1-80; "Consonant clusters in Tai," *Language*, vol. 30 (1954), pp. 368-379; "The Tibetan inscription of the Sino-Tibetan treaty of 821-822," *T'oung Pao*, vol. 44 (1955), pp. 1-99; "Siamese wan and waan," *Language*, vol. 32 (1956), pp. 81-82; "Classification by vocabulary: Tai dialects," *Anthropological Linguistics*, vol. 1 (1959), pp. 15-21; "A tentative classification of Tai dialects" in: Stanley Diamond (editor), *Culture in History: Essays in Honor of Paul Radin* (New York: 1960), pp. 951-959; "The Tai and the Kam-Sui languages," *Lingua*, vol. 14 (1965), pp. 148-179; "Some tonal irregularities in the Tai languages" in: R. Jakobson and S. Kawamoto (editors), *Studies in General and Oriental Linguistics* (Tōkyō: 1970), pp. 415-422; "Languages and dialects of China," *Journal of Chinese Linguistics*, vol. 1 (1973), pp. 1-13; "Tai languages" in: *The New Encyclopaedia Britannica* (Chicago: 1974), vol. 17, pp. 989-992; *A Handbook of Comparative Tai* (Honolulu: 1977).

SOURCES: Pang-hsin Ting, "Academic contributions of Dr. Fang Kuei Li," *Journal of Chinese Linguistics*, vol. 16 (1988), pp. 167-172; "Biographical sketch of Fang-Kuei Li" in: T. Gething, J. Harris and P. Kullavanijaya (editors), *Tai Linguistics in Honor of Fang-Kuei Li* (Bangkok: 1976).

Thomas W. Gething

Li Ji (Li Chi). Archaeologist. Born in Zhongxiang, Hubei (China) 2 June 1896, died in Taipei (Taiwan) 1 August 1979. After graduating from Tsinghua Academy, Li Ji studied psychology and sociology at Clark University and then anthropology at Harvard, where he earned a doctorate in 1923. After his return to China he taught at Nankai University and at Tsinghua Academy's new Graduate Research Institute. During 1925-1926 he excavated a Neolithic Yangshao Culture site in Xiaxian, southern Shanxi, becoming the first Chinese scholar to undertake modern archaeological fieldwork. In 1928 he was appointed by the Academia Sinica to the new post of archaeology department chairman and excavation project director at Anyang, the recently discovered center of the 3,000-plus-year-old Shang dynasty, which produced the oracle bone inscriptions that were the first written documents in the eastern half of Asia. Li applied Western archaeological methods at Anyang, recruiting and training the first generation of Chinese archaeologists and setting the tone and priorities of the study of the Anyang finds. His methodology, and above all his ceramic and bronze vessel nomenclature and typology, still dominate the whole field of archaeology in China. The Sino-Japanese War, breaking out in 1937, virtually put an end to any significant fieldwork by Li Ji's department, and after 1949 he went to Taiwan with the Nationalist government. Outside his Anyang work, Li Ji was engaged in many other significant archaeological activities—first during the war in the Southwest and, after 1949, in Taiwan where he founded the Department of Archaeology and Anthropology at National Taiwan University, the first university program in China to train professional archaeologists. But, above all, from 1928 until his death in 1979, he devoted much of his time to the excavation, care, transport, study and publication of the 1928-1937 Anyang material, and his Anyang work established his status as the father of modern Chinese archaeology.

MAJOR WORKS: *Xiyincun Shiqiandi Yicun* [*Prehistoric Remains at Xiyincun*] (Peking: 1927); *The Formation of Chinese People: An Anthropological Inquiry* (Cambridge, Mass.: 1928); *Yinxu Qiwu Jiabian: Taoqi (Shangji)* [*Yinxu Artifacts, Volume I, Pottery, Part 1*] (Taipei: 1956); *The Beginnings of Chinese Civilization* (Seattle: 1957); *Archaeologia Sinica*, n.s., 1-5 (1964-1972); *Anyang Excavations* (Seattle: 1977).

SOURCE: Li Guangmo, "Li Ji zhuan lue" ["A brief biography of Li Ji"], *Zhongguo Xiandai Shehuikexuejia Zhuanlue*, 3 (1984), pp. 153-173.

K.C. Chang

Lilientalowa, Regina. Ethnographer. Born in Zawichost k/Sandomierz (Poland) 14 June 1877, died in Warsaw (Poland) 4 December 1924. Lilientalowa was largely self-taught but supplemented her knowledge by taking secret advanced scientific courses for women. Under the influence of LUDWIK KRZYWICKI she developed and expanded her academic interests in the field of Jewish folk culture and ritual. Over time she changed her primary research interests from the description of modern Jewish cultural life to the past and worked to analyze the customs and rituals occurring in recorded form (e.g., in the *Talmud* and *Bible*). She compiled her own field material. Her studies dealt primarily with folklore, but they also consisted of material related to Jewish folk art. Lilientalowa was also a translator of stories and song-texts from Yiddish into Polish.

MAJOR WORKS: "Życie pozagrobowe i świat przeszły w wyobrażeniu ludu żydowskiego" ["The afterlife and the life of the past in the Jewish folk imagination"], *Lud*, vol. 8 (1902), pp. 350-353; "Dziecko żydowskie" ["The Jewish child"], *Materiały Antropologiczno-Archeologiczne i Etnograficzne*, vol. 7, no. 2 (1904), pp. 141-173 [tr.: "Das Kind bei den Juden," *Mitteilungen zur jüdischen Volkskunde*, vol. 10, no. 2 (1908), pp. 41-55]; "Święta żydowskie w przeszłości i teraźniejszości" ["Jewish holidays of the past and present"] [3 parts], *Rozprawy Akademii Umiejętności Wydział Filologiczny*, vol. 45 (1909), pp. 191-288; vol. 52 (1913), pp. 270-380; vol. 58, no. 5 (1920), pp. 1-103; *Kult ciał niebieskich u starożytnych Hebrajczyków i szczątki tego kultu u współczesnego ludu żydowskiego* [*Cult of the Heavenly Bodies among the Ancient Hebrews and Vestiges of that Cult Among Contemporary Jewish Folk*] (Lwów and Warsaw: 1921); *Kult wody u starożytnych Hebrajczyków i szczątki tego kultu u współczesnego ludu żydowskiego* [*The Cult of Water among Ancient Hebrews and Vestiges of that Cult among Contemporary Jewish Folk*] (Warsaw: 1930).

SOURCES: Giza Fränklowa, "Regina Lilientalowa," *Lud*, vol. 26 (1927), pp. 119-121; Wiesław Bieńkowski, "Lilientalowa z Eigerów, Regina" in: *Polski słownik biograficzny* [*Polish Biographical Dictionary*], vol. 17 (Wrocław: 1972), pp. 334-335.

Maria Niewiadomska and Iwona Grzelakowska

[Translation from Polish: Joel Janicki]

Lilly, Eli. Industrialist, philanthropist, archaeologist. Born in Indianapolis (Indiana) 1 April 1885, died in Indianapolis (Indiana) 24 January 1977. A pharmacist by vocation, president of an international pharmaceutical firm (Eli Lilly and Company), and an archaeologist by avocation, Eli Lilly possessed the uncommon combination of substantial financial resources and real historical sensitivity, which, when applied to anthropology/archaeology, had significant impact on the growth of the discipline in the eastern United States.

At age forty-five, in 1929, intrigued by materials derived from local prehistoric sites, he began purchasing artifacts for a private collection. However, unable to find satisfactory answers to questions concerning their age, use and ethnic association, Lilly within three years turned from a dilettante collector to a valued associate of a small group of individuals then attempting to elevate archaeology to a level of academic respectability. Not content to be simply a patron who made it possible for others to do anthropological/archaeological research, he participated actively. Always interested in Indiana, his home state, he initially set about compiling a bibliography and synthesis of what was known about state prehistory (*Prehistoric Antiquities of Indiana*) in an effort to raise public awareness. Then a major research project focused on the Walam Olum, mnemonic signs painted on bark, which were thought to record in allegorical form the migration history of the Delaware Indians. Reputedly, these had been collected by C. Rafinesque in Indiana in the early 19th century. Inspired by EDWARD SAPIR's work on aboriginal time perspective, Lilly brought together a team of anthropologists from the major fields of anthropology, whose purpose was to determine whether the Walam Olum could illuminate culture history. And for nearly two decades he funded scholarships; research in linguistics, archaeology, physical anthropology and ethnology; and archival investigations. He wrote a substantial portion of the final report (*Walam Olum or Red Score*). Though the validity of the Walam Olum may be questioned, the financial support provided abetted the growth of the discipline and several members of the research team formed the nucleus of the Department of Anthropology, Indiana University, founded in 1947.

Heinrich Schliemann was a boyhood idol, and, because Schliemann had spent several crucial months in Indianapolis pursuing a divorce, finding a new spouse and preparing for his Homeric field research, Lilly assembled, edited, and published the correspondence from that period (*Schliemann in Indianapolis*).

He also provided funds for the purchase of Angel Mounds State Memorial, a large Mississippian town located near Evansville (Indiana), and supported thirty years of fieldwork and the construction of interpretive facilities there. Also, the Glenn A. Black Laboratory of Archaeology, Indiana University, was the result of his beneficence. Lilly's long-time partnership with GLENN A. BLACK founded the archaeological research program in Indiana, which continues.

MAJOR WORKS: *Prehistoric Antiquities of Indiana* (Chicago: 1937); (with C.F. Voegelin and Erminie Voegelin) *Walam Olum or Red Score: the Migration Legend of the Lenni Lenape or Delaware Indians* (Chicago and Crawfordsville, Indiana: 1954); "Pictograph concordance with bibliography" in: *Walam Olum or Red Score: the Migration Legend of the Lenni Lenape or Delaware Indians* (Chicago and Crawfordsville, Indiana: 1954), pp. 226-239; "Speculations on the chronology of the Walam Olum and migration of the Lenni Lenape" in: *Walam Olum or Red Score: the Migration Legend of the Lenni Lenape or Delaware Indians* (Chicago and Crawfordsville, Indiana: 1954), pp. 273-285; *Schliemann in Indianapolis* (Indianapolis: 1961).

SOURCES: James B. Griffin, "A commentary on an unusual research program in American anthropology" in: untitled dedication booklet for the Glenn A. Black Laboratory of Archaeology (Bloomington: 1971); Lana Ruegamer, *A History of the Indiana Historical Society, 1830-1980* (Indianapolis 1980); James H. Madison, "Eli Lilly: archaeologist" (Bloomington: 1988) (= *Glenn A. Black Laboratory of Archaeology, Indiana University, Research Reports*, no. 8); James H. Madison, *Eli Lilly: a Life, 1885-1977* (Indianapolis: 1989).

James H. Kellar

Lin Yuehua (also: Lin Yüeh-hwa, Lin Yao-hua).

Ethnographer, anthropologist, sociologist. Born in Gutian, Fujian province (China) 27 March 1910. In 1932 Lin was graduated from Yanjing University in the capital, then Beiping, and from 1937 to 1940 he studied in the United States at Harvard University, where he received the degree of doctor of philosophy. After returning to China in 1941, Lin became a professor and then head of the Department of Sociology at Yanjing University. From 1952 he worked at the Central Nationalities College, where in 1983 he established the first department of anthropology in the country. Lin completed a series of expeditions to Yunnan, Sichuan and Tibet; to Northwest and Northeast China; to the island of Hainan and other places. He conducted research on the family and social organization of the Han and of the peoples of Southwest China. A large part of his work also deals with the history of primitive society and theories of ethnography.

MAJOR WORKS: "Miao-Man peoples of Kweichow," *Harvard Journal of Asiatic Studies*, vol. 3 (1940), pp. 261-345; "Kinship systems of the Lolo," *Harvard Journal of Asiatic Studies*, vol. 9 (1946), pp. 81-100; *Liangshan Yi jia* [*The Liangshan Yi*] (Peking: 1947); *The Golden Wing: a Sociological Study of Chinese Familism* (London: 1947); "Nekotorye nasushchnye problemy, stoiashie pered kitaiskimi étnografami v sviazi s resheniem natsional'nogo voprosa v KNP," *Sovetskaia étografiia*, no. 3 (1956), pp. 79-91; (with N.N. Cheboksarovyi) "Khoziaistvenno-kul'turnye tipy Kitaia," *Trudy Instituta étnografii AN SSSR*, vol. 23 (1961), pp. 5-46; *The Lolo of Liang Shan* (New Haven: 1961); (editor) *Yuanshi shehui shi* [*A History of Primitive Society*] (Peking: 1984); *Minzu xue yanjiu* [*Researches in Ethnography*] (Peking: 1985); (editor) *Minzu xue rumen* [*Introduction to Ethnography*] (Peking: 1990).

SOURCE: Zhang Kungshao, "Lin Yaohua" in: *Zhongguo da baike quanshu* [*Great Chinese Encyclopedia*], vol. "Minzu" ["Ethnos"] (Beijing and Shanghai: 1986), p. 250.

A.M. Reshetov
[Translation from Russian: Ruth Dunnell]

Lindblom, Gerhard K.

Ethnographer. Born in Åby (Sweden) 26 August 1887, died in Stockholm (Sweden) 14 June 1969. Lindblom obtained his B.A. (*fil. kand.*) in Uppsala in 1908, his M.A. (*fil. lic.*) in 1915 and his doctorate the year after, in 1916. Lindblom was thus the first Swedish Ph.D. (*fil. dr.*) in ethnography.

He started his museum career as an assistant (*e. amanuens*) at the Ethnographical Museum of Stockholm in 1912. He became a museum curator in 1923 and a professor of ethnography at the University of Stockholm (at that time Stockholms Högskola) in 1928. This position was at the time combined with the directorship of the Ethnographical Museum, and Lindblom held this double chair until his retirement in 1954. (The new subject "*Allmän och jämförande etnografi*" was taught actively by Lindblom only after 1933).

Lindblom took a special interest in African ethnography and linguistics and made several trips to Africa. His first major expedition was to British and German East Africa in 1910-1912. A large portion of that time was spent among the Kamba people of Kenya. Another trip took him to Kenya and Uganda in 1930. A third expedition was to Libya in 1938.

Lindblom was inspired by the German-Austrian Cultural-Historical School of ethnographic research. Thus, he emphasized cultural history and the study of diffusion. His rich bibliography testifies to a special interest in hunting and trapping methods. Nevertheless, he also published on African linguistics, Kamba folklore and general ethnographic issues.

Lindblom held several honorary positions; he was the Swedish representative at international ethnographic and anthropological congresses (e.g., Copenhagen, 1938; Brussels, 1948; and Vienna, 1952). He was also the president of the Swedish Anthropological and Geographical Society (SSAG) during 1933-1934.

In addition to publishing scholarly works, Lindblom became well known to the general public through his popular books on Africa. The Swedish image of Africa and Africans has been much influenced by Gerhard Lindblom.

MAJOR WORKS: *Afrikanska strövtåg* (Stockholm: 1914); *Outlines of a Tharaka Grammar* (Uppsala: 1914) (= *Archives d'études orientales*, vol. 9); *The Akamba in British East Africa* [3 parts] (Uppsala: 1916) (= *Archives d'études orientales*, vol. 17); *I vildmark och negerbyar à Mount Elgon och annorstädes i Ostafrika* (Uppsala: 1921); *Negerhistorier kring lägerelden* (Uppsala: 1922); *Afrika. I. De geografiska upptäckternas historia* (Uppsala: 1924); *Jakt- och fångstmetoder bland afrikanska folk* [3 vols.] (Stockholm: 1925-1926); *Kamba Folklore* [3 vols.] (Uppsala: 1928-1935) (= *Archives d'études orientales*, vol. 20, nos. 1-3).

SOURCES: Anita Jacobsson-Widding. "Från antropologi till kulturantropologi," *Ymer*, årgång 102 (1982), pp. 19-34; Sigvald Linné, "Gerhard Lindblom, 1887-1969," *Ethnos*, supplement to vol. 34 (1969), pp. 7-12; "Gerhard Lindblom: bibliography," *Ethnos*, supplement to vol. 34 (1969), pp. 35-43.

Jan-Åke Alvarsson

Ling Shun-Sheng (Ling Chunsheng). Anthropologist, sociologist. Born in Wujin County, Jiangsu Province (China) 18 January 1901, died in Taipei (Taiwan) 21 July 1978. Ling received a *doctorat ès lettres* from the University of Paris in 1929 and returned to China soon afterward to the Academia Sinica where he spent much of his time doing research and writing and where he ultimately established the Institute of Ethnology in 1965. He was a pioneer in introducing modern ethnographic fieldwork methods to China. In 1930 Ling conducted fieldwork among the Hezhe, a fishing-and-hunting people living along the lower Sungari River, and published the first ethnography ever written by a Chinese anthropologist, *Sung-hua chiang hsia yu ti Ho-chê-ts'u* [*The Hezhe of Lower Sungari River*]. This book was used extensively as the standard ethnographic textbook by subsequent anthropologists.

During World War II when the Nationalist Government was forced by the Japanese to move to western China, Ling shifted his ethnographic research to the Miao in western Hunan Province. The major change of his research direction occurred, however, after 1949 when the Nationalist Government moved to Taiwan after its losses to the Chinese Communists. On the basis of his familiarity with China's traditional customs and material culture, plus occasional observations in Taiwan, Ling began to make cross-cultural comparisons of specific artifacts or customs as they appeared in China, Southeast Asia, Mesopotamia, Egypt, India, the Pacific Islands and the New World. This endeavor lasted until the end of his life and covered a broad range of topics: teknonymy, bone-washing, Patu, Kava-drinking, dog sacrifice, earth altars, phallic worship, head hunting, bark cloth, printing, pyramidal platforms, outrigger canoes, turtle sacrifice and so on. Comparative studies of similar cultural traits among these regions demonstrated, he believed, prehistoric contacts and hence provided the basis of a grand theory that was diffusionist in nature. The Austronesian people, who used to inhabit the east coast of Asia and who acquired many cultural traits from the ancient Chinese, had emigrated by boat to the islands of the Pacific and Indian Oceans. Ling argued that their influence could be seen as far west as the east coast of Africa and as far east as the Pacific Coast of the Americas. This diffusionist view, however, has not been embraced by most of Ling's followers in Taiwan.

MAJOR WORKS: *Recherches ethnographiques sur les Yao dans la Chine du sud* (Paris: 1929); *Sung-hua chiang hsia yu ti Ho-chê-ts'u* [*The Hezhe [Goldi] of Lower Sungari River*] (Peking: 1934); *Pien chiang wên hua lun chi* [*Essays on Border Region Cultures*] (Taipei: 1953); *Chung T'ai wên hua lun chi* [*Essays on Sino-Thai Cultures*] (Taipei: 1958); *Shu p'i pu yin wên t'ao yü tsao chih yin shua shu fa ming* = *Bark Cloth Impressed Pottery, and the Inventions of Paper and Printing* (Taipei: 1963) [in Chinese; title page also in English]; *T'ai-wan yü Tung-nan Ya Chi hsi-nan T'ai-p'ing-yang to shih p'êng wên hua* [*Megalithic Cultures in Taiwan, East Asia and Southwest Pacific Regions*] (Taipei: 1967); *Mei-kuo tung nan yu Chung-kuo hua tung ti ch'iu tun wên hua* = *The Mound Cultures of East China and Southeastern North America* (Taipei: 1968) [in Chinese; title page also in English]; *Chung-kuo yüan ku yü T'ai-p'ing Yin-tu liang yang ti fan fa, ko ch'uan, fang chou ho lou ch'uan ti yen chiu* = *Study of the Raft, Outrigger, Double and Deck Canoes of Ancient China, the Pacific and the Indian Oceans* (Taipei: 1970) [in Chinese; summaries in English]; *Chung-kuo yü Hai-yang-chou ti kuei chi wên hua* = *Turtle Sacrifice in China and Oceania* (Taipei: 1971) [in Chinese; title page also in English].

Huang Shu-min

Linné, Sigvald. Ethnographer, archaeologist. Born in Stockholm (Sweden) 14 April 1899, died in Stockholm (Sweden) 23 December 1986. Linné attained his M.A. (*fil. lic.*) in Göteborg in 1925 and Ph.D. (*fil. dr.*) in 1929; he was appointed a docent and a professor of ethnography in Stockholm in 1934.

As a young science student, Linné traveled to Göteborg, partly to attend the Göteborgsutställningen (Göteborg Exhibition). There he heard about the famous ethnographer, ERLAND NORDENSKIÖLD, and through this scholar he was attracted to the study of the American Indians and finally "converted" to ethnography and archaeology by Nordenskiöld (who had gone in the same direction two decades earlier).

Under the supervision of his mentor, he wrote his first major work on the technique of South American ceramics, presented as an M.A. thesis in 1925. In this work, the scientific background of Linné is evident, and, surprisingly enough, this work is still often referred to after half a century.

In 1927 Linné accompanied Nordenskiöld on his expedition to Panama and Colombia. Linné served as head of the archaeological research work. The results of the expedition were published in his doctoral thesis, *Darien in the Past.*

This was only the first in a long series of trips and field visits to Central America; however, Mexico was the country that captured his major interest. Linné was there in 1932, 1934-1935, 1939, 1947-1948 and 1956. Fieldwork was combined with a scrutiny of archives and libraries, yet Linné never compromised his firm methodological convictions in all these tasks.

Regionally, he concentrated on Teotihuacán (*Archaeological Research at Teotihuacan, Mexico*), Puebla and Tlaxcala (*Mexican Highland Cultures*) as well as on the Mexican highland cultures in general. In his bibliographical works he wrote on Zapotecan archaeology (*Zapotecan Antiquities*) as well as on the mid-16th-century map of Mexico City, kept at the University Library of Uppsala (*Valle y la ciudad de México en 1550*). Linné made a significant contribution to the study of Mesoamerican ethnography and pre-Columbian archaeology in these publications.

In 1929 Linné moved to Stockholm and became a museum assistant at the Statens Etnografiska Museum (State Ethnographical Museum) of Stockholm. In 1953 he was appointed museum curator at the same institution, and, the year after, in 1954, he became its director, a position that he held until his retirement.

MAJOR WORKS: *The Technique of South American Ceramics* (Göteborg: 1925) (= *Göteborgs kungl. vetenskaps- och vitterhets-samhälles handlingar*, 4:e följden, vol. 29, no. 5); *Darien in the Past: the Archaeology of Eastern Panama and Northwestern Colombia* (Göteborg: 1929) (= *Göteborgs kungl. vetenskaps- och vitterhets-samhälles handlingar*, 5:e följden, ser. A, vol. 1, no. 3); *Archaeological Research at Teotihuacán, Mexico* (Stockholm: 1934) (= *Riksmuseet etnografiska avdelning*, n.s., no. 1); *Zapotecan Antiquities* (Stockholm: 1938) (= *Riksmuseet etnografiska avdelning*, n.s., no. 4); *Mexican Highland Cultures* (Stockholm: 1942); *El Valle y la Ciudad de México en 1550* (Stockholm: 1948) (= *Riksmuseet etnografiska avdelning*, n.s., no. 9) (2nd ed., Stockholm: 1988); (with Hans-Diedrich Disselhof) *Alt Amerika: die Hochkulturen der neuen Welt* (Baden-Baden: 1960) [part of series, *Kunst der Welt*].

SOURCES: Ulla Wagner and Staffan Brunius, "In memoriam: Sigvald Linné," *Ethnos*, vol. 53 (1988), pp. 124-125; Staffan Brunius, "Presentación" to: Sigvald Linné, *El Valle y la Ciudad de México en 1550* (2nd ed., Stockholm: 1988), pp. i-iii.

Jan-Åke Alvarsson

Linton, Ralph. Anthropologist, ethnologist. Born in Philadelphia (Pennsylvania) 27 February 1893, died in New Haven (Connecticut) 24 December 1953. Linton came from an old Quaker family. He received his B.A. from Swarthmore College in 1915 and his M.A. from the University of Pennsylvania in 1916. He then studied at Columbia and Harvard, receiving a Ph.D. from the latter in 1925 with the thesis, *The Material Culture of the Marquesas Islands.* His teaching career brought him to the University of Wisconsin (1928-1937) and Columbia University (1937-1946). In 1946 he accepted the Sterling Professorship in Anthropology at Yale University where he taught until his death in 1953. Linton was president of the American Anthropological Association (1946), vice-president of the American Association for the Advancement of Science (1937) and for many years chairman of the Division of Anthropology in the National Academy of Sciences. He received the Viking Fund Medal in 1951 and was chosen as the 1954 winner of the Huxley Medal.

Linton's first academic interests focused on archaeology. Between 1912 and 1919 he took part in numerous archaeological expeditions both within and outside the United States. Of particular scientific interest were expeditions to New Jersey, in 1915, where Linton excavated a site dated around 2000 B.C. and to Mesa Verde National Park where he excavated and identified the first Basket Maker III Structure. In 1920 Linton participated in a two-year archaeological expedition in the Marquesas sponsored by the Bernice P. Bishop Museum of Honolulu. The time spent in Polynesia was decisive for Linton's scientific activity. It was at that time that he oriented himself toward cultural anthropology. However, he never abandoned his archaeological interests. Back from Polynesia, Linton was employed by the Field Museum of Natural History of Chicago as Assistant Curator of North American Ethnology. In the fall of 1925 the Museum entrusted him with an ethnographic expedition to Madagascar. He spent about a year and a half in the island, partly with his second wife Margaret McIntosh Linton, visiting many regions, acquainting himself with various ethnic groups and assembling an imposing collection of artifacts purchased for the museum. His major anthropological work, *The Tanala: a Hill Tribe of Madagascar*, was a result of this expedition. On his return journey Linton went to Rhodesia to view the Zimbabwe archaeological site.

The scientific work of Ralph Linton has not received unanimous academic approval. More than once it has been judged unreliable and more in the character of literary production than exacting research. In spite of this Linton remains a key figure in modern cultural anthropology. In his work *The Study of Man*, Linton elaborated on his concepts of status and role, which led him to ascertain the link existing between societal culture and the individual personality. These themes were dealt with again and analyzed in Linton's later works, *The Cultural Background of Personality* and *Culture and Mental Disorder*. Linton's merit is that of having harmonized the different schools of American anthropology and of having given unity to the discipline.

The autobiographical words he wrote for *Twentieth Century Authors* a few months before his death bear witness to his strong and personal attitudes about his profession and his own society: "Fortunately, as an ethnologist I have always been able to combine business with pleasure and have found my greatest satisfaction in friendship with men of many different races and cultures. I consider as my greatest accomplishment that I am an adopted member of the Comanche tribe, was accepted as a master carver by the Marquesas natives and executed commissions for them in their own art, am a member of the native Church of North America (Peyote) according to the Quapaw rite, became a properly accredited *ombiasy nkazo* (medicine man) in Madagascar, and was even invited to join the Rotary Club of a Middle Western city."

MAJOR WORKS: *The Tanala: a Hill Tribe of Madagascar* (Chicago: 1933); *The Study of Man: an Introduction* (New York: 1936); (editor) *Acculturation in Seven American Indian Tribes* (New York: 1940); (editor) *The Cultural Background of Personality* (New York: 1945); (editor) *The Science of Man in World Crisis* (New York: 1945); *The Tree of Culture* (New York: 1955); *Culture and Mental Disorder* (Springfield, Ill.: 1956).

SOURCES: "Ralph Linton dies," *The New York Times* (25 December 1953), p. 17; John Gillin, "Ralph Linton, 1893-1953," *American Anthropologist*, vol. 56 (1954), pp. 274-281; "Linton, Ralph" in: S.J. Kunitz (editor), *Twentieth Century Authors: a Biographical Dictionary of Modern Literature*, 1st suppl. (New York: 1955), pp. 586-587; Clyde Kluckhohn, "Ralph Linton," *National Academy of Sciences, Biographical Memoirs*, vol. 31 (1958), pp. 236-253; Lauriston Sharp, "Linton, Ralph" in: David A. Sills (editor), *International Encyclopedia of the Social Sciences* (New York: 1968-1979), vol. 9, pp. 386-390; Adelin Linton and Charles Wagley, *Ralph Linton* (New York and London: 1971); John Witthoft, "Linton, Ralph" in: *Dictionary of American Biography*, supplement 5 (New York: 1977), pp. 434-436.

Liliana Mosca
[Translation from Italian: Gianna Panofsky]

Lipkind, William. Anthropologist. Born in New York (New York) 17 December 1904, died in New York (New York) 2 October 1974. William Lipkind studied at the City College of New York (A.B., 1927) and Columbia University (Ph.D, 1937). Before he turned to anthropology, he pursued courses in English, history and law. He taught at Ohio State University, Hunter College and New York University.

Lipkind's introduction to fieldwork came during the summer of 1936 when, for his dissertation, FRANZ BOAS sent him to Winnebago, Nebraska, to investigate the Winnebago language and to review PAUL RADIN's relevant investigations. His next fieldwork was in Brazil where he spent 1937-1938 with the Carajá, studying their language and culture. At the same time he investigated the languages and cultures of neighboring peoples, including the Cayapó.

Lipkind eventually became a civilian employee of the federal government and worked with military intelligence in Europe. After returning to the United States in 1947, his activity in anthropology was largely confined to teaching. His publications consisted mostly of children's literature.

MAJOR WORKS: *Winnebago Grammar* (New York: 1945); "The Carajá" in: Julian H. Steward (editor), *Handbook of South American Indians* (Washington: 1948) (= *Bureau of American Ethnology Bulletin*, no. 143, vol. 3), pp. 179-191; "Carajá cosmology," *Journal of American Folklore*, vol. 53 (1940), pp. 248-251.

SOURCE: Lipkind papers in the National Anthropological Archives; "William Lipkind, anthropologist," *New York Times* (3 October 1974), p. 46.

James R. Glenn

Lips, Julius Ernst. Ethnologist, sociologist, jurist. Born in Saarbrücken (Germany) 8 September 1895, died in Leipzig (German Democratic Republic) 21 January 1950. According to Lips himself, his first academic position after his graduation from the University of Leipzig in 1921 was as amanuensis to ethnology professor Karl Weule (1864-1926). After writing a dissertation in law, the ambitious Lips, who came from a family of modest means, went to the Rautenstrauch-Joest-Museum für Völkerkunde (Rautenstrauch-Joest Ethnographic Museum) in Cologne as a research assistant to FRITZ GRAEBNER. There he aligned himself with the tradition of the Cologne School of *Kulturkreislehre* developed by Willy Foy (1873-1929) and (especially) by Graebner. He enriched it, however, with his own ideas and, after becoming museum director in 1928, he developed his concept of "dynamic ethnology" (see, for example, his article "Ethnopolitik und Kolonialpolitik").

As a museum director he broke new ground in popularizing ethnology through exhibitions and lecture series. After his *Habilitation* in 1927 he founded the Department of Ethnology at the University of Cologne and in 1930 was appointed associate professor of ethnology and sociology. In 1933 his membership in the Socialist Party led to suspension from his posts by the National Socialist city government. After attempting in vain to ingratiate himself with the new regime, in 1934 Lips and his wife Eva (1906-1988) fled the escalating persecutions by emigrating, first to France then to the United States. From 1934 to 1948 he taught and conducted research at Columbia University, Howard University and the New School for Social Research. During these years he and his wife undertook fieldwork among the Montagnais-Naskapi Indians of Labrador and in 1947 among the Ojibwa in Minnesota. While in exile, Lips proved himself a consistent anti-fascist in his writings, as a speaker and supporter of the appeals of the Deutsch-Amerikanischer Kulturverband and as chairman of the Council for a Democratic Germany. As a result, his German citizenship was revoked in 1938. In 1948 Lips was called to Leipzig to take the professorial chair for ethnology and comparative legal ethnology and soon was elected rector of the university, but he died of intestinal cancer shortly thereafter.

Lips's ethnological publications especially include the fields of technology (e.g., *Fallensysteme der Naturvölker*), legal ethnology (e.g., *Naskapi Law*) and economic ethnology (e.g., *Erntevölker*), in which he introduced the new term *Erntevölker*. The high point of his creativity was his book on the ethnology of art, *The Savage Hits Back*, which, in reversing the traditional viewpoint of ethnology, risked a bold interpretation of native depictions of Europeans with the inference that the indigenous people in these works of art drew caricatures of the white man.

Julius Lips was not only an ethnologist. In his youth he also was active in student affairs, and he wrote a novel and a drama. His wife, who collaborated in almost all of his research and publication, succeeded him as professor at Leipzig and worked through the fieldwork notes left unpublished at his unexpected death.

MAJOR WORKS: "Die gleichzeitige Vergleichung zweier Strecken mit einer Dritten nach dem Augenmaß (zum Drei-Reize Problem in der Psychophysik)," *Archiv für die gesamte Psychologie*, vol. 40, Heft 3-4 (1920), pp. 193-267 [dissertation]; *Die internationale Studentenbewegung nach dem Kriege* (Leipzig: 1921); *Fallensysteme der Naturvölker* (Leipzig: 1926); *Die Stellung von Thomas Hobbes zu den politischen Parteien der großen englischen Revolution* (Leipzig: 1927); *Einleitung in die vergleichende Völkerkunde* (Leipzig: 1928); "Kamerun" in: E. Schultz-Ewerth and L. Adam (editors), *Das Eingeborenenrecht* (Stuttgart: 1930-1931), pp. 127-209; "Ethnopolitik und Kolonialpolitik," *Koloniale Rundschau*, Schlußheft (1932), pp. 530-538; *The Savage Hits Back* (London and New Haven: 1937) [German ed. of original manuscript: (Leipzig: 1983)]; *Tents in the Wilderness* (Philadelphia: 1942; London: 1944); *The Origins of Things* (New York and London: 1946); *Naskapi Law: Law and Order in a Hunting Society* (Philadelphia: 1947) (= *Transactions of the American Philosophical Society*, vol. 38, no. 4); *Forschungsreise in die Dämmerung* (Weimar: 1950); *Die Erntevölker, eine wichtige Phase in der Entwicklung der menschlichen Gesellschaft* (Berlin: 1953) (= *Berichte über die Verhandlungen der sächsischen Akademie der Wissenschaften zu Leipzig, Philologisch-historische Klasse*, 101, no. 1); (editor and co-author) *Führer des Rautenstrauch-Joest Museums* (Cologne: 1927); (editor) *Ethnologica*, vols. 3 and 4.

SOURCES: Lips file in the university archives, Cologne; archives of the Rautenstrauch-Joest Museum in the historical archives of the city of Cologne; Rolf Herzog, "Lips, Julius" in: *Neue Deutsche Biographie* (Berlin: 1953-), vol. 14, pp. 672-673; Eva Lips, *Zwischen Lehrstuhl und Indianerzelt* (Berlin [East]: 1965); "Lips, Julius Ernst" in: Herbert A. Strauss and Werner Röder (editors), *International Biographical Dictionary of Central European Emigrés* (Munich and New York: 1980-1983), vol. 2, part 2, pp. 735-736.

Lothar Pützstück
[Translation from German: Sem C. Sutter]

Lisiſsian, S.D. (Stepan Danilovich).

Ethnographer, geographer, regional specialist, literary scholar. Born in Tbilisi (Georgia, Russia) 23 September 1865, died in Erevan (Armenian S.S.R.) 4 January 1947. Lisiſsian was the founder of Soviet Armenian ethnography. From 1928 to 1947 he headed the Department of Ethnography at the Gosudarstvennyĭ istoricheskiĭ muzeĭ Armenii (Armenian State Historical Museum), which now bears his name. He also worked as a professor in the Institut istorii (Institute of History) of the Academy of Sciences of the Armenian S.S.R.

In his research, Lisiſsian elucidated all sides of the economic, material, social, familial and religious life of the Armenians in the historically and ethnographically separate regions of Armenia. He revealed their local characteristics and at the same time showed the historical-cultural unity of the Armenian ethnic group as a whole. In 1980 the archival office of the Institut arkheologii i ètnografii (Institute of Archaeology and Ethnography) of the Academy of Sciences of the Armenian S.S.R. was named for Lisiſsian and his daughter S.S. Lisiſsian.

MAJOR WORKS: "K izucheniiu armianskikh krest'ianskikh zhilishch: karabakhskiĭ karadam," *Izvestiía Kavkazskogo istoriko-arkheologicheskogo Instituta v Tiflise* vol. 3 (1925), pp. 97-108; "Iz materialov po izucheniiu zhilishch Armenii," *Izvestiía Kavkazskogo istoriko-arkheologicheskogo Instituta v Tiflise* vol. 6 (1927), pp. 119-140; "Armianskaia ètnografiía za 15 let," *Sovetskaía ètnografiía*, no. 5 (1936), pp. 270-274; "Sviatyni u perevalov," *Sovetskaía ètnografiía*, no. 5 (1936), pp. 200-212; "Ocherki ètnografii dorevoliutsionnoĭ Armenii," *Trudy Instituta ètnografii AN SSSR*, vol. 26 (1955), pp. 182-264; (with others) "Armiane" in: *Narody Kavkaza*, vol. 2 (Moscow: 1962), pp. 435-601.

SOURCE: S.D. Eremian, D.S. Vardumian and L.M. Bardanian, "S.D. Lisiſsian," *Materialy k biobibliografii uchenykh ArmSSR*, no. 41 (Erevan: 1987) [contains bibliography].

A.M. Reshetov
[Translation from Russian: Thomas L. Mann]

Lisiſsian, S.S. (Srbui Stepanovna).

Ethnographer, folklorist. Born in Tbilisi (Georgia) 28 June 1893, died in Erevan (Armenian S.S.R.) 28 August 1979. Lisiſsian was the greatest researcher of Armenian dance folklore. She held a doctorate in historical sciences. The dance notation that she developed made it possible to record with mathematical precision the position of the body in space at every moment during the process of a dance. As a researcher Lisiſsian gave special attention to the genesis of Armenian dance and theatrical folklore. She developed an analysis of traditional dance steps, focusing on the "semantics" of movement and viewing each element of the dance as a manifestation of an ethnic group's language of movement. Through the study of the genesis of the dance she attempted to penetrate the essence of "primitive" thought. Lisiſsian was the originator in Soviet scholarship of a new field, ethnochoreography. She also gave much energy to the publication of the works of her father, S.D. Lisiſsian, such as his monograph *Armiane Zangezura* (1969).

MAJOR WORKS: *Zapis' dvizheniĭa (kinetografiĭa)* (Moscow: 1940); *Starinnye plĭaski i teatral'nye predstavleniĭa armĭanskogo naroda* [2 vols.] (Erevan: 1958-1972); *Narody Kavkaza*, vol. 2 (Moscow: 1962); *Tanĭseval'nyĭ i teatral'nyĭ fol'klor armĭanskogo naroda* (Moscow: 1964); *Armĭanskie starinnye plĭaski* (Erevan: 1983).

SOURCES: "S. Lisifŝian (nekrolog), *Sovetskaĭa ėtnografiĭa*, no. 2 (1980), pp. 188-189; Ė.Kh. Petrosĭan, "Nauka byla ee zhizn'fŭ," *Sovetskiĭ balet*, no. 4 (1982), p. 31.

A.M. Reshetov
[Translation from Russian: Thomas L. Mann]

Locke, John. Philosopher, man of affairs. Born in Somerset (England) 29 August 1632, died at Oates (England) 28 October 1704. Raised a liberal Puritan, he was educated and taught at Oxford. Trained in medicine, he was deeply influenced by the new sciences. In 1665 he became physician and advisor to the first Earl of Shaftesbury, a leader of the Whigs before 1689. He was arguably the most influential of modern philosophers and, with Descartes, the most representative. His *tabula rasa* epistemology and social philosophy articulated modern progress as a project. In a widely realized elaboration of dualism, social relations were functionally defined and the Protestant conscience was reconceived as the private mind of the rational, self-governing citizen. His influence on anthropology is massive but contextual. Efforts to induce moral law from a "state of nature" informed modern images of the savage—of lost harmony, of brutal or childish ignorance. Natural rights of improving labor justified European claims to uncultivated "waste" overseas. As Enlightenment deism faded, Locke's empiricist derivation of rationality became a natural history of human development that conditioned social Darwinism and Victorian paternalism. Anthropology took shape in that framework and, though evolutionism is eclipsed, Lockean assumptions about functional external orders and interior mental representations persist.

MAJOR WORKS: *An Essay Concerning Human Understanding* (London: 1690; J. Yolton, editor, London: 1961); *Two Treatises of Government* (London: 1690; P. Laslett, editor, Cambridge: 1960); *Some Thoughts Concerning Education* (London: 1693; J. Axtell, editor, Cambridge: 1968); *A Letter Concerning Toleration* (London: 1689).

SOURCES: M. Cranston, *John Locke, a Biography* (London: 1957); B. Russell, *A History of Western Philosophy* (New York: 1945), pp. 596-647; P. Alexander, *Ideas, Qualities and Corpuscles: Locke and Boyle on the External World* (Cambridge: 1985); J. Dunn, *The Political Thought of John Locke* (Cambridge: 1969); R. Needham, "Locke in the huts of the Indians" in: *Examplars* (Berkeley: 1985), pp. 57-64; J. Yolton (editor), *John Locke: Problems and Perspectives* (Cambridge: 1969). T. de Zengotita, "The functional reduction of kinship in the social thought of John Locke" in: George Stocking, Jr. (editor), *Functionalism Historicized* (Madison: 1984) (= *History of Anthropology*, vol. 2), pp. 10-30.

Thomas de Zengotita

Lohest, Max. Mining engineer, geologist, archaeologist. Born in Liège (Belgium) 8 September 1857, died in Liège (Belgium) 6 December 1926. As a professor of geology at the University of Liège, Lohest devoted the greater part of his studies to the evolution of the Paleozoic landscapes of Belgium, their stratigraphy, petrography and tectonics. In anthropology, in collaboration with MARCEL DE PUYDT, he carried out the 1885-1886 excavations in the cave at Spy (Betche-al-Rotche Cavern, Namur) which led to the discovery of two fairly complete Neanderthal skeletons. For the first time in the history of human paleontology, despite the difficulty of working the deposits, the discovery was accompanied by a precise stratigraphic determination, permitting the definitive establishment of the Mousterian age of the remains of the Spy cavern.

Lohest collaborated in a large number of other excavations in the caves of Belgium with JULIEN FRAIPONT, Tihon, Braconnier and Servais. He also served as one of the promoters of the creation of a school of anthropology at the University of Liège in order to correct a deficiency in the official program of the university.

MAJOR WORKS: (with Marcel De Puydt) "L'homme contemporain du mammouth à Spy, province de Namur (Belgique)," *Annales de la Fédération archéologique et historique de Belgique*, vol. 2 (1887), pp. 205-240; (with Julien Fraipont) "La race humaine de Néanderthal ou de Canstadt en Belgique," *Archives de Biologie*, vol. 7 (1887), pp. 587-757.

SOURCES: Charles Fraipont, "Max Lohest," *Bulletin de l'Institut archéologique liégeois*, vol. 51 (1927), pp. 71-82; P. Fourmarier, "Notice sur Max Lohest," *Annuaire de l'Académie royale de Belgique*, vol. 119 (1953), pp. 279-386; A. Leguebe, "Importance des découvertes de Néandertaliens en Belgique pour le développement de la paléontologie humaine," *Bulletin de la Société royale belge d'Anthropologie et de Préhistoire*, vol. 97 (1986), pp. 13-31.

André Leguebe
[Translation from French: Timothy Eastridge and Robert B. Marks Ridinger]

Lombroso, Cesare. Medical doctor, pathologist, criminologist. Born in Verona (Italy) 6 November 1835, died in Turin (Italy) 9 October 1909. Lombroso was the founder of the school of criminal anthropology. He proposed an anthropological explanation of deviance. He believed that criminality was organically determined. On the basis of painstaking anthropometric and cranioscopic surveys, he described the "delinquent man" as a precise anthropological type, eventually supporting a relationship between crime and primitivism (having embraced the thesis of "reversion," he attributed the origin of deviant behavior to the coming to the surface of ancestral anatomic characteristics). His attempt to found penal law on a scientific base was the object of lively debates both in Italy and abroad.

Lombroso became a professor at a clinic of mental diseases in Pavia in 1867 and then a professor of legal medicine in Turin. It was not until 1905 that he obtained (at the University of Turin) a teaching post in criminal anthropology.

A friend of PAOLO MANTEGAZZA when the latter was still teaching in Pavia, Lombroso had collaborated on *Igea*, a medical journal founded by Mantegazza in 1862 and directed by him until 1873. A little later he was one of the founders of the Società Italiana di Antropologia ed Etnologia (Italian Society of Anthropology and Ethnology), promoting with Mantegazza the *Raccolta* (collecting) of materials for Italian ethnology (1871) and formulating the questions on mental pathology for the *Istruzioni* of 1873. In the same year in which, with R. Garofalo and E. Ferri, he founded the *Archivio di Psichiatria, Antropologia criminale e Scienze penali per servire allo studio dell'uomo alienato e delinquente* (1880), he left the Società Italiana di Antropologia ed Etnologia, apparently in response to the criticisms that Mantegazza had made of his experiments on sensitivity to pain, in reality—in all probability—because of academic and personal rivalry. From that moment the two scholars did not spare each other from criticisms and reciprocal attacks.

Despite his more or less institutional estrangement from the world of ethno-anthropological studies, Lombroso would continue his interest in "primitives" and in the "popular world," making continuous—although uncritical and self-serving—use of ethnographic data in all of his criminological works (e.g., in *L'uomo delinquente studiato in rapporto all'antropologia, alla medicina legale e alle discipline carcerarie*) and significant incursions into "demology." Lombroso's demo-ethno-anthropological interests were, in fact, quite precocious, as is demonstrated by the "demological" flavor of his 1862 reportage on Calabria, his studies on races (*L'uomo bianco e l'uomo di colore*), his debate with GIUSEPPE PITRÈ on "popular prison songs" ("La poesia e il crimine" and "Sui canti carcerari e criminali in Italia" and Pitrè, "Sui canti popolari italiani di carcere"), and his research on tattooing and on crime in popular consciousness. His studies on prison "palimpsests," and on the relationship between folklore and crime and between races and criminality were also quite ethnographic in their approach.

MAJOR WORKS: *Genio e follia* (Milan: 1864); *L'uomo bianco e l'uomo di colore: letture sull'origine e le varietà delle razze umane* (Padova: 1871); *L'uomo delinquente studiato in rapporto all'antropologia, alla medicina legale e alle discipline carcerarie* (Milan: 1876); "La poesia e il crimine," *Rivista Europea*, anno 7, vol. 1 (3 February 1876), pp. 475-480; "Sui canti carcerari e criminali in Italia: lettera al prof. G. Pitrè," *Rivista Europea*, anno 7, vol. 3 (1 June 1876), pp. 155-159; "Il delitto nella coscienza popolare," *Archivio di Psichiatria, Antropologia criminale e Scienze penali per servire allo studio dell'uomo alienato e delinquente*, vol. 3 (1882), pp. 451-456; *Palimsesti del carcere, raccolta unicamente destinata agli uomini di scienza* (Turin: 1888); (with R. Laschi) *Il delitto politico e le rivoluzioni in rapporto al diritto, alla antropologia criminale ed alla scienza di governo* (Turin: 1890); *Le più recenti scoperte ed applicazioni della psichiatria ed antropologia criminale* (Turin: 1893); "Palisesti del carcere," *Archivio di Psichiatria, Antropologia criminale e Scienze penali per servire allo studio dell'uomo alienato e delinquente*, vol. 14 (1893), pp. 454-455; *L'uomo di genio* (Turin: 1894); *In Calabria, 1862-1897: studi con aggiunte del Dr. G. Pelaggi* (Catania: 1898); "Folklore e crimini," *Archivio di Psichiatria, Antropologia criminale e Scienze penali per servire allo studio dell'uomo alienato e delinquente*, vol. 19 (1898), pp. 141-142; "Razze e criminalità," *Archivio di Psichiatria, Antropologia criminale e Scienze penali per servire allo studio dell'uomo alienato e delinquente*, vol. 24 (1903), pp. 245-248; *Ricerche sui fenomeni ipnotici e spiritici* (Turin: 1909).

SOURCES: *L'opera di Cesare Lombroso nella scienza e nelle sue applicazioni* (Bologna: 1908); L. Bulferetti, *Cesare Lombroso* (Turin: 1975); E. Ehrenfreund, "Bibliografia degli scritti di P. Mantegazza," *Archivio per l'Antropologia e l'Etnologia*, vol. 56 (1926), pp. 11-176; G. Lombroso Ferrero, *Cesare Lombroso nella vita e nelle opere* (Bologna: 1921); P. Mantegazza, "Protesta contro alcune affermazioni fatte nell'ultimo Congresso di Antropologia Criminale in Roma," *Archivio per l'Antropologia e l'Etnologia*, vol. 16 (1886), pp. 598-600; G. Pitrè, "Sui canti popolari italiani di carcere," *Rivista Europea*, anno 7, vol. 2, fasc. 2 (April 1876), pp. 320-323; S. Puccini, "Antropologia positivista e femminismo: teorie scientifiche e luoghi comuni nella cultura italiana tra '800 e '900," *Itinerari*, no. 3 (1980), pp. 217-244; and no. 1-2 (1981), pp. 187-238; R. Villa, *Il deviante e i suoi segni: Lombroso e la nascita dell'antropologia criminale* (Milan: 1985).

Sandra Puccini and Giorgio de Finis
[*Translation from Italian: CW and Gianna Panofsky*]

Lorenz, Konrad Zacharias. Zoologist, ethologist. Born in Vienna (Austria) 7 November 1903, died in Vienna (Austria) 27 February 1989. Lorenz, a Nobel laureate, was renowned for his pioneering studies in animal behavior that gave rise to the discipline of ethology. His philosophical contributions laid the foundations of a biological epistemology.

Although zoology was his main interest from childhood days, Lorenz studied medicine at the University of Vienna, in accordance with his father's wishes. (His father, Adolf Lorenz, was a medical doctor of high reputation and the founder of the orthopedics department at the University of Vienna.) After receiving his M.D. in 1928 Lorenz studied zoology and received his Ph.D. at the University of Vienna in 1933. In 1940 Lorenz was appointed Professor of Philosophy at the University of Königsberg. He was the last to hold the Immanuel Kant chair. In 1942 he was inducted into the army as a medical doctor and soon thereafter became a prisoner of war in Russia. He returned to Austria in 1948, lectured at the University of Vienna and established the Institut für Vergleichende Verhaltensforschung (Institute for Comparative Behavioral Research) under the auspices of the Austrian Academy of Sciences. In 1950 he was appointed head of a Research Institute for Behavioral Physiology of the Max Planck Society. In 1957 this institute moved from Westphalia to Bavaria (Seewiesen), where Lorenz worked until he retired in 1973. In that same year he, NIKOLAAS TINBERGEN and Karl von Frisch received the Nobel Prize for medicine. He moved back to his home in Altenberg near Vienna in 1973 where he was head of the Research Unit for Ethology of the Austrian Academy of Sciences until his death. He had a field station in Grünau sponsored by the academy where he continued his work on geese.

During his years as a medical student he worked as an assistant to Ferdinand Hochstetter, from whom he gained a comprehensive knowledge of comparative and functional anatomy. While still a student, he published his first work on jackdaws in 1927. In his papers on the ethology of the social corvidae ("Beiträge zur Ethologie sozialer Corviden"), the species-specific behavior patterns of birds ("Betrachtungen über das Erkennen der arteigenen Triebhandlungen bei Vögeln") and the companion in the bird's world ("Der Kumpan in der Umwelt des Vogels"), he presented the first detailed outline of ethology. He thus initiated the "objectivistic study of instinct" (Tinbergen). Following the lead of Charles Darwin, Oskar Heinroth and Charles-Otis Whitman, Lorenz regarded movement patterns as stable characteristics of organisms and made them the subject of his studies. However, he was not only interested in the comparative morphology of movement patterns to trace their phylogeny but also looked at behavior as a functional whole within an evolutionary framework. Questions of motivation, learning and the stimuli that trigger behavior also aroused his interest. He developed the concept of the innate template, which was reformulated by Tinbergen and specified to be those mechanisms through which certain behaviors are released by incoming key stimuli. His observations about the spontaneity of the actions of animals led him to integrate Erich von Holst's discoveries of central automatism—now termed central generator systems—into a theory of a central excitatory potential underlying innate motor patterns. With the discovery of imprinting, Lorenz contributed to learning theory by providing the experimental evidence for an innate learning disposition. He integrated the observations of pioneers of behavioral research with his observations, and this synthesis gave birth to ethology, defined as the biology of behavior. His findings contributed significantly to understanding human behavior.

The concepts of this new field evoked vigorous discussion. Some traditional behaviorists felt their stimulus-response psychology and their environmentalistic views endangered. The concept of the innate was hotly disputed in the 1950s when, as Daniel Lehrmann has pointed out, the term *innate* was only negatively defined as that which is not learned. This caused Lorenz to think his original ideas over from the perspective that every adaptation constitutes a hypothesis about this world. Thus, the fin that a fish develops within the egg as well as its motor patterns of swimming that develop while still in the egg are expressions of the hypothesis that after hatching the fish will move about in the water, a hypothesis that has stood the test of phylogeny. Every adaptation thus mirrors facets of the outer world relevant to survival, and in order for adaptation to occur we have to assume that at some time in the past interaction between the organism and those features of the environment that are "depicted" or "mirrored" by its adaptations must have taken place. By depriving the developing individual of the information relevant to the adaptation in question, one can indeed find out whether this information has been acquired during phylogeny or whether each individual had to acquire the information by learning. The innate was thus positively defined as "phylogenetically adapted." Phylogenetic adaptations have since been shown to determine the behavior of animals and man in well defined ways, and accompanying concepts such as central generators, innate releasing mechanisms and imprinting have been analyzed down to the neuronal level.

Closely linked to the question of adaptedness is the question of to what extent adaptations, including the human mind, mirror the "reality" of the outer world. Here Lorenz' and Sir Karl Popper's trains of thought met in a common pathway. Both interpreted adaptations as hypotheses about the external world formed by organisms. They fit the mesocosmos to which organisms adapted, since they were tested by selection and thus mirror reality in ways relevant to survival ("hypothetical realism").

Lorenz was active and brilliant until shortly before his death. The year before he died, his long-expected book on the behavior of greylag geese was published.

MAJOR WORKS: "Beobachtungen an Dohlen," *Journal für Ornithologie*, vol. 75 (1927), pp. 511-519; "Beiträge zur Ethologie sozialer Corviden," *Journal für Ornithologie*, vol. 79 (1931), pp. 67-127; "Betrachtungen über das Erkennen der arteigenen Triebhandlungen bei Vögeln," *Journal für Ornithologie*, vol. 80 (1932), pp. 50-98; "Der Kumpan in der Umwelt des Vogels," *Journal für Ornithologie*, vol. 83 (1935), pp. 137-215, 289-413 [tr.: "The companion in the bird's world," *The Auk*, vol. 54 (1937), pp. 245-273]; "Über den Begriff der Instinkthandlung," *Folia biotheoretica*, Series B 2 (1937), pp. 17-50; "Über die Bildung des Instinktbegriffes," *Naturwissenschaften*, vol. 25 (1937), pp. 289-300, 307-318, 324-331; (with N. Tinbergen) "Taxis und Instinkthandlung in der Eirollbewegung der Graugans," *Zeitschrift für Tierpsychologie*, vol 2 (1938), pp. 1-29; "Durch Domestikation verursachte Störungen arteigenen Verhaltens," *Archiv für angewandte Psychologie und Charakterkunde*, 59 (1940), pp. 1-81; "Vergleichende Bewegungsstudien an Anatinen," *Journal für Ornithologie*, vol. 89 (1941), pp. 194-293 [publication in honor of Oskar Heinroth] [tr.: "Comparative studies on the behaviour of *anatinae*," *Avicultural Magazine*, vols. 57, 58, 59 (1951-1953)]; "Die angeborenen Formen möglicher Erfahrung," *Zeitschrift für Tierpsychologie*, vol. 5 (1943), pp. 235-409; *Er redete mit dem Vieh, den Vögeln und den Fischen* (Vienna: 1949) [tr.: *King Solomon's Ring* (London: 1952)]; "Ganzheit und Teil in der tierischen und menschlichen Gemeinschaft," *Studium Generale*, vol. 9 (1950), pp. 455-499; *So kam der Mensch auf den Hund* (Vienna: 1950) [tr.: *Man Meets Dog* (New York: 1965)]; "Gestaltwahrnehmung als Quelle wissenschaftlicher Erkenntnis," *Zeitschrift für experimentelle und angewandte Psychologie*, vol. 6 (1959), pp. 118-165 [tr.: "Gestalt perception as fundamental to scientific knowledge," *General Systems*, vol. 7 (1962), pp. 37-56]; "Phylogenetische Anpassung und adaptive Modifikation des Verhaltens," *Zeitschrift für Tierpsychologie*, vol. 18 (1961), pp. 139-187 [tr.: *Evolution and Modification of Behavior* (Chicago: 1967)]; *Das sogenannte Böse: Zur Naturgeschichte der Aggression* (Vienna: 1963) [tr.: *On Aggression* (New York: 1974); *Die Rückseite des Spiegels* (Munich: 1973) [tr.: *Behind the Mirror* (New York: 1977)]; *Vergleichende Verhaltensforschung: Grundlagen der Ethologie* (New York, etc.: 1978) [tr.: *The Foundations of Ethology* (New York, etc.: 1981)]; *Der Abbau des Menschlichen* (Munich: 1983); *Hier bin ich–Wo bist du?* (Munich: 1989).

SOURCES: Irenäus Eibl-Eibesfeldt, *Grundriss der vergleichenden Verhaltensforschung* (Munich: 1967; 7th rev. ed., Munich: 1987) [tr.: *Ethology: the Biology of Behavior* (New York: 1970; 2nd ed., New York: 1975)]; Irenäus Eibl-Eibesfeldt, *Liebe und Hass* (Munich: 1970; 13th ed., Munich: 1987) [tr.: *Love and Hate: the Natural History of Behavior Patterns* (New York: 1972)]; Irenäus Eibl-Eibesfeldt, *Krieg und Frieden aus der Sicht der Verhaltensforschung* (Munich: 1975); Irenäus Eibl-Eibesfeldt, *Die Biologie des menschlichen Verhaltens: Grundriss der Humanethologie* (Munich: 1984; 2nd ed., Munich: 1986) [tr.: *Human Ethology* (New York: 1989)]; Irenäus Eibl-Eibesfeldt, *The Biology of Peace and War* (New York: 1979); Daniel S. Lehrmann, "A critique of Konrad Lorenz' theory of instinctive behavior," *Quarterly Review of Biology*, vol. 28 (1953), pp. 337-363; Nikolaas Tinbergen, *The Study of Instinct* [based on a series of lectures given at the American Museum of Natural History in 1947] (Oxford: 1951; New York and Oxford: 1969); Donald A. Dewsbury (editor), *Leaders in the Study of Animal Behavior: Autobiographical Perspectives* (Lewisburg, Pa. and London: 1985), pp. 69-91.

Irenäus Eibl-Eibesfeldt

Loria, Lamberto. Traveler, ethnographer, folklorist. Born in Alexandria (Egypt) 12 February 1855, died in Rome (Italy) 4 April 1913. Loria graduated with a degree in mathematics but devoted much of his life to ethnography and travel. In 1883 he visited the Caucasus and Lapland. Between 1886 and 1889 he went several times to New Guinea and resided there from 1891 to 1898.

These travels, sponsored by the Società Geografica Italiana (Italian Geographic Society) and the Società Italiana di Antropologia ed Etnologia (Italian Society for Anthropology and Ethnology) but generally self-financed, resulted in a rich collection for the Museo Preistorico-Etnografico (Prehistoric and Ethnographic Museum) of Rome and the Museo Nazionale di Antropologia (National Anthropological Museum) of Florence. He wrote only brief and fragmentary notes on his experiences, and his field notes are still unpublished.

During a trip to Calabria, southern Italy, in 1905, he discovered the wealth of Italian popular traditions whose importance had not gone unnoticed by those who held an evolutionary view of cultural phenomena. This new interest was reinforced when Loria met Aldobrandino Mochi, an anthropologist and a pupil of PAOLO MANTEGAZZA, in the course of a journey in Eritrea. Mochi had long been devoted to the study of Italian popular culture and the collection of popular artifacts. Loria's contribution to *Istruzioni per lo studio della Colonia Eritrea* shows that he did not abandon ethnology but in 1906 joined forces with Mochi and founded the Museo di Etnografia Italiana (Museum of Italian Ethnography) which imparted a systematic character to research in the field of Italian regional cultures and the collection of artifacts through an established network of co-workers. Subsequently, together with Mochi and the historian Francesco Baldasseroni, he established the Società di Etnografia Italiana (Italian Ethnographic Society), which was responsible for exhibiting the material collected for the museum in Rome in 1911 and for organizing the first Congress of Italian Ethnography. The congress drew the participation of all the major representatives of the discipline and marked the transition from the positivist to the modern age of Italian scholarship. Among the subjects discussed were the theory and methods of museology in light of the need to organize the Museo di Etnografia Italiana, which still lacked a proper home. After a long series of delays the museum finally found a home in Rome in 1956 and was named Museo di Arti e Tradizioni Popolari (Museum of the Popular Arts and Traditions).

Loria also founded *Lares*, an ethnographic journal, which was published between 1912 and 1914 and restarted after World War I.

Shortly before his death, Loria expressed, in his article, "L'etnografia, strumento di politica interna e coloniale," his interpretation of applied ethnography, which while echoing the ideas of GIOVENALE VEGEZZI RUSCALLA and ANGELO DE GUBERNATIS also anticipated the ideas of modern applied anthropology.

The major features of positivist ethno-anthropology are represented in Loria's work. These include overlap among the different fields of enquiry including the physical and the cultural domain. One can also detect the evolutionist's inclination to study primitive societies and the subordinate classes of the West as "living fossils."

Loria's contributions stand out as milestones in the scientific and documentary legacy of Italian anthropological studies.

MAJOR WORKS: "Isterismo tra i selvaggi," *Archivio di Psichiatria, Antropologia criminale e Scienze penali*, vol. 16 (1895), pp. 168-169; *La Nuova Guinea Britannica ed i suoi abitanti* [Conference, Rome, 5 April 1898]; "Appunti di psicologia papuana" in: *Atti del V Congresso Internazionale di Psicologia, Roma* (Rome: 1905), pp. 53-58; "Com'è sorto il Museo di Etnografia Italiana" in: *Atti del VI Congresso Geografico Italiano, Firenze* (Florence: 1907), pp. 11-16; *Caltagirone: cenni etnografici* (Florence: 1907); "Come si deve usare la macchina fotografica" in: Società di Studi Geografici e Coloniali and Società Italiana di Antropologia, Etnologia e Psicologia Comparata, *Istruzioni per lo studio della colonia Eritrea* (Florence: 1907), pp. 10-13; (with Aldobrandino Mochi and Rufillo Perini) "Etnografia" in: Società di Studi Geografici e Coloniali and Società Italiana di Antropologia, Etnologia e Psicologia Comparata, *Istruzioni per lo studio della colonia Eritrea* (Florence: 1907), pp. 136-182; "L'etnografia, strumento di politica interna e coloniale," *Lares*, vol. 1 (1912), pp. 73-79.

SOURCES: Angelo Colini, "Collezione etnografica della Penisola Sud-Est della Nuova Guinea formata dal dott. L. Loria," *Bollettino della Società Geografica Italiana*, ser. 3, vol. 4 (1891), pp. 830-840; Francesco Baldasseroni, "Lamberto Loria," *Lares*, vol. 2, no. 1 (1913), pp. 3-16; Raffaele Corso, "Valutazione dell'opera di L. Loria," *Il Folklore Italiano*, vol. 1, no. 1 (1925), pp. 121-123; Luigi Lombardi-Satriani, "Realtà meridionale e conoscenza demologica: linee per una storia degli studi demologici dagli anni postunitari alla conquista della Libia," *Problemi del Socialismo*, vol. 20, no. 16 (1979), pp. 41-66; Luigi Lombardi-Satriani, "Introduzione" to: Lamberto Loria, *Il paese delle figure: Caltagirone* (Palermo: 1981), pp. 1-5; Sandra Puccini, "Evoluzionismo e positivismo nell'antropologia italiana (1869-1911)" in: Pietro Clemente [et al.], *L'antropologia italiana: un secolo di storia* (Bari: 1905), pp. 99-148.

Sandra Puccini
[Translation from Italian: Gianna Panofsky]

Lothrop, Samuel Kirkland. Archaeologist. Born in Milton (Massachusetts) 6 July 1892, died in New York (New York) 10 January 1965. Born into a wealthy and influential family, Lothrop attended Harvard University, graduating in 1915. He was a student of ALFRED M. TOZZER and did his first archaeology under ALFRED V. KIDDER in the summer following his graduation. For the period 1915-1917, Lothrop was a research associate of Harvard's Peabody Museum, traveling in Central America and the Caribbean in order to visit archaeological excavations and examine museum collections. In the process he became familiar with the material culture of the two areas.

After service as a second lieutenant during World War I, Lothrop returned to Harvard and took his Ph.D. in 1921. From 1919 until 1924 he was an archaeologist for the Washington-based Carnegie Institute, while from 1924 to 1930 he was on the staff of the Museum of the American Indian, in New York. Lothrop was independently wealthy and did not need these positions for economic reasons; however, he did benefit by such employment in three ways. The various institutions for which he worked bore the expenses of his excavations, gave him intellectual credibility through affiliation and generally published the results of his labors. When in 1930 the Museum of the American Indian could not afford to continue its monograph series, Lothrop left it for the Peabody Museum; there he was research associate and sometime curator of Andean archaeology. The Peabody remained his base officially until his retirement in 1957, and effectively until his death.

Lothrop, unencumbered by teaching duties, spent a great deal of his time in the field. His excavations took place in the Yucatán peninsula, Guatemala, Costa Rica, Argentina, El Salvador, Peru, Puerto Rico, Chile and especially Panama and the Canal Zone. In 1937 he was one of the founders of the Institute of Andean Research, an organization to which he devoted much time. He was also one of the best-known Americans in the international community of archaeological scholars, particularly those who met in the triennial Congress of Americanists.

Rarely interested in theoretical matters, Lothrop specialized in two great areas as an archaeologist. One was the development of specific cultures over time, while the other—his primary focus—was decorative material culture. He was an acknowledged expert on metallurgy, particularly the use of gold by prehistoric Central American societies, and also interested himself in pottery and stone work. Perhaps his most significant other contribution was as an explorer and survey archaeologist in the southern portion of Central America.

In the period following his official retirement, Lothrop was given the A.V. Kidder Medal by the Society for American Archaeology, the Royal Anthropological Institute's Huxley Medal, the Loubat Prize from Columbia University and the Viking Fund Medal. In 1951 he was elected to the National Academy of Sciences.

MAJOR WORKS: "The architecture of the ancient Mayas," *The Architectural Record*, vol. 57 (1925), pp. 491-509; *Pottery of Costa Rica and Nicaragua* (New York: 1926); *Polychrome Guanaco Cloaks of Patagonia* (New York: 1927); *The Indians of Tierra del Fuego* (New York: 1928); "Aboriginal navigation off the West Coast of South America," *Journal of the Royal Anthropological Institute*, vol. 62 (1932), pp. 229-256; *Atitlán: an Archaeological Study of Ancient Remains on the Borders of Lake Atitlán, Guatemala* (Washington: 1933) (= *Carnegie Institution Publications*, no. 444); *Inca Treasure; as Depicted by Spanish Historians* (Los Angeles: 1938); "The southeastern frontier of the Maya," *American Anthropologist*, vol. 41 (1939), pp. 42-54; "The archaeology of Panama" in: Julian H. Steward (editor), *Handbook of South American Indians*, vol. 4 (Washington: 1949), pp. 143-167; "Gold artifacts of Chavin style," *American Antiquity*, vol. 16 (1951), pp. 226-240; "Early migrations to Central and South America," *Journal of the Royal Anthropological Institute*, vol. 91 (1961), pp. 97-123 [Huxley Memorial Lecture, 1960]; "Archaeology of lower Central America" in: Robert Wauchope (editor), *Handbook of Middle American Indians*, vol. 4 (Austin: 1966), pp. 180-208.

SOURCES: Dudley T. Easby, Jr., "Samuel Kirkland Lothrop, 1892-1965," *American Antiquity*, vol. 31 (1965), pp. 256-261; Gordon R. Willey, "Samuel Kirkland Lothrop," *National Academy of Sciences, Biographical Memoirs*, vol. 48 (1976), pp. 252-272.

David Lonergan

Lowie, Robert H. Anthropologist, ethnographer. Born in Vienna (Austria) 12 June 1883, died in Berkeley (California) 21 September 1957. After attending primary school in his native city, he came to the United States in 1893. City College of New York granted him a B.A. in 1901 and Columbia a Ph.D. in anthropology in 1908. In 1906, while connected with the American Museum of Natural History, he began extensive fieldwork on several Indian reservations, chiefly among the Crow of Montana. From 1921 until his retirement in 1950, he taught anthropology at Berkeley. Central to his scientific work was a lasting interest in the philosophy of science. His mentors, Ernst Haeckel (1834-1919) and, to a greater extent, Ernst Mach (1838-1916), exerted a profound influence on his way of approaching problems. The constant preoccupation with ascertaining the facts, the careful distinction between them and their interpretation, the necessity of grounding theory on the solid foundation of precise, accurate and complete data were the chief hallmarks of his scholarly output as well as of his university teaching. Hence his deeply felt aversion to sweeping and premature generalizations.

Throughout his life he was especially concerned with kinship and social institutions, either based on blood ties, like the family and lineage, or of wider scope, like associations and military societies among the Plains Indians. *Primitive Society*, a critique of LEWIS HENRY MORGAN's views and conclusions on social evolution, was his major contribution to this field, superseded only in the late 1940s by the works of GEORGE PETER MURDOCK and CLAUDE LÉVI-STRAUSS.

In *The Origin of the State* he explored the factors which may have led to its appearance in acephalous societies, i.e., those lacking a centralized source of power and authority. From his concern with primitive peoples he moved later to a consideration of complex societies, chiefly European. The last chapter of *Social Organization* is devoted to the Hapsburg empire, of which he was born a citizen. *Toward Understanding Germany* is a notable instance of inquiry into social institutions spanning two centuries. To date, no other European country has received similar treatment by anthropologists.

Lowie's catholic interests are evidenced by his concern with almost all sub-divisions of anthropology, although he tended to neglect economic factors, since his fieldwork was done long after the bison herds had been decimated and the traditional way of life of the Plains Indians had been dramatically disrupted by the might of the invading whites. His abiding interest in ethnography, first of all North American, later South American as well, was extended to the whole world by careful reading and study of all available sources. Because of his perfect command of German and, later, English, he was at home in two different worlds and literatures. Goethe and Shakespeare were always at the heart of his literary interests. His very early acquaintance with literature quite possibly influenced his concern with the oral traditions of the American Indians.

Lowie's work on the history of anthropological theories, written half a century ago, is virtually the last in the English-speaking world to pay serious attention to sources in German. For him, anthropology was not a discipline bound by the use of English, as is more and more the trend today. Lowie felt it essential to keep in touch with scholars of other countries, languages or schools, and the references in his books, papers and reviews are an impressive testimony to his wide-ranging approach. His political views also had an impact on his writings. A socialist in his youth, he voted for Eugene V. Debs several times in presidential elections and was, like FRANZ BOAS, charged with the stigma of being pro-

German during World War I. He grew more and more disillusioned with the way scholars on opposing sides behaved toward one another. The last two chapters of *Are We Civilized?* are a poignant demonstration of his position and of the spirit of enlightenment (*Aufklärungsgeist*) inculcated in him when he was still a young boy in Vienna by his maternal grandfather, Dr. Israel Kohn. The tragedy of World War II and the horror of the Holocaust inspired his superb chapter on Germans and Jews in *Toward Understanding Germany*. It stands as an example of objective analysis of social relations and as a passionate plea for future mutual respect.

MAJOR WORKS: *Culture and Ethnology* (New York: 1917); *Primitive Society* (New York: 1920); *Primitive Religion* (New York: 1924); *The Origin of the State* (New York: 1927); *Are We Civilized?: Human Culture in Perspective* (New York: 1929); *An Introduction to Cultural Anthropology* (New York: 1934); *The Crow Indians* (New York: 1935); *The History of Ethnological Theory* (New York: 1937); *The German People: a Social Portrait to 1914* (New York: 1945); *Social Organization* (New York: 1948); *Indians of the Plains* (New York: 1954); *Toward Understanding Germany* (Chicago: 1954); *Robert H. Lowie, Ethnologist: a Personal Record* (Berkeley: 1959); *Lowie's Selected Papers in Anthropology* (edited by Cora DuBois) (Berkeley: 1960).

SOURCES: Robert F. Murphy, *Robert H. Lowie* (New York: 1972); Marvin Harris, *The Rise of Anthropological Theory: A History of Theories of Culture* (New York: 1968), pp. 343-372; Paul Radin, "Robert H. Lowie," *American Anthropologist*, vol. 60 (1958), pp. 358-361; William D. Hohenthal, "Robert H. Lowie," *Revista do Museu Paulista*, vol. 11 (1959), pp. 241-246; Harold E. Driver, "Lowie, Robert H." in: David L. Sills (editor), *International Encyclopedia of the Social Sciences* (New York: 1968-1979), vol. 9, pp. 480-483; Julian H. Steward, "Robert Harry Lowie," *National Academy of Sciences, Biographical Memoirs*, vol. 44 (1974), pp. 175-183; Robert H. Lowie papers, Alfred L. Kroeber papers and Dept. of Anthropology records at the Bancroft Library, University of California, Berkeley.

Piero Matthey

Lubbock, John (often known as Lord Avebury). Amateur anthropologist, ethologist, natural historian. Born in London (England) 30 April 1834, died at Kingsgate Castle, Kent (England) 28 May 1913. Lubbock was the son of Sir John William Lubbock, baronet, a leading banker as well as treasurer of the Royal Society. Lubbock was educated at Eton from 1845 until 1849, at which time, not yet fifteen, he began to work in his father's bank. Formal education ended at that point, but his lifelong interests in science and natural history were already formed. His boyhood home was very near that of Charles Darwin, who befriended both the elder and the younger Lubbock, and strongly influenced the latter's thought.

Lubbock prospered in the banking business and as an amateur scientist. He succeeded his father as baronet in 1865. As a banker, and as a liberal member of Parliament (1870, 1874, 1880-1900), he was dedicated to honesty and reform; he also served as president of the Royal Anthropological Institute and of the Ethnological Society of London, as vice-chancellor of the University of London and as trustee of the British Museum. In 1900 he was made the first Baron Avebury.

Lubbock was a staunch defender of his friend Darwin's *Origin of Species* and himself proposed numerous theories of evolution in anthropology. He took accounts of various archaeological excavations throughout Europe and North America and synthesized from them an evolutionary overview of human development and was influential in defining archaeology as an emerging science rather than a hobby for careless collectors of artifacts.

Lubbock held that social evolution had progressed naturally from primitives to civilization and coined the terms "paleolithic" and "neolithic" to help clarify the distribution of culture types in space and time. His evolutionary viewpoint was widely accepted, with some modifications, by many anthropologists, while his spirited and knowledgable defense of Darwin helped make evolution and natural selection generally acceptable to the British intelligentsia.

In addition to anthropology, Lubbock wrote widely in entomology, botany and other areas of natural science and published several books of popular philosophy.

MAJOR WORKS: *Prehistoric Times* (London: 1865); *The Origin of Civilization* (London: 1870); *Marriage, Totemism, and Religion* (London: 1911).

SOURCES: Jacob W. Gruber, "Lubbock, John" in: David L. Sills (editor): *International Encyclopedia of the Social Sciences* (New York: 1968-1979), vol. 9, pp. 487-488; C. Hercules Read, "Lord Avebury," *Man,* vol. 13 (1913), pp. 97-98; "Lubbock, Sir John" in: *Dictionary of National Biography,* 3rd supplement (Oxford: 1927), pp. 345-347.

David Lonergan

Luce, Gordon Hannington. Linguist, epigraphist, art historian, poet. Born in Gloucester (England) 20 January 1889, died at St. Lawrence, Jersey (Channel Islands, United Kingdom) 3 May 1979. Luce devoted most of his long scholarly career to the study of the early historical origins of contemporary Burma.

Luce, son of Reverend John J. Luce, attended Emmanuel College, Cambridge University, on scholarship. The young classics major received First Class honors in 1911, and in 1912 he took a "First" in Part Two of the Cambridge English Tripos. In 1912 Luce joined the Indian Educational Service and was named as a professor of English literature at Government College, Rangoon. The first of his many contributions to the *Journal of the Burma ResearchsBe Society* was published in 1916. About 1920 Luce returned to England for studies in Oriental languages at the University of London and later at the Sorbonne (Paris). Among his teachers and mentors were Charles Otto Blagden, Louis Finot and Paul Pelliot. Following appointment in 1922 as lecturer in English at the new University of Rangoon, Luce began systematic research on the early inscriptions of Burma, with emphasis on writings in Mon, Pyu and Old Burmese. The first of five portfolio volumes of *Inscriptions of Burma* was published in 1933. Luce's studies were disrupted during World War II (when many of his research papers were lost) and again in 1964 when he (along with others) was required to leave Burma. Luce (with his wife, Daw Tee Tee) then settled in a farmhouse on Jersey, the Channel Islands. A synthesis of knowledge on medieval Burma, incorporating decades of research by Luce, and prepared with assistance of the Burma Archaeological Department, was published in 1970 in three folio volumes. The focus of *Old Burma-Early Pagan* is the dynastic period beginning about 1057 A.D.—a "golden century." Two additional monographs (based on manuscript notes) were published after Luce's death.

Luce was honored with the C.B.E. (Commander of the British Empire) in 1952. An honorary Doctorate of Literature was conferred by the University of Rangoon in 1957. Luce's career has been described in articles by colleagues D.G.E. Hall and Hugh Tinker.

MAJOR WORKS: (translator, with Pe Maung Tin) *The Glass Palace Chronicle of the Kings of Burma* (London: 1923); *Inscriptions of Burma* [5 vols.] (London: 1933-1956) (= *University of Rangoon Oriental Studies Publication*, no. 2); *Old Burma-Early Pagan* [3 vols.] (Locust Valley, N.Y.: 1970) (= *Artibus Asiae*, supplementum 25); *A Comparative Word-List of Old Burmese, Chinese and Tibetan* (London: 1981); *Phases of Pre-Pagan Burma: Languages and History* [2 vols.] (Oxford: 1985); "Economic life of the early Burman," *Journal of the Burma Research Society*, vol. 30 (1940), pp. 283-335; "A century of progress in Burmese history and archaeology," *Journal of the Burma Research Society*, vol. 32 (1948), pp. 79-94; "Rice and religion: a study of old Mon-Khmer evolution and culture," *Journal of the Siam Society*, vol. 63 (1965), pp. 139-152; "Sources of early Burma history" in: C.D. Cowan and O.W. Wolters (editors), *Southeast Asian History and Historiography: Essays Presented to D.G.E. Hall* (Ithaca: 1976), pp. 31-42.

SOURCES: Ba Shin and A.B. Griswold, "Works of Mr G.H. Luce: a selected bibliography" in: Ba Shin, Jean Boisselier and A.B. Griswold (editors), *Essays offered to G.H. Luce by his Colleagues and Friends in Honour of his Seventy-fifth Birthday* (Ascona, Switzerland: 1966), vol. 1, pp. xi-xvi (= *Artibus Asiae*, supplementum 23); D.G.E. Hall, "Gordon Hannington Luce," *Bulletin of the School of Oriental and African Studies*, vol. 43 (1980), pp. 581-588; Nai Pan Hla, "Gordon Hannington Luce, 1889-1979," *Journal of the Burma Research Society*, vol. 62, no. 1-2 (December 1979), pp. [214]-234; H.L. Shorto, "Gordon H. Luce: Old Burma-Early Pagan," *Bulletin of the School of Oriental and African Studies*, vol. 35 (1972), pp. 181-183; Hugh Tinker, "The place of Gordon Luce in research and education in Burma during the last decade of British rule," *Journal of the Royal Asiatic Society* (1986), pp. 174-190.

Lee S. Dutton

Lukas, Johannes. Africanist. Born at Fischern, near Karlsbad (Austria-Hungary, now Czechoslovakia) 7 October 1901, died in Hamburg (Germany) 4 August 1980. Prior to 1925, Lukas studied music as well as Semitic philology, Egyptology and African philology in Vienna. From 1927 until 1932 he served as *Wissenschaftlicher Hilfsarbeiter* (research assistant) at the Museum für Völkerkunde (Ethnographic Museum) in Vienna; he also worked as a private tutor in Cairo in 1928 and 1929. He spent 1932-1933 conducting fieldwork in northeastern Nigeria with the assistance of the International African Institute of London; this was followed by a brief period of residency at the School of Oriental and African Studies. In the same year he accepted a teaching position with the Seminar for African Languages in Hamburg, at which he was given the rank of *Wissenschaftlicher Hilfsarbeiter*. He obtained his *Habilitation* in 1937 with a work on the Logone language, and in 1941 he was hired as *außerordentlicher Professor* at the Auslands-Hochschule (Foreign Institute) of the University of Berlin, from which he was called up for military service one year later. A second residency at the School of Oriental and African Studies in 1949 followed his return to Hamburg, and from 1954 to 1970 he served as the director of the Seminar for African Languages, to whose name he appended the phrase "and Cultures" in 1956.

The linguistic researches completed by Lukas during 1951-1952, 1957-1958, 1961-1962 and 1971-1973 in northeastern Nigeria, northern Cameroon and Chad established the existence of a region that could be regarded as a boundary zone between the Sūdānic and Bantu languages. In addition to the so-called "Eastern Saharan" language group (presently termed Saharan), he devoted himself in particular to research on the Chado-Hamitic or Chadic language family (both of whose technical names he had originated). Over some thirty years he laid the groundwork for a separate branch of study of the Hamito-Semitic languages, which would subsequently become known as Chadic. He propounded the thesis that these originally Hamitic languages had become intermixed with those of the Sūdān. Besides studying the Chado-Hamitic/Chadic and Eastern Saharan, Lukas dealt with the phenomenon of tonality in the languages of Africa. After 1949 Lukas was a co-editor of the journal *Afrika und Übersee* and after 1963 editor of the series *Afrikanistische Forschungen*, which he founded.

MAJOR WORKS: "Genesis der Verbalformen im Kanuri und Teda," *Wiener Zeitschrift für die Kunde des Morgenlandes*, vol. 34 (1927), pp. 87-104; "Kanuri Texte," *Mitteilungen des Seminars für Orientalische Sprachen*, vol. 32 (1929), pp. 41-92; *Die Sprache der Kaidi-Kanembu in Kanem* (Berlin: 1931) (= *Zeitschrift für Eingeborenen-Sprachen*, Beiheft 13); "Die Gliederung der Sprachenwelt des Tschadsee-Gebietes in Zentralafrika," *Forschungen und Fortschritte*, vol. 10 (1934), pp. 356-357; *Die Logone-Sprache im Zentralen Sudan: mit Beiträgen aus dem Nachlaß von Gustav Nachtigal* (Leipzig: 1936) (= *Abhandlungen für die Kunde des Morgenlandes*, vol. 21, no. 6); "Hamitisches Sprachgut im Sudan," *Zeitschrift der Deutschen Morgenländischen Gesellschaft*, vol. 90 (1936), pp. 579-588; *Zentralsudanische Studien* (Hamburg: 1937); *A Study of the Kanuri Language* (London: 1937); "Der hamitische Gehalt der tschadohamitischen Sprachen," *Zeitschrift für Eingeborenen-Sprachen*, vol. 28 (1937-1938), pp. 286-299; *Die Sprache der Buduma im Zentralen Sudan: auf Grund eigener Studien und des Nachlasses von G. Nachtigal* (Leipzig: 1939) (= *Abhandlungen für die Kunde des Morgenlandes*, vol. 24, no. 2); "Umrisse einer ostsaharanischen Sprachgruppe," *Afrika und Übersee*, vol. 36 (1951-1952), pp. 3-7; "Verbalwurzel und Verbalaffixe im Maba (Waddai)," *Afrika und Übersee*, vol. 36 (1951-1952), pp. 93-98; "Das Nomen im Tiv," *Anthropos*, vol. 47 (1952), pp. 147-176; "Über die Verwendung der Partikel *sai* im Haussa," *Afrikanistische Studien*, no. 26 (1955), pp. 108-117; "Der II. Stamm des Verbums im Hausa," *Afrika und Übersee*, vol. 47 (1963), pp. 162-186; "Nunation in afrikanischen Sprachen," *Anthropos*, vol. 63 (1968), pp. 97-114; "Tonpermeable und tonimpermeable Konsonanten im Bolanci (Nordnigerien)" in: *Ethnological and Linguistic Studies in Honour of N.J. van Warmelo* (Pretoria: 1969) (= *South Africa Ethnological Publications*, no. 57), pp. 133-138; *Studien zur Sprache der Gisiga* (Glückstadt: 1970); "Die unabhängigen Personalpronomina in der westzentralsaharanischen Sprachgruppe," *Afrika und Übersee*, vol. 61 (1978), pp. 279-294.

SOURCES: H. Jungraithmayr, "Johannes Lukas (1901-1980)," *Zeitschrift der Deutschen Morgenländischen Gesellschaft*, vol. 133 (1983), pp. 1-4; Hermann Jungraithmayr, "Lukas, Johannes" in: H. Jungraithmayr and W.J.G. Möhlig (editors), *Lexikon der Afrikanistik* (Berlin: 1983), pp. 149-150; H. Meyer-Bahlburg, "Johannes Lukas, 7. Oktober 1901-4. August 1980," *Afrika und Übersee*, vol. 63 (1980), pp. 161-169; V. Six and N. Cyffer, E. Wolff, L. Gerhardt and H. Meyer-Bahlburg (editors), *Afrikanische Sprachen und Kulturen: ein Querschnitt (Johannes Lukas zum 70. Geburtstag gewidmet)* (Hamburg: 1971) (= *Hamburger Beiträge zur Afrika-Kunde*, vol. 14).

Herrmann Jungraithmayr
[Translation from German: Robert B. Marks Ridinger]

Luschan, Felix von. Physician, anthropologist, ethnologist, archaeologist. Born in Hollabrunn (Austria) 11 August 1854, died in Berlin (Germany) 7 February 1924. A man of extraordinarily broad education (his academic degrees are M.D., Litt.D. and D.Sc. from the University of Vienna as well as a D.Phil. from the University of Munich), Luschan was first noted for his excavations in Sendschirli (Zinzirli, Turkey; *Die Ausgrabungen in Sendschirli*). More than thirty years of detailed archaeological and anthropometric fieldwork led him to establish a diachronic anthropological classification of the inhabitants of Asia Minor (*Die anthropologische Stellung der Juden, The Early Inhabitants of Western Asia*). Subsequently, he developed a liberal race theory in which he introduced the word *Pygmäen* (pygmies) and the notion of "convergence" into anthropological terminology (*Die Nilländer; Wissen der Gegenwart; Zusammenhänge und Convergenz*). Luschan denied the existence of an anthropologically uniform "Jewish race," ridiculing the theory that the Germans were of Aryan origin by proving that the distinctive features of the so-called "Jewish type" descended directly from the ancient Hittites, who belonged to the ancient Armenian race and, thus, were the closest relatives of the "Aryans." He also strongly objected to the popular classification of human races as "superior" and "inferior" on the basis of color or other criteria (with special reference to Africans). Luschan dismissed such terms as "fetish" and "savages," claiming that the only savages in Africa were the whites (*Anthropological View of Race*; *Anleitungen für ethnographische Beobachtungen*; *Völker, Rassen, Sprachen*). The work he did while full professor of anthropology at the University of Berlin from 1909 to 1922 foreshadowed the disciplines of anthropobiology and human genetics.

His radical social Darwinism did not contribute to his popularity, and today Luschan's fame relies chiefly on his activities as curator and later director (1885-1910) of the Berlin Museum für Völkerkunde (Ethnographic Museum), for whose ethnographic holdings he had provided unprecedented scientific descriptions and for which he acquired the most complete collection of Benin art ever assembled. By 1901 he had established himself as an expert on Benin with several publications, wherein he emphasized its genuine African origin and its value for world culture ("Die Altertümer von Benin"; "Bruchstück einer Beninplatte"; *Über die alten Handelsbeziehungen von Benin*; *Karl Knorrsche Sammlung von Benin Altertümern*). His "Altertümer von Benin" remains the standard reference work on this subject.

MAJOR WORKS: "Die physischen Eigenschaften der wichtigsten Menschenrassen," *Wiener medizinische Wochenschrift*, nos. 39-42 (1882); *Die Nilländer* (Leipzig: 1884); "Die anthropologische Stellung der Juden," *Neue Freie Presse* [Vienna] (1892); *Wissenschaftliche Monographie von Ausgrabungen in Senddschirli* (Berlin: 1893, 1898, 1902, 1911, 1943); "Die Altertümer von Benin," *Verhandlungen der Berliner Gesellschaft für Anthropologie, Ethnologie und Urgeschichte* (1898), pp. 146-164 and plates IV-VI; *Über die alten Handelsbeziehungen von Benin* (Berlin: 1899) (= *Verhandlungen des 7. internationalen Geographen-Kongresses*); "Bruchstück einer Beninplatte," *Globus*, vol. 78, no. 19 (1900), pp. 306-307 ["Sonder-Abdruck"]; *Karl Knorrsche Sammlung von Benin Alterttümern* (Stuttgart: 1901) (= *Jahresbericht des Württembergischen Vereins für Handelsgeographie*); *Anleitung für ethnographische Beobachtungen und Sammlungen in Afrika und Oceanien* (Berlin: 1899-1906); *The Early Inhabitants of Western Asia* (London: 1911); *Anthropological View of Race* (New York: 1915); *Zusammenhänge und Konvergenz* (Berlin: 1916; 2nd ed., Vienna: 1918) (= *Jahrbuch der königliche preußischen Kunstsammlungen*, Heft 1 and 2); *Die Altertümer von Benin* (Berlin and Leipzig: 1919); *Völker, Rassen, Sprachen* (Berlin: 1922).

SOURCES: "Luschan, Felix von" in: Richard Wrede (editor), *Das geistige Berlin* (Berlin: 1898), vol. 3, p. 790 [reprinted in *Deutsches Biographisches Archiv* [microfiche] (Munich and New York: 1982-1984)]; "Luschan, Felix von" in: J. Pagel (editor), *Biographisches Lexikon hervorragender Ärtze des 19. Jahrhunderts* (Berlin and Vienna: 1900), pp. 321-322 [reprinted in *Deutsches Biographisches Archiv* [microfiche] (Munich and New York: 1982-1984)]; A.A. Goldenweiser, "Das Prinzip der begrenzten Möglichkeiten in der Entwicklung der Kultur" in: Carl Schmitz (editor), *Historische Völkerkunde* (Frankfurt: 1967), pp. 293-331, esp. p. 293; Fritz Kiffner, "Die Bibliographie Felix von Luschans," *Zeitschrift für Ethnologie*, vol. 83 (1958), pp. 285-295 and vol. 85 (1960), pp. 118-119; Kurt Krieger, "Abteilung Afrika" in: "Hundert Jahre Museum für Völkerkunde Berlin," *Baessler Archiv*, n.F., vol. 21 (1973), pp. 105-118; Walter Hirschberg, "Luschan, Felix von" in: *Österreichisches Biographisches Lexikon*, vol. 5 (Vienna: 1972), pp. 372-373; personal communications from Angelika Tunis and Marion Melk-Koch; Hans Virchow, "Gedächtnisrede auf Felix von Luschan," *Zeitschrift für Ethnologie*, vol. 56 (1924), pp. 112-117; "Luschan, Felix v." in: *Wer ist's*, vol. 4 (Leipzig: 1909), p. 869.

Malgorzata Irek

m

MacFarlane, Roderick Ross. Factor, collector. Born in Stornoway (Scotland) 1 November 1833, died in Winnipeg (Manitoba) 12 April 1920. MacFarlane was employed by the Hudson's Bay Company for forty-one years, rising to the position of Chief Factor. He spent sixteen years in the Mackenzie River District (present-day Northwest Territories), where he collected many valuable specimens of Inuit and northern Indian material culture. The Smithsonian Institution received 600 specimens of native dress and technology from MacFarlane, and many of the specimens from his collections can still be found at the Smithsonian. Besides being one of the largest individual collections made to a museum, MacFarlane's specimens of Inuit culture represent some of the earliest anthropological accessions made by a North American museum.

SOURCES: *Annual Report of the Smithsonian Institution* (Washington: 1860-1871); accession records, Anthropology Department, Smithsonian Institution; Collected notes, lists and catalogues on birds, MacFarlane papers, Smithsonian Institution Archives; Hudson's Bay Company correspondence collection, Smithsonian Institution archives; biographical file, Hudson's Bay Company Archives, Provincial Archives of Manitoba; R.R. MacFarlane, "Retired Chief Factor R. MacFarlane" in: F.H. Schofield (editor), *The Story of Manitoba* (Winnipeg: 1913), vol. 3; Roderick MacFarlane, *A Brief Sketch of the Life and Services of Retired Chief Factor R. MacFarlane, 1852-1913* [Provincial Archives of Manitoba]; E.O. Hohn, "Roderick MacFarlane of Anderson River and Fort," *The Beaver* (winter 1963), pp. 22-29.

Debra Lindsay

Machado y Alvarez, Antonio (Antonio Demófilo Machado y Alvarez). Folklorist. Born in Santiago de Compostela (Spain) 6 April 1846, died in Seville (Spain) 4 February 1893. Machado y Alvarez received graduate degrees in philosophy, letters and law from the University of Seville. He pioneered folklore study in Spain, a field to which he turned after his early research on popular national literature. In this research, influenced by the principles of the German philosopher, Karl Christian Friedrich Krause, he tried to discover the "spirit of the people." His later evolution to a positivist viewpoint led him to import from England the recently born discipline of folklore, defined as the study of popular knowledge created and maintained in the lowest social strata. This concept widened his field of interest beyond popular literature to customs and traditional beliefs, which, to evolutionists, were survivals of past civilizations.

In 1881, inspired by the English model, Machado created the Sociedad del Folk-Lore Español (Spanish Folklore Society) which sought to assemble, classify and study the material of popular Spanish culture. This ambitious project, which Machado y Alvarez and his colleagues directed from Andalucía, led to the creation of several regional societies throughout the length of the country as well as the publication of numerous scientific folklore journals and of the eleven volumes of the *Biblioteca de las tradiciones populares españolas.*

Machado y Alvarez was at the head of the folklore movement in Spain, which ran parallel to similar developments throughout Europe. It is necessary to stress his *scientific* concept of folklore since it involved the same theoretical orientation in which anthropology was born at the end of the 19th century and was quite different from the romantic current in folklore studies. In continuous contact with the European folklore movement, Machado contributed to numerous foreign publications.

In many theoretical discussions an attempt was made to separate the study of folklore from other disciplines that were also born or developed in the heat of the evolutionary environment. One must note the 1884 controversy with the English researchers George Laurence Gomme and Edwin Sidney Hartland in which Machado y Alvarez insisted on a folklore that was less archaeological and more centered on the study of cultural traits of contemporary peoples.

Besides his theoretical contributions and his works on mythology and techniques for gathering data, Machado did personal research centered primarily in Andalucía, undertaking to define some of cultural norms of this region. On this theme, his work *Cantes flamencos* deserves note. A great expert on the work of the English anthropologist, E.B. TYLOR, Machado translated Tylor's *Anthropology* into Spanish.

MAJOR WORKS: "Apuntes para una articulo literario," *Revista Mensual de Filosofía Literatura y Ciencias de Sevilla*, vol. 1 (1869), pp. 294-298; "Dos cuentos populares," *La Enciclopedia* (Seville: 1879), vol. 3, pp. 488-489; *Colección de enigmas y adivinanzas en forma de diccionario* (Seville: 1880); *Colección de cantes flamencos* (Seville: 1881); *Adivinanzas francesas y españolas* (Seville: 1881); "Juegos infantiles españoles" in: *El folk-lore andaluz* (Seville: 1882), vol. 5, pp. 158-171; "El folk-lore de los colores," *Boletin Bético-Extremeño*, vol. 2 (1883), pp. 299-305; *Post-scriptum a la obra de Cantos populares español* (Seville: 1883); "Breves indicaciones acerca del significado y alcance de término folk-lore," *Boletin Folklórico Español*, no. 5 (1885), pp. 41-43; and no. 7 (1885), pp. 49-51; (with various co-authors) *Biblioteca de la tradiciones populares* (Madrid: 1884-1886).

SOURCES: Alejandro Guichot y Sierra, *Noticia histórica del folklore* (Seville: 1922); Encarnación Aguilar Criado, *Los primeros estudios sobre la cultura popular andaluza* (Seville: 1990); Antonio Sendras y Burín, "Antonio Machado y Alvarez: estudio biográfico," *Revista de España*, nos. 140-141 (1892), pp. 140-141; Isidoro Moreno Navarro, "La antropología en Andalucía: desarrollo histórico y estado actual de las investigaciones," *Etnica*, no. 1 (1971), pp. 109-144; Moreno Navarro,

"Primer descubrimiento consciente de la identidad andaluza" in: *Historia de Andalucía* (Madrid: 1981), vol. 8, pp. 233-251; José Blas Vega and Eugenio Cobos, "Antonio Machado Alvarez 'Demófilo': estudio preliminar" in: *El folklore andaluz* (Seville: 1981), pp. x-xlv [originally 1882]; E. Aguilar Criado, "Los origenes de la antropología en Andalucía: la *Revista mensual de filosofía, literatura y ciencias de Sevilla*" in: Salvador Rodríguez Becerra (editor), *Antropología cultural de Andalucía* (Seville: 1984), pp. 177-184.

Encarnación Aguilar Criado
[Translation from Spanish: Margo L. Smith]

Mackenzie, Sir *Alexander.* Fur trader, explorer. Born in Stornoway (Scotland) 1764, died near Dunkeld (Scotland) 12 March 1820. Mackenzie joined a Montréal-based fur trading company, Finlay and Gregory, in 1779. He became a wintering partner and was assigned charge of a post at Île à la Crosse (in northern Saskatchewan) during 1785-1787. After the company coalesced with the North West Company in 1787, Mackenzie worked in the Lake Athabasca area and, together with Peter Pond, founded Fort Chipewyan (in northeastern Alberta). Mackenzie is best known for two voyages of discovery—one to the Arctic Ocean in 1789 and one to the Pacific Ocean during 1792-1793. He was the first European to explore the Mackenzie River to the Arctic Ocean and to cross the full width of North America. Though he was primarily a businessman, on these expeditions he also collected and recorded his findings on the cultures and characteristics of the native peoples he encountered. Mackenzie made comparative observations and sometimes rated groups according to how "susceptible of civilization" they were. His writings are a useful source of information on the Bella Coola, Algonquian, Cree, Dene and other native groups. Mackenzie recognized the destructiveness of the intense competition between fur companies, both for the traders and for the Indians, and argued for a merger twenty years before the amalgamation of the North West and Hudson's Bay Companies in 1821. When he went to London in 1799 Mackenzie worked on a long-planned account of his travels. *The Voyages* were published in London in 1801. A French translation and two editions in German appeared in 1802 and an abridged translation in Russian in 1808. Mackenzie married and retired to Scotland in 1812.

MAJOR WORKS: *Voyages from Montréal, on the River St. Laurence, through the Continent of North America, to the Frozen and Pacific Oceans; in the Years 1789 and 1793; with a Preliminary Account ... of the Fur Trade of that Country* (edited by William Combe) (London: 1801); *Exploring the Northwest Territory: Sir Alexander Mackenzie's Journal of a Voyage by Bark Canoe from Lake Athabasca to the Pacific Ocean in the Summer of 1789* (edited by T.H. McDonald) (Norman: 1966); *The Journals and Letters of Sir Alexander Mackenzie* (edited by W. Kaye Lamb) (Cambridge: 1970); *Alexander Mackenzie's Voyage to the Pacific Ocean in 1793* (edited by M.M. Quaife) (Chicago: 1931).

SOURCES: W. Kaye Lamb, "Introduction" to: *The Journals and Letters of Sir Alexander Mackenzie* (Cambridge: 1970), pp. 1-53; Thomas Bredin, *From Sea to Sea: Alexander Mackenzie* (Toronto: 1970); Roy Daniells, *Alexander Mackenzie and the North West* (London: 1969); J.K. Smith, *Alexander Mackenzie, Explorer: the Hero Who Failed* (Toronto and New York: 1973); M.S. Wade, *Mackenzie of Canada: the Life and Adventures of Alexander Mackenzie, Discoverer* (Edinburgh and London: 1927); Arthur P. Woollacott, *Mackenzie and his Voyageurs: by Canoe to the Arctic and the Pacific, 1789-1793* (London: 1927); H.H. Wrong, *Sir Alexander Mackenzie, Explorer and Fur Trader* (Toronto: 1927); Michael Bliss, "Conducted tour: Alexander Mackenzie finds the Arctic Ocean, with a lot of help," *The Beaver*, vol. 69, no. 2 (1989), pp. 16-24.

Frieda Esau Klippenstein

Maesen, Albert A.L. Ethnographer, art historian. Born in Antwerp (Belgium) 2 March 1915. Maesen studied art history and ethnology at the University of Ghent. During 1938-1939 he did fieldwork among the Senufo in Ivory Coast, focusing on sculpture. This work led to his Ph.D. in 1946 at Ghent University. In 1941 he started working as a freelance collaborator at the Congo Museum in Tervuren and became department head there in 1949. After the restructuring of what became known as the Musée d'Afrique Centrale (Museum of Central Africa) in 1962, he headed its department of cultural anthropology, ending his career as director of the Museum in 1980. From 1952 to 1985 he also taught cultural anthropology and ethnic art at the University of Louvain, and from 1964 to 1968 he was a part-time visiting professor at the Lovanium University in Kinshasa (Zaïre).

During 1953-1955 Maesen did fieldwork on the arts and culture of Southern Zaïre, for example, among the Holo and Lulua. In 1967 he did similar fieldwork in Ivory Coast (Senufo), in West-Central Cameroon (Bamileke and Bamum) and in Western Zaïre. Between 1970 and 1972 he made several visits to Nigeria to do fieldwork with the Jukun and the Mumuye. He was also a guest lecturer at the Institut des Musées Nationaux du Zaïre (Institute of National Museums of Zaïre). Later, he did contract work for the Musée Cheikh Anta Diop of the Institut Fondamental d'Afrique Noire (IFAN) in Dakar and the Musée National Côte d'Ivoire in Abidjan.

As a museologist, Maesen was first and foremost, although not exclusively, interested in the arts and material culture of Africa. He focused on the Senufo first, then the Holo and Mumuye and other West and Central African peoples. He is also one of the most knowledgeable scholars on the traditional sculpture of Zaïre of which he studied both the morphology and the functional meaning in different societies.

From 1938 on he was the closest collaborator of FRANS M. OLBRECHTS and contributed substantially to the latter's pathbreaking book on the plastic arts of Zaïre. Maesen was also interested in methodological problems in the study of African art. Although he did not publish extensively, his influence on his colleagues was considerable, mostly through his museum activities, his teaching, and his many contacts and visits abroad.

MAJOR WORKS: (with F.M. Olbrechts) *Plastiek van Kongo* (Antwerp: 1946) [tr.: *Les arts plastiques du Congo* (Brussels: 1954); *Congolese Sculpture* (New Haven: 1982)]; "Un art traditionel au Congo Belge: la sculpture" in: *Les arts au Congo Belge et au Ruanda-Urundi* (Brussels: 1950), pp. 9-33; "Les Holo du Kwango: notes succinctes," *Reflets du Monde* [Brussels], no. 9 (May 1956), pp. 31-44; *Arte del Congo* (Rome: 1959); "Styles et expériences stylistiques dans la plastique concolaise," *Problèmes de l'Afrique centrale*, vol. 12, no. 44 (1959), pp. 84-93; *Kunst fra Congo* (Oslo: 1960); *Umbangu: art du Congo au Musée royal de l'Afrique centrale* (Brussels: 1960); (with H. Van Geluwe) *Art d'Afrique dans les collections belges: Musée royal de l'Afrique centrale, Tervuren, 29 juin au 30 octobre 1963* (Tervuren: 1973); "Congo art and society" in: *Art of the Congo: Objects from the Collection of the Koninklijk Museum voor Midden-Afrika / Musée royal de l'Afrique centrale, Tervuren, Belgium* (Minneapolis: 1967), pp. 15-71; "Le masque korubla chez les Sénoufo orientaux," *Critice d'arte africana* [Florence], vol. 46, fasc. 178 (1981), pp. 85-96; "Statuaire et culte de fécondité chez les Lulua de Kasaï (Zaïre)," *Quaderni Poro* [Milan], vol. 3 (1982), pp. 49-58; "Lo scultore i Africa nera" in: E. Bassiani (editor), *La grande scultura dell'Africa nera* (Florence: 1989), pp. 34-43.

Herman Burssens

Maine, Sir ***Henry Sumner.*** Legal historian, theorist, colonial statesman. Born in Kelso, Roxburgh (Scotland) 15 August 1822, died in Cannes (France) 3 February

1888. Maine is distinguished as the founder of anthropological jurisprudence as an aspect of the study of comparative law. His major work, *Ancient Law: Its Connection with the Early History of Society, and Its Relation to Modern Ideas*, was first published in 1861 and remains a viable classic to this day, contrasting the importance of the kinship group as the significant legal entity and the dominance of private law in the social systems of ancient (primitive) societies as against the prevalence of public law in later Roman and modern law. In the infancy of jurisprudence, he wrote, it is the person who suffered a wrong, or delict, and who is conceived to have been injured—not the state. As society develops, however, the state reduces away the legal powers of the kinship group in a process through which the individual becomes increasingly free to make his own legal commitments independently of his kinship membership in a movement "from Status to Contract." Maine formulated this movement within the framework of a scheme of social evolution in which regulation of human behavior was first achieved through *themistes* (divinely inspired judgments), then by means of codes that through the ages became modifiable by means of the use of equity, fictions and legislation. Maine's enduring contribution to modern social science methodology is in his formulation of the concept of ideal polar types and its uses in the comparative analysis of social phenomena.

Maine was a member of the Supreme Council of India, Lecturer in Jurisprudence and Civil Law at the Middle Temple, London, and Regius Professor of Law, the University of Cambridge.

MAJOR WORKS: *Ancient Law: Its Connection with the Early History of Society, and Its Relations to Modern Ideas* (London: 1861); *Village-Communities in the East and West, to Which Are Added Other Lectures, Addresses and Essays* (London: 1871); *Lectures on the Early Histories of Institutions* (London: 1875).

SOURCES: Mountstuart E. Grant Duff, *Sir Henry Maine: a Brief Memoir of His Life* (New York: 1892); E. Adamson Hoebel, "Status and contract in primitive law" in: F.S.C. Northrop and H.H. Livingston (editors), *Cross-Cultural Understanding: Epistemology in Anthropology* (New York: 1964), pp. 284-294.

E.A. Hoebel

Mair, Lucy Philip. Anthropologist. Born in London (England) 18 January 1901, died in London (England) 1 April 1986. Mair graduated in Classics from Newnham College, Cambridge, in 1923, and then worked for five years for Sir Gilbert Murray. During this period she wrote her first book, an account of the League of Nations' protection of minorities. In 1927 she joined the London School of Economics (LSE) in the Department of International Relations and was drawn into the seminars held by BRONISLAW MALINOWSKI. She went to Uganda in 1931 and did fieldwork that resulted in her Ph.D. in anthropology in 1932. She became Lecturer in Colonial Administration at LSE where she remained until her retirement in 1968, apart from work at the Royal Institute for International Affairs during the war and a brief period (1945-1946) training Australian administrators who were to work in Papua New Guinea. Mair was Reader in Colonial Administration from 1946, Reader in Applied Anthropology from 1956 and Professor from 1963. After her retirement she visited New Guinea again and held honorary posts at the Universities of Durham and Kent. She ceased teaching in her seventy-eighth year but continued writing until her death.

Mair wrote that "Malinowski sent me to study social change because, he said, I didn't know enough anthropology for fieldwork of the standard type. Nobody today regards the study of social change as an occupation for the half-baked" (*Anthropology and Social Change*, p. 8). In fact, Mair's work was always concerned with contemporary experience. She never attempted a reconstruction of "pre-contact" society, and administrators, missionaries, traders as well as elected leaders and modernizing chiefs figure in her first-hand accounts of Africa and Papua New Guinea (as they notably do not in the work of many of her contemporaries). She worked intensively on politics, on land tenure (e.g., "Modern developments in African land tenure" and "Land tenure in the Gold Coast") and marriage (e.g., "Marriage and family in the Dedza district" and *African Marriage and Social Change*) as well as on issues of administration and development that involved the practical problems of making new social orders.

In her first work Mair remarked that the League of Nations could prevent the extermination of minorities but could do nothing about people's grievance that they were governed by people whom they thought inferior: a grievance, she said, found in all societies. In her work after the war she was equally short with those who argued that colonial administrations assured fairness and justice: Any European able to choose between good government and self-government would have no doubt which to choose; why should it be different for colonial subjects? ("Self-government or good government?").

On the other hand, colonial authorities and later the leaders of new nations had real and practical problems to solve, and the decisions they made would be consequential. They should be informed about their own people, about how others had confronted similar issues (*The New Africa* and *New Nations*). Much of Mair's work from the 1940s and 1950s is devoted to reviews of contemporary processes in which she brings anthropological understanding to bear on issues that were important to administrators. They needed to know what was happening to chiefs, what the effects of recent policies were on marriage or land tenure, and what anthropologists were up to and what they could offer (e.g., "What anthropologists are after"). She wrote on these issues with great clarity for an interested audience of non-anthropologists, developing a style of synthesis and exposition that stood her in good stead also in her writing for academic audiences. She was not ashamed to address layman's questions and to illuminate them in a forthright and jargon-free way.

No doubt at this time, too, Mair developed her short way with theoretical disputes: she made up her mind, came to a conclusion, then passed to more important matters. In many cases her "own mind" was strikingly original, but her contribution is sometimes underestimated because she did not engage in detailed theoretical discussion. Some of these papers are collected in the two volumes (*Studies in Applied Anthropology, Anthropology and Social Change*) published by the Athlone Press and are still valuable. In later years, when colonial administrators were widely and routinely criticized, Mair refused to agree that they had always done wrong; and in any case the important point was, that they *thought* they were doing good. Irony—the more or less compassionate confrontation of people's intentions and aspirations with the consequences of their actions—permeates Mair's work on development and administration from the 1930s until her last book (*Anthropology and Development*).

She argued that "applied" anthropology is not a separate branch of the discipline: it was not as if there is a category of pure anthropologists who worked out the principles of the science that can then be used as rules of thumb by social engineers. Applied anthropologists had to know anthropology. She read widely and deeply and was concerned with the latest developments in ethnography and theory until the year of her death. Her *Introduction to Social Anthropology* is a survey of the whole discipline, remarkable for its mastery of the field and of developing discussions as well as for its theoretical inexplicitness. From 1962 she began to publish a series of syntheses, representing her understanding of the state of anthropological knowledge. These works pass for summaries but contain significant and original intellectual contributions. *Primitive Government* is the first general anthropology book to contain a discussion of the forms of patronage and of their role in state formation. The chapter "What are husbands for?" in *Marriage* reviews that issue in a way that anticipates some later claims by feminist anthropologists.

Mair never married. She was one of a generation of early woman graduates from Cambridge who came to maturity in the 1920s. That background is essential for understanding some of the crucial aspects of her character and action: her cleverness and integrity were formed in a period in which women were under pressure to use their new opportunities to prove themselves the equals of men, in the face of sometimes derisive scepticism. Among those dedicated women the pursuit of anything other than excellence was a betrayal. The pressure was reinforced for some among them by the devastation of the marriageable cohort of young men in World War I: Mair's twenty-first birthday was in 1922, and too many of the men who had come of age in the preceding decade were dead.

Nevertheless, the pressure to vie with men in a world devastated of men by men presented her as well as other women of acute intelligence with a major and, as it seems in retrospect, formative contradiction. Her intellectualism, her dedication to rationality in public affairs, her sense of duty to work for the betterment of the human condition were always tinged with irony and with an awareness that justice and good sense were not promised, but had to be achieved against most odds.

MAJOR WORKS: "Native land tenure in East Africa," *Africa*, vol. 4 (1931), pp. 314-329; "What anthropologists are after," *Uganda Journal*, vol. 7 (1939), pp. 85-92; "Modern developments in African land tenure," *Africa*, vol. 18 (1948), pp. 184-189; "Self-government or good government?" *World Affairs*, n.s., vol. 2 (1948) [reprinted in: *Anthropology and Social Change* [see below], pp. 111-119]; "Marriage and family in the Dedza district of Nyasaland," *Journal of the Royal Anthropological Institute*, vol. 81 (1951), pp. 103-119; "Land tenure in the Gold Coast," *Civilisations*, vol. 2 (1952), pp. 183-188; "General characteristics of African family and marriage" in: A.W. Phillips (editor), *A Survey of African Marriage and Family Life* (London: 1953), pp. 1-171; *Free Consent in African Marriage* (London: 1958); *Studies in Applied Anthropology* (London: 1961) (= *London School of Economics Monographs on Social Anthropology*, vol. 16); *Primitive Government* (London: 1962); *New Nations* (London: 1963); *An Introduction to Social Anthropology* (Oxford: 1965; 2nd ed., Oxford: 1972); *The New Africa* (London: 1967); *Witchcraft: an Introductory Survey* (London: 1969); *Anthropology and Social Change* (London: 1969); *Marriage* (London: 1972); *Anthropology and Development* (London: 1984).

SOURCE: John Davis (editor) *Choice and Change: Essays in Honour of Lucy Mair* (London: 1974) [contains bibliography of Mair's work, pp. 4-6].

John Davis

Majumdar, Dhirendra Nath. Anthropologist, sociologist. Born in Patna (India) 3 June 1903, died in Lucknow (India) 31 May 1960. Majumdar was one of the first formally trained anthropologists of India: he received his M.A. from Calcutta University

(1924) and Ph.D. from Cambridge (1935). In 1928 he joined the economics department of Lucknow University where he taught courses in comparative economics, which he was able to expand gradually into introductory courses in general anthropology. In 1950 he was appointed full professor of anthropology. A year later, the University created a department of anthropology, the third in the country, and made him its head. By then Majumdar had acquired an international reputation for his contributions to cultural anthropology (monographic studies and numerous research papers on Hos, Korwas, Khasas, etc. in central and northern India) as well as to physical anthropology (anthropometric and serological studies in eastern, northern and western India).

Majumdar was an evolutionist and a functionalist in his approach to the study of culture, but this did not preclude him from taking a deep interest in processes of cultural dynamics. He neither infantalized tribal people nor romanticized them. According to him, they needed to be "rehabilitated" (he preferred the notion of "rehabilitation" to that of "upliftment") and brought into the modern mainstream; but this did not mean that they had to be culturally uprooted. Indeed, tribal cultures had much to offer to modern society.

The last decade of his life was perhaps the most active and innovative. He made field studies of Hindu village communities and of urbanization in the context of the socio-economic development plans of the government in the years following independence in 1947. In the process he came closer to sociology. Throughout, he remained committed to the notion of anthropology as fieldwork-based practical knowledge of man in his biological and cultural aspects. The strength of his considerable published work lay in its descriptive detail, wide scope, and concern with solving problems; its weakness stemmed from a lack of interest in theory. Apart from his own published work, his lasting contributions include the training of a large number of students and the 1947 founding of *The Eastern Anthropologist*, a major journal.

MAJOR WORKS: *A Tribe in Transition* (Calcutta and London: 1937); *Fortunes of Primitive Tribes* (Lucknow: 1944); *The Affairs of a Tribe* (Lucknow: 1950); (with T.N. Madan) *An Introduction to Social Anthropology* (Bombay: 1956); *Caste and Communication in an Indian Village* (Bombay: 1958); *Social Contours of an Industrial City* (Bombay: 1960); (with C.R. Rao) *Race Elements in Bengal* (Bombay: 1960); *Races and Cultures of India* (Bombay: 1961); *Himalayan Polyandry* (Bombay: 1962).

SOURCES: T.N. Madan, "Dhirendra Nath Majumdar, 1903-1960," *American Anthropologist*, vol. 63 (1961), pp. 369-374; T.N. Madan, "Majumdar, D.N." in: David L. Sills (editor), *International Encyclopedia of Social Sciences* (New York: 1968-1979), vol. 9, pp. 540-541; T.N. Madan, *Culture and Development* (Delhi: 1983); T.N. Madan and G. Sarana (editors), *Indian Anthropology: Essays in Memory of D.N. Majumdar* (Bombay: 1962).

T.N. Madan

Maksimov, A.N. (Aleksandr Nikolaevich).
Ethnographer. Born in Orel (Russia) 1 August 1872, died in Moscow (Russian S.F.S.R.) 24 June 1941. From 1919 to 1930 Maksimov was a professor at Moscow University.

His major research was devoted primarily to questions of the history and theory of the family, kinship and economics. Maksimov's characteristics as a scholar were his deep erudition, his conscientious and painstaking research, his critical understanding of the works of his predecessors, his desire to exhaust all material on a research problem and, together with that, his originality and care in synthesizing. In his works analysis definitely predominated over synthesis.

> MAJOR WORKS: "K voprosu o metodakh izucheniîa istorii sem'i," *Ètnograficheskoe obozrenie*, no. 4 (1899), pp. 1-35; *Russkie inorodfsy* (Moscow: 1901); *Chto sdelano po istorii sem'i* (Moscow: 1901); "Iz istorii sem'i u russkikh inorodfšev," *Ètnograficheskoe obozrenie*, no. 1 (1902), pp. 41-76; "Gruppovoĭ brak," *Ètnograficheskoe obozrenie*, no. 3 (1908), pp. 1-48; "Teoriîa rodovogo byta" in: *Sbornik v chest' 70-letiîa prof. D.N. Anuchina* (Moscow: 1913), pp. 333-350; "Skotovodstvo malokul'turnykh narodov," *Uchenye zapiski Instituta istorii*, vol. 2 (Moscow: 1927), pp. 3-24; "Proiskhozhdenie olenevodstva," *Uchenye zapiski Instituta istorii*, vol. 6 (Moscow: 1928), pp. 3-37; "Nakanune zemledeliîa," *Uchenye zapiski Instituta istorii*, vol. 8 (Moscow: 1929), pp. 21-34; *Materinskoe pravo v Avstralii* (Moscow and Leningrad: 1930).

> SOURCE: S.A. Tokarev, "A.N. Maksimov (nekrolog i spisok rabot)," *Sovetskaîa ètnografiîa*, no. 6-7 (1947), pp. 330-335 [contains bibliography].

A.M. Reshetov
[Translation from Russian: Thomas L. Mann]

Maksimov, S.V. (Sergeĭ Vasil'evich).

Ethnographer. Born in the small settlement of Parfent'evo, Kostroma Province (Russia) 1831, died in St. Petersburg (Russia) 3 June 1901. In the 19th century Maksimov played an important role in the development of the unique Russian ethnographic tradition.

As a young man, Maksimov turned briefly to government service and then to journalism because his Upper Volga landholding family had become impoverished as a result of the economic crisis that, in the early 19th century, affected not only most of the small landholding estates but all of the Russian Empire. His early provincial and later formal medical-surgical education (1850-1855) did not have direct application to his life's work. Even before formal schooling, in the late 1840s, he had fallen under the influence of other writers of the same background from Kostroma—e.g., A.F. Pisemskiĭ and A.A. Potekhin. In their writing and discussion circles, these way-of-life writers realistically and sympathetically portrayed the *narod* (the "folk," peasantry and other unprivileged social groups). Maksimov himself precociously wandered on foot in the countryside before he was twenty, much like P.V. Kireevskiĭ, P.M. ÎAzykov, P.I. ÎAkushkin and so many others, gathering popular legends, expressions and songs, and he published his findings in journals and in the encyclopedic dictionary of V.I. DAL'.

The milieu of Maksimov from which a unique Russian ethnographic tradition emerged had several components. His circles of friends came out of the soil of struggle between Slavophiles and Westerners, a struggle between those who sought for the Russian people a natural and self-guided development with attention to popular ways and means (including Russian Orthodox religiosity) and those who, following Western models, advocated secularism, revolution and internationalism. Maksimov (and, indeed, all Russians) were heir to this debate. As a result, Maksimov's ethnography shows a special ambivalence about Western-defined "progress" and "civilization" and an early attachment to popular culture and concern for its erosion.

When he first began working as ethnographer in the 1850s, Maksimov worked within a developing scientific and artistic framework that included both scholarly work in natural history and folkloric taxonomy as well as the government ministries' scientific and statistical investigations of the 1830s and 1840s. For example, from 1848 to 1852 V.I.

Nadezhdin had initiated a prolonged ethnographic investigation of the Russian people through the ethnographic section of the Imperial Russian Geographic Society and enlisted hundreds of educated Russians in the provinces to investigate. Nadezhdin's program was in step with contemporary anthropological categories: it included anthropometry, linguistics, domestic economy, social organization, cultural diffusion and folklore.

In the reform era, the new Tsar's brother, Naval Minister Grand Duke Konstantin Nikolaevich (also head of the Geographic Society) commissioned first Pisemskiĭ and Potekhin and then Maksimov and four others to carry out the Ethnographic Expedition of 1855-1862 to investigate the popular way of life along rivers and seas. They developed an early form of ethnographic fieldwork and occasionally concerned themselves with methodology and objectivity. They attempted to make a place for themselves among the people they studied as well as among their educated city audiences and hoped to mediate between the two cultures. Maksimov, especially, recognized the methodological problems posed by the unique politics of ethnography at work in the Russian empire. With Maksimov and others, "way-of-life writing" became ethnography. (It is interesting to note that only later in the 1860s and 1870s was any kind of formal university ethnographic training offered in the empire.)

Maksimov surveyed extensively the way of life of the peoples of the empire's periphery: in the Far North, from Lapland eastward and down the great northern rivers of Siberia, to the Far East as well as in southwestern Siberia and Belorussia. Such early sources on popular life in the 19th century are currently proving to be critical for both Western and Soviet historians of Russian society, and the recent revival of interest of Soviet folklorists and anthropologists in such sources has led to new editions of early ethnography (e.g., *God na severe*, 1984).

MAJOR WORKS: *Sobranie sochinenii* (edited by P.V. Bykov) [20 vols.] (St. Petersburg: 1908-1913); *God na severe* (St. Petersburg: 1859, 1864, 1871, 1890; Arkhangelsk: 1984); *Ssyl'nye i tiur'ma* (St. Petersburg: 1862; later ed. [*Sibir' i katorga*], St. Petersburg: 1871); *Na vostoke, poezdka na Amur v 1860-61 godakh* (St. Petersburg: 1864).

SOURCES: M.K. Azadovskiĭ, *Istoriĭa russkoĭ fol'kloristiki* [2 vols.] (Moscow: 1858-1863); P. Christoff, *The Third Heart* (The Hague: 1970); Giuseppe Cocciara, *Storia del folklore in Europa* (Turin: 1952) [tr.: *The History of European Folklore* (Philadelphia: 1981)]; Sergeĭ. Plekhanov, "Literaturnoe ėkspedifsiĭa" in: *God na Severe* (Arkhangelsk: 1984), pp. 5-19; A.A. Pypin, *Istoriĭa russkoĭ ėtnografii* [4 vols.] (St. Petersburg: 1890-1892); P.P. Semenov Tian-Shanskiĭ, *Istoriĭa poluvekovoĭ deĭatel'nosti Imperatorskogo Russkogo Geograficheskogo Obshchestva, 1845-1895* (St. Petersburg: 1896), vol. 1; ĬŪ.M. Sokolov, *Russkiĭ fol'klor* (Moscow: 1941) [tr.: *Russian Folklore* (New York: 1950; New York: 1966)]; S.A. Tokarev, *Istoriĭa russkoĭ ėtnografii (dookt[ĭa]br'ski[ĭ] period)* (Moscow: 1966); L.D. Alekseeva, "Moskovskiĭ Universitet i stanovlenie prepodavaniĭa ėtnografii v dorevolĭŭfsionnoĭ Rossii," *Vestnik Moskovskogo Universiteta*, seriĭa 8: *Istoriĭa*, vol. 6 (1983), pp. 54-62.

Catherine Clay

Maler, Teobert. Archaeologist. Born in Rome (Italy) 12 January 1842, died in Mérida (Mexico) 22 November 1917. After attending secondary school in Baden-Baden (Germany), Maler studied architecture and engineering at the Polytechnic College in Karlsruhe and worked for a year as an architect in Vienna. In 1864 he accompanied Archduke Maximilian (later Emperor Maximilian of Mexico) as a cadet and served in the

Imperial Mexican Army, eventually as captain, until the capitulation in 1867. Thereafter, Maler traveled throughout southern Mexico and in 1874 began photographing city scenes, buildings and Indians. In 1875 he directed excavations in Tehuantepec. The gold objects discovered there are today in the Museum für Völkerkunde (Ethnographic Museum), Berlin. Following this he explored the Maya ruins in Chiapas, Yucatán and El Petén (Guatemala), some one hundred sites in all. At times he worked on behalf of the Peabody Museum of American Archaeology and Ethnology of Harvard University.

Maler's archaeological work was distinguished by the high technical quality of his photography and by his scale drawings of buildings. By limiting himself to nondestructive documentation, he proved himself a responsible and farsighted researcher. Through his photographs of the Chilam Balam books, colonial documents that have since partially disappeared, Maler carried out pioneering work in documenting Indian cultures at a time when photographic documentation of manuscripts was by no means customary.

MAJOR WORKS: "Découverte d'un tombeau royal zapotèque à Tehuantepec en 1875," *La Nature*, vol. 7 (1879), pp. 22-24; "Yukatekischische Forschungen," *Globus*, vol. 35, no. 3 (1879), pp. 41-43; vol. 68, no.16 (1895), pp. 247-259; no.18, pp. 277-292; vol. 81, no. 1 (1902), pp. 14-15; no. 13/14, pp. 197-230; *Researches in the Central Portion of the Usumtsintla Valley* (Cambridge, Mass.: 1901-1903) (= *Memoirs of the Peabody Museum of American Archaeology and Ethnology, Harvard University*, vol. 2, nos. 1 and 2); *Explorations of the Upper Usumatsintla and Adjacent Regions* (Cambridge, Mass.: 1908-1910) (= *Memoirs of the Peabody Museum of American Archaeology and Ethnology, Harvard University*, vol. 4, nos. 1-3); *Explorations in the Department of Petén, Guatemala* (Cambridge, Mass.: 1911-1913) (= *Memoirs of the Peabody Museum of American Archaeology and Ethnology, Harvard University*, vol. 5, no. 1); *Bauten der Maya* (edited by Gerdt Kutscher) (Berlin: 1971); *Peninsula Yucatán* (edited by Hanns J. Prem) (Berlin: in preparation).

SOURCES: Archives of the Peabody Museum of Archaeology and Ethnology, Harvard University; Archives of the Iberoamerikanisches Institut and Museum für Völkerkunde, both parts of the Stiftung Preußischer Kulturbesitz, Berlin; Archives of the Hamburgisches Museum für Völkerkunde; R. Andrée, "Teobert Maler und seine Erforschung der Ruinen der Mayas," *Globus*, vol. 68, no. 16 (1895), pp. 245-247; Capitan, "Theobert Maler," *Journal de la Société des Américanistes de Paris*, n.s. vol. 11 (1919), pp. 636-637; W. Pferdekamp, *Auf Humboldts Spuren: Deutsche im jungen Mexiko* (Munich: 1958), pp. 205-210; G. Kutscher, Introduction to: Teobert Maler, *Bauten der Maya* (Berlin: 1971), pp. 9-19; C. A. Echánove Trujillo, *Dos héroes de la arqueología maya: Frédéric de Waldeck y Teobert Maler* (Mérida: 1974); Matthias Strecker, "Teobert Maler: unveröffentichter Nachlass," *Mexicon*, vol. 2, no. 6 (1981), pp. 91-93; Berthold Riese, "Maler ... Teobert" in: *Neue Deutsche Biographie* (Berlin: 1953-), vol. 15, pp. 726-727.

Berthold Riese
[Translation from German: Sem C. Sutter]

Malfatti, Bartolomeo. Historian, geographer, ethnographer. Born in Trento (Austria-Hungary, now in Italy) 23 February 1828, died in Florence (Italy) 1892. Malfatti studied law at the Universities of Vienna and Berlin where he also attended the lessons of the geographer Carl Ritter (1779-1859). When he returned to Italy he spread the concept of a "human" geography free, however, of the deterministic components that characterized the work of Ritter. It was his study of the interaction between the natural habitat and the history and character of peoples that led Malfatti to his interest in ethnography. Both ethnography and geography guided his important historical research (e.g., *Imperatori e Papi*).

At the end of the 1860s Malfatti was appointed to the chair of geography (the first in Italy) at the University of Milan. In 1869 he gathered in one volume, *Scritti geografici ed etnografici*, the articles previously published in various scholarly journals. Subsequently he taught a course in ethnography at the University of Rome and in 1878 he was offered the chair of geography and ethnography at the University of Florence. That year he completed the first ethnographic manual published in Italy.

Although close to the positions of the anthropological school headed by PAOLO MANTEGAZZA and the circle of the evolutionist theoreticians, Malfatti did not share the holistic framework that the Florentine professor impressed upon the discipline. His Middle European training and his early contacts with the philological-linguistic and philosophical schools of thought then predominant in Northern Italy (that were associated with Carlo Cattaneo, Carlo Tenca and GIOVENALE VEGEZZI RUSCALLA) led him to conceive an ethnographic discipline free from physical anthropology and all biological determinism and closer to the human sciences than to the natural sciences. Malfatti defined ethnography as the historical science of peoples: its role would be to study human societies in order to reconstruct their gradual evolution. He postulated the psychic oneness of the human mind. This led him to study socio-cultural phenomena with the aim of deriving the underlying laws that regulate the unfolding of cultural diversity.

Malfatti enriched the evolutionist social sciences of his day by introducing on the one hand the humanistic-philological tendency whose roots lay in Italian culture in the early 19th century and on the other the rigorous methods of study typical of positivism.

MAJOR WORKS: *Scritti geografici ed etnografici* (Milan: 1869); *Imperatori e Papi ai tempi della Signoria dei Franchi in Italia* (Milan: 1876); *Etnografia* (Milan: 1878; new ed., Rome: 1982-1983).

SOURCES: Francesco Ambrosi, *Scrittori e artisti trentini* (Trento: 1883); Giovanni Marinelli, *Scritti minori* (Florence: 1908); Attilio Mori, "Malfatti, Bartolomeo" in: *Enciclopedia italiana*, vol. 22 (Milan: 1934), p. 16; Raffaele Corso, *Etnografia: prolegomeni* (Naples: 1940); Benedetto Croce, *Storia della storiografia italiana nel secolo XIX* (Bari: 1947); Pietro Gribaudi, *Scritti di varia geografia* (Turin: 1955); Sandra Puccini, "La natura e l'indole dei popoli: B. Malfatti e il primo manuale italiano di etnografia (1878)," *Giornale critico della Filosofia italiana*, vol. 67, fasc. 1 (January-April 1988), pp. 81-104.

Sandra Puccini
[Translation from Italian: Gianna Panofsky]

Malinowski, Bronislaw (Polish form of name: Bronisław Kasper Malinowski). Social anthropologist. Born in Kraków (Poland, Austria-Hungary) 7 April 1884, died in New Haven (Connecticut) 16 May 1942. One of the founding fathers of British social anthropology, Malinowski had a profound influence on the discipline though his innovative field research, his theoretical writings and his inspired teaching. His early studies at the Jagiellonian University in Kraków were in mathematics, physics and philosophy, and his doctorate earned him the highest honors in the Austrian Empire. He then turned his interests to anthropology and after a period of study in Germany he went to England in 1910 to become a student of ethnology under C.G. SELIGMAN and EDWARD WESTERMARCK at the London School of Economics. In 1914 he accompanied members of the British Association for the Advancement of Science to Australia, where (despite his status as an enemy alien) he was permitted to remain for the duration of the World War I. It was during three expeditions to the Australian colony of Papua (the first to Mailu, the second and third to the Trobriand Islands) that he conducted the intensive fieldwork that was to become the hallmark of British anthropology. In 1922 Malinowski declined the offer of a professorial chair at his alma mater, the Jagiellonian University, and he spent most of the next sixteen years at the London School of Economics where he was appointed Lecturer in 1922, Reader in 1924 and foundation Professor of Anthropology in 1927. Malinowski went to Yale University on sabbatical leave in 1938; and, when World War II broke out in Europe, he decided to remain in America. In 1940 he conducted fieldwork in Oaxaca, Mexico. Just before his sudden death in 1942 he was appointed to a permanent professorship at Yale.

Together with A.R. RADCLIFFE-BROWN, Malinowski presided over a major paradigm shift in British anthropology: from the speculatively historical or diachronic study of customs and cultural traits as "survivals" (whether in the evolutionist or diffusionist mode) to the ahistorical, synchronic study of social "institutions" within bounded, functioning societies. The shift was marked by the collection and synthesis of new kinds of data by increasingly professional investigators and by a corresponding shift from the library armchair to the ethnographer's tent. Although others of his generation also conducted intensive fieldwork, none were so ambitiously innovative as Malinowski. He propagated "a new line of anthropological fieldwork: the study by direct observation of the rules of custom as they function in actual life" (*Crime and Custom*, p. 125). Thus, through his example and teaching, fieldwork became the constitutive experience of social anthropology, an essential rite of passage for entry to the profession.

Malinowski's theoretical stance was characterized by a commitment to Machian positivism, Durkheimian holism and a conviction that the key to the understanding of any culture lay in the interrelation of its constituent elements. In a word, his formal contribution lay in his functionalism, and it is this pragmatic, hard-working doctrine with which he is usually associated. His functionalism was essentially an appeal for contextualized empirical data, quantitative as well as qualitative, purified of spurious historical speculations. Hence his stress on the synchronic study of a society or culture in which all "institutions" are functionally related to one another. Malinowski taught the importance of studying social behavior and social relations in their concrete cultural contexts; the observable differences between norms and action (between what people say they do and what they actually do) he regarded as crucial.

In the 1920s and 1930s, an era of colonial stagnation, Malinowski's sociological functionalism was highly influential. As a methodological prescription it clearly worked, though it ran into obvious analytical difficulties when applied to situations of social or cultural change. But in the general form in which he developed cultural functionalism toward the end of his life (as a "scientific theory of culture" based on primary and derived biological needs) it did not long survive him. The utilitarian notion of culture as an "instrumental apparatus" was ultimately stultifying.

Malinowski is better remembered as an incomparable ethnographer, one who sought "the native's point of view" through "the intensive study of a restricted area" and a mastery of the local vernacular. Despite many flaws and omissions, his celebrated Trobriand corpus remains one of the most comprehensive in world ethnography, and his classic *Argonauts of the Western Pacific* remains one of the most widely read. His enduring conceptual contributions lay in the areas of kinship and marriage (e.g., the concept of "sociological paternity"); in magic, ritual language and myth (e.g., the idea of "myth as social charter"); and in economic anthropology (notably the fruitful concept of "reciprocity"). All these contributions have been fully absorbed by social anthropology, while his grand theory of culture is all but forgotten.

Malinowski was a charismatic and paradoxical personality who created intense loyalty (and sometimes strong antipathy) in his students. A brilliant and challenging teacher, he trained a generation of talented anthropologists in his Socratic seminars at the London School of Economics. It was mainly these disciples who, established in key academic positions in Britain and throughout the Commonwealth, gave the discipline its distinctive intellectual profile.

Malinowski relished polemic, outside as well as inside academe. As a pundit and publicist he wrote and lectured on marriage and the family, changing sexual mores, and other social issues of the day. He did much to bring the scientific study of man to public attention, and he greatly modified popular views about "the savage" and the nature of "primitive culture."

A true cosmopolitan, a scientific humanist, a romantic positivist, a rationalist and political liberal, Malinowski also wrote forcefully against the doctrines of totalitarianism. His prodigious gift for languages aided the international scope of his scholarship and facilitated the immense range of his personal contacts. Recent re-evaluation by Polish scholars of Malinowski's earliest work in philosophy has restored his reputation in his homeland and placed him firmly in the mainstream of modernist European thought.

MAJOR WORKS: *The Family among the Australian Aborigines: a Sociological Study* (London: 1913); *Argonauts of the Western Pacific* (London: 1922); *Crime and Custom in Savage Society* (London: 1926); *Sex and Repression in Savage Society* (London: 1927); *The Sexual Life of Savages in Northwestern Melanesia* (London: 1929); *Coral Gardens and their Magic* [2 vols.] (London: 1935); *The Foundations of Faith and Morals* (London: 1936); *Freedom and Civilization* (New York: 1944); *A Scientific Theory of Culture and Other Essays* (Chapel Hill: 1944); *The Dynamics of Culture Change: an Inquiry into Race Relations in Africa* (New Haven: 1945); *Magic, Science and Religion and Other Essays* (Boston: 1948); *Sex, Culture and Myth* (New York: 1962); *A Diary in the Strict Sense of the Term* (London: 1967).

SOURCES: Raymond Firth (editor), *Man and Culture: an Evaluation of the Work of Bronislaw Malinowski* (London: 1957); Roy Ellen, Ernest Gellner, Grazyna Kubica and Janusz Mucha (editors), *Malinowksi Between Two Worlds: the Polish Roots of an Anthropological Tradition* (Cambridge: 1988); Adam Kuper, *Anthropology and Anthropologists: the Modern British School* (London: 1983); Michael W. Young (editor), *The Ethnography of Malinowski: the Trobriand Islands, 1915-18* (London: 1979); Michael W. Young (editor), *Malinowski among the Magi: "The Natives of Mailu"* (London: 1988); Raymond Firth, "Bronislaw Malinowski" in: Sydel Silverman (editor), *Totems and Teachers: Perspectives on the History of Anthropology* (New York: 1981), pp. 100-139; Edmund Leach, "On the 'Founding Fathers,'" *Current Anthropology*, vol. 7 (1966), pp. 560-576; George W. Stocking, Jr., "The ethnographer's magic: fieldwork in British anthropology from Tylor to Malinowski" in: George W. Stocking, Jr. (editor), *Observers Observed* (Madison: 1983) (= *History of Anthropology*, vol. 1), pp. 70-120; Michael W. Young, "Malinowski and the function of culture" in: Diane J. Austin-Broos (editor), *Creating Culture: Profiles in the Study of Culture* (Sydney: 1987), pp. 124-140.

Michael W. Young

Malleret, Louis. Museum director, archaeologist, historian, administrator. Born in Clermont-Ferrand (France) 28 November 1901, died at Louveciennes, Yvelines Département (France) 16 March 1970. As a young man Malleret was a language teacher at the École Normale Supérieure of Saint-Cloud. Perhaps in search of adventure, he set out for a new career in colonial Indochina, arriving at Saigon in October 1929. The following year, Malleret was teaching at the École Primaire Supérieure de Garçons (Saigon). In 1930 he became librarian of the Société des Études Indochinoises. Malleret immersed himself in the colonial literature on Indochina. This self-guided study resulted in a literature survey that was published in Paris in 1934: *L'exotisme indochinois dans la littérature française depuis 1860.* In 1935 he was named director of the Musée Blanchard de la Brosse (Saigon Museum). This position opened many opportunities for archaeological, historical and ethnographic research. In 1936 an historical and archaeological study of the ancient fortifications of Saigon was completed, and the following year an annotated portfolio on the ethnic groups of French Indochina was published.

By 1938 Malleret had become interested in the archaeological investigation of the region of southern Indochina from the Mekong Delta to the Gulf of Siam. In 1942 workers began to uncover the site of the ancient port city of Oc Eo. Excavations continued there until 9 March 1945 when work was abruptly halted. Publication of findings from this major site was delayed by Malleret's appointment in 1946 as administrator of the École Française d'Extrême-Orient. From 1950 until 1956 he was director of this organization—a position that, during this time of conflict, brought many administrative problems. In 1949 Malleret's two-volume report on the Oc Eo excavations was submitted as a doctoral thesis to the Faculty of Letters, University of Paris. In 1959 the same text was published by the École Française d'Extrême-Orient as volume 1, parts 1 and 2, of *L'archéologie du Delta du Mekong.*

Malleret returned to France in 1957 to devote his attention to unfinished writing and research, particularly to the completion of his major work, the multi-volume report on the excavations at Oc Eo. *L'archéologie du Delta du Mekong* was published in four volumes (with three volumes of plates) between 1959 and 1965. This site report clearly associated Oc Eo with the early Indianized culture (2nd to the 5th century) known in Chinese sources as Funan. Objects excavated at Oc Eo included brick and granite structures, Brahman and Buddhist sculptures, Indian seals and Roman coins. These finds demonstrated extensive Indian influence on Funan culture and established trading links between Funan and South Asia and the Mediterranean region. Malleret was unable to continue excavations in the Oc Eo area after 1949 although some additional data were gathered by means of aerial photography.

Malleret received a doctoral degree from the University of Paris in 1949. During his later years, he resumed work on a biography of the 18th-century French traveler, Pierre Poivre. An annotated edition of a Poivre travel manuscript was published in 1968. Malleret's lengthy biography of Pierre Poivre was incomplete at the time of Malleret's death in 1970. Editing of this text was later completed by Malleret's wife.

Malleret's major contribution to Southeast Asian archaeology was the discovery and excavation of Oc Eo. He did not have the benefit of formal training in archaeology, and his excavation technique has been subject to some criticism. The Oc Eo finds have nevertheless been recognized as a substantial contribution to the understanding of Indian cultural influence in Southeast Asia. Some 175 books, articles and other writings were produced by Malleret between 1931 and 1968.

MAJOR WORKS: *L'exotisme indochinois dans la littérature française depuis 1860* (Paris: 1934); *L'Indochine française en face du Japon* (Paris: 1947) [published under the pseudonym, André Gaudel]; *Récentes découvertes concernant l'archéologie du Fou-Nan* [thesis] (Paris: 1959); *L'archéologie du Delta du Mekong* [7 vols.] (Paris: 1959-1965); *Un manuscrit inédit de Pierre Poivre: les mémoires d'un voyageur: texte reconstitué et annoté par Louis Malleret* (Paris: 1968); *Pierre Poivre* (Paris: 1974); "Éléments d'une monographie des anciennes fortifications et citadelles de Saigon," *Bulletin de la Société des Études indochinoises,* n.s., vol. 10, no. 4 (1935), pp. [5]-108; "À la recherche de Prei Nokor: note sur l'emplacement présumé de l'ancien Saigon khmer," *Bulletin de la Société des études indochinoises,* n.s., vol. 17, no. 2 (1942), pp. 19-34; "La Cochinchine dans le passé," *Bulletin de la Société des Études indochinoises,* n.s., vol. 13, no. 3 (1942), pp. 1-133; "Ouvrages circulaires en terre dan l'Indochine méridionale," *Bulletin de l'École française d'Extrême-Orient,* vol. 49 (1959), pp. 409-434.

SOURCES: Jean Filliozat, "Louis Malleret (1901-1970)," *Bulletin de l'École française d'Extrême-Orient,* vol. 58 (1971), pp. [1]-15 [contains bibliography]; Edmond Saurin, "La vie et l'oeuvre de Louis Malleret (1901-1970)," *Bulletin de la Société des Études indochinoises,* n.s., vol. 46, no. 1 (1971), pp. [7]-20; "Société des Études indochinoises ... liste des membres, 1930," *Bulletin de la Société des Études indochinoises,* n.s., vol. 5, no. 1-2 (1930), p. 155; Jeremy H.C.S. Davidson, "Archaeology in Southern Viet-Nam since 1954" in: R.B. Smith and W. Watson (editors), *Early South East Asia: Essays in Archaeology, History, and Historical Geography* (New York: 1979), pp. 215-222.

Lee S. Dutton

Malý, Jiří. Physical anthropologist, physician. Born at Mělník, Bohemia (Austria-Hungary, now Czechoslovakia) 6 November 1899, died in Prague (Czechoslovakia) 7 July 1950. A professor of anthropology at Charles University in Prague, Malý was originally a physician at a children's clinic of the university. In 1924 he became assistant to JINDŘICH MATIEGKA at the Institute of Anthropology. In 1927 he attained the rank of associate professor of anthropology and from 1934 served as a visiting professor and, later, as full professor and head of the Institute.

Malý graduated from a gymnasium in Bohemia and during his college years assisted Matiegka with research in a local ossuary. At Matiegka's urging, he attended the medical school of Charles University in Prague. During a study trip to the United States (made at the invitation of ALEŠ HRDLIČKA) he participated in a journey to Alaska to study Eskimos and Indians in the Yukon delta and the influence of the American environment on the physical characteristics of Czech and Slovak immigrants. Beginning in 1924 his works began to appear in the journal *Anthropologie,* of which he became co-editor in 1932. His subjects of research included deformed skulls of Indians from Bolivia, the skeleton of a wounded gorilla, the development of Slovak children, participants in the mass sport event Spartakiad and bones of famous people in Czech history (especially some Czech kings and the poet Karel Hynek Mácha). He also described a rare find of two human skeletons in the Dolní Věstonice dating from the times of the mammoth hunters.

During World War II, when Czech schools were closed, he retired and worked in the Institute of Pedagogy in Prague. At the end of the war in May 1945, he immediately resumed his lectures at the Department of Natural Sciences of Charles University and again undertook work on the idea of Hrdlička's Museum of Man. He also lectured to students in other departments including those of ethnography and physical education.

A great supporter of his work was his wife Ludmila Čížková-Malá, a former assistant to Matiegka. This family tradition has been continued by their daughter, Helena Malá, Ph.D., associate professor of the anthropology department of the Faculty of Natural Sciences at Charles University. Malý served as the inspiration for the first post-war generation of Czechoslovak anthropologists. He died in the midst of his work at the age of fifty-one.

MAJOR WORKS: "Staropražské lebky a kosti" ["Skulls and bones of Old Prague"], *Anthropologie*, vol. 3, no. 2 (1925), pp. 156-176; "Uměle deformované lebky z Tiahuanaco v Bolívii" ["Artificially deformed skulls from Tihuanaco in Bolivia"], *Anthropologie*, vol. 4, no. 4 (1926), pp. 251-348; "Vzrůst dětí na Podkarpatské Rusi" ["Growth of children in Carpatho-Russia"], *Anthropologie*, vol. 8, no. 2 (1930), pp. 149-173; "Kostry středoafrických Pygmejů z poříčí Ituri" ["The bones of Central African Pygmies from the Ituri Delta"], *Anthropologie*, vol. 16 (1938), pp. 1-60; "Lebky fosilního člověka z Dolních Věstonic" ["Skulls of the fossil man from Dolni Věstonice"], *Anthropologie*, vol. 17 (1939), pp. 171-192; "Ostatky K.H. Máchy a jeho tělesný zjev" ["Remains of K.H. Mácha and his physical appearance"], *Anthropologie*, vol. 18 (1940), pp. 36-53.

SOURCE: Ferdinand Škaloud, *Vzpomínka na profesora MUDr. Jiřího Malého k výročí nedožitých 75. narozenin* [*Memories of Prof. Dr. Jiří Malý at the Anniversary of his 75th Birthday*] (Prague: 1974) (= *Zprávy Československé společnosti antropologické při CSAV*, vol. 27, no. 1-2).

M. Prokopec
[Translation from Czech: Jitka Hurych]

Mandelbaum, David G.. Social-cultural anthropologist. Born in Chicago (Illinois) 22 August 1911, died in Berkeley (California) 19 April 1987. The first American social and cultural anthropologist to conduct fieldwork in India, Mandelbaum is best remembered for his holistic approach to the study of Indian civilization, his inspirational role in the development of South Asian studies in America and his enduring commitment to teaching.

After studying with MELVILLE HERSKOVITS at Northwestern University, and receiving an A.B. in anthropology in 1932, Mandelbaum pursued graduate studies with EDWARD SAPIR, who had recently established a program at Yale. Under the guidance of LESLIE SPIER, CLARK WISSLER and Sapir, Mandelbaum completed his doctoral dissertation, a descriptive ethnography of the Plains Cree of Saskatchewan, in 1936. His dissertation was republished more than forty years later and remains a standard reference on the subject.

During 1937-1938 Mandelbaum began the ethnographic work for which he is most widely known, among the Kota in the Nilgiri Hills of southern India, and also worked among the tribes of Travancore and the Jews of Cochin. After returning from India, Mandelbaum was on the faculty of the University of Minnesota until coming to Berkeley in 1946. But during World War II Mandelbaum spent time in India and Burma as an officer in the Office of Strategic Services. Although he retired in 1978, Mandelbaum continued to research and publish as professor emeritus until his death. He held office in a number of professional organizations including the American Anthropological Association, the American Institute of Indian Studies, the Association for Asian Studies and the Society for Applied Anthropology.

Squarely within an "American" tradition of anthropological scholarship, Mandelbaum shared the intellectual concerns of the Boasians—and especially those of his teacher Edward Sapir. A lifelong preoccupation with the role of the individual in shaping society and culture coupled with an interest in characterizing the encompassing units within which an individual lives led to an approach, prevalent in nearly all Mandelbaum's work, that attempted to balance attention to the ideal structures of a society (its "rules" as derived by the analyst) with discussion of actual behavior. Mandelbaum was careful to note the diverse and the exceptional in any group or phenomenon he attempted to characterize and brought an extraordinary clarity to explanations of the different levels at which a society operates—the village, tribe or caste, region or civilization. Mandelbaum tended to view Indian society as a constellation of "systems" (e.g., the caste system), but this did not keep him from dealing substantively with issues of social and cultural change.

Throughout his career, but especially from the 1950s until his death, Mandelbaum pursued the problems connected with characterizing the ethnographically diverse and sociologically complex. In a quest to develop a holistic approach to the study of Indian society, Mandelbaum organized interdisciplinary seminars, conferences and other forums for scholars to meet and exchange ideas. The growth of area studies in America was partly due to these efforts of Mandelbaum as well as those of such colleagues as ALFRED L. KROEBER, ROBERT REDFIELD and MILTON B. SINGER.

Mandelbaum was also concerned with practical problems. He wrote about culturally conditioned aspects of responses to illness and stress and on such problems as leadership and morale for the Department of Defense, piloted educational projects sponsored by the National Science Foundation and served on the National Commission for UNESCO. He also wrote about such issues as racism, alcoholism, the nuclear threat, energy, population and gender.

MAJOR WORKS: "The Jewish way of life in Cochin," *Jewish Social Studies*, vol. 1 (1939), pp. 423-460; "Culture change among the Nilgiri tribes," *American Anthropologist*, n.s., vol. 43 (1941), pp. 19-26; (editor) *Selected Writings of Edward Sapir* (Berkeley: 1949); "Psychiatry in military society" [2 parts], *Human Organization*, vol. 13 (1954), pp. 5-15; vol. 14 (1955), pp. 19-25; "The world and world-view of the Kota" in: McKim Marriott (editor), *Village India* (Chicago: 1955), pp. 223-254; *Society in India* [2 vols.] (Berkeley: 1970); *The Plains Cree: an Ethnographic, Historical and Comparative Study* (Regina: 1979) (= *Canadian Plains Studies*, no. 9); *Women's Seclusion and Men's Honor: Sex Roles in North India, Bangladesh and Pakistan* (Tucson: 1988).

SOURCES: Gerald D. Berreman, Murray B. Emeneau and George M. Foster, "David Mandelbaum, 1911-1987: Professor of Anthropology, Emeritus, Berkeley" [unpublished manuscript] (Berkeley: [ca. 1987]); Gerald D. Berreman, Elizabeth Colson and Milton Singer, "David Mandelbaum (1911-1987)," *American Anthropologist*, vol. 90 (1988), pp. 410-415. Milton Singer, "David Mandelbaum and the rise of South Asian Studies: a reminiscence" in: Paul Hockings (editor), *Dimensions of Social Life* (Berlin: 1987), pp. 1-6; Paul Hockings (editor), *Dimensions of Social Life: Essays in Honor of David G. Mandelbaum* (Berlin: 1987); Dennis Templeman, "David Mandelbaum, Professor of Anthropology: a profile," *Center for South and Southeast Asia Studies Review*, vol. 1, no. 2 (1978), pp. 3-4.

Richard Kent Wolf

Manker, Ernst M. Ethnographer. Born in Sweden 20 March 1893, died in Stockholm (Sweden) 1972. Manker took his B.A. (*fil. kand.*) in Göteborg in 1924. He became the second curator at the Nordic Museum of Stockholm in 1939, museum curator in

1945 and first curator at the same museum in 1957, a position he held until his retirement in 1961.

Manker made his first field trip to Lapland, which was to become the major interest in intellectual life, in 1926. Several years later, he was appointed the director of the Archaeological and Ethnographic Field Survey of Lapland (1948-1956), a project under the auspices of the Nordic Museum of Stockholm.

Manker earned a position as the foremost scholar of his time on the Swedish Saami. He published widely and received international recognition. He was, for example, an honorary member of the Royal Anthropological Institute in London.

His popular works in Swedish also shed light on the Saami. For many in his Swedish audience, this meant a first acquaintance with this neighboring ethnic minority that earlier had had a mystic air about it.

MAJOR WORKS: *En stallo i Jokkmokk* (Stockholm: 1928); *Bönder och nomader* (Uppsala: 1931); *Rajden går* (Stockholm: 1934); *Die Lappische Zaubertrommel* [2 vols.] (Stockholm: 1938-1950) (= *Acta Lapponica*, vol. 6); *Menschen und Götter in Lappland* (Zürich: 1950); *The Nomadism of the Swedish Mountain Lapps* (Stockholm: 1953) (= *Acta Lapponica*, vol. 7); *Les Lappons des montagnes suédoises* (Paris: 1954).

SOURCE: Gösta Berg, "In memoriam, Ernst Manker," *Ethnos*, vol. 37 (1972), pp. 168-170.

Jan-Åke Alvarsson

Mantegazza, Paolo. Physician, anthropologist, ethnologist. Born in Monza (Italy) 31 October 1831, died near La Spezia (Italy) 28 August 1910. Mantegazza is considered to be the founder of Italian anthropology.

Having graduated in medicine at the University of Pavia in 1850, in 1855 he left for Argentina and stayed there for three years, working as a doctor and traveling through the less accessible regions of the country. His passion for travel began to grow at that time (he went to Siberia in 1879 and to India between 1881 and 1882), but most of all he developed an interest in anthropology.

Upon his return to Italy he was named professor of general pathology at the University of Pavia. In 1869 he was called to Florence to occupy the first Italian chair of anthropology and ethnology; in addition, in 1871 he founded the Museo Nazionale di Antropologia (National Museum of Anthropology)—the first in Italy—and the Società Italiana di Antropologia ed Etnologia (Italian Society of Anthropology and Ethnology) (after 1878 expanded to include the name of "Psicologia Comparata" ("Comparative Psychology"), along with its journal, *L'Archivio*. These institutions, under Mantegazza's direction, were the most important centers of the 19th century for scholarly discussions (which were not without polemics) and for the promotion of essential research on Italian society and the standardization of the methodology of observation. Among the first achievements of these institutions were the *Raccolta*, a collection of materials on Italian ethnology compiled in 1871, the *Inchiesta*, a study of superstitions in Italy undertaken in 1887, and the *Concorso* of 1895, which produced an ethnographic map of Italy. The institutions provided their most useful tool to aid research in the detailed *Istruzioni* (instructions) oriented toward the study of the comparative psychology of the races of man, which were drawn up in 1871 by Mantegazza together with Charles Letourneau and ENRICO HILLYER GIGLIOLI.

Mantegazza was among the first Italian supporters of Darwin, even though he did not refrain from criticizing some of Darwin's concepts. Both Mantegazza's works and the institutions he founded reflect the influence of evolutionism, and evolutionism pervades his basic concept of the study of anthropology. General anthropology as conceived by Mantegazza is in fact "the natural history of man," which includes a diversity of specializations united by the common goal of analyzing all human manifestations (physical and psychological, social and cultural) of the past and present, of both civilized and primitive societies; these elements should be linked together by the positivist method and by the guiding concept of evolution through increasingly complex phases of development.

Even if it was not outwardly proclaimed, it appears evident in scientific practice that the diverse fields brought together by this heuristic vision of anthropology are all dominated by the study of man's physical and racial characteristics. Thus it happens that even in his strictly scientific activities Mantegazza maintained an interest in the popular diffusion of his ideas, which gained him much fame and success abroad. In all his vast production, his efforts in ethnology, psychology and folklore are subordinate to medical and biological considerations, which prevail even in his interpretations of cultural phenomena.

Already in the last years of Mantegazza's life his broad and all-encompassing conception of anthropology was beginning to wane. On the other hand, empirical practice and academic organization in Italian anthropology maintained a link between the physical and cultural aspects throughout the first half of the 20th century; it is through this dependence of ethnology on physical anthropology that the field conserved a part of Mantegazza's legacy.

MAJOR WORKS: *Rio de la Plata e Tenerife: viaggi e studii* (Milan: 1867); *Quadri della natura umana: feste ed ebbrezze* [2 vols.] (Milano: 1871); "L'elezione sessuale e la neogenesi: lettera a C. Darwin," *Archivio per l'Antropologia e l'Etnologia*, vol. 1 (1871), pp. 306-325; "Sulla monogenesi, complemento della teoria darwiniana," *Rendiconti del Regio Istituto lombardo di Scienze, Lettere ed Arti* [Milan], 39 (1871), vol. 4, p. 307; "L'uomo e gli uomini: saggio di una etnologia naturale," *Archivio per l'Antropologia e l'Etnologia*, vol. 6 (1876), pp. 30-46; "Studi antropologici ed etnologici sulla Nuova Guinea," *Archivio per l'Antropologia e l'Etnologia*, vol. 7 (1877), pp. 137-172 and 307-348; *Un viaggio in Lapponia con l'amico Sommier* (Milan: 1880); *India* (Milan: 1884); *Gli amori degli uomini: saggio di una etnologia dell'amore* (Milan: 1886); "Darwin dopo cinquant'anni," *Archivio per l'Antropologia e l'Etnologia*, vol. 34 (1904), pp. 311-322.

SOURCES: Paolo Mantegazza, "Trent'anni di storia della Società di Antropologia, Etnologia e Psicologia comparata," *Archivio per l'Antropologia e la Etnologia*, vol. 30 (1901), pp. 1-7; Abele De Blasio, *Biografia di Paolo Mantegazza* (Naples: 1905); Erasmo Ehrenfreund, "Bibliografia degli scritti di P. Mantegazza," *Archivio per l'Antropologia e la Etnologia*, vol. 56 (1926), pp. 11-176 [bibliography]; Sergio Sergi, "Le scienze antropologiche in Italia durante il primo centenario della sua unità" in: *Atti del I Congresso di Scienze Antropologiche Etnologiche e di Folklore* (Turin: 1961), pp. 24-42; Giovanni Landucci, *Darwinismo a Firenze: tra scienza e ideologia (1860-1900)* (Firenze: 1977); Sandra Puccini, "Antropologia positivista e femminismo: teorie scientifiche e luoghi comuni nella cultura italiana tra '800 e '900," *Itinerari*, no. 3 (1980), pp. 217-144; and n.s., nos. 1-2 (1981), pp. 187-283; Sandra Puccini, "Evoluzionismo e positivismo nell'antropologia italiana (1869-1911)" in: Pietro Clemente [et al.], *L'antropologia italiana: un secolo di storia* (Bari: 1985), pp. 97-148; Giovanni Landucci, *L'occhio e la mente: scienza e filosofia nell'Italia del secondo Ottocento*

(Florence: 1987), esp. "P. Mantegazza e la storia naturale dell'uomo" and "Biografia di P. Mantegazza," pp. 137-200 and 281-288.

Sandra Puccini
[Translation from Italian: Chris Nissen]

Manuel, E. Arsenio. Anthropologist, educator. Born in Quezon (Philippines) 14 December 1909. Manuel is best known to anthropologists for his writings on the Manuvu and the songs and epics of Mindanao. He has also engaged in research in various other fields of knowledge, including law, linguistics, archaeology, folklore, biography and bibliography. He has devoted the major part of his long and distinguished career to serving as a professor of anthropology at the University of the Philippines. He was a long-time research assistant of the late H. OTLEY BEYER.

Manuel studied law at the University of Manila, later finishing an M.A. in anthropology at the University of the Philippines and a Ph.D. in anthropology at the University of Chicago under FRED EGGAN. His major contributions to anthropology lie in his research, publications and teaching. His work on a dictionary of Philippine biography has been a landmark in Philippine scholarship, and his original research on the songs and folk epics of Mindanao as well as his publication on the social organization of the Manuvu community are major contributions to Philippine anthropology.

He has also done research in the field of custom law, morphology and morphemes of Philippine languages, especially Tagalog Tayabas in Luzon. He has conducted fieldwork in archaeology in the central Philippines. He is a founding member of the Philippine Folklore Society and is one of its most prolific authors.

MAJOR WORKS: *Upland Bagobo Narratives* (Quezon City: 1962); *Bagobo Riddles* (Quezon City: 1962); *Philippine Folklore Bibliography: a Preliminary Survey* (Quezon City: 1965); *Pre-Proto-Philippinensian* (Manila: 1966); *Agyu: the Ilianon Epic of Mindanao* (Manila: 1969); *Manuvu Social Organization* (Quezon City: 1973); *Tuwang Attends a Wedding* (Quezon City: 1975).

SOURCES: "Manuel, E. Arsenio" in: Sol Tax (editor), *Fifth International Directory of Anthropologists* (Chicago: 1975), p. 247; Mario D. Zamora (editor), *Studies in Philippine Anthropology (in Honor of H. Otley Beyer)* (Quezon City: 1967).

Mario D. Zamora

Maquet, Jacques Jérôme. Anthropologist. Born in Brussels (Belgium) 4 August 1919. Maquet studied at the University of Louvain (Belgium) from 1942 to 1946. He was student at Harvard University from 1946 until 1948 and finished his Ph.D. at the University of London in 1952. He came to the United States in 1967 and became a naturalized citizen in 1974. In 1973 he became *docteur-ès-lettres* at the Sorbonne. He has held the following positions: field anthropologist for the Institut de Recherches Scientifiques de l'Afrique Centrale (Institute of Scientific Research in Central Africa) (1949-1951); head of the same institute (1951-1957); professor at the State University of the Congo in Elisabethville (1957-1960); research director at the École Pratique des Hautes Études, VIème section, University of Paris (1961-1968); professor of anthropology at Case Western Reserve University (1968-1971); professor at University of California, Los Angeles (1971-).

Maquet's works are dominated by two parallel concerns. An ethnographic approach the aim of which is intra-cultural, qualitative discrimination and interpretation alternates with an ever-recurring theoretical inclination to build grand explanatory schemes based on correlations of quantifiable cross-cultural variations of phenomena.

Maquet started his ethnographic fieldwork as an anthropologist for the Institut de Recherches Scientifiques de l'Afrique Centrale in the Belgian colony, Rwanda. His focus can best be described as explorations in political anthropology: he investigated the system of government, the social hierarchy, and the feudal institution of the *ubuhake* in the traditional kingdom of Rwanda. This resulted in (a) two major publications covering all aspects of political relations and social reproduction, (b) a number of articles focusing on specific aspects of Rwandan feudalism, such as political participation and land tenure, and (c) several comparative articles culminating in his *Pouvoir et société en Afrique*.

1971 was an important year for Maquet, not only in terms of his academic career—he became professor at UCLA—but also from an intellectual point of view. With the publication of *Introduction to Aesthetic Anthropology* Maquet succeeded in applying his theoretical affinities with the cultural materialism of Pitirim Sorokin to aesthetics in general and African art in particular. This theoretical leap had been prepared carefully. Already in his Ph.D. dissertation on the sociology of knowledge he had investigated Sorokin's macro-historical cycles of three cultural premises. Maquet retained from this the more general notion that there is a correspondence between world views and aesthetic configurations that can be demonstrated by statistical correlations. In 1962 he proposed an outline for analyzing and comparing African cultural traits. He distinguished six kinds of civilizations on the African continent, each named after its most characteristic "tool" or "institution." He introduced each civilization by contemplating its characteristic art forms. These cultural expressions became the framework for further analysis of the economic systems, family and political institutions, myths and religious beliefs of each geo-cultural entity.

Although he continued to stress the importance of finding correlations between the sculptural tradition on the one hand and the productive system, social organization and collective representations on the other hand (cf. "Problématique d'une sociologie," p. 129), his approach became more and more interpretative, that is, he argued that works of art, styles and aesthetic experiences are culturally constructed, imagined realities that should be made understandable in "emic" terms (*The Aesthetic Experience*, pp. 245-251).

From 1971 onward his work was almost entirely devoted to the study of "the aesthetic phenomenon." His theory rests on the assumption that aesthetic attitudes and interests are universal, whereas the domain of aesthetic praxis, institutions and products—the aesthetic locus—has a culture-specific structuration and localization. Maquet rewrote and expanded his aesthetic theory in his 1986 book, *The Aesthetic Experience*. Comparing this to the earlier version (*Introduction to Aesthetic Anthropology*), we can detect a growing interest in the subjective side of art appreciation. As he himself admitted this new focus on contemplation results from more recent trips to South and Southeast Asia and meditation practices in Sri Lanka, Thailand and Burma (cf. "Expressive space and Theravada values," *Buddhist Studies in Honour of Walpola Rahula, Scholar and Shaman*).

One of Maquet's most well known contributions to art anthropology is his "art by metamorphosis" thesis. By pointing to the political and historical exigencies leading to the metamorphosis (aesthetic enfranchisement) of African ritual sculpture into art objects,

Maquet succeeded in demystifying the Western discovery of African art at the beginning of this century. As a consequence, he stipulated the problematic character of "universal art." His latest study is an attempt to explore the epistemological and methodological requisites of aesthetic anthropology.

MAJOR WORKS: *The Sociology of Knowledge: a Critical Analysis of the Systems of Karl Mannheim and Pitirim A. Sorokin* (Boston: 1951); *Le système des relations sociales dans le Ruanda ancien* (Tervuren: 1954) (= *Annales du Musée Royal du Congo Belge, Sciences de l'Homme. Ethnologie,* vol. 1); *The Premise of Inequality in Ruanda: a Study of Political Relations in a Central African Kingdom* (London: 1961); *Afrique: les civilisations noires* (Geneva: 1962); *Pouvoir et société en Afrique* (Paris: 1971); *Introduction to Aesthetic Anthropology* (Malibu: 1971; 2nd ed., Malibu: 1979); *The Aesthetic Experience: an Anthropologist Looks at the Visual Arts* (New Haven: 1986).

SOURCES: J.J. Maquet, "Problématique d'une sociologie de la sculpture traditionnelle" in: *Colloque, 1er Festival mondial des Arts nègres, Dakar* (Dakar: 1966), pp. 125-146; J.J. Maquet, *Pouvoir et société en Afrique* (Paris: 1971); J.J. Maquet, "Expressive space and Theravada values: a meditation monastery in Sri Lanka," *Ethos,* vol. 3, no. 1 (1975), pp. 1-21; J.J. Maquet, "Art by metamorphosis," *African Arts,* vol. 12, no. 4 (1979), pp. 33-37, 90-91; J.J. Maquet, "Bhavana in contemporary Sri Lanka: the idea and practice" in: S. Balasooriya [et al.] (editors), *Buddhist Studies in Honour of Walpola Rahula* (London and Sri Lanka: 1980), pp. 139-153; Larry Peters (editor), *Scholar and Shaman: Introduction to Ecstasy and Healing in Nepal* (Malibu: 1981).

Karel Arnaut

Marett, R.R. (Robert Ranulph).

Anthropologist, college rector, barrister. Born on Jersey (Channel Islands, United Kingdom) 13 June 1866, died in Oxford (England) 18 February 1943. Marett was influential in the development of social anthropology in Britain, and a leading theorist on primitive religion.

Born into a wealthy and respected family, Marett attended Balliol College, Oxford, from 1885 until 1888, taking a degree in Classics. He then studied law, and was admitted to the bar in Jersey by 1891. However, in the same year he was elected a fellow of Exeter College, Oxford, and so did not begin the practice of law.

In 1893 Marett won the Green moral philosophy prize with an essay on the ethics of primitives and was made both a tutor in philosophy and the sub-rector of Exeter College. His writings brought him to the attention of E.B. TYLOR, who became his friend and mentor at Oxford. For the 1899 meeting of the British Association, Marett prepared a paper on "pre-animistic religion," which carried Tylor's minimal definition of religion one step further. Marett hypothesized that proto-religions consisted of belief in impersonal forces not necessarily conceived of as supernatural entities. Evidently this reflected his own rather diffuse, non-theological religious feelings; Marett consistently emphasized feelings and actions over the thoughts or rationales of religious actors. He also condemned approaches to primitive religion that assumed an intellectual basis for cultic acts; members of these religions, he thought, were much more certain of how to perform a ritual than of any reason why the ritual should have taken any particular form.

Marett was a founding member of Oxford's anthropology diploma committee in 1905, personally responsible for the teaching of social anthropology. He became the secretary of the committee in 1907, retaining the position until 1927. In 1909 he founded the Oxford University Anthropological Society and the next year was appointed reader in social anthropology, a position he held until his seventieth year.

Marett, R.R.

Intrigued by the archaeology of continental Europe, Marett led the excavation of a Mousterian cave near his home on Jersey. The project, which lasted from 1912 to 1915, was his only first-hand field research of any kind. In 1913 he was awarded a D.Sc. and in 1928 he became rector of Exeter. When in 1934 A.R. RADCLIFFE-BROWN was appointed to the first chair of social anthropology at Oxford and was unable to occupy the post for a year, Marett was Oxford's first anthropology professor, if only in a caretaker role.

MAJOR WORKS: *The Threshold of Religion* (London: 1900); *Anthropology* (New York: 1912); *Psychology and Folklore* (London: 1920); *Faith, Hope and Charity in Primitive Religion* (Oxford: 1932); *Sacraments of Simple Folk* (Oxford: 1933); *Head, Heart and Hands in Human Evolution* (London: 1935); *Tylor* (New York: 1936).

SOURCES: T.K. Penniman, "Robert Ranulph Marett," *Man*, vol. 44 (1944), pp. 33-35; J.N. Mavrogordato, "Marett, Robert Ranulph" in: *Dictionary of National Biography*, 6th supplement (Oxford: 1959), pp. 572-574; M.J. Ruel, "Marett, Robert Ranulph" in: David L. Sills (editor), *International Encyclopedia of the Social Sciences* (New York: 1968-1979), pp. 565-567.

David Lonergan

Margulan, A.Kh. (Al'keĭ Khakanovich). Ethnographer, archaeologist, folklorist, historian. Born in Pavlodarskaĭa oblast' (Kazakhstan) 11 May 1904, died in Alma-Ata (Kazakh S.S.R.) 12 January 1985. Margulan was an academician of the Academy of Sciences of the Kazakh S.S.R. and the director of the department of ethnology of the Institut istorii, arkheologii i etnografii (Institute of History, Archaeology and Ethnography) of the Academy of Sciences of the Kazakh S.S.R. from 1956 to 1978.

The range of Margulan's scholarly interests was wide: he defended both a candidate's dissertation in history, *Istoricheskoe znachenie ĭarlykov i paĭsze* [*The Historical Meaning of Edicts and Talisman-symbols of Investiture*], and a doctoral dissertation in philology, *Ėpicheskie skazanii kazakhskogo naroda* [*Epic Legends of the Kazakh People*]. He devoted much energy to studies of the history of Kazakh folk architecture and of the material and non-material culture of the Kazakhs. He also wrote a great deal on the archaeology of central Kazakhstan. Margulan was one of the founders of archaeology in Kazakhstan. He made a significant contribution to the study of the national legacy of the Kazakh scholar Chokan Valikhanov, preparing an edition of his works for publication in the *Kazakhskaĭa sovetskaĭa ėnt͡siklopedii͡a* (he was a member of the editorial board and the author of more than 100 articles for this encyclopedia). Many of his works were published only in the Kazakh language.

MAJOR WORKS: "Naĭmany" in: S.I. Rudenko (editor), *Kazakhi: sbornik stateĭ antropologicheskogo otri͡ada kazakhskoĭ ėkspedit͡sii AN SSSR, 1927 g.* (Leningrad: 1930), pp. 329-334; "O kharaktere i istoricheskoĭ obuslovlennosti kazakhskogo ėposa," *Izvestii͡a Kazakhskogo filiala AN SSSR, serii͡a istoricheskai͡a*, no. 2 (1946), pp. 75-81; *Iz istorii gorodov i stroitel'nogo iskusstva drevnego Kazakhstana* (Alma-Ata: 1950); "Kul'tura plemen i narodnosteĭ Kazakhstana v VI-XII vekakh" in: *Istorii͡a kazakhskoĭ SSR* (Alma-Ata: 1957), pp. 71-111; "Kul'tura kazakhskogo naroda v XV-XVII vekakh" in: M.O. Auezov [et al.] (editors), *Istorii͡a Kazakhskoĭ SSR* (Alma-Ata: 1957), pp. 180-218; *Kazakhskai͡a i͡urta i ee ubranstvo* (Moscow: 1964); (co-author), *Drevni͡ai͡a kul'tura T͡Sentral'nogo Kazakhstana* (Alma-Ata: 1966); *Doislamskai͡a arkhitektura Kazakhstana* (Moscow: 1968); *Begazy-dandybaevskai͡a kul'tura T͡Sentral'nogo Kazakhstana* (Alma-Ata: 1979).

SOURCES: Zh.M. Abil'din (editor), *A.Kh. Margulan* (Alma-Ata: 1984) (= *Materialy k bibli-ografii uchenykh Kazakhstana*); "A.Kh. Margulin (nekrolog)," *Vestnik AN Kazakhskoĭ SSR*, no. 3 (1985), p. 67; *Izvestiĭa AN Kazakhskoĭ SSR,. ser. obshchestv. nauk*, no. 1 (1985), pp. 89-90.

A.M. Reshetov
[Translation from Russian: Thomas L. Mann]

Martin, Paul S. Archaeologist. Born in Chicago (Illinois) 20 November 1899, died in Tucson (Arizona) 20 January 1974. Martin received a Ph.D. in anthropology from the University of Chicago in 1929 and spent most of his career at Field Museum of Natural History, Chicago, where he served as Chief Curator of Anthropology (1935-1964), and Chief Curator Emeritus (1964-1974). He was also Lecturer in Anthropology at the University of Chicago (1955-1974).

Martin is known for his vigorous and systematic approach to archaeological research in the American Southwest. Between 1930 and 1955 he conducted research on Mogollon and pre-Mogollon sites in New Mexico, demonstrating the distinctiveness of the Mogollon culture. After 1956 Martin moved to east-central Arizona where he directed his research toward relationships between the prehistoric Mogollon culture and the historic Zuni Indians. Throughout his career he assisted in the training of students through their participation in his research, training that was formalized after 1965 with undergraduate research participation grants from the National Science Foundation. During his career he assisted in the training of nearly fifty individuals who became professional archaeologists. In an important late publication, *The Archaeology of Arizona* (with Fred T. Plog), Martin produced a major areal synthesis incorporating the tenets of the "new archaeology," a processual rather than a cultural history. Martin served as president of the Society for American Archaeology during 1965-1966 and in 1968 received the seventh Alfred Vincent Kidder Award from the American Anthropological Association for outstanding contributions to American archaeology.

MAJOR WORKS: (with Lawrence Roy and G. von Bonin) *Lowry Ruin in Southwestern Colorado* (Chicago: 1936) (= *Field Museum of Natural History, Anthropological Series*, vol. 23, no. 1); *The SU Site, Excavations at a Mogollon Village, Western New Mexico, 1939* (Chicago: 1940) (= *Field Museum of Natural History, Anthropological Series*, vol. 32, no. 1); (with George I. Quimby and Donald Collier) *Indians before Columbus* (Chicago: 1947); (with John B. Rinaldo, Elaine A. Bluhm, Hugh C. Cutler, and R.T. Grange) *Mogollon Cultural Continuity and Change* (Chicago: 1952) (= *Fieldiana: Anthropology*, vol. 40); (with John B. Rinaldo) *Excavations in the Upper Little Colorado Drainage* (Chicago: 1960) (= *Fieldiana: Anthropology*, vol. 51, no. 1); "The revolution in archaeology," *American Antiquity*, vol. 36 (1971), pp. 1-8; (with Fred T. Plog) *The Archaeology of Arizona: a Study of the Southwestern Region* (New York: 1973).

SOURCES: William A. Longacre, "Paul Sidney Martin, 1899-1974," *American Anthropologist*, vol. 78 (1976), pp. 90-92, Dorothy K. Washburn, Review of *The Archaeology of Arizona* by Paul S. Martin and Fred T. Plog, *American Antiquity*, vol. 41 (1976), p. 243.

James W. VanStone

Mason, Otis Tufton. Anthropologist, museum curator and administrator, teacher. Born in Eastport (Maine) 10 April 1838, died in Washington (D.C.) 5 November 1908. Mason received a bachelor's degree from Columbian College (now George Washington University) in 1861 and taught in the preparatory department of the college until 1884. His original interest was in classical studies, but around 1873, as a volunteer at the Smithsonian Institution, he was urged by Joseph Henry and Spencer F. Baird to take up North American ethnology. In 1884 Mason was appointed to the regular staff of the Smithsonian as curator of ethnology. During 1902-1903 he was acting head curator of the Department of Anthropology, and during 1904-1908 he was the head curator.

Much of Mason's museum career was devoted to the classification, description and exhibit of ethnological specimens. Derived from this work were his many publications on such subjects as weapons, basketry, transportation, tools, human migration, race, agriculture and invention. In addition, he prepared guides for making scientific collections of anthropological materials and summarized developments in anthropology in such serials as *Harper's Record of Science and Industry, American Naturalist,* and *Annual Reports of the Smithsonian Institution.* He worked on a synonymy of American Indian tribal names that was eventually merged with the work of others in the *Handbook of American Indians North of Mexico.* Although Mason's work focused primarily on the American Indian, he also studied and wrote on aspects of many other cultures.

Mason was a proponent of the theory that evolution was the major factor in culture history, and he has received attention in part because of his disputes with FRANZ BOAS over the emphasis placed on this concept in ethnological exhibits at the United States National Museum. Mason was also among the first to advance the culture area concept, which grew from his interest in the influence of environment on culture as a determinant in the particular expression of a group's stage of evolutionary development.

MAJOR WORKS: *Ethnological Directions Relative to the Indian Tribes of the United States* (Washington: 1875); "Influence of environment upon human industries or arts," *Annual Report of the Smithsonian Institution* (1895), pp. 636-666; "Aboriginal American harpoons: a study in ethnic distribution and invention," *Annual Report of the United States National Museum* (1900), pp. 189-304; "Aboriginal American basketry: study in a textile art without machinery," *Annual Report of the United States National Museum* (1900), pp. 171-458; (contributor) Frederick Webb Hodge (editor), *Handbook of American Indians North of Mexico* (Washington: 1907-1910) (= *Bureau of American Ethnology Bulletin,* no. 30).

SOURCES: John Buttner-Janusch, "Boas and Mason: particularism versus generalization," *American Antiquity,* vol. 59 (1957), pp. 318-324; Carol Beth Hetler, *Otis Tufton Mason and the Organizing of Washington Anthropology, 1870-1895* [unpublished M.A. thesis, George Washington University] (Washington: 1978); Walter Hough, "Otis Tufton Mason," *American Anthropologist,* n.s., vol. 10 (1908), pp. 661-667; Aleš Hrdlička, "Obituary of Otis T. Mason," *Science,* vol. 28 (1908), pp. 746-748; Mason papers in the Smithsonian Institution National Anthropological Archives; Charles D. Walcott, "Obituary of Otis T. Mason," *Annual Report of the Smithsonian Institution* (1909), p. 32.

James R. Glenn

Matiegka, Jindřich. Physical anthropologist, physician. Born in Benešov near Prague (Austria, now Czechoslovakia) 31 March 1862, died in Mělník (Czechoslovakia) 4 August 1941. Matiegka was the first professor of anthropology at Charles University in Prague.

Matiegka first worked as a medical doctor in the country and then as a general practitioner in the city of Prague. In 1895 he prepared an exhibit on "Man" at the ethnographic exposition in Prague with anthropological and demographic data about the population of Bohemia and the development of adolescents. From 1897 he was a docent (associate professor) of anthropology in the Department of Philosophy at Charles University and from 1908 served as visiting professor of anthropology and demography. He was promoted to full professor in 1918 and later became provost of Charles University.

He became interested in anthropology through research on bones that were found in the area of the Elbe River where he worked as a medical doctor, an area of "Unetic" and other Neolithic cultures. He was promoted under the influence of Lubor Niederle, who saw in him someone destined and qualified to establish a department of anthropology at the university, something that Niederle himself originally had hoped to do. In addition to studying bones from archaeological excavations and Czech ossuaries (for twelve years Matiegka spent his vacations studying bones in the ossuary at Mělník), Matiegka researched contemporary populations. In 1910 (with professor of psychiatry I.K. Herfort, Professor Čada and professor of education J. Dolenský) he established the Institute for Research on the Child (also known as the Institute of Pedagogy) and served as its director for many years. In 1918 he established the modern Institute of Anthropology with excellent facilities in the Faculty of Natural Sciences of Charles University. His friend ALEŠ HRDLIČKA provided him with advice and financial assistance. Matiegka (together with Professor Pantoflíček) applied a method of stereophotogrammetry to anthropology in 1911 and in 1921 published a paper on a method that described the physical construction of the human body *in vivo* with reference to external proportions. In 1923 he started the journal *Anthropologie* of which he was the main editor (later co-editor with JIŘÍ MALÝ) until his death.

Another of his publications was a series, *Antropologická knihovna* [*Library of Anthropology*], established with Hrdlička and published by Charles University. From 1934 on he worked assiduously toward the establishment of a Museum of Man at Charles University for which a separate building was planned and which was supported by the Hrdlička foundation. Matiegka was extremely industrious and enthusiastic about his scientific discipline, and, as a teacher, scientist and private individual, he was liked and respected. Many of his students entered the field of anthropology, including VOJTĚCH SUK, Jiří Malý (his successor), Božo Škerlje from Ljubljana, JINDŘICH VALŠÍK, K. Stolyhwo from Kraków, demographer F.J. Netušil and others.

Matiegka managed to realize most of his plans. It was unfortunate that, due to the events of World War II, the public was not given the Museum of Man to which Matiegka had dedicated so much of his energy.

MAJOR WORKS: *Crania Bohemica. 1. Böhmens Schadel aus dem VI-XII. Jahrhundert* (Prague: 1891); *Vzrůst, vývin, tělesné vlastnosti a zdravotní poměry mládeže Královského hlavního města Prahy* [*Growth, Development, Physical Characteristics and Health Status of the Youth of Prague*] (Prague: 1897) (= *Rozpravy České akademie pro vědy, slovesnost a umění*, třída 2, vol. 6, no. 17); "The testing of physical efficiency," *American Journal of Physical Anthropology*, vol. 4 (1921), pp. 223-230; *Somatologie školní mládeže* [*Somatology of School Children*] (Prague: 1927); *Všeobecná nauka o plemenech* [*General Study of Races*] (Prague: 1929); *Tělesné pozůstatky českých králů a jejich rodin* [*Bodily Remains of Czech Kings and Their Families*] (Prague: 1932); "Tělesná povaha dnešního lidu československého" ["Physical characteristics of current population of Czechoslovakia"], *Čs. vlastivěda*, vol. 2 (1933), pp. 193-259; *Homo predmostensis. I. Skulls* (Prague: 1934); (with P. Šebesta) *Anthropologie středoafrických Pygmeju* [*Anthropology of Central African Pygmies*] (Prague: 1936); *Homo predemostensis. II. Ostatní části kostrové* (Prague: 1938).

SOURCE: Jiří Malý, *Jindřich Matiegka* (Prague: 1949), pp. 3-39.

M. Prokopec
[Translation from Czech: Jitka Hurych]

Matorin, N.M. (Nikolaĭ Mikhaĭlovich). Ethnographer, scholar of religion, folklorist, organizer of scientific and museum work. Born in Tverskaia guberniia (Russia) 5 (17) August 1898, executed by firing squad in Leningrad (Russian S.F.S.R.) 11 October 1936. Matorin was a professor at Leningrad University, director of the Muzeĭ antropologii i etnografii (Museum of Anthropology and Ethnography) of the Soviet Academy of Sciences, deputy director of the Institut po izucheniiu narodov (Institute for the Study of Peoples) of the Soviet Academy of Sciences, first director of the Institut ètnografii (Institute of Ethnography) of the Soviet Academy of Sciences, and managing editor of the journal *Sovetskaia ètnografiia* (1931-1933).

Matorin made a major contribution to the study of the ethnography of the peoples of the Volga basin, but his primary scholarly achievement was the study of the theoretical and actual problems of religion among the world's peoples and of the role of religion in the life of society. At the end of the 1920s and beginning of the 1930s, Matorin organized a seminar of young scholars of religion who had studied sectarian movements. The scope of his scholarly interests was unusually wide, ranging from the problems of prehistoric times to the ethnographic present.

MAJOR WORKS: *Religiia u narodov Volzhsko-Kamskogo kraia prezhde i teper'* (Moscow: 1929); *Zhenskoe bozhestvo v pravoslavnom kul'te: Piatnitsa-Bogoroditsa: ocherk po sravnitel'noĭ morfologii* (Moscow: 1931); *Pravoslavnyĭ kul't i proizvodstvo* (Moscow and Leningrad: 1931); "Sovremennyĭ ètap i zadachi sovetskoĭ ètnografii," *Sovetskaia ètnografiia*, no. 1-2 (1931), pp. 3-38; "15 let sovetskoĭ ètnografii," *Sovetskaia ètnografiia*, no. 5-6 (1932), pp. 1-14; (general editor) *Leningradskie rabochie o derevne* (Leningrad: 1925); *Pervobytnoe obshchestvo* (Moscow: 1932).

SOURCES: G.A. Nosova, "N.N. Matorin kak issledovatel' religii," *Voprosy nauchnogo ateizma*, no. 7 (1969), pp. 366-386; A.M. Reshetov, "N.N. Matorin: pedagog, organizator nauki, issledovatel'" in: O.V. Lysenko (editor), *Polevye issledovaniia Gosudarstvennogo Muzeia ètnografii narodov SSSR, 1985-1987 gg.* (Leningrad: 1989), pp. 23-25.

A.M. Reshetov
[Translation from Russian: Thomas L. Mann]

Matsumura, Akira. Physical anthropologist. Born in Tōkyō (Japan) 1 August 1880, died in Tōkyō (Japan) 21 May 1936. Matsumura entered the specialized course in anthropology at the University of Tōkyō Faculty of Science in 1900. Following the completion of his studies, he traveled widely in Japan in 1907, visiting remote corners of the country with a view toward inaugurating comprehensive somatological studies, a plan that proved to be too ambitious and was never fulfilled. In 1911 he began the extensive study of head shapes and body lengths in men and women students, clarifying regional differentiation in Japanese physical types. In 1924 he received a Ph.D. in science, and in 1925 became an associate professor at the University of Tōkyō. He also served as secretary-general of the Anthropological Society of Tōkyō.

In addition to his work with the anthropology of living Japanese, he carried out fieldwork in Micronesian ethnology and in the archaeology of the Ryūkyū Islands. In 1926 he supervised the Ubayama shell mound excavation, which for some time thereafter remained a model of scientific excavation.

MAJOR WORKS: *A Gazetteer of Ethnology* (Tōkyō: 1908); "Contributions to the ethnography of Micronesia," *Journal of the College of Science, Imperial University of Tōkyō*, vol. 40, art. 7 (1918), pp. 1-174; "On the cephalic index and stature of the Japanese and their local differences," *Journal of the Faculty of Science, Imperial University of Tōkyō*, section V, vol. 1 (1925), pp. 1-312; (editor) *Nihon Minzoku* [*People of Japan*] (Tōkyō: 1935).

SOURCE: Akiyoshi Suda, "Matsumura Akira Sensei den ryakuki" ["Dr. A. Matsumura, his life and works"], *Journal of the Anthropological Society of Tōkyō*, vol. 51 (1936), pp. 357-373.

Bin Yamaguchi
[*Translation from Japanese: Theodore Welch*]

Matteucci, Pellegrino. Medical doctor, naturalist, explorer. Born in Ravenna (Italy) 10 October 1850, died in London (England) 8 August 1881. After taking his degree Matteucci dedicated himself to traveling and to the study of natural science. His deep Catholic faith did not prove an obstacle to his sincere interest in the positions expressed in the works of Charles Darwin, PAUL BROCA and ARMAND DE QUATREFAGES, from which he derived a method much influenced by positivism. Having failed in his attempt to be included in the expedition to the equatorial lakes organized by the Società Geografica Italiana (Italian Geographical Society) in 1876, Matteucci was invited the following year by Romolo Gessi (1831-1881), an Italian explorer who had been in Africa for some years, to join an expedition to Kaffa, following the course of the Blue Nile. Matteucci was a tireless chronicler of his voyages. After the publication of his account of his first experience, he was commissioned by the Società di Esplorazione Commerciale in Africa (Society for Commercial Exploration in Africa), formed in Milan in 1879, to facilitate the introduction of Italian commercial products as far as the Kingdom of Shoa. Together with his colleagues Giuseppe Vigoni (1846-1914) and Gustavo Bianchi (1845-1884), at the end of 1879 Matteucci left Italy, but upon his arrival in Massawa he decided to change his destination because of the confused political situation in Ethiopia. The expedition was directed therefore toward Debra Tabor and gathered much useful information.

When he returned to Italy, Matteucci prepared a plan for the crossing of the African continent from Khartoum to the Gulf of Guinea. The Società Geografica Italiana and the Italian government financed the undertaking which in July of 1881 brought Matteucci to the Atlantic Coast of Africa; from there the expedition reembarked for Great Britain. The following month the explorer died in London from a disease he had contracted during the crossing.

Matteucci was an avid reader of the works of foreign authors; this interest can be attested to by the citations and comparisons he makes to support his theories concerning the classification of races and their origins. One can see a particular example of this tendency in his observations regarding the Akka pygmies. With all the peoples he encountered Matteucci never ceased to consider language, religion, physical appearance, social organization and customs together with history and geography.

MAJOR WORKS: *La Spedizione Italiana all'Africa Equatoriale: considerazioni di Pellegrino Matteucci* (Bologna: 1875); *Gli Akka e le razze africane* (Bologna: 1877); *Sudan e Gallas* (Milan: 1879); *In Abissinia* (Milan: 1880).

SOURCES: Cesare Cesari, *I viaggi africani di Pellegrino Matteucci* (Milan: 1932); Mario Longhena, *Scritti di Pellegrino Matteucci raccolti ed annotati* (Ravenna: 1965); Elia Millosevich, *Le principali esplorazioni geografiche italiane nell'ultimo cinquantennio* (Milan: 1911); Sandra Puccini, "Gli Akka' del Miani: una storia etnologica nell'Italia di fine secolo (1872-1883). Parte prima: dall'Africa selvaggia all'Europa degli scienziati (1872-1874)," *L'Uomo*, vol. 8, no. 1 (1984), pp. 29-58; Silvio Zavatti, *Dizionarfio generale degli esploratori* (Milan: 1939).

Massimo Guerra
[Translation from Italian: Chris Nissen]

Maudslay, Alfred Percival. Archaeologist. Born in London (England) 18 March 1850, died in Hereford (England) 22 January 1931. Maudslay was the grandson of the celebrated engineer Henry Maudslay. After education at Harrow School and Cambridge University, Maudslay began the study of medicine but abandoned it and entered the Colonial Service, serving in Fiji and Tonga (1875-1880). There he became interested in ethnography and archaeology.

Resigning from the service in 1880, Maudslay left for Guatemala to reconnoitre Maya ruins, and visited Quirigua, Copán, Tikal and Yaxchilán: he was the first to describe the latter. In six further expeditions (1882-1894) Maudslay made site-plans and recorded sculpture at Chichen Itzá and Palenque in addition to the four sites mentioned. His was the first scientifically accurate work in the Maya area, and his presentation of sculpture by means of both photographs and drawings (done from originals or from his own plaster-casts) set the standard for all later workers.

Maudslay's importance lies in (a) his having perceived the need for conscientious data-gathering well before museums or academic institutions were ready to send teams into the field, and (b) his having the ability and the money to perform this service in exemplary fashion. Maudslay also made a full translation of the *Historia* by Bernal Diaz (1496-1584) and was at work on a translation of the *Relación de las cosas de Yucatán* by Bishop Diego de Landa (1524-1579) when he died.

MAJOR WORKS: "Explorations in Guatemala and examination of the newly discovered Indian Ruins of Quirigua, Tikal and the Usumacinta," *Proceedings of the Royal Geographical Society*, n.s. vol. 5 (1883), pp. 185-204; *Biologia Centrali-Americana (Archaeology)* [5 vols.] (London: 1889-1902); (with Ann C. Maudslay) *A Glimpse at Guatemala* (London: 1899); (translator) *The True History of the Conquest of New Spain by Bernal Diaz del Castillo* [5 vols.] (London: 1908-1916); *A Note on the Position and Extent of the Great Temple Enclosure of Tenochtitlán* (London: 1912); *Life in the Pacific Fifty Years Ago* (London: 1930).

SOURCES: Autobiographical data in works cited above; Alfred M. Tozzer, "Alfred Percival Maudslay," *American Anthropologist*, n.s., vol. 33 (1931), pp. 403-413; Ian Graham, "Alfred Maudslay and the discovery of the Maya" *British Museum Yearbook*, no. 2 (1977), pp. 126-155.

Ian Graham

Mauss, Marcel. Sociologist, ethnologist. Born in Epinal (France) 10 May 1872, died in Paris (France) 1 February 1950. Mauss is best known to anthropologists for his theories on exchange, reciprocity and total social facts.

Mauss studied philosophy at Bordeaux and the history of religion at the École Pratique des Hautes Études where he became professor of primitive religion. He taught also at the Collège de France and was co-founder of the Institut d'Ethnologie of the University of Paris. In his youth he was active in the French socialist movement.

Mauss closely collaborated with his uncle Émile Durkheim (e.g., "De quelques formes primitives de classification") and with young scholars (e.g., with Henri Hubert, "Essai sur la nature et la fonction du sacrifice") grouped around *L'année sociologique*, the journal in which Durkheim's ideas and sociological methods were expounded. Upon Durkheim's death, Mauss became the journal's editor and the leader of the group. One of the earliest advocates of a close relationship between anthropology and psychology, Mauss's ethnological studies are concrete applications of Durkheimian rules of sociological research, particularly the concentration on typical, well studied facts and on relating the "collective representations" of the group to its social structure. One of the best examples of this approach is his study of the Eskimos (*Essai sur les variations saisonnières des sociétés eskimos*, part 7 of *Sociologie et anthropologie*) with Henri Beuchat, where winter grouping is related to the development among the Eskimos of a strong religious and moral unity of mind and summer dispersal is related to moral and religious impoverishment of the community and individual. Many of his other writings are on the sociology of religious phenomena such as sacrifice, magic, prayer, death and mourning rituals. Mauss's best known work is *The Gift*, an essay on primitive systems of exchange that are, in theory, voluntary, spontaneous and disinterested but are, in fact, obligatory and interested. Focusing on the three obligations of giving, receiving and repaying, Mauss sees the exchange of goods and persons as the structure, at once religious, legal, moral and economic, that supports and strengthens social bonds in primitive societies. In the "Conclusion" of this work, Mauss recommends a return to "the spirit of the gift" by modern societies.

It is difficult to separate Mauss's influence in anthropology from that of Durkheim. Inasmuch as he explored and applied Durkheim's ideas of "total systems," Mauss greatly influenced functional anthropologists like BRONISLAW MALINOWSKI and A.R. RADCLIFFE-BROWN as well as structuralists like CLAUDE LÉVI-STRAUSS. In France, Mauss's most direct influence was felt by a generation of ethnographers (MARCEL GRIAULE, LOUIS DUMONT, ROGER BASTIDE, MAURICE LEENHARDT), historians (Lucien Febvre, Marc Bloch) and psychologists (Charles Blondel).

MAJOR WORKS: (with Henri Hubert) "Essai sur la nature et la fonction du sacrifice," *L'année sociologique*, vol. 2 (1989), pp. 29-138 [tr.: *Sacrifice: Its Nature and Function* (Chicago: 1964)]; (with Émile Durkheim) "De quelques formes primitives de classification," *L'année sociologique*, vol. 6 (1901-1902), pp. 1-72 [tr.: *Primitive Classification* (Chicago: 1968)]; "Essai sur le don, forme et raison de l'échange dans les sociétés archaïques," *L'année sociologique*, 2nd sér., vol. 1 (1923-1924), pp. 30-186 [tr.: *The Gift* (New York: 1967)]; "Une catégorie de l'esprit humain: la notion de personne, celle de 'moi,'" *Journal of the Royal Anthropological Institute*, vol. 68 (1938), pp. 263-281 [tr.: "A category of the human mind: the notion of person, the notion of 'self,'" in: Marcel Mauss, *Sociology and Psychology: Essays* (London: 1979), pp. 57-94]; *Sociologie et anthropologie* (edited by Claude Lévi-Strauss) (Paris: 1950); *Oeuvres* (edited by Victor Karady) [3 vols.] (Paris: 1968); *Sociology and Psychology: Essays* (London: 1979).

SOURCES: Jean Cazeneuve, *La sociologie de Marcel Mauss* (Paris: 1968); C. Dubar, "La méthode de Marcel Mauss," *Revue française de sociologie*, vol. 10 (1969), pp. 515-521; Marshall Sahlins, "Philosophie politique de *L'Essai sur le don*," *L'Homme*, vol. 8 (1968), pp. 4-21 [tr.: *Stone Age Economics* (Chicago: 1972), pp. 168-183]; Claude Lévi-Strauss, "Introduction à l'oeuvre de Marcel Mauss" in: Marcel Mauss, *Sociologie et anthropologie* (Paris: 1950), pp. ix-lii [tr.: *Introduction to the Work of Marcel Mauss* (London: 1988)]; Manuel Moreno, "Mauss' methodology reconsidered," *Journal of Anthropology*, vol. 4 (1984), pp. 101-122; Victor Karady, "Introduction" to: Marcel Mauss, *Oeuvres* (Paris: 1968), vol. 1, pp. 1-53; Valerio Valeri, "Marcel Mauss e la nuova antropologia," *Critica storica*, vol. 5 (1966), pp. 677-703; Steven Lukes, "Mauss, Marcel" in: David L. Sills (editor), *International Encyclopedia of the Social Sciences* (New York: 1968-1979), vol. 10, pp. 78-82.

Manuel Moreno

McAllister, J. Gilbert. Ethnologist, archaeologist. Born in San Antonio (Texas) 26 January 1904. McAllister received his bachelor's degree at the University of Texas in 1928 and did graduate work in anthropology at the University of Chicago receiving his Ph.D. in 1935.

In 1929 he went to Hawaii where he joined the staff of the Bernice P. Bishop Museum and spent three years on an archaeological survey of Oahu and Kahoolawe Islands. He went on in his career to specialize in the social organization of the Plains Indians of North America.

MAJOR WORKS: *Archaeology of Oahu* (Honolulu: 1934); *Kiowa-Apache Social Organization* (Chicago: 1937).

SOURCES: "Report of the Director for 1929," *Bernice P. Bishop Museum, Bulletin*, no. 78 (1930), p. 10; "Report of the Director for 1930," *Bernice P. Bishop Museum, Bulletin*, no. 82 (1931), p. 9; "Report of the Director for 1931," *Bernice P. Bishop Museum, Bulletin*, no. 94 (1932), p. 8; "Report of the Director for 1932," *Bernice P. Bishop Museum, Bulletin*, no. 106 (1933), p. 8; "McAllister, J. Gilbert" in: *International Directory of Anthropologists* (Washington: 1938), pp. 63-64; "McAllister, J. Gilbert" in: *International Directory of Anthropologists* (2nd ed., Washington: 1940), pp. 94-95; "McAllister, J. Gilbert" in: *International Directory of Anthropologists* (3rd ed., Washington: 1950), p. 116; "McAllister, J. Gilbert" in: Sol Tax (editor), *Fifth International Directory of Anthropologists* (Chicago: 1975), p. 236.

Thomas L. Mann

McGee, W.J. (William John). Anthropologist, geologist, hydrologist. Born in Farley (Iowa) 17 April 1853, died in Washington (D.C.) 4 September 1912. McGee spent his early years on his family's farm and was largely self-educated. He excelled in mathematics, working for several years as a professional surveyor; he also briefly pursued careers in law and as an inventor. In 1878 McGee's interest in geology led him to join the American Association for the Advancement of Science. In the same year he began presenting papers in anthropology.

After conducting a topographic survey of northeast Iowa, McGee was appointed geologist in the U.S. Geological Survey, under JOHN WESLEY POWELL. McGee spent seven years on one project, mapping the southeastern United States. In 1893 he moved to the Bureau of American Ethnology (BAE), again under Powell, and the following year became Ethnologist in Charge.

In 1894 and 1895 McGee visited Tiburon Island in the Gulf of California to map it and to perform ethnographic research among its inhabitants, the Seri Indians. Unable to make contact with the Seri on Tiburon, McGee questioned more acculturated Seri of mainland Sonora about traditional life ways.

After a decade at the BAE McGee resigned to head the anthropology department of the Louisiana Purchase Exposition, held in St. Louis in 1904. He also was appointed director of the St. Louis Public Museum, but the latter project never got beyond the planning stages. By 1907 McGee had joined both the U.S. Department of Agriculture, where he served as a soil specialist, and the federal Inland Waterways Commission, of which he was secretary and vice-chair, appointed by President Theodore Roosevelt.

McGee was a prolific scholar in many disciplines, but his importance to anthropology was chiefly due to his organizational and leadership abilities. He played a major role in the Anthropological Society of Washington, serving as its president from 1898 until 1900, and was one of the founders of the American Anthropological Association. In 1902 he became the Association's first president. McGee was also a vice-president of the Archaeological Institute of America, a founder of the Geological Society of America, vice-president of the National Geographic Society and one of the editors of *National Geographic* magazine. In 1901 he was awarded an honorary LL.D. by Cornell College of Iowa, in recognition of his many achievements.

McGee died in 1912 after a long battle with cancer, leaving his body to medical science. Dr. Edward Spitzka of Philadelphia received McGee's brain (along with that of Powell, which had been left to McGee) for scientific study.

MAJOR WORKS: "Man and the glacial period," *American Anthropologist*, vol. 5 (1892), pp. 85-95; "Comparative chronology," *American Anthropologist*, vol. 5 (1892), pp. 327-344; "The beginning of agriculture," *American Anthropologist*, vol. 8 (1895), pp. 350-375; "Expedition to Papagueria and Seriland," *American Anthropologist*, vol. 9 (1896), pp. 93-98; "The science of humanity," *American Anthropologist*, vol. 9 (1896), pp. 241-272; "The beginning of marriage," *American Anthropologist*, vol. 9 (1896), pp. 371-383; "National growth and national character," *National Geographic Magazine*, vol. 10 (1899), pp. 186-206; "The beginning of mathematics," *American Anthropologist*, n.s., vol. 1 (1899), pp. 646-674; "Anthropology and its larger problems," *Science*, vol. 21 (1905), pp. 770-784.

SOURCES: Frederick Webb Hodge, "W.J. McGee," *American Anthropologist*, vol. 14, n.s. (1912), pp. 683-687; "Dr. McGee, noted geologist, dead," *The New York Times* (5 September 1912), p. 9; Andrew S. Goudie, "W.J. McGee," *Geographers: Biobibliographical Studies*, vol. 10 (1986), pp. 111-116.

David Lonergan

McIlwraith, T.F. (Thomas Forsyth).

Anthropologist, curator. Born in Hamilton (Ontario) 9 April 1899, died in Toronto (Ontario) March 29 1964. McIlwraith is best known to anthropologists as the author of *The Bella Coola Indians*, but he spent most of his career as an administrator and teacher, establishing anthropology as an academic discipline in Canada and building the ethnological collections at the Royal Ontario Museum.

Trained in Cambridge under A.C. HADDON and W.H.R. RIVERS following World War I, McIlwraith belonged to that small cadre of students developing new methods of intensive ethnographic fieldwork. He spent two seasons with the Nuxalk (Bella Coola) Indians in British Columbia from 1922 to 1924, not only witnessing their winter ceremonies but participating as a prompter and dancer. He accepted a position at the University of Toronto in 1925, becoming the first full-time academic anthropologist in Canada. With the creation of the Department of Anthropology in 1936, McIlwraith became Head and Professor, guiding the development of the department until his retirement in 1963. With PHILLEO NASH and Norman Emerson, he introduced the first field school in archaeology in Canada, and in 1939 he co-hosted with C.T. Loram of Yale University an innovative conference on American Indian welfare. McIlwraith published mostly in Canadian scholarly journals, contributing articles on archaeology, the history of anthropology in Canada and native peoples.

> MAJOR WORKS: (with C.T. Loram) *The North American Indian Today* (Toronto: 1943); *The Bella Coola Indians* (Toronto: 1948); "On the location of Cahiague," *Transactions of the Royal Society of Canada*, vol. 46, series 3 (1947), pp. 99-102; "Ethnology, anthropology and archaeology," *Canadian Historical Review*, vol. 6-35 (1925-1954).

> SOURCES: John Barker, "T.F. McIlwraith and anthropology at the University of Toronto, 1925-63, *Canadian Review of Sociology and Anthropology*, vol. 24 (1987), pp. 253-268; John Barker (editor), "'At home with the Bella Coola Indians' by T.F. McIlwraith," *BC Studies*, vol. 75 (1987), pp. 43-60; Michael Levin, Gail Avrith and Wanda Barrett, *An Historical Sketch, Showing the Contribution of Sir Daniel Wilson and Many Others to the Teaching of Anthropology at the University of Toronto* (Toronto: 1984).

John Barker

McLennan, John Ferguson. Lawyer, ethnologist. Born in Inverness (Scotland) 14 October 1827, died in Hayes Common, Kent (England) 16 June 1881. McLennan's theories on social evolution, kinship and the origin of religion contributed to the development of social anthropology.

McLennan was called to bar in 1857 and made parliamentary draftsman for Scotland in 1871. McLennan's first major work, *Primitive Marriage*, was published in 1865. In it he put forward theories based on his own legal and literary studies. These theories were founded on what he thought was a universal theme—marriage by capture—which he explained further by coining the words exogamy (out-marriage) and endogamy (in-marriage). He went on to hypothesize on the development of the family, which he believed had evolved from a stage of promiscuity to mother-right (matriarchy) and, finally, to father-right (patriarchy). A similar idea was also advanced by JOHANN JAKOB BACHOFEN. McLennan was also responsible for introducing the concept of "totemism" into anthropological theory. He regarded totemism as the most primitive form of religion. The adoption of a plant or animal as a symbol of the unity of a particular group provided the beginning of the idea of kinship or family. Later, through exogamy, these symbols were dispersed through the female line.

> MAJOR WORKS: *Primitive Marriage: an Inquiry into the Origin of the Form of Capture in Marriage Ceremonies* (Edinburgh: 1865); "Bride catching," *Argosy*, vol. 2 (1866), pp. 31-42; "Kinship in ancient Greece," *Fortnightly Review*, vol. 4 (1866), pp. 560-588, 682-691; "The worship of animals and plants," *Fortnightly Review*, n.s., vol. 6 (1868), pp. 407-427, 562-582; n.s., vol. 7 (1870), pp. 194-216; "Exogamy and endogamy," *Fortnightly Review*, n.s., vol. 21 (1877), pp. 884-895; "The levirate and polyandry," *Fortnightly Review*, n.s., vol. 21 (1877), pp. 694-707; *The Patriarchial Theory* (edited and completed by Donald McLennan) (London: 1885); *Studies in Ancient History: Comprising a Reprint of Primitive Marriage* (London: 1886); *Studies in Ancient History: Second Series* (edited and completed by Eleanora A. McLennan and Arthur Platt) (London: 1896).

> SOURCES: "M'Lennan, John Ferguson" in: *Encyclopaedia Britannica* (9th ed., New York: 1878), vol. 15, pp. 162-163; Alfred C. Haddon with the help of A. Hingston Quiggen, *History of Anthropology* (London: 1910), pp. 132-133; J.R. Fox, "McLennan, John Ferguson" in: David L. Sills (editor), *International Encyclopedia of the Social Sciences* (New York: 1968-1979), vol. 9, pp. 517-519; T.K. Penniman, *A Hundred Years of Anthropology* (New York: 1970), pp. 119-121; Murray J. Leaf, *Man, Mind and Science: a History of Anthropology* (New York: 1979), pp. 1, 112-115, 124; E.E. Evans-Pritchard, "McLennan (1827-1881)" in: *A History of Anthropological Thought*

(London: 1981), pp. 61-68; "McLennan, John Ferguson" in: *The New Encyclopaedia Britannica* (Chicago: 1986), vol. 7, p. 642.

Michele Calhoun

Mead, Margaret. Anthropologist. Born in Philadelphia (Pennsylvania) 16 December 1901, died in New York (New York) 15 November 1978. Mead was preeminently a cultural anthropologist who continually drew on and contributed to others of the human disciplines in her research in the field and at home. She was also one of the most skilled communicators of her generation in speech as in writing.

Based throughout her professional life at the American Museum of Natural History in New York City, she had unusual freedom to choose the direction of her research activities, to lecture, to teach and to participate actively in scientific work outside the museum. In doing so, she carried her mode of thinking, her skills as an observer and interpreter, and the questions raised through her field research into analyses in complex settings and then, implicitly, into new fieldwork.

She was eloquent, superbly organized and convincing as a speaker on ceremonial occasions; as a lecturer speaking to an education audience; as a member of a working committee or of a small, scientific study group; as an informant or an advocate; and above all as a teacher in a classroom or in a one-on-one relationship with a student. She enjoyed her students and her audiences—readers as well as listeners and fellow discussants. They held her attention as she held theirs.

Mead became an anthropologist at an important turning point in American anthropology. FRANZ BOAS's formulation of the fourfold program had taken hold and, under his guidance, students went to the field to explore within the framework of ethnography specific cultural and personality problems viewed through the life in ongoing small societies. Mead's career choice had been psychology until, studying under Boas, she chose cultural anthropology as the science that offered the variety and complexity that attracted her to the study of human behavior.

In all, Mead carried out field research in eight societies—five at varying length and depth, depending on the availability of field funds: (Samoa (1925-1926), alone; Manus (1928-1929) and Arapesh (1931-1932), together with Reo Fortune; and Bali (1936-1938), Iatmul (1938) and Bali again, briefly (1939), together with GREGORY BATESON). Mead also worked briefly among the Omaha (a summer project, 1930) and in Mundugumor and Tchambuli (today, Chambri) (1932-1933), all with Reo Fortune.

Her most complex and innovative work was the research carried out in Bali, a literate society, where Mead and Bateson worked in three contrasting settings using photography—still and cine—to capture style and motion. Periodically, they joined with Jane Belo and the musicologist, Colin McPhee, and also with Katherine Mershon, formerly a dancer, in a collaboration that provided a unique interweaving of talent and viewpoint.

However, her work at Peri Village in Manus was the most enduring and, perhaps, the most fruitful, field research. In 1953, after twenty-four years, Mead returned to Manus—this time with a student fieldworker and his wife, Lenore, who for the most part worked another nearby village—to study the radical changes the Manus themselves had brought about in response to wartime experiences in the Admiralty Island area. Thereafter,

Mead made six field trips to Peri Village (twice with Barbara Roll, who has carried on the research) to continue to record the lives of three generations of a people "who have skipped over thousands of years of history in just the last twenty-five years" (Mead, 1956, p. 8).

As Nancy McDowell pointed out: "One of Mead's major interests [was] in pattern ... . Her keen sense and use of personality and individual differences ... heighten our awareness of the pattern, its complexity, and the relationship between it and deviation ... . The continual interplay between pattern and individual relates to another striking characteristic of Mead's ethnography: the extent to which her concern is predominantly with process and system. Her descriptions are never static, always dynamic ... [S]he sees a fluid, dynamic, processual system, something we are only now beginning to appreciate fully" (p. 283).

Nevertheless, by 1939, Mead had moved from that first period of her life work that was essentially related to active field research with its possibilities for insight as well into the life of our own time and place.

Thereafter, her life fell into three quite distinct, yet wholly integrated, periods. First, the war and early post-war years, during which, as Executive Secretary of the Committee on Food Habits of the National Research Council in Washington (where, indeed, a great number of anthropologists were at work), she brought together a team, each member of which, having specialized skills and research abilities, contributed to a new form of applied anthropology related to the country's current needs. At the same time, Mead herself cooperated in other governmental projects and traveled up and down the nation and, once, to England to help work out the misinterpreted relations of American GIs and English girls.

During the second period, 1946-1952, the project, Research in Contemporary Cultures, initiated by RUTH BENEDICT, became Mead's major responsibility, as active participant and as director of research by some 120 people on eight cultures (China, Czechoslovakia, the East European Jewish *shtetl*, France, Poland, pre-Soviet Great Russia, Syria and, for one year, Germany) with the research aim of analyzing cultural regularities in the characters of individuals, members of societies inaccessible to direct observation.

In the same period, Mead was increasingly in demand as a speaker and began her program of graduate school teaching. But most challenging was her membership in a series of small study groups, each made up members of several disciplines, that met annually for intense discussion of a set of related problems, for example, one known as Problems of Consciousness, another as Discussions on Child Development.

The last period, a long one, can be seen as the high point in her career, the culmination of her complex activities. She held high office in the organizations of her peers. Honors accumulated and, belatedly, she was admitted to the fold of the National Academy of Sciences. After more than forty years she was at last able to bring together a team to produce her own hall in the museum, the Hall of the Pacific. Requests for articles, learned and popular, were numerous, and for seventeen years she wrote a monthly column for a popular magazine. After almost a lifetime of political inactivity, she consented to testify on a great variety of topics before committees of Congress. In her last years, in addition to her many students, she preferred, as a speaker, to address audiences of students and other young people and she did so frequently, challenging them to face a new and very difficult future. In the last year of her life, she wrote once again—with some hope—on the subject of culture and commitment (*Culture and Commitment*).

MAJOR WORKS: *Coming of Age in Samoa* (New York: 1928); *Growing Up in New Guinea: a Comparative Study in Primitive Education* (New York: 1930); *Sex and Temperament in Three Primitive Societies* (New York: 1935); *And Keep Your Powder Dry: an Anthropologist Looks at America* (New York: 1942; rev. ed., New York: 1965); *Male and Female* (New York: 1949); *New Lives for Old: Cultural Transformations, Manus, 1928-1953* (New York: 1956); *An Anthropologist at Work: the Writings of Ruth Benedict* (Boston: 1959); *Ruth Benedict* (New York: 1974); *Culture and Commitment: The New Relationships between the Generations in the 1970s* (revised and updated ed., New York: 1978); (with Rhoda Métraux) *Aspects of the Present* (New York: 1980).

SOURCES: Joan Gordan (editor), *Margaret Mead: the Complete Bibliography* (The Hague: 1976); Margaret Mead, *Blackberry Winter: My Earlier Years* (New York: 1972); Margaret Mead, *Letters from the Field, 1925-1975* (New York: 1977); Margaret Mead, *Margaret Mead, Some Personal Views* (edited by Rhoda Métraux) (New York: 1979); "In memoriam, Margaret Mead (1901-1978)," *American Anthropologist*, vol. 82 (1980), pp. 261-373 [which includes the following two works]; Nancy McDowell, "The oceanic ethnography of Margaret Mead," *American Anthropologist*, vol. 82 (1980), pp. 278-302; Rhoda Métraux, "Margaret Mead: a biographical sketch," *American Anthropologist*, vol. 82 (1980), pp. 262-269; Allyn Moss, *Margaret Mead: Shaping a New World* (Chicago: 1963); Robert Cassidy, *Margaret Mead: a Voice for the Century* (New York: 1982); Mary Catherine Bateson, *With a Daughter's Eye: a Memoir of Margaret Mead and Gregory Bateson* (New York: 1984); Jane Howard, *Margaret Mead, a Life* (New York: 1984); Phyllis Grosskurth, *Margaret Mead* (Harmondsworth: 1989)

Rhoda Métraux

Meek, Charles Kingsley. Anthropologist, colonial administrator. Born in Larne (Northern Ireland) 24 June 1885, died in Eastbourne (England) 27 March 1965. Meek was a distinguished pioneer of anthropological studies in Nigeria. He is best known to anthropologists for his service as a social anthropologist in Nigeria.

Meek was educated in Rothesay Academy, Bedford School, Glasgow University. His early training was in anthropology. He had a brilliant record in his undergraduate days and graduated with a B.A. in theology in 1910 at Brasenose College, Oxford.

Meek entered the Colonial Administrative Service and was posted to Nigeria in 1912. His interest in social anthropological studies led to his appointment as the Commissioner of the Decennial Census in Northern Nigeria in 1921. His first scholarly work focused on the social groupings of the Nigerian tribes. This book, *The Northern Tribes of Nigeria*, was a report of the census survey that was regarded as the first systematic attempt at a decennial census. The work's descriptions of the various Nigerian tribal groups, many not known before, made the report a valuable, informative and educational document to the outside world. The book was one of the first detailed scholarly accounts of the diverse peoples of West Africa.

Meek was appointed to one of the two posts of government anthropologist established in Nigeria. Some of his noteworthy achievements include his two publications in one year, namely: *Tribal Studies in Northern Nigeria* and *A Sudanese Kingdom*, which is a study of divine kingship among the Jukun-speaking peoples in Nigeria.

Meek served for eighteen years, rendered invaluable service to the cause of African research and established a high reputation in Northern Nigeria. He was promoted to the rank of resident and transferred from Northern to Southern Nigeria in 1929. As a government anthropologist and a senior administrative officer, Meek assisted in the investigations to prepare proposals for reconstruction after a women's riot at the close of 1929 in the southeastern part of Nigeria. He resigned from the Colonial Service in 1933 due to ill health.

The rest of his life was devoted to research and field study. In recognition of his good record of anthropological research, Meek was granted leave by Oxford University to enable him to work for a D.Sc. degree, which he later obtained. He lectured in the University of London, School of Hygiene and Tropical Medicine, during 1938-1939. He was elected to a senior research fellowship in 1943 and in 1947 was appointed lecturer in anthropology at Oxford University.

After retirement in 1950 his college in Oxford elected him tutor and retained his membership on the governing body of the college. He left Oxford in 1957. As an outstanding academic Africanist, he was invited to contribute the first article to the first issue of the *Journal of African History* (1960).

His wealth of experience in Nigeria was put at the disposal of other colleagues through his various lectures and publications on and about Nigeria. His academic contributions to research studies after retirement were recognized by various institutes and organizations. The Royal Anthropological Society awarded him the Society's Welcome Gold Medal in 1936.

Meek was a fellow of the Royal Anthropological Institute and the Royal Geographical Society and was also a member of Royal Societies Club, Union Society, Oxford.

MAJOR WORKS: *The Northern Tribes of Nigeria: an Ethnographical Account of the Northern Provinces of Nigeria together with a report on the 1921 Decennial Census* (London: 1925); *A Sudanese Kingdom: an Ethnographical Study of the Jukun-Speaking Peoples of Nigeria* (London: 1931); *Tribal Studies in Northern Nigeria* [2 vols.] (London: 1931); *Nigeria: Report on Social and Political Organisation in the Owerri Division* (Lagos: 1934); *Law and Authority in a Nigerian Tribe: a Study in Indirect Rule* (New York: 1937); (with W.M. Macmillan and E.R.J. Hussey) *Europe and West Africa* (London: 1940); *Colonial Law: a Bibliography with Special Reference to Native African Systems of Law and Land Tenure* (London: 1948): *Land Law and Customs in the Colonies* (London: 1946) [revised ed. published as: *Land Tenure and Land Administration in Nigeria and the Cameroons* (London: 1957)]; "The Niger and the classics: the history of a name," *Journal of African History*, vol. 1 (1960). pp 1-17.

SOURCES: *The Author's and Writer's Who's Who and Reference Guide: First Post-War Edition* (London: 1948-1949); C.K. Meek, *Law and Authority in Nigerian Tribe: a Study in Indirect Rule* (New York: 1937); Sir Hugh Clifford, "Preface" to: C.K. Meek, *The Northern Tribes of Nigeria* (London: 1925), pp. v-vi; S.M. Jacobs, *Census of Nigeria, 1931* (London: 1933), vol. 1, p. 11; "Meek, Charles Kingsley" in: T. Williams and C.S. Nicholls (editors), *The Dictionary of National Biography, 1961-1970* (Oxford: 1981), pp. 747-748; [Obituary], *The Sunday Times* [London] (14 April 1965), p. 14; "Dr. Meek and Nigeria, from a correspondent," *West Africa*, no. 2499 (24 April 1965), p. 452; [Obituary], *The Brazen Nose* [Brasenose College magazine, Oxford] (1965); *Colonial Office List* (1932); "Meek, Charles Kingsley, M.A. (Oxon), F.R.A.I." in: *Who Was Who in Literature, 1906-1934* (Detroit: 1979), p. 765.

Margaret O. Oyesola

Meinhof, Carl (Carl Friedrich Michael Meinhof). Linguist, theologian. Born in Barzwitz bei Rügenwalde (Germany) 23 July 1857, died in Greifswald (Germany) 10 February 1944. Meinhof studied theology, Hebrew and German at the Universities of

Halle, Erlangen and Greifswald. In connection with these studies he worked as a lecturer at gymnasia and after 1886 as a clergyman as well. His groundbreaking works in comparative Bantu philology originated during this period of time. During 1902-1903 Meinhof traveled to East Africa. After his return to Germany, he served as an instructor at the Seminar for Oriental Languages in Berlin and received the title of professor there in 1905. From 1909 on Meinhof presided over the Seminar for Colonial Languages at the Colonial Institute in Hamburg where he founded, in 1910, the Laboratory of Phonetics and the *Zeitschrift für Eingeborenen-Sprachen*, later known as *Afrika und Übersee*. His second trip to Africa, made in 1914 in company with AUGUST KLINGENHEBEN, took him to the province of Kordofan in the Sudan. In 1919 Meinhof became *Ordentlicher Professor* for African languages at the newly founded University of Hamburg. He made a lecture tour to South Africa in 1927, returning via East Africa in 1928. He was awarded the rank of professor emeritus in 1930. In addition, Meinhof received a doctorate in law (University of Edinburgh, 1910), a doctorate in theology (University of Greifswald, 1911) and a doctorate in philosophy *honoris causa* (University of Leipzig, 1927).

Meinhof may be considered one of the founders of modern African linguistic science, especially in the area of comparative Bantu philology. Under the influence of the "young grammarians," particularly the comparative grammar of the Indo-Germanic languages of AUGUST SCHLEICHER, Meinhof conceived the idea of "Ur-Bantu," which he reconstructed, first inductively, through a minute phonetic and semantic analysis of the modern Bantu languages available to him, then deductively, using further comparative philological investigations as a third level of control. As a result of his East African journey, he wrote several detailed linguistic descriptions that appeared between 1904 and 1907 in the *Mitteilungen des Seminars des Orientalische Sprachen*. In addition, Meinhof defined and made more precise many of the phonetic laws of the Bantu languages. With regard to the classification of Bantu languages, Meinhof first took the position that a comprehensive classification of this language family was premature on the basis of the then-contemporary state of research. In 1912 Meinhof's controversial work *Die Sprachen der Hamiten* appeared. In it he attempted "to establish the characteristic peculiarities of the Hamitic languages" and, further, advocated the view that African languages constituted the preliminary stages of the Hamitic languages. In this scheme a special role devolved upon Fulfulde as a "proto-Hamitic" language. In his final works on this theme (*Die Entstehung der flektierenden Sprachen* and *Die Entstehung der Bantusprachen*) Meinhof partially retracted this thesis. In addition to all these activities, he also concerned himself with the analysis of the Kordofanian and Khoisan language families. The extremely broad framework of his African work was also marked in shorter articles, such as those on tonal pitch in Ewe, on the language of Meroë, or on Libyan inscriptions. He was also interested in the problems of language teaching and wrote textbooks on Nama, Herero, Swahili and Douala. His lectures in Hamburg between 1910 and 1914 on contemporary African linguistic research, African poetry, the religions of Africa and the use of law in Africa—as well as his anthologies of African folk-tales—illustrate his efforts to make not only languages but also other aspects of African cultures comprehensible to a broader public. His commitment to this mission resulted in a great number of articles and lectures. Meinhof's methods and his teaching style, as well as his strong personality, imprinted themselves decisively on the development of African philological studies in Germany.

MAJOR WORKS: *Grundriß einer Lautlehre der Bantusprachen nebst einer Anleitung zur Aufnahme von Bantusprachen* (Leipzig and Berlin: 1899; 2nd ed., Berlin: 1910); *Grundzüge einer vergleichen Grammatik der Bantusprachen* (Berlin: 1906 (= *Abhandlungen für die Kunde des Morgenlandes*, vol. 11, no. 2); 2nd ed., Hamburg: 1948); *Lehrbuch der Nama-Sprache* (Berlin: 1909); *Die Sprache der Herero in Deutsch-Sudwestafrika* (Berlin: 1909; 2nd ed., Berlin: 1937); *Die moderne Sprachforschung in Afrika* (Berlin: 1910) [Hamburg lectures]; *Die Dichtung der Afrikaner* (Berlin: 1911); *Die Sprachen der Hamiten* (Hamburg: 1912); *Die Sprache der Duala in Kamerun* (Berlin: 1912); *Afrikanische Religionen* (Berlin: 1912); *Afrikanische Rechtsgebräuche* (Berlin: 1914); *Der Koranadialekt des Hottentottischen* (Berlin: 1930); *Die libyschen Inschriften* (Leipzig: 1931); *Die Entstehung der flektierenden Sprachen* (Berlin: 1936); (with N.J. van Warmelo) *Introduction to the Phonology of the Bantu Languages* (Berlin: 1932).

SOURCES: Gudrun Miehe, "Meinhof, Carl Friedrich Michael" in: H. Jungraithmayr. and W.J.G. Möhlig (editors), *Lexikon der Afrikanistik* (Berlin: 1983), pp. 161-162; A. Klingenheben, "Überblick über das literarische Schaffen Meinhofs" in: *Brevier Meinhof: Festgabe zum 80. Geb. Meinhofs* (Berlin: 1937), pp. 15-27; J. Lukas, "Carl Meinhof," *Zeitschrift für Eingeborenen-Sprachen*, vol. 34 (1943-1944), pp. 81-93; C. Doke [et al.], "In memory of Carl Meinhof," *African Studies*, vol. 5 (1946), pp. 73-81; D. Westermann, "Carl Meinhof zum Gedächtnis," *Zeitschrift für Phonetik*, vol. 1 (1947), pp. 68-71.

G. Miehe and K. Winkelmann
[Translation from German: Robert B. Marks Ridinger]

Mejía Xesspe, M. Toribio. Archaeologist, writer. Born in Toro, Arequipa (Peru) 16 April 1896, died in Lima (Peru) 2 November 1983. Mejía is most remembered for his complementary association with Peruvian archaeologist JULIO C. TELLO. During Tello's lifetime Mejía was his principal field assistant. Following Tello's death, Mejía compiled and edited a portion of Tello's voluminous field notes into monographs published through the Universidad Nacional Mayor de San Marcos (San Marcos University).

In 1924 Mejía enrolled in Tello's seminar in general anthropology at San Marcos. Although he had become a police officer after moving to Lima in 1920, Mejía changed careers in 1925 when he assumed the first of many positions in archaeological museums as an assistant at the Museo de la Universidad (University Museum). The following year, he became an assistant at the Museo de Arqueología Peruana (Museum of Peruvian Archaeology), which was reorganized as the Museo Nacional del Perú (National Museum of Peru) in 1931. He was promoted to conservator, then inspector general and subsequently to assistant director, a post he held until his retirement in 1966. He held the chair for Inka (Inca) archaeology at Universidad Nacional Mayor de San Marco from 1946 to 1953, after which he began publishing his edited versions of Tello's field and museum notes. His personal writings were mostly newspaper articles about archaeological sites and indigenous cultures of Peru and short articles recalling his fieldwork with Tello, which were included in the edited volumes.

He worked with Tello in excavations and reconnaissance at Paracas, Chavín and other Marañón Valley sites, Sechín and other Casma Valley sites, Nazca and Pachacamac. Mejía is credited with an interpretation of the famous Nazca (Nasca) lines as ceremonial roads bound up with a hydrological/agricultural cult. He later worked at Ancón and in the Palpa Valley on his own and accompanied the First University of Tōkyō Mission to the Andes in its explorations of the Tumbes area in 1957.

Mejía could speak Quechua and was proud of his indigenous ancestry, a pride he shared with Tello. It was Mejía's editorship and publication of his mentor Tello's documents (listed below) that has made them widely available to recent generations of students of Peruvianist archaeology.

> MAJOR WORKS: "Acueductos y caminos antiguos de la Hoya del Rio Grande de Nasca," *Actas y Memorias del XXVII Congreso International de Americanistas* (Lima: 1942), vol. 1, pp. 559-569; "Apuntes biográficos sobre el Dr. Julio C. Tello," *Revista del Museo Nacional de Antropología y Arqueología*, vol. 2 (1948), pp. 35-49; "Historia de la expedición arqueológica al Marañón de 1937" in: Julio C. Tello, *Arqueología del Valle de Casma* (Lima: 1956), pp. 319-337; "Prefacio" to: Julio C. Tello, *Paracas* (Lima: 1959), pp. v-vi; (Julio C. Tello, with revision by Toribio Mejía Xesspe) *Chavín, cultura matriz de la civilización andina* (Lima: 1960); "Julio C. Tello" in: *Biblioteca Hombres del Peru*, 3rd serie, vol. 28 (1964), pp. 51-111; (Julio C. Tello, with selection and prologue by Toribio Mejía Xesspe) *Paginas escogidas* (Lima: 1967); (with Julio C. Tello) *Historia de los museos nacionales del Peru, 1822-1946* (Lima: 1967) (= *Arqueológicas* , vol. 10); (with Julio C. Tello) *Paracas, II parte: cavernas y necropolis* (Lima: 1979); "Cultura Pukina" in: Roswith Hartmann and Udo Overem (editors), *Festschrift für Hermann Trimborn* (St. Augustin, Germany: 1979) (= *Amerikanistische Studien = Estudios Americanistas*, vol. 2), pp. 40-47.

> SOURCES: Rogger Ravines, "Toribio Mejía Xesspe (1896-1983)," *Revista del Museo Nacional*, vol. 47 (1984), pp. 333-340; "Mejía Xesspe, Toribio" in: *Enciclopedia ilustrada del Perú* (Lima: 1987), pp. 1311-1312.

Kathryn M. Cleland

Mellink, Machteld J. Prehistorian, educator. Born in Amsterdam (Netherlands) 26 October 1917. A scholar of the ancient Near East, Mellink has worked primarily in Asia Minor as an astute and systematic investigator and chronicler of the region's past.

Mellink was educated in the Netherlands at the University of Amsterdam and Utrecht University where she received her Ph.D. in 1943. After the war, she joined the excavations at Tarsus in southeastern Turkey directed by Hetty Goldman where she worked until 1949. That same year Mellink became a member of the faculty of Bryn Mawr College (Pennsylvania). She was Chairperson of the Department of Classical and Near Eastern Archaeology from 1955 to 1983 and retired from teaching in 1988. She was also a Research Associate (1955-1982) at the University Museum of Archaeology and Anthropology, University of Pennsylvania, where she received an honorary L.L.D. in 1987. As a teacher and mentor, she is held in high esteem by several generations of American and Turkish students, a number of whom are prominent in the field today.

Mellink's work focuses on ancient Anatolia. She has contributed substantially both to documenting the region's own independent cultural development and to tracing its relations with its neighbors in the Aegean and the Near East as a whole. She participated in the University Museum's excavations at Gordion in central Turkey from their beginning in 1950 until 1974 and was Chair of the Publications Committee from 1976 to 1982. The site yielded important information about the previously little-known Phrygians and the recovery in 1957 of the rich royal tomb believed to be that of King Midas.

In 1963 Mellink began her own work for Bryn Mawr at Karataş-Semayük in southwestern Turkey. Her imaginative and systematic efforts there have contributed substantially toward our understanding of Early Bronze Age life in southwestern Anatolia. By pursuing both archaeological and physical-anthropological investigations, she has addressed many important questions concerning the population, its local traditions and its relations with other areas of Anatolia and abroad. The cemetery remains, among the largest in western Anatolia, were skillfully studied by J. LAWRENCE ANGEL and yielded valuable information on health, longevity and population change. In 1969 Mellink expanded her work to include the archaic and Greco-Persian painted tombs nearby, confirming a long-standing tradition of wall-painting in Anatolia and eastern Greece.

In addition to her other responsibilities, Mellink is a mainstay in a number of professional societies. She was President of the Archaeological Institute of America from 1981 to 1984 and of the American Research Institute in Turkey from 1988. Within the international world of prehistorians, she is a skilled and highly respected member.

MAJOR WORKS: *Hyakinthos* (Utrecht: 1943); "Archaeology in Asia Minor," *American Journal of Archaeology* (1955-present); *A Hittite Cemetery at Gordion* (Philadelphia: 1956); (editor and contributor), *Dark Ages and Nomads c. 1000 B.C.: Studies in Iranian and Anatolian Archaeology* (İstanbul: 1964); (with J. Filip) *Frühe Stufen der Kunst* (Berlin: 1974); (contributor) R.S. Young, *Gordion Excavations*. I. *Three Great Early Tumuli* (Philadelphia: 1981); (editor) *Troy and the Trojan War* (Bryn Mawr, Pennsylvania: 1986).

SOURCES: "Excavations at Karataş-Semayük," *American Journal of Archaeology* (1964-1977, 1980); *Who's Who in America* (1984-85 and 1989-90); Jeanny Vorys Canby [et al.] (editors), *Ancient Anatolia: Aspects of Change and Cultural Development: Essays in Honor of Machteld J. Mellink* (Madison: 1986); personal communication from Machteld J. Mellink.

Margaret R. Dittemore

Merriam, C. Hart. Naturalist, government administrator. Born in New York (New York) 5 December 1855, died in Berkeley (California) 19 March 1942. Merriam studied at Yale University and took an M.D. degree at the College of Physicians and Surgeons in New York. As a young man he traveled widely, serving as a naturalist with the U.S. Geological Survey of the Territories (Hayden Survey) in 1872 and the U.S. Fish Commission in 1875. In private medical practice from 1879 to 1885, he nevertheless found time to continue travel and scientific study. In 1885 he was appointed head of the U.S. Department of Agriculture's Division of Ornithology and Mammalogy, which became the U.S. Biological Survey in 1896. In 1910 Merriam retired from government service to pursue ethnological and zoological studies in the Far West using a fund set up for him by Mrs. E.H. Harriman. His main anthropological work was in recording linguistic and ethnographic data in California and neighboring states and in forming a very large collection of American Indian baskets. Much of his material was published posthumously.

MAJOR WORKS: *The Dawn of the World: Myths and Weird Tales Told by the Mewan Indians of California* (Cleveland: 1910); *An-nik-a-del: the History of the Universe as Told by the Modeś-se Indians of California* (Boston: 1928); *Studies of California Indians* (edited by the staff of the University of California Department of Anthropology) (Berkeley: 1955); *Ethnographic Notes on California Indian Tribes* (edited by Robert F. Heizer) (Berkeley: 1966) (= *Report of the University of California Archaeological Survey*, no. 68, part 3); *Chumash Place Names Lists* (Berkeley: 1975); *Indian Names for Plants and Animals Among Californian and Other Western North American Tribes* (Socorro, New Mexico: 1979).

SOURCES: Charles L. Camp, "C. Hart Merriam, 1855-1942," *California Historical Society Quarterly*, vol. 21 (1942), pp. 284-286; A.K. Fisher, "Obituaries: Clinton Hart Merriam," *Journal of the Washington Academy of Sciences*, vol. 32 (1942), pp. 318-320; Robert F. Heizer, "C. Hart Merriam" in: Wilcomb Washburn (editor), *History of Indian-White Relations* (Washington: 1988) (= William C. Sturtevant (general editor), *Handbook of North American Indians*, vol. 4), pp. 667-668; A.L. Kroeber, "C. Hart Merriam as anthropologist" in: *Studies of California Indians* (Berkeley: 1955), pp. vii-xiv; Wilfred H. Osgood, "Biographical memoir of Clinton Hart Merriam, 1855-1942,"

Biographical Memoirs of the Washington Academy of Sciences, vol. 24 (1947), pp. 1-26; Kier B. Sterling, *Last of the Naturalists: the Career of C. Hart Merriam* (New York: 1977).

James R. Glenn

Métraux, Alfred. Field ethnologist, linguist, applied anthropologist. Born in Lausanne (Switzerland) 5 November 1905, died in Paris (France) 12 April 1963. Métraux was by choice a field ethnologist who combined his fieldwork with intensive scholarly research. He was a gifted and trained linguist, competent in five European languages, who also read Greek for pleasure throughout his life. His linguistic training, necessary for fieldwork, was equally essential to his use of diverse sources, particularly complex early archival data.

During his childhood, Métraux lived in Mendoza (western Argentina), where he became aware of Indian peoples about whom very little was known and determined even then to study their lives. After he returned to Europe, he entered the Classical Gymnasium of Lausanne and, in Paris, studied at the École Nationale des Chartres, the École Nationale des Langues Orientales (*Diplôme,* 1925), the École Pratique des Hautes Études (*Diplôme,* 1927) and the Sorbonne (*Docteur ès lettres,* 1928). He also studied with ERLAND NORDENSKIÖLD in Göteborg and, still in his student years, began a scholarly correspondence with JOHN MONTGOMERY COOPER—the first of many in his lifetime with scholars the world over.

His professional life was cosmopolitan. He founded and for six years (1928-1934) directed the Institute of Ethnology, University of Tucumán, and began short, difficult field studies, principally with the Chiriguano Indians, but also with other groups. In 1934 he returned to Paris, his chosen intellectual home. There he joined the Franco-Belgian expedition to Easter Island as ethnographer and linguist, together with Henri Lavachéry, who was primarily the archaeologist. They worked for six months (July 1934-January 1935) on Easter Island and on the return voyage visited Pitcairn, Tahiti, the Tuamotus, the Marquesas and the Hawaiian Islands. In Paris he helped mount the great Easter Island exhibition at the Musée d'Ethnographie (Paris). During 1936-1938, as a Fellow of the Bernice P. Bishop Museum in Honolulu, he analyzed the data—drawing on his own research and also on many other sources—for his volume on Easter Island.

During 1938-1939 and 1940-1941, he was visiting professor at Yale University and also worked with LEONARD BLOOMFIELD on an analysis of Quechua. In the year between (1939-1940), he carried out field studies in Argentina and Bolivia as a Guggenheim Fellow. Then, in the summer of 1941, he began new field research in Haiti.

Thereafter (1941-1945) he was on the staff of the Bureau of American Ethnology, Smithsonian Institution, as co-editor, with JULIAN H. STEWARD, and author of twenty articles in the *Handbook of South American Indians.* Then, early in 1945, he joined a U.S. Bombing Survey international team sent abroad to study the first responses of Germans to defeat.

In 1946, after travel in South America (Brazil, Argentina, Chile and Peru), Métraux joined the United Nations in the Department of Social Affairs, directed by Alva Myrdal. However, in 1947, he was assigned to UNESCO so that he could participate in the

Hylean-Amazon project and also, in 1948, to undertake for three years the direction of the UNESCO's fundamental education pilot study in Marbial, Haiti.

In 1950, permanently assigned to UNESCO, Métraux functioned both as an administrator in Paris and as an active consultant in the field as, for example, when he carried out, together with International Labor Office personnel, a study of the internal migrations of Aymara and Quechua Indians in Peru and Bolivia.

In 1962 Métraux retired from UNESCO. He planned a last field study with student collaborators in a remote region of Argentina and expected thereafter to teach in Paris together with lifelong friends and younger colleagues.

Métraux described himself as a field ethnologist. His work was neglected for some years. Now it is recognized as an invaluable base on which to build new knowledge and new theory.

MAJOR WORKS: *La religion des Tupinamba et ses rapports avec des autres tribus Tupi-Guarani* (Paris: 1928); "Études sur la civilisation des Indiens Chiriguano," *Revista del Instituto de Etnología de la Universidad Nacional de Tucumán*, vol. 1 (1930), pp. 295-480; *Myths and Tales of the Matako Indians* (Göteborg: 1939) (= *Etnologiska Studier*, vol. 9); *Ethnology of Easter Island* (Honolulu: 1940); *The Native Tribes of Eastern Bolivia and Western Mato Grosso* (Washington: 1942) (= *Bureau of American Ethnology, Bulletin*, no. 134); *Myths of the Toba and Pilaga Indians of the Gran Chaco* (Philadelphia: 1946); *Le vaudou haïtien* (Paris: 1958) [tr.: *Voodoo in Haiti* (London and New York: 1959)].

SOURCES: Charles Wagley, "Alfred Métraux, 1902-1963," *American Anthropologist*, vol. 66 (1964), pp. 603-613; Claude Lévi-Strauss [et al.], "Hommage à Alfred Métraux," *L'Homme*, vol. 4 (1964), pp. 5-19; Claude Tardits, "Bibliographie d'Alfred Métraux," *L'Homme*, vol. 4 (1964), pp. 49-62.

Rhoda Métraux

Miklukho-Maklaĭ, N.N. (Nikolaĭ Nikolaevich). Ethnographer, anthropologist, traveler. Born in St. Petersburg (Russia) 17 July 1846, died in St. Petersburg (Russia) 14 April 1888. Miklukho-Maklaĭ lived alone among the Papuas of New Guinea from September 1871 to December 1872 and came to learn their language and enjoy their trust. He gathered and summarized information about their customs and culture and wrote the first major ethnography of this people. His work also contributed to the development of ethnographic fieldwork.

In addition, Miklukho-Maklaĭ conducted ethnographic and anthropological research in other areas of Oceania and Southeast Asia.

MAJOR WORKS: *Sobranie sochineniĭ* [5 vols., 6 books] (Moscow and Leningrad: 1950-1954); *Chelovek s luny: dnevniki, stat'i, pis'ma N.N. Miklukho-Maklaĭa* (Moscow: 1982); *Travels to New Guinea: Diaries, Letters, Documents* (compiled, with a foreward and commentary by D. Tumarkin) (Moscow: 1982).

SOURCES: D.N. Anuchin, "N.N. Miklukho-Maklaĭ: ego zhizn', puteshestviĭa i sud'ba ego trudov" in: *Zemlevedenie*, no. 3-4 (1923), pp. 3-80; ĬA.ĬA. Roginskiĭ and S.A. Tokarev, "N.N. Miklukho-Maklaĭ kak ĕtnograf i antropolog" in: N.N. Miklukho-Maklaĭ, *Sobranie sochineniĭ*, vol. 2 (Moscow and Leningrad: 1950), pp. 683-738; N.A. Butinov, *N.N. Miklukho-Maklaĭ: velikiĭ russkiĭ uchenyĭ-gumanist* (Leningrad: 1971); N.A. Butinov, *Put' k Beregu Maklaĭa* (Khabarovsk: 1975); B.N. Putilov, *N.N. Miklukho-Maklaĭ: straniĭsy biografii* (Moscow: 1981); B.N. Putilov, *N.N.*

Miklukho-Maklaï: puteshestvennik, uchenyï, gumanist (Moscow: 1985); E.S. Thomassen, *A Biographical Sketch of Nicholas de Miklouho-Maclay* (Brisbane: 1882).

A.M. Reshetov
[Translation from Russian: Thomas L. Mann]

Modigliani, Elio. Naturalist, ethnographer, traveler. Born in Florence (Italy) 13 June 1860, died in Florence (Italy) 6 August 1932. Modigliani came from a rich and aristocratic family. After taking a degree in law from the University of Pisa in 1883, he dedicated himself entirely to the natural sciences and in particular to the study of man, in order to understand the peoples both of Italy and of distant countries.

He prepared seriously for his journeys of exploration under some of the leading scholars of the time, GIACOMO DORIA, Odoardo Beccari, PAOLO MANTEGAZZA and ENRICO HILLYER GIGLIOLI.

Modigliani's three journeys (financed by his personal fortune) were carried out in a very short space of time (between 1886 and 1893) and always in the same general regions: Sumatra (where he explored the regions inhabited by the Batak) and several islands in the Malay Archipelago (Nias, Engano and the tiny island of Sipura in the Mentawai group). On his first two expeditions Modigliani remained for long periods of time among the natives and utilized his knowledge of botany, zoology, ethnography and anthropology to amass extensive collections that were donated to the Museo Civico di Storia Naturale (Civic Museum of Natural History) in Genoa (directed by Doria) and the Museo Nazionale di Antropologia (National Museum of Anthropology) in Florence (headed by Mantegazza) and that have continued to be studied, especially in recent years, by both Italian and foreign scientists.

His closely made ethno-anthropological observations were gathered together in his 1890 volume on Nias (*Un viaggio a Nias*) and in several works of lesser stature.

Modigliani's third voyage (to the Mentawai Islands) was concluded in an unexpected and dramatic manner. Modigliani fell ill and was forced to return to Italy after eight months' stay at Sipura. There, he received numerous honors. He was made an honorary associate of the Società Geografica Italiana (Italian Geographical Society), received an order of knighthood (the rank of Commander of Orange Nassau) from the government of the Netherlands and appointed president of the Società Italiana di Antropologia ed Etnologia (Italian Society for Anthropology and Ethnology) for the year 1911-1912. The remainder of his long life was dedicated to the classification and ordering of the materials assembled in the course of his expeditions.

Modigliani was among the first ethnographic travelers of the 19th century to use photographic representation scientifically and to use "relief" techniques in physical anthropology such as *gesso* masks "from life."

He also stressed precise and exhaustive descriptions of populations with special attention to their physical qualities and those elements of material culture (such as tools, clothing, dwellings and weapons) that could aid in determining their place in a general system of classification for the human races that would conform with the ideas of evolutionism and scientific positivism.

MAJOR WORKS: *Un viaggio a Nias* (Milan: 1890); *Fra i Batacchi indipendenti: viaggio del dott. Elio Modigliani, pubblicato per cura della Società Geografica Italiana in occasione del I Congresso Geografico Italiano* (Rome: 1892*); L'Isola delle Donne: viaggio ad Engano* (Milan: 1894); "Appunti etnologici su Sipora (Isole Mentawei)," *Archivio per l'Antropologia e la Etnologia*, vol. 61 (1931), pp. 29-75.

SOURCES: Enrico Hillyer Giglioli, "Modigliani's exploration of Nias," *Nature*, vol. 41 (1890), pp. 587-591; Enrico Hillyer Giglioli, "Dr. Modigliani's recent explorations in Central Sumatra and Engano," *Nature*, vol. 46 (1892), pp. 565-585; Enrico Hillyer Giglioli, "Notes on the ethnographical collections formed by Dr. Modigliani in Sumatra and Engano," *Internationales Archiv für Ethnographie*, vol. 6 (1893), pp. 4-25; vol. 7, pp. 109-118; Sandra A. Niessen, "Modigliani's batak textiles: evaluation of a collection," *Archivio per l'Antropologia e la Etnologia*, vol. 118 (1988), pp. 57-91; Sandra Puccini, "Elio Modigliani: esplorare, osservare, raccogliere nell'esperienza di un etnografo dell'Ottocento," *La Ricerca Folklorica*, no. 18 (ottobre 1988), pp. 25-40; Nello Puccioni, "Necrologio di E. Modigliani," *Archivio per l'Antropologia e la Etnologia*, vol. 62 (1932), pp. 5-11; Decio Vinciguerra, "Elio Modigliani: cenni biografici," *Annali del Museo Civico di Storia Naturale di Genova*, vol. 56 (23 January 1933), pp. 1-8.

Sandra Puccini
[Translation from Italian: Robert B. Marks Ridinger]

Montagu, Ashley. Anthropologist, socio-biologist, philosopher, humanist. Born in London (England) 28 June 1905. A genius of prodigious scholarly output, Montagu exerted a profound influence on the social consciousness of his contemporaries. Mainly through his work on "race," "race" relations, child development, aggression and human development, he has shared his research and ideas with a very wide public, while he has remained mostly aloof from the strictly academic environment.

Francis Ashley Montagu attended the Central Foundation School in London and University College before becoming a student at the University of Florence, Italy and Columbia University in the city of New York where he obtained a doctorate in anthropology in 1937 under FRANZ BOAS. He has lived in the United States since 1930. He was Assistant Professor of Anatomy in the Graduate School of Medicine, New York University, from 1931 to 1938 and Associate Professor at Hahnemann College and Hospital in Philadelphia from 1938 to 1949. Between 1949 and 1955 he was Professor and Chair of the Department of Anthropology at Rutgers University.

Montagu's work has focused on some of the overriding interests of humanity: the interaction of genetic and environmental forces in human behavior, the concepts of race, gender, aggression and cooperation, reproductive development and so on. He was responsible for the original draft of the UNESCO *Statement on Race* that appeared in an expanded commentary by Montagu in 1951. This work is credited for having introduced the use of the term "ethnic group" in place of the discredited and fallacious term "race." On the subject of aggression Montagu was among the first scientists to differ with the widely held belief that aggression is the natural drive of human behavior.

MAJOR WORKS: *Man's Most Dangerous Myth: the Fallacy of Race* (New York: 1942); *Statement on Race* (New York: 1951); *Culture and Human Development* (Englewood Cliffs, N.J.: 1975); *The Nature of Human Aggression* (Oxford: 1976); (editor) *Science and Creationism* (Oxford: 1984); *Growing Young* (2nd. ed., Granby, Mass.: 1989).

SOURCES: "Montagu, Ashley" in: Sol Tax (editor), *Fifth International Directory of Anthropologists* (Chicago: 1975), p. 265; Steven Harnad, "Montagu, Ashley" in: David L. Sills (editor), *International Encyclopedia of the Social Sciences* (New York: 1968-1979), vol. 18, pp. 535-

537; "Montagu, (Montague Francis) Ashley," *Current Biography* (1967), pp. 294-297; "Montagu, Prof. Ashley," *Who's Who* (London: 1988), pp. 1242-1243; "Montagu, Ashley," *Who's Who in America* (1988-1989), p. 2188; "Montagu, Ashley" in: *The New Encyclopaedia Britannica* (Chicago: 1986), vol. 8, p. 274; "Philosophy of the branches of knowledge" in: *The New Encyclopaedia Britannica* (Chicago: 1986), vol. 25, esp. p. 687.

Hans E. Panofsky

Mooney, James. Ethnologist. Born in Richmond (Indiana) 10 February 1861, died in Washington (D.C.) 22 December 1921. Mooney was the son of Irish immigrants, and his formal education was limited to the public schools of Richmond, Indiana. As a boy, he developed an interest in American Indians, read widely about them and eventually began to compile a synonymy of tribal names. After working as a teacher and newspaperman, he came to the attention of JOHN WESLEY POWELL, director of the Smithsonian Institution's Bureau of American Ethnology (BAE), who employed him in 1885. At the BAE Mooney acquired such a breadth and depth of knowledge that he was recognized as one of the most outstanding authorities on American Indians.

Mooney was among early fieldworkers who sought long association with the subjects of his research. His work with the Cherokee began in 1887 and continued for the rest of his life. His other chief concern was the Kiowa tribe, who were also studied over many years. He also spent considerable amounts of time studying and collecting among the Arapaho, Cheyenne, Apache, Dakota, Plains Apache, Wichita and Comanche and lesser amounts with the Hopi, Paiute, Shoshoni, Caddo and small groups in northern Mexico and in the Southeast. His publications and fieldwork reveal additional interests in southern mountain people, the Irish, Florida aborigines, and missionary efforts among the Indians.

Mooney's investigations led him to several cross-cultural studies, including most notably investigations of the ghost-dance religion and the use of peyote. His study of the American population at contact, published posthumously, was considered authoritative for several decades. His considerable breadth of knowledge is reflected in the variety of his articles in the *Handbook of American Indians North of Mexico* and in the exhibits he prepared for several international expositions.

While in his early work Mooney revealed the influence of Powell's evolutionary theories, as he developed, his broader ideas focused on geographically based culture regions. Particularly, he felt these were important in forming a strategy to allow a few scientists to deal meaningfully with the great multiplicity of Indian tribes. Mooney's studies themselves tended to be particularistic with a strong historical element. He carried this to a point that his work with a given tribe sometimes came to concentrate on one or a few features, although these were usually phenomena of broad significance for that group.

From deeply and personally felt pro-Irish loyalties, Mooney had an almost instinctive sympathy for oppressed peoples, and this led to great understanding and respect for Indian hopes and aspirations and for their cultures. Although such sympathies caused some problems with government officials and even some Indians, they more significantly provided for great rapport with his subjects and, in some instances, considerable enhancement of his writings as works of literature.

MAJOR WORKS: *Linguistic Families of Indian Tribes North of Mexico* (Washington: 1885); "Sacred formulas of the Cherokees," *Annual Report of the Bureau of American Ethnology*, vol. 7

(1891), pp. 301-397; *The Siouan Tribes of the East* (Washington: 1894) (= *Bureau of American Ethnology Bulletin*, no. 22); "The ghost-dance religion, and the Sioux out-break of 1890," *Annual Report of the Bureau of American Ethnology*, vol. 14 (1896), vol. 2, pp. 641-1110; "Calendar history of the Kiowa Indians," *Annual Report of the Bureau of American Ethnology*, vol. 17 (1900), vol. 1, pp. 129-445; "Myths of the Cherokee," *Annual Report of the Bureau of American Ethnology*, vol. 19 (1900), vol. 1, pp. 1-548; *The Cheyenne Indians* (Washington: 1907) (= *Memoirs of the American Anthropological Association*, vol. 1, pp. 357-442); (contributor) Frederick Webb Hodge (editor), *Handbook of American Indians North of Mexico* (Washington: 1907-1910) (= *Bureau of American Ethnology Bulletin*, no. 30) *The Aboriginal Population of America North of Mexico* (Washington: 1928) (= *Smithsonian Miscellaneous Collections*, vol. 70); *The Swimmer Manuscript, Cherokee Sacred Formulas and Medicinal Prescriptions* (revised and completed by Frans M. Olbrechts) (Washington: 1932) (= *Bureau of American Ethnology Bulletin*, no. 99).

SOURCES: William Mann Colby, *Routes to Rainy Mountain: a Biography of James Mooney, Ethnologist* [unpublished Ph.D. dissertation, University of Wisconsin] (Madison: 1978); "James Mooney" in: Wilcomb Washburn (editor), *History of Indian-White Relations* (Washington: 1988) (= William C. Sturtevant (general editor), *Handbook of North American Indians*, vol. 4), pp. 669-670; L.G. Moses, *Indian Man: a Biography of James Mooney* (Urbana: 1984); Althea Bass, "James Mooney in Oklahoma," *Chronicles of Oklahoma*, vol. 32 (1954), pp. 246-262; John C. Ewers, "Introduction" to reprint of: James Mooney, *The Calendar History of the Kiowa Indians* (Washington: 1979); Walter Hough, "James Mooney" in: Allen Johnson and Dumas Malone, *Dictionary of American Biography*, vol. 13 (1934), pp. 110-111; Mooney manuscripts in the Smithsonian Institution National Anthropological Archives; L.G. Moses, "James Mooney and the peyote controversy," *Chronicles of Oklahoma*, vol. 56 (1978), pp. 127-144; John R. Swanton, "James Mooney," *American Anthropologist*, vol. 24 (1922), pp. 209-214, Anthony F.C. Wallace, "Introduction" to reprint of: James Mooney, *The Ghost Dance Religion* (Chicago and London: 1965); Ira Jacknis, "James Mooney as an ethnographic photographer," *Visual Anthropology*, vol. 3 (1990), pp. 179-212.

James R. Glenn

Moora, Kh.A. (Khaari Al'bertovich) (Estonian form of name: H. Moora). Ethnographer, archaeologist, historian. Born in the Kuremaa district of the Tartussk district (Estonia, Russia) 2 March 1900, died in Tallinn (Estonian S.S.R.) 2 May 1968. Prior to World War II, Moora's scholarly activity was concentrated primarily in archaeology. After 1945 he took an active role in the establishment of the Éstonskiĭ narodnyĭ muzeĭ (Estonian National Museum) and in the development of Estonian Soviet ethnography. After 1947 he played a leadership role in the Archaeology Section of the Institut istorii (Institute of History) of the Academy of Sciences of the Estonian S.S.R. where, in 1952, an ethnographic group was organized that was later reorganized into the Section of Archaeology and Ethnography. After 1957 Moora became an active member of the Academy of Sciences of the Estonian S.S.R.

Moora made a major contribution to the study of the ethnogenesis of the Estonian people and their social and cultural history. Under his leadership and with his participation such fundamental works as *Istoriia Éstonskoĭ SSR*, *Éstonskaia narodnaia odezhda* and the articles on the Estonians for the volume *Narody Evropeĭskoĭ chasti SSSR* were prepared. He also compiled a series of works with his spouse, the ethnographer Khil'da Aleksandrovna Moora.

MAJOR WORKS: "Voprosy étnogeneza narodov Sovetskoĭ Pribaltiki po dannym arkheologii," *Kratkie soobshcheniia Instituta étnografii*, vol. 12 (1950), pp. 29-37; "Vozniknovenie klassovogo obshchestva v Pribaltike (po arkheologicheskim dannym)," *Sovetskaia arkheologiia*, vol. 27 (1953), pp. 105-132; "Nekotorye voprosy étnogeneza éstonskogo naroda v svete arkheologicheskikh dannykh,"

Sovetskai͡a arkheologii͡a, vol. 21 (1954), pp. 95-118; (contributor) *Ėstonskai͡a narodnai͡a odezhda* (Tallinn: 1957; Tallinn: 1961); "O drevneĭ territorii rasselenii͡a baltiĭskikh plemen," *Sovetskai͡a arkheologii͡a*, no. 2 (1958), pp. 9-33; (with Kh.A. Moora), "K voprosu ob istoriko-kul'turnykh podoblastĭakh i raĭonakh Pribaltiki," *Sovetskai͡a ėtnografii͡a*, no. 3 (1960), pp. 21-51; (contributor) V. Maamiagi [et al.] (editors), *Istorii͡a Ėstonskoĭ SSR* [3 vols.] (Tallinn: 1961); (contributor) "Ėstonĭsy" in: V.A. Aleksandrov [et al.] (editors), *Narody evropeĭskoĭ chasti SSSR*, vol. 2 (Moscow: 1964), pp. 209-310; (with Kh.A. Moora), "Iz ėtnicheskoĭ istorii vodi i izhori" in: (co-editor with L. Jaanits) *Iz istorii slavi͡ano-pribaltiĭsko-finskikh otnoshenii = Slaavi-läänemeresoome suhete ajaloost* (Tallinn: 1965), pp. 209-310.

SOURCES: "Kharri Moora," *Sovetskai͡a ėtnografii͡a*, no. 4 (1968), pp. 184-186; "Spisok osnovnykh rabot Kh.A. Moora," *Sovetskai͡a ėtnografii͡a*, no. 4 (1968), pp. 186-189.

A.M. Reshetov
[Translation from Russian: Thomas L. Mann]

Morgan, Lewis Henry. Lawyer, anthropologist. Born near Aurora (New York) 21 November 1818, died in Rochester (New York) 17 December 1881. Morgan was educated at Cayuga Academy in Aurora and Union College, Schenectady, from which he graduated in 1840, after which he read law and was admitted to the bar. He moved to Rochester in 1844 and resided there until his death. As a lawyer for Rochester investors in railroads and iron smelting works in the Upper Peninsula of Michigan, Morgan made a modest fortune, which permitted him in the 1860s to devote himself fully to scholarship.

Morgan was an inveterate organizer of and participant in literary and scientific societies. After graduation from Union he and a group of young men founded the Grand Order of the Iroquois (or New Confederacy of the Iroquois), a secret society which resembled a social fraternity but with a constitution patterned on that of the Iroquois League. This organization gave Morgan a vehicle from which to develop a scholarly interest in the Indians. He came to know Ely S. Parker, a young Seneca (later to become an adjutant general on the staff of Ulysses S. Grant, and subsequently Commissioner of Indian Affairs in Grant's administration), who became his collaborator in Iroquois ethnology. In 1854 Morgan formed The Club of Rochester (often called the Pundit Club), before which many of his ethnological papers were first read. He joined the American Association for the Advancement of Science (AAAS) in 1856, presiding over the newly created anthropology section in 1875 and becoming president of the AAAS in 1879. He was made a member of the National Academy of Sciences in 1875.

Morgan's fieldwork among the Iroquois led to articles on social structure and religion in the *North American Review* and reports on material culture describing objects he had collected for the New York State Museum. These he gathered together in his first book, *League of the ... Iroquois*, in which the structure of the Iroquois league is shown to rest on "the family relationships" through a system of clan-based chiefs. It remains the best overall ethnography of the Iroquois, though Morgan himself thought it showed signs of haste, apparently referring to the integration of the parts, not their substance. He had written it to bring his youthful Indian researches to a conclusion as he turned to the business of raising a family and developing his legal practice. But after joining the AAAS he returned to Indian ethnology, seeking to show that some features of Iroquois life were part of a pattern universal in the Americas and hence proving the unity of the American Indians, a proof that had eluded Americanist philology.

Morgan's subsequent ethnology grew out of his early encounter with two features of Iroquois life that had made a deep impression on him—matrilineal clans and the classificatory character of the kinship terminology. Morgan's fieldwork among the Ojibwa of Michigan showed that, although they did not have matrilineal clans, their kinship terminology had classificatory features as did the Iroquois, suggesting that two peoples whose languages' philologists had not shown to be historically connected could be proved to be related by the comparison of their kinship terminologies. If this "new instrument for ethnology," the comparative study of kinship semantics, could establish Amerindian unity, perhaps it could also provide the proof of their Asian origin, putting to rest the competing theory of their derivation from the lost tribes of Israel. Morgan sought out a missionary to South India, home on furlough, and got an incomplete but accurate account of the Tamil kinship terminology, which showed striking similarities to the semantic patterning of Iroquois. The circular and questionnaire on kinship terms Morgan developed and sent to informants around the world, some with the help of the Smithsonian Institution, contains the first formulation of the conception of the kinship project (including a number of remarkable predictions as to the structure of the remaining Tamil terms to be collected) that eventuated in his masterwork, the massive *Systems of Consanguinity and Affinity*. In this book Morgan went well beyond his original purpose of demonstrating Amerindian unity and Asian origin and created the analytical tools that form the basis of modern kinship studies. As MEYER FORTES noted, Morgan originated the conception of kinship data as forming a system, directed analysis to the comparison of underlying ideas or semantic patterns rather than vocabularies, abstracted "indicative features" of terminologies as the beginning of analysis and focused attention on the connection between classificatory terminology and certain forms of social organization.

In the *Systems*, the dominant form of historicism was a genealogism patterned on comparative philology, that is, an elucidation of "genetic" relations of co-descent between kinship systems similar to one another. At the highest level of integration the kinship systems of the Americas, Asia and Oceania were all seen as examples of the unitary "classificatory" kinship system and hence historically related to one another, and opposed to the "descriptive" system of Europe and the Near East, to which they could not be shown to be related. The revolutionary expansion of ethnological time occasioned by the discovery of tools in association with long extinct animals came about as Morgan was writing his book, and it encouraged him in the direction of evolutionism. He resolved the final puzzle of the relationship of the two systems by historicising it, such that the classificatory system became an earlier evolutionary stage of the descriptive. An evolutionary series of supposed marriage rules, from primitive promiscuity to modern monogamy, inferred from the terminologies, became the "conjectural solution" of the classificatory system first announced in an 1868 article.

From this point on, evolutionism displaced genealogism as the dominant mode of historicism for Morgan. *Ancient Society*, his most far-reaching work of synthesis, is an outstanding example of the evolutionism so characteristic of high Victorian anthropology. Here Morgan purported to show "the lines of human progress from savagery through barbarism to civilization" by tracing the growth of intelligence through inventions and discoveries and through the growth of the ideas of government, the family and property. Especially important in it are his incorporation of kinship data on Australia (from LORIMER

FISON) into the general treatment of kinship and the bringing of the Iroquois matrilineal clan to bear on the study of the Greek and Roman *gens*. Marx studied the book closely for the flood of light it seemed to throw on the newly expanded prehistoric period of history, and after his death Friedrich Engels published a radical reading of Morgan in his *Der Ursprung der Familie*.

The whole of Morgan's writing subsequent to his initiation into Iroquois ethnology was governed by the attempt to generalize his Iroquois findings to a larger field of significance, as he did in the *Systems* and in *Ancient Society*. He had come to believe that the Iroquois exemplified a common pattern of American Indian life that proved historic unity, a pattern consisting not only of classificatory kinship terminology and matrilineal clans, but of many other things including the manner of bestowing and changing names, the dance, burial customs, domestic architecture and even such curious details as the custom of sleeping in the nude. He argued that Aztec society is to be understood as a part of this pattern; not in terms of the European feudal system with its kings, empires, vassals and palaces (characteristic of contemporary writing on the Aztecs), but in terms of the Iroquois sachems, confederacy, matrilineal clans and longhouses, or the "joint tenement" structures of the Pueblo Indians. "Montezuma's dinner" is a notable polemic on those lines. Several of his later publications, including *Houses and House-life of the American Aborigines* (which appeared in the last year of his life), elucidate the architectural component of this common pattern, showing how Indian dwellings follow kinship structures and arranging architectural types into an evolutionary sequence. Beyond the unity of the American peoples, Morgan adhered strongly to the (religiously orthodox) belief in the unity of the human race and vigorously opposed polygenism. In respect of the relation of humankind to other animals he expressed the less popular view, in *The American Beaver and His Works* and his shorter writings on animal psychology, that the mental activity of the higher animals shows no sharp discontinuity from that of humans.

Morgan's work had a considerable effect when it appeared, especially on JOHANN JAKOB BACHOFEN, JOHN MCLENNAN and JOHN LUBBOCK, and to a lesser extent on HENRY SUMNER MAINE and Charles Darwin. Although he did not hold a university post, he may be said to have had three students who were significant figures in the following generation: Fison, the Australianist; ADOLPH BANDELIER, the specialist on Mesoamerican and Southwestern history and archaeology; and JOHN WESLEY POWELL, head of the Bureau of (American) Ethnology and leading classifier of American languages in his day. In the profession generally his most durable contribution is the kinship work in the *Systems*, which has had a major influence on W.H.R. RIVERS, A.R. RADCLIFFE-BROWN and CLAUDE LÉVI-STRAUSS.

MAJOR WORKS: *League of the Ho-dé-no-sau-nee, or Iroquois* (Rochester: 1851); "Circular in reference to the degrees of relationship among different nations," *Smithsonian Miscellaneous Collections*, vol. 2 (1862), pp. 5-33; *The American Beaver and His Works* (Philadelphia: 1868); "A conjectural solution of the origin of the classificatory system of relationship," *Proceedings of the American Academy of Arts and Sciences*, vol. 7 (1868), pp. 436-477; *Systems of Consanguinity and Affinity of the Human Family* (Washington: 1871); "Australian kinship; with appendices, by Rev. Lorimer Fison," *Proceedings of the American Academy of Arts and Sciences*, vol. 8 (1872), pp. 412-438; "Montezuma's dinner," *North American Review*, vol. 122 (1876), pp. 265-308; *Ancient Society, or Researches in the Lines of Human Progress from Savagery through Barbarism to Civilization* (New York: 1877); *Houses and House-life of the American Aborigines* (Washington: 1881).

SOURCES: Lewis Henry Morgan Papers, University of Rochester Library; Leslie A. White (editor), *Lewis Henry Morgan, the Indian Journals, 1859-62* (Ann Arbor: 1959); Carl Resek, *Lewis Henry Morgan, American Scholar* (Chicago: 1960); Meyer Fortes, *Kinship and the Social Order: the Legacy of Lewis Henry Morgan* (Chicago: 1969); Thomas R. Trautmann, *Lewis Henry Morgan and the Invention of Kinship* (Berkeley: 1987); John Wesley Powell, "Sketch of Lewis H. Morgan, President of the American Association for the Advancement of Science," *The Popular Science Monthly*, vol. 18 (1880), pp. 114-121; Elisabeth Tooker, "The structure of the Iroquois league: Lewis H. Morgan's research and observations," *Ethnohistory*, vol. 30 (1983), pp. 141-154; Elisabeth Tooker, "Foreword" to: Lewis Henry Morgan, *Ancient Society* (Tucson: 1985), pp. xv-xxviii; Friedrich Engels, *Der Ursprung der Familie, des Privateisgenthums und des Staats, im Anschluss an L.H. Morgan's Forschungen* (Zürich: 1884) [tr.: *The Origin of the Family, Private Property and the State, in the Light of the Researches of Lewis H. Morgan* (New York: 1940)].

Thomas R. Trautmann

Morley, Sylvanus Griswold. Archaeologist, epigrapher, cultural anthropologist. Born in Chester (Pennsylvania) 7 June 1883, died in Santa Fe (New Mexico) 2 September 1948. By the time he was fifteen, Morley already had an interest in the ancient peoples of the Americas. Following training as an engineer at the Pennsylvania Military Academy, he entered Harvard in 1904, coming under the influences of FREDERIC WARD PUTNAM, curator of the Peabody Museum, and ALFRED TOZZER. During his period of study he began to establish a network of contacts among leading figures in Central American studies, such as Edward H. Thompson, and made his first visit to Mexico in 1907. This trip served as an introduction to a large number of the more important Maya sites including Uxmal, Mayapan and Chichen Itzá.

Practical experience in field surveying and recording was gained in an apprenticeship under Edgar Hewett in the McElmo Canyon region of southwestern Colorado and adjacent portions of the Four Corners region. The summer of 1908 included work at the ruins of Spruce Tree House and Cliff Palace at Mesa Verde and the ruins at Puye, New Mexico. From 1908 to 1914 he worked closely with Hewett in various capacities, making trips to measure buildings at Uxmal, to inspect the walled city of Tulum and to carry out reconnaissance of the sites of Quirigua and Yaxchilan.

Morley's appointment to the staff of the Carnegie Institution of Washington in 1914 inaugurated a twenty-six-year association focusing on intensive excavation and restoration of sites in the Maya area. Morley's particular field of interest lay in the hieroglyphic texts and calendrical inscriptions from all known Maya sites. This research culminated in the publication of two volumes, *An Introduction to the Study of Maya Hieroglyphs* and *The Inscriptions of Petén*. Together, these collections established the groundwork for all later study of Mayan writing and preserved many date glyphs since eroded. Prior to the granting of a concession to the Carnegie Institution in 1923 for extensive excavation and stabilization at Chichen Itzá, Morley centered his attention upon locating new Initial Series and Supplementary Series glyphs to establish a relative chronology for the known Maya sites. Underlying these efforts was a view that, by explaining the growth and decline of the Maya (whom he regarded as having developed their cultural achievements in relative isolation), it would be possible to determine whether societies obeyed underlying laws or simply grew without pattern. This was a position he maintained until his death.

Morley was also influential in attracting to the field of Maya studies many individuals for whom he served as mentor, among them FRANS BLOM, Tatiana Proskouriakoff,

Gustav Stromsvik and EARL HALSTEAD MORRIS. Between 1924 and 1940, his research interests focused on continuing the excavation of the ruins of Uaxactun, expanding the ongoing work at Chichen and recording epigraphic materials for all known Maya centers. His final publication, *The Ancient Maya*, was an attempt to synthesize his knowledge of Maya civilization and present the achievements of that culture to the general public. At his death he was Director of the Museum of New Mexico and the School of American Research in Santa Fe. His significance for Mesoamerican archaeology lies in his unceasing efforts to publicize current work to both the professional and lay publics and to analyze the hieroglyphics as guides to site chronology.

> MAJOR WORKS: *An Introduction to the Study of Maya Hieroglyphs* (Washington: 1915) (= *Bureau of American Ethnology, Bulletin*, no. 57); *The Inscriptions at Copán* (Washington: 1920); *Guide Book to the Ruins of Quirigua* (Washington: 1935) (= *Carnegie Institution of Washington, Supplementary Publication*, no. 16); *The Inscriptions of Petén* [5 vols.] (Washington: 1938) (= *Carnegie Institution of Washington, Publication*, no. 437); *The Ancient Maya* (Stanford: 1946).

> SOURCES: Robert L. Brunhouse, *Sylvanus G. Morley and the Ancient Mayas* (Norman: 1971); J. Eric S. Thompson, "Sylvanus Griswold Morley, 1883-1948" *American Anthropologist*, vol. 51 (1949), pp. 293-297; Arthur J.O. Anderson (editor), *Morleyana: a Collection of Writings in Memoriam, Sylvanus Griswold Morley, 1883-1948* (Santa Fe: 1950); Ralph L. Roys and Margaret W. Harrison, "Sylvanus Griswold Morley, 1883-1948" *American Antiquity*, vol. 14 (1949), pp. 215-221; Alfred V. Kidder, "The diary of Sylvanus G. Morley," *American Philosophical Society Proceedings*, vol. 103 (1959), pp. 778-782.

Robert B. Marks Ridinger

Morris, Earl Halstead. Archaeologist, conservator. Born in Chama (New Mexico) 24 October 1889, died in Boulder (Colorado) 24 June 1956. Although Morris was originally interested in the field of psychology, a chance encounter with Edgar Hewett sparked a lifelong fascination with the archaeology of the U.S. Southwest. As early as 1912, Morris took part in excavations in southwestern Colorado and at Quirigua, Guatemala. Between 1912 and 1931 he worked almost exclusively for the University of Colorado Museum with later joint excavations for the Carnegie Institution of Washington, D.C., the School of American Archaeology and the American Museum of Natural History. His work at clearing and restoring the Great Kiva at the Aztec ruins in San Juan County, Colorado, and to survey archaeological sites of the La Plata District, Colorado, are only two of the projects described in more than sixty articles and reviews in the field of regional archaeology. In Mesoamerica, Morris worked not only at Quirigua but also led the excavation and restoration of the Temple of the Warriors at Chichén Itzá, Yucatán, Mexico. Between 1937 and 1955 he summarized and reviewed the progress being made in studies of Southwestern archaeology in the *Year Book* of the Carnegie Institution of Washington. His work in this area is further reflected in the large artifactual collections amassed by him at the University of Colorado Museum and his painstaking detail in analysis of excavation materials. Works for which he is best known are *Archaeological Studies in the La Plata District*, *The Temple of the Warriors* and his accounts of various projects at Aztec, New Mexico, and in Canyon del Muerto. Morris's chief importance for American archaeology lies in his setting up of a framework of regional survey against which later discoveries could be measured and in his demonstrating effective methods of site stabilization and control.

MAJOR WORKS: "The ruins at Aztec," *El Palacio*, vol. 4, no. 3 (1917), pp. 43-69. "Preliminary account of the antiquities of the region between the Mancos and La Plata Rivers in Southwestern Colorado," *Thirty-Third Annual Report of the Bureau of American Ethnology* (Washington: 1919), pp. 155-206; *The Temple of the Warriors at Chichén Itzá, Yucatán* (Washington: 1931); *Archaeological Studies in the La Plata District, Southwestern Colorado and Northwestern New Mexico* (Washington: 1939).

SOURCES: *The Earl Morris Papers* (Boulder: 1963); *Earl H. Morris Photographic Portfolio* (Austin: 1985); *Among Ancient Ruins: the Legacy of Earl H. Morris* (Boulder: 1985); "Earl Halstead Morris, 1889-1956," *American Anthropologist*, vol. 59 (1957), pp. 521-523; A.V. Kidder, "Earl Halstead Morris, 1889-1956," *American Antiquity*, vol. 22 (1957), pp. 390-397; Hugo G. Rodeck, "Earl Morris and the University of Colorado Museum: an Appreciation," *Southwestern Lore*, vol. 22, no. 3 (December 1956), pp. 32-39; Elizabeth Ann Morris, "A bibliography of Earl H. Morris," *Southwestern Lore*, vol. 22, no. 3 (December 1956), pp. 40-43.

Robert B. Marks Ridinger

Morselli, Enrico. Anthropologist, neurologist, psychiatrist. Born in Modena (Italy) 17 July 1852, died in Genoa (Italy) 18 February 1929. As an evolutionist and one of the most renowned advocates of the positivist approach to the study of man, Morselli contributed significantly if not entirely originally to the advancement of the positivistic sciences in Italy.

Having obtained a degree in medicine (1874) in his native city, Morselli first practiced in Florence and was then director of psychiatric hospitals in Macerata (appointed 1877) and Turin (appointed 1880). His academic career was initially in psychiatry and neuropathology (University of Genoa, 1889) and was later extended to experimental psychology (Genoa, 1905-1910). In addition, from 1888, Morselli lectured on anthropology at the University of Turin (where CESARE LOMBROSO also taught) and somewhat later in Genoa. Among Morselli's interests were forensic medicine, philosophy, metaphysics and psychoanalysis; with Ardigò, Canestrini, Boccardo, and GIUSEPPE SERGI he directed the journal *Rivista di filosofia scientifica* (1881-1891) and founded *Psiche* with R. Assagioli in 1911.

Through his regular reviews in *Rivista analitica* Morselli helped introduce in Italy the ideas of HERBERT SPENCER, E.B. TYLOR, JOHN LUBBOCK, JOHN MCLENNAN, WILHELM WUNDT and of Charles Darwin himself, whose obituary he wrote and—in the argument on neogenesis—some of whose positions he defended against the view of his own teacher, PAOLO MANTEGAZZA.

Morselli was also curator of the Section on Anthropology at the Esposizione Generale Italiana (Turin, 1884) at a time when the anthropological disciplines were first being acknowledged as a legitimate subfield within the natural and biological sciences. Indeed, anthropology was viewed by the positivist Morselli as the "natural history of mankind" and thus but a branch of biology (while races, peoples and "types" were to be the objects of such related disciplines as ethnology, ethnography and anthropography, respectively).

His main contributions to anthropology can be found in *Critica e riforma del metodo in antropologia* and more significantly in the two-volume work, *Antropologia generale*, which appeared in the same year as the First Congress of Italian Ethnography of 1911. It was in that transitional year that Morselli's "physical" naturalist's orientation—and, indeed, the entire positivist orientation of Italian anthropology—were effectively criticized. Aldobrandino Mochi in particular stressed the need to distinguish "anthropology," a natural science, from "ethnology," a sociocultural discipline.

MAJOR WORKS: *Critica e riforma del metodo in antropologia fondata sulle leggi statistiche e biologiche dei valori seriali e sullo esperimento* (Rome: 1880); "Darwin," *Rivista analitica*, vol. 1 (July 1881-June 1882), p. 613; *Manuale di semeiotica delle malattie mentali* [2 vols.] (Milan: 1885-1894); *Psicologia e spiritismo* (Turin: 1906); *Antropologia generale: l'uomo secondo la teoria dell'evoluzione* (Turin: 1911); *Le nevrosi traumatiche* (Turin: 1913); *L'uccisione pietosa* (Turin: 1925); *Sessualità umana secondo la psicologia, la biologia e la sociologia* (Turin: 1931).

SOURCES: M. David, *La psicoanalisi nella cultura italiana* (Turin: 1966); P. Guarnieri, *La psichiatria antropologica di Enrico Morselli* (Milan: 1986); G. Landucci, *L'occhio e la mente* (Florence: 1987); S. Puccini, "Evoluzionismo e positivismo nell'antropologia italiana" in: Pietro Clemente [et al.], *L'antropologia italiana: un secolo di storia* (Bari: 1985), pp. 97-148; L. Rossi, *Enrico Morselli e la scienza dell'uomo nell'età del positivismo* (Reggio-Emilia: 1984); P. Rossi (editor), *L'età del positivismo* (Bologna: 1986).

Giorgio de Finis
[Translation from Italian: Paolo Gnecco]

Morton, Samuel George. Physician, geologist, physical anthropologist. Born in Philadelphia (Pennsylvania) 26 January 1799, died in Philadelphia (Pennsylvania) 15 May 1851. Morton studied medicine under the noted Philadelphia physician Dr. Joseph Parrish and at the University of Pennsylvania. Considering his medical training in Philadelphia inadequate, Morton enrolled at the University of Edinburgh in 1820 where, in addition to medicine, he attended lectures in geology and phrenology. Morton spent 1822 in Paris studying clinical medicine and then returned to Edinburgh taking a degree in medicine in 1823. On his return to Philadelphia, Morton practiced medicine and taught at Pennsylvania College where he lectured on anatomy and began his cranial studies. In 1839 he published his major work *Crania Americana* in which he theorized that the Indians of both North and South America were a distinct race and that all races could be ranked by cranial size and intelligence. His cranial researches led him to polygenism and, as a prominent member of the so-called American School of Anthropology, Morton in his works buttressed the school's arguments of innate racial inferiority and polygenism.

MAJOR WORKS: *Crania Americana; or, A Comparative View of the Skulls of Various Aboriginal Nations of North and South America, to which is Prefixed an Essay on the Varieties of the Human Species* (N.p.: 1839); *Brief Remarks on the Diversity of the Human Species, and on Some Kindred Subjects* (Philadelphia: 1842); *An Inquiry into the Distinctive Characteristics of the Aboriginal Race of America* (Boston: 1842); *Crania Aegyptica; or, Observations on Egyptian Ethnography Derived from Anatomy, History, and the Monuments* (Philadelphia: 1844); "Study of ancient crania," *The Boston Medical and Surgical Journal*, vol. 31 (1844), pp. 422-423; *A Letter to Rev. John Bachman, D.D., on the Question of Hybridity in Animals, Considered in Reference to the Unity of the Human Species* (Charleston: 1850).

SOURCES: Robert E. Bieder, *Science Encounters the Indian, 1820-1880: the Early Years of American Ethnology* (Norman: 1986), pp. 55-103; Robert E. Bieder, "Samuel G. Morton: nineteenth-century craniology and the American Indian," *Les Américains et les autres: Actes du GRENA Groupe de Recherche et d'Études Nord-Américaines, 1981* (Aix-en-Provence: 1982), pp. 7-19; Stephen Jay Gould, *The Mismeasure of Man* (New York: 1981); Sanford Hunt, "Samuel George Morton" in: Samuel D. Gross (editor), *Lives of Eminent American Physicians and Surgeons of the Nineteenth Century* (Philadelphia: 1861), pp. 582-604; Henry S. Patterson, "Memoir of the life and scientific labors of Samuel George Morton" in: J.C. Nott and George R. Glidden, *Types of Mankind: or Ethnological Researches, Based upon the Ancient Monuments, Paintings, Sculptures, and Crania of*

Races, and upon their Natural, Geographical, Philological, and Biblical History (Philadelphia: 1854), pp. xvii-lvii; William Stanton, *The Leopard's Spots: Scientific Attitudes Toward Race in America, 1815-59* (Chicago: 1960).

Robert E. Bieder

Moser, Oskar. Folklorist, researcher of buildings and tools. Born in Sachsenburg, Kärnten (Corinthia) (Austria) 20 January 1914. Moser was a student of German studies, Romance-language studies and folklore at the University of Graz under K. Polheim. He graduated in 1938. He obtained his *Habilitation* in folklore in 1962 at the University of Graz, where he held a chair from 1971 to 1984. Moser was also active in popular education and participated in the construction of the Kärntner Freilichtsmuseum (Corinthian Open-Air Museum).

His first scholarly works were on popular drama and on peasant furniture. Later he worked on vernacular architecture in Inner Austria. With this Moser carried on the "Graz School," which had been founded by Rudolf Meringer and VIKTOR GERAMB and constituted one of the fundamental traditions in comparative tool and architecture studies within European ethnology. Moser's research on tools made clear the relationship between the historical development of work tools and economic factors. His contribution to the field of European vernacular-architecture studies is the detailed examination of Inner Austrian "house landscapes" and his precise research on contruction with regard to work and production techniques. His international reputation is also based on his works on popular narrative.

MAJOR WORKS: *Die Kärntner Rätsel von "Reiter" und Sieb* (Klagenfurt: 1974); *Das Bauernhaus und seine landschaftliche und historische Entwicklung in Kärnten* (Klagenfurt: 1974); *Das Pfettenstuhldach: eine Dachbauweise im östlichen alpinen Übergangsbereich* (Vienna: 1976); *Riß und Arl im Kärntner Nockgebiet: Topographie der altständigen Pfluggeräte in den südlichen Ostalpen* (Vienna: 1981); *Kärntner Bauernmöbel* (Klagenfurt: 1982); *Materialen zur Geschichte und Typologie der Getreidewinde* (Vienna: 1984).

SOURCES: H. Eberhart [et al.] (editors), *Bauen, Wohnen, Gestalten: Festschrift für Oskar Moser* (Trautenfels: 1984); Eva Kausel (editor), *Volkskundlicher in und aus Österreich (unter Berücksichtigung von Südtirol)* (Vienna: 1987), pp. 88-90.

Elisabeth Katschnig-Fasch
[Translation from German: Robert B. Dean]

Moszyński, Kazimierz. Ethnologist, cultural historian, linguist. Born in Warsaw (Poland) 5 March 1887, died in Kraków (Poland) 30 March 1959. Moszyński studied in Zürich and Kraków (the Academy of Fine Arts). Contact with the Young Poland circle awoke his interest in folk culture. His first ethnographic and linguistic studies were conducted in the Ukraine and Belorussia. In 1922 he became assistant and then director of the Workshop on Slavic Ethnology at the Anthropological Institute of the Scientific Society of Warsaw. Between 1926 and 1959 (with a hiatus during the war) he directed the Departments of Ethnology and Ethnography at the University of Vilnius and Jagiellonian University. He was a member of the Polish Academy of Knowledge and, after the war, of the Polish Academy of Sciences. He was a co-organizer of the Institute of the History of Material Culture of the Polish Academy of Sciences created in the years 1953-1954.

Moszyński was an outstanding expert in the field of Polish and Slavic ethnography. He was an authority both in Slavistics and in non-European ethnography. He was also a specialist in Finno-Ugric studies, a theoretician of culture and a methodologist. Combining interests in folk culture with the world view of an evolutionary naturalist, he sought out in culture the traces of primary states of the development of thought and human creativity. Moszyński strove for the reconstruction of the characteristic features of the development of folk culture, conceived as a unity. In his search for cultural archaisms, he conducted systematic fieldwork that revealed expert knowledge of sources by means of the "atlas" system throughout all of Poland and the Balkans. He was the author of the famous *Atlas kultury ludowej w Polsce* [*The Atlas of Folk Culture in Poland*]. In his investigations he made use of his own method of critical evolutionism which linked the methods of comparative history, geography and linguistics in an eclectic manner.

> MAJOR WORKS: *Badania nad pochodzeniem i pierwotną kulturą Słowian* [*Studies on the Origin and Primary Culture of Slavs*] (Kraków: 1925); *Kultura ludowa Słowian* [*Folk Culture of the Slavs*] [3 vols.] (Kraków: 1929-1939); *Atlas kultury ludowej w Polsce* [*The Atlas of Folk Culture in Poland*] [3 vols.] (Kraków: 1934); *Ludy zbieracko-łowieckie* [*Folk as Hunters and Gatherers*] (Kraków: 1951); *Ludy pasterskie* [*Pastoral Folk*] (Kraków: 1953); *Pierwotny zasięg języka prasłowiańskuego* [*The Original range of Proto-Slavic Language*] (Wrocław and Kraków: 1957); *Człowiek: wstęp do etnografii ogólnej i etnologii* [*Man: Introduction to General Ethnography and Ethnology*] (Wrocław: 1958); *O sposobach badania kultury materialnej Prasłowian* [*On the Research Methods of the Material Culture of the Proto-Slavs*] (Wrocław: 1962).

> SOURCES: Kazimierz Moszyński, *Życie i twórczość* [*Life and Works*] (Wrocław: 1976); Anna Kutrzeba-Pojnarowa, "Kazimierz Moszyński (5 III 1887-30 III 1959)," *Kwartalnik Historyczny*, vol. 68 (1961), pp. 284-288; Anna Kutrzeba-Pojnarowa, *Kultura ludowa i jej badacze* [*Folk Culture and Its Researchers*] (Warsaw: 1977).

Maria Niewiadomska and Iwona Grzelakowska
[Translation from Polish: Joel Janicki]

Mouhot, Henri (Alexandre Henri Mouhot). Naturalist, explorer. Born in Montbéliard (France) 15 May 1826, died near Luang Prabang (Laos) 10 November 1861. Mouhot is remembered for his narrative account of explorations in Indochina between 1858 and 1861, and especially for his on-site description (during a visit in 1860) of the ancient Khmer ruins of Angkor. Early in his career, Mouhot displayed a great interest in travel. He spent some ten years in Russia as an educator and French tutor to the nobility. In 1856 he settled in England, where he took up studies in the fields of zoology and natural history. Two years later, with encouragement of the Royal Geographical Society (London), he embarked on an ambitious zoological expedition to the interior of Indochina. Between 1858 and 1861, he undertook four expeditions to interior regions of Siam, Cambodia and Laos. In January 1860 he reached the site of the ancient Khmer capital of Angkor, which he studied for three weeks, recording his observations in his journal. These three chapters in Mouhot's diary have been described by LOUIS MALLERET as the first attempt at a scientific account of Angkor and of the civilization of the Khmers. Mouhot described the exceptional craftsmanship and imposing scale of the monuments and the evident Indian influence on reliefs and sculptures. He also called attention to the presence of numerous Sanskrit inscriptions. Mouhot died of a fever in October 1861 in the vicinity of Luang Prabang, northern Laos. He was buried on the banks of the Nam Khan River. Mouhot's diary was recovered and was first published in installments in the Parisian journal *Tour du Monde* (1863, nos. 196-204). An English translation was published (in a two-volume edition) in 1864, and the French book edition was published in 1868. Mouhot's description of the monuments of Angkor quickly aroused the interest of European scholars and archaeologists. Louis Delaporte, Étienne Aymonier, GEORGE COEDÈS and Philippe Stern are among those who would subsequently add to the appreciation of Angkor and of the Indianized civilization of the Khmer.

MAJOR WORKS: *Voyage dans les Royaumes de Siam, de Cambodge, de Laos et autres parties centrales de l'Indo-Chine: relation extrait du journal et de la correspondance de l'auteur par Ferdinand de Lanoye* (Paris: 1868) [tr.: *Travels in the Central Parts of Indo-China (Siam), Cambodia, and Laos during the Years 1858, 1859, and 1860 by the Late Henri Mouhot* [2 vols.] (London: 1864)]; *Henri Mouhot's Diary: Travels in the Central Parts of Siam, Cambodia, and Laos During the Years 1858-1961* (Kuala Lumpur: 1966).

SOURCES: Louis Malleret, "Le centenaire de la mort d'Henri Mouhot (1826-1861)," *Bulletin de la Société des Études Indochinoises*, n.s., vol. 36 (1961), pp. 681-687; Christopher Pym, "Introduction" to: *Henri Mouhot's Diary: Travels in the Central Parts of Siam, Cambodia and Laos During the Years 1858-1861* (Kuala Lumpur: 1966), pp. xi-xxii; "Mouhot, (Alexandre-)Henri" in: *The New Encyclopaedia Britannica* (Chicago: 1987), vol. 8, p. 369.

Lee S. Dutton

Mountford, Charles Percy. Ethnologist, anthropologist, photographer. Born in Hallett, near Peterborough (South Australia) 8 March 1890, died in Adelaide (South Australia) 16 December 1976. Mountford, educated at state schools, had no formal academic training. Employed as a telegraphic mechanic, in 1920 he transferred to Darwin (Northern Territory) where he first met Aborigines. He subsequently obtained a Diploma of Anthropology (Cambridge, 1959), an M.A. (University of Adelaide, 1964), and two Hon.D.Litt. degrees (University of Melbourne, 1973, and University of Adelaide, 1976).

Mountford's first contribution (in conjunction with N.B. Tindale, 1926) focused on rock engravings. Continuing research in this direction as an Honorary Associate in Ethnology at the South Australian Museum, he became an authority on Aboriginal art. He accompanied three expeditions of the Board for Anthropological Research, the University of Adelaide, between 1935 and 1937. It was in the Western Desert of Central Australia, including Mt. Olga and Ayers Rock (Uluru), that Mountford obtained Aboriginal material for three books that enhanced his reputation. One of these, *Brown Men and Red Sand*, had wide circulation and was responsible for stimulating interest in Aborigines both locally and overseas. Mountford's writing was of significance to Australian Aboriginal studies primarily because there were few trained anthropologists working in this field at that time and because the traditional life of Aborigines was radically changing. His work probably made more of an impact than did that of a number of professional anthropologists because he provided them with opportunities to interpret and analyze the data he presented so attractively.

Mountford embarked on a lecture tour in the United States, Canada and the United Kingdom in 1945. As a result, he was able to arrange an American-Australian Scientific Expedition to Arnhem Land (1948) sponsored by the National Geographic Society of America, the Smithsonian Institute of Washington, D.C., and the Commonwealth of

Australia. From this research came two large volumes—one on *Art, Myth and Symbolism* and the other on *Anthropology and Nutrition*, both edited by him. This was followed by a period among the Tiwi of Bathurst and Melville Islands (1954). In short, Mountford was the last of the amateurs who left their indelible mark on Australian Aboriginal anthropology.

MAJOR WORKS: *The Art of Albert Namatjira* (Melbourne: 1944); *Brown Men and Red Sand* (Melbourne: 1948); (editor) *Records of the American-Australian Scientific Expedition to Arnhem Land* [4 vols.] 1, *Art, Myth and Symbolism;* 2, *Anthropology and Nutrition* (Melbourne: 1956-1960); *The Tiwi: Their Art, Myth and Ceremony* (London and Melbourne: 1958); *Ayers Rock: Its People, Their Beliefs and Their Art* (Sydney: 1965); *Winbaraku and the Myth of Jarapiri* (Adelaide: 1968); *Nomads of the Australian Desert* (Adelaide: 1976).

SOURCE: M. Lamshed, *"Monty": the Biography of C.P. Mountford* (Adelaide: 1972); *Who's Who in Australia, 1974* (Melbourne: 1974).

Ronald M. Berndt

Mühlmann, Wilhelm Emil. Anthropologist, sociologist. Born in Düsseldorf (Germany) 1 October 1904, died in Wiesbaden (Germany) 11 May 1988. From 1925 to 1931 Mühlmann studied physical anthropology with the then-leading anthropologist Eugen Fischer (1874-1967); he also studied philosophy and sociology at various German universities, receiving a Ph.D. in 1932 and a *Habilitation* in 1938 from the University of Berlin under RICHARD THURNWALD. He worked for short terms as curator of anthropological museums in Berlin, Hamburg and Breslau but lived most of the time in Berlin where he held courses as *Privatdozent* and published prolifically on topics of physical anthropology (*Rassen- und Völkerkunde*, 1936) and political anthropology (*Krieg und Frieden*, 1940), which, however, were not completely in the mainstream of Nazi ideology.

His *Methodik der Völkerkunde* was a major contribution, introducing concepts of "intentionality" into anthropological thinking and reasoning, thus applying contemporary philosophical theory, mainly of the phenomenological school (Edmund Husserl (1859-1938)). During World War II Mühlmann was largely freed from active military service and was thus able to pursue his anthropological studies. Also during his Berlin years he engaged in a historical case study in political anthropology focusing on Tahitian secret societies that resulted in several publications after 1932, culminating in his *Arioi und Mamaia*. His *Geschichte der Anthropologie* is outstanding for its comprehensiveness, including not only traditional anthropological disciplines (such as ethnography, physical anthropology and anthropological theory) but also psychology, philosophy and political theory. This unusually comprehensive view is also reflected in his programmatic essay *Umriß und Probleme einer Kulturanthropologie*.

In 1950 Mühlmann was appointed professor of *Völkerpsychologie* (anthropology) and sociology at Mainz and later Heidelberg Universities. He pursued his long-standing interest in political anthropology focusing on chiliastic movements (*Chiliasmus und Nativismus*) and inter-ethnic relationships (*Rassen, Ethnien, Kulturen*). His concepts of *interethnisches Gefälle* (inter-ethnic gradient) and *interethnischer Druck* (inter-ethnic pressure) testify to his innovative perception of social processes, although ethnographic data do not always bear out his theories, as Wolfgang Rudolph pointed out in 1972.

His last major publications (*Die Metamorphose der Frau* and *Pfade in die Weltliteratur*) apply in a *tour de force* anthropological concepts (mainly from the domains of shamanism and psychology) to the personalities and writing of two major authors of world literature, Miguel de Cervantes Saavedra (1547-1616) and Annette von Droste-Hülshoff (1797-1848).

Mühlmann's importance for German anthropology lies in the fact that he was the first leading anthropologist in post-war Germany to reintroduce a socially, psychologically and philosophically founded discipline on the lines of his teachers Thurnwald and Alfred Vierkandt (1867-1953) when most anthropologists in Germany were adherents of the Cultural-Historical School in the tradition of LEO FROBENIUS, FRITZ GRAEBNER and WILHELM SCHMIDT. Mühlmann thus greatly stimulated the re-integration of German anthropology into the international scholarly discourse.

MAJOR WORKS: *Methodik der Völkerkunde* (Stuttgart: 1938); *Geschichte der Anthropologie* (Bonn: 1948; 2nd revised ed., Frankfurt and Bonn: 1968; 3rd ed., Wiesbaden: 1984); *Arioi und Mamaia: eine ethnologische, religionssoziologische und historische Studie über polynesische Kultbünde.* (Wiesbaden: 1955) (= *Studien zur Kulturkunde*, 14); *Chiliasmus und Nativismus: Studien zur Psychologie, Soziologie und historische Kasuistik der Umsturzbewegungen* [some parts written by his students; all introductory, summary and theoretical contributions by Mühlmann] (Berlin: 1961; 2nd. ed., Berlin: 1964); *Homo Creator: Abhandlung zur Soziologie, Anthropologie und Ethnologie* [collected papers] (Wiesbaden: 1962); *Rassen, Ethnien, Kulturen. Moderne Ethnologie* (Neuwied and Berlin: 1964) (= *Soziologische Texte*, 24) [collected and revised papers]; *Die Metamorphose der Frau: Weiblicher Schamanismus und Dichtung* (Berlin: 1981; 2nd. ed., Berlin: 1984); *Pfade in die Weltliteratur* (Königstein: 1984).

SOURCES: Wilhelm Emil Mühlmann, *Dreizehn Jahre* (Hamburg: 1947) [autobiography, 1933-1945]; Horst Reimann and Ernst Wilhelm Müller (editors), *Entwicklung und Fortschritt: Soziologische und ethnologische Aspekte des soziokulturellen Wandels* (Tübingen: 1969) [Festschrift for his 65th birthday]; Ursula Schlenther, *Zur Geschichte der Völkerkunde an der Berliner Universität von 1810 bis 1945* (Berlin [East]: 1961); Horst Reimann and Klaus Kiefer, *Wilhelm Emil Mühlmann, Bibliographie, 1928-1964* (Wiesbaden: 1964); Berthold Riese's personal acquaintance with Mühlmann since 1965; Horst Reimann, *Bibliographie, 1965-1984, Wilhelm Emil Mühlmann* (Augsburg: 1984); Horst Reimann, "Zum 80. Geburtstag von Wilhelm Emil Mühlmann," *Kölner Zeitschrift für Soziologie und Sozialpsychologie*, vol. 37 (1985), pp. 178-181; Horst Reimann, "In Memoriam Wilhelm Emil Mühlmann," *Kölner Zeitschrift für Soziologie und Sozialpsychologie*, vol. 40 (1988), pp. 611-612; Ernst Wilhelm Müller, "Wilhelm Emil Mühlmann," *Zeitschrift für Ethnologie*, vol. 114 (1990), pp. 1-12.

Berthold Riese

Munkácsi, Bernát. Linguist, anthropologist. Born in Nagyvárad (Austria-Hungary, now Oradea, Rumania) 12 March 1860, died in Budapest (Hungary) 21 September 1937. Munkácsi was a researcher of Finno-Ugric and also Turkic and Caucasian languages and cultures.

He collected linguistic and folklore material among the Votiaks (Udmurts) in Russia in 1885 and undertook a sixteen-month expedition to the Voguls (Mansi) of north-west Siberia during 1888-1889 to translate the texts left by ANTAL REGULY. Munkácsi's material is a basic source of Vogul folklore and religion. During 1914-1918 he recorded folklore from Votiak and Osetian war prisoners in Hungary. Investigating the alien influences on Ugrian cultures, he made a major contribution to the study of early ethnic contacts of the Finno-Ugrian peoples with Turkic, Aryan and Iranian groups.

MAJOR WORKS: *Votják népköltészeti hagyományok* [*Votiak Oral Tradition*] (Budapest: 1887); *Vogul népköltési gyűjtemény* [*Collection of Vogul Folk Poetry*], vol. i (Budapest: 1892-1902), vol. ii/1 (Budapest: 1910-1921), vol. ii/2 (Budapest: 1892-1921), vol. iii/1 (Budapest: 1893); (with Kálmán Béla), vol. iii/2 (Budapest: 1952); vol. iv/1 (Budapest: 1896); (with Kálmán Béla), vol. iv/2 (1963); (with D.R. Fuchs), *Volksbräuche und Volksdichtung der Wotjaken* (Helsinki: 1952); *Árja és kaukázusi elemek a finn-magyar nyelvekben* [*Aryan and Caucasian Elements in Finno-Hungarian Languages*], vol. 1 (Budapest: 1901).

SOURCES: *Magyar Nyelvőr*, vol. 59 (Budapest: 1930) [this volume of the journal is wholly devoted to Munkácsi]; Munkácsi Noémi, *Egy nagy magyar nyelvész* [*A Great Hungarian Linguist*] (Budapest: 1943); Kálmán Béla, *Munkácsi Bernát* (Budapest: 1981); Gulya János and Oláh Éva, "Munkácsi Bernát munkássága (bibliográfia)" ["The life work of Bernát Munkácsi (bibliography)"], *A Magyar Tudományos Akadémia Nyelv-és irodalomtudományok osztályának közleményei*, vol. 24 (1967), pp. 397-413 [includes full bibliography of Munkácsi's works and translations into German].

Éva Schmidt

Murdock, George Peter. Anthropologist. Born in Meriden (Connecticut) 11 May 1897, died in Devon (Pennsylvania) 29 March 1985.

Murdock is probably best known to anthropologists for his efforts to foster worldwide cross-cultural tests of explanations of cultural variation. He believed that the comparative method is indispensable to the scientific study of human behavior. Accordingly, he spent much of his life creating, distributing and studying the growing body of information on the cultures of the world.

To facilitate empirical tests of possible explanations, he founded and was primarily responsible for developing the Human Relations Area Files (HRAF), a worldwide ethnographic archive. From its beginnings at Yale in the 1930s when it was called the Cross-Cultural Survey, and since the establishment in 1949 of the inter-university and now international consortium that is the Human Relations Area Files, Inc., the HRAF Archive has become an enormous and annually growing microfiche collection of original pages of ethnographic text, indexed and grouped for the retrieval of particular kinds of information. As of 1990, the Archive contained nearly 800,000 text pages of information on 335 cultures or ethnic groups, many described at two or more points in time. The indexing is done according to an extensive classification of the topics that are likely to be found in ethnographic documents (more than 700 categories are listed in Murdock [et al.]'s *Outline of Cultural Materials*).

The HRAF Archive provides original texts that cross-cultural researchers code themselves. But Murdock also pioneered the publication of coded data on the societies of the world. He personally did much of this coding, which he published for a number of worldwide samples. These samples (and their precoded data) have been used frequently by researchers, often as lists to sample from in order to code additional variables; the two most commonly used are the *Ethnographic Atlas* and the "Standard cross-cultural sample."

Murdock is also known for his pioneering cross-cultural research on kinship classification and other aspects of marriage, family and kinship. His major publication in this area, *Social Structure*, used a sample of 250 cultures to test various theories about variation in social organization. This work stimulated a large number of cross-cultural studies over the next forty years.

MAJOR WORKS: (with C.S. Ford, A.E. Hudson, R. Kennedy, L.W. Simmons, and J.W.M. Whiting) *Outline of Cultural Materials* (New Haven: 1938; 5th revised ed., New Haven: 1987); *Social Structure* (New York: 1949); *Outline of World Cultures* (New Haven: 1954; 6th revised ed.,

New Haven: 1983); *Africa: Its Peoples and Their Culture History* (New York: 1959); *Ethnographic Atlas* (Pittsburgh: 1967); (with Douglas White) "Standard cross-cultural sample," *Ethnology*, vol. 8 (1969), pp. 329-369; *Theories of Illness: a World Survey* (Pittsburgh: 1980); *Atlas of World Cultures* (Pittsburgh: 1981).

SOURCES: Ward H. Goodenough, "Murdock, George P." in: David L. Sills (editor), *International Encyclopedia of the Social Sciences* (New York: 1968-1979), vol. 18, pp. 554-559; Ward H. Goodenough, "George Peter Murdock's contributions to anthropology: an overview," *Behavior Science Research*, vol. 22 (1988), pp. 1-9; Alexander Spoehr, "George Peter Murdock (1897-1985)," *Ethnology*, vol. 24 (1985), pp. 307-317; John W.M. Whiting, "George Peter Murdock (1897-1985)," *American Anthropologist*, vol. 88 (1986), pp. 682-686.

Melvin Ember

Murie, James R. (Pawnee name: Sakuuru' Taa', "Coming Sun"). Ethnologist, informant. Born in Grand Island (Nebraska) 1862, died in Pawnee (Oklahoma) 18 November 1921. The son of a Pawnee woman and a white man, Murie became the foremost recorder of ethnological material on 19th-century Pawnee culture and society.

In 1883, after graduating from boarding school at Hampton Institute in Virginia, Murie returned to Pawnee where he worked intermittently for the rest of his life as a clerk and in various capacities for the Pawnee tribe. When FRANCIS LAFLESCHE, a Hampton schoolmate, introduced Murie to anthropologist ALICE C. FLETCHER, Murie embarked on a quest to preserve a record of the traditional culture of his people. From 1898 to 1902 he collaborated with Fletcher on a study of the Hako, the Pawnee calumet adoption ceremony. In 1899 he began to work with GEORGE A. DORSEY of the Field Columbian Museum, taking primary responsibility for collecting Pawnee mythology (Dorsey, *Traditions of the Skidi Pawnee* and *The Pawnee: Mythology*). Murie also recorded a large collection of Skiri texts on wax cylinders, transcribed it in Pawnee and translated it into English (unpublished). Dorsey and Murie enlisted the aid of FRANZ BOAS to guide them in developing an appropriate orthography and an understanding of the sound system of the language. Dorsey and Murie also drafted a massive monograph on the society and religion of the Skidi Pawnee, which has not yet been published. During the summers of 1903 and 1905 Murie recorded Arikara mythology and ceremonies on the Fort Berthold Reservation in North Dakota (Dorsey, *Traditions of the Arikaras*). As a part of his studies, Murie also collected artifacts for the Field Museum. In 1910, after Dorsey had stopped working on the Pawnee, Murie was hired as a part-time field researcher for the Bureau of American Ethnology, focusing on Pawnee ceremonies. In 1912 Murie began collaborating with CLARK WISSLER of the American Museum of Natural History, starting with a study of Pawnee societies and collecting specimens for the museum. From 1914 until just before his death, Murie worked on a comprehensive study, *Ceremonies of the Pawnee*, a monumental record of native American ritual. Much of the material he recorded was not published during his lifetime, and the extent of his invaluable contribution to American Indian ethnology is only slowly being appreciated.

MAJOR WORKS: (contributor) Alice C. Fletcher, *The Hako: a Pawnee Ceremony* (Washington: 1904) (= *Annual Report of the Bureau of American Ethnology*, vol. 22, part 2, pp. 13-368); (contributor) George A. Dorsey, *Traditions of the Skidi Pawnee* (Boston: 1904); (contributor) George A. Dorsey, *Traditions of the Arikara* (Washington, D.C.: 1904); (contributor) George A. Dorsey, *The*

Pawnee: Mythology (Washington: 1906); *Pawnee Indian Societies* (New York: 1914) (= *Anthropological Papers of the American Museum of Natural History,* vol. 11, part 7, pp. 543-644); *Ceremonies of the Pawnee* (edited by Douglas R. Parks) [2 vols.] (Washington: 1981) (= *Smithsonian Contributions to Anthropology,* no. 27).

SOURCE: Douglas R. Parks, "James R. Murie, Pawnee, 1862-1921" in: Margot Liberty (editor), *American Indian Intellectuals* (St. Paul: 1978) (= *1976 Proceedings of the American Ethnological Society*), pp. 75-89.

Douglas R. Parks

Murko, Matija. Linguist, literary historian, ethnologist/folklorist. Born in Drstelja pri Ptuju (Austria, now Slovenia) 10 February 1861, died in Prague (Czechoslovakia) 11 February 1951. Murko studied Germanics and Slavistics at the University of Vienna and graduated in 1886. He was a professor of Slavistics in Graz, Leipzig and Zagreb and, from 1920, at the newly established Department for South Slavic Languages and Literature at Charles University in Prague. His areas of specialization were Slavic literature and the comparative study of South Slavic and Slovenian literature.

He became interested in ethnology after he visited the ethnographic exhibit at Prague in 1895. This exhibit was the result of some of the first systematic research on ethnology in Eastern Europe, and it exerted great influence on the development of ethnology in Slovenia. Murko researched material culture and folk poems. He wrote about the vernacular architecture of the Slovenians, Croatians and Serbians based on literature and on his own fieldwork. This work was the first of its type. He was interested especially in kitchens and the hearth, and he studied the vocabulary used in different regions, categorizing it linguistically. He dealt with folk poetics giving special attention to the epic poems of the Serbs and Croatians. He traveled often to the South Slavic regions, collecting poems, taking photographs and researching everyday life. He was the first person to make recordings of the poems. He was also the co-founder of the philological and cultural-historical publication, *Wörter und Sachen.*

MAJOR WORKS: "Narodopisna razstava češkoslovanska v Pragi" in: *Letopis Matice Slovenske* (Ljubljana: 1986); "Zur Geschichte des volkstümlichen Hauses bei den Südslawen," *Mitteilungen der Anthropologischen Gesellschaft in Wien,* vol. 35 (1905), pp. 308-330; and and vol. 36 (1906), pp. 12-40 and 92-129; "Das Grab als Tisch," *Wörter und Sachen,* vol. 2 (1910), pp. 79-160; *La poésie populaire épique en Yougoslavie* (Paris: 1929).

SOURCES: Joža Glonar, "Matija Murko" in: Franc Ksaver Lukman (editor), *Slovenski biografiski leksikon,* vol. 2, zvezek [fasc.] 6 (Ljubljana: 1935), pp. 169-175; France Kotnik, "Pregled slovenskega narodopisja," *Narodopisje Slovencev,* vol. 1 (1944), pp. 21-52; Ivan Grafenauer, "Matiji Murku (1861-1952) v spomin," *Slovenski etnograf,* vol. 5 (1952), pp. 197-207; Anton Slodnjak, *Uvod. M. Murko: izbrano delo* (Ljubljana: 1962); Vilko Novak, *Raziskovalci slovenskega življenja* (Ljubljana: 1986).

Mojca Ravnik
[Translation from Slovene: Corrine Leskovar]

Murray, Margaret Alice. Egyptologist, historian of religions. Born in Calcutta (India) 13 July 1863, died in London (England) 13 November 1963. Murray was the daughter of a paper mill manager in Calcutta; on both sides, her family had been in India for generations as missionaries, traders, and employees of the East India Company.

Murray visited Britain with her parents on several occasions, staying three years at one point, but did not leave India for good until her father's retirement in 1887. At the age of twenty she had volunteered as a nurse in Calcutta for three months, but parental opposition prevented further training at that time. Back in Britain, Murray found that she was barred from the profession of nursing by arbitrary height requirements; she was quite short, yet had been the sole healthy nurse in a major hospital during an epidemic in Calcutta.

In 1891, when Murray was twenty-eight, her father died, which gave her a greater degree of personal freedom. She spent a lengthy period in Madras, visiting her married sister. The latter urged her to find some sort of career and suggested studying Egyptology with FLINDERS PETRIE. In January 1894 Murray began as an undergraduate in Egyptology at University College, London.

Within a year Murray had made such progress in reading Egyptian hieroglyphs that Petrie assigned her a research project on the inheritance of property in early Egypt, a paper that was published before the end of 1895. Murray did not take a degree but was shortly appointed lecturer in Egyptology and taught the course on hieroglyphics. She assisted Petrie on excavations in Egypt for several years starting in 1902 but by around 1907 was kept in London by her greatly increased teaching duties. Murray wrote a number of monographs between 1900 and 1922, when she was elected a fellow of University College.

During the same period she became interested in anthropology and studied under C.G. SELIGMAN (who was also greatly interested in Egypt). Murray worked quietly but firmly for equality of the sexes in such organizations as the British Association. Murray has been credited with effecting considerable change in her lifetime; she was often the first woman to achieve certain goals, such as directing an archaeological dig.

Egypt was too distant for the kind of brief excavations that she could direct during summer terms, so Murray worked in Malta during 1921-1923, in Britain in 1925 and in the Balearic Islands during 1930-1931.

She was appointed assistant professor in 1924, elected to the Folklore Society in 1927 and retired from University College with an honorary D.Litt. in 1935 at the age of seventy-two. Murray, rather than settling down to a less active existence, seized the opportunity to return to Egyptian archaeology. She excavated with Petrie in Palestine in 1935 and 1936 and directed an excavation in Petra in 1937. Her final season as a field archaeologist was in 1938 when she worked on a Bronze Age site in Palestine.

While Murray was an influential teacher and prolific author in Egyptology, her greatest recognition came for her studies of European witchcraft; among other startling and generally unaccepted conclusions was the claim that Joan of Arc was a witch (i.e., a leader of a pagan cult).

Murray was president of the Folklore Society from 1953 to 1955. Her autobiography, *My First Hundred Years*, went through two editions in July 1963. She died four months later.

MAJOR WORKS: (editor and major contributor) *The Osireion at Abydos* (London: 1904); *Ancient Egyptian Legends* (London: 1913); *The Witch-cult in Western Europe* (Oxford: 1921); *Egyptian Sculpture* (New York: 1930); *The God of the Witches* (London: 1931); *Egyptian Temples* (London: 1931); (with J.C. Ellis) *A Street in Petra* (London: 1940); *Egyptian Religious Poetry* (London: 1949); *The Splendour that Was Egypt* (New York: 1949); *The Divine King in England* (London: 1954); *The Genesis of Religion* (London: 1963).

SOURCES: "Dr. Margaret Murray's hundredth birthday," *Man*, vol. 63 (1963), p. 106; Margaret Murray, *My First Hundred Years* (London: 1963); "Dr. Margaret Murray," *The Times* [London] (15 November 1963), p. 21; "Murray, Margaret Alice," *Contemporary Authors*, vol. 5-8 (1969), pp. 809-810.

David Lonergan

Mussolini, Gioconda. Anthropologist. Born in São Paulo (Brazil) 15 November 1913, died in São Paulo (Brazil) 28 May 1969. Mussolini belonged to the pioneering generation of social scientists who introduced modern anthropology and sociology to Brazil and who established the Faculdade de Filosofia, Ciências e Letras (Faculty of Philosophy, Sciences and Letters) at the University of São Paulo on the eve of World War II.

Above all a teacher, Mussolini was trained at a government normal school. She worked as a school teacher while studying in the Political and Social Sciences Section of the Faculdade de Filosofia, Ciências e Letras of the University of São Paulo, from which she graduated in 1937. In 1941 she entered the Escola Livre de Sociologia e Política (Free School of Sociology and Political Science) of São Paulo from which she obtained her M.A. in 1945 with the thesis *Os meios de defesa contra a moléstia e a morte em duas tribos brasileiras: Kaingang de Dugue de Caxias e Bororó Ocidental*, written under the guidance of HERBERT BALDUS. In her professional training she was influenced by EMÍLIO WILLEMS and ROGER BASTIDE, scholars with whom she studied and, later, worked as assistant and collaborator. She also studied with CLAUDE LÉVI-STRAUSS and A.R. RADCLIFFE-BROWN, among other foreign professors who taught in São Paulo during the war and shortly after it.

She was probably the first Brazilian woman to choose anthropology as her career and profession. Her principal intellectual contribution was as a teacher, and she trained more than a generation of anthropologists. She possessed a special interest in psychology and physical anthropology, as a function of which she gave a number of courses and conferences.

Her professional career at the University of São Paulo began in 1938 in the Department of Sociology where she was researcher and later teaching assistant (Bastide was a professor in this department from 1943 to 1945). In 1944 she was transferred to anthropology as the second assistant to Willems and was promoted in 1957 to first assistant to fill the vacancy of EGON SCHADEN when he was promoted to interim professor. She remained in this position until 1964 when she was named head of the anthropology department for the evening course of study. In 1969 the college decided not to reappoint her to that post because she did not have the doctorate as required by the university. Two months later, she died.

Her name is intimately associated with the study of the way of life of small fishing villages on the north coast of the state of São Paulo and the social and cultural transformations resulting from the introduction of new fishing technology and the growth of the market economy. She gave particular attention to the migration of fishermen and their families from the small towns to the large urban centers. She began her research in 1945 when she participated in a project coordinated by Willems that resulted in the book *Cunha: tradição e transição em uma cultura rural do Brasil*. She followed the process of social change in that region until the late 1960s, publishing several articles and producing a large volume of still unpublished notes. Her field notes were deposited in the college where she taught.

In close connection with her classroom work, she carefully translated more than fifty articles for use by students and researchers and two books as well: *Race Relations* by Otto Klineberg and *The Meaning of Evolution* by G.G. Simpson. Some of these articles, to which she added commentaries and many bibliographic suggestions for the reader, were gathered together in the volume *Evolução, raça e cultura*, which still influences Brazilian anthropology students.

MAJOR WORKS: "Notas sobre os conceitos de moléstia, cura e morte entre os índios Valpidiana," *Sociologia*, vol. 6, no. 2 (1944), pp. 134-155; "O cerco de tainha na Ilha de São Sebastião," *Sociologia*, vol. 7, no. 3 (1945), pp. 135-147; "O cerco flutuante: uma rede de pesca japonesa que teve a Ilha de São Sebastião com centro de difusão no Brasil," *Sociologia*, vol. 8 no. 3 (1946), pp. 172-181 [also in: *Paulistania* (October-December 1949)]; "Os pasquins do litoral norte do Estado de São Paulo e suas peculiaridades na Ilha de São Sebastião," *Revista do Arquivo Municipal*, vol. 34 (1950), pp. 5-68; (with Egon Schaden) *Povos e trajes da América Latina* (São Paulo: 1951); (with Emílio Willems) *Buzios Island: a Caiçara Community in Southern Brazil* (New York: 1952) (= *Monographs of the American Ethnological Society*, no. 20); "Die Lebensweise der brasilianischen Küstenbevölkerung," *Staden-Jahrbuch: Beiträge zur Brasilkunde*, vol. 2 (1954), pp. 13-32 [tr.: "Aspectos da cultura e da vida social no litoral brasileiro," *Revista de Antropologia*, vol. 1 (1953), pp. 81-97]; "Persistência e mudança em sociedades de 'Folk' no Brasil," *Anais do XXXI Congresso Internacional de Americanistas (1954)* (São Paulo: 1954), vol. 2, pp. 333-355; entries on Antonio Candido, Florestan Fernandes, Emílio Willems, Oliveira Vianna and Arthur Ramos in: Wilhelm Bansdorf (editor), *Internationales Soziologenlexikon* (Stuttgart: 1959); "Os japoneses e a pesca comercial no litoral-norte de São Paulo," *Revista do Museu Paulista*, vol. 14 (1963), pp. 283-297; *Evolução, raça e cultura: leituras de antropologia física* (São Paulo: 1969); *Ensaios de antropologia indígena e caiçara* (edited by Edgard Carone) (Rio de Janeiro: 1980) (= *Coleção estudos brasileiros*, vol. 38).

SOURCES: Archives of the University of São Paulo; Claude Lévi-Strauss, *Tristes tropiques* (Paris: 1955); F. Fernandes, "Nota da editôra" in: Gioconda Mussolini, *Evolução, raça e cultura: leituras de antropologia física* (São Paulo: 1969), pp. xi-xx; Antonio Candido, "Prefácio" to: Gioconda Mussolini, *Ensaios de antropologia indígena e caiçara* (edited by Edgard Carone) (Rio de Janeiro: 1980) (= *Coleção estudos brasileiros*, vol. 38), pp. 9-13.

Antônio Augusto Arantes
[Translation from Portuguese: Margo L. Smith]

n

Nadel, S.F. (Siegfried Frederick). Anthropologist, philosopher, scientist, psychologist. Born in Vienna (Austria) 24 April 1903, died in Canberra (Australian Capital Territory) 14 January 1956. Nadel received a doctoral degree in psychology and philosophy (1925) from the University of Vienna; he had also received earlier training in musical composition and conducting. Anthropology studies at the London School of Economics with BRONISLAW MALINOWSKI and C.G. SELIGMAN were a prelude to much productive fieldwork. He worked with the Nupe and related groups in northern Nigeria (1934-1936) and with the Nuba of the Anglo-Egyptian Sudan (1938-1940). A deeply moral man, he enlisted in the Sudan Defence Force, desiring a personal involvement with the destruction of the Nazi forces. During his army career (1941-1946) he was Secretary for Native Affairs in the British Military Administration in Asmara and received a gazetted commendation "for outstanding service." After the war he spent a year as a Lecturer at the London School of Economics, after which he was appointed Reader in Anthropology and Head of the Department at King's College, Newcastle, University of Durham. In 1950 he accepted the Chair in Anthropology at the new Australian National University, a post he held until his death.

Linguistic talents, sociability, great energy and a sharp analytical mind worked together to produce outstanding ethnographic writings, most of which artfully interlaced hard facts with insightful theory. Two works, *The Foundations of Social Anthropology* and *A Theory of Social Structure*, established Nadel as a major theoretician who attempted to develop a new synthesis of social sciences. Anthropology, Nadel argued, is a science and therefore must go beyond description to explanation; further, and consistent with cybernetic theory, in order to explain human behavior one must posit purpose. Human action, in response to two basic problems, has two "ulterior purposes": to satisfy human needs and to satisfy social system "needs." In *Foundations*, individual needs are given priority over system "needs." However, in *A Theory of Social Structure*, a brilliant conceptual scheme transforms matters of priority into more useful questions of interlinkage. The key lies in a systematic analysis of individuals as actors in role relationships. A complete description requires consideration of three aspects of roles: the allocation principles, the authority lodged in roles, and the degree to which roles command resources and benefits. The latter, are usefully classified into six types: material wealth; social dignity; cognitive values; emotional, sensual and aesthetic gratification; moral values; and transcendental values. Nadel's model, still in need of further elaboration at the time of his death, holds the promise of bringing "social structure," a highly abstract and frequently used concept, out of the sphere of armchair theorizing and into the world of empirical research. The death of Nadel at the height of his intellectual powers was a serious loss to anthropology. His challenge remains a modern goal: to link the "Study of Man with the whole universe of scientific knowledge."

MAJOR WORKS: "Nupe state and community," *Africa*, vol. 8 (1935), pp. 257-303; "Gunnu: a fertility cult of the Nupe in Northern Nigeria," *Journal of the Royal Anthropological Institute of Great Britain and Ireland*, vol. 67 (1937), pp. 91-130; *A Black Byzantium: the Kingdom of Nupe in Nigeria* (Oxford: 1942); *The Nuba: an Anthropological Study of the Hill Tribes in Kordofan* (Oxford: 1947); *The Foundations of Social Anthropology* (London and Glencoe, Ill.: 1951); "Witchcraft in four African societies: an essay in comparison," *American Anthropologist*, n.s., vol. 54 (1952), pp. 18-29; *Nupe Religion* (Glencoe, Ill.: 1954); *The Theory of Social Structure* (London and Glencoe, Ill.: 1957).

SOURCES: R. Dahrendorf, "S.F. Nadel" in: Wilhelm Bernsdorf (editor), *Internationales Soziologen-Lexikon* (Stuttgart: 1959), p. 410; Raymond Firth, "Siegfried Frederick Nadel: 1903-1956," *American Anthropologist*, n.s., vol. 59 (1957), pp. 117-124; Meyer Fortes, "Siegfried Frederick Nadel, 1903-1956: a Memoir" in: S.F. Nadel, *The Theory of Social Structure* (London and Glencoe, Ill.: 1957), pp. ix-xvi; Morris Freilich, "Toward a model of social structure," *Journal of the Royal Anthropological Institute of Great Britain and Ireland*, vol. 94 (1964), pp. 183-200; Morris Freilich, "Nadel, Siegfried" in: David L. Sills (editor), *International Encyclopedia of the Social Sciences* (New York: 1968-1979), vol. 11, pp. 1-3; E.R. Leach, Review of *The Foundations of Social Anthropology*, *Africa*, vol. 21 (1951), pp. 243-244.

Morris Freilich

Nash, Philleo. Anthropologist, public official, cranberry grower. Born in Wisconsin Rapids (Wisconsin) 25 October 1909, died in Marshfield (Wisconsin) 12 October 1987. Respected among his colleagues as an applied anthropologist, Nash was the only member of his profession to head the Bureau of Indian Affairs. He was unique, also, in holding high elective office at the state level and in serving two American presidents as a principal advisor on civil rights and minority affairs.

Nash began the formal study of anthropology at the University of Wisconsin, from which he received a baccalaureate degree in 1932; RALPH LINTON was one of his professors. He enrolled as a graduate student at the University of Chicago and began his first important research among Native Americans in 1934. This research, directed by LESLIE SPIER, was on the Klamath Indian Reservation in Oregon and led to a dissertation and, in 1937, a doctoral degree. A condensed version of the dissertation entitled "The place of religious revivalism in the formation of the intercultural community on Klamath Reservation" was published in *Social Anthropology of North American Tribes: Essays in*

Social Organization, Law and Religion. This volume, edited by FRED EGGAN, was presented to A.R. RADCLIFFE-BROWN in 1937 on the occasion of his accepting the chair of social anthropology at Oxford University.

After receiving his doctorate, Nash accepted an appointment at the University of Toronto where he lectured in anthropology and was Assistant Keeper of Ethnological Collections of the Royal Ontario Museum. He remained in Toronto until 1941, when he returned to Wisconsin to help manage the family cranberry marsh and to teach at the University of Wisconsin. In 1942, shortly after the outbreak of World War II, he began work for the Office of War Information. Four years later, President Franklin D. Roosevelt named him a special assistant for minority affairs. He continued in this position during the administration of President Harry S. Truman, with whom he worked closely on matters having to do with civil rights.

Following Truman's departure from the White House, Nash returned again to Wisconsin, where he became active in politics. From 1959 to 1961 he held the office of Lieutenant Governor. He went to Washington in 1961 to serve on a special task force on Indian affairs appointed by Secretary of the Interior Stewart L. Udall. When the task force finished its work in the summer of 1961, President John F. Kennedy appointed him Commissioner of Indian Affairs. After Kennedy's assassination, President Lyndon B. Johnson kept Nash in this post, which he held until 1966. Retired from government service, he returned to academic life and taught at American University from 1971 to 1977. Nash spent the final ten years of his life in Wisconsin.

During his career, Nash held several elected positions in professional societies, among them President of the Society for Applied Anthropology, Treasurer of the American Anthropological Association, and Secretary of the Anthropology Section of the American Association for the Advancement of Science. He was a recipient of the Bronislaw Malinowski Award of the Society for Applied Anthropology and of the Distinguished Service Award of the American Anthropological Association.

MAJOR WORKS: "The place of religious revivalism in the formation of the intercultural community on Klamath Reservation" in: Fred Eggan (editor), *Social Anthropology of North American Tribes: Essays in Social Organization, Law, and Religion* (Chicago: 1937), pp. 377-442; "An introduction to the problem of race tension" in: C.T. Loram and T.F. McIlwraith (editors), *The North American Indian Today* (Toronto: 1943), pp. 331-335; "Applied anthropology and the concept of guided acculturation" in: James E. Officer and Francis McKinley (editors), *Anthropology and the American Indian* (San Francisco: 1973), pp. 23-34; "Anthropologist in the White House," *Practicing Anthropology*, vol. 1, no. 3 (1979), pp. 3, 23-24; "Science, politics, and human values," *Human Organization*, vol. 45 (1986), pp. 189-201.

SOURCES: Margaret Connel Szasz, "Philleo Nash" in: Robert M. Krasnicka and Herman J. Viola (editors), *The Commissioners of Indian Affairs 1842-1977* (Lincoln, Nebr.: 1979), pp. 311-323; James E. Officer, "Philleo Nash (1909-1987)," *American Anthropologist*, vol. 90 (1988), pp. 952-956; Ruth H. Landman and Katherine Spencer Halpern (editors), *Applied Anthropologist and Public Servant: the Life and Work of Philleo Nash* (Washington: 1989) (= *NAPA Bulletin*, no. 7). Documents related to Nash's years of public service are in the Truman Library in Independence, Missouri, and in the Stewart L. Udall Archive of the University of Arizona Library. Tape recordings of interviews with Nash are in the John F. Kennedy Library in Boston.

James E. Officer

Nelson, Edward W. Naturalist, ethnographer, government administrator, meteorological observer, rancher. Born in Manchester (New Hampshire) 8 May 1855, died in Washington (D.C.) 19 May 1934. Edward William Nelson's early education was in the public schools of Franklin County (New York) and Chicago (Illinois). He attended Northwestern University in 1875 and the Johns Hopkins University during 1876-1877. He received an honorary M.A. from Yale University and an Sc.D. from George Washington University, both in 1920.

Nelson gained field experience as a naturalist with Samuel Garman and Edward Drinker Cope in Nevada, Utah and California in 1872. Thereafter he began correspondence with the naturalist HENRY WETHERBEE HENSHAW, who urged him to contact Spencer F. Baird, of the Smithsonian Institution. Thus Nelson came within the circle of naturalists that Baird guided in the collection of specimens and data. In 1877 Baird secured Nelson an appointment as a private (weather observer) in the U.S. Signal Corps with assignment to St. Michael, Alaska, and Nelson continued there until 1881. While in Alaska he traveled widely—along the coast from the mouth of the Kuskokwim River to Barrow and the islands of the Bering Sea and Siberia and in the Alaskan interior mainly in the region of the lower Yukon River. In those lands he carried out his only anthropological work, amassing the almost 10,000 items that form one of the earliest, richest and best documented collections of native Alaskan material culture. He also collected considerable data on Eskimo and Northern Athabaskan cultures. Most of his artifacts and photographs are now in the Smithsonian. His ethnographic data appear to have survived mainly in his anthropological publications; repeated attempts to locate a cache of original field notes have failed.

When Nelson returned from Alaska, he developed tuberculosis and sought rest and clean air in the West, working there as a rancher. In 1890 he resumed his biological work for the U.S. government, exploring widely in California and Mexico. By 1916 he had become Chief of the U.S. Bureau of Biological Survey, a position he held until he retired in 1927.

MAJOR WORKS: *Report upon Natural History Collection Made in Alaska Between the Years 1877 and 1881* (Washington: 1887) (= *Sen. Misc. Doc.*, 156, 49th Cong., 1st Sess.); "The Eskimo about Bering Strait," *Annual Report of the Bureau of American Ethnology*, vol. 18 (1899), pp. 3-518.

SOURCES: Jenks Cameron, *The Bureau of Biological Survey* (Baltimore: 1929); Henry B. Collins, "The man who buys good-for-nothing things" in: William W. Fitzhugh and Susan A. Kaplan, *Inua: Spirit World of the Bering Sea Eskimo* (Washington: 1982), pp. 29-37; Edward A. Goldman, "Edward William Nelson—naturalist, 1855-1834," *The Auk*, vol. 52 (1935), pp. 135-148; Margaret Lantis, "Edward William Nelson," *Anthropological Papers of the University of Alaska*, vol. 3 (1954), pp. 5-16; Paul Oesher, "Nelson and Goldman," *Cosmos Club Bulletin*, vol. 5 (1951), pp. 2-6; Witmer Stone, "Nelson, Dr. Edward William" in: T.S. Palmer, *Biographies of the Members of the American Ornithologists' Union* (Washington: 1954), pp. 418-419; Tom Sexton, "A guide to the photographs of Edward W. Nelson" [copy available for examination at the Smithsonian Institution National Anthropological Archives]; James W. VanStone, *E.W. Nelson's Notes on the Indians of the Yukon and Innoko Rivers, Alaska* (Chicago: 1978) (= *Fieldiana Anthropology*, vol. 70; = *Field Museum of Natural History Publication*, no. 1281).

James R. Glenn

Nelson, George. Fur trader, writer. Born probably in Montréal (Québec) 4 June 1786, died in Sorel (Québec) 13 July 1859. The eldest child of an English-born schoolmaster, Nelson entered the Canadian fur trade in 1802 as an apprentice clerk in the XY Company, trading among the Ojibwa of northern Wisconsin. When that company was absorbed in the North West Company in 1804, Nelson was posted to the Lake Winnipeg region (Manitoba) where he spent most of his subsequent career. After the North West and Hudson's Bay companies merged in 1821, he continued as a clerk in the new firm but was retired in 1823 as one of many employees found redundant after the merger. His later life in Québec was marked by poverty and the early deaths of his Ojibwa wife and all but one of their eight children.

Nelson's writings (none of which were published in his lifetime) are a rich collection of on-the-spot fur trade journals and letters as well as reminiscences set down in the last twenty-five years of his life. Fluent in the Ojibwa language and familiar with Cree, he recorded as much as he could learn about Northern Algonquian life, mythology and religion as well as the everyday details of his trading relations with groups and individuals (whom he generally named). He never explored the north on the scale of a SAMUEL HEARNE, ALEXANDER MACKENZIE or DAVID THOMPSON; nor did he attain fame or career success. But his detailed documentation of the Lake Winnipeg region and its people in the early 1800s constitutes a unique ethnohistorical record of an area he came to know in depth. Outstanding among his papers is his 1823 letter-journal written at Lac la Ronge (Saskatchewan) in which he sympathetically recorded more details on Algonquian religion and myth than any other fur trader of his period (*"The Orders of the Dreamed"*). Although reflecting the cultural and religious biases of his time, Nelson's concern for accuracy, his listening ability, his critical stance toward his own culture and the extent to which he was moved and impressed by the Indian ceremonials he witnessed set him apart from most writers of his century.

MAJOR WORKS: Richard Bardon and Grace Lee Nute (editors), "A winter in the St. Croix Valley, 1802-1803," *Minnesota History*, vol. 28 (1947), pp. 1-14, 142-159, 225-240 [reminiscences by G. Nelson]; Jennifer S.H. Brown and Robert Brightman (editors), *"The Orders of the Dreamed": George Nelson on Cree and Northern Ojibwa Religion and Myth, 1823* (Winnipeg and St. Paul: 1988); unpublished MSS, Metropolitan Public Library of Toronto.

SOURCES: Jennifer S.H. Brown, "Man in his natural state: the Indian worlds of George Nelson" in: Thomas C. Buckley (editor), *Rendezvous: Selected Papers of the Fourth North American Fur Trade Conference, 1981* (St. Paul: 1984), pp. 199-206; Sylvia Van Kirk, "George Nelson's 'wretched' career, 1802-1823" in: Thomas C. Buckley (editor), *Rendezvous: Selected Papers of the Fourth North American Fur Trade Conference, 1981* (St. Paul: 1984), pp. 207-214; Sylvia Van Kirk and Jennifer S.H. Brown, "George Nelson" in: *Dictionary of Canadian Biography* (Toronto: 1985), vol. 8, pp. 652-654; Sylvia Van Kirk, "This rascally and ungrateful country: George Nelson's response to Rupert's Land" in: Richard C. Davis (editor), *Rupert's Land: a Cultural Tapestry* (Waterloo: 1988), pp. 113-130; Jennifer S.H. Brown, "From Sorel to Lake Winnipeg: George Nelson as an ethnohistorical source" in: Barry M. Gough (editor), *New Directions in Ethnohistory: Papers of the Second Laurier Conference* (Ottawa: forthcoming) (= *Canadian Museum of Civilization, Mercury Series*).

Jennifer S.H. Brown

Nelson, Nels Christian. Archaeologist. Born near Fredericia (Denmark) 9 April 1875, died in New York (New York) 5 March 1964. Nelson is best remembered for his contributions to stratigraphic techniques. In 1912 Nelson toured European archaeological sites and, while visiting Castillo Cave (Spain), he spent several weeks excavating in the well stratified Paleolithic remains. In his subsequent excavations at San Cristobal pueblo (New Mexico) in 1914, Nelson developed a method of imposing artificial levels to determine minute chronological changes. At that time, the cultural chronology of the American Southwest was utterly unknown, and Nelson's painstaking excavations and analysis of the recovered ceramics provided the first solid chronological framework. This research in the Galisteo Basin is generally acknowledged as the first significant stratigraphic archaeology in the Americas.

Nelson's earliest contribution was an archaeological survey of the shell middens surrounding the San Francisco Bay (California). Walking more than 3,000 miles, he recorded 425 prehistoric shell mounds. His unusually complete report described the location of these sites relative to natural resources, listed the animal bones recovered, and pondered the ecological adaptation implied by such a bayside lifeway. Since most of these sites are now destroyed, Nelson's map and description, originally published in 1909, remain an irreplaceable resource to California archaeology.

After obtaining employment at the American Museum of Natural History, Nelson began working in the American Southwest, where he introduced his important innovations in stratigraphic excavation. In the next few years, he excavated caves in Kentucky and Missouri and more shell mounds in Florida. Nelson accompanied an American Museum of Natural History expedition to the Gobi desert in 1925. Nelson typified early-20th-century museum-based archaeology. He continued to be a force in American archaeology until his retirement in 1943.

MAJOR WORKS: "Shellmounds of the San Francisco Bay Region," *University of California Publications in American Archaeology and Ethnology*, vol. 7 (1909), pp. 310-356; "Pueblo ruins of the Galisteo Basin, New Mexico," *Anthropological Papers of the American Museum of Natural History*, vol. 15, no. 1 (1916); "Chronology of the Tano ruins," *American Anthropologist*, vol. 18 (1916), pp. 159-180.

SOURCES: Leslie Spier, "N.C. Nelson's stratigraphic technique in the reconstruction of prehistoric sequences in Southwestern America" in: S.A. Rice (editor), *Methods in Social Science* (Chicago: 1931), pp. 275-283; Richard B. Woodbury, "Nels C. Nelson and chronological archaeology," *American Antiquity*, vol. 25 (1960), pp. 400-401; Gordon R. Willey and Jeremy A. Sabloff, *A History of American Archaeology* (New York: 1980), pp. 85-89; David Hurst Thomas, *Archaeology* (2nd ed., New York: 1989), pp. 35-37, 270-275, 316-320.

David H. Thomas

Newman, Stanley S. Linguist, anthropologist, poet. Born in Chicago (Illinois) 18 July 1905, died 26 August 1984. Newman grew up speaking Czech and English and learned German during an extended visit to Prague when he was eight. He entered the University of Chicago in 1924. At a meeting of the University Poetry Club he met EDWARD SAPIR, and he later took Sapir's course on the "Psychology of Culture." In the summer of 1930 Newman took his first field trip to California to study the Yokuts language and collect the data on Yawelmani Yokuts that formed the basis of his dissertation. When Sapir moved to Yale the following year, Newman followed and soon completed his doctorate. He remained at Yale for the next five years, working on English grammar, phonetic symbolism and the speech of psychotic patients. He also gathered data on different Yokuts dialects and on Bella Coola.

During World War II Newman worked with Henry Lee Smith in the Language Section of the Army Service Forces and was put in charge of courses in "Reverse English" (today, TESOL). At the end of the war, Newman was transferred to the Institute of Social Anthropology of the Smithsonian Institution. He was sent to Mexico City to teach linguistics at the Escuela Nacional de Antropología e Historia and to conduct research on Nahuatl and Otomi. After three productive years in Mexico, Newman accepted a position at the University of New Mexico in 1949. In Albuquerque he taught a variety of courses in general anthropology and linguistics. He also undertook studies of two Pueblo Indian languages of New Mexico (Laguna Keresan and Zuni). During the 1950s Newman was invited to teach at the summer institutes of the Linguistic Society of America. He also participated in an early conference of linguists and psychologists. During the 1960s Newman became a co-editor of the *Southwestern Journal of Anthropology* (now the *Journal of Anthropological Research*).

Newman's imaginative research and teaching were always grounded in a mastery of linguistic details and cultural patterns. When his grammar of Yokuts was first published, many readers considered it "too abstract," yet it is today recognized as a classic. Newman retired from teaching in 1971, but he continued work on his Salish materials. His contribution to linguistics was recognized when a special issue of the *International Journal of American Linguistics* was dedicated to him in 1975, and in 1984 he became President-elect of the Linguistic Society of America.

MAJOR WORKS: *Yokuts Language of California* (New York: 1944) (= *Viking Fund Publications in Anthropology*, vol. 2); *Zuni Dictionary* (Bloomington: 1958) (= *Indiana University Research Center in Anthropology, Folklore, and Linguistics Publication*, no. 6); *Zuni Grammar* (Albuquerque: 1965) (= *University of New Mexico Publications in Anthropology*, no. 14); *How I Discovered Linguistics* [mimeo manuscript] (1984); "The development of Sapir's psychology of human behavior" in: W. Cowan, M.K. Foster, and K. Koerner (editors), *New Perspectives in Language, Culture, and Personality* (Amsterdam and Philadelphia: 1986), pp. 405-431.

SOURCES: Philip Bock and Harry Basehart, "Stanley S. Newman (1905-1984)," *American Anthropologist*, vol. 88 (1986), pp. 151-153; Michael Silverstein, "Stanley Newman," *Language*, vol. 63 (1987), pp. 346-360; Mary Ritchie Key and Henry M. Hoenigswald (editors), *General and Amerindian Ethnolinguistics: In Remembrance of Stanley Newman* (Berlin and New York: 1989) [contains bibliography, pp. 33-40].

Philip K. Bock

Nicolucci, Giustiniano. Physician, physical anthropologist. Born in Isola del Liri (Italy) 12 March 1819, died in Isola del Liri (Italy) 15 June 1904. Nicolucci graduated from the University of Naples in medicine and practiced this profession for some time in his home town while concurrently pursuing studies and research on craniology and prehistoric archaeology. In 1857 he published *Delle razze umane: saggio etnologico*, the first systematic Italian treatment of ethnology (which was seen as a physical, racial and paleontological study of humanity). This volume was the result of Nicolucci's research in several Italian museums and laboratories combined with his knowledge of ancient history, archaeology and the most recent international studies in anthropology. In this book, Nicolucci embraced the monogenetic belief concerning the origin of man as the one most in agreement with his religious orientation. In the years following the appearance of this text, he continued his research and excavations, demonstrating through fossil findings the gradual evolution and, most importantly, the antiquity of the human species, which was unequivo-cably older than that estimated by Biblical chronologies. However, Nicolucci was always extremely cautious in his treatment of Darwin's theories ("Darwinismo e antropologia" and "Darwinismo secondo i più recenti studi").

Nicolucci was largely an independent scholar who only began teaching anthropo-logy at the University of Naples in 1880. Even after his late recognition, he remained on the margins of both the scientific debate and the statutory construction of studies. He be-longed more to the 18th-century school of erudite encyclopedism than to that of the new theories. He established no school and was only formally tied to the Società di Antropologia of PAOLO MANTEGAZZA where he was the absentee vice-president be-ginnning in 1879.

During his long and extensive research in paleontology and prehistoric archaeo-logy Nicolucci had much contact with Heinrich Schliemann (from whom he received several Trojan objects), and he gathered a notable collection of prehistoric, osteological and ethnographic objects that he sent in part to the Hunter Museums of London and Harvard Museum in the United States. The rest of his collection was placed in the Cabinet of Anthropology at the University of Naples where it was completely abandoned after his death.

MAJOR WORKS: *Delle razze umane: saggio etnologico* [2 vols.] (Naples: 1857-1858); *Catalogo della collezione di oggetti preistorici dell'età della pietra posseduti da G. Nicolucci in Isola del Liri* (Naples: 1877); *Prolusione al corso di antropologia, dettato nella R. Università di Napoli, recitata il 22 aprile 1880* (Naples: 1880) [reproduced in: Francesco Fedele (editor), *G. Nicolucci: alle origini dell'antropologia moderna* (Isola del Liri: 1985), pp. 221-230]; "Il Darwinismo e l'antropologia," *L'Anomalo* (1884), pp. 27-35; "Il Darwinismo secondo i più recenti studi," *Rendiconto dell'Accademia delle Scienze fisiche e matematiche di Napoli*, vol. 25 (1886), pp. 223-230; *Antropologia dell'Italia nell'Evo antico e nel moderno* (Naples: 1887); *I nostri vicini d'Africa* (Naples: 1890).

SOURCES: Riccardo Riccardi, *Saggio di un catalogo bibliografico antropologico italiano: cenni storici intorno all'antropologia e biografici intorno ad alcuni antropologi italiani* (Modena: 1883); Vincenzo Giuffrida-Ruggeri, "A sketch of the anthropology of Italy," *Journal of the Royal Anthropological Institute of Great Britain and Ireland*, vol. 48 (1918), pp. 80-102; Francesco Fedele (editor), *G. Nicolucci: alle origini dell'antropologia moderna* (Isola del Liri: 1985); Sandra Puccini, "Gli studi demo-etno-antropologici dell'Ottocento e G. Nicolucci," *La ricerca folklorica*, no. 12 (October 1985), pp. 131-135; Francesco Fedele and Alberto Baldi (editors), *Alle origini dell'antropologia italiana: G. Nicolucci e il suo tempo* (Naples: 1988).

Sandra Puccini
[Translation from Italian: Phyllis Liparini]

Nigra, Costantino. Politician, savant with literary and historical interests in dialectology and popular poetry. Born in Villa Castelnuovo, Aosta (Italy) 11 June 1828, died in Rapallo (Italy) 1 January 1907. Nigra had a distinguished diplomatic and political career in the first years of the Kingdom of Italy. He was also, with ALESSANDRO D'ANCONA, one of the first scholars of popular Italian literature to adopt philological-comparative methods with a positivist character.

Nigra believed that a fundamental distinction ought to be made between the "poetic content" of a text and the way in which it is communicated, i.e., its metric, formal aspects. It was to this second element that Nigra applied his own analytic criteria, going so far as to construct his "theory of the ethnic substratum." According to this theory, popular poetry was an expression of the "ethnic base" which, in Romance-language populations, went back to pre-Latin culture. After the fall of the Roman Empire, the "ethnic base" affected the development of each of the various Romance dialects and languages, influencing, for example, the metric peculiarities of each dialect's poetry.

Through a detailed comparison of collections of regional poems—at the time already available in considerable number—Nigra reached the conclusion that in the Italian population one could identify two distinct ethnic substrata. The first, located in the northern regions, was thought to be of Celtic origin and was marked by the production of historical narrative *canzoni*. The second, located in south-central Italy, was instead considered to be of indigenous Italic origin and was characterized by its lyrical love poetry. Comparing these two thematic orders with the corresponding metric forms of expression, Nigra associated the *canzoni* of the Italian North with French-Hispanic poetic tradition.

The theory of the ethnic substratum sparked lively discussions in academic circles. In terms of methodology, it is even today recognized for its having made a clear distinction between the contents and the form of the poetic text (to which little attention had been paid until that time) and for its having applied philological analysis and comparison rigorously.

One can say that, with the works of Nigra and D'Ancona, Italian studies on popular Italian poetry entered definitively into the orbit of European debate, having by now completely abandoned the criteria of aesthetic content that had characterized studies in the romantic tradition.

MAJOR WORKS: *Canzoni popolari del Piemonte* [6 parts] (Turin: 1856-1862); "La poesia popolare italiana," *Romania*, vol. 5 (1876), pp. 417-452; *Canti popolari del Piemonte* (Turin: 1888); *Rappresentazioni popolari in Piemonte: il Natale in Canavese* (Turin: 1894).

SOURCES: A.M. Cirese, *Cultura egemonica e culture subalterne* (Palermo: 1980); G. Grana (editor), *Letteratura italiana: i criteri* (Milan: 1969).

Gianni Vanucci
[Translation from Italian: CW and Paolo Gnecco]

Nimuendajú, Curt (Curt (or Kurt) Un(c)kel before 1910). Ethnographer. Born in Jena, Saxony (Germany) 17 April 1883, died in Santa Rita (Brazil) about 10 December 1945. Orphaned from the first year of his life, Unckel was brought up by his grandmother in Jena and at age sixteen entered the factory of Carl Zeiss in his home town as a mechanics apprentice. Social welfare and educational opportunities offered by his employer fostered Unckel's intellectual interests, in spite of a lack of formal graduation from high school. He emigrated in 1903 to Brazil and only two years later was already fully immersed in ethnographic research among Guaraní Indians in southern and southeastern Brazil. He was adopted by the subgroup of Apapocuvá-Guaraní into the tribe and received the Indian name "Nimuendajú" which he henceforeward used as his second name, dropping his birthname "Unckel." His fieldwork resulted in one of his major and most influential works ("Die Sagen von der Erschaffung und Vernichtung der Welt").

An untiring fieldworker until his death, Nimuendajú studied, collected artifacts from and published substantially on fifty different Indian tribes of Brazil. His outstanding ethnographic skills were recognized by leading institutions. The ethnographic museums at

Göteborg, Leipzig, Dresden and Hamburg, the Carnegie Institution of Washington and the University of California at Berkeley (in this chronological sequence) commissioned artifact collections, monographs and general research by Nimuendajú. From these commissions he made his and his wife's living in Belém do Pará. When in 1934 his German patrons where not able or willing to continue the cooperation, it was of great help that through the good services of ROBERT H. LOWIE, Nimuendajú was selected as a contributor to the *Handbook of South American Indians*. He contributed thirteen tribal monographs to the *Handbook*, all translated from the German or Portuguese original, edited and sometimes co-authored by Lowie. The collaboration with Lowie lasted throughout the last decade of Nimuendajú's life and produced further important monographs (e.g., *The Tukuna*).

Nimuendajú's most influential study is his early research on the decline of traditional nativism among the Tupí-Guaraní. This was the basis for several subsequent studies by ALFRED MÉTRAUX that he published in his comprehensive work on pre-Columbian migratory movements in Lowland South America ("Migrations historiques des Tupi-Guarani," *Journal de la Société des Américanistes de Paris*, n.s., vol. 19 (1927), pp. 1-45) and also by EGON SCHADEN ("Paradiesmythen im Leben der Guaraní-Indianer," *Staden Jahrbuch*, vol. 3 (1955), pp. 151-162). Nimuendajú's monograph still stands as the classic case study for the theory of nativism (see, e.g., WILHELM EMIL MÜHLMANN, *Chiliasmus und Nativismus* (Berlin: 1961)). Nimuendajú must also be credited with the discovery and first adequate description of the complex social organization (dual organization, age sets, secret societies) among the Gê Indians of eastern Brazil (who were only superficially known and who were thought to be socially "primitive" as a correlate of their nomadic life style and reduced group sizes). His field methods are outstanding in their balance between "going-native" and rigorous observation and documentation (including material, intellectual, social and linguistic aspects) and through the fact that he re-studied many tribes over an extended period of time.

MAJOR WORKS: "Die Sagen von der Erschaffung und Vernichtung der Welt als Grundlagen der Religion der Apapocuvá-Guaraní," *Zeitschrift für Ethnologie*, vol. 46 (1914), pp. 284-403; *Die Palikur-Indianer und ihre Nachbarn* (Göteborg: 1926) (= *Göteborgs Kungl. Vetenskaps- och Vitterhets-Samhälles Handlingar*, 4th series, vol. 31, no. 2); *The Apinaye'* (Washington: 1939) (= *Catholic University of America, Anthropological Series*, no. 8); *The Eastern Timbirá* (Berkeley: 1946) (= *University of California Publications in American Archaeology and Ethnology*, no. 41); thirteen articles on different Brazilian tribes in: Julian H. Steward (editor), *Handbook of South American Indians* (Washington: 1948), vol. 3; *The Tukuna* (Berkeley: 1952) (= *University of California Publications in American Archaeology and Ethnology*, no. 45); "Mitos indígenas inéditos na obra de Curt Nimuendajú," *Revista do Patrimonio*, vol. 21 (1986), pp. 64-112.

SOURCES: Pola Brückner, *Eine Frau ging in den Urwald*. (Berlin: 1939); Nemas Pereira [i.e., Herbert Baldus], "Curt Nimuendajú: síntesis de uma vida e de uma obra," *Sociologia*, vol. 8 (1946), pp. 45-52; Robert H. Lowie, *Ethnologist* (Berkeley and Los Angeles: 1959), pp. 119-126; Egon Schaden, "Curt Nimuendajú, quarenta anos a serviço do índio brasileiro e ao estudo de suas culturas" *Problemas Brasileiros: Revista Mensal de Cultura*, vol. 11, no. 124 (1973), pp. 119-126.

Berthold Riese

Nina Rodrigues, Raimundo. Physician, expert in forensic medicine, anthropologist, psychiatrist. Born in the state of Maranhão (Brazil) 4 December 1862, died in Paris (France) 17 July 1906. Nina Rodrigues is well known to those interested in the study of race relations as the father of Afro-Brazilian studies. He was the first person to observe and record the religious practices of Brazilians of African descent systematically, and it is because of his writing on race that his name survives.

Nina Rodrigues's main impact in his lifetime, however, was as a physician turned expert in forensic medicine. His contributions to the Brazilian criminal code in the early years of the new Republic (*As raças humanas e a responsabilidade penal no Brasil*) and to the civil code (*O alienado no direito civil brasileiro*) earned him a reputation in forensic circles well outside the Medical Faculty in Bahia. His publications in French (some never translated into Portuguese) also made him known to a wide circle of experts in forensic anthropology. In fact, it was while traveling to an International Health Congress in Italy, at the age of forty-four, that he died in Paris, after finally meeting the specialists in French forensic medicine whom he had admired at a distance.

A skilled polemicist, Nina Rodrigues wrote about many of the questions put to the medical profession in his day. He wrote about public health, beriberi, hysteria and leprosy and about some famous criminal cases; he also wrote extensively on the destiny of the insane in Brazilian asylums. He also intervened in the politics of the Medical School in Bahia. His polemical style is exemplified by the censorship evoked in response to an evaluation he wrote of the faculty and the School—published seventy years after his death.

In addition to writing, he actively participated in establishing professional associations and of medical journals and was a member of the Medico-Legal Society of New York and of the Société Medico-Psychologique of Paris.

Heavily influenced by HERBERT SPENCER, as were many of his contemporaries, Nina Rodrigues began his studies of the black population of Brazil as a physical anthropologist and a disciple of CESARE LOMBROSO and his Italian school of criminal anthropology. He changed his views concerning the social and cultural productions of Africans after encountering the contemporary works of Gabriel de Tarde, A. Ellis, ANDREW LANG, JAMES G. FRAZER and E.B. TYLOR. After slavery was abolished in Brazil in 1888, Nina Rodrigues spoke of ethnicity rather than race, to emphasize not only the presence of European immigrants in Brazil but also the diversity resulting from their—and the slaves'—settlement in Brazil. But his preferred theme was the miscegenation of blacks and whites and its result, the mulatto.

Although he remained skeptical to the end about the possibility of blacks' "whitening" (biologically or culturally)—then a strong belief among Brazilian intellectuals—he was a brave champion of blacks' right to their primitiveness. That is, he protested the hypocrisy of the white liberals who granted the slaves their freedom but at the same time persecuted the African religious cults in the name of civilization and ignored the ethnic diversity of the country. Both of his books on blacks in Brazil (*O animismo fetichista dos negros baianos* and *Os Africanos no Brasil*) reflect the prejudices of the time, but both are fine descriptions, elegantly written, of the religious associations, the language, the oral literature and the art of the blacks in Bahia.

MAJOR WORKS: *As raças humanas e a reponsabilidade penal no Brasil* (Bahia: 1894); "Métissage, dégénerescence et crime," *Archives d'anthropologie criminelle* (Lyon: 1899), pp. 1-40; *L'animisme fétichiste des nègres de Bahia* (Bahia: 1900); *O alienado no direito civil brasileiro* (Bahia: 1901); "Atavisme psychique et paranoia" in: *Archives d'anthropologie criminelle* (Lyon: 1902), pp.

325-355; *Os Africanos no Brasil* (São Paulo: 1932); *As collectividades anormaes* (Rio de Janeiro: 1939).

SOURCES: Arthur Ramos, "Afranio Peixoto e a escola de Nina Rodrigues" in: Arthur Ramos, *Loucura e crime* (Porto Alegre: 1937), pp. 188-204; Alcantara Machado, "Nina Rodrigues," *Arquivos de Medicina Legal e Identificação*, no. 18 (1940), pp. 272-280; Edison Carneiro, "Nina Rodrigues" in: E. Carneiro, *Ladinos e crioulos* (Rio de Janeiro: 1964), pp. 209-272; Lamartine de Andrade Lima, "Roteiro de Nina Rodrigues," *Ensaios/Pesquisas*, vol. 2 (1980), pp. 1-12; Mariza Corrêa, *As ilusões da liberdade: a escola Nina Rodrigues e a antropologia no Brasil.* [unpublished Ph.D. thesis, University of São Paulo] (São Paulo: 1982).

Mariza Corrêa

Nordenskiöld, Baron *Erland* (Nils Erland Herbert Nordenskiöld). Ethnographer, anthropologist, archaeologist. Born in Tveta (Sweden) 19 July 1877, died in Göteborg (Sweden) 5 July 1932. Nordenskiöld was the son of the famous Adolf Erik "Vega" Nordenskiöld (who completed the first successful navigation of the Northeast Passage) and inherited the title of "baron." He took his B.A. (*fil. kand.*) at the University of Uppsala in 1890 and got his (honorary) doctorate in 1916 at the University of Göteborg. He became a museum curator at the Ethnographical Museum of Göteborg in 1913 and a professor of ethnography at the University of Göteborg in 1923, a position that he held until his premature death in 1932. In 1926 he also taught for some time at the University of California as a visiting professor.

Nordenskiöld continued the explorative attempts of his family and made several expeditions, especially to South and Central America. He started out as a zoologist and went to Patagonia in 1899 to continue the explorations of his cousin Otto Nordenskiöld. He was still primarily a zoologist at the time of the Swedish Chaco-Cordillera Expedition (1901-1902), an expedition that he led and in which both ERIC BOMAN and ERIC VON ROSEN participated. During this expedition, however, his ethnographic interest took over, and he returned to Sweden as an anthropologist-to-be.

From then on, his expeditions were all ethnographic or archaeological investigations. During 1904-1905 he excavated at several sites in the Bolivian and Peruvian Andes. During his prolonged Chaco-Amazon expedition (1908-1909), he emulated modern anthropological "fieldwork" through his repeated, long stays with the Chorote and the Chiriguano Indians, peoples about whom he published copiously in years to come.

During 1913-1914 he brought his wife, Olga Nordenskiöld, with him on an Argentinian/Bolivian expedition in which he returned to several of the Indian peoples he had met on previous trips. He also "rediscovered" the most important Inca ruins of Bolivia, Incallajta, and mapped them and the surrounding area. His final expedition, in 1927, took him to the Chocó and the Cuna Indians of Colombia and Panama, and thus he initiated the last phase of his Americanist research. This period reached its peak with the visit of a Cuna Indian, Ruben Perez Kántule, whom Nordenskiöld brought to the Ethnographical Museum of Göteborg as an assistant. In this respect, as in many others, Nordenskiöld was a pioneering force, well ahead of his time.

Nordenskiöld has been called "the foremost scholar of South American ethnography and culture history of his time" (Fock). He pioneered in methods of mapping distribution of many ethnographic elements in South, Central and North American cultures.

Through the use of extensive bibliographical and ethnographic material, he was able to develop a remarkably clear reconstruction of cultural history in an area of considerable complexity.

Nordenskiöld was a prolific writer and his major work is the ten-volume series called *Comparative Ethnographical Studies* in which he analyzes the material and spiritual culture of several Amerindian peoples and makes extensive comparative studies.

Nordenskiöld tried to relate material culture to the natural environment and historical situation of the peoples studied. He openly questioned the *Kulturkreis* theory, which postulates early diffusion of cultural elements from a primeval area of human development. He suggested that if the alleged Asian or Oceanian influences were authentic, they dated from an early age and that the impetus to high civilization of Central and South America was entirely Amerindian.

He also showed that the cultures of the Amazon rain forest had been less affected by Inca imperialism than the more easily reached Chaco peoples. And he demonstrated that the Chaco Indians must have had a common origin with the Patagonian peoples like the Ona. The Andean and Amazonian influences on the Chaco cultures involved isolated incorporations, e.g., the use of certain "luxury articles." Furthermore, he hinted at a close relationship between the Chaco/Patagonian Indians and several North American plains peoples.

In the latter volumes of the *Comparative Ethnographical Studies* Nordenskiöld takes up linguistics and language history to show how trade routes and cultural influence may have spread over the Americas; this is manifested in the the *quipus* (Andean knot-records) and Cuna pictorial writings. A look at Andean astronomy and a survey of Amerindian endemic inventions are two other noteworthy contributions of these works.

Among his purely archaeological works, the description of urn burials and mounds in Bolivia ("Urnengräber und Mounds") should be mentioned. Furthermore, he wrote on the eastern distribution of the Tiahuanaco culture ("Die östliche Ausbreitung der Tihuanacokultur") and the little noticed archaeology of the Amazon (*L'archéologie du bassin de l'Amazone*).

Nordenskiöld was also a good popular writer, and several of his books were semipopular in character. Through these (notably *Indianlif: El Gran Chaco, Sydamerika, Indianer och Hvita i Nordöstra Bolivia,* and *Forskningar och äventyr i Sydamerika*), as well as through his dedicated popular museum work, he influenced the Swedish attitude toward Amerindians in a positive way. As an inspiring supervisor, he also formed a "school" of ethnographers in Sweden and other places. Among Nordenskiöld's disciples were ALFRED MÉTRAUX, Sven Lovén, SIGVALD LINNÉ, KARL GUSTAV IZIKOWITZ, STIG RYDÉN and S. HENRY WASSÉN.

MAJOR WORKS: *Indianlif: El Gran Chaco, Sydamerika* (Stockholm: 1910; 2nd ed. [*Indianliv i El Gran Chaco Sydamerika)*], Stockholm: 1926) [tr.: *Indianerleben* (Leipzig: 1912)]; *Indianer och Hvita i Nordöstra Bolivia* (Stockholm: 1911); *De sydamerikanska indianernas kulturhistoria* (Stockholm: 1912); "Urnengräber und Mounds im bolivianischen Flachlande," *Baessler Archiv*, vol. 3 (1912), pp. 205-255; *Forskningar och äventyr i Sydamerika* (Stockholm: 1915); "Die östliche Ausbreitung der Tihuanacokultur in Bolivien und ihr Verhältnis zur Aruakkultur in Mojos," *Zeitschrift für Ethnologie*, vol. 49 (1917), pp. 10-20; *Comparative Ethnographical Studies* [10 vols.] (Göteborg: 1918-1938); *L'archéologie du bassin de l'Amazone* (Paris: 1930).

SOURCES: Kaj Birket-Smith. "Nordenskiöld, Erland" in: David L. Sills (editor), *International Encyclopedia of the Social Sciences* (New York: 1968-1979), vol. 8, pp. 203-204; "Nordenskiöld,

(Nils) Erland (Herbert)" in: *The New Encyclopaedia Britannica* (Chicago: 1986), vol. 8, p. 759; S. Henry Wassén "Four Swedish anthropologists in Argentina in the first decades of the 20th century: bio-bibliographical notes," *Folk*, vol. 8-9 (1966/67), pp. 343-350; Niels Fock, "Erland von Nordenskiöld" in: Johannes Wilbert and Karin Simoneau (editors), *Folk Literature of the Mataco Indians* (Los Angeles: 1982) (= *UCLA Latin American Studies Publication*, no. 52), p. xvi.

Jan-Åke Alvarsson

Nordenskiöld, Gustaf (Erik Adolf Gustaf Nordenskiöld). Amateur geologist and archaeologist. Born in Stockholm (Sweden) 29 June 1868, died in Mörsil, Jämtland (Sweden) 6 June 1895. Nordenskiöld's parents were Baron A.E. Nordenskiöld and Anna Maria Mannerheim, daughter of the Finnish president, the famous entomologist Count Carl Mannerheim. His brother was the ethnologist ERLAND NORDENSKIÖLD. Gustaf Nordenskiöld attended Uppsala University where he studied chemistry and minerology and from which he received a Ph.D. in 1889.

Nordenskiöld undertook an expedition to Spitsbergen in the summer of 1890 with two other young scientific researchers, Baron A. Klinkowström and J.A. Björling. The most important result of this expedition was a valuable collection of Miocene plant fossils.

In 1891 Nordenskiöld began a "recreational" journey, intending to travel around the world. He travelled to Paris and on to North America. By chance, he made a trip to the remarkable ruins in the Mesa Verde canyons and was so taken by these grand reminders of a unique culture that he decided to change his travel plans in order to spend the remaining six months of his journey in examining them. He made his headquarters at the Alamo Ranch of Benjamin K. Wetherill, father of the Wetherill brothers (see ALFRED WETHERILL).

When Nordenskiöld arrived in Colorado in the summer of 1891 he was untrained in anthropology. Nevertheless, he conducted the first scientific archaeological investigation of the prehistoric culture of the Mesa Verde. Drawing upon a standard geological concept wherein the oldest deposits are assumed to comprise the lowest strata with more recent materials above them, Nordenskiöld routinely recorded the vertical position of features and specimens. This technique is known as stratigraphy. Nordenskiöld anticipated by several decades the widespread application of stratigraphy to southwestern American archaeology.

Nordenskiöld reported the results of his ethnological examinations in his impressive work, *The Cliff Dwellers of the Mesa Verde*. He also wrote *Från fjärran västern: minnen från Amerika*, which was based on articles about his journeys originally published in a Swedish newspaper.

Nordenskiöld assembled a collection of approximately 600 artifacts in Mesa Verde. Today, the collection's home is the National Museum of Finland.

During the interval between his return home and his death he worked on the crystallography of minerals and the photography of snowflakes.

He died of tuberculosis.

MAJOR WORKS: *Ruiner af klippboningar i Mesa Verde* (Stockholm: 1892) [tr.: *The Cliff Dwellers of the Mesa Verde-Southwestern Colorado, Their Pottery and Implements* (Chicago: 1892; reprinted, New York: 1973; Glorieta, N.M.: 1979; Mesa Verde: 1990)]; *Från fjärran västern minnen från Amerika.* (Stockholm: 1892) [tr.: *From the Far West: Memories from America* (Mesa Verde: 1991)].

SOURCES: Olof W. Arrhenius, *Stones Speak and Waters Sing: the Life and Works of Gustaf Nordenskiöld* (edited by Robert H. Lister and Florence C. Lister) (Mesa Verde: 1984); Benjamin Alfred Wetherill, *The Wetherills of the Mesa Verde: Autobiography of Benjamin Alfred Wetherill* (edited by Maurine S. Fletcher) (Rutherford, N.J.: 1977); *Letters of Gustaf Nordenskiöld Written in the Year 1891 and Articles from the Journals Ymer and the Photographic Times* (edited by Irving L. Diamond and Daniel M. Olson) (Mesa Verde: 1991) [contains bibliography].

Irving L. Diamond

Novitskiĭ, G.I. (Grigoriĭ Il'ich). Ethnographer. Born middle 17th century, died at the end of the first decade of the 18th century. Novitskiĭ was a representative of the Ukrainian Kazak nobility and was exiled to Siberia for belonging to Ivan's Mazepa movement against Peter I. During 1712-1715 he took part in the missionary expeditions which were under the control of the Metropolitan Filofeĭ, going to the the middle and lower Ob River to the region of the Khanty, Ostiaks, Mansi and Voguls. These expeditions were undertaken under the direct order of Peter I (1710). Novitskiĭ gathered unique material on the economic system, way of life, material culture, customs and beliefs of the Khanty and Mansi, which he summarized in the Russian ethnographic monograph (one of the first in world literature), *Kratkoe opisanie o narode Ostiatskom* (1715). Novitskiĭ's original text was published for the first time in 1884, but its contents had gone into wide scientific circulation in Russia and abroad. It was first published in German in 1720.

MAJOR WORKS: (contributor) Johann Berhard Müller, *Leben und Gewohnheiten der Ostjaken* (Berlin: 1720); *Kratkoe opisanie o narode ostiatskom* (with introduction by L.N. Maĭkov) (St. Petersburg: 1884 (= *Pamiatniki drevneĭ pis'mennosti*, vol. 53); new ed., Novosibirsk: 1941).

SOURCE: S.A. Tokarev, *Istoriia russkoĭ étnografii (dooktiabr'skiĭ period)* (Moscow: 1966), pp. 76-78.

A.M. Reshetov
[Translation from Russian: Thomas L. Mann]

Nuttall, Zelia. Anthropologist, archaeologist. Born in San Francisco (California) 6 September 1857, died in Coyoacán (Mexico) 12 April 1933. The daughter of an American mother and an Irish father, Nuttall spent much of her youth in Europe and was educated in Germany, France, Italy, Switzerland, and Great Britain. In 1876 her family returned to San Francisco after eleven years abroad; in 1880 Nuttall met and married the French anthropologist Alphonse Pinart, with whom she traveled in the Caribbean and from whom she learned the rudiments of anthropology. A daughter was born to them in 1882, and they were legally separated in 1884, to be divorced four years later.

Nuttall visited Mexico for the first time in 1884, becoming intrigued with the terracotta figurines excavated in central Mexico. She collected a number of these and began to write papers on Mexican prehistory. From 1886 to 1899 she lived in Dresden, but from 1902 to the end of her life she occupied Casa Alvarado, the site of the mansion of the conquistador Pedro de Alvarado, in a suburb of Mexico City.

Although her primary interest was in the archaeology of Mexico, Nuttall also investigated numerous cross-cultural phenomena. In such publications as *The Fundamental Principles of Old and New World Civilizations*, her mastery of several European languages stood her in good stead as she marshalled arguments from many earlier writings. The idea expressed in that work is that both Old and New World at one time had a religion based on the worship of the North Star, as symbolized by the swastika; like many other of Nuttall's theories, it was not widely accepted and was soon forgotten.

The source of Nuttall's lasting fame lay in the several codices and manuscripts that she rediscovered and authenticated, dealing with Prehispanic Mexico and the history of the New World. Two of these, the *Codex Maglibecchiano* and the *Codex Nuttall,* are important sources of data on pre-Conquest times. Among Nuttall's other interests were the Aztec calendar and Central American astronomy.

Nuttall was a fellow of the American Anthropological Association, the American Ethnological Society, the Royal Anthropological Institute, the American Geographical Society and numerous other groups. She was awarded gold medals for her contributions to anthropology by the Historical Exposition of 1892 in Madrid, the Columbian Exposition of 1893 in Chicago and the Buffalo (New York) Exposition of 1901. Nuttall was also an Honorary Professor of Anthropology at the National Museum of Mexico and Honorary Assistant in Mexican Archaeology at the Peabody Museum of Harvard University.

MAJOR WORKS: "The terra cotta heads of Teotihuacán," *American Journal of Archaeology,* vol. 2 (1886), pp. 157-178, 318-330; "Note on ancient Mexican folklore," *Journal of American Folklore,* vol. 8 (1895), pp. 117-129; "Ancient Mexican superstitions," *Journal of American Folklore,* vol. 10 (1897), pp. 265-281; *The Fundamental Principles of Old and New World Civilizations* (Cambridge, Mass.: 1901) (= *Peabody Museum Publications,* no. 2); "The periodical adjustments of the ancient Mexican calendar," *American Anthropologist,* n.s., vol. 6 (1904), pp. 486-500; "The Island of Sacrificios," *American Anthropologist,* n.s., vol. 12 (1910), pp. 257-295; "The Aztecs and their predecessors in the Valley of Mexico," *Proceedings of the American Philosophical Society,* vol. 65 (1926), pp. 245-255.

SOURCES: Alfred M. Tozzer, "Zelia Nuttall," *American Anthropologist,* n.s., vol. 35 (1933), pp. 475-482; Ross Parmenter, "Nuttall, Zelia Maria Magdalena" in: Edward T. James [et al.] (editors), *Notable American Women, 1607-1950,* vol. 2 (Cambridge, Mass.: 1971), pp. 640-642.

David Lonergan

Nygylev, Maksim. Ostiak (Khanty) epic singer. Born in Khorumpaul, region of Sygva River, Northwest Siberia (Russia) ca. 1770. Russian colonization caused serious changes in the status of Ob-Ugrian peoples and triggered a flow of migration to the still lightly colonized northern and eastern territories. At the turn of the 19th century all this resulted in a decline in traditional religious practices. Seeing no interest among the younger generation, Nygylev, the best singer of the Sygva Ostiaks, decided to give all his knowledge to the Hungarian researcher, ANTAL REGULY. During 1844-1845, in the course of a few weeks, he dictated more than eighty sheets of sacral heroic poetry (nearly the size of the *Kalevala*) and thus saved the biggest corpus of the ancient oral tradition. In forty years his group was entirely replaced by the Vogul (Mansi) population.

SOURCE: Németh Imre, *Az ősi szó nyomában* [*On the Trail of Ancient Words*] (Budapest: 1970), pp. 332-340.

Éva Schmidt

O

Oberg, Kalervo. Anthropologist, civil servant. Born in Nanaimo (British Columbia) 15 January 1901, died in Corvallis (Oregon) 11 July 1973. In government service for over twenty years, Oberg was a longtime applied anthropologist.

Oberg earned a B.A. in economics from the University of British Columbia in 1928 and an M.A. in 1930 from the University of Pittsburgh before turning to anthropology. He studied under A.R. RADCLIFFE-BROWN at the University of Chicago, obtaining his Ph.D. in 1933 with a dissertation on the Tlingit of southeastern Alaska. Oberg next spent two postdoctoral periods at the London School of Economics, 1933-1934 and 1936-1937, between which he was engaged in fieldwork in Uganda.

After a fruitless search for a permanent teaching position, Oberg joined the civil service in the United States. (He became a naturalized American citizen in 1944.) From 1939 to 1942 he worked for the Soil Conservation Service (Department of Agriculture), where his fieldwork experience and knowledge of economics were first adapted to the ends of applied anthropology (though it was not yet called by that name). Oberg next worked for the wartime Institute of Inter-American Affairs, first in Ecuador (1942) and then in Peru (1943). After a brief period in Washington, D.C., he was sent to Brazil by the Smithsonian Institute. He taught at the Escola Livre de Sociologia e Política (Free School of Sociology and Political Science) in São Paulo from 1946 to 1952 and then was a social science consultant in Rio de Janeiro until 1955. At that point Oberg joined what is now known as the Agency for International Development, remaining in Brazil until 1959 in its Community Development Division.

After his retirement from government service, Oberg taught at Cornell (1963-1965), the University of Southern California (1965-1967) and Oregon State University

(1967-1973, on a part-time basis). Few anthropologists have been able to bring so much first-hand experience of applied anthropology to academe or could claim to have done such extensive fieldwork on three different continents. Oberg's publication record suffered from the small amount of writing time a civil service career permits; in addition, his post-retirement teaching career was too episodic to allow much influence on graduate students. For these reasons, his impact on the scholarly discipline of anthropology, and specifically on its applied branch, was considerably muted.

MAJOR WORKS: "Crime and punishment in Tlingit society," *American Anthropologist*, n.s., vol. 36 (1934), pp. 145-156; "The kingdom of Ankole in Uganda" in: Meyer Fortes and E.E. Evans-Pritchard (editors), *African Political Systems* (London: 1940), pp. 121-162; (with A.G. Harper and A.R. Cordova) *Man and Resources in the Middle Rio Grande Valley* (Albuquerque: 1943); *The Terena and the Caduveo of Southern Mato Grosso, Brazil* (Washington: 1949); *Indian Tribes of Northern Mato Grosso, Brazil* (Washington: 1953); "Types of social structure among the lowland tribes of South and Central America," *American Anthropologist*, vol. 57 (1955), pp. 472-487; "A community improvement project in Brazil" in: B.D. Paul (editor), *Health, Culture, and Community* (New York: 1955), pp. 349-376; *The Social Economy of the Tlingit Indians of Alaska* (Seattle: 1973).

SOURCE: Marlin R. McComb and George M. Foster, "Kalervo Oberg, 1901-1973," *American Anthropologist*, vol. 76 (1974), pp. 357-360.

David Lonergan

Obrębski, Józef. Sociologist, ethnologist, researcher of non-European cultures. Born in Teplik (Russia) 18 February 1905, died in New York (New York) 28 December 1967. Obrębski studied at the Jagiellonian University and the London School of Economics. He was a student of KAZIMIERZ MOSZYŃSKI and BRONISLAW MALINOWSKI. He obtained his doctorate in 1934, became an assistant professor in 1945 and eventually a professor of sociology in the United States.

Obrębski investigated the archaic culture of the Slavs in the Balkans (1927-1933) and in Polasie (1934). He also conducted research in Jamaica (1946-1948). A scholar of problems of ethnicity, he combined the perspectives of the empirical ethnographer, of the historian of the ancient and modern countryside, of the sociologist, and also of the theoretician of societal structures and traditional cultural transformations. He pointed out the necessity of investigating social attitudes and opinions as the basis for distinguishing ethnic groups (besides objective descriptions of their cultural inventory). He formulated theories concerning the conditions of the occurrence of cultural change and the theory of the formation of group, regional and national consciousness.

MAJOR WORKS: "Rolnictwo ludów wschodniej części Półwyspu Bałkanskiego" ["The folk agriculture of the Eastern Region of the Balkan Peninsula"], *Lud Słowiański*, vol. 1, no. 1 (1929), pp. 10-54; vol. 1, no. 2 (1930), pp. 147-187; vol. 2, no. 1 (1931), pp. 9-27; vol. 2, no. 2 (1931), pp. 133-148; "Problem grup etnicznych w etnologii i jego socjologiczne ujęcie" ["The problem of ethnic groups in ethnology and its sociological conception"], *Przegląd Socjologiczny*, vol. 4 (1936), pp. 177-196; "Teoria ekonomiczna i metoda socjologiczna w badaniach społeczeństw pierwotnych" ["Economic theory and sociological method in the investigations of primitive societies"], *Przegląd Socjologiczny*, vol. 81 (1946), pp. 84-102; "Obrzędowa i społeczna struktura wsi macedońskiej" ["Ritual and social structure of a Macedonian village"], *Etnografia Polska*, vol. 16 (1972), pp. 201-213 [tr.: *Ritual and Social Structure in a Macedonian Village* (Amherst: 1977)]; *The Changing Peasantry of Eastern Europe* (Cambridge, Mass.: 1976).

SOURCES: Anna Kutrzeba-Pojnarowa, "Pozycja Józefa Obrębskiego w etnografii polskiej" ["The place of Józef Obrębski in Polish ethnography"], *Etnografia Polska*, vol. 16 (1972), pp. 215-219; Anna Kutrzeba-Pojnarowa, *Kultura ludowa i jej badacze* [*Folk Culture and Its Researchers*] (Warsaw: 1977).

Maria Niewiadomska and Iwona Grzelakowska
[Translation from Polish: Joel Janicki]

Ogburn, William F. (William Fielding). Cultural sociologist, demographer, economist. Born in Butler (Georgia) 1886, died in Tallahassee (Florida) 27 April 1959. Ogburn taught high school for a few years after receiving a B.S. from Mercer University and before pursuing graduate training in sociology at Columbia University with Franklin Giddings. He earned his Ph.D. in 1912; taught anthropology, economics, sociology and history courses at Princeton, Reed, and the University of Washington; and put in World War I service with the National War Labor Board before succeeding Giddings as chair of the Department of Economics and Sociology at Barnard College in 1919. Like other Giddings students such as Howard Odum, Frank Hankins, John Gillin, Malcolm Willey and F. Stuart Chapin, Ogburn was keenly interested in explaining cultural process and in increasing the use of quantitative methods in the social sciences. Ogburn was a part of the Boasian circle both socially and intellectually. He was especially close to ROBERT H. LOWIE and EDWARD SAPIR and encouraged by mail Sapir's first reading of Freud during the late 1910s. MARGARET MEAD began her professional social science career as Ogburn's assistant in editing the *Journal of the American Statistical Association* and was introduced to psychoanalytic ideas in his course on psychological aspects of culture. Before moving to the University of Chicago in 1927 he spent time in Vienna with leading psychoanalysts, including Freud, and in Paris with French ethnologists, notably MARCEL MAUSS. Together with ALEXANDER GOLDENWEISER, Ogburn edited *The Social Sciences and Their Interrelations*. At Chicago, where he taught until his retirement in 1951, he encouraged systematic inquiry such as SOL TAX's *Penny Capitalism*, for which he wrote an (unpublished) preface, and Ellen Black Winston's comparison of rates of psychosis in the United States and in Margaret Mead's Samoan data.

In his major theoretical work, *Social Change*, Ogburn introduced the concept of cultural lag: "Material culture changes force changes in other parts of culture such as social organization and customs, but these latter parts of culture do not change as quickly. They lag behind the material-culture changes." Ogburn was fascinated by the repercussions of technological changes on family structures and other parts of culture. With a very holistic conception of culture (presumably reinforced by discussion with A.R. RADCLIFFE-BROWN at Chicago) he was able to impress students by relating long chains of unanticipated social consequences of new technologies, such as railroads or airplanes. Although culture lag is Ogburn's most popular formulation, and although he wrote and talked often about adjustments of the rest of culture to technological changes, he did not consider lags to be "a fundamental part of the theory of social evolution" because cultures either adjust to the diffusion of technical innovations or reject the innovation. For explaining social evolution rather than the social problems of adjustment, Ogburn felt that other, more quantifiable factors were sufficient: "The problem of social evolution is solved by four factors: invention, exponential accumulation, diffusion and adjustment. My contribution has been largely in the factor of exponential accumulation and also in the development of the factor of invention."

Although a major advocate of quantification in the study of social trends, Ogburn constantly stressed the limitations of statistics and cautioned against mindless extrapolation of trend lines.

MAJOR WORKS: *Social Change* (New York: 1922; New York: 1950); (with Dorothy S. Thomas) "Are inventions inevitable? a note on social evolution," *Political Science Quarterly*, vol. 37 (1922), pp. 83-98; (co-editor with Alexander Goldenweiser) *The Social Sciences and Their Interrelation* (Boston: 1927); *Recent Social Trends* (New York: 1933); *The Social Effects of Aviation* (Boston: 1946); (with M.F. Nimkoff) *Technology and the Changing Family* (Boston: 1955).

SOURCES: Otis Dudley Duncan (editor), *William F. Ogburn on Culture and Social Change* (Chicago: 1964); Toby E. Huff, "Theoretical innovation in science: the case of William F. Ogburn," *American Journal of Sociology*, vol. 79 (1973), pp. 261-277; A.J. Jaffe, "Ogburn, William Fielding" in: David L. Sills (editor), *International Encyclopedia of the Social Sciences* (New York: 1968-1979), vol. 11, pp. 277-281.

Stephen O. Murray

Okladnikov, A.P. (Aleksei Pavlovich). Archaeologist, ethnographer, historian. Born in Siberia (Russia) 3 October 1908, died in Moscow (Russian S.F.S.R.) 18 November 1981. Okladnikov worked primarily in Leningrad at the Institut arkheologii (Institute of Archaeology) of the Soviet Academy of Sciences. In 1961 he went to Novosibirsk where he established and headed the Institut istorii, filologii i filosofii (Institute of History, Philology and Philosophy) of the Siberian division of the Soviet Academy of Sciences. He remained there for the rest of his life.

Okladnikov was interested in an extremely varied and diverse set of geographic and academic areas. He worked in Pribaĭkal, ĪAkutiĭa, the Altaĭ, Primor'e, Central Asia, Mongolia and Alaska. He possessed a shrewd and rich intuition and was exceptionally conversant with all areas of archaeology, ethnography and history and had the ability to make exact appraisals and broad generalizations, encompassing vast geographic and temporal frames. He paid special attention to the material and spiritual life of primitive societies and the question of the origin of their beliefs, religions and art. He was the author of appoximately 1,000 scholarly works.

MAJOR WORKS: *Ocherki po istorii zapadnykh burĭat-mongolov (XVII-XVIII vv.)* (Leningrad: 1937); "Drevnie shamanskie izobrazhneniĭa iz Vostochnoĭ Sibiri," *Sovetskaĭa arkheologiĭa*, no. 10 (1948), pp. 203-225; *Proiskhozhdenie ĭakutskogo naroda* (Moscow and Leningrad: 1951); *Dalekoe proshloe Primor'ĭa* (Vladivostok: 1959); *Drevnee poselenie na poluostrove Peschanom u Vladivostoka* (Moscow and Leningrad: 1963); *Olen' Zalotye Roga: rasskazy ob okhote za naskal'nymi risunkami* (Leningrad and Moscow: 1964); *Liki derevnego Amura: petroglify Sakachi-Alĭana* (Novosibirsk: 1968); *TSentral'noaziatskiĭ ochag pervobytnogo iskusstva* (Novosibirsk: 1972); *Petroglify Baĭkala: pamĭatniki drevneĭ kul'tury narodov Sibiri* (Novosibirsk: 1974); *Paleolit TSentral'noĭ Azii* (Novosibirsk: 1981); *Petroglify Mongolii* (Leningrad: 1981); *Paleolit Mongolii* (Novosibirsk: 1986).

SOURCES: V.E. Larichev, *A.P. Okladnikov: issledovatel' drevnikh kultur' Azii* (Irkutsk: 1958); *Aleksei Pavlovich Okladnikov* (Moscow: 1981) (= *Materialy k bibliografii uchenykh SSSR, seriĭa istorii*, no. 13); V.P. Alekseev and I.S. Gurvich, "A.P. Okladnikov (nekrolog)," *Sovetskaĭa ėtnografiĭa*, no. 2 (1982), pp. 168-172.

A.M. Reshetov

[Translation from Russian: Helen Sullivan]

Olbrechts, Frans M. Anthropologist, museum administrator. Born in Malines (Belgium) 16 February 1899, died in Aachen (Germany) 24 March 1958. Olbrechts was trained in Germanic philology at Louvain University (Ph.D., 1925) and, as a fellow of the Commission for the Relief of Belgium Educational Foundation, in anthropology as a post-doctoral student at Columbia University. He became a curator in ethnography at the Musées Royaux d'Art et d'Histoire (Royal Art and History Museums) in 1929 and professor at the University of Ghent in 1932. In 1947 he was appointed director of the Musée du Congo Belge (Museum of the Belgian Congo) at Tervuren.

Olbrechts' first scholarly interests were in folk beliefs and his dissertation concerned Flemish magical formulas. While he was at Columbia, FRANZ BOAS arranged for him to work during 1926-1927 with a collection of formulas in Cherokee syllabary that had been collected much earlier by JAMES MOONEY of the Bureau of American Ethnology. Olbrechts carried out investigations that placed the manuscripts into a cultural context. In 1928 he studied the Tuscarora language, and in 1929 he conducted general investigations into the ethnography of the Onondaga.

Next, Olbrechts devoted himself mainly to museum work, which included the cataloging of a large collection of the Museés Royaux d'Art et d'Histoire. In the course of his work, he made trips to West Africa to collect specimens. With this, his interest turned to Africa, particularly the art of the continent. At the end of his life, he was the outstanding authority on the art of the Belgian Congo, having carried out detailed studies of its structure and its anthropological significance. In reference to his *Plastiek van Congo*, William Fagg stated that it was "the most systematic work yet produced for any large field of African Art" (quoted in the English translation of Olbrechts' book).

MAJOR WORKS: *Het roode land der zwarte karialieden* (Leuven: 1935); *Maskers en dansers in de Ivoorkust* (Leuven: 1940); *Bijdrage voor de kennis van de chronologie der afrikannsche plastiek* (Brussels: 1941); (with Albert A.L. Maesen) *Plastiek van Congo* (Antwerp: 1946) [tr.: *Les arts plastiques du Congo belge* (Brussels: 1959); *Congolese Sculpture* (New Haven: 1982)]; *Some Masterpieces of African Art from the Collection of the Royal Museum of Belgian Congo, Tervuren* (Tervuren: 1952).

SOURCES: Daryll Forde, "Frans Olbrechts," *Africa*, vol. 28 (1958), pp. 6-7; Melville J. Herskovits, "Frans Olbrechts in America," *Congo-Tervuren*, vol. 3 (1957), pp. 45-54; B. Holas, "Frans M. Olbrechts," *Institut français d'Afrique noire, Bulletin*, sér. b, vol. 21 (1959), pp. 240-241; A. Maesen, "Notes sur la vie et la pensée de Frans M. Olbrechts," *Congo-Tervuren*, vol. 3 (1957), pp. 7-22; Olbrechts' papers concerning his Cherokee work in the Smithsonian Institution National Anthropological Archives.

James R. Glenn

Ol'derogge, D.A. (Dmitrĭ Alekseevich). Africanist. Born in Vilnius (Lithuania, then part of Russia) 23 May 1903, died in Leningrad (Russian S.F.S.R.) 30 April 1987. Ol'derogge was the son of a military man. The family moved to St. Petersburg in 1906. Ol'derogge lost his father at the age of fifteen and, after approximately two years' service in the Red Army, entered the University of what had now become Petrograd. He began as an Egyptologist but his teachers included scholars such as V.V. Struve and V.V. Bartol'd. After graduation in 1925, Ol'derogge began work in the African section of the Muzeĭ Antropologii i Ėtnografii (Museum of Anthropology and Ethnography) and was initiated into museum work and ethnography by L.ÍA. (LEO) SHTERNBERG. He remained associated with this museum for the rest of his life.

Ol'derogge studied abroad, mainly in Germany during 1927-1928 and began publishing in the African field on his return in 1929. From 1946 he held the Chair of African Studies at Leningrad University. He lived through the worst initial period of the siege of Leningrad, joining the local defense unit, and the Africanist office was turned into a military strongpoint. In July 1942, on the orders of the Presidium of the Academy of Sciences, he was evacuated to Tashkent, and he returned to Leningrad in 1944 so as to work on the re-establishment of the Museum.

He defended his doctoral dissertation in 1945. It was never published in its entirety, but some of the ideas contained in it were published in the main Soviet anthropological journal in 1946. These ideas had a a certain affinity with those later due to be made famous by the work of CLAUDE LÉVI-STRAUSS. An even earlier version of Ol'derogge's ideas on kinship was formulated in a paper he presented in May 1942, during the siege; this manuscript did not survive, but a reconstruction of it was published in 1978.

Throughout his life Ol'derogge never published a full book. On the other hand, his output of articles was phenomenal. There were well over 200 of them. More remarkable than their quantity was their range and their quality. He was at home in history, linguistics, kinship studies (where he would perhaps have most claimed originality) and other fields.

When he died, he had witnessed the start, but certainly not the full flowering, of the Gorbachevian liberalization. His life spanned the period from the Russo-Japanese War to Perestroika.

He eventually became the undisputed leader of Soviet African studies. The significance of his work lies not only in his innovation in the field of kinship, which the political climate prevented him from following up properly, but above all in the stimulus his wide-ranging brilliance provided for African studies in the Soviet Union. He maintained high scholarly standards even if, like any man who survived the Stalinist period, he was obliged on occasion to compromise. He knew this and could express himself with wry bitterness. His intellectual distinction and fame protected him in some measure, but in some measure only: in his last years, after 1968, he was not allowed to travel, though he received many invitations from abroad. He was brilliant in conversation, erudite yet quite free of pedantry. He was made Corresponding Member of the Soviet Academy of Sciences in 1960, this being a rank one level below full membership. The fact that a man of his distinction, who unquestionably towered over Africanists in the Soviet Union, did not achieve the rank in the Academy that he deserved constitutes eloquent testimony about the ambiguity of his relationship to the establishment of his time.

MAJOR WORKS: *Épigamiīa: izbrannye stat'i* (Moscow: 1983) [collection of thirteen of Ol'derogge's most important articles].

SOURCE: ÍŪ.V. Bromley (editor), *Osnovye problemy Afrikanistiki: étnografiīa, istoriīa, filologiīa k 70-letīū chlena-korespondenta AN SSSR D.A. Ol'derogge* (Moscow: 1973) [Festschrift for Ol'derogge, containing a bibliography of his writings up to the date of publication of the volume].

Ernest Gellner

Oliver, Douglas L. Anthropologist, historian. Born in Ruston (Louisiana) 10 February 1913. Oliver received an undergraduate degree in anthropology from Harvard University and a D.Phil. from the University of Vienna. He taught at Harvard from 1948 to 1973. In 1969 he was appointed to a Pacific Islands chair in anthropology at the University of Hawaii and taught there (initially half-time) until 1978. Oliver's first major contribution to anthropology came in the form of a fine-grained ethnography of Siwai-speakers of Bougainville Island, whom he studied during 1938-1939. His *A Solomon Island Society* is widely regarded as the classic description of "big-man" leadership in Melanesia, a topic that still generates theoretical attention and debate. World War II and its aftermath took him into other areas of the Pacific, and his *The Pacific Islands* surveyed the cultures and history of the entire region for the educated general reader. In 1954-1959 he organized a team of researchers to study modern culture in the Society Islands; since that time, his own research has been increasingly devoted to history. In the 1980s, an ever-growing number of historians and anthropologists, including some of Oliver's students, has sought to blend the two disciplines in order to illuminate what is still a relatively little-known part of the world. Oliver's contribution to this effort is as distinctive as was his earlier ethnography and has produced, since his retirement from teaching, encyclopedic treatments of traditional island cultures, as well as a more conventionally historical monograph about Captain William Bligh.

MAJOR WORKS: *Studies in the Anthropology of Bougainville, Solomon Islands* (Cambridge, Mass.: 1949); *The Pacific Islands* (Cambridge, Mass.: 1951; 3rd ed., Honolulu: 1989); *A Solomon Island Society* (Cambridge, Mass.: 1955); *Bougainville: a Personal History* (Honolulu: 1973); *Ancient Tahitian Society* (Honolulu: 1974); *Two Tahitian Villages* (Laie, Hawaii: 1981); *Return to Tahiti: Bligh's Second Breadfruit Voyage* (Honolulu: 1988); *Oceania: the Native Cultures of Australia and the Pacific Islands* (Honolulu: 1988).

SOURCES: Robert D. Craig and Russell T. Clement, *Who's Who in Oceania, 1980-81* (Laie, Hawaii: 1980); *Rank and Status in Polynesia and Melanesia: Essays in Honor of Professor Douglas Oliver* (Paris: 1978).

Eugene Ogan

Olson, Ronald Leroy. Anthropologist. Born in Mankato (Minnesota) 8 December 1895, died in Escondido (California) 1 August 1979. Olson was a specialist in the cultures of the Northwest Coast. He did fieldwork in a greater number of Northwest societies than any other member of his generation.

A lumberjack in the Northwest for several years before his military service in World War I, Olson returned from France an invalid due to tuberculosis. After long treatment, he was able in 1921 to begin attending college. He studied anthropology at the University of Washington under LESLIE SPIER, taking a B.A. in 1925 and an M.A. the next year. Moving to Berkeley for doctoral study, he worked under ALFRED L. KROEBER and finished a dissertation on the diffusion of clan and moiety organization in native North America by 1929.

For the next two years Olson was employed by the American Museum of Natural History, primarily to engage in archaeology in Peru. In 1931, however, he was chosen by Kroeber as the fourth member of the Berkeley anthropology department; this was a controversial appointment. The department at that time was made up of only three instructors, of whom one (E.W. GIFFORD) was primarily a museum curator. Olson was older and less socially sophisticated than many of the other junior anthropologists avid for the post; Kroeber picked him because of his broad range of interests and his superior abilities as an instructor of undergraduates. Olson brought Berkeley's introductory course in anthropology to new heights of enrollment.

Olson was a popular and influential professor among the department's graduate students as well. He taught there for twenty-five years during a period of growth and greatness, retiring in 1956. He frequently spent his summers on the Northwest Coast, and wrote on the Quinault (Coast Salish), the Tlingit (Athabaskan) and four different groups of the Kwakiutl (Wakashan). Unwilling to accept the widespread view that the Northwest had been adequately studied by FRANZ BOAS, JOHN REED SWANTON and others of the late 19th and early 20th centuries, Olson recorded a large amount of data on the flourishing mid-century cultures. Worthwhile in their own right, his studies also provide a basis for comparison over time.

MAJOR WORKS: *Adze, Canoe, and House Types of the Northwest Coast* (Seattle: 1927); *Clan and Moiety in Native America* (Berkeley: 1933); *The Quinault Indians* (Seattle: 1936); *Social Life of the Owikeno Kwakiutl* (Berkeley: 1954); *Social Structure and Social Life of the Tlingit in Alaska* (Berkeley: 1967).

SOURCES: A.L. Kroeber, "Ronald Leroy Olson, retired, 1956," *Kroeber Anthropological Society Papers*, vol. 16 (1957), pp. 1-4; Omer C. Stewart, "Memorial to Ronald L. Olson (1895-1979)," *Journal of California and Great Basin Anthropology*, vol. 2 (1980), pp. 162-164; Philip Drucker, "Ronald Leroy Olson, 1895-1979," *American Anthropologist*, vol. 83 (1981), pp. 605-607.

David Lonergan

Omwake, H. Geiger. Public school teacher and administrator, archaeologist. Born in Mercersburg (Pennsylvania) 1907, died in Washington (D.C.) 31 December 1967. Henri Geiger Omwake was educated at Franklin and Marshall College, the University of Pennsylvania and Duke University. Until he retired in 1963, he was primarily a public school official in Delaware. He also became a leading archaeologist in his state through his spare-time work on surveys and excavations and his activities with several archaeological societies. He was one of the main organizers of the Archeological Society of Delaware (in 1933), the Sussex Society of Archaeology and History (in 1948), and the Kent Archaeological Society (in 1965). He was also active with the Maryland Archaeological Society. Omwake's study of pipes of European manufacture and their significance in American archaeological sites, a study begun in the 1940s, brought him recognition on a national level.

MAJOR WORKS: (with T. Dale Stewart) "The Townsend Site near Lewes, Delaware," *The Archeolog* [Sussex Society for Archaeology and History], vol. 15 (1963), pp. 1-69; "Date-bore correlation in English white kaolin pipe stems, yes or no?" *Archaeological Society of Virginia, Quarterly Bulletin*, vol. 11 (1956), pp. [2-14].

SOURCES: L.T. Alexander, "H. Geiger Omwake," *Bulletin of the Archaeological Society of Delaware* (fall 1967), p. 7; Virginia C. Jones, "In memoriam: Henri Geiger Omwake," *Maryland Archeology*, vol. 4 (March 1968), p. 4; Omwake papers and collections file in the Smithsonian Institution National Anthropological Archives; Richard C. Quick, "H. Geiger Omwake's archeologi cal writings: a commemorative bibliography, 1934-1972," *Bulletin of the Archaeological Society of Delaware*, n.s., no. 11 (1978), pp. 1-16.

James R. Glenn

Opler, Morris E. (Morris Edward). Anthropologist. Born in Buffalo (New York) 16 May 1907. Opler received his B.A. (sociology) and M.A. (anthropology) degrees from the University of Buffalo, where he was a student of LESLIE A. WHITE. He received his Ph.D. in anthropology from the University of Chicago in 1933, working first under EDWARD SAPIR and finishing under A.R. RADCLIFFE-BROWN. One of Opler's major influences on anthropology was as the teacher of many academic anthropologists. His main teaching posts were at Cornell University, where he was Professor of Anthropology and Asian Studies from 1948 until his retirement in 1969, and the University of Oklahoma, Norman, from 1969 until 1977. After his second retirement, Opler vigorously continued his research and writing. Among his many professional distinctions, he was First Vice-President (1946-1947) of the American Folklore Society and President of the American Anthropological Association (1962-1963).

As an ethnologist, Opler's field research focused primarily on the Apache of the American Southwest and the peoples of India, although he also wrote about the Third Reich, Japan, China and American culture. During World War II, he worked as a Social Science Analyst at the Manzanar Japanese relocation camp in California and assisted the Japanese American Citizens League and the American Civil Liberties Union, researching and writing briefs in defense of Japanese-American civil rights. This was work that held strong emotional value for Opler.

A voluminous writer, Opler is best known as an ethnographer and critic. His ethnographic publications reveal his great care for detail, the breadth of his research interests and his desire to preserve his informants' points of view. Reflecting this, one of his abiding interests has been the depiction of culture through the vehicles of folklore and to a lesser extent biography. A particular theoretical theme of Opler's work is the significant role he gives individuality and human volition in explanations of cultural and social history ("Some implications of culture theory for anthropology and psychology"). This perspective sets him against unilineal evolutionists and other biological and cultural determinists (e.g., "The human being in cultural theory"). Beginning in 1945, a second theoretical concern of Opler's is his development of the concept of cultural themes ("Themes as dynamic forces in culture"). The design of this approach is to provide an economic way of characterizing cultures. Themes are the primary postulates that typify indigenous perspectives and compel behavior in a culture. Finally, throughout his career, Opler has expressed dissatisfaction with single-causation explanations, putting him in conflict with the culturology of White, the social determinism of Radcliffe-Brown, and the "culture-reflects-a-single-dominant-personality" depictions of RUTH BENEDICT.

The Apache are the primary concern of both Opler's pre-Cornell (e.g., *An Apache Life-Way: the Economic, Social, and Religious Institutions of the Chiricahua Indians*) and post-Cornell publications (e.g., *Apache Odyssey: a Journey Between Two Worlds*). While at Cornell, Opler wrote some of his finest critical work and focused his ethnographic attention on the Indian subcontinent. During his tenure he developed and directed the Cornell

India Program, which involved the intensive multi-disciplinary study of village India and made Cornell one of the leading U.S. centers of South Asian studies.

MAJOR WORKS: "A summary of Jicarilla Apache Culture," *American Anthropologist*, n.s., vol. 38 (1936), pp. 202-223; *An Apache Life-Way: the Economic, Social, and Religious Institutions of the Chiricahua Indians* (Chicago 1941); "Themes as dynamic forces in culture," *The American Journal of Sociology*, vol. 51 (1945), pp. 198-206; "Some implications of culture theory for anthropology and psychology," *American Journal of Orthopsychiatry*, vol. 18 (1948), pp. 611-621; (with Rudra Datt Singh) "Two villages of Eastern Uttar Pradesh (U.P.), India: an analysis of similarities and differences," *American Anthropologist*, vol. 54 (1952), pp. 179-190; "The extensions of an Indian village," *Journal of Asian Studies*, vol. 16 (1956), pp. 5-10; "Component, assemblage, and theme in cultural integration and differentiation," *American Anthropologist*, vol. 61 (1959), pp. 955-964; "The human being in culture theory," *American Anthropologist*, vol. 66 (1964), pp. 504-528; "The themal approach in cultural anthropology and its application to North Indian data," *Southwestern Journal of Anthropology*, vol. 24 (1968), pp. 215-227; *Apache Odyssey: a Journal Between Two Worlds* (New York: 1969).

SOURCES: Mario D. Zamora, J. Michael Mahar and Henry Orenstein (editors), *Themes in Culture: Essays in Honor of Morris E. Opler* (Quezon City: 1971); Gerry C. Williams (general editor) and Carolyn Peel (associate editor), *Essays in Anthropology in Honor of Morris Edward Opler* (Norman: 1977) (= *Papers in Anthropology*, vol. 18, no. 2).

Mattison Mines

Oracion, Timoteo S. Anthropologist, educator, administrator. Born in Tanjay, Negros Oriental (Philippines) 22 August 1911. Oracion is best known to anthropologists for his writings on the Negritos, Magahats and Bukidnons of Negros Oriental. His early training, however, was in education, and, in his long academic career at Silliman University and later at Foundation University, he served as a professor of education, anthropology and sociology.

Oracion finished at the Cebu Normal School in 1934. He obtained a bachelor's degree (1947) and an M.A. (1951) in education at Silliman. His earlier acquaintance with the Negritos and other ethnic minorities in his province led him to anthropology. In 1952 he obtained an M.A. in anthropology at the University of Chicago under FRED EGGAN with the thesis, *An Introduction to the Culture of the Magahats of the Upper Tayabanan River Valley, Tolong, Negros Oriental.* In 1970, on a Ford Foundation grant, he finished his Ph.D. degree in anthropology at San Carlos University, Cebu.

He was a classroom teacher between 1930 and 1941. Then he served in the Armed Forces of the Philippines (AFP) and the U.S. Armed Forces in the Far East (USAFFE) as Captain of the Infantry from 1941 to 1946. Currently, he is a major on reserve.

Since 1946 he has been a professor of education, anthropology and sociology at Silliman and Foundation Universities. He was founding chair of the anthropology-sociology department at Silliman and is graduate school dean at Foundation. He was a Fulbright scholar at the University of Chicago (1948-1949), UNESCO fellow at the International Institute for Child Study, Bangkok, Thailand (1956-1957), and a delegate to the UNESCO conference, 2-16 July 1970, in Dar-es-Salaam, Tanzania, on "the influence of colonialism on the artist, his milieu and his public in developing countries." He was consultant to the Commission on National Integration, member of the National Presidential Action Commission on Land Problems provincial chapter and a staff consultant/representative for the Negros area of the Research Center for National Defense and Development. Oracion was an elected member of the Dumaguete Legislative Council from 1980-1987. He was likewise consultant on herbal medicine in Negros and ran a radio broadcast for three years on "Folk Medicine/Herbal Medicine" over Radio Station DYSR, Silliman Radio.

Oracion's major contributions to anthropology are in teaching, research, publication, and public service. He was the first Filipino to teach anthropology in Negros Oriental. Oracion has conducted pioneering research among the Negritos, Magahats and Bukidnons (he published the first article on this people). Oracion likewise has the distinction of being a pioneer in anthropology in the Visayan Islands.

MAJOR WORKS: "An adult education program for the Bukidnons of Southern Negros Island, Philippines," *Asian Profile*, vol. 1 (1973), pp. 385-408; "Notes on the culture of Negritos on Negros Island," *Silliman Journal*, vol. 7 (1960), pp. 201-208; "Notes on the social structure and social change of the Negritos on Negros Island," *Philippine Sociological Review*, vol. 2 (1963), pp. 57-67; "The Bais Forest Preserve Negritos: some notes on their rituals and ceremonials" in: Mario D. Zamora (editor), *Studies in Philippine Anthropology (in Honor of H. Otley Beyer)* (Quezon City: 1967), pp. 419-442.

SOURCES: "Oracion, Timoteo S." in: Sol Tax (editor), *Fifth International Directory of Anthropologists* (Chicago: 1975), p. 288; Mario D. Zamora (editor), *Studies in Philippine Anthropology (in Honor of H. Otley Beyer)* (Quezon City: 1967), pp. 419-442; Mario D. Zamora, "Timoteo S. Oracion: a pioneer in Philippine anthropology," *Asian Profile*, vol. 12 (1984), pp. 23-27.

Mario D. Zamora

Orel, Boris. Man of letters, publicist, ethnologist/folklorist, puppeteer. Born in Brnca pri Beljaku (Austria-Hungary) 2 March 1903, died in Ljubljana (Slovenia) 5 February 1952. Orel researched material culture, customs and cults, mythology and ancient religions. After the Liberation he became director of the Ethnographic Museum in Ljubljana. He organized a method of systematic field research to be used by ethnological teams in heretofore overlooked Slovenian regions. From this work were developed the first questionnaires for fieldwork done by Slovenian ethnologists. Orel also founded a new journal, *Slovenski etnograf*, and edited its first fifteen volumes, which played an important role in the development of Slovenian ethnology.

MAJOR WORKS: "Slovenski ljudski običaji," *Narodopisje Slovencev*, vols. 1 (1944), pp. 263-349 and 2 (1952), pp. 134-165; "Ralo na Slovenskem," *Slovenski etnograf*, vols. 8 (1955), pp. 31-68 and 14 (1961), pp. 15-40; *Bloške smuči: vprašanje njihovega nastanka in razvoja* (Ljubljana: 1964).

SOURCES: Marija Makarovič, "Življenje in delo Borisa Orla," *Slovenski etnograf*, vol. 16-17 (1963-1964), pp. 7-22; Vilko Novak, *Raziskovalci slovenskega življenja* (Ljubljana: 1986).

Mojca Ravnik
[Translation from Slovene: Corrine Leskovar]

P

Palerm, Angel. Anthropologist, historian of civilizations. Born in Eivissa (Spain) 11 September 1917, died in Mexico City (Mexico) 17 June 1980. Gifted with an extraordinary ability to make connections between political and historical questions and ethnographic detail, Palerm developed the critical *usefulness* of anthropology. Leading the last thrust of evolutionary theory, he repeatedly associated the study of the bases of civilization with the practical problems of development and social welfare.

Follower of the concept of empirical and systematic construction of theory, Palerm achieved a teaching, organizational and research role whose influence has not been limited to Mexico. In dialogue with anthropological luminaries such as Eric Wolf, John Murra or Sidney Mintz, Palerm contributed efficaciously to the maintenance of a critical and universal anthropology. His contribution can be considered to lie in the classical arena of the social sciences, falling between multilineal evolution and critical Marxism. His most original theories have three foci: those that explain the systematic relationship between the political order of the ancient empires and their modes of production, it being understood that this relationship is the result of long evolution; those that locate peasant society conceptually; and those that analyze topics of political economy, evaluating *apparently* anachronistic economic systems of the past. This last aspect places Palerm outside the narrow evolutionary circle and puts him face to face with solutions of profound scope in the presence of the long-standing ecological problematic.

MAJOR WORKS: (with Isabel Kelly) *The Tajin Totonac* (Washington: 1952) (= *Smithsonian Institution Publication*, no. 13); *Introducción a la teoria etnológica* (Mexico City: 1967); *Productividad agricola: un estudio sobre México* (Mexico City: 1968); *Agricultura y civilización en Mesoamérica* (Mexico City: 1972); *Agricultura y sociedad en Mesoamérica* (Mexico City: 1972);

Obras hidráulicas prehispánicas en el sistema lacustre del Valle de México (Mexico City: 1973); *Historia de la etnología: los precursores* (Mexico City: 1974); *Historia de la etnología: los evolucionistas* (Mexico City: 1976); *Modos de producción y formaciones socioeconómicas* (Mexico City: 1976); *Historia de la etnología: Tylor y los profesionales británicos* (Mexico City: 1977); *Antropología y marxismo* (Mexico City: 1980).

SOURCES: Neus Escandell and Ignasi Terradas (editors), *Història i antropologia a la memòria d'Angel Palerm* (Barcelona: 1984); Susana Glantz (editor), *La heterodoxia recuperada: en torno a Angel Palerm* (Mexico City: 1987).

Ignasi Terradas
[Translation from Spanish: Margo L. Smith]

Palmer, Edward. Naturalist, archaeological fieldworker, physician. Born near Wilton, County Norfolk (England) in 1830 or 1831, died in Washington (D.C.) 10 April 1911. Palmer came to the United States in 1849 and soon fell under the influence of Jared Potter Kirtland, who encouraged his interest in biology. Practical experience came in 1852 when he joined the Thomas Jefferson Page expedition to the Rio de la Plata and its tributaries as a hospital steward and collector of biological specimens. During 1856-1857, he attended the Cleveland Homeopathic College briefly. Other than this, he was largely self-trained in both medicine and natural history.

In his scientific work, Palmer was essentially a collector of botanical specimens. Until 1868, he carried out this work while supporting himself as a private physician, U.S. Army surgeon, and, for a brief period, Indian agency doctor. Later, he became a scientific assistant and a professional collector, working for several U.S. government agencies, including the Department of Agriculture and the Smithsonian Institution, and for the Peabody Museum at Harvard University and other private and state scientific organizations. Most of his work was carried on in the area that includes Arkansas and Kansas and extends west to California in the United States and extensively into Mexico. He also worked in Maine, Florida, Idaho and the Bahamas. In anthropology, he made a large collection of artifacts from Indians he encountered. He also collected many ethnobotanical specimens.

Beginning in 1875, Palmer carried out archaeological work, mainly in Utah, Texas and Mexico. During 1881-1884 he was an archaeological field assistant for the Mounds Survey of the Smithsonian Institution's Bureau of American Ethnology; he worked in Arkansas, other southeastern states and Indiana.

MAJOR WORKS: "Arkansas mounds: observation and results of excavations made around the mounds in various parts of the state," *Publications of the Arkansas Historical Association*, vol. 4 (1917), pp. 390-448 [Palmer's notes published posthumously]; "Customs of the Coyotero Apaches," *Zoe*, vol. 1 (1890), pp. 161-172; "Food products of the North American Indians," *Report of the Commission of Agriculture* (1871), pp. 404-428; "Remarks concerning two divisions of Indians inhabiting Arizona, New Mexico, Utah, and California," *American Naturalist*, vol. 11 (1877), pp. 735-747.

SOURCES: Janice J. Beaty, *Plants in His Pack: a Life of Edward Palmer, Adventurous Botanist and Collector* (New York: 1964) [biography for children]; Walter Hough, "Edward Palmer," *American Anthropologist*, n.s., vol. 13 (1911), p. 173; Marvin D. Jeter, "Edward Palmer's 1882 excavation at the Tillar Site (3DR1), Southeast Arkansas" [unpublished paper in the Smithsonian Institution National Anthropological Archives]; Roger McVaugh, *Edward Palmer: Plant Explorer of the American West* (Norman: 1956); "Edward Palmer" in: Wilcomb Washburn (editor), *History of Indian-White Relations* (Washington: 1988) (= William C. Sturtevant (general editor), *Handbook of*

North American Indians, vol. 4), p. 674; Palmer papers in the Smithsonian Institution National Anthropological Archives [which include William E. Safford's unpublished manuscript, "Edward Palmer: botanical explorer"].

James R. Glenn

Parsons, Elsie Clews (née Elsie Worthington Clews). Folklorist, anthropologist. Born in New York (New York) 27 November 1874, died in New York (New York) 19 December 1941. Trained in sociology at Barnard College by Franklin Giddings, Parsons gathered life histories of 787 public relief recipients for her 1897 M.A. thesis. Her 1899 Ph.D. dissertation was entitled *The Educational Legislation and Administration of the Colonies*. She married alderman and future reformist Republican congressman Herbert Parsons in 1900. She wrote a number of works of quasi-scientific social criticism of American institutions, particularly the family, and translated Gabriel Tarde's *Les lois d'imitation*.

After the United States became involved in World War I, involvement that Parsons actively opposed, she was introduced to Boasian anthropology by ROBERT H. LOWIE and ALFRED L. KROEBER and began to collect African-American folklore. She maintained the Columbia commitment to comparison as she began annual fieldwork in New Mexico pueblos in 1915. In addition to her own assiduous collection and comparison of African-American and Pueblo cosmologies and folklore, Parsons, through the Southwest Foundation, supported fieldwork by others, including RALPH BEALS, RUTH BENEDICT, ESTHER GOLDFRANK, E. ADAMSON HOEBEL and LESLIE A. WHITE. She also underwrote production of the *Journal of American Folklore* for many years. Along with her encyclopedic, comparativist work on Pueblo religions, she produced major communities-studies of acculturation within peasant villages in Mexico and Ecuador. She endeavored to distinguish traits that were indigenous from those that were Spanish in origin. At the time of her death she was the first woman president of the American Anthropological Association.

> MAJOR WORKS: *The Family* (New York: 1906); *Mitla: Town of Souls* (Chicago: 1936); *Pueblo Indian Religion* [2 vols.] (Chicago: 1939); *Peguche: a Study of Andean Indians* (Chicago: 1945).

> SOURCES: Judith Friedlander, "Elsie Clews Parsons" in: Ute Gacs [et al.] (editors), *Women Anthropologists: a Biographical Dictionary* (New York: 1988), pp. 282-290; Louise Lamphere, "Feminist anthropology: the legacy of Elsie Clews Parsons," *American Ethnologist*, vol. 16 (1989), pp. 518-533; Peter H. Hare, *A Woman's Quest for Science* (Buffalo: 1985); Leslie Spier and Alfred Kroeber, "Elsie Clews Parsons," *American Anthropologist*, vol. 45 (1943), pp. 244-255; Nancy Oestreich Lurie, "Parsons, Elsie Clews" in: David L. Sills (editor), *International Encyclopedia of the Social Sciences* (New York: 1968-1979), vol. 11, pp. 426-428.

Stephen O. Murray

Patai, Raphael. Anthropologist, folklorist, historian of religion. Born in Budapest (Hungary) 22 November 1910. Patai is best known to anthropologists for his studies of the cultural history of the Jews and the Arabs, Hebrew mythology, Jewish folk religion and the mentality of the Arabs and Jews.

His early training was in rabbinic studies and Semitic languages and literatures. He served as a research fellow in Jewish anthropology at the Hebrew University of

Jerusalem (1943-1947) and from 1948 taught the anthropology of the Middle East at several U.S. universities, including the University of Pennsylvania, Columbia, Princeton and Ohio State University. His first scholarly works, written in Hebrew, focused on Palestinology, ancient Palestinian folklore, and ancient Jewish customs, beliefs, and legends.

Patai was a pioneer in academic anthropology and folklore in Palestine where he lived from 1933 to 1947. In 1944 he founded the Palestine Institute of Folklore and Ethnology in Jerusalem, served as its director of research until 1948, and edited its journal, *Edoth (Communities): a Quarterly for Folklore and Ethnology* and its two monograph series. He carried out fieldwork among the Persian and Kurdish Jews in Jerusalem and (1948) among the "Indian Jews" of Mexico. His programmatic essay, "Ha-folḳlor yeha-etnologyah shel ᶜAm Yiśra'el: beᶜayot ye-tafḳidim," became a guideline for some members of the young generation of folklorists and anthropologists who developed these fields after the independence of Israel in 1948. His *Madaᶜ ha-Adam: Mavo le-Antropologyah* was the first, and is to this day the only, Hebrew introductory text in anthropology. Arriving in the United States in 1947 on a Viking Fund (later Wenner-Gren Foundation) fellowship, Patai became one of the first scholars to teach the anthropology of the Middle East and of Israel in U.S. universities.

MAJOR WORKS: *Adam ya-Adamah* [2 vols.] (Jerusalem: 1942-1943); "Ha-folḳlor yeha-etnologyah shel ᶜAm Yiśra'el: beᶜayot ye-tafḳidim," *Edoth*, vol. (1945), pp. 1-12 [tr.: "Problems and tasks of Jewish folklore and ethnology," *Journal of American Folklore*, vol. 59 (1946), pp. 25-39]; *Man and Temple in Ancient Jewish Myth and Ritual* (Edinburgh: 1947; expanded ed., New York: 1967); *Madaᶜ ha-Adam: Mavo le-Antropologyah* [2 vols.] (Tel Aviv: 1947); *Israel between East and West: a Study in Human Relations* (Philadelphia: 1953; revised ed., Westport, Conn.: 1970); *The Kingdom of Jordan* (Princeton: 1958); *Sex and Family in the Bible and the Middle East* (New York: 1959); *Golden River to Golden Road: Society, Culture and Change in the Middle East* (Philadelphia: 1962; 2nd ed., Philadelphia: 1967; 3rd ed., Philadelphia: 1969; 3rd ed. [with title *Society, Culture and Change in the Middle East*], Philadelphia: 1971); (with Robert Graves) *Hebrew Myths* (New York: 1964); *The Hebrew Goddess* (New York: 1967; 2nd ed., New York: 1978; 3rd ed., Detroit, 1990); *Tents of Jacob: the Diaspora Yesterday and Today* (Englewood Cliffs, N.J.: 1971); *Encyclopaedia of Zionism and Israel* [2 vols.] (New York: 1971); *Myth and Modern Man* (Englewood Cliffs, N.J.: 1972); *The Arab Mind* (New York: 1973; rev. ed., New York: 1983); (with Jennifer Patai) *The Myth of the Jewish Race* (New York: 1975; rev. ed., Detroit: 1989); *The Jewish Mind* (New York: 1978); *The Messiah Texts* (Detroit and New York: 1973); *Gates to the Old City* (New York: 1980); *The Vanished Worlds of Jewry* (London and New York: 1981); *On Jewish Folklore* (Detroit: 1983); *The Seed of Abraham: Jews and Arabs in Conflict* (New York and Salt Lake City: 1986); *Apprentice in Budapest: Memories of a World That Is No More* (Salt Lake City: 1988).

SOURCES: Howard M. Sachar, "Raphael Patai: an appreciation" in: Victor D. Sanua (editor), *Fields of Offerings: Studies in Honor of Raphael Patai* (New York: 1983), pp. 17-18; Haim Schwarzbaum, "The oeuvre of Raphael Patai" in: Victor D. Sanua (editor), *Fields of Offerings: Studies in Honor of Raphael Patai* (New York: 1983), pp. 19-28; "Patai, Raphael, 1910-," *Contemporary Authors*, vol. 29-32 (1978), pp. 514-515; "Patai, Raphael" in: *Encyclopaedia Judaica* (Jerusalem: 1972), p. 178; "Patai, Raphael" in: *American Jewish Biographies* (New York: 1982), pp. 312-313.

Paulme, Denise. Jurist, ethnographer. Born in Paris (France) 4 May 1909. The research of Paulme is centered on fieldwork, data gathering, erudite ethnography and the study of a sizable corpus of African oral literature. Conducted without regard to the theoretical debates that excited French ethnologists (notably the debates between Marxists and structuralists in the field of anthropology after World War II), her work is characterized by the dialectic movement that had been previously noted by MARCEL MAUSS and that must accompany every study of social facts: if knowledge of context clarifies the meaning of a story, of a ritual or of an object, the opposite is just as true: understanding particular phenomena helps to deepen one's knowledge of context.

In 1927 Paulme had already begun to study law. Through her study of the history of law, she became interested in the institutions of primitive law and enrolled in the Institut d'Ethnologie of the University of Paris where she took courses from Mauss and graduated in 1932, the same year she obtained her law degree (*License en droit*).

She was a frequent visitor to the Musée d'Ethnographie du Trocadéro (Museum of Ethnography of the Trocadéro), and she participated in its reorganization under the direction of PAUL RIVET and GEORGES HENRI RIVIÈRE. She received a grant from the Rockefeller Foundation in 1934 and participated in the Sahara-Soudan mission under the direction of MARCEL GRIAULE. Accompanied by the linguist and ethnographer Deborah Lifchitz, she then spent nine months living among the Dogon in what is now Mali collecting materials for her law dissertation, which she defended in 1940. In 1938 she became assistant at the Muséum National d'Histoire Naturelle (National Museum of Natural History) and curator in the Black Africa Department of the Musée de l'Homme before becoming *Directeur d'études* (professor) at the École Pratique des Hautes Études (Social Sciences Section) in 1958. With her husband ANDRÉ SCHAEFFNER, she visited Black Africa several more times to conduct fieldwork among the Kissi and the Baga of Guinea and among the Bété and the Lagoon peoples of the Ivory Coast. During the same period she helped form an institutional basis for African ethnological research by participating in the creation of the Centre d'Études Africaines of the École Pratique des Hautes Études and by collaborating in the foundation of the *Cahiers d'études africaines*.

Paulme's work was at first centered on judicial ethnology and on tribal monographs, of which *Organisation sociale des Dogon de Sanga* and *Les gens du riz* are the most refined examples, but the focus of her later work turned toward the ethnology of art and, starting in the early 1960s, to the more specialized domains of social and symbolic life. Her works on rituals and syncretic cults, particularly her investigations of the status of women in West Africa, of associations and age-classes and of African oral literature—to which she devoted herself after her retirement in 1979—may be considered as pioneer research. Each of her later works represents an advance whose theoretical scope and heuristic value have helped train an entire generation of French Africanist researchers who have studied in the sixth section of the École Pratique des Hautes Études (now called the École des Hautes Études en Sciences Sociales).

MAJOR WORKS: *Organisation sociale des Dogon de Sanga* (Paris: 1940; 2nd ed., revised and expanded, Paris: 1988); *Les civilisations africaines* (Paris: 1953); *Les gens du riz: Kissi de Haute-Guinée française* (Paris: 1954); *Les sculptures de l'Afrique noire* (Paris: 1956); *Une société de Côte d'Ivoire, hier et aujourd'hui: les Bété* (Paris and The Hague: 1962); *La mère dévorante: essai sur la morphologie des contes africains* (Paris: 1976); *La statue du commandeur: essais d'ethnologie* (Paris: 1984); (editor) *Manuel d'ethnographie de Marcel Mauss* (Paris: 1947; 2nd ed., Paris: 1989); (editor) *Femmes d'Afrique noire* (Paris and The Hague: 1960); (editor) *Classes et associations d'âge en Afrique de l'Ouest* (Paris: 1971).

SOURCES: Marc Augé, *Le dieu objet* (Paris: 1988); "Gens et paroles d'Afrique: écrits pour Denise Paulme," *Cahiers d'études africaines*, vol. 19 (1979), pp. 73-76; Geneviève Calame-Griaule (editor), *Langages et cultures africaines* (Paris: 1977); Annie Dupuis (editor), "Correspondance de Deborah Lifchitz et Denise Paulme avec Michel Leiris, Sanga 1935," *Gradhiva*, no. 3 (1987), pp. 44-58.

Jean Jamin
[*Translation from French: Timothy Eastridge*]

Pei Wenzhong (Pei Wen-Chung). Palaeolithic archaeologist, palaeoanthropologist. Born in Fengnan, Hebei (China) 19 January 1904, died in Peking (China) 18 September 1982. Pei graduated from the Department of Geology, Peking University, in 1927. He studied in the field at Choukoutien with C.C. Young, Davidson Black and Pierre Teilhard de Chardin and with the Abbé HENRI BREUIL in Paris, where he received a doctorate before returning to China in 1937. He engaged in archaeological field research at Choukoutien, at Yangshao village (the first Neolithic site in China, discovered in the early 1920s by J.G. Andersson), at Djalainor in Manchuria, at the limestone caves of Guangxi, and in Gansu. He taught at Yenching University and, after the founding of the People's Republic of China in 1949, joined the staff of the Institute of Vertebrate Paleontology and Palaeoanthropology of the Chinese Academy of Sciences, with which he remained affiliated until his death.

In the fields of paleolithic archaeology and paleoanthropology, Pei was the most important and influential scholar in China. He and his junior associate, Jia Lanpo, trained every palaeolithic archaeologist working in China today; and he was also responsible, as director of short-term training institutes in Peking in the early 1950s, for the training of a whole generation of museum curators and local archaeologists. He is widely known as the discoverer of the first Peking Man skull in Choukoutien in 1929 when he was field director at that site for the Laboratory of Cenozoic Research. His interests, however, were broad. He was the first scholar to pay serious attention to the Choukoutien cultural deposits; he investigated many Neolithic sites; he proposed the concept of a Mesolithic stage in China's southwest; and he was a profoundly influential synthesizer of Chinese prehistory. His vision of China's archaeological potential and his immense contributions to the field made Pei Wenzhong one of the very foremost movers behind China's rapid progress and astonishing achievements in archaeology in the three decades since 1949.

MAJOR WORKS: "An account of the discovery of an adult Sinanthropus Skull in the Chou Kou Tien Deposit," *Bulletin of the Geological Society of China*, vol. 8 (1929), pp. 203-205; (with P. Teilhard de Chardin) "The lithic industry of the *Sinanthropus* deposits in Choukoutien," *Bulletin of the Geological Society of China*, vol. 11 (1932), pp. 315-358; *Zhoukoukian Dongxue Caijueji* [*Choukoutien excavations*] (Peiping: 1934) (= *Geological Memoirs*, series B, no. 7); "Preliminary note on some incised, cut and broken bones found in association with *Sinanthropus* remains and lithic artifacts from Choukoutien," *Bulletin of the Geological Society of China*, vol. 12 (1934), pp. 105-108; "On a Mesolithic industry of the caves of Kwangsi," *Bulletin of the Geological Society of China*, vol. 14 (1935), pp. 393-408; "An attempted correlation of Quaternary geology, palaeontology, and prehistory in Europe and China," *Institute of Archaeology, University of London, Occasional Papers*, no. 2 (1939), *Geochronological Table*, no. 1, pp. 3-16; "A preliminary study of a new palaeolithic station known as Locality 15 within the Choukoutien Region," *Bulletin of the Geological Society of China*, vol. 19 (1939), pp. 147-187; "The Upper Cave industry of Choukoutien," *Palaeontologia Sinica*, series D, no. 9 (1939), pp. 1-41; *Zhongguo Shiqian Shiqi Zhi Yanjiu* [*A Study of the Prehistoric Period in China*] (Shanghai: 1948); (with Ju-kang Woo) *Ziyang Ren* [*Tzu-yang Palaeolithic Man*] (Peking: 1957) (= *Institute of Vertebrate Palaeontology, Academia Sinica, Memoir*, no. 1); *Liujiang Jüyuandong Di Faxian He Guangxi Quita Shandong Di Tancha* [*Excavation of Liucheng Gigantopithecus Cave and Exploration of Other Caves in Guangxi*] (Peking: 1965) (= *Institute of Vertebrate Palaeontology and Palaeoanthropology, Academia Sinica, Memoir, 7*).

SOURCE: An Zhimin, "Pei Wenzhong xiansheng zhuanlue" ["A brief biography of Pei Wenzhong"], *Kaogu Xuebao*, 1 (1983), pp. 1-5.

K.C. Chang

Péristiany, Jean George. Social anthropologist, sociologist, diplomat. Born in Athens (Greece) 4 September 1911, died in Paris (France) 27 October 1987. Péristiany is best known for his work on Mediterranean societies and for the various symposia that he helped organize on the common customs and modes of thought in Mediterranean societies.

Originally trained in law, he studied at the Faculté de Droit in Paris, earning a Docteur en Droit in 1937. His interest in law among tribal peoples led him into social anthropology. He studied with BRONISLAW MALINOWSKI in London and under R.R. MARETT at Oxford where he received his D.Phil. in 1938. He conducted fieldwork among the Kipsigis of Kenya during 1937-1938, concentrating particularly on their systems of customary law. He returned to Africa in 1946 for fieldwork among the pastoral Pokot and also served as a sociologist for the government of Kenya. He became lecturer in social anthropology at the University of London and at Cambridge University from 1946 to 1948, and then senior university lecturer at Oxford from 1948 to 1963.

While at Oxford the focus of his research shifted from Africa to the Mediterranean, and he became associated with efforts to extend the methods of social anthropology to his native Greece and to other Mediterranean countries. His own work focused on the common institutions and dominant cultural motifs found throughout the region. He was particularly concerned with the system of social sanctions—the preoccupation of males with personal honor and of females with sexual shame—encountered in village communities from Turkey to Portugal. He saw this concern for personal reputation as a means by which small, face-to-face communities exercise control over the behavior of their members. This concern, therefore, was an expression of his lifelong interest in informal legal sanctions that he brought to anthropology from his early training in law. His most influential publications were devoted to the polarity of honor and shame, and he served as editor of significant collections of papers on rural social change in the Mediterranean and on Mediterranean family types.

Péristiany's influence on anthropology was due as much to his organizational talents as to his writings. In 1960 he was appointed UNESCO professor of sociology, and he established UNESCO centers for the social sciences in Athens, Greece and in Nicosia, Cyprus. As director of these centers he convened various conferences that served as catalysts for scholarly exchange on all aspects of Mediterranean social anthropology and sociology.

In 1978 he entered the Cypriot diplomatic corps and eventually served as ambassador to France, Spain and Portugal.

MAJOR WORKS: *The Social Institutions of the Kipsigis* (London: 1939); *La vie et le droit coutumier des Kipsigis du Kenya* (Paris: 1939); (editor and contributor) *Honour and Shame: the Values of Mediterranean Society* (Chicago: 1966); (editor and contributor) *Contributions to Mediterranean Sociology: Mediterranean Rural Communities and Social Change* (Paris: 1968); (editor) *Mediterranean Family Structures* (Cambridge: 1976).

SOURCES: "Peristiany, Jean Georg," *Contemporary Authors* (1968), p. 332; "Péristiany (Jean, Georges)" in: *Who's Who in France, 1981-1982* (Paris: 1981), p. 1171; "Prof Jean Peristiany," *The Times* [London] (4 November 1987), p. 18 [obituary].

Richard A. Barrett

Peter, Prince of Greece and Denmark. Anthropologist, banker. Born in Paris (France) 3 December 1908, died in London (England) 15 October 1980. Prince Peter is best known for his psychoanalytically inspired work on Himalayan polyandry (*A Study of Polyandry*). Though his first training was in law, he was soon attracted to both psychoanalysis and anthropology, his mother being the well known psychoanalyst Marie Bonaparte; a meeting with GÉZA RÓHEIM in 1928 confirmed his decision to become an anthropologist. He studied with BRONISLAW MALINOWSKI at the London School of Economics during 1934-1935, and in 1937 he left for fieldwork in the Himalayas, which was followed by a study of the Todas in the Nilgiri Hills, South India. World War II forced him to suspend his anthropological studies, but he resumed fieldwork in India in 1949. He spent the years 1950-1957 doing anthropometric studies of Tibetans in Kalimpong, northeastern India. When forced to leave Kalimpong for political reasons, he settled in Denmark, completed his dissertation in London in 1959 and was awarded an honorary doctorate at the University of Copenhagen in 1960. He devoted the last twenty years of his life to banking (in the mornings) and anthropology (in the afternoons).

Prince Peter was a witty and engaging lecturer with a very outspoken loyalty both to the people he had been studying and to his Malinowskian and psychoanalytic background. His study of Himalayan polyandry remains a classic in its field.

MAJOR WORKS: *The Eternal Question* (Copenhagen: 1952); *A Study of Polyandry* (The Hague: 1963); (with J. Balslev Jørgensen) "Physical anthropological observations on 5000 Tibetans" in: *Anthropological Researches from the 3rd Danish Expedition to Central Asia* (Copenhagen: 1966) (= *Historisk-Filosofiske Skrifter, Kongelige Danske Videmkabernes Selskab*, vol. 4, no. 4).

SOURCES: Mogens Mugge Hansen (editor), *Venner af Prins Peter* (Copenhagen: 1978); David G. Mandelbaum, "Prince Peter of Greece and Denmark, 1908-1980," *American Anthropologist*, vol. 83 (1981), pp. 616-617; Finn H. Lauridsen, "Peter, prins" in: *Dansk Biografisk Leksikon* (Copenhagen: 1982), vol. 11, pp. 258-259.

Jan Ovesen

Petri, Helmut. Anthropologist. Born in Cologne (Germany) 7 November 1907, died in Cologne (West Germany) 21 June 1986. Petri studied in Berlin and Rome and at the University of Vienna (with WILHELM SCHMIDT, WILHELM KOPPERS and ROBERT VON HEINE-GELDERN) and gained his D.Phil. (1933) with a thesis entitled *Geldformen der Südsee*. Appointed curator at the Vienna Naturhistorisches Museum (Museum of Natural History) (1933-1935), he later joined the staff of LEO FROBENIUS at the Forschungsinstitut für Kulturmorphologie (Research Institute of Cultural Morphology) at the University of Frankfurt on Main, focusing on Australian and Pacific areas. He was awarded his *Habilitation* (1949) for his thesis on *Der australischen Medizinmann*. In 1958 he became Professor and Director of the Institut für Völkerkunde (Institute of Ethnology) at the University of Cologne, retiring as Emeritus Professor in 1973.

Petri's first field research (1938-1939) was carried out in the Northwest Kimberleys (Western Australia). However, World War II interrupted his professional career and it was not until 1954-1955 that he returned to his research in Aboriginal Australia. One result of this was *Sterbende Welt in Nordwest-Australien*. This significant anthropological study made an impact on German anthropology, which had virtually ignored Australian Aboriginal social studies from the early part of this century. Between 1960 and 1984 Petri made ten field trips to the Kimberleys, which provided him with a large amount of valuable data that needed to be written up. His list of publications demonstrates his contribution to Aboriginal studies, especially on religion and ritual. He was responsible for editing and expanding on Ernest Worms' writing in *Die Religionen der Südsee und Australiens*. His *Sterbende Welt* signaled a concern for the problems of changes facing Aborigines; his pessimistic view at that time gave way later to a more optimistic interpretation of current events.

Although Petri made regular excursions with his students to Mediterranean villages and various European museums and retained his interests in South American and Mexican ethnology and prehistory—a heritage of his early training in Vienna—he remained consistent in regard to his Australian Aboriginal research. His interests were widespread, and he did not restrict himself to the perimeters of his own discipline.

MAJOR WORKS: "Kúrangara: neue magische Kulte in Nordwest-Australien," *Zeitschrift für Ethnologie*, vol. 75 (1950), pp. 43-51; *Sterbende Welt in Nordwest-Australien* (Braunschweig: 1954); "Die Alterklasse der Vorinitiation bei Eingeborenengruppen Nordwest-Australiens," *Ethnologica*, vol. 2 (1960), pp. 132-145; "Kosmogonie unter farbigen Völkern der westlichen Wüste Australiens," *Anthropos*, vol. 60 (1965), pp. 469-479; "'Wandji-Kuran-Gara,' ein mythischer Traditionskomplex aus der westlichen Wüste Australiens," *Baessler Archiv*, vol. 15 (1967), pp. 1-34; (editor, with H. Nevermann and E. Worms) *Die Religionen der Südsee und Australiens* (Stuttgart: 1968); (with Gisela Petri-Odermann) "Nativismus und Millenarismus im gegenwärtigen Australien" in: Eike Haberland [et al.] (editors), *Festschrift für Ad. E. Jensen* (Munich: 1964), pp. 461-466; (with Gisela Petri-Odermann) "Stability and change: present-day historic aspects among Australian Aborigines" in: R.M. Berndt (editor), *Australian Aboriginal Anthropology: Modern Studies in the Social Anthropology of Australian Aborigines* (Nedlands: 1970), pp. 248-276.

SOURCES: K. Tauchmann (editor), *Festschrift zum 65. Geburtstag von Helmut Petri* (Cologne: 1973); R.M. and C.H. Berndt, "Helmut Petri, 1907-1986," *Australian Aboriginal Studies*, no. 1 (1987), pp. 97-98.

Ronald M. Berndt

Petrie, Sir *William Matthew Flinders.* Archaeologist, Egyptologist. Born in Charlton (England) 3 June 1853, died in Jerusalem (Palestine) 28 July 1942. Despite his lack of formal education, Petrie became the first professor of Egyptology in England, holding the Edwards Chair at University College London from 1892 to 1933. Fascinated with the past from an early age, he worked for years with his civil engineer father surveying sites in England, including Stonehenge. He went to Egypt in 1880 to survey the Giza pyramids accurately as a test of the theories of divine inspiration put forward by astronomer Piazzi Smyth, an old friend of the Petrie family. His measurements showed that no such unit as the "pyramid inch" existed, thus destroying the basis for Smyth's entire conceptual framework.

Having become interested in all the history of Egypt during the three seasons of the survey, Petrie made the recovery of its past his life's work. Returning almost every season from 1881 to 1926, he excavated at dozens of sites, trained scores of young archaeologists and published more than a thousand titles, of which fully 10% were books, primarily excavation reports. Although he was an early excavator for the Egypt Exploration Fund, most of his work was through his own Egyptian Research Account, later expanded into the British School of Archaeology in Egypt. In 1926 he shifted his excavations permanently to Palestine, where he had worked briefly in 1890 and where he continued in active fieldwork until the age of eighty-five.

Petrie made several important contributions to the field of archaeology. Contrary to practices common in his day, he recorded all finds, both spectacular and humble, broken and complete. This concentration on the totality of remains allowed him to interpret past history more realistically than the previous emphasis on major finds had allowed. He also insisted on publishing his finds immediately following each field season. Although this was novel for the time, his excavation reports would be judged rather sketchy by modern standards. It must be kept in mind that in attempting to gain an overview of all Egyptian history, Petrie shifted sites almost annually, precluding the detailed analysis of a single area. Perhaps his most significant contribution was the excavation and analysis of the predynastic cultures (which he did not immediately recognize as such) that preceded the development of pharaonic society. His development of "sequence dates" based on a comparative study of the pottery and other items from his predynastic graves (*Diospolis Parva*) was the forerunner of the modern relative dating technique of seriation.

MAJOR WORKS: *Inductive Metrology* (London: 1877); *The Pyramids and Temples of Gizeh* (London: 1883); *Tanis. Part I, 1883-4* (London: 1885); (with E. Gardner [et al.]) *Naukratis. Part I, 1884-5* (London: 1886); *Hawara, Biahmu and Arsinoe* (London: 1889); (with A.H. Sayce [et al.]) *Illahun, Kahun and Gurob, 1889-90* (London: 1894); *A History of Egypt* [3 vols.] (London: 1894-1905); (with J.E. Quibbell [et al.]) *Naqada and Ballas, 1895* (London: 1896); *The Royal Tombs of the First Dynasty, 1900, Pt. 1* (London: 1900); (with F.Ll. Griffith) *The Royal Tombs of the Earliest Dynasties, 1901, Pt. II* (London: 1901); (with A.C. Mace) *Diospolis Parva: the Cemeteries of Abadiyeh and Hu, 1898-9* (London: 1901); (with A.E. Weigall) *Abydos, Pt. I* (London: 1902); (with F.Ll. Griffith) *Abydos, Pt. II* (London: 1903); *Methods and Aims in Archaeology* (London: 1904); *The Arts and Crafts of Ancient Egypt* (London: 1909); *Egypt and Israel* (London: 1911); *Prehistoric Egypt* (London: 1920); *Social Life in Ancient Egypt* (London: 1923); *Ancient Gaza: Tell el Ajjul* [5 vols.] (London: 1931-1952); *Seventy Years in Archaeology* (London: 1931); *Egyptian Architecture* (London: 1938); *The Making of Egypt* (London: 1939); *Wisdom of the Egyptians* (London: 1940).

SOURCES: W.M. Flinders Petrie, *Ten Years Digging in Egypt* (London: 1892); W.M. Flinders Petrie, *Seventy Years in Archaeology* (London: 1931); Margaret S. Drower, *Flinders Petrie: a Life in Archaeology* (London: 1985); Warren R. Dawson and Eric P. Uphill, *Who Was Who in Egyptology* (London: 1972), pp. 228-230; John David Wortham, *The Genesis of British Egyptology* (London: 1971), pp. 113-126; S.R.K. Glanville, "Flinders Petrie: the scientific classification of archaeological material," *Proceedings of the Royal Institution of Great Britain*, vol. 32 (1942), pp. 344-359; Eric P. Uphill, "A bibliography of Sir William Matthew Flinders Petrie (1853-1942)," *Journal of Near Eastern Studies*, vol. 31 (1972), pp. 356-379.

Carter Lupton

Pettazzoni, Raffaele. Ethnologist, historian of religions. Born in San Giovanni Persiceto, near Bologna (Italy) 3 February 1883, died in Rome (Italy) 8

December 1959. Pettazzoni studied at the University of Bologna, taking a degree in letters with a thesis entitled *Le origini dei Kabiri nelle isole del Mar Tracio.*

Religious philosophy remained his principal field of study, and he was responsible for the foundation of the first secular chair for the history of religions in Italy at the University of Rome in 1923. He was granted the title of Accademico d'Italia in 1933, and in 1937 he was appointed to the chair of ethnology at the University of Rome. He was elected president of the International Association for the History of Religions (IAHR) in 1950.

Pettazzoni's research has made an important contribution to the history of European ethno-anthropological studies. He was one of the first scholars in a Catholic country to maintain that one should consider religious phenomena in their psychological and social context, abandoning the traditional theological approach. In one of his first works, which was appreciated by JAMES G. FRAZER, Pettazzoni dealt with the concept of Supreme Beings among ethnologically significant peoples: by applying his comparative method, Pettazzoni attempted to demonstrate that such divinities could not be considered "pure" or "primordial" manifestations of monotheism—as the theories of WILHELM SCHMIDT and the Cultural-Historical School of Vienna had maintained—but ought instead to be interpreted as a product of specific aesthetic and perceptual phenomena. He made this point again in his last work (*L'onniscienza di dio*) in which, still using the comparative method, he classified the different types of Supreme Being (Earth Mother, Celestial God, Lord of the Animals) and placed them according to their relationship to the various means of subsistence (agriculture, herding, hunting). Using analogous criteria he dealt with the theme of the confession of sins, analyzing practically every documented instance of this practice around the world and described it in terms of magic and ritual. In this case he regarded the word as an instrument for the ritualized expulsion of impurity.

In the area of methodology Pettazzoni made a significant contribution, seeking to reconcile the use of the comparative method to an ethnology based on historicist rather than evolutionary principles. He maintained that such a result could be obtained by basing the comparison on the examination of the historical development of analogous phenomena, instead of only on their morphological affinities.

Pettazzoni was one of the few Italian scholars in the ethno-anthropological field to be well known in Europe before World War II, despite the fact that he was the target of polemics within his own country originating from philosophical circles, that, then, followed the theories of Benedetto Croce and were particularly reluctant to embrace the social sciences.

MAJOR WORKS: *L'Essere Celeste nelle credenze dei popoli primitivi* (Rome: 1922); *La religione di Zarathustra* (Bologna: 1920); *La religione nelle Grecia antica fino ad Alessandro* (Bologna: 1921); *I misteri* (Bologna: 1924); *Miti e leggende* (Turin: 1948-1966); *Essays on the History of Religions* (Leiden: 1954); *The All-Knowing God: Researches into the Early History of Religions* (London: 1956) [also: *The All-Knowing God* (New York: 1978)]; (founder) *SMSR (Studi e Materiali di Storia delle Religioni)* (Rome: 1925-); (founder) *Numen* (Leiden: 1954-).

SOURCES: G. Cocchiara, *Storia degli studi di tradizioni populari in Italia* (Palermo: 1947); E. DeMartino, *Naturalismo e storicismo nella etnologia* (Bari: 1941); M. Gandini, "Il contributo di Raffaele Pettazzoni agli studi storico-religioni," *Strada maestra*, vol. 2 (1969), pp. 1-48; M. Eliade,

"The history of religions in retrospect, 1912-1962," *Journal of Bible and Religion*, vol. 31 (1963), pp. 98-109; P. Clemente [et al.], *L'antropologia italiana: un secolo di storia* (Bari: 1985).

Gianni Vannucci
[Translation from Italian: Chris Nissen]

Pierson, Donald. Social anthropologist, sociologist. Born in Indianapolis (Indiana) 3 September 1900. Pierson received an A.B. from the College of Emporia in 1927, an A.M. from the University of Chicago in 1933 and a Ph.D. from the University of Chicago in 1939. As Research Assistant, Social Science Research Committee, University of Chicago, he engaged in research on race relations in Bahia, Brazil (1935-1939). He was professor of sociology and social anthropology, Escola Livre de Sociologia e Política (Free School of Sociology and Political Science), São Paulo, Brazil (1939-1955), and also organizer and director of the Department of Sociology and Anthropology and organizer and dean of the Graduate Division of the Social Sciences (1943-1957). As an anthropologist of the Institute of Social Anthropology, Smithsonian Institution, he engaged in a program of research and training in research, again in collaboration with the Escola Livre. He has also been Visiting Professor, Escuela Nacional de Antropología (National School of Anthropology), Mexico (1960 and 1961); Guggenheim Research Fellow, Portugal and Spain (1963-1964); Fulbright Lecturer, Instituto Superior de Ciências Sociais e Política Ultramarina (Higher Institute of Overseas Social and Political Sciences), Lisbon, Portugal (1966); and Doctor *Honoris Causa*, Federal University of Bahia (1986).

Pierson played a crucial role in the development of social anthropology and sociology in Brazil, which were not included in the curriculum of some Brazilian educational institutions until the 1930s. Most of Pierson's major research projects were designed and carried out in collaboration with undergraduate and graduate students with the purpose of linking classroom instruction with actual fieldwork. Pierson also supervised the translation, publication and distribution of a number of standard works in the social sciences. His own book on theory and research had an unprecedented success in Brazil and is still widely used in Brazilian educational institutions.

MAJOR WORKS: *O homem no vale de São Francisco* [3 vols.] (Rio de Janeiro: 1972); *Cruz das Almas: a Brazilian Village* (Washington: 1951); *Teoria e pesquisa em sociologia* (São Paulo: 1945); *Negroes in Brazil: a Study of Race Contact at Bahia* (Chicago: 1942; 2nd revised ed., Carbondale: 1966); (with Mario Wagner Vieira de Cunha) "Research and research possibilities in Brazil, with particular reference to culture and cultural change" *Acta Americana*, vol. 5., nos. 1-2 (1947), pp. 18-82; "Obstaculos no caminho de uma verdadeira ciência social," *Universitas*, nos. 6-7 (1970), pp. 407-416; "Exame crítico da ecologia humana," *Sociologia*, vol. 10, no. 4 (1948), pp. 227-241; "National images in Portugal and Spain" in: *Memoriam: Antonio Jorge Dias* (Lisbon: 1974), vol. 2, pp. 357-372 ; "Life in a Brazilian village," *Völkerkundliche Abhandlungen*, vol. 1 (1964), pp. 407-416; "Habitações em São Paulo: estudo comparativo," *Revista do Arquivo Municipal*, vol. 91 (1942), pp. 199-238; "Race relations in Portuguese America" in: Andrew W. Lind (editor), *Race Relations in World Perspective* (Honolulu: 1955), pp. 433-462; "Race prejudice as revealed in the study of racial situations," *International Social Science Bulletin*, vol. 2 (1950), pp. 467-478.

SOURCE: Donald Pierson, "Algumas atividades no Brasil em prol da antropologia e outras ciências" in: Mariza Corrêa (organizer), *História da antropologia no Brasil (1930-1960): testemunhos* (Campinas and São Paulo: 1987), vol. 1, pp. 29-116.

Emilio Willems

Pigorini, Luigi. Paleoethnologist. Born in Fontanellato, Parma (Italy) 10 January 1842, died in Padua (Italy) 1 April 1925. Pigorini was one of the pioneers of Italian prehistory as well as of ethnographic museology.

He graduated in 1865 in political science and began his archaeological activity working with the naturalist Pellegrino Strobel in excavations of prehistoric *terramare* in the Po Valley. His extensive research on the *terramare* civilization led Pigorini to become the spokesman of the so-called "Pigorinian" hypothesis, which involved the notion that Italian cultural development in the prehistoric age had been in part determined by the immigration into the peninsula of Transalpine populations. This thesis would have among its most significant opponents GIUSEPPE SERGI.

In 1867 Pigorini took up a position at the Museo Nazionale (National Museum) in Parma, where he eventually became director. For the 5th International Congress of Anthropology and Prehistoric Archeology in Bologna in 1871, he organized the National Exposition of Prehistoric Antiquities, at which he proposed the institution of an Italian museum of prehistory and ethnography. (Such a museum was founded in Rome by royal decree 25 July 1875, the present-day Museo Preistorico Etnografico Luigi Pigorini). The tasks of the new institution, as well as of its *Bulletino di Paletnologia italiana*, a periodical founded by Pigorini with Strobel and Gaetano Chierici in the same year, were to collect the remains of the ancient civilizations of Italy and contribute to the progress of the new science of prehistory. Pigorini's work reflected the traditional chronologic and geographic categories of 19th-century evolutionary museography. He organized his museum into two major sections, one prehistoric, the other ethnographic, ethnography like folklore having a fundamental role in Pigorini's evolutionist conception. The material objects of present-day "savages" and the costumes of the "lower orders" of the civilized nations were combined—thanks to the analogic method and to comparison—with those of prehistoric men, the object of paleoethnology.

Donations of numerous travelers enriched the holdings of the new national museum, among which those of LAMBERTO LORIA from New Guinea and ENRICO HILLYER GIGLIOLI are particularly noteworthy. The museum became a center of research.

From 1876, for forty years, Pigorini occupied the chair of paleoethnology at the University of Rome, the first to be instituted in Italy.

In 1912 he was nominated a senator of the Kingdom.

MAJOR WORKS: (with P. Strobel) "Le Terramare e le Palafitte del Parmense," *Atti della Società italiana di scienze naturali*, vol. 6 (Milano: 1864); "Epoche preistoriche in Italia: l'epoca del bronzo nelle terramare dell'Emilia," *Nuova Antologia*, vol. 15 (1870), pp. 347-362; *Relazione sulla Esposizione italiana d'Antropologia e d'Archeologia preistoriche in Bologna nel 1871* (Bologna: 1871); "Il Museo Nazionale Preistorico ed Etnografico a Roma," *Bullettino di Paletnologia Italiana*, vol. 2 (1876), p. 33; "Note per la storia della paletnologia italiana," *Bullettino di Paletnologia Italiana*, vol. 5 (1879), p. 1; "Primo anno del corso di paletnologia nell'Università di Roma," *Bullettino di Paletnologia Italiana*, vol. 8, fasc. 7, 8, 9 (1882); "La Scuola paletnologea italiana," *Nuova Antologia*, vol. 75 (1884), pp. 434-447; "Museo Preistorico ed Etnografico di Roma," *Archivio per l'Antropologia e l'Etnologia*, vol. 31 (1901), p. 313; "Le più antiche civiltà dell'Italia," *Bullettino di Paletnologia Italiana*, vol. 29 (1903), p. 189; "Preistoria" in: *Cinquanta anni di storia italiana (1860-1910)* (Rome: 1911); "Bibliografia paletnologica italiana dal 1860 al 1874," *Bullettino di Paletnologia Italiana*, vol. 42 (1916), pp. 49, 115.

SOURCES: *Un maestro di scienza e d'italianità* (Rome: 1925); E. Bassani, "Origini del Museo preistorico etnografico 'Luigi Pigorini' di Roma," *Belfagor*, vol. 32, no. 4 (31 July 1977), pp. 445-

458; R. Bonghi, "Un nuovo museo preistorico in Roma," *Archivio per l'Antropologia e la Etnografia*, vol. 1 (1876), pp. 464-468; Raffaele Corso, "Un museo che ci manca," *Giornale d'Italia* (27 July 1923); Raffaele Corso, "L'indirizzo paletnologico: L. Pigorini: il Museo de Etnografia Italiana" in: *Problemi di etnografia* (Naples: 1956), pp. 103-105; C. Marchesetti, *Commemorazione di Luigi Pigorini* (Trieste: 1926); G. Sergi, "Luigi Pigorini," *Rivista di Antropologia*, vol. 26 (1925), pp. 519-520.

Giorgio de Finis
[Translation from Italian: CW]

Piłsudski, Bronisław Piotr. Ethnographer, museologist. Born in Zułów (Lithuania, then in Russia) 21 October 1866, died in Paris (France) 17 May 1918. Piłsudski began his studies in Petersburg. For his participation in the assassination attempt on Tsar Aleksandr II he was sentenced to fifteen years of hard labor on Sakhalin Island. After several years he was granted permission to settle freely. He worked as a teacher, and he undertook meteorological and botanical observations. He grew closer to the autochthonous people and became acquainted with the Oroche (Orok), Gilyak and Ainu languages. The primary direction of his interests was the collection of the folklore of the Gilyak people (Nivokh). In 1899 he became employed as a curator for a museum in Vladivostok. In 1902 he obtained partial citizenship rights. In 1903, on the recommendation of the Academy of Sciences, he began a three-year research project on the Ainu of Sakhalin Island. His interests were concentrated on the history of the ancient inhabitants of the island, their religious beliefs and rituals, folklore and languages. In 1907 he returned to Poland and published the results of his investigations. He was an organizer of ethnographic study in Podhale and the founder of the Folk Studies Division of the Tatra Society in Zakopane and the founder of the publication *Rocznik Podhalański*. After 1914 he spent much time abroad (Vienna, Freiburg, Paris). He left behind a legacy of valuable material on the small ethnic groups of the northeast extremes of Siberia (Ainu, Gilyaks, Oroches). Piłsudski was also an initiator of modern ethnographic museology.

MAJOR WORKS: "Szamanizm u tubylców na Sachalinie" ["Shamanism among the inhabitants of Sakhalin Island"], *Lud*, vol. 15 (1909), pp. 261-274; vol. 16 (1910), pp. 117-132; *Materials for the Study of the Ainu Language and Folklore* (Kraków: 1911); "Poezya Gilaków" ["Poetry of the Gilyak"] *Lud*, vol. 17 (1911), pp. 95-124; "Trąd wśród Gilaków i Ajnów" ["Leprosy among the Gilyak and Ainu"], *Lud*, vol. 18 (1912), pp. 79-91; *Krzyże litewskie [Lithuanian Crosses]* (Kraków: 1922).

SOURCES: Wacław Sieroszewski, "Bronisław Piłsudski," *Rocznik Podhalański*, vol. 1 (1914-1921), pp. 3-30; Witold Armon, "Piłsudski, Bronisław Piotr" in: *Polski słownik biograficzny [Polish Biographical dictionary]*, vol. 26 (Wrocław: 1981), pp. 305-308; Henryk Swienko, "Wkład Bronisława Piłsudskiego do etnografii religioznawczej" ["The contribution of Bronisław Piłsudski to the ethnography of religious studies"], *Studia Religioznawcze*, vol. 14 (1979), pp. 77-98.

Maria Niewiadomska and Iwona Grzelakowska
[Translation from Polish: Joel Janicki]

Pinto, Edgar Roquette-. See: *Roquette-Pinto, Edgar.*

Pitrè, Giuseppe. Physician, folklorist. Born in Palermo (Italy) 22 December 1841, died in Palermo (Italy) 9 April 1916. Pitrè is recognized in Italy as one of the founding fathers of folklore as a distinct discipline with its own methods and objectives.

In Italy in the 1870s, the study of the popular traditions, concentrating chiefly on oral traditions (fables, songs, poems and proverbs), was considered a marginal field and subordinate to such disciplines as philology, literary history and dialectology. Pitrè attempted to call this field of study "demopsychology," which was the official title of the chair he occupied at the University of Palermo from 1910 to 1916.

Initially, his works were concerned with the many common themes in native Italian folklore: the songs, fables and riddles current among the population of Sicily. Consequently, his early works strongly exhibited the influence of romanticism that had previously characterized this field of study in Italy. His interests subsequently expanded to all aspects of folk culture, festivals, games, customs, costumes, magical and religious concepts, the family and housing. He dedicated himself assiduously to the collection of handmade objects of the country peasants and in 1909 founded the Museo Etnografico Siciliano (Museum of Sicilian Ethnography) in Palermo, which bears his name today.

At the same time, and with similar fervor, he was developing contacts with the anthropological schools of other countries. His work was significantly influenced by F. Max Müller's *Comparative Mythology* (1856) and E.B. TYLOR's *Primitive Culture* (1871). To provide a framework for his expanded interests he occupied himself with the journal *Archivio per lo Studio delle Tradizioni Popolari*, which he had founded in 1882 with the help of Salvatore Salomone-Marino. This was the first scientific periodical in Italy focusing on either "demology" (folklore) or ethnology that was open to international contributors.

> MAJOR WORKS: *Biblioteca delle tradizioni popolari siciliane* [25 vols.] (Palermo: 1870-1913; reprinted, Bologna: 1970); (founder and director, with S. Salvatore-Marino) *Archivio per lo studio delle tradizioni popolari* [24 vols.] (Palermo: 1882-1909; reprinted, Bologna: 1968); *Bibliografia delle tradizioni popolari d'Italia* (Turin and Palermo: 1894); *Catalogo illustrato della Mostra Etnografica Siciliana, Esposizione Nazionale di Palermo 1891-1892* (Palermo: 1892; reprinted, Palermo: 1968); *Per la inaugurazione del corso di Demopsicologia nella Regia Università di Palermo: Prelezione del Prof. G. Pitrè* (Palermo: 1911).

> SOURCES: Giuseppe Bonomo, "Introduzione e commento" to: G. Pitrè, *Che cos'è il folklore?* (reprint of 1911 edition, Palermo: 1965); *Pitrè e S. Salomone-Marino* (Palermo: 1968) [acts of the conference held at Palermo to mark the 50th anniversary of Pitrè's death, November 1966]; Alberto M. Cirese, "Giuseppe Pitrè" in: Gianni Grana (editor), *Letteratura Italiana: i critici* (Milan: 1969), vol. 1, pp. 279-300; Giuseppe Bonomo, *Pitrè, la Sicilia e i Siciliani* (Palermo: 1989).

> *Paola de Sanctis Ricciardone*
> *[Translation from Italian: Robert B. Marks Ridinger]*

Pitt-Rivers, Augustus Henry Lane-Fox. Archaeologist, military general. Born in Branham Park, Yorkshire (England) 14 April 1827, died on his estate at Rushmore, Wiltshire (England) 4 May 1900. Pitt-Rivers graduated from the Royal Military Academy at Sandhurst in 1841 and rose to the rank of Lieutenant-General. He served briefly in the Crimea but, due to illness, was sent back to England, where for a few years more he served in military administration. During those years, Pitt-Rivers became involved in evaluating new military rifles for the service and, as a result of his acquired expertise, in 1853 he wrote the basic manual on rifle drill for the army. While working with the firearms Pitt-Rivers acquired an extensive collection of various types, which he analyzed and displayed in chronological sequence to demonstrate their historical development. He did the same with other types of weapons and gradually collected and analyzed a great many ethnographic artifacts in similar fashion. He was influenced by Charles Darwin's *Origin of Species* and, on the basis of Darwin's principles, developed his own ideas on the evolution of culture. He lectured on his ideas, displaying his large collection of ethnographic objects arranged according to his own principles of classification, and became a respected member of England's scientific community by the 1870s. He donated his collection of about 14,000 ethnographic artifacts to the University of Oxford where it still exists as the Pitt-Rivers Museum.

In 1880 Pitt-Rivers inherited a large estate. It was there, on its grounds and with ample private funds, that he put into practice for the first time a scientific approach to systematic excavation, detailed recording (not all of which were published during his lifetime), and careful preservation of prehistoric artifacts. This approach was unique in his century, as was his insistence on gathering not just the much-prized art objects which others looted from burial tombs but also the commonplace pieces found in excavated dwelling sites, which he considered much more revealing of the life of the former inhabitants. For all these contributions he is known as the father of scientific archaeology.

MAJOR WORKS: *Excavations in Cranborne Chase, near Rushmore, on the Borders of Dorset and Wilts, 1880-1896* [4 vols.] (London: 1887-1898); *King John's House, Tollard Road, Wilts.* (London: 1890); *The Evolution of Culture and Other Essays* (edited by J.L. Myers) (Oxford: 1906) [includes: "Primitive warfare" (1867-1869); "Early modes of navigation" (1874); "Principles of classification" (1874); and "On the evolution of culture" (1875)].

SOURCES: *Catalogue of the Correspondence and Papers of Augustus Henry Lane-Fox Pitt-Rivers* (London: 1976); Michael Wilman Thomas, *General Pitt-Rivers' Evolution and Archaeology in the Nineteenth Century* (Brandon-on-Avon: 1977); Mark Bowden, *General Pitt-Rivers: the Father of Scientific Archaeology* (Salisbury: 1984); R. Bradley, "Archaeology, evolution and the public good: the intellectual development of General Pitt-Rivers" in: *Proceedings of the Summer Meeting of the Royal Archaeological Institute* (Weymouth: 1983), pp. 1-9.

Thomas L. Mann

Piwocki, Franciszek Ksawery. Art historian, ethnographer. Born in Lwów, Galicia (Austria-Hungary, now in the U.S.S.R.) 19 November 1901, died in Warsaw (Poland) 14 December 1974. Piwocki studied at the University of Lwów. From 1927 he was affiliated with museums, at first in Lwów and later in Warsaw as the director of the Państwowe Muzeum Etnograficzne (State Ethnographic Museum) during the years 1946-1968. In 1946 he was named professor at the Academy of Fine Arts.

A theoretician and historian of art, Piwocki did not limit himself to offical art but embraced folk, naive and amateur art in his studies. He helped to confer an independent artistic and cultural status on folk art in Polish culture. He also made contributions in such "practical" areas as the preservation of folk art and ethnographic museology.

MAJOR WORKS: *Drzeworyt ludowy w Polsce* [*Folk Woodcarving in Poland*] (Lwów: 1934); *O historycznej genezie polskiej sztuki ludowej* [*On the Historical Genesis of Polish Folk Art*] (Warsaw: 1953); "Sztuka ludowa w nauce o sztuce" ["Folk art in the study of art"], *Lud*, vol. 51 (1968), pp. 359-389; *Sztuka żywa: szkice z teorii i metodyki historii sztuki* [*Living Art: Sketches of the Theory and Methodology of the History of Art*] (Wrocław: 1970).

SOURCES: *Granice sztuki: z badań nad teorią i historią sztuki, kulturą artystyczną oraz sztuką ludową* [*The Limits of Art: from the Investigations of the Theory and History of Art, Artistic Culture and Folk Art*] (Warsaw: 1972); Jacek Olędzki, "Ksawery Piwocki (1901-1974)," *Etnografia Polska*, vol. 20 (1976), pp. 11-15; Kazimierz Pietkiewicz, "Ksawery Piwocki (1901-1974)," *Lud*, vol. 60 (1974), pp. 363-367.

Maria Niewiadomska and Iwona Grzelakowska
[*Translation from Polish: Joel Janicki*]

Pol, Wincenty. Poet, geographer, ethnographer. Born in Lublin (Russia, now in Poland) 20 April 1807, died in Kraków, Galicia (Austria-Hungary, now in Poland) 2 December 1872. Pol studied in Lwów and Vilnius. He made a series of trips through Europe (Italy, France, Switzerland, Austria, Galicia) making ethnogeographic observations. Ultimately he became affiliated with the University of Kraków where he was awarded an honorary doctorate and an independent chair in geography.

Through his lectures at the university the patriotic poet propagated the idea of Polishness. Pol put great stock in the knowledge obtained from the personal examination of folk culture. He expanded his inquiry into anthropo-geography, history and ethnographical linguistics. He determined the place of ethnography as a separate science, considering it as a widely embracing general geography. He introduced ethnography as a lecture course at the university and argued for wide-ranging studies in the field, the goal of which would be the isolation of types examined in terms of origin and nationality and also their mutual relationship. Pol initiated the discipline of anthropo-geography in Poland, emphasized the problems of the links between man and his natural environment and introduced studies on the territorial differentiation of folk culture.

MAJOR WORKS: *Volkslieder der Polen gesammelt und übersetzt* (Leipzig: 1833); *Pieśń o ziemi naszej* [*Song of Our Land*] (Poznań: 1843); *Rzut oka na umiejętność geografii ze stanowiska uniwersyteckiego wykładu* [*A Glance at Geographical Knowledge from the Perspective of the University Lecture*] (Kraków: 1850); *Rzut oka na północne stoki Karpat* [*A Glance at the Northern Slopes of the Carpathians*] (Kraków: 1851); *Obrazy z życia i natury* [*Images from Life and Nature*] (Kraków: 1869); *Dzieła wierszem i prozą* [*Works in Verse and Prose*] (Lwów: 1875-1878).

SOURCES: Anna Kutrzeba-Pojnarowa, *Kultura ludowa i jej badacze* [*Folk Culture and its Researchers*] (Warsaw: 1977); Stefan Majchrowski, *Wincenty Pol: szkic biograficzny* [*Wincenty Pol: Biographical Sketch*] (Lublin: 1982); Kazimiera Zawistowicz-Adamska, *Wincenty Pol: badacz kultury ludowej* [*Wincenty Pol: Investigator of Folk Culture*] (Warsaw: 1966).

Maria Niewiadomska and Iwona Grzelakowska
[*Translation from Polish: Joel Janicki*]

Polanyi, Karl. Economic historian. Born in Budapest (Hungary) 25 October 1886, died in Pickering, a suburb of Toronto (Ontario) 23 April 1964. Polanyi was an economic historian known to anthropologists for his work in economic anthropology. He studied law and philosophy in Budapest, served as an officer in World War I and then worked in journalism as foreign affairs editor of Vienna's *Österreichische Volkswirt* throughout the 1920s. He emigrated to England in 1933 where he became intensely interested in the origins of the British Industrial Revolution and the enormity of its economic and social consequences. This was the subject of his first book, *The Great Transformation*, written while he was a resident scholar at Bennington College in Vermont between 1940 and 1943.

The eminent American economist, John Maurice Clark, was sufficiently impressed by *The Great Transformation* to invite Polanyi to Columbia University as a visiting professor of economic history in 1947 (when Polanyi was already 61). Polanyi had to retire from teaching at Columbia in 1953 but remained there for another four years to supervise a research project jointly undertaken with the anthropologist CONRAD M. ARENSBERG which was published as *Trade and Market in the Early Empires*, the book by which Polanyi is best known to anthropologists. His third book, *Dahomey and the Slave Trade*, was published posthumously.

Polanyi's work has inspired a good deal of research and publication by constituencies of academics in economic anthropology, economic archaeology, economic history, comparative economic systems, and Third World development. They employ Polanyi's paradigm in their analysis of pre-industrial economies throughout the world and in their analysis of the modern growth and development of such economies. In response to this interest, the Karl Polanyi Institute of Political Economy was established at Concordia University (Montréal, Québec) in the 1980s. The Institute organized conferences on Polanyi's work in Budapest (1986), Montréal (1988) and Milan (1990).

Polanyi's work remains controversial among anthropologists and others because it is one of three rival theoretical systems employed to analyze the structure and performance of early and primitive economies, the other two being conventional micro-economics ("formalism") and Marxian analysis.

Polanyi invented a conceptual vocabulary of socio-economic terms to specify the core attributes of the two kinds of aboriginal (pre-colonial) tribal economies studied by anthropologists, stateless tribal economies (e.g., Trobriands, Nuer, Kwakiutl) and tribal kingdoms (e.g., Dahomey, Asante, Inca): "reciprocity," "redistribution," "special-purpose money," "port of trade," "politically administered trade." He argued that the differences between such aboriginal tribal economies and modern industrial capitalism were more important than their similarities; that the absence not only of machine technology but also of economy-wide land, labor, and product markets and of modern cash, meant that such tribal economies were controlled by and direct expressions of lineage and political organization—that tribal economies are "embedded" in their societies; and that, the further back one goes into pre-industrial economic history, the more such early economies resemble those studied by anthropologists, a conclusion shared by such eminent economic historians as M.I. Finley (*The Ancient Economy* (Berkeley: 1973)) and Philip Grierson ("The origins of money," *Research in Economic Anthropology*, vol. 1 (1978), pp. 1-35). Polanyi's work is thought to be particularly illuminating on the nature of early money uses and the organization of early foreign trade.

MAJOR WORKS: *The Great Transformation* (New York: 1944); (with C.M. Arensberg and H.W. Pearson) *Trade and Market in the Early Empires* (Glencoe, Ill.: 1957); *Dahomey and the Slave Trade* (Seattle: 1966); *Primitive, Archaic, and Modern Economies: Essays of Karl Polanyi* (edited by George Dalton) (New York: 1968); *The Livelihood of Man* (edited by Harry W. Pearson) (New York: 1977).

SOURCES: Lucette Valensi [et al.], "Economic anthropology and history: the work of Karl Polanyi" in: George Dalton (editor), *Research in Economic Anthropology* (Greenwich, Conn.: 1981), vol. 4, pp. 1-94; Kari Polanyi-Levitt and Marguerite Mendell, "Karl Polanyi: a biographical sketch," *Telos* (1987), pp. 121-131; George Dalton and Jasper Köcke, "The work of the Polanyi Group: past, present, and future" in: Sutti Ortiz (editor), *Economic Anthropology* (New York: 1983), pp. 21-50; S.C. Humphreys, "History, economics, and anthropology: the work of Karl Polanyi," *History and Theory*, vol. 8 (1969), pp. 165-212; A.M. Sievers, *Has Market Capitalism Collapsed? a Critique of Karl Polanyi's New Economics* (New York: 1949); Louis Dumont, "Préface" to: *La grande transformation* (Paris: 1983), pp. i-xix; Y. Garlan, "L'oeuvre de Polanyi: la place de l'économie dans les sociétés anciennes," *La Pensée*, no. 171 (1973), pp. 119-127; Hans Zeisel, "Polanyi, Karl" in: David L. Sills (editor), *International Encyclopedia of the Social Sciences* (New York: 1968-1979), vol. 12, pp. 172-174.

George Dalton

Poniatowski, Stanisław. Anthropologist, ethnologist. Born in Ceranów (Poland) 6 October 1884, died in the concentration camp at Litomierzyce (now Czechoslovakia) 7 January 1945. Poniatowski studied mechanics at the Warsaw Polytechnic and archaeology and ethnology at the University of Zürich. He obtained his doctorate in 1911, and in 1934 he was appointed associate professor at the University of Warsaw. He directed the Division of Ethnology at the Institute of Anthropological Studies (to 1935), as well as the Department of Ethnology and General Ethnography at the University of Warsaw.

Poniatowski was an organizer of Polish scientific ethnography. He developed his interests in four areas: methodology, religious studies, investigation of cultural spheres (or circles) and material culture. He was a representative of the Cultural-Historical School. His studies focused on the analysis of the structure, function and ideology of cultural artifacts with a view to establishing their relative chronology and cultural origin. The goal of much of his work was the elucidation of the genesis of particular artifacts and also folk groups. Poniatowski conducted research not only in Poland but also in the Trans-Amur region in Eastern Siberia (1914).

> MAJOR WORKS: "O metodzie historicznej w etnologii" ["On the historical method in ethnology"], *Przegląd Historyczny*, vol. 1 (1919), pp. 303-319; *Zadanie i przedmiot etnologii* [*The Task and Subject of Ethnology*] (Warsaw: 1922); *Materials to the Vocabulary of the Amur Golds* (Warsaw: 1923); *Geneza łuku triumfalnego* [*The Genesis of the Triumphal Arch*] (Warsaw: 1930); *Etnografia polski* [*Polish Ethnography*] (Warsaw: 1932); *Pochodzenie ludów aryjskich* [*Origin of the Aryan Peoples*] (Warsaw: 1932); "Mahabvrata: metoda badania genezy wytworów kulturowych" ["Mahabarata: investigative method of the genesis of cultural artifacts"], *Lud*, vol. 36 (1946), pp. 107-162; "Dziennik wyprawy do kraju Goldów i Oroczonów" ["Journal of the expedition to the lands of the Golds and Oroches in 1914"], *Lud*, vol. 50 (1964-1965), pp. 7-120.

> SOURCES: Edward Bulanda, "Pamięci wybitnego etnologa polskiego prof. dr Stanisława Poniatowskiego" ["In memory of the outstanding Polish ethnologist, Dr. Stanisław Poniatowski"], *Lud*, vol. 36 (1939-1945), pp. 19-32; Małgorzata Terlecka (editor), *Historia etnografii polskiej* [*History of Polish Ethnography*] (Wrocław: 1973); Janina Rosen-Przeworska, "Poniatowski, Stanisław" in: *Polski słownik biograficzny* [*Polish Biographical Dictionary*], vol. 27 (Wrocław: 1983), pp. 487-489.

Maria Niewiadomska and Iwona Grzelakowska
[Translation from Polish: Joel Janicki]

Pope, Saxton Temple. Surgeon, professor of medicine, amateur ethnologist. Born in Fort Stockton (Texas) 4 September 1875, died in San Francisco (California) 8

August 1926. Pope was the son and grandson of military surgeons and spent much of his youth on frontier army posts. He obtained his medical degree from the University of California in 1899 and practiced as a surgeon until 1912, when he joined the medical school from which he had graduated. Pope was a very popular professor and a surgeon of renown.

His interest in anthropology came about in 1912 through a chance observation of Ishi, the Yahi Indian, practicing with a bow. Ishi began his residence at the University of California's museum, in San Francisco, in 1911, under the auspices of ALFRED L. KROEBER, THOMAS TALBOT WATERMAN and E.W. GIFFORD, the anthropology faculty at the time. Pope had learned archery from reservation Indians in the 1880s and was intrigued by what he saw of Ishi's stance and style. They became good friends; through Ishi, Pope met Kroeber and the other anthropologists and became a frequent visitor to the museum.

Pope and Ishi practiced with their bows in Golden Gate Park, near the museum and the medical school's hospital. Ishi made many bows and arrows for Pope, and the latter was led to examine the museum's considerable collection of archery equipment. In 1914 Pope, Kroeber and Waterman took Ishi on a month-long hunting trip to his home area in northern California, near Mount Lassen. Pope also was Ishi's personal physician from 1912 until 1916, when the last Yahi died of tuberculosis.

Pope published a number of works on archery and was partially responsible for its resurgence as a sport in the middle 20th century. He compared different cultures' archery equipment and techniques and experimented with various materials in bow construction. One of the most useful experiments he performed, from the perspective of later researchers, was the testing of museum specimen bows that are now far too old and brittle to be bent.

MAJOR WORKS: *Yahi Archery* (Berkeley: 1918) (= *University of California Publications in American Archaeology and Ethnology*, vol. 13, no. 3, pp. 103-152); *The Medical History of Ishi* (Berkeley: 1920) (= *University of California Publications in American Archaeology and Ethnology*, vol. 13, no. 5, pp. 175-213); *A Study of Bows and Arrows* (Berkeley: 1923) (= *University of California Publications in American Archaeology and Ethnology*, vol. 13, no. 9, pp. 329-414); *Hunting with the Bow and Arrow* (San Francisco: 1923).

SOURCES: A.L. Kroeber, "Saxton Temple Pope," *American Anthropologist*, vol. 29 (1927), pp. 341-342; "Pope, Saxton Temple" in: *The National Cyclopaedia of American Biography*, vol. 20 (New York: 1929), pp. 434-435; Theodora Kroeber, *Ishi in Two Worlds* (Berkeley: 1962).

David Lonergan

Potapov, L.P. (Leonid Pavlovich). Ethnographer, historian, museum director, Turkologist. Born in Barnaul, Altaï (Russia) 6 July 1905. Potapov was a doctor of historical sciences and a professor. He worked in Leningrad at the Gosudarstvennyĭ muzeĭ étnografii narodov SSSR (State Museum of the Ethnography of the Peoples of the U.S.S.R.) and the Institut étnografii (Institute of Ethnography) of the Soviet Academy of Sciences as director of the Siberian department and deputy director for scientific work.

Much of Potapov's scholarly work is devoted to the reconstruction of the history of the nonliterate peoples of Siberia—the Kazakhs, Shor (Shorians), Altaïs, Tuvinians and others. He wrote about the nomads' patriarchal family structure, their traditions of land- and cattle-ownership, shamanism, material culture, and present-day ethnography, as well as the problem of national consolidation. Potapov was an experienced museum worker. He was the author of more than 200 scholarly works. In addition, he participated in and guided the preparation of a series of major overviews.

MAJOR WORKS: "Okhotnich'i pover'ía i obríády u altaĭskikh tíurkov" in: *Kul'tura i pis'mennost' Vostoka*, vol. 5 (Baku: 1929), pp. 123-149; *Ocherk istorii Oĭrotii: Altaĭtsy v period russkoĭ kolonizaísii* (Novosibirsk: 1933); *Razlozhenie rodovogo stroía u severnykh altaĭtsev: material'noe proizvodstvo* (Moscow and Leningrad: 1935); *Ocherki po istorii Shorii* (Moscow and Leningrad: 1936); "Obríad ozhivleníía shamanskogo bubna u tíukoíazychnykh plemen Altaía," *Trudy Instituta ètnografii AN SSSR*, vol. 1 (1947), pp. 159-182; *Ocherki po istorii altaĭtsev* (Novosibirsk: 1948; reprinted, Moscow and Leningrad: 1953); *Kratkie ocherki istorii i ètnografii khakasov, XVII-XIX vv.* (Abakan: 1952); *Narody ÍUzhnoĭ Sibiri* (Novosibirsk: 1953); "O sushchnosti petriarkhal'no-feodal'nykh otnosheniĭ u kochevykh narodov Sredneĭ Azii i Kazakhstana," *Voprosy istorii*, no. 6 (1954), pp. 73-89; *Proiskhozhdenie i formirovanie khakasskoĭ narodnosti* (Abakan: 1957); (with M.G. Levin) "Vvedenie" to: *Istoriko-ètnograficheskiĭ atlas Sibiri* (Moscow and Leningrad: 1961), pp. 3-11; *Ètnicheskiĭ sostav i proiskhozhdenie altaĭtsev* (Leningrad: 1969); *Ocherki narodnogo byta tuvintsev* (Moscow: 1969); "Mify altae-saíanskikh narodov kak istoricheskiĭ istochnik" in: N.S. Modorov (editor-in-chief) *Voprosy arkheologii i ètnografii Gornogo Altaía* (Gorno-Altaĭsk: 1983), pp. 96-110.

SOURCES: "Spisok osnovnikh rabot L.P. Potapova," *Sovetskaía ètnografiía*, no. 6 (1975), pp. 197-198; and no. 3 (1985), pp. 115-117 [bibliography]; S.M. Abramzon and V.P. D'íakonova, "K 70-letiíu L.P. Potapova," *Uchenye zapiski Tuvinskogo nauchno-issledovatel'skogo Instituta íazyka, literatury i istorii* [Kyzyl], no. 17 (1975), pp. 242-247.

A.M. Reshetov
[Translation from Russian: Thomas L. Mann]

Potekhin, I.I. (Ivan Izosimovich). Ethnographer, historian, Africanist.

Born in Krivosheino, Eniseĭskaía Guberniía, Krasnoíarskiĭ Kraĭ (Russia) 1 (14) October 1903, died in Moscow (Russian S.F.S.R.) 17 September 1964. A doctor of historical sciences and a professor, Potekhin was one of the creators of the Soviet school of Africanists. He served as deputy director of the Institut ètnografii (Institute of Ethnography) of the Soviet Academy of Sciences (1949-1959) and as the first director of the Institut Afriki (Institute of Africa) of the Soviet Academy of Sciences (1959-1964). He was one of the principal authors and the editor of the volume, *Narody Afriki*. The author of more than 200 works, he devoted much of his research to the national and social-economic development of African societies.

MAJOR WORKS: "Voennaía demokratiía matabele," *Trudy Instituta ètnografii AN SSSR*, vol. 12 (1951), pp. 234-254; *Formirovanie natsional'noĭ obshchnosti íuzhnoafrikanskikh bantu* (Moscow: 1955) (= *Trudy Instituta ètnografii AN SSSR*, vol. 29); *Rodovye otnosheniía v sisteme sotsial'nykh otnosheniĭ sovremennoĭ afrikanskoĭ derevni* (Moscow: 1956); "O feodalizme u ashanti," *Sovetskaía ètnografiía*, no. 6 (1960), pp. 86-91; "Problemy bor'by s perezhitkami proshlogo na afrikanskom kontinente," *Sovetskaía ètnografiía*, no. 4 (1964), pp. 186-195; (co-editor, with D.A. Ol'derogge) *Narody Afriki* (Moscow: 1954).

SOURCES: "Ivan Izosimovich Potekhin," *Sovetskaía ètnografiía*, no. 6 (1964), pp. 171-173; "Spisok osnovnykh pechatnykh rabot I.I. Potekhina," *Sovetskaía ètnografiía*, no. 6 (1964), p. 173-175 [bibliography].

A.M. Reshetov
[Translation from Russian: Thomas L. Mann]

Powdermaker, Hortense. Anthropologist, union organizer, educator. Born in Philadelphia (Pennsylvania) 24 December 1896, died in Berkeley (California) 15 June 1970. Powdermaker is best known for her wide-ranging field studies and for her application of the anthropological method to the study of social issues and popular culture in the United States. Her early training in history and the humanities at Goucher College was complemented by an interest in socialism and community activism. Following graduation in 1920, Powdermaker took a job with the Amalgamated Clothing Workers of America and she went to Cleveland and Rochester as a union organizer.

In 1925 Powdermaker began her anthropological studies at the London School of Economics under the mentorship of BRONISLAW MALINOWSKI. Soon after earning her doctorate in 1928 she embarked on her first field expedition to New Ireland where she conducted a general ethnographic study of a stoneage village, published in 1933 as *Life in Lesu*. When she returned from the field Powdermaker was hailed in a flurry of news articles in New York City as a brave, young female "explorer," and as "the first woman to risk her life for so long a time among the cannibal Melanesians" (*New York Evening Journal* (15 July 1920), p. 1, second news section). The irony is that Powdermaker's own efforts were aimed at demystifying and de-sensationalizing western views of "primitive" peoples.

Powdermaker was an early proponent of psychological anthropology and of critical reflexivity through self-analysis applied to the entire field research and ethnographic writing endeavor. She used anthropology as a source of cultural critique and was arguably the first anthropologist to conduct fieldwork in a modern community: Sunflower County, Mississippi (1932-1933). Powdermaker maintained cordial relations with both whites and blacks while studying the psychological costs to both groups of accommodation to the South's race-caste system. The resulting monograph, *After Freedom*, was followed by a textbook for high school teachers and students, *Probing Our Prejudices*.

A lifelong fan of the cinema (even grade "B" movies entertained her during the stressful field research in Mississippi), Powdermaker went to Hollywood (1946-1947) to initiate a path-breaking study of the conflicts between business and art in the film world. *Hollywood, the Dream Factory* explored the power dynamics that influenced the nature and quality of American film. This only partly successful study led to another major fieldwork venture (1953-1954) aimed at exploring the effects of the mass media on "modernizing" African migrant workers in the copper belt of Northern Rhodesia, published as *Copper Town: Changing Africa*. The work, however, for which Powdermaker is best known is her candid and often self-critical autobiographical account of the practice of anthropology: *Stranger and Friend: the Way of an Anthropologist*.

The founder of the department of Anthropology and Sociology at Queens College in New York City, Powdermaker was a challenging teacher of African ethnography, field methods, and culture and personality. She mentored a number of eminent anthropologists through an intellectual style that was witty, cosmopolitan, and irreverent. Of all her many awards she most treasured her Distinguished Teaching Award from the Queens College Alumni Association. Powdermaker served as President of the American Ethnological Association. After she retired from teaching in 1967 Powdermaker moved to Berkeley, California, where she lived in the Kroeber "compound" until her death. She was involved in a study of Berkeley youth culture and in the early stages of writing a book on gender and culture when she died of a heart attack after returning home from the movies.

MAJOR WORKS: *Life in Lesu: the Study of a Melanesian Society in New Ireland* (New York: 1933); *After Freedom: a Cultural Study in the Deep South* (New York: 1939); "The channeling of Negro aggression by the cultural process," *American Journal of Sociology*, vol. 48 (1943), pp. 122-130; *Probing Our Prejudices* (New York: 1944); "An anthropologist looks at the race problem," *Social Action*, vol. 11 (1945), pp. 5-13; *Hollywood, the Dream Factory: an Anthropologist Studies the Movie Makers* (Boston: 1950); *Mass Communications Seminar: Edited Proceedings of an Interdisciplinary Seminar Held May 11-13, 1951 under the Auspices of the Wenner-Gren Foundation for Anthropological Research* (New York: 1953); "An anthropological approach to the problem of obesity," *Bulletin, New York Academy of Medicine*, vol. 36 (1960), pp. 5-14; *Copper Town: Changing Africa, the Human Situation on the Rhodesian Copperbelt* (New York: 1962); *Stranger and Friend: the Way of an Anthropologist* (New York: 1966): "Field work" in: David L. Sills (editor), *International Encyclopedia of the Social Sciences* (New York: 1968-1979), vol. 5, pp. 418-424.

SOURCES: "Woman finds tribe having no religion," *New York Times* (15 July 1930), p. 25; "Woman back after living a year in cannibal tribe," *The New York Telegram* (14 July 1930), p. 22; "Expert explorer," *New York Evening Journal* (15 July 1930); "Hortense Powdermaker is dead: an authority on varied cultures," *New York Times* (17 June 1970), p. 47; "Hortense Powdermaker," *Baltimore Evening Sun* (17 June 1970); Eric Wolf, "Hortense Powdermaker, 1900-1970," *American Anthropologist*, vol. 73 (1971), pp. 783-786; George Traeger, "Hortense Powdermaker: a tribute," *American Anthropologist*, vol. 73 (1971), pp. 786-787; Sydel Silverman, "Hortense Powdermaker" in: Ute Gacs [et al.] (editors), *Women Anthropologists: a Biographical Dictionary* (New York: 1988), pp. 291-296.

Nancy Scheper-Hughes

Powell, John Wesley. Anthropologist, geologist, philosopher. Born in Mt. Morris (New York) 24 March 1834, died in Haven (Maine) 23 September 1902. Powell grew up in the midwestern United States and fought in the Civil War, in which he lost his right arm at the battle of Shiloh. During and immediately following his famous explorations of the Colorado River canyons (1869-1876) Powell did sporadic fieldwork among the Numic peoples (Shoshone, Ute, Paiute) of the Great Basin and Grand Canyon regions. While he emphasized language and mythology, Powell's interests extended to most aspects of social life: kinship terminology, ceremonialism, curing practices, material culture; he even noted treatment of children, the aged and the insane. His linguistic and ethnographic manuscripts remained unpublished, however, for nearly a century. His influence in anthropology consequently lay in his strong unilinear evolutionism and his founding of the Smithsonian's Bureau of American Ethnology, which he directed from 1879 to 1902. Heavily influenced by Charles Darwin, HERBERT SPENCER, LEWIS HENRY MORGAN and his own geological observations, Powell developed a rigid and comprehensive view of human social and mental evolution. He formulated his opinions in essays between 1882 and 1898 and in the Bureau of American Ethnology's *Annual Reports*, and he attempted to institutionalize his evolutionism through the bureau. With "mind" as the universal agency of development, he envisioned lines of human activity running from savagery to civilization; each culture-grade was a stage of human mental growth with characteristic and corresponding "inventions" predictable at each stage—kinship, property, art, political organization, philosophy, religion, etc. To varying degrees he imposed his framework on his bureau workers; but most took him on their own terms. He supported FRANZ BOAS's collection of texts and encouraged publication with interlinear translations for future reference. His permanent contributions to anthropology through the BAE included, in addition, the Cyrus Thomas survey of North American Indian mounds; vigorous collection of Native American vocabularies; the 1891 linguistic map of North America; sponsorship of the fieldwork of FRANK HAMILTON CUSHING, MATILDA COXE STEVENSON, JAMES MOONEY, Victor and Cosmos Mindeleff, William Henry Holmes and many others; an early rationale for applied government anthropology (for improved reservation conditions); and the model of federal, public support of linguistics, archaeology and ethnographic fieldwork and lobbying for preservation of antiquities.

> MAJOR WORKS: (with G.W. Ingalls) *Report of Special Commissioners J.W. Powell and G.W. Ingalls on the Condition of the Ute Indians of Utah; the Pai-Utes of Utah, Northern Arizona, Southern Nevada, and Southeastern California; the Go-Si-Utes of Utah and Nevada; the Northwestern Shoshones of Idaho and Utah; and the Western Shoshones of Nevada; and Report Concerning Claims of Settlers in the Mo-a-pa Valley (Southeastern Nevada)* (Washington: 1874); "An overland trip to the Grand Canyon," *Scribner's Monthly*, vol. 10 (1875), pp. 659-678; "The ancient province of Tusayan," *Scribner's Monthly*, vol. 11 (1875), pp. 193-213; "Sketch of Lewis H. Morgan," *Popular Science Monthly*, vol. 18 (1881), pp. 114-121; "Darwin's contributions to philosophy," *Proceedings of the Biological Society of Washington*, vol. 1 (1882), pp. 60-70; "Human evolution," *Transactions of the Anthropological Society of Washington*, vol. 2 (1883), pp. 176-208; "From savagery to barbarism," *Transactions of the Anthropological Society of Washington*, vol. 3 (1885), pp. 173-196; "Museums of ethnology and their classification," *Science*, vol. 9 (1887), pp. 612-614; "Competition as a factor in human evolution," *American Anthropologist*, vol. 1 (1898), pp. 297-321; Introductions to the *Annual Report of the Bureau of American Ethnology* (1879-1902).

> SOURCES: Wallace Stegner, *Beyond the Hundredth Meridian* (Boston: 1954); William C. Darrah, *Powell of the Colorado* (Princeton: 1951); Curtis M. Hinsley, *Savages and Scientists: the Smithsonian Institution and the Development of American Anthropology, 1846-1910* (Washington: 1981); Don D. and Catherine S. Fowler, *The Anthropology of the Numa: John Wesley Powell's Manuscripts on the Numic Peoples of Western North America, 1868-1880* (Washington: 1971); Don D. Fowler and John Matley, *Material Culture of the Numa: the Powell Collection, 1868-1876* (Washington: 1975); Don D. Fowler, Robert C. Euler, and Catherine S. Fowler, *John Wesley Powell and the Anthropology of the Canyon Country* (Washington: 1969).

Curtis Hinsley

Preuß, Konrad Theodor. Anthropologist, historian of religions. Born in Preußisch-Eylau (Germany) 2 June 1869, died in Berlin (Germany) 8 June 1938. Preuß was educated as a school teacher and through additional studies received a Ph.D. in ethnology in 1894 from the University of Königsberg. From 1895 until the end of his life he was employed at the Berlin Museum für Völkerkunde (Ethnographic Museum). His first field research (1905-1907) was done among Mexican Indians (Cora, Huichol, Mexicano). Only a portion of the results were published (*Die Nayarit-Expedition*) due to a second field trip to Colombia in 1913-1919, during which Preuß did archaeological investigations of the San Agustín culture and ethnographical fieldwork among Uitoto and Kágaba Indians. Three sizeable publications were the outcome of his Colombian years. His field methodology encompassed long-term residence among the groups studied and a focus on oral lore recorded and published in the indigeneous languages. In following these principles Preuß was far ahead of his time and most of his fellow ethnographers. His conception of primitive religion, for which his fieldwork served as empirical background, started off with criticism of E.B. TYLOR's theory of animism. For some time he followed LUCIEN LÉVY-BRUHL's theory of the primitive mind but then proceeded to the theory of a primeval

"*Hochgottglaube*" (belief in a high god) along the lines of ANDREW LANG and the Vienna School (WILHELM SCHMIDT and WILHELM KOPPERS). Although important at his time, these and Preuß's own contributions to the theory of religion are now considered obsolete. His *Habilitation* under EDUARD SELER in 1921 opened university teaching for him. However, he was not an inspired teacher. Later during his life Preuß focused on early colonial pictorial and textual documents from Mexico in the Nahuatl language, which he considered major ethnographic sources worth publishing, translating and commenting on as he had done earlier with his own field recordings. Most of these studies were co-authored with Ernst Mengin (1893-1973). They greatly stimulated subsequent ethnohistorical studies in Mexico and Germany. Preuß's editorship of the controversial *Lehrbuch für Völkerkunde* (1937) was formal only, since the original editor, Leonhard Adam (1891-1960), being a "non-Aryan," was not permitted to appear as such in the imprint in Nazi Germany.

MAJOR WORKS: "Der Ursprung der Religion und Kunst," *Globus*, vol. 86 (1904), pp. 333-337, and vol. 87 (1905), pp. 325-327; *Die Nayarit-Expedition: Textaufnahmen und Beobachtungen unter mexikanischen Indianern*. Vol. 1. *Die Religion der Cora-Indianer* (Leipzig: 1912) [following volumes were never published, but some of the materials have been edited posthumously; see below]; "Forschungsreise zu den Kágaba-Indianern der Sierra Nevada de Santa Marta in Columbien," *Anthropos*, vols. 14-22. (1919-1927) [separately printed as a book in 1926-1927]; *Religion und Mythologie der Uitoto* [2 vols.] (Göttingen: 1921-1923); *Monumentale vorgeschichtliche Kunst: Ausgrabungen im Quellgebiet des Magdalena in Kolumbien und ihre Ausstrahlung in Amerika* [2 vols.] (Göttingen: 1929) [tr.: *Arte monumental prehistórico: excavaciones hechas en el Alto Magdalena y San Agustín* (Bogotá: 1931; 2nd ed., Bogotá: 1974)]; *Der religiöse Gehalt der Mythen* (Tübingen: 1933) (= *Sammlung gemeinverständlicher wissenschaftlicher Vorträge*, vol. 162); (with Ernst Mengin) *Die mexikanische Bilderhandschrift Historia Tolteca-Chichimeca* (Berlin: 1937-1938) (= *Baessler Archiv*, Beiheft 9 and vol. 21, pp. 1-66); *Nahua-Texte aus San Pedro Jícora in Durango* [3 vols.] (edited by Elsa Ziehm) (Berlin: 1968-1975).

SOURCES: Archives of the Museum für Völkerkunde, Berlin-Dahlem; *Minerva, Jahrbuch der gelehrten Welt*, vol. 15 (1905/1906) and vol. 16 (1906/1907); H. Jungbluth, *Konrad Theodor Preuß und seine religionsgeschichtlichen Grundanschauungen* [Ph.D. dissertation] (Bonn: 1933); R. Thurnwald, "Nachruf auf K.Th. Preuß," *Archiv für Religionswissenschaften*, vol. 36 (1939), pp. 181-189; F.R. Lehmann, "K.Th. Preuß," *Zeitschrift für Ethnologie*, vol. 71 (1940), pp. 145-150; H. Snethlage, "Konrad Theodor Preuss," *Ethnologischer Anzeiger*, vol. 4, part 2 (1944), pp. 261-267 [unreliable bibliography]; Berthold Riese, *Indianische Handschriften und Berliner Forscher* (Berlin: 1988), pp. 41-43.

Berthold Riese

Propp, V.IA. *(Vladimir IAkovlevich)*. Folklorist, ethnographer. Born in St. Petersburg (Russia) 17 (29) April 1895, died in Leningrad (Russian S.F.S.R.) 22 August 1970. Propp was a doctor of the philological sciences and a professor at Leningrad University.

Propp made a substantial contribution to the study of the origin, history and nature of the principal genres of Russian folklore: the folktale, the epic poem, the historical song, annual ritual folklore, wedding songs, lyrical folk poetry, legends and so forth. He preferred the structural-typological method of analysis of the folktale. Propp believed that one of the most important features of folklore was its organic and deeply ethnographic nature. In this connection, the monograph of Propp, *Istoricheskie korni volshebnoĭ skazki* [*The Historical Roots of the Magic Folktale*], was more important for the Russians than *The Golden Bough* of JAMES G. FRAZER was for western Europeans. Propp argued that the esthetics of folklore and its specific character are genetically and historically conditioned by connections with various phenomena of folk customs and life. He developed principles that now constitute an important part of the methodology of scholarly folklore studies. Propp was a staunch supporter of the comparative-historical method in the study of folklore. His work defined an entire direction in the contemporary study of folk literature.

MAJOR WORKS: *Morfologiia skazki* (Leningrad: 1928; Moscow: 1969) [tr.: *Morphology of the Folktale* (Bloomington: 1958; Austin: 1968); *Morphologie du conte* (Paris: 1970)]; *Istoricheskie korni volshebnoĭ skazki* (Leningrad: 1946; Leningrad: 1986); *Russkiĭ geroicheskiĭ ėpos* (Leningrad: 1955; Moscow and Leningrad: 1958); *Russkie agrarnye prazdniki (opyt istoriko-ėtnograficheskogo issledovaniia)* (Leningrad: 1963); "Prinfsipy klassifikafsii fol'klornykh zhanrov," *Sovetskaia ėtnografiia*, no. 4 (1964), pp. 147-154; "Zmeeborstvo Georgiia v svete fol'klore" in: B.N. Putilov and K.V. Chistov (editors), *Fol'klor i ėtnografiia russkogo Severa* (Leningrad: 1973), pp. 160-178; *Fol'klor i deĭstvitel'nost': izbrannye stat'i* (Moscow: 1976).

SOURCES: B.N. Putilov, "V.IA. Propp," *Sovetskaia ėtnografiia*, no. 1 (1971), pp. 178-180; B.N. Putilov, "Problemy fol'klora v trudakh V.IA. Proppa" in: *Tipologicheskie issledovaniia po fol'kloru: sbornik pamiati V.IA. Proppa* (Moscow: 1975), pp. 7-15; "Bibliografiia trudov V.IA. Proppa" in: *Tipologicheskie issledovaniia po fol'kloru: sbornik pamiati V.IA. Proppa* (Moscow: 1975), pp. 16-25 [bibliography]; V.K. Chistov, "V.IA. Propp: legendy i fakty," *Sovetskaia ėtnografiia*, no. 6 (1981), pp. 52-64.

A.M. Reshetov
[Translation from Russian: Thomas L. Mann]

Purkyně, Jan Evangelista. Physician, physiologist, anthropologist, anatomist, histologist, embryologist. Born 18 December 1787 in Libochovice, Bohemia (Austria, now in Czechoslovakia), died in Prague (Austria-Hungary, now in Czechoslovakia) 28 July 1869. Purkyně was one of the greatest natural scientists of the 18th and 19th centuries. In 1987, in honor of the 200th anniversary of his birth, Purkyně's name was placed on the UNESCO calendar.

Purkyně studied at the philosophical and medical faculties of Charles University in Prague. His doctoral dissertation was on the theme *Přispěvky k poznání vidění ze subjektivního hlediska* [*Subjective Contributions to the Knowledge of Vision*]. His inaugural dissertation (*Habilitationsschrift*), *Commentatio de examine physiologico organi visus et systematis cutanei*, is among Purkyně's most pioneering works. In 1823 he was named a professor of physiology and pathology at the University of Wrocław (then Breslau), and in 1827 he became a dean of the medical faculty of that university, where he founded the world's first physiological institute. He became in 1829 a member of the Academia Leopoldine Carolina Naturae Curiosorum, in 1832 a member of the Royal Academy of Sciences in Berlin, in 1836 a corresponding member of the Imperial Academy of Sciences in St. Petersburg, in 1850 a member of the Royal Society in London and a professor of physiology at the university in Prague. In 1853 Purkyně founded the Czech journal of natural history *Živa* and in 1862 *Časopis lékařů českých* [*Journal of Czech Physicians*], both of which have continued their publication through the present day. In 1860 Purkyně became a member of the Academy of Sciences in Vienna and in 1861 a corresponding member of the Academy of Sciences in Paris and founded the Spolek českych lekařů (Czech Medical Society), which even today brings together Czech physicians and natural scientists.

The importance of Purkyně to anthropology consists, above all, in his morphological-physiological approach to science and mankind. His lecture at the university in Wrocław in 1828, *Antropologie co vstupná nauka veškeré fyziologie (Anthropology—the Introductory Science for General Physiology)*, characterizes this approach. His work in anthropology concerns itself with the areas of somatometry (cranioscopy, organometry), the composition of the human body, typology, physiognomy, evolutionary anthropology and, above all, functional anthropology (dynamometry, spirometry, changes in blood circulation under stress). Other discoveries of Purkyně include those in the area of vision (entropic phenomena, Purkyně's blood-vessel image, the construction of the kinesiscope and Purkyně's pherolyt, the description of chromosy, the discovery of the displacement of the sensitivity curve of the eye toward the shorter wave lengths of low light intensity named the Purkyně effect, the discovery of the third and fourth images reflected from the front and rear surfaces of the cornea, the principles of tachyscopy, the bimicroscopy of the eye and the fundamentals of the development of opthalmoscopy). Purkyně also made discoveries in the area of hearing (analysis of the third tone of Tertini, bone and air sound conduction, analysis of biaural hearing); in the area of blood circulation (the suction power of the heart, the demonstration of the heart beat using a kinesiscope, Purkyně's fibers in the conduction system of the heart); in the area of respiration (the construction of the first spirometer); in the area of digestion (the description of the microscopic structure of the gastric mucosa and stomach glands, an explanation of the movement of cilia); in the area of histology and anatomy (new methods of fixation of tissues, tissue staining, analysis of the demineralization of bones and teeth, the perfection of microscopic study techniques, the discovery of the sweat glands, the discovery of osteocytes, a description of chondrocytes and dental root canals); in the area of embryology (the discovery of germinal vesicles), and in the area of the nervous system (the principles of the theory of neurology, the discovery of the Purkyně cell in the cerebellum and the Purkyně axis cylinders, the discoveries of the causes of vertigo and the postural mechanisms, and the pre- and post-rotational nystagmus, a description of disturbances of movement coordination due to cerebellar lesions, the perception of heat and cold, the two phases of sleep, the classification of dreams, the definition of the three main elements of speech, the discovery of hypopharyngeal resonance). Purkyně is highly esteemed in contemporary preventive medicine as the founder of blood circulation tests, which in their perfected form have become today's diagnostic tests in the prevention of cardiovascular diseases.

MAJOR WORKS: *Beiträge zur Kenntniss des Sehens in subjectiver Hinsicht* (Prague: 1819); *Commentatio de examine physiologico organi visus et systematis cutanei* (Bratislava: 1823); *Ueber das indirekte Sehen* (Wrocław: 1824); *Beobachtungen und Versuche zur Physiologie der Sinne* (Prague: 1823-1825); *Neue Beiträge zur Kenntniss des Sehens in subjektiver Hinsicht* (Berlin: 1825); *Ueber Verhalten und Bildung des Tartinischen dritten Tones, der beim Intonieren zweier anderer zu gleicher Zeit zu hörer ist* (Nürnberg: 1826); *Ueber das Verhältniss der Physiologie und Pathologie* (Wrocław: 1829); *Symbolae od ovi avium historiam ante incubationem* (Leipzig: 1830); *Neueste Resultate seiner Untersuchungen über die physiologisch-psychische Thäthigkeit des Gesichtssinnes* (Wrocław: 1830); *De cellulis antherarum fibrosis nec non de granorum pollinarium formis* (Bratislava: 1830); *Mikroskopische Beobachtungen über den Bau des Narbenkanals* (Wrocław: 1831); *De phenomeno generali et fundamentali motus vibratorii continui in membranis cum externis tum internis animalium plurimorum et superiorum et inferiorum ordinum obvii* (Bratislava: 1835); *Badania w przedmiocie mowy ludskiej [Research on the Features of Human Language]* (Kraków: 1835); *Über den Bau der Magen-Drüsen und die Natur des Verdauungsprozesses* (Prague: 1838);

Über die gangliöse Natur bestimter Hirntheile (Prague: 1838); *Ueber Saugkraft des Herzens* (Wrocław: 1843); *Ueber Struktur der Zähne des Menschen und der Tiere* (Wrocław: 1844); *Ueber die Strukturverhältnisse des Fasergewebes des Herzens* (Wrocław: 1845); *Über den Begriff der Physiologie, ihre Beziehung zu den übrigen Naturwissenschaften und zu anderen wissenschaftlichen und Kunst-Gebieten, die Methoden ihrer Lehrer und Praxis, über die Bildung den Physiologen, über Errichtung physiologischer Institute* (Prague: 1852); *Die Typologie der Sinne im allgemeinen, nebst einem Beispiel eigenthümlicher Empfindungen der Rückenhaut beim Gebrauch des Regenbandes* (Prague: 1854); *J.E. Purkyně: opera omnia* [7 vols.] (Prague: 1918-1958); *J.E. Purkyně: opera selecta* (Prague: 1948).

SOURCES: K. Amerling, *Jan Evangelista Purkyně* (Prague: 1918) (= *Duch a svět*, no. 37); L. Borovanský and K. Weigner, "Anatomické práce Jana Ev. Purkyně" ["Anatomical work of Jan Ev. Purkyně"] in: *Jan. Ev. Purkyně, 1787-1937: sborník statí* [*Jan. Ev. Purkyně, 1787-1937: Collection of Articles*] (Prague: 1937), pp. 3-31; K. Bross, *Jan Ev. Purkyně: życie i dzieło: medycyna prakticzna* [*Jan Ev. Purkyně: Life and Work: Practical Medicine*] (Poznań: 1937); Russell Burton Opitz, "Johannes Evangeliste Purkinje," *Journal of the American Medical Association*, vol. 32 (1899), pp. 812-814; Erich Ebstein, "Purkinje: der Begründer der physiologischen Institute in Braslau und Prag," *Hippokrates*, vol. 3 (1931), pp. 502-528; O.V. Hykeš, *Jan Evangelista Purkyně a moderní lékařství: spolek čes. lékařů* [*Jan Evangelista Purkyně and Modern Medicine: Czech Medical Association*] (Prague: 1936); O.V. Hykeš, "Ce qui a été écrit sur les travaux scientifiques de Jan Evangelista Purkyně (Purkinje) par les biologistes," *Biologické listy*, vol. 14 (1929), pp. 33-70; Z.S. Katznelson, *Sto let uchenii o kletke* (Moscow: 1939); F. Krause, *Weg und Welt der Goetheanisten Johannes Evangelista Purkyně* (Basel: 1936); V. Kuthan, E. Trávníčková and S. Trojan, *Pamětní spis k 200. výročí narození Jana Evangelisty Purkyně* [*Commemorative Publication for the 200th Anniversary of the Birth of Jan Evangelista Purkyně*] (Prague: 1987); V. Laufberger, *Co daly naše země Evropě a lidstvu* [*What Our Country Has Given to Europe and Mankind*] (Prague: 1940); J. Malý, "Význam Jana. Ev. Purkyně pro antropologii" ["The importance of Jan Ev. Purkyně to anthropology"] in: *Jan Evangelista Purkyně, 1787-1937: sborník statí* (Prague: 1937), pp. 70-83; R. Michalowski, *Jan Ex. Purkyně a rozwój teoretycznych nauk lekarskich* [*Jan Ex. Purkyně and the Development of the Theoretical Sciences of Medicine*] (Warsaw: 1938); B. Němec and O. Matoušek (editors), *Jan Evangelista Purkyně* (Prague: 1955); V.V. Novotný, "The functional anthropology at time of J.E. Purkyně and today" in: *Methods of Functional Anthropology* (Prague: 1990); J. Psotníčková, *Jan Evangelista Purkyně* (Prague: 1955); *Purkyňova společnost: in memoriam Joh. Ev. Purkyně* [*The Purkyně Society: in Memory of Joh. Ev. Purkyně*] (Prague: 1937); E. Rádl, "Jana Evangelisty Purkyně práce histologické" ["The histological work of Jan Evangelista Purkyně"], *Věstník Královské české společnosti nauk* (Prague: 1900), pp. 1-51; V. Robinson, *Pathfinders in Medicine* (2nd ed., New York: 1929); *Societas medicorum bohemorum: Joanni Ev. Purkyně, physiologi excellentissimo diem semisaecularem summorum in medicina honorum in alma antiquissima univeristate pragena celebrati gratulantur Societas medicorum bohemorum* (Prague: 1868); F.K. Studnička, "Joh. Ev. Purkinjes histologische Arbeiten," *Anatomischer Anzeiger*, vol. 82 (1936), pp. 41-66; F.K. Studnička, "Purkyně et la théorie cellulaire" in: *Purkyňova společnost: in memoriam Joh. Ev. Purkyně* (Prague: 1937), pp. 66-75; E. Thomsen, "Über Johannes Evengelista Purkyně und seine Werke," *Skandinavisches Archiv für Physiologie*, vol. 37 (1919), pp. 1-116; C. Wurzbach, "Joh. Ev. Purkinje: Bibliograph," *Lexikon des Kaiserthums Oesterreich*, vol. 24 (1872), p. 95; E. Vlček, "Jan Evangelista Purkyně a začátky české antropologie" ["Jan Evangelista Purkyně and the beginning of Czech anthropology"], *Zprávy čs. spolecnosti antropologické*, vol. 22 (1969), pp. 37-41.

V. V. Novotný
[Translation from Czech: June Pachuta Farris]

Putilov, B.N. (Boris Nikolaevich). Folklorist, ethnographer. Born in Northern Caucasus (Russia) 14 September 1919. After finishing at Leningrad Pedagological Institute, Putilov worked in the Groznyĭ Pedagological Institute from 1943 to 1954 and was the director of the folklore section of the Institut Russkoĭ literatury (Institute of Russian Literature) of the Soviet Academy of Sciences from 1954 to 1967. He became the chief research assistant and director of the general ethnography group of the Institut étnografii (Institute of Ethnography) of the Soviet Academy of Sciences in 1967.

Putilov's main interests were always the essence, nature and specific character of folklore as a phenomenon of popular culture. He worked primarily on the folklore of Slavic countries; he also did research on the peoples of Oceania and the non-Slavic peoples of the U.S.S.R. Putilov's research was based on historical-typological theory, to the development of which he made a significant contribution. A certain portion of his research was devoted to the examination of oral folklore as an organic part of folklore reality: folklore as the most important phenomenon of non-material culture, interpreting folklore facts with the methodologies of ethnography and so forth. In his Slavic scholarship, Putilov concentrated primarily on the history of the epic of the Slavic peoples. Putilov is credited with a new reading of the full range of epic subjects, their hidden semantics and subtexts. Putilov's influence in the textual study of folklore is considerable. He was the author of more than 400 works.

MAJOR WORKS: *Pesni grebenskikh kazakov* (Groznyĭ: 1946); *Istoricheskie pesni na Tereke* (Groznyĭ: 1948); *Russkie istoriko-pesennyĭ fol'klor XIII-XVI vekov* (Moscow and Leningrad: 1960); *Narodnye istoricheskie pesni* (Moscow and Leningrad: 1962); *Slavi͡anskai͡a istoricheskai͡a ballada* (Moscow and Leningrad: 1965); *Russkiĭ i i͡uzhnoslavi͡anskiĭ geroicheskiĭ épos: sravnitel'no-tipologicheskoe issledovanie* (Moscow: 1971); *Metodologii͡a sravnitel'no-istoricheskogo izuchenii͡a fol'klora* (Leningrad: 1976); *Pesni I͡Uzhnikh moreĭ* (Moscow: 1978); *Mif–obri͡ad–pesni͡a Novoĭ Gvineĭ* (Moscow: 1980); *N.N. Miklukho-Maklaĭ: strani͡sy biografii* (Moscow: 1981); *Geroicheskiĭ épos chernogori͡sev* (Leningrad: 1982); *Geroicheskiĭ épos i deĭstvitel'nost'* (Leningrad: 1988).

SOURCES: E.I. Shastina (editor), *B.N. Putilov: bibliografii͡a (1940-1987)* (Irkutsk: 1987) [bibliography]; V.P. Vladimir͡sev and G.G. Shapovalova, "14 senti͡abri͡a 1979 goda ... ," *Russkiĭ fol'klor*, vol. 20 (Leningrad: 1981), pp. 197-198; "Spisok osnovnykh rabot B.N. Putilova," *Sovetskai͡a étnografii͡a*, no. 5 (1979), pp. 184-187; and no. 6 (1979), pp. 129-130.

A.M. Reshetov
[Translation from Russian: Thomas L. Mann]

Putnam, Frederic Ward. Archaeologist, museum anthropologist, zoologist. Born in Salem (Massachusetts) 16 April 1839, died in Cambridge (Massachusetts) 14 August 1915. After early training under Henry Wheatland at the Essex Institute in Salem, Putnam studied with Louis Agassiz and Asa Gray at Harvard. After the revolt of Agassiz's students in 1863, Putnam returned to Salem, where he founded and published *The American Naturalist*, directed the new (1868) Peabody Academy of Science and pursued a career in ichthyology and herpetology. After the death of JEFFRIES WYMAN in 1874, Putnam returned to Cambridge as director and curator of the Peabody Museum of American Archaeology and Ethnology at Harvard. He became Peabody Professor of Anthropology as well in 1887 and held all three positions until retirement in 1909. He served as Permanent Secretary of the American Association for the Advancement of Science (AAAS) from 1873 to 1898 and President of AAAS in 1898-1899. He was a founding member of the Archaeological Institute of America (1879) and was largely responsible for its early work in the western hemisphere. From 1891 to 1894 he served as Chief of the Department of Ethnology of the World's Columbian Exposition in Chicago, directing the work of FRANZ BOAS, ALICE C. FLETCHER, ZELIA NUTTALL, Marshall Saville, George Byron Gordon, GEORGE A. DORSEY, Warren K. Moorehead and many others. From 1894 to 1903 he served as curator of anthropology at the American Museum of Natural History. He brought Boas to New York, and together they supervised the Jesup North Pacific Expedition and the Hyde Expeditions to the American Southwest. In 1903 he founded the Department of Anthropology at the University of California, Berkeley and served as Professor of Anthropology and Director of the Anthropological Museum there until 1909. He was elected to the National Academy of Sciences in 1884.

Putnam was a major institution-builder in early American anthropology, and his significance derived primarily from his organizational abilities, his support for and influence on younger men and women (especially Boas and ALFRED M. TOZZER), his pioneering work in preserving Serpent Mound in southern Ohio and other sites and his popularization of North American archaeology. He and Boas jointly trained the next generation of anthropologists in the four-field tradition by dividing the labor: archaeology at Harvard, linguistics and ethnography at Columbia, physical (biological) anthropology at both. His own archaeological fieldwork of the 1880s in southern Ohio (preceded by explorations in Kentucky and Tennessee and followed a decade later by work in California) established field methods on a new plane, with emphasis on attention to context (spatial, stratigraphic) of specimens, careful recording of the excavation process, viewing each site as a complex unit for purposes of study and conservative excavation techniques. Deeply embroiled in the controversies of his generation over "ancient man" in North America, Putnam cautiously supported the claims of Charles C. Abbott and others for a presence of 10,000 or more years. Permanently influenced by his early zoological training under Agassiz, Putnam evinced always a preference for close description of the artifactual base and a reluctance to make broader generalizations.

MAJOR WORKS: *Archaeology* (Washington: 1879) (= *Report of the U.S. Geographical Survey West of the 100th Meridian* [Wheeler survey], vol. 7); (with A.S. Packard) *The Mammoth Cave and Its Inhabitants* (Salem: 1879); "Archaeological explorations in Tennessee," *Peabody Museum Annual Report*, vol. 11 (1880), pp. 305-360; "Sketch of Hon. Lewis H. Morgan," *Proceedings of the American Academy of Arts and Sciences*, vol. 27 (May 1882), pp. 429-436; "The Altar Mounds of the Turner Group in Ohio," *Peabody Museum Annual Report*, vol. 17 (1886), pp. 554-562; "Conventionalism in ancient American art," *Bulletin of the Essex Institute*, vol. 18 (1886), pp. 155-167; "The proper method of exploring an earthwork," *Ohio Archaeological and Historical Quarterly*, vol. 1 (1887), pp. 60-62; "Palaeolithic man in Eastern and Central North America," *Proceedings of the Boston Society for Natural History*, vol. 23 (1888), pp. 421-449; "The Serpent Mound of Ohio," *Century Illustrated Monthly Magazine*, vol. 39 (1890), pp. 871-888; (with C.C. Willoughby) "Symbolism in the art of ancient America," *Proceedings of the American Association for the Advancement of Science*, vol. 44 (1895), pp. 301-322; "Archaeological and ethnological research in the United States," *Proceedings of the American Antiquarian Society*, vol. 24 (1902), pp. 461-470; (with A.L. Kroeber) *The Department of Anthropology of the University of California* (Berkeley: 1905); *Annual Reports of the Peabody Museum of Archaeology and Ethnology* (1875-1909).

SOURCES: Franz Boas (editor), *Putnam Anniversary Volume: Anthropological Essays Presented to Frederic Ward Putnam in Honor of his 70th Birthday* (New York: 1909); Franz Boas, "Frederic Ward Putnam," *Science*, n.s., vol. 42, no. 1080 (10 September 1915), pp. 330-332; Ralph W. Dexter, "Contributions of Frederic Ward Putnam to Ohio archaeology," *The Ohio Journal of Science*, vol. 65 (1965), pp. 110-117; Ralph W. Dexter, "Frederic Ward Putnam and the development of Museums of Natural History and Anthropology in the United States," *Curator*, vol. 9 (1966), pp. 150-155; Ralph W. Dexter, "Putnam's problems popularizing anthropology," *American Scientist*, vol. 54 (1966), pp. 315-332; Ralph W. Dexter, "Contributions of Frederic Ward Putnam to the development of anthropology in California," *Science Education*, vol. 50 (1966), pp. 314-318; Ralph W. Dexter, "The role of F.W. Putnam in founding the Field Museum," *Curator*, vol. 13 (1970), pp. 21-26; Ralph W. Dexter, "The Putnam-Abbott correspondence on Palaeolithic Man in North America,"

Twelfth International Congress of the History of Sciences, vol. 9 (Paris: 1971), pp. 17-21; Ralph W. Dexter, "The role of F.W. Putnam in developing anthropology at the American Museum of Natural History," *Curator*, vol. 9 (1976), pp. 303-310; Ralph W. Dexter, "The Putnam-Metz correspondence on mound explorations in Ohio," *Ohio Archaeologist*, vol. 32, no. 4 (1982), pp. 24-28; Ralph W. Dexter, "F.W. Putnam's scientific studies at Mammoth Cave (1871-1881)," *The NSS Bulletin*, no. 46 (April 1984), pp. 10-14; Ralph W. Dexter, "F.W. Putnam at the Serpent Mound in Adams County, Ohio: a historical review," *Journal of the Steward Anthropological Society*, vol.18 (1988-89), pp. 141-150; Roland B. Dixon, "Frederic Ward Putnam," *Harvard Graduates Magazine*, vol. 24 (1915), pp. 304-308; C.M. Hinsley, "From shell-heaps to stelae: early anthropology at the Peabody Museum" in: G.W. Stocking (editor), *Objects and Others: Essays on Museums and Material Culture* (Madison: 1985) (= *History of Anthropology*, vol. 3), pp. 49-74; C.M. Hinsley, "The museum roots of Harvard anthropology, 1866-1915" in: Clark A. Elliott and Margaret Rossiter (editors), *Science at Harvard University: Historical Perspectives* (Bethlehem: 1991); A.L. Kroeber, "Frederic Ward Putnam," *American Anthropologist*, vol. 17 (1915), pp. 712-718; Joan Mark, *4 Anthropologists: an American Science in its Early Years* (New York: 1980); Joan Mark, *A Stranger in Her Native Land: Alice Fletcher and the American Indians* (Lincoln: 1989); Edward S. Morse, "Frederic Ward Putnam, 1829-1915," *National Academy of Sciences, Biographical Memoirs*, vol. 16 (1935), pp. 125-153; Stephen Williams (editor), *The Selected Archaeological Papers of Frederic Ward Putnam, 1844-1915* (New York: 1973) (= *Antiquities of the New World: Early Explorations in Archeology*, vol. 5).

Curtis Hinsley

q

Quatrefages, Armand de (Jean-Louis Armand de Quatrefages de Breau).
Physician, zoologist, anthropologist. Born in Bertezenne, Gard (France) 10 February 1810,
died in Paris (France) 12 January 1892. Following the beginning of a career dedicated essentially to zoology, in 1855 Quatrefages was named to the chair of anthropology at the
Muséum d'Histoire Naturelle (Museum of Natural History) in Paris, a new name for the
chair of anatomy and human natural history that had been vacated by Augustin Serres.
Quatrefages's efforts over the next several years consisted primarily of specifying the various problems posed by the study of man from the perspective of a naturalist.

In the *Rapport sur les progrès de l'anthropologie en France*, published on the occasion of the Universal Exposition in Paris in 1867, Quatrefages gave an overview of all
available sources of information. In his work, *L'unité de l'espèce humaine*, he took a position in favor of monogenism and against polygenism, which had come into great favor
during the first half of the 19th century. In his opinion, the idea of good and evil and the
belief in a divinity present among all men and belonging to man alone, justified the recognition of a "human kingdom" in addition to those of animal, vegetable and mineral. From
1873 on, he began the publication in fascicles of *Crania ethnica*, which was principally the
work of THÉODORE HAMY.

It was in the influence of environment that Quatrefages sought an explanation of
human racial diversity, and it was through the facts of geography and migration that he explained the populating of the world from a unique center of human origins, probably located in the higher regions of Asia.

For all his firmly anti-transformist position, Quatrefages was very quickly won
over to the idea of the ancientness of the appearance of man. In a series of articles subse-

quently published as part of his works, he fought the theory of the primate origin of man and the ideas of Darwin.

MAJOR WORKS: *L'unité de l'espèce humaine* (Paris: 1861); *Métamorphoses de l'homme et des animaux* (Paris: 1862); *Histoire de l'homme* (Paris: 1867-1868); *Rapport sur les progrès de l'anthropologie* (Paris: 1868); *Charles Darwin et ses précurseurs français: étude sur le transformisme* (Paris: 1870); *La race prussienne* (Paris: 1871); *Crania ethnica* [2 vols.] (Paris: 1882); *Hommes fossiles et hommes sauvages* (Paris: 1884); *Les polynésiens et leurs migrations* (Paris: 1886); *Les pygmées des anciens d'après la science moderne* (Paris: 1887); *Histoire générale des races humaines* (Paris: 1887-1889); *Les émules de Darwin* [2 vols.] (Paris: 1894); numerous contributions to the following journals: *Revue des Deux Mondes, Revue des Cours scientifiques* and *Journal des Savants*.

SOURCES: E. Hamy, *Leçon d'ouverture au cours d'anthropologie du Museum d'Histoire naturelle (31 mai 1892)* (Paris: 1892) [also in: *Les émules de Darwin* (Paris: 1894)]; A.G. Malard, "Liste des ouvrages et mémoires publiés de 1822 à 1891 par A. de Quatrefages," *Nouvelles Archives du Museum d'Histoire naturelle, Bulletin*, 3rd sér., vol. 4 (1892), pp. 1-49; *À la mémoire de Jean-Louis-Armand de Quatrefages de Breau* (Lille: s.d.); G. Hervé and L. de Quatrefages, "Armand de Quatrefages," *Bulletin de la Société française d'histoire de la médicine*, vol. 20 (1926), pp. 309-330; vol. 21 (1927), pp. 17-35 and 200-231; A. Leguebe, "The dawn of anthropology in France," *Man*, vol. 17 (1982), pp. 348-350.

André Leguebe
[*Translation from French: Timothy Eastridge and Robert B. Marks Ridinger*]

Quetelet, Adolphe (Lambert Adolphe Jacques Quetelet). Mathematician, astronomer, statistician. Born in Ghent (Belgium) 22 February 1796, died in Brussels (Belgium) 17 February 1874. Quetelet, the founder and director of the Observatory of Belgium and the permanent secretary of the Académie Royale de Sciences, des Lettres et de Beaux-Arts of Brussels, played a key role in the development of the sciences in Belgium.

In the course of planning the construction of the observatory, Quetelet traveled to various other European cities, making the acquaintance of numerous prominent individuals, among them, Laplace, Poisson and Fourier. While developing his research in astronomy, he became involved with the field of statistics through publications relating to birth rates, mortality and criminality, progressively orienting purely descriptive statistics toward a scientific analysis of the characteristics of human societies. He was also engaged in the amassing of official statistics, and the Commission Centrale de Statistique was considered a model by many foreign statisticians. He was the initiator of the Congrès Internationaux de Statistique, and contributed to the establishment of guidelines for improving the quality of census data.

Quetelet extended his analysis to numerous other mensurations, such as height, weight, limbs, head growth and dynamometry. Impressed by the consistency and frequency of certain observations, he sought to establish social laws comparable to physical laws.

His most essential contribution was his application of probability to the interpretation of data for phenomena that were not susceptible to experimental verification, particularly those pertaining to human nature. This explains the importance he accorded to making a great number of observations that would reduce the significance of random events and his attachment to the idea of the "average man," a notion that was the object of numerous criticisms.

Although the concepts of error and variability remained confused in Quetelet's works, it was in these works that, for the first time, the law of probability of error became a law of nature itself.

MAJOR WORKS: *Instructions populaires sur le calcul des probabilités* (Brussels: 1828) [tr.: *Popular Instructions on the Calculation of Probabilities* (London: 1839)]; *Sur l'homme et le développement de ses facultés, ou essai de physique sociale* (Paris: 1835); *Lettres à S.A.R le duc régnant de Saxe-Cobourg et Gotha sur la théorie des probabilités, appliquée aux sciences morales et politiques* (Brussels: 1846) [tr.: *Letters Addressed to H.R.H. the Grand Duke of Saxe-Cobourg and Gotha on the Theory of Probabilities, as Applied to the Moral and Political Sciences* (London: 1849)]; *Physique sociale ou essai sur le développement des facultés de l'homme* (Brussels: 1869); *Anthropométrie ou mesure des différentes facultés de l'homme* (Brussels: 1870).

SOURCES: Edouard Mailly, "Essai sur la vie et les ouvrages de L.A.J. Quetelet," *Annuaire de l'Académie royale de Belgique*, vol. 41 (1875), pp. 109-297; G.F. Knapp, "Bericht über die Schriften Quetelet's zur Social Statistik und Anthropologie," *Jahrbuch für Nationalökonomie und Statistik*, vol. 17 (1871), pp. 167-174, 342-358, and 427-445; F.H. Hankins, *Adolphe Quetelet as a Statistician* (New York: 1908) (= *Studies in History, Economics and Public Law,* vol. 31, no. 4); J.M. Joly and P. Dagnelie, "Adolphe Quetelet, 1796-1874" in: R.C. Olby (editor), *Early Nineteenth Century European Scientists* (Oxford: 1967), pp. 153-179; Académie Royale de Belgique, *Mémorial Adolphe Quetelet, 1796-1874* [4 vols.] (Brussels: 1974); Theodore M. Porter, "The mathematics of society: variation and error in Quetelet's statistics," *British Journal for the History of Science,* vol. 18 (1985), pp. 51-69; M.P. Johnston, *The Origins of Adolphe Quetelet's Social Physics* (Cambridge, Mass.: 1976).

André Leguebe
[Translation from French: Timothy Eastridge and Robert B. Marks Ridinger]

r

Radcliffe-Brown, A.R. (Alfred Reginald). Anthropologist, comparative sociologist. Born in Birmingham (England) 17 January 1881, died in London (England) 24 October 1955. Radcliffe-Brown is best known for the theoretical perspective that came to be called "structural-functionalism" and for helping to establish anthropology as a discipline in the United Kingdom and the British Commonwealth. He was also influential in establishing his theoretical perspective in the United States, where it coexisted with and competed against the school of thought begun by FRANZ BOAS.

Radcliffe-Brown was born Brown, and some of his earlier works were published under this surname. He adopted the name Radcliffe Brown, later Radcliffe-Brown, in the early 1920s, and finally changed his name by deed poll in 1926. Radcliffe-Brown began his university career in 1901 at Cambridge, where friends called him "Anarchy Brown" because of his political inclinations. He knew personally the anarchist writer Peter Kropotkin, whose ideas anticipated Radcliffe-Brown's notion of society as a self-regulating system. At Cambridge Radcliffe-Brown had intended to study natural science but changed to moral science, a course that included philosophy, economics and psychology. All these influences are evident in his writing (as either positive or negative influences) and in his conception of anthropology as "a natural science of society."

After completing his bachelor's degree in 1904 Radcliffe-Brown did postgraduate work with W.H.R. RIVERS and subsequently conducted fieldwork in the Andaman Islands (1906-1908) and Western Australia (1910-1911). During World War I, he served as Director of Education in the Kingdom of Tonga. Among numerous academic appointments, he held foundation chairs of social anthropology at the Universities of Cape Town (1920-1925), Sydney (1926-1931), Chicago (1931-1937) and Oxford (1937-1946) as well as shorter-term senior posts at Yenching, São Paulo, Farouk I (Alexandria, Egypt) and Rhodes (Grahamstown, South Africa).

It has been said that Radcliffe-Brown's primary influence was as a teacher rather than as a writer. He possessed a charismatic personality and was a brilliant lecturer, generally performing without any notes whatsoever. He published little for a person of his stature, but all his writings (often first delivered as public lectures) exhibit a simple clarity and conversational style rare in the social sciences. His writings also exhibit a consistency in theoretical viewpoint through some four decades of active scholarship. Early in his career, Radcliffe-Brown turned against the prevalent historicist debates over diffusion and evolution. In his famous 1924 paper, "The mother's brother in South Africa" (included in *Structure and Function in Primitive Society*), he argued against conjectural history and in favor of a synchronic approach to the explanation of social institutions. In his own Australian ethnography his concerns were similar. He advocated a comparative perspective and sought to explain the diversity in Aboriginal kinship systems in terms of the full complex of Aboriginal social structure as it was found at the time.

Radcliffe-Brown's approach differed from the prevailing one in North America during his time there. Indeed, in his *History of Ethnological Theory*, ROBERT H. LOWIE included him, along with Émile Durkheim and his associates in Paris, under the heading "French Sociology." While the classification of kinship terminologies, descent structures, etc., was as great a concern for Radcliffe-Brown as it was in American anthropology, Radcliffe-Brown was careful to distinguish classification (which involves relations of similarity and difference) from the notion of system (which involves relations of interconnectedness). This distinction is especially clear in a set of impromptu seminars that were presented at Chicago in 1937. A transcription of these seminars (which FRED EGGAN called "the essential Radcliffe-Brown") was published after Radcliffe-Brown's death under the title *A Natural Science of Society*.

Radcliffe-Brown's work is often compared with that of BRONISLAW MALINOWSKI, but, unlike Malinowski (who enthusiastically adopted the label "functionalist"), Radcliffe-Brown sought an anthropology without separate schools of thought. The two also differed in their conception of "function." For Malinowski, the term implied responses to individual, biological needs, while for Radcliffe-Brown it suggested relations between institutions (marriage, bridewealth, etc.) within the larger systems (kinship, economic, etc.) which make up a society.

Radcliffe-Brown's work is regarded by many today as oversimplistic and excessively positivistic. His defenders, however, point out that his influence has been so great as to be almost unnoticed. The vision of anthropology he had is implicit in modern methods of data analysis, and the vocabulary of anthropology still retains many of the concepts he introduced to the subject. In spite of the consistency of his approach through the decades, his essay "The comparative method in social anthropology" anticipates French structuralism and, in particular, CLAUDE LÉVI-STRAUSS's theory of totemism. Two essay collections by Radcliffe-Brown's students pay tribute to his ideas (an American collection edited by Fred Eggan and a British one edited by MEYER FORTES). A volume of his own essays (*Structure and Function in Primitive Society*) was published in 1952, and two further volumes (*Method in Social Anthropology* and *The Social Anthropology of Radcliffe-Brown*) were published posthumously.

MAJOR WORKS: "Three tribes of Western Australia," *Journal of the Royal Anthropological Institute*, vol. 43 (1913), pp. 143-194; *The Andaman Islanders* (Cambridge: 1922); "The mother's brother in South Africa," *South African Journal of Science*, vol. 21 (1924), pp. 542-555; *The Social Organization of Australian Tribes* (Sydney: 1931); "The comparative method in social anthropology," *Journal of the Royal Anthropological Institute*, vol. 81 (1951), pp. 15-22; *Structure and Function in Primitive Society* (London and Glencoe, Ill.: 1952); *A Natural Science of Society* (Chicago: 1957); *Method in Social Anthropology* (edited by M.N. Srinivas) (Chicago: 1958); *The Social Anthropology of Radcliffe-Brown* (edited by Adam Kuper) (London: 1977).

SOURCES: Fred Eggan (editor), *Social Anthropology of North American Tribes* (Chicago: 1937); Meyer Fortes (editor), *Social Structure: Studies Presented to A.R. Radcliffe-Brown* (Oxford: 1949); Robert H. Lowie, *The History of Ethnological Theory* (New York: 1937); Adam Kuper, *Anthropologists and Anthropology: the British School, 1922-72* (London: 1973); Meyer Fortes, "Radcliffe-Brown's contributions to the study of social organization," *British Journal of Sociology*, vol. 6 (1955), pp. 16-30; Meyer Fortes, "Alfred Reginald Radcliffe-Brown, F.B.A., 1881-1955: a memoir," *Man*, vol. 56 (1956), article no. 172, pp. 149-153; Raymond Firth, "Alfred Reginald Radcliffe-Brown, 1881-1955," *Proceedings of the British Academy*, vol. 42 (1956), pp. 287-302; A.P. Elkin, "A.R. Radcliffe-Brown, 1881-1955," *Oceania*, vol. 26 (1956), pp. 239-251; W.E.H. Stanner, "Radcliffe-Brown, A.R." in: David L. Sills (editor), *International Encyclopedia of the Social Sciences* (New York: 1968-1979), vol. 13, pp. 285-290; I. Schapera, "A.R. Brown to Radcliffe-Brown," *Anthropology Today*, vol. 5, no. 5 (October 1989), pp. 10-11.

Alan Barnard

Radin, Paul. Anthropologist. Born in Łódź (Poland, then in Russia) 2 April 1883, died in New York (New York) 21 February 1959. Radin is best known for his voluminous corpus of work dealing with the Winnebago tribe of Wisconsin and Nebraska and for his writings on American Indian religion, literature, myth and philosophy.

Radin and his family immigrated to the United States in 1884 when he was one year old. His father, Adolph Moses Radin, was a Reform rabbi, an intellectual and scholar, the product of the Jewish Haskalah of mid-19th-century Europe.

Initially interested in zoology, which he studied at Columbia University, Radin became increasingly influenced by the historian James Harvey Robinson. At the time that Radin was at Columbia, Robinson was teaching history and doing so from a broadly liberal and humanist perspective that appealed to Radin. From 1905 to 1907 Radin was in Europe attending the University of Munich and then the University of Berlin. It was there after he had studied under such men as Johannes Ranke at Munich and EDUARD SELER at Berlin that his focus shifted to the study of anthropology. Radin returned to America and was one of the anthropologists who studied under FRANZ BOAS. He obtained his doctorate in 1910, taking a second minor in history under James Harvey Robinson.

Radin's split with the school of Boas came primarily over the question of methodology. Distrusting the "quantitative" method, he preferred to approach ethnology from a "historical" perspective. He openly stated this in his *The Method and Theory of Ethnology: an Essay in Criticism* in which he critiqued the methodology of his peers, among them ROBERT H. LOWIE and EDWARD SAPIR, with whom he maintained lifelong friendships in spite of their differences over method. Radin stressed the individual as the essential component of society, holding that the individual formulated change, introduced innovations, new techniques, new thoughts and new religious concepts. Thus, rather than being molded by their culture, individuals were themselves the instruments of culture change. He states this in his *World of Primitive Man*.

Radin was never affiliated for a long period with any one academic institution, and his ideas were disseminated through his writings and, in Europe, through his frequent lectures at such universities as Oxford, Manchester and the four major Swedish universities as well as at the Jungian Eranos Conferences at Ascona, Switzerland, and the Jung Institute in Zürich. Students who worked with him at those American universities in which he did teach remember him as a Socratic teacher who was at his best with small groups of students in an informal setting. In all, Radin is better known and more widely read in Europe than in America. Observers have argued that, because of his refusal to be allied for long periods with any particular university, Radin was not fully in touch with the currents of the anthropology of his time. Defenders argue that this very refusal to be confined within one academic institution permitted him to devote more time to the development of his own work.

MAJOR WORKS: *The Autobiography of a Winnebago Indian* (Berkeley: 1920); *The Winnebago Tribe* (Washington: 1923); *Primitive Man as Philosopher* (New York: 1927); *Social Anthropology* (New York: 1932); *The Method and Theory of Ethnology: an Essay in Criticism* (New York: 1933); *Primitive Religion: Its Nature and Origin* (New York: 1937) [tr.: *La religion primitive: sa nature et son origine* (Paris: 1941)]; *The Road of Life and Death: a Ritual Drama of the American Indians* (New York: 1945); *The World of Primitive Man* (New York: 1953) [tr.: *Gott und Mensch in der Primitiven Welt* (Zürich: 1953)]; *The Trickster* (New York: 1956) [tr.: *Der Gottliche Shelm: ein Indianischer Mythenzyklus* (Zürich: 1954)]; *Le fripon divin: un mythe indien* (Geneva: 1958)].

SOURCES: Stanley Diamond, "Paul Radin" in: Sydel Silverman (editor), *Totems and Teachers: Perspectives on the History of Anthropology* (New York: 1981), pp. 67-99; Cora DuBois, *Culture in History: Essays in Honor of Paul Radin* (New York: 1960); Mary Sacharoff-Fast Wolf, *Paul Radin: New Perspectives on Ethnology* (San Francisco: forthcoming); Mary Sacharoff-Fast Wolf, taped interviews, correspondence and other Radin archival material donated by Mrs. Doris Woodward Radin.

Mary Sacharoff-Fast Wolf

Radlov, V.V. (Vasiliĭ Vasil'evich). Ethnographer, archaeologist, Turkologist, traveler, museologist. Born in Berlin (Germany) 5 April 1837, died in Petrograd (Russia) 12 May 1918. Radlov received his doctorate in the spring of 1858 with a dissertation on the influence of religion on the people of Asia. In the summer of that same year he arrived for service in Leningrad. From 1859 to 1871 he lived in the Altaĭ, where he gathered material on the ethnography, languages and folklore of the Turkic peoples of that region. From 1871 to 1884 Radlov worked in Kazan' and from 1884 until his death he lived in St. Petersburg. Between 1885 and 1890 he was director of the Aziatskiĭ Muzeĭ (Asiatic Museum), and between 1894 and 1918 he was director of the Muzeĭ Antropologii i Ėtnografii (Museum of Anthropology and Ethnography).

Radlov made a significant contribution to the study of the ethnogenesis and ethnic composition of the Turkic peoples. He is noted for his conclusion that the inhabitants of the steppes during the Iron Age did not only raise cattle but were also occupied with farming. In addition, it was under his leadership that runic inscriptions were discovered by the Orkhonskiĭ Expedition.

MAJOR WORKS: *Obraztsy narodnoĭ literatury tiurkskikh plemen* (St. Petersburg: 1866-1907); *Etnographische Übersicht der Türkenstämme Sibiriens unde der Mongolei* (Leipzig: 1883) [tr.: *Ėtnograficheskiĭ obzor turetskikh plemen Sibirii i Mongolii* (Irkutsk: 1929)]; *Aus Sibirien* [2 vols.] (Leipzig: 1884) [tr.: *Iz Sibiri; stranitsy dnevnika* (Moscow: 1989)]; *Ėtnograficheskiĭ obzor tiurkskikh plemen IUzhnoĭ Sibiri i Dzhungarii* (Tomsk: 1887); *Opyt slovarĭa tiurkskikh narechiĭ* [4 vols.] (St.

Petersburg: 1888-1911); "Sibirskie drevnosti: iz putevnykh zapisok po Sibiri," *Zapiski russkogo arkheologicheskogo obshchestva*, vol. 7 (St. Petersburg: 1896); *Atlas drevnosteĭ Mongolii* [4 parts] (St. Petersburg: 1892-1899).

SOURCES: S.I. Vaĭnsteĭn and S.G. Klĭashtornyĭ, "V.V. Radlov i istoriko-geograficheskoe izuchenie tĭurkskikh narodov" in: *Tĭurkologicheskiĭ sbornik: 1971* (Moscow: 1972), pp. 20-31; N.A. Dulina (compiler), "Khronologicheskiĭ perechen' trudov V.V. Radlova i literatura o nem" in: *Tĭurkologicheskiĭ sbornik: 1971* (Moscow: 1972), pp. 261-277.

A.M. Reshetov
[Translation from Russian: Thomas L. Mann]

Raglan, Lord ***FitzRoy Richard Somerset*** (usually referred to as Lord Raglan). Soldier, politician, anthropologist. Born in London (England) 10 June 1885, died in Usk, Monmouthshire (England) 14 September 1964. Raglan was heir to the third Baron Raglan; his great-grandfather was the British general known for ordering the Charge of the Light Brigade during the Crimean War. Following family tradition, Raglan was educated at Eton and the British military academy, Sandhurst. From 1904 to 1922 he served in the Grenadier Guards, retiring at the rank of major when he succeeded his father as baron.

During a varied military career, Raglan was exposed to a number of non-Western cultures. He served in India and Afghanistan, was aide-de-camp to the governor of Hong Kong, was seconded to the Egyptian Army from 1913 to 1919 (spending several years as District Commissioner for Mongolla Province, the Sudan) and acted as political officer in Palestine for the last few years of his career.

Upon his return to civilian life, Raglan took up the management of the family's 1,100-acre estate in Monmouthshire. While he inherited a title and famous name with the land, little money accompanied it; at least in part for economic reasons, Raglan began writing books and articles at that point. A paper that he wrote in 1918 on the Lotuko tribe of the Sudan attracted the attention of C.G. SELIGMAN, already several years into his survey of that country. Seligman encouraged Raglan in his anthropological endeavors; at that time, it was not unusual to become a recognized anthropologist without a moment's formal training in the subject.

As an anthropologist, Raglan represented largely 19th-century trends and interests, bringing an impressive scholarship (and the mastery of several languages) to bear on folklore and mythology. He traced themes in folklore from much earlier ritual but was not at all interested in the meaning or significance of myths and rites as handed down or performed in the everyday life of a community. A diffusionist, Raglan rejected the idea that myths represent even a garbled rendition of history. He argued persuasively that preliterate societies were unable to retain knowledge of the past beyond a few generations; hero myths, rather than reflecting a demi-god made from some historical person, represent a humanized version of a formerly important god.

In addition to the numerous honors and positions more or less automatically bestowed on him by virtue of his title, Raglan was elected to the council of the Royal Anthropological Institute in 1930 and was president of the anthropological section of the British Society in 1933, the Folklore Society from 1945 to 1947, and the Royal Anthropological Institute in 1955-1957. He long served on the council of the National Museum of Wales and was its president from 1957 until 1962.

MAJOR WORKS: *Jocasta's Crime* (London: 1933); *The Science of Peace* (London: 1933); *If I Were Dictator* (London: 1934); *The Hero* (London: 1936); *How Came Civilization?* (London: 1939); *Death and Rebirth* (London: 1945); *The Origins of Religion* (London: 1949); *The Temple and the House* (London: 1964).

SOURCES: C. Daryll Forde, "Lord Raglan, 1884-1964," *Man*, vol. 64 (1964), pp. 181-182; "Lord Raglan, 79, dies in Wales," *New York Times* (15 September 1964), p. 37; "Raglan, Fitzroy [sic], 1885-1964," *Contemporary Authors*, vol. 5-8 (1969), p. 927.

David Lonergan

Ramos, Arthur (Arthur Ramos de Araújo Pereira). Anthropologist, physician, educator. Born in Pilar (Brazil) 7 July 1903, died in Paris (France) 31 October 1949. Although Ramos carried out studies in the areas of psychoanalysis, education, and public health, he is exclusively associated today with his research and reflections on the Afro-Brazilians. Two well defined phases may be distinguished in his output on this population. In the first, Ramos proposed a kind of re-examination of the biological work of RAIMUNDO NINA RODRIGUES (a pioneer in the scientific study of Brazilians of African descent) with the notion of substituting the ideas of the Italian and French schools of criminology and psychoanalysis; this was a theoretical and methodological perspective that he never completely abandoned. In the second phase of his work, Ramos focused on the Afro-Brazilians and their life style from a cultural viewpoint, under the delayed influence of the theory of acculturation. Of the three principal proponents of this theory—RALPH LINTON, ROBERT REDFIELD and MELVILLE J. HERSKOVITS—it was the latter (who conducted research in Brazil) who most influenced Ramos.

In Ramos's later writings one notes an attempt to consider the question of the Afro-Brazilians as a structural problem and hardly at all a matter of culture. This writing foreshadowed Brazilian sociological studies of the 1950s. It would be these studies (which Ramos himself planned while he was Director of the Social Sciences Division of UNESCO) that would call into question all of his cultural work.

MAJOR WORKS: *Educação e psicanálise* (São Paulo: 1934); *O negro brasileiro* (Rio de Janeiro: 1934); *O folclore negro no Brasil* (Rio de Janeiro: 1935); *Introdução à psicologia social* (Rio de Janeiro: 1936); *As culturas negras no novo mundo* (Rio de Janeiro: 1937); *The Negro in Brazil* (Washington: 1939); *A criança problema* (São Paulo: 1939); *A aculturação negra no Brasil* (Rio de Janeiro: 1942); *Introdução à antropologia brasileira* (Rio de Janeiro: 1943); *O negro na civilização brasileira* (Rio de Janeiro, [1971]).

SOURCES: Emílio Willems, "Arthur Ramos" in: *Dicionário de sociologia* (São Paulo: 1950); Anisio Teixeira [et al.], *Arthur Ramos* (Rio de Janeiro: 1952); Marilu Gusmão, *Arthur Ramos: o homem e a obra* (Maceió: 1974); Mariza Corrêa, *As ilusões da liberdade: a Escola Nina Rodrigues e a antropologia do Brasil* [unpublished Ph.D. dissertation] (São Paulo: 1982); Waldir Freitas de Oliveira and Vivaldo da Costa Lima, *Cartas de Edison Carneiro a Arthur Ramos* (São Paulo: 1987); João Baptista Borges Pereira, *Arthur Ramos* (São Paulo: forthcoming).

João Baptista Borges Pereira
[Translation from Portuguese: Robert B. Marks Ridinger]

Rasmussen, Knud (Knud Johan Victor Rasmussen). Arctic explorer, ethnographer. Born in Jakobshavn (Greenland) 7 July 1879, died in Copenhagen (Denmark) 21 December 1933. Rasmussen's maternal grandmother was a native Greenlander, and he spent his childhood in Greenland. After his school education in Denmark he participated in his first Arctic expedition to the Thule area during 1902-1904. In 1906 he returned, this time with dog sledges, carrying provisions to the Polar Eskimos, with whom he spent two years. In 1909 he founded the polar station at Thule, and from there he led the First Thule Expedition (1912) across the inland ice to Independence Fjord and the Second Thule Expedition (1916-1918) to the areas between Independence Fjord and Greenland's northwest coast. The "Fourth Thule Expedition" was his individual ethnographic research trip to eastern Greenland, where he collected a large amount of folklore. The famous Fifth Thule Expedition ("from Greenland to the Pacific") from 1921 to 1924, with the participation of KAJ BIRKET-SMITH and Therkel Mathiassen, among others, was his greatest achievement, the fulfillment of his childhood ambition to accomplish a comprehensive scholarly survey of the various Inuit groups.

Rasmussen's life was totally committed to the Inuit Arctic. Even during his lifetime he became something of a legend; his personal qualities—modesty, selflessness, thoughtfulness and physical and mental endurance—made it a privilege to work with him, and among the Inuit his reputation acquired the proportions of that of a culture hero. His pioneering ethnographic works on Inuit intellectual culture remain unparalleled, and both these and his popular writings convey his deep respect, admiration and affection for the Inuit and their culture. He was awarded honorary doctorates at the Universities of Copenhagen (Denmark) and Edinburgh (Scotland).

MAJOR WORKS: (with Laugé Koch, C.H. Ostenfeld, M.P. Porsild and Thorild Wulff) *Grønland Langs Polhavet: Udforskningen af Grønland fra Melvillebugten til Kap Morris Jesup, Skildring af den II. Thule-Ekspedition 1916-18* (Copenhagen: 1919) [tr.: *Greenland by the Polar Sea: the Story of the II. Thule Expedition from Melville Bay to Cape Morris Jesup* (London: 1921)]; *Myter og Sagn fra Grønland*, I: *Østgrøenlændere* (Copenhagen: 1921); *Myter og Sagn fra Grønland*, II: *Vestgrønlændere* (Copenhagen: 1924); *Myter og Sagn fra Grønland*, III: *Kap York-Distriktet og Nordgrønland* (Copenhagen: 1925); *Fra Grønland til Stillehavet, Rejser og Mennesker: Fra V. Thule-Ekspedition 1921-1924* [2 vols.] (Copenhagen: 1925-1926) [tr.: *Across Arctic America: Narrative of the Fifth Thule Expedition* (New York: 1927)]; *Festens Gave: Eskimoiske Alaska-Eventyr* (Copenhagen: 1929) [tr.: *The Eagle's Gift, Alaska Eskimo Tales* (New York: 1932)]; *Intellectual Culture of the Iglulik Eskimos* (Copenhagen: 1929) (= *Report of the Fifth Thule Expedition 1921-1924*, vol. 7, no. 1); *Observations on the Intellectual Culture of the Caribou Eskimos* (Copenhagen: 1930) (= *Report of the Fifth Thule Expedition 1921-1924*, vol. 7, no. 2); *Iglulik and Caribou Eskimo Texts* (Copenhagen: 1930) (= *Report of the Fifth Thule Expedition 1921-1924*, vol. 7, no. 3); *The Netsilik Eskimos, Social Life and Spiritual Culture*, I-II (Copenhagen: 1931) (= *Report of the Fifth Thule Expedition 1921-1924*, vol. 8, nos. 1-2); *Intellectual Culture of the Copper Eskimos* (Copenhagen: 1932) (= *Report of the Fifth Thule Expedition 1921-1924*, vol. 9).

SOURCES: Therkel Mathiassen, *Med Knud Rasmussen blandt Amerikas Eskimoer: Minder fra 5. Thule-ekspedition* (Copenhagen: 1926); Peter Freuchen, *Knud Rasmussen som jeg husker ham* (Copenhagen: 1934) [tr.: *I Sailed with Rasmussen* (New York: 1958)]; Kaj Birket-Smith, *Knud Rasmussen's Saga* (Copenhagen: 1936); H. Ostermann, "Rasmussen, Knud Johan Victor" in: *Dansk Biografisk Leksikon* (Copenhagen: 1982), vol. 12, pp. 40-43; Inge Kleivan and Ernest S. Bruch Jr. (editors), *L'oeuvre de Knud Rasmussen = The Works of Knud Rasmussen* (Québec: 1988) (= *Études Inuit = Inuit Studies*, vol. 12, no. 1-2) [issue devoted to the work of Knud Rasmussen, with comprehensive bibliography].

Jan Ovesen

Rassers, W.H. (Willem Huibert). Ethnologist, Orientalist. Born in Roosendaal (Netherlands) 16 September 1877, died in Leiden (Netherlands) 15 May 1973.

In 1896 Rassers became a student of Dutch language and literature at Leiden University. Probably influenced by the Sanskrit scholar H. Kern he became interested in Oriental studies and in 1899 took his *Candidaats* examination in the languages and literature of the East Indian Archipelago (Indonesia). However, due to health problems, he did not pursue his studies for nearly eighteen years. But in 1918 he returned to Leiden and took his *Doctoraal* examination. In 1922 at the age of forty-five he was awarded a cum laude doctorate for his thesis on the Javanese Pañji-novel (*De Pandji-roman*).

In 1918, shortly after his final examination, he was appointed as conservator of the Malay-Polynesian section at the National Ethnographic Museum in Leiden. In 1937 he was appointed Director of the Museum, a post he filled until he retired in 1943. His career was uneventful. Rassers never made a name as a museum anthropologist, nor did he ever do any fieldwork. In fact, he never was in Indonesia or any other part of the non-Western world. Though he did teach Malay, Javanese and ethnology at the Protestant Mission School in Oegstgeest (Netherlands), he never lectured at the university and had no ambitions for an academic career.

Yet Rassers left an indelible imprint on the development of the Leiden structuralist tradition in anthropology. This was effected principally through his publications, mainly on the ethnology of Java. Although few in number and spread over a time span of twenty years, they were of very high quality and influenced not only anthropologists (e.g., J.P.B. DE JOSSELIN DE JONG) but also historians, linguists, students of literature, archaeologists and students of native law (*adatrecht*). In 1959 his most important articles were translated and published in the bundle *Pañji, the Culture Hero*. With this publication Rassers emerged for a much wider public as a pioneer and forerunner of modern structuralism.

Inspired by *De quelques formes primitives de classification* by Émile Durkheim and MARCEL MAUSS (1903), Rassers was one of the very first Dutch ethnologists to explore intensively the idea of the unity of myth, rite, material culture and social structure. He showed that the form of a myth (the Pañji-novel), a rite (the *wayang*) or an object (the Javanese *kris*) and the way in which they are told, enacted or used, are not coincidental; they mirror the social structure in which they originated. In their turn they shape the present-day reality and the way new ideas are accepted and incorporated in culture. This kind of argumentation became essential in the Leiden structuralist tradition and also one of the points on which it was most severely criticized.

MAJOR WORKS: *De Pandji-roman* (Leiden and Antwerp: 1922); "Over den zin van het Javaansche drama," *Bijdragen tot de Taal-, Land- en Volkenkunde*, vol. 81 (1925), pp. 311-384 [tr.: "On the meaning of Javanese drama" in: W.H. Rassers, *Pañji, the Culture Hero: a Structural Study of Religion in Java* (The Hague: 1969), pp. 1-62]; "Ciwa and Boeddha in den Indischen Archipel," *Gedenkschrift, uitgegeven ter gelegenheid van het 75-jarig bestaan van het Koninklijk Instituut voor Taal,- Land- en Volkenkunde* (The Hague: 1926), pp. 221-253 [tr.: "Siva and Buddha in the East Indian Archipelago" in: W.H. Rassers, *Pañji, the Culture Hero: a Structural Study of Religion in Java* (The Hague: 1959), pp. 63-92]; "Religionen der Naturvölker Indonesiens," *Archiv für Religionswissenschaft*, vol. 25 (1927), pp. 130-193; "Naar aanleiding van eenige maskers van Borneo," *Nederlandsch-Indië Oud en Nieuw*, vol. 13, no. 2 (1928), pp. 35-64; "Over den oorsprong van het Javaansche tooneel," *Bijdragen tot de Taal-, Land- en Volkenkunde*, vol. 88 (1931), pp. 317-450 [tr.: "On the origin of the Javanese theatre" in: W.H. Rassers, *Pañji, the Culture Hero: a Structural Study of Religion in Java* (The Hague: 1959), pp. 93-215]; "Inleiding tot een bestudeering van de Javaansche kris," *Mededeelingen Koninklijke Nederlandse Akademie van Wetenschappen, afdeeling Letterkunde*, n.r., vol. 1(8) (1938), pp. 425-483; "Tooneel" in: *Encyclopaedie van Nederlandsch Oost-Indie*, supplement, vol. 8 (The Hague: 1939), pp. 1630-1632; "On the Javanese kris," *Bijdragen tot de Taal-, Land- en Volkenkunde*, vol. 99 (1940), pp. 501-582; "Kabadjan," *Bijdragen tot de Taal-, Land- en Volkenkunde*, vol. 100 (1941), pp. 377-403; *Pañji, the Culture Hero: a Structural Study of Religion in Java* (The Hague: 1959).

SOURCES: G.W. Locher, "Willem Huibert Rassers," *Bijdragen tot de Taal-, Land- en Volkenkunde*, vol. 130 (1974), pp. 1- 15; A. Teeuw, "Herdenking van Willem Huibert Rassers (16 september 1877—15 mei 1973)," *Jaarboek Koninklijke Nederlandse Akademie van Wetenschappen* (1973), pp. 214-221.

S.R. Jaarsma and J.J. de Wolf

Rattray, Robert Sutherland. Anthropologist, lawyer. Born 1881, died in Farmoor (England) 14 May 1938. Following service in the Boer War in South Africa and with the Great Lakes Corporation in Nyasaland (now Malawi), Rattray obtained a diploma in anthropology at Exeter College, Oxford, where he studied with R.R. MARETT. In 1918 he was called to the Bar at Gray's Inn. He was a member of the colonial service in Togoland (now Togo) and Gold Coast (now Ghana), where he became the first head of a new anthropology department, in 1921, assigned to find out why indirect rule was not working in Ashanti. Rattray also was an aviator; he was the first to fly solo from England to the Gold Coast in 1929 and died prematurely in a glider accident in 1938. For more than thirty years Rattray was a fellow of the Royal Anthropological Institute, which recognized his accomplishments with the award of the Rivers Medal in 1933.

Rattray was best known as an African ethnographer and linguist. From his first residence in Central Africa where, prior to his anthropological training, he learned the Nyanja language, collected folklore and translated it in *Some Folk-Lore Stories and Songs in Chinyanja*, he made detailed studies of the cultures of peoples among whom he lived. His greatest accomplishment was his trilogy on the Ashanti: *Ashanti, Religion and Art in Ashanti* and *Ashanti Law and Constitution*, which resulted from his need to learn about the whole culture in order to understand Ashanti politics and law. Rattray's work was marked by its thoroughness, linguistic competence and sympathy with the people. He also wrote a novel about the Ashanti, *The Leopard Priestess*, in which he told a real story using dialogue spoken by his informants to portray individuals and how Africans think. At the time of his death he was planning a sequel which he hoped to have made into a film.

MAJOR WORKS: *Some Folk-Lore Stories and Songs in Chinyanja* (London: 1907); *Hausa Folk-Lore, Customs, Proverbs* (Oxford: 1913); *Ashanti Proverbs* (Oxford: 1916); *An Elementary Môle Grammar* (Oxford: 1918); *Ashanti* (Oxford: 1923); *A Short Manual of the Gold Coast* (London: 1924); *Religion and Art in Ashanti* (Oxford: 1927); *Ashanti Law and Constitution* (Oxford: 1929); *Akan-Ashanti Folk-Tales* (Oxford: 1930); *The Tribes of the Ashanti Hinterland* (Oxford: 1932); *The Leopard Priestess* (London: 1934).

SOURCES: Melville J. Herskovits, "Robert Sutherland Rattray," *American Anthropologist*, n.s., vol. 41 (1939), pp. 130-131; Edwin W. Smith, "Robert Sutherland Rattray," *Man*, vol. 38 (1938), pp. 107-108; "Rattray, Captain Robert Sutherland" in: *Who Was Who, 1929-1940* (London: 1941), p. 1124.

Nancy J. Schmidt

Ratzel, Friedrich. Geographer, anthropogeographer. Born in Karlsruhe (Germany) 30 August 1844, died near Lake Starnberg (Germany) 9 August 1904. Ratzel is generally considered one of the most important of 19th-century geographers. In an era when geography and ethnology were not clearly separated disciplines, he also played a key role in the development of ethnology in the German-speaking world.

Ratzel's university training was originally in zoology. For some years (1869-1875) after graduating he traveled extensively. He then returned for his *Habilitation* in geography at the University of Munich. For the rest of his life he taught, first at the Technische Hochschule in Munich, then at the University of Leipzig.

Within geography, he is perhaps best known for his speculations on the influence of environment on human life. His writing and teaching had considerable influence on geography both in the German-speaking world and in the United States. The American environmentalist Ellen Church Semple was one of his students. Ratzel is also known to geographers for his thoughts on political geography; he was a great supporter of German colonialism and the inventor of the concept *"Lebensraum."* In addition, he was evidently the originator of the term "anthropo-geography." In English this word is now little used (except by the Library of Congress in its system of subject headings). But Ratzel's use of the term suggests his role as one of the most forthright 19th-century proponents of a distinctive discipline of human geography.

Historians of anthropology think of him quite differently. He is remembered as having, along with FRITZ GRAEBNER, LEO FROBENIUS and WILHELM SCHMIDT, helped to originate the Cultural-Historical School. His particular contribution was the notion of the culture area (later the *Kulturkreis*, although Ratzel rarely used this term himself). He also wrote at length on diffusion. Delineating diffusion routes later became an obsession of the Cultural-Historical School.

His "culture-area" idea has had some importance in American anthropology too, although not everyone who used the concept would have known it came from Ratzel. Among those who have made use of the concept self-consciously are CLARK WISSLER, ALFRED L. KROEBER and HAROLD DRIVER. But, in fact, every scholar or museum curator who has invoked names of cultural regions like "Melanesia," "Mesoamerica" or "Northwest Coast" has (unconsciously at least) been making use of the "culture-area" idea.

MAJOR WORKS: *Städte und Culturbilder aus Nordamerika* (Leipzig: 1876) [tr.: *Sketches of Urban and Cultural Life in North America* (New Brunswick: 1988)]; *Die Vereinigte Staaten von Nord-Amerika* [2 vols.] (Munich: 1878-1880); *Anthropo-Geographie, oder Gründzeuge der Anwendung der Erdkunde auf die Geschichte* (Stuttgart: 1882); *Völkerkunde* [3 vols.] (Leipzig: 1885-1888; revised ed. [2 vols.], Leipzig and Vienna: 1894) [tr.: *The History of Mankind* [3 vols.] (London: 1896-1898)]; *Anthropogeographie. Zweiter Teil. Die geographische Verbreitung des Menschen* (Stuttgart: 1891; revised ed., Engelhorn: 1912; 3rd ed., Engelhorn: 1922); *Politische Geographie* (Oldenburg: 1897).

SOURCES: Günther Buttmann, *Friedrich Ratzel: Leben und Werk eines deutschen Geographen, 1844-1904* (Stuttgart: 1977) (= *Grosse Naturforscher*, vol. 40) [contains nearly complete bibliography of works by and about Ratzel]; Mark Bassin, "Friedrich Ratzel, 1844-1904," *Geographers: Biobibliographical Studies*, vol. 11 (1987), pp. 123-132; Roy Ellen, "Persistence and change in the relationship between anthropology and human geography," *Progress in Human Geography*, vol. 12 (1988), pp. 229-262; Marvin Mikesell, "Geographic perspectives in anthropology," *Annals of the Association of American Geographers*, vol. 57 (1967), pp. 617-634; Robert Heine-Geldern, "One hundred years of ethnological theory in the German-speaking countries: some milestones," *Current Anthropology*, vol. 5 (1964), pp. 407-418; Ellen Church Semple, *Influences of Geographic Environment: on the Basis of Ratzel's System of Anthropogeography* (New York: 1911).

Rau, Charles. Archaeologist, museum curator. Born in Verviers (Belgium) 1826, died in Philadelphia (Pennsylvania) 25 July 1887. Little is known about Rau's early life except that he lived as a boy in Heidelberg, became an apprentice in the iron industry in Siegen in 1839 and was later a mining superintendent in Remagen. A university education is assumed and, by report, he attended Heidelberg University, although the records of that institution have failed to substantiate this. In 1882 he received an honorary Ph.D. from the University of Freiburg in Baden. Rau immigrated to the United States in 1848 and settled in Belleville, Illinois. There he taught languages in order to support himself, and he carried out investigations of nearby archaeological sites in Missouri and Illinois. He also amassed an archaeological collection. Beginning in 1859 he began to publish reports of his work regularly and to prepare general articles on ancient American industries. In 1863 he moved to New York and, while still teaching, continued to prepare publications on American and European archaeology that brought him recognition as one of the leading archaeologists of the United States.

In 1875 Rau was engaged to prepare the joint Smithsonian Institution-Bureau of Indian Affairs exhibit for the Centennial Exposition in Philadelphia. In 1881 he was appointed curator in the Department of Archaeology of the United States National Museum, his being the first permanent anthropology curatorship at the Smithsonian Institution. He continued in the position until his death.

In his work with exhibits for the Centennial Exposition, Rau formed a classificatory scheme for ethnological materials derived from European models. For archaeological classification, the scheme stressed aspects of manufacture including materials, methods and forms in that order of importance.

MAJOR WORKS: *The Archaeological Collection of the United States National Museum* (Washington: 1876) (= *Smithsonian Contributions to Knowledge*, vol. 22, article 2); *Articles on Anthropological Subjects Contributed to the Annual Reports of the Smithsonian Institution from 1863 to 1877* (Washington: 1882); *Early Man in Europe* (New York: 1876); *The Palenque Tablet in the United States National Museum, Washington, D.C.* (Washington: 1879) (= *Smithsonian Contributions to Knowledge*, vol. 22, article 5); *Prehistoric Fishing in Europe and North America* (Washington: 1884) (= *Smithsonian Contributions to Knowledge*, vol. 25, article 1).

SOURCES: Rau papers in the Smithsonian Institution National Anthropological Archives and unpublished finding aid to them by Carol Day; Walter Hough, "Charles Rau" in: Allen Johnson and Dumas Malone, *Dictionary of American Biography*, vol. 8 (1960), p. 3889; Thomas G. Tax, *The Development of American Archaeology, 1800-1879* [unpublished Ph.D. dissertation, University of Chicago] (Chicago: 1973).

James R. Glenn

Redfield, Robert. Anthropologist. Born in Chicago (Illinois) 4 December 1897, died in Chicago (Illinois) 16 October 1958. Redfield developed concepts that brought into a single purview preliterate tribes, folk peasantries and complex civilizations. He was associated all his life with the University of Chicago, as student, professor and dean. The son of a lawyer, Redfield married Margaret Park (daughter of the sociologist Robert E. Park) before graduating in law. A summer visit to Mexico turned him to anthropology. His Ph.D. dissertation (1928) reported fieldwork in a community in Mexico; *Tepoztlán* received immediate attention as a pioneer study of the "folk" community as a way of life. After extended fieldwork with his family in Yucatán, he showed through comparison of tribe, village, town and city how the growth of a small isolated community into a large heterogeneous society involves social disorganization and the substitution of formal institutions for a "moral order."

In 1947, about seventeen years after Redfield published his study of Tepoztlán, the anthropologist OSCAR LEWIS made a series of revisits to the village together with his wife and several experts. Lewis published a comprehensive monograph about his revisits under the title *Life in a Mexican Village*. The monograph created a stir among anthropologists because it not only described where the later observations agreed with Redfield's earlier report but also where they disagreed.

Both anthropologists acknowledged the differences between the two books and also agreed that the time lapse between them and Lewis's use of more experts and informants did not suffice to explain the differences. The disagreement became a classic example of how two ethnographies of the same village could select different "facts" and stimulated use of the method of restudy.

In a more explicit and general discussion of this issue in his Uppsala lectures on *The Little Community*, Redfield endorsed Lewis's method of restudying a community at a later date to take direct account of historical changes, as he had done in a restudy of Chan Kom (*A Village that Chose Progress*) and also described the interesting and difficult proposal that a single investigator use alternative, contrasting types of society and culture to guide the concrete questions put to particular observations, as he had done in his Yucatán comparisons.

Redfield also drew the important conclusion from this discussion that anthropologists must recognize that "the personal interests and personal and cultural values of the investigator influence the content of the description of the community" (*The Little Community*, p. 136).

From 1951 through 1958 Redfield directed an interdisciplinary and international research project, supported by the Ford Foundation, to develop methods for characterizing and comparing living civilizations, in general and with special reference to China, India, Islam, America and Europe. Much of his travel, teaching and writing during this period was devoted to the project, which was based at the University of Chicago and was continued after Redfield's death in 1958 until 1961 by MILTON B. SINGER, who had been its associate director.

One of Redfield's chief goals in the project was to modify in some degree "the separateness with which the study of Western civilization has been carried on, and of supplementing, through a more central vision, the efforts made in UNESCO and elsewhere to develop a world community of ideas." By bringing both the learned "great traditions" and the "little traditions" of the folk of different civilizations into greater comparability at the level of systematic thought and scholarly research, Redfield hoped to advance mutual understanding between the peoples of the world in a "conversation of cultures" and a "civilization of the dialogue."

In anthropology and in other social science disciplines, the Redfield project helped move teaching and research dominated by positivistic, causal and functional models toward more humanistic models that added history, analysis of cultural symbolism and ethical and esthetic valuations. It also transformed the ideal-type theory of a folk-urban continuum into empirical studies of how civilizations, historically grounded in peasant communities and cultures, have been modernizing and trying to recover their great and little traditions at the same time.

This extension of anthropological perspective and method, which Redfield called a "social anthropology of civilizations" to distinguish it from ALFRED L. KROEBER's comparative macro-history of civilizations, has stimulated many new programs for interdisciplinary and intercultural teaching and research about different civilizations at the University of Chicago and at other universities and colleges.

The making and use of nuclear bombs at the end of World War II has given such educational programs a special urgency and relevance for the conduct of international relations, Redfield believed. The comparative study of civilizations provided, he felt, both a hearing aid and a psychic radar with which to listen to the persistent characteristics of other nations, their changing moods, and their universal human nature, in short, the means for conducting a conversation of cultures that would bypass the use of nuclear weapons as instruments of foreign policy.

MAJOR WORKS: *Tepoztlán: a Mexican Village: a Study of Folk Life* (Chicago: 1930); (with Alfonso Villa Rojas) *Chan Kom: a Maya Village* (Washington: 1934) (= *Carnegie Institution of Washington, Publications*, no. 448); *The Folk Culture of Yucatan* (Chicago: 1941); *A Village That Chose Progress: Chan Kom Revisited* (Chicago: 1950); *The Primitive World and Its Transformations* (Ithaca, N.Y.: 1953); *The Little Community* (Chicago: 1955); *Peasant Society and Culture: an Anthropological Approach to Civilization* (Chicago: 1956); *Human Nature and the Study of Society* (edited by Margaret Park Redfield) (Chicago: 1962); *The Social Uses of Social Science* (edited by Margaret Park Redfield) (Chicago: 1963).

SOURCES: Richard H. Davis, *South Asia at Chicago: a History* (Chicago: 1985); Charles M. Leslie, "Redfield, Robert" in: David L. Sills (editor), *International Encyclopedia of the Social Sciences* (New York: 1968-1979), vol. 13, pp. 350-353; Oscar Lewis, *Life in a Mexican Village: Tepoztlán Restudied* (Urbana: 1951); Milton Singer, "Robert Redfield's development of a social anthropology of civilizations" in: John V. Murra (editor), *American Anthropology: the Early Years* (St. Paul: 1976) (= *1974 Proceedings of the American Ethnological Society*), pp. 187-260; Asael T. Hansen, "Robert Redfield, the Yucatan Project, and I" in: John V. Murra (editor), *American Anthropology: the Early Years* (St. Paul: 1976) (= *1974 Proceedings of the American Ethnological Society*), pp. 167-186; Charles M. Leslie, "The hedgehog and the fox" in: John V. Murra (editor), *American Anthropology: the Early Years* (St. Paul: 1976) (= *1974 Proceedings of the American Ethnological Society*), pp. 146-166; Milton Singer, "Robert Redfield, 1897-1958" (forthcoming); Milton Singer, "A conversation of cultures: the United States and Southern Asia" in: Margaret Case and Gerald Barrier (editors), *Aspects of India: Essays in Honor of Edward Cameron Dimock, Jr.* (Delhi: 1986), pp. 153-171; Milton Singer (editor), *Nuclear Policy, Culture and History* (Chicago: 1988); Milton Singer, "Foreword" to: A.L. Kroeber, *An Anthropologist Looks at History* (edited by Theodora Kroeber) (Berkeley and Los Angeles: 1963), pp. v-xiv; George W. Stocking, Jr., "The ethnographic sensibility of the 1920s" in: George W. Stocking, Jr. (editor), *Romantic Motives* (Madison: 1989) (= *History of Anthropology*, vol. 6), pp. 30-35; George W. Stocking, Jr., *Anthropology at Chicago: Tradition, Discipline, Department* (Chicago: 1979); Sol Tax, "Redfield, Robert" in: *Encyclopaedia Britannica* (Chicago: 1971), vol. 19, p. 30. Robert Redfield's papers and correspondence have been deposited in Special Collections of the Joseph Regenstein Library, University of Chicago.

Milton B. Singer
(with first paragraph by Sol Tax)

Reed, Charles A. Physical anthropologist, zoologist, anatomist. Born in Portland (Oregon) 6 June 1912. Reed's eclectic education and farm background in Oregon have had a profound influence on his contributions to science. He went from geology to history to geography and taught zoology while an undergraduate at the University of Oregon. His formal education ended when he received a doctorate in zoology from the University of California, Berkeley (1943). He made the transfer from zoology to anthropology by way of archaeology. With ROBERT J. BRAIDWOOD at Jarmo, in Iraq, he was in charge of identifying nonhuman bones for signs of domestication. The presence of a zoologist on an archaeological dig of this importance was the key to adding breadth and depth to the total field results. It also made possible the future examination of data from other expeditions. Another season with Braidwood, this time in Iran, sparked Reed's continuing interest in the origins of agriculture. Eventually this was to culminate in a well known conference at the Ninth International Congress of Anthropologists and Ethnologists in Chicago, 1973, from which came a large volume, *Origins of Agriculture*, edited by Reed. While at Yale University from 1962 to 1965, Reed spent three long seasons working on late Pleistocene sites in Nubia and Upper Egypt, examining the range of animals found at preagricultural and predomestication levels. In 1970 he returned to Turkey with Braidwood, checking on finds of nonhuman bones, both domesticated and hunted, on an archaeological site. In 1966 Reed returned to the University of Illinois, Chicago, and in 1967 joined the newly formed Department of Anthropology as the acting head. He retired in 1980 but has remained as an active Professor Emeritus.

His imaginative sense of imagery and whimsey in nonscientific writing is not well known but very real (see his "Answer to Virginia").

MAJOR WORKS: (editor) *Origins of Agriculture* (The Hague: 1977); (edited with Linda Braidwood, Robert Braidwood, Bruce Howe, and Patty Jo Watson) *Prehistoric Archeology along the Zagros Flanks* (Chicago: 1983) (= *University of Chicago Oriental Institute Publications*, no. 105); "Locomotion and appendicular anatomy in three soricoid insectivores," *American Midland Naturalist*, vol. 45 (1951), pp. 513-671; (with Robert Braidwood) "The achievement and early consequences of food-production: a consideration of the archaeological and natural-historical evidence," *Cold Spring Harbor Symposia in Quantitative Biology*, vol. 22 (1957), pp. 19-31; "A review of the archaeological evidence on animal domestication in the prehistoric Near East," *Studies in Ancient Civilizations*, vol. 31 (1960), pp. 119-145; "A natural history of the Kurkur Oasis, Libyan Desert, Western Governate, Egypt. I. Introduction," *Postilla, Yale Peabody Museum*, no. 84 (1964), pp. 1-20; "Origins of agriculture: discussion and some conclusions" in: Charles Reed (editor), *Origins of Agriculture* (The Hague: 1977), pp. 879-953; "Answer to Virginia," *Perspectives in Biology and Medicine*, vol. 26 (1982), pp. 39-45; "Energy traps and tools" in: Phillip V. Tobias (editor), *Hominid Evolution: Past, Present and Future* (New York: 1985), pp. 89-97.

SOURCES: "Reed, Charles A." in: *Who's Who in America* (44th ed., Chicago: 1986-1987), p. 2304; "Reed, Charles A." in: *American Men and Women of Science* (16th ed., New York: 1986), *Physical and Biological Section*, vol. 6, p. 90.

Justine Cordwell

Reguly, Antal. Traveler, anthropologist, linguist. Born in Zirc (Hungary) 13 July 1819, died in Buda (Hungary) 23 August 1858. Reguly was one of the founders of scholarly research among eastern Finno-Ugrian peoples.

Searching for the origin and national identity of Hungarians, he undertook an eight-year journey (1839-1847) to several linguistically related peoples. He developed a complex concept of anthropology. His ideal was the joint examination of all fields of ethnic existence (including, e.g., physical anthropology, natural environment, history, spiritual culture and comparative and typological linguistics). He believed in the value of long-term fieldwork with full language competence. His goal was the achievement of a "brotherly," near-assimilated status in the given society. He gained such a status not only among the Finns but also among the hardly accessible sub-Arctic societies of the Voguls (Mansi) and Ostiaks (Khanty) in northwest Siberia. He recorded a rich collection of the disappearing archaic folklore of these peoples. He also collected data among the Lapps (Saami), Cheremis (Mari), Mordvins and Chuvash. After his untimely death, several generations of Hungarian scholars, including, for example, BERNÁT MUNKÁCSI, worked on translating and publishing his legacy.

> MAJOR WORKS: (completed by Hunfalvy Pál) *A vogul föld és nép* [*The Vogul Land and People*] (Budapest: 1864); (with Pápay József) *Osztják népköltési gyüjtemény* [*Collection of Ostiak Folk Poetry*] (Budapest and Leipzig: 1905); (with Pápay József, Zsirai Miklós and Fokos Dávid) *Osztják hősénekek* [*Ostiak Heroic Songs*] [3 vols.] (Budapest: 1944-1965) [contains German translations].

> SOURCES: Pápay József, "Reguly Antal emlékezete = Anton Reguly's Gedächtnis" in: *Osztják népköltési gyüjtemény* (Budapest and Leipzig: 1905), pp. i-lxxxii; J. Kodolányi Jr. "Antal Reguly" in: Vilmos Diószegi (editor), *Popular Beliefs and Folklore Tradition in Siberia* (Budapest: 1968), pp. 17-26.

Éva Schmidt

Reichard, Gladys Amanda. Ethnologist, linguist. Born in Bangor (Pennsylvania) 17 July 1893, died in Flagstaff (Arizona) 25 July 1955. After teaching school, Reichard attended Swarthmore College (B.A., 1919), concentrating in Latin and classics. She then studied with FRANZ BOAS, with whom she was closely associated until his death, receiving an M.A. (1920) and Ph.D. (1923) from Columbia University. Her mentor PLINY EARLE GODDARD introduced her in 1923 to the Southwest and the Navajo, her lifetime focus, and established her interest in linguistics. Although she started with research in Navajo social organization, by 1930 she had turned to Navajo religion, publishing a two-volume work in 1950, the culmination of her research. From her long friendship with a Navajo medicine man and his family she produced three semipopular books in the 1930s concerned with weaving and women's roles and became a weaver herself. Her linguistic work, always a part of any research she engaged in, resulted in *Navaho Grammar* and a Navajo dictionary (manuscript in the Museum of Northern Arizona archives) as well as her dissertation on Wiyot and a Coeur d'Alène grammar. At the time of her death she was engaged in a comparative study of Salish.

Reichard's lifelong professional association with Barnard College began in 1923 when she was appointed as an instructor in one of the few independent undergraduate anthropology departments and the only one for many years in a women's school. She became full professor in 1951. She served in several association positions as secretary: American Ethnological Society (1924-1926), American Folklore Society (1924-1936), Section H of the American Association for the Advancement of Science (1945) and New York Linguistic Circle (1945-1947). In 1940 she agreed to act as interim editor of the *Journal of American Folklore*. A Guggenheim fellowship (1926-1927) took her to Germany, where she studied Melanesian design. Her two-volume book on the subject brought her the Morrison Prize of the New York Academy of Sciences. Her obituarist, Marian Smith, points out that

"Reichard's work was so richly intensive that her contributions went far beyond that usually associated with ethnography."

MAJOR WORKS: *Social Life of the Navajo Indians* (New York: 1928) (= *Columbia Contributions to Anthropology*, vol. 7); *Melanesian Design* (New York: 1932) (= *Columbia Contributions to Anthropology*, vol. 18); *Spider Woman: a Story of Navajo Weavers and Chanters* (New York: 1934); *Navajo Shepherd and Weaver* (New York: 1936); *Dezba: Woman of the Desert* (New York: 1939); *Navajo Medicine Man: Sandpaintings and Legends of Miguelito* (New York: 1939); *Prayer: the Compulsive Word* (New York: 1944) (= *American Ethnological Society Monograph*, no. 7); *Navajo Religion: a Study of Symbolism* (New York: 1950); *Navaho Grammar* (New York: 1950) (= *American Ethnological Society Publication*, no. 21).

SOURCES: Marian W. Smith, "Gladys Armanda [sic] Reichard," *American Anthropologist*, vol. 58 (1956), pp. 913-916 [contains complete bibliography]; Esther S. Goldfrank, "Gladys Amanda Reichard," *Journal of American Folklore*, vol. 69 (1956), pp. 53-54; Eleanor Leacock, "Gladys Amanda Reichard" in: Ute Gacs [et al.] (editors), *Women Anthropologists: a Biographical Dictionary* (New York: 1988), pp. 303-309; Barnard College, *Gladys A. Reichard, 1893-1955* (New York: 1956); "Gladys A. Reichard, 1893-1955" in: Barbara A. Babcock and Nancy J. Parezo, *Daughters of the Desert* (Albuquerque: 1988), pp. 46-51; William H. Lyon, "Gladys Reichard at the frontiers of Navajo culture," *American Indian Quarterly*, vol. 13 (1989), pp. 137-163.

Nathalie F.S. Woodbury

Reinfuss, Roman. Ethnographer. Born in Przeworsk, Galicia (Austria-Hungary, now in Poland) 27 May 1910. Reinfuss studied law and later (1936-1945) ethnography at Jagiellonian University. While studying law he began an ethnographic analysis of Lemkovian folk culture and started to publish his findings. He also established contact with the Muzeum Etnograficzne (Ethnographic Museum) in Kraków and in 1936 began work there, simultaneously studying ethnography under KAZIMIERZ DOBROWOLSKI. In 1945, with a master's degree in ethnography, he founded, together with other members of Jagiellonian University, the University of Wrocław. For many years he chaired the Department of Ethnography, which he himself had founded. Between 1957 and 1967 he chaired the Department of Ethnography in Lublin. He remained closely connected to Kraków. It was in Kraków in 1946 that he obtained his doctorate and where, in 1953, he was appointed assistant professor. In 1955 he became associate professor and in 1971 full professor. He has been affiliated with the Laboratory of the Documentation of Art in Kraków continuously since 1946.

Reinfuss initiated and directed collective investigations in traditional folk art and its contemporary transformations. He considers his investigations of the links between art and material culture, the emergence of crafts in the village, and the connections between the socio-economic situation of the village and its creativity as his most important contributions.

MAJOR WORKS: "Budownictwo ludow na zachodniej Łemkowszczyźnie" ["Folk architecture in western Lemkovian regions"], *Lud*, vol. 33 (1934), pp. 83-112; "Etnograficzne granice Łemkowszczyzny" ["The ethnographic limits of the Lemkovian folk culture"], *Ziemia*, vol. 26, no. 10-11 (1936), pp. 240-253; "Łemkowie (opis etnograficzny)" ["The Lemkovians: ethnographic description"], *Wierchy*, vol. 14 (1936), pp. 1-24; *Stroje górali szczawnickich* [*Costumes of the Szczawnian Mountain Folk*] (Lublin: 1949); *Polskie druki ludowe na płotnie* [*Polish Folk Printing on Canvas*] (Warsaw: 1953); *Ludowe skrzynie malowane* [*Traditional Painted Boxes*] (Warsaw: 1954); *Garncarstwo ludowe* [*Folk Pottery*] (Warsaw: 1955); *Szopka krakowska* [*The Krakovian Christmas Manger*] (Kraków: 1958); *Malarstwo ludowe* [*Folk Painting*] (Kraków: 1960); *Polska sztuka ludowa*

[Polish Folk Art] (Kraków: 1960); *Ludowe kafle malowane [Painted Folk Tiles]* (Kraków: 1966); *Meblarstwo ludow w Polsce [Folk Furniture in Poland]* (Wrocław: 1977); *Ludowe kowalstwo artysty-cze [Artistic Folk Ironwork]* (Wrocław: 1980).

SOURCES: Zofia Cieśla-Reinfussowa, "Bibliografia prac Romana Reinfussa" ["Bibliography of the works of Roman Reinfuss"], *Lud*, vol. 64 (1980), pp. 53-66; Jerzy Czajkowski, "Roman Reinfuss (w rocznicę urodzin i 50 rocznicę pracy naukowej)" ["Roman Reinfuss (on his 70th birthday and the 50th anniversary of his scientific work)"], *Acta Scansenologica*, vol. 1 (1980), pp. 9-16; Aleksander Jackowski, "Roman Reinfuss i sztuka ludowa" ["Roman Reinfuss and folk art"], *Polska Sztuka Ludowa*, vol. 34 (1980), pp. 131-136.

Maria Niewiadomska and Iwona Grzelakowska
[Translation from Polish: Joel Janicki]

Reinisch, Simon Leo. Egyptologist, Africanist. Born in Osterwitz (Austria) 26 October 1832, died at Lankowitz (Austria) 24 December 1919. Starting in 1846, Reinisch attended the gymnasium in Graz and, after 1854, the University of Vienna where he was employed as a *wissenschaftlicher Hilfsarbeiter* (research assistant) in the library. In 1859, he received his doctorate from the University of Tübingen and in 1861 qualified as a lecturer at Vienna with a *Habilitationsschrift* on the history of the ancient East, including Egypt. In 1865, he cataloged the Egyptian collection of the Emperor Maximilian at Miramar Castle. He followed Maximilian to Mexico in 1866 after a prolonged sojourn in Egypt. While in Mexico he carried out linguistic as well as historical studies and assembled a large document collection. After his return Reinisch became *außerordentlicher Professor* in the field of Egyptian languages and classical studies at the University of Vienna in 1868; he was named *ordentlicher Professor* in 1873. During 1875-1876 and 1879-1880 he conducted field research in the Sudan and Eritrea, studying several Cushitic languages and Nubian. In 1879 he was made a corresponding member of the Academy of Sciences, which granted him regular membership in 1884. From 1890 to 1891 he served as dean of the Faculty of Philosophy (Arts) and subsequently (1896-1897) as rector of the University of Vienna. He was awarded the title *"Kaiserlicher Hofrat"* (approximately, "Privy councillor") prior to his retirement in 1903.

Reinisch, together with J. Karabaček (1845-1918), D.H. Müller (1846-1912) and others, was editor of the *Wiener Zeitschrift für die Kunde des Morgenlandes* (volumes 1-18) and may be regarded as the founder of Austrian Egyptology, with particular emphasis in the field of Cushitic studies. His works, which demonstrated the substantial relationship of the African (particularly Cushitic) languages both with each other and with ancient Egyptian, are still recognized as highly reliable and valuable.

MAJOR WORKS: *Grammatik und Wörterbuch der Barea-Sprache* (Vienna: 1874); *Die Sprache der Irob-Saho* (Vienna: 1878); *Die Nuba-Sprache* (Vienna: 1879); *Die Kunama-Sprache* (Vienna: 1881-1890); *Die Bilin-Sprache* (Vienna: 1882-1887); *Die Chamir-Sprache* (Vienna: 1884); *Die Quara-Sprache* (Vienna: 1885); *Die Afar-Sprache* (Vienna: 1885-1887); *Die Kafa-Sprache* (Vienna: 1888); *Texte der Saho-Sprache* (Vienna: 1889-1890); *Die Beḍauye-Sprache in Nordost-Afrika* (Vienna: 1893); *Wörterbuch der Beḍauye-Sprache* (Vienna: 1895); *Die Somali-Sprache* [3 vols.] (Vienna: 1900-1903); *Das persönliche Fürwort und die Verbalflexion in den chamito-semitischen Sprachen* (Vienna: 1909); *Die sprachliche Stellung des Nuba* (Vienna: 1911).

SOURCES: C. Conti-Rossini, "Leo Reinisch (necrologia)," *Revista degli Studi Orientali*, vol. 8 (1920), pp. 691-692; Hermann Jungraithmayr, "Reinisch, Leo" in: H. Jungraithmayr and W.J.G. Möhlig (editors), *Lexikon der Afrikanistik* (Berlin: 1983), pp. 201-202; H. Junker, "Nachruf auf Leo

Reinisch" in: *Almanach der Österreichischen Akademie der Wissenschaften* (Vienna: 1920), pp. 3-11; C. Meinhof, "Hofrat Prof. Dr. Leo Reinisch +," *Zeitschrift für Eingeborenen-Sprachen*, vol. 10 (1919-1920), p. 1; H. Mukarovsky (editor), *Leo Reinisch: Werk und Erbe* (Vienna: 1987); Ferdinand Anders, "Der steirische Vater der Afrikanistik: Maximilian von Mexico als großer Förderer," *Die Presse* [Vienna] (23-24 October 1982).

Rudolf Leger
[Translation from German: Robert B. Marks Ridinger]

Ribeiro, René. Physician, psychiatrist, anthropologist. Born in Recife (Brazil) 3 January 1914. Ribeiro received his M.D. from the Federal University of Pernambuco in 1936 and an M.A. in anthropology from Northwestern University in 1949. Ribeiro was one of the physicians who began teaching anthropology in the colleges of philosophy that were founded in the 1940s in Brazil and later integrated into the universities. He became instructor of psychiatry in 1937 at the Federal University of Pernambuco and University Professor of Anthropology there in 1957. Between 1976 and 1978 he served as president of the Brazilian Anthropological Association.

Ribeiro's experience in psychiatry as clinician and as hospital director awoke his interest in the problem of the supernatural, principally as it was manifested in the possession "phenomenon" in Xangô animist cults. He observed responses on psychological tests, particularly the Rorschach test, administered to *mães de santo* (cult priestesses) in a trance. Research on that cult stimulated the anthropological study of religion in general and questions about personality and psychosocial adjustment, cross-cultural psychiatry, messianism, race relations and the position of the Afro-Brazilian in Brazilian society. Ribeiro is the author of the pioneering and original analysis of the *amaziado* (mistress) relationship and of works on crime and violence. He is an authority on the relation between psychiatry and anthropology.

MAJOR WORKS: *As esquizofrenias: estudo estatístico e sua aplicação à higiene mental* (Recife: 1937); "On the *amaziado* relationship and on other aspects of the family in Recife (Brazil)," *American Sociological Review*, vol. 10 (1945), pp. 44-51; *Cultos afrobrasileiros do Recife: um estudo de ajustamento social* (Recife: 1952); "Projective mechanisms and the structuralization of perception in Afrobrazilian divination," *Revue d'Ethopsychologie normale et pathologique*, vol. 1, no. 2 (1955); *Religião e relações raciais* (Rio de Janeiro: 1956); "Personality and the psychosexual adjustment of Afro-Brazilian cult members," *Journal de la Société des Américanistes*, vol. 58 (1969), pp. 109-120; *Serviço social psiquiátrico* (São Paulo: 1973); *Antropologia da religião e outros estudos* (Recife: 1982); *O Negro na atualidade brasileira* (Lisbon: 1988).

Thales de Azevedo
[Translation from Portuguese: Margo L. Smith]

Riehl, Wilhelm Heinrich. Cultural historian, folklorist, ethnographer, sociologist, novelist. Born at Bieberich am Rhein (Germany) 6 May 1823, died in Munich (Germany) 16 November 1897. Riehl's significance for European ethnology lies chiefly in his ethnographic work (his use of qualitative methods such as observation and direct interviewing), his cultural analyses and his programmatic essay "Die Volkskunde als Wissenschaft," which contributed to his image as "the father of German folklore."

At first, Riehl studied theology with the intention of becoming a minister. Following his examinations in 1844, he resolved—stimulated in part by the lectures of

Ernst Moritz Arndts (1769-1860)—to devote himself completely to research on the German people. After approximately ten years of journalistic activity, Riehl was summoned to Bavaria by King Maximilian II to assume the position of chief correspondence editor of the Ministry of Foreign Affairs and an honorary professoriate in the Faculty of Political Science at the University of Munich. While at Munich, he delivered lectures in the areas of political science, social science, folklore, the history of culture and the state, the ethnography of Germany, etc. In 1859 he was made *ordentlicher Professor* for cultural history and statistics (in political science), giving lectures after 1876-1877 at the Königliche Musikschule (Royal School of Music) in Munich on the history of music. In 1885 Riehl became the director of the Bayerisches Nationalmuseum (National Museum of Bavaria) and chief conservator of the artistic works and antiquities of Bavaria.

Riehl's scientific goal was the exploration of the "natural laws of folk life." This investigation of folk life—as he recorded in his *Wanderbuch*—was based on direct interviews and observations undertaken during his travels, augmented by literary studies. In his monograph, *Die Pfälzer,* Riehl combined the description of the land, settlement patterns, history, art forms, social and political structure, religious life, the dietary habits and regional costume into a complete ethnographic picture of Palatinate culture.

With regard to theory, Riehl proceeded from the position that topography limited an economy, and economy limited the life of a society. Consequently, the tripartite geographic division of Germany into Tiefland, Mittelgebirge and Hochgebirge was reflected not only in climate but also in the political division, diet, modes of life and customs of the inhabitants. In "Die Volkskunde als Wissenschaft" he firmly opposed the pointless accumulation of data, stating that such collection should be directed to painting a broad portrait, classification and comparison. Riehl's differentiated observations by region, social strata and urban vs. rural areas are also of importance.

In Riehl's view, the scientific study of *Volkskultur* (folk culture) should be utilized for sociopolitical objectives. These goals are especially evident in the works *Die bürgerliche Gesellschaft* and *Die Familie,* in which he speaks firmly in favor of conservation and against liberalism and emancipation. He explained social phenomena as a consequence of "naturally" occurring polarities (such as masculine vs. feminine, potential energy vs. kinetic energy) whose overthrow did not appear desirable to him. Riehl opposed the individualized society of early capitalism. The sociopolitical agenda of his writings and the picture they propounded of *Volkskultur* as an "organic whole" led to a heightened interest in Riehl's work during the period of the National Socialist government.

MAJOR WORKS: *Die Naturgeschichte des Volkes als Grundlage einer deutschen Socialpolitik.* Vol. 1. *Land und Leute* (Stuttgart: 1854); Vol. 2. *Die bürgerliche Gesellschaft* (Stuttgart: 1851); Vol. 3. *Die Familie* (Stuttgart: 1855); Vol. 4: *Wanderbuch* (Stuttgart: 1869); *Die Pfälzer, ein rheinisches Volksbild* (Stuttgart: 1857); *Culturstudien aus 3 Jahrhunderten* (Stuttgart: 1859); "Die Volkskunde als Wissenschaft" in: *Culturstudien aus 3 Jahrhunderten* (Stuttgart: 1859), pp. 205-229; *Die deutsche Arbeit* (Stuttgart: 1861); (with others) *Bavaria: Landes- und Volkskunde des Königreichs Bayern* [3 vols.] (Munich: 1860).

SOURCES: Wolfgang Brückner, "Riehl und die Folgen," *Jahrbuch für Volkskunde,* vol. 7 (1984), pp. 67-79; Viktor von Geramb, *Wilhelm Heinrich Riehl: Leben und Wirken* (Salzburg: 1954); Helge Gerndt, "Abschied von Riehl—in allen Ehren," *Jahrbuch für Volkskunde,* vol. 2 (1979), pp. 77-88; Eberhard Gothein, "Wilhelm Heinrich Riehl," *Preußische Jahrbücher,* 92 (April 1898), pp. 1-27; Klaus Guth, "Wilhelm Heinrich Riehl und kein Ende ... ?," *Jahrbuch für Volkskunde,* vol. 2 (1979), pp. 73-76; Gerhard Heilfurth, "Über Riehls 'Handwerksgeheimnisse des Volksstudiums,'"

Hessische Blätter für Volkskunde, vol. 60 (1969), pp. 29-38; Antonie Hornig, *Wilhelm Heinrich Riehl und König Max II von Bayern* [dissertation] (Munich: 1938); Konrad Köstlin, "Anmerkungen zu Riehl," *Jahrbuch für Volkskunde*, vol. 7 (1984), pp. 81-95; Otto Lauffer, "Wilhelm Heinrich Riehl und die Museumsarbeit," *Niederdeutsche Zeitschrift für Volkskunde*, vol. 19 (1941), pp. 121-125; Georg von Mayr, "Riehl, Wilhelm Heinrich," *Biographisches Jahrbuch und deutscher Nekrolog*, vol. 3 (Berlin: 1900), pp. 400-414; Hans Moser, "Wilhelm Heinrich Riehl und die Volkskunde: eine wissenschaftsgeschichtliche Korrektur," *Jahrbuch für Volkskunde*, vol. 1 (1978), pp. 9-66; Robert Müller-Sternberg, *W.H. Riehls Volkslehre: ihre geistesgeschichtlichen Grundlagen und zeitgeschichtlichen Grenzen* (Leipzig: 1939) (= *Form und Geist*, vol. 41); Bernhard J. Chr. Schmidt, *W.H. Riehl: seine geistige Entwicklung bis zur Übernahme seiner Professur in München* [dissertation] (Strasbourg: 1913); Florian Simhart, "Wilhelm Heinrich Riehls 'Wissenschaft vom Volke' als konzeptioneller Rahmen seiner Landes und Volkskunde," *Zeitschrift für bayerische Landesgeschichte*, vol. 40, Heft 2/3 (1977), pp. 445-500; Henry Simonsfeld, "Riehl, Wilhelm Heinrich" in: *Allgemeine deutsche Biographie*, vol. 53 (Leipzig: 1907), pp. 362-383; Henry Simonsfeld, *Wilhelm Heinrich Riehl als Kulturhistoriker* (Munich: 1898); Klara Trenz, *Wilhelm Heinrich Riehls "Wissenschaft vom Volke" unter besonderer Heranziehung seiner Darstellung des saarpfälzischen Volkstums* (Berlin: 1937); Günter Voigt, "Zur weltanschaulichen Entwicklung Wilhelm Heinrich Riehls: eine Säkularbetrachtung," *Deutsches Jahrbuch für Volkskunde*, vol. 4 (1958), pp. 287-300; Günter Wiegelmann, "Riehls Stellung in der Wissenschaftsgeschichte der Volkskunde," *Jahrbuch für Volkskunde*, vol. 2 (1979), pp. 89-102.

Dorothea Schell
[Translation from German: Robert B. Marks Ridinger]

Ritzenthaler, Robert Eugene. Anthropologist, ethnologist. Born in Milwaukee (Wisconsin) 11 November 1911, died in Milwaukee (Wisconsin) 15 March 1980. Ritzenthaler received a Ph.M. from the University of Wisconsin-Madison (1940) and a Ph.D. from Columbia University (1950), both in anthropology. His positions as an aide and later department head of the anthropology section at the Milwaukee Public Museum gave him the opportunity to become actively involved in research and collecting activities in many parts of the world. His first fieldwork was among the Oneida Indian people of Wisconsin in 1939. Subsequent fieldwork was undertaken among the Ojibwa during the summers of 1941, 1942 and 1944. An interest in tribal economics took him to the island of Palau in 1948 where he was part of the Coordinated Investigation of Micronesian Anthropology headed by GEORGE PETER MURDOCK. His research resulted in a monograph that describes the different kinds and uses of money and illuminates Palauan culture as a whole. The Palau research was followed by two summer seasons of archaeological work in Wisconsin at the Aztalan site in 1949 and the Oconto site in 1951. *Cameroons Village* was published as a result of fieldwork done in what was then the still functioning Kingdom of the Bafut people. He also published an article on a Cameroon woman's organization empowered to punish certain kinds of offenders.

Ritzenthaler avoided the broad hypothesizing that attracted many of his contemporaries, referring to himself as "a simple ethnologist" interested in recording data rather than building theories. Many times he became interested in significant questions and trends long before their importance was generally recognized. For example, his Ojibwa studies produced some of the earliest publications on the impact of World War II on an Indian community. He also analyzed the processes whereby English surnames were acquired by Indian people and the effects of the introduction of a small industry on an Indian reservation as well as cross-cultural comparisons of attitudes toward health and disease. With

Mary Sellers, he undertook one of the first systematic studies of Indian people in an urban situation. As in his work among the Bafut, he drew special attention to women's activities well before women's studies had become a popular subject. While he considered ethnology his primary field, he made notable contributions in archaeology, particularly concerning the Old Copper Culture of Wisconsin. He served as president of the Wisconsin Archaeological Society in 1951 and edited its journal from 1952 to 1972. He was active in the Central States Anthropological Society and served as its president during 1959-1960.

MAJOR WORKS: "The impact of war on an Indian community," *American Anthropologist*, n.s., vol. 45 (1943), pp. 325-326; "The acquisition of surnames by the Chippewa Indians," *American Anthropologist*, n.s., vol. 47 (1945), pp. 175-177; "The impact of a small industry on an Indian community," *American Anthropologist*, vol. 55 (1953), pp. 143-148; "Chippewa preoccupation with health," *Milwaukee Public Museum Bulletin*, vol. 19 (1953), pp. 157-257; *Native Money of Palau* (Milwaukee: 1954) (= *Milwaukee Public Museum Publications in Anthropology*, no. 1); (with Mary Sellers) "Indians in an urban setting," *Wisconsin Archaeologist*, vol. 36 (1955), pp. 147-161; (with Frederick Peterson) *The Mexican Kickapoo Indians* (Milwaukee: 1956) (= *Milwaukee Public Museum Publications in Anthropology*, no. 2); "Anlu: a woman's uprising in the British Cameroons," *African Studies*, vol. 19 (1960), pp. 151-156; (with Pat Ritzenthaler) *Cameroons Village: an Ethnography of the Bafut* (Milwaukee: 1962) (= *Milwaukee Public Museum Publications in Anthropology*, no. 8); (with Pat Ritzenthaler) *The Woodland Indians of the Western Great Lakes* (Garden City: 1970).

SOURCE: Nancy O. Lurie, "Robert Eugene Ritzenthaler, 1911-1980," *American Anthropologist*, vol. 83 (1981), pp. 608-611.

Donald J. Terras

Rivers, W.H.R. (William Halse Rivers).

Social anthropologist, physician, neurologist, experimental psychologist, psychiatrist. Born in Chatham (England) 12 March 1864, died in Cambridge (England) 4 June 1922. Rivers is perhaps best remembered for his contributions to rigorous analysis of kinship patterns and the social organization of nonindustrial societies. He is regarded as a key figure in the development of British social anthropology.

Rivers' academic background was largely in medicine. He received his M.D. in 1888. From 1893 until his death, he was a member of St. John's College, Cambridge University. He came to Cambridge to teach physiology, then was director of the psychology laboratory, then Praelector of Natural Science Studies. He never taught anthropology as such, although he did have some anthropology pupils, e.g., A.R. RADCLIFFE-BROWN.

Rivers' comparative studies of visual perception and of neural pain mechanisms, the latter in collaboration with Henry Head (1904-1907), are landmarks in neurological research. During World War I, Rivers served as a military psychiatrist; as such, he treated and later befriended Siegfried Sassoon. He also became a close friend of Robert Graves.

In 1898 Rivers joined the Cambridge Anthropological Expedition to Torres Straits in charge of psychological studies. As an aid to investigating the islanders' psychological functions, he devised the "genealogical method" of tracing and defining kin. This became standard procedure in anthropological inquiry. Increasingly drawn into anthropology, Rivers during 1901-1902 sojourned with a hill tribe of southwestern India. The resulting ethnography, *The Todas*, is considered a classic. During 1907-1908 and 1914-1915 he conducted ethnological surveys in Melanesia. Material from the earlier survey provided the data for the two-volume *History of Melanesian Society*.

In 1911 Rivers turned from acceptance of social evolutionism, as then understood, toward adherence to the Egypt-oriented "heliocentric" hypothesis of G. ELLIOT SMITH; however, in later years his involvement with these ideas diminished as he developed interests in political dynamics and also in subliminal and unconscious motivations as factors in social action. He was one of the earliest of established scholars in Britain to examine, with critical care and interest, the formulations of both Freud and Jung.

During 1921-1922 Rivers was president of the (British) Folk-Lore Society; he was elected president of the Royal Anthropological Institute in 1922. In that year he died suddenly, not long after declaring as a Labour Party candidate for Parliament.

The posthumous repute of Rivers suffered from his association with Elliot Smith's heliocentric views and also from his venture into the "conjectural history" of Melanesian society, an enterprise strongly deprecated by British anthropologists. However, the penetrating quality of his analyses and his willingness to take up a wide variety of issues have won admiration. He was also, in his last years, one of the first European social scientists to consider the consequences of European contact and exploitation on nonindustrialized colonial peoples.

A restless intellectual adventurousness combined with methodological rigor characterizes Rivers' work. Although trained as a scientist, he was very much a humanist.

Considering his versatility and productiveness, it is worth noting that Rivers' career in anthropology could hardly have totalled more than a dozen years; that is, about half of his working time between 1898 and 1922.

MAJOR WORKS: *The Todas* (London: 1906); "The disappearance of useful arts" in: O. Castrén [et al.] (editors), *Festskrift Tillägnad Edvard Westermarck ...* (Helsingfors: 1912), pp. 109-130; *Kinship and Social Organization* (London: 1914); *The History of Melanesian Society* (Cambridge: 1914); *Dreams and Primitive Culture* (Manchester: 1917-18); "The psychological factor" in: W.H.R. Rivers (editor), *Essays on the Depopulation of Melanesia* (Cambridge: 1922), pp. 84-113; *Conflict and Dream* (London: 1923); *Psychology and Politics* (London: 1923); *Social Organization* (London: 1924).

SOURCES: Frederic C. Bartlett, "W.H.R. Rivers," *The Eagle*, no. 62 (1969), pp. 156-160; Robert Graves, *Good-Bye to All That* (London: 1929); Ian Langham, *The Building of British Social Anthropology* (Dordrecht, Holland: 1981); Jeremy MacClancy, "Unconventional character and disciplinary convention: John Layard, Jungian and anthropologist" in: George W. Stocking, Jr. (editor), *Malinowski, Rivers, Benedict and Others* (Madison: 1986) (= *History of Anthropology*, vol. 4), pp. 50-71; Charles S. Myers, "The influence of the late W.H.R. Rivers" in: W.H.R. Rivers, *Psychology and Politics* (London: 1923), pp. 147-181; Siegfried Sassoon, *Sherston's Progress* (London: 1936); Richard Slobodin, *W.H.R. Rivers* (New York: 1978); Anthony R. Walker, *The Toda of South India: a New Look* (Delhi: 1986).

Richard Slobodin

Rivet, Paul. Physician, physical anthropologist, politician. Born in Wasigny, Ardennes (France) 7 May 1876, died in Paris (France) 21 March 1958. Rivet was primarily responsible for the professionalization of French ethnology between the two world wars. Despite the extremely diverse aspects of his works, they nevertheless lack the conceptual force, theoretical rigor and rhetorical elegance of the works of Émile Durkheim and MARCEL MAUSS and were not as influential as those of LUCIEN LÉVY-BRUHL. However, it is with Mauss, a Durkheimian sociologist, and with Lévy-Bruhl, a philosopher, that Rivet collaborated in the creation of the Institut d'Ethnologie of the University of Paris in 1925.

Rivet thus brought together within one institution three currents that had characterized the history of anthropology in France since the beginning of the 19th century: the philosophical, the anthropological (physical) and the sociological.

A military doctor (1897), Rivet went to Ecuador in 1901 as part of a French geodesic expedition to measure an arc of the meridian. He remained there until 1906, collecting materials valuable to the fields of anthropology, archaeology and linguistics and to the ethnography of Ecuadorian peoples. Elected professor at the Muséum National d'Histoire Naturelle in 1928, Rivet changed the title of his chair from "Chair of Anthropology" (founded by ARMAND DE QUATREFAGES in 1855) to "Chair of Ethnology of Present and Fossil Man." Named director of the Musée d'Ethnographie du Trocadéro in 1929, he merged it with the Muséum and proceeded to reorganize it with the help of GEORGES HENRI RIVIÈRE. This was the origin of the Musée de l'Homme, founded by Rivet in 1937.

In his most well known work (and his most controversial), *Les origines de l'homme américain*, Rivet upholds the theory that transpacific migrations took place that enabled oceanic peoples (Melano-Polynesian and Australian) to occupy part of the American continent in relatively recent times. Based on the study of archaeological remains and on the discovery of linguistic analogies, the latter theory thus challenges the theory of an indigenous source or of an Asiatic origin.

A Dreyfusard like Lévy-Bruhl, with whom Rivet became associated a few years before World War I, a socialist like Mauss, a great admirer of Jean Jaurès since 1914 and, later, closely tied to Léon Blum, and an activist in the Front populaire (1936), Rivet was involved in a political career the intensity of which makes it difficult to distinguish the aspects of his thought that are due to his role as a politician from those due to his role as a scientist. Conseiller municipal of Paris (1935) and a member of the resistance network of the Musée de l'Homme (1940), Rivet was dismissed by the Vichy government and hunted by the Gestapo. He fled to South America where he spent the war years. After the Liberation, Rivet returned to France and became a socialist representative (1944-1951).

Rivet was a militant anti-racist and anti-fascist. With Alain and Paul Langevin, he founded the Comité de Vigilance des Intellectuels Antifascistes in 1934, the year he planned to make the future Musée de l'Homme a weapon against prejudice and a bastion of anti-racism and began to conceive of ethnology as a "discipline of vigilance" that set itself the goal of understanding and explaining the mores of others while at the same time reforming mores at home. However, his political involvement and his socialist alliances led him, in 1956, to support the hardline policy of France toward Algeria. As a delegate of France to the session of the United Nations in New York in 1957, he became, according to d'Harcourt, the "pilgrim of French policy amidst American friends."

MAJOR WORKS: "L'étude des civilisations materielles: ethnographie, archéologie, préhistoire," *Documents*, 3 (1929), pp. 130-134; "Les données de l'anthropologie" in: G. Dumas (editor), *Nouveau traité de psychologie* (Paris: 1930), pp. 55-100; "Ce qu'est l'ethnologie" in: *L'encyclopédie française*, vol. 7 (*L'espèce humaine*) (Paris: 1936), 7.06.1-7.08.16; *Trois lettres, un message, une adresse* (Mexico City: 1944); *Les origines de l'homme américain* (Mexico City: 1943; Paris: 1957); (with René Verneau) *Ethnographie ancienne de l'Équateur* (Paris: 1912); (with Georges Henri Rivière) "La réorganisation du Musée d'ethnographie du Trocadéro," *Bulletin du Muséum national d'Histoire naturelle*, 2nd sér., vol. 2 (1930), pp. 478-487; (with Henri Arsandaux) *Métallurgie précolombienne* (Paris: 1946); (with Guy de Créqui-Monfort) *Bibliographie des langues aymará et kičua*

[4 vols.] (Paris: 1951-1956) (= *Travaux et mémoires de l'Institut d'ethnologie, Université de Paris,* 51); (editor with Georges Henri Rivière) *Bulletin du Musée d'ethnographie du Trocadéro (1931-1935)* (Paris: 1989).

SOURCES: Anonymous, "Biographie de Paul Rivet, fondateur du Musée de l'Homme" in: *Miscellanea Paul Rivet, Octogenario dicata* [2 vols.] [31st Congress of Americanists] (Mexico City: 1958), pp. xxiii-xxvii; Pierre Champion, "Introduction" to: *Catalogue de l'exposition Paul Rivet (1876-1958), fondateur du musée de l'Homme* (Paris: 1976); Raoul Girardet, *L'idée coloniale en France, de 1871 à 1962* (Paris: 1972); Raoul d'Harcourt, "Paul Rivet, 1876-1958," *Journal de la Société des Américanistes,* vol 47 (1958), pp. 7-11; Jean Jamin, "Le Musée d'ethnographie en 1930: l'ethnologie comme science et comme politique" in: Georges Henri Rivière, *La muséologie selon Georges Henri Rivière: cours de muséologie, textes et témoignages* (Paris: 1988), pp. 110-121; "L'anthropologie et ses acteurs" in: Ch. Descamps (editor), *Les enjeux philosophiques des années 50* (Paris: 1989), pp. 99-114; Victor Karady, "Durkheim et les débuts de l'ethnologie universitaire," *Actes de la recherche en sciences sociales,* no. 74 (1988), pp. 21-32.

Jean Jamin
[Translation from French: Timothy Eastridge]

Rivière, Georges Henri. Museologist, ethnologist. Born in Paris (France) 5 June 1897, died in Louveciennes, Yvelines (France) 24 March 1985. Rivière is known above all for his museum work in which he had two apparently contradictory aims: placing objects on display in context and exhibiting them in austere—even puritanical—presentations. The "anti-aestheticism" which he displayed when he mounted ethnographic exhibits—whether temporary or permanent—had the effect of breaking with the evolutionary presentation schemas that had prevailed until then. Instead of an archaeological or genealogical conception of the ethnographic object, he substituted an "environmental" conception.

Even if Rivière, more concerned with "making" than writing, did not leave behind any book, his influence remains profound, and many of the questions he posed are still important. He was perhaps one of the few museum curators to suggest for anthropology the means to surmount its almost congenital incapacity to utilize the collections gathered in museums in its name.

Son of an official of the city government of Paris and nephew of the painter Henri Rivière who developed his taste for the "object," Rivière was in turn an organist, a jazz pianist, a lover of popular shows, a secretary of the celebrated collector David Weill, a habitué of Parisian society as well as of avant-garde literary and artistic circles, and a founder of *Documents*, a journal directed from its 1929 creation by Georges Bataille and which had among its collaborators savants, painters, poets and writers most of whom were dissidents of the surrealist movement. With only a *baccalauréat* and a diploma from the École du Louvre, Rivière had no university education. This did not prevent PAUL RIVET from recruiting him as *sous-directeur* (assistant director) of the Musée d'Ethnographie du Trocadéro (Ethnographic Museum of Trocadéro) in 1929, having discerned in him talents as an organizer and a sense of the "object." His talents would totally renew ethnographic museography in France where little had happened in the years since THÉODORE HAMY's first attempts at systematization in 1878.

From 1929 to 1935 Rivière took an active and decisive role in the reorganization of the Musée d'Ethnographie du Trocadéro and in the building of the Musée de l'Homme, which opened its gates in 1937. That same year he founded the Musée des Arts and

Traditions Populaires and became its first curator. In 1948 he participated in the creation of the International Council of Museums (ICOM) and was its director until 1966. At the same time he was also the principal driving force behind the development of the ethnology of France: he was responsible for the conception and direction of a major interdisciplinary survey on a French region, Aubrac, which would run more than eight volumes and took on the qualities of a manifesto. It prefigured the founding of the Centre d'Ethnologie Française, a laboratory affiliated with the Centre National de la Recherche established in 1967 at the Musée des Arts et Traditions Populaires.

Loyal to the legacy of Rivet, Rivière was always concerned with the relationship of fieldwork, museography and popular education. His conception of "ecomuseums"—defined as "museums rooted in society," which he developed and put into practice from 1967—was aimed at involving the local population in the conservation and management of its cultural and natural heritage. Rivière believed that the museum environment should be "transparent" and enlightening. Objects in museums were to be liberated "from the tyranny of taste, masterpieces and rarity." To attach these objects to the life of man in society is the only means of suggesting their profound meaning or understanding the message of those who made them. The ethnological approach whose goal is precisely to discover the relations among men as well as those between man and nature extends into all areas of "plastic expression." In displaying different notions of self such as different manners of using and transforming nature, the ethnographic museum should serve less to educate than to stimulate. Its goal is to increase sensitivity and to sharpen reflection on the human condition.

MAJOR WORKS: (with Alfred Métraux) *Les arts anciens de l'Amérique* (Paris: 1928); "Le Musée d'ethnographie du Trocadéro," *Documents*, 1 (1929), pp. 54-58; "Religion et 'Folies-Bergère'," *Documents*, 4 (1929), pp. 37-38; (co-editor with Paul Rivet) *Bulletin du Musée d'ethnographie du Trocadéro* (Paris: 1930-1935; reprinted, Paris: 1988); (with Paul Rivet) "La réorganisation du Musée d'ethnographie du Trocadéro," *Bulletin du Musée d'ethnographie du Trocadéro*, no. 1 (1930), pp. 3-11; "Les musées de folklore à l'étranger et le futur Musée des Arts et Traditions populaires," *Revue de Folklore français et de Folklore colonial*, vol. 7 (1936), pp. 58-71; "My experience at the Musée d'ethnologie" in: *The Huxley Memorial Lecture, 1968* (London: 1968), pp. 17-21; "Musées et autres collections publiques d'ethnographie" in: J. Poirier (editor), *Ethnologie générale* (Paris: 1968), pp. 472-493; "Avant-propos" to volumes 2-6 of: *L'Aubrac, étude ethnologique, linguistique, agronomique et économique d'un établissement humain* (Paris: 1970-1982); "Role of museums of art and of human and social sciences," *Museum*, vol. 25 (1973), pp. 26-44; "Essai d'une définition du jazz," *Jazz Magazine*, 319 (1983), p. 41; "Lettres de Georges Henri Rivière à Paul Rivet," *Gradhiva*, no. 1 (1986), pp. 22-27.

SOURCES: Isac Chiva, "Georges Henri Rivière: un demi-siècle d'ethnologie de la France," *Terrains*, 5 (1985), pp. 76-83; *La muséologie selon Georges Henri Rivière: cours de muséologie, textes et témoignages* (Paris: 1989); André Desvallées, "Les écomusées" in: *Universalia* (Paris: 1980); Jean Jamin, "Les objets etnographiques sont-ils des choses perdues?" in: Jacques Hainard and Roland Kaehr (editors), *Temps perdu, temps retrouvé: voir les choses du passé au présent* (Neuchâtel: 1985), pp. 51-74; Jean Jamin, "Tout était fétiche, tout devint totem," preface to the new edition of: *Bulletin du Musée d'ethnographie du Trocadéro* (Paris: 1988), pp. viii-xxii; Henry-Pierre Jeudi, *Mémoires du social* (Paris: 1986); Michel Leiris, "Présentation" to: "Religion et 'Folies-Bergère'," *L'Homme*, 96 (1985), pp. 137-140.

Jean Jamin

[Translation from French: Philippe Forêt and CW]

Robecchi Bricchetti, Luigi. Engineer, explorer. Born in Pavia (Italy) 21 May 1855, died in Pavia (Italy) 31 May 1926. After completing his studies, Robecchi Bricchetti dedicated himself to exploration. In 1888 he visited Egypt, where he planned an itinerary that in 1889 brought him across the Libyan desert to the oasis of Siwa. Robecchi Bricchetti's interests were primarily directed toward the Somalian territories (today comprising Ethiopia, Somalia and Kenya), whose interior was to a great extent unexplored; as the first explorer to travel through these places he made a decisive contribution to our knowledge of them and provided fundamental information concerning the geography of the region and the customs and languages of the indigenous peoples.

Robecchi Bricchetti's Somalian voyages began in 1888 with the exploration of the Harer region, followed two years later by an excursion along the coast from Obbia to Alula on the Gulf of Aden. A collection of skulls made during the journey was donated to the Museo Antropologico (Anthropology Museum) in Rome.

In 1891 he guided an expedition organized by the Società Geografica Italiana (Italian Geographical Society): after leaving Mogadishu he made the first internal crossing of the Somalian territory, following a route that took him once more to Aden.

Robecchi Bricchetti's experiences opened the way to journeys that, in the years immediately following, were undertaken by other Italian explorers with varying success.

In 1903 the Società Antischiavistica d'Italia (Italian Antislavery Society) entrusted Robecchi Bricchetti with the mission of conducting research on the incidence of the slave trade in the Somalian region; he concentrated his efforts in the Benadir territory. His letters from the journey provide a document of considerable interest, as they reveal a disquieting aspect of life in the Italian protectorate of Somalia. In fact the explorer, opposed to the silence from official sources, denounced the complicity of both the Italian authorities and the Società Anonima Commerciale del Benadir (Trade Company of Benadir, Ltd.) in the perpetuation of the slave trade.

Robecchi Bricchetti's writings provided numerous references to the customs and habits of the Somalian people; he described both daily material life and cultural rituals. His accounts provided important documentation. Of particular interest are some indigenous songs, recorded in their original form, a Somali-Italian dictionary, some photographic data, and detailed engravings. His engineering studies contributed to his ability to make accurate observations concerning geography, geology, meteorology, zoology and botany.

MAJOR WORKS: *All'oasi di Giove Ammone* (Milan: 1889); *I nostri protetti* (Pavia: 1894); *I nostri protetti, Abissini e Somali* (Rome: 1895); *Tripolitania* (Rome: 1896); "La prima traversata della peninsola dei Somali: estratti del giornale di viaggio," *Bollettino della Società Geografica Italiana*, vol. 30 (1892), pp. 465-539, 708-729, 802-842, 961-989; *Note sulle lingue parlate Somali, Galla e Harari* (Naples: 1898); *Nell'Harrar* (Milan: 1899); *Nel paese degli aromi* (Milan: 1903); *Dal Benadir* (Milan: 1904).

SOURCES: Elia Millosevich, *Le principali esplorazioni geografiche italiane nell'ultimo cinquantennio* (Milan: 1911); Gino Pellaci, *Luigi Robecchi Bricchetti, 1855-1926* (Pavia: 1934); Nello Puccioni, "Per Luigi Robecchi-Bricchetti," *Bollettino della Società Geografica Italiana*, ser. 6, vol. 3 (1926), pp. 503-510; Francesco Surdich, "L'immagine dell'Africa e dell'Africano nelle relazioni di Luigi Robecchi Bricchetti," *Miscellanea di storia delle esplorazioni*, vol. 5 (Genoa: 1980)

(= *Studi di storia delle esplorazioni*, 9), pp. 195-225; Silvio Zavatti, *Dizionario generale degli esploratori* (Milan: 1939).

Massimo Guerra
[Translation from Italian: Chris Nissen]

Roberts, Frank H.H., Jr. Archaeologist, government administrator. Born in Centerburg (Ohio) 11 August 1897, died in Washington (D.C.) 23 February 1966. Frank Roberts (strictly speaking he was not a "Jr.") was trained in English, history and political science at the University of Denver, obtaining a B.A. in 1919 and an M.A. in 1921. He received a Ph.D. in anthropology from Harvard University in 1927. He was an instructor in archaeology at the University of Denver (1921-1924); assistant curator at the Colorado State Museum (1923); and archaeologist with the Bureau of American Ethnology (BAE) (1926-1964). Roberts became the assistant chief of the BAE in 1944; associate director of the BAE and director of the BAE's River Basin Surveys in 1947; and director of the BAE in 1958.

Except for excavations of mounds in the Shiloh National Military Park in Tennessee under United States Work Projects Administration auspices (1933-1934), Roberts' early fieldwork was carried out in the Southwest. He worked in the Piedra-Pagosa region of the San Juan River (1921-1922 and 1928); in Chaco Canyon (1925-1927 and 1940-1941); at Kiathuthlunna in Arizona (1929); at the Village of the Great Kivas on the Zuni Reservation (1930); and along the Whitewater River near Allantown in Arizona (1931-1933). He regularly prepared publications based on his fieldwork, including an outline for a seriation scheme for Southwestern house types and syntheses of Southwestern archaeology.

It has been pointed out that throughout his early work Roberts' primary interest was "the early structure and sequences of Southwestern culture." This interest prepared the way for what became Roberts' ultimate concern: the problem of early man in America. Invited in 1927 to inspect the newly discovered Folsom site, in time Roberts was convinced of the error in scientific thought about the relatively recent arrival of man in the New World. Increasingly drawn into the problem, he came to devote most of his fieldwork to it. Between 1934 and 1940 he worked at Lindenmeier, a Folsom site in northern Colorado. In 1941 he worked at Folsom sites near San Jon in New Mexico, in 1943 at the Clear Fork site in Texas and in 1961 in the Agate Basin in Wyoming. In addition to these, Roberts carried out many inspections of reported sites of early human activity in North America.

Roberts was an advisor to the Carnegie Institution of Washington in excavations at Chichen Itzá and Uxmal and to the Wetherill Mesa Project of the National Park Service. He was the American representative to the League of Nations International Conference of Archeologists at Cairo in 1937 and the International Commission for Sites and Monuments during 1939-1942. During World War II, he worked for the Ethnogeographic Board and prepared a book on Egypt and the Suez Canal. He was a member of the National Council for Historical Sites and Buildings and National Research Council. He was a founding member of the Society for American Archaeology and served as its president in 1950. Much of his later life (1947-1969) was devoted to the organization and administration of the Smithsonian's River Basin Surveys, the salvage archaeological project that operated primarily in the Missouri Basin, the southeastern states, Texas, and the states along the Northwest Coast.

MAJOR WORKS: *Shabik'eshchee Village: a Late Basket Maker Site in the Chaco Canyon, New Mexico* (Washington: 1929) (= *Bureau of American Ethnology Bulletin*, no. 92); *Early Pueblo Ruins in the Piedra District, Southwestern Colorado* (Washington: 1930) (= *Bureau of American Ethnology Bulletin*, no. 96); *The Ruins of Kiatuthlanna, Eastern Arizona* (Washington: 1931) (= *Bureau of American Ethnology Bulletin*, no. 111); *The Village of the Great Kivas on the Zuni Reservation, New Mexico* (Washington: 1932) (= *Bureau of American Ethnology Bulletin*, no. 100); "A survey of Southwestern archaeology," *American Anthropologist*, vol. 17 (1935), pp. 1-33; "Archaeology in the Southwest," *American Antiquity*, vol. 3 (1937), pp. 3-33; *Archeological Remains in the Whitewater District, Eastern Arizona*, Part 1, *House Types* (Washington: 1939) (= *Bureau of American Ethnology Bulletin*, no. 121); *Archeological Remains in the Whitewater District, Eastern Arizona*. Part 2. *Artifacts and Burials* (Washington: 1940) (= *Bureau of American Ethnology Bulletin*, no. 126); "Developments in the problem of the North American Paleo-Indian," *Smithsonian Miscellaneous Collections*, vol. 100 (1940), pp. 51-116; (with Edwin N. Wilmsen) *Lindenmeier, 1934-1974: Concluding Report on Investigations* (Washington: 1978).

SOURCES: Gordon R. Willey and Jeremy A. Sabloff, *A History of American Archaeology* (London: 1974); Neil M. Judd, "Frank H.H. Roberts, Jr., 1897-1966," *American Anthropologist*, vol. 68 (1966), pp. 1226-1232; Roberts papers and vertical file in the Smithsonian Institution National Anthropological Archives; Janette Saquet, *Register to the Papers of Frank Harold Hanna Roberts* (Washington: 1983); Robert L. Stephenson, "Frank H.H. Roberts, Jr., 1897-1966," *American Antiquity*, vol. 32 (1967), pp. 84-94; Omer Stewart and John Greenway, "Frank Harold Hanna Roberts: an appreciation," *Southwestern Lore*, vol. 25 (1959), pp. 1-6; Edwin N. Wilmsen and Frank H.H. Roberts, Jr., "Introduction" to: *Lindenmeier, 1934-1974* (Washington: 1978), pp. 1-21.

James R. Glenn

Rodrigues, Raimundo Nina. See: *Nina Rodrigues, Raimundo.*

Róheim, Géza. Folklorist, ethnographer, psychoanalyst, psychoanalytical anthropologist. Born in Budapest (Hungary) 12 September 1891, died in New York (New York) 7 June 1953. In the first phase of his professional career—between 1913 and 1925—Róheim became involved in research on 19th-century Hungarian folklore and myth, and the results of his studies in establishing historical-period associations of Hungarian folk beliefs and folk customs are still considered valid. At the same time he was also interested in the field of ethnology. He explained contemporary popular beliefs by general ethnological concepts. Early in his professional life (1915-1916) he became acquainted with the views of Sigmund Freud and came into close contact with representatives of the Budapest psychoanalytical school: Vilma Mészáros, Sándor Ferenczi, Géza Révész, Róbert Bak and, somewhat later, Imre Hermann and others. He attempted through ethnographic methods to justify the theorems of the Freudian system. In 1921 he received the Freud award for outstanding contributions in this field, and, starting in the early 1920s, he worked as a practicing psychoanalyst.

During 1928-1931 he carried out ethnological and psychoanalytical research in Somalia, in Central Australia, in New Guinea, and with the Yuma Indians in the U.S. Southwest. This latter research expedition became the turning point in his career. He was the first professional ethnologist who was also a skilled psychoanalyst scientifically apply-

ing psychoanalytical procedures to ethnological work (such as analysis of dreams, of chil-
drens' games, observation of sexual behavior, etc.).

When he returned to Budapest (1931-1938) he resumed his psychoanalysis practice
in the Hungarian Psychoanalytical Society and at the same time developed the ethnological
findings of his fieldwork. Analysis of his observations led to the formation of a more precise theory. The precept of his theory is that the reason and basis for the advent of civilization is the connection between the evolutionary and general effect of the Oedipus Complex
and man's biological and social characteristics. In his works, using different angles of approach, he repeatedly sought the roots of various social phenomena and institutions within
the different phases of development of the human psyche.

To escape the fascist regime, he emigrated from Hungary to the United States in
1938. At first he worked at the Worcester State Hospital, but in 1940 he moved to New
York. In 1947 he completed his work on the dreams of the New Mexico Navajo Indians.
Beginning in 1947 he published the monographic series *Psychoanalysis and Social
Sciences*, which since 1960 has appeared under the title *Psychoanalytical Study of Society*,
edited by Warner Muensterberger. In the last phase of his professional career he returned
to his favorite topic, the study of Hungarian mythology. Similarly noteworthy is his theory
on dreams as outlined in his last work, a theory that is on the one hand in complete agreement with Freud's *Traumdeutung* (dream interpretation), while on the other hand quite
original in the interpretation of dreams as they relate to man's cultural circumstances.

Over the course of his career, Róheim's horizon of inquiry spread into all areas of
European culture, from classical antiquity to contemporary folk culture, from the Jewish
historical tradition to Vogul mythology, as well as to the study of the myths of the indigenous peoples of Central Australia. He combined his aptitude as a keen observer with his
ability to bring forth daring new theories. He was the first psychoanalyst of his generation
to contribute directly to the development of the psychoanalytic system of thought while simultaneously balancing the orthodox theoretical viewpoint with flexibility and openness.

MAJOR WORKS: *Magyar néphit és népszokások* [*Hungarian Folk Beliefs and Customs*]
(Budapest: 1925) [tr. of chs. 6-8: "Hungarian calendar customs," *Journal of the Royal
Anthropological Institute*, vol. 56 (1926), pp. 361-384]; "Die Psychoanalyse primitiver Kulturen,"
Imago, vol. 18 (1932), pp. 297-563 [tr.: "Psycho-analysis of primitive cultural types," *The
International Journal of Psycho-Analysis*, vol. 13 (1932), pp. 1-224]; *The Riddle of the Sphinx, or
Human Origins* (London: 1934); *The Origin and Function of Culture* (New York: 1943); *The Eternal
Ones of the Dream: Psychoanalytic Interpretation of Australian Myth and Ritual* (New York: 1950);
The Gates of the Dream (New York: 1952); *Hungarian and Vogul Mythology* (New York: 1954);
Children of the Desert [2 vols.] (vol. 1, New York: 1974; vol. 2, Sydney: 1988).

SOURCES: Roger Dadoun, *Géza Róheim et l'essor de l'anthropologie psychoanalytique* (Paris:
1972); Georges Devereux, "Géza Róheim," *American Anthropologist* vol. 55 (1953), p. 420; Weston
La Barre, "Géza Róheim, psychoanalysis and anthropology" in: Franz Alexander, Samuel Eisenstein,
and Martin Grotjahn (editors), *Psychoanalytic Pioneers* (New York and London: 1966), pp. 272-281;
Paul A. Robinson, *The Freudian Left: Wilhelm Reich, Géza Róheim, Herbert Marcuse* (New York,
Evanston and London: 1969); G.B. Wilbur and W. Muensterberger (editors), *Psychoanalysis and
Culture: Essays in Honor of Géza Róheim* (New York: 1951); Kincső Verebélyi, "On the 85th an-
niversary of Géza Róheim, the Hungarian forerunner of psychoanalytic anthropology," *Acta
Ethnographica*, vol. 26 (1977), pp. 199-218.

Kincső Verebélyi
[Translation from Hungarian: Ildiko D. Nowak]

Roquette-Pinto, Edgar. Anthropologist, physician, educator. Born in Rio de Janeiro (Brazil) 25 September 1884, died in Rio de Janeiro (Brazil) 18 October 1954. Roquette-Pinto is known nationally for having devoted his life to elementary education among the Brazilian populace. His work as a popular educator was inspired by his prior training in medicine and anthropology.

Educated in medicine, in 1905 he shifted his interests and devoted himself to the study of physiology and the racial composition of the Brazilian population. At this time many Brazilian intellectuals considered Brazil to be a backward and unhealthy country because of its racial miscegenation and believed that Brazil was incapable of modernization because the population was composed of *mestiços*—the result of the intermixture of three races: whites (European colonizers), blacks (African slaves) and Indians (native to the area). Roquette-Pinto, through his medical and anthropological research, attempted to show that Brazil was backward and unhealthy because of its social disorganization, not because of racial miscegenation. He developed a typology of the Brazilian population, which he divided into four groups: leucoderms (whites), faioderms (mixture of blacks and whites), xantoderms (mixture of whites and Indians), and melanoderms (blacks). A staunch nationalist, he attempted to show via this classification that none of these types was biologically inferior and therefore could not be held responsible for the backwardness of the country.

After defending his doctoral thesis in medicine, Roquette-Pinto became assistant professor of anthropology at the Museu Nacional (National Museum) in Rio de Janeiro in 1906. In 1911 he went to London as one of the Brazilian delegates to the World Congress on Race. In 1912, accompanying the Rondon expedition, he traveled through the Serra do Norte (Rondônia) and studied the Parecis and Nhambiquara Indians. Between 1926 and 1935 he was director of the Museu Nacional.

In 1923 he founded the Rádio Sociedade (Radio Society) of Rio de Janeiro, which was devoted exclusively to popular education. At the beginning of the 1930s he traveled to Europe to study the use of mass communication in education in national-socialist Germany and in Mussolini's Italy. In 1936 he founded the Instituto Nacional de Cinema Educativo (National Institute of Educational Film), which was also dedicated to popular education. In that same year he left all his professional activities in anthropology to devote himself to elementary education among the Brazilian people. He believed he had been born with the mission of saving the country from misery, ignorance and backwardness and decided that the isolated work of a researcher in medicine and anthropology was insufficient to help the country develop. He considered himself an educator of the masses, maintaining that the "new education" would save Brazil. However, Roquette-Pinto only came to be considered an educator of the people inasmuch as medicine and anthropology proved that the population was not biologically inferior.

MAJOR WORKS: *Etnographia americana: o exercício da medicina entre os indígenas da América* (Rio de Janeiro: 1906); *Etnografia indígena do Brasil: estado atual dos nossos conhecimentos* (Rio de Janeiro: 1909); *Rondônia* (Rio de Janeiro: 1917) [tr.: *Rondonia: eine Reise in das Herzstück südamerikas* (Vienna: 1954)]; *Conceito atual da vida* (Rio de Janeiro: 1922); *Seixos rolados: estudos brasileiros* (Rio de Janeiro: 1927); *Ensaios de antropologia brasiliana* (Rio de Janeiro: 1933); *Samambaia* (Rio de Janeiro: 1934); *Ensaios brasilianos* (Rio de Janeiro: 1940).

SOURCES: Francisco Venâncio Filho, "A radiocultura no Brasil (ao Prof. Roquette-Pinto)" in: *Educar-se para educar* (Rio de Janeiro: 1931); Fernando de Azevedo, "Edgar Roquette-Pinto," *Revista de antropologia*, vol. 2 (1954), pp. 87-100; Ernest Feder, *Erinnerungen an Roquette-Pinto*

(Rio Grande do Sul: 1956); Álvao Lins, *Discurso de posse na Academia brasileira: estudo sobre Roquette-Pinto* (Rio de Janeiro: 1956); Luis de Castro Faria, *A contribuição de E. Roquette-Pinto para a antropologia brasileira* (Rio de Janeiro: 1959); José Bento Monteiro Lobato, "Rondônia" in: *Idéias de Jéca Tatú* (São Paulo: 1967); Beatriz Roquette-Pinto Bojunga, "E. Roquette-Pinto" in: Francisco de Assis Barbosa (editor), *Retratos de família* (Rio de Janeiro: 1968), pp. 165-176; Roberto Ruiz de Rosa Metheus, *Edgar Roquette-Pinto: aspectos marcantes de sua vida e obra* (Brasília: 1984).

João Baptista Cintra Ribas

[Translation from Portuguese: Margo L. Smith]

Rosen, Eric von (Eric Carl Gustaf Bloomfield von Rosen). Ethnographer, explorer. Born in Stockholm (Sweden) 2 June 1879, died 25 April 1948. Von Rosen came from a wealthy family and inherited the title of count. He studied ethnography at the University of Stockholm (at that time the Ethnographical Department of the Swedish Riksmuseum) under the museum director, Professor Hjalmar Stolpe. He also received an honorary doctorate from the University of Cologne.

During 1901-1902 von Rosen took part in the Swedish Chaco-Cordillera Expedition, led by ERLAND NORDENSKIÖLD (an expedition that he also partially financed). In 1909 he led his second exploratory trip, this time to the White Nile. His most important field trip, however, was to be the Swedish Rhodesia-Congo Expedition during 1911-1912. On this trip he visited the "people of the Marshes," the Batua (Batwa), and brought back unique documentation in the form of excellent photographs and large ethnographic collections which he gave to the museums of Göteborg and Stockholm.

Von Rosen was a typical ethnographer, placing more emphasis in documentation than in analysis. He was also an excellent photographer and had a flair for drawing; thus his works are all well illustrated and in this way his basic work on peoples such as the Chorote and the Batwa is invaluable.

Von Rosen's genuine interest in ethnography was noted also after his death. His funeral service at Helgesta church commenced to the tunes of an Inca march recorded by him in the Tarija Valley, Bolivia, in 1902.

MAJOR WORKS: *The Chorotes Indians in the Bolivian Chaco* (Stockholm: 1904); *Från Kap till Alexandria* (Stockholm: 1912); *Träskfolket: Svenska Rhodesia-Kongo-expeditionens etnografiska forskningsresultat* (Stockholm: 1916); *En förgången värld: forskningar och äventyr bland Andernas högfjäll* (Stockholm: 1919); *Bland Indianer: forskningar och äventyr i Gran Chaco* (Stockholm: 1921); *Ethnographical Research Work during the Swedish Chaco-Cordillera Expedition* (Stockholm: 1924); *Popular Account of Archaeological Research of the Swedish Chaco-Cordillera Expedition, 1901-1902* (Stockholm: 1924); *Did Prehistoric Egyptian Culture Spring from a Marsh Dwelling People?* (Stockholm: 1929); *Un mundo que se va: exploraciones y aventuras entre las altas cumbres de la cordillera de los Andes* (Tucumán: 1957).

SOURCES: S. Henry Wassén. "Four Swedish anthropologists in Argentina in the first decades of the 20th century: bio-bibliographical notes," *Folk*, vol. 8-9 (1966/67), pp. 343-350; Gerhard Lindblom, "In memoriam: Eric von Rosen, 1879-1948," *Ethnos*, vol. 14 (1949), pp. 192-197.

Jan-Åke Alvarsson

Ross, Bernard Rogan. Trader, ethnographer. Born in Ireland 25 September 1827, died in Toronto (Ontario) 21 June 1874. Ross was chief trader with the Hudson's Bay Company and field ethnographer for the Smithsonian Institution from 1859 to 1866.

Between 1861 and 1869 Ross sent the Smithsonian 195 specimens of dress and technology belonging to the Inuit, Chipewyan, Kutchin and Slave Indians and specimens of native crania. He also sent northern anthropological specimens to the Royal Industrial Museum of Scotland (Royal Scottish Museum). Ross wrote a descriptive account of the "Eastern Tinneh," which forms one installment of an ethnographic trilogy published by the Smithsonian in 1866. His essay appears with W.L. HARDISTY's description of the Loucheux and with Strachan Jones' article on the Kutchin (Jones and Hardisty were fellow officers with the Hudson's Bay Company). All three accounts are important because they are some of the earliest recorded descriptions of these northern peoples and because they took their form and substance in response to "scientific" needs. They are concrete examples of the transformation that occurred, at mid-century, in the methods of collecting and recording ethnographic data. They conform to the criteria set out in the Smithsonian "Instructions" (1863) for ethnological studies and illustrate the innovations in the compilation of data associated with the first stage in the development of an empirically oriented methodology.

> MAJOR WORKS: "On the Indian tribes of McKenzie River District and the Arctic Coast," *The Canadian Naturalist and Geologist*, vol. 4 (1859), pp. 190-195; "The Eastern Tinneh," *Annual Report of the Smithsonian Institution* (1866), pp. 304-311.

> SOURCES: Strachan Jones, "The Kutchin tribes," *Annual Report of the Smithsonian Institution* (1866), pp. 320-327; accession records, Anthropology Department, Smithsonian Institution; collected notes, lists and catalogues on Birds, Ross papers, Smithsonian Institution Archives; Hudson's Bay Company correspondence collection, Smithsonian Institution Archives; *Bernard Rogan Ross Notebook*, Smithsonian Institution Archives; Hartwell Bowsfield, "Ross, Bernard Rogan" in: *Dictionary of Canadian Biography* (Toronto: 1966-), vol. 10, p. 629; Debra Lindsay, "The Hudson's Bay Company-Smithsonian connection and fur trade intellectual life: Bernard Rogan Ross, a case study" in: Bruce Trigger, Toby Morantz and Louise Dechene, *Le castor fait tout* (Montréal: 1987), pp. 587-617.

Debra Lindsay

Rouch, Jean. Anthropologist, filmmaker. Born in Paris (France) 31 May 1917. Known to anthropologists as an ethnographer of the Songhay and as the author of 125 films on Songhay and Dogon ritual and West African labor migration, Rouch is also recognized for his contributions to the *cinéma direct* movement and to the development of indigenous cinema in Africa. Since 1987 Rouch has been president of the Cinématheque Française.

Rouch saw Robert Flaherty's film, *Nanook of the North*, in 1924. He attended the Lycée Henri IV and the École des Ponts et Chaussées in Paris. In 1941 he obtained an engineering post in French West Africa. He became interested in the rituals of the workmen under his direction and began collaborating with Damouré Zika in ethnographic work on Songhay religion and magic, the subject of his dissertation (1960) and of numerous short films. After World War II Rouch studied anthropology at the University of Paris under MARCEL GRIAULE, the ethnographer of the Dogon. With Griaule's colleague, Germaine Dieterlen, he later filmed the sexentenary Sigi ritual (1966-1973) and the Dama of Ambara (1974).

In 1949 Rouch received the first of many film prizes, at Jean Cocteau's Festival du Film Maudit, for *Initiation à la danse des possedés*. In 1952 he was named Secretary-

General of the newly constituted Comité International du Film Ethnographique et Sociologique, with headquarters at the Musée de l'Homme in Paris. His controversial 1954 film, *Les maîtres fous*, showing a ritual of the Hauka cult in Accra, won a prize at the Venice Film Festival and influenced Jean Genet in the writing of his play, *Les nègres*. In 1957 Rouch worked with a Vietnam veteran from Niger, Oumarou Ganda, in Abidjan on *Moi, un noir*, a dramatization of the situation of migrant laborers. Ganda later directed several films, including the story of the veteran Cabascabo. In Niger, where he held the post of director of research at the Institut Français de l'Afrique Noire, Rouch encouraged the work of other African filmmakers, notably Moustapha Alassane.

In Paris, where he was a director of research at the Centre National de la Recherche Scientifique, Rouch taught courses in visual anthropology at the University of Paris (Nanterre). He also taught during the 1980s at Harvard University.

Rouch's 1960 film with the sociologist Edgar Morin, *Chronique d'un été*, drew international attention to the cinéma-verité technique of filmmaking, which used the portable Éclair camera and synchronized Nagra tape recorder with nonprofessional actors in an update of the Soviet filmmaker Dziga Vertov's *Kino pravda* series. However, Rouch remained aloof from schools of filmmaking or anthropology, preferring instead to be iden- tified as a *griot* or, in the words of a West African joke that he likes to tell on himself, as "Jean-Jacques Roucheau." His 1984 film, *Dionysos*, posited the necessity of a cult of na- ture in industrial society. In *Liberté, égalité, fraternité ... et après?*, filmed in France dur- ing the bicentennial of the 1789 Revolution, Rouch posed a solution to the historic clash between Napoléon and Toussaint l'Ouverture.

MAJOR WORKS: [Films are listed by date of production, which is followed by a bracketed note about the place of production.] *Les maîtres fous* [film] (1954) [Gold Coast]; (with Damouré Zika, Lam Ibrahima Dia, and Illo Gaoudel) *Jaguar* [film] (1954) [French West Africa, Togo, Gold Coast]; *Moi, un noir* [film] (1957) [Ivory Coast]; *La religion et la magie Songhay* (Paris: 1960); (with Edgar Morin) *Chronique d'un été* [film] (1960) [France]; "Le film ethnographique" in: *Ethnologie générale* (Paris: 1968) (= *Encyclopédie de la Pléiade*, vol. 24), pp. 429-471; *Premier catalogue sélectif inter- national de films ethnographiques sur l'Afrique noire* (Paris: 1967); *Petit à petit* [film] (1969) [Niger, France]; "Cinq regards sur Dziga Vertov" in: Georges Sadoul, *Dziga Vertov* (Paris: 1971), pp. 11- 14; (with Germaine Dieterlen) *Funerailles à Bongo: le vieil Anai* [film] (1972) [Mali]; *Tourou et Bitti, les tambours d'avant* [film] (1973) [Niger]; "The camera and man" in: Paul Hockings (editor), *Principles of Visual Anthropology* (The Hague: 1975), pp. 83-102; (with John Marshall) *Margaret Mead: a Portrait by a Friend* [film] (1977) [U.S.A.]; *Dionysos* [film] (1984) [France]; *Liberté, égal- ité, fraternité ... et après?* [film] (1989) [France].

SOURCES: Pascal-Emanuel Gallet (editor), *Jean Rouch: une rétrospective* (Paris: 1981) [authorized portrait]; Mick Eaton (editor), *Anthropology--Reality--Cinema: the Films of Jean Rouch* (London: 1979) [not always reliable]; Teshome Gabriel, *Third Cinema in the Third World* (Ann Arbor: 1982) [critical view].

Emilie de Brigard

Rousseau, Jean-Jacques. Moral philosopher, social critic, man of letters. Born in Geneva (Switzerland) 28 June 1712, died in Ermenonville (France) 2 July 1778. Rousseau is arguably the most controversial and enigmatic of the great moderns; no other has provoked so much contradictory interpretation while inspiring such intensity of per- sonal attachment and antipathy. Rousseau was, in effect, the first modern critic of modernity, the first to call for and embody an alternative to the Enlightenment notion of social progress.

In histories of anthropology, Rousseau is often associated with the Enlightenment's noble savage or with Romantic primitivism. Both themes undoubtedly conditioned the discipline's development, but Rousseau's anthropological speculations (as opposed to interpretations of them) do not actually belong with either. The Enlightenment's noble savage was the epitome of natural reason espousing natural law; Romanticism's primitives enjoyed spontaneous community in nature. But Rousseau's primitives, as described in the *Discours sur les sciences et les arts* and the *Discours sur l'origine de l'inégalité*, were barely sentient, isolated brutes destined to enjoy a transient moment of social happiness in the bosom of the nuclear family before descending into the morass of self-love, greed, inequality and hypocrisy that accompanied economic and social development.

It remains true, however, that Rousseau conceived a systematic consideration of primitive society in search of natural moral forms and, in that posture, he can rightly be said to embody the Romantic effort to recover for the future what alienated moderns believed had been lost. His *Confessions* established alienation as a literary posture and his life became the paradigm of modern authenticity, of secular sainthood validated by suffering and even madness, consecrated to art and truth in a world of Philistine artifice. The *Contrat social* and *Émile* are best understood as attempts to articulate social principles and practices that might heal that alienation; their object was what prompted Rousseau's anthropological turn in the first place. Insofar as anthropology is an expression of modernity's uncertainty about its own direction and entitlement, insofar as anthropology embodies a submission of the imperial *cogito* to the claims of civilization's victims, and insofar as Rousseau was the first to systematically express and embody the impulse to anthropology so conceived, he deserves the title conferred upon him by CLAUDE LÉVI-STRAUSS: "fondateur des sciences de l'homme" ("founder of the sciences of man") (1962).

MAJOR WORKS: *Discours sur les sciences et les arts* (Geneva: 1750) [tr.: "Discourse on the arts and sciences" in: *The Essential Rousseau* (New York: 1974)]; *Discours sur l'origine et les fondamens* [sic] *de l'inégalité* (Amsterdam: 1755) [tr.: "Discourse on the origin and basis of inequality among men" in: *The Essential Rousseau* (New York: 1974)]; *Émile* (Paris: 1762) [tr.: *Emile* (New York: 1979)]; *Contrat social* (Paris: 1772) [tr.: "The social contract" in: *The Essential Rousseau* (New York: 1974)]; *Confessions* (Geneva: 1781) [tr.: *The Confessions* (Harmondsworth: 1953)]. For the authoritative edition of the original works see: *Oeuvres complètes de J.J. Rousseau* (Paris: 1884-1887).

SOURCES: Émile Durkheim, *Montesquieu and Rousseau: Forerunners of Sociology* (Ann Arbor: 1960); Ernst Cassirer, *The Question of Jean-Jacques Rousseau* (Bloomington: 1963); Victor Goldschmidt, *Anthropologie et politiques: les principes du systeme de Rousseau* (Paris: 1974); Paul A. Cantor, *Creature and Creator: Myth-making and English Romanticism* (Cambridge: 1984); Asher Horowitz, *Rousseau, Nature, and History* (Toronto: 1987); Claude Lévi-Strauss, "Jean-Jacques Rousseau, fondateur des sciences de l'homme" in: *Jean-Jacques Rousseau* (Neuchâtel: 1962), pp. 239-248 [tr.: "Jean-Jacques Rousseau, founder of the sciences of man" in: Claude Lévi-Strauss, *Structural Anthropology*, vol. 2 (New York: 1976), pp. 33-43]; T. de Zengotita, "Speakers of being: romantic refusion and cultural anthropology" in: George W. Stocking, Jr. (editor), *Romantic Motives:*

Essays on the Anthropological Sensibility (Madison: 1989) (= *History of Anthropology*, vol. 6), pp. 74-123.

Thomas de Zengotita

Royce, C.C. (Charles C.). Sailor, clerk, farmer, historian. Born in Defiance (Ohio) 22 December 1845, died in Washington (D.C.) 11 February 1923. Little is known of Royce's early life. He joined the staff of the Bureau of Indian Affairs (BIA) after serving in the U.S. Navy during the Civil War. While at the BIA, he began privately working on an historical study of American Indian land cessions, and he became associated as a collaborator with the Bureau of American Ethnology (BAE) in 1879, receiving support for his apparently voluminous correspondence and travels. In 1883 he was appointed as a BAE ethnologist. He served for slightly longer than one year, during which he completed his anthropological work. He then turned to a job in a bank and eventually became the manager of a fruit farm in California

Royce's book on Indian land cessions is considered a basic tool for those involved in American Indian affairs and it is frequently cited in legal cases. It has undoubtedly been the most directly useful volume in governmental affairs to be produced by the BAE. Very little of Royce's related correspondence or notes are extant.

MAJOR WORKS: "The Cherokee Nation of Indians: a narrative of their official relations with the colonial and federal governments," *Annual Report of the Bureau of American Ethnology*, vol. 5 (1887), pp. 121-378; "Indian land cessions in the United States," *Annual Report of the Bureau of American Ethnology*, vol. 18, part 2 (1902), pp. 521-964.

SOURCES: Records of the Bureau of American Ethnology and Royce vertical file in the Smithsonian Institution National Anthropological Archives; Herman J. Viola, "Biographical notes" in: C.C. Royce, *The Cherokee Nation of Indians* (Chicago: 1975), pp. 257-258.

James R. Glenn

Rubieri, Ermolao. Man of letters, specialist in Italian folk poetry. Born in Prato, Province of Florence (Italy) 21 February 1818, died in Florence (Italy) 23 October 1879. Rubieri is among the pioneering scholars whose scientific enquiry centered on Italian folk literature. Under the influence of Romanticism and the enthusiasm for national unification, he analyzed folk poetry as an unparalleled repository of folk culture capable of revealing the psychological and ethical foundations of popular traditions, institutions and rituals.

In his major work, *Storia della poesia popolare italiana*, Rubieri furnished a developmental history of the genre from as far back as Etruscan and Roman times. The analytic criteria adopted by Rubieri assumed that three major aspects could be studied in the folk poetry of Italy. The first, which Rubieri considered extrinsic to poetry, concerned metric forms and their historical development. The latter aspects, which Rubieri regarded as intrinsic to folk poetry, were the psychological and ethical contents, both rich sources of information on the character of popular culture. Because of his emphasis on the common traits of these regional poetic manifestations, Rubieri contributed to the weakening of the trend, begun by COSTANTINO NIGRA, that identified in Italy two distinct and separate traditions within the linguistic and literary areas: a Celtic tradition in the north and an Italic tradition in the center and south.

Although Rubieri shared the climate and the ideals of the romantic age, his scientific research helped to discredit the stereotype that associated folk cultures with the ideals of moral purity, patriotism, family values and religion. He did not hesitate to point out elements like irreverence, superstition, aversion to military service and discomfort with conjugal bonds. Moreover, he formulated a basic distinction between folk poetry and popularized poetry, the former being a collective, instinctive and anonymous creation of the common folk, the latter being composed for popular consumption by literate authors.

The work of Rubieri remained unrecognized in his own time because of the great importance assigned to the philological methods of positivism. It was rediscovered later by Benedetto Croce.

MAJOR WORKS: *Sulle condizioni agrarie, economiche e sociali della Sicilia e della Maremma Pisana* (Florence: 1968); *Storia della poesia popolare italiana* (Florence: 1877).

SOURCES: A.M. Cirese, *Cultura egemonica e culture subalterne* (Palermo: 1980); G. Cocchiara, *Storia del folklore in Italia* (Palermo: 1981).

Gianni Vanucci
[Translation from Italian: Gianna Panofsky]

Rubin, Vera (née Vera Dourmashkin). Anthropologist. Born in Moscow (Russia) 6 August 1911, died in New York (New York) 7 February 1985. Rubin's family came to the United States when she was a year old, and she grew up in a middle-class environment where learning was prized. She attended New York University, earning a bachelor's degree in French by 1930; however, she postponed graduate work in Columbia University's anthropology department until the late 1940s when her children had entered high school.

At Columbia she studied with MARGARET MEAD, RUTH BENEDICT and JULIAN H. STEWARD, who served as her doctoral advisor. She earned her Ph.D. in 1952. Unable to find a full-time position in New York City, Rubin taught part-time at Hunter College and New York University. She also engaged in unpaid research on mental health for Cornell University's medical school in New York City.

Following the lead of her mentor Steward, Rubin became interested in the peoples of the Caribbean, specializing in the English-speaking islands. In 1955, using her own funds, Rubin began the Research Institute of the Study of Man in the Tropics (later simply the Research Institute of the Study of Man, or RISM). The institute's original aim was to prepare students for research in the Caribbean region; it was housed at Columbia, and Rubin was made a research associate of the anthropology department. She directed RISM for the rest of her life, developing major research projects to be carried out in the Caribbean, engaging in research herself, and participating in influential graduate seminars at Columbia. Her earlier interests in culture's effects on mental health were further developed in Caribbean research, which included ground-breaking studies of the effects of marijuana use in Jamaica.

Rubin was also influential in an organizational and editorial capacity. She led a number of Caribbeanist and other conferences and edited or co-edited nine volumes of proceedings between 1957 and 1981. Her research interests expanded to encompass studies of longevity, race relations and many other topics. Rubin was president of the Society for Applied Anthropology and chair of the anthropology section of the New York Academy of Sciences, among other honors. Her most lasting influence is likely to be on the development of research and communication in and on the Caribbean.

MAJOR WORKS: *Fifty Years in Rootville* (Boston: 1951); "Family attitudes and aspirations of Trinidad youth" in: *Proceedings, Second Caribbean Conference for Mental Health* (St. Thomas: 1959), pp. 59-91; "The adolescent: his expectations and his society" in: *Proceedings of the Third Caribbean Conference for Mental Health* (Jamaica: 1961), pp. 56-71; "The anthropology of development," *Biennial Review of Anthropology* (1961), pp. 120-159; "Culture, politics and race relations," *Social and Economic Studies*, vol. 11 (1962), pp. 433-455; (with Marisa Zavalloni) *We Wish to be Looked Upon* (New York: 1969); (editor) *Cannabis and Culture* (The Hague: 1975); (with Lambros Comitas) *Ganja in Jamaica* (The Hague: 1975).

SOURCES: Lucie Wood Saunders, "Vera Dourmashkin Rubin" in: Ute Gacs [et al.] (editors), *Women Anthropologists: a Biographical Dictionary* (New York: 1988), pp. 316-321.

David Lonergan

Ruscalla, Giovenale Vegezzi. See: *Vegezzi Ruscalla, Giovenale.*

Rydén, Stig. Ethnographer, archaeologist. Born in Helsingborg (Sweden) 19 January 1908, died in Stockholm (Sweden) 12 April 1965. He obtained his "GCE" at Advanced Level in Göteborg in 1928 and was attracted to ethnography by ERLAND NORDENSKIÖLD at the Ethnographical Museum of Göteborg. In 1929 he received his first position at the museum as an assistant to Nordenskiöld.

Inspired by Nordenskiöld, and invited by ALFRED MÉTRAUX in Tucumán, Rydén made his first field trip to the Argentinian Gran Chaco and adjacent archaeological sites in 1932. He followed Nordenskiöld, his mentor and professor, in the type of fieldwork he carried out as well as in his popular account of it (*Chaco*). Like Nordenskiöld, he saw the Indians as individuals and his portrait of the Chulupi Indian boy, Taáá, is a charming account on par with Nordenskiöld's best.

His field experiences were rich but straining. Rydén suffered from diabetes and the expedition was carried out with a very limited budget. Furthermore, it coincided with the Chaco War. Thus, Rydén could report on the direct and indirect effects on the Indians.

Rydén's ethnographical work on the Gran Chaco is concentrated to the period just after his trip to Argentina (1933-1936). Thereafter, he concentrated on the archaeology of South America and recording his notes on his field material from La Candelaria. Rydén had spent two months digging at this site in 1932. Later, Walter Kaudern supported this research by printing the results in his *Etnologiska Studier*.

In July 1938 Rydén initiated his second expedition to South America, this time to carry out archaeological research in the highlands of Bolivia. He worked on a Titicaca island, at Tiahuanaco and adjacent sites, as well as in northern Chile. After finishing this work, he went for a brief field study to the Siriono and the More of the Bolivian lowlands. More than a decade later (1951-1952) he returned to Bolivia for a follow-up study of the archaeological part of the second trip.

In January 1956 Rydén left Göteborg to work with SIGVALD LINNÉ at the Ethnographical Museum of Stockholm. In 1961 he was appointed Reader in Ethnography at the University of Stockholm. Here, Rydén published his major work on archaeology (*Andean Excavations*), and here he stayed until his death in 1965.

Rydén dedicated his whole adult life to the study of the history and culture of the South American Indians. A Bolivian scholar, Ponce Sangines, summarized Rydén's contributions as "pertinently important to the archaeology and ethnography of our country."

MAJOR WORKS: *Chaco* (Göteborg: 1936); *Archaeological Researches in the Department of La Candelaria* (Göteborg: 1936) (= *Etnologiska Studier*, vol. 3); *A Study of the Siriono Indians* (Göteborg: 1941); *Contributions to the Archaeology of the Rio Loa Region* (Göteborg: 1944); *Archaeological Researches in the Highlands of Bolivia* (Göteborg: 1947); *Decoración por impresión a cordel en la cerámica chaqueña* (Buenos Aires: 1948) (= *Archivos Ethnos*, ser. B, no. 1); "A study of South American Indian traps," *Revista do Museo Paulista*, vol. 4 (1950), pp. 247-532; *Andean Excavations* (Stockholm: 1957) (= *Monograph Series*, no. 4); *Andean Excavations*, no. 2 (Stockholm: 1959) (= *Monograph Series*, no. 6); *The Banks Collection* (Stockholm: 1963) (= *Monograph Series*, no. 8).

SOURCES: Sigvald Linné. "In memoriam: Stig Rydén," *Ethnos*, vol. 30 (1965), pp. 163-166; Carlos Ponce Sangines, "Bio-bibliografia de Stig Rydén" in: Stig Rydén, *Los Indios Moré: notas etnográficas* (La Paz: 1958); S. Henry Wassén, "Four Swedish anthropologists in Argentina in the first decades of the 20th century: bio-bibliographical notes," *Folk*, vol. 8-9 (1966/67), pp. 343-350.

Jan-Åke Alvarsson

S

Sandin, Benedict. Folklorist, ethnohistorian, ethnologist, museum curator. Born in Kerangan Pinggai, Paku (Sarawak, now Malaysia) 18 October 1918, died in Kerangan Pinggai (Malaysia) 7 August 1982. Sandin entered government service as a Sarawak "native officer" in 1941. After serving briefly with the Information Office (where he edited the first Iban-language news magazine) he joined the Sarawak Museum in 1952, becoming its first Sarawakian curator and government ethnologist (1966-1973).

Sandin was a gifted ethnographer and prolific author, particularly in his native Iban, and his years with the Sarawak Museum were highly productive. Two concerns predominated in his work. The first was religion, which he characteristically approached through textual recording. Tapping a major source of Iban cultural identity, he recorded in particular the great bardic chants (e.g., *Pengap Gawai Batu, Gawai Antu, Gawai Burong*) sung during major ritual cycles to invoke the cosmic journeyings of the gods and spirit-heroes. He also recorded the poem of lamentation sung for the dead (*Leka Sabak*) and wrote at length on myth (e.g., *Raja Durong*), augury and divination.

Sandin's second major concern was with oral narrative and historical tradition. His best-known work, *The Sea Dayaks of Borneo before White Rajah Rule*, drew particularly on indigenous genealogies to reconstruct the proto-historic migrations of the Iban prior to European penetration. The book remains a standard work and an important source for subsequent debates concerned with the interrelations of warfare, swidden ecology, and expansive tribal migration. As museum curator, Sandin actively assisted a generation of scholars, and through his collaboration with the historian Robert Pringle (*Rajahs and Rebels*), added an authentic Iban voice to our understanding of indigenous responses to colonial rule in northern Borneo.

MAJOR WORKS: *Raja Durong* (Kuching: 1964); *Tusun Pendiau* (Kuching: 1966) [tr.: *Iban Way of Life* (Kuching: 1976)]; *The Sea Dayaks of Borneo before White Rajah Rule* (London: 1967); *Pengap Gawai Batu* (Kuching: 1968); *Leka Sabak* (Kuching: 1968); *Gawai Antu* (Kuching: 1972); *Gawai Burong: the Chants and Celebrations of the Iban Bird Festival* (Penang: 1977); *Iban Adat and Augury* (Penang: 1980); *Living Legends: Borneans Telling Their Tales* (Kuala Lumpur: 1980).

SOURCES: Robert Pringle, "Introduction" to: *The Sea Dayaks of Borneo* (London: 1967), pp. xiii-xx; Clifford Sather, "Benedict Sandin, 1918-1982," *Sarawak Museum Journal*, vol. 29 (1981), pp. 101-136.

Clifford Sather

Santandrea, Stefano. Missionary, ethnologist. Born in Imola (Italy) 16 February 1904, now living in Verona (Italy). After having completed his studies in theology at Verona, Santandrea spent a year in Britain learning English. From 1928 to 1957 he lived in the region of Baḥr al-Ghazāl in the Sudan except for brief rest periods in Italy. From 1958 to 1972 he was responsible for the library of the Combonian headquarters in Rome. In 1972 he was called back to Verona.

During his long stay in the Sudan, Santandrea produced numerous interesting articles on ethnographic and linguistic subjects that published in several journals (*Anthropos*, *Africa* [London], *Annali Lateranensi*, *Sudan Notes and Records*). Other works from the same period include: *L'Africano fotografato a casa sua*, particularly interesting for its 180 illustrations; *Bibliografia di studi africani della Missione dell'Africa Centrale*, and *Comparative Outline-Grammar of Ndogo-Sere-Tagbu-Bai-Bviri*, a comparative grammar and dictionary of the five languages.

After his return to Italy, Santandrea devoted himself to the organization of his ethnographic data and observations in more systematic works. He described the history and ethnography of the Sudan in *Tribal History of the Western Bahr el Ghazal* and *Ethno-Geography of the Bahr el Ghazal (Sudan)*. In these works Santandrea attempted to reconstruct the historical, cultural and religious history of the people he studied. In his last work, *Religion among the Bahr el Ghazal Luo (Sudan)*, Santandrea pursued this theme, trying to prove the substantial identity between the Christian God and the Supreme Being of the Luo, thus supporting the thesis of primordial monotheism.

MAJOR WORKS: *L'africano fotografato a casa sua* (Verona: 1938); "Il gruppo Ndogo del Bahr el Ghazal," *Annali Lateranensi*, vol. 2 (1938), pp. 175-353; *Bibliografia di studi africani della Missione dell'Africa Centrale* (Verona: 1948); *Comparative Linguistics: Indri-Togoyo-Feroge-Mangaya-Mondu* (Verona: 1948); *Comparative Outline-Grammar of Ndogo-Sere-Tagbu-Bai-Bviri* (Verona: 1961); *A Tribal History of the Western Bahr el Ghazal* (Verona: 1964); *Languages of the Banda and Zande Groups* (Naples: 1965); "Aggiornamenti sul gruppo Ndogo," *Annali Lateranensi*, vol. 29 (1965), pp. 45-243; *Note grammaticali e lessicali sul gruppo Feroge e sul Mondu* (Naples: 1969); *Ethno-Geography of the Bahr el Ghazal (Sudan)* (Bologna: 1981); *Religion among the Bahr el Ghazal Luo, Sudan: Notes on Spirits* (Verona: 1983).

SOURCES: "Comboniani," *Nigrizia*, no. 2 (1967), pp. 37-38; A. Rosa Leone, "La chiesa, i cattolici e le scienze dell'uomo, 1860-1920" in: Pietro Clemente [et al.], *L'antropologia italiana: un secolo di storia* (Bari: 1985), pp. 51-96.

Massimo Guerra
[Translation from Italian: Gianna Panofsky]

Santoli, Vittorio. Philologist, Germanist, literary historian, folkorist. Born in Pistoia (Italy) 11 March 1901, died in Pisa (Italy) 1971. Santoli taught German literature at the University of Cagliari in 1935 and at the University of Florence during 1936-1937. He was a member of the Accademia della Crusca (Crusca Academy), the most prestigious of the Italian philological institutions.

Together with GIUSEPPE VIDOSSI he belonged to the Italian school of philology that (during the World War II period) was instrumental in moving the study of folk literature from the domain of aesthetics to that of historical, geographic and linguistic analysis.

Santoli dealt with folk literature as a historical body of texts that differed from high literature especially in its relationship with its public and in that its texts underwent continuous reinterpretation and modification. He believed that it was necessary to ground the analysis of folk literature on specific criteria that would take these differences into account. Although he shared the methods promoted by COSTANTINO NIGRA, Santoli came to different conclusions, favoring a reconstruction of the regional texts in all their variants ("Cinque canti popolari della raccolta Barbi") rather than the subdivisions of Italian folk literature into linguistic areas.

Santoli accepted and perfected, in a philological sense, the distinction already formulated by ERMOLAO RUBIERI between folk poetry and popularized poetry (*I canti popolari italiani*). He remarked that folk texts cannot be reconstructed in their original versions and that relative chronology was the only possible goal.

Along these lines he devoted particular attention to the linguistic implications that the common life in the trenches created for the soldiers speaking the dialects of the different Italian regions during World War I. He was among the first to share and spread, in the field of "demology" (folklore studies), Antonio Gramsci's theory on the circulation and stratification processes of culture.

MAJOR WORKS: "Cinque canti popolari della Raccolta Barbi," *Annali della Scuola Normale Superiore di Pisa*, ser. 2, vol. 7 (1938), pp. 109-193; *I canti popolari italiani: ricerche e questioni* (Florence: 1940); "Gli studi di letteratura popolare" [originally 1950] in: *I canti popolari italiani* (enlarged ed., Florence: 1968); "Tre osservazioni su Gramsci e il folklore," *Società*, vol. 7 (1951); "La duplice genealogia e l'unità istituzionale del folklore," *Il Tesaur*, vol. 10, no. 1 (1958), pp. 1-2.

SOURCES: G. Cocchiara, *Storia del folklore in Italia* (Palermo: 1981); A.M. Cirese, *Cultura egemonica e culture subalterne* (Palermo: 1980); A.M. Cirese, "Vittorio Santoli" in: G. Grana (editor), *Letteratura italiana: i critici* (Milan: 1969), pp. 3648-3658.

Gianni Vanucci
[Translation from Italian: Gianna Panofsky]

Sapir, Edward. Linguist, anthropologist. Born in Lauenberg (Germany) 26 January 1884, died in New Haven (Connecticut) 6 February 1939. Sapir was raised in New York City, where he attended public schools and Columbia University. A brilliant student of languages, he intended at first to specialize in Germanic and Indo-European philology, but early in his graduate work he was attracted to FRANZ BOAS's program of field research in American Indian linguistics. Under Boas's sponsorship Sapir carried out field studies of Wishram Chinook (1905), Takelma (1906) and Yana (1907-1908), receiving his doctorate from Columbia in 1909 with a dissertation on Takelma grammar. He then taught briefly at the University of Pennsylvania (1908-1910), where he carried out research on Southern Paiute.

Sapir's most productive years as an ethnologist and linguist were spent in Ottawa, where from 1910 to 1925 he was Chief Ethnologist for the Geological Survey of Canada. He undertook a rigorous program of linguistic fieldwork, the highlights of which were major studies of Nootka (1910-1914), Sarcee (1922) and Kutchin (1923). Besides many descriptive monographs and papers, Sapir published during this period several pioneering works on genetic relationship, which culminated in a classification of North American Indian languages that reduced their immense diversity to six large stocks. He also joined with ALFRED L. KROEBER, ROBERT H. LOWIE, PAUL RADIN and others in defining the theoretical goals of ethnology in strongly historical terms, and his short monograph on *Time Perspective in Aboriginal American Culture* is generally regarded as the clearest statement of this position. During the second half of his Ottawa period, beginning about 1917, Sapir became deeply interested in poetry, aesthetics, and other aspects of cultural creativity; he wrote a considerable amount of verse, much of which was published, and contributed reviews and essays to a wide range of literary and intellectual journals. With the publication of *Language* in 1921 he also acquired a worldwide reputation as a general linguist.

After the early 1920s Sapir's enthusiasm for data-oriented studies of American Indian linguistics and ethnology slackened, and he began to search for a broader field in which to exercise his talents. The opportunity came in 1925 when he was invited to join the Department of Anthropology and Sociology at the University of Chicago. He was soon an academic figure of near-legendary proportions, attracting a brilliant circle of students. Although an important part of his teaching was in technical linguistics, he also offered wide-ranging courses in language and culture theory. In 1931 he left Chicago for the Sterling Professorship of Anthropology and Linguistics at Yale, remaining there until his death in 1939.

Beginning in his Chicago years, but especially at Yale, Sapir was concerned with the development of a psychologically realistic theory of culture, being especially influenced by the interactionalist psychiatrist, Harry Stack Sullivan. Although he continued American Indian research with field studies of Hupa (1927) and Navajo (1929) and trained a number of students in this tradition, much of his creative energy during his last decade went into research and teaching in cultural psychology. Sapir planned a book on the psychology of culture and talked seriously of establishing an institute for cultural psychiatry in collaboration with Sullivan, but he died before either of these projects could be realized.

Even during his lifetime Sapir was called a supreme linguistic genius, and few in a position to judge would dispute that assessment. All of his linguistic work is characterized by profound structural insight and brilliant clarity of statement. His phonological and grammatical analyses foreshadowed FERDINAND DE SAUSSURE's structuralism, embodying (often without formalizing) many of the insights that crystalized in the autonomous science of linguistics in the 1930s. Sapir's studies of Takelma and Southern Paiute came to be regarded as the classic models of linguistic description, a view still widely held. Since many of the linguists of the "Bloomfieldian" school were in fact originally students of Sapir's at Chicago or Yale, Sapir's ideas as much as LEONARD BLOOMFIELD's helped shape the American school of linguistics that emerged in the post-World War II decades. Although with the rise of generative linguistics in the 1960s Sapir's direct influence appeared to wane, certain aspects of his grammatical technique, particularly his "processual" treatment of phonology, were much discussed. More recently, his work has again attracted the attention of theoreticians (cf. the sections on Sapir in *Phonology in the Twentieth Century*, by Stephen R. Anderson).

As a historical linguist, Sapir's influence has been more limited but equally persistent. While his six-stock quasi-typological classification of North American Indian languages is his most-remembered historical hypothesis, his detailed studies of the comparative linguistics of Uto-Aztecan and Athabaskan are more typical of his historical work, which is characterized by the rigorous use of the neogrammatical comparative method. MORRIS SWADESH and MARY R. HAAS, particularly the latter, carried on historical work in Sapir's style in the 1940s and 1950s, and more recently a vigorous resurgence of detailed comparative work among individual families of American Indian languages (surveyed in *The Languages of Native America*, edited by Lyle Campbell and Marianne Mithun (Austin: 1979)) owes much to Sapir's substantive and methodological contributions. The classificatory proposals made by Swadesh, beginning in the 1950s, embracing worldwide networks of relationship, and similar recent work by JOSEPH H. GREENBERG (cf. *Language in the Americas* (Stanford: 1987)), were also influenced by some of Sapir's ideas, but are less firmly rooted in the main tradition of his historical work.

As a cultural theorist Sapir was underappreciated, in fact virtually isolated among his contemporaries. In the words of his friend Harry Stack Sullivan, Sapir's was "a genius largely wasted on a world not yet awake to the value of the very great." His concern with psychological realism, while superficially similar to Boas's, was deeply interwoven with structuralist insights deriving from his linguistic work. He was especially fascinated by the theoretical problems posed by the integration of cultural traits in individual personalities, and in some respects his ideas adumbrate the concerns of modern cognitive science. An early but important statement of his views is "Do we need a 'superorganic'?," a critique of Kroeber's identification of culture as an independent object of study. Several of his students at Chicago and Yale, most notably STANLEY NEWMAN and BENJAMIN LEE WHORF, shared his broad interests, but no "Sapir School" survived his death and the relationship between Sapir's thought and the "culture and personality" movement of the 1940s is probably not as important as some have claimed. His enduring influence on anthropological and psychological theory has been felt less through his students than through his writings, especially the volume of *Selected Writings of Edward Sapir*, edited by DAVID G. MANDELBAUM. The entire corpus of Sapir's work is being published in a multi-volume standard edition.

MAJOR WORKS: *Wishram Texts* (Leiden: 1909) (= *Publications of the American Ethnological Society*, vol. 2); *Takelma Texts* (Philadelphia: 1909) (= *Anthropological Publications of the University Museum*, vol. 2, no. 1); *Yana Texts* (Berkeley: 1910) (= *University of California Publications in American Archaeology and Ethnology*, vol. 9, no. 1); *The Takelma Language of Southwestern Oregon* (Washington: 1912) (= *Bureau of American Ethnology Bulletin*, 40, part 2, pp. 1-296) [published also as part of: *Handbook of American Indian Languages* (Washington: 1922)]; "Southern Paiute and Nahuatl: a study in Uto-Aztecan," *Journal de la Société des Américanistes de Paris*, vol. 10 (1913), pp. 379-425 and vol. 11 (1914), pp. 443-488; *Notes on Chasta Costa Phonology and Morphology* (Philadelphia: 1914) (= *Anthropological Publications of the University Museum*, vol. 2, no. 2); *Abnormal Types of Speech in Nootka* (Ottawa: 1915) (= *Memoir of the Canadian Geological Survey*, no. 62, Anthropological Series, no. 5); *Time Perspective in Aboriginal*

American Culture (Ottawa: 1915) (= *Memoir of the Canadian Geological Survey*, no. 90, *Anthropological Series*, no. 13); *The Position of Yana in the Hokan Stock* (Berkeley: 1917) (= *University of California Publications in American Archaeology and Ethnology*, vol. 13, no. 1); *Language: an Introduction to the Study of Speech* (New York: 1921); (with Morris Swadesh) *Nootka Texts: Tales and Ethnological Narratives with Grammatical Notes and Lexical Materials* (Philadelphia: 1939) (= *Anthropological Records*, vol. 3, no. 3); *Navaho Texts, with Supplementary Texts by Harry Hoijer* (edited by Harry Hoijer) (Philadelphia: 1942); (with Leslie Spier) *Notes on the Culture of the Yana* (Berkeley: 1943); "Do we need a 'superorganic'?" *American Anthropologist*, n.s., vol. 19 (1917), pp. 441-447; *Selected Writings of Edward Sapir* (edited by David G. Mandelbaum) (Berkeley: 1949); *The Collected Works of Edward Sapir* (editor-in-chief, Philip Sapir) (Berlin and New York: 1989-).

SOURCES: E.F. Konrad Koerner (editor), *Edward Sapir: Appraisals of His Life and Work* (Amsterdam and Philadelphia: 1984) [reprints a comprehensive collection of obituaries and commentaries on Sapir's work]; Regna Darnell, *Edward Sapir: Linguist, Anthropologist, Humanist* (Berkeley: 1990) [the first full biography of Sapir]; Victor Golla (editor), *The Sapir-Kroeber Correspondence: Letters Between Edward Sapir and A.L. Kroeber, 1905-1925* (Berkeley: 1984) [Sapir's extensive correspondence with A.L. Kroeber, covering a wide range of linguistic, anthropological and intellectual topics]; William Cowan, Michael K. Foster and E.F. Konrad Koerner (editors), *New Perspectives in Language, Culture, and Personality* (Amsterdam and Philadelphia: 1986) [the published proceedings of a major conference held in Ottawa on the centenary of Sapir's birth in 1984, containing a number of essays by linguists, anthropologists, psychiatrists, and others assessing the importance of Sapir's work and thought in many fields]; Stephen R. Anderson, *Phonology in the Twentieth Century* (Chicago: 1985).

Victor Golla

Sarkar, Sasanka Sekhar. Anthropologist, geneticist, demographer. Born in Moydah, 24-Parganas, West Bengal (India) 30 March 1908, died in Calcutta (India) 9 March 1969. Sarkar is best known for his pioneering efforts to apply physical anthropology to the welfare of society in modern India, which gained political independence during his lifetime. His formal education was acquired at the University of Calcutta (Honours in Anthropology, 1928; M.Sc., 1931; D.Sc., 1949) and at the Kaiser Wilhelm Institute of Anthropology in Berlin (1938-1939). Although his training was rooted in the earlier anthropological traditions of racial classification and typology, Sarkar emerged as India's leading scholar in human genetics (twin studies, dermatoglyphics, serology), demography (fertility, menarcheal age, mortality) and application of human biology to resolution of social problems (birth control, sex education, food resources). However, the interpretations of South Asia's ancient peoples held by Eugen Fischer, Mortimer Wheeler, John Marshall, B.S. Guha and his other mentors influenced Sarkar's anthropological approach to the racial affinities of prehistoric and contemporary populations of the subcontinent. Throughout his career he contended that a basic Australoid racial element formed the substratum of peoples inhabiting the peninsular region of India in earlier and present times. Successive waves of foreign invaders (including the ancient Iranians from Tepe Hissar) accounted for the present biological diversity of his country, the population of which he classified into six racial groups: Australoid, Indo-Iranian, Irano-Scythian, Mundari, Malayo-Polynesian and Mongoloid. He argued for the presence of an ancient Negrito racial element in India, but later rejected this idea.

Sarkar received a Senior Research Fellowship that supported him at the Bose Institute, Calcutta, while he was conducting anthropological studies among the Maler and other tribal populations of the Rajmahal Hills, Bihar (1933-1937). The Griffith Memorial

Prize was awarded by the University of Calcutta in recognition of his serological research among the Santal Parganas, Bihar. His work in Berlin ended with the outbreak of World War II, when he rejoined the Bose Institute in 1940. He was on the staff of the Anthropological Survey of India, Calcutta, in 1947 when he directed the Human Biology Section and carried out research in the Andaman and Nicobar Islands. From 1953 until the time of his death, Sarkar was affiliated with the Department of Anthropology, University of Calcutta, as Senior Research Fellow, Lecturer and, after 1966, Reader. He was made a Fellow of the National Institute of Sciences, Delhi (1958), and held membership in the Asiatic Society of Bengal, the Society for the Study of Human Biology and the International Association of Human Biologists.

MAJOR WORKS: "Blood grouping investigations in India with special reference to Santal Parganas, Bihar," *Transactions of the Bose Research Institute*, vol. 12 (1936-1937), pp. 89-103; "The place of human biology in anthropology and its utility in the service of the nation," *Man in India*, vol. 31 (1951), pp. 1-20; *The Aboriginal Races of India* (Calcutta: 1954); *A Laboratory Manual of Somatology* (Calcutta: 1957); "Human skeletal remains from Brahmagiri," *Bulletin of the Department of Anthropology, Government of India*, vol. 9 (1960), pp. 5-25; *Ancient Races of Punjab, Baluchistan and Sind* (Calcutta: 1964); *Ancient Races of the Deccan* (Calcutta: 1972).

SOURCE: "Introduction" to: A. Basu, A.K. Ghosh, S.K. Biswas and R. Ghosh (editors), *Physical Anthropology and Its Expanding Horizons: S.S. Sarkar Memorial Volume* (Bombay: 1973), pp. 1-16.

Kenneth A.R. Kennedy

Sauer, Carl. Geographer. Born in Warrenton (Missouri) 1889, died in Berkeley (California) 18 July 1975. Sauer is often considered the most distinguished American geographer of the 20th century. His work intersected in many areas with that of anthropologists.

Sauer came from a religious family of German stock and grew up largely in small-town Missouri. There is some reason to believe that the traditional rural values inculcated during his childhood played a considerable role in his thinking. His graduate education at the University of Chicago emphasized botany and geology and a rather deterministic kind of human geography. His first teaching job was at the University of Michigan. In 1923 he became professor of geography at the University of California, Berkeley, and spent the rest of his professional career there, building a department of considerable renown.

Sauer's interests were wide-ranging, but most of his writing can be classified as "historical geography." Among the subjects with which he dealt were prehistoric settlements in Mexico, early agriculture, the exploration of the New World and man-land relationships.

Sauer had intellectual ties with many scholars outside geography. At Berkeley he developed close relationships with ALFRED L. KROEBER and (to a lesser extent) ROBERT H. LOWIE. These contacts may have stimulated Sauer in his battle with environmental determinism, the notion that environmental factors determine ways of life, which in the 1920s still played a considerable role in American academic geography. Much of Sauer's writing stressed the importance of cultural factors; this viewpoint was expressed most clearly in *The Morphology of Landscape*. Sauer also influenced many anthropologists, not only Kroeber but also JULIAN H. STEWARD and others who dealt with "ecological" factors in human life. Sauer's work on the early diffusion of agriculture and on American Indians was of particular interest to many anthropologists. With anthropologist William L. Thomas, he organized the landmark 1955 Symposium on Man's Role in Changing the Face of the Earth.

MAJOR WORKS: *The Morphology of Landscape* (Berkeley: 1928) (= *University of California Publications in Geography*, vol. 2, no. 2); *The Distribution of Aboriginal Tribes and Languages in Northwestern Mexico* (Berkeley: 1934); *Agricultural Origins and Dispersals* (New York: 1952; 2nd ed., Cambridge, Mass.: 1969); (co-editor with William L. Thomas, Jr. [et al.]) *Man's Role in Changing the Face of the Earth* (Chicago: 1956); "Homestead and community in the Middle Border" in: H.W. Ottoson (editor), *Land Use Policy in the United States* (Lincoln: 1963), pp. 65-85; *Land and Life: a Selection from the Writings of Carl Sauer* (edited by John Leighly) (Berkeley: 1963); *The Early Spanish Man* (Berkeley: 1966); *Northern Mists* (Berkeley: 1968).

SOURCES: John Leighly, "Carl Ortwin Sauer, 1889-1975," *Geographers: Biobibliographical Studies*, vol. 2 (1976), pp. 99-105 [includes bibliography]; James J. Parsons, "Carl Ortwin Sauer, 1889-1975," *Geographical Review*, vol. 66 (1976), pp. 83-89; James J. Parsons, "Sauer, Carl O." in: David L. Sills, *The International Encyclopedia of the Social Sciences* (New York: 1968-1979), vol. 14, pp. 17-19; Martin S. Kenzer (editor), *Carl Sauer: a Tribute* (Corvallis: 1987); Robert Goper West, *Carl Sauer's Fieldwork in Latin America* (Ann Arbor: 1979); Roy Ellen, "Persistence and change in the relationship between anthropology and human geography," *Progress in Human Geography*, vol. 12 (1988), pp. 229-262.

Saussure, Ferdinand de. Indo-Europeanist, general linguist. Born in Geneva (Switzerland) 26 November 1857, died in Château Vufflens near Geneva (Switzerland) 22 February 1913. Saussure is best known for *Cours de linguistique générale*, the posthumous compilation of his lecture notes on general linguistics, edited by his former students and first published in 1916. (It has since been translated into more than a dozen languages, including—in order of their first appearance—Japanese, German, Russian, Spanish, English, Polish, Italian and Hungarian.) However, during his lifetime, Saussure was most widely known for his masterly *Mémoire* of 1879 which included an audacious reconstruction of the Proto-Indo-European vowel system. It is generally agreed that his *Cours* ushered in a revolution in linguistic thinking during the 1920s and 1930s that still is felt in many quarters. Saussure is universally regarded as "the father of structuralism."

Although from a distinguished Geneva family that—beginning with Horace Bénédict de Saussure (1740-1799), whose picture adorns the Swiss twenty-franc note—can boast of several generations of natural scientists, Saussure was early drawn to language study, producing an "Essai pour réduire les mots du grec, du latin et de l'allemand à un petit nombre de racines" at the age of fourteen or fifteen (published in *Cahiers Ferdinand de Saussure*, vol. 32 (1978), pp. 77-101). Enrolling at the University of Leipzig in the fall of 1876, he published his *Mémoire* just over two years later, at age twenty-one. In this 300-page work Saussure assumed, on purely theoretical grounds, the existence of an early Proto-Indo-European sound of unknown phonetic value (designated *A) which would develop into various phonemes of the Indo-European vocalic system, depending on its combination with various "sonantal coefficients." Saussure was thus able to explain a number of puzzling questions of Indo-European ablaut. But the real proof of Saussure's hypotheses came many years later, after the decipherment of Hittite and its identification as an Indo-European language, and after the Polish scholar Jerzy Kuryłowicz (1895-1978) in 1927 pointed to Hittite cognates that contained the sound corresponding to Saussure's *A and that were identified as laryngeals, sounds previously not found in any of the other Indo-European languages, including Sanskrit and Greek.

Since the 1920s, however, Saussure's influence and fame have been almost exclusively connected with the book he never wrote, *Cours de linguistique générale*, which was largely based on notes carefully taken down by a number of his students during the series of lectures given at the University of Geneva during 1907-1911. (He had returned to the University of Geneva as a professor of Sanskrit and comparative grammar in 1891, after receiving his doctorate at Leipzig in 1880 and after having taught in Paris for ten years.) One of those students was Albert Riedlinger (1883-1978), whose name appears on the title page of the *Cours*; but the *Cours* was put together by Saussure's successors, Charles Bally (1865-1947) and Albert Sechehaye (1870-1946), though neither of them had attended the lectures as is frequently, and erroneously, stated in the literature. (It should also be mentioned that the *Cours* was never published in Geneva but in Lausanne and Paris, and not in 1915, but in 1916, i.e., exactly 100 years after FRANZ BOPP's (1791-1867) *Conjugationssystem*, which is usually regarded as the beginning of comparative-historical Indo-European linguistics.)

The ideas advanced in the *Cours* produced a veritable revolution in linguistic science; historical-comparative grammar, which had dominated linguistic research since the early 19th century, soon became a mere province of the field. Saussure's general theory of language was seen as assigning pride-of-place to the non-historical, descriptive and "structural" approach (Saussure himself did not use "structural" in a technical sense), thus leading to a tremendous body of work concerned with the analysis of the linguistic system of language and its function and a neglect of questions of language change and linguistic evolution, a situation still characteristic of the current linguistic scene, particularly in the framework associated with Noam Chomsky. Since the 1920s a variety of important schools of linguistic thought developed in Europe that can be traced back to proposals made in the *Cours*, schools usually identified with the respective centers from which they emanated—Geneva, Prague, Copenhagen, Paris. In North America, too, through the work of LEONARD BLOOMFIELD, Saussure's ideas became stock-in-trade among linguists, descriptivists, structuralists and generativists.

At the core of Saussure's linguistic theory is the assumption that language is a system of interrelated terms, which he called "*langue*" (in contradistinction to "*parole*," the individual speech act or speaking in general). This "*langue*" is the underlying code ensuring that people can speak and understand each other; it has a social underpinning and is an operative system embedded in the brain of everyone who has learned a given language. The analysis of this system, Saussure maintains, is the true object of linguistics. The system is a network of relationships he characterized as syntagmatic (i.e., items are arranged in a sequential, linear order) and associative, later termed "paradigmatic" (i.e., the organization of units on the basis of grammatical and semantic relations). Saussure's emphasis on language as "a system of (arbitrary) signs" and his characterization of linguistics as the central part of an overall science of sign relations or "*sémiologie*" led to the development of a field of inquiry more frequently called (following Charles Sanders Peirce's terminology) "semiotics," which deals with sign systems in literature and other forms of art, including music and architecture.

Many ingredients of Saussure's general theory of language have often been taken out of context and incorporated into theories outside of linguistics, at times quite arbitrarily, especially in works by French writers engaged in "structuralist" anthropology (e.g., CLAUDE LÉVI-STRAUSS) and philosophy (e.g., Louis Althusser), literary theory (e.g., Jacques Derrida), psychoanalysis (e.g., Jacques Lacan) and semiotics (e.g., Roland Barthes) and their various associates and followers. The trichotomies (usually reduced to dichotomies) which have become current in 20th-century thought, far beyond their original application, are *langage-langue-parole* (i.e., language in all its manifestations or "speech"; language as the underlying system; and "speaking"), *signe-signifié-signifiant* (sign, signified, and signifier), synchrony vs. diachrony ("panchrony" would be a combination of these two perspectives) and syntagmatic vs. paradigmatic relations.

MAJOR WORKS: *Mémoire sur le système primitif des voyelles dans les langues indo-européennes* (Leipzig: 1879; reprinted, Hildesheim: 1968) [partial tr.: "Memoire on the primitive system of vowels in the Indo-European language" in: Winfred P. Lehmann (editor), *A Reader in Nineteenth-Century Historical Indo-European Linguistics* (Bloomington and London: 1967), pp. 218-224]; *Cours de linguistique générale* (edited by Charles Bally and Albert Sechehaye, with the collaboration of Albert Riedlinger) (Lausanne and Paris: 1916; 2nd ed., Paris: 1922; 3rd and last corrected ed.: Paris: 1931; 4th ed.: Paris: 1949; 5th ed.: Paris: 1960, etc.) [tr: (1) by Wade Baskin, *Course in General Linguistics* (London and New York: 1959; reprinted, New York: 1966; rev. ed., London: 1974); and (2), by Roy Harris, *Course in General Linguistics* (London: 1983) on the basis of the 1972 ed. of the *Cours*]; *Recueil des publications scientifiques* (edited by Charles Bally and Leopold Gautier) (Lausanne and Heidelberg: 1922; reprinted, Geneva: 1970) [includes a reprint of the *Mémoire*, Saussure's 1880 dissertation (pp. 269-338) and all of his published papers]; *"Cours de linguistique générale* (1908-1909): introduction," *Cahiers Ferdinand de Saussure*, vol. 15 (1957), pp. 6-103 [published from students' notes by Robert Godel]; *Cours de linguistique générale* [4 fascs.] (Wiesbaden: 1967-1974) ["édition critique" prepared by Rudolf Engler]; *Cours de linguistique générale* (Paris: 1972; reprinted, with a "postface" by Louis-Jean Calvet, Paris: 1985) [contains biographical and critical notes by Tullio De Mauro].

SOURCES: Robert Godel, *Les sources du Cours de linguistique générale de F. de Saussure* (Geneva: 1957); Rudolf Engler, *Lexique de la terminologie saussurienne* (Antwerp and Utrecht: 1968); E.F. Konrad Koerner, *Bibliographia Saussureana, 1870-1970: an Annotated, Classified Bibliography on the Background, Development and Actual Relevance of Ferdinand de Saussure's General Theory of Language* (Metuchen, N.J.: 1972); E.F. Konrad Koerner, *Contribution au débat post-saussurien sur le signe linguistique: introduction générale et bibliographie annotée* (The Hague: 1972); E.F. Konrad Koerner, *Ferdinand de Saussure: Origin and Development of his Linguistic Thought in Western Studies of Language: a Contribution to the History and Theory of Linguistics* (Braunschweig: 1973) [trs.: *Ferdinand de Saussure* (Budapest: 1982); *Ferdinand de Saussure* (Tōkyō: 1982); *Ferdinand de Saussure* (Madrid: 1982)]; Rudolf Engler, "European structuralism: Saussure," *Current Trends in Linguistics*, vol. 13 (*Historiography of Linguistics*) (1975), pp. 829-886; Rudolf Engler, "Bibliographie saussurienne," *Cahiers Ferdinand de Saussure*, vol. 30 (1976), pp. 100-138; vol. 31 (1977), pp. 279-306; vol. 33 (1978), pp. 79-145; vol. 40 (1986), pp. 131-200; Konrad Koerner, *Saussurean Studies = Études saussuriennes* (Geneva: 1988) [includes (pp. 137-153) an appraisal of Saussure's *Mémoire*]; Remo Gmür, *Das Schicksal von F. de Saussure's "Mémoire": eine Rezeptionsgeschichte* (Bern: 1986) [cf. the review by Henry M. Hoenigswald in *Historiographia Linguistica*, vol. 16 (1989), pp. 192-194].

E. F. Konrad Koerner

Schaden, Egon. Anthropologist. Born in São Bonifácio, municipality of Palhoça, State of Santa Catarina (Brazil) 4 July 1913, now living in São Paulo (Brazil). Born and reared in a pioneer area of German colonization in southern Brazil, Schaden finished his formal training in philosophy at the University of São Paulo in 1937. Before his appointment to lecture in anthropology at his alma mater in 1943, he had already published papers on the native peoples of Santa Catarina, carried out fieldwork among descendants of German immigrants, and translated into Portuguese two classic German sources on Brazilian Indians—KARL VON DEN STEINEN'S *Unter den Naturvölkern Zentral-Brasiliens* and Fritz Krause's *In den Wildnissen Brasiliens*. Ethnology and acculturation were to remain his chief concerns and form the core of his scientific work, while a lasting interest in the history of anthropological thought prompted several interpretative essays on the significance of the early German expeditions to the interior of Brazil.

From 1952 until his retirement in 1967, Schaden directed the Department of Anthropology at the University of São Paulo, lecturing at the same time on Brazilian anthropological issues at other institutions, especially abroad—in Germany, France, Switzerland, Colombia and Paraguay. After acting as head of the Department of Anthropology of the University of the Andes in Colombia (1968-1969), Schaden became interested in the anthropology of communication, a subject he lectured on from 1970 to 1983 both at the University of São Paulo and in Canada and Japan.

Schaden acted primarily as a professor, lecturing on the physical, cultural and linguistic aspects of humankind, establishing the foundations of anthropological inquiry, especially during the earlier part of his academic career when the discipline was still fighting for status among university studies. But Schaden is best known for his researches on Guaraní religion, mythology and ways of life; with CURT NIMUENDAJÚ and León Cadogan he wrote the basic sources for modern investigations among this people. Schaden was instrumental in bringing Cadogan's accomplishments to the attention of the scholarly world: much of Cadogan's work was published in the *Revista de Antropologia*, a bi-annual periodical founded by Schaden and directed by him from 1953 to 1978. His editorial activities are also linked to the *Staden-Jahrbuch*, which he founded in 1953 as an annual publication on Brazilian themes for German-speaking readers.

Schaden's contribution to anthropology in Brazil is, however, mainly of a theoretical character. While not bound by any single intellectual trend, his writings do show a decided functionalist approach, particularly when he discusses mythology. His 1964 book, apart from its specific contribution to the understanding of interethnic phenomena, subsumed what had been done and what could be done with the concept of acculturation, eventually closing the chapter of cultural change studies from this perspective in Brazil.

MAJOR WORKS: *Ensaio etno-sociológico sobre a mitologia heróica de algumas tribos indígenas do Brasil* (São Paulo: 1945); *Aspectos fundamentais da cultura guarani* (São Paulo: 1945); "Aculturação de alemães e japoneses no Brasil," *Revista de Antropologia*, vol. 4 (1956), pp. 41-46; *Aculturação indígena: ensaio sobre fatores e tendências da mudança cultural de tribos índias em contacto com o mundo dos brancos* (São Paulo: 1964); "Educação indígena," *Revista do Arquivo Municipal*, vol. 186 (1976), pp. 7-31; "O índio e sua imagem do mundo: subsídios para um estudo de antropologia simbólica," *Revista de Antropologia*, vol. 21 (1978), pp. 33-43; "A antropologia da comunicação e a cultura eurotropical do Brasil," *Seminário de Tropicologia*, vol. 11 (1978), pp. 289-322; "A religião guarani e o cristianismo: contribuição ao estudo de um processo histórico de comunicação intercultural," *Revista de Antropologia*, vol. 25 (1982), pp. 1-24.

SOURCES: Thekla Hartmann and Vera Penteado Coelho (editors), *Contribuições à antropologia em homenagem ao Professor Egon Schaden* (São Paulo: 1981), esp. pp. 13-25; Egon Schaden,

"Os primeiros tempos da antropologia em São Paulo," *Anuário Antropológico*, vol. 82 (1984), pp. 251-258.

Thekla Hartmann

Schaeffner, André. Ethnologist, historian and sociologist of music. Born in Paris (France) 5 February 1895, died in Paris (France) 10 August 1980. Schaeffner, along with GEORGES HENRI RIVIÈRE and MICHEL LEIRIS, was recognized by CLAUDE LÉVI-STRAUSS to be one of those to whom French ethnology owes its original character, described by Lévi-Strauss in 1986 as: "Art as much as science, passionately attentive to both the new and the old, refusing to withdraw into itself, seeking out new resemblances between plastic arts and music, knowledge and poetry, reverence of facts and poetic imagination."

Schaeffner devoted himself to the history of music and to comparative musicology at the beginning of the 1920s. A student of Salomon Reinach at the École du Louvre and of Vincent d'Indy at the Schola Cantorum de Paris, his earliest works were concerned with the reciprocal influences of the German, French, Italian and Russian musical traditions in the 19th century, with the history and fabrication of the harpsichord, and with the African origins of jazz; the latter interest led him to specialize in ethnomusicology. A friend of Rivière, who became assistant director of the museum of ethnography of the Trocadéro in 1929, Schaeffner was called upon by its director, PAUL RIVET, to help reorganize the aforementioned museum where he founded the first ethnomusicology department in France, which he directed until his retirement in 1965. Schaeffner thereby helped make ethnomusicology an independent discipline. Having graduated from the Department of Religious Sciences at the École Pratique des Hautes Études where, after 1930, he had enrolled in the courses of MARCEL MAUSS, in 1941 Schaeffner was named director of research at the Centre National de la Recherche Scientifique and completed several missions in West Africa (among the Dogon of Mali, the Kissi and Baga of Guinea, the Bété of the Ivory Coast) during which he gathered data that enabled him to constitute a history and sociology of African music. He was also president of the Société Française de Musicologie and a member of the Académie Charles Cros.

In his important and varied work, Schaeffner attempted to demonstrate that the study of esthetic phenomena cannot be separated from the study of the societies in which these phenomena occur. He was able to demonstrate that every division in the usage of musical instruments in so-called primitive societies corresponds to a division of the society itself or corresponds to a distinction between rituals that members of society observe or have observed in the past. Schaeffner was one of the first to apply the methods of ethnomusicology to the study of more complex types of music. This explains the double aspect of part of his research, which is at times oriented toward popular or traditional music, and is at other times oriented toward the learned music of advanced societies. As early as 1930, he established with the help of Curt Sachs the terminology pertaining to the study of musical instruments. He also proposed a new classification of musical instruments that he continued to refine. This classification has become the reference work used for classification and analysis in the field of ethnomusicology.

MAJOR WORKS: (with André Coeuroy) *Le jazz* (Paris: 1926; revised ed., Paris: 1988); *Strawinsky* (Paris: 1931); *Origine des instruments de musique: introduction ethnologique a l'histoire de la musique occidentale* (Paris: 1936; 2nd ed., with index, Paris and the Hague: 1980); *Les Kissi: une société noire et ses instruments de musique* (Paris: 1951); *Essais de musicologie et autres fantaisies* (Paris: 1980); "Musique savante, musique nationale, musique populaire" (edited by Jean Jamin), *Gradhiva*, no. 6 (1989), pp. 68-88; (editor) *Dictionnaire de musique de Hugo Riemann* (Paris: 1931); (editor) *Claude Debussy: lettres inédites à André Caplet* (Monaco: 1957); (editor) *F. Nietszche: lettres à Peter Gast* (Monaco: 1957); (editor) *Segalen et Debussy* (Monaco: 1961).

SOURCES: Geneviève Dournon, *Guide pour la collecte sur le terrain* (Paris: 1981); Jean Jamin, "André Schaeffner (1895-1980)," *Objets et mondes*, vol. 20, no. 3 (1980), pp. 131-135; Claude Lévi-Strauss, "Allocution à l'occasion de l'hommage à Georges Henri Rivière rendu par le Musée des Arts et Traditions populaires (26 novembre 1986)," *Ethnologie française*, vol. 2 (1986), pp. 127-133; Gilbert Rouget, "In memoriam: André Schaeffner (1895-1980)," *Ethnomusicology*, vol. 25 (1981), pp. 99-101; François Lesure and Gilbert Rouget (editors), *Les fantaisies du voyageur: XXXIII variations Schaeffner* (Paris: 1982) (= *Revue de musicologie*, vol. 68, nos. 1-2); Gilbert Rouget, "L'ethnomusicologie" in: Jean Poirier, *Ethnologie générale* (Paris: 1968), pp. 1339-1390.

Jean Jamin
[Translation from French: Timothy Eastridge]

Schapera, Isaac.

Schapera, Isaac. Social anthropologist. Born in Garies (South Africa) 23 June 1905. Schapera is known primarily for his extensive and meticulously detailed ethnographic and historical research on the Tswana peoples of Botswana (the former Bechuanaland Protectorate).

Initially trained by A.R. RADCLIFFE-BROWN at Cape Town, Schapera became the first of many South African students in social anthropology at the London School of Economics, studying under C.G. SELIGMAN and BRONISLAW MALINOWSKI. His voluminous Tswana corpus—based on forty-five months of field research with various Tswana peoples between 1929 and 1943—encompasses virtually the entire spectrum of Tswana social and cultural life during the first half of the 20th century, with the partial exception of religion and symbolism. Although Schapera has tended to avoid explicit theoretical statements or comparative generalizations, his work has had considerable impact on social anthropological studies beyond Southern Africa; his *Handbook of Tswana Law and Custom*, for example, has served as a model for subsequent constitutional studies in Africa and elsewhere.

One of the pioneers of anthropological engagement with oral sources and the documentary historical method, Schapera has long argued for understanding the social field as a dynamic unity, a changing system of social relations encompassing villagers, migrant laborers, labor recruiters, urban political economy, colonial administrators and missionaries. Although a number of Schapera's works were commissioned by the Bechuanaland colonial government, his work has been acclaimed by recent writers for its careful documentation of the exploitative dimensions of colonial culture and political economy.

Schapera has also worked extensively on the early history of exploration and of missionization in Southern Africa, editing and publishing a wide range of travel, missionary and administrative literature.

MAJOR WORKS: *The Khoisan Peoples of South Africa* (London: 1930); *A Handbook of Tswana Law and Custom* (London: 1938); *Married Life in an African Tribe* (London: 1940); *Native Land Tenure in the Bechuanaland Protectorate* (London: 1943); *Migrant Labour and Tribal Life* (London: 1956); *Praise-Poems of Tswana Chiefs* (Oxford: 1965); *Tribal Innovators: Tswana Chiefs and Social*

Change, 1795-1940 (London: 1970); *Rainmaking Rites of Tswana Tribes* (Leiden: 1971); (editor) *Western Civilization and the Natives of South Africa: Studies in Culture Contact* (London: 1934); *The Bantu-Speaking Tribes of South Africa* (London: 1937).

SOURCES: Adam Kuper, *Anthropologists and Anthropology: the British School: 1922-1972* (London: 1973); Meyer Fortes, "Isaac Schapera: an appreciation" in: M. Fortes and S. Patterson (editors), *Studies in Social Anthropology* (London: 1975), pp. 1-6; Max Gluckman, "Anthropology and apartheid: the work of South African anthropologists" in: M. Fortes and S. Patterson (editors), *Studies in Social Anthropology* (London: 1975), pp. 21-39; Jean Comaroff and John Comaroff, "On the founding fathers: fieldwork and functionalism: a conversation with Isaac Schapera," *American Ethnologist*, vol. 15 (1988), pp. 554-565.

Mark Auslander

Schebesta, Paul Joachim. Missionary, ethnographer, linguist. Born in Groß-Peterwitz, Silesia (Germany) 20 March 1887, died in Vienna (Austria) 17 September 1967. Schebesta studied philosophy and theology at the missionary training academy of St. Gabriel in Mödling near Vienna. He was ordained in 1911 and became a member of the Society of the Divine Word. He set out in 1912 to serve as a missionary in Mozambique, where (until his internment by the Portuguese in 1916) he carried out linguistic and ethnographic studies. In 1918, at the suggestion of Father WILHELM SCHMIDT, he was appointed to the editorial staff of the journal *Anthropos*, where he represented Africanist interests until 1923. During 1924 and the first half of 1925 Schebesta carried out research on the Semang of the Malay Peninsula, living among them in their jungle settlements. After obtaining his doctorate in ethnography and Egyptology in 1926 in Vienna, he conducted his first two expeditions (1929-1930 and 1934-1935, respectively) to the central African Pygmies of the Ituri Forest. In 1938 and 1939, Schebesta traveled to the Philippines to study the Negrito population there and also made a second visit to the Semang. His third and fourth journeys to the Ituri Pygmies occurred during 1949-1950 and 1954-1955. Both trips placed an emphasis on linguistic research.

As an academic instructor Schebesta conducted courses in ethnology, religious studies and linguistics at the seminar for missionaries and priests at St. Gabriel in Mödling and at the Hochschule für Welthandel (Institute of World Trade) in Vienna. Schebesta's most notable contributions to scholarship were the ethnological, anthropological and linguistic studies of surviving primitive peoples in remote parts of Southeast Asia and in the Lake Albert region of eastern Zaïre. The chief value of this research lay in its contribution to an understanding of the languages and settlement history of these populations.

MAJOR WORKS: "Eine Bantu-Grammatik aus dem 17. Jahrhundert: Arte da Lingua de Cafre," *Anthropos*, vol. 16 (1919-1920), pp. 764-787; "Grammatical sketch of the Jahai dialect, spoken by a Negrito tribe of Ulu Perak and Ulu Kelantan, Malay Peninsula," *Bulletin of the School of Oriental Studies*, vol. 4 (1926-1928), pp. 803-826; *Die Bambuti-Pygmäen vom Ituri* [2 vols.] (Brussels: 1938-1950) [tr.: *Les Pygmées* (Paris: 1940)]; *Die Negrito Asiens* [2 vols.] (Vienna-Mödling: 1952-1957); "La langue des Pygmées," *Zaïre*, vol. 3 (1949), pp. 119-128; "Das Problem der Pygmäensprachen," *Wiener Beiträge zur Kulturgeschichte und Linguistik*, vol. 9 (1952), pp. 426-451; "Das Problem des Urmonotheismus: Kritik einer Kritik," *Anthropos*, vol. 49 (1954), pp. 689-697.

SOURCES: Anton Vorbichler, "Schebesta, Paul" in: H. Jungraithmayr and W.J.G. Möhlig (editors), *Lexikon der Afrikanistik* (Berlin: 1983), pp. 208-209; R. Rahmann, "Vier Pioniere der Völkerkunde: den Patres Paul Arndt, Martin Gusinde, Wilhelm Koppers und Paul Schebesta zum siebzigsten Geburtstag," *Anthropos*, vol. 52 (1957), pp. 263-276; Anton Vorbichler, "Professor Dr. Paul Schebesta SVD +," *Anthropos*, vol. 62 (1967), pp. 665-685; Anton Vorbichler and Wilhelm

Dupré, "Vorwort" to: *Festschrift Paul J. Schebesta zum 75. Geburtstag* (Vienna-Mödling: 1963) (= *Studia Instituti Anthropos*, vol. 18), pp. vii-xi.

Rudolf Leger

[Translation from German: Robert B. Marks Ridinger]

Schellhas, Paul. Judge, Mayanist. Born in Berlin (Germany) 16 November 1859, died in Berlin (Germany) 25 April 1945. Schellhas studied law and entered the Prussian civil service as judge, which remained his lifelong career. Impressed by the pictorial Maya manuscript *Codex Dresdensis* when visiting Dresden in 1885, Schellhas dedicated his spare time mainly to Maya research. He was encouraged in this research by the then-leading Mayanist scholar and chief librarian in Dresden ERNST WILHELM FÖRSTEMANN. Schellhas identified name glyphs for Maya gods and mythical animals and made a systematic inventory and description of the nearly thirty deities represented in the pre-Hispanic Maya pictorials. His system is still in use today, only slightly modified and added to by J. ERIC THOMPSON in 1950 and Günter Zimmermann (1914-1972) in 1956. Until his death, Schellhas was convinced that the Maya glyphs would never be completely deciphered, due to their ideographic nature. In this attitude he stood well within the mainstream of contemporary theory (EDUARD SELER and Thompson). The opposing phoneticist theory, reformulated by Yuri Knorowzow (1922-), gained credence only thirty years later in the work of David Kelley (1924-), Floyd Lounsbury (1914-) and others.

MAJOR WORKS OF ANTHROPOLOGICAL IMPORT: "Die Göttergestalten der Mayahandschriften," *Zeitschrift für Ethnologie*, vol. 24 (1892), pp. 101-121 [plus revised eds. as pamphlets, Dresden: 1897 and Berlin: 1904] [tr.: *Representation of Deities of the Maya Manuscripts* (Cambridge: Mass.: 1904) (= *Papers of the Peabody Museum of American Archaeology and Ethnology*, vol. 4, no. 1)]; *An den Grenzen unseres Wissens: dunkle Gebiete der Menschheitsgeschichte, allgemein verständlich dargestellt* (Vienna: 1908); "Fünfzig Jahre Mayaforschung: ein Epilog," *Zeitschrift für Ethnologie*, vol. 69 (1937), pp. 365-389.

SOURCES: Franz Termer, "Paul Schellhas zum 80. Geburtstag," *Forschungen und Fortschritte*, vol. 15 (1939), pp. 406-407; Franz Termer, "In memoriam: Paul Schellhas, 1859-1945," *Ethnos*, vol. 11 (1946), pp 182-186; Berthold Riese, *Indianische Handschriften und Berliner Forscher* (Berlin: 1988), pp. 23-24.

Berthold Riese

Schleicher, August. Linguist. Born in Meiningen (Germany) 19 February 1821, died in Jena (Germany) 6 December 1868. Schleicher was initially trained in philology and textual criticism by the great classicist Friedrich Ritschl at Bonn, where he obtained a doctorate in 1845. He began teaching at the University of Prague in 1850, where he specialized in Slavic and Lithuanian. In 1852 he published a comparative grammar of the Slavic languages, including both phonology and morphology. In the summer of the same year he traveled to Lithuania and mastered the language in a few months. On his return he published the first grammatical account of Lithuanian and a collection of folkloric material. In 1857 he received an honorary professorship at Jena, where he remained until his death. He then turned from Slavic and Lithuanian to general and comparative linguistics. His most influential publication was a two-volume compendium of comparative Indo-European, which began to appear in 1861. It was a concise summation of everything that was known at that time about Proto-Indo-European and its subsequent development. Schleicher inaugurated the convention, still observed today, of identifying any unattested forms reconstructed by the linguist by means of an asterisk.

Schleicher regarded linguistics as one of the natural sciences and human speech as a material object no less substantial than human nerves and bones. Individual languages are, he thought, organisms that develop in accordance with ascertainable laws and like other organisms are destined to age, decay and die. Human beings are defined as much by their native languages as by the complexion of their skulls. He regarded Proto-Indo-European as qualitatively different from and superior to the languages that developed from it—linguistic change being, according to him, a constant process of degeneration. He felt that the goal of linguistics is to discover developmental laws and that linguists should therefore be both philologists and anthropologists.

Schleicher's theories were repudiated by the next generation of linguists, who preferred to regard linguistics as a cultural instead of a natural science and language as an external product of the physiological and psychic nature of human beings. Schleicher's close identification of linguistic development with Darwin's notion of evolution was likewise rejected. His method of representing linguistic development by the family-tree diagram is still used, although the genealogical metaphor has been complemented by the notion of linguistic changes as analogous to waves radiating out geographically, an idea popularized by his student Johannes Schmidt.

MAJOR WORKS: *Zur vergleichenden Sprachengeschichte* (Bonn: 1848); *Die Sprachen Europas in systematischer Übersicht* (Bonn: 1850); *Handbuch der litauischen Sprache* [2 vols.] (Prague: 1856-1857); *Litauische Märchen, Sprichworte, Rätsel und Lieder* (Weimar: 1857); *Zur Morphologie der Sprache* (St. Petersburg: 1859) (= *Mémoires de l'Académie impériale des sciences de St. Pétersbourg*, ser. 7, vol. 1, no. 7); *Die deutsche Sprache* (Stuttgart: 1860); *Compendium der vergleichenden Grammatik der indogermanischen Sprachen* [2 vols.] (Weimar: 1861-1862; 4th ed., Weimar: 1876) [tr.: *A Compendium of the Comparative Grammar of the Indo-European, Sanskrit, Greek and Latin Languages* (London: 1874-1877)]; *Die Darwinsche Theorie und die Sprachwissenschaft* (Weimar: 1863; 3rd ed., Weimar: 1873) [tr.: *Darwin Tested by the Science of Language* (London: 1869)]; *Über die Bedeutung der Sprache für die Naturgeschichte des Menschen* (Weimar: 1865).

SOURCES: Salomon Lefmann, *August Schleicher: Skizze* (Leipzig: 1870); Vittore Pisani, "Schleicher, August" in: *Enciclopedia italiana* (Rome: 1926-1938), vol. 31, p. 103; Johannes Schmidt, "Schleicher, August" in: *Allgemeine deutsche Biographie* (Berlin: 1875-1912), vol. 31, pp. 402-416.

W. Keith Percival

Schmerling, Philippe-Charles. Physician, paleontologist. Born in Delft (Netherlands) 24 February 1791, died in Liège (Belgium) 6 November 1836. Following service as a medical officer in the army of the Netherlands from 1813 to 1816, Schmerling set up a medical practice in Venloo. In 1821 he settled in Liège, where he obtained the title of Doctor of Medicine from the University of Liège in 1825. He was named Professor of Geology at the university in 1835.

In the course of his medical practice, Schmerling spent much time as a working quarryman at Chokier cavern, whose fossil deposits induced him to begin a systematic exploration of the caves of the Liège region of Belgium. He explored more than forty caves in the valleys of the Meuse (such as Chokier, Engis and Engihoul), the Ourthe (notably Remouchamps) and the Vesdre (in particular Fond-de-Forêt and Goffontaine) in less than three years. His discoveries were published in several notes and chiefly in his *Recherches sur les ossemens fossiles* accompanying an atlas of more than sixty extinct species. Schmerling's research interest was specifically in the pathological characteristics of each species.

Besides this important paleontological work—which Charles Lyell admired but which was very much in the tradition of the times—Schmerling reported the discovery, under a layer of brecchia at Engis and at Engihoul, of human remains among those of extinct animals.

The importance of Schmerling's work lies in the fact that, in opposition to most of the dominant opinions of his time, he affirmed the existence of a fossil species of man on the basis of his discoveries and described objects fashioned by human agency (bone punches and needles and flints that could have been used as knives or arrowheads). Schmerling also came into possession of a fragmentary infant skull (later reconstructed by professor of mineralogy P. Davreux) that was recognized in 1935 as that of a Neanderthal child.

MAJOR WORKS: "Notes sur les cavernes à ossemens fossiles découvertes jusqu'à ce jour dans la province de Liège" in: Vander Maelen (editor), *Dictionnaire géographique de la province de Liège* (Brussels: 1832); *Recherches sur les ossemens fossiles découverts dans les cavernes de la province de Liège* [2 vols.] (Liège: 1833-1834).

SOURCES: C. Morren "Notice sur la vie et les travaux de P.C. Schmerling," *Annuaire de l'Académie royale de Bruxelles*, vol. 4 (1838), pp. 130-150; Charles Lyell, *The Antiquity of Man* (London: 1863), pp. 68-69; Philip Shorr, "The genesis of prehistorical research," *Isis*, vol. 23 (1935), pp. 425-443; S. De Laet, "Philippe-Charles Schmerling (1791-1836)" in: G. Daniel (editor), *Towards a History of Archaeology* (London: 1981), pp. 112-119; Léon Fredericq, "Schmerling (Philippe-Charles)" in: *Biographie nationale* [Brussels], vol. 21 (1911), pp. 728-734; D.K. Grayson, *The Establishment of Human Antiquity* (New York: 1983), pp. 108-112; A. Leguebe, "Importance des découvertes de Néandertaliens en Belgique pour le développement de la paléontologie humaine," *Bulletin de la Société royale belge d'Anthropologie et de Préhistoire*, vol. 97 (1986), pp. 13-31.

André Leguebe
[Translation from French: Timothy Eastridge and Robert B. Marks Ridinger]

Schmidt, Max. Ethnologist, jurist, political economist, museologist. Born in Altona (Germany) 16 December 1874, died in Asunción (Paraguay) 26 October 1950. In the first half of the century, Schmidt was a leading figure in the study of South American Indian cultures, especially those of central Brazil, the upper reaches of the Paraguay River and the Chaco region. He was not one of ethnology's great architects, as Baldus pointed out in Schmidt's obituary, but was, rather, a distinguished craftsman in his judicious discussion of the materials at his disposal, most of which he himself assembled in the course of his expeditions.

In 1899 the University of Erlangen granted Schmidt the title of *Doctor Juris Utriusque* for his thesis on Roman law. But in his very first paper he had already discussed law among South American Indian populations. He set out for Berlin where he studied ethnology with KARL VON DEN STEINEN and EDUARD SELER; at the same time he worked at the American Section of the Museum of Ethnology and prepared his first expedition to

Mato Grosso (Brazil), which he carried through in 1900 and 1901, primarily in the Upper Xingu area. When he returned he applied himself to the study of the available collections, while holding assistant and managing positions in the museum. His second expedition to Mato Grosso (1910) resulted in masterly works on the Guató and the Paressi-Kabiši of the upper Paraguay.

In 1914 Schmidt did fieldwork among the Toba and the Kainguá of Paraguay. He earned a D.Phil. degree with his dissertation on the Aruak, submitted in 1916 to the University of Leipzig. In it, he discussed the problem of the Aruak expansion over wide areas of the continent and their peaceful conquest of alloglottic tribes with whom they mingled, forming a higher stratum.

In 1921 Schmidt was appointed professor at the University of Berlin. His last expedition in Brazil, from 1926 to 1928, took him once again to Mato Grosso where he resumed the study of tribes he had visited before: this gave him occasion for a comparative vision of cultural and interethnic situations in a diachronic perspective, mainly concerning the Bakairí in contact with the world of the white man. Even before that, in his 1905 book, he had already included a pioneer chapter on acculturative phenomena among the Upper Xingu tribes since the arrival of the first German expeditions.

Schmidt's first theoretical contributions were on the ethnology of law, a subject he dealt with from the beginning of his career and which he took up several times. Later on he advocated an increasingly broad and integrative vision, which was subsumed in a masterly way in the first part of his 1924 compendium. His aim was a comprehensive concept of the "sciences of man" and, through it, a systematization that would overcome former fetters. In his 1920-1921 work he had already stated the principles of an "ethnological political economy" conceived as existing on the borderland of traditional ethnology and political economy; this was understood as the domain in which the social processes link with all of Nature's manifestations.

Worth mentioning in the scientific make-up of Schmidt is his interdisciplinary approach to most of the subjects he broached. In terms of object, theory or method he did not let himself be restricted by the somewhat rigid boundaries between the sciences. He was not committed to any school of ethnological thought and repudiated the interference of ideologies or value judgments in scientific work. Although stating that ethnology should be based on the point of view of the natural sciences, he often used the historical perspective in his writings. As to method, it should derive from the deductive sciences, while contents should be based on a thorough knowledge of concrete facts. In short, he sided with the axiomatic statement that no good ethnology exists without good ethnography.

One of Schmidt's favorite themes was the origin of ornamental art. Various anthropologists (A.A. Gerbrands, for instance) took exception to his thesis that geometric patterns derive for the most part from the technique of basketry, this being determined by the forms (pinnulated or flabelliform) of the palm leaves used as raw material; but it appears that so far no one has succeeded in refuting Schmidt's proposition. Even von den Steinen, who favored a psychological form of explanation, had no objection to Schmidt's. Later on, while studying art in the context of the Peruvian high cultures, Schmidt tackled the subject again in relation to weaving and wrote one of the most solid studies on the art of Inca culture.

After his retirement from the University of Berlin (1929), Schmidt lived for two years in Brazil, then settled in Paraguay where he stayed until his death. There he worked on his unpublished materials while organizing a museum of ethnology. In 1935 he visited several Chaco tribes, and in 1944 he started lecturing at the National University of Asunción.

MAJOR WORKS: *Indianerstudien in Zentralbrasilien: Erlebnisse und ethnologische Ergebnisse einer Reise in den Jahren 1900-1901* (Berlin: 1905); "Über altperuanische Gewebe mit scenenhaften Darstellungen," *Baessler-Archiv,* vol. 1 (1910), pp. 1-61; "Die Paressi-Kabiši: ethnologische Ergebnisse der Expedition zu den Quellen des Jaurú und Juruena im Jahre 1910," *Baessler-Archiv,* vol. 4 (1914), pp. 167-250; "Die Guató und ihr Gebiet: ethnologische und archäologische Ergebnisse der Expedition zum Caracará-Fluss in Matto Grosso," *Baessler-Archiv,* vol. 4 (1914), pp. 251-283; *Die Aruaken: ein Beitrag zum Problem der Kulturverbreitung* (Leipzig: 1917); *Grundriss der ethnologischen Volkswirtschaftslehre* (Stuttgart: 1920-1921); "Das Haus im Xingú-Quellgebiet" in: Walter Lehmann (editor), *Festschrift Eduard Seler* (Stuttgart: 1922), pp. 441-470; *Die materielle Wirtschaft bei den Naturvölkern* (Leipzig: 1923); *Völkerkunde* (Berlin: 1924); "Ergebnisse meiner zweijährigen Forschungsreise in Matto-Grosso: September 1926 bis August 1928," *Zeitschrift für Ethnologie,* vol. 60 (1928), pp. 85-124; *Kunst und Kultur von Peru* (Berlin: 1929).

SOURCES: Max Schmidt, "Autobiografia," *Revista de Antropologia,* vol. 3 (1955), pp. 115-124; Herbert Baldus, "Max Schmidt, 1874-1950," *Revista do Museu Paulista,* n.s., vol. 5 (1951), pp. 253-260; Herbert Baldus, *Bibliografia crítica da etnologia brasileira,* vol.1 (São Paulo: 1954), pp. 14-15 [et passim]; A.A. Gerbrands, *Art as an Element of Culture, Especially in Negro-Africa* (Leiden: 1957), pp. 32-35; Egon Schaden, "O estudo do índio brasileiro—ontem e hoje," *Revista de História,* vol.5 (1952), pp. 385-401.

Egon Schaden

Schmidt, Wilhelm. Linguist, ethnologist, specialist in studies of religion. Born in Hörde, Westphalia (Germany) 16 February 1868, died in Fribourg (Switzerland) 10 February 1954. In 1883 Schmidt entered the Missionary Society of the Divine Word (*Societas Verbi Dei,* SVD) and was ordained in 1892. From 1893 to 1895, he studied at the University of Berlin, specializing in the Semitic languages. In 1895 he was named Professor to the Mission Seminary of St. Gabriel at Mödling (near Vienna) where he remained until 1938. Beginning in 1921, he also delivered lectures at the University of Vienna and, after leaving Austria in 1938, at the University of Fribourg in Switzerland until 1951. In 1906 he founded *Anthropos: International Review of Ethnology and Linguistics* and, in 1931, the Anthropos Institute, where he remained director until 1950. Between 1927 and 1939, he also served as director of the Museo Missionario-Etnologico Lateranense (Pontifical Museum of the Lateran) in Rome.

It was through submissions of new language materials from missionaries in New Guinea that he first concerned himself with linguistics. His first work on Oceanic languages appeared in 1899. Schmidt became well known for his work on the "Austronesian" (formerly Malayo-Polynesian) languages (which he gathered together with several of the languages of Southeast Asia, the "Austro-Asiatic" languages, into one great language family, the "Austral") as well as for his pioneering work on the divisions of the Australian languages, and for his attempt to place language families and cultural units within a common framework. However, his interests shifted more and more to the areas of ethnology and the study of religion. In ethnology, he became best known as the founder of the "Vienna Cultural-Historical School." Stimulated by Leo Frobenius, Fritz Graebner and other German ethnologists, he integrated the nonliterate peoples into a world-spanning system of *Kulturkreisen,* or culture circles, whose relative age would be established above all by their geographic distribution. In religious studies his name is linked with the attempt to determine the most ancient religious form on the basis of relative cultural age.

Stimulated by ANDREW LANG (who had ascertained the existence of the Supreme Being among the Australian peoples), Schmidt investigated the religions of primitive hunters and gatherers in his greatest work, *Der Ursprung der Gottesidee,* and drew the conclusion that, since in many of these religions the Supreme Being assumed such a prominent position with respect to other venerated beings, one had to speak of "monotheism." This monotheism had been maintained in a relatively pure form among the nomadic herding cultures, while in other culture circles it had been driven into the background or disappeared completely.

Schmidt's cultural-historical reconstructions, which he wished to set in the place of unilinear evolution, proved to be too inflexible and schematic. Although his systematization was totally discarded by many, others pointed out that the cultural forms he had devised retained a certain typological value. His works on religion may be similarly evaluated. Despite the fact that his historical, philosophical and theological conclusions are questionable, his investigations retain their value in the study of religion in that they helped to direct attention to the belief in a High God among preliterate peoples. Thus, his work remains as a noteworthy stage of research.

MAJOR WORKS: *Die Stellung der Pygmäenvölker in der Entwicklungsgeschichte des Menschen* (Stuttgart: 1910); *Der Ursprung der Gottesidee* [12 vols.] (Münster.: 1912-1955); (with Wilhelm Koppers) *Völker und Kulturen: 1. Gesellschaft und Wirtschaft der Völker* (Regensburg: 1924); *Die Sprachfamilien und Sprachenkreise der Erde* (Heidelberg: 1926); *Handbuch der vergleichenden Religionsgeschichte* (Münster: 1930) [tr.: *Origine et évolution de la religion* (Paris: 1931); *The Origin and Growth of Religion* (London: 1931); *Manual de historia comparada de las religiones* (Bilbao, Madrid, and Barcelona: 1932; 1941); *Manuale di storia comparata delle religioni* (Brescia: 1934; 1938; 1943; 1949); *Pi-chiao tsung-chiao shih* (Peking: 1948)]; *Handbuch der Methode der kulturhistorischen Ethnologie* (Münster: 1937); [tr.: *The Culture Historical Method of Ethnology* (New York: 1939)]; *Das Eigentum auf den ältesten Stufen der Menschheit* [3 vols.] (Münster: 1937-1942); *Das Mutterrecht* (Mödling bei Wien: 1955); *Wege der Kulturen: Gesammelte Aufsätze* (St. Augustin bei Bonn: 1964).

SOURCES: Wilhelm Koppers (editor) *Festschrift: publication d'hommage offerte au P.W. Schmidt [zum 60. Geburtstag]* (Vienna: 1928); Fritz Bornemann, "Verzeichnis der Schriften von P.W. Schmidt, S.V.D. (1868-1954)," *Anthropos,* vol. 49 (1954), pp. 397-432; Joseph Henninger, "P. Wilhelm Schmidt, S.V.D. (1868-1954): eine biographische Skizze," *Anthropos,* vol. 51 (1956), pp. 19-60; Joseph Henninger, "Schmidt, Wilhelm" in: David L. Sills (editor), *The International Encyclopedia of the Social Sciences* (New York: 1968), vol. 14, pp. 56-58; Jacques Waardenburg, *Classical Approaches to the Study of Religion* [2 vols.] (The Hague and Paris: 1973-1974), vol. 1 ("Introduction" and "Anthropology"), pp. 264-286; vol. 2 ("Bibliography"), pp. 251-258; Fritz Bornemann, *P. Wilhelm Schmidt, S.V.D., 1868-1954* (Rome: 1982); Ernest Brandewie, *Wilhelm Schmidt and the Origin of the Idea of God* (New York and London: 1983); Joseph Henninger, "Schmidt, Wilhelm" in: Mircea Eliade (editor-in-chief), *The Encyclopedia of Religion* (New York and London: 1987), vol. 13, pp. 113-115 [plus additional sources cited in Bornemann and Brandewie].

Joseph Henninger
[Translation from German: Robert B. Marks Ridinger]

Schneider, David M. Cultural and social anthropologist. Born in Brooklyn (New York) 11 November 1918. Schneider is best known for his studies of American and Yapese kinship, his contributions to the study of kinship as a symbolic system, and his theoretical work on symbolic anthropology.

Schneider first turned to anthropology as an undergraduate at Cornell University where he studied with LAURISTON SHARP. From Cornell, Schneider went to Yale, where he worked briefly with Geoffrey Gorer and GEORGE PETER MURDOCK. But the major portion of Schneider's graduate training was at Talcott Parsons' Department of Social Relations at Harvard, where Schneider went in 1946, the year the department was inaugurated. He studied primarily with Parsons and with CLYDE KLUCKHOHN. The latter supervised his dissertation fieldwork on the Yap Islands of Micronesia. This fieldwork marked a first turning point in Schneider's interests: from psychoanalytically informed studies of the relationship between the individual personality and culture to structural-functionalist studies of kinship and social organization. Schneider completed his dissertation in 1949.

Over the next fifteen years, Schneider earned a reputation as one of the foremost American scholars in the field of comparative kinship studies. He taught during this period at the London School of Economics, Harvard, Berkeley and the University of Chicago. In 1954 he organized a major conference on matrilineal systems of kinship that resulted in *Matrilineal Kinship*, a collection of theoretical essays.

In the 1960s, however, Schneider repudiated structural-functionalism and began to advocate a radically particularist approach that emphasized the explication of categories recognized within a particular culture. This theoretical shift was crystallized in Schneider's famous studies of American kinship, which analyzed it as a "system of symbols and meanings"—the salient cultural symbols (e.g., blood, love, money, marriage) applied by people in defining types and qualities of relationships and the shared cultural meanings associated with the symbols. These studies, emblematic of a theoretical movement known as "symbolic anthropology," were predicated on a rigorous distinction between the "cultural system" (consisting of ideological structures through which actions acquire social meaning) and the "social system" (consisting of concrete social arrangements whose import may only be understood with reference to the cultural system)—a distinction deriving from Talcott Parsons' "theory of action."

In his later years Schneider increasingly came to see major theoretical constructs of anthropological science (e.g., the "genealogical grid") as reflections or reifications of the cultural system of Western culture. He strongly supported the cultural anthropological study of Western culture as a way of gaining perspective on the theoretical categories used by anthropologists in the analysis of radically different cultures and societies.

Over the course of more than twenty-five years of teaching at the University of Chicago, Schneider's work with several dozen graduate students helped establish the importance of a symbolic approach in anthropology. He retired from the University of Chicago in 1985 and joined the faculty of the University of California, Santa Cruz.

MAJOR WORKS: (with George C. Homans) *Marriage, Authority and Final Causes: a Study of Unilateral Cross-Cousin Marriage* (Glencoe, Ill.: 1955); (with Kathleen Gough) *Matrilineal Kinship* (Berkeley: 1961; 2nd ed., Berkeley: 1973); "Double descent on Yap," *Journal of the Polynesian Society*, vol. 71 (1962), pp. 1-24; *American Kinship: a Cultural Account* (Englewood Cliffs, N.J.: 1968; 2nd ed., Chicago: 1980); "What is kinship all about?" in: Priscilla Reining (editor), *Kinship*

Studies in the Morgan Centennial Year (Washington: 1972), pp. 32-63; (with Raymond T. Smith) *Class Differences and Sex Roles in American Kinship and Family Structure* (Englewood Cliffs, N.J.: 1973); "Notes toward a theory of culture" in: Keith H. Basso and Henry A. Selby (editors), *Meaning in Anthropology* (Albuquerque: 1976), pp. 197-220; *A Critique of the Study of Kinship* (Ann Arbor: 1984).

SOURCES: Adam Kuper, *The Invention of Primitive Society: Transformations of an Illusion* (London and New York: 1988), pp. 241-243; Ira R. Bashkow, "The dynamics of rapport in a colonial situation: David Schneider's fieldwork on the islands of Yap" in: George W. Stocking, Jr. (editor), *Colonial Situations: Essays in the Contextualization of Ethnographic Knowledge* (Madison: in press) (= *History of Anthropology*, vol. 7).

Ira R. Bashkow

Schoolcraft, Henry Rowe. Indian agent, ethnologist, explorer. Born in Guilderland (New York) 28 March 1793, died in Washington (D.C.) 10 December 1864. Schoolcraft, largely self-educated, left New York to explore the mineral regions of Missouri after a series of failed ventures in glass-making. His book recounting these travels, *A View of the Lead Mines of Missouri*, attracted the attention of Secretary of War, John C. Calhoun, who appointed Schoolcraft to the position of geologist on the 1820 government expedition to Lake Superior and the Mississippi River under the command of Lewis Cass and in 1822 to the position of Indian agent at Sault Ste. Marie, Michigan Territory. There Schoolcraft married Jane Johnson, a mixed-blood Ojibwa; from her and her family, he acquired much of his information on Ojibwa language and culture. Sensitive about his lack of linguistic training, Schoolcraft turned from Ojibwa linguistics and concentrated on recording the legends of the Ojibwa and Ottawa. He concluded in *Algic Researches*, his first major ethnological work, that the legends revealed an Indian mentality that was decidedly Oriental and thus, he believed, nearly impervious to change. Schoolcraft moved to New York in 1842 and sought to make a living as a writer. In this he failed, however. He was one of the founding members of the American Ethnological Society and an important resource on Great Lakes Indian ethnology. A religious experience in the 1830s awakened in Schoolcraft a conviction that ethnology should serve the interests of religion. His last work, a multi-volume compilation of ethnographic and historical data that was written with government support, attacked polygenists. Although he was pessimistic regarding the Indians' future, Schoolcraft nevertheless argued that greater religious and scientific efforts ought to be made to civilize them.

MAJOR WORKS: *A View of the Lead Mines of Missouri* (New York: 1819); *Travels in the Central Portions of the Mississippi Valley* (New York: 1825); *Narrative of an Expedition through the Upper Mississippi to Itasca Lake* (New York: 1834); *Algic Researches, Comprising Inquiries Respecting the Mental Characteristics of the North American Indians* [2 vols.] (New York: 1839); *Oneota, or Characteristics of the Red Race of America* (New York: 1845); *Notes on the Iroquois* (Albany: 1847); *Personal Memoirs of a Residence of Thirty Years with the Indian Tribes on the American Frontier* (Philadelphia: 1851); *Historical and Statistical Information respecting the History, Condition and Prospects of the Indian Tribes of the United States* [6 vols.] (Philadelphia: 1851-1857).

SOURCES: Robert E. Bieder, *Science Encounters the Indian, 1820-1880: the Early Years of American Ethnology* (Norman: 1986), pp. 146-193; John Finley Freeman, "Religion and personality in the anthropology of Henry Schoolcraft," *Journal of the History of the Behavioral Sciences*, vol. 1 (1965), pp. 301-313; Philip P. Mason (editor), *Schoolcraft's Expedition to Lake Itasca* (East Lansing: 1958); William L. Mentor (editor), *Narrative Journal of Travels* (East Lansing: 1953); Chase S.

Osborn and Stellanova Osborn, *Schoolcraft-Longfellow-Hiawatha* (Lancaster, Pa.: 1942); Roy Harvey Pearce, *The Savages of America* (Baltimore: 1953).

Robert E. Bieder

Schultz, Harald. Ethnographer, photographer, filmmaker. Born in Porto Alegre, Rio Grande do Sul (Brazil) 22 February 1909, died in São Paulo (Brazil) 8 January 1965. Schultz is known for his well documented field research, the great majority of which was published in the *Revista do Museu Paulista* (*nova série*), of the University of São Paulo.

His career began in photography. The camera was an extension of his personality. He was also a born naturalist, a constant observer of flora and fauna and of the people who live intimately with nature.

Schultz's romanticism was stimulated by the presence of an old champion of causes, the then-General Mariano Cândido da Silva Rondon, whose pro-indigenist actions led to the founding of an organization for the protection of the Brazilian Indians, the SPI, Serviço de Proteção aos Índios (Indian Protection Service), later FUNAI, Fundação Nacional do Índio (National Indian Foundation).

It was as an employee of this organization that Schultz began learning the techniques of field research, under the guidance of another luminary of Brazilian ethnology, CURT NIMUENDAJÚ. Perfecting his study of ethnology as an independent student of HERBERT BALDUS at the Escola Livre de Sociologia e Política (Free School of Sociology and Politics) in São Paulo in 1946 and part of 1947, he continued to develop his study and research projects together with Baldus as Assistant in Ethnology at the Museu Paulista (Paulista Museum) until his death.

As an artist Schultz was above all concerned with the transmission of reality, that is, with the documentation of observed phenomena. Besides the ethnographic collections that constitute an important part of the Museu Paulista holdings, Schultz left a photographic archive that includes scenes of daily life and rituals among fourteen Brazilian tribes—approximately 12,000 black-and-white negatives and 10,000 color slides. The fifty ethnographic films he made were edited by the Institut für den Wissenschaftlichen Film (Institute for Scientific Film) in Göttingen (Germany).

Among his scientific publications are articles published in *National Geographic Magazine* and books on the Indians, notably *Vinte três índios resistem à civilização* and *Hombu*, a collection of photographs published simultaneously in Amsterdam, Rio de Janeiro, New York and Paris.

Schultz's works also include recordings of songs and other materials, now found in the Musée de l'Homme in Paris.

Schultz's role in ethnology can be characterized by his impulse to augment and deepen our knowledge of the facts. With his empirical orientation—from which CLAUDE LÉVI-STRAUSS was able to profit in writing *Mythologiques*—Schultz was one of the researchers who, through his collecting and disseminating of primary materials, most contributed to building up a rich documentary foundation for Brazilian ethnology.

MAJOR WORKS: *Vinte três índios resistem à civilização* (São Paulo: 1954); *Hombu: Indian Life in the Brazilian Jungle* (New York: 1962).

SOURCE: Herbert Baldus, *Bibliografia crítica da etnologia brasileira* (vol. 1, São Paulo: 1954; vol. 2, Hannover: 1968; vol. 3, Berlin: 1984) [contains more complete bibliography].

Vilma Chiara

[Translation from Portuguese: Margo L. Smith]

Schultze Jena, Leonhard (the "Jena" was added in 1912). Zoologist, geographer, philologist. Born in Jena (Germany) 28 May 1872, died in Marburg (Germany) 28 March 1955. Schultze Jena was born into an academic family of high status in Jena. He started with studies in medicine in Lausanne, Kiel and Jena, and switched to biological sciences and chemistry after receiving his first medical degree (*"Physikum"*). In 1896 he successfully concluded his university education with an D.Sc. in zoology from the University of Jena. Schultze Jena's career is exceptional in that he consecutively worked in four distinct scientific fields, namely: zoology, where he obtained his first employment as assistant to Ernst Haeckel (1834-1919); physical anthropology, for which he did field studies in South Africa; geography, of which he was professor from 1908, first in Jena, later in Kiel, and from 1913 until retirement in 1937 at Marburg University; and non-European philology, to which he made his major contributions. The regions of his anthropological fieldwork were also exceptionally diverse: South Africa (1903-1905), New Guinea (1910-1911), Europe (1915-1919, 1922, 1951) and Mesoamerica (1929-1931).

Schultze Jena's major anthropological contributions lay in the study of languages, in the recording and translation of indigeneous religious texts and in the ethnographic study of rituals. This inclination materialized first with his study of a Melanesian language based on his own fieldwork (*Zur Kenntnis ... Tumelo*) and reached a climax in his three-volume *Indiana* publication in which he presented studies of Mesoamerican languages—Mixtec, Tlapanec, Nahua, Pipil and Quiché—and which included important ethnographic observations as well. After his retirement, Schultze Jena continued his philological work with translations and editions of early colonial Mesoamerican Indian literatures, all published as monographs in the series *Quellenwerke*, founded by his friend WALTER LEHMANN of the Iberoamerikanisches Institut (Ibero-American Institute) in Berlin. Of these, the *Popol Vuh*, published in 1944, stands out due to Schultze Jena's intuitive comprehension of the Quiché text which stemmed in part from knowledge gained during his linguistic and ethnographic fieldwork. The work includes an analytical dictionary and an excellent German translation that has not been surpassed even by later Guatemalan and North American editions, specifically Adrian Recinos' of 1953 and Munro Edmonson's of 1971. Schultze Jena's later editions of Nahuatl texts, mainly from the corpus of the Franciscan friar Bernardino de Sahagún (1499-1590), are not as reliable, since Schultze Jena lacked first-hand experience with that language, which he learned at a rather advanced age and only by reading documents. However, for several years, Schultze Jena's were the only modern editions and translations of those important sources. His anthropogeographic study of the Balkans (*Makedonien*) is important, too, since it thoroughly documents this southern European region in a decisive epoch (1915-1922) of political and social change.

MAJOR WORKS OF ANTHROPOLOGICAL IMPORT: *Aus Namaland und Kalahari* (Jena: 1907); *Zur Kenntnis der melanesischen Sprache von der Insel Tumelo* (Jena: 1911); *Forschungen im Innern der Insel Neuguineas* (Berlin: 1914); *Makedonien: Landschafts- und Kulturbilder* (Jena: 1927); *Zur Kenntnis des Körpers der Hottentotten und Buschmänner* (Jena: 1928); *Indiana* [3 vols.] (Jena:

1933-1938); *Popol Vuh: das heilige Buch der Quiché-Indianer von Guatemala* (Stuttgart: 1944; 2nd ed., Berlin: 1972) (= *Quellenwerke zur alten Geschichte Amerikas aufgezeichnet in den Sprachen der Eingeborenen*, 2); *Wahrsagerei, Himmelskunde und Kalender der alten Azteken* (Stuttgart: 1950) (= *Quellenwerke zur alten Geschichte Amerikas aufgezeichnet in den Sprachen der Eingeborenen*, 4); *Gliederung des alt-aztekischen Volks in Familie, Stand und Beruf* (Stuttgart: 1950) (= *Quellenwerke zur alten Geschichte Amerikas aufgezeichnet in den Sprachen der Eingeborenen*, 5); *Alt-Aztekische Gesänge* (Stuttgart: 1957) (= *Quellenwerke zur alten Geschichte Amerikas aufgezeichnet in den Sprachen der Eingeborenen*, 6).

SOURCES: F. Termer, "Leonhard Schultze Jena (28.5.1872-29.3.1955)," *Petermanns Geographische Mitteilungen*, vol. 99 (1955), pp. 212-213; Gerdt Kutscher, "Leonhard Schultze Jena," *Baessler Archiv*, n.F., vol. 3 (1955), pp. 249-252; Hermann Trimborn, "Leonhard Schultze Jena," *Marburger Gelehrte* (1977), pp. 479-500 [includes full bibliography].

Berthold Riese

Schweinfurth, Georg. Geographer, botanist, explorer. Born in Riga (Latvia, then in Russia) 29 December 1836, died in Berlin (Germany) 19 September 1925. Following attendance at gymnasia in Riga and Lindenruh, Schweinfurth, starting in 1857, studied natural sciences in Heidelberg, Munich and Berlin. Between 1863 and 1866 he carried out his first great journey, exploring the geography of plant life in the coastal regions between the Nile Valley and the Red Sea. With the financial assistance of the Berlin Academy of Sciences (the Humboldt Foundation), he returned to the Upper Nile region between 1868 and 1871 for the purpose of "botanical investigation of the section of the river called the Baḥr al-Ghazāl. In addition, geographical and ethnographic researches are also to be carried out as the opportunity arises" (Schweinfurth, 1925, p. 3). On 5 January 1869 he left Khartoum for the hitherto unexplored country of the Mangbetu, where he discovered the westward flowing Uelle River and, with it, the watershed between the Nile and Congo drainages. On this journey, in addition to collecting ethnographic, botanical and zoological materials, Schweinfurth also assembled linguistic data, particularly on the Bongo, Sandéh (Zande), Dyur (Shilluk) and Dinka languages. (These collections and notes were destroyed in a warehouse fire after his return.)

When he returned to Germany in 1872, he was granted a doctorate by the University of Heidelberg, and the following year he worked with Gerhard Rohlfs on the geographic investigation of the Kharga Oasis. His two-volume masterpiece *The Heart of Africa* (for which the London Geographical Society granted him its gold author's medal) appeared in 1874 in English and German, and subsequently in French, Italian and Turkish translations. In 1875, at the suggestion of Khedive Ismail, he founded the Egyptian Geographical Society in Cairo and served as president until 1876. He also became director of the Egyptian Museum, and in this role Schweinfurth supported and undertook further journeys of exploration, paying particular attention to the Arabian Desert and Fayyūm. In 1880 the Prussian minister of culture awarded him the academic rank of professor without portfolio (*Prädikat Professor*), and in 1888 he moved back to Berlin. Despite this, until 1914 he continued to carry out research trips to the countries of North Africa, focusing primarily on Egypt and Yemen.

MAJOR WORKS: "Aufzählung und Beschreibung der Acacien-Arten des Nilgebiets," *Linnéa*, n.F., vols. 1-3 and 4 (1867), pp. 309-376; "Linguistische Ergebnisse einer Reise nach Central-Afrika," *Zeitschrift für Ethnologie*, vol. 4, suppl. (1872), pp. 1-82; *The Heart of Africa* [2 vols.] (London: 1874) [tr.: *Im Herzen von Afrika* [2 vols.] (Leipzig: 1874)]; "The flora of ancient Egypt,"

Nature, vol. 28 (1883), pp. 109-114; "Abyssinische Pflanzennamen," *Abhandlungen der Königlichen Akademie der Wissenschaften zu Berlin* (1893), pp. 1-84; "Sammlung arabisch-äthiopischer Pflanzen," *Bulletin de l'herbier Boissier* (Genève), vol. 2, append. 2 (1894), pp. 1-113; vol. 4, append. 2 (1896), pp. 114-266; and vol. 7, append. 2 (1899), pp. 267-340; "Recherches sur l'âge de la pierre dans la haute Égypte," *Annales du Service des Antiquités Égyptiennes (Le Caire)* (1904), pp. 9-64.

SOURCES: K. Guenther. *Georg Schweinfurth: Lebensbild eines Afrikaforschers* (Stuttgart: 1954); S. Hillelson, "Obituary Georg Schweinfurth," *Sudan Notes and Records*, vol. 8 (1925), pp. 243-245; Hermann Jungraithmayr, "Schweinfurth, Georg" in: H. Jungraithmayr and W.J.G. Möhlig (editors), *Lexikon der Afrikanistik* (Berlin: 1983), pp. 214-215; *Meyers Grosses Konversations-Lexikon* (6th ed., Leipzig: 1907); G. Schweinfurth, *Afrikanisches Skizzenbuch* (Berlin: 1925); C. Weidmann, *Deutsche Männer in Afrika* (Lübeck: 1894).

Rudolf Leger

[Translation from German: Robert B. Marks Ridinger]

Seler, Eduard. Americanist, archaeologist. Born in Crossen, Niederlausitz (Germany) 5 December 1849, died in Berlin (Germany) 23 November 1922. After studying natural sciences and mathematics at the Universities of Breslau (now Wrocław) and Berlin, Seler earned his living as a private tutor and, after successfully passing his state-exams, as a high school teacher in Berlin until recurrent illness forced him to abandon teaching. In 1884 Seler married Caecilie Sachs, daughter of his physician, and through this marriage acquired considerable material wealth, which enabled him to pursue his anthropological interests and studies. In that year he also entered the Berlin Museum für Völkerkunde (Ethnographic Museum) at the level of *wissenschaftlicher Hilfsarbeiter* (research assistant) and pursued his professional career in that museum, reaching the position of departmental director in 1904. In 1887 Seler received a Ph.D. from the University of Leipzig with his dissertation on the *Conjugationssystem der Maya Sprachen*, an outstanding and lucidly written contribution to comparative grammar of Mayan languages. In the same year he made the first of a total of six extended field trips to the Americas, all of which he undertook with his wife. Seler received his *Habilitation* in 1894 with a monograph on the iconography, hieroglyphs and general content of the small collection of ancient Mexican manuscripts that had been brought to Berlin by ALEXANDER VON HUMBOLDT early in the 19th century (*Die mexikanischen Bilderhandschriften*). This and other Mexican studies earned him a professorship at the University of Berlin, sponsored by the Duc Florimond de Loubat (1831-1927), several prizes, and in 1908 full membership of the Prussian Academy of Sciences. During the last decade of his life Seler was president of the Berlin Anthropological Society and editor of the *Zeitschrift für Ethnologie*. In 1902 he started revising and editing his own collected papers (*Gesammelte Abhandlungen*). This process was continued after his death by his wife and former pupils.

Seler's foremost contribution to science was his methodical use of ethnohistorical sources (mostly in the Nahuatl language) to elucidate pre-Columbian iconography in pictorial manuscripts, stone sculpture and architecture (*Gesammelte Abhandlungen*). Seler was an empiricist who handled factual information from all anthropological domains (viz., archaeology, linguistics, ethnohistory and to a lesser degree ethnography and physical anthropology), integrating them in his studies with the goal of reconstructing segments of past cultures. This research strategy made his studies superior to the more speculative and factually limited writings of his predecessors and many of his contemporaries (e.g., Charles Étienne Brasseur de Bourbourg (1814-1874) and ADOLPH BANDELIER). He also made major contributions to the study of deity and animal figures in the Maya manuscripts, elaborating on PAUL SCHELLHAS' earlier, more limited, efforts (*Die Tierbilder*). Seler was one of the most prolific collectors of archaeological and botanical specimens for the Berlin Museums. His impact on German anthropology is especially notable, since he was a gifted teacher and occupied the only specialized professorship in "Americanistics" that existed at the time. By virtue of his writings and teaching he is considered the founder of empirical Mexican studies as an anthropological subdiscipline in Germany, and this influence is still present in that German universities at Berlin, Hamburg and Bonn offer full academic careers in *"(Alt)amerikanistik."* Internationally his monumental and profusely illustrated *Gesammelte Abhandlungen* and his commentaries on all important Mexican pictorials (*Codex Borgia*), including the definition of the Borgia-Group of manuscripts as a stylistic unit, are most influential (cf. Karl A. Nowotny, *Tlacuillolli* (Berlin: 1961)). Some of his interpretations about astral mythology, much *en vogue* in his time, are considered speculative today; and he was not prepared to study these pictorials as possible historical chronicles, as some are now classified.

MAJOR WORKS: *Das Konjugationssystem der Maya-Sprachen.* [Ph.D. dissertation] (Berlin: 1887; reprinted in: *Gesammelte Abhandlungen*, vol. 1 (1902), pp. 65-126; *Die mexikanischen Bilderhandschriften Alexander von Humboldts in der königlichen Bibliothek zu Berlin* [Habilitationsschrift; 2 vols.] (Berlin: 1893-1894) [tr.: "Alexander von Humboldt's picture manuscripts in the Royal Library at Berlin" in: *Mexican and Central American Antiquities, Calendar Systems and History* (translated under the supervion of Charles P. Bowditch) (Washington: 1904) (= *Bureau of American Ethnology, Bulletin* 28), pp. 123-229]; "Die Ausgrabungen am Orte des Haupttempels in Mexiko," *Mitteilungen der Anthropologischen Gesellschaft in Wien*, vol. 31 (1901), pp. 113-137; reprinted in: *Gesammelte Abhandlungen*, vol. 2 (1904), pp. 767-904) [tr.: "Las escavaciones en el sitio del Templo Mayor de México," *Anales del Museo Nacional de México*, vol. 7 (1903), pp. 235-256 and "El Cuauhxicalli del Telpochcalli del Templo Mayor de México," *Anales del Museo Nacional de México*, vol. 7 (1903), pp. 260-262]; *Die alten Ansiedlungen von Chaculá im Distrikt Nentón des Departamentos Huehuetenango der Republik Guatemala* (Berlin: 1901); *Codex Borgia: eine altmexikanische Bilderschrift der Bibliothek der Congregatio de Propaganda Fide* [3 vols.] (Berlin: 1904-1909) [tr.: *Codice Borgia* (Mexico City: 1963)]; *Gesammelte Abhandlungen zur Amerikanischen Sprach-und Alterthumskunde* [5 vols. and index vol.] (Berlin: 1902-1923; reprinted with new index vol., Graz: 1961-1967); "Altmexikanischer Schmuck und soziale und militärische Rangabzeichen," *Zeitschrift für Ethnologie*, vol. 21 (1889), pp. 69-85 and vol. 23 (1891), pp. 114-144 (reprinted in: *Gesammelte Abhandlungen*, vol. 2 (1904), pp. 509-619); "Die Tierbilder der mexikanischen und der Maya-Handschriften," *Zeitschrift für Ethnologie*, vol. 41 (1909), pp. 209-257, 301-451, 784-846 and vol. 42 (1910), pp. 31-97, 242-287 (1910) (reprinted in: *Gesammelte Abhandlungen*, vol. 4 (1923), pp. 453-758); *Beobachtungen und Studien in den Ruinen von Palenque* (Berlin: 1915) (= *Abhandlungen der königlich-preußischen Akademie der Wissenschaften Berlin, philhist. Klass*, 5) [tr.: *Observations and Studies in the Ruins of Palenque* (Pebble Beach, Calif.: 1977)]; *Einige Kapitel aus dem Geschichtswerk des Fray Bernardino de Sahagun* (posthumously edited by Caecilie Seler-Sachs, Walter Lehmann and Walter Krickeberg) (Stuttgart: 1927).

SOURCES: Eduard Seler, *Reisebriefe aus Mexiko* (Berlin: 1889); Caecilie Seler-Sachs, *Auf alten Wegen in Mexiko und Guatemala: Reiseerinnerungen und Eindrücke aus den Jahren 1895-1897* (Berlin: 1900); Caecilie Seler-Sachs, Walter Lehmann and Walter Krickeberg (editors), *Festschrift Eduard Seler* (Stuttgart: 1922) [includes bibliography]; Konrad Theodor Preuß, "Die wissenschaftliche Lebensarbeit Eduard Selers," *Zeitschrift für Ethnologie*, vol. 55 (1923), pp. 1-6; Otto Quellet, [obituary], *Iberoamerikanisches Archiv*, vol. 1 (1924), pp. 33-39; *El México antiguo*, vols. 7-8 (1949) [commemorative volumes]; Eduard Seler, *Gesammelte Abhandlungen* (Graz: 1967) [index volume (edited by Ferdinand Anders) includes bibliography, portraits and listings of archival material, pp. 1-54]; Henry Bigger Nicholson. "Eduard Georg Seler, 1849-1922" in: *Handbook of Middle American Indians* (Austin: 1973), vol. 13, pp. 348-369 [biography and selected bibliography]; Berthold Riese, *Indianische Handschriften und Berliner Forscher* (Berlin: 1988), pp. 43-45 and Abb. 30.

Berthold Riese

Seligman, Brenda Z. (née Brenda Z. Salaman). Anthropologist. Born in London (England) 1882, died in London (England) 2 January 1965. Born into the well-to-do Salaman family, Seligman initially intended to become a physician, like her older brother, and attended a premedical course at Bedford College. She quit in 1905 to marry C.G. SELIGMAN, one of her brother's friends and an established physician and pioneering anthropologist.

With her husband, Seligman went to Ceylon (modern Sri Lanka) to study the Vedda in 1906 and 1907. At first merely a research assistant to her husband, Seligman quickly became intrigued with the variety of lifeways seen in Ceylon and was informally trained as an ethnologist while in the field. Her research specializations were kinship and descent as well as marriage and the family areas that would not have been as accessible to a male researcher working alone.

Seligman accompanied her husband on all his future fieldwork, which included three long periods spent in the Sudan. She acted both as hostess and intellectual preceptor to generations of anthropologists and colonial administrators at the Seligman home in Toot Baldon, Oxfordshire, which was recognized as one of the chief anthropological gathering places. After her husband's death in 1940, Seligman turned the house into a receiving center for children sent out from London into the countryside in flight from German air attacks on the city.

Though her husband was professor of anthropology at the University of London and she was his collaborator in both research and writing, Seligman never held an academic post. She was elected a fellow of the Royal Anthropological Institute in 1923 and subsequently served as vice-president of the organization; in 1963 she was the first person to receive the Institute's Patron's Medal, in large part due to her unpublicized philanthropy.

In 1959 Seligman was elected president of the Association of Social Anthropologists, a clear indication of the respect in which she was held by the anthropologists of the United Kingdom.

Seligman and her husband had acquired a world-famous collection of Asian art, including bronzes, jades, sculptures, weapons and ceramics. At her husband's death, Seligman donated the latter two categories to the British Museum; the remainder she willed to the Museum as well, with the proviso that the objects first be temporarily lent to the U.K. Arts Council for display in many locations throughout Europe.

MAJOR WORKS: (with C.G. Seligman) *The Veddas* (Cambridge: 1911); (with C.G. Seligman) "The Kababish, a Sudan Arab tribe," *Harvard African Studies*, vol. 2 (1918), pp. 105-186; "Bilateral descent and the formation of marriage classes," *Journal of the Royal Anthropological Institute*, vol. 57 (1927), pp. 349-375; "Asymmetry in descent, with special reference to Pentecost," *Journal of the Royal Anthropological Institute*, vol. 58 (1928), pp. 533-558; (with C.G. Seligman) "The Bari," *Journal of the Royal Anthropological Institute*, vol. 58 (1928), pp. 409-479; "Incest and descent: their influence on social organization," *Journal of the Royal Anthropological Institute*, vol. 59 (1929), pp.

231-272; (with C.G. Seligman) *Pagan Tribes of the Nilotic Sudan* (London: 1932); "The problem of incest and exogamy: a restatement," *American Anthropologist*, vol. 52 (1950), pp. 305-316.

SOURCES: Meyer Fortes, "Brenda Zara Seligman, 1882-1965: a memoir," *Man*, vol. 65 (1965), pp. 177-181; "Mrs. Brenda Seligman," *The Times* [London] (6 January 1965), p. 13; Basil Gray, "Mrs. Brenda Seligman," *The Times* [London] (8 January 1965), p. 13; "Brenda Seligman," *Oriental Art*, vol. 11 (1965), p. 189.

David Lonergan

Seligman, C.G. (Charles Gabriel). Physician, anthropologist. Born in

London (England) 24 December 1873, died in Oxford (England) 19 September 1940. Seligman studied medicine at St. Thomas' Hospital in London, taking his M.D. in 1896. His early researches were in pathology, an area in which he maintained an interest for many years. In 1897 he was a staff physician of the hospital, but the following year a growing interest in tropical diseases led him to join the Cambridge-sponsored anthropological expedition to Torres Straits, under the leadership of A.C. HADDON. Seligman was not initially encouraged to accompany the expedition, but in the end was permitted to go at his own expense.

While in Torres Straits region, Seligman was influenced by the investigations of Haddon, W.H.R. RIVERS and the other members of the expedition. He added anthropometric and ethnographic research to his medical studies but was not a very important contributor to the Haddon-dominated six-volume *Report* series issued by Cambridge over many years.

Seligman returned to St. Thomas' Hospital in 1899, to continue his research in pathology. By 1904 he had obtained funding from a wealthy American, Major Cooke Daniels, to organize and lead an anthropological expedition to coastal New Guinea. This was the turning point in Seligman's career; after 1904 anthropology, rather than medicine, was the dominant intellectual focus of his life. The periods of research spent in Torres Straits and New Guinea gave rise to Seligman's first major publication, *The Melanesians of British New Guinea*, a pioneering effort at classification of peoples by geographic, linguistic, cultural and physical evidence.

In 1905 Seligman married Brenda Z. Salaman (see BRENDA Z. SELIGMAN), who was to be his research partner for all subsequent fieldwork. In 1906 the Seligmans were invited to study the Vedda of Ceylon (now known as Sri Lanka); their later periods of fieldwork were spent in the Sudan, during 1909-1910, 1911-1912 and 1921-1922.

Seligman was offered a readership in anthropology at the University of London and in 1913 was given the professorship there. He was honored with election to the Royal College of Physicians in 1911, the Royal Society in 1919 and the presidency of the Royal Anthropological Institute from 1923 to 1925. He was awarded the two most prestigious awards of the R.A.I., the Rivers and Huxley medals, in 1925 and 1932, respectively.

Among Seligman's students at the University of London were BRONISLAW MALINOWSKI, ISAAC SCHAPERA, S.F. NADEL, E.E. EVANS-PRITCHARD, MEYER FORTES, and RAYMOND FIRTH. Seligman's protégés were renowned for their achievements as ethnographers, and Seligman himself was more concerned with ethnographic accuracy and detail than with theoretical questions. However, much of his work was of a peripatetic survey sort, conducted through interpreters or in pidgin dialects. He also obtained a good deal of information from experienced missionaries and colonial administrators but was skeptical of the biased interpretations that sometimes accompanied their observations. Seligman's work had the effect of providing a basis for later, more impressively trained fieldworkers (often his own students) whose research went beyond his, sometimes to produce anthropological classics.

MAJOR WORKS: *The Melanesians of British New Guinea* (Cambridge: 1910); (with Brenda Z. Seligman) *The Veddas* (Cambridge: 1911); "Anthropology and psychology: a study of some points of contact," *Journal of the Royal Anthropological Institute*, vol. 54 (1924), pp. 13-46; "The unconscious in relation to anthropology," *British Journal of Psychology*, vol. 18 (1928), pp. 373-387; *Races of Africa* (Oxford: 1930); (with Brenda Z. Seligman) *Pagan Tribes of the Nilotic Sudan* (London: 1932); *Egypt and Negro Africa: a Study in Divine Kingship* (London: 1934).

SOURCES: Melville J. Herskovits, "Charles Gabriel Seligman," *American Anthropologist*, vol. 43 (1941), pp. 159-162; Charles S. Myers, "Seligman, Charles Gabriel" in: *Dictionary of National Biography*, 5th supplement (London: 1949), p. 802; Meyer Fortes, "Seligman, C.G." in: David L. Sills (editor), *International Encyclopedia of the Social Sciences* (New York: 1968-1979), vol. 14, pp. 159-162; Raymond Firth, "Seligman's contributions to Oceanic anthropology," *Oceania*, vol. 45 (1975), pp. 272-282.

David Lonergan

Şenyürek, S. Muzaffer. Paleoanthropologist. Born in İzmir (Turkey) 15 November 1915, died in Ankara (Turkey) 23 September 1961. Şenyürek received his degree from Harvard University. After his return to Turkey in 1942, he speedily went through the academic ranks to become an "Ordinarius Professor" in 1958, the second and last anthropologist to achieve this rank in Turkey, the pioneer being ŞEVKET AZİZ KANSU. Şenyürek's life ended at the age of forty-six in a plane crash that occurred while he was returning from an excavation.

Şenyürek spent his life as an untiring researcher and teacher of human paleontology and primatology at the Anthropological Institute at the Faculty of Languages, History and Geography in Ankara. He founded the Chair of Paleoanthropology and served a term as Dean of this institution. He was internationally acclaimed as an authority in his field, with his cranial equilibrium index, his revolutionary views on taurodontism, and his claim that the *Australopithecus*, *Plesianthropus* and *Paranthropus* found in South Africa were, in fact, not apes but hominids. Another specialization was the physical appearance of early Anatolians, their life span, the pathology of their skeletons, and the relationship of their age to the erosion of their teeth. His identification as Neanderthal of the teeth found in Karain (Antalya, Turkey) by İSMAİL KILIÇ KÖKTEN as well as the fossil man in Tangier was of great significance. He also attempted to develop a map of the regions likely to have been inhabited by anthropoid apes and prehistoric man in Anatolia, besides studying the fossil fauna found during the excavations in Anatolia, thus contributing to evolutionary paleontology and paleobiology.

MAJOR WORKS: "Cranial equilibrium index," *American Journal of Physical Anthropology*, vol. 4 (1938), pp. 23-41; "The dentition of Plesianthropus and Paranthropus," *Annals of the Transvaal Museum*, vol. 20, no. 3 (1941), pp. 203-302; "Anadolu Bakır Çağı ve Eti sekenesinin kraniyolojik tetkiki" ["A craniological study of the Hittites and Copper-Age inhabitants of Anatolia"], *Belleten*, vol. 5, no. 17-18 (1941), pp. 219-253; "A note on the duration of life of the ancient inhabitants of Anatolia," *American Journal of Physical Anthropology*, vol. 5 (1947), pp. 55-56; "Anadolu'nun eski sakinlerinde taurodontism" ["Taurodontism in the ancient inhabitants of

Anatolia"], *Belleten*, vol. 13, no. 50 (1949), pp. 215-227; "Türk Tarih Kurumu adına yapılan Karain kazısında bulunan iki fosil dişe dair kısa ön rapor" ["A preliminary report of the two fossil teeth discovered at the Karain excavation"], *Belleten*, vol. 13, no. 52 (1949), pp. 833-836; "A study of the Pontian fauna at Gökdere (Elmadağ) south-east of Ankara," *Belleten*, vol. 16, no. 64 (1952), pp. 449-492; "Order of eruption of the permanent teeth in Chalcolithic and Copper-Age inhabitants of Anatolia," *Belleten*, vol. 20, no. 77 (1956), pp. 1-28; "Hatay vilayetinin Paleolitik kültürleri" ["The Paleolithic cultures of Hatay, Turkey"], *Belleten*, vol. 22, no. 86 (1958), pp. 171-201; *A Study of the Deciduous Teeth of the Fossil Shanidar Infant: a Comparative Study of the Milk Teeth of Fossil Men* (Ankara: 1959).

SOURCES: Aydın Sayılı, "Ordinaryüs Prof. Dr. Muzaffer Şenyürek (1915-1961)," *Belleten*, vol. 26, no. 101 (1962), pp. 181-200; Aygen Erdentuğ, "A.Ü.D.T.C.F. antropoloji bibliyografyası (1935-1983)" ["Bibliography of anthropology, D.T.C.F., Ankara University (1935-1983)"], *Antropoloji*, no. 12 (1985), pp. 489-496.

Aygen Erdentuğ

Sergi, Giuseppe. Anthropologist. Born in Messina (Italy) 20 March 1841, died in Rome (Italy) 17 October 1936. Sergi came to anthropology from philosophy by way of linguistics, classical philology, pedagogy, psychology and sociology. All of his interests were influenced by evolutionist theory, and all of his work was set in a positivist scientific framework. In this intellectual journey he was quite close to the School of Criminal Anthropology, arguing for and embellishing the notions of CESARE LOMBROSO—as in the case of the presumed psychophysical inferiority of women (*Se vi sono donne di genio*). In his approach to socio-cultural problems, he and the anthropologists of criminality shared both political positions (the scientific socialism of the end of the century) and certain fields of study (the "stratification" of character, delinquency, and degeneration). Along with ENRICO MORSELLI, Sergi was among those who—starting in the 1880s—helped to introduce to Italy the work of HERBERT SPENCER, and he never stopped declaring himself a convinced disciple of Darwin.

From 1880 to 1884 Sergi held the chair in anthropology at the University of Bologna. From there he went to Rome where he taught the same subject until 1916. From 1879 to 1893 he played a role in the Società di Antropologia ed Etnologia (Society of Anthropology and Ethnology), adopting the broad and comprehensive vision assigned to the discipline by PAOLO MANTEGAZZA. In 1893, at the International Congress of Anthropology in Moscow, he presented an innovative proposal concerning human race classification based not on the cephalic index but on cranial morphology and on the polygenetic hypothesis of the origin of man. His ideas received a warm international welcome but, at the same time, immediately inspired bitter arguments in Italian anthropological circles. This led Sergi to break with the school of Mantegazza and to found (still in 1893) a new institution, the Società Romana di Antropologia (Roman Anthropological Society), of which he was president until his death.

Even though Sergi was one of the very few Italian exponents of positivist studies with humanistic (rather than medical) training, he practiced an essentially biological anthropology. He was concerned only marginally with cultural phenomena and emphasized, rather, the study of the origin and evolution of the races, above all of the Mediterranean race (but also of the Aryans and the Britons) whose history he traced, whose diffusion he delineated, and whose morphological characteristics he described, demonstrating the

Mediterranean race's anthropological closeness to the population of North Africa. The last thirty years of his life he dedicated to perfecting his classification system.

Nevertheless, Sergi's infrequent incursions into socio-cultural areas (if one can forget the biological reductionism that, even outside Italy, suggests ties to the work of Spencer) are rich with lucid and original ideas. This is the case with respect to his clear vision of anthropology (*Antropologia e scienze antropologiche*), his definition of ethnocentrism and the connection he described between racial and cultural polygenesis (*L'evoluzione umana individuale e sociale*) and, finally, his rigorous consideration of the processes of acculturation ("Differenze nei costumi dei popoli").

MAJOR WORKS: *Elementi di psicologia* (Milan: 1879) [tr.: *La psychologie physiologique* (Paris: 1888)]; *Antropologia e scienze antropologiche* (Messina: 1889); *Se vi sono donne di genio* (Turin: 1894); *Origine e diffusione della stirpe mediterranea: induzioni antropologiche* (Rome: 1895) [tr.: *The Mediterranean Race: a Study of the Origin of European peoples* (London: 1901)]; *Africa: antropologia della stirpe camitica (specie euroafricana)* (Turin: 1897); *Specie e varietà umane: saggio d'una sistematica antropologica* (Turin: 1898); *L'evoluzione umana individuale e sociale* (Turin: 1904) [tr.: *La evolución humana individual y social* [2 vols.] (Barcelona: 1905)]; "Differenze nei costumi dei popoli e loro resistenza ad un rapido cambiamento," *Rivista Italiana di Sociologia*, vol. 15 (911), pp. 1-7; *Hominidae: l'uomo secondo le origini, l'antichità, le variazioni e la distribuzione geografica: sistema naturale di classificazione* (Turin: 1911).

SOURCES: Paolo Mantegazza, "Trent'anni di storia della Società Italiana di Antropologia, Etnologia e Psicologia Comparata," *Archivio per l'Antropologia e l'Etnologia*, vol. 30 (1901), pp. 1-7; Aldobrandino Mochi, "La discriminazione delle forme craniensi ed il sistema del Sergi," *Archivio per l'Antropologia e l'Etnologia*, vol. 37 (1908), pp. 87-126; Gioacchino Sera, "L'attuale controversia su poligenismo e monogenismo in Italia," *Archivio per l'Antropologia e l'Etnologia*, vol. 39 (1910), pp. 97-108; Società Romana di Antropologia, "G. Sergi (necrologio)," *Rivista di Antropologia*, vol. 46 (1936), pp. vi-xlvii, Sandra Puccini, "Antropologia positivista e femminismo: teorie scientifiche e luoghi comuni nella cultura italiana tra '800 e '900," *Itinerari*, no. 3 (1980), pp. 217-244 and nos. 1-2 (1981), pp. 187-238; Sandra Puccini, "Evoluzionismo e positivismo nell'antropologia italiana (1869-1911)" in: Pietro Clemente [et al.], *L'antropologia italiana: un secolo di storia* (Bari: 1905), pp. 99-148; Renzo Villa, *Il deviante e i suoi segni: Lombroso e la nascita dell'antropologia criminale* (Milan: 1985).

Sandra Puccini
[Translation from Italian: CW]

Serrurier, Lindor. Ethnologist, physical anthropologist. Born in Wijk bij Duurstede (Netherlands) 1846, died in Batavia (Indonesia) 7 July 1901. Serrurier's main contributions to anthropology lie in the organizational sphere: the development of museum collections, the publication of scientific journals and the founding and support of scientific societies. He studied law at Leiden University but, after meeting J.J. Hoffmann, concentrated on the study of the Japanese language. During 1877-1878 he attended the École d'Anthropologie in Paris to study with PAUL BROCA and Paul Topinard. He edited the Japanese dictionaries of his teacher and published extensively on Japanese language, culture and history as well as Indonesian cultures. His major ethnological work was a monograph on *Wayang purwa*, in essence a comparative study of shadow-plays in Southeast Asia, which went through many editions.

From 1881 to 1896 he directed the National Museum of Anthropology in Leiden, eventually resigning because the government refused to increase its funding. With HERMAN F.C. TEN KATE he founded the short-lived physical anthropology periodical *Notices an-*

thropologiques in 1884. He also took the initiative in founding the journal *Internationales Archiv für Ethnographie* in 1888. Two years later he was the main force behind the founding of the interdisciplinary Society for the Propagation of Natural Research in the Dutch Colonies, which, in time, sent out several scientific expeditions to Indonesia. In this capacity he wrote a manual for travelers with directives for gathering scientific data in tropical areas, notably in the fields of physical anthropology and ethnology (*De pionier*). During his long stay in Indonesia he invigorated the Batavian Society of Arts and Sciences and promoted archaeological research on Java. He also pioneered the idea of "culture areas" in the Netherlands.

> MAJOR WORKS: (with Johann Joseph Hoffman) *Japansch-Nederlandsch woordenboek* [3 vols.] (Leiden: 1881-1892) [tr.: *Japanese-English Dictionary* (London: 1892)]; (editor) *Notices anthropologiques* [3 vols.] (Leiden, 1884-1886); *De pionier: handleiding voor verzamelen en waarnemen in tropische gewesten* (Leiden: 1891); *Museum of pakhuis* (Leiden: 1893); *De Wajang poerwa, eene ethnologische studie* (Leiden: 1896).

> SOURCES: H.F.C. ten Kate, *Lindor Serrurier herdacht* (Tōkyō: 1902); A.A.W. Hubrecht "In memoriam, Mr. L. Serrurier," *De Gids*, vol. 65, no. 3 (1901), pp. 539-547.

Pieter Hovens

Setzler, Frank M. Archaeologist, museum curator and administrator. Born in Fremont (Ohio) 21 September 1902, died in Culver (Indiana) 13 February 1975. As a student at Ohio State University, Setzler carried out archaeological work under Henry C. Shetrone, but transferred and received his bachelor's degree from the University of Chicago in 1928. He continued there as a graduate student until 1930. He was awarded an Sc.D. degree by Indiana University in 1971.

During 1928-1930 Setzler was the state archaeologist of Indiana. In 1930 he was appointed an assistant curator of archaeology in the Smithsonian Institution's U.S. National Museum. He became head curator of the Department of Anthropology in 1937 and continued there until 1961. He served as Smithsonian Institution liaison officer for the Civil Works Administration and as consultant to the Work Projects Administration, and he directed eleven projects in the southeastern states and California. After retiring from the Smithsonian, he served in 1961 as director of the Southeast Museum on North American Indians in Marathon (Florida).

As a fieldworker, Setzler was primarily interested in Hopewellian mounds in the Midwest and Southeast. He worked at sites at Marksville, Louisiana; Proctorville, Ohio; Cumberland Island, Florida; and the Kincaid site in Illinois; as well as at other sites in Maryland, West Virginia and Virginia. From 1931 to 1933, working in the Big Bend area of Texas, he was involved in attempting to find links between Mexican Indian cultures and those of the Mississippi Valley. In addition, he carried out archaeological reconnaissance along the Yampa and Green Rivers in Colorado and Utah and worked at a historical site at Marlborough Town in Virginia. In the 1940s, he was deputy leader of an expedition to Arnhem Land in Australia where he carried on archaeological and ethnological work.

Along with JULIAN H. STEWARD, Setzler was one of the anthropologists who during the 1930s sought to direct the field of archaeology toward a broad understanding of cultures and of culture change. Setzler's publications themselves, however, have been criticized as being more historically than anthropologically oriented and as consisting largely of trait lists (Brose).

MAJOR WORKS: "The archeology of the Whitewater Valley," *Indiana History Bulletin*, vol. 7 (1930), pp. 353-549; "The archaeology of Randolph County and Fudge Mound," *Indiana History Bulletin*, vol. 9 (1931), pp. 1-52; (with Julian H. Steward) "Function and configuration in archaeology," *American Antiquity*, vol. 4 (1938), pp. 4-10; "Archaeological perspectives in the Northern Mississippi Valley" in: Smithsonian Institution, *Essays in Historical Anthropology of North America* (Washington: 1940) (= *Smithsonian Miscellaneous Collections*, vol. 100), pp. 253-290; (with Jesse D. Jennings) *Peachtree Mound and Village Site, Cherokee County, North Carolina* (Washington: 1941) (= *Bureau of American Ethnology Bulletin*, no. 131).

SOURCES: Davis S. Brose, "The Northeastern United States" in: James E. Fitting, *The Development of American Archaeology* (University Park, Penn.: 1973), pp. 84-115; Gordon R. Willey and Jeremy A. Sabloff, *A History of American Archaeology* (London: 1974); Jean R. Hailey, "Anthropologist Frank M. Setzler dies," *Washington Post* (20 February 1975), p. E6; James H. Kellar, "Frank M. Setzler, 1902-1975," *Indiana Archaeological Bulletin*, vol. 1 (1975), p. 62; Edwin Austin Lyon II, *New Deal Archaeology in the Southeast: WPA, TVA, NPS, 1934-1943* [unpublished Ph.D. dissertation, Louisiana State University] (Baton Rouge: 1982); Setzler papers and vertical file in the Smithsonian Institution National Anthropological Archives.

James R. Glenn

Seweryn, Tadeusz. Ethnographer, museologist, regionalist. Born in Żabno, Galicia (Austria-Hungary, now in Poland) 21 August 1894, died in Kraków (Poland) 17 January 1975. In 1913 Seweryn began studies simultaneously at Jagiellonian University and the Kraków Academy of Fine Arts. In 1930 he obtained his doctorate at Jagiellonian University. In 1937 he was appointed assistant professor at the University of Poznań and in 1954 he became a full professor. Between 1937 and 1965 he directed the Muzeum Etnograficzne (Ethnographic Museum) in Kraków.

An expert in folk art, and particularly in painting and sculpture, Seweryn conducted a great deal of fieldwork in Mazovia, the region around Kraków, in Kaszubia, and in the Hucul area of the Eastern Carpathian Mountains. In researching folk art, Seweryn did not stop at pure description but tried to establish the genesis of various forms of folk creativity and techniques. After 1945 he expanded his interests to include the topics of Old Polish graphic arts and folk hunting.

MAJOR WORKS: *O Chrystusie frasobliwym: figury - legendy -świątkarze* [*On the Care-worn Christ. Figures, Legends and Chapel Carvings*] (Kraków: 1926); *Krakowskie skrzynie malowane* [*Krakovian Painted Boxes*] (Kraków: 1928); *Pokucka majolika kudowa* [*Folk-Forged Majolica*] (Kraków: 1929); *Polskie malarstwo ludowe* [*Polish Folk Painting*] (Kraków: 1937); *Staropolska grafika ludowa* [*Old Polish Folk Graphic Arts*] (Warsaw: 1956); *Kapliczki i krzyże przydrożne w Polsce* [*Chapels and Roadside Crosses in Poland*] (Warsaw: 1958); "Łowieckie sposoby wabienia" ["Hunting-lure methods"], *Lud*, vol. 45 (1958-1959), pp. 223-262; *Rola drzeworytu ludowego w polskiej kulturze ludowej* [*The Role of Folk Woodcarving in Polish Folk Culture*] (Kraków: 1970).

SOURCE: Bolesław Łopuszański, "Tadeusz Seweryn (1894-1975)," *Lud*, vol. 60 (1976), pp. 355-363.

Maria Niewiadomska and Iwona Grzelakowska
[*Translation from Polish: Joel Janicki*]

Shapiro, Harry Lionel. Physical anthropologist, human biologist, forensic anthropologist. Born in Boston (Massachusetts) 19 March 1902, died in New York (New York) 7 January 1990. A student of E.A. HOOTON, Shapiro earned his Ph.D. in physical anthropology at Harvard University in 1926. His thesis centered on genetic studies of the Norfolk Island descendants of the H.M.S. Bounty mutineers and set the pattern for his career studying the effects of population mixture.

In 1926 Shapiro became an assistant curator in the Department of Anthropology at the American Museum of Natural History. During 1934-1935 he conducted fieldwork on the genetics of the Pitcairn Islanders, where nine Bounty mutineers had settled with Tahitian wives. The results were published in 1936 in *The Heritage of the Bounty.* His study of Japanese migrants to Hawaii, published in 1939 as *Migration and Environment,* was an early and influential study of selective biological factors in human migration and the effects of new environments on migrants. Shapiro conducted field research in many parts of the world on the biology of both living and dead populations, and this resulted in the publication of 138 books and articles.

Shapiro was chairman and curator of the anthropology department at the American Museum from 1942 to 1970, when he retired. In 1946 he was a consultant to the American Graves Registration Command and devised a method for identifying unknown war dead. At the museum, Shapiro was the curator for the Hall of the Biology of Man (1960-1983). At the 1964 New York World's Fair, he curated the "Triumph of Man" exhibition.

He held professorships at Columbia University, the University of Pittsburgh, Lehman College, and the University of Hawaii. Shapiro's honors included election to the National Academy of Sciences (1949), election to the American Academy of Arts and Sciences (1964), and the Theodore Roosevelt Distinguished Service Medal (1964). Among the offices he held were Chairman of the anthropology section of the New York Academy of Sciences (1939), Vice-President of the American Association of Physical Anthropology (1941-1942), President of the American Ethnological Society (1942-1943), President of the American Anthropological Association (1948) and President of the American Eugenics Society (1955-1962).

Shapiro's association with FRANZ WEIDENREICH inevitably involved him in unsuccessful attempts to recover the *Homo erectus* fossils discovered at Zhoukoudian in China and lost during World War II. His experiences regarding the affair were published in 1974 in *Peking Man.*

After his retirement from the American Museum in 1970, Shapiro was a curator emeritus in the Department of Anthropology.

MAJOR WORKS: *The Heritage of the Bounty: the Story of Pitcairn Island through Six Generations* (New York: 1936); *Migration and Environment* (New York: 1939); *Race Mixture* (Paris: 1953); (editor) *Man, Culture and Society* (New York: 1956); *Aspects of Culture* (New Brunswick: 1956); *The Jewish People: a Biological History* (Paris: 1960); *Peking Man* (New York: 1975).

SOURCES: Harry L. Shapiro, "The role of the American Museum of Natural History in 20th-century paleoanthropology" in: Eric Delson (editor), *Ancestors: the Hard Evidence* (New York: 1985), pp. 6-8; Paul F. Beelitz, "The 'Ancestors' Project," *Curator,* vol. 29, no. 1 (1986), pp. 46-47.

Paul F. Beelitz

Sharp, Lauriston. Anthropologist. Born in Madison (Wisconsin) 24 March 1907. Lauriston Sharp is best known for his research among the Yir Yoront of Cape York Peninsula, Australia, carried out in the 1930s, and his extensive studies in Thailand in the years after World War II. Throughout his long career two central themes informed his teaching and research. One was the insistence that the peoples ordinarily studied by anthropologists be viewed always in the larger cultural context of the time and region in which they live. The other was that social scientists have a responsibility to put to practical use the results of their research on changing cultural behavior or to make them available to those who will.

His father, Frank Chapman Sharp, was a professor of philosophy at the University of Wisconsin, where Sharp took his B.A. in that discipline in 1929. This humanistic training had a profound impact on his teaching and writing. Following his graduation, Sharp stayed on at Wisconsin as Freshman Dean during 1929-1930, the second year of RALPH LINTON's tenure there. Sharp attended Linton's lectures and early in 1930 signed on with an expedition to North Africa organized by the Logan Museum, Beloit College, whose members included SOL TAX and John P. Gillin. Hoping to undertake research in Southeast Asia, then virtually unknown to anthropology, on the advice of ROBERT H. LOWIE, Sharp went to study with ROBERT VON HEINE-GELDERN at the University of Vienna, earning the Certificate in Anthropology in 1931. In the fall of that year he entered Harvard University's doctoral program, studying under ROLAND B. DIXON, ALFRED M. TOZZER and E.A. HOOTON. Sharp joined the faculty of Cornell University in 1936 and in the following year received his Ph.D. from Harvard University. With the exception of sixteen months during 1945-1946, with the Division of Southeast Asian Affairs of the Department of State, he taught at Cornell until his retirement in 1973. He holds the title of Goldwin Smith Professor of Anthropology and Asian Studies emeritus.

During his tenure at Cornell, Sharp was instrumental in assembling a group of anthropologists who shared his view that the scholar ought to contribute knowledge and skills to the development of public policy. They were ALLAN R. HOLMBERG, MORRIS E. OPLER, John Adair, and Alexander H. Leighton. The department they established quickly became a center for research in the anthropology of cultural change or development. Field stations were established in Thailand, Peru, India and the Canadian Maritimes and on the Navajo Reservation. The research carried out by many of the department's doctoral candidates during this period under the aegis of the Cornell University Studies in Culture and Applied Science focused on the impact of the forces of modernization on indigenous societies. Sharp also played a major role in setting up both Cornell's Southeast Asia Program and Center for International Studies. The Southeast Asia Program remains today the premier center in the United States for research and study of that area for scholars and students from all over the world. In 1989, in recognition of his manifold contributions, Sharp was presented the Bronislaw Malinowski Award of the Society for Applied Anthropology.

The long series of papers based on his Australian research, particularly those on totemism ("The social organization of the Yir-Yoront Tribe," "Ritual life and economics of the Yir-Yoront," *Tribes and Totemism in North-east Australia*) are classics of the period, but he is best known for the repeatedly reprinted "Steel axes for Stone Age Australians," a paper that offers a paradigmatic case of the socio-cultural and especially ideological ramifications of the introduction of new technology. Almost as well known and as frequently reprinted are two other papers, "People without politics" and "Cultural continuities and discontinuities in Southeast Asia," the latter his Presidential Address to the Association for Asian Studies. The results of Sharp's own research in Thailand are reported in two books (*Siamese Rice Village* and *Bang Chan*), the second written in collaboration with Lucien M. Hanks, Jr. Through these publications on the Thai rice village of Bang Chan and his many papers on Thai society and culture, Sharp left an indelible imprint on a field of study that he himself largely helped define.

MAJOR WORKS: "The social organization of the Yir-Yoront Tribe, Cape York Peninsula" *Oceania*, vol. 4 (1934), pp. 404-431; "Ritual life and economics of the Yir-Yoront of Cape York Peninsula" *Oceania*, vol. 5 (1934), pp. 19-42; "Semi-moieties in North-western Queensland" *Oceania*, vol. 6 (1935), pp. 158-174; *Tribes and Totemism in North-east Australia* (Sydney: 1939); "Notes on Northeast Australian totemism" in: Carleton S. Coon and James M. Andrews, IV (editors), *Studies in the Anthropology of Oceania and Asia* (Cambridge, Mass.: 1943) (= *Papers of the Peabody Museum of American Archaeology and Ethnology, Harvard University*, vol. 20), pp. 66-71; "Steel axes for Stone Age Australians" in: Edward H. Spicer (editor), *Human Problems in Technological Change* (New York: 1952), pp. 69-90; "People without politics" in: Verne F. Ray (editor), *Systems of Political Control and Bureaucracy in Human Societies* (Seattle: 1958) (= *Proceedings of the 1958 Annual Spring Meeting of the American Ethnological Society*), pp. 1-8; "Cultural continuities and discontinuities in Southeast Asia," *Journal of Asian Studies*, vol. 22 (1962), pp. 3-11; (with Hazel M. Hauck, Kamol Janlekha and Robert B. Textor) *Siamese Rice Village: a Preliminary Study of Bang Chan: 1948-1949* (Bangkok: 1953); (with Lucien M. Hanks) *Bang Chan: Social History of a Rural Community in Thailand* (Ithaca: 1978); "The Far and the Near: can we get here from there?" *Human Organization* (forthcoming).

SOURCES: Robert J. Smith (editor), *Social Organization and the Applications of Anthropology* (Ithaca: 1974); G. William Skinner and A. Thomas Kirsch (editors), *Change and Persistence in Thai Society* (Ithaca: 1975); Stanley J. O'Connor, "Lauriston Sharp and Southeast Asian Studies at Cornell," *Arts and Sciences Newsletter, Cornell University*, vol. 3 (fall 1981), pp. 4 and 6.

Robert J. Smith

Shepard, Anna Osler. Archaeologist, ceramic technologist, petrographer. Born in Merchantville (New Jersey) 9 May 1903, died in Boulder (Colorado) 19 July 1973. Shepard, more than any other person, pioneered the application of the techniques of optical petrography to the study of prehistoric pottery. Her classic study of Pecos and Rio Grande pottery demonstrated the value of petrographic analysis in archaeology and showed that much of the utilitarian pottery found at Pecos had been made elsewhere. She made technological analyses of prehistoric pottery from the Southwest and Mesoamerica, carried out studies of modern Indian pottery techniques in both areas, clarified the principles of symmetry in design analysis, and reconstructed the technology used to produce the unique Plumbate ware of Guatemala. She communicated her ideas about the value of technological analyses of potsherds most successfully through her enduring and oft-reprinted book, *Ceramics for the Archaeologist.*

MAJOR WORKS: "The technology of Pecos pottery" in: A.V. Kidder and A.O. Shepard, *The Pottery of Pecos* (New Haven: 1936), vol. 2, pp. 389-587; *Rio Grande Glaze Paint Ware: a Study Illustrating the Place of Ceramic Technological Analysis in Archaeological Research* (Washington: 1942) (= *Contributions to American Anthropology and History*, vol. 7, no. 39; *Carnegie Institution of Washington, Publication*, no. 528); *Plumbate: a Mesoamerican Tradeware* (Washington: 1948) (= *Carnegie Institution of Washington, Publication*, no. 473); *The Symmetry of Abstract Design with Special Reference to Ceramic Decoration* (Washington: 1948) (= *Contributions to American Archaeology and History*, vol. 9, no. 47; = *Carnegie Institution of Washington, Publication*, no.

574); *Ceramics for the Archaeologist* (Washington: 1956; reprinted numerous times, with a new foreword after 1968) (= *Carnegie Institution of Washington, Publication*, no. 609).

SOURCES: Elizabeth Ann Morris, "Anna O. Shepard, 1903-1973," *American Antiquity*, vol. 39 (1974), pp. 448-451; Raymond H. Thompson, "Shepard, Kidder, and Carnegie" in: R.L. Bishop and F.W. Lange (editors), *Ceramic Analysis and Social Inference: the Legacy of Anna O. Shepard* (Boulder: in press).

Raymond H. Thompson

Sheppard, Mubin (Malayan title: Tan Sri Dato' Haji). Civil servant, author, ethnographer, museum director. Born in Wouldham, Kent (England) 21 June 1905, now living in Malaysia. Although Sheppard was born in England, his parents were of Anglo-Irish heritage and Sheppard spent much of his childhood and youth in southern Ireland. He was educated at Marlborough College and at Magdalene College, Cambridge University (M.A., Honours in History). He entered the competitive civil service examination in 1927 and in January 1928 became a cadet in the Malayan Civil Service, serving in a variety of government posts prior to the Japanese occupation of Malaya in February 1942. During the war years (1942-1945) he was interned in Singapore.

In March 1946 Sheppard was named as the first Director of Public Relations of the Federation of Malaya. From 1950 to 1956 he was British Adviser in Kelantan and Negeri Sembilan. Sheppard's longstanding ties to Malaya led to his adoption of Malayan citizenship following the independence of the Federation in 1957. Sheppard founded the National Archives of Malaya (1959) and, while serving as Director of Museums (1960-1963), established the National Museum in Kuala Lumpur.

Since retirement from the civil service (1964), Sheppard has been active in voluntary service, occupying key positions in the Ex-Services Association of Malaysia, the Muslim Welfare Organisation of Malaysia, the Malaysian Branch of the Royal Asiatic Society and the Heritage of Malaysia Trust.

Sheppard's writings on Malay traditional culture, folklore, crafts and history have been disseminated in numerous publications. A major study of Malay traditional arts, *Taman Indera: a Royal Pleasure Ground*, was published in 1972. A 1978 monograph, *Living Crafts of Malaysia*, combines biographical and artistic information concerning ten folk artists of Malaysia. Sheppard has contributed to the development of Malaysian studies as editor of the *Journal of the Malaysian Branch, Royal Asiatic Society*. A detailed account of Sheppard's years of government service is presented in his *Taman Budiman: Memoirs of an Unorthodox Civil Servant*. Sheppard's awards and honors include: the Hon. D.Litt. (University Sains Malaysia, Penang, 1984); Tun Razak Award (1984); C.M.G. and M.B.E. (British Military); P.S.M. (title: Tan Sri, Malaysian, 1969); D.J.P.D. and D.S.N.S. (Negeri Sembilan); and D.P.M.S. (Selangor).

MAJOR WORKS: *The Magic Kite and Other Ma'yong Stories* (Singapore: 1960); *Taman Indera: a Royal Pleasure Ground: Malay Decorative Arts and Pastimes* (Kuala Lumpur: 1972); *Living Crafts of Malaysia* (Singapore: 1978); *Taman Budiman: Memoirs of an Unorthodox Civil Servant* (Kuala Lumpur: 1979); *Tunku: a Pictorial Biography* [2 vols.] (Petaling Jaya: 1984-1987).

Dato' M. Noordin Keling

Shirokogorov, S.M. (Sergeĭ Mikhaĭlovich). Ethnographer, scholar of religion, physical anthropologist, linguist. Born in Suzdal' (Russia) 2 July 1887, died in Beijing (China) 19 October 1939. Shirokogorov worked in Leningrad in the Muzeĭ antropologii i ètnografii (Museum of Anthropology and Ethnography) (1911-1917); in Vladivostok University (1918-1922); and in China (1922-1939), first in Shanghai, afterward primarily in Beijing.

Shirokogorov was the preeminent researcher of the ethnography of the Tungus-Manchurian peoples. In the course of several expeditions he gathered unique scientific material on the language, folklore, ethnography and physical anthropology of the Oroches, Manchurians, Dakhur and others. He also is credited with the first scientific definition of the concept of "ethnicity" and with the first attempt to outline typological indications of ethnicity. According to Shirokogorov, "an *ethnos* is a group of people speaking one language, acknowledging a common origin and possessing a complete set of customs and a way of life which protects and sanctifies traditions and sets the group apart from other similar groups. That is ethnographic unity—the object of the science of ethnography." His fundamental research, devoted to the analysis of the social organization of the Tungus and Manchurians and Tungus-Manchurian shamanism, is still important for scholarship.

MAJOR WORKS: "Zadachi antropologii v Sibiri," *Sbornik Muzeĭa antropologii i ètnografii,* vol. 3 (Petrograd: 1916), pp. 15-48; "Opyt issledovaniĭa osnov shamanstva y tungusov," *Uchenye zapiski istoriko-filologicheskogo fakul'teta vo Vladivostoke,* vol. 1, no. 1 (1919), pp. 47-168 [tr.: "Versuch einer Erforschung der Grundlagen des Schamentums bei den Tungusen," *Baessler-Archiv: Beiträge zur Völkerkunde,* vol. 18 (1935), pp. 41-96]; *Ètnos: issledovanie osnovnykh prinĭsipov izmeneniĭa ètnicheskikh i ètnograficheskikh ĭavleniĭ* (Vladivostok: 1922) (= *Izvestiĭa Vostochnogo fakul'teta Gosudarstvennogo dal'nevostochnogo universiteta,* vol. 67) [also reprinted separately, Shanghai: 1923]; "Ethnological investigations in Siberia, Mongolia and Northern China," *The China Journal* [Shanghai], no. 5 (1923), pp. 513-522; no. 6 (1923), pp. 611-621; "Social organization of the Manchus: a study of the Manchu clan organization," *Journal of the North China Branch of the Royal Asiatic Society* [Shanghai], extra vol. 6 (1924); *Social Organization of the Northern Tungus, with Introductory Chapters Concerning Geographical Distribution and History of These Groups* (Shanghai: 1929); *Psychomental Complex of the Tungus* (London: 1935); *A Tungus Dictionary: Tungus-Russian and Russian-Tungus* (Tōkyō: 1944-1954).

SOURCES: I.I. Serebrennikov, "In memoriam (Professor S.M. Shirokogoroff)," *The China Journal,* vol. 22, no. 5 (May 1940), pp. 205-209; A.M. Reshetov, "S.M. Shirokogorov, ego zhizn' i trudy (k 100-letiĭu so dnĭa rozhdeniĭa)" in: O.V. Lysenko (editor), *Polevye issledovaniĭa Gosudarstvennogo Muzeĭa ètnografii narodov SSSR 1985-1987 gg.* (Leningrad: 1989), pp. 25-27.

A.M. Reshetov
[Translation from Russian: Thomas L. Mann]

Shternberg, Leo (Russian form of name: Lev ĬAkovlevich Shternberg). Technologist, ethnographer. Born in Zhitomir (Ukraine) 21 April (4 May) 1861, died near Leningrad (Russian S.F.S.R.) 14 August 1927. After completing university studies in Odessa, Shternberg was exiled to Sakhalin for revolutionary activities. There he became interested in the Gilyak and Ainu. He returned to Russia in 1897 where he began an association with the Museum for Anthropology and Ethnography of the Imperial (later Soviet) Academy of Sciences that lasted for the rest of his life. He inaugurated annual collecting expeditions to the peripheries of the Soviet Union, and established a Division for the Evolution and Typology of Culture in which objects from all parts of the world were grouped according to Marxist culture-historical categories. In 1915 he became Professor and Dean of the Ethnographic Faculty of the Geographical Institute, which merged with the University of Leningrad. With WALDEMAR BOGORAS he founded the Northern Faculty of the Oriental Institute of Leningrad. He was chairman of the Siberian division of the Committee for the Investigation of the Peoples of the U.S.S.R. and also of the Jewish Historico-Ethnographic Society.

His pioneering work on Gilyak phonology, kinship systems and folklore demonstrated an affinity between Gilyak and the Athabaskan languages of North America. More dubious though, in the opinion of later anthropologists, was his attempt to prove that the Ainu language and culture are Austronesian. His work on folklore extended to the history of religion (with a special focus on divine election) and combined the method of cutting and pasting pieces of diverse cosmologies exemplified by JAMES G. FRAZER with the evolutionary typologizing of LEWIS HENRY MORGAN.

MAJOR WORKS: "Die Religion der Giljaken," *Archiv für Religionswissenschaft*, vol. 8 (1905), pp. 244-274 and 456-473; "Divine election in primitive religion," *Comte-rendu de la XXIe session, Congrès international des Américanistes* (Göteborg: 1925), vol. 2, pp. 472-512; "Der Adlerkult bei den Völkern Siberiens," *Archiv für Religionswissenschaft*, vol. 28 (1930), pp. 125-153; *Sem'ia i rod u narodov Severo-vostochnoi Azii* (Leningrad: 1933); *Pervobytnaia religiia v svete etnografii* (Leningrad: 1936).

SOURCES: Chester S. Chard "Sternberg's materials on the sexual life of the Gilyak." *Anthropological Papers of the University of Alaska*, no. 10 (1961), pp. 13-24; Nina I. Gagen-Torn, *Lev Iakovlevich Shternberg* (Moscow: 1975); Eugen Kagaroff, "Leo Sternberg," *American Anthropologist*, n.s., vol. 31 (1929), pp. 568-571.

Stephen O. Murray

Siebold, Philipp Franz von. Natural historian, physician, ethnographer. Born in Würzburg (Germany) 17 February 1796, died in Munich (Germany) 18 October 1866. After studying medicine and natural history at the University of Würzburg and influenced by the scientific work of ALEXANDER VON HUMBOLDT, von Siebold was sent to Japan by the Dutch East Indian colonial government to study that country and its people in order to facilitate current and future trade. From 1823 to 1829 and again from 1859 to 1862 he lived in Japan, studying the country's geography, botany and zoology as well as all aspects of Japanese culture. He gathered data as well as specimens in all fields to bring back to the Netherlands where he intended to found a Japanese museum. He lived and worked in Deshima, Nagasaki and at the Shōgun's court at Edo. He enlisted the service of Japanese draftsmen to make drawings of scenes of everyday life and of craftsmen to build scale models of houses, temples and ships. Von Siebold energetically pursued his ethnographic, geographic and scientific investigations in spite of the numerous Tokugawa restrictions on the activities or movements of foreigners. On one occasion he was arrested by the Japanese authorities when imperial maps of Japan were found in his possession. He was eventually banished from Japan and returned to Holland. In 1837 he submitted a plan for an ethnographical museum to the Dutch king, proposing the systematic arrangement of artifacts for scientific study and public education, the objects to be displayed within their cultural context. This novel approach was based on von Siebold's insights into the structural coherence of cultural complexes. That same year the government bought his collections and a Japanese Museum was opened in Leiden, the first anthropological museum in the world. Von Siebold's advice on museum matters was repeatedly requested by later founders of ethnographical museums in Copenhagen and Paris. The Japanese Museum gradually developed into the National Museum of Ethnology by the inclusion of von Siebold's non-Japanese East Asian and North American collections as well as collections from the Dutch East Indies and other parts of the world. The Japanese collection brought together during von Siebold's second stay in East Asia was acquired by the king of Bavaria and is now in the State Museum of Ethnology in Munich.

MAJOR WORKS: *Nippon* [20 vols.] (Leiden: 1832-1858) [partial tr.: *Voyage au Japon* (Paris: 1838); *Manners and Customs of the Japanese* (New York: 1841)]; *Lettre sur l'utilité des musées ethnographiques et sur l'importance de leur création* (Paris: 1843); *Guide to the Collection of Objects Pertaining to the Sciences, Arts, Crafts and Industrial Products of Japan* (Amsterdam: 1863).

SOURCES: W. Bijleveld, *Von Siebold* (Leiden: 1932); W. Rassers, *Overzicht van de geschiedenis van het Rijksmuseum voor Volkenkunde, 1837-1937* (Leiden: 1937); *Philipp Franz von Siebold* (Leiden: 1978); W. van Gulik, "Von Siebold and his Japanese collection in Leiden" in: W. Otterspeer (editor), *Leiden Oriental Connections* (Leiden: 1989), pp. 378-391.

Pieter Hovens and Willem van Gulik

Singer, Milton B. Anthropologist, social scientist. Born in a small village about 320 kilometers southeast of Warsaw (Poland) 15 July 1912, now living in Chicago (Illinois). Singer came to the United States with his family as a child. He was naturalized a U.S. citizen at about eight years of age and grew up mostly in Detroit. He attended the University of Texas where he received a B.A. (1934) and an M.A. (1936) in psychology and philosophy. While he was at Texas, in 1935, he married a fellow student, Helen Singer, a native Texan who studied economics and wrote poetry and who has shared his work and interests since that time. He completed his Ph.D. in philosophy at the University of Chicago under the direction of the famous logical positivist Rudolf Carnap (1891-1970); his dissertation was on formal method in mathematical logic. Philosophy, and the work of Charles Sanders Peirce (1839-1914), established two of Singer's enduring concerns, philosophical and semiotic anthropology. In addition to semiotic anthropology, an analytical method largely created and defined by Singer, his major contribution lies in his interpretation of the relations between nations as a conversation of cultures with particular attention to South Asia and the United States.

While working on his doctorate, he took part in a number of seminars on social science methods with University of Chicago economists. This subspecialty led to his first faculty appointment at the University of Chicago, in 1941, teaching social sciences at the university's College during the period of Robert Maynard Hutchins' radical experiments with the undergraduate curriculum. His achievement as a teacher was recognized in 1948 when he was given the university's highly prized Quantrell Award for Excellence in Undergraduate Teaching. The integrated, interdisciplinary curriculum at Chicago expanded his knowledge of the social sciences and led to publications on culture and personality and to an acquaintance with ROBERT REDFIELD. In 1951 Singer joined Redfield as associate director of a major project on the comparison of cultures and civilizations, as a part of which he undertook fieldwork in Madras City during 1954-1955; he continued this work during 1960-1961 and 1964. A principal product of this period was an analysis of the positive role of traditional institutions and beliefs in urbanization and modernization in India, a special form of the process M.N. SRINIVAS called "Sanskritization."

Throughout his professional career Singer has been a member of the faculty of the University of Chicago. Singer's academic appointments at Chicago, after his instructorship in the social sciences in the College (1941), included the Paul Klapper chair (1952) and a professorship in the Department of Anthropology (1954).

The choice of India as an accessible example of a living civilization that clearly contrasted with the European and American traditions led Singer to attend the lectures of W. Norman Brown (1892-1975) and Stella Kramrisch (1898-) at the University of Pennsylvania as well as those of DAVID G. MANDELBAUM at the University of California at Berkeley. After his first visit to India he began the work that led to the establishment at Chicago of a program in Southern Asian studies, which Singer directed throughout its formative period. Beginning about 1970, responding to renewed student interest, he turned his attention to American culture and to new fieldwork in W. LLOYD WARNER's "Yankee City." He devised a new conception of cultural symbolism based on the semiotics of Peirce and used it to address the issue of identities of Americans and Indians.

In 1979 Singer became Professor Emeritus at Chicago. In the following years, while continuing to develop semiotic analysis, Singer also initiated a broadly interdisciplinary project on culture and nuclear policy that addressed issues of the most far-reaching consequences for the future of humanity. This project was co-sponsored during 1987-1990 by the University's Center for International Studies and the Council for Advanced Studies on Peace and International Cooperation as well as by the not-for-profit Center for Psychosocial Studies, for which Singer has been research consultant since 1979.

Singer was elected a fellow of the American Academy of Arts and Sciences in 1972. He was chosen as the Distinguished Lecturer of the American Anthropological Association in 1978. And he received the Distinguished Scholar Award of the Association for Asian Studies in 1984.

MAJOR WORKS: (with Gerhart Piers) *Shame and Guilt: a Psychoanalytical and a Cultural Study* (New York: 1953); (with Robert Redfield) "The cultural role of cities," *Economic Development and Cultural Change*, vol. 3 (1954), pp. 53-72; (editor) *Traditional India: Structure and Change* (Philadelphia: 1959); (editor) *Krishna: Myths, Rites and Attitudes* (Honolulu: 1966); (co-editor with Bernard S. Cohn) *Structure and Change in the Indian Society* (Chicago: 1968); "The concept of culture" in: David L. Sills (editor), *International Encyclopedia of the Social Sciences* (New York: 1968-1979), vol. 3, pp. 527-543; *When a Great Tradition Modernizes: an Anthropological Approach to Indian Civilization* (New York: 1972; Chicago: 1980); (editor) *Entrepreneurship and Modernization of Occupational Cultures in South Asia* (Durham, N.C.: 1973); "A neglected source of structuralism: Radcliffe-Brown, Russell and Whitehead," *Semiotica*, vol. 48 (1984), pp. 11-96; *Man's Glassy Essence: Explorations in Semiotic Anthropology* (Bloomington: 1984); (editor) *Nuclear Policy, Culture and History* (Chicago: 1988); "Pronouns, persons and the semiotic self" in: Benjamin Lee and Greg Urban (editors), *Semiotics, Self, and Society* (Berlin: 1989), pp. 229-296; *Semiotics of Cities, Selves and Cultures: Explorations in Semiotic Anthropology* (Berlin: 1991).

SOURCES: Richard H. Davis, *South Asia at Chicago: a History* (Chicago: 1985); Murray J. Leaf, "Singer, Kant, and the semiotic self" in: Benjamin Lee and Greg Urban (editors), *Semiotics, Self, and Society* (Berlin: 1989), pp. 171-192 [and other material in this Festschrift volume including Singer's reply to Leaf]; Thomas A. Sebeok, "Semiotics in the United States" in: Thomas A. Sebeok and Jean Umiker-Sebeok (editors), *The Semiotic Web, 1989* (Berlin: 1990), pp. 320-322; Milton B. Singer, "Robert Redfield's development of a social anthropology of civilizations" in: John V. Murra (editor), *American Anthropology: the Early Years* (St. Paul: 1976) (= *1974 Proceedings of the American Ethnological Society*), pp. 187-260.

Ralph W. Nicholas

Škaloud, Ferdinand. Stomatologist, physical anthropologist. Born in Jičín, Bohemia (Austria-Hungary) 29 October 1903, died in Prague (Czechoslovakia) 18 October 1984. Škaloud received his Ph.D. at the Faculty of Natural Sciences at Charles University in 1926 and his M.D. at the Faculty of Medicine in 1932. The most important of Škaloud's works are related to the stomatologic development of children, with an anthropologic orientation as evidenced in several of his papers on such subjects (stomatology is the study of the mouth). Also important are his works on the significance of vitamin A for the cutting through and condition of teeth, which was based on a rich experimental material.

During the 1930s, Škaloud devoted more time to the studies of orthodontic problems. He also tried to solve some methodological problems of instrument technology in orthodontics. He formulated a pioneering theory of the adaptation of teeth and jaws under the influence of functional load, not only in contemporary humans but also in fossil man. As a clinician he advocated surgical treatment of anomalies of the teeth and jaws and prevention of disorders. He was a proponent of good nutrition for children and authored tables determining the "tooth age" of a child, examining some 30,000 school children to determine the frequencies of functional orthodontic anomalies. His textbook of orthodontics (published with M.A. Wachsmann) was up-to-date from the methodological point of view and after World War II was enlarged, updated and translated into Polish.

MAJOR WORKS: (with M. Adam Wachsmann) *Učebnice orthodontie* [*Textbook of Orthodontics*] (Prague: 1955) [tr.: *Podrzecsnik ortodoncyi* (Warsaw: 1957)]; *Prevence poruch orofaciální soustavy* [*Prevention of Disorders of the Orofacial System*] (Prague: 1955); "Prevention of disturbances of the natural functions of the orofacial system," *Acta Universitatis Carolinae, Medica,* vol. 14 (1968), pp. 93-98.

K. Hajniš
[Translation from Czech: Jitka Hurych]

Skeat, Walter-William. Ethnographer, colonial administrator, writer. Born in Cambridge (England) 14 October 1866, died in Devon (England) 24 July 1953. Among anthropologists Skeat is best known as the author of the first comprehensive and systematic descriptions of Malay and Malayan aboriginal customs and beliefs.

After graduating in classics at Cambridge, Skeat served as a colonial administrator in Selangor (western Malaya) from 1891 to 1897. He was then joint leader (with F.F. Laidlaw) of a scientific expedition to northeastern Malaya and the adjoining area of Thailand during 1899-1900. Poor health forced his retirement from the Federated Malay States (FMS) Civil Service, but for some years he wrote books and also articles on Malaya and Thailand both for learned journals and for more popular publications. From 1914 to 1934 he was an "official guide-lecturer" in the ethnographic and historical sections of the British Museum in London. Late in life he wrote an account of his expedition of 1899-1900. In 1899 he presented to the Museum of Archaeology and Ethnology at Cambridge his large collection of Malay and Malayan aboriginal artifacts.

In the methodology of his ethnographic fieldwork, Skeat followed the lead of his friend and mentor, A.C. HADDON, who founded (in 1900) and was head (until 1925) of the Department of Anthropology at Cambridge. In so far as Skeat adopted any conceptual approach, he applied the theory of "animism" developed by E.B. TYLOR. K.M. Endicott, in *An Analysis of Malay Magic* (Oxford: 1970), draws extensively on Skeat's *Malay Magic* as a unique source of valuable data and analyzes it in terms of modern theory.

MAJOR WORKS: *Malay Magic* (London: 1900); (with C.O. Blagden) *Pagan Races of the Malay Peninsula* (London: 1906); "Reminiscences of the [Cambridge] Expedition," *Journal of the Malayan Branch of the Royal Asiatic Society*, vol. 26, pt. 4 (1953), pp. 9-147. His more popular works include: *Fables and Folk-Tales from an Eastern Forest* (Cambridge: 1901) [which Rudyard Kipling acknowledged as a model for his *Just So Stories*].

SOURCES: F.F. Laidlaw, "Obituary—W.W. Skeat 1866-1953," *Journal of the Malayan Branch of the Royal Asiatic Society*, vol. 26, pt. 1 (1953), pp. 225-228; C.A. Gibson-Hill, "Introduction" [to Skeat's account of his expedition], *Journal of the Malayan Branch of the Royal Asiatic Society*, vol. 26, pt. 3 (1953), pp. 5-8; J.M. Gullick, "W.W. Skeat and Malayan ethnography: an appreciation," *Journal of the Malaysian Branch of the Royal Asiatic Society*, vol. 61 (1988), pp. 117-152; J.M. Gullick, "The Skeat Collection and Malayan ethnography," *Journal of the Anthropological Society of Oxford*, vol. 20, no. 3 (1989), pp. 197-208. Skeat's surviving papers are at the Institute of Social Anthropology at Oxford.

John M. Gullick

Smith, Sir *Grafton Elliot.* Anatomist, anthropologist, Egyptologist. Born in Grafton (New South Wales) 15 August 1871, died in London (England) 1 January 1937. Smith began his studies in Sydney and later went to England. His professional posts were at the Cairo School of Medicine (1900-1909), the University of Manchester (1909-1919) and University College, London (1919-1936). Trained in anatomy, his interests gradually broadened from physical anthropology to cultural history. After his initial work on the brains of Australian marsupials, he became involved in the study of the human brain and its evolution. He was a major figure in the study of early man and his development. While in Egypt, Smith analyzed the human remains recovered during the original archaeological survey of Nubia. He also studied the royal mummies of the New Kingdom and became the leading expert on this topic in the early 20th century. Most of his studies in this field were the result of dissection, though he did use radiology on occasion. Despite the lack of modern technology, which of course limited his results as well as his sample, many of his findings are still valid. His studies of Egyptian mummies led him to comparisons with mummies from other areas of the world. Believing that all mummified humans were ultimately derived from the Egyptian example, he finally concluded that all cultures owed their origins to the civilization of the Nile (*The Migrations of Early Culture*). The Egyptians, who Smith believed had essentially developed civilization for the first and only time, proceeded to spread its benefits across the globe through migration and colonization. Although this English Diffusionist School, of which Smith was a major leader, had some adherents during and after World War I, notably W.J. Perry (*The Children of the Sun*) and W.H.R. RIVERS, it was never in the mainstream of anthropological theory. Recent apologists have argued that criticisms of Smith's diffusionism were extreme and have suggested that careful study of his writings in this field would warrant a re-evaluation of his position.

MAJOR WORKS: "Studies in the morphology of the human brain, with special reference to that of the Egyptians. No. 1. The occipital region" in: *Records of the Egyptian Government School of Medicine* (Cairo: 1904), pp. 125-173; "A contribution to the study of mummification in Egypt ...," *Mémoires présentés a l'Institut Égyptien*, vol. 5 (1908), pp. 3-57; (with F. Wood-Jones) *Archaeological Survey of Nubia, 1907-1908. 2. Report on the Human Remains* [2 vols.] (Cairo: 1910); *The Royal Mummies* (Cairo: 1912); *The Migrations of Early Culture* (Manchester: 1915); *Evolution of the Dragon* (London: 1919); *The Ancient Egyptians and the Origin of Civilization* (2nd ed., London: 1923); *The Evolution of Man* (London: 1924); (with W.R. Dawson) *Egyptian Mummies* (London: 1924); *In the Beginning: the Origin of Civilization* (New York: 1928); *Human History* (New York: 1929); *Diffusion of Culture* (London: 1933).

SOURCES: Warren R. Dawson, *Sir Grafton Elliot Smith: a Biographical Record by His Colleagues* (London: 1938); T. Wingate Todd, "The scientific influence of Sir Grafton Elliot Smith," *American Anthropologist*, vol. 39 (1937), pp. 523-526; Warren R. Dawson and Eric P. Uphill, *Who Was Who in Egyptology* (London: 1972), pp. 273-274; Marvin Harris, *The Rise of Anthropological Theory* (New York: 1968), pp. 380-382; A.P. Elkin and N.W.G. Macintosh (editors), *Grafton Elliot Smith: the Man and His Work* (Sydney: 1974).

Carter Lupton

Smith, Marian Wesley. Anthropologist. Born in New York (New York) 10 May 1907, died in New York (New York) 2 May 1961. Smith was educated at Columbia University where she earned bachelor's (1929) and master's (1934) degrees in philosophy and a doctorate in anthropology (1938). She was FRANZ BOAS's last graduate student and in many ways was typical of the Boasians. Her dissertation was an examination of Plains Indian warfare, while her early fieldwork was restricted to Boas's preferred region, the Northwest Coast. Smith was trained in all areas of anthropology and published and/or taught in cultural anthropology, linguistics, archaeology, physical anthropology and folklore.

Between the late 1930s and 1951, Smith was honored by her fellow anthropologists with the posts of secretary-treasurer, vice-president, president, and editor of the American Ethnological Society; vice-president of the American Folklore Society; and secretary of the anthropology section of the American Association for the Advancement of Science. She was also a visiting professor at Vassar University, the University of Washington, New York University, the University of Pennsylvania and the University of California at Berkeley. During the same period, Columbia University, her full-time employer, refused to promote her from instructor to assistant professor, much less bestow tenure upon her.

In 1952 Smith married a British businessman whom she had met in Pakistan (her research having led her to India, to study the Sikh religion). Relocating in London, Smith was elected a fellow of the Royal Anthropological Institute before the end of the year and made its honorary secretary in 1956. From 1952 until her death she was also a member of the anthropology faculty of the London School of Economics. In Britain Smith involved herself energetically in editorial work, leading symposia, fund-raising and other activities. The painful disease of the lymphatic system that finally killed her in 1961 had plagued her since 1949; that, and the partial paralysis of one leg due to childhood polio, make her many achievements all the more impressive. Her health, and a blatant case of gender discrimination, robbed Smith of what might have been a brilliant career, rather than merely a remarkably productive one.

MAJOR WORKS: "The war complex of the Plains Indians," *American Philosophical Society Proceedings*, vol. 78 (1938), pp. 425-464; *The Puyallup-Nisqually* (New York: 1940); (editor) *Indians of the Urban Northwest* (New York: 1949); *Archaeology of the Columbia-Fraser Region* (Menasha, Wisconsin: 1950) (= *Memoirs of the Society for American Archaeology*, no. 6-7); (co-editor, with S. Stansfeld Sargent) *Culture and Personality* (New York: 1949); (editor) *Asia and North America: Transpacific Contacts* (Salt Lake City: 1953).

SOURCES: Lord Raglan, Raymond Firth, and William Fagg "Marian Wesley Smith, 1907-1961," *Man*, vol. 61 (1961), pp. 176-178; A.E. Mourant, "Dr. Marian W. Smith," *Nature*, vol. 192 (1961), p. 917; Frederica de Laguna, "Marian Wesley Smith, 1907-1961," *American Antiquity*, vol. 27 (1962), pp. 567-569.

David Lonergan

Smith, Stephenson Percy. Ethnologist, historian, surveyor. Born in Beccles, Suffolk (England) June 1840, died in New Plymouth (New Zealand) 19 April 1922. Smith migrated to New Plymouth with his family in 1850 and four years later joined the survey department, rising through the ranks to become Surveyor-General of New Zealand in 1889. Much of Smith's surveying work was carried out in the rugged interior of the North Island where he had frequent contact with Maori, learned their language and began to record their tribal history and lore. He was instrumental in founding the Polynesian Society at Wellington in 1892 and edited the *Journal of the Polynesian Society*, a quarterly publication, for the next thirty years. He published a great deal of his material on Maori history in the *Journal* or the Society's *Memoirs*.

Smith was one of a small band of amateur ethnologists, including Abraham Fornander of Hawaii, who applied diffusionist theory to trace the origins of the Polynesians back to India or the Middle East and their migrations through Southeast Asia into the Pacific. Smith and other New Zealand scholars argued, on the basis of flimsy connections in language, myths and legends, that the Maori, a branch of the Polynesians, were descended from Aryans (or a cognate people) who had migrated eastward into the Pacific. Moreover Smith, with Fornander, used collections of genealogies, in this case derived from elders in Rarotonga and New Zealand, to provide a chronological framework for the migration, starting from India in 450 B.C. and culminating in the final wave of migrants to New Zealand—the so-called Great Fleet—in 1350, a chronology that was unquestioned in New Zealand until recently. He first expounded the theory in "Hawaiki, the original home of the Maori," serialized in *The Journal of the Polynesian Society* during 1898-1899 and subsequently expanded into a separate book, *Hawaiki*, which went through several editions.

Smith was also responsible for collecting and publishing in the *Journal* Maori oral traditions relating to their warfare and internal migrations in New Zealand in the late 18th and early 19th century, material that was also gathered together into several standard monographs. Like many collectors of his time, Smith had great faith in his informants: the more esoteric the lore he extracted from them, the more authentic he imagined it to be. When he got hold of a collection of manuscripts written by a part-Maori scribe from some oral traditions, recited by Maori elders, Smith hastily published them as *The Lore of the Whare-wananga* (the Maori School of Learning) in 1913 and 1915. Later scholars, starting with TE RANGI HIROA (Peter H. Buck), have cast considerable doubt on the authenticity of these recorded traditions. But in his lifetime Smith and his works were unchallenged. He must be chiefly remembered for steering the Polynesian Society through the first third of its first hundred years.

MAJOR WORKS: *Hawaiki: the Whence of the Maori* (Christchurch: 1898); *The Peopling of the North* (Wellington: 1898); *History and Traditions of the Taranaki Coast* (New Plymouth: 1910); *Maori Wars of the Nineteenth Century* (Christchurch: 1910); *The Lore of the Whare-wananga* [2 vols.] (New Plymouth: 1913-1915).

SOURCES: D.R. Simmons, *The Great New Zealand Myth* (Wellington: 1976); M.P.K. Sorrenson, *Maori Origins and Migrations* (Auckland: 1979); A.G. Bagnall, "Smith, Stephenson Percy (1840-1922)" in: *An Encyclopaedia of New Zealand* (Wellington: 1966), vol. 3, pp. 265-266; "The late Stephenson Percy Smith, president and founder of the Polynesian Society and editor of its journal," *Journal of the Polynesian Society*, vol. 31 (1922), pp. 68-84.

M.P.K. Sorrenson

Smith, William Robertson. Historian of religions, Orientalist, theologian. Born in Keig (Scotland) 8 November 1846, died in Cambridge (England) 31 March 1894. The son of a Free Church minister, Smith early determined to follow his father's occupation. He was privately tutored at home and entered the University of Aberdeen at the age of fifteen. Interested in both natural science and Semitic languages, Smith became proficient in both areas. He graduated in 1865, traveled in Europe and then attended Edinburgh's New College, a Free Church theological school, from 1866 until 1870.

Shortly before Smith's ordination in 1870, he was appointed to the professorship of Oriental languages at Free Church College of Aberdeen. This was a testimonial to his maturity and scholarship—he was not yet twenty-four years old. While at Aberdeen Smith began to practice the new Biblical criticism that he had encountered in Germany and Holland, treating the Old Testament as a series of quasi-historical documents from which one could learn a great deal about an ancient religion. By 1877 he found it necessary to demand a formal trial for heresy, due to the hostility directed at him by some of his colleagues and students. Smith was in a form of academic limbo for several years, and by the spring of 1881 he was dismissed from his professorship.

Having been associated since 1870 with the editors of the forthcoming ninth edition of the *Encyclopaedia Britannica*, Smith was chosen in 1881 to succeed the ailing Professor Spencer Baynes as its editor-in-chief. He was a capable and hardworking editor, himself writing dozens of major entries, and remained with the project until its culmination in 1888.

In 1883 Smith was appointed to the lord almoner's professorship of Arabic at Cambridge; in 1885 he was elected a fellow of Christ's College, while the next year he became chief librarian of Cambridge. In 1889 he was appointed to the better paid Adams professorship of Arabic, which he kept until his death.

Smith was a pioneer in the sociological analysis of religion. He held that religious beliefs were part of an individual's social milieu, thus that one was born into a religion and that volition had no part in the process of acquiring beliefs. Early religions were dominated by public rituals rather than beliefs or theology; religion was fully interpenetrated by political institutions, serving to enforce public social and religious conformity. (This was a point that Smith could undoubtedly appreciate, after being hounded from Aberdeen.) He was a devout Christian who did not feel that analysis of belief systems in their geographical and chronological contexts should undermine religious faith.

MAJOR WORKS: *The Old Testament in the Jewish Church* (Edinburgh: 1881); *The Prophets of Israel* (Edinburgh: 1882); *Kinship and Marriage in Early Arabia* (Cambridge: 1885); *Lectures on the Religion of the Semites* (Edinburgh: 1889).

SOURCES: E.L. Peters, "Smith, William Robertson" in: David L. Sills (editor), *The International Encyclopedia of the Social Sciences* (New York: 1968-1979), vol. 14, pp. 329-335; John Sutherland Black, "Smith, William Robertson" in: *The Dictionary of National Biography*, vol. 18 (Oxford: 1917), pp. 568-570; T.O. Beidelman, "Smith, William Robertson" in: Mircea Eliade (editor), *The Encyclopedia of Religion* (New York: 1987), vol. 13, pp. 366-367.

David Lonergan

Snethlage, Maria Emília.

Snethlage, Maria Emília. Zoologist, explorer, ethnologist. Born in Kraatz, near Berlin (Germany) 13 April 1868, died in Porto Velho, formerly Mato Grosso, today Rondônia (Brazil) 25 November 1929. Snethlage was a woman of great will power who, at the end of the 19th and the beginning of the 20th century, broke through the old tradition of female subjugation and successfully made her way in the world. She acquired solid academic training at the Universities of Berlin, Jena and Freiburg, obtaining a doctorate at Freiburg in 1904. Between 1890 and 1899 she was the headmistress of schools in Germany, Switzerland, England and Ireland. She spoke fluent French and English and, later, Portuguese. She was always especially interested in zoology, particularly ornithology.

At the age of thirty-seven Snethlage contracted with EMÍLIO GOELDI to work at the Museu Paraense Emílio Goeldi (Emílio Goeldi Pará Museum). She arrived on 15 August 1905. She was active, intelligent, attractive, amiable and audacious, and she became well known in all of Amazônia and throughout Brazil. In her bold explorations, Snethlage contacted or lived with diverse indigenous groups, some of whom, such as those from the region between the Tapajós and Xingu Rivers south of Pará, had previously been little known. Beginning in 1908, while continuing her ornithological work, she began her ethnographic and linguistic studies of the Indians. Snethlage worked at the Pará Museum until 1921 when she transferred to the Museu Nacional (National Museum) in Rio de Janeiro. Her professional activity was completely focused on the exploration of all the regions of Brazil, where her laboratory was nature. From 1914 to 1921 she was director of the Goeldi Museum, the first woman to hold such a post in South America. Her last field trip was to have been to the Madeira and Branco Rivers near the Brazilian-Colombian-Venezuelan frontier, but she never got there, dying alone in Porto Velho at sixty-two years of age. Until the end of her life Snethlage was an intransigent defender of the rights of the Brazilian Indians and of their culture, toward whom she maintained a feminine affection.

MAJOR WORKS (IN ANTHROPOLOGY): *Zur Ethnographie der Chipaya und Curuahé* (Berlin: 1910); *A travessia entre o Xingú e o Tapajóz* (Belém: 1912); *Vocabulario comparativo dos Índios Chipayas e Curuahé* (Belém: 1912); *Nature and Man in Eastern Pará, Brazil* (New York: 1917); *Die Indianersträmme am Mittleren Xingu* (Berlin: 1920/21); *Die Flüsse Iriri und Curua im Gebiete des Xingu* (Berlin: 1925).

SOURCES: Humberto de Campos, "Emília Snethlage," *Revista Brasileira de Letras*, vol. 32 (1930), pp. 345-349; Hélio F. Camargo, "Pequena contribução ao estudo da história do Museu Paraense Emílio Goeldi," *Ciência e Cultura*, vol. 3 (1951), pp. 61-68; Alípio Miranda Ribeiro,

"Discurso de recepção da Dra. Emília Snethlage na Academia Brasileira de Ciências em sessão de 28 de outubro de 1926," *Boletim do Museu Nacional*, vol. 12 (1936), pp. 77-85; Heinrich Snethlage, "Dr. Emílie Snethlage zum Gedächtnis," *Journal für Ornithologie*, vol. 78 (1930), pp. 123-124; Osvaldo R. da Cunha, "Maria Emília Snethlage (1868-1929): a primeira mulher cientista na Amazônia," *O Liberal* (Belém) (15 November 1985); Osvaldo R. da Cunha, "Maria Elizabeth Emília Snethlage (1868-1929)" in: *Talento e atitude: estudos biográficos do Museu Emílio Goeldi*, vol. 1 (Belém: 1989), pp. 83-102.

Osvaldo Rodrigues da Cunha
[Translation from Portuguese: Margo L. Smith]

Sokolov, B.M. (Boris Matveevich). Ethnographer, folklorist, literary critic, museum curator. Born in Nezhin (Ukraine, Russia) 8 (20) April 1889, died in Moscow (Russian S.F.S.R.) 30 June 1930. Together with his twin brother ĨUriĭ Matveevich, also a folklorist and literary critic (who died in Kiev 15 January 1941), Sokolov made significant contributions to the collection and study of the folklore of the peoples of the U.S.S.R. as well as to an understanding of the relationship between folklore and literature. From 1926 to 1928 the Sokolov brothers carried on a three-year expedition "in the footsteps of" Pavel Nikolaevich Rybnikov (1831-1885) and Aleksandr Fedorovich Gil'ferding (1831-1872), which afforded them the opportunity to study changes in the long-forgotten *epos* discovered some sixty years earlier. Their expedition attracted the attention of Soviet and foreign scholars. Their main contribution was in the popularization of folk art and folklore.

Sokolov was the head of the Moscow Muzeĭ narodov SSSR/ĨSentral'nyĭ muzeĭ narodovedeniĩa (Museum of the Peoples of the U.S.S.R./Central Museum of Ethnology) and headed the journal *Ėtnografiĩa* from 1925 to 1930.

MAJOR WORKS: "Gogol'—ėtnograf: interesy i zanĩatiĩa N.V. Gogolĩa ėtnografieĭ," *Ėtnograficheskoe obozrenie*, no. 2-3 (1910), pp. 59-119; *Byliny: istoricheskiĭ ocherk, teksty i kommentarii* (Moscow: 1918); "Ėtnograficheskoe izuchenie Saratovskogo kraĩa," *Saratovskiĭ ėtnograficheskiĭ sbornik*, vol. 1 (1922), pp. 3-49; *Ocherki razvitiĩa noveĭsheĭ russkoĭ poėzii* (Saratov: 1923); *Sobirateli narodnykh pesen* (Moscow: 1923); "Neskol'ko ocherednykh voprosov sovremennogo kraevedeniĩa," *Nauka i iskusstvo*, vol. 1 (1923), pp. 54-60; "Narodnye russkie verovaniĩa, kul't i obrĩady v muzeĭnoĭ ėkspoziĩsii" in: V.V. Bogdanov and S.P. Tolstov (editors), *Kul'tura i byt naseleniĩa ĨSentral'no-promyshlennoĭ oblasti* (Moscow: 1929), pp. 41-45; (with ĨUriĭ Sokolov] *Skazki i pesni Belozerskogo kraĩa* (Moscow: 1915); (with ĨUriĭ Sokolov) *Poėziĩa derevni: rukovodstvo dlĩa sobiraniĩa proizvedeniĭ russkoĭ slovesnosti* (Moscow: 1926).

SOURCES: Ė. Pomeranĩseva and V. Chicherov, "Boris Matveevich Sokolov (1889-1930)," *Sovetskaĩa ėtnografiĩa*, no. 4 (1955), pp. 97-105; Ė.V. Pomeranĩseva, "Sokolovy ..." in: A.A. Surkov (editor-in-chief), *Kratkaĩa literaturnaĩa ėnĩsiklopediĩa*, vol. 7 (Moscow: 1972), pp. 48-49.

A.M. Reshetov
[Translation from Russian: Helen Sullivan]

Sousberghe, Léon de. Priest, writer on legal matters (*juriste*), ethnologist. Born near Ciney, Province of Namur (Belgium) 25 October 1903. After his primary and secondary studies, which were interrupted by the exile of his family to France and Great Britain during World War I, de Sousberghe pursued studies in philosophy and law at the Catholic University of Louvain. He received his Ph.D. in 1927 after the presentation of a thesis on property in natural law. He then went to Vienna where, in the anti-Semitic climate of the time, he followed the teachings of WILHELM SCHMIDT. After returning to Belgium, he joined the Company of Jesus in 1930 and was ordained in 1936. He participated on several occasions in archaeological excavations in the French Basque country where he became acquainted with Teilhard de Chardin (although he did not adopt his ideas). During World War II, he was a military chaplain and then a war prisoner. After the war, Father de Sousberghe remained for two years a chaplain for displaced persons.

In 1950 de Sousberghe began a career as an ethnologist. He became reacquainted with ethnology in the lecture halls of London where DARYLL FORDE was teaching; he did not, however, share the enthusiasm of Rodney Needham and EDMUND LEACH for *Les structures élémentaires de la parenté* of CLAUDE LÉVI-STRAUSS. His first ethnological publication—a critique of PLACIDE TEMPELS' *La philosophie bantoue*—dates from 1951. In it he expressed the ideas to which he remains faithful to this day: "To try to define Bantu knowledge as a speculative system is to repeat the error of LUCIEN LÉVY-BRUHL who *identifies* coherent thought and philosophic system."

From 1951 to 1953 and from 1955 to 1957 de Sousberghe lived in what is now Zaïre, first at Totschi then at Gungu (in the Kwango District). There, for a time under the aegis of the Institut de Recherche Scientifique en Afrique Centrale (IRSAC), he studied first and foremost the Pende, then neighboring ethnic groups as well. De Sousberghe remains the foremost authority on the Pende. He has worked on their ethnography and the interpretation of their kinship and marriage structures and has paid some attention to their art. His analysis of kinship and marriage structures was inspired by the hypotheses of ROBERT RATTRAY and opposed those of Lévi-Strauss. His position aroused the criticisms of Needham and, above all, of L. de Heusch.

In 1960 the Company of Jesus assigned de Sousberghe to Mexico. His stay there, devoted primarily to teaching, resulted in two publications on kinship structures among the Tetztlal.

In 1962 he returned to Zaïre where he taught at Lovanium and again took up his Pende studies. An assignment in Bujumbura provided an opportunity for comparative study of the social structures of the populations of Burundi and Rwanda. Study at the archives of the Musée Royal de l'Afrique Centrale (Royal Museum of Central Africa) at Tervuren permitted an extension of these studies to the Sena of Mozambique. From these comparative studies and using the approach pioneered by MARCEL MAUSS, de Sousberghe formulated what he called the "principle of immutability" of alliance.

MAJOR WORKS: *Structures de parenté et de l'alliance d'après les formules pende (ba-Pende, Congo-Belge)* (Brussels: 1955); *Les danses rituelles mungonge et kela des ba-Pende* (Brussels: 1956); *L'art pende* (Brussels: 1960); *Pactes de sang et pactes d'union dans la mort chez quelques peuplades du Kwango* (Brussels: 1960); *Deux palabres d'esclaves chez les Pende (Province de Léopoldville)* (Brussels: 1961); *Les unions entre cousins croisés: une comparaison des systèmes du Rwanda-Burundi et du Bas-Congo* (s.l.: 1968); *L'indissolubilité des unions entre apparentés au Bas-Zaïre* (Uppsala: 1976); *Don et contre-don de la vie: structure élémentaire de parenté et union préférentielle* (St. Augustin bei Bonn: 1986).

SOURCE: Interview with Léon de Sousberghe.

Danielle de Lame
[Translation from French: CW]

650

Soustelle, Jacques. Anthropologist, archaeologist, politician. Born in Montpellier (France) 3 February 1912, died in Neuilly-sur-Seine (France) 7 August 1990. Soustelle's training as a philosopher and his first fieldwork experiences in Mexico among the Otomi-Pame and the Lacandón Maya (1932-1939) led him to create a body of work in which he strongly stressed cultural relativism and wrote at length on the notion of "civilization." His early participation in World War II and the responsibilities assigned to him brought an end to his museum duties (he was *sous-directeur* of the Musée de l'Homme in Paris) and subsequently led him to participate actively in French political life while continuing to pursue his university career (as *Directeur d'études* at the École Pratique des Hautes Études and the École des Hautes Études en Sciences Sociales). He became a member of the Académie Française in 1983. He was president of the Group PACT (European Study Group on Physical Chemistry and Mathematical Techniques Applied to Archaeology) and of the Centre Universitaire Européen pour les Biens Culturels, organizations created in Strasbourg and in Ravello (Italy) under the aegis of the Council of Europe.

Rejecting his training in philosophy, and inspired by the ideas and methods of MARCEL MAUSS and PAUL RIVET, Soustelle opted for an anthropology free of all dogmatism. His fieldwork, as well as the influence of scholars and researchers in many disciplines, such as M. Cohen, Hermann Beyer, Roberto J. Weitlaner, MANUEL GAMIO, ALFONSO CASO and IGNACIO BERNAL, led him to undertake research in Mexico that had a multidisciplinary character, in which he combined, above all, archaeology, ethnology and linguistics. His work, always marked by an interest in the history of research in Mexico and the role in it of travelers and patrons, contributed enormously to an understanding of the great civilizations of Mesoamerica (the Olmecs, Teotihuacán, the Aztecs, the Maya, etc.). Soustelle was one of the first to describe the original and eminent part played by ancient Mexico in the intellectual and artistic heritage of humankind.

His book *La vie quotidienne* still serves as a major reference for scholars of Mexico at the same time that it presents a vivid portrait accessible to the public at large. His study of the cosmological thought of the ancient Mexicans *(La pensée cosmologique des anciens Mexicains)* in which he tried to sketch the indigenous notions of time, space and colors and his scientific approach—always based on cultural relativism—also contributed to the development of cognitive anthropology. His duties as a public figure led him to act assiduously for the recognition of archaeology and of ethnology by the French and, more recently, European political authorities.

MAJOR WORKS: *La famille Otomi-Pame du Mexique central* (Paris: 1937); "La culture matérielle des Lacandons," *Journal de la Société des Américanistes,* n.s., vol. 29 (1937), pp. 1-95; *La pensée cosmologique des anciens Mexicains* (Paris: 1940); "Observations sur le symbolisme du nombre 5 chez les anciens Mexicains" in: *XXVIII Congrès des Américanistes* (Paris: 1947), pp. 495-503; *La vie quotidienne des Aztèques à la veille de la Conquête espagnole* (Paris: 1955); *L'art du Mexique ancien* (Paris: 1966; Paris: 1977); *Les quatre soleils* (Paris: 1967); *Les Aztèques* (Paris: 1970); *La recherche française en archéologie et anthropologie* (Paris: 1975); *L'univers des Aztèques* (Paris: 1979); *Les Olmèques* (Paris: 1979); *Les Maya* (Paris: 1982).

Dominique Fournier
[Translation from French: CW]

Sparrman, Anders. Naturalist, explorer. Born in Tensta, twenty kilometers north of Uppsala (Sweden) 27 February 1748, died in Stockholm (Sweden) 9 August 1820. Sparrman was a disciple of the famous Swedish botanist Carl von Linné (1707-1778) and started traveling at a very young age. On his first long voyage he went to China as a seventeen-year-old "ship's doctor" in 1765, and he brought back important collections of natural history material, including ethnographic collections.

In 1772 he traveled to the Cape Province of southern Africa and from there he participated in the second circumnavigation of the earth by James Cook. In 1775 he returned to the Cape and in 1776 he was back in Sweden, again with important collections of, among many other things, ethnographic material from, for example, the South Seas. It is from this trip that we have his major work (*Resa till Goda Hopps-Udden: södra pol-kretsen*). During 1787-1788 he participated in a colonizing venture to southern Africa. It failed, but Sparrman brought back more knowledge about this part of the world.

Sparrman became a member of the Royal Scientific Academy of Sweden in 1776 and the curator of their collections in 1780. In this function, he was the first director of the ethnographic collections that were later to become the Ethnographical Museum of Sweden in Stockholm. He was appointed a professor and a deputy of the Collegium Medicum in 1790.

MAJOR WORK: *Resa till Goda Hopps-Udden: södra pol-kretsen* ... [2 vols.] (Stockholm: 1783) [tr.: *A Voyage to the Cape of Good Hope* ... (London: 1785-1786; reprinted, Cape Town: 1975)].

SOURCE: Vernon S. Forbes, "Foreword" to: Anders Sparrman, *A Voyage to the Cape of Good Hope* ... (Cape Town: 1975), pp. 1-25.

Jan-Åke Alvarsson

Speck, Frank G. Ethnologist, folklorist. Born in Brooklyn (New York) 8 November 1881, died in Philadelphia (Pennsylvania) 6 February 1950. Speck was raised in Hackensack, New Jersey, the son of a stockbroker. He attended Columbia University with the intention of becoming a minister, but his fascination with native American languages brought him to the attention of FRANZ BOAS, with whom he began studying anthropology in 1904. Speck obtained his M.A. under Boas the next year and continued his graduate education at Columbia until 1907. In that year he was offered a research fellowship by the University of Pennsylvania, which enabled him to undertake fieldwork among the Yuchi Indians of Oklahoma. Speck received his Ph.D. in 1908 and remained affiliated with the University of Pennsylvania for the rest of his life. He was chairman of the Department of Anthropology for most of his career, and was largely responsible for the development of its graduate program. Speck was also the founder of the Philadelphia Anthropological Society, and at various times associate editor of *American Anthropologist*, vice-president of the American Anthropological Association, and president of the American Folklore Society.

Speck's special province was the study of the Algonquian peoples, though this was not an exclusive interest. He carried out fieldwork among many tribes and linguistic groups, at first primarily in New England and subsequently throughout eastern North America. At a time when many anthropologists disdained the idea of research into the lifeways of relatively acculturated tribes, Speck sought to document them fully. In this he was far ahead of his time.

His research was permeated with the question of man's relation to the natural world, and his botanical and zoological knowledge was great. (Speck published more than a dozen articles and a monograph on natural history.) Ethnobiology, material culture and the uses of the environment are major themes in Speck's work. His knowledge of a variety of Algonquian languages gave him a feel for nuances in myths and other texts that he collected, as well as in everyday conversations during fieldwork. Little of Speck's attention was on linguistics per se; rather, for him language was a key to understanding the ethos or a people—a trait rare in the Americanists of his generation.

Speck typically eschewed theoretical concerns, preferring to amass the detailed ethnographic descriptions without which later generations would not truly understand the past. A self-aware romantic, Speck much disliked the tenor of 20th-century civilization, and preferred the company of his Algonquian friends to that of his fellow citizens of Philadelphia.

Although he produced an impressive number of publications, Speck was a careful and methodical researcher. He spent many periods of varying lengths in the field, often departing with little warning to his colleagues and students. In this, his choice of a specialization in eastern North America was wise. His frequent brief trips from Philadelphia, or from his summer home in Massachusetts, were highly productive. He also did a great deal of collecting for many different anthropological museums during these trips.

Speck was well aware of the ongoing effects of acculturation in the lifeways of his beloved eastern woodlands peoples and was highly successful in his self-appointed role of salvage ethnographer. This is not to say that his task was merely one of recording; he was a careful and incisive interpreter as well. Without his work later studies of Algonquian and other eastern North American peoples would have been much diminished.

MAJOR WORKS: *Family Hunting Territories and Social Life of Various Algonkian Bands of the Ottawa Valley* (Ottawa: 1915); "Kinship terms and the family band among the Northeastern Algonkian," *American Anthropologist*, vol. 20 (1918), pp. 143-161; "The functions of wampum among the Eastern Algonkian," *Memoirs of the American Anthropological Association*, vol. 6 (1919), pp. 3-71; *Beothuk and Micmac* (New York: 1922); "Symbolism in Penobscot art," *Anthropological Papers of the American Museum of Natural History*, vol. 29 (1927), pp. 25-80; *A Study of the Delaware Indian Big House Ceremony* (Philadelphia: 1931); *Naskapi: the Savage Hunters of the Labrador Peninsula* (Norman: 1935); *Penobscot Man: the Life History of a Forest Tribe in Maine* (Philadelphia: 1940); (with Alexander General) *Midwinter Rites of the Cayuga Long House* (Philadelphia: 1949).

SOURCES: A. Irving Hallowell, "Frank Gouldsmith Speck, 1881-1950," *American Anthropologist*, vol. 53 (1951), pp. 67-87; Horace P. Beck, "Frank G. Speck," *Journal of American Folklore*, vol. 64 (1951), pp. 415-418; Loren Eiseley, *All the Strange Hours* (New York: 1975).

David Lonergan

Spencer, Sir **Baldwin** (Walter Baldwin Spencer). Biologist, anthropologist, academic administrator. Born in Manchester (England) 23 June 1860, died in Navarin Island (Chile) 14 July 1929. Spencer was influential in making available Australian field data to European social theorists. Graduating in science at Oxford in 1884, he assisted E.B. TYLOR in the transfer of AUGUSTUS LANE-FOX PITT-RIVERS' ethnographic collection to its Oxford museum. Appointed foundation professor of biology at the University of Melbourne (1887-1919), he contributed significant taxonomic and biogeographic studies of

Australian fauna, both popularizing science and encouraging research. As honorary director of the National Museum of Victoria (1899-1923), he applied Pitt-Rivers' classificatory concepts to Aboriginal objects, as exemplified by his *Guide*.

Spencer first experienced Aboriginal society in 1894 when on a scientific expedition to central Australia. At Alice Springs he met the postmaster, F.J. Gillen, and established a congenial partnership that diverted his career into ethnography. Their *Native Tribes of Central Australia* was the first of four joint publications on societies stretching from Lake Eyre to the Gulf of Carpentaria. It constituted the most intensive Australian fieldwork before the 1930s. Spencer was based in Darwin during 1912 as Special Commissioner to advise the Commonwealth government on Aboriginal administrative and welfare policies.

As an evolutionary biologist and a capable artist, he applied his observational skills to describing Aboriginal societies, but social Darwinism suffused his picture. Although concentrating on esoteric themes such as initiation, marriage rules and beliefs, his linguistic experience was slight, so he was dependent on English-speaking informants. Spencer was contacted by JAMES G. FRAZER in 1897 while still preparing *Native Tribes* for publication. Frazer acted as his mentor thereafter, and Spencer dedicated *The Arunta* to "Our Master Sir James Frazer." Before Frazer's intervention, Spencer had concluded that totemic ceremonies were increase rites but thereafter adopted Frazer's definition that such rituals were "magical rather than religious." In this evolutionary model, Aboriginal mentality and cognitive systems reflected primitive survivals—"a relic of the early childhood of mankind."

Publication of the first *Native Tribes* profoundly influenced contemporary interpretations of European Paleolithic art and models of social and religious origins. Spencer's work served, in Australia, to provide academic respectability for popular racial prejudice, justifying authoritarian social control. In the history of ethnographic film, Spencer's movies and wax cylinder sound recordings are second only to A.C. HADDON's initiative in Torres Strait. His still photographs are an unrivalled archive of Aboriginal life. He was the first person to collect Aboriginal bark paintings on a large scale and to describe them, while extensive ethnographic collections initially assembled for his museum were exchanged internationally. Spencer's research virtually stamped the Aranda people as the type of Aboriginal Australian, so that a minority of arid country dwellers overshadowed knowledge concerning divergent societies of the majority inhabiting more congenial coastal regions.

MAJOR WORKS: (with F.J. Gillen) *Native Tribes of Central Australia* (London: 1899); *Guide to the Australian Ethnographical Collection* (Melbourne: 1901); (with F.J. Gillen) *The Northern Tribes of Central Australia* (London: 1904); *The Native Tribes of the Northern Territory* (London: 1914); (with F.J. Gillen) *The Arunta* [2 vols.] (London: 1927); *Wanderings in Wild Australia* [2 vols.] (London: 1928).

SOURCES: D.J. Mulvaney and J.H. Calaby, *"So Much That Is New": Baldwin Spencer 1860-1929, a Biography* (Melbourne: 1985); R.R. Marett and T.K. Penniman (editors), *Spencer's Last Journey, Being the Journal of an Expedition to Tierra del Fuego* (Oxford: 1931); R.R. Marett and T.K. Penniman (editors), *Spencer's Scientific Correspondence* (Oxford: 1932).

D.J. Mulvaney

Spencer, Herbert. Anthropologist, sociologist, philosopher. Born in Derby (England) 27 April 1820, died in Brighton (England) 8 December 1903. Spencer's main contribution to science was to formulate the concept of evolution in a comprehensive and systematic way and apply it to a broad range of phenomena, especially to human societies.

Spencer's interest in biology led him to reject special creation and to espouse organic evolution as early as 1852 in his article "The development hypothesis."

In 1858 Spencer conceived the idea of surveying all of nature from an evolutionary perspective and carried this out in his ten-volume *Synthetic Philosophy* (1862-1896). In the first volume of this work, *First Principles*, he developed the general concept of evolution, step by step. Subsequent volumes applied evolution to biology, psychology and, especially, anthropology (although Spencer called it sociology). His three-volume work, *The Principles of Sociology*, dealt with the evolution of human societies, not only in its broadest aspects but also in its specific details.

Spencer can also be considered the father of functionalism in the social sciences. As early as 1860, in "The social organism," he described societies as functioning systems, similar to animal organisms, and in later works he continued to pursue the organic analogy.

Just prior to beginning *The Principles of Sociology*, Spencer took time out to write *The Study of Sociology*, in which he noted the pitfalls facing anyone attempting to study human societies scientifically but argued that it was valid and fruitful nonetheless.

To prepare for writing *The Principles of Sociology*, Spencer began collecting a large body of comparative cultural data from many societies, both ethnographic and historical. The facts thus gathered were used not only as illustrative material for *The Principles of Sociology* but were also published separately in a standardized and compact form in a series of large format volumes called *Descriptive Sociology*, eight volumes of which were published during Spencer's lifetime and another nine after his death.

Spencer was enormously influential during his day, sharing with Darwin the distinction of having made evolution a master principle in the interpretation of nature, thus bringing about a profound transformation in human thought.

MAJOR WORKS: *Social Statics* (London: 1850); *Education* (London: 1861); *The Principles of Psychology* (London: 1855); "Progress: its law and cause," *Westminster Review*, n.s., vol. 11 (1857), pp. 445-485; *First Principles* (London: 1862); *The Principles of Biology* [2 vols.] (London: 1864-1867); *The Study of Sociology* (London: 1873); *Descriptive Sociology* [17 vols., of which 3 were revisions of earlier vols.] (London: 1873-1934); *The Principles of Sociology* [3 vols.] (London: 1876-1896); *Essays: Scientific, Political, & Speculative* [3 vols.] (London: 1890); *The Principles of Ethics* [2 vols.] (London: 1879-1893).

SOURCES: Herbert Spencer, *An Autobiography* (London: 1904); David Duncan (editor), *Life and Letters of Herbert Spencer* [2 vols.] (New York: 1908); F. Howard Collins, *An Epitome of the Synthetic Philosophy* (London: 1889); William H. Hudson, *An Introduction to the Philosophy of Herbert Spencer* (London: 1894); William James, "Herbert Spencer," *The Critic*, vol. 44, no. 6 (1904), pp. 21-24; J. Arthur Thomson, *Herbert Spencer* (London: 1906); Raphael Meldola, *Evolution: Darwinian and Spencerian* (Oxford: 1910); Josiah Royce, *Herbert Spencer: an Estimate and Review* (New York: 1904); Jay Rumney, *Herbert Spencer's Sociology* (New York: 1934); J.D.Y. Peel, *Herbert Spencer: the Evolution of a Sociologist* (New York: 1971); James G. Kennedy, *Herbert Spencer* (Boston: 1978); Jonathan H. Turner, *Herbert Spencer: a Renewed Appreciation* (Beverly Hills: 1985); Robert L. Carneiro, "Editor's introduction" in: Robert L. Carneiro (editor), *The Evolution of Society: Selections from Herbert Spencer's Principles of Sociology* (Chicago: 1967), pp. ix-lvii; Robert L. Carneiro, "Structure, function, and equilibrium in the evolutionism of Herbert Spencer," *Journal of Anthropological Research*, vol. 29 (1973), pp. 77-95; Robert L. Carneiro,

"Herbert Spencer's *The Study of Sociology* and the rise of social science in America," *Proceedings of the American Philosophical Society*, vol. 118 (1974), pp. 540-554; Robert L. Carneiro, "Herbert Spencer as an anthropologist," *The Journal of Libertarian Studies*, vol. 5 (1981), pp. 153-210.

Robert L. Carneiro

Spicer, Edward Holland. Cultural and applied anthropologist, linguist, archaeologist, ethnohistorian, theoretician, humanist, poet. Born in Cheltenham (Pennsylvania) 29 November 1906, died in Tucson (Arizona) 5 April 1983. Spicer spent fifty years of his life studying the culture, language and history of the Yaqui Indians of Sonora and Arizona, as well as other Southwestern Indian tribes, although he had started his professional career as a Southwestern archaeologist. Most of his fieldwork was effected in conjunction with his wife, Rosamond B. Spicer, also an anthropologist. They had three children.

During thirty-four years as professor of anthropology at the University of Arizona, Spicer wrote numerous books and articles on the Yaqui, on culture change, on ethnicity, on the ethnohistory of southwest United States and northwest Mexico, on linguistics and on other subjects. During World War II he was employed as Community Analyst by the War Relocation Authority and published on the subject of Japanese-Americans and the War Relocation Authority. Partially as a result of this experience he developed a keen interest in applied anthropology and community development. He said, "One learns from all kinds of people, one goes to ordinary people for the cultural essentials." His principal theoretical contributions were in the field of acculturation and assimilation, cultural and developmental change and persistent cultural systems.

For a considerable part of his career, Spicer was an active contributor to the work of the American Anthropological Association, serving as council member, editor of *American Anthropologist* and president and chairman of the Publications Policy Committee. He also participated in the development of the Society for Applied Anthropology. He was active in civil rights and community affairs, particularly historic preservation and community development in his own neighborhood. Spicer's ideas became known through his numerous writings, seminars at many colleges and universities and frequent public lectures. His ideas were also spread by the many students who had passed through his classes. His ideas on cultural change and "enduring peoples" are a part of the body of anthropological theory much used today.

MAJOR WORKS: *Tuzigoot: the Excavation and Repair of a Ruin on the Verde River Near Clarkdale, Arizona* (Berkeley: 1935); *Pascua, a Yaqui Village in Arizona* (Chicago: 1940); "The use of social scientists by the War Relocation Authority," *Applied Anthropology*, vol. 5 (1946), pp. 16-36; (editor and contributor) *Human Problems in Technological Change: a Casebook* (New York: 1952); *Potam, a Yaqui Village in Sonora* (Washington: 1954) (= *American Anthropologist*, vol. 56, no. 4, part 2; *Memoir*, no. 77); (editor and author of three chapters) *Perspectives in American Indian Culture Change* (Chicago: 1961); *Cycles of Conquest: the Impact of Spain, Mexico, and the United States on the Indians of the Southwest* (Tucson: 1962); "Acculturation," "Cahita Indians," and "Papago Indians" in: *Encyclopaedia Britannica* (14th ed., Chicago: 1962); "Ways of life" in: Russell C. Ewing (editor), *Six Faces of Mexico* (Tucson: 1966), pp. 65-102; "Acculturation" in: David L. Sills (editor), *International Encyclopedia of the Social Sciences* (New York: 1968), vol. 1, pp. 21-27; (with Katherine Luomala, A.T. Hansen and Marvin K. Opler) *Impounded People: Japanese Americans in the Relocation Centers* (Tucson: 1969); "Persistent cultural systems," *Science*, vol. 174 (19 Nov. 1971), pp 795-800; (co-editor with Raymond H. Thompson) *Plural Society in the Southwest*

(Albuquerque: 1975); "Social and cultural change" in: *Encyclopaedia Britannica* (Chicago: 1974), vol. 16, pp. 920-923; (editor) *Ethnic Medicine in the Southwest* (Tucson: 1976); *The Yaquis: a Cultural History* (Tucson: 1980); "American Indians," and "American Indians, federal policy toward" in: Stephan Thernstrom (editor), *Harvard Encyclopedia of American Ethnic Groups* (Cambridge, Mass.: 1980), pp. 58-122; *People of Pascua* (edited by Kathleen M. Sands and Rosamond B. Spicer) (Tucson: 1988).

SOURCES: Spicer Collection in the Archives of the Arizona State Museum, Tucson, Arizona; Spicer materials in the possession of Rosamond B. Spicer; Edward H. Spicer, *Finding my Way* (Tucson: 1982) [chapter 1 of planned autobiography]; Watson Smith, "The archaeological legacy of Edward H. Spicer," *The Kiva*, vol. 49, nos. 1-2 (1983), pp. 75-79; René Koenig, "Nekrologe: in memoriam Edward Holland Spicer (19.11.1906-4.4.1983)," *Kölner Zeitschrift für Soziologie und Sozialpsychologie*, vol. 4 (1983), pp. 822-824; Art Gallaher, "Obituary," *American Anthropologist*, vol. 86 (1984), pp. 380-385; "Ned Spicer," *Old Fort Lowell Gazette*, vol. 3 (1983), p. 4; Gilbert Kushner, "Elegy for a teacher," *Anthropology and Humanism Quarterly*, vol. 9, no. 3 (1984), pp. 9-14; "Edward Holland Spicer," *Southwestern Missions Research Center Newsletter*, no. 17 (July 1983), p. 55; "Anthropologist Edward Spicer," *Arizona Alumnus* (June 1983); "Edward Spicer wins spot among the stars," *Lo Que Pasa* (29 August 1983); "Edward H. Spicer," *Arizona Daily Star* (7 April 1983); "Noted UA anthropologist Edward H. Spicer dies," *Arizona Daily Star* (6 April 1983); "Renowned Southwestern anthropologist Spicer dies," *Lo Que Pasa* (11 April 1983); "Edward Holland Spicer, noted anthropologist, dies," *Tucson Daily Citizen* (6 April 1983); "Dr. Edward Spicer: UA anthropologist," *Arizona Republic* (6 April 1983); Rosamond B. Spicer, "Living in Pascua: looking back fifty years" in: Edward H. Spicer, *People of Pascua* (edited by Kathleen M. Sands and Rosamond B. Spicer) (Tucson: 1988), pp. xxiii-xlvi; Rosamond B. Spicer, "A full life well-lived," *Journal of the Southwest*, vol. 32 (1990), pp. 3-17; William Y. Adams, "Edward Spicer, historian," *Journal of the Southwest*, vol. 32 (1990), pp. 18-26; James E. Officer, "Edward H. Spicer and the application of anthropology," *Journal of the Southwest*, vol. 32 (1990), pp. 21-35; Mona Lange McCroskey, *Annotated Bibliography of the Published Works of Edward Holland Spicer (1906-1983)* [unpublished M.A. thesis, University of Arizona] (Tucson: 1990).

Rosamond B. Spicer

Spier, Leslie. Anthropologist. Born in New York (New York) 13 December 1893, died in Albuquerque (New Mexico) 3 December 1961. Spier began his association with anthropology in 1913 when the Public Service Commission of New Jersey (for which he worked as a junior engineer) assigned him to the New Jersey Archaeological and Geological Survey for the summer. By 1915, when he received a Bachelor of Science in engineering from the College of the City of New York, Spier had taken part in excavations and site surveys in Delaware and New York as well as New Jersey and was deeply interested in archaeology. That fall he entered the graduate program in anthropology at Columbia University where he studied with FRANZ BOAS.

From 1916 until 1920, when he obtained his doctorate, Spier was assistant in anthropology at the American Museum of Natural History. There he worked under CLARK WISSLER and ROBERT H. LOWIE, both of whom sparked his interest in Native American cultures. His years at Columbia and the museum produced a major change in Spier; initially attracted to anthropology by the subfield of archaeology, he grew less satisfied with the latter's scientific rigor as he became more knowledgeable. From 1919 on, he scarcely wrote a line in archaeology, directing his efforts into physical anthropology (specifically, human growth and development) and ethnology. By 1929 he had moved away from physical anthropology as well.

Spier's dissertation, *The Sun Dance of the Plains Indians*, was an indication of the directions his career would subsequently take. He specialized in North American Indian cultures, doing fieldwork among many tribes of the Northwest Coast and Southwest cultural regions, and he frequently concerned himself with problems of historical reconstruction. Another main interest was kinship studies. In his dissertation Spier attempted to establish the origins of the Sun Dance, a religious ritual involving self-torture, by carefully comparing the distribution among many Plains tribes of various cultural traits associated with the practice. However, in later years he cautioned that, while specific historical developments could be studied in this fashion, the broad generalizations some scholars inferred from cultural element distributions were attempts to derive too much from often equivocal data.

With his then wife, fellow Boasian ERNA GUNTHER, Spier went to Seattle in 1920 to take up a position at the University of Washington. During his decade there they both did considerable fieldwork among the Coast Salish peoples of Western Washington. Spier also frequently taught summer courses at Columbia and the University of California at Berkeley; he later extended his visiting professorships to the University of California at Los Angeles and to Harvard. When the couple separated, Spier taught at the University of Oklahoma from 1927 to 1929 before formally resigning his position at Washington. He briefly taught at the University of Chicago before going to Yale as a research associate in 1932. He stayed on as a professor until 1939.

In 1925 Spier had founded a monograph series, the *University of Washington Publications in Anthropology*, which he edited until 1931. He was even more active as an editor during the 1930s. He edited the *American Anthropologist* from 1934 to 1938, founded the *General Series in Anthropology* in 1934, and founded, and edited from 1936 to 1938, the *Yale University Publications in Anthropology*. That decade also saw the end of his formal fieldwork while he was still a relatively young man.

In 1939 Spier moved to the University of New Mexico where he remained until his retirement in 1955. He continued his editorial labors there, founding both the *Southwestern Journal of Anthropology* (now the *Journal of Anthropological Research*) and the *University of New Mexico Publications in Anthropology* monograph series in 1944; he edited both until his death in 1961. However, teaching had the greatest emphasis during the latter half of Spier's career. His broad knowledge of anthropology, coupled with his extreme care as a researcher and writer, influenced generations of students at a number of universities.

Spier was president of the American Anthropological Association in 1943, and vice-president of the anthropological section of the American Association for the Advancement of Science in 1943 and 1946. He was awarded the Townsend Harris medal in 1946 as well as the Viking Fund medal in 1960 and was elected to the National Academy of Sciences and the American Philosophical Society (1946), the Academy of Arts and Sciences (1953) and the California Academy of Sciences (1955).

MAJOR WORKS: *An Outline of a Chronology of Zuni Ruins* (New York: 1917) (= *American Museum of Natural History, Anthropological Papers*, vol. 18, part 3); *The Sun Dance of the Plains Indians: Its Development and Diffusion* (New York: 1921) (= *American Museum of Natural History, Anthropological Papers*, vol. 16, pp. 421-527); *The Distribution of Kinship Systems in North America* (Seattle: 1925) (= *University of Washington, Publications in Anthropology*, vol. 1, pp. 89-112); *The Ghost Dance of 1870 among the Klamath of Oregon* (Seattle: 1927) (= *University of Washington, Publications in Anthropology*, vol. 2, pp. 39-56); *Havasupai Ethnography* (New York: 1928) (= *American Museum of Natural History, Anthropological Papers*, vol. 29, pp. 81-392); (with Edward

Sapir) *Wishram Ethnography* (Seattle: 1930) (= *University of Washington, Publications in Anthropology*, vol. 3, pp. 151-299); *Klamath Ethnography* (Berkeley: 1930) (= *University of California, Publications in American Archaeology and Ethnology*, vol. 30); *Yuman Tribes of the Gila River* (Chicago: 1933); *The Prophet Dance of the Northwest and Its Derivatives: the Source of the Ghost Dance* (Menasha, Wisconsin: 1935); *Cultural Relations of the Gila River and Lower Colorado Tribes* (New Haven: 1936) (= *Yale University Publications in Anthropology*, no. 3).

SOURCES: "Viking Awards, 1960," *American Anthropologist*, vol. 63 (1961), pp. 835-837; Walter W. Taylor, "Leslie Spier, 1893-1961," *American Antiquity*, vol. 28 (1963), pp. 379-381; Harry W. Basehart and W.W. Hill, "Leslie Spier, 1893-1961," *American Anthropologist*, vol. 67 (1965), pp. 1258-1277; Ruth Bunzel, "Spier, Leslie" in: David L. Sills (editor), *The International Encyclopedia of the Social Sciences* (New York: 1968-1979), vol. 15, pp. 130-131.

David Lonergan

Spinden, Herbert Joseph. Archaeologist, ethnologist. Born in Huron (South Dakota) 16 August 1879, died in Beacon (New York) 23 October 1967. Spinden took his B.A., M.A. and Ph.D. from Harvard University in 1906, 1908 and 1909, respectively, but had lived an adventurous life before beginning college at the age of twenty-three. In 1900 he took part in the Gold Rush in Nome, Alaska, and he had also held surveying jobs for railroads in several western states.

As an undergraduate Spinden excavated a Mandan village site in North Dakota and during 1907-1909 was a graduate teaching fellow in the Harvard Department of Anthropology, one of his few periods as an instructor. Interested in ethnology as well as archaeology, he did fieldwork among the Tewa Indians of the U.S. Southwest at intervals between 1909 and 1913. His first position after leaving Harvard in 1909 was assistant curator of anthropology at the American Museum of Natural History, where he stayed until 1921. During this period Spinden also involved himself in Mesoamerican archaeology, which became his chief interest. He discovered a number of previously lost ruins on the Yucatán peninsula and elsewhere in Central America and became an expert on the Maya and their art.

In 1921 Spinden was hired as curator of Mexican anthropology at Harvard's Peabody Museum. Two years earlier he had deciphered the Maya dating system, which has allowed dependable dates to be assigned to Maya stelae and other monuments; his discovery was a major achievement in the historical reconstruction of Maya culture.

Spinden served as curator of anthropology at the Buffalo (New York) Museum from 1926 to 1929, at which point he moved to the Brooklyn Museum, where he remained until retirement in 1951. He was president of the American Anthropological Association during 1936-1937 and was a fellow of the American Academy of Arts and Sciences and the Royal Geographical Society. In addition to his curatorial work and archaeological research, Spinden was a visiting professor in Mexico, Peru, Argentina and Chile. He was also president of the New York-based Explorers' Club.

MAJOR WORKS: (with George F. Will) *The Mandans* (Cambridge, Mass.: 1906) (= *Papers of the Peabody Museum, Harvard University*, vol. 3, no. 4); *The Nez Percé Indians* (Lancaster, Penn.: 1908) (= *Memoirs of the American Anthropological Association*, vol. 2, pp. 165-274); *A Study of Maya Art* (Cambridge, Mass.: 1913) (= *Memoirs of the Peabody Museum*, vol. 6); *Ancient Civilizations of Mexico and Central America* (New York: 1917); *The Reduction of Mayan Dates* (Cambridge, Mass.: 1924) (= *Papers of the Peabody Museum of Archaeology and Ethnology*, vol. 6, no. 4); *Songs of the Tewa* (New York: 1933).

SOURCES: "Spinden, Herbert Joseph" in: *The National Cyclopaedia of American Biography*, vol. E (New York: 1938), p. 73; "Dr. Spinden dead, Indian authority," *The New York Times* (24 October 1967), p. 44.

David Lonergan

Squier, Ephraim George. Journalist, diplomat, archaeologist, ethnologist. Born in Bethlehem (New York) 17 June 1821, died in Brooklyn (New York) 17 April 1888. Self-educated, Squier first worked as a journalist in New York and Connecticut before moving in 1845 to southern Ohio where he published a newspaper and, in 1847 and 1848, served as clerk of the Ohio House of Representatives. There Squier became interested in the region's mounds and with Dr. Edwin H. Davis excavated mounds along the Ohio River. From their investigations they concluded that the mounds were of considerable antiquity, that the builders were Indians, that they may have had contact with the civilizations of Central and South America and that they were an agricultural people more advanced in the arts of civilization and religious expression than contemporary Indians of the region. The careful research of Squier and Davis impressed Joseph Henry of the Smithsonian Institution who published their *Ancient Monuments of the Mississippi Valley* as the first volume of the Smithsonian's *Contributions to Knowledge* series. Squier's subsequent work on the New York mounds was also published by the Smithsonian. In 1848 Squier was in New York City where, as a member of the American Ethnological Society, he became still more interested in Indian legends and the ethnological study of religious symbols and their evolution. In subsequent articles and in *The Serpent Symbol*, Squier considered "religious ideas" significant because they revealed paths of intellectual development as well as a people's progress in civilization. Squier held several diplomatic posts between 1849 and 1870 including missions to Nicaragua, Honduras and Peru. While in Peru, Squier explored and mapped the pre-Columbian Chimú capital of Chan-Chan. His investigations in Peru were published in *Peru: Incidents of Travel and Exploration in the Land of the Incas*. Today Squier is primarily noted for his contributions to American archaeology, but he was also an ethnologist whose studies of Indian legends and religious symbols led him to advocate strongly the theory of independent development of Indian civilization.

MAJOR WORKS: (with E.H. Davis) *Ancient Monuments of the Mississippi Valley* (Washington: 1848) (= *Smithsonian Contributions to Knowledge*, vol. 1); "New Mexico and California," *American Review*, n.s., vol. 2 (1848), pp. 503-28; "Manabozho and the Great Serpent," *American Review: a Whig Journal*, vol. 8 (1848), pp. 392-398; "Historical and mythological traditions of the Algonquins," *American Review*, n.s., vol. 3 (1849), pp. 273-293; *Aboriginal Monuments of the State of New York* (Washington: 1849) (= *Smithsonian Contributions to Knowledge*, vol. 2); "American ethnology: being a summary of some of the results which have followed the investigation of this subject," *American Review*, n.s., vol. 3 (1849), pp. 385-398; *The Serpent Symbol, and the Worship of the Reciprocal Principles of Nature in America* (New York: 1851) (= *American Archaeological Researches*, vol. 1); *Nicaragua: its People, Scenery, Monuments, and the Proposed Interoceanic Canal* [2 vols.] (London: 1852); "Observations on the archaeology and ethnology of Nicaragua," *Transactions of the American Ethnological Society*, vol. 3 (1853), pp. 85-158; *Peru: Incidents of Travel and Exploration in the Land of the Incas* (New York: 1877).

SOURCES: Robert E. Bieder and Thomas G. Tax, "From ethnologists to anthropologists: a brief history of the American Ethnological Society" in: John V. Murra (editor) *American Anthropology: the Early Years* (St. Paul: 1976) (= *1974 Proceedings of the American Ethnological*

Society), pp. 3-22; Robert E. Bieder, *Science Encounters the Indian, 1820-1880: the Early Years of American Ethnology* (Norman: 1986), pp. 104-145; Leo Duel, *Conquistadors Without Swords: Archaeologists in the Americas* (New York: 1967); William Stanton, *The Leopard's Spots: Scientific Attitudes Toward Race in America, 1815-59* (Chicago: 1960), pp. 82-89; Thomas G. Tax, *The Development of North American Archeology 1800-1879* [Ph.D. dissertation, University of Chicago] (Chicago: 1973); Thomas G. Tax, "E. George Squier and the mounds, 1845-1850" in: Timothy H.H. Thoresen (editor), *Toward a Science of Man: Essays in the History of Anthropology* (The Hague: 1975), pp. 99-124; Gordon R. Willey and Jeremy A. Sabloff, *A History of American Archaeology* (London: 1974).

Robert E. Bieder

Srinivas, M.N. Social anthropologist, sociologist. Born in Mysore City, Mysore State (India) 16 November 1916. Srinivas is one of the founders of sociology and social anthropology in India. He was trained under G.S. GHURYE at Bombay and then under A.R. RADCLIFFE-BROWN and E.E. EVANS-PRITCHARD at Oxford. Initially he taught at Oxford (1948-1951), but he has spent the rest of his working life in India and continues to be active.

Srinivas has written books and papers on many aspects of Indian society and culture but is best known for his work on religion, village community, caste, social change and methodology. While most of his writings are based on intensive fieldwork in South India in general, and in Coorg, and Rampura (pseudonym) village in Karnataka State in particular, his writings on Indian society at large provide syntheses of his personal observation and knowledge and the existing literature on many different parts of the country. "Sanskritization" and "dominant caste," two of the several new concepts he has developed, have been used by a wide range of scholars to understand Indian society and culture, past and present, and have even become part of the public discourse in India. His distinction between the "book view" and "field view" in the study of civilizations has also become important.

During his long teaching career, he founded two new departments of sociology—the first at the Maharaja Sayajirao University of Baroda and the second at the University of Delhi where he introduced new ideas of teaching sociology and social anthropology and pioneered research in a number of new fields by encouraging his students to work in them. Several of his students have achieved an international reputation in sociology and social anthropology.

Srinivas has, in his research and teaching and in numerous writings, strongly supported integration between sociology and social anthropology and between contemporary and historical studies. He would not describe himself as belonging to any "school" or "ism," except empiricism. His writings are free from jargon and from references to grand sociological theories. His empiricism is related to his view that for many years to come deeper insights into Indian society will come from field studies, particularly intensive studies, although he is not averse to using data from macro-surveys and to arriving at overall perspectives of social processes.

While Srinivas would not agree with the view of some of his critics that he is a structural-functionalist, he has frequently stated that the ideas of social structure and function have profoundly influenced his work. He has said that the full potential and implications of the idea of social structure have not yet been worked out. While he has not propounded any general anthropological theory of his own, his discussions of the contributions of Radcliffe-Brown and Evans-Pritchard, including his editorial introduction to Radcliffe-Brown's posthumous work, *Method in Social Anthropology*, have provided illuminating commentaries on theoretical developments in anthropology. And in fieldwork he has demanded from his students not only methodological competence but also the sensitivity of a novelist.

Srinivas has worked hard to disseminate the knowledge and insights of anthropology among ordinary citizens by writing in newspapers and magazines and by speaking in public forums. He has played an important role in strengthening professional associations and has influenced the policies of the government and other public bodies by working on many committees and commissions while consistently refusing administrative and lucrative international positions. He is one of the few social scientists who have built institutions in addition to contributing to scholarship.

MAJOR WORKS: *Religion and Society among the Coorgs of South India* (Oxford: 1952); (editor) *India's Villages* (Calcutta: 1955); (editor) A.R. Radcliffe-Brown, *Method in Social Anthropology* (Chicago: 1959); *Caste in Modern India and Other Essays* (Bombay: 1962); *Social Change in Modern India* (Berkeley: 1966); "Itineraries of an Indian social anthropologist," *International Social Science Journal*, vol. 25 (1973), pp. 129-148; *The Remembered Village* (Berkeley and Delhi: 1976); (editor with S. Seshaiah and V.S. Parthasarathy) *Dimensions of Social Change in India* (Delhi: 1977); (editor with A.M. Shah and E.A. Ramaswamy) *The Fieldworker and the Field* (Delhi: 1979); "My Baroda days," *Journal of the Maharaja Sayajirao University of Baroda*, vol. 30 (1981), pp. 171-182; (with T.S. Epstein, M.N. Panini and V.S. Parthasarathy) *Basic Needs Viewed from Above and from Below: the Case of Karnataka State, India* (Paris: 1983); *The Dominant Caste and Other Essays* (Delhi: 1987); *The Cohesive Role of Sanskritization and Other Essays* (Delhi: 1989).

SOURCES: M.N. Srinivas, "Itineraries of an Indian social anthropologist," *International Social Science Journal*, vol. 25 (1973), pp. 129-148; M.N. Srinivas, "My Baroda days," *Journal of the Maharaja Sayajirao University of Baroda*, vol. 30 (1981), pp. 171-182; "A review symposium on M.N. Srinivas's *The Remembered Village*," *Contributions to Indian Sociology*, n.s., vol. 12 (1978), pp. 1-152.

A.M. Shah

St. John, Sir *Spenser Buckingham.*

Author, explorer, diplomat. Born in St. John's Wood, London (England) 22 December 1825, died in Pinewood Grange, Surrey (England) 2 January 1910. St. John's father, James Augustus St. John, was a writer and traveler whose career included a stint in London as assistant editor of the *Oriental Herald and Colonial Review*. St. John was educated in private schools. He displayed an early interest in the then little-known and distant island of Borneo and studied the Malay language while at home in England. In 1847 St. John met Sir James Brooke, first Rajah of Sarawak, during the latter's visit to London. St. John was to become closely associated with Rajah Brooke. In 1848 St. John accompanied Brooke to Borneo as the latter's private secretary. St. John spent the next thirteen years in the north and west regions of Borneo (present-day Sabah, Sarawak and Brunei). In 1856 he was appointed Consul-General in Brunei. He eagerly led an expedition into the then largely unexplored rainforest. St. John's narrative of his Borneo and Sulu explorations, *Life in the Forests of the Far East,* was published in London in 1862. This account of the Sea Dayaks, Land Dayaks, and other Borneo peoples was a pioneering contribution to Borneo ethnography. The Malay and Chinese populations of coastal Borneo figure only incidentally in the very readable narrative; these groups having been described by other authors. The work includes an account of the author's ascent of Mount Kinabalu. St. John returned to England in 1859. His later diplomatic career took him to stations in Haiti and elsewhere in the Americas. In an introduction to the 1974 reprint edition of *Life in the Forests of the Far East*, TOM HARRISSON (former curator of the Sarawak Museum) praised this work for its balance and attention to detail.

MAJOR WORK: *Life in the Forests of the Far East* [2 vols.] (London: 1862; reprinted, Kuala Lumpur: 1974).

SOURCES: "St. John, Sir Spenser Buckingham" in: Sir Sidney Lee (editor), *Dictionary of National Biography. Supplement, 1901-1911* (London: 1927), pp. 249-250; Tom Harrisson, "Introduction" to: *Life in the Forests of the Far East* (Kuala Lumpur, 1974), vol. 1, pp. [v]-xvi; Nicholas Tarling, "Spenser St. John and his *Life in the Forests of the Far East*," *Sarawak Museum Journal*, n.s., vol. 23, no. 44 (July-December 1975), pp. [293]-305.

Lee S. Dutton

Stanner, W.E.H. (William Edward Hanley). Anthropologist. Born in Sydney (New South Wales) 1906, died in Canberra (A.C.T.) 1981. Enrolling at Sydney University in 1929, Stanner took an undergraduate course from the foundation professor, A.R. RADCLIFFE-BROWN. After the latter's departure, Stanner conducted fieldwork among Aborigines in the Northern Territory under the direction of A.P. ELKIN. In 1936 he went to the London School of Economics to complete his doctoral dissertation under the direction of BRONISLAW MALINOWSKI. The outbreak of World War II interrupted post-doctoral research in Kenya, and Stanner returned home to participate in the war effort. In 1946 he toured the insular Pacific, studying problems of reconstruction. In 1947 he took up the directorship of the East African Research Institute in Makerere, Uganda, but he resigned after a year. In 1950 he took a chair in Comparative Social Institutions at the newly formed Australian National University in Canberra. Here he remained until his retirement in 1971, although he remained active in Aboriginal affairs and in the Australian Institute of Aboriginal Studies until his death in 1981.

Throughout his career Stanner divided his energies between academic anthropology and the problems of colonial policy and Aboriginal affairs. As an academic anthropologist he attempted to develop a form of transactionalism out of the thought of Radcliffe-Brown and to redefine the Durkheimian distinction between the sacred and the profane. These ideas were most effectively applied to the study of Australian Aboriginal religion in articles written between 1958 and 1967. Stanner participated in the debate on Aboriginal policy as early as the 1930s and in the late 1960s and early 1970s raised public understanding to a new level through his radio broadcasts and public lectures. As a member of the governmental Council for Aboriginal Affairs he played a role in the redefinition of policy during the early 1970s, helping to bring about the recognition of Aboriginal land rights in the Northern Territory.

MAJOR WORKS: *South Seas in Transition* (Sydney: 1953); *On Aboriginal Religion* (Sydney: 1963); *After the Dreaming* (Sydney: 1968); *White Man Got No Dreaming* (Canberra: 1979).

SOURCES: Daine E. Barwick, Jeremy Beckett and Marie Reay, "W.E.H. Stanner: an Australian anthropologist" in: Diane E. Barwick, Jeremy Beckett and Marie Reay (editors), *Metaphors of Interpretation: Essays in Honour of W.E.H. Stanner* (Canberra: 1985), pp. 1-52.

Jeremy Beckett

Starcke, Carl Nicolai. Philosopher, educationalist, politician. Born in Copenhagen (Denmark) 29 March 1858, died in Copenhagen (Denmark) 7 March 1926. In Denmark, Starcke is best known as a politician and as one of the founders, in 1919, of a Georgeist political party, following his disappointment with other liberal parties on the question of land rent. His academic career culminated in his appointment, in 1916, as professor of philosophy at the University of Copenhagen. But in his earlier years he had been an active pedagogical reformer, staunchly critical of the authoritarian school system of his day. His educational commitment was accompanied by a lifelong interest in comparative family structures.

In his work on the primitive family (*Die primitive Familie in ihrer Entstehung und Entwicklung*) Starcke dismissed JOHN F. MCLENNAN's and LEWIS HENRY MORGAN's evolutionary schemes (e.g., the sequence from promiscuity via matriliny to patriliny) on the grounds that the explanation of existing customs should be sought in existing circumstances, and only if this is impossible may we have recourse to historical explanations that must then be based on definite historical accounts ("If this main principle is not accepted, we shall be led astray by every idle delusion"). Starcke argued that descent systems were to be explained by existing legal, economic and residential factors and had nothing to do with the status of the child with regard to the procreative roles of the mother and father. With respect to kinship terminology, Starcke was equally critical of Morgan's evolutionism; nomenclature, he argued, was the faithful reflection of the juridical relations among kinsmen, and "there is nothing to show that the social order changes more quickly and easily than the nomenclature."

These arguments have a strikingly "modern," functionalist tenor and, indeed, Starcke was later to be praised by A.R. RADCLIFFE-BROWN as being "the first to maintain the position which has always been my own."

MAJOR WORKS (OF ANTHROPOLOGICAL RELEVANCE): *Die primitive Familie in ihrer Entstehung und Entwicklung* (Leipzig: 1888) [tr.: *The Primitive Family in Its Origin and Development* (London: 1889; Chicago and London: 1976)]; *Samvittighedslivet: en Fremstilling af Principperne for menneskeligt Samfundsliv* [2 vols.] (Copenhagen: 1894-1897); *La famille dans les différentes sociétés* (Paris: 1899); *Lovene for Samfundsudviklingen og de sociale Idealer* (Copenhagen: 1927) [tr.: *Laws of Social Evolution* (London: 1932)] [the latter contains a comprehensive bibliography].

SOURCES: Rodney Needham, "Editor's introduction" in: Carl Nicolai Starcke, *The Primitive Family in Its Origin and Development* (Chicago and London: 1976), pp. ix-xxxi; Helge Larsen, "Starcke, Carl Nicolai" in: *Dansk Biografisk Leksikon* (Copenhagen: 1983), vol. 13, pp. 634-635.

Jan Ovesen

Starr, Frederick. Anthropologist, educator. Born in Auburn (New York) 2 September 1858, died in Tōkyō (Japan) 14 August 1933. Starr began his career in geology at the University of Rochester in upstate New York. After two years he transferred to

Lafayette College in Easton, Pennsylvania, where he received his bachelors and masters. He was awarded a doctoral degree in geology in 1885.

In 1884 he moved to Cedar Rapids, Iowa, to join the faculty of Coe College where he taught his first anthropology course and the first anthropology course offered in the state. From this point, his professional career focused on anthropology and museums. During his four years in Iowa he accomplished significant work in Iowa archaeology that is still considered valuable today. He played a significant role in the administration of the Davenport Academy of Sciences, which published his most widely praised works (*Bibliography of Iowa Antiquities* and *Summary of the Archaeology of Iowa*).

In 1888 Starr moved back to his home state where he accepted the position of registrar and professor of geognosy at Chautauqua Institute. This was a most important move for Starr. Here, he met William Rainey Harper who was soon to become the first president of the newly established University of Chicago. In selecting his faculty, Harper chose Starr to be the anthropologist in the Department of Sociology and Anthropology, a post he held for thirty-one years.

Starr's primary interests were in physical anthropology. Some of the theories he supported took environmental determinism to new extremes. For example, he believed that Europeans were becoming "red men." He was one of the first anthropologists to work in the Congo but he is known more for his award-winning photographs than for his anthropological studies.

Starr had dreams of starting a renowned department of anthropology and a great museum at the University of Chicago with the collections that were assembled for the World's Columbian Exposition in 1893. The separate department was never established during his tenure, and the Exposition collections were used to establish a new city museum, the Field Columbian Museum, later the Field Museum of Natural History. Starr has been greatly criticized for his administrative ineptitude and for his inability to establish a significant graduate program. However, his achievements lay in his teaching abilities and strategies that created public interest in the infant science of anthropology, his prolific writings and his work in new areas of the world.

MAJOR WORKS: *Bibliography of Iowa Antiquities* (Davenport, Iowa: 1895); *Some First Steps in Human Progress* (Chautauqua, N.Y.: 1895); *Summary of the Archaeology of Iowa* (Davenport, Iowa: 1895); *American Indians* (Boston: 1899); *Indians of Southern Mexico* (Chicago: 1899); *Notes upon the Ethnography of Southern Mexico* (Davenport, Iowa: 1900); *Strange Peoples* (Boston: 1901); *The Physical Characters of the Indians of Southern Mexico* (Chicago: 1902); *Notes upon the Ethnography of Southern Mexico*, part 2 (Davenport, Iowa: 1904); *The Truth about the Congo* (Chicago: 1907); *A Bibliography of Congo Languages* (Chicago: 1908); *In Indian Mexico* (Chicago: 1908); *Congo Natives: an Ethnographic Album* (1912); *Liberia: Description, History, Problems* (Chicago: 1913).

SOURCE: Nancy Evans, *Frederick Starr: Missionary for Anthropology* [unpublished masters thesis, Indiana University] (Bloomington: 1987).

Nancy L. Evans

Stefansson, Vilhjalmur. Anthropologist, explorer, Arctic expert. Born in Arnes (Manitoba) 3 November 1879, died in Hanover (New Hampshire) 26 August 1962.

Better known as an explorer and writer than as an anthropologist, Stefansson willingly left academe and became a popularizer and celebrity.

Stefansson's parents were Icelandic immigrants to Canada, who migrated once again (this time to North Dakota, motivated by poor harvests) while he was still an infant. The family anglicized its surname shortly after arriving in the New World, and Vilhjalmur Stefansson was first named William Stephenson; as a college junior he changed his name back to what he felt his parents should have called him. His nationality was also subject to alteration, being Canadian at birth, American as an infant, Canadian again in 1913 and American from World War II until his death. The two later changes were made at the request of the governments involved, while he was employed by them.

Three years into his studies at the University of North Dakota, Stefansson was expelled for rowdy behavior. He graduated in 1903 from the University of Iowa and was sent by influential Unitarian ministers to the Harvard Divinity School. By 1904 he was a doctoral student in Harvard's anthropology department, where his lifelong fascination with the variety of human diets was given a scholarly basis.

Stefansson visited Iceland to do research in physical anthropology during the summers of 1904 and 1905. His fluency in the language gave him unprecedented access to oral and written sources of data. When the University of Chicago's polar expedition called for an anthropologist with Arctic experience, Stefansson's work in Iceland earned him the post. He spent the winter of 1906-1907 with the Inuit (Eskimo) of northwestern Canada and—after the Chicago expedition fell apart—obtained funding from the American Museum of Natural History for a longer stay among the Inuit. Stefansson's first independent (two-man) expedition lasted approximately four years. Popular books and articles resulting from his expeditions made Stefansson well known in the United States and Canada.

His next expedition was financed by the Canadian government. The Canadian Arctic Expedition (1915-1918), which included DIAMOND JENNESS as ethnologist, demonstrated Stefansson's lack of ability in (and even lack of concern for) leadership. The expedition was a fiasco, but it helped Stefansson put forth his ideas about the need for Arctic explorers to adopt the Inuit (meat- and fat-rich) diet and modes of travel.

When he returned to New York, Stefansson launched a successful career as a platform lecturer and was awarded gold medals by the American, National, Royal and Philadelphia Geographic Societies. He was subsequently given honorary degrees by eight universities in Canada, Iceland and the United States.

Stefansson was several times involved in efforts to develop various areas of the Arctic economically. These all ended badly; one, the colonization of Wrangell Island, ultimately cost four lives. During the 1930s and 1940s, Stefansson was a consultant to a number of private concerns and government agencies on subjects such as polar air routes and Arctic survival. He also worked for the American government on the never-published *Encyclopedia Arctica*. As that project required cooperation with Soviet scholars at a time of increasing fear of domestic as well as Russian communism, it was abandoned when already nearing completion. Subsequently, Stefansson was the target of an inept "witch-hunt," perhaps because of his close friendship with the distinguished scholar Owen Lattimore, who had amazingly been named by Senator Joseph McCarthy as the Soviet Union's chief espionage agent in the United States.

Stefansson's most lasting contribution was the assembling of a huge private library of Arctic studies, once housed in the Manhattan apartment he shared with Harvard classmate HERBERT SPINDEN. The collection was eventually purchased by a philanthropist and donated to Dartmouth College where it now forms the nucleus of a world-renowned special library collection. Stefansson accompanied his books to Dartmouth and spent his last years associated with the university.

MAJOR WORKS: "Icelandic beast and bird lore," *Journal of American Folklore*, vol. 19 (1906), pp. 300-308; "Suitability of Eskimo methods of winter travel in scientific exploration," *Bulletin of the American Geographical Society*, vol. 40 (1908), pp. 210-213; *My Life with the Eskimos* (New York: 1913); *The Friendly Arctic* (New York: 1921); *Hunters of the Great North* (New York: 1922); *Arctic Manual* (New York: 1944); *Not by Bread Alone* (New York: 1946).

SOURCES: William R. Hunt, *Stef: a Biography of Vilhjalmur Stefansson* (Vancouver, B.C.: 1986); Vilhjalmur Stefansson, *Discovery* (New York: 1964).

David Lonergan

Steinen, Karl von den. Ethnographer. Born in Mühlheim/Ruhr (Germany) 7 March 1855, died in Kronberg/Taunus (Germany) 7 November 1929. Von den Steinen had been educated as a medical doctor specializing in psychiatry when in 1880, sojourning in Honolulu (Hawaii), he met ADOLF BASTIAN, then director of the Berlin Museum für Völkerkunde (Ethnographic Museum). Four years later, after successfully completing a south polar expedition, he organized his first ethnographical expedition into the interior of Brazil with Wilhelm von den Steinen, his cousin and a lifelong illustrator of ethnographic and archaeological publications. During 1887-1888 a second similar expedition with Paul Ehrenreich (1855-1914) followed. Back in Berlin von den Steinen obtained his *Habilitation* and started teaching at the University of Marburg but, two years later, returned to Berlin to join the staff of the Ethnographic Museum there. In 1890 he was appointed editor of the important exploration journal *Das Ausland*. In 1886 and 1894 von den Steinen published two books on his Brazilian fieldwork. They are landmarks in early ethnography and linguistic exploration of the virtually unknown regions of the Alto Xingu and Mato Grosso. His revision of classification of the Caraib, Gê and Tupi languages is a major contribution to American Indian linguistics. His ethnographic and linguistic data on the Bakairí tribe (published separately in 1912) are the only scholarly works on that tribe prior to its assimilation into the Brazilian folk culture. Von den Steinen inaugurated a Berlin-based tradition of German ethnographic expeditions into this region that has been carried on into the present (the last expedition, in 1983, was headed by Günther Hartmann (1924-)). His ethnographic publications were also instrumental in the creation of a Xingu Indian reservation by Brazilian state authorities.

During 1897-1898 von den Steinen traveled to the Marquesas Islands (Polynesia) and dedicated the rest of his life to the visual and oral art of this Polynesian culture. The gradual shift of his regional interests toward Oceania is reflected in his renouncing the directorship of the American Section at the Berlin Ethnographic Museum in 1906. The definitive three-volume monograph on his Polynesian research, *Die Marquesaner und ihre Kunst*, was published shortly before his death and is considered an outstanding contribution.

MAJOR WORKS: *Durch Central-Brasilien* (Leipzig: 1886); "Sambaki-Untersuchungen in der Provinz Santa Catharina (Brasilien)," *Zeitschrift für Ethnologie*, vol. 19 (1887), pp. 445-450; *Zweite Schingú-Expedition 1887-1888: die Bakaírí-Sprache: Wörterverzeichnis, Sätze, Sagen, Grammatik* (Leipzig: 1892); *Unter den Naturvölkern Zentral-Brasiliens: Reiseschilderungen und Ergebnisse der Zweiten Schingú-Expedition 1887-1888* (Berlin: 1894; reprint, New York: 1968); *Die Marquesaner und ihre Kunst: Studien über die Entwicklung primitiver Südseeornamentik* [3 vols.; I: *Tatauierung*; II: *Plastik*; III: *Die Sammlungen*] (Berlin: 1925-1928); "Marquesanische Mythen," *Zeitschrift für Ethnologie*, vol. 65 (1933), pp. 1-44 and 326-373; vol. 66 (1934), pp. 191-240.

SOURCES: *Minerva Jahrbuch der Gelehrten Welt*, vol. 10 (1900/1), pp. 88 and 93 and vol. 14 (1904/5), p. 109; H. Plischke, "Steinen, Karl v.d." in: *Deutsches Biographisches Jahrbuch*, vol. 11 (1929), pp. 291-292; E. Nordenskjöld, "Nécrologie: Karl von den Steinen," *Journal de la Société des Américanistes*, vol. 22 (1929), pp. 221-227; Gustav Roessler, "Der Anteil der deutschen völkerkundlichen Erforschung des tropischen Südamerika vom Ende des 19. Jahrhunderts bis zum Beginn des Weltkrieges," *Göttinger Völkerkundliche Studien* (1939), pp. 268-288; Günther Hartmann, *Xingu* (Berlin: 1986), pp. 13-15, 39-43, 46-53; Günther Hartmann, *Keramik des Alto Xingu, Zentral-Brasilien* (Berlin: 1986), pp. 8, 9, 13-14, 153-154 and cat. nos. 1-86.

Berthold Riese

Steinmetz, S.R. (Sebald Rudolph). Ethnologist, sociologist. Born in Breda (Netherlands) 6 December 1862, died in Amsterdam (Netherlands) 5 December 1940. Steinmetz's work as an ethnologist can be compared with that of other "armchair" anthropologists who tried to reconstruct evolutionary sequences of particular institutions. His main contribution in this field was a study of the development of penal law.

Steinmetz studied law at Leiden University; and, after his final examination in 1886, he continued his studies at Leipzig, where WILHELM WUNDT and FRIEDRICH RATZEL were among his teachers. Having returned to Leiden in 1888 he presented the second volume of his studies on the origins and early development of legal punishment as his Ph.D. thesis in 1892. His choice of subject had been much influenced by G.A. WILKEN, who had argued the value of ethnology for the comparative study of law. From E.B. TYLOR Steinmetz adopted the statistical method for the analysis of correlations between functionally related phenomena. Although Steinmetz had a keen eye for the interconnectedness of social phenomena, he tended toward psychological reductionism when looking for ultimate explanations.

Steinmetz did some teaching at Utrecht and Leiden Universities, but it was not until 1908 that he acquired a tenured position at Amsterdam. There he had to teach geography as well as ethnology. However, in his opinion social life was certainly not determined by environmental factors and had to be the subject of a separate branch of scientific description, which he dubbed sociography when applied to civilized peoples, in the same way that ethnography was concerned with the observation and recording of the way of life of primitive peoples. The inductive generalizations based on such empirical research constituted the sciences of sociology and ethnology. Steinmetz put much store by a comprehensive coverage of all known facts. Before World War I he even tried to set up an equivalent of the Human Relations Area Files, but, lacking funds, the project was never completed.

A number of dissertations were completed under Steinmetz's supervision according to his methodological principles and statistical methods, but only one of them had a lasting impact: H.J. Nieboer's *Slavery as an Industrial System*, which was completed in 1900. In the Netherlands his influence as a sociologist has been much greater than that exerted by him as an ethnologist. A high proportion of the sociological chairs established after 1945, when sociology became an autonomous subject at Dutch universities, were occupied by his former students.

MAJOR WORKS: *Ethnologische Studien zur ersten Entwicklung der Strafe*, vol. 2 (Leiden: 1892); *Ethnologische Studien zur ersten Entwicklung der Strafe nebst einer psychologischen Abhandlung über Grausamkeit und Rachsucht*, vol. 1 (Leiden: 1894); "Endokannibalismus," *Mitteilungen der Anthropologischen Gesellschaft in Wien*, vol. 26 (1896), pp. 1-60; "Classification des types sociaux et catalogue de peuples," *L'Année sociologique*, vol. 3 (1898/99) [articles reprinted in *Gesammelte kleinere Schriften zur Ethnologie und Soziologie* [2 vols.] (Groningen: 1928-1930)].

SOURCES: Marcel Mauss, "La religion et les origines du droit pénal d'après un livre recent," *Revue de l'histoire des religions*, vol. 34 (1896), pp. 269-295; vol. 35 (1897), pp. 31-60; W.A. Bonger, "De plaats van Steinmetz in de geschiedenis der maatschappelijke wetenschappen in Nederland," *Mensch en Maatschappij*, vol. 9 (1933), pp. 2-10; J.J. Fahrenfort, "Steinmetz als ethnoloog," *Mensch en Maatschappij*, vol. 9 (1933), pp. 11-16; J.J. Fahrenfort, "S.R. Steinmetz als volkenkundige," *Mens en Maatschappij*, vol. 38 (1963), pp. 24-32; J.P. Kruijt, "De betekenis van Steinmetz voor de sociografie en sociologie," *Mens en Maatschappij*, vol. 38 (1963), pp. 32-40; E.W. Hofstee, "Steinmetz, Sebald Rudolph" in: J. Charité (editor), *Biografisch woordenboek van Nederland* (Amsterdam: 1985), vol. 2, pp. 535-536; E.E. Evans-Pritchard, *A History of Anthropological Thought* (London: 1981), pp. 187-188.

S.R. Jaarsma and J.J. de Wolf

Stephens, John Lloyd. Traveler, archaeologist. Born in Shrewsbury (New Jersey) 25 November 1805, died in New York (New York) 12 October 1852. Stephens wrote widely about his extensive travels in the Middle East and Mesoamerica. His work on the Maya ruins is particularly renowned.

Stephens was trained as a lawyer, but in the course of a trip to Europe and the Near East during 1834-1835, discovered a taste for travel and a gift for writing. In 1836 he traveled to Egypt and to what is now Jordan; he described this trip in *Incidents of Travel in Egypt, Arabia Petraea and the Holy Land*. In 1836 he met FREDERICK CATHERWOOD in London. The two struck up a long-term friendship, and their collaboration on a travel book about Eastern Europe (Stephens wrote the text; Catherwood illustrated it) set the pattern for their later, more famous work in Central America.

Their initial travel in Central America was to some extent justified by Stephens' appointment as chargé d'affaires. These journeys—to Copán and Palenque (1839-1840) and later to Chichen Itzá, Uxmal and elsewhere (1840-1841)—resulted in the most accurate and most enticingly written descriptions of these ruins that had ever appeared, and they awakened scholars' interest in the ruins to such an extent that they can be said in many respects to have laid the groundwork for later, more formal archaeological research.

Stephens spent the last years of his life first in the steamship, later in the railway business.

MAJOR WORKS: *Incidents of Travel in Egypt, Arabia Petraea and the Holy Land* [2 vols.] (New York: 1837); *Incidents of Travel in Central America, Chiapas and Yucatán* [2 vols.] (New York: 1841); *Incidents of Travel in Yucatán* [2 vols.] (New York: 1843).

SOURCES: Victor W. von Hagen, *Maya Explorer: John Lloyd Stephens and the Lost Cities of Central America and Yucatán* (Norman: 1947); Victor W. von Hagen, *Frederick Catherwood, Archt.* (New York: 1950); Victor W. von Hagen, *Search for the Maya: the Story of Stephens and Catherwood* (Westmead: 1973).

Stern, Bernhard J. Sociologist, anthropologist. Born in Chicago (Illinois) 19 June 1894, died in New York (New York) 22 November 1956. While working on a B.A. and M.A. at the University of Cincinnati (1913-1917) Stern studied at the Hebrew Union College and became a Reform rabbi. After studying at the University of Berlin and at the London School of Economics and giving up aspirations to become a medical doctor, Stern entered graduate school at Columbia in 1924, where he studied with FRANZ BOAS and WILLIAM F. OGBURN and wrote a doctoral thesis on social resistance to medical innovations that was published in 1927. As an Assistant Professor of Sociology at the University of Washington (1927-1930), he did fieldwork among the Lummi, co-authored an anthropology textbook with MELVILLE JACOBS, wrote books on race and on the family and began research on the ideas of LEWIS HENRY MORGAN. From 1931 until his death Stern was a lecturer in sociology and anthropology at Columbia. Also in 1931 he joined the *Encyclopedia of the Social Science*s project as an assistant editor. In 1936 Stern was one of the founders of the Marxist journal, *Science and Society*. Stern pioneered a history-oriented medical sociology in addition to doing archival research on 19th-century American social science. Although he was not promoted to a rank commensurate with his scholarly accomplishments at Columbia, he was defended by the institution when attempts were made to have him dismissed during the red-baiting 1950s.

MAJOR WORKS: *Social Factors in Medical Progress* (New York: 1927); *Lewis Henry Morgan: Social Evolutionist* (Chicago: 1931); *The Lummi Indians of Northwest Washington* (New York: 1934); (with Melville Jacobs) *General Anthropology* (New York: 1947; 2nd ed., New York: 1952); *Historical Sociology: the Selected Papers of Bernhard J. Stern* (New York: 1959).

SOURCES: Samuel W. Bloom, "The intellectual in a time of crisis: the case of Bernhard J. Stern," *Journal of the History of the Behavioral Sciences*, vol. 26 (1990), pp. 17-37; Robert Merton and William Goode, "Bernhard J. Stern," *American Sociological Review*, vol. 22 (1957), pp. 460-461.

Stephen O. Murray

Stevenson, Matilda Coxe (née Matilda Coxe Evans). Ethnologist. Born in San Augustine (Texas) 12 May 1849, died in Oxon Hill (Maryland) 24 June 1915. Stevenson was born into a prosperous family and trained by governesses at home and as a student at Miss Anable's Academy in Philadelphia. She also read law while she clerked for her father, an attorney, and she studied chemistry and geology with N.M. Mew, of the U.S. Army Medical School. After marrying James Stevenson, executive officer of the U.S. Geological Survey of the Territories (Hayden Survey), Stevenson accompanied her husband in his fieldwork and began to study some of the Indian groups they encountered. She continued this after her husband joined JOHN WESLEY POWELL's Bureau of American Ethnology (BAE). Their first BAE-sponsored trip in 1879 introduced her to the Zuni, who became long-time subjects of her research. Although it was originally anticipated that she would complement her husband's ethnographic investigations through the study of women and children, she was the one who became an active student of ethnology. Her interests eventually focused on Pueblo religion, including secret organizations and ceremonies.

James Stevenson died in 1888, and Matilda Stevenson—childless, capable and politically influential—obtained employment at the BAE to continue their work. In 1881 she took up the study of the Hopi and by the end of her life had worked at Zia, Jemez, Cochiti,

Santa Clara, San Juan, San Ildefonso, Nambe and Taos. In her later years she was engaged in a general comparative study of Pueblo religion, especially that of the Tewa. A believer in the need for long-term fieldwork if a culture was to be truly and thoroughly understood by an outsider, she was never satisfied with the completeness of her inquiries and, consequently, she failed to publish much of the data recorded during her fieldwork.

Stevenson served as a champion as well as an example of women's suitability for anthropological research. She was founder and first president of the Women's Anthropological Society of America, one of the first female members of the Anthropological Society of Washington and a fellow of the American Association for the Advancement of Science. She became the only professional female employee on the regular rolls of the BAE. She also served as a judge at the World's Columbian Exposition and was on the Board of Lady Managers of the Louisiana Purchase Exposition, for which she also prepared an exhibit on Zuni symbolism.

On a negative side, Stevenson was well known for being contentious, and she was sometimes imperious and high-handed in dealing with her Indian hosts, possibly to the point of having brought injury to the cause of anthropology. One researcher has explained that "so single-minded did she become in her quest, in her dedication to the science of anthropology, that she developed a reputation for being pigheaded, humorless, insensitive, and overbearing" (Parezo). At the same time, however, she was quite capable of cordiality and long-lasting friendships with some informants.

MAJOR WORKS: "The Sia," *Annual Report of the Bureau of American Ethnology*, vol. 11 (1894), pp. 3-157; "The Zuni Indians," *Annual Report of the Bureau of American Ethnology*, vol. 23 (1904), pp. 1-608.

SOURCES: William Henry Holmes, "Matilda Coxe Stevenson," *American Anthropologist*, vol. 18 (1916), pp. 552-559; Nancy O. Lurie, "Matilda Coxe Evans Stevenson" in: Edward T. James [et al.], *Notable American Women, 1607-1905* (Cambridge, Mass.: 1971), pp. 373-374; Matilda Coxe Stevenson manuscripts and papers in the Smithsonian Institution National Anthropological Archives; Nancy J. Parezo, "Matilda Coxe Evans Stevenson" in: Ute Gacs [et. al.] (editors), *Women Anthropologists: a Biographical Dictionary* (New York: 1988), pp. 337-343.

James R. Glenn

Steward, Julian H. Anthropologist. Born in Washington (D.C.) 31 January 1902, died in Urbana (Illinois) 6 February 1972. Steward received a B.A. in zoology and geology from Cornell University in 1925 and a Ph.D. in anthropology from the University of California, Berkeley, in 1929. After early university teaching positions, Steward in 1935 accepted a post in the Bureau of American Ethnology of the Smithsonian Institution; he became director of its Institute of Social Anthropology in 1943. He subsequently served as professor of anthropology at Columbia University from 1946 to 1952 and as research professor of anthropology at the University of Illinois from 1952 until his retirement in 1970.

One of the great anthropological theorists of the 20th century, Steward is best known for his ideas on "cultural ecology." This theory holds that a society's environmental resources in conjunction with the technology available to exploit them determine the forms of labor used by the group, which in turn exert profound influence on the entire social system. He applied this theory, using a method that was both comparative and historical, in a search for scientifically verifiable laws of social causality. This inquiry led

Steward to formulate a theory of "multilinear evolution," which outlined several possible paths societies have taken in the course of orderly progression toward greater complexity.

In a parallel progression, he began his ethnographic career among the Western Shoshone, one of the world's simplest societies, and culminated it with major programs of research on the nature of complex cultures, starting with his pioneering analysis of Puerto Rican society and ending with a four-continent, cross-cultural inquiry into modernization of peasant societies. Today most anthropologists work in complex societies, and cultural ecology remains one of the discipline's major interests. The contributions of Julian Steward are lasting and pervasive.

MAJOR WORKS: *Basin-Plateau Aboriginal Sociopolitical Groups* (Washington: 1938); (editor) *Handbook of South American Indians* [6 vols.] (Washington: 1946-1950); *Area Research: Theory and Practice* (New York: 1950); *Theory of Culture Change* (Urbana: 1955); *The People of Puerto Rico* (Urbana: 1956); (with Louis C. Faron) *Native Peoples of South America* (New York: 1959); (editor) *Contemporary Change in Traditional Societies* [3 vols.] (Urbana: 1967); *Evolution and Ecology: Essays on Social Transformation* (Jane C. Steward and Robert F. Murphy, editors) (Urbana: 1977).

SOURCES: Robert Manners (editor), *Process and Pattern in Culture: Essays in Honor of Julian H. Steward* (Chicago: 1967); Marvin Harris, *The Rise of Anthropological Theory* (New York: 1968); Robert Manners, "Julian Haynes Steward," *American Anthropologist*, vol. 75 (1973), pp. 886-903; Robert F. Murphy, "Introduction: the anthropological theories of Julian H. Steward" in: Julian H. Steward, *Evolution and Ecology: Essays on Social Transformation* (Jane C. Steward and Robert F. Murphy, editors) (Urbana: 1977), pp. 1-39.

Robert F. Murphy

Stokes, John F.G. Anthropologist, historian. Born 1875, died 9 September 1960. Stokes joined the Bernice P. Bishop Museum in 1899 as one of the earliest members of the research staff. He served at one time or another as librarian, curator and researcher until he left the museum in 1929. He was a founding member of the Anthropological Society of Hawaii. He wrote articles on the culture of the native Hawaiians during his time at the museum; fishing techniques, handicrafts and artwork were topics of particular interest to him. He also did an ethnological survey of the Austral Islands group south of Tahiti. After 1929 he continued to be an active participant in the work of the Hawaiian Historical Society.

MAJOR WORKS: *An Account of the Polynesian Race: Its Origins and Migrations, and the Ancient History of the Hawaiian People to the Times of Kamehameha I* [3 vols.] (London: 1878-1885).

SOURCES: E.H. Bryan, "Biography of J.F.G. Stokes" [manuscript, Bernice P. Bishop Museum] (September 1960); "[Obituary]," *Honolulu Advertiser* (11 September 1960), p. 7.

Thomas L. Mann

Strong, William Duncan. Anthropologist, archaeologist. Born in Portland (Oregon) 30 January 1899, died in Kent (New York) 29 January 1962. Strong's family was active in the early history of the Oregon and Washington territories where it had formed a sympathetic, "long and warm association" with the native Americans. Given this impetus, he earned his Ph.D. in anthropology at the University of California, Berkeley in 1926 where he studied with ALFRED L. KROEBER. It was at Berkeley that he became fully convinced that ethnology and archaeology should be complementary disciplines. Strong's first major publications dealt with ethnological research in the southwestern United States and California, but his first expression of an integrated anthropological approach is seen in the work he carried out with Waldo R. Wedel in Nebraska. To this day, their study remains an important example of the direct-historical method. Carried out during Strong's tenure at the Smithsonian Institution in Washington, D.C., this investigation led to the realization that the historically well known nomadic Plains Indians had been sedentary agriculturalists before the introduction of horses in Late Prehistoric times. By selecting specific sites in order to test and extend back in time contemporary ethnological or historical interpretations, Strong and Wedel were able to build an integrated and continuous developmental sequence. This fieldwork, highly innovative at the time, is still very relevant to the recent controversies on the limitations and proper uses of ethnological analogy in archaeology.

After further work in Honduras and the Great Plains, Strong was appointed to the Department of Anthropology at Columbia University in New York City where he participated in projects carried out by the Institute of Andean Research. In 1943 he was the first to define broadly one of the major traits of post-World War II archaeological research; that is, the study of cultural change from a regional to a continental framework in terms of culture process and culture history. This comparative, historical-developmental perspective led not only to various interpretive models of Andean prehistory by Strong, WENDELL CLARK BENNETT, RAFAEL LARCO HOYLE, JULIAN H. STEWARD and GORDON R. WILLEY but also eventually to a scheme for the entire American continent proposed by Philip Phillips and Gordon R. Willey. Strong remained in the mainstream of archaeological research throughout his career and his work still constitutes an excellent illustration of the advantages of a broad anthropological approach, enriching both ethnology and archaeology through mutual theoretical stimulation and data correlation.

MAJOR WORKS: "The Plains Culture area in the light of archaeology," *American Anthropologist*, n.s., vol. 35 (1933), pp. 271-287; *An Introduction to Nebraska Archaeology* (Washington: 1935); "Anthropological theory and archaeological fact" in: *Essays in Anthropology in Honor of Alfred Louis Kroeber* (Berkeley: 1936), pp. 359-370; "From history to prehistory in the Northern Great Plains" in: *Essays in Historical Anthropology of North America in Honor of John R. Swanton* (Washington: 1940) (= *Smithsonian Miscellaneous Collections*, vol. 100), pp. 353-394; *Cross Sections of New World Prehistory: a Brief Report on the Work of the Institute of Andean Research, 1941-1942* (Washington: 1943); "Cultural epochs and refuse stratigraphy in Peruvian archaeology," *Society for American Archaeology, Memoirs*, no. 4 (1948), pp. 93-102; "Cultural resemblances in nuclear America: parallelism or diffusion?" in: Sol Tax (editor), *The Civilizations of Ancient America: Selected Papers of the International Congress of Americanists, 29th* (Chicago: 1951), pp. 271-279; (with Clifford Evans, Jr.) *Cultural Stratigraphy in the Virú Valley, Northern Peru: the Formative and Florescent Epochs* (New York: 1952); "Knickerbocker views of the Oregon country: Judge William Strong's narrative, with a foreword by William Duncan Strong," *Oregon Historical Quarterly*, vol. 62 (1961), pp. 271-287.

SOURCES: Julian H. Steward, *Theory of Culture Change* (Urbana: 1955); Gordon R. Willey and Jeremy A. Sabloff, *A History of American Archaeology* (2nd ed., San Francisco: 1980); Gordon R. Willey and Philip Phillips, *Method and Theory in American Archaeology* (Chicago: 1958); Jacques Bordaz, "Strong, William Duncan" in: David L. Sills (editor), *International Encyclopedia of the Social Sciences* (New York: 1968-1979), vol. 15, pp. 348-350; Ralph Solecki and Charles Wagley, "William Duncan Strong: 1899-1962," *American Anthropologist*, n.s., vol. 65 (1963), pp. 1102-1111; Gordon R. Willey, "Archeological theories and interpretations: New World" in: *Anthropology Today: an Encyclopedic Inventory* (Chicago: 1953), pp. 361-385; Alison Wylie, "The reaction against analogy" in: Michael B. Schiffer (editor), *Advances in Archaeological Method and Theory*, vol. 8 (New York: 1985), pp. 63-111.

Jacques Bordaz

Struck, Bernhard (Bernhard Friedrich Eduard Struck). Anthropologist, linguist. Born in Heidelberg (Germany) 28 August 1888, died in Jena (German Democratic Republic) 8 October 1971. Struck studied geography, ethnology, anthropology and natural sciences in Heidelberg and later in Berlin, where he also occupied himself with African languages under CARL MEINHOF. Between 1908 and 1909 Struck worked as a research assistant in the African division of the Museum für Völkerkunde (Ethnographic Museum) in Berlin. From 1913 on he worked at the Zoologisches und Anthropologisches Museum (Zoological and Anthropological Museum) in Dresden, where he became curator in 1923. He was awarded his doctorate in 1921 at the University of Tübingen and obtained his *Habilitation* in anthropology and ethnology at the Technische Hochschule in Dresden in 1924; he served there as *außerordentlicher Professor* without portfolio until 1933. In 1937 he became *ordentlicher Professor* in anthropology and ethnology at Jena. During 1930-1931 Struck, together with H.A. Bernatzik, made a research trip to Portuguese Guinea (modern Guinea-Bissau).

Struck's object of research—to pursue as broadly as possible the history of cultures and belief systems, especially those of the African peoples—becomes evident in the broad thematic sweep of his works. Through a painstaking analysis of all publications available to him he was able to achieve new insights. His general survey works are frequently cited as models of their genre, for example, *Die Sprachverhältnisse in Moyen Congo, Somatischen Typen und Sprachgruppen in Kordofan, Chronologie der Beninaltertümer*, and *Systematik der nilotischen Völker und ihrer Abteilungen*. The logical consequence of such mastery of the literature was a series of comprehensive bibliographies on the Bantu languages of British East Africa, Swahili, Northern Nigeria and the Southern Sudan. Struck also prepared case studies on linguistic materials that others placed at his disposal, such as those on the Fipa and the language of the Tatoga and Iraku. Struck was the first to recognize the unity of the branches of the extant languages of Togo, which he termed the "semi-Bantu of Central Togo." In his work *Einige Sudan-Wortstämme* he also undertook for the first time a classification of the Sudanic languages using lexicostatistics (even though he felt this method inappropriate). With regard to the question of the relationship between the Sūdānic and the Bantu languages, Struck advanced the theory in his essay, *Der Schlüssel der Sudansprachen*, published in 1913, that "Ur-Bantu" and "Ur-Sūdānic" were separate descendents of a more ancient basal language family, which he termed "Ur-Nigritic."

MAJOR WORKS: "Collection towards a bibliography of Bantu languages of British East Africa," *Journal of African Languages*, vol. 6 (1907), pp. 390-404; "Suaheli-Bibliographie mit einer Einführung in die moderne Suaheli-Literatur," *Orientalistischer Literaturbericht*, no. 1, 3 (1909), pp. 61-92; "Über die Sprachen der Tatoga und Irakuleute" in: F. Jaeger, *Das Hochland der Riesenkrater und die umliegenden Hochländer Deutsch Ostafrikas* (Berlin: 1911), pp. 107-132; "Linguistic bibliography of Northern Nigeria," *Journal of the African Society*, vol. 11 (1911), pp. 47-61 and 213-230; "Die Fipasprache," *Anthropos*, vol. 6 (1911), pp. 951-993; "Einige Sudan-Wortstämme," *Zeitschrift für Kolonialsprachen*, vol. 2 (1911-1912), pp. 233-253 and 309-323; "Die Sprachverhältnisse im Moyen Congo," *Koloniale Rundschau* (1912), pp. 204-225; "Linguistische Kongostudien,"

Mitteilungen des Seminars für Orientalische Sprachen, vol. 16 (1913), pp. 93-113; "Der Schlüssel der Sudansprachen," *Allgemeine Missionszeitung*, vol. 11-12 (1913), pp. 1-25; "Die Gbaya-Sprache," *Mitteilungen des Seminars für Orientalische Sprachen*, vol. 16 (1918), pp. 53-100; "Somatische Typen und Sprachgruppen in Kordofan," *Zeitschrift für Eingeborenen-Sprachen*, vol. 52 (1920), pp. 129-170; "Chronologie der Beninaltertümer," *Zeitschrift für Ethnologie*, vol. 55 (1923), pp. 113-166; "A bibliography of the languages of the Southern Sudan," *Sudan Notes and Records*, vol. 9 (1928), pp. 217-226; "Systematik der nilotischen Völker und ihrer Abteilungen" in: H. Bernatzik, *Zwischen Weissem Nil und Belgisch-Kongo* (Vienna: 1929), pp. 125-129.

SOURCES: E. Dammann, "In memoriam Bernhard Struck," *Afrika und Übersee*, vol. 5 (1971-1972), pp. 241-242; Gudrun Miehe, "Struck, Bernhard Friedrich Eduard" in: H. Jungraithmayr and W.J.G. Möhlig (editors), *Lexikon der Afrikanistik* (Berlin: 1983), pp. 230-231; Gudrun Miehe, "In memoriam Bernhard Struck," *Africana Marburgensia*, vol. 5, no. 2 (1972), pp. 66-69.

G. Miehe and K. Winkelmann
[Translation from German: Robert B. Marks Ridinger]

Suk, Vojtěch. Anthropologist, traveler. Born in Prague (Czechoslovakia) 18 August 1879, died in Brno (Czechoslovakia) 8 March 1967. Suk attended the University of Zürich, where he was awarded his Ph.D. in anthropology, ethnology and zoology after defending his dissertation on the myology of primates. Later, he broadened his education through the study of medicine at Charles University in Prague where he received his M.D. in 1922. In 1919 he was promoted to the Faculty of Natural Sciences of Charles University, and, after establishing the Institute of Anthropology at the Faculty of Natural Sciences at the University in Brno in 1923, he became a university professor there. Professor Suk devoted his attention primarily to problems relating to the biology of different ethnic groups. He studied the influence of the environment on the growth of children in central Europe and central Africa, health conditions of Huculs in the Carpatho-Ukraine from an anthropological point of view, Eskimos in Labrador, and also general questions of physical anthropology (such as serology, physiological variability and physical structure and its classification, which he interpreted from an evolutionary point of view).

Between the two world wars his interest was concentrated on pedagogical questions and problems of social hygiene. With his conceptual focus on human biology, his views emphasizing synthesis and his consistently anti-racist attitude, he was a pioneer of several trends in physical anthropological research.

MAJOR WORKS: "Beiträge zur Myologie d. Primaten," *Gegenbaurs Morphologisches Jahrbuch*, no. 45 (1913), pp. 267-294; and no. 47 (1915), pp. 355-418; "Chrup školní mládeže pražské z hlediska antropologického" ["Teeth of school youth in Prague from an anthropological point of view"], *Biologické listy a lékařské rozhledy* (Prague: 1916); "Eruption and decay of permanent teeth in Whites and Negroes ... ," *American Journal of Physical Anthropology*, vol. 24 (1919), pp. 351-388; "Health status of students after physical training and after brain work," *Anthropologie*, vol. 7 (1929), pp. 130-168; *Contribution of the Study of Blood Groups in Czechoslovakia* (Brno: 1930) (= *Spisy vydávané přírodovědeckou fakultou Masarykovy University v Brně*, no. 124); "Congenital pigment spots in Eskimo children," *Anthropologie*, vol. 6 (1928), pp. 28-34; *Fallacies of Anthropological Identifications and Reconstructions: a Critique Based on Anatomical Dissection* (= *Spisy vydávané přírodovědeckou fakultou Masarykovy University v Brně*, no. 207); "Race and racismus," *Práce Brněnské základny ČSAV*, vol. 27 (1955), pp. 157-192.

SOURCES: A. Lorencová and J. Beneš, "Prof. MUDr. et RNDr. V. Suk, DrSc," *Anthropologie*, vol. 5, no. 3 (1967), pp. 67-69; M. Dokládal, "Vědecký odkaz profesora V. Suka" ["Scientific heritage of Professor V. Suk"], *Zprávy antropologické společnosti při ČSAV*, vol. 20, no. 3 (1967), pp. 36-37; E. Vlček (editor), "Czechoslovak anthropologist contributes to the world science," *Národní muzeum Praha* (1970), pp. 18-29.

J. Beneš
[*Translation from Czech: Jitka Hurych*]

Sundkler, Bengt. Theologian, church historian. Born in Degerfors (Sweden) 7 May 1909. Sundkler was the son of a merchant. He obtained his "GCE" at advanced level in Umeå in 1928 and received his B.D. (*teol. kand*) in 1931, his Master of Divinity (*teol. lic.*) in 1936 and his Doctorate of Divinity in 1937. He was appointed docent of mission history in 1945 and professor of ecclesiastical history in 1949.

Sundkler served as a missionary of the Swedish Lutheran Church in South Africa from 1937 to 1942. He was the director of a theological seminary in Tanganyika in 1944 and 1945, and he was appointed the bishop of Bukoba in 1961. Sundkler has become known to an international public through his works on the indigenous churches of South Africa (e.g., *The Christian Ministry in Africa*). His latest scholarly contribution is a major work on Church history in Africa (in press).

MAJOR WORKS: *Bantu Prophets in South Africa* (London: 1948; 2nd ed., London and New York: 1960); *Ung kyrka i Tanganyika* (Stockholm: 1948); *Missionsforskningens arbetsuppgifter* (Uppsala: 1952); *Church of South India: the Movement towards Union, 1900-1947* (London: 1954); (co-editor with Gudmar Sommerström) *Svensk missionsatlas* (Stockholm: 1957); *The Christian Ministry in Africa* (Uppsala and London: 1960); *The Church History of Africa* (in press).

Jan-Åke Alvarsson

Sundt, Eilert Lund. Demographer, anthropologist, sociologist, social reformer, editor, clergyman. Born in Farsund (Norway) 8 August 1817, died in Eidsvoll (Norway) 13 June 1875. In 1835 Sundt entered the University of Christiania (Oslo) where he was caught up in the national romantic movement that esteemed authentic folk traditions and was to influence his career as a social researcher and social reformer. He graduated at the top of his class in 1846, winning a scholarship for further study of ecclesiastical history. However, he wanted neither the life of a professor nor that of a clergyman. Instead, after a field study of Gypsy culture in 1847 and 1848, he developed an unprecedented research career, supported continuously from 1850 to 1869 with government stipends. An indefatigable field worker, he traveled throughout the country, studying the culture and living conditions of the peasantry, working class, and minority groups of Norway. His life program encompassed a series of interrelated topics of contemporary public concern, among them, population growth and marriage practices of the lower classes, urban poverty, rural-urban migration, morality and social control, housing conditions, technological change, working conditions for women, and alcohol use. His methods ranged from sophisticated statistical analysis of large questionnaire surveys to sensitive case studies of particular individuals and families. His books, written for a popular audience, are sprinkled with dialogue between the author and his informants. "Sundt's law," his most noted demographic generalization, relates marriage rates in the population to earlier fertility rates.

Sundt's work was controversial. He rejected both economic determinism as a causal explanation and class conflict as a mechanism for eventual social betterment. At the same time his interpretations did not reinforce the stereotypes held by the middle and professional classes. Increasingly sensitive to the historical and cultural context of peasant and working class practices, Sundt revealed the logic behind customs that seemed "immoral" or "backward" to the middle class. His defense of peasant cooking and hygienic practices embroiled him in highly public controversies. His support in Parliament declined and his stipend was eliminated in 1869, forcing him to take a position as a clergyman in Eidsvoll and to restrict, but not eliminate, his field research. Sundt was a leader in two social reform organizations, the Workers' Association of Christiana and the Society for the Promotion of Popular Enlightenment, and edited the journal of the latter organization.

Writing in a minor European language, outside of a university context and without students or collaborators to carry on his work, Sundt's influence outside of Scandinavia has been minimal until a post-war revival of interest in his work, marked by the English translation of *Om giftermaal i Norge*, his most important book, and the reissuing of a selection of his other works. In addition to the contribution to applied statistics and demography for which he is best known, Sundt anticipated, more or less explicitly, the functionalist argument concerning the interrelatedness of cultural elements, the ethnographer's use of observation and informal interviews, the historicist's emphasis on cultural continuity, the relativist's insistence on the contextual importance of values, the urbanist's concern with the breakdown of social order in cities, the structural sociologist's deductions about the consequences of social scale and differentiation, the social network analyst's search for interactional linkages among units and the symbolic anthropologist's exegesis of relations among symbolic categories.

MAJOR WORKS: *Beretning om fante- eller landstrygerfolket i Norge* (Christiania: 1850); *Om dødelighheden i Norge* (Christiania: 1855); *Om giftermaal i Norge* (Christiania: 1855; Oslo: 1967) [tr.: *On Marriage in Norway* (Cambridge: 1980)]; *Om sædeligheds-tilstanden i Norge* (Christiania: 1857) (Oslo: 1968); *Om Piperviken og Ruseløkbakken: Undersøgelser om arbeidsklassens kaar og sæder i Christiania* (Christiania: 1858; Oslo: 1975); *Om Røros og Omegn* (Christiania: 1858; Oslo: 1975); *Om ædrueligheds-tilstanden i Norge* (Christiania: 1859); *Om bygnings-skikken paa landet i Norge* (Christiania: 1862); *Om husfliden i Norge* (Christiania: 1867); *Om renligheds-stellet i Norge* (Christiania: 1869).

SOURCES: Martin Allwood, *Eilert Sundt: a Pioneer in Sociology and Social Anthropology* (Oslo: 1957); H.O. Christophersen, *Eilert Sundt: en dikter i kjensgjerninger* (Oslo: 1962); Nils Christie, *Eilert Sundt som fanteforsker og sosialstatistiker* (Oslo: 1958) (= *Instituttet for Sosiologi, Stensilserie*); Michael Drake, "Introduction" to: *On Marriage in Norway* (Cambridge: 1980), pp. xiii-xxi; Michael Drake, "T.R. Malthus and Eilert Sundt" in: *Population and Society in Norway, 1735-1865* (Cambridge: 1969), pp. 19-40; Helge Refsum, "Eilert Sundt" in: *Norsk Biografisk Leksikon* (Oslo: 1923-), vol. 15 (1966), pp. 276-293; Arthur Hillman, "Eilert Sundt: pioneer student of family and culture in Norway" in: Thomas D. Eliot, Arthur Hillman [et al.], *Norway's Families* (Philadelphia: 1960), pp. 36-46; Johan Vogt, "Sundt, Eilert Lund" in: David L. Sills (editor), *International Encyclopedia of the Social Sciences* (New York: 1968-1979), vol. 15, pp. 409-411; Francis Bull, "Sundt, Eilert Lund" in: E.R.A. Seligman (editor), *Encyclopaedia of the Social Sciences* (New York: 1930-1935), vol. 14, pp. 468-469; Gudmund R. Iversen, "Eilert Sundt som statistiker," *Tidsskrift for samfunnsforskning*, vol. 24 (1983), pp. 577-591; Douglas Caulkins, "The Norwegian connection: Eilert Sundt and the idea of social networks in 19th century ethnology," *Connections*, vol. 3, no. 2 (1981), pp. 28-31.

Douglas Caulkins

Suzuki, Hisashi. Physical anthropologist. Born in Hatogaya (Japan) 24 March 1912. Following his graduation from the University of Tōkyō Faculty of Medicine in 1936, Suzuki studied physical anthropology under Professor Emeritus YOSHIKIYO KOGANEI after entering the Department of Anatomy. In 1943 he transferred to the Department of Anthropology in the Faculty of Science, becoming head of that department in 1955. He retired from the University of Tōkyō in 1972 and, in that year, established the Department of Anthropology at the National Science Museum, becoming its founding director. From 1970 to 1976 he served as president of the Anthropological Society of Nippon.

In 1953 he excavated the medieval burial site of Zaimokuza in Kamakura, discovering many skeletal remains, thereby demonstrating brachycephalization in the Japanese people from medieval to modern times. From 1958 to 1960 he investigated the remains of the Tokugawa *shōguns* and their wives throughout the dynasties and clarified physical aspects of the peerage in early modern times.

After 1957 he expanded his investigations in the search for Pleistocene hominid fossils within the Japanese archipelago. This work included the discoveries of the specimens termed Mikkabi Man, Hamakita Man, and Minatogawa Man—concerning all of which full detailed accounts were recorded. In 1961 he formed an expedition that went to Israel to excavate Amud Cave in the Lake Tiberias region, where he discovered a relatively complete Neanderthal skeleton.

MAJOR WORKS: (with Hitoshi Watanabe [et al.]) *Kamakura Zaimokuza Hakken no Chūsei Iseki to Sono Jinkotsu* [*Medieval Japanese Skeletons from the Burial Site at Zaimokuza, Kamakura City*] (Tōkyō: 1956) [with English summary]; (with Kyōsuke Yajima, Tomoyuki Yamanobe [et al.]) *Zōjōji Tokugawa Shogunbo to Sono Ihin/Itai* [*Studies on the Graves, Coffin Contents and Skeletal Remains of Tokugawa Shoguns and their Families at the Zōjōji Temple*] (Tōkyō: 1967) [with English summary]; (with Fuyuji Takai [et al.]) *The Amud Man and his Cave Site* (Tōkyō: 1970); "Racial history of the Japanese" in: I. Schwidetsky (editor), *Rassengeschichte der Menschheit, Asien I* (Vienna: 1981), pp. 7-69; (with Kazuro Hanihara [et al.]) *The Minatogawa Man* (Tōkyō: 1982) (= *The University Museum, University of Tōkyō, Bulletin,* no. 19); "Pleistocene man in Japan," *Journal of the Anthropological Society of Nippon,* vol. 90, supplement (1982), pp. 11-26.

SOURCES: Hisashi Suzuki, "Watakushi no jinruigaku 50-nen" ["Fifty years as an anthropologist"], *Shinzenkagaku to Hakubutsukan,* vol. 43 (1976), pp. 30-37; Kazuo Terada, "Suzuki Higashi Sensei no koki o iwattei" ["A short biography of Professor Hisashi Suzuki in commemoration of his seventieth birthday"], *Journal of the Anthropological Society of Nippon,* vol. 90, supplement (1982), pp. 1-10.

Bin Yamaguchi
[Translation from Japanese: Theodore Welch]

Swadesh, Morris. Linguist, anthropologist. Born in Holyoke (Massachusetts) 22 January 1909, died in Mexico City (Mexico) 20 July 1967. Swadesh studied linguistics under EDWARD SAPIR at the University of Chicago, taking his bachelor's and master's degrees in 1930 and 1931, respectively. He then followed Sapir to Yale, where he received his Ph.D. in linguistics in 1933 with a dissertation on the Nootka language of Vancouver Island, British Columbia. Swadesh continued to be associated with Yale over the next several years, as an American Council of Learned Societies fellow (studying variations in spoken English) and, during 1936-1937, as an instructor of linguistics. He was appointed an associate professor of anthropology at the University of Wisconsin in 1937 and remained there for two years.

In 1939 Swadesh was approached by representatives of the Mexican government who asked him to take charge of a literacy project among Tarascan-speakers of Michoacán state. Swadesh became professor of anthropology at the Instituto Politécnico Nacional de México (National Polytechnic Institute of Mexico) and learned both Spanish and Tarascan in record time. (It is indicative of both his linguistic gifts and his determination that Swadesh published a major book in Spanish before the end of 1941.)

With the United States' entry into World War II, Swadesh became a language instructor for the Army and later for the Office of Strategic Services. He rose to the rank of first lieutenant and taught Russian, Chinese, Spanish and Burmese from 1942 until 1946. From that year to 1948 he was a Guggenheim fellow, studying Nootkan once again, followed by a year as an associate professor of anthropology at the City College of New York. The period from 1949 until 1954 was spent on his major research project, lexicostatistical analyses of American Indian and Eskimo languages, under the auspices of the American Philosophical Society. From 1955 until his death, Swadesh was professor at the Escuela Nacional de Antropología e Historia (National School of Anthropology and History) in Mexico City. He was also a frequent visiting professor at universities in North, Central and South America.

Lexicostatistics was a major innovation in linguistics, as it depended on analysis of certain kinds of differentiation between related languages to yield an approximate date for those languages' separation from a single, earlier form. Swadesh applied his theory to languages from many parts of the New World.

Another major interest of Swadesh's was in the area of language teaching methods. His career presented him with a number of opportunities to practice and observe the teaching of many different languages, both in spoken and written forms. He published primers with titles like *Talking Russian Before You Know It* and *Chinese in Your Pocket*.

Swadesh was an important theorist in linguistics and linguistic anthropology, with remarkably broad interests. He produced more than 20 books and monographs and well over 100 articles, on topics including such varied languages as Tarascan, Russian, Gur (a West African language family), Eskimo and Chitimacha—to mention only a few. His prolificacy with regard to languages was an enabler of his broad theoretical concerns. In his last years he took up the problem of ultimate origins of language, a subject too vast for anyone less broadly grounded in the varieties of human speech.

MAJOR WORKS: "The phonemic principle," *Language*, vol. 10 (1934), pp. 117-129; *La nueva filología* (Mexico City: 1941); "On the analysis of English syllabics," *Language*, vol. 23 (1947), pp. 137-150; "Motivations in Nootka warfare," *Southwestern Journal of Anthropology*, vol. 4 (1948), pp. 76-93; "Salish internal relationships," *International Journal of American Linguistics*, vol. 16 (1950), pp. 157-167; "Lexicostatistical dating of prehistoric ethnic contacts with special reference to North American Indians and Eskimos," *Proceedings of the American Philosophical Society*, vol. 96 (1952), pp. 452-463; "Time depths of American linguistics groupings," *American Anthropologist*, vol. 56 (1954), pp. 361-377; (with Edward Sapir) *Native Accounts of Nootka Ethnography* (Bloomington: 1955); "Linguistic relations across Bering Strait," *American Anthropologist*, vol. 64 (1962), pp. 1262-1291; "Origen y evolución del lenguaje humano," *Anales de Antropología*, vol. 2 (1965), pp. 61-88 .

SOURCES: Juan Jose Rendon, "Mauricio Swadesh, 1909-1967," *América Indígena*, vol. 27 (1967), pp. 735-746; Norman A. McQuown, "Morris Swadesh, 1909-1967," *American Anthropologist*, vol. 70 (1968), pp. 755-756.

David Lonergan

Swanton, John Reed. Ethnohistorian, ethnologist. Born in Gardiner (Maine) 19 February 1873, died in Newton (Massachusetts) 2 May 1958. Swanton earned a B.A. from Harvard in 1896, an M.A. in 1897 and a Ph.D. in 1900. Along with ROLAND B. DIXON, Swanton spent the last two years of his graduate work studying with FRANZ BOAS at Columbia. After some fieldwork on Vancouver Island (primarily among the Haida Tlingit), Swanton took up a position at the Bureau of American Ethnology of the Smithsonian Institution and remained there through the end of World War II.

Swanton focused on migrations of Native Americans, particularly in the Southeast. He critically reviewed documents left by explorers, travelers and missionaries for information on the social structure and tribal distinctions in that area and championed ethnohistorical research at a time when other Boas students refused to consider data not gathered by professionally trained anthropologists. Swanton's work on social structure was taken as disproving 19th-century evolutionist claims on the order of "structuration." In addition to critically sorting through historical documents for ethnological data, Swanton collected a basic lexicon from the last speakers of Muskogean and Tunica and classified North American kinship systems.

MAJOR WORKS: "The social organization of American tribes," *American Anthropologist*, vol. 7 (1905), pp. 663-673; *Indian Tribes of the Lower Mississippi Valley and Adjacent Coast of the Gulf of Mexico* (Washington: 1911) (= *Bureau of American Ethnology Bulletin*, no. 43); (with Roland B. Dixon) "Primitive American history," *American Anthropologist*, vol. 16 (1914), pp. 376-412; *Final Report of the United States De Soto Expedition Commission* (Washington: 1939); *Source Material on the History and Ethnology of Caddo Indians* (Washington: 1942) (= *Bureau of American Ethnology Bulletin*, no. 132); *Indians of the Southeastern United States* (Washington: 1952) (= *Bureau of American Ethnology Bulletin*, no. 145).

SOURCES: Alfred L. Kroeber, *Essays in Historical Anthropology of North America* (Washington: 1940) (= *Smithsonian Miscellaneous Collections*, vol. 100); William N. Fenton, "John Reed Swanton," *American Anthropologist*, vol. 61 (1959), pp. 663-668; Stephen O. Murray, "Historical inferences from ethnohistorical data," *Journal of the History of the Behavioral Sciences*, vol. 19 (1983), pp. 335-340.

Stephen O. Murray

t

Tangco, Marcelo V. Anthropologist, educator, administrator. Born in the Philippines 16 January 1893, died in Manila (Philippines) 27 August 1987. Tangco is best known in the Philippines for his writings on the Christian peoples of the Philippines. He was the country's first professional anthropologist, the first physical anthropologist and the first full professor and head, Department of Anthropology, University of the Philippines.

Tangco graduated from the Manila High School in 1913. He received his A.B. and High School Certificate from the University of the Philippines in 1916 and the B.S.E. degree from the same institution in 1918. From 1921 until 1925 he was a fellow of the University of the Philippines at Harvard University and the University of California at Berkeley. He finished an M.A. at Harvard in 1922 and also did two years of postgraduate studies at Berkeley.

Tangco taught at the Manila High School from 1916 until 1918. He became an assistant instructor at the University of the Philippines in 1918 and an instructor until 1945. Promoted to Associate Professor in 1946, he became full Professor and head of the Department of Anthropology in 1954, holding these positions until his retirement in 1958. In 1963, the University of the Philippines designated him Professor Emeritus.

Tangco was a member of the First Independence Congress in 1930 and was appointed translator (from English to Tagalog) of the Community Assembly Lectures for the enlightenment of the masses from 1932 to 1935 by former Governor General Theodore Roosevelt.

From among skeletal remains of soldiers of several nationalities exhumed from Bataan, Tangco identified and selected the remains of a Filipino soldier who was honored as the Unknown Filipino Soldier during the Philippine Independence anniversary celebration in 1950. In 1955 Tangco helped survey centers of Asian studies in the United States, Europe and Southeast Asia for the purpose of organizing an Institute of Asian Studies at the University of the Philippines. He was a co-founder of the Institute and a member of its faculty. From 1948 to 1953 he was a member of the Philippine Board of Pardons and Paroles. On 9 April 1958, after forty-two years of active service, Tangco retired from the University of the Philippines.

Tangco won honors and awards including the University of the Philippines Board of Regents Diploma of Merit, the U.P. Education Alumni Association Diploma of Merit, and a symposium in his honor on "National Identity and National Integration"; papers from that symposium were published in the 1966-1967 issue of the journal *Lipunan* (Society), published by the Asian Center, University of the Philippines.

Tangco's major contributions to anthropology are in teaching, administration, publication and public service. He was a pioneer in the professionalization of anthropology in the Philippines. His publications on the Christian peoples of the Philippines, on the history of anthropology, on textbook-writing and on deviant behavior have been landmarks in the field.

> MAJOR WORKS: *The City Boys Reformatory: a Study of Juvenile Delinquency in the Philippines* (Manila: 1918); *The Treatment of Delinquent Boys* (Manila: 1918); *Habitual Criminals* (Manila: 1920); *An Outline of Lectures in General Anthropology* (Manila: 1931); *Cultural Traits in Connection with the Crises of Life in Pre-Spanish Philippines* (Manila: 1932); *Anthropology and the Philippines* (Manila: 1940); *The Christian Peoples of the Philippines* (Quezon City: 1951).

> SOURCE: Mario D. Zamora, "A new frontier: a Philippine founder's career, or is the native father legitimate?" *Social Change in Modern Philippines*, vol. 2 (1983), pp. 137-147.

Mario D. Zamora

Tax, Sol. Anthropologist, ethnographer. Born Chicago (Illinois) 30 October 1907, now living in Chicago. Tax's career has included extensive components of research, teaching, publishing, conference-organizing, and other forms of service to the discipline.

Tax grew up mainly in Milwaukee, Wisconsin. There he displayed early editorial and organizational talents while a member of the "Newsboys' Republic." As an undergraduate at the University of Wisconsin in Madison, Tax studied anthropology with RALPH LINTON, whose student and friend he became. For his Ph.B. degree (University of Wisconsin, Madison, 1931) he submitted a thesis, *A Re-Interpretation of Culture, with an Examination of Animal Behavior*, which sought to integrate cultural and biological aspects of anthropology.

Tax was a member of two archaeologically oriented field schools in 1930: the Logan Museum Archaeological Expedition to Algeria and the American School of Prehistoric Research in Europe. However, his participation in 1931 in the Summer Ethnology Program at the Mescalero Indian Reservation, directed by RUTH BENEDICT, was his first extensive ethnological experience and the beginning of a lifelong association with American Indians, especially the Mesquakie, the Maya of Guatemala and the Chicago Indian community.

Tax conducted research for his doctoral dissertation (1932-1934) under the direction of A.R. RADCLIFFE-BROWN at the University of Chicago. He worked among the Central Algonquin peoples, focusing on questions about the history and meaning of kinship. While doing this work, he developed the ego-less kinship chart and the notion that kinship relations were based on accommodation among universal rules and principles present in small societies. Thus, he anticipated the later development of componential analysis in kinship.

After successfully defending his dissertation in 1935, Tax was employed as an ethnologist by the Carnegie Institution of Washington under the supervision of ROBERT REDFIELD. In October 1934 Tax and his wife (née Gertrude Jospe Katz) left the United States to begin research in Guatemala. Tax conducted seven years of intensive research in the Highlands of Guatemala, then largely undescribed except in travel literature. During this period Don Sol and Doña Luna, as their Indian friends called them, conducted research on the economy, ethnic relations, and world view of the Lake Atitlán area. This work provided the basic understanding of Highland Guatemala that guided anthropological work in the area well into the 1970s.

Following work in Guatemala, Tax spent one year as Visiting Professor at the Instituto Nacional de Antropología e Historia (National Institute of Anthropology and History) in Mexico and initiated fieldwork in Chiapas. After returning to the United States and joining the faculty at the University of Chicago, Tax restarted his work with North American Indians. Beginning in 1948 with a project originally intended to serve as an ethnographic field school, Tax's work began to combine research with assistance.

Together with his students Tax developed an approach which insisted that research and practical assistance were equal imperatives in anthropological work. This approach, called "action anthropology," incorporated the principles (a) that people should be free to make their own decisions and hence mistakes and (b) that the proper role of the anthropologist is to facilitate communication and decision-making, not to direct it. Action anthropology engaged Tax's research and creative efforts among Native Americans, especially the Mesquakie in Iowa and in Fort Berthold, Rapid City and Chicago, and the Cherokee of Eastern Oklahoma, and to some extent characterized his approach to other areas of his career.

Tax was constantly involved in organizing professional conferences. Many of these proved to be seminal in their influence. Among the more significant conferences he organized were: the Viking Fund Seminar on Middle American Ethnology (which resulted in *Heritage of Conquest*) (1949); the Wenner-Gren International Symposium on Anthropology (1952-1953); the Darwin Centennial Celebration (which resulted in the three-volume *Evolution after Darwin*) (1958); the Conference on the Origin of Man (1964); the Conference on Man the Hunter (1965); the Conference on the Draft (which resulted in *The Draft: a Handbook of Facts and Alternatives*) (1966); and the Community Service Workshops (which resulted in *The People versus the System*) (1966-1967).

Tax also served as associate editor (1948-1953) and then editor (1953-1956) of *American Anthropologist*. At the request of the Wenner-Gren Foundation in 1958, Tax became founding editor of *Current Anthropology*. In designing and running this journal Tax conceived of anthropology as a community of scholars with whom he could work in the style of action anthropology. Thus, he emphasized self-determination and discussion and debate in the development of the journal, eventually designing the innovative and much copied *CA Treatment*, in which articles, comments on them by qualified colleagues and authors' replies to those comments appear together in a single issue.

Tax was appointed Associate Professor of Anthropology at the University of Chicago in 1944 and full Professor in 1948. He served as Associate Dean of the Social Sciences (1948-1953), Director of the Ford Foundation Self Study of the University's Behavioral Sciences (1953-1954), Chairman of the Board of University Publications (1956-1958), Chairman of the Department of Anthropology (1955-1958), and Dean of the University of Extension (1963-1968). Tax was Visiting Professor of Anthropology at the University of California at Berkeley during the summer of 1950 and a Fellow of the Center for Advanced Study in the Behavioral Sciences in 1969-1970.

Tax was President of the American Anthropological Association and of the International Union of Anthropological and Ethnological Sciences. He was also a founding member of the Chicago Anthropological Society and of the Library-Anthropology Resource Group. Tax served as an officer of the American Folklore Society, the Society for Applied Anthropology, the American Association for the Advancement of Science, the Central States Anthropological Society and the National Academy of Sciences.

Tax has invested his energies in using anthropology to better the human condition. He has served as a consultant to numerous governmental and private efforts, ranging from Hyde Park Community Council, through the Illinois State Museum and the Smithsonian Institution to the U.S. National Committee on UNESCO.

Tax has been honored by citations and medals from the governments of Czechoslovakia and Santander, Spain. He has received honorary degrees from Beloit College, Wilmington College and the University of the Valley of Guatemala. His contributions to anthropology have been recognized with honorary memberships in the Royal Anthropological Institute of Great Britain and the national anthropological societies of Chile, Hungary, and Slovakia.

Tax is the recipient of the Viking Fund Medal and Award, the Malinowski Award of the Society of Applied Anthropology, and the Distinguished Service Award of the American Anthropological Association.

The publication of the papers from the Ninth International Conference of Anthropological and Ethnological Sciences, of which he was president, in the nearly 100 volumes of the *World Anthropology Series*, of which he was editor, indicates the breadth of concern, creative acumen and vigor of Tax's anthropological career.

MAJOR WORKS: "An Algerian Passover," *The American Hebrew* (23 April 1931), pp. 548ff.; "The municipios of the Midwestern Highlands of Guatemala," *American Anthropologist*, n.s., vol. 39 (1937), pp. 423-444; "Some problems of social organization" in: Fred Eggan (editor), *Social Anthropology of the North American Tribes* (Chicago: 1937), pp. 1-32; "World view and social relations in Guatemala," *American Anthropologist*, n.s., vol. 43 (1941), pp. 27-42; "Action anthropology," *America Indígena*, vol. 12 (1952), pp. 103-109; (editor) *Heritage of Conquest: the Ethnology of Middle America* (New York: 1952); *Penny Capitalism: a Guatemalan Indian Economy* (Washington: 1953); (with others, editor) *An Appraisal of Anthropology Today* (Chicago: 1953); (editor) *Evolution after Darwin* (Chicago: 1960); (editor) *Horizons of Anthropology* (Chicago: 1964); *The Draft: a Handbook of Facts and Alternatives* (Chicago: 1967); (editor) *The People versus the System: a Dialogue in Urban Conflict* (Chicago: 1968); "Pride and puzzlement: a retro-introspective record of 60 years of anthropology," *Annual Review of Anthropology*, vol. 17 (1988), pp. 1-21.

SOURCES: Robert Hinshaw, "Tax, Sol" in: David L. Sills (editor), *International Encyclopedia of the Social Sciences* (New York: 1968-1979), vol. 18, pp. 760-763; Robert Hinshaw (editor), *Currents in Anthropology: Essays in Honor of Sol Tax* (The Hague: 1979); Allan Coult, "Lineage solidarity, transformational analysis, and the meaning of kinship terms," *Man*, vol. 2 (1967), pp. 26-

46; Fred Gearing, *The Face of the Fox* (Chicago: 1970); Fred Gearing, Robert McC. Netting and Lisa Peattie, *Documentary History of the Fox Project* (Chicago: 1960); Robert A. Rubinstein, "Reflections on action anthropology: some developmental dynamics of an anthropological tradition," *Human Organization*, vol. 45 (1986), pp. 270-275; Robert A. Rubinstein (editor), *Fieldwork: the Correspondence of Robert Redfield and Sol Tax* (Boulder: 1991).

Robert A. Rubinstein

Te Rangi Hiroa (Peter Henry Buck). Anthropologist, museum director, medical administrator, politician. Born in Urenui (New Zealand) ca. 1877, died in Honolulu (Hawaii) 1 December 1951. The son of a Maori mother and an Anglo-Irish father, Buck was educated at Te Aute College and the Otago Medical School and devoted his early life to the service of his Maori people, first as a medical officer (1905-1911), briefly as a politician (1911-1914), then, after war service, as Director of Maori Hygiene (1919-1927). During this time he developed a keen interest in the ethnology of the Maori and the Cook Islanders. In 1927, when he was about fifty, Buck was appointed Research Fellow at the Bishop Museum, initially for five years, but he stayed on at the Museum, spending two years as visiting Professor at Yale and becoming Director of the Museum in 1936, remaining in that position until his death.

Although he came into professional anthropology in middle age, Buck's interests covered a broad range of sub-disciplines, at least in so far as they applied to Maori and other Polynesian peoples of the Pacific. He was interested in and wrote extensively on myths and legends, poetry and language, origins and migrations, anthropometry, social organization, acculturation and material culture. Like his alter ego, the Maori scholar and statesman, Sir Apirana Ngata, with whom he kept up a lengthy academic correspondence during the years at the Bishop Museum, Buck believed that his Maori ancestry and upbringing gave him a special insight into the psychology of his people, which no purely European anthropologist could develop. Both men were critical of anthropologists like LUCIEN LÉVY-BRUHL who believed that they could understand "how natives think."

Nevertheless, Buck's main contributions to Pacific anthropology lay in the field of material culture. He produced a succession of monographs, starting with *The Evolution of Maori* and concluding with the posthumously published *Arts and Crafts of Hawaii*. Each was based on close observation of techniques in the field, which in turn were described and illustrated with fine line drawings. But Buck was much more than a craftsman: he was a popular lecturer whose sparkling humor often punctuated his writings. He is best known for his popular surveys of Polynesian and Maori origins and migrations, *Vikings of the Sunrise* and *The Coming of the Maori*, each of which went through numerous editions.

MAJOR WORKS: *The Coming of the Maori* (Nelson, New Zealand: 1925; rev. ed., Wellington: 1949); *The Evolution of Maori Clothing* (New Plymouth: 1926); *The Material Culture of the Cook Islands (Aitutaki)* (New Plymouth: 1927); *Samoan Material Culture* (Honolulu: 1930); *Vikings of the Sunrise* (New York: 1938); *Anthropology and Religion* (New Haven: 1939); *Arts and Crafts of the Cook Islands* (Honolulu: 1944); *An Introduction to Polynesian Anthropology* (Honolulu: 1945); *The Material Culture of Kapingamarangi* (Honolulu: 1950); *Arts and Crafts of Hawaii* (Honolulu: 1957).

SOURCES: J.B. Condliffe, *Te Rangi Hiroa: the Life of Sir Peter Buck* (Christchurch: 1971); M.P.K. Sorrenson (editor), *Na To Hoa Aroha: From Your Dear Friend: the Correspondence between Sir Apirana Ngata and Sir Peter Buck, 1925-50* [3 vols.] (Auckland: 1986-1988); M.P.K. Sorrenson "Polynesian corpuscles and Pacific anthropology: the home-made anthropology of Sir Apirana Ngata and Sir Peter Buck," *Journal of the Polynesian Society*, vol. 91 (1982), pp. 7-27; Katherine Luomala,

"Necrology: Peter Henry Buck (Te Rangi Hiroa)," *Bernice P. Bishop Museum Bulletin*, no. 208 (1952), pp. 36-44; "Tributes to and speeches by Sir Peter Buck," *Journal of the Polynesian Society*, vol. 60 (1951), pp. 223-254; Eric Ramsden, *A Memoir ... Te Rangihiroa* (Wellington: 1954).

M.P.K. Sorrenson

Tello, Julio Cesar. Archaeologist, museum director, physician. Born in Huarochiri (Peru) 11 April 1880, died in Lima (Peru) 3 June 1947. Tello, the first Peruvian archaeologist to apply scientific methods to excavation, is best known for his theory of the autochthonous highland origins of Andean civilization and for his powerful influence over Peruvian archaeology during his lifetime. For a generation following his death, his influence continued through the students he had trained at the Universidad Nacional Mayor de San Marcos (National University of San Marcos).

Matrilineally descended from an Inka (Inca) lord of Huarochiri, Tello was symbolically connected by many Peruvians with the archaeological past. He and his family worked especially hard to enable him to pursue his education in Lima at the Colegio de Osma, where he was befriended by author Ricardo Palma, then through the doctoral degree at San Marcos, which he entered in 1901. During his years as a university student, Tello supported himself by working as a conservator in the Biblioteca Nacional (National Library) and Museo Raimondi (Raimondi Museum). By 1909 he had completed the *bachiller* in medicine, the *titulo médico-cirujano*, and had produced a thesis on syphilis in ancient Peru that was well received by the medical community. He was awarded a scholarship to study at Harvard and cancelled his planned medical internship in Peru to take advantage of it. At Harvard, he studied with FRANZ BOAS, ALEŠ HRDLIČKA and FREDERIC WARD PUTNAM and was awarded a master's degree in anthropology in 1911. He traveled subsequently to France, England and Germany, where he studied and met with museum officials to learn more about preservation and display of archaeological materials.

Tello returned to Peru in 1913 and became director of the archaeological section of the Museo de Historia Nacional (Museum of Natural History), which was soon renamed the Museo de Antropología y Arqueología (Museum of Anthropology and Archaeology).

He was awarded the degree *doctor de ciencias naturales* (doctor of natural sciences) by the University of San Marcos in 1918 after presenting a thesis on cranial trephination in prehistoric Peru. He was appointed director of the Museo Universitario (University Museum) at San Marcos in 1923, then director of the Museo Arqueológico Nacional (National Archaeological Museum) in 1924. He was named *catedrático* (professor) of general archaeology at San Marcos in 1923, then *catedrático* of American and Peruvian archaeology in 1928, a position he held for life. Tello was also briefly *catedrático* of anthropology at Pontífica Universidad Católica (Pontifical Catholic University) (1931-1933). He often accompanied foreign archaeologists or anthropologists in the field (e.g., Hrdlička in 1913 and ALFRED L. KROEBER in 1926).

Tello's involvement in national politics ultimately hurt him financially, although he was able to remain prominent in Peruvian archaeology through the leaner years. He ran unopposed as candidate for deputy to the National Congress from Huarochiri in 1917. He continued to be re-elected through 1928, during which time he was politically allied with President Augusto Bernardino Leguía. When Leguía was ousted in 1930, Tello lost his job as museum director, although he was retained there, unsalaried, as research associate. He was reinstated as director in the newly consolidated Museo de Antropología (Anthropology Museum) at Magdalena Viejo (Pueblo Libre), which was developed in the late 1930s, and later of the Museo Nacional de Antropología y Arqueología (National Museum of Anthropology and Archaeology) (1945), which marked consolidation of several museums at the Magdalena Viejo site. He was a professor at San Marcos throughout this time and continued there and at the museum until his death. He was an honorary curator of archaeology at Harvard University, a fellow of the Royal Anthropological Institute, London, and an executive board member of the Institute of Andean Research.

His early fieldwork focused on highland areas (e.g., Rio Marañón, 1916, and Ancash, 1919), where he was the first scientifically trained person to encounter Chavín and Chavínoid materials. He undertook or participated in many other expeditions that are too numerous to list. By the time he worked on the coast in the 1930s (principally in the Casma and Nepeña Valleys), his understanding of Chavín culture from highland sites had led him to his theories about the highland origins of Andean civilization, which he later published (*Origen y desarrollo de la civilización andina*).

Tello did not like academic writing, although he gave papers at international conferences and frequently wrote newspaper articles on archaeological topics. He willed his field notes to San Marcos for others to publish. M. TORIBIO MEJÍA XESSPE developed six monographs from this material before his death in 1983.

MAJOR WORKS: *La antigüedad de la sífilis en el Perú* (Lima: 1909); *Introducción a la historia antigua del Perú* (Lima: 1921); *Antiguo Perú, primera época* (Lima: 1929); *Origen et desarollo de las civilizaciones prehistóricas andinas* (Lima: 1942); *Wira-Kocha* (Lima: 1949); and posthumous works edited by Toribio Mejía Xesspe: *Arqueología del Valle de Casma* (Lima: 1956); *Paracas* (Lima: 1959); *Chavín, cultura matriz de la civilización andina* (Lima: 1960); *Paracas II* (Lima: 1979); *Paginas escogidas* (Lima: 1967).

SOURCES: Samuel K. Lothrop, "Julio C. Tello, 1880-1947," *American Antiquity*, vol. 14 (1948), pp. 50-56; "Doctor J. C. Tello dies, archaeologist, 67," *New York Times* (5 June 1947), p. 26; "Tello, Julio C." in: *Enciclopedia ilustrada del Perú* (Lima: 1987), vol. 6, pp. 2063-2064; Teofilo Espejo Nuñez, *Formación universitaria de Julio C. Tello (1900-1912)* (Lima: 1959); Nicolas A. Puga Arroyo, *Julio C. Tello (referencias y anecdotas)* (Trujillo: 1960).

Kathryn M. Cleland

Tempels, Placide (or: Placied Tempels). Priest, missionary, amateur ethnologist. Born in Berlaar, Province of Anvers (Belgium) 18 February 1906, now living in Belgium. Tempels was not a professional ethnologist, but nevertheless one of his publications had a broad impact on anthropology. When Tempels was working as a Flemish missionary in the former Belgian Congo (now Zaïre), the failure of Christian evangelization convinced him of the need for a more profound knowledge of "his" Bantu in order to permit a more efficacious preaching of the gospel. His interest resulted in *La philosophie bantoue*, a work of enormous importance for African studies and anthropology in general. This publication elicited a host of reactions from different factions involved (especially Church authorities, Africanists and Africans themselves). The initial appreciation was markedly different from the more recent criticism.

The basic idea of Tempels' study is that the Bantu (actually he only treats the Luba of the Kasai) do not think in static Western categories but that Bantu philosophy is basically dynamic; it is a philosophy of force(s) (*muntu*) in which "being is force" and the basic principle is "vital force." Starting from this powerful though relatively simple ontological premise, he systematically developed a coherent philosophical system—including epistemology, the notion of a person and ethics—that would be characteristic of all Bantu speaking people.

In the epoch his book was written (1944-1945), Tempels' treatment of an African system of thought as coherent and systematic was absolutely revolutionary. Together with MARCEL GRIAULE, whose famous conversations with a Dogon sage (*Dieu d'eau*) were published in the same year, Tempels is beyond doubt the initiator of the study of African thinking as a genuine philosophical system. It is therefore not surprising that at the outset the book was received as a rehabilitation of African wisdom and Africans in general; it seemed a refutation of the more general inferiorizing image of the "savage" who had to be "civilized" and taught "logical reasoning" (LUCIEN LÉVY-BRUHL's famous idea of a "prelogical reasoning" dates from the same epoch!), an idea that legitimized the colonial enterprise. However, close scrutiny of the undertone of Tempels' book led to a somewhat different and more balanced evaluation. Was the final objective of his study not the establishment of a Christian culture in Africa, be it on the basis of African cultural principles? Only from this perspective can we understand his emphasis on the idea of a unique deity, or his insistence on the numerous parallellisms he sees between African and Christian philosophy. Philosophical notions identical to Christian ones are, according to Tempels, present in Africa although in an embryonic way and have to be "developed from within" to allow for the development of African Christianity. Nowhere does Tempels question the colonial endeavor for reasons of principle, and he insists on the crucial role missionaries have in accomplishing the civilizing process. No wonder that Tempels was soon considered by the African elites as an ideologist of a Christian-inspired colonialism, who did not care about *négritude*. Although he initially received some approval from the Church, as soon as his efforts to reorient evangelization on the basis of the principles outlined in his *La philosophie bantoue* led directly to the emergence of a charismatic movement, the Jamaa (of which Tempels was the spiritual leader), the Church authorities intervened firmly and he was expelled to an outlying district of Belgium.

A similar ambiguity characterized the academic reactions to Tempels' view of African philosophy. At the time of its publication, the book received unanimously positive reactions, and it initiated the study of African systems of thought as philosophy. But very soon, Tempels' early followers, such as Alexis Kagame, John Mbiti—both priests like Tempels with a proselytic attitude—and Paulin Hountondji, all of them Africans, disagreed with Tempels on both scientific and ideological grounds.

Their criticisms are reasonable, but they did not affect the core of Tempels' argument concerning the African dynamic philosophy of force(s). It is true that his book was far too ambitious and that the proselytic undertone hindered a sound scientific attitude, but it was nevertheless a first formulation of what could be considered characteristic of African thinking. The merits of Tempels' broad vision far outweighed the deficiencies stressed by some. The book laid the foundations of a subdiscipline—ethnophilosophy—and the continued interest in this subfield make his study classic, though controversial.

MAJOR WORK: *Bantoe-filosofie* (Antwerp: 1946) [tr.: *La philosophie bantoue* (Elisabethville: 1945 [sic]); Paris: 1949); *Bantu Philosophy* (Paris: 1952; Paris: 1959)].

SOURCE: A.J. Smet, *Le père Placide Tempels et son oeuvre oublié* (Kinshasa: 1976).

Dirk Verboven

Terent'eva, L.N. (Lïudmila Nikolaevna). Ethnographer, sociologist, museum worker. Born in Barnaul, Altaï (Russia) 1910, died in Moscow (Russian S.F.S.R.) 9 June 1982. Terent'eva was director of the Section on the Ethnography of the Peoples of the Volga Region, the European North, and the Baltic Region and deputy director of the Institut ètnografii (Institute of Ethnography) of the Soviet Academy of Sciences. She had considerable experience in field ethnography and museum work. One of the leading Soviet specialists on the ethnography of the peoples of the Baltic region, Terent'eva directed work on the *Istoriko-ètnograficheskiï atlas Pribaltiki*. The author of more than 100 works, she is particularly associated with Soviet studies of the ethnographic aspects of family and marriage.

MAJOR WORKS: "Opyt izuchenïa sem'i i semeïnogo byta latyshskogo kolkhoznogo krest'ïanstva," *Sovetskaïa ètnografïïa*, no. 3 (1958), pp. 53-71; *Kolkhoznoe krest'ïanstvo Latvii (istoriko-ètnograficheskaïa monografïïa po materialam kolkhozov Ekabpilsskogo raïona Latviïskoï SSR)* (Moscow: 1960) (= *Trudy Instituta ètnografii AN SSSR*, vol. 59); "Opredelenie svoeï nafsional'noï prinadlezhnosti podrostkami v nafsional'no-smeshannykh sem'ïakh," *Sovetskaïa ètnografïïa*, no. 3 (1969), pp. 20-30); *Ètnicheskie profsessy i sem'ïa* (Moscow: 1972); *Formirovanie ètnicheskogo samosoznanïïa v nafsional'no-smeshannykh sem'ïakh v SSSR* (Moscow: 1974); (with O.A. Ganfskaïa) "Mezhètnicheskie braki i ikh rol' v ètnicheskikh profsessakh" in: ÏU.V. Bromleï [et al.] (editors), *Sovremennye ètnicheskie profsessy v SSSR* (Moscow: 1975), pp. 458-480; (2nd ed., Moscow: 1977), pp. 460-483; "Kartografirovanie kul'tury naselenïa Latgalii v svïazi s istorieï ee formirovanïïa" in: M.A. Borodina (editor-in-chief) *Areal'nye issledovanïïa v ïazykoznanii i ètnografii* (Leningrad: 1977), pp. 200-211; (co-editor with S.I. Bruk [et al.]) *Istoriko-ètnograficheskiï atlas Pribaltiki* (Vilnius: 1985-).

SOURCES: "Lïudmila Nikolaevna Terent'eva (1910-1982)," *Sovetskaïa ètnografïïa*, no. 5 (1982), pp. 169-171; "Spisok osnovnykh rabot," *Sovetskaïa ètnografïïa*, no. 5 (1982), pp. 171-172 [bibliography].

A.M. Reshetov
[Translation from Russian: Thomas L. Mann]

Tereshkin, N.I. (Nikolaï Ivanovich). Linguist. Born near River Sogom, Northwest Siberia (Russia) 24 December 1913, died in Leningrad (Russian R.F.S.S.R.) 28 February 1986. Tereshkin was born to an Ostiak (Khanty) hunter's family which, at the time of his birth, was fleeing from famine. As both his parents died, he remained completely alone in the forest at the age of two. He was rescued and reared by a stepmother near the Irtysh estuary. Having passed the special education program for northern minorities, he became the first scholar of his people. He was the only competent collector of the Ostiak oral tradition in the post-World-War-II period.

SOURCE: M.P. Vakhrusheva, "Pervyï iz khanty," *Prosveshchenie na Kraïnem Severe*, vol. 15 (1967), pp. 148-151.

Éva Schmidt

Tessmann, Günther. Ethnologist, linguist, biologist. Born in Lübeck (Germany) 2 April 1884, died in Curitiba (Brazil) 15 November 1969. Following two years training at the Kolonialschule in Witzenhausen, in 1904 Tessmann journeyed for the first time to Cameroon, undertaking several trips into the Basa and Ewondo linguistic areas as well as the previously unexplored back country of Rio Muni (now part of Equatorial Guinea). He returned to Lübeck in 1907 and was put in charge of the Lübeck Pangwe expedition (1907-1909) and, in 1913, of the Ssanga-Lobaje expedition, which had to be abruptly broken off due to the outbreak of World War I. Between 1922 and 1926, he undertook research journeys among the Indians in the Upper Amazon regions of Peru. In 1930 Tessmann received the degree of Doctor of Philosophy *honoris causa* from the University of Rostock. He moved to Brazil in 1936.

In addition to the comprehensive monographs on the Pangwe, the Bubi of the island of Fernando Po and the Baja and Bafia, his publications also included linguistic materials on such languages as Mbaka-Limba, Mbum and Laka. His notes on the cult languages Labi and To attracted particular attention. In 1932 there appeared a complete classification of the peoples and languages of Cameroon in which Tessmann sought to represent the complex relationships of the ethnic groups of Cameroon primarily on the basis of lexical evidence. In addition, Tessmann's study of Indian tribes of the eastern slope of the Central Andes resulted in the most comprehensive monograph (*Indianer Nordost Perus*) of that little-known culture area of lowland South America.

Besides his ethnological and linguistic studies Tessmann was also renowned for his investigations of fauna and flora.

MAJOR WORKS: *Die Pangwe* (Berlin: 1913); "Sprichwörter der Pangwe, Westafrika," *Anthropos*, vol. 8 (1913), pp. 402-426; *Die Bubi Fernando Poo* (Hagen-Darmstadt: 1923); *Menschen ohne Gott* (Stuttgart: 1928); *Die Indianer Nordost-Perus* (Hamburg: 1920); "Die Sprachen der Mbaka-Limga, Mbum and Lakka," *Mitteilungen des Seminars für Orientalische Sprachen*, vol. 34 (1930), pp. 55-82; "Die drei Sprachen des Bajastammes: To, Labi, Baja," *Mitteilungen des Seminars für Orientalische Sprachen*, vol. 34 (1931), pp. 70-115; "Die Völker und Sprachen Kameruns," *Petermanns Geographische Mitteilungen*, vol. 78 (1932), pp. 113-120 and 184-190; *Die Bafia und die Kultur der Mittelkamerun-Bantu* (Stuttgart: 1934); *Die Baja* [2 vols.] (Stuttgart: 1934-1937).

SOURCES: Gudrun Miehe, "Tessmann, Günter" in: H. Jungraithmayr and W.J.G. Möhlig (editors), *Lexikon der Afrikanistik* (Berlin: 1983), pp. 239-240; H.-O. Neuhoff, "Lebensweg und Veröffentlichungen Dr. Günter Tessmanns," *Afrika Heute* (1969), pp. 117-120; Thomas Klockmann, "Vom Geheimnis menschlicher Gefühle: Günther Tessmanns Pangwe-Monographie im Lichte seiner Lebenserinnerungen sowie neuerer Forschungen," *Wiener ethnohistorische Blätter*, no. 29 (1986), pp. 3-20; Thomas Klockmann, *Günther Tessmann: König im weißen Fleck: das ethnologische Werk im Spiegel der Lebenserinnerungen: ein biographisch-werkkritischer Versuch* [dissertation] (Hamburg: 1988).

G. Miehe, K. Winkelmann and Berthold Riese
[*Translation from German: Robert B. Marks Ridinger*]

Theuws, Jacques A. (pseudonym, when writing as a novelist: Jac. Bergeyck). Ethnographer, priest. Born in Lommel (Belgium) 15 November 1914. Theuws entered the order of the Franciscan Fathers in 1934 and studied philosophy and theology. In 1942 he continued his studies at the University of Louvain, graduating with a thesis about religion and ethnography in the work of LEO BITTREMIEUX. He left for Africa as a missionary in 1947 and was stationed in Katanga (now Shaba, Zaïre). He did extensive fieldwork on the

Luba of Katanga and obtained a Ph.D. at the University of Louvain in 1953. He returned to Katanga for fieldwork among the Luba between 1953 and 1961; in between, he returned to the Universities of Louvain and of Witwatersrand (South Africa) to lecture and write. He lectured at Oxford from 1961 to 1962, at the Louvanium University in Kinshasa from 1962 to 1965 and at the University of Lubumbashi from 1966 to 1969. In 1969 he was guest professor at the University of Calgary (Alberta) and from 1972 until 1980 served as professor at the University of Windsor (Ontario). He has been retired since 1980.

The general focus of his research was the world view of the Luba. Theuws wanted to know above all how the Luba conceive of their own history and of their place in the world. The emphasis was on traditional beliefs, reached primarily through the study of indigenous texts. The methodological and theoretical concerns of fieldwork were highlighted, and the relationships among language, thought and culture were central.

Theuws, who was a confrater of PLACIDE TEMPELS, occasionally wrote about religious matters as well. Some of his articles dealt with the Jamaa movement in Katanga as well as with problems of contemporary missionary work. His institutional affiliations were primarily with the Catholic University of Louvain and with the Central African Museum in Tervuren.

A second but certainly no less important part of Theuw's work is his fictional writing under the pseudonym of Jac. Bergeyck. The same themes of Luba world view and Luba behavior are central in not less than seven novels. All of them have become well known to the Dutch and Flemish literary audience. Finally, Theuws published four poetry collections (in English, French and Dutch). They deal with deep religious and cosmological experiences rather than with the African context.

MAJOR WORKS: *Textes Luba* (Brussels: 1954); *De Luba mens* (Brussels: 1962); *The "Jamaa"-Movement in Katanga* (London: 1962); (with J. Jacobs and A. Burssens) *De Negro-Afrikaanse mens en zijn cultuur* (Brugge: 1965); *Word and World: Luba Thought and Literature* (Zürich: 1983). NOVELS: *De Levende Doden* (Antwerp: 1960); *Het Levende Beeld* (Antwerp: 1962); *Het Stigma* (Leuven: 1970); *De Pofadders* (Brussels: 1975); *Een Tuin die niet van Eden was* (Leuven: 1985); *Het Orakel* (Leuven: 1987); *Verhalen uit Kongo* (Leuven: s.d). POETRY: *Transcendentale Meditaties = Transcendental Meditations* (Windsor, Ontario: 1980); *Les heures de Thèbes* (Paris: 1988); *Vesperaal* (Mechelen: 1986); *Playing the Trumpet from my Window* (Windsor, Ontario: 1989).

Rik Pinxten

Thomas, W.I. (William Isaac).

Thomas, W.I. (William Isaac). Physical anthropologist, sociologist, social psychologist. Born in rural Virginia 13 August 1863, died in Berkeley (California) 5 December 1947. Thomas enrolled at the University of Tennessee in 1880, and in 1886 he received the first doctorate it ever granted. He began teaching (English, Greek, natural history) before the all-but-obligatory year of study in Europe. During the 1888-1889 academic year, he studied folk psychology and ethnology with Heymann Steinthal (1823-1899) and Moritz Lazarus (1824-1903) in Göttingen and Berlin. At the University of Chicago he took more courses in biology and psychology from Adolf Meyer (1866-1950) and Jacques Loeb (1859-1924) than courses in the Department of Sociology and Anthropology in which he enrolled after beginning to teach natural history at Oberlin College. His graduate work at Chicago was that of a physical anthropologist. After earning a second doctorate in 1895 (with a thesis entitled *On a Difference of the Metabolism of the*

Sexes) he was advanced from the rank of Lecturer to that of Assistant Professor at Chicago (he was promoted to the rank of Associate Professor in 1900, to full Professor in 1910).

Thomas listed FRANZ BOAS as having had more influence on him than his teachers of sociology. He was also influenced by some of the same German "folk psychologists" who were Boas's formative influences (e.g., WILHELM WUNDT, ADOLF BASTIAN and Heymann Steinthal). Thomas was on terms of mutual regard with Boasians and drew heavily on their ethnography for his ethnology. Thomas's 1909 *Source Book for Social Origins* included a chapter by Boas. At the time he was preparing that volume, Thomas had not yet cast off the influences of HERBERT SPENCER and FRIEDRICH RATZEL. Thomas wrote about race and sex in increasingly more Boasian (i.e., less Spencerian) terms during the first decade of the 20th century.

During the 1910s Thomas collaborated with Florian Znaniecki in a large-scale study of cultural and individual disorganization and reorganization of Polish peasants to Chicago, pioneering the use of life history materials as well as analysis of peasants and urban acculturation.

If Thomas's academic career had not been permanently disrupted by his summary, politically motivated firing by Chicago in 1918, a revised version of his *Source Book* would probably have appeared during the early 1920s, along with other works of Boasian synthesis. By 1937, the time *Primitive Behavior* actually appeared, the Boasian message had been received and the work had little influence on professional social scientists, despite considerable sales.

As a leading figure in national research councils after his dismissal from the University of Chicago in 1918, Thomas dominated the symposia from which "culture and personality" work derived. He organized a symposium on the unconscious, and he was the dominant fomenter of interdisciplinary investigation of personality during the 1920s. Supported by Rockefeller Foundation funds, he planned investigation of personality during the 1920s. He also planned to follow his earlier monumental work on Polish immigrants with a contrast between Swedish and Sicilian personality and culture, alongside his long-running analysis of Jewish immigrants. Thomas and his second wife, the demographer Dorothy Swaine Thomas, studied delinquent and nondelinquent American children during the 1920s and early 1930s, formulating the famous formula "If men define their situations as real, they are real in their consequences." W.I. Thomas also unofficially aided Dorothy Thomas in administering her University of California, Berkeley, study of incarcerated Japanese-Americans during World War II and remained active and curious until his death in 1947.

Thomas was a major influence on those who developed symbolic interactionism and quantitative attitude measurement, as well as the Yale behaviorist work of the Institute for Human Relations, where the Thomases were in the mid-1930s, the Human Relations Area Files, and two generations of Boasians. He was also a recurrent participant in the EDWARD SAPIR-John Dollard seminar on the impact of culture on personality at Yale (which he may originally have proposed to Rockefeller funders). Although it is difficult to determine where the center of Thomas's thought was, its peripheries were everywhere in inter-war American social sciences.

MAJOR WORKS: *Source Book for Social Origins* (Chicago: 1909); (with Florian Znaniecki) *The Polish Peasant in America and Europe* [2 vols.] (Boston: 1918-1920); "Life history" [originally written in 1927], *American Journal of Sociology*, vol. 79 (1973), pp. 246-250; *The Unadjusted Girl* (Boston: 1928); (with Dorothy Swaine Thomas) *The Child in America* (New York: 1928); *Primitive Behavior* (New York: 1937).

SOURCES: Herbert Blumer, *An Appraisal of Thomas and Znaniecki's The Polish Peasant in Europe and America* (New York: 1939) (= *Social Science Research Council, Bulletin*, no. 44); Morris Janowitz, *W.I. Thomas on Social Organization and Social Personality* (Chicago: 1966); Stephen O. Murray, "W.I. Thomas, behaviorist ethnologist," *Journal of the History of the Behavioral Sciences*, vol. 24 (1988), pp. 381-391; Edmund H. Volkart, "Aspects of the theories of W.I. Thomas," *Social Research*, vol. 20 (1953), pp. 345-357; Florian Znaniecki, "W.I. Thomas as a collaborator," *Sociology and Social Research*, vol. 32 (1948), pp. 765-767; E.H. Volkart, "Thomas, W.I." in: David L. Sills (editor), *International Encyclopedia of the Social Sciences* (New York: 1968-1979), vol. 16, pp. 1-6.

Stephen O. Murray

Thompson, David. Fur trader, explorer, surveyor, mapmaker. Born in London (England) 30 April 1770, died in Longueuil (Canada East, now Québec) 10 February 1857. David Thompson began a seven-year apprenticeship with the Hudson's Bay Company in 1784 and after 1797 took on mapping assignments for the North West Company. Thompson explored the Black River Route to Lake Athabasca (1796), surveyed much of present day Manitoba and Saskatchewan (1797), located the source of the Mississippi (1798), crossed the Rockies to the Columbia (1807), charted the Columbia River from its source to the Pacific Ocean (1811) and surveyed the Canada-U.S. boundary (1817-1826). His maps provided the first comprehensive view of vast territories that became part of Canada after 1869.

Thompson also made an important contribution to the record of early contact between Europeans and the indigenous peoples. During his extensive travels he attempted a systematic study of the cultural attributes and distinctions of the native groups he encountered. Master of several languages (including Cree and Piegan), Thompson interviewed natives for their stories and explanations and recorded several partial vocabularies. He chose older people to interview in order to "avoid opinions learned from white men." Thompson appreciated the differences between indigenous groups and never lumped them together as "Indians." Instead, he used a comparative method to distinguish groups and describe the social and political relationships between them. Thompson admired their practical skills and abilities and was anxious to learn from them. He worked to refute the common stereotypes of the North American Indians as inferior to Europeans. He was also critical of "civilized men" who confidently predicted that the North American Indian "must soon cease to exist, and give place to the White Man."

Thompson retired to Canada in 1812 and in his later years experienced business failures and financial difficulties. He turned to writing the narrative of his explorations in western Canada. Thompson's *Narrative*, written in direct consultation with his fur trade journals, includes chapters on the Mandan, Cree, Piegan, Kootenay, Assiniboine, Chipewyan and others and was obscure until it was first published in 1916.

MAJOR WORKS: *A Brief Narrative of the Journeys of David Thompson, in North-Western America ...* (edited by J.B. Tyrrell) (Toronto: 1888); *David Thompson's Narrative of His Explorations in Western North America, 1784-1912* (edited by J.B. Tyrrell) (Toronto: 1916); *Travels in Western North America, 1784-1812* (edited by Victor G. Hopwood) (Toronto: 1971); *New Light on the History of the Greater North West: the Manuscript Journals of Alexander Henry and of David Thompson* (edited by Elliott Coues) (New York: 1897); "David Thompson's account of his first attempt to cross the Rockies" (edited by F.W. Howay), *Queen's Quarterly*, vol. 40 (1933), pp. 333-356; *Journal of the International Boundary Survey, 1817-1827: Western Lake Erie, Aug-Sept 1819* (edited by C.E. Leverette) (London, Ontario: 1974); *Journals Relating to Montana and Adjacent Regions, 1808-1812* (edited by M.C. White) (Missoula, Montana: 1950); *Documents Relating to the North West Company* (edited by Stewart Wallace) (Toronto: 1934).

SOURCES: J.B. Tyrrell, "Introduction" to: *David Thompson's Narrative ...* (Toronto: 1916) (= *Publications of the Champlain Society*, vol. 12), pp. xxiii-lxiv; J.B. Tyrrell, "David Thompson and the Rocky Mountains," *Canadian Historical Review*, vol. 15 (1934), pp. 39-45; J.B. Tyrrell, "David Thompson and the Columbia River," *Canadian Historical Review*, vol. 18 (1937), pp. 12-27; R. Glover, "Introduction" to: *David Thompson's Narrative, 1784-1812* (Toronto: 1962) (= *Publications of the Champlain Society*, vol. 12), pp. xi-lxxii; Victor G. Hopwood, "Introduction" to: David Thompson, *Travels in Western North America, 1784-1812* (Toronto: 1971), pp. 1-39; C.N. Cochrane, *David Thompson, the Explorer* (Toronto: 1924); James K. Smith, *David Thompson: Fur Trader, Explorer, Geographer* (Toronto: 1971); A.S. Morton, *David Thompson* (Toronto: 1930); John Nicks, "Thompson, David" in: *Dictionary of Canadian Biography* (Toronto: 1966-), vol. 8, pp. 878-884.

Frieda Esau Klippenstein

Thompson, Sir *John Eric Sidney.* Born in London (England) 31 December 1898, died in Cambridge (England) 9 September 1975. Archaeologist, anthropologist. Thompson devoted his life to the study of Maya culture and was able to decipher early Maya glyphs extensively and establish that they contain historical as well as ritualistic and religious records. He also discovered that present-day Mexican Indians preserve many ancestral customs. Thompson became the leading English ethnographer of the Maya people.

Among the Maya sites for which Thompson wrote separate publications, we find Coba, Quirigua, Palenque, the Usumacinta Valley, Chichen Itzá, Piedras Negras and Naranjo. At least fourteen of the twenty early (1925-1962) publications of Thompson listed in *Enciclopedia de México* deal with calendrical materials.

Thompson studied anthropology at Cambridge University and, after graduation, joined the Carnegie Institution excavation in the Yucatán in 1926. His first Maya fieldwork was in British Honduras with T.A. Joyce. He was Assistant Curator in charge of Central and South American archaeology and ethnology at the Chicago Natural History Museum from 1926 to 1935, and he worked with the Carnegie Institution of Washington from 1935 to 1958.

Thompson was Honorary Professor at the Museo Nacional de México (National Museum of Mexico) (from 1941) and Honorary Curator, Middle-American Archaeology, Chicago Natural History Museum (from 1945). He was President of the Thirty-Second International Congress of Americanists (1952), Consejero of the Centro de Investigaciones Antropológicas Mexicanas (Center of Mexican Anthropological Investigations) (after 1953) and an Honorary Fellow of Fitzwilliam College, Cambridge (1973). He received the Rivers Memorial Medal of the Royal Anthropological Institute (1945), the Viking Fund Medal for Anthropology, New York (1955), the Encomienda de Isabel la Católica (1964), the Order of the Aztec Eagle (1965), the Huxley Memorial Medal (1966) and the Sahagún Medal, Mexico (1972). He received an L.L.D. from the University of Yucatán (1959), a D.Lit. from the University of Pennsylvania (1962) and from Tulane University (1972), and an Hon. Litt.D. from Cambridge University (1973).

Thompson's work has been honored by the governments of Spain and Mexico, and he was the first New World archaeologist to be knighted in Great Britain (1975).

MAJOR WORKS: "The meaning of the Mayan monthly," *Man*, vol. 25 (1925), pp. 121-123; *Correlation on the Mayan and European Calendars* (Chicago: 1927) (= *Field Museum of Natural History Publications, Anthropology Series*, vol. 27); *The Civilization of the Mayas* (Chicago: 1927; many later eds., e.g., Chicago: 1958; Chicago: 1973); (with Thomas Gann) *History of the Maya from the Earliest Times to the Present Day* (New York: 1931); *Mexico before Cortes: an Account of the Daily Life, Religion, and Ritual of the Aztecs and Kindred Peoples* (New York and London: 1933); "The dates of the Temple of the Cross, Palenque," *Maya Research*, vol. 3 (1936), pp. 287-293; *Excavations at San José, British Honduras* (Washington: 1939) (= *Carnegie Institution of Washington, Publication*, no. 506); "Pitfalls and stimuli in the interpretation of history through loan words," *Philological and Documentary Studies*, vol. 1, no. 2 (1943), pp. 17-26; *Maya Hieroglyphic Writing* (Washington: 1950) (= *Carnegie Institution of Washington, Publication*, no. 589); *The Rise and Fall of Maya Civilization* (Norman: 1954; 2nd ed., Norman: 1966); (editor), Thomas Gage, *The English-American, His Travail by Land and Sea* (Westport, Conn.: 1958; later ed.: *Thomas Gage's Travels in the New World*, Norman: 1981); *A Catalog of Maya Hieroglyphs* (Norman: 1962); *Maya Archaeologist* (Norman: 1963); *Maya History and Religion* (Norman: 1970) [tr.: *Historia y religión de los Mayas* (Mexico City: 1977)]; *A Commentary on the Dresden Codex: a Maya Hieroglyphic Book* (Philadelphia: 1972) (= *Memoirs of the American Philosophical Society*, vol. 93).

SOURCES: Norman Hammond (editor), *Social Process in Maya Prehistory: Studies in Honour of Eric Thompson* (London and New York: 1977); "Sir Eric Thompson (1885-1975)," *Archaeology*, vol. 29 (1976), p. 57; "Thompson, John Eric Sydney" in: *Enciclopedia de México* (Mexico City: 1987-1988), vol. 13, p. 7681; "Thompson, Sir (John) Eric (Sidney)" in: *Who Was Who, 1971-1980* (London: 1981), p. 788.

Francis X. Grollig, S.J.

Thompson, Laura Maud. Anthropologist. Born in Honolulu (Hawaii) 23 January 1905. Thompson received a B.A. from Mills College, California, in 1927 and a Ph.D. in anthropology from the University of California, Berkeley, in 1933. Between 1927 and 1933 she also attended graduate school in anthropology at Radcliffe College and served first as an assistant ethnologist and then as a graduate fellow at the Bishop Museum in Hawaii. In 1941 she carried out post-doctoral work at the University of Chicago. Thompson has held positions as professor and visiting professor in the anthropology departments of numerous universities throughout the country. In 1973 she was awarded an honorary L.L.D. from Mills College, California.

Co-founder of the Society of Applied Anthropology in 1941, Thompson became interested in practical applications of anthropology during her earliest fieldwork, an expedition to the Lau Islands of Fiji during 1933-1934. Thompson presented her findings from that study in a form intended for use by administrators interested in the peoples' government and economic development, an approach now known as "administrative anthropology." Thompson conducted her second field study in the Marianas Islands of Guam during 1938-1939. She was responding to an invitation from the island's naval governor to evaluate the local educational system, thereby applying anthropological research to the area of education.

Thompson is also well known for her work as Coordinator of the Indian Personality, Education, and Administration Research Project (IPEA, also known as the Indian Education and Government Study), which was initiated by the Bureau of Indian Affairs in 1941 and ran until September 1947. The IPEA involved an intensive study of eleven communities of five native American groups: the Hopi, Navaho, Papago, Sioux and United Pueblos. The aim of this long-range, multidisciplinary research project was to improve welfare and develop local autonomy by increasing the effectiveness of Indian Affairs policies and programs. The study was an innovative attempt to use social science research to guide the creation and implementation of social policy.

Still active in the fields of theoretical and applied anthropology, Thompson received the Malinowski Award from the Society for Applied Anthropology in 1979.

MAJOR WORKS: *The Native Culture of the Marianas Islands* (Honolulu: 1945) (= *Bishop Museum Bulletin*, no. 185); *Guam and Its People* (San Francisco: 1945; 3rd ed., revised, Princeton: 1947); *Culture in Crisis: a Study of the Hopi Indians* (New York: 1950); *Personality and Government: Findings and Recommendations of the Indian Administration Research* (Mexico: 1951); *Toward a Science of Mankind* (New York: 1961); (with Alice Joseph) *The Hopi Way* (Chicago: 1944; revised ed., New York: 1967); "Applied anthropology and the development of a science of mankind" in: Morton H. Fried (editor), *Readings in Anthropology* (New York: 1968), vol. 2, pp. 594-614; *The Secret of Culture* (New York: 1969); *Fijian Frontier* (San Francisco: 1940; revised ed., New York: 1972).

SOURCE: Laura Maud Thompson Collection in the National Anthropological Archives and correspondence with Laura Thompson.

Kathleen T. Baxter

Thomsen, Christian Jürgensen. Antiquary, archaeologist. Born in Copenhagen (Denmark) 29 December 1788, died in Copenhagen (Denmark) 21 May 1865. In 1816 Thomsen was appointed National Antiquary (or "Secretary to the Royal Commission for the Keeping of Antiquities," as it was then called). In this capacity he first endeavored to introduce some orderliness into the nation's rather haphazard collection of archaeological specimens; while doing this work he devised the periodization into stone, bronze and iron ages, and he arranged the archaeological collection according to this periodization. The system was devised in 1818, though he did not publish it until 1836.

In 1839 Thomsen was appointed curator of the Museum of Art, where he first concentrated his efforts on the ethnographical collection. In shaping the collection he put the emphasis on acquiring and showing ordinary artifacts rather than rarities and on organizing them according to the "principle of the progression of culture." In 1841 he managed to have the collection opened to the public, and he thereby became the founder of the world's first public ethnographic museum.

Thomsen never published much; he said of himself, "The talent for writing has been denied me; it is in other ways that I have sought to make myself useful." And, indeed, his work as a museum organizer may be said to equal several volumes of written work.

MAJOR WORK: *Ledetraad til Nordisk Oldkyndighed* (Copenhagen: 1836).

SOURCES: Glyn Daniel, *The Origins and Growth of Archaeology* (Harmondsworth: 1967); Ole Klindt-Jensen, *A History of Scandinavian Archaeology* (London: 1975); Poul Kjærum, "Thomsen, Christian Jürgensen" in: *Dansk Biografisk Leksikon* (Copenhagen: 1983), vol. 14, pp. 481-485.

Jan Ovesen

Thomson, Donald (Donald Finlay Fergusson Thomson). Anthropologist, naturalist, photographer. Born in Brighton (Victoria) 26 June 1901, died in Melbourne (Victoria) 12 May 1970. Thomson received his doctorate in anthropology from the University of Cambridge in 1950 after having taken a B.Sc. (1925) and a D.Sc. (1934) at the University of Melbourne and two diplomas in anthropology, one from the University of Sydney in 1928 and the other from Cambridge in 1939.

Although known as an anthropologist Thomson was at heart a naturalist who brought to all his ethnographic field research a natural science approach to observation. He was also a talented linguist, not only making accurate transcriptions of the Aboriginal dialects he worked with but also—long before the establishment of ethnosemantics—understanding the importance of constructing glossaries of key indigenous terms and concepts. His most referred-to works are his analysis of the impact of seasonal variation on the material culture and land use of Cape York Aborigines, which has been widely taken up by ethno-archaeologists, and his monograph on ceremonial exchange in Arnhem Land. He was also an active campaigner for Aboriginal rights and awarded the Wellcome Gold Medal in 1939 for application of modern scientific methods to problems of native administration as a result of work in Arnhem Land during a period of unrest. He was one of the very few anthropologists to work beyond the frontier in Australia for any extended period.

The outstanding monument to his lifetime of ethnographic research is the Donald Thomson Collection housed in the Museum of Victoria, Melbourne. This is made up of more than 5,700 items of material culture collected principally from Cape York and Arnhem Land before World War II; 7,000 pages of field notes; 11,000 superb ethnographic photographs, reflecting his lifelong interest in photography; and 2,000 zoological and botanical items.

MAJOR WORKS: "Ceremonial presentation of fire in north Queensland," *Man*, vol. 32 (1932), pp. 162-166; "The hero cult, initiation and totemism on Cape York," *Journal of the Royal Anthropological Institute*, vol. 63 (1933), pp. 453-537; *Birds of Cape York Peninsula* (Melbourne: 1935); "The joking relationship and organized obscenity in north Queensland," *American Anthropologist*, n.s., vol. 37 (1935), pp. 460-490; "Fatherhood in the Wik Monkan tribe," *American Anthropologist*, n.s., vol. 38 (1936), pp. 374-393; "The seasonal factor in human culture," *Proceedings of the Prehistoric Society*, vol. 5 (1939), pp. 209-221; "Arnhem Land: explorations among an unknown people (in three parts)," *Geographical Journal*, vol. 112 (1948), pp. 146-64; vol. 113 (1949), pp. 1-8; vol. 114 (1949), pp. 53-67; *Economic Structure and the Ceremonial Exchange Cycle in Arnhem Land* (Melbourne 1949); "Some wood and stone implements of the Bindibu tribe of central Western Australia," *Proceedings of the Prehistoric Society*, vol. 30 (1964), pp. 400-422.

SOURCES: "Introduction" to: Donald Thomson, *Mammals and Fishes of Northern Australia* (edited and annotated by J.M. Dixon and L. Huxley) (Melbourne: 1985), pp. 1-10; C. Hogarth, *Donald Thomson in Irian Jaya* [unpublished graduate diploma thesis, James Cook University] (Townsville: 1984); N. Peterson, "Donald Thomson: a biographical sketch" in: N. Peterson (editor), *Donald Thomson in Arnhem Land* (Melbourne: 1983), pp. 1-18.

Nicolas Peterson

Thurnwald, Richard. Anthropologist, sociologist. Born in Vienna (Austria) 19 September 1869, died in Berlin (Germany) 19 January 1954. Thurnwald was educated in law (he received his Dr.Jur. in 1891) and occupied administrative posts in Austria until he moved to Berlin to dedicate himself to the study of Oriental languages and cultures. In his early years there he was active as co-founder of a *rassenhygienische Bewegung* (race-hygienic movement), centering on a rather opaque nonbiological, philanthropic concept of "race" formulated by Alfred Ploetz (1860-1940); its precursors lay in the anti-alcohol movement. Thurnwald's early association with the Museum für Völkerkunde (Ethnographic Museum) as *Volontär* (volunteer) and with its director FELIX VON LUSCHAN led to two expeditions to New Guinea, Melanesia and Micronesia during 1906-1909 and 1912-1917, which resulted in museum collections and two major ethnographic publications (*Forschungen auf den Salomon Inseln* in 1912-1913 and *Bánaro Society* in 1916) which were highly praised by his contemporaries (among them BRONISLAW MALINOWSKI) for their focus on social relations and their systematic treatment of institutions. Thurnwald's concept of "reciprocity," developed in those studies but not comprehensively published until 1936, is now considered a key idea in anthropological theory.

Back in Germany Thurnwald successfully obtained his *Habilitation* from the University of Halle and was appointed professor of anthropology at the University of Berlin (1925), where he lectured on *Völkerpsychologie* (ethnopsychology), social and political systems, religion and art. Interested in colonial and applied anthropology since his formative years, and joined by his wife Hilde Thurnwald, he engaged in a third field trip to East Africa (*Black and White in East Africa*), then under British colonial administration. He also held lecturing positions at Yale University, Harvard and other U.S. East Coast institutions (1931-1936), and was an outspoken anti-Nazi. However, his efforts to stay in the United States were unsuccessful and he returned to Berlin in 1936 to resume his teaching duties there. From then on he served without break under Nazi, Soviet and finally U.S. governments as university professor in Berlin beyond the usual age of retirement. He and his wife Hilde are the post-war founders of the Institute of Ethnology at the Free University in Berlin. His founding of the journal *Sociologus* in 1931 and his outside contacts during the Nazi regime as well as his role in re-establishing anthropology in Berlin after 1945 characterize Thurnwald as a key figure in mid-20th-century German anthropology, although his influence on contemporary German anthropology was largely transmitted indirectly through his pupil WILHELM E. MÜHLMANN rather than through his own writing.

MAJOR WORKS: "Bosnien und Hercegovina: Gewerbe und Handel" in: *Bosnien und Hercegovina* (Vienna: 1901) (= *Die Österreichisch-ungarische Monarchie in Wort und Bild*, vol. 22), pp. 487-499; "Staat und Wirtschaft in Babylon zu Hammurabis Zeit," *Jahrbücher für Nationalökonomie und Statistik*, vol. 26 (1903), pp. 644-675 and vol. 27 (1904), pp. 64-88 and 191-202; *Forschungen auf den Salomo-Inseln und dem Bismarck-Archipel* [2 vols.] (Berlin 1912-1913); *Bánaro Society* (Lancaster: 1916) (= *Memoirs of the American Anthropological Association*, vol. 3, pp. 249-391) [rev. German ed.: "Die Gemeinde der Bánaro," *Zeitschrift für vergleichende Rechtswissenschaft*, vol. 38 (1920), pp. 362-474 and vol. 39 (1921), pp. 68-219]; *Die menschliche Gesellschaft in ihren ethnosoziologischen Grundlagen* [5 parts, each part published under separate title] (Berlin: 1931-1934); *Black and White in East Africa* (London: 1935); "Gegenseitigkeit im Aufbau und Funktionieren der Gesellungen und deren Institutionen" in: *Reine und angewandte Soziologie: eine Festgabe für Ferdinand Tönnies zu seinem achtzigsten Geburtstage* (Leipzig: 1936), pp. 275-297 [reprinted in: Richard Thurnwald, *Grundfragen menschlicher Gesellung* (Berlin: 1957), pp. 82-103].

SOURCES: W.E. Mühlmann, "Richard Thurnwald zum 70. Geburtstag," *Archiv für Anthropologie, Völkerforschung und kolonialen Kulturwandel*, n.F., vol. 25 (1939), pp. 65-70; *Beiträge zur Gesellungs- und Völkerwissenschaft: Professor Dr. Richard Thurnwald zu seinem achtzigsten Geburtstag gewidmet* (Berlin: 1950) [Festschrift]; Robert Lowie, "Richard Thurnwald, 18.9.1869-19.1.1954," *Sociologus*, n.F., vol. 4 (1954), pp. 2-5; Oswin Köhler, "Völkerwissenschaft und Völkerverständigung: zur 100. Wiederkehr des Geburtstages von Richard Thurnwald,"

'Apartheids-Projekt' für die koloniale Expansion des deutschen Faschismus in Afrika," *Ethnographisch-archäologische Zeitschrift*, vol. 18 (1977), pp. 617-649; R. König, "Richard Thurnwalds Beitrag zur Theorie der Entwicklung," *Kölner Zeitschrift für Soziologie und Sozialpsychologie*, Sonderheft 26 (1984), pp. 364-379; Marion Melk-Koch, *Auf der Suche nach der menschlichen Gesellschaft: Richard Thurnwald* (Berlin: 1990) (= *Veröffentlichen des Museums für Völkerkunde*, n.F., no. 46).

Berthold Riese

Tillema, Hendrik Freerk. Hygienist, pharmacist, traveler, photographer, filmmaker. Born in Echten, Friesland (Netherlands) 5 July 1870, died in Bloemendaal (Netherlands) 26 November 1952. Tillema is best known for his writings about and photographs of the peoples of the Netherlands East Indies (now the Republic of Indonesia). Tillema originally qualified in pharmaceutics at the State Universities of Leiden and Groningen.

His early career began as a pharmacist in Semarang, Java, in 1895. He established a successful business there, diversifying into the large-scale production of mineral water. During his residence in Java, and especially following the cholera epidemic in Semarang in 1910, he developed an interest in matters of public health and hygiene. He published his first major illustrated book (*Van wonen en bewonen*) in 1913; it provided detailed data on housing conditions in Semarang and its environs.

Tillema retired a wealthy man in mid-1914 and returned to Holland. He devoted the rest of his life to research and writing on hygiene and native ways of life in the Indies. He was primarily a propagandist, advocating greater Dutch public awareness of the peoples of Indonesia and the conditions under which they lived. He wrote many popular articles in newspapers and magazines. Between 1915 and 1923 he produced his six-volume encyclopedia, *Kromoblanda*, on housing conditions, sanitation, diet, disease, clothing and child-care in the Indies. In this reference work there is the first direct evidence of Tillema's interest in ethnography and the importance for him of studying local customs and practices in an effort to improve the physical and material well-being of indigenous populations.

Most importantly he undertook and personally financed three expeditions in the East Indies. During 1924-1925 he traveled through the archipelago from Sumatra in the west to New Guinea in the east. During 1927-1928 and 1931-1932 he visited the various territories of Dutch Borneo and made two ethnographic films (*Langs Borneo's breede stroomen* and *Apo-Kajan*). His most well known photographs of such Borneo tribes as the Kenyahs and Punans were published in his book *Apo-Kajan* in 1938.

Naturally he was attracted to the visual aspects of native cultures: arts, crafts, costumes and adornments, housing, rituals and technology. He also recognized the need to understand these different modes of life in their own terms and record them visually before they were radically altered by the forces of modernization.

In recognition of his scientific and practical work, especially in the field of hygiene, on behalf of the peoples of the East Indies, the University of Groningen conferred on him an Honorary Doctorate in Medicine in 1940. His photographs, films and library were donated to the Rijksmuseum voor Volkenkunde (State Ethnographical Museum) in Leiden in 1942.

MAJOR WORKS: *Van wonen en bewonen, van bouwen, huis en erf* (Tjandi-Semarang: 1913); *Kromoblanda: over 't vraagstuk van 'het Wonen' in Kromo's groote land* [6 vols.] (The Hague: 1915-1923); *Zonder tropen geen Europa* (Bloemendaal: 1926); *Langs Borneo's breede stroomen* [film] (Haarlem: 1928); *Apo-Kajan* [film] (Haarlem: 1932); *Apo-Kajan: een filmreis naar en door Centraal-Borneo* (Amsterdam: 1938) [tr.: *A Journey among the Peoples of Central Borneo in Word and Picture* (Singapore: 1989)]; *Ons Indisch boekje* [3 parts] (Assen: 1940-1941).

SOURCES: J. Keuning, "Dr. H.F. Tillema: zijn streven en werk," *Indonesie*, vol. 6 (1953), pp. 472-477; Victor T. King, "The Tillema Collection in Leiden," *Indonesia Circle*, No. 43 (June 1987), pp. 3-13; "Hendrik Tillema and Borneo," *Borneo Research Bulletin*, vol. 19 (1987), pp. 3-15; Victor T. King, "Editor's introduction" to: H.F. Tillema, *A Journey among the Peoples of Central Borneo in Word and Picture* (edited by Victor T. King) (Singapore: 1989), pp. 1-27; Noto Soeroto, "H.F. Tillema," *Nederlandsch-Indië Oud en Nieuw*, vol. 6 (1922), pp. 355-358; G.L. Tichelman, "5 July 1870-26 November 1952: in memoriam Dr. H.F. Tillema," *Oost en West*, vol. 46 (1953), p. 5; P. van der Wielen, "Hendrik Freerk Tillema: een overzicht van zijn leven en van zijn levenswerk," *Oost en West*, vol. 40 (1940), pp. 20-22.

Victor T. King

Tinbergen, Nikolaas (Niko Tinbergen). Biologist, ethologist. Born in The Hague (Netherlands) 15 April 1907, died in Oxford (England) 21 December 1988. Tinbergen received his education at Leiden University, where he carried out his early research. In 1949 he moved to Oxford (England) where he established an important center for ethology. His work has resulted in numerous prizes and honors including, in 1973, the award of the Nobel Prize for Physiology and Medicine, which he shared with KONRAD LORENZ and Karl von Frisch (1886-1982). In his empirical and theoretical contributions Tinbergen demonstrated that questions about the causation, development, function and evolution of behavior were logically distinct, but inter-fertile. His work on animal behavior has been characterized primarily by an emphasis on simple experiments under field conditions. He worked especially with the three-spined stickleback and the herring gull. Of special importance are his studies of the nature of the stimuli that release "instinctive" behavior, of the evolution of behavior and of the nature of motivational systems. During 1932-1933 Tinbergen and his wife Elizabeth Amélie spent fourteen months living with Eskimos in Greenland and acquired an interest in the hunter-gatherer way of life.

Although Tinbergen has not published in anthropological journals, his papers have included numerous discussions about the applications of principles derived from the study of animals to human behavior. These provided a major stimulus to the new discipline of human ethology. For instance his work on social releasers and on the evolutionary processes involved in ritualization constituted a major contribution to the foundation of the comparative study of human expressive movements, and his work on animal motivation helps to throw light on the problem of human aggression. More important, ethological principles that he elaborated are now being used by his students and others to counter the "cultural imperialism" of many anthropological interpretations. In recent years the Tinbergens have applied principles derived from ethology to the study of childhood autism and produced important evidence for a new form of treatment.

MAJOR WORKS: "An objectivistic study of the innate behavior of animals," *Bibliotheca Biotheoretica*, series D1 (1942), pp. 39-98; "Social releasers and the experimental method required for their study," *Wilson Bulletin*, vol. 60 (1948), pp. 6-51; *The Study of Instinct* (Oxford: 1951, 1969); "'Derived' activities: their causation, biological significance, origin and emancipation during evolution," *Quarterly Review of Biology*, vol. 27 (1952), pp. 1-32; *The Herring Gull's World: a Study of the Social Behaviour of Birds* (London: 1953, 1961); *Social Behaviour in Animals, with Special Reference to Vertebrates* (London: 1953); *Curious Naturalist* (London: 1958); "Comparative studies of the behavior of gulls (Laridae): a progress report," *Behaviour*, vol. 15 (1959), pp. 1-70; "On aims and methods of ethology," *Zeitschrift für Tierpsychologie*, vol. 20 (1963), pp. 410-433; "On war and peace in animals and man: an ethologist's approach to the biology of aggression," *Science*, vol. 160 (1968), pp. 1411-1418; "Functional ethology and the human sciences," *Royal Society of London Proceedings*, series B, vol. 182 (1972), pp. 385-410; *The Animal in Its World: Explorations of an Ethologist, 1932-72* [2 vols.] (London: 1972-1973); (with E.A. Tinbergen) *"Autistic" Children: New Hope for a Cure* (London: 1983).

SOURCE: R.A. Hinde, "Tinbergen, Nikolaas" in: David L. Sills (editor), *International Encyclopedia of the Social Sciences* (New York: 1968-1979), vol. 18, pp. 770-775.

R.A. Hinde

Titiev, Mischa. Anthropologist. Born in Kremenchug (Russia) 11 September 1901, died in Ann Arbor (Michigan) 17 August 1978. Titiev's family moved from Russia to Boston in 1907. He studied English at Harvard, taking a B.A. in 1923 and an M.A. in 1924. At the point of beginning dissertation research in 1925, he became interested in anthropology and changed majors. After earning his doctorate in 1935, he was briefly an archaeologist and curator for the National Park Service. In 1936 he was hired by the anthropology department at the University of Michigan (he was well known by LESLIE A. WHITE as a result of their mutual interest in the pueblos of the U.S. Southwest), and there he remained for his entire teaching career.

Titiev conducted research in Oraibi of the Hopi Third Mesa during 1932-1934 and made repeated return visits over the next three decades. During World War II he served as a research analysis officer for the Office of Strategic Services in India. Following the war he considerably widened his research horizons. He did fieldwork among the Japanese of Peru in 1948 and then among the Araucanian Indians of Chile. His growing interest in the Japanese led to his involvement in the creation of the Japanese Study Center at the University of Michigan and to his directing a field research center in Japan in 1951. Three years later he was a Fulbright Professor at the Australian National University.

Long-term familiarity with the Hopi of Oraibi allowed Titiev both to describe their culture as it was and to analyze the process of cultural change thoroughly. (The period between his first visit to Oraibi and his last publication on the pueblo was forty years.) Among his special interests were religion, ceremonialism and kinship systems.

MAJOR WORKS: "The influence of common residence on the unilateral classification of kindred," *American Anthropologist*, vol. 45 (1943), pp. 511-530; *Old Oraibi* (Cambridge: 1944); "The religion of the Hopi Indians" in: Vergilius Ferm (editor), *Forgotten Religions* (New York: 1950), pp. 365-378; *Araucanian Culture in Transition* (Ann Arbor: 1951); *The Science of Man* (New York: 1954); *Introduction to Cultural Anthropology* (New York: 1959); "A fresh approach to the problem of magic and religion," *Southwestern Journal of Anthropology*, vol. 16 (1960), pp. 292-298; *The Hopi Indians of Old Oraibi: Change and Continuity* (Ann Arbor: 1972).

SOURCE: Joseph G. Jorgensen, "Mischa Titiev, 1901-1978," *American Anthropologist*, vol. 81 (1979), pp. 342-344.

David Lonergan

Tokarev, S.A. (Sergeĭ Aleksandrovich). Ethnographer, specialist in religious studies, historian. Born in Tula (Russia) 16 December 1899, died in Moscow (Russian S.F.S.R.) 19 April 1985. After finishing at Moscow University in 1925, Tokarev began a teaching career and then worked at the TSentral'nyĭ Muzeĭ narodovedeniĭâ (Central Museum of Ethnology) (1928-1941). He received his doctorate in history in 1940, was a professor at Moscow University and head of the Ethnography Section there from 1956 to 1973. He was also head of the Section for the Ethnography of the Peoples of America, Australia and Oceania from 1943 to 1957 and served as head of the Section on the Ethnography of Non-European Peoples from 1957 to 1987 at the Institut ètnografii (Institute of Ethnography) of the Soviet Academy of Sciences.

Tokarev had extremely wide-ranging scholarly interests. He became so important a figure that B.A. Rybakov said of him: "In Moscow there are three ethnographic institutions: the Institute of Ethnography of the Soviet Academy of Sciences, the Ethnographic Section of the History Department of Moscow University and Sergeĭ Aleksandrovich Tokarev." As a scholar Tokarev not only broadened his own interests until he encompassed practically all areas of ethnographic study but he also contributed substantially to world scholarship. He was an academician-encyclopediast.

MAJOR WORKS: "O sistemakh rodstva avstraliĭŝev," *Ètnografiĭâ*, no. 1 (1929), pp. 23-53; "Rodovoĭ stroĭ v Melanezii," *Sovetskaĭâ ètnografiĭâ*, no. 2 (1933), pp. 39-73; no. 3-4 (19433), pp. 28-87; and no. 5-6 (1933), pp. 14-47; *Dokapitalisticheskie perezhitki v Oĭrotii* (Moscow and Leningrad: 1936); *Ocherki istorii ĭâkutskogo naroda* (Moscow: 1940); *Obshchestvennyĭ stroĭ ĭâkutov XVII-XVIII vv.* (ĬAkutsk: 1945); "K postanovke problem ètnogeneza," *Sovetskaĭâ ètnografiĭâ*, no. 3 (1949), pp. 12-36; *Narody Avstralii i Okeanii* (Moscow: 1956); *Religioznye verovaniĭâ vostochnoslavĭânskikh narodov XIX—nachala XX vv.* (Moscow and Leningrad: 1957); *Ètnografiĭâ narodov SSSR: istoricheskie osnovy byta i kul'tury* (Moscow: 1958); *Religiĭâ v istorii narodov mira* (Moscow: 1964; Moscow: 1965; Moscow: 1976); *Rannye formy religii i ikh razvitie* (Moscow: 1964); "Problema tipov ètnicheskikh obshchnosteĭ," *Voprosy filosofii*, no. 2 (1964), pp. 43-53; *Istoriĭâ russkoĭ ètnografii (dooktĭâbr'skiĭ period)* (Moscow: 1966); *Istoki ètnograficheskoĭ nauki (do serediny XIX v.)* (Moscow: 1978); *Istoriĭâ zarubezhnoĭ ètnografii* (Moscow: 1978); "Obychai i obrĭâdy kak ob˘ekt ètnograficheskogo issledovaniĭâ," *Sovetskaĭâ ètnografiĭâ*, no. 3 (1980), pp. 26-36; (editor-in-chief) *Mify narody mira* [2 vols.] (Moscow: 1980-1982).

SOURCES: "Spisok pechatnykh rabot S.A. Tokareva (k 80-letiĭû so dnĭâ rozhdeniĭâ)," *Sovetskaĭâ ètnografiĭâ*, no. 3 (1980), pp. 182-188 [bibliography]; S.A. Arutĭûnov and N.L. Zhukovskaĭâ, "Zasedanie Uchenogo Soveta Instituta ètnografii AN SSSR, posvĭâshchennoe 80-letiĭû S.A. Tokareva," *Sovetskaĭâ ètnografiĭâ*, no. 3 (1980), pp. 133-135; V.P. Alekseev, "Pamĭâti S.A. Tokareva," *Sovetskaĭâ ètnografiĭâ*, no. 4 (1980), pp. 168-172.

A.M. Reshetov
[Translation from Russian: Helen Sullivan]

Tolstov, S.P. (Sergeĭ Pavlovich). Ethnographer, archaeologist, historian, Orientalist. Born in St. Petersburg (Russia) 25 January 1907, died in Moscow (Russian S.F.S.R.) 28 December 1976. Tolstov was a professor at Moscow University, an honored associate member of the Academy of Sciences of the Uzbek S.S.R., an associate member of the Soviet Academy of Sciences, director of the Institut ètnografii (Institute of Ethnography) of the Soviet Academy of Sciences (1942-1966), and chief editor of the journal *Sovetskaĭâ ètnografiĭâ* (1946-1966). Under his leadership during 1954-1966 the publication of the fundamental eighteen-volume series *Narody mira* was accomplished. He also led the Khorezm archaeological-ethnological expedition.

His interests included theoretical problems. In 1932 basic concepts of economic-cultural types and historical-ethnographic regions were formulated by him for the first time. Tolstov made a substantial contribution to the study of the ethnography of the nomads, seminomads and settled peoples of Central Asia, especially to the problems of their ethnogenesis and to the development of the bases of paleoethnography; he attached great importance to the use of ethnographic materials in historical reconstruction during the analysis of archaeological data.

MAJOR WORKS: "K étnologicheskoĭ sistematike élementov veliko-russkoĭ kul'tury zhilishcha v Srednei Rossii" in: V.V. Bogdanov and S.P. Tolstov (editors), *Kul'tura i byt naseleniĭa TSentral'no-Promyshlennoĭ oblasti* (Moscow: 1929), pp. 75-88; "Problemy dorodovogo obshchestva," *Sovetskaĭa étnografiĭa*, no. 3-4 (1931), pp. 69-103; "Ocherki pervonachal'nogo islama," *Sovetskaĭa étnografiĭa*, no. 2 (1932), pp. 24-82; "Perezhitki totemizma i dual'noĭ organizaĭsii u turkmen" in: F.K. Kiparisov (editor), *Problemy istorii dokapitalisticheskikh obshchestv*, no. 9-10 (Leningrad: 1935), pp. 3-41; "K voprosu o periodizaĭsii istorii pervobytnogo obshchestva," *Sovetskaĭa étnografiĭa*, no. 1 (1946), pp. 25-30; "Étnografiĭa i sovremennost'," *Sovetskaĭa étnografiĭa*, no. 4 (1946), pp. 3-11; "Sovetskaĭa shkola v étnografii," *Sovetskaĭa étnografiĭa*, no. 4 (1947), pp. 8-28; *Drevniĭ Khorezm* (Moscow: 1948); *Po sledam drevnekhorezmiĭskoĭ ĭsivilizaĭsii* (Moscow: 1948); "Opyt primeneniĭa aviaĭsii v arkheologicheskikh rabotakh Khorezmskoĭ ékspediĭsii," *Vestnik AN SSSR*, no. 6 (1948), pp. 54-68; "Sorok piat' let sovetskoĭ étnografii," *Sovetskaĭa étnografiĭa*, no. 5 (1957), pp. 31-55; "Osnovnye teoreticheskie problemy sovremennoĭ sovetskoĭ étnografii," *Sovetskaĭa étnografiĭa*, no. 6 (1960), pp. 10-23; *Po drevnim del'tam Oksa i ĬAksarta* (Moscow: 1962).

SOURCES: T.A. Zhdanko, ĬU.A. Rapoport, N.N. Cheboksarov, "S.P. Tolstov," *Sovetskaĭa étnografiĭa*, no. 1 (1967), pp. 130-138; T.A. Zhdanko, M.A. Itina, "S.P. Tolstov," *Sovetskaĭa étnografiĭa*, no. 2 (1977), pp. 3-14; "Tolstov, S.P." in: B.V. Lunin (editor), *Bibliograficheskie ocherki o deĭateliĭakh obshchestvennikh nauk Uzbekistana*, vol. 2 (Tashkent: 1977), pp. 164-168.

A.M. Reshetov
[Translation from Russian: Thomas L. Mann]

Toschi, Paolo. Historian, folklorist, linguist. Born in Lugo, near Ravenna (Italy) 8 May 1893, died in Rome (Italy) 1974. Toschi studied linguistics and letters and received his degree from the University of Florence. From 1933 on Toschi was professor of traditional folk literature at the University of Rome. From 1930 to 1943 and again in 1948 he was on the editorial board of *Lares*, a journal of demology, i.e., folklore studies. He directed the organization of material for Rome's Museo delle Arti e Tradizioni Popolari (Museum of Folk Arts and Traditions) and was also a member of numerous cultural institutions, including the International Folk Music Council and the International Society for Folk Narrative Research.

Toschi produced numerous works of classification and bibliographical collection, applying the classic criteria of positivistic comparativism, partially enriched by an aesthetic sensitivity tied to the literary criticism of Benedetto Croce. His prinicipal areas of study were traditional dramatic-religious manifestations, folk art and poetry and the organization and didactics of folklore study.

With regard to sacred dramatizations, his contribution is important because it surpassed the schematism of philological classification by reintegrating religious texts into the sphere of their original ritual contexts (*Le origini del teatro italiano*). Besides a simple analysis of the poetic texts, Toschi added, at least at the level of classification, the use of analogies between the typical aspects of the sacred representations of different regional areas and the corresponding forms of the sacred art that shared the same inspirational motives, aims and functions. He dedicated particular attention to the taxonomic order of the constitutive elements of the religious rites—for example, procession, song, narration, etc.—and devoted attention to structural elements such as the reoccurence, transference of content from one rite to another, and equivalency of elements found in different rites. By applying the classical criteria used in comparative historical reconstruction, Toschi was able to discover the common origin of sacred and profane rites from pagan antiquity, making evident the agrarian character of the great traditional feasts, the deep affinity between the calendar cycles of very different peoples living substantial distances from each other, the ritual aspects of purification from sin and the propitiation of fate found in them.

In the field of folk poetry Toschi established an order for the formation, transmission and elaboration of songs (*Fenomenologia del canto popolare* and *Rappresaglia di studi di letteratira popolare*). Applying historical and philological criteria, he reduced the distance between the folk and literary components, refuting the concept of a collective and anonymous creation. Among his works, the most important are his bibliographic studies of Italian folklore up to 1940 (*Bibliografia delle tradizioni dal 1916 al 1940*) and his research on folk art (*Stampe popolari italiane dal XV al XX secolo* and *Tradizioni, vita ed arti popolari.*)

MAJOR WORKS: *Saggi sull'arte popolare* (Rome: 1945); *Bibliografia delle tradizioni popolari d'Italia dal 1916 al 1940* (Florence: 1946); *Fenomenologia del canto popolare* (Rome: 1947-1949); *Romagna tradizionale: usi, costumi, credenze, e pregiudizi* (Bologna: 1952); *Le origini del teatro italiano* (Turin: 1955); *Rappresaglia di studi di letteratura popolare* (Florence: 1957); *Fabri del folklore: ritratti e ricordi* (Rome: 1958); *Guida allo studio delle tradizioni popolari* (Turin: 1962); *Stampe popolari italiane dal XV al XX secolo* (Milan: 1964); *Tradizioni, vita ed arti popolari* (Milan: 1964; 2nd ed., Milan: 1967).

SOURCES: A.M. Cirese, *Cultura egemonica e culture subalterne* (Palermo: 1980); G.B. Bronzini, "Paolo Toschi" in: G. Grana, *Letteratura italiana: i critici* (Milan: 1969), pp. 2791-2806.

Gianni Vanucci
[Translation from Italian: Phyllis Liparini]

Tout, Charles. See: *Hill-Tout, Charles.*

Tozzer, Alfred Marston.

Tozzer, Alfred Marston. Anthropologist, archaeologist, ethnologist, linguist. Born in Lynn (Massachusetts) 4 July 1877, died in Cambridge (Massachusetts) 4 October 1954. Tozzer is best known for his Mesoamerican research and, in particular, for his work with Maya culture from an archaeological, ethnological and linguistic perspective. His monograph *Comparative Study of the Mayas and the Lacandones* was a landmark Maya ethnology that showed his interest in archaeological/ethnological connections. Subsequently, several substantial monographs on Mesoamerican site excavations were published, including *Tikal* and *Nakum*. These studies used comparative methods and noted the correlation of hieroglyphic inscriptions with architecture. His major archaeological monograph *Chichen Itzá and Its Cenote of Sacrifice*, published posthumously in 1957, is a synthesis of the preconquest history of the Yucatán. His translation and annotation of Landa's *Relación de las cosas de Yucatán* is an essential source for the ethnology of 16th-century Yucatán. Included in Tozzer's annotations, which are more extensive than the original text, is a compendium of all that was known of Maya ethnohistory at the time Tozzer prepared it. Tozzer's linguistic research is also important, and his grammar of the Mayan language was published in 1921.

The older son of a pharmacist and a drug store proprieter in Lynn, Massachusetts, Tozzer went to high school in Lynn and graduated from Harvard University, receiving the degrees of A.B. in 1900, A.M. in 1901, and Ph.D. in 1904. Tozzer's first ethnographic and linguistic work was in 1901 among the Navajo in New Mexico. Later that year he took his first field trip to the Yucatán and subsequently spent four years on a traveling fellowship of the Archaeological Institute. His ethnographic and linguistic work during this time with the Lacandón and the Yucatán Maya provided material for his doctoral dissertation. In 1904 Tozzer began his long and distinguished teaching career at Harvard University and in 1905 first offered his famous seminar on the Maya, "Anthropology 9." His first archaeological fieldwork was undertaken in 1907 in New Mexico and during 1909-1910 Tozzer became the director of the Peabody Museum American Expedition in Guatemala. In 1913 he was appointed curator of Middle-American archaeology and ethnology at the Peabody Museum and in April of that year he married Margaret Castle of Honolulu. During 1913-1914, Tozzer took a leave of absence from Harvard to succeed FRANZ BOAS as the director of the International School of Archaeology and Ethnology in Mexico. In this capacity, he excavated a Toltec site in the Valley of Mexico, his last fieldwork in Mesoamerica (reported in 1921).

After serving two years during World War I as a Captain in the Air Services, Tozzer returned to Harvard where he held various teaching and executive posts. He soon became chair of the Department of Anthropology, actively participated in the administrative affairs of Radcliffe College and the Peabody Museum, became Professor of Anthropology in 1921, and served as librarian of the Peabody Museum Library (1934-1948). Tozzer received many academic honors, including election to the American Academy of Arts and Sciences (1911), American Philosophical Society (1937), and National Academy of Sciences (1942). He was president of the American Anthropological Association for two terms (1928 and 1929) and was the first recipient of the Alfred Vincent Kidder medal for distinction in American archaeology. During World War II, Tozzer ran the Honolulu Office of Strategic Services, supervising radio broadcasts to eastern Asia and Indonesia and analyzing intercepted Japanese radio messages. He returned to Harvard in 1945 as the John E. Hudson Professor of Archaeology and in July 1948 became Professor Emeritus.

Possibly Tozzer's greatest contribution was as a teacher. A student of FREDERIC WARD PUTNAM, he started teaching early and was an inspiration to a whole generation of students. Tozzer was a gifted and dynamic teacher whose influence on Maya archaeology was profound. Many of his students were highly individualistic and the wide range of their interests is represented in the Festschrift volume, *The Maya and Their Neighbors*, which was dedicated to Tozzer in 1940. Tozzer and his students were largely responsible for establishing the structure of Maya studies and Mesoamerican archaeology in the early 20th century.

MAJOR WORKS: *A Comparative Study of the Mayas and the Lacandones* (New York: 1907); *A Preliminary Study of the Prehistoric Ruins of Tikal, Guatemala* (Cambridge, Mass.: 1911) (= *Memoirs of the Peabody Museum, Harvard University*, vol. 5, no. 2); *A Preliminary Study of the Prehistoric Ruins of Nakum, Guatemala* (Cambridge, Mass.: 1913) (= *Memoirs of the Peabody Museum, Harvard University*, vol. 5, no. 3); *Excavations of a Site at Santiago Ahuitzotla, D.F. Mexico* (Washington: 1921) (= *Bureau of American Ethnology, Bulletin*, no. 74); *A Maya Grammar; with Bibliography and Appraisement of Works Noted* (Cambridge, Mass.: 1921) (= *Papers of the Peabody Museum, Harvard University*, vol. 9); *Social Origins and Social Continuities* (New York: 1925); *Landa's Relación de las Cosas de Yucatán, a Translation (with 1154 Notes and Syllabus)* (Cambridge, Mass.: 1941) (= *Papers of the Peabody Museum, Harvard University*, vol. 18); *Chichen Itzá and Its Cenote of Sacrifice: a Comparative Study of Contemporaneous Maya and Toltec* (Cambridge, Mass.: 1957) (= *Memoirs of the Peabody Museum, Harvard University*, vols. 11-12).

SOURCES: S.K. Lothrop, "Alfred Marston Tozzer," *American Anthropologist*, vol. 57 (1955), pp. 614-618; Philip Phillips, "Alfred Marsten Tozzer," *American Antiquity*, vol. 21 (1955), pp. 72-80 [contains complete bibliography]; Barbara J. Price, "Alfred M. Tozzer" in: David L. Sills (editor), *International Encyclopedia of the Social Sciences* (New York: 1968-1979), vol. 16, pp. 116-118; Herbert Joseph Spinden, "Alfred Marston Tozzer," *National Academy of Sciences, Biographical Memoirs*, vol. 30 (1957), pp. 383-397; Evon Z. Vogt, "Alfred Marston Tozzer and Maya social anthropology" in: *The Maya and Their Neighbors* [suppl. 1] (Cambridge, Mass.: 1975), pp. 22-33; Gordon Randolph Willey, "Alfred Marston Tozzer" in: Gordon Randolph Willey, *Portraits in American Archaeology: Remembrances of Some Distinguished Americanists* (Albuquerque: 1988), pp. 266-290; Gordon R. Willey, "Alfred Marston Tozzer and Maya archaeology" in: *The Maya and Their Neighbors* [suppl. 1] (Cambridge, Mass.: 1975), pp. 3-10; *The Maya and Their Neighbors* (Cambridge, Mass.: 1940).

Lynne M. Schmelz-Keil

Tsuboi, Shōgoro. Anthropologist. Born in Edo [now Tōkyō] (Japan) 22 February 1863, died in St. Petersburg [now Leningrad] (Russia) 26 May 1913. Tsuboi studied biology at the Imperial University (now the University of Tōkyō), graduated in 1886, and immediately entered graduate study, specializing in anthropology. While still in the University in 1884, he organized the Anthropological Association (predecessor to the Anthropological Society of Nippon) and in 1886 established the society journal that developed into the *Tōkyō Jinrui Gakkai Zasshi* [*Journal of the Anthropological Society of Tōkyō*] and then into the *Jinruigaku Zasshi* [*Journal of the Anthropological Society of Nippon*]. In 1888 he did research on the Hokkaidō Ainu with YOSHIKIYO KOGANEI and from 1889 to 1892 studied in London, exploring widely in the scholarship of British anthropology. When he returned to Japan, he assumed a professorship in anthropology at his alma mater, thus providing a solid basis for the study of anthropology in his country and the rigorous dissemination of anthropological knowledge.

Tsuboi believed that Japan's Stone Age inhabitants were "Korobokkuru," a legendary dwarf people who appear in Ainu folktales as the aboriginals of Hokkaidō. He contributed to a great dispute that led to the development of many studies, arguing with Koganei and others concerning the relationship between the early Japanese and the Ainu. Because he died relatively young, he took his arguments with him to the grave, and his theories did not have time to mature. At a time when archaeology and folk studies were the parameters of a broad-based anthropological discipline, the *Tōkyō Jinrui Gakkai Zasshi*, under Tsuboi's editorship, provided a valuable forum for anthropological sciences in a wide sense.

MAJOR WORKS: *Kamban Kō [About Signboards]* (Tōkyō: 1887); *Haniwa Kō [About Haniwa]* (Tōkyō: 1901); *Jinruigaku Sōwa [Anthropological Lectures]* (Tōkyō: 1907).

SOURCES: "Tsuboi Rigakuhakushi kinengō" ["Special number issued in memory of the late Dr. Tsuboi"], *Journal of the Anthropological Society of Tōkyō*, vol. 28 (1913), pp. 623-714; Tadashi Saito (editor), *Tsuboi Shogoro Shū [Collected Works of Shogoro Tsuboi]* (Tōkyō: 1971-1972).

Bin Yamaguchi
[Translation from Japanese: Theodore Welch]

Tullio-Altan, Carlo. Anthropologist. Born in San Vito al Tagliamento, Pordenone (Italy) 30 March 1916. Tullio-Altan is best known for his cultural-anthropological and historical-anthropological studies of modern Italian society. While rejecting the cultural determinism sometimes associated with the work of ALFRED L. KROEBER, Tullio-Altan has underscored the value of a cultural-anthropological perspective in the study of complex societies.

After completing studies in law (University of Rome, 1939), Tullio-Altan was attracted by the historicist philosophy of Benedetto Croce and oriented his subsequent research toward questions in the history and philosophy of religions and ancient civilizations. In the 1950s he undertook ethnological studies in Vienna, Paris and London. He was professor of cultural anthropology at the Universities of Pavia (appointed 1963) and Florence (1971-1978) and is currently at the University of Trieste. He was among the promoters of the Primo Convegno Nazionale di Antropologia Culturale delle Società Complesse (First National Conference on the Cultural Anthropology of Complex Societies), held in Rome in 1987.

Tullio-Altan's ethno-anthropological research on Italian society dates from the 1960s, at which time he conducted an extensive survey of the value systems of the younger generation. This was followed by a series of historical-anthropological investigations of the "crisis" and the social and cultural late development ostensibly afflicting Italian society, which then brought him to studies of Italian ideologies of the 19th and 20th centuries. From these he has turned more recently to the issue of symbolic experience, focusing on both the variety of its cultural manifestations and the nature of its epistemological grounding.

Tullio-Altan has consistently rejected unidimensional paradigms and ahistorical approaches to the understanding of social and cultural facts, seeing instead a necessary multiplicity of interacting factors as the source of an always complex historical dynamic. His opposition to structuralism even in its heyday took the form of an adherence to the functionalist positions of BRONISLAW MALINOWSKI. Similarly, his espousal of Marxian theory has been colored by his interest in the work of the *Annales* school of historiography in France.

MAJOR WORKS: *Lo spirito religioso del mondo primitivo* (Milan: 1960); *Antropologia funzionale* (Milan: 1967); *Manuale di antropologia culturale* (Milan: 1971); (with A. Marradi and R. Cartocci) *Valori, classi sociali, scelte politiche: indagine sulla gioventù degli anni Settanta* (Milan: 1976); (with R. Cartocci) *Modi di produzione e lotte di classe in Italia* (Milan: 1978); *Antropologia, storia e problemi* (Milan: 1983); *La nostra Italia: arretratezza socioculturale, clientelismo, trasformismo e ribellismo dall'Unità ad oggi* (Milan: 1986); *Populismo e trasformismo: saggio sulle ideologie italiane* (Milan: 1989).

SOURCES: G. de Finis and S. Puccini, "Le società complesse: il peso del passato," *MondOperaio*, no. 10 (1987), pp. 130-132 [interview with Tullio-Altan]; P. Ignazi, "Populismo e trasformismo nell'analisi di Tullio-Altan," *Il Mulino*, no. 5 (1989), pp. 864-870; C. Rossetti, "L'antropologia della storia," *Il Mulino*, no. 1 (1985), pp. 29-43.

Giorgio de Finis
[Translation from Italian: Paolo Gnecco]

Tunakan, Seniha (née Seniha Hüsnü). Biologist, physical anthropologist. Born in İstanbul (Turkey) 14 March 1908. Tunakan received her degree from Frederick Wilhelm University in Berlin (1941). On her return to Turkey she was appointed Assistant to the Anthropological Institute, chaired by ŞEVKET AZİZ KANSU, at the Faculty of Languages, History and Geography (D.T.C.F.) in Ankara where she received her ensuing professional titles and continued teaching until her retirement in 1973. Her works on the anthropomorphology of several early Anatolian peoples, the palm prints of Turkish children, the palm and finger-prints of Turkish criminals, the Mongolian spot on Turkish neonates, and the genetics of Turkish twins were pioneer studies on the morphology and genetics of the Turkish people. Her work on Turkish palm prints and twins illustrates the similarities between the Turks and the races of Eastern Europe.

MAJOR WORKS: (with Şevket Aziz Kansu) "Alacahöyük (1943-45) kazılarında çıkarılan Kalkolitik, Bakır ve Tunç çağlarına ait halkın antropolojisi" ["The anthropology of the remains of the peoples of the Chalcolithic, Copper and Bronze Ages found in the 1943-45 excavations at Alacahöyük"], *Belleten*, vol. 10, no. 40 (1946), pp. 539-555; (with Şevket Aziz Kansu) "Karaoğlan höyüğünde çıkarılan Eti, Frig, ve Klasik devir iskeletlerinin antropolojik incelenmesi" ["An anthropological study of the Hittite, Phrygian, and Classic Period skeletons found in the tumulus at Karaoğlan"], *Belleten*, vol. 12, no. 48 (1948), pp. 749-774; "Türklerde ve Türk suçlularında el ayasındaki dört parmak çizgisi (maymun çizgisi) üzerinde araştırma" ["Research on the four-finger line of the palms of Turks and criminal Turks"], *A.Ü.D.T.C.F. Dergisi*, vol. 12, no. 1-2 (1954), pp. 117-126; "Memleketimizde ikiz doğumu çoğunluğu üzerinde ilk deneme" ["A report on the multitude of twin births in Turkey"], *A.Ü.D.T.C.F. Dergisi*, vol. 13, no. 3 (1955), pp. 17-19; "Türk suçlularında parmak izlerinin karşılaştırmalı incelenmesi" ["A comparative study of the fingerprints of Turkish criminals"], *A.Ü.D.T.C.F. Dergisi*, vol. 18, no. 1-2 (1960), pp. 85-91; "Türk suçlularında el ayasının karşılaştırmalı incelenmesi" ["A comparative palm study of Turkish criminals"], *Antropoloji*, no. 4 (1969), pp. 1-26.

SOURCE: Aygen Erdentuğ, "A.Ü.D.T.C.F. antropoloji bibliyografyası (1935-1983)" ["Bibliography of anthropology, D.T.C.F., Ankara University (1935-1983)"], *Antropoloji*, no. 12 (1985), pp. 496-498.

Aygen Erdentuğ

Turney-High, Harry Holbert. Anthropologist. Born in Kansas City (Missouri) 11 February 1899, died in Columbia (South Carolina) 2 October 1982. After taking his M.A. and Ph.D. at the University of Wisconsin, Turney-High taught at the University of South Dakota and at DePauw University before becoming sociology department head at the University of Montana (1927-1942). He served in Europe during World War II as an officer in the Military Police, becoming a colonel by 1946. Later that year Turney-High became chair of the sociology-anthropology department at the University of South Carolina, a post he retained until his retirement in 1964.

Turney-High's early research was on the Indians of the western United States, facilitated by his long stay in Montana. However, his war service influenced later research. During 1949-1950 he returned to Europe, where he undertook research as a Fulbright scholar; this resulted in a ground-breaking monograph on Walloon villagers in Belgium. Another influential study of the 1940s was his book on primitive war (a major interest of his). Turney-High remained an active researcher in retirement, publishing his seventh and last book at the age of eighty-two.

MAJOR WORKS: *The Flathead Indians of Montana* (Menasha: 1937); *Ethnography of the Kutenai* (Menasha: 1941); *General Anthropology* (New York: 1949); *Primitive War* (Columbia: 1949); *Chateau-Gerard* (Columbia: 1953); *Man and System* (New York: 1968); *The Military: the Theory of Land Warfare as Behavioral Science* (West Hanover, Massachusetts; 1981).

SOURCE: "Turney High, Harry Holbert" in: *Who's Who in America* (New York: 1976), pp. 3189-3190.

David Lonergan

Tylor, Sir *E.B. (Edward Burnett).* Anthropologist, lecturer, administrator. Born in Camberwell, London (England) 2 October 1832, died in Wellington (England) 2 January 1917. Tylor was the evolutionary anthropologist who is best remembered for his formulation of the "doctrine of survivals" and the "theory of animism." Considered by many to be the founder of modern anthropology, he played a major role in the gradual acceptance of anthropology as a scientific discipline. Tylor's two-volume work entitled *Primitive Culture*, in which he set out to demonstrate the continuous and progressive evolution of human culture and religion, influenced anthropological study not just during his lifetime but well into the 20th century.

The son of a prosperous Quaker brassfounder, Tylor never obtained a university education. Instead, at age sixteen he entered the family business, from which he was forced to resign a few years later due to poor health. It was during his recuperative travels in the United States and Cuba in 1856 that he chanced to meet Henry Christy, a Quaker banker who had already established a reputation as an archaeologist and ethnologist. Tylor accompanied Christy on a six-month archaeological expedition to Mexico and it was there that his ideas on culture and the prehistoric origins of man began to germinate and take shape.

Though evidence of his anthropological interest can already be seen in *Anahuac*, Tylor's account of his Mexican trip published in 1861, it was not until 1865 that his first major anthropological work, *Researches into the Early History of Mankind*, appeared. In it Tylor showed through examination of language, myths, rites, customs and beliefs that the human mind works in similar ways under similar conditions, thus allowing for either an evolutionary or diffusionist explanation for certain cultural phenomena. The development of his ideas on religion and culture culminated in 1871 with the publication of *Primitive Culture*, in which Tylor not only established and defended the doctrine of cultural evolution but also developed an elaborate theory of religion as well. The publication of *Primitive Culture* represented the high point in Tylor's career and he was honored for it by being elected a fellow of the Royal Society.

The only book-length work Tylor wrote after *Primitive Culture* was an anthropology textbook published in 1881. However, he continued to be a prolific writer of journal articles and reviews as well as a frequent lecturer. In addition, he concentrated much effort toward the advancement of anthropology as a scientific discipline. Even though Tylor did not have a university degree, he was very highly regarded by his professional colleagues. He was appointed keeper of the University Museum at Oxford in 1883 and shortly afterward was appointed a reader in anthropology; in 1896 he became Oxford's first professor of anthropology. Twice he served as president of the Royal Anthropological Institute and was the first president of the anthropological section of the British Association for the Advancement of Science. Among the many honors he received toward the end of his life was a volume of anthropological essays presented to him by his colleagues in honor of his seventy-fifth birthday and the conferring of knighthood in 1912.

MAJOR WORKS: *Anahuac: Or, Mexico and the Mexicans, Ancient and Modern* (London: 1861); *Researches into the Early History of Mankind and the Development of Civilization* (London: 1865); *Primitive Culture: Researches into the Development of Mythology, Philosophy, Religion, Art, and Custom* [2 vols.] (London: 1871); *Anthropology: an Introduction to the Study of Man and Civilization* (London: 1881); "On a method of investigating the development of institutions: applied to laws of marriage and descent," *Journal of the Royal Anthropological Institute of Great Britain and Ireland*, vol. 18 (1889), pp. 245-272.

SOURCES: R.R. Marett, *Tylor* (New York: 1936); Elvin Hatch, *Theories of Man and Culture* (New York and London: 1973); George W. Stocking, Jr., "Tylor, Edward Burnett" in: David L. Sills (editor), *International Encyclopedia of the Social Sciences* (New York: 1968-1979), vol. 16, pp. 170-177; Abram Kardiner and Edward Preble, "Edward Tylor" in: *They Studied Man* (Cleveland and New York: 1961), pp. 56-77; Robert H. Lowie, "Edward B. Tylor," *American Anthropologist*, n.s., vol. 19 (1917), pp. 262-268; Andrew Lang, "Edward Burnett Tylor" in: H. Balfour [et al.], *Anthropological Essays Presented to Edward Burnett Tylor in Honour of His 75th Birthday* (Oxford: 1907), pp. 1-15; Barbara W. Freire-Marreco, "A bibliography of Edward Burnett Tylor from 1861 to 1907" in: H. Balfour [et al.], *Anthropological Essays Presented to Edward Burnett Tylor in Honour of His 75th Birthday* (Oxford: 1907), pp. 375-409.

Maija M. Lutz

U

Udziela, Seweryn. Ethnographer. Born in Stary Sacz, Galicia (Austro-Hungarian Empire, now in Poland) 24 December 1857, died in Kraków (Poland) 26 September 1937. After graduation from the Teachers' College in Tarnów, Udziela began work as a teacher, then (for thirty-three years) worked as a school inspector. But he considered himself an ethnographer and regionalist from early youth.

In 1888 Udziela initiated the systematic collection of ethnographic materials from the Małopolska region. He conducted fieldwork during his inspection trips. Thanks to his position as school inspector he was able to find numerous co-workers among the teachers.

Udziela's works were primarily concerned with folk literature, beliefs and magical practices, certain aspects of material culture (folk costume and the artwork related to it, as well as architecture) and also native and seasonal ritual. He treated phenomena in a descriptive manner without attempting to explain them or to determine their development and significance. He proposed dress and architecture as criteria for the division into ethnographic groups. He was one of the founders of the the Polskie Towarzystwo Ludoznawcze (Polish Society of Folk Studies) as well as a reviewer, reporter and editor (1904-1905) for *Lud*. Udziela was also the founder and curator of the Muzeum Etnograficzne (Ethnographic Museum) in Kraków (which is now named for him).

MAJOR WORKS: *Lud polski w powiecie ropczyckim* [*Polish Folk in the Ropczyce District*] (Kraków: 1892); *Topograficzno-etnograficzny opis wsi polskich w Galicji* [*Topographic-Ethnographic Description of Polish Villages in Galicia*] (Kraków: 1901); "O potrzebie zestawienia i uporządkowania opowiadań ludowych" ["On the need for the arrangement and ordering of folk tales"], *Lud*, vol. 11 (1905), pp. 389-393; *Hafty ludu krakowskiego* [*Krakovian Folk Weavings*] (Kraków: 1906); "Etnograficzne ugrupowania i rozmieszczenia rodów górali polskich" ["Ethnographic groupings and the distribution of clans of Polish mountain folk"], *Przegląd*

Geograficzny (1918), pp. 80-91; *Krakowiacy [Krakovians]* (Kraków: 1924); "Ocieka: zapiski etnograficzne z lat 1899-1907" ["Ocieka: ethnographic notebooks from the years 1899-1907"], *Lud*, vol. 23 (1924), pp. 127-146; *Dwory [Manor Houses]* (Kraków: 1925); *Ludowe stroje krakowskie i ich krój [Krakovian Folk Costumes and their Style]* (Kraków: 1930); *Ziemia łemkowska przed półwieczem [A Half-Century of the Lemkovian Land]* (Lwów: 1934).

SOURCE: Kazimierz Dobrowolski [et al.], "Seweryn Udziela," *Lud*, vol. 35 (1937), pp. 5-41.

Maria Niewiadomska and Iwona Grzelakowska
[Translation from Polish: Joel Janicki]

Uhle, Max. Archaeologist. Born in Dresden (Germany) 25 March 1856, died in Loben, Upper Silesia (Germany) 11 May 1944. Uhle studied philology at Göttingen and Leipzig. His dissertation was on pre-classical Chinese. Uhle began his professional career in the ethnological museums of Dresden, Leipzig and Berlin, where he became familiar with pre-Columbian archaeology. In 1892, he published a joint monograph with Alphons Stübel on Tiahuanaco. His studies on the stylistic and chronological differences between the art of Tiahuanaco and that of the Inca formed the basis of his later more elaborate archaeological framework for the cultures of the Andes. That same year Uhle took his first journey of exploration to America on behalf of the Berlin Museum für Völkerkunde (Ethnographic Museum). His objective was the historical investigation of the Incas' methods of conquest. On this journey, he also carried out linguistic researches among the Uro and Aymara in Bolivia. In succeeding years, Uhle concerned himself with the archaeological exploration of the cultures of coastal Peru. He directed excavations at Ancón, at Pachacamac (this on behalf of the University of Pennsylvania where, during 1897-1899, he put the finishing touches on his notes and conducted lectures), during 1899-1901 in the Moche Valley, the Chincha Valley, Huamachuco, Ica and Pisco. Following a lengthy stay in California (where he was employed at the University of California at Berkeley during 1901-1903) further excavations were carried out at Nazca (Ocucaje), Ancón, Chancay, Supe, Cuzco and Nievería.

In his excavations, Uhle repeatedly succeeded in uncovering the ceramics of previously unknown cultures and in placing them in their correct chronological sequence. Examples of this are the Nazca ceramics in the areas of Chincha and Ica and the Chavín pottery of Ancón. Uhle belongs to a group of archaeologists who, at the end of the 19th and the beginning of the 20th centuries, commenced a systematic investigation of the pre-Spanish cultures of South America. Uhle properly interpreted the historical significance and cultural relationships of the artifacts he found. Uhle was the first to develop a general framework of the historical and chronological cultural sequences in the Andean region. The definition of the term "cultural horizon" (as the Andean sequence was called) arose from insights gained by Uhle during his excavations at Pachacamac (later, it was further formulated by the American, John Rowe).

In the period between 1906 and his return to Germany in 1933 Uhle carried out other excavations at Arica in Chile and Esmeraldas and Manabí in Ecuador. He also dedicated himself to the building of various archaeological collections. From 1906 to 1909 he served as the Director of the Museo Nacional de Historia (National Historical Museum) in Lima. After 1912 he was involved with the construction of an archaeological museum in Santiago de Chile (serving as professor at the University of Santiago) and after 1919 was employed as a lecturer at the University of Quito, arranging archaeological collections located there. In Germany Uhle collaborated with the Ibero-Amerikanisches Institut (Ibero-American Institute) of Berlin; he was also a professor at the University of Berlin, where he lectured on Andean archaeology exclusively. In his old age Uhle received countless honors, making his last journey to Lima in 1939.

MAJOR WORKS: (with A. Stübel) *Die Ruinenstätte von Tiahuanaco im Hochlande des alten Perú* (Leipzig: 1892); *Pachacamac* (Philadelphia: 1903); "Die Ruinen von Moche," *Journal de la Société des Américanistes*, vol. 10 (1913), pp. 95-117; "Zur Chronologie der alten Culturen von Ica," *Journal de la Société des Américanistes*, vol. 10 (1913), pp. 341-367; "Muschelhügel von Ancón, Peru" in: *Proceedings of the International Congress of Americanists* (London: 1912), sess. 18, pp. 22-45.

SOURCES: Hans-Dietrich Disselhoff, "Max Uhle (1856-1944) zum Gedächtnis," *Zeitschrift für Ethnologie*, vol. 81 (1956), pp. 307-310; Gerdt Kutscher, "Max Uhle zum Gedächtnis," *Ibero-Amerikanisches Archiv*, vol. 18 (1944), pp. 1-8; John Howland Rowe, *Max Uhle, 1856-1944: a Memoir of the Father of Peruvian Archaeology* (Berkeley: 1954).

Frauke Johanna Riese
[Translation from German: Robert B. Marks Ridinger]

Uhlenbeck, C.C. (Christiaan Cornelis).

Ethnolinguist. Born in Voorburg (Netherlands) 18 October 1866, died in Lugano (Switzerland) 12 August 1951. Uhlenbeck is best known for his studies of Indo-Germanic and aboriginal North American languages.

Uhlenbeck studied linguistics and history at the University in Leiden starting in 1885 under Johan Kern (1833-1917), Matthias de Vries (1820-1892), Robert Fruin (1823-1899) and Samuel Cosijn (1820-1901). For a short time he was a teacher at a high school, but subsequently he studied the Russian archives for the Dutch government, learning Russian at the same time. In 1893 he was appointed professor of Sanskrit at the Municipal University of Amsterdam. In 1899 he succeeded Cosijn at the University of Leiden as professor of Old Germanic languages. He conducted linguistic fieldwork among the Basques in Spain (1906) and the Blackfeet in the United States (1910 and 1911, assisted by J.P.B. DE JOSSELIN DE JONG).

Uhlenbeck's scientific work is characterized by a broad comparative and typological approach. He was an opponent of the neo-grammarian school. In his comparative work he emphasized lexical similarities, also keeping areal features and borrowing in mind. He discussed the possibility of distant genetic relationships between diverse languages such as Basque and Caucasian and Eskimo and Indo-European. He stressed the contributions archaeology and ethnology could make to linguistics. In his typological work he discussed the passiveness of transitive (mainly ergative) and other constructions and similarities of possessive constructions with intransitivity. He published numerous treatises on the phonology, morphology and grammar of Basque, Indo-European, Eskimo and Algonquian languages, notably Blackfoot. Uhlenbeck was one of the few European scientists who dared to venture into the field of North American Indian languages, which remained his favorite specialization for a quarter of a century.

MAJOR WORKS: *Manual of East Indian Phonology* (London: 1898); *Beiträge zu einer vergleichenden Lautlehre der Baskischen Dialekte* (Berlin: 1903); *Die einheimischen Sprachen Nord-Amerikas bis zum Rio Grande* (Vienna: 1908); *Original Blackfoot Texts* (Amsterdam: 1911); *An English-Blackfoot Vocabulary* (Amsterdam: 1930); *Eskimo en Oer-Indogermaansch* (Amsterdam:

1935); *A Blackfoot-English Vocabulary* (Amsterdam: 1934); *A Concise Blackfoot Grammar* (Amsterdam: 1938).

SOURCES: J.P.B. de Josselin de Jong, "In memoriam: Christianus Cornelius Uhlenbeck," *Lingua*, vol. 3 (1953), pp. 243-268; V. Pisani-Christianus, "Cornelius Uhlenbeck," *Paideia*, vol. 7 (1952), pp. 81-88; P. Swiggers, "C.C. Uhlenbeck and the scientific study of Algonkian languages," *European Review of Native American Studies*, vol. 2, no.1 (1988), pp. 7-8.

Pieter Hovens and Peter Bakker

Umaru, Alhaji (also known as Imam Imoru; full Arabized name: ᶜUmar ibn Abū Bakr ibn ᶜUthmān ibn ᶜAlī al-Kabbawī al-Kanawī). Poet, informant, Muslim scholar, religious leader. Born in Kano (Nigeria) 1858, died at Kete-Krachi (Ghana) 1934. At the age of seven Umaru was sent to a Koranic school in the Magoga quarter of Kano city. Having memorized the *Qur'ān* in 1870 he began advanced Islamic studies and continued them through some twenty years. He studied Muslim theology (*tauḥīdī*), Koranic commentaries (*tafsīrī*), the Maliki code of law (*fikihu*), the Arabic language, the historical traditions of Islam and the Muslim world and related subjects. Between the ages of seven and twenty-five he participated occasionally in his father's trading travels to Salaga. In 1883, after his father's death, Umaru migrated to Sokoto and spent the period between 1883 and 1891 there, studying in the towns of that region—Sokoto, Gwandu and Argungu. From there he traveled west to the lands of Zabarma, Songhay, Dendi, Gurma, Mossi and Gurunsi. In 1892 he settled in the trading town of Salaga (where his brothers and a sister were living) and established his own Islamic school. After the Salaga civil war and the destruction of the town by German colonial forces, in 1896 Umaru was forced to move to Kete-Krachi, a trading center that developed after Salaga's decline. Welcomed by his students, friends and relatives, soon he was given the office of Imam. While staying in Kete Krachi he traveled from time to time and visited the Dagomba kingdom and the kingdom of Maprusi. Between 1913 and 1918 he made a pilgrimage to Mecca, having changed there his religious affiliation from the Qadiriyya to the Tijaniyya brotherhood.

Umaru served as an informant to G.A. Krause (1850-1938), Adam Mischlich (1864-1948) and ROBERT RATTRAY. On their initiative, he wrote in Ajami numerous Hausa fables, stories and chronicles and provided them with source materials on Hausa material and spiritual culture and on socio-economic relations in Central and Western Sūdān.

He may also have written as many as 120 poems, both in Hausa and in Arabic. More than twenty of them are well known to scholars. These poems can be thematically grouped into political poems (e.g., lamenting the arrival of the Christians and listing towns and states conquered by them), religious poems (homilies and polemics), praise poems (including those secular in character), thanksgiving poems, elegies and elaborations of the Arabic prototypes. Umaru also became famous as a gifted translator of the works of the pre-Muslim Arabic poet Imru'l-Qays into Hausa. His poetry might be described as the vehicle of social commentary, social criticism and reflection on the history of his time. Umaru's writings would seem to be as significant for the understanding of the recent social and political history of Central and Western Sūdān as the writings of Wells and Bennett for the history of Britain. From the literary point of view, his creative output indicates that the interrelations between the Hausa and Arabic literary traditions are less close than it was believed. It suggests that the secular stream in Hausa learned poetry began to develop much earlier than many Hausaists believe. The example of Umaru's poetry makes it evident that Hausa literate verse has been influenced to some extent by the oral genres.

MAJOR WORKS: *Talᶜ al-munāfiᶜa fī dhikr al-munāzaᶜa* (1898) [*Useful Information concerning the Dispute*] [tr.: G.G. Martin, "Two poems by Al-Ḥajj ᶜUmar of Kete-Krachi" in: I.A. Braimah and J.R. Goody, *Salaga: the Struggle for Power* (London: 1967), pp. 193-198]; *Tanbīh al-ikhwān fī dhikr al-aḥzān* (ca. 1896) [*A Warning to the Brethren concerning Afflictions*] [tr.: B.G. Martin, "Two poems by Al-Ḥajj ᶜUmar of Kete-Krachi" in: I.A. Braimah and J.R. Goody, *Salaga: the Struggle for Power* (London: 1967), pp. 198-209]; *Mashraᶜ mā' al-khabar* (1899) [*Access to the Sea of Knowledge*] [partial tr. with commentary: Stanisław Piłaszewicz, *Alhadżi Umaru (1858-1934): poeta ludu Hausa* (Warsaw: 1981), pp. 65-71]; *Nazm al-la'ālī bi-akhbar wa tanbīh al-kirām* (1900-1901) [*Pearl Necklace of Information and a Warning to the Noble People*] [partial tr. with commentary: Stanisław Piłaszewicz, *Alhadżi Umaru (1858-1934): poeta ludu Hausa* (Warsaw: 1981), pp. 71-79]; *Zuwan Nasarā* (1903) [*The Arrival of the Christians*] [tr. with commentary: Stanisław Piłaszewicz, "'The arrival of the Christians': a Hausa poem on the colonial conquest of West Africa," *Africana Bulletin*, vol. 22 (1975), pp. 55-129]; *Wāḳar talaucī da wadātā* (1903) [*The Song of Poverty and Wealth*] [tr. with commentary: Stanisław Piłaszewicz, "'The Song of Poverty and Wealth': a Hausa poem on social problems," *Africana Bulletin*, vol. 21 (1974), pp. 67-115; tr. in: Jack Goody, *Cooking, Cuisine and Class* (Cambridge: 1982), pp. 194-203; also: M.B. Duffiel, "Hausa poems as sources for social and economic history," *History in Africa*, vol. 13 (1986), pp. 35-88]; *Kalmōmī miyāgū* (1903) [*Evil Words: a Homily*] [partial tr. with commentary: Stanisław Piłaszewicz, "Homiletic poetry of Al-Ḥāji ᶜUmaru," *Africana Bulletin*, vol. 30 (1981), pp. 73-109]; *Nā fārā da dūnan Ta'ālā* (between 1904 and 1919) [*I Begin in the Name of God the Most-High*] [partial tr. with commentary: Stanisław Piłaszewicz, *Alhadżi Umaru (1858-1934): poeta ludu Hausa* (Warsaw: 1981), pp. 177-193; *Al-Sarḥat al-warīqah fī ᶜilm al-wathīqat* (1889-1890) [*The Thornless Leafy Tree concerning the Knowledge of Letter-Writing*] [tr. in: *Research Bulletin* [Ibadan], no. 9-10 (1973-1974), pp. 1-68]; manuscripts on Hausa customs and habits [see: Adam Mischlich, "Über Sitten und Gebräuche der Haussa. 1. Ursprung der Gausaner. 2. Länder der Hausaner. 3. Die sieben echten Haussastaaten," *Mitteilungen des Seminars für Orientalische Sprachen*, vol. 10 (1907), pp. 155-181; vol. 11 (1908), pp. 1-81; and vol. 12 (1909), pp. 215-274]; manuscripts on Hausa material culture [texts in Roman script and tr.: Adam Mischlich, *Über die Kulturen in Mittel-Sudan* (Berlin: 1942)]; historical manuscripts [tr.: H. Sölken, "Die Geschichte von Kabi nach Imam Umaru," *Mitteilungen des Instituts für Orientforschung*, vol. 7 (1959), pp. 123-162; "Die Geschichte von Ada," *Mitteilungen des Ausland-Hochschule an der Universität Berlin*, vol. 40 (1933), pp. 144-169; "Afrikanische Dokumente zur Frage der Entstehung der hausanischen Diaspora in Oberguinea," *Mitteilungen des Ausland-Hochschule an der Universität Berlin*, vol. 42 (1939), pp. 1-127].

SOURCES: D.E. Ferguson, *Nineteenth Century Hausaland: Being a Description by Imam Imoru of the Land, Economy and Society of his People* [unpublished Ph.D. dissertation] (Los Angeles: 1973); Stanisław Piłaszewicz, *Alhadżi Umaru (1858-1934): poeta ludu Hausa: studiem historyczno-literackie* (Warsaw: 1981); Stanisław Piłaszewicz, "From Arabic to Hausa: the case of the Hausa poet Alhaji Umaru," *Recznik Orientalistyczny*, vol. 46 (1988), pp. 97-104; Robert S. Rattray, "Hausa poetry" in: E.E. Evans-Pritchard, Raymond Firth, Bronislaw Malinowski and Isaac Schapera (editors), *Essays Presented to C.G. Seligman* (London: 1934), pp. 255-265; H. Sölken, "Die Geschichte von Ada," *Mitteilungen des Ausland-Hochschule an der Universität Berlin*, vol. 40 (1933), pp. 144-169; H. Sölken, "Zur Biographie des Imām ᶜUmaru von Kete Kratyi," *Africana Marburgensia*, vol. 7 (1959), pp. 24-30; Adam Mischlich, *Über die Kulturen im Mittel-Sudan* (Berlin: 1942); Ivor Wilks, "The growth of Islamic learning in Ghana," *Journal of the Historical Society of Nigeria*, vol. 2 (1963), pp. 409-418; T. Hodgkin, "The Islamic literary tradition in Ghana" in: M. Lewis (editor), *Islam in Tropical Africa* (London: 1966), pp. 442-462; B.C. Martin, "Two poems by Al-Ḥajj ᶜUmar of Kete-Krachi" in: I.A. Braimah and J.R. Goody, *Salaga: the Struggle for Power* (London: 1967), pp. 185-209.

Stanisław Piłaszewicz

Unckel, Kurt. See: *Nimuendajú, Curt.*

Underhill, Ruth. Born in Ossining (New York) 22 August 1883 (1884?), died in Denver (Colorado) 14 August 1984. After a twenty-year career in social work, Underhill wanted "to know more about PEOPLE" and enrolled at Columbia University in 1930 to study anthropology. RUTH BENEDICT encouraged her to study culture as it is expressed in individual personalities. Underhill's first weeks among the Tohono O'Odham "were spent almost entirely among women," the most important of whom was Chona. Chona's story, *Autobiography of a Papago Woman*, was the first published life history of a Southwestern Indian woman. Underhill returned repeatedly to the "hard-working but poetic" Papago who came to value her and her efforts "to capture the spirit of their people" (*Papago Woman*).

Underhill's fifty-year career in anthropology included thirteen years traveling to the reservations of the Southwest as a consultant for the Bureau of Indian Affairs. In this capacity, she wrote study books for Indian children as well as several books and pamphlets interpreting the Indians of the Southwest to the general public.

MAJOR WORKS: *Autobiography of a Papago Woman*, Memoir of the American Anthropological Association, no. 46 (1936); *First Penthouse Dwellers in America* (New York: 1938); *Singing for Power* (Berkeley: 1938); *Pueblo Crafts* (Phoenix: 1944); *Papago Indian Religion* (New York: 1939) (= *Columbia University Contributions to Anthropology*, no. 30); *Ceremonial Patterns in the Greater Southwest* (New York: 1948) (= *American Ethnological Society Monograph*, no. 13); *People of the Crimson Evening* (Phoenix: 1951); *Red Man's America: a History of Indians in the United States* (Chicago: 1953); *The Navajos* (Norman: 1956); *Indians of the Southwest* (Garden City, N.Y.: 1961); *Papago Woman* (New York: 1979) [revised and expanded edition of *Autobiography of a Papago Woman*].

SOURCES: Barbara A. Babcock and Nancy J. Parezo, *Daughters of the Desert: Woman Anthropologists and the Native American Southwest, 1880-1989: an Illustrated Catalogue* (Albuquerque: 1988), pp. 72-75, 239-240.

Barbara A. Babcock and Nancy J. Parezo

Unkel, Kurt. See: ***Nimuendajú, Curt.***

V

Vaillant, George C. Anthropologist, archaeologist. Born in Boston (Massachusetts) 5 April 1901, died in Devon (Pennsylvania) 13 May 1945. Vaillant is known above all for fundamental stratigraphic work in the Basin of Mexico, where, in the 1930s, he created a sequence founded on quantified pottery and figurine data. He thus greatly improved the chronology then available for this key region of Mesoamerica. Only the early portion of his sequence, based on work at the Preclassic sites of Zacatenco, Ticomán and El Arbolillo, was ever published in full. An overview of his entire chronology, however, appears in his classic *Aztecs of Mexico*. Many of his ceramic counts and tabulations for the Classic (Teotihuacán, Atzcapotzalco) and Postclassic (Chiconautla, Nonoalco) periods were later made available in summary graphic form (Tolstoy, 1958).

Prior to his work in Central Mexico, Vaillant wrote a pioneering study of the chronological significance of Maya ceramics, which served as his doctoral thesis at Harvard in 1927. Though unpublished it enjoyed wide circulation. Like his friend, Miguel Covarrubias, Vaillant was among the few at the time to recognize the significance of the emerging Olmec style. He claimed correctly that it was chronologically early and that its epicenter would eventually be found in Veracruz.

In his research Vaillant gave priority to problems of chronology and culture history. He acquired his approach to these problems and his field techniques in the Southwestern United States, where he participated in work by ALFRED V. KIDDER at Pecos. A key problem on Vaillant's agenda was Herbert Spinden's influential "Archaic hypothesis," which Vaillant set out to test and correct. In dealing with the later periods of the Central Mexican sequence Vaillant sought to relate archaeology to the events and descriptions of Colonial sources and Mexican traditions. Though his espousal of ADOLPH

BANDELIER's views on the nature of Aztec society and his identification of Teotihuacán as "Toltec" have been superseded, he tackled important ethnohistorical questions, some of which remained unanswered as of 1990.

MAJOR WORKS: *Excavations at Zacatenco* (New York: 1930) (= *Anthropological Papers of the American Museum of Natural History*, vol. 32, part 1); *Excavations at Ticomán* (New York: 1930) (= *Anthropological Papers of the American Museum of Natural History*, vol. 32, part 2); *Excavations at El Arbolillo* (New York: 1930) (= *Anthropological Papers of the American Museum of Natural History*, vol. 35, part 1); "A correlation of archaeological and historical sequences in the Valley of Mexico," *American Anthropologist*, n.s., vol. 40 (1938), pp. 535-573; "Tiger masks and platyrrhine bearded figures from Middle America" in: *XXVII Congreso Internacional de Americanistas* (Mexico City: 1939), vol. 2, pp. 131-135; *Aztecs of Mexico* (New York: 1941).

SOURCES: A.V. Kidder, "George Clapp Vaillant, 1901-1945," *American Anthropologist*, n.s., vol. 47 (1945), pp. 589-602; P. Tolstoy, *Surface Survey of the Northern Valley of Mexico: the Classic and Post-classic Periods* (Philadelphia: 1958) (= *Transactions of the American Philosophical Society*, vol. 48, part 5).

Paul Tolstoy

Vakarelski, Khristo Tomov. Ethnographer, Slavicist, philologist, translator. Born in Momina Klisura, Pazardzhik Region (Bulgaria) 15 December 1896, died in Sofia (Bulgaria) 26 November 1979. Vakarelski is among the best known of Slavic ethnographers and is universally considered the most distinguished researcher of Bulgarian folk culture. During the course of half a century he exerted a strong influence on Bulgarian ethnography and published more than 1000 scholarly books and articles.

Born into a peasant family, Vakarelski left his home village to study Slavic philology at the University of Sofia. He was later advised by the well known folklorist, I.D. Shishmanova, to study ethnography in Poland, where he worked under renowned Polish ethnographers EUGENIUSZ FRANKOWSKI and STANISŁAW PONIATOWSKI. This, in addition to later contacts with KAZIMIERZ MOSZYŃSKI, were to have an enormous influence on the nature of his future work in ethnography. Until his death he maintained an active contact with Polish ethnographic centers and, during the course of many trips, he became acquainted with the work of many other centers, including Hungary, Austria, Finland and Czechoslovakia. From 1927 to 1941 he was curator at the National Ethnographic Museum in Sofia.

The Polish ethnographer Moszyński had a particularly strong influence on Vakarelski's work. Both men made use of typological-geographic, etymological and historical methods of interpretation of cultural phenomena. This is best seen in Vakarelski's milestone work, *Etnografia Bulgarii* (first published in Poland and later in an expanded version in Bulgaria), which was compiled from numerous articles he had written on the folk culture of Bulgaria and culminated many years of research. It contains a vast collection of ethnographic material from all regions of Bulgaria presented in an analytical form that shows the ethnic and cultural processes at work throughout the 1,300-year history and development of the country.

Vakarelski took a mainstream European academic approach in this ethnographic work. Evolutionists exerted a strong influence on the way he approached cultural phenomena. Vakarelski tended to study cultural phenomena largely through objects, believing that objects (together with their functions) constituted important documents of human activity.

In discussing material culture he particularly recognized the influence of the specific geographic surroundings and ecological conditions out of which it grew. He also felt that true understanding of the peasant classes should spring from direct observation and looked disapprovingly on "desk research"—i.e., analysis of cultural phenomena on the basis of written source materials.

MAJOR WORKS: *Etnografia Bulgarii* (Wrocław: 1965) [expanded Bulgarian ed.: *Etnografiia na Bulgariia* (Sofia: 1977)]; "Starinnite elementi v bulgarskite narodni obichai" in: Krustiu Miiâtev (editor), *Prez vekovete* (Sofia: 1938), pp. 246-281; *Kniga na narodnata lirika* (Sofia: 1946); "Die bulgarischen wandernden Hirtenhutten," *Acta Ethnographica* [Budapest], vol. 5 (1956), pp. 1-82; and vol. 6 (1958), pp. 1-40; *Bulgarische Volkskunde* (Berlin: 1969); *Dobrudzha* (Sofia: 1964).

SOURCES: Mieczysław Gładysz, "Christo Tomov Vakarelski (1896-1979)," *Etnografia Polska*, vol. 25. no. 2 (1981), pp. 47-51; Khristo Vakarelski, *Etnografia Bulgarii* (Wrocław: 1965); *Izvestiia na Etnografskiia Institut i Muzeï*, vol. 6 (1963) [contains bibliography].

Dennis Koliński

Valcárcel, Luis E. Historian, educator, archaeologist, journalist, political figure. Born in Ilo (Peru) 8 February 1891, died in Lima (Peru) 26 December 1987. Valcárcel is best known to anthropologists for his studies of the prehistoric and historic cultures of Peru from a holistic perspective, studies that drew on multiple archaeological, ethnohistoric, historic and ethnographic lines of evidence and that were based on his belief in the cultural unity underlying the diversity of indigenous peoples of Peru. He is also remembered for directing national museums concerned with field research in archaeology and culture history, for providing official cooperation and support for Peruvian and foreign anthropologists and archaeologists working in Peru and for initiating and directing journals reporting their scientific research.

Valcárcel's most significant archaeological fieldwork was at Sacsahuamán (primarily during 1933-1935), near Cuzco, his type site for a scheme of cultural evolution in terms of Paleo-, Meso-, and Neo-Andean cultures. As a champion of *Indigenismo*, a popularly based civil-rights movement, he sought to explain the devolution of Inka (Inca) civilization into the marginal way of life of modern *campesinos*, the mostly indigenous peasantry. This concern was fundamental to his teaching, writing and politics.

Educated at Universidad San Antonio Abad, Cuzco, he received the *bachiller* (bachelor's degree) in three fields, "letters," economic and political sciences and jurisprudence, and doctorates in letters and jurisprudence between 1913 and 1916. He was affiliated with Peruvian universities for most of the period 1911-1961. He became *catedrático* (professor) in Peruvian history and art at the Universidad Nacional del Cuzco (National University of Cuzco) (1917), where he founded and headed the institution's Museo Arqueológico (Archaeological Museum) (1923-1930). It was while in Cuzco that he began contributing newspaper articles about the sites and legends of prehistoric cultures and the problems of contemporary indigenous peoples.

Valcárcel moved to Lima in 1930 to direct the Museos Bolivariano and Arqueología Peruana (renamed the Museo Nacional del Perú (National Museum of Peru) in 1931). With Jorge C. Muelle and Eugenio Yavcovleff, he founded the scientifically oriented *Revista del Museo Nacional* (1932). He later initiated other journals, including *Folklore Americano* and *Etnología y Arqueología*. He began teaching at the Universidad

Nacional Mayor de San Marcos (National University of San Marcos) in 1931 and became dean of the Faculty of Letters in 1956. The Instituto de Etnología (Institute of Ethnology) at San Marcos, which was subsequently headed by Valcárcel, was established by law while he was serving as Peru's Minister of Education during 1945-1946, during which time he also founded the Museo de la Cultura Peruana (Museum of Peruvian Culture), which he later directed from 1946 to 1966. He retired from San Marcos in 1961, but remained an active writer and defender of archaeological sites against destruction, notably in the case of Pachacamac (near Lima) in a joint effort with Arturo Jiménez Borja during 1962-1963.

Although his scholarly writings about indigenous prehistoric and historic peoples are the most important to anthropologists, Valcárcel was known among the Peruvian intelligentsia for his historical writings (e.g., *Historia del Perú antiguo: a través de la fuente escrita*) and to the general public for his newspaper features about indigenous Peruvians, their prehistory, folkloric heritage, and disadvantaged conditions in modern times. His autobiography (*Memorias*) recounts the intellectual and political history of Peru in the 20th century by one who played multiple roles in both.

MAJOR WORKS: *Del ayllu al imperio* (Lima: 1925); *Tempestad en los Andes* (Lima: 1927); "Sajsawaman redescubierto: estudio arqueológico y histórico," *Revista del Museo Nacional*, vol. 3 (1934), pp. 3-36 and 211-233; vol. 4 (1935), pp. 161-203; *Cuzco, capital arqueológico de Sudamérica* (Lima 1934); *Mirador indio* [2 vols.] (Lima: 1937-1941); *Historia de la cultura antigua del Perú* [2 vols.] (Lima: 1943-1948); *Ruta cultural del Perú* (Mexico City: 1945); *Etnohistoria del Perú antiguo* (Lima: 1959); *Historia del Perú antiguo: a través de la fuente escrita, historiadores de los siglos XVI, XVII, XVIII* (Buenos Aires: 1964); (with José Matos Mar, José Deustua C. and José Luis Renique) *Memorias* (Lima: 1981).

SOURCES: Luis E. Valcárcel with José Matos Mar, José Deustua C., and José Luis Renique, *Memorias* (Lima: 1981). Jorge C. Muelle, "Homenaje al Dr. Valcárcel," *Revista del Museo Nacional*, vol. 30 (1960), pp. 366-372; Luis E. Valcárcel, "Autobiográfica: discurso del Dr. Luis E. Valcárcel en la actuación de homenaje que le ofreció la Facultad de Letras de la Universidad Nacional de San Marcos," *Revista del Museo Nacional*, vol. 31 (1962), pp. 10-14; Izumi Shimada, "Obituary, Luis Eduardo Valcárcel Vizcarra," *Willay*, vol. 28 (1988), pp. 1-4; "Valcárcel, Luis E." in: *Enciclopedía illustrada del Perú* (Lima: 1987), vol. 6, pp. 2177-2178; "In memoriam," *Revista del Museo Nacional*, vol. 49 (1986-87 [1988]), pp. 9-11; "Luis E. Valcárcel revindicó con sus obras la cultura andina," *El Comercio* (27 December 1988).

Kathryn M. Cleland

Valšík, Jindřich Antonín. Physical anthropologist, physician, pediatrician. Born in Prague (Austria-Hungary, now Czechoslovakia) 25 August 1903, died in Bratislava (Czechoslovakia) 10 February 1977. Valšík graduated from the Charles University in Prague both from the Medical School (1927) and the Faculty of Sciences (1930). In 1938 he obtained the *venia docendi* for anthropology, in 1957 the title of Professor and in 1965 the degree of Doctor of Biological Sciences (Dr.Sc.). From the time he worked in the health service until 1948, he was engaged in intensive anthropological research. Most of the papers he published in that period (the first in 1924) dealt with methodological, genetic and ethnological aspects of dermatoglyphics, as well as with their practical application in the assessment of paternity. Nevertheless, Valšík's contributions to other fields of anthropology (human genetics, auxology, ethnology) were also remarkable.

In 1953 Valšík was invited to the Comenius University in Bratislava, where he finally had the opportunity to work in the field of anthropology and to found a department according to his own ideas. At this period his research was directed toward various aspects of the normal growth and development of children and youth. Valšík gained the greatest recognition as a result of these studies. The topics of the papers concerned, among other things, the genetic and environmental factors influencing the maturation of girls, primarily the onset of menarche. Valšík collected material from Slovakia and from many other countries. He made several interesting observations about the seasonal occurrence of menarche in both urban and rural areas, for example about the connection between the month of menarche onset and the month of birth. Another important problem in the development of children studied by Valšík was the eruption of the permanent dentition as well as changes occurring in the sequence of tooth eruption and factors influencing it.

In his numerous ethnological investigations (among Montenegrans, Lusatian Serbians, Greeks, Nubians, Russian immigrants in Northeast Poland, Romanians, Gypsies), Valšík expressed his unambiguous opposition to racism. He took part in the work of the Experts Committee of UNESCO that elaborated *The Statement on Human Races* in 1964, dealing with the problems of the biological aspects of the human race concept.

Besides his numerous domestic distinctions Valšík's extensive scientific and organizational activity was appreciated internationally. He was member of Société d'Anthropologie de Paris, the Polish Towarzystwo Anthropologiczne, the Royal Anthropological Institute, the International Association of Human Biology, the Association on Dermatoglyphics, the Société de Biométrie Humaine, the Anthropologische Gesellschaft in Vienna and the Association of Current Anthropology. Valšík was the representative of Czechoslovakia at the Permanent Counsel of International Congress of Anthropological and Ethnographical Sciences, where he accomplished much.

MAJOR WORKS: "Příspěvek k poznání papilárních linii lidské dlani a pravidel jejich frekvence a dědění" ["Contribution to the knowledge of the epidermic ridges on the human palm and of the regularity of their occurrence and heredity"], *Anthropologie* [Prague], vol. 2 (1924), pp. 17-39; "Pokus o nové vyjádření formulí papillárních linií lidské dlaně" ["Genetic expression of papillary formulas on the lines of the human hand"], *Časopis lékařů českých*, vol. 67 (1928), pp. 281-283; "Papillární číslo v dermatoglyfice" ["Papillar number in dermatoglyphics"], *Časopis lékařů českých*, vol. 71 (1932), pp. 1165-1168; "Sexual maturation in Central Europe" in: *Compte rendu de la 1ère Session du Congrès International des Sciences Anthropolgiques et Ethnologiques* (London: 1934), pp. 93-94; "Études anthropologiques sur les Monténégrins du Dourmitor," *L'Anthropologie*, vol. 47 (1937), pp. 339-354; "Tempy prorezyvaniā postaſannykh zubov" in: *Sovremennaiā antropologiā* (Moscow: 1964) (= *Trudy Moskovskogo obshchestva ispytateleĭ prirody*, no. 14), pp. 35-41; "The seasonal rhythm of menarche," *Human Biology*, vol. 2 (1965), pp. 75-90; "La standardisation des méthodes dans l'étude de la puberté chez la femme," *Biotypologie*, vol. 3 (1965), pp. 93-97; "Dreißig Jahre Menarcheforschung," *Acta Facultatis Rerum Naturalium Universitatis Comenianae-Anthropologie*, vol. 10 no. 8 (1966), pp. 325-342; "On the Egyptian Nubians," *Current Anthropology*, vol. 9 (1968), p. 220; "M- and M-types in the eruption of first permanent teeth," *The Anthropologist*, special vol. (1968); "Biology of man in Africa," *Materiały i Prace Antropologiczne*, vol. 78 (1970), pp. 93-98; "Correlation of permanent dentition with stature and weight in Nubian children," *Scripta Medica*, vol. 45 (1972), pp. 149-153; "The seasonal rhythm of menarche and climate," *International Journal of Biomedicine*, supplement (1972), pp. 120-121.

SOURCES: K. Žlábek, "Život a dílo prof. Valšíka" ["Life and work of Professor Valšík"], *Acta Facultatis Rerum Naturalium Universitatis Comenianae-Anthropologie*, vol. 10 (1965), pp. 1-13; M. Pospíšil, M., "Profesor Valšík," *Acta Facultatis Rerum Naturalium Universitatis Comenianae-Anthropologie*, vol. 23 (1976), pp. 1-7; Z. Kroupova, "Publikačná činnost prof. Valšíka"

["Publications of Professor Valšík"], *Acta Facultatis Rerum Naturalium Universitatis Comenianae-Anthropologie*, vol. 23 (1976), pp. 9-19.

Z. Siegelová

Van Gennep, Arnold. See: *Gennep, Arnold van.*

Van Wing, Joseph.

Jesuit missionary, ethnographer. Born in Herk-de-Stad (Belgium) 1 April 1884, died in Drongen (Belgium) 30 July 1979. Van Wing was a self-taught ethnographer of the Eastern matrilineal Kongo, a local variation of the Kongo culture extending throughout Lower Zaïre, the south of the Republic of Congo, and northwestern Angola. He obtained his data from meeting with elders and (more often) from catechists and school teachers, interviewing within the community of those converted to the Catholic church. He was influenced by the French Sociological School and by the *Anthropos* and Vienna School. Van Wing's major focus was on the educational, initiatory, religious, socio-political and judicial institutions that form the individual's psychology, his duties and loyalty toward the matriclan. He offered unique information on the *kimpasi* collective cult for enhancing reproduction in society and nature (*De geheime sekte van 't Kimpasi*) and on puberty rituals ("Nzo longo"). With C. Penders, he edited the oldest Kongo lexicon of the Capuchin missionary Joris de Geel, who died in the Congo in 1652 (*Le plus ancien dictionnaire bantu*). Starting in 1952, he was a lecturer at the Africanist Institute, University of Leuven.

As a Catholic missionary of the pioneer type (1911-1945), holding many executive functions in the Jesuit Missions in Zaïre and, from 1945 onward, representing the Catholic Missions to Belgian governmental institutions, Van Wing basically had a missionary intent. Such is also the evaluation by Kongo scholars who criticize his opposition to indigenous belief systems and his negative stance toward fertility rituals and marriage practices (Ngimbi [et al.], 1983). He aimed to "free" the Kongo individual through evangelization and school education (from 1945 he forcefully defended the creation of a university in the Belgian Congo) as well as through encouraging wide-spread literacy, private enterprise, property-ownership (he was against the colonial appropriation of land), monogamous marriage and health care. Because he believed the Kongolese to be enmeshed in collectivity and their ancestral past ("Une évolution de la coutume Bakongo"), he aimed to "emancipate their capacity for free choice and justice," and hoped that what he called a genuine African humanism would develop. He believed that traditional Kongolese beliefs about child-rearing, seniority, corporate clan organization and conformism, as well as ancestral cults and omnipresent envy and sorcery and dependence on "fetishes," sustained their collectivism. Kimbanguist prophetic movements also curtailed the emancipation of the individual ("Le kibangisme").

In 1956, voicing in "Duidelijke taal" the expectations of major Kongolese leaders-to-be, whose confidence he enjoyed, he shocked many Belgian governors by warning them that "the complete emancipation of the Kongo is ineluctable and within a short delay." From 1960 onward, blindness slowed his intellectual productivity.

MAJOR WORKS: *De geheime sekte van 't Kimpasi* (Brussels: 1920) [also an abridged translation in 1938 and 1959]; "Nzo longo, ou les rites de puberté chez les Bakongo," *Congo*, année 1, tome 2 (1920), pp. 229-246; année 2, tome 2 (1921), pp. 48-59, 365-389; *Études Bakongo: histoire et sociologie* (Brussels: 1921); *Études Bakongo II, religion et magie* (Brussels: 1938; revised ed. [*Études Bakongo: sociologie, religion et magie*], Brugge: 1959); "Une évolution de la coutume Bakongo," *Congo*, année 7, tome 2 (1926), pp. 353-359; (with C. Penders) *Le plus ancien dictionnaire bantu = Het oudste bantu woordenboek Vocabularium P. Georgii Gelensis O.F.M. Cap* (Louvain: 1928); "Bakongo incantations and prayers," *Journal of the Royal Anthropological Institute of Great-Britain and Ireland*, vol. 60 (1930), pp. 401-423; "Bakongo magic," *Journal of the Royal Anthropological Institute of Great-Britain and Ireland*, vol. 71 (1941), pp. 85-97; "Duidelijke taal: inleiding op het manifest van 'Conscience africaine'," *Die Linie* (17 August and 14 September 1956), pp. 10-11 (also published as a booklet: *Kongo-documenten* or *Congo-documents* (both: Brussels: 1956)); "Le kibangisme vu par un témoin," *Zaïre*, vol. 12 (1958), pp. 563-618.

SOURCES: Ngimbi Nseka [et al.], *Actualité et inactualité des "Études Bakongo" du Père J. Van Wing* (Mayidi, Zaïre: 1983); J. van de Casteele, *Bibliographie Joseph Van Wing s.j., 1884-1970* (Heverlee, Belgium: 1987).

René Devisch

Vasil'ev, V.P. (Vasiliĭ Pavlovich).

Sinologist, historian, teacher. Born in Nizhniĭ Novgorod (Russia) 20 February 1818, died in St. Petersburg (Russia) 21 April 1900. Vasil'ev spent ten years operating a mission to China. He was a professor at Kazan' University (from 1851), then at St. Petersburg University (from 1855), and was an academician of the Petersburg Academy of Science (from 1886).

In his study of Chinese Confucian civilization, Vasil'ev was one of the first in Russian and world Sinology to discuss critically the meaning not only of Confucian morality, virtues and humanism, but also of the conservative-dogmatic principles of the social-family structure and the administrative-political system of China. He believed China to be backward and saw Confucianism as the cause. He was a supporter of the theory of the autochthonous evolution of the Chinese people. Vasil'ev contributed greatly to the study of Chinese religion and literature. He left behind a great wealth of unpublished scholarly writing, vastly exceeding his publications in scale.

MAJOR WORKS: "Opisanie Man'chzhurii," *Zapiski Geograficheskogo Obshchestva*, vol. 12 (1857), pp. 1-109; *Buddizm, ego dogmaty, istoriĭa i literatura* (St. Petersburg: 1857-1869); *Svedeniĭa o man'chzhurakh vo vremĭa dinastiĭ Ĭuan' i Min* (St. Petersburg: 1863); *Analiz kitaĭskikh ieroglifov* [2 [arts] (St. Petersburg: 1866-1898); *O dvizhenii magometanstva v Kitae* (St. Petersburg: 1867); *Religii Vostoka: konfuĭsianstvo, buddizm, daosizm* (St. Petersburg: 1873); *Ocherk istorii kitaĭskoĭ literatury* (St. Petersburg: 1880); *Geografiĭa Tibeta* (St. Petersburg: 1895); *Otkrytie Kitaĭa* (St. Petersburg: (1900).

SOURCES: L.S. Vasil'ev (editor), *Istoriĭa i kul'tura Kitaĭa: sbornik pamĭati akademika V.P. Vasil'eva* (Moscow: 1974); P.E. Skachkov, *Ocherki po istorii russkogo kitaevedeniĭa* (Moscow: (1977), pp. 204-214, 216-232.

A.M. Reshetov
[Translation from Russian: Alexander Kemel]

Vasilevich, G.M. (Glafira Makar'evna).

Ethnographer, folklorist, linguist. Born in St. Petersburg (Russia) 15 March 1895, died in Leningrad (Russian S.F.S.R.) 21 April 1971. Vasilevich was a doctor of historical sciences, taught Tungus-Manchurian ethnography and language in the *vuzy* (higher educational institutions) of Leningrad, and worked in the Siberia section of the Institut ètnografii (Institute of Ethnography) of the Soviet Academy of Sciences.

Vasilevich did fundamental research on the ethnography of the Tungus (Évenki): she studied problems of their ethnography, economy, social structure, ancestral composition, material and non-material culture, folklore and shamanism. She was deeply interested in the general problems of Tungus-Manchurian and Altai ethnography. She wrote textbooks and taught literature in the Évenki language. She also trained Évenki scholars. Vasilevich was the author of approximately 200 works.

MAJOR WORKS: *Sbornik materialov po étnograficheskomu (tungusskomu) fol'kloru*, no. 1 (Leningrad: 1936); "Drevneĭshie étnonimy Azii i nazvaniĭa évenkiĭskikh rodov," *Sovetskaĭa étnografiĭa*, no. 4 (1946), pp. 34-49; (with M.G. Levin), "Tipy olenevodstva i ikh proiskhozhdenie," *Sovetskaĭa étnografiĭa*, no. 1 (1951), pp. 63-87; *Évenkiĭsko-russkiĭ slovar'* (Moscow: 1958); "K voprosu o klassifikaĭsii tunguso-manchzhurskikh ĭazykov," *Voprosy ĭazykoznaniĭa*, no. 2 (1960), pp. 43-49; "Évenki," *Narody Sibiri* (Moscow: 1956), pp. 701-741; "Tungusskaĭa kolybel' (v svĭazi s problemoĭ étnogeneza tunguso-manchzhurov)," *Sbornik Muzeĭa antropologiii i étnografii* vol. 19 (Moscow and Leningrad: 1960), pp. 15-28; (with M.G. Levin), "Olennyĭ transport" in: M.G. Levin and L.P. Potapov (editors), *Istoriko-étnograficheskiĭ atlas Sibiri* (Moscow and Leningrad: 1961), pp. 11-54; *Istoricheskiĭ fol'klor évenkov: skazaniĭa i predaniĭa* (Moscow and Leningrad: 1966); *Évenki: istoriko-étnograficheskie ocherki (XVIII–nachalo XX v.)* (Leningrad: 1969).

SOURCES: N.N. Stepanov, "G.M. Vasilevich," *Izvestiĭa Vsesoĭuznogo Geograficheskogo obshchestva*, vol. 87, no. 4 (1965), pp. 380-381; Ch.M. Taksami, "G.M. Vasilevich (nekrolog)," *Sovetskaĭa étnografiĭa*, no. 5 (1971), pp. 184-187.

A.M. Reshetov
[Translation from Russian: Thomas L. Mann]

Veblen, Thorstein. Economist, philosopher, social theorist, social critic. Born in rural Cato Township (Wisconsin) 30 July 1857, died in Stanford (California) 3 August 1929. Veblen received his Ph.D. from Yale University before further formal graduate training in economics at Cornell University. He taught, in turn, at the Universities of Chicago, Stanford, Missouri and, finally, at the New School for Social Research. In most instances, he either voluntarily left these institutions under of cloud of opprobrium or was dismissed for what has been referred to as his unacceptable "domestic economy," which included a series of adulterous affairs and a divorce from his first wife. His earliest publications were technical essays in philosophy and economics.

His first book, *The Theory of the Leisure Class*, appeared in 1899. This readable volume, introducing the memorable phrase, "conspicuous consumption," established his popular reputation as an acerbic critic of American manners and morals. Although remembered primarily for this tone, the discussion included serious considerations of the emergence of private property, reciprocity, rank and privilege, gender relations, the evolution of political systems, culture change and the symbolism of goods. Many of these original concerns are still maintained in the anthropological commentary on the meaning of social reciprocity and symbolic analysis with particular reference to the classic examples of the Trobriand *kula* and the Northwest coast *potlatch* system. In these instances his insights, though often diluted, remain the framework for the interpretation of the seemingly bizarre display and exchange of material culture. Many of his subsequent publications, 10 other books and more than 150 articles, reviews and essays, continued his comparative interest in the production and consumption patterns of complex societies. In addition to the United States, his purview included the then emerging economic and political significance of

Imperial Germany and Japan. These works clearly identify Veblen as the original cultural analyst of modern industrial societies and demonstrated his knowledge of history and politics wedded to a sophisticated grasp of classical economic and social theory. However, Veblen's often decidedly subjective tone, usually positive in the consideration of simple societies and negative in relation to complex ones, has led to an overall relative neglect by contemporary social anthropology, which strives for a less value-laden interpretation of cultural systems. His influence remains more pronounced in modern sociology, which occasionally lends itself to explicit subjective commentary on the nature of Western society.

It is not easy to summarize the life and work of this eccentric and iconoclastic genius who, in his own time and after, inspired so much in the way of emotional reactions from colleagues. Yet, his often profound influence continues to be felt in contemporary social science. As Coser suggests, he makes us think about our ourselves and society more than any other social theorist.

MAJOR WORKS: *The Theory of the Leisure Class* (New York: 1899; new ed., New York: 1918); *The Theory of Business Enterprise* (New York: 1904); *The Instinct of Workmanship and the State of Industrial Arts* (New York: 1914); *Imperial Germany and the Industrial Revolution* (New York: 1915); *The Place of Sciences in Modern Civilization* (New York: 1919); *The Vested Interests and the State of the Industrial Arts* (New York: 1919); *The Engineers and the Price System* (New York: 1921); *Absentee Ownership and Business Enterprise in Recent Times* (New York: 1923).

SOURCES: Lewis Coser, *Masters of Sociological Thought* (New York: 1971); R.L. Duffus, *Innocents at Cedro: a Memoir of Thorstein Veblen and Others* (New York: 1944); John Diggins, *The Bard of Savagery: Thorstein Veblen and Modern Social Theory* (New York: 1978); Joseph Dorfman, *Thorstein Veblen and His America* (New York: 1934); Arthur K. Davis, "Veblen, Thorstein" in: David L. Sills (editor), *International Encyclopedia of the Social Sciences* (New York: 1968-1979), vol. 16, pp. 303-308; Max Lerner, *The Portable Veblen* (New York: 1957); David Reisman, *Thorstein Veblen* (New York: 1953).

W. Arens

Vegezzi Ruscalla, Giovenale. Philologist, linguist, ethnographer. Born in Turin (Italy) 1799, died in Turin (Italy) 1884. Vegezzi Ruscalla belonged to that early 19th-century Northern Italian cultural milieu that, caught between Enlightenment and Romanticism but already anticipating positivism, approached linguistic studies with philological rigor despite an overriding interest in the question of national unification. Other names tied to this intellectual atmosphere are Carlo Cattaneo (1801-1869), Graziadio Isaia Ascoli (1829-1907), Bernardino Biondelli (1804-1886), BARTOLOMEO MALFATTI and COSTANTINO NIGRA.

Between 1830 and 1850 Vegezzi Ruscalla had undertaken the collection of Italian dialects, enlarging the scope of his research in succeeding years to the Romance languages in general. Mostly self-taught, he nevertheless held the chair in Romanian at the University of Turin.

He arrived at ethnology through his studies on ethno-linguistic minorities (the Basques, the Romansch-speakers and the Serbo-Dalmatians of Molise). These studies led him to propose a link between nation and language and to consider linguistic uniformity as a fundamental element of nationality (*Che cos'è nazione*). The connection to the process of Italian political unification is obvious.

But above all Vegezzi Ruscalla was the first Italian scholar to use and to define the terms "ethnography" (*etnografia*) and "ethnology" (*etnologia*), to specify precisely their research scope and to urge their academic institutionalization. For Vegezza Ruscalla ethnology was the "science of nations"; it studied and compared ethnic aggregations of a physical and moral character ("ethnic societies," to use his vocabulary) with the goal of reconstructing their origins and researching their character and history. Ethnology for Vegezzi Ruscalla was therefore as different from ethnography, which was only a description of peoples, as it was from "anthropology" (*antropologia*, i.e., physical anthropology), which occupied itself with the physical characteristics of single individuals and belonged therefore to the natural sciences. Ethnography and ethnology on the other hand fell—like linguistics and history—among the "moral sciences" ("Della convenienza di un corso di etnologia," pp. 83 and 85; *Le colonie Serbo-dalmate*, p. 5). In addition, Vegezzi Ruscalla stressed to those in power the importance of basing laws on ethnological knowledge in order to put them in harmony with diverse populations ("Etnocrazia e autonomia," pp. 12 and 14). Finally, with great lucidity, he warned scholars of all types against prejudice in dealing with other peoples, assigning as a fundamental quality to the new discipline the role of dispassionate and objective observation of the values and faults of various human groups. All of these positions (from the connection between language and culture to the applied use of social sciences) appeared again and again in Italian ethnology in the second half of the 19th century, without, however, succeeding in overcoming the dominant biological focus in studies on man in the positivist age.

MAJOR WORKS: "Del clima e del carattere delle nazioni," *Il Cimento*, vol. 2 (1853), pp. 654-670; *Che cos'è nazione* (Turin: 1854); "I Romanci: cenno etnografico," *Rivista Contemporanea*, vol. 13, anno 6 (1858), pp. 46-58; "Della convenienza di un corso di etnologia," *Rivista Contemporanea*, vol. 14, anno 7 (1859), pp. 81-88; *Le colonie Serbo-dalmate del Circondario di Larino, Provincia di Molise: studio etnografico* (Turin: 1864); "Etnocrazia e autonomia," *Nuove Effemeridi Siciliane* (May-June 1869), pp. 3-16.

SOURCES: B. Biondelli, *Saggio sui dialetti Gallo-italici* (Milan: 1853); Teodoro Onciulescu, "Contributo alla storia della filologia romanza in Italia: G. Vegezzi Ruscalla," *Rendiconti della R. Accademia di Archeologia, lettere ed Arti di Napoli*, 18 (1937), pp. 233-265; Sebastiano Timpanaro, *Classicismo e Illuminismo nell'Ottocento italiano* (Pisa: 1865); Tullio De Mauro, *Storia linguistica dell'Italia unita* (Bari: 1963; 2nd, revised ed., Bari: 1970); Alberto Mario Cirese, *Mondo culto e mondo popolare dall '400 all'800* (edited by Sandra Puccini) (Rome: 1981-1982); Sandra Puccini, "La natura e l'indole dei popoli: B. Malfatti e il primo manuale italiano di etnografia (1870)," *Giornale critico della Filosofia italiana*, vol. 67, fasc. 1 (January-April 1988), pp. 81-104.

Sandra Puccini
[Translation from Italian: CW]

Velten, Carl. Linguist, colonial official. Born in Fluterschen, Rhine Province (Germany) 4 September 1862, died after 1935. After completing the study of modern languages at the Universities of Bonn and Würzburg (and obtaining a doctorate of philosophy at the latter), Velten prepared himself for colonial service from 1891 to 1893 at the Seminar for Oriental Languages in Berlin. From 1893 to 1896 he served as an interpreter for the imperial governor of German East Africa (now Tanzania). Between 1896 and 1921 he held the chair in Swahili at the Seminar for Oriental Languages. Between 1898 and 1919

Velten served as co-editor of the *Mitteilungen des Orientalischen Seminars, Abteilung III, Afrikanische Studien.*

Velten above all contributed much to the knowledge of the customs, laws and history (as well as the poetry and oral traditions) of the Swahili-speaking peoples through numerous textual collections, often with translations. In addition, he published grammars, manuals and dictionaries for Swahili as well as grammatical sketches on the Hehe, Kani and Nyamwezi languages.

MAJOR WORKS: "Die Sprache der Wahehe," *Mitteilungen des Seminars für Orientalische Sprachen,* vol. 2 (1899), pp. 65-241; "Kikami, die Sprache der Wakami in Deutsch-Ostafrika," *Mitteilungen des Seminars für Orientalische Sprachen,* vol. 3 (1900), pp. 1-56; *Grammatik des Kinyamuesi* (Göttingen: 1901); *Desturi za Wasuaheli* (Göttingen: 1903); *Praktische Suaheli-Grammatik nebst einem Deutsch-Suaheli-Wörterverzeichnis* (Leipzig: 1904); *Prosa und Poesie der Suaheli* (Berlin: 1907); *Suaheli-Wörterbuch, Suaheli-Deutsch* (Berlin: 1910); *Suaheli-Wörterbuch, Deutsch-Suaheli* (Magliaso: 1933).

SOURCE: Ernst Dammann, "Velten, Carl" in: H. Jungraithmayr and W.J.G. Möhlig (editors), *Lexikon der Afrikanistik* (Berlin: 1983), p. 257.

G. Miehe and K. Winkelmann
[Translation from German: Robert B. Marks Ridinger]

Veniaminov (Popov), I.E. (Ivan Evseevich) (religious name: Innokentiĭ). Scholar, ethnographer, linguist, church official, missionary. Born in Anginsk, Irkutsk district (Russia) 26 August 1797, died in Moscow (Russia) 31 March 1879. Veniaminov was an honored member of Moscow University and the ethnographic department of the Obshchestvo lĭubitelĭ estestvoznaniĭa, antropologii i ėtnografii (Society of Friends of Science, Anthropology and Ethnography). Known to scholarship as Innokentiĭ, he became Metropolitan of Moscow and Kolomna at the end of his life and was canonized by the Russian Orthodox Church on 6 October 1977. The author of the first monographic description of the native North American population, he was a prominent official of Russian America.

MAJOR WORKS: *Zapiski ob ostrovakh Unalashkinskogo otdela* [3 vols.] (St. Petersburg: 1840); *Zamechaniĭa o koloshenskom i kad'ĭanskom ĭazykakh i otchasti o prochikh rossiĭsko-amerikan-skikh, s prisovokupleniem rossiĭsko-koloshenskogo slovarĭa, soderzhashchego bolee 1000 slov, iz koikh na nekotorye sdelany poĭasneniĭa* (St. Petersburg: 1846); *Pis'ma Innokentiĭa, mitropolita moskovskogo i kolomenskogo, 1828-1878,* vol. 1 (St. Petersburg: 1897).

SOURCES: M.V. Stepanova, "I. Veniaminov kak ėtnograf," *Trudy Instituta ėtnografii AN SSSR,* vol. 2 (1947), pp. 294-314; A.A. Arsen'ev, "Ėtnograficheskoe nasledie I.E. Veniaminova," *Sovetskaĭa ėtnografiĭa,* no. 5 (1979), pp. 76-89.

A.M. Reshetov
[Translation from Russian: Thomas L. Mann]

Veth, Pieter Johannes. Ethnologist. Born in Dordrecht (Netherlands) 2 December 1814, died in Arnhem (Netherlands) 14 April 1895. Veth studied theology and Asian, classical and modern languages at the Leiden University. He taught Malayan at the Royal Military Academy and Hebrew and Arabic at the Universities of Franeker and Amsterdam. In 1864 he became a member of the Royal Academy of Sciences and professor of Indonesian languages, geography and ethnology at the National Institute for the Education of Colonial Civil Servants in Leiden. In 1873 he was among the founders of the Royal Netherlands Geographical Society. As its chairman he was instrumental in the organization of several multi-disciplinary scientific expeditions to Sumatra, Timor and Angola. In 1877 he received an appointment at Leiden University, becoming the first professor of (Indonesian) ethnology in the Netherlands.

Veth published multi-volume monographs on the geography, history and cultures of Borneo and Java. His Indonesian specialization was further exemplified by his publications on Islam, native political systems, *adat* law and archaeology. Africa became his second geographical field of specialization. Veth published a bibliography and articles on African history and languages. In addition he wrote about colonial native policies, the history of religion, ethnographic collections and modern European literature.

Veth was a typical mid-19th-century encyclopedic scholar, an armchair ethnologist who never visited the regions he wrote about. Instead he compiled comprehensive surveys on Indonesian islands and their native inhabitants. He combined his Protestant religious conviction with humanitarian ideals, which resulted in his strong opposition to slavery and to the exploitation of native peoples in overseas colonies. He therefore advocated the improvement of the education of colonial civil servants and a just treatment of native peoples.

MAJOR WORKS: *Borneo's Wester-afdeeling* [2 vols.] (Zaltbommel: 1854-1856); *Java: geografisch, ethnologisch, historisch* [3 vols.] (Haarlem: 1873-1884); *Treasury of Languages or Rudimentary Dictionary of Universal Philology* (London: 1873); (with M.C. Kan) *Bibliographie van Neederlandsche boeken over Afrika* (Utrecht: 1876); *Ontdekkers en onderzoekers* (Leiden: 1884); (with J.F. Snelleman) *Daniel Veth's reizen in Angola* (Haarlem: 1887).

SOURCE: "Pieter Johannes Veth" in: *Jaarboek van de Koninklijke Akademie van Wetenschappen* (1896), pp. 1-42.

Pieter Hovens

Vidossi, Giuseppe. Philologist, dialectologist. Born in Capodistria (Austria-Hungary, now Yugoslavia) 1878, died in Turin (Italy) 1969. Vidossi attended the University of Vienna majoring in Romance philology and completed his studies at the University of Florence. In 1939 he became a member of the board of directors of the review *Archivio Glottologico Italiano* and in 1941 he accepted the chair of Romance philology at the University of Turin.

His works, among which are many short papers, are collected in one volume (*Saggi e scritti minori di folklore*).

Vidossi's research moved in three directions. First were the methodological and historical writings and those concerned with the problems of applied philology in the study of dialects and oral culture. In these Vidossi placed himself as an intermediary between Italian and German scholarship ("Zur Geschichte der italienischen Volkskunde"). He introduced in Italy the morphological-structural perspective of V.ĨA. PROPP ("Nuovi orientamenti nello studio delle tradizioni popolari"). He also wrote a historical study of the relationship between Italian folk culture and high literature ("Poesia popolare e poesia d'arte").

Vidossi's linguistic and dialectological studies led him in a second direction: the path of linguistic geography that had already been sketched out by Matteo Bartoli (1873-

1946). This consisted of mapping out areas of dialect diffusion, making assumptions analogous to those adopted by the Cultural-Historical School of Vienna that Vidossi extended to folklore data (*Lineamenti di linguistica spaziale*, "Geografia linguistica e demologica"). Along these lines he contributed some of his fundamental studies for the preparation of the *Atlante linguistico italiano* and for a similar work in demology.

Vidossi's third direction involved works dealing with specific linguistic and demological phenomena of which Vidossi was able to trace either the origin or the inspiration by way of a comparative, historical and geographical analysis ("Echi romani del Natale cristiano").

MAJOR WORKS: "Poesia popolare e poesia d'arte," *Folklore italiano*, vol. 6 (1931), pp. 106-133; "Le norme areali ed il folklore" [originally 1933] in: G. Vidossi, *Saggi e scritti minori di folklore* (Turin: 1960), pp. 148-154; "L'atlante demologico tedesco," *Bollettino dell'atlante linguistico italiano*, vol. 1, no. 2 (1934), pp. 77-94; "Nuovi orientamenti nello studio delle tradizioni popolari" in: *Atti del III Congresso di Arti e Tradizioni popolari, Trento, settembre 1934* (Rome: 1936), pp. 194ff.; "Echi romani nel Natale cristiano," *Minerva*, vol. 47 (1937), pp. 737-739; "Zur Geschichte der italienischen Volkskunde," *Zeitschrift für Volkskunde*, vol. 48 (1939), pp. 7-17; "Geografia linguistica e demologica," *Rivista Geografica Italiana*, vol. 48 (1941), pp. 272-282; *Lineamenti di linguistica spaziale* (Milan: 1943); *Saggi e scritti minori di folklore* (Turin: 1960).

SOURCES: P. Toschi, "Introduzione" to: G. Vidossi, *Saggi e scritti minore di folklore* (Turin: 1960), pp. ix-xiv; A.M. Cirese, *Cultura egemonica e culture subalterne* (Palermo: 1980); G. Cocchiara, *Storia del folklore in Europa* (Turin: 1952).

Gianni Vanucci
[Translation from Italian: Gianna Panofsky]

Villa Rojas, Alfonso. Ethnographer, anthropologist. Born in Mérida (Mexico) 31 January 1906. Villa Rojas is widely recognized for his contribution to the ethnography of tropical Mexico, particularly of the Maya of Quintana Roo. He began his career as an anthropologist while a teacher in rural Chan Kom, where he was associated with ROBERT REDFIELD in the study of Chan Kom in 1930 and in the exploration of the Yaxuná-Cobá Causeway. Both publications (by the Carnegie Institution of Washington, D.C.) gave him early international fame. As an anthropology student at the University of Chicago during 1933-1935, he knew A.R. RADCLIFFE-BROWN and BRONISLAW MALINOWSKI, both of whom strongly influenced his professional work. He returned to Yucatán to study the hamlet of Tusik (which belonged to the chiefdom of X-Cacal) in light of Redfield's model of the "folk-urban continuum" in Yucatán. His ethnography of this semi-autonomous community, heir to a rebel tradition from the Caste Wars, is a classic text of contemporary anthropology.

Villa Rojas held many public offices where he was responsible for applying anthropological knowledge to the improvement of the social conditions of the Indians. He directed a program of ethnographic studies of the Indians affected by the construction of a hydroelectric dam on the Papaloapan River (1949-1952). He assumed the directorship of the Centro Coordinador Indigenista Tzetltal-Tzotzil (Tzetltal-Tzotzil Indian Coordinating Center) in San Cristóbal de las Casas (1955). He was director of anthropological research at the Interamerican Indian Institute (1967-1970) and sub-director of the Instituto Indigenista Nacional (National Indianist Institute) (1970-1976).

At present he is a researcher at the Universidad Nacional Autónoma de México (Autonomous National University of Mexico).

MAJOR WORKS: (with Robert Redfield) *Chan Kom: a Maya Village* (Washington: 1932) (= *Carnegie Institution of Washington, Publication*, no. 448); *Yaxuná-Cobá Causeway* (Washington: 1934) (= *Carnegie Institution of Washington, Publication*, no. 436); (with Robert Redfield) *Notes on the Ethnography of Tzeltal Communities of Chiapas* (Washington: 1939) (= *Carnegie Institution of Washington, Publication*, no. 509); "Kinship and Nagualism in a Tzeltal community, Southeastern Mexico," *American Anthropologist*, vol. 49 (1947), pp. 578-587; *The Maya of East Central Quintana Roo* (Washington: 1945) [tr.: *Los elegidos de Dios* (Mexico City: 1978)]; *Los mazatecos y el problema indígena de la cuenca del Papaloapan* (Mexico City: 1955); "The Maya of Yucatán," "Maya lowlands: the Chontal, Chol and Kekchi," and "The Tzeltal" in: Robert Wauchope (general editor), *Handbook of Middle American Indians*, vol. 7 (Austin: 1969), pp. 230-243 and 195-225; "En torno a la nueva tendencia ideológica de antropólogos e indigenistas," *América Indígena*, vol. 29 (1969), pp. 787-804; "Fieldwork in the Mayan region of Mexico" in: George M. Foster [et al.] (editors), *Long-Term Field Research in Social Anthropology* (New York: 1979), pp. 45-64.

SOURCES: Paul Sullivan, *Unfinished Conversations* (New York: 1989); Heber Morales Mendoza, "Alfonso Villa Rojas" in: Carlos García Mora (general coordinator), *La antropología en México* (Mexico City: 1987-1988), vol. 11, pp. 487-500.

Roberto Melville
[Translation from Spanish: Margo L. Smith]

Violant i Simorra, Ramón. Folklorist, ethnographer, museologist. Born in Sarroca de Bellera, Catalonia (Spain) 1903, died in Barcelona (Spain) 1956. Violant i Simorra worked as a tailor, first in his home town and later in Barcelona, until 1940 when he was named conservator of the Ethnography Section of the Museo de Industrias y Artes Populares (Museum of Crafts and Popular Arts) in Barcelona. He also collaborated with the Centro de Etnología Peninsular del Consejo Superior de Investigaciones Científicas (Center of Peninsular Ethnography, Superior Council of Scientific Research).

His interest in ethnography arose in 1921 when he moved to Barcelona and came into contact with the important Catalonian folklore movement and with tourist societies. Self-taught, he experienced different influences, among which two should be cited. With Fritz Krüger (*Die Hochpyrenäen*), founder of the *Wörter und Sachen* ethnolinguistics school in Hamburg, he maintained a close friendship; Krüger played a fundamental role in arousing his interest in material culture. The influence of JAMES G. FRAZER, through his major work, *The Golden Bough*, is especially noticeable on those of Violant i Simorra's works that are most folkloric in orientation, such as *El llibre de Nadal*. Violant i Simorra, finding himself tightly bound to the folkloristic movement, can be considered the first Catalonian ethnographer, thanks to his careful monographs about different aspects of material culture, especially in the Pyrenees. In works such as *El Pirineo español*, he attempted ethnological syntheses.

Violant i Simorra's museum work is distinguished by its didactic approach and by the modernity of his results, aspects especially manifest in the exhibit known as the *Casa pallaresa*, which shows domestic life and the work cycle of a herding family in the Catalan Pyrenees.

Violant i Simorra's career passed through three principal stages. The first developed during the 1930s when Violant i Simorra wrote a series of monographs, published in the form of articles, about his native Pyrenees region, Pallars (these were republished copied posthumously in his *Obra oberta*). The second, which occurred during the 1940s, reflected principally Violant i Simorra's museum period and culminated in the publication of *El Pirineo español* in 1949. During the third stage, ended by his premature death, Violant i Simorra showed a greater interest in comparative studies of symbolic aspects of culture. At this time he presented a new attempt at ethnological synthesis in *Etnografia de Reus i la seva comarca*.

MAJOR WORKS: *El llibre de Nadal: costums, creences, significats i orígens* (Barcelona: 1948); *Art popular decoratiu a Catalunya* (Barcelona: 1948); *El Pirineo español: vida, usos, costumbres, creencias y tradiciones de una cultura milenaria que desaparece* (Madrid: 1949); *Etnografia de Reus i la seva comarca: el Camp, la Conca de Barberà, el Priorat* (Reus: 1955-1959); *Obra oberta* [4 vols.] (Barcelona: 1949-1982) [collection of articles].

SOURCES: Ramona Violant, "Ramon Violant i Simorra: esbós biogràfic" in: *Etnologia pallaresa: homenatge a Ramon Violant i Simorra* (La Pobla de Segur: 1981), pp. 17-19; Llorenç Prats, "La transición del folklore a la etnografía en Cataluña: la obra de Ramón Violant i Simorra," *Ethnica*, vol. 16 (1980), pp. 105-120; Llorenç Prats, Dolors Llopart, Joan Prat, *La cultura popular a Catalunya: estudiosos i institucions, 1853-1981* (Barcelona: 1982); Dolors Llopart, "La Casa pallaresa i les sales annexes de l'antic Museu d'Indústries i Arts Populars del Poble Espanyol de Montjuïc (Barcelona): l'obra museogràfica de Ramon Violant i Simorra" in: *I Jornades sobre el Patrimoni Etnològic a les Terres de Ponent i l'Alt Pirineu* (in press).

Llorenç Prats
[Translation from Spanish: Margo L. Smith]

Vladimirtsov, B.IA. (Boris IAkovlevich). Orientalist, Mongolian specialist, ethnographer, folklorist, linguist, historian. Born in Kamenets-Podol'skiĭ (Ukraine) 20 July 1884, died in Leningrad (Russian S.F.S.R.) 17 August 1931. Vladimirtsov was an academician of the Soviet Academy of Sciences (1929), a professor at Leningrad University and the director of the ethnologic-linguistic group of the Mongolian Commission. During the course of an expedition to Mongolia, he gathered unique linguistic, folkloristic and ethnographic material. Later, he proposed an ethnographic classification of the Mongolian peoples. Vladimirtsov's research encompassed the epoch of the social development of the Mongols and the inception of Mongol nomadic feudalism. He also studied theater and religion in nomadic societies.

MAJOR WORKS: "Otchet o komandirovke k dérbétam Kobdinskogo okruga letom 1908," *Izvestiia Russkogo komiteta dlia izucheniia Sredneĭ i Vostochnoĭ Azii*, no. 9 (St. Petersburg: 1909), pp. 47-60; "Turetskiĭ narodets khotony," *Zapiski Vostochnogo otdeleniia Russkogo arkheologicheskogo obshchestva*, vol. 23 (1916), pp. 265-290; *Buddizm v Tibete i Mongolii* (Petrograd: 1919); *Chingis-Khan* (Berlin, Petrograd and Moscow: 1922); "Tibetskie teatral'nye predstavleniia," *Vostok*, vol. 3 (1923), pp. 97-107; *Mongolo-oĭratskiĭ geroicheskiĭ èpos: perevod, vstupitel'naia stat'ia i primechaniia* (Petrograd and Moscow: 1923); "O dvukh smeshannykh iazykakh Zapadnoĭ Mongolii," *IAfeticheskiĭ sbornik*, no. 2 (1923), pp. 32-52; *Obraztsy mongol'skoĭ narodnoĭ slovesnosti (Severo-Zapadnaia Mongoliia)* (Leningrad: 1926); "Ètnologo-lingvisticheskie issledovaniia v Ugre, Urginskom i Kenteĭskom paĭonakh," *Severnaia Mongoliia*, vol. 2 (1927), pp. 1-42; *Sravnitel'naia grammatika mongol'skogo pis'mennogo iazyka i khalkhaskogo narechiia: vvedenie i fonetika* (Leningrad: 1929); *Obshchestvennyĭ stroĭ mongolov: mongol'skiĭ kochevoĭ feodalizm* (Leningrad: 1934).

SOURCES: N.P. Shastina, "B.IA. Vladimirtsov (1884-1931)" in: G.D. Sanzheev (editor-in-chief), *Filologiia i istoriia mongol'skikh narodov, pamiati akademika B.IA. Vladimirtsova* (Moscow: 1958), pp. 3-11; A.M. Reshetov, "Akademik B.IA. Vladimirtsov kak ètnograf" in: V.M. Solntsev (editor), *Vsesoíūznaíã nauchnaíã konferenísíīã, posvíãshchennaíã 100-letíīū so dníã rozhdeníã akademika B.ÍĀ Vladimirísova* (Moscow: 1984), pp. 6-8.

A.M. Reshetov
[*Translation from Russian: Thomas L. Mann*]

Voegelin, C.F. (Charles Frederick). Anthropologist, linguist, editor. Born in New York (New York) 14 January 1906, died in Honolulu (Hawaii) 22 May 1986. Voegelin is best known for his role in the development of structural linguistics in the United States from the 1930s onward and for his work on American Indian languages. Although his B.A. (Stanford University) was in psychology, his Ph.D. (University of California, Berkeley) was in anthropology, with a primary interest in language. He spent most of his career teaching and developing a program in anthropology at Indiana University (1941-1976).

Voegelin's initial training in anthropology was at the University of California, Berkeley, under ALFRED L. KROEBER. Berkeley offered no formal training in linguistics or language study at that time; the tradition was to send the student into the field to work things out for himself. Voegelin did have the advantage of summer field schools in Santa Fe, New Mexico, and on the Umatilla Indian Reservation in Oregon. He did the fieldwork for his dissertation on Tübatulabal in eastern California. He subsequently worked with EDWARD SAPIR at Yale and at summer linguistic institutes during the 1930s and was one of the small group of scholars instrumental in working out the structuralist theories of language that were developed by Sapir and by LEONARD BLOOMFIELD.

Throughout his career Voegelin was interested in language structure, particularly that of the languages of the aboriginal Americans. He studied more than a dozen of these languages and is best known for his work on those of the Tübatulabal, Hopi, Delaware and Shawnee. In the mid-1950s he organized a field school at Flagstaff, Arizona, for his students from Indiana University and, over the years, arranged for them to work on virtually every language spoken in Arizona and New Mexico. This increased his own familiarity with the Indians' languages. Besides his work in structuralist theory, he was keenly interested in semantics (hence his *Hopi Domains*), comparative linguistics and especially language typology. He always based theoretical ideas on data, particularly from the languages he knew well, insisting that theory without a variety of supporting data was of limited value.

One of Voegelin's major accomplishments, and the one of which he was probably most proud, was his revival in 1944 of the *International Journal of American Linguistics* after the death in 1942 of its previous editor FRANZ BOAS. He improved its quality and added low-cost supplements over the years, enhancing its status as one of the major linguistic journals in the world. To help ensure the preservation of materials on American Indian languages, he founded the Archives of Languages of the World at Indiana University in 1953. In the 1960s he organized the Conference on American Indian Languages, with annual meetings, to enable the community of scholars interested in these languages to exchange ideas and make their data available to others.

MAJOR WORKS: *Tübatulabal Grammar* (Berkeley: 1935) (= *University of California Publications in American Archaeology and Ethnology*, vol. 34, pp. 55-190); *Tübatulabal Texts* (Berkeley: 1935) (= *University of California Publications in American Archaeology and Ethnology*, vol. 34, pp. 191-246); (with Morris Swadesh) "A problem in phonological alternation," *Language*, vol. 15 (1939), pp. 1-10; (with Z.S. Harris) "Linguistics in ethnology," *Southwest Journal of Anthropology*, vol. 1 (1945), pp. 455-465; "Delaware, an Eastern Algonquian language" in: Cornelius Osgood (editor), *Linguistic Structures of Native America* (New York: 1946) (= *Viking Fund Publications in Anthropology*, no. 6), pp. 130-157; (with Florence M. Voegelin) *Hopi Domains: a Lexical Approach to the Problem of Selection* (Bloomington: 1957) (= *Indiana University Publications in Anthropology and Linguistics*, memoir 14; (with F.M. Voegelin and Kenneth L. Hale) *Typological and Comparative Grammar of Uto-Aztecan: 1 (Phonology)* (Bloomington: 1962) (= *Indiana University Publications in Anthropology and Linguistics*, memoir 17); (with F.M. Voegelin) *Classification and Index of the World's Languages* (New York: 1977).

SOURCES: M. Dale Kinkade, "Charles Frederick Voegelin (1906-1986)," *American Anthropologist*, vol. 91 (1989), pp. 727-729; Robert A. Black (compiler), "C.F. Voegelin: bibliography" in: M. Dale Kinkade, Kenneth L. Hale and Oswald Werner (editors), *Linguistics and Anthropology: in Honor of C.F. Voegelin* (Lisse: 1975), pp. 11-26.

M. Dale Kinkade

Voegelin, Erminie Wheeler. See: *Wheeler-Voegelin, Erminie.*

Volkov, F.K. *(Fedor Kondrat'evich).* Physical anthropologist, ethnographer, archaeologist, literary scholar. Born in Poltavskaiã guberniiã (Ukraine) 17 March 1847, died near Gomel' (Belorussian S.S.R.) on a journey to Kiev 29 June 1918. From 1879 to 1887 Volkov lived in Romania and in Switzerland; from 1887 to 1905 he worked in Paris. From 1905 to 1917 he was curator of the ethnography department of the Russkiĭ muzeĭ (Russian Museum) in St. Petersburg.

Besides his primary interest in the ethnography and physical anthropology of the Ukrainians, Volkov studied the wedding ceremonies of the Slavs, including the marriage customs of expatriate Ukrainians and also the various methods of burial as well as the economy and way of life of the peoples of the world. As a scholar he belonged to the evolutionary school. Possessing deep multifaceted understanding of the ethnography of the peoples of the world, he advocated the development of comparative ethnography. He often appeared in the press, acquainting the scholarly community with the achievements of ethnography.

MAJOR WORKS: "Rites et usages nuptiaux en Ukraine," *L'Anthropologie*, vol. 13-4 (1891-1892); "Paleoliticheskaiã stoiãnka v s. Mezine, Chernigovskoĭ gubernii" in: *Trudy chetyrnadtsatogo arkheologicheskogo s'ezda v Chernigove, 1909*, vol. 3 (Moscow: 1911), pp. 262-270; "Ėtnograficheskie osobennosti ukrainskogo naroda" and "Antropologicheskie osobennosti ukrainskogo naroda" in: F.K. Volkov and M.S. Grushevskiĭ [et al.] (editors), *Ukrainskiĭ narod v proshlom i nastoiãshchem*, vol. 2 (Petrograd: 1916), pp. 427-647; "Variations squelettiques du pied chez les primates et dans les races humaines," *Bulletins et Mémoires de la Société d'Anthropologie de Paris*, sér. 5, vol. 4 (1903), pp. 632-708; and vol. 5 (1904), pp. 1-50, 201-331 and 720-725.

SOURCES: D.F. Zolotarev, "F.K. Volkov," *Russkiĭ istoricheskiĭ zhurnal*, no. 5 (1918), pp. 353-365; D.N. Anuchin, "F.K. Volkov (1847-1918)," *Russkiĭ antropologicheskiĭ zhurnal*, vol. 12, no. 3-4 (1923), pp. 78-79; O.O. Franko, "Narodoznavchi pratsi F.K. Volkova," *Narodna tvorchist' ta étnografiiã*, no. 6 (1989), pp. 15-26; A.D. Franko and O.E. Franko, "Fedor Kondrat'evich Vovk (Volkov): biograficheskiĭ ocherk," *Sovetskaiã étnografiiã*, no. 1 (1990), pp. 86-95.

A.M. Reshetov
[Translation from Russian: Thomas L. Mann]

Vorob'ev, N.I. (Nikolaĭ Iosifovich). Ethnographer, geographer. Born in Khvalynsk, Saratovskiĭ Guberniĭa (Russia) December 1895, died in Kazan' (Russian S.F.S.R.) 29 September 1967. Vorob'ev held a doctorate in history and was a professor at Kazan' University as well as head of the Archaeology and Ethnography Section of the Institut îazyka, literatury i istorii (Institute of Language, Literature and History) at the Kazan' branch of the Soviet Academy of Sciences. He was also an honorary member of the Geograficheskoe obshchestvo (Geographic Society) of the Soviet Union.

Vorob'ev was the author of a great many studies of the people of Povolzh'e, primarily the Kazan' Tatars and the Chuvash. It was characteristic of his work to focus on the geographic environment and its influence on economic activities and the life style of the population. Vorob'ev gave particular attention to the analysis of the evolution of Tatar culture and Tatar ethnicity from ancient times to the present. He refuted the theory that the Kazan' Tatars originated from the Golden Horde and demonstrated the genetic tie between the Kazan' Tatars and the ancient agricultural and nomadic peoples of the steppe. He made important contributions to the development of a Tatar museum, founding the Ethnographic Section of the Gosudarstvennyĭ muzeĭ Tatarskoĭ ASSR (State Museum of the Tatar A.S.S.R.).

MAJOR WORKS: *Materialy po bytu russkogo starozhil'cheskogo naseleniîa Vostochnoĭ Sibiri: naselenie Prichun'skogo kraîa* (Kazan': 1926); *Material'naîa kul'tura kazanskikh tatar* (Kazan': 1930); "Proiskhozhdenie kazanskikh tatar po dannym ètnografii," *Sovetskaîa ètnografiîa*, no. 3 (1946), pp. 75-86; "Ètnogenez chuvashskogo naroda po dannym ètnografii," *Sovetskaîa ètnografiîa*, no. 3 (1950), pp. 66-78; "K voprosu ob ètnograficheskom izuchenii kolkhoznogo krest'îanstva," *Sovetskaîa ètnografiîa*, no. 1 (1952), pp. 142-146; *Kazanskie tatary* (Kazan': 1953); (with A.R. L'vovaîa, N.R. Romanov and A.R. Smirnov) *Chuvashi: ètnograficheskoe issledovanie*, part 1 (Cheboksary: 1956); (with E.P. Busygin and N.V. Zorin) *Ètnograficheskiĭ muzeĭ Kazanskogo universiteta* (Kazan': 1957); (with E.P Busygin) *Khudozhestvennye promysly Tatarii v proshlom i nastoîâshchem* (Kazan': 1957); "Povolzhskie tatary" in: V.A. Aleksandrov [et al.] (editors), *Narody evropeĭskoĭ chasti SSSR*, vol. 2 (Moscow: 1956), pp. 634-681; "Chuvashy" in: V.A. Aleksandrov [et al.] (editors), *Narody evropeĭskoĭ chasti SSSR*, vol. 2 (Moscow: 1956), pp. 598-633.

SOURCE: E.P. Busygin, N.V. Zorin and L.N. Terent'eva, "N.I. Vorob'ev (nekrolog)," *Sovetskaîa ètnografiîa*, no. 1 (1968), pp. 203-205.

A.M. Reshetov
[Translation from Russian: Helen Sullivan]

Vroklage, B.A.G. (Bernardus Andreas Gregorius). Ethnologist, philosopher, theologian. Born in Oldemarkt (Netherlands) 28 December 1897, died in Nijmegen (Netherlands) 7 October 1951. Having joined the Society of the Divine Word (S.V.D.) in 1919, Vroklage was ordained as a Roman Catholic priest in 1924. After teaching philosophy and theology at his own missionary college in Teteringen for a few years, he went to Rome to resume his studies at the Angelicum and was awarded a doctorate in theology in 1932. He then went on to study ethnology at the University of Vienna, where he took his doctorate in 1934 with a thesis concerning social relations on Borneo. During the next two years he worked on a major publication in which he reviewed a considerable part of the ethnographic literature on Borneo, Celebes and the Moluccas (*Die sozialen Verhältnisse Indonesiens*).

From October 1936 until autumn 1938 Vroklage did fieldwork on Timor and Flores (Indonesia). Some of the material he gathered was used by physical anthropologists at Leiden University and resulted in several articles and a dissertation. His ethnographic material, however, remained largely unpublished through lack of funds. An extensive three-part description of the Belu (Timor) was published posthumously (*Ethnographie der Belu in Zentral Timor*).

Starting in 1939 Vroklage lectured on ethnology and the science of religions at Teteringen. In 1948 he was appointed to a part-time professorate in ethnology at the Catholic University in Nijmegen (Netherland), a post he held until his death in 1951.

In his work and teachings he was a follower of his Viennese mentor WILHELM SCHMIDT and his Cultural-Historical School. On the whole the Dutch academic establishment was severely critical of this perspective. Over the years Vroklage distanced himself somewhat from the extremes of the concept of *Kulturkreisen* (culture circles) and in the end used them as a welcome but hypothetical means of categorizing ethnographic material. In the same way he distanced himself from the conception of an original monotheism. In his teachings he expressed the need for correct and scientific conceptualization and tried to create some order out of the chaos of religious concepts in the ethnographic literature. Also, he constantly pointed out the differences in meaning for the primitive mentality of notions like shame, sin, guilt, redemption, etc.

Vroklage published extensively both on ethnographic subjects and on the missionary sciences. He acted as co-editor for the *Internationales Archiv für Ethnographie* and starting in 1935 was actively involved as a member of the Anthropos Institute in the publication of *Anthropos: Internationales Zeitschrift für Völker- und Sprachkunde*.

MAJOR WORKS: "Magie und Soziologie in Indonesien," *Mitteilungen der Anthropologischen Gesellschaft in Wien* vol. 65 (1935), pp. 267-275; *Die sozialen Verhältnisse Indonesiens: eine kulturgeschichtliche Untersuchung*, Band I, *Borneo, Celebes und Molukken* (Munster: 1936); "Enkele aanteekeningen over in de laatste jaren ontdekte stammen in het mandaatgebied van Nieuw Guinee," *Tijdschrift van het Koninklijk Nederlandsch Aardrijkskundig Genootschap*, vol. 53 (1936), pp. 886-893; "Ethnologisch en Anthropologisch Onderzoek op Centraal Timor," *Koloniaal Missie Tijdschrift*, vol. 22 (1939), pp. 372-375; (with J.A.J. Barge) "Contributions to the anthropology of Timor and Flores (Dutch East Indies) after data collected by Dr. B.A.G. Vroklage S.V.D.," *Acta Neerlandica Morphologiae Normalis et Pathologicae*, vol. 4 (1942), pp. 329-356; vol. 5 (1943), pp. 119-130, 213-228, and 262-273; *De physische anthropologie van de bevolking van Oost-Dawan (Noord-Midden-Timor), naar de gegevens van B.A.G. Vroklage* (edited by H.J. Lammers) (Nijmegen and Leiden: 1948); *Primitieve mentaliteit en zondebesef bij de Beloenezen en enige andere volken* (Roermond and Maaseik: 1949); *Ethnographie der Belu in Zentral-Timor* [3 vols.] (Leiden: 1952); "Bride price or dower," *Anthropos*, vol. 47 (1952), pp. 133-146; "Die grossfamiliale und Verwandtschaftsexogamie in Belu, Zentraltimor (Indonesien)," *Internationales Archiv für Ethnographie*, vol. 46 (1952), pp. 163-191.

SOURCES: A. Mulders, "In memoriam: Prof. Dr. B.A.G. Vroklage S.V.D.," *Het Missiewerk*, vol. 30 (1951), pp. 235-238; "In Memoriam: Prof. Dr. B.A.G. Vroklage S.V.D. (born 28th December 1897, died 7th October 1951)," *Internationales Archiv für Ethnographie*, vol. 46 (1952), pp. 2-3; F. Bornemann, "In Memoriam: B.A.G. Vroklage S.V.D., 1897-1951," *Anthropos*, vol. 48 (1953), pp. 292-295; L.F. Triebels, "De beginjaren van de culturele antropologie in Nijmegen," *Antropologische Verkenningen*, vol. 7, no. 1/2 (1988), pp. 118-122.

S.R. Jaarsma and J.J. de Wolf

W

Wagley, Charles William. Anthropologist. Born in Clarksville (Texas) 9 November 1913. Wagley began his student life in Kansas City, Missouri, and attended the University of Oklahoma and Columbia College (B.A., 1936). He received a Ph.D. in 1941 from the graduate school of Columbia University, where he was a student of FRANZ BOAS; at Columbia he was also influenced by RUTH BENEDICT, RALPH LINTON, RUTH BUNZEL and ALEXANDER LESSER. For his doctorate, he undertook ethnological research in 1937 in Guatemala, writing about the economy, social life and religion of an indigenous community there. He returned to the field in 1956 to re-examine these problems from the point of view that "understanding a society depends on knowledge of the past, on the outcomes we observe in the present, and on the nature of the situation and its current tendencies."

Wagley began his career as a teacher and researcher at Columbia College (1940-1941). In 1949 he was promoted to full professor at Columbia University and became Franz Boas Professor in 1967. He moved to the University of Florida in 1971 as Graduate Research Professor of Anthropology and Latin American Studies, a position he occupied until he retired in 1984 with the title Professor Emeritus. He also served as Visiting Lecturer in the Anthropology Department at the Museu Nacional (National Museum) in Rio de Janeiro (1941-1942), staff member of the John Simon Guggenheim Foundation (1945-1947) and Director of the Institute of Latin American Studies at Columbia University (1961-1969).

The focus of his research was on the study of Brazilian Indians. During more than fifteen months during 1939-1940 he undertook research among the Tapirapé Indians of central Brazil; this was followed by identical work among the Tenetehara Indians in Maranhão. His knowledge of these Tupi-speaking tribes served as his credentials when he collaborated on the *Handbook of South American Indians* and wrote the chapter "The Indian heritage of Brazil" in *Brazil, Portrait of Half a Continent.*

Wagley also worked on modern Brazilian society, publishing pioneering studies on regionalism and the cultural unity of Brazil (e.g., in *Social Forces*) that were assembled into a book (*An Introduction to Brazil*) in which he analyzed Brazilian identity as a culture, society and people. His knowledge was derived from his experiences as professor at the Museu Nacional on several occasions; from participation in the Brazilian anthropology meetings; from campaigns in education, public health and economy; from the training of North American, Latin American and Brazilian students in anthropology; and from marriage into a Brazilian family. Cecilia, his wife, collaborated with him in fieldwork. He directed extensive research in the communities of Bahia from the comparative perspective. He undertook observational travel to Portugal and Lusophone Africa (Angola, Mozambique and Guinea-Bissau), while conducting a series of conferences for the Instituto Superior de Estudos Ultramarinos (Higher Institute of Overseas Studies) in Lisbon in 1960. His view of Latin America is the product of his trips, sojourns and scientific contacts.

Wagley's fluency in the spoken Portuguese of Brazil and his having lived with Brazilian social scientists, combined with his direct knowledge of the regional literature (romance, tales, folklore), explain his stature among highly regarded Brazilianists. A statement he made in relation to one of his books could be extended to all of his work: "It should be clear that my book on Itá (Amazônas) is not a study in the vein of modern social science, although it uses the framework of social anthropology. As I look back, I know now that I am essentially a humanist; and I realize that this was a humanistic book with a humanistic message." This feature is manifested even more clearly in *Welcome of Tears.*

MAJOR WORKS: *Economics of a Guatemalan Village* (Washington: 1941) (= *Memoirs of the American Anthropological Association*, no. 58); "Regionalism and cultural unity in Brazil," *Social Forces*, vol. 26 (1948), pp. 457-464; (with Eduardo Galvão) chapters in: Julian H. Steward (editor), *Handbook of South American Indians* (Washington: 1948); *The Social and Religious Life of a Guatemalan Village* (Washington: 1949) (= *Memoirs of the American Anthropological Association*, no. 71) [tr.: *Santiago Chimaltenango: estudio antropologico-social de una comunidad indígena de Huehuetenango* (Guatemala City: 1957)]; "The Indian heritage of Brazil" in: T. Lynn Smith and Alexander Marchant (editors), *Brazil, Portrait of Half a Continent* (New York: 1951), pp. 104-124; (with Eduardo Galvão) *The Tenetehara Indians of Brazil: a Culture in Transition* (New York: 1949); (editor and contributor) *Race and Class in Rural Brazil* (Paris: 1952); *Amazon Town: a Study of Man in the Tropics* (New York: 1953; revised ed., London: 1976) [tr.: *Uma comunidade amazônica* (São Paulo: 1957)]; (with Marvin Harris) *Minorities in the New World* (New York: 1958); *An Introduction to Brazil* (New York: 1963; revised ed., New York: 1971); *The Latin American Tradition: Essays on the Unity and Diversity of Latin American Culture* (New York and London: 1968); *Welcome of Tears: the Tapirapé Indians of Central Brazil* (New York: 1977) [tr.: *Lágrimas de boas vindas* (São Paulo: 1988)].

Thales de Azevedo
[*Translation from Portuguese: Margo L. Smith*]

Waligórski, Andrzej. Ethnologist, sociologist. Born in Kraków, Galicia (Austria-Hungary, now in Poland) 12 December 1908, died in Kraków (Poland) 8 August 1974. Waligórski studied linguistics and philosophy at Jagiellonian University and social anthropology under BRONISLAW MALINOWSKI at the University of London, obtaining his doctorate in 1938. For a short time he worked at the State Institute of Village Culture in

Warsaw. During World War II he worked at the Royal Institute for International Affairs in London. In the years 1946-1948 Waligórski conducted fieldwork among the Luo, working through an extension of the University of London. In 1948 he returned to Poland and began work at Jagiellonian University; from 1962 he was director of the Institute of Ethnography and Sociology of African Peoples in Kraków; and from 1973 he served as director of the Division of Culture and Education of the Institute of Sociology. In 1955 he was named assistant professor and in 1969 associate professor.

Waligórski wrote on the cultural and social problems of Africa, especially focusing on the Luo. His theoretical interests included the problems of the theory of culture, the functional method of Malinowski and the history of cultural anthropology. He pursued social anthropology, working on the borders of ethnography and ethnology. Waligórski linked the functionalism of Malinowski with Marxist sociological theory.

MAJOR WORKS: "Studia nad więzią terytorialną i rodzinną wschodnioafrykańskiego plemienia Luo" ["Studies on the territorial link and the native East-African Tribe Luo"], *Etnografia Polska*, vol. 7 (1963), pp. 299-362; *Społeczność afrykańska w procesie przemian, 1890-1949: studium wschodnioafrykańskiego plemienia Luo* [*African Society in the Process of Transformation, 1890-1949: Study of the East-African Tribe Luo*] (Warsaw: 1969); "Kierunek ewolucyjny w etnografii (1860-1890)" ["Evolutionary direction in ethnography (1860-1890)"], *Zeszyty Naukowe Uniwersytetu Jagiellońskiego Prace Etnograficzne*, vol. 5 (1971), pp. 7-49; *Antropologiczna koncepcja człowieka* [*The Anthropological Conception of Man*] (Warsaw: 1973); "Roczny cykl produkcyjny chłopskiej zagrody zachodniokenijskich Luo" ["The annual production cycle of the peasant farm of the Western Kenyan Luo"], *Lud*, vol. 58 (1974), pp. 41-72; "Malinowski w trzydzieści lat później" ["Malinowski thirty years later"], *Studia Socjologiczne*, vol. 53, no. 2 (1974), pp. 5-26.

SOURCES: Leszek Dzięgiel, "Andrzej Waligórski," *Lud*, vol. 59 (1975), pp. 347-349; Barbara Olszewska-Dyoniziak, "Profesor Andrzej Waligórski," *Zeszyty Naukowe Uniwersytetu Jagiellońskiego Prace Etnograficzne*, vol. 9 (1976), pp. 11-17.

Maria Niewiadomska and Iwona Grzelakowska
[Translation from Polish: Joel Janicki]

Warner, W. Lloyd. Social anthropologist. Born in Redlands (California) 26 October 1898, died in Chicago (Illinois) 23 May 1970. Warner was one of the best known American social anthropologists. He is perhaps most renowned for his application of anthropological ideas to the study of American society.

Warner first became acquainted with anthropology at the University of California, Berkeley, from which he obtained an A.B. (1925) and where he was particularly influenced by ROBERT H. LOWIE, ALFRED and Theodora KROEBER and (during their visits to Berkeley) BRONISLAW MALINOWSKI and A.R. RADCLIFFE-BROWN. The latter played some role in his decision to do doctoral research among the Murngin in Australia, research that resulted in several classic papers.

Warner became Assistant Professor at Harvard in 1929. It was there that he first extended his classic anthropological training to the study of American society on a large scale. The best-known product of this research is the Yankee City series, a five-volume study of Newburyport, Massachusetts, but Warner also participated in or inspired other studies of the contemporary world, many of which had practical significance. He is considered one of the originators of industrial anthropology.

Much of his research was published during his twenty-four years at the University of Chicago starting in 1935. During these years he also contributed to several government research studies on aspects of American society. His last teaching position (from 1959) was at Michigan State University.

Much of his writing—his work on the Murngin, on Yankee City and on various features of U.S. society—focused on the ways in which societally determined status dominated individual lives and the relationship between individuals and the institutional settings in which they found themselves. His work has been criticized for its ahistorical character.

MAJOR WORKS: *A Black Civilization: a Social Study of an Australian Tribe* (New York and London: 1937; rev. ed., New York: 1964); *The Social Life of a Modern Community* (New Haven: 1941) [1st vol. of *Yankee City Series*]; *The Status System of a Modern Community* (New Haven: 1942) [2nd vol. of *Yankee City Series*]; *The Social Systems of American Ethnic Groups* (New Haven: 1945) [3rd vol. of *Yankee City Series*]; *The Social System of the Modern Factory* (New Haven: 1947) [4th vol. of *Yankee City Series*]; *American Life: Dream and Reality* (Chicago: 1953; rev. ed., Chicago: 1962); *The Living and the Dead: a Study of the Symbolic Life of Americans* (New Haven: 1959) [5th vol. of *Yankee City Series*]; (co-editor) *The Emergent American Society*. Vol. 1. *Large-Scale Organizations* (New Haven: 1967).

SOURCES: Solon T. Kimball, "Warner, W. Lloyd" in: David L. Sills (editor), *International Encyclopedia of the Social Sciences* (New York: 1969-1978), vol. 18, pp. 791-795; Dietrich Herzog, *Klassengesellschaft ohne Klassenkonflikt: eine Studie über William Lloyd Warner und die Entwicklung der neuen amerikanischen Stratifikationsforschung* (Berlin: 1965) (= *Soziologische Abhandlungen*, Heft 5).

Wassén, S. Henry. Ethnographer, anthropologist. Born in Göteborg (Sweden) 24 August 1908. Wassén took his "GCE" at Advanced level in 1928 and obtained his M.A. (*fil. lic.*) in ethnography in 1936.

Wassén was only a young man when he started his museum career at the Ethnographical Museum of Göteborg in 1930, employed as an assistant to the famous Swedish ethnographer ERLAND NORDENSKIÖLD. Wassén was to become the most genuine disciple of Nordenskiöld, publishing some of his Cuna material posthumously, continuing his regional interest in Panama and Colombia and dedicating his entire life to the service of the Ethnographical Museum of Göteborg.

When Nordenskiöld was partially bedridden by the illness that would take his life, Wassén intensified his interest in the Cuna through his acquaintance with the Cuna Indian visiting the Göteborg Museum, Perez Kántule. In 1947 Wassén also led an expedition to the Cunas (as well as to the Chocó). All this taken together has made Wassén the foremost ethnographic authority on the Cunas. He has published several important works on this people (*Original Documents from the Cuna Indians of San Blas, Panama; Contributions to Cuna Ethnography*). He also published several works on the Chocó Indians of Colombia (*Notes on the Southern Groups of Chocó Indians in Colombia; Apuntes sobre grupos meridionales de indígenas Chocó en Colombia*). Later, his interest focused on Amerindian drugs (*The Use of Some Specific Kinds of South American Indian Snuff and Related Paraphernalia; A Medicine-Man's Implements and Plants in a Tiahuanacoid Tomb in Highland Bolivia*).

In 1968 Wassén became the director of the Ethnographical Museum of Göteborg, a position that he held until his retirement in 1973.

MAJOR WORKS: *Notes on the Southern Groups of Chocó Indians in Colombia* (Göteborg: 1935) (= *Etnologiska Studier*, no. 1, pp. 35-182); *Original Documents from the Cuna Indians of San Blas, Panama* (Göteborg: 1938) (= *Etnologiska Studier*, no. 6); *Contributions to Cuna Ethnography* (Göteborg: 1949) (= *Etnologiska Studier*, no. 16); *The Use of Some Specific Kinds of South American Indian Snuff and Related Paraphernalia* (Göteborg: 1965) (= *Etnologiska Studier*, no. 28); (editor and contributor) *A Medicine-Man's Implements and Plants in a Tiahuanacoid Tomb in Highland Bolivia* (Göteborg: 1972) (= *Etnologiska Studier*, no. 32); *Apuntes sobre grupos meridionales de indígenas Chocó en Colombia* (Bogotá: 1988).

Jan-Åke Alvarsson

Wasson, R. Gordon (Robert Gordon). Ethnomycologist. Born in Great Falls (Montana) 22 September 1898, died in Binghamton (New York) 23 December 1986. Wasson was the founder of the interdisciplinary field of ethnomycology and produced a number of influential works on the subject.

Wasson was educated at Columbia University's School of Journalism and was successively an instructor of English at Columbia, a journalist and editorial writer and a banker. In 1927 he married a Russian-born pediatrician, Valentina Pavlovna Guercken, with whom he began a lifelong investigation of various cultures' uses of, and attitudes toward, mushrooms. Eventually this led them to the discovery of the use of hallucinogenic mushrooms in curing rituals among the Mazatec people of Mexico and to the publication of their two-volume work *Mushrooms, Russia, and History* in 1957. Shortly afterward, Valentina Wasson died.

Wasson collaborated with numerous specialists, himself remaining a learned generalist. His collaborators included Vedic scholar Wendy Doniger O'Flaherty, ethnobotanist Richard Evans Schultes, chemist Albert Hofmann (the discoverer of LSD-25), and mycologist Roger Heim. Wasson's next major work was the identification, now widely accepted, of the hallucinogenic mushroom *Amanita muscaria* as the mysterious soma in the *Rig Veda*.

Wasson and his wife had much earlier speculated that the frequent occurrence of either strong mycophilia or strong mycophobia (terms they coined) in various cultures implied an Ur-religion based on the use of hallucinogenic mushrooms; in *Amanita muscaria*, Wasson thought that he had found that mushroom, at least for Eurasia. Subsequently Wasson would attempt to identify hallucinogens involved in the Eleusinian mysteries and the mushroom that supposedly made up the last supper of the Buddha. These were both less likely, and less significant, attempts than his earlier identification of soma had been.

Wasson's long fascination with ethnomycology (another of his neologisms) has had salutary effects on anthropology and on a number of other disciplines on which it impinged. Wasson himself was an amateur scholar in the finest sense of the word, someone whose lack of institutional affiliation, and willingness to finance his own research, enabled him to spend decades in his investigations. Under no pressure to publish, Wasson wrote most of his works after his retirement from banking.

However, as a generalist he also frequently lacked linguistic or ethnological knowledge in depth, which led him on occasion to conclusions that some specialists remain unwilling to endorse.

MAJOR WORKS: *Soma: Divine Mushroom of Immortality* (New York: 1968); *The Wondrous Mushroom: Mycolatry in Mesoamerica* (New York: 1980); (with V.P. Wasson) *Mushrooms, Russia, and History* (New York: 1957); (with A. Hofmann and C.A.P. Ruck) *The Road to Eleusis* (New York: 1978).

SOURCES: Christopher Brown, "R. Gordon Wasson," *Economic Botany*, vol. 41 (1987), pp. 469-473; Donald H. Pfister, "R. Gordon Wasson—1898-1986," *Mycologia*, vol. 80 (1988), pp. 11-13.

David Lonergan

Waterman, Thomas Talbot. Anthropologist. Born in Hamilton (Missouri) 23 April 1885, died in Honolulu (Hawaii) 6 January 1936. A clergyman's son who originally intended to enter the Episcopal ministry, Waterman discovered anthropology during his undergraduate years at the University of California. A student of ALFRED L. KROEBER's, he became the older man's protégé, first as an assistant in the Museum of Anthropology in San Francisco (1907-1909), then progressively Instructor (1910-1914), Assistant Professor (1914-1918) and finally Associate Professor (1920-1921) at Berkeley. A creative and popular teacher, he was Kroeber's principal collaborator in designing the Berkeley anthropology curriculum that became the model for departments throughout the United States. After leaving California in 1921 for a short-lived position with the Heye Foundation (he had earlier been at the University of Washington for two years, 1918-1920), Waterman's career fell into unproductive disarray. Most of his last decade was spent in Hawaii.

Waterman's scholarly work was largely devoted to ethnographic detail rather than to theoretical issues. While his name is most often remembered in the context of his work with Ishi, the Yana Indian who lived at the Museum of Anthropology from 1911 to 1916, his studies of the Yurok and Tolowa of northwestern California were of greater significance. No ethnographer has better captured the flavor of traditional northwest California society than did Waterman in his sketch, "All is trouble along the Klamath," and his *Yurok Geography* remains one of the most important ethnographic statements on the region. Waterman's brief period of teaching in Washington also resulted in important work on the Indians of Puget Sound and the Makah.

MAJOR WORKS: "The explanatory element in the folk-tales of the North American Indian," *Journal of American Folk-Lore*, vol. 27 (1914), pp. 1-54; *The Yana Indians* (Berkeley: 1918) (= *University of California Publications in American Archaeology and Ethnography*, vol. 13, no. 2); *Yurok Geography* (Berkeley: 1920) (= *University of California Publications in American Archaeology and Ethnography*, vol. 16, no. 5); *Whaling Equipment of the Makah Indians* (Seattle: 1920) (= *University of Washington Publications in Political and Social Science*, vol. 1, no. 1); (with A.L. Kroeber) *Source Book in Anthropology* (Berkeley: 1920; 2nd ed., New York: 1931); "All is trouble along the Klamath: a Yurok idyll" in: Elsie Clews Parsons (editor), *American Indian Life* (New York: 1922), pp. 289-296; "Village sites in Tolowa and neighboring areas of Northwestern California," *American Anthropologist*, n.s., vol. 27 (1925), pp. 528-543.

SOURCE: A.L. Kroeber, "Thomas Talbot Waterman," *American Anthropologist*, n.s., vol. 39 (1937), pp. 527-529.

Victor Golla

Weber-Kellermann, Ingeborg. Folklorist, Europeanist, ethnologist. Born in Berlin (Germany) 26 June 1918. Weber-Kellermann's significance lies above all in her research on customs and family and in her studies of the relationships within ethnic groups, for which she developed new ways of stating the problems and new approaches. In all her work, she tried to place cultural phenomena in their social and economic context.

Weber-Kellermann graduated in 1940 from Berlin, having worked under Adolf Spamer. She worked until 1960 at the Volkskundliches Institut (Folklore Institute) at the Academy of Sciences in Berlin. She then moved to Marburg where she obtained her *Habilitation* in the area of harvest customs in the rural communities of the 19th century. The data for her investigation derived from the 1865 questionnaires of the Grimm school's Wilhelm Mannhardt, which she freed of mythological ballast and put into an economic and social context. In 1968 she obtained a professorship in folklore and European ethnology and culture research at Marburg.

With her historical-social-economic approach, Weber-Kellerman interpreted customs as codes, social facts and signs through which the social life of groups was expressed and through which distinct ways of thought and ways of behavior made themselves known. Even for the investigation of clothing, by stressing the interactions of fashion and tradition, she put new a new stress on cultural interpretation. Her works on the social history of the family, women and childhood, in which she did not limit herself to statistical material but turned above all to normative and qualitative data, attracted considerable attention.

MAJOR WORKS: *Erntebrach in der ländlichen Arbeitswelt des 19. Jahrhunderts auf Grund der Mannhardtbefragung in Deutschland von 1865* (Marburg: 1965); *Die deutsche Familie: Versuch einer Sozialgeschichte* (Frankfurt am Main: 1974); *Deutsche Volkskunde zwischen Germanistik und Sozialwissenschaften* (Stuttgart: 1969); *Das Weihnachtsfest: eine Kultur- und Sozialgeschichte der Weihnachtszeit* (Lucerne: 1978); *Die Kindheit: Kleidung und Wohnung, Arbeit und Spiel: eine Kulturgeschichte* (Frankfurt am Main: 1979); *Frauenleben im 19. Jahrhundert: Empire und Romantik, Biedermeier, Gründerzeit* (Munich: 1983).

SOURCES: Adalhart Zippelius, "Ingeborg Weber-Kellermann zum 26.6.1978" in: A. Bummer [et al.] (editors), *Brauch–Familie–Arbeitsleben: Schriften von Ingeborg Weber-Kellermann* (Marburg: 1978), pp. 199-207; Rolf W. Brednich (editor), *Grindriß der Volkskunde: Einführung in die Forschungsfelder der Europäischen Ethnologie* (Berlin: 1988).

Adelheid Schrutka-Rechtenstamm
[Translation from German: Robert B. Dean]

Weidenreich, Franz. Physician, anatomist, anthropologist. Born in Edenkoben (Germany) 7 June 1873, died in New York (New York) 11 July 1948. Weidenreich attended the Gymnasium at Landau, then spent six years studying medicine in Munich, Kiel, Berlin and Strasbourg. After receiving his M.D. in 1899 from Strasbourg he taught anatomy there and was appointed professor of anatomy in 1904. By 1914 he had published fifty-four papers, mostly concerned with blood, although he was very much interested in bone and connective tissue. His anthropological interests commenced with a paper on the chin ("Zur Kinnbildung beim Menschen") and on upright posture ("Über das Hüftbein und das Becken der Primaten"). The advent of World War I interrupted Weidenreich's work and when the French took over Strasbourg he was dismissed from his professorship. In 1921 Weidenreich became Professor of Anatomy at Heidelberg. His interest in blood continued, but his interest in bone and evolution became much more pronounced. His publications on the foot, the skull, domestication and race foreshadowed the basic thinking of all of his later work. In 1928 he described the Ehringsdorf skull and in the same year moved to Frankfurt. There he continued writing about blood, bone, teeth and connective tissue; in addition he wrote about fossil man and the evolution of the hand and foot. His Jewish family background and his work on race brought Weidenreich into conflict with the German authorities, and in 1934 he left Germany to accept a visiting professorship at the University of Chicago. In 1935 he became Professor of Anatomy at Peking Union Medical College and honorary director of the Cenozoic Research Laboratory. There he prepared a series of monographs on mandibles (*The Mandibles of Sinanthropus Pekinensis*), dentition (*The Dentition of Sinanthropus Pekinensis*), extremity bones (*The Extremity Bones of Sinanthropus Pekinensis*) and the skull (*The Skull of Sinanthropus Pekinensis*). In 1941 Weidenreich moved again, and he spent his final years at the American Museum of Natural History in New York. Weidenreich's writings the last ten years of his life dealt exclusively with human evolution, but they were enriched by the profound anatomical understanding he had derived from his earlier work.

Many of Weidenreich's last papers, especially the monograph *Giant Early Man*, were concerned with *Pithecanthropus erectus* from Java. The original specimens of Peking Man were lost during World War II, but the Dutch paleontologist G.H.R. von Koenigswald (1902-1982), having survived his experiences in a Japanese prison camp, managed to obtain original specimens of *Pithecanthropus* and he brought them to Weidenreich in New York.

Weidenreich's views on human evolution were summarized in a series of six lectures and later published in *Apes, Giants and Man* and in a review article, "The trend of human evolution." He believed that human evolution was fundamentally orthogenetic in character, that the principal trends that changed ancestral ape to man were interconnected and consisted of bipedalism, increased brain size and decreased face size and decreased massiveness in the final giant man, ancient man, modern man series. Weidenreich, along with most European and German paleoanthropologists, did not accept Piltdown man, maintaining that the lower jaw was that of an ape. Nor did he ever accept Pleistocene *Homo sapiens*. He believed that mankind comprised only one species from before the time of Java man. Although he saw continuity of structural differences in each of the major geographical areas of the Old World, he believed that there had been genetic connections among all the areas throughout the Pleistocene period (*Apes, Giants and Man*). Contrary to the misrepresentations of his views on the origin of races, he never proposed a multilineal sequence of human evolution.

Weidenreich's fossil descriptions remain unequaled. His general chronological arrangement of their forms still appears to be essentially correct, although recent discoveries of jaws show *Gigantophithecus* to be an ape and not, as Weidenreich had suspected, an early man.

Probably no other person contributed more to the study of human evolution than did Weidenreich. In spite of persecution, the loss of academic positions for political reasons and great personal difficulties, he remained a generous and friendly individual. He welcomed colleagues and students who wanted to see his collection. Weidenreich exerted a profound influence in the few years he was in the United States.

MAJOR WORKS: "Zur Kinnbildung beim Menschen," *Anatomischer Anzeiger*, vol. 25 (1904), pp. 314-319; "Über das Hüftbein und das Becken der Primaten und ihre Umformung durch den aufrechten Gang," *Anatomischer Anzeiger*, vol. 44 (1913), pp. 397-513; *Der Schädelfund von Weimar-Ehringsdorf* (Jena: 1928); *The Mandibles of Sinanthropus Pekinensis: a Comparative Study*

(Beijing: 1936) (= *Palaeontologia Sinica*, series D 7, fasc. 3); *Observations on the Form and Proportions of the Endocranial Casts of Sinanthropus Pekinensis, Other Hominids and Great Apes: a Comparative Study of Brain Size* (Beijing: 1936) (= *Palaeontologia Sinica*, series D 7, fasc. 4); *The Dentition of Sinanthropus Pekinensis: a Comparative Odontography of the Hominids* (Beijing: 1937) (= *Palaeontologia Sinica*, n.s. D, no. 1, whole series no. 101); *The Extremity Bones of Sinanthropus Pekinensis* (Beijing: 1941) (= *Palaeontologia Sinica*, n.s. D, no. 5, whole series no. 116); *The Skull of Sinanthropus Pekinensis: a Comparative Study on a Primitive Hominid Skull* (Beijing: 1943) (= *Palaeontologia Sinica*, n.s. D, no. 10, whole series no. 127); *Giant Early Man from Java and South China* (New York: 1945) (= *American Museum of Natural History, Anthropological Papers*, vol. 40, part 1); "The brachycephalization of recent mankind," *Southwest Journal of Anthropology*, vol. 1 (1945), pp. 1-54; *Apes, Giants and Man* (Chicago: 1946); "The trend of human evolution," *Evolution*, vol. 1 (1947), pp. 221-236; "Facts and speculations concerning the origin of *Homo sapiens*," *American Anthropologist*, n.s., vol. 49 (1947), pp. 187-203; *The Shorter Anthropological Papers of Franz Weidenreich Published in the Period 1939-1948: a Memorial Volume* (compiled by S.L. Washburn and Davida Wolffson) (New York: 1949).

SOURCE: S.L. Washburn, "Weidenreich, Franz" in: David L. Sills (editor), *International Encyclopedia of the Social Sciences* (New York: 1968-1979), vol. 16, pp. 502-503.

S.L. Washburn

Weiss, Richard. Folklorist. Born in Stuttgart (Germany) 9 November 1907, died in Russo (Switzerland) 29 July 1962. Weiss's significance lies in his calling special attention, after 1945, to the functional relations of folklore. He established new standards for folklore research and, in particular, research on vernacular architecture (*Hausforschung*).

He completed his studies (in German and history) at the Universities of Zürich, Heidelberg and Paris. Stimulated by a fellowship from the *Atlas der deutschen Volkskunde* spent in Berlin under Adolf Spamer (1933-1934), he sketched out with Paul Geiger a similar project for Switzerland. He obtained his *Habilitation* in Zürich, where he was active as a *Privatdozent*, until he became the first Swiss professor of folklore (1945).

In 1946 his *Volkskunde der Schweiz* appeared. This book gave post-war German-language folklore both an impulse and a direction and was influential even outside Switzerland.

Weiss dealt with the contemporary world in his research and took up such subjects as the city, workers and refugees. Before that time, these had not been part of the folklore canon at all.

With his functional approach he was interested above all in people. The function of things and the question of the representation of things by people were significant for him. Also important was his definition of *Volk*, which for him could no longer be described as a social group but rather was something to which *everyone* belonged.

MAJOR WORKS: *Das Alpwesen Graubündens* (Erlenbach-Zürich: 1941); *Volkskunde der Schweiz* (Erlenbach-Zürich: 1946); *Häuser und Landschaften der Schweiz* (Erlenbach-Zürich: 1959); *Einführung in den Atlas der schweizerischen Volkskunde* (Basel: 1950).

SOURCES: Hans Trümpy, "Volkskundliche Forschung und Lehre an den deutsch-schweizerischen Universitäten und die schweizerische Gesellschaft für Volkskunde" in: W. Brückner and K. Beitl (editors), *Volkskunde als akademische Disziplin: Studien zur Institutionausbildung* (Vienna:

1983), pp. 63-76; Karl Meuli, "Richard Weiss, 9. November 1907-29. Juli 1962," *Schweizerisches Archiv für Volkskunde*, vol. 57 (1961), pp. 185-199.

Adelheid Schrutka-Rechtenstamm
[*Translation from German: Robert B. Dean*]

Weitzner, Bella. Ethnologist, museum curator. Born in New York (New York) 1891, died in New York (New York) 3 April 1988. Weitzner spent eighty-one years with the American Museum of Natural History. She started there in 1908 as secretary to CLARK WISSLER and retired in 1956 as associate curator, continuing to work in the anthropology department with the title of curator emeritus. She was one of the very few people at the museum to achieve curatorial rank without formal training. Weitzner's editorial skill and knowledge of the collections made her an invaluable asset to all the scientific staff. The anthropology publications during her tenure all benefited greatly from her attention and she was, informally, a superb teacher and guide to volunteers and visiting scholars who came to the department.

SOURCES: N.F.S. Woodbury, "Bella Weitzner," *Anthropology Newsletter*, vol. 29, no. 6 (September 1988), p. 4; "Bella Weitzner, 97, ex-curator of Museum," *The New York Times* (9 April 1988), p. 12.

Nathalie F.S. Woodbury

Weltfish, Gene (Gene Regina Weltfish). Anthropologist. Born in New York (New York) 7 August 1902, died in New York (New York) 2 August 1980. Weltfish's family was impoverished at the death of her father, a lawyer. From the age of fourteen, she held a clerical job and went to night school; she graduated from high school at the age of sixteen nonetheless. Weltfish began college as a journalism major at Hunter and graduated in 1925 from Barnard College. While at Barnard she took courses in philosophy from John Dewey and in anthropology from FRANZ BOAS. Her exposure to anthropology led her to graduate work at Columbia where she became one of Boas's star pupils.

Weltfish finished her doctoral dissertation (on Native American basketry and art; the latter was a lifelong interest) in 1929 but was not awarded her degree until twenty-one years later, in 1950. Until that time, Columbia required that a dissertation be published before the degree was bestowed, and Weltfish could not underwrite the expensive publication process.

In 1928 she began a long-term research project on the Pawnee Indians in Oklahoma. Synthesizing archaeological, ethnohistoric, and ethnographic data, Weltfish produced a masterful recreation of Pawnee life ways, *The Lost Universe*, which was completed in the 1960s. She was employed by the Bureau of American Ethnology during 1930-1931 to work on Pawnee texts taken down long before by JAMES R. MURIE. During the early 1930s, Weltfish was often in Oklahoma, doing fieldwork with her then-husband, anthropologist and Boasian ALEXANDER LESSER.

Weltfish was hired as an instructor of anthropology by Columbia in 1935 and soon became involved in the university's School of General Studies. One of her pioneering courses there, strongly in the Boasian tradition, was on race relations. As World War II developed, she became a major figure in anthropology at Columbia. She was also active in the effort to eradicate racism in the United States through education. Her efforts to further the cause of social justice resulted in Weltfish's being elected one of the four vice-presidents of the Women's International Democratic Federation and, later, president of the Congress of American Women in the post-war period.

In 1952 Weltfish was fired by Columbia (to be precise, her contract was not renewed) following an investigation into her politics by Senator Joseph McCarthy's Internal Security Committee. *The Races of Mankind*, which she co-authored with RUTH BENEDICT, and which had been widely used as an educational resource by the United States Army during the war, was now labeled "subversive." Boas and Benedict, her former mentors, were no longer present to aid Weltfish, and, after seventeen years as an instructor at Columbia, she was still untenured. The university administration declared that political questions were unrelated to their actions and let her go.

Weltfish worked on her Pawnee studies in New York City, but under the auspices of the University of Nebraska from 1954 to 1958 and then for two years on a Bollingen Foundation grant. In 1961 she was finally able to find another teaching post, at Fairleigh Dickinson University in New Jersey. She remained there until her retirement in 1972.

Weltfish was a founder of the Gerontological Society of New Jersey and after retirement became a visiting professor of gerontology at Rutgers University. She was also a part-time instructor of anthropology at the New School for Social Research.

Her career, while it doubtless provided many satisfactions, was blighted by her dismissal from Columbia in 1952; that politically expeditious act was made possible, or at least much easier, by her lack of tenure at the age of forty-nine after many years of honorable service to the university and to her discipline.

MAJOR WORKS: "Prehistoric North American basketry techniques and modern distributions," *American Anthropologist*, vol. 32 (1930), pp. 435-495; (with Ruth Benedict) *The Races of Mankind* (New York: 1943); *The Origins of Art* (Indianapolis: 1953); "The question of ethnic identity: an ethnological approach," *Ethnohistory*, vol. 6 (1959), pp. 321-346; *The Lost Universe* (New York: 1965); "The Plains Indians: their continuity in history and their Indian identity" in: E. Leacock and N.O. Lurie (editors), *North American Indians in Historical Perspective* (New York: 1971), pp. 200-227; *Work, an Anthropological View* (Saratoga Springs: 1974); *Aesthetics, the Dimension of Beauty in the Human Being* (Saratoga Springs: 1980).

SOURCES: Ruth E. Pathe, "Gene Weltfish" in: Ute Gacs [et al.] (editors), *Women Anthropologists: a Biographical Dictionary* (New York: 1988), pp. 372-381; Douglas R. Parks and Ruth E. Pathe, "Gene Weltfish, 1902-1980," *Plains Anthropologist*, vol. 30 (1985), pp. 59-64.

David Lonergan

Westermann, Diedrich Hermann.

Westermann, Diedrich Hermann. Missionary, Africanist. Born in Baden, near Bremen (Germany) 24 June 1875, died in Baden, near Bremen (Germany) 31 May 1956. Westermann had an intensive and fruitful career in several branches of African studies. Together with CARL MEINHOF he was in fact the founder of German African studies.

After a brief career at the post office, Westermann entered the service of the Norddeutsche Missionsgesellschaft (North German Mission Society) in 1895, which sent him to study in Basel and Tübingen. From 1901 to 1903 he served as a missionary in Togo where—in addition to other African languages—he learned and studied Ewe thoroughly. The most important scholarly results of this first African residence were an Ewe dictionary

(*Wörterbuch der Ewe-Sprache*), an Ewe grammar (*Grammatik der Ewe-Sprache*), a Fulani handbook (*Handbuch der Ful-Sprache*), and a Hausa grammar (*Die Sprache der Haussa in Zentralafrika*). After his return Westermann taught at the Oriental Seminar in Berlin and, together with J. Spieth, translated the Bible into Ewe. In 1908 Westermann resigned from the Mission and was named Professor at the Seminar for Oriental Languages in Berlin. In 1925 he was appointed to the Chair in African Languages and Cultures at the same institution. He became *Emeritus* in 1950.

His two major works in linguistics were *Die Sudansprachen* and *Die westlichen Sudansprachen und ihre Beziehungen zum Bantu*. In these works he was the first to apply the cultural-historical method to the exceptionally complicated language belt between the equator and the Sahara. Many separate studies date from this period, among others, works on the Shilluk (*A Short Grammar of the Shilluk Language* and *The Shilluk People*), the More or Mossi ("Die Mossi-Sprachengruppe"), the Grussi languages ("Die Grussisprachen"), the Zarma-Songhay ("Ein Beitrag zur Kenntnis des Zarma-Songhai"), the Gola (*Die Gola-Sprache in Liberia*), the Guang (*Die Sprache der Guang in Togo*), the Kpelle (*Die Kpelle-Sprache in Liberia*), the Edo ("Das Edo in Nigerien"), and the West Atlantic languages (*Die westlichen Sudansprachen*). The 1930s and 1940s were allocated more to general African interests and broad themes. During this period he wrote the text *Practical Phonetics for Students of African Languages* with I.C. Ward and also published *The African To-day*, "Charakter und Einteilung der Sudansprachen," *Africa and Christianity*, "Die Sprachen," *Afrika als europäische Aufgabe*, and *Sprachbeziehungen und Sprachverwandtschaft in Afrika*. Westermann crowned his life's work with two books, namely *Geschichte Afrikas* and the *Wörterbuch der Ewe-Sprache*, a monumental work of African linguistics.

Westermann was extremely active in the politics and organization of scholarship. He was the co-founder and first director of the International African Institute in London (1926); he transformed the "Lepsius" alphabet into what was applied in many places as the "Westermann script"; in 1928 he participated in the founding of the journal, *Africa*, which he edited until 1940; the Ethnographic Survey of Africa and the *Handbook of African Languages* were also both instigated by him; from 1937 to 1944, together with E. Zwirner, he edited the *Archiv für vergleichende Phonetik* and from 1947 until his death the *Zeitschrift für vergleichende Phonetik und allgemeine Sprachwissenschaft*. Köhler wrote that "Westermann's work and eminent contribution to our knowledge of African languages and cultures was based on a contribution of linguistic and anthropological research ... Seeing Africa as an indivisible whole is the characteristic outlook of the Westermann school" (1956, p. 218).

MAJOR WORKS: *Wörterbuch der Ewe-Sprache* [2 vols.] (Berlin: 1905-1906); *Grammatik der Ewe-Sprache* (Berlin: 1907); *Handbuch der Ful-Sprache: Wörterbuch, Grammatik, Übungen und Texte* (Berlin: 1909); *Die Sprache der Haussa in Zentralafrika* (Berlin: 1911) (= *Deutsche Kolonialsprachen*, 3); *Die Sudansprachen: eine Sprachvergleichende Studie* (Hamburg: 1911); *A Short Grammar of the Shilluk Language* (Berlin: 1911); *The Shilluk People: Their Language and Folklore* (Berlin: 1912); "Die Mossi-Sprachengruppe im westlichen Sudan," *Anthropos*, vol. 8 (1913), pp. 467-504 and 810-830; "Die Grussisprachen im westlichen Sudan," *Zeitschrift für Kolonialsprachen*, vol. 4 (1913-1914), pp. 161-180 and 312-332; vol. 5 (1915), pp. 45-76; "Ein Beitrag zur Kenntnis des Zarma-Songai am Niger," *Zeitschrift für Eingeborenen-Sprachen*, vol. 11 (1920/21), pp. 188-220; *Die Gola-Sprache in Liberia: Grammatik, Texte und Wörtherbuch* (Hamburg: 1921); *Die Sprache der Guang in Togo und auf der Goldküste und fünf andere*

Togosprachen (Berlin: 1922); *Die Kpelle-Sprache in Liberia: Grammatische Einführung, Texte und Wörterbuch* (Berlin: 1924) (= *Beiheft zu Zeitschrift der Eingeborenen-Sprachen*, no. 6); "Das Edo in Nigerien: seine Stellung innerhalb der Kwa-Sprachen," *Mitteilungen des Seminars für Orientalische Sprachen*, vol. 29 (1926), pp. 32-60; *Die westlichen Sudansprachen und ihre Beziehungen zum Bantu* (Berlin: 1927); *A Study in the Ewe Language* (London, New York and Toronto: 1930) (with I.C. Ward) *Practical Phonetics for Students of African Languages* (London: 1933); *The African To-day* (London: 1934); "Charakter und Einteilung der Sudansprachen," *Africa* vol. 8 (1935), pp. 129-148; *Africa and Christianity* (London: 1937); "Die Sprachen" in: H. Baumann, R. Thurnwald and D. Westermann (editors), *Völkerkunde von Afrika* (Essen: 1940), pp. 375-433; *Afrika als europäische Aufgabe* (Berlin: 1941); *Sprachbeziehungen und Sprachverwandtschaft in Afrika* (Berlin: 1949) (= *Sitzungsberichte der Deutschen Akademie der Wissenschaften zu Berlin, Philisophische-historische Klasse*, Jahrgang 1948, 1); *Geschichte Afrikas: Staatenbildung südlich der Sahara* (Cologne: 1952); *Wörterbuch der Ewe-Sprache* (Berlin: 1954).

SOURCES: E. Dammann, "Zum 80. Geburtstag von Diedrich Westermann," *Mitteilungen der Norddeutschen Missionsgesellschaft*, 5/6 (1955), pp. 17-19; E. Dammann, "Zum Gedächtnis an Diedrich Westermann," *Evangelische Missionszeitschrift*, vol. 13 (1956), pp. 123-125; E. Dammann, "Die Bedeutung von Diedrich Westermann," *Internationales Afrika Forum*, vol. 12 (1976), pp. 174-180; U. Feyer, "Diedrich Westermann zum 80. Geburtstag," *Forschungen und Fortschritte*, vol. 29 (1955), pp. 253-254; U. Feyer, "Diedrich Westermann," *Zeitschrift für Phonetik, Sprachwissenschaft und Kommunikationsforschung*, vol. 9 (1956), pp. 199-201; D. Forde, "Diedrich Westermann, 24 June 1875—31 May 1956," *Africa*, vol 26 (1956), pp. 329-331; R. Hartmann, "Nachruf auf Diedruch Westermann," *Jahrbuch der Deutschen Akademie der Wissenschaften zu Berlin* (1956), pp. 530-531; U. Hintze, "Diedrich Westermann: Schriftenverzeichnis und einige biographische Daten," *Mitteilungen des Instituts für Orientforschung*, vol. 5 (1957), pp. 45-83; H. Höftmann, "Westermanns sprachwissenschaftliches Werk: eine kritische Analyse," *Wissenschaftliche Zeitschrift der Humboldt-Universität zu Berlin*, vol. 25 (1976), pp. 183-188; O. Köhler, "Professor Diedrich Westermann," *African Studies*, vol. 15 (1956), pp. 217-218; J. Lukas, "In memoriam Diedrich Westermann," *Afrika und Übersee*, vol. 41 (1957), pp. 1-2; E. Ramsauer, "Erinnerungen an Diedrich Westermann," *Jahrbuch der Norddeutschen Missionsgesellschaft, Bremen* (1975), pp. 76-82; A. Rüger, "Diedrich Westermanns Beitrag zur Geschichtsschreibung über Afrika," *Wissenschaftliche Zeitschrift der Humboldt-Universität zu Berlin*, vol. 25 (1976), pp. 197-202; W. Rusch and J. Sellnow, "Diedrich Westermann und die Ethnographie," *Wissenschaftliche Zeitschrift der Humboldt-Universität zu Berlin*, vol. 25 (1976), pp. 191-195; Hermann Jungraithmayr, "Westermann, Diedrich Hermann" in: H. Jungraithmayr and W.J.G. Möhlig (editors), *Lexikon der Afrikanistik* (Berlin: 1983), pp. 265-268.

Hermann Jungraithmayr
[Translation from German: CW]

Westermarck, Edvard Alexander (used "Edward Westermarck" for most English-language publications). Anthropologist, philosopher, sociologist. Born in Helsinki (Finland) 20 November 1862, died in Lappvik (Finland) 3 September 1939. Although Westermarck received his doctorate from the University of Helsinki and later taught there as well as at the Åbo Akademi (Turku, Finland), his intellectual orientation was toward Britain: the chief influences on his thought were David Hume, W. ROBERTSON SMITH, Charles Darwin and JAMES G. FRAZER; he served as the first professor of sociology at the London School of Economics; and he wrote his major works in English. The main areas of his research were the history of marriage, the civilization of Morocco and the moral ideas. His initial curiosity about the origin of sexual modesty culminated in his classic comparative study, *The History of Human Marriage*, where he argued against the prevailing view (held by JOHANN JAKOB BACHOFEN, LEWIS HENRY MORGAN, JOHN LUBBOCK and others) that early peoples were sexually promiscuous. Not content with armchair study in the British Museum, he became one of the earliest fieldworkers; and his linguistically sensitive investigations of Moroccan customs were much praised by his pupil BRONISLAW MALINOWSKI. Fascinated by the tenacity of ethical disagreement, Westermarck sought to determine whether it was caused by "defective knowledge" or had "a merely sentimental origin." In *The Origin and Development of the Moral Ideas* and again in *Ethical Relativity* he defended a subjectivist, but nevertheless non-nihilistic, conception of morality. Late in his life he engaged in a controversy with Freud over the Oedipus complex and also analyzed the retributive nature of Christian ethics. Although he left behind no formal school of disciples, Westermarck was responsible for teaching many notable British and Finnish anthropologists. His autobiography modestly depicts a bachelor who studied marriage, a proper European who studied Morocco, a relativist who studied morality, and a disbeliever who studied religion. In recent years, countering earlier attacks by critics like Émile Durkheim and W.H.R. RIVERS, there has been a revival of interest in Westermarck, attesting to the continuing importance of his work.

MAJOR WORKS: *The History of Human Marriage* (London: 1891; rev. ed. [3 vols.], London: 1921); *The Origin and Development of the Moral Ideas* [2 vols.] (London: 1906-1908); *Marriage Ceremonies in Morocco* (London: 1914); *Ritual and Belief in Morocco* [2 vols.] (London: 1926); *A Short History of Marriage* (London: 1926); *Minnen ur mitt liv* (Helsinki: 1927) [tr.: *Memories of My Life* (London: 1929)]; *Wit and Wisdom in Morocco* (London: 1930); *Ethical Relativity* (London: 1932); *Early Beliefs and Their Social Influence* (London: 1932); *Pagan Survivals in Mohammedan Civilisation* (London: 1933); *Three Essays on Sex and Marriage* (London: 1934); *The Future of Marriage in Western Civilisation* (London: 1936); *Christianity and Morals* (London: 1939).

SOURCES: Rolf Lagerborg, *Edvard Westermarck och verken från hans verkstad under hans tolv sista år* (Helsinki: 1951); Timothy Stroup, *Westermarck's Ethics* (Turku: 1982); Timothy Stroup (editor), *Edward Westermarck: Essays on His Life and Works* (Helsinki: 1982); Ronald Fletcher, "Edward Westermarck" in: Ronald Fletcher, *The Making of Sociology: a Study of Sociological Theory* (London and New York: 1971), vol. 2, pp. 84-122; J.L. Mackie, "Westermarck, Edward Alexander" in: Paul Edwards (editor), *The Encyclopedia of Philosophy* (New York: 1967), vol. 8, pp. 284-286.

Timothy Stroup

Wetherill, Alfred (Benjamin Alfred Wetherill). Rancher, archaeologist/anthropologist, photographer, trader, amateur botanist, postmaster, railroader. Born in Diamond Island (Kansas) 25 June 1861, died in Tulsa (Oklahoma) 5 January 1950. With minimal formal education, Wetherill and his brothers Richard, John and Clayton were nonetheless well versed, with a curiosity that enabled them to evaluate and analyze the prehistoric Anasazi remains found in the Four Corners region (the point where the states of Arizona, Colorado, New Mexico and Utah meet). When ranch work permitted, the brothers, with brother-in-law Charles Mason, searched for the lost cities of the Mesa Verde in southwestern Colorado. About 1886 Wetherill looked up from a canyon bottom to see an abandoned city high in the nearly sheer cliff face, the "great blue vault" hanging above him "like a mirage," the "solemn grandeur" breathtaking. Fatigue prevented him from reaching the ruin, leaving it for Richard and Charles to discover it again from the mesa top on 8 December 1888. Peering through sifting snow across the canyon abyss, Charles Mason likened it to a palace, bringing forth the name "Cliff Palace." Ranching was then neglected, but many discoveries resulted. By comparison between the structures and contents of the Four Corners ruins, the family developed the classification "Basket Makers" for the earliest peoples, "Cliff Dwellers" for the Mesa Verde occupants, and "Village Dwellers" for the community house clusters such as Chaco Canyon, becoming authorities on the ancient peoples. Criticized at times, they were defended by T. Mitchell Prudden as being "early impressed with the scientific aspects" of the great ruins, preserving them from harm though they were "ignored by the government and sorely threatened by the tourists." McNeil Camp observed that the Wetherills, "keen of intellect, received a free university education in archaeology, ethnology and kindred subjects from the world's best minds of the time." William H. Jackson, subsequently credited with making the first pictures of the major ruins, declined the honor, writing that he never even saw them until three years after the "Wetherill boys happened onto them." The Wetherills, said to have been the first to use stratigraphy in the Southwest, probably followed Al Wetherill, for in the catalog accompanying a collection made during 1888-1889 by Wetherill and others, one entry lists "6 pieces of broken pottery taken from a 1 foot thick strata of ashes, charcoal, etc., overlaid by about 8 feet of adobe or clay exposed in an arroyo." The entry precedes by two years the work of Gustaf Nordenskiöld who is said to have instructed the Wetherills in archaeology. In his old age, Wetherill found that the National Park Service-Department of the Interior publications called them "vandals" and deleted his discovery of Cliff Palace. Inquiry producing rebuff, he laboriously set about gleaning journals and diaries to substantiate his claims, but these were dismissed as irrelevant by the authorities. Wetherill's autobiography was produced posthumously.

MAJOR WORK: *The Wetherills of the Mesa Verde: Autobiography* (edited and annotated by Maurine S. Fletcher) (Rutherford, N.J.: 1977).

SOURCES: McNeil Camp, *Durango (Colorado) Herald* (31 August 1952), p. 8; Ella D. and Herbert C. Cantelow, "Biographical notes on persons in whose honor Alice Eastwood named native plants," *Leaflets of Western Botany*, vol. 8, no. 5 (1957), pp. 83-101; Frederick Hastings Chapin, "Cliff dwellings of the Mancos Cañons," *American Antiquarian and Oriental Journal*, vol. 12, no. 4 (1890), p. 195; Alice Eastwood, "Report on a collection of plants from San Juan County, Southeastern Utah," *California Academy of Sciences Proceedings*, 2nd ser., vol. 6 (1896), pp. 270-329; Jesse Walter Fewkes, "Antiquities of the Mesa Verde National Park: Cliff Palace," *Smithsonian Bureau of American Ethnology Bulletin*, no. 51 (1911), pp. 11-12; Clarence S. Jackson, *Picture Maker of the Old West: William H. Jackson* (New York: 1947); William H. Jackson, letter to Herbert Lee Cowing (n.d.); Alfred V. Kidder, *An Introduction to the Study of Southwestern Archaeology* (New Haven: 1924); Charles Christopher Mason, "The story of the discovery and early exploration of the cliff houses at the Mesa Verde," *The Denver (Colorado) Post* (1 July 1917), section 2, p. 6; Robert H. Lister, "Interpretive foreward" to: Gustaf Nordenskiöld, *The Cliff Dwellers of the Mesa Verde* (Glorietta, N.M.: 1979 [originally: Stockholm: 1893]), pp. 31-36; State Historical Society of Colorado, "Ancient Aztec relics catalogue," *The Herald* [Durango] (1889); U.S. Department of the Interior, *Mesa Verde National Park, Colorado* (Washington: 1912, 1914-1919, 1923-1942, 1945, 1948, 1951, 1952, 1953-1955, 1957-1958, 1960, 1963, 1965); Benjamin Alfred Wetherill, *The Wetherills of the Mesa Verde* (Rutherford, N.J.: 1977); *Biographical Sketches and Letters of T. Mitchell Prudden, M.D.* (New Haven: 1927).

Maurine S. Fletcher

Wheeler-Voegelin, Erminie. Ethnohistorian, anthropologist, folklorist. Born in Berkeley (California) 2 April 1903, died in Great Falls (Virginia) 10 July 1987. Wheeler-Voegelin was a pioneer in emphasizing the importance of using historical documents, along with ethnographic fieldwork and archaeological data, to reconstruct the history of societies lacking printed archives. She was the founder of the American Society for

Ethnohistory and editor of the journal *Ethnohistory* the first eleven years of the society's existence (1954-1964).

A specialist in North American Indians, Wheeler-Voegelin's research included native groups living in California and Oregon, the northern plains, Ohio Valley and the Great Lakes areas of the United States. She first followed the cultural elements distribution procedure for studying Indian society, a method advocated by ALFRED L. KROEBER, her mentor at the University of California, Berkeley. Her first major research was an analysis of mythological elements common to the Kiowa, Arapaho, Gros Ventre, Cheyenne and Blackfeet. She continued graduate study at Yale University in 1939, becoming the first woman to receive a doctoral degree in anthropology from that institution.

During the 1930s and 1940s, Wheeler-Voegelin pursued fieldwork among the Tübatulabal of California, the Shawnee, the Delaware, and the Miami in Oklahoma, the Blackfeet in Alberta, and the Ottawa and Chippewa of the Upper Peninsula of Michigan and Ontario, often in conjunction with the parallel linguistic research of her husband, C.F. VOEGELIN. Bloomington, Indiana, became a research and teaching base for the Voegelins when C.F. Voegelin joined the faculty of Indiana University in 1941. Both were members of the team coordinated by ELI LILLY, president of an Indianapolis pharmaceutical firm, to develop a new translation and interpretation of the "Walum Olam," a pictographic account of Delaware tribal history collected in the White River district of Indiana in 1822. Each received a Guggenheim Fellowship in 1947.

Wheeler-Voegelin's award was granted to enable her to pursue her broad studies in the unwritten history and mythology of American Indians and Eskimos. In 1948 she became president of the American Folklore Society and for the period 1949-1951 served as executive secretary for the American Anthropological Association. She received the Chicago Folklore Society prize in 1950 and was named a Fellow of the American Association for the Advancement of Science.

An innovative change in career direction occurred in 1953 when Wheeler-Voegelin became assistant director of a new Indiana University project to investigate the Indian history of "The Old Northwest," the area of the United States northwest of the Ohio River to the Mississippi River headwaters. The conference group she organized to promote research, meeting first in 1954, marked the genesis of the present American Society for Ethnohistory. In 1956 she became Director of the Great Lakes-Ohio Valley Research Project and a full professor in the Department of History, a position she held until her retirement in 1969. In her new position, she introduced the first formal course on ethnohistory offered in any history department in the United States.

Under the direction of Wheeler-Voegelin, the research project became a training ground for anthropology students. The staff prepared thirty-four substantial reports for federal government use in litigating cases brought before the Indian Claims Commission, established in the Department of Justice in 1946. Most of the reports appeared in the multi-volume *American Indian Ethnohistoric Series*, a reference work published in 1974.

MAJOR WORKS: *Tübatulabal Ethnography* (Berkeley: 1938) (= *Anthropological Records*, vol. 2, no. 1); "The Shawnee female deity in historical perspective," *American Anthropologist*, vol. 46, no. 3 (1944), pp. 370-375; "Anthropology in American universities," *American Anthropologist*, vol. 52 (1950), pp. 350-391; *Pitt River Indians of California* (New York: 1974) (= *California Indians*, vol. 3); *Anthropological Report on the Ottawa, Chippewa, and Potawatomi Indians* (New York:

1974); *Ethnohistory of Indian Use and Occupancy of Ohio and Indiana prior to 1795* (New York: 1974) (= *Indians of Ohio and Indiana Prior to 1795*, vol. 2).

SOURCES: "Voegelin, Erminie Brooke Wheeler" in: Melville J. Herskovits (editor), *International Directory of Anthropologists* (3rd ed., Washington: 1950), p. 189; David R. Miller, *A Guide to the Ohio Valley-Great Lakes Ethnohistory Archive* (Bloomington: 1979) (= *Glenn A. Black Laboratory of Archaeological Research Reports*, no. 4); Helen Hornbeck Tanner, "Erminie Wheeler-Voegelin, founder of the American Society for Ethnohistory, 1903-1988," *Ethnohistory*, vol. 38, no. 1 (1991), pp. 58-72.

Helen Hornbeck Tanner

White, Leslie A. Cultural anthropologist. Born in Salida (Colorado) 19 January 1900, died in Lone Pine (California) 31 March 1975. White was best known as an ethnological theorist who vigorously espoused cultural evolutionism, culturology, cultural determinism and cultural materialism, contributing to the development of these fields.

White studied psychology at Columbia University (B.A., 1923; M.A., 1925) and anthropology at the University of Chicago (Ph.D., 1927). After teaching for three years at the University of Buffalo and serving as curator of anthropology at the Buffalo Museum of Science (1927-1930), he went to the University of Michigan where he taught from 1930 until his retirement in 1970.

During the late 1920s, White became interested in the work of LEWIS HENRY MORGAN, finding in Morgan's neglected evolutionism much that was still sound and illuminating. He eventually became the leading Morgan scholar in the world, editing Morgan's letters and journals and writing an introduction to the definitive edition of *Ancient Society*.

In a series of trenchant essays beginning in the late 1930s and culminating in his book *The Evolution of Culture*, White argued that the evolutionary approach was indispensable to anthropology and answered in detail the objections raised against it by members of the Boas school (see FRANZ BOAS). He also maintained that the harnessing of energy was the prime mover of cultural evolution. Largely through White's efforts, by the late 1960s, cultural evolutionism was again generally accepted in American anthropology, especially among archaeologists.

White saw in the ability to use symbols, which he considered unique to the human species, the basis of all culture. He propounded what he called culturology, the science that studies culture as a distinct class of phenomena, independent of biology and psychology, with laws of its own. His views on culturology were most fully set forth in *The Science of Culture*.

Over and above his contributions to particular theories, White was very influential in reinstilling vigorous theorizing into American ethnology, where it had been discouraged and constrained during the ascendancy of Franz Boas' historical particularism.

Though known principally as a theorist, White did extensive fieldwork as well, especially among the Keresan-speaking Pueblos of New Mexico, publishing five monographs on them.

MAJOR WORKS: *The Science of Culture* (New York: 1949); *The Evolution of Culture* (New York 1959); *Ethnological Essays* (edited by Beth Dillingham and Robert L. Carneiro) (Albuquerque: 1987); *The Pueblo of San Felipe* (Menasha, Wisc.: 1932) (= *American Anthropological Association, Memoir*, no. 38); *The Pueblo of Sia, New Mexico* (Washington: 1962) (= *Smithsonian Institution,*

Bureau of American Ethnology, Bulletin, no. 184); (editor) *Pioneers in American Anthropology: the Bandelier-Morgan Letters, 1873-1883* [2 vols.] (Albuquerque: 1940); (editor) *Lewis Henry Morgan: the Indian Journals, 1859-1862* (Ann Arbor: 1959); *The Ethnography and Ethnology of Franz Boas* (Austin: 1963) (= *Texas Memorial Museum Bulletin,* no. 6); *The Social Organization of Ethnological Theory* (Houston: 1966) (= *Rice University Studies,* vol. 52, no. 4); (with Beth Dillingham) *The Concept of Culture* (Minneapolis: 1973); *The Concept of Cultural Systems* (New York: 1975).

SOURCES: Harry Elmer Barnes, "Foreword" to: Gertrude E. Dole and Robert L. Carneiro (editors), *Essays in the Science of Culture in Honor of Leslie A. White* (New York: 1960), pp. xi-xlvi; Robert L. Carneiro, "Leslie A. White" in: Sydel Silverman (editor), *Totems and Teachers: Perspectives on the History of Anthropology* (New York: 1981), pp. 209-251, 293-297; Robert L. Carneiro, "White, Leslie Alvin" in: David L. Sills (editor), *International Encyclopedia of the Social Sciences* (New York: 1968-1979), vol. 18, pp. 803-807; Elvin Hatch, *Theories of Man and Culture* (New York: 1975), pp. 128-161; Elman R. Service, "Leslie Alvin White, 1900-1975," *American Anthropologist* (1976), vol. 78, pp. 612-617; Richard K. Beardsley, "An appraisal of Leslie A. White's scholarly influence," *American Anthropologist,* vol. 78 (1976), pp. 617-620; A.L. Kroeber, "White's view of culture," *American Anthropologist,* vol. 50 (1948), pp. 405-415; Richard A. Barrett, "The paradoxical anthropology of Leslie White," *American Anthropologist,* vol. 91 (1989), pp. 986-999.

Robert L. Carneiro

Whiting, Alfred Frank. Ethnobotanist, anthropologist, museum administrator. Born in Burlington (Vermont) 22 May 1912, died in Flagstaff (Arizona) 1 May 1978. Alfred Whiting was trained as a botanist at the University of Vermont (B.S., 1933) and the University of Michigan (M.A., 1934). He was trained in anthropology and botany at the University of Chicago (1937-1940, 1942-1944). His appointments included curator of botany at the Museum of Northern Arizona (1935-1937), assistant professor of anthropology at the University of Oregon (1944-1947), teacher at Santa Cruz Valley School (1950-1951), anthropologist with the U.S. Trust Territory of the Pacific Islands on Ponape Island (1952-1954), curator of anthropology at the museum of Dartmouth College (1955-1974) and adjunct assistant professor in Dartmouth's Department of Anthropology (1966-1974), and research ethnobotanist at the Museum of Northern Arizona (1974-1978).

In his fieldwork, Whiting's emphasis was usually ethnobotany, but he also took a broad interest in the cultures he was studying. This work began with a University of Michigan expedition to San Luis Potosí, Mexico, in 1935. Following that, he carried out a survey of the Hopi crops with Volney Jones and collected wild plants in the Hopi area while he was at the Museum of Northern Arizona. During 1940-1941 he investigated the ethnobiology of the Havasupai. Periodically throughout the remainder of his career, Whiting returned to the Southwest to continue his studies among several tribes, including the Apache and Papago, and to collect specimens for his museum.

Whiting's work on Ponape was different in that it focused primarily on social relations and demography. He also became involved in archaeological work when, in 1960, he provided information about the burial ground Nan Matol for use by Saul Riesenberg and Clifford Evans.

MAJOR WORKS: *Ethnobotany of the Hopi* (Flagstaff: 1939) (= *Museum of Northern Arizona Bulletin,* no. 15); "The origin of corn: an evaluation of fact and theory," *American Anthropologist,* vol. 46 (1944), pp. 500-515; "The present status of ethnobotany in the Southwest," *Economic Botany,* vol. 20 (1966), pp. 316-325; "Leaves from a Hopi doctor's casebook," *Bulletin of the New York Academy of Medicine,* vol. 47 (1971), pp. 125-146.

SOURCES: Katharine Bartlett, "Alfred F. Whiting," *Journal of Ethnobiology*, vol. 1 (1981), pp. 1-5; P. David Seaman, "A. F. Whiting Indian Archives contents summary" [copy available at the Smithsonian Institution National Anthropological Archives]; Whiting papers in the Smithsonian Institution National Anthropological Archives.

James R. Glenn

Whiting, John W.M. Anthropologist. Born in Chilmark, Martha's Vineyard (Massachusetts) 12 June 1908. Whiting's career began with an ethnographic report on the Kwoma, a Sepik River tribe in New Guinea. Parts of the ethnography concentrated on a theoretical problem: how does the culture-less infant learn to be a member of its society? This work was predictive of Whiting's future: his writings have been dominated by theoretical interest, and socialization of the young was one of the problems recurrently addressed.

Most characteristic of his publications, from 1953 on, has been "holocultural" research based on the myriad ethnographies that constitute a permanent reservoir of data for anthropologists and other social scientists. For a typical holocultural study, a worldwide sample of societies are chosen on which the ethnographies contain adequate information on the cultural feature relevant to the topics of study. Each society is classified or rated on the pertinent features, and the correlations among the various features are then assessed. Whiting first applied this method to testing whether a people's unrealistic responses to illness are correlated with crucial aspects of how they were treated in childhood. The former variables were taken to index adult personality traits; the latter variables, factors of experience that shape personality. Thus the holocultural study provided a tentative test of the universality of hypotheses derived from psychoanalytic and psychological theories of development and learning. Whiting found the same general kind of significance in later holocultural study of conscience and other mechanisms of self-control; of sexual identity and its relation to initiation ceremonies and *couvade*; of aloofness versus intimacy of marital pairs; and of adolescent sexual behavior. These holocultural studies also serve to place problems of our society in a worldwide perspective and to improve understanding of those problems' sources and possible solutions.

Both theoretical and practical interests have motivated Whiting's extension of his research to studies of individual behavior within specific cultural settings, partly on the topics of his earlier holocultural studies.

His research and writing have been conducted in the gregarious style that is natural to his personality, so that he has had many collaborators, including his students and his wife, anthropologist Beatrice B. Whiting. Collaboration with him has been an important influence on the later work of former students and other associates, as suggested by the papers in the Festschrift published in 1973 as number 4 of the first volume of *Ethos*.

From 1949 on, Whiting has been on the faculty of Harvard University; from 1966 to 1973, he also served as Director of the Child Development Research Unit of the University of Nairobi. His formative years from 1931 to 1947 (with time out for military service) as undergraduate, graduate student and researcher at the Institute of Human Relations, had been spent at Yale University and had been followed by two years of research in developmental psychology at the Iowa Child Welfare Research Station. He has been influenced by a variety of intellectual forebears, often thought to offer incompatible approaches, and with great originality has brought them together in his research on personal and cultural development, achieving a remarkable synthesis of the best of what they each had to offer.

MAJOR WORKS: *Becoming a Kwoma* (New Haven: 1941); (with Irvin L. Child) *Child Training and Personality: a Cross-Cultural Study* (New Haven: 1953); "Effects of climate on certain cultural practices" in: Ward H. Goodenough (editor), *Explorations in Cultural Anthropology* (New York: 1964), pp. 511-544; (with Eleanor Hollenberg Chasdi, Helen Faigin Antonovsky, and Barbara Chartier Ayres) "The learning of values" in: Evon Z. Vogt and Ethel M. Albert (editors), *People of Rimrock: a Study of Values in Five Cultures* (Cambridge, Mass.: 1966), pp. 83-125; (with Beatrice B. Whiting) "Aloofness and intimacy of husbands and wives: a cross-cultural study," *Ethos*, vol. 3 (1975), pp. 183-207; "A model for psycho-cultural research" [Distinguished Lecturer Address presented at the 1973 Annual Meeting of the American Anthropological Association, New Orleans] in: P. Herbert Leiderman, Steven R. Tulkin and Anne Rosenfeld (editors), *Culture and Infancy* (New York: 1977), pp. 29-48; "Environmental constraints on infant care practices" in: Ruth H. Munroe, Robert L. Munroe and Beatrice B. Whiting (editors), *Handbook of Cross-Cultural Human Development* (New York: 1981), pp. 155-179; (with Victoria K. Burbank and Mitchell S. Ratner) "The duration of maidenhood across cultures" in: Jane B. Lancaster and Beatrix A. Hamburg (editors), *School Age Pregnancies and Parenthood* (New York: 1986), pp. 273-302; *The Career of an Anthropologist* (Eleanor H. Chasdi, editor) (forthcoming).

SOURCES: Irvin L. Child, "Whiting, John W.M." in: David L. Sills (editor), *International Encyclopedia of the Social Sciences* (New York: 1968-1979), vol. 18, pp. 807-809; Marvin Harris, *The Rise of Anthropological Theory* (New York: 1968), pp. 449-463; George D. Spindler, *The Making of Psychological Anthropology* (Berkeley: 1978); Eleanor H. Chasdi, "Biographical introduction" to: Eleanor H. Chasdi (editor), *The Career of an Anthropologist* (forthcoming).

Irvin L. Child

Whorf, Benjamin Lee. Chemical engineer, linguist, anthropologist. Born in Winthrop (Massachusetts) 24 April 1897, died in Wethersfield (Connecticut) 26 July 1941. Trained in chemical engineering at the Massachusetts Institute of Technology, Whorf worked professionally as a fire-prevention specialist for the Hartford Fire Insurance Company throughout his life. Whorf's linguistic work was avocational.

Concerned with the conflict between science and religion, Whorf began to study Hebrew in order to do a careful linguistic analysis of the Old Testament. Later, as his interest in languages deepened, he turned his attention to American Indian languages which led to the rekindling of a childhood interest in Mexican antiquities. Whorf eventually published papers on Mesoamerican history, a grammatical sketch of Milpa Alta Aztec (Nahuatl), and a series of studies of Mayan hieroglyphics that attempted to revive the thesis that Mayan writing was in part phonologically based. All this work is still of contemporary relevance including the Mayan thesis, which was spurned by professionals at the time but is now widely accepted.

Beginning in 1930 Whorf had sustained contact with EDWARD SAPIR at Yale University. Under Sapir's guidance Whorf's linguistic work became more professional and he undertook a detailed study of Hopi, a language genetically related to Aztec. He subsequently made a number of original contributions to general linguistics including influential characterizations of grammatical categories in terms of formal qualities (e.g., "overt" versus "covert") and substantive type (e.g., "status" in Hopi). (Much of this work shows the influence of LEONARD BLOOMFIELD.) The Hopi work led to an important descriptive sketch of that language and to an improved characterization of the Uto-Aztecan group of languages. However, Whorf is best known for his use of Hopi to explore certain of Sapir's suggestions about the influence of language diversity on thought—what is often termed the Sapir-Whorf hypothesis or the linguistic relativity principle.

In Whorf's view, each language refers to an infinite variety of experiences with a finite array of formal categories (both lexical and grammatical) by grouping experiences together as analogically "the same" for the purposes of speech. The categories in a language also interrelate in a coherent way, reinforcing and complementing one another, so as to constitute an overall interpretation of experience. These linguistic classifications vary considerably across languages not only in the basic distinctions they recognize but also in the assemblage of these categories into a coherent system of reference. Thus the system of categories each language provides to its speakers is not a common, universal system but a particular "fashion of speaking."

Whorf argued that these linguistic categories influence habitual thought by serving as a guide to the interpretation of experience. Speakers tend to assume that the categories and distinctions of their language are entirely natural and given by external reality and thus can be used as a guide to it. When speakers attempt to interpret an experience in terms of a category available in their language, they unwittingly involve other language-specific meanings implicit in that particular category and in the overall configuration of categories in which it is embedded. In Whorf's view, language does not blind speakers to some obvious reality but rather suggests associations among elements of experience which are not necessarily entailed by those elements alone. Because language is such a pervasive and transparent aspect of behavior, speakers do not understand that the associations they "see" are from language but rather assume that they are "in" the external situation and patently obvious to all. In the absence of another language (natural or artificial) with which to talk about experience, speakers will not be able to recognize the conventional nature of their linguistically based understandings. Whorf argues that, by influencing everyday habitual thought, language can come to influence cultural institutions generally including philosophical and scientific activity.

Although Whorf's thesis has had wide impact on thinking in the humanities and social sciences, it has not been extensively investigated empirically. Existing empirical research has been of three types: attacks on his Hopi analyses, tests of his claims using lexical categories (especially words for colors) and, finally, tests of his claims using grammatical categories. The results of such research remain controversial because of methodological weaknesses in the studies and because of their dubious applicability to Whorf's actual claims. In large part, therefore, acceptance or rejection of his proposals remains more a matter of personal and professional outlook than solid evidence. Many philosophers, psychologists and linguists in the generative tradition tend to be hostile to his views. Scholars in literary studies, comparative linguistics, folklore and anthropology tend to be more receptive.

In recent years with the advance of symbolic and critical approaches in the human disciplines there has been a substantial renewal of interest in Whorf's work. There have also been important attempts to broaden the relativity thesis by joining it with research in the British (e.g., Basil Bernstein, M.A.K. Halliday), Soviet (e.g., L.S. Vygotskiĭ, M.M. Bakhtin) and American (e.g., Dell Hymes, Paul Friedrich, Michael Silverstein) traditions on the diverse functions of language both within and across cultures. This work suggests that the influence of linguistic structure on thought is mediated by (and therefore contingent on) particular cultural uses of language.

MAJOR WORKS: *Language, Thought, and Reality: Selected Writings of Benjamin Lee Whorf* (edited by John Carroll) (Cambridge, Mass.: 1956) [contains a bibliography of Whorf's writings]; "The Milpa Alta dialect of Aztec, with notes on the Classical and the Tepoztlan dialects" in: Harry Hoijer (editor), *Linguistic Structures of Native America* (New York: 1946), pp. 367-397; "The Hopi language, Toreva dialect" in: Harry Hoijer (editor), *Linguistic Structures of Native America* (New York: 1946), pp. 158-183. Unpublished manuscript materials are available in the Yale, Chicago, and Harvard University libraries.

SOURCES: Harry Hoijer (editor), *Language in Culture* (Chicago: 1954); Peter Rollins, *Benjamin Lee Whorf: Transcendental Linguist* [unpublished Ph.D. dissertation, Harvard University; vol. 3 reprints some of Whorf's unpublished materials] (Cambridge, Mass.: 1972); Peter Rollins, *Benjamin Lee Whorf: Lost Generation Theories of Mind, Language, and Religion* (Ann Arbor: 1980) [reproduces main arguments of the preceding]; Julia Penn, *Linguistic Relativity versus Innate Ideas: the Origins of the Sapir-Whorf Hypothesis in German Thought* (The Hague: 1972); Helmut Gipper, *Gibt es ein sprachliches Relativitätsprinzip?: Untersuchungen zur Sapir-Whorf-Hypothese* (Frankfurt am Main: 1972) [partly reproduced in English as "Is there a linguistic relativity principle?" in: Rik Pinxton (editor), *Universalism versus Relativism in Language and Thought* (The Hague: 1977), pp. 217-228)]; Ekkehart Malotki, *Hopi Time: a Linguistic Analysis of the Temporal Concepts in the Hopi Language* (Berlin: 1983); Paul Friedrich, *The Language Parallax: Linguistic Relativism and Poetic Indeterminacy* (Austin: 1986); John Lucy, *Grammatical Categories and Cognitive Processes* [2 vols.] (Cambridge: in press); John Carroll, "Introduction" in: John Carroll (editor), *Language, Thought, and Reality: Selected Writings of Benjamin Lee Whorf* (Cambridge, Mass.: 1956), pp. 1-34; Dell Hymes, "Two types of linguistic relativity" in: William Bright (editor), *Sociolinguistics, Proceedings of the UCLA Sociolinguistics Conference (1964)* (The Hague: 1966), pp. 114-165; Michael Silverstein, "Language structure and linguistic ideology" in: P. Clyne, W. Hanks, and C. Hofbauer (editors), *The Elements: a Parasession on Linguistic Units and Levels* (Chicago: 1979), pp. 193-247; John Lucy, "Whorf's view of the linguistic mediation of thought" in: Elizabeth Mertz and Richard Parmentier (editors), *Semiotic Mediation: Sociocultural and Psychological Perspectives* (New York: 1985), pp. 73-97.

John A. Lucy

Wijesekera, Nandadeva. Anthropologist, archaeologist, art historian, philologist, public servant. Born in Kalutara District, Western Province (Sri Lanka) 11 December 1908, now living in Colombo (Sri Lanka). Although Wijesekera is a scholar of considerable versatility, his intellectual focus has been in the field of anthropology. His early training as an Indo-Aryanist at Cambridge University, where he won the Tripos in Anthropology and Archaeology and later obtained his M.A., laid the foundation for a lifelong commitment to anthropology.

Wijesekera pioneered anthropological research in Sri Lanka with a comprehensive ethnological work, *People of Ceylon.* His book attracted considerable attention and stimulated some controversy because Wijesekera challenged the accepted unilinear interpretations of the origins of the Sinhalese, the major community in Sri Lanka, which laid claims to a strictly Indo-Aryan origin. Wijesekera brought to light the complexity of the forces that led to the establishment of the early settlements and the final evolution of the ethnological structure of Sri Lanka as it now exists. His work, *Veddas in Transition,* was in many ways a sequel to *The People of Ceylon.* It was an in-depth study of a group of people who had retained their identity and traditional way of life until modern times but who found it increasingly difficult to do so. Wijesekera brought studies of the Vedda from the domain of the romantic to that of objective social-science scholarship. Wijesekera's work as an art historian, which culminated in a study that won the Ph.D. in Calcutta, also contained anthropological insights. The burdens of public service, including an ambassadorship to Burma, were no doubt a distraction.

Late in his active career he essayed into the field of demonology and magic, Sri Lanka providing the ideal setting for such studies.

MAJOR WORKS: *People of Ceylon* (Colombo: 1949); *Early Sinhalese Painting* (Maharagama, Ceylon: 1959) [based on Calcutta University thesis]; *Early Sinhalese Sculpture* (Colombo: 1962); *Veddas in Transition* (Colombo: 1964); *Sir D.B. Jayatilake: a Biography and Assessment of the Man and His Work* (Colombo: 1973); *Selected Writings* (Colombo: 1983); *Heritage of Sri Lanka* (Colombo: 1984); *Anthropological Gleanings from Sinhala Literature* (Colombo: 1984); *Deities and Demons: Magic and Masks* [2 parts] ([Colombo]: 1987-1988).

SOURCES: *The Ceylon Civil List* (Colombo: 1959), p. 129; Wimal G. Balagalle, "Doctor Nandadeva Wijesekera" (Colombo: 1985) [transcript of talk given on the occasion of the conferment of the Hon. D.Litt. degree by Sri Jayawardena University].

Swarna Wickremeratne

Wilken, G.A. (George Alexander). Ethnologist, colonial administrator. Born in Menado (Dutch East Indies, now Indonesia) 13 March 1847, died in Leiden (Netherlands) 1 July 1891. Wilken was the first Dutch ethnologist in the 19th century to be widely recognized outside his own country. He worked mainly with Indonesian material, which he interpreted in an evolutionary fashion.

Wilken was the son of a Protestant missionary who worked in the Minahasa (northern Sulawesi). He spent his childhood with his parents, but in 1859 he was sent to Holland for further education. In 1868 he passed the colonial civil service examination and for the next twelve years he worked in the Dutch East Indies as an administrator on the island Buru and in parts of northern Sulawesi and western Sumatra. During these years he published a short ethnography of Buru and articles on land tenure in the Minahasa.

When on leave in Holland he devoted himself to linguistic studies at Leiden University and published articles on primitive marriage and the origins of family life, on Indonesian kinship and on customary law concerning marriage and inheritance in Indonesia. He applied current evolutionary notions to Indonesian data, thus furnishing disparate ethnographic facts from many parts of the archipelago with a unified framework, however speculative this may appear from a late-20th-century vantage point. E.B. TYLOR's influence is especially apparent in Wilken's work on animism in Indonesia.

The high professional quality of his work was recognized at home, where he received a doctorate *honoris causa* from Leiden University in 1884 and was appointed as professor of ethnology at the same university in 1885. He also drew attention from abroad when his treatise on matriarchy among the ancient Arabs involved him in a polemic with W. ROBERTSON SMITH, while his ideas on totemism earned him the approval of Tylor.

In his inaugural lecture he demonstrated the usefulness of ethnology for the comparative study of jurisprudence. He also forcefully drew attention to the importance of customary law and religion (*adat*) for a colonial administration based on trust and understanding. After a few hectic years in which Wilken wrote much on various aspects of culture and society in Indonesia, he died in 1891.

MAJOR WORKS: "Bijdrage tot de kennis der Alfoeren van het eiland Boeroe," *Verhandelingen van het Bataviaasch Genootschap van Kunsten en Wetenschappen*, vol. 38 (1875), pp. 1-57; "Over de primitieve vormen van het huwelijk en den oorsprong van het gezin," *De Indische Gids*, vol. 2, no. 2 (1880), pp. 601-665; pp. 1177-1206; vol. 3, no. 2 (1881), pp. 232-289; "Over de verwantschap en het huwelijks- en erfrecht bij de volken van het Maleische ras," *De Indische Gids*, vol. 5, no. 1 (1883), pp. 656-765; "Het matriarchaat bij de oude Arabieren," *De Indische Gids*, vol. 6, no. 1 (1884), pp. 89-133; "Het animisme bij de volken van den Indischen Archipel," *De Indische Gids*, vol. 6, no. 1 (1884), pp. 925-1001; vol. 6, no. 2 (1884), pp. 19-101; vol. 7, no. 1 (1885), pp. 13-59 and 191-243; "Plechtigheden en gebruiken bij verlovingen en huwelijken bij de volken van den Indischen Archipel," *Bijdragen van het Koninklijk Instituut voor de Taal-, Land- en Volkenkunde van Nederlandsch Indie*, 5e reeks, vol. 1 (1885), pp. 140-220; and vol. 4 (1889), pp. 380-463; "Het shamanisme bij de volken van den Indischen Archipel," *Bijdragen van het Koninklijk Instituut voor de Taal-, Land-, en Volkenkunde van Nederlandsch Indie*, 5e reeks, vol. 2 (1887), pp. 427-497; "De couvade bij de volken van den Indischen Archipel," *Bijdragen van het Koninklijk Instituut voor de Taal-, Land- en Volkenkunde van Nederlandsch Indie*, 5e reeks, vol. 4 (1889), pp. 250-266; "Huwelijken tusschen bloedverwanten," *De Gids*, vol. 54, no. 2 (1890), pp. 478-521; "Eene nieuwe theorie over den oorsprong der offers," *De Gids*, vol. 55, no. 3 (1891), pp. 535-572 [all these articles are reprinted in: F.D.E. van Ossenbruggen (editor), *De verspreide geschriften van Prof. Dr. G.A. Wilken* [4 vols.] (The Hague: 1912)].

SOURCES: T.H. der Kinderen, "Levensbericht van Dr. G.A. Wilken," *Bijdragen van het Koninklijk Instituut voor de Taal-, Land- en Volkenkunde van Nederlansch Indie*, 5e reeks, vol. 7 (1892), pp. 139-156; H.H. Juynboll, "Wilken (George Alexander)" in: P.C. Molhuysen and P.J. Blok (editors), *Nieuw Nederlandsch Biografisch Woordenboek* (Leiden: 1914), vol. 3, p. 1425; R.M. Koentjaraningrat, *Anthropology in Indonesia* (The Hague: 1975), pp. 28-41.

S.R. Jaarsma and J.J. de Wolf

Wilkes, Charles. U.S. naval officer, explorer. Born in New York (New York) 3 April 1798, died in Washington (D.C.) 8 February 1877. Wilkes was commander of the first (1838-1842) U.S. naval exploring expedition to Antarctica, the South Seas and the Pacific—officially known as the U.S. South Seas Exploring Expedition. The idea of such an expedition had been debated in Congress for many years. Its major objective was to aid navigation and commerce by performing marine surveys and other studies. On the recommendation of scientific advisors, numerous scientific projects were added to the expedition's already ambitious mission. Nine civilian scientists and artists were selected to accompany the expedition. Among these were James D. Dana, HORATIO HALE, Titian Peale and Charles Pickering. Wilkes's monumental five-volume account, published in 1845, contains an abundance of ethnographic data on the peoples encountered during four years of Pacific Basin exploration. Official scientific reports were also written by Hale and other "scientifics." Hale, who accompanied the expedition as philologist, described the migration of Pacific peoples on the basis of linguistic evidence in his *Ethnography and Philology*. Some 2,500 ethnographic pieces were gathered by Wilkes, Hale, Pickering and other "Ex.Ex." (Exploring Expedition) personnel. Numerous Polynesian and Pacific Northwest Coast Indian artifacts were assembled—the collection of Fiji artifacts is one of the most important of its kind. Many additional objects were acquired privately as "curiosities" by scientifics and seamen alike. In 1985 some 1,600 Wilkes Expedition cultural artifacts remained in collections of the Smithsonian Institution. The expedition, Wilkes, and several of the scientifics have been subjects of many historical or biographical studies. A book-length bibliography of Wilkes Expedition official publications was prepared by Daniel C. Haskell in 1942.

MAJOR WORKS: *Narrative of the United States Exploring Expedition During the Years 1838, 1839, 1840, 1841, 1842* [5 vols. and atlas] (Philadelphia: 1845); *Autobiography of Rear Admiral Charles Wilkes, U.S. Navy 1798-1877* (edited by William James Morgan [et al.]) (Washington: 1978).

SOURCES: Herman J. Viola and Carolyn Margolis (editors), *Magnificent Voyagers: the U.S. Exploring Expedition, 1838-1842* (Washington: 1985); Horatio Emmons Hale, *Ethnography and Philology* (Philadelphia: 1846); Daniel Carl Haskell, *The United States Exploring Expedition, 1838-1842, and its Publications* (New York: 1942); Daniel Henderson, *The Hidden Coasts: a Biography of Admiral Charles Wilkes* (New York: 1953); David B. Tyler, *The Wilkes Expedition: the First United States Exploring Expedition (1838-1842)* (Philadelphia: 1968); Harley Harris Bartlett, "The reports of the Wilkes Expedition, and the work of the specialists in science," *Proceedings of the American Philosophical Society*, vol. 82, no. 5 (1940), pp. 601-705; "Wilkes, Charles" in: *National Cyclopaedia of American Biography*, vol. 2 (New York: 1921), pp. 105-106.

Lee S. Dutton

Willems, Emílio. Anthropologist, sociologist. Born in Cologne (Germany) 18 August 1905. Willems received a Certificate in Economics in 1928 and a Ph.D. in social sciences in 1931 from the University of Berlin. Because of economic and political conditions in Germany at that time, Willems emigrated to Brazil in 1931. He taught Latin, French and English in secondary schools in the states of Santa Catarina, Paraná and São Paulo. With a *livre-docente* in 1937, he became Assistant Professor of Educational Sociology at the Federal University of São Paulo (1937-1941) then Professor of Anthropology at that university (1941-1949) and also at the Escola Livre de Sociologia e Política (Free School of Sociology and Political Science) of São Paulo (1941-1949). With Romano Barreto in 1939 he founded, and edited for many years, the pioneer journal, *Sociologia.* He was Professor of Anthropology, Vanderbilt University (1941-1974).

He has also been: Visiting Professor of Anthropology, Michigan State University (1952); University of Michigan (1952-1953); University of Cologne, Germany (1956, 1962, 1967); University of Chile (1959); Federal University of São Paulo (1960); and National University of Colombia (1962-1963).

Grants and fellowships received have included: Guggenheim Foundation (1950); UNESCO (1952); Social Science Research Council (1954); Rockefeller Foundation (1959-1960); Fulbright Commission (1950, 1960); Ford Foundation (1962-1963); National Science Foundation (1967); Latin American Center, Vanderbilt University (1970-1971).

Soon after arriving in Brazil in 1931 Willems became particularly interested in the acculturation of German and, later, Japanese immigrants, as well as in other aspects of social and cultural change. Influenced by ROBERT REDFIELD and JULIAN H. STEWARD, he carried out community studies in the state of São Paulo. After being invited to join the Institute of Brazilian Studies at Vanderbilt in 1949, he made periodic trips abroad to carry on research, including a follow-up study of acculturation among German immigrants, southern Brazil (1952); studies of the structure of the Portuguese family, Portugal (1954); of the development of Protestantism, Brazil, Chile (1959-1960); and of cultural change, San Andrés, Colombia (1962-1963). In 1970-1971 he traveled briefly in Brazil, Argentina, Chile, Peru, Ecuador and Colombia, gathering data on urban development with special attention to the emergence and growth of "shanty towns."

His extensive publications (in English, Portuguese, German, Spanish and French) evidence an increasingly broad range of research interests that have included, in addition to

761

those mentioned above, the general characteristics of Latin American culture; feudal remnants in its bureaucratic portion; social and cultural continuity and change, especially on Latin American frontiers; Latin American social stratification; social differentiation in colonial Brazil; the rise of a rural middle class in Brazilian frontier society; the relation of urban underclasses to acculturation in Latin America; minority sub-cultures in present-day Brazil; racial attitudes in Brazil; the family in Brazil and Portugal; the relation of Protestantism to class structure in Chile and to cultural change in Brazil and Chile; religious mass movements and cultural change in Brazil; authority validation in the Pentecostal sects of Brazil and Chile; the physical anthropology of Brazil and Mexico; change in social structure and function among the rural peoples of five European countries; economic organization; primitive law; education; recreation and Prussian militarism.

MAJOR WORKS: *A aculturação dos alemães no Brasil* (São Paulo: 1946); *Aspectos da aculturação dos japoneses no Estado de São Paulo* (São Paulo: 1948); *Cunha, tradição e transição em uma cultura rural do Brasil* (São Paulo: 1948); *A família portuguesa comtemporânea* (São Paulo: 1955); *Followers of the Faith: Culture Change and the Rise of Protestantism in Brazil and Chile* (Nashville, Tenn.: 1967); *Latin American Culture: an Anthropological Synthesis* (New York: 1975); *A Way of Life and Death* (Nashville, Tenn.: 1986); "Race attitudes in Brazil," *American Journal of Sociology*, vol. 54 (1949), pp. 402-408; "Acculturative aspects of the Feast of the Holy Ghost in Brazil," *American Anthropologist*, n.s., vol. 51 (1949), pp. 400-405; "San Andrés: continuity and change in the culture of a Caribbean island," *Völkerkundliche Abhandlungen*, vol. 1 (1964), pp. 315-328; "Peasantry and city: cultural persistence and change in historical perspective: a European case," *American Anthropologist*, vol. 72 (1970), pp. 528-544; "Barackensiedlungen und Urbanisierung in Lateinamerika," *Kölner Zeitschrift für Soziologie und Sozialpsychologie*, vol. 23 (1971), pp. 727-744; "Die Barackensiedlungen Lateinamerikas als städtische 'Frontier'," *Kölner Zeitschrift für Soziologie und Sozialpsychologie*, vol. 32 (1980), pp. 281-285.

SOURCE: Emílio Willems, "Dezoito anos no Brasil: resumo de atividades didáticas e científicas" in: Mariza Corrêa (organizer), *História da antropologia no Brasil (1930-1960): testemunhos* (Campinas and São Paulo: 1987), vol. 1, pp. 117-127.

Donald Pierson

Willey, *Gordon Randolph*. Archaeologist. Born in Chariton (Iowa) 7 March 1913. Willey's bachelor's and master's degrees were from the University of Arizona (1935, 1936) and his Ph.D. from Columbia University (1942). He was an instructor at the Department of Anthropology, Columbia University (1942-1943), and spent several years as Senior Anthropologist at the Bureau of American Ethnology (1943-1950). He came to Harvard University in 1950 as the Bowditch Professor of Mexican and Central American Archaeology, a position he held until 1983 when he became Senior Professor in Anthropology. He retired in 1987 as Bowditch Professor Emeritus.

Willey has done important archaeological work in North, Middle and South America. His *Archaeology of the Florida Gulf Coast* established the basic space-time structure of this region of the United States. His *Primitive Settlement Patterns in the Belize Valley* marked the beginning of settlement-pattern investigation in the Maya Lowlands. His *Prehistoric Settlement Patterns in the Virú Valley, Peru* was arguably the first major settlement pattern survey in New World archaeology and has formed the basis for many later studies.

His work has always had a strong theoretical component. He has made a particularly influential contribution to the study of ancient settlement patterns. He has been concerned with hemisphere-wide archaeological synthesis, as in *Introduction to American Archaeology* and other works. In books like *Method and Theory in American Archaeology*, he wrote at length on the question of theory in archaeology.

In recent years he has become more interested in the history of American archaeology (*A History of American Archaeology, Portraits of American Archaeologists*).

MAJOR WORKS: *Excavations in the Chancay Valley, Peru* (New York: 1943) (= *Columbia Studies in Archaeology and Ethnology*, vol. 1); *Archeology of the Florida Gulf Coast* (Washington: 1949) (= *Smithsonian Miscellaneous Collections*, vol. 113); *Prehistoric Settlement Patterns in the Virú Valley, Peru* (Washington: 1953) (= *Bureau of American Ethnology Bulletin*, no. 155); (with J.M. Corbett) *Early Ancon and Early Supe Culture: Chavín Horizon Sites of the Central Peruvian Coast* (New York: 1954) (= *Columbia Studies in Archaeology and Ethnology*, vol. 3); (with C.R. McGimsey) *The Monagrillo Culture of Panama* (Cambridge, Mass.: 1954) (= *Peabody Museum Papers in Archaeology and Ethnology*, vol. 49, no. 2); (with Philip Phillips) *Method and Theory in American Archeology* (Chicago: 1958); (co-edited with R.J. Braidwood) *Courses toward Urban Life: Archaeological Considerations of Some Cultural Alternates* (New York: 1962) (= *Viking Fund Publications in Anthropology*, no. 32); *An Introduction to American Archaeology* [2 vols.] (Englewood Cliffs, N.J.: 1966-1971); (with J.A. Sabloff) *A History of American Archaeology* (London and New York: 1974); (editor) *Archaeological Researches in Retrospect* (Cambridge, Mass.: 1974); *Lowland Maya Settlement Patterns: a Summary Review* (Albuquerque: 1981); *Portraits of American Archaeologists* (Albuquerque: 1989).

SOURCES: Richard M. Leventhal and Alan L. Kolata (editors), *Civilization in the Ancient Americas: Essays in Honor of Gordon R. Willey* (Cambridge, Mass.: 1983); Evon Z. Vogt and Richard M. Leventhal (editors), *Prehistoric Settlement Patterns: Essays in Honor of Gordon R. Willey* (Albuquerque and Cambridge, Mass.: 1983) [contains bibliography].

Wissler, Clark. Anthropologist, ethnographer, museum curator, teacher. Born in Wayne County (Indiana) 18 September 1870, died in New York (New York) 25 August 1947. Wissler was born on a farm near Cambridge City and christened Clarkson Davis Wissler. He received his A.B. and A.M. in psychology from Indiana University in 1897 and 1899, respectively. His graduate studies at Columbia University were under the psychologist James McKeen Cattell. He received his Ph.D. in psychology there in 1901. His interest in anthropology stemmed from his rural boyhood when a neighbor interested him in Indian life and he tramped the fields searching for arrowheads, from William L. Bryan, a professor at Indiana University, who had studied under WILHELM WUNDT in Germany, and from Cattell. In Wissler's last year of graduate work, he took three courses in anthropology, one taught jointly by FRANZ BOAS and Livingston Farrand; the other two, by Boas and Farrand, respectively. Anthropology was part of the Psychology Department at Columbia until 1902 when it became a separate department. By 1902 Wissler was pursuing an anthropological career at the American Museum of Natural History where he was first an assistant to Boas, the Assistant Curator, and eventually Curator and Chair of the Department of Anthropology. During this time he carried out and directed extensive fieldwork among the Plains Indians of North America, in particular coming to know the Blackfeet well.

Wissler's theoretical orientation was nomothetic, that is, he was looking for general statements and scientific laws. He was the first anthropologist after E.B. TYLOR and the first American anthropologist to define culture, pointing out several of its characteristics that are today generally accepted. He was the first anthropologist to perceive the normative aspect of culture, to define it as learned behavior, and to describe it as a complex of ideas. His best known theoretical contributions are the concepts of culture area, age area, culture pattern and universal pattern of culture. The culture area concept is regarded as the most important. The concepts of the culture area and the universal culture pattern established a theoretical basis for cross-cultural comparison and the building of theories. In the early decades of the 20th century, these contributions brought anthropology beyond 19th-century evolutionary theories and away from the particularistic Boasian style of anthropology. The universal pattern of culture still merits attention in any consideration of the relationship of biology, psychology and culture.

Wissler held the following positions: teacher at Hagerstown High School in Indiana (1887-1892) and principal at that same institution (1892-1893); Instructor in Psychology and Education at Ohio State University (1897-1899); Instructor in Pedagogy at New York University (1901-1902); Assistant at Columbia University (1903-1905); Lecturer at Columbia (1905-1909); Assistant to Boas, Assistant Curator to Curator at American Museum of Natural History (1902-1942); Head, Department of Anthropology (1905-1942); and Professor of Anthropology at Yale University (1924-1940).

MAJOR WORKS: "Material culture of the Blackfoot Indians," *Anthropological Papers of the American Museum of Natural History*, vol. 5 (1910), pp. 1-175; "The Social life of the Blackfoot Indians," *Anthropological Papers of the American Museum of Natural History*, vol. 7 (1911), pp. 1-64; "Ceremonial bundles of the Blackfoot Indians," *Anthropological Papers of the American Museum of Natural History*, vol. 7 (1912), pp. 65-289; "Societies and dance associations of the Blackfoot Indians," *Anthropological Papers of the American Museum of Natural History*, vol. 11 (1913), pp. 359-460; "General discussion of shamanistic and dancing societies," *Anthropological Papers of the American Museum of Natural History*, vol. 11 (1916), pp. 853-876; "The sun dance of the Blackfoot Indians," *Anthropological Papers of the American Museum of Natural History*, vol. 16 (1918), pp. 223-270; *The American Indian* (New York: 1917); *Man and Culture* (New York: 1923); *The Relation of Nature to Man in Aboriginal America* (New York: 1926); "The contribution of James McKeen Cattell to American anthropology," *Science*, vol. 99 (1944), pp. 232-233.

SOURCES: D.R. Barton. "Biographer of the Indian: a biographical sketch of Clark Wissler, 1870-1947," *Natural History*, vol. 45, no. 4 (1940), pp. 246-249, 253-254; George F. Carter, "Clark Wissler, 1870-1947," *Annals of the Association of American Geographers*, vol. 38 (1948), pp. 145-146; Stanley A. Freed and Ruth S. Freed, "Clark Wissler and the development of anthropology in the United States," *American Anthropologist*, vol. 85 (1983), pp. 800-825; A.L. Kroeber, "The culture-area and age-area concepts of Clark Wissler" in: Stuart A. Rice (editor), *Methods in Social Science: a Case Book* (Chicago: 1931), pp. 248-265; A.L. Kroeber, "In memory of Clark Wissler" in: *Memorial Service for Dr. Clark Wissler* [manuscript, 1948; American Museum of Natural History, Dept. of Anthropology Archives], pp. 1-4 (appended); Robert H. Lowie. "Supplementary facts about Clark Wissler," *American Anthropologist*, vol. 51 (1949), pp. 527-528; George P. Murdock, "Remarks" in: *Memorial Service for Dr. Clark Wissler* [manuscript, 1958; American Museum of Natural History, Dept. of Anthropology Archives], pp. 7-10; James S. Reed, *Clark Wissler: a Forgotten Influence in American Anthropology* [unpublished Ph.D. dissertation, Department of Anthropology, Ball State University] (Muncie: 1980); George W. Stocking, Jr., "Wissler, Clark" in: *Dictionary of American Biography*, supplement 4 (1946-1950) (New York: 1974), pp. 906-909; Mary V. Wissler [Clark Wissler's daughter and Librarian at American Museum of Natural History] (compiler), *Clark Wissler: a Bibliography, 1897-1947* [manuscript, 1969; American Museum of Natural History Library].

Stanley A. Freed and Ruth S. Freed

Wölfel, Dominik Josef. Ethnologist, linguist. Born in Vienna (Austria) 25 May 1888, died in Vienna (Austria) 27 April 1963. As the twelfth child of a civil servant, Wölfel did not have access to higher education. After a period of individual study he became first a teacher of languages and subsequently entered the Austrian Ministry of Trade in 1916 as a translator. In 1919 he studied anthropology and ethnology with Father WILHELM SCHMIDT as a special university student in Vienna and, following completion of his qualifying examinations, was awarded a doctorate in 1925 with a dissertation on trepanation. The next year he entered the service of the Museum für Völkerkunde (Ethnographic Museum) in Vienna where he worked first as an assistant and later as a curator. From 1939 to 1945 he was placed on pension for political reasons. Through the help of the Berlin anthropologist E. Fischer, Wölfel was able to undertake research trips after 1930, visiting the most important archival collections in Europe as well as the Canary Islands, with whose investigation he chiefly concerned himself. In 1931, he was made an honorary member of the Instituto de Estudios Canarios (Institute of Canarian Studies) and the Museo Canario (Museum of the Canaries). Because of wartime conditions, Wölfel was obliged to decline a chair at the University of San Fernando, La Laguna, Tenerife, offered to him in 1941, although the university nonetheless named him as an adjunct professor. In 1945 he became a *Privatdozent* at the University of Vienna and resumed his position at the Museum für Völkerkunde. A severe heart condition as well as progressive impairment of vision forced him to abandon his teaching duties in 1953. In 1960 the University of La Laguna awarded him an honorary doctorate.

Using ethnological and linguistic methods, Wölfel sought to solve the problems of the megalithic cultures and to reconstruct the prehistoric cultural strata. He viewed the European megalithic as the most significant level of high culture and its religion (defined by ancestral worship and belief in a supreme god) as the world's most ancient. For him, languages were both the point of departure and the source of pivotal information. Wölfel compared the language of the original inhabitants of the Canary Islands especially with the Berber languages (but also with ancient Egyptian, Hausa and the Cushitic languages) to see if commonly inherited cultural elements could be deduced. In his hypothesis of an Atlanto-Libyan linguistic unity stretching from North Africa to pre-Indo-Germanic Europe, Wölfel contributed to research into the substrata of European languages. While well aware that many of his proposals were contestable, Wölfel nonetheless performed a valuable service in demonstrating cultural-historical connections between Europe and Africa.

MAJOR WORKS: "Die Trepanation," *Anthropos*, vol. 20 (1925), pp. 1-50; "La Curia Romana y la Corona de España en la defensa de los aborígines Canarios," *Anthropos*, vol. 25 (1930), pp. 1011-1083; "Los Gomeros vendidos por Pedro de Vera y doña Beatriz de Bobadilla," *El Museo Canario*, vol. 1 (1933), pp. 5-84; "Historische Anthropologie in ihrer Anwendung auf die Kanarischen Inseln," *Eugen-Fischer-Festband, Zeitschrift für Morphologie und Anthropologie*, vol. 34 (1934), pp. 493-503; "Nord- und Weißafrika" in: H.A. Bernatzik (editor), *Illustrierte Völkerkunde*, vol. 1 (Leipzig: 1939); *Die kanarischen Inseln und ihre Ureinwohner* (Leipzig: 1940); *Eurafrikanische Wortschichten als Kulturschichten* (Salamanca: 1955); "Weißafrika von den Anfängen bis zur Eroberung durch die Araber" in: *Oldenbourgs Abriß der Weltgeschichte: Abriß der Geschichte antiker Randkulturen* (Munich: 1961), pp. 193-257; *Monumenta Linguae Canariae: die Kanarischen Sprachdenkmäler: eine Studie zur Vor- und Frühgeschichte Weißafrikas* (edited by A. Closs) (Graz: 1965).

SOURCES: F. Anders, "Dominik Wölfel (1888-1963)," *Wiener Völkerkundliche Mitteilungen*, vol. 11 (1964), pp. 1-6; Hermann Jungraithmayr, "Wölfel, Dominik Josef" in: H. Jungraithmayr and W.J.G. Möhlig (editors), *Lexikon der Afrikanistik* (Berlin: 1983), pp. 268-269.

Herrmann Jungraithmayr and Rudolf Leger
[Translation from German: Robert B. Marks Ridinger]

Woodbury, Nathalie F.S. Anthropologist, editor, association administrator. Born in Humboldt (Arizona) 25 January 1918. Woodbury was educated at Barnard College (A.B., 1939) where she studied with ethnographer GLADYS REICHARD, and at Columbia University (A.B.D., 1943). Originally interested in archaeology, she turned to ethnology but then took up archaeology again after her marriage to RICHARD B. WOODBURY.

In 1940 she was a member of a Columbia University field party to the Comanche, which focused on ethnolinguistics. That same year she produced an annotated bibliography on North American Indian art for the Indian Arts and Crafts Board. During World War II she worked in intelligence in New York and taught part-time at Hunter College, New York University and Brooklyn College. Later she taught at Eastern New Mexico College, the University of Arizona and the University of Kentucky. During 1948-1949 she took part with her husband in the excavation and restoration of Zaculeu, a Maya site in highland Guatemala.

During the 1950s Barnard College recognized her administrative talents with appointments as Acting Chair of Anthropology (1954-1956) and Assistant Dean of Students (1956-1958). During 1954-1958 she was assistant editor of *American Antiquity*, becoming an associate editor in 1958. She was co-editor with R.B. Woodbury of *Abstracts of New World Archaeology* (1960-1964). Later she was associate editor of *American Anthropologist* (1973-1975), editor of *Guide to Departments of Anthropology* (1968-1974) and of the *Bulletins* and *Newsletter* of the American Anthropological Association (1968-1974). Since 1978 she has provided the obituaries of the profession for the *Anthropology Newsletter*, and in 1984 she began her monthly column, "Past is present," which deals with the history of anthropology.

Beginning in 1958 Woodbury served in a number of offices in professional societies, applying anthropological insights to their problems. She was Secretary (1960-1966) and Treasurer (1978-1979) of the American Ethnological Society, Treasurer of the Society for American Archaeology (1965-1967), Secretary (1970-1975) and Board member (1975-1978) of the American Anthropological Association. These were critical years during which anthropology in the United States grew from a small coterie of scholars to a profession enrolling thousands of practitioners.

For her work with professional associations she has received Distinguished Service Awards from the American Anthropological Association (1978) and the Society for American Archaeology (1988, with her husband). The latter organization also honored her with a Presidential Recognition Award (1988) and its 50th Anniversary Award (1986).

Woodbury's business card identifies her as a "facilitator" and this is an apt description for her role in anthropological organizations where her work has influenced the course of American anthropology during the second half of the 20th century.

MAJOR WORKS: (collaborator with Irwin T. Saunders [et al.], editors), *Societies Around the World* (New York: 1953); "The history of Zaculeu" in: Richard B. Woodbury and Aubrey S. Trik,

The Ruins of Zaculeu, Guatemala (Boston: 1953), pp. 9-20; (with Richard B. Woodbury) "Zuni prehistory and El Morro National Monument," *Southwestern Lore*, vol. 21 (1956), pp. 56-60; (with Watson Smith and Richard Woodbury) *The Excavation of Hawikuh by Frederick Webb Hodge* (New York: 1966) (= *Museum of the American Indian, Contributions*, no. 20); (with R.B. Woodbury) "Women of vision and wealth: their impact on Southwestern anthropology" in: A.V. Poore (editor), *Reflections: Papers on Southwestern Culture History in Honor of Charles H. Lange* (Santa Fe: 1988) (= *Papers of the Archaeological Society of New Mexico*, vol. 14), pp. 45-56.

SOURCE: "Nathalie Woodbury, 1918-" in: Barbara A. Babcock and Nancy J. Parezo, *Daughters of the Desert* (Albuquerque: 1988), pp. 154-155.

Alice B. Kehoe

Woodbury, Richard B. Anthropologist. Born in West Lafayette (Indiana) 16 May 1917. Woodbury was educated at Harvard (B.S., 1939; Ph.D., 1949). His lifelong interest in Southwest U.S. archaeology dates from 1938 when he served as a member of the Peabody Museum Awatovi Expedition to the Hopi area. During World War II he served in the U.S. Army Air Corps as a weather observer. From 1947 to 1950 he was archaeologist for the United Fruit Company's Zaculeu Project in Highland Guatemala then taught anthropology at the University of Kentucky (1950-1952) and Columbia University's graduate school (1952-1958). In 1959 he joined the University of Arizona's research program in arid lands, focusing on prehistoric water management in the Southwest. From 1963 to 1969 he was curator of North American archaeology and anthropology at the Smithsonian Institution, heading its Office of Anthropology in 1966 and 1967. In 1969 he was invited to establish a new anthropology department at the University of Massachusetts, Amherst, where he continued until his retirement as Professor Emeritus in 1981.

Woodbury, besides research and teaching, has had an extensive editorial role, as editor of *American Antiquity* (1954-1958), founder and editor of *Arid Lands Newsletter* in 1959 and *Abstracts of New World Archaeology* in 1960, and editor-in-chief of *American Anthropologist* (1975-1978). He was on the planning committee for the Southwest volumes of the *Handbook of North American Indians* and edited two symposium volumes on arid lands.

Woodbury's field research includes site surveying in northwest Florida, excavation of Adena remains in Kentucky, research on Zuni prehistory in New Mexico, prehistoric irrigation in Oaxaca and Hohokam irrigation canals in southern Arizona, as well as excavation and restoration of a highland Maya site in Guatemala.

He has been active in professional societies and organizations, including the American Anthropological Association (Executive Board, 1963-1966), the Archaeological Institute of America (Executive Committee, 1965-1976), the Human relations Area File (Executive Committee of the Board, 1968-1970), the Division of Anthropology and Psychology of the National Research Council (Executive Committee, 1955-1957), the Society for American Archaeology (Treasurer, 1953-1954; Editor, 1954-1958; President, 1958-1959), the Archaeological Conservancy (Board of Directors founding member, 1978-1984), and the Museum of Northern Arizona (Board of Trustees, 1983-1989).

He has received the following awards and honors: the Museum of Northern Arizona Fellowship (1985), the Society for American Archaeology's 50th Anniversary Award "for outstanding contributions to American archaeology" (1985), the Distinguished

Service Award of the Society for American Archaeology (with N.S.F. Woodbury, 1988), and the A.V. Kidder Award for Eminence in the Field of American Archaeology, presented by the American Anthropological Association (1989). The citation for the Kidder Award notes that Woodbury "pioneered new research directions in the Southwest" and that "his publications are a model of insight, scholarship and timeliness."

MAJOR WORKS: (with Aubrey S. Trik) *The Ruins of Zaculeu, Guatemala* (Boston: 1953); *Prehistoric Stone Implements of Northeastern Arizona* (Cambridge, Mass.: 1954) (= *Papers of the Peabody Museum of American Archaeology and History*, vol. 34; = *Reports of the Awatovi Expedition*, no. 6); (with Watson Smith and N.S.F. Woodbury) *The Excavation of Hawikuh by Frederick Webb Hodge* (New York: 1966); (with J.A. Neely) "Water controls of the Tehuacan Valley" in: *The Prehistory of the Tehuacan Valley*, vol. 4 (Austin: 1972), pp. 81-153; *Alfred V. Kidder* (New York: 1973); *Sixty Years of Southwestern Archaeology: a History of the Pecos Conference* (in press).

SOURCE: "Woodbury, Richard B." in: *Who's Who in America* (Wilmette, Ill.: 1988), pp. 3363.

Nathalie F.S. Woodbury

Worcester, Dean Conant. Statesman, anthropologist, zoologist, ornithologist. Born in Thetford (Vermont) 1 October 1866, died in Manila (Philippine Islands) 2 May 1924. Worcester, who was from an old New England family, attended Thetford Academy and Newton (Massachusetts) High School. The decision to enroll at the University of Michigan was to have a major influence on the future administrator's career. In 1887, while an undergraduate in Ann Arbor, Worcester joined a zoological expedition to the Philippine Islands under the direction of Professor Joseph B. Steere. Worcester completed the A.B. degree in 1889. In 1890 he returned to the Philippines as a member of the Louis Menage expedition directed by Dr. Frank S. Bourns. He traveled widely in the Visayas and in other islands, collecting ornithological and mammalian specimens and gaining a knowledge of Philippine geography and cultures. His first book, *The Philippine Islands and Their People*, a popular success, brought its author to the attention of President William McKinley. Worcester was appointed by McKinley to the first Philippine Commission, marking a decisive turn in his career. As Secretary of the Interior of the Insular government, he administered the bureaus of non-Christian tribes, health, public lands, forestry, mining, agriculture, fisheries, government laboratories, as well as others. A decisive and often controversial administrator, he displayed a special interest in the welfare of the non-Christian tribes but was criticized by Filipino nationalists and advocates of independence. In 1906 his "The non-Christian tribes of Northern Luzon" was published. In 1913 he left government service, moving to Mactan in the central Visayas where he became engaged in a number of successful agricultural and business activities. The first edition of *The Philippines Past and Present* was published in 1914. Worcester's contributions to Philippine anthropology include his activities in the field of applied anthropology, his varied writings and publications, as well as his support of ethnographic research both during his tenure as Secretary of the Interior and during his later years.

MAJOR WORKS: *The Philippine Islands and Their People* (New York: 1898); "The non-Christian tribes of Northern Luzon," *Philippine Journal of Science*, vol. 1 (1906), pp. 791-875; *The Philippines Past and Present* (New York: 1914; revised 2nd ed., New York: 1930).

SOURCES: Ralston Hayden, "Biographical sketch" in: Dean Conant Worcester, *The Philippines Past and Present* (New York: 1930), pp. [1]-79; Karl L. Hutterer, "Dean C. Worcester and Philippine anthropology," *Philippine Quarterly of Culture and Society*, vol. 6, no. 3 (September 1978), pp. 125-156; Resil B. Mojares, "Worcester in Cebu: Filipino response to American business, 1915-1924," *Philippine Quarterly of Culture and Society*, vol. 13, no. 1 (March 1985), pp. 1-13; "Worcester, Dean Conant" in: *National Cyclopaedia of American Biography*, vol. 20 (New York: 1929), p. 246.

Lee S. Dutton

Wu Wenzao. Ethnographer, sociologist. Born in Jiangyang, Jiangsu province (China) 12 April 1901, died in Beijing (China) 1985. From 1923 until 1929 Wu Wenzao studied in the United States and defended a doctoral dissertation at Columbia University on the problem of opium in China in the social ideas and activities of the English. After his return to China Wu first taught at Qinghua and then transferred to Yanjing University, where at that time his wife Si Bingxin, the noted children's writer, worked. Wu Wenzao gave courses on the history of Western social thought, the sociology of the family and anthropology. He set for himself the task of domesticating ethnography and sociology. This meant working out an effective theory with the help of which it would be possible to study the Chinese situation and train independent scientific cadres for this task.

Wu Wenzao himself sent the young scholars LIN YUEHUA to Fuzhou to study Chinese lineage organization; FEI HSIAO-T'UNG (Fei Xiaotong) to Jiangsu province to study the problems of the agricultural economy; and Li Yu to Shanxi to study social organization. He regularly kept the Chinese scholarly community acquainted with the state of ethnography in the United States, England, France and Germany. After the victory of the Revolution in 1949, Wu Wenzao returned to China from Japan in 1951 and after 1953 worked at the Central Nationalities College. From 1957 to 1979 he was persecuted as a "bourgeois rightist element." After his rehabilitation and right up until his death Wu took an active role in graduate study programs to train new scientific cadres. Wu is widely recognized as having made an outstanding contribution to the development of Chinese ethnography.

MAJOR WORKS: "Xiandai faguo shehuixue" ["Contemporary French sociology"], *Shehuixue gan* [*Journal of Sociology*], vol. 3, no. 2 (1932); and vol. 4, no. 2 (1934); "Deguo zhidu shehuixue xuepai" ["The German school of systematic sociology"], *Shehuixue za* [*World of Sociology*], vol. 8 (1934); "Gonglunbai shehui renleixue di youlai yu xianzhuang" ["The origin and contemporary situation of functional anthropology"], *Minzuxue yanjiu jikan* [*Journal for Ethnographic Research*], vol. 1 (1936), pp. 123-144; "Xin jinhua lunshi xi" ["A preliminary analysis of the theory of neo-evolutionism"], *Minzuxue yanjiu* [*Research in Ethnography*], vol. 7 (1984), pp. 290-304.

SOURCES: Chen Yongling, "Wu Wenzao" in: *Zhongguo da baike quanshu* [*Great Chinese Encyclopedia*], vol. "Minzu" ["Ethnos"] (Beijing and Shanghai: 1986), pp. 462-463; Lin Yaohua, Chen Yongling and Wang Qinren, "Wenzao zhuanlüe" ["A short biography of Wenzao"], *Minzu yanjiu*, no. 4 (1987), pp. 38-44; M.V. Krĭukov, "Kitaĭskaĭa shkola sofsiolokal'nykh issledovaniĭ" in: M.V. Krĭukov and I. Zel'nov (editors), *Svod ètnograficheskikh ponĭatiĭ i terminov: ètnograficheskie subdisfsipliny, shkoly i napravleniĭa metody* (Moscow: 1988), pp. 203-204.

A.M. Reshetov
[Translation from Russian: Ruth Dunnell]

Wundt, Wilhelm. Psychologist, physiologist, philosopher. Born in Neckerau/Mannheim (Germany) 16 August 1832, died in Leipzig (Germany) 31 August 1920. After earning the M.D. degree from the University of Heidelberg, Wundt served as assistant in the physiology laboratory of Hermann von Helmholtz before being named professor of anthropology and psychology. He immediately set himself the task of developing a comprehensive system of scientific psychology with an appropriate methodology. As he conceived it, only physiological individual psychology, limited to sensory perceptions, can work with individual laboratory experiments. General psychology, based on the more complicated forms of individual thought, requires statistical analyses to prove its legitimacy. And the "objective cultural forms" of larger sociocultural collectivities are only ascertainable through comparative historical observation. Wundt saw language (and art), myth (and religion) and customs (including law and institutions) as universal, primary forms of cultural development, which he later analyzed comprehensively in his mature work, the ten-volume *Völkerpsychologie*.

Wundt is considered the last great constructor of systems in the 19th century. He wanted to unite the sciences and humanities and conceived a philosophy that built on the conclusions of the modern sciences and was purified of theology and metaphysics. However, his comprehensive system remained a torso. His originality is particularly evident in cross-fertilizations between disciplines in the natural sciences (physiology and psychology), the humanities (cultural history and philology) and the social sciences (statistics, ethnology and sociology). Today Wundt is perceived only as the founding father of experimental individual psychology, since he established the first psychological laboratory in the world in 1879 at the University of Leipzig, where he had been appointed professor of philosophy in 1875. But by doing so, he also paved the way for cultural anthropology: from his insight that it is scientifically improper to apply results of experiments in individual psychology to social and historical phenomena, he developed an ethnopsychological concept of general cultural genesis, the results of which, conversely, must be connected to psychological analysis. He expressly rejected, however, a universal concept of evolution that organizes cultural forms in a progressive and value-laden order from primitive to advanced societies. Following Darwin, he defined evolution as the development of new cultural forms through adaptation to new situations. He also replaced the Hegelian metaphysical construct of national spirit (*Volksgeist*) with the notion of actuality (*Aktualitätsgedanken)*, the nature of a thing as realized in existence; national soul (*Volksseele*) and collective will (*Gesamtwille*) manifest themselves in constantly new "creative syntheses" as direct actualization of concrete collective experiences.

It was this "Leipzig School" approach to the development of structures and to collective psychology with which Émile Durkheim and MARCEL MAUSS and others in France sought to come to terms in their works on myth, religion and ethics. In the United States, Wundt's influence was considerable. His students (James McKeen Cattell, Frank Angell, E.B. Titchener and G. Stanley Hall, among others) occupied all of the important research centers for individual psychology; in social psychology, William James (who held high hope for Wundt's renewal of philosophy) and James Mark Baldwin (a student of Wundt) developed the concept of the "social self" in response to Wundt's ideas; and George Herbert Mead took his concept of "language as gesture" from Wundt's *Lautgebärde*. In its German reception—by Felix Krueger (psychology), Willy Hellpach (social psychology), or Alfred Vierkandt (sociology), for example—Wundt's macroconcept of cultural anthropology tended to fade behind a social-ontological individualism that was clearly typical of the generation of German scholars that succeeded him.

MAJOR WORKS: *Vorlesungen über die Menschen- und Thierseele* [2 vols.] (Leipzig: 1863) [tr.: *Lectures on Human and Animal Psychology* (London and New York: 1894)]; *Grundzüge der physiologischen Psychologie* (Leipzig: 1874) [tr.: *Principles of Physiological Psychology* (London and New York: 1904)]; *Logik: eine Untersuchung der Prinzipien der Erkenntnis und der Methoden wissenschaftlicher Forschung* [2 vols.] (Stuttgart: 1883); *Ethik: eine Untersuchung der Tatsachen und Gesetze des sittlichen Lebens* (Stuttgart: 1886) [tr.: *Ethics: an Investigation of the Facts and Laws of the Moral Life* [3 vols.] (London: 1897); *Grundriß der Psychologie* (Leipzig: 1896) [tr.: *Outlines of Psychology* (London and New York: 1897)]; *System der Philosophie* (Leipzig: 1897); *Einführung in die Psychologie* (Leipzig: 1911) [tr.: *An Introduction to Psychology* (London: 1912)]; *Elemente der Völkerpsychologie: Grundlinien einer psychologischen Entwicklungsgeschichte der Menschheit* (Leipzig: 1912) [tr.: *Elements of Folk Psychology: Outlines of a Psychological History of the Development of Mankind* (London: 1916)]; *Völkerpsychologie: eine Untersuchung der Entwicklungsgesetze von Sprache, Mythus und Sitte* [10 vols.] (Leipzig: 1900-1920) [tr. of parts of vols. 1 and 2: *The Language of Gesture* (The Hague: 1973)].

SOURCES: Wilhelm E. Mühlmann, *Geschichte der Anthropologie* (Frankfurt/Main: 1968); Wilhelm Wundt, *Erlebtes und Erkanntes* [autobiography] (Stuttgart: 1920); Carl F. Graumann, "Experiment, Statistik, Geschichte," *Psychologische Rundschau*, vol. 3 (1980), pp. 73-83; Jan Jacob de Wolf, "Wundt and Durkheim: a reconsideration of a relationship," *Anthropos*, vol. 82 (1987), pp. 1-23; R.W. Rieber (editor), *Wilhelm Wundt and the Making of a Scientific Psychology* (New York and London: 1980); Georg Eckart and Lothar Sprung (editors), *Advances in the History of Psychology* (Berlin [East]: 1983); W.G. Bringmann and E. Scheerer (editors), "Wundt centennial issue," *Psychological Research*, vol. 42 (1980), pp. 1-189.

Elfriede Üner
[Translation from German: Sem C. Sutter]

Wyman, Jeffries. Anthropologist, comparative anatomist, biologist, teacher, curator. Born in Chelmsford (Massachusetts) 11 August 1814, died in Cambridge (Massachusetts) 4 September 1874. A greatly respected man of science in late 19th-century America, Wyman graduated from Harvard in medicine in 1837 and returned there in 1847 to teach anatomy. Wyman was a member of numerous prestigious associations, including the National Academy of Sciences, the American Association for the Advancement of Science and the American Academy of Arts and Sciences. Like many scientists of the day, Wyman was not a theorizer but a gatherer of interesting data who left interpretation to others. In some of his research, however, Wyman addressed two of the burning questions of his time, spontaneous generation and biological evolution.

In the 1860s Wyman conducted experiments, similar to those done by Louis Pasteur in France, which proved to him that spontaneous generation was not possible. Some of Wyman's other work was cited by Charles Darwin as evidence supporting his theory of natural selection (1866). As president of the Boston Society of Natural History, he presided over the famous Louis Agassiz-William Rogers debate on Darwinian evolution in early 1860. The evidence indicates that Wyman probably supported evolution, but he was not a vocal proponent. Wyman influenced anthropology primarily through his work as Hersey Professor of Anatomy and as the first director of the Peabody Museum of Archaeology and Ethnology at Harvard. He taught such notable men as FREDERIC WARD PUTNAM, the founder of American archaeology, and William James, the founder of

American psychology. Among his contributions to anthropology was his work in primatology. Wyman, with Thomas Savage, gave the first scientific description of the gorilla
("Notice of the external characters and habits ..."). Wyman also wrote numerous other articles on primate anatomy. As director of the Peabody Museum he labored to build the
collection and conducted archaeological investigations. With his student and friend
Putnam, he searched for the remains of primitive humans in America. Wyman described
many anatomical anomalies among ancient and modern human remains and investigated the
relationship between the development of the embryo and its adult form. Unlike most of his
contemporaries, Wyman declined to infer racial rankings from his study of comparative
anatomy. Instead he felt that the differences between what were termed the "lower races"
and non-human primates far outweighed any similarities. He never assumed any race to be
less than fully human.

MAJOR WORKS: (with Thomas Savage) "Notice of the external characters and habits of
troglodytes gorilla," *Boston Journal of Natural History*, vol. 5 (1847), pp. 417-422; "Notes on the
cells of the bee," *Proceedings of the American Academy of Arts and Sciences*, vol. 7 (1866), pp. 68-
83; "Observations on crania," *Proceedings of the Boston Society of Natural History*, vol. 11 (1868),
pp. 440-462; "On the fresh-water shell-heaps of the St. John's River, East Florida," *American
Naturalist*, vol. 2 (1869), pp. 293-403, 449-463; "Observations on crania and other parts of the
skeleton," *Fourth Annual Report of the Peabody Museum* (1871), pp. 10-24.

SOURCES: Asa Gray, "Jeffries Wyman," *Proceedings of the Boston Society of Natural History*,
vol. 17 (1874), pp. 96-124; Oliver Wendell Holmes, "Professor Jeffries Wyman: a memorial outline," *Atlantic Monthly*, vol. 34 (1874), pp. 611-623; Alpheus S. Packard "Memoir of Jeffries
Wyman, 1814-1874," *National Academy of Sciences, Biographical Memoirs*, vol. 2 (1878), pp. 75-
126; Bert G. Wilder, "Sketch of Dr. Jeffries Wyman," *Popular Science Monthly*, vol. 6 (January
1875), pp. 355-360.

Joyce L. Ogburn

X

Xesspe, M. Toribio Mejía. See: *Mejía Xesspe, M. Toribio.*

Xia Nai. Archaeologist. Born in Wenzhou (China) 7 February 1910, died in Beijing (China) 19 June 1985. Xia Nai, the architect of Chinese archaeology from 1950 until his death, graduated from Tsinghua University in 1934 with a major in economic history. He engaged in fieldwork at the 3,000-plus-years-old Shang capital at Anyang, and then studied Egyptology and classical archaeology in England, earning the Ph.D. degree in Egyptology from the University of London in 1946. In the meantime, in 1943, he had returned to China where he joined the staff of the Central Museum and then the Department of Archaeology of the Institute of History and Philology, Academia Sinica, where he later became Acting Director. On the founding of the People's Republic of China, in 1949, Xia taught for one year at Zhejiang University and then was appointed a Deputy Director of the new Institute of Archaeology, the Chinese Academy of Sciences. From 1962 until 1982 he was Director of the Institute, and from 1982 until his death he retained the title of Honorary Director, assuming the first Vice-Presidency of the Chinese Academy of Social Sciences. Xia had become a member of the Academy in 1955 and a member of the Communist Party in 1959, but he was first and foremost an original scholar of the first order. He was the first archaeologist to reverse—through the finding of Yangshao culture sherds in the fill of a Qijia culture burial—the chronology of those two cultures, thus setting Chinese Neolithic archaeology on the right track toward its phenomenal development. He had a lifelong interest in China's Northwest, in the Silk Road, and in East-West communication in general, and he is known for his substantial and original works of synthesis.

He was highly regarded not only within his own country but also internationally, being the recipient of honors and memberships from learned societies all over the world. Xia Nai can claim enormous credit for China's archaeological achievements and for the training of the new generation of Chinese archaeologists. He was involved in the founding of the Archaeology Program at Peking University and of the short-term Training Institutes for Cultural Relics Workers in the early 1950s. Above all, during his later years, he exerted preeminent influence on China's archaeological policy, plans, priorities and standards.

MAJOR WORKS: *Kaoguxue Lunwenji* [*Collection of Archaeological Papers*] (Beijing: 1961); *Kaoguxue yu Kejishi* [*Archaeology and the History of Science and Technology*] (Beijing: 1971); *Zhongguo Wenming di Qiyuan* [*The Origin of Chinese Civilization*] (Beijing: 1985).

SOURCES: Wang Zhongshu, "A brief biography of Mr. Xia Nai," *Kaogu Xuebao* (1985), pp. 407-415; K.C. Chang, "Xia Nai," *American Anthropologist*, vol. 88 (1986), pp. 442-444.

K.C. Chang

Z

Zawistowicz-Adamska, Kazimiera. Ethnographer. Born in Haniebno (Ukraine, Russia) 19 March 1897, died in Łódź (Poland) 8 July 1984. Zawistowicz-Adamska was a journalism student (1920-1923), but between 1923 and 1929, at the Polish Free University and the University of Warsaw, she studied ethnography, ethnology and related fields under the direction of STANISŁAW PONIATOWSKI, STEFAN ZYGMUNT CZARNOWSKI, LUDWIK KRZYWICKI and Włodzimierz Antoniewicz, obtaining her doctorate in 1929. Zawistowicz-Adamska engaged in many trips and studies abroad. She studied in Paris under MARCEL MAUSS (1930-1931); she participated in the ethnographic investigations of the Ethnological Institute of the Sorbonne in the Basque Country; and in Finland and Estonia she conducted ethnological-archaeological studies on Slav-Finnish cultural relations (1931-1932). Between 1932 and 1939 she conducted research on the folk culture of village society in Poland and wrote a monograph on Zaborów (1937-1938). After World War II she took part in the organization of the Department of Ethnography at the University of Łódź, remaining there as director until her retirement (1967). She was appointed assistant professor in 1952, associate professor in 1955 and full professor in 1962. During the years 1954-1972 she was the director of the Ethnographic Laboratory of the Institute of the History of Material Culture of the Polish Academy of Sciences.

Zawistowicz-Adamska was a representative of the sociological-historical method of research. The research she conducted was concerned with the economic and social-cultural aspects of the regions of Central Poland and the problems of the traditional and contemporary forms of mutual help, various types of cooperative economic activity, the influence of extra-agricultural occupations, and social bonds and their transformations. She attached particular value to field research. She was an organizer and an outstanding teacher and social worker.

MAJOR WORKS: *Sagi estońskie [Estonian Sagas]* (Kraków: 1929); *Zawarcie małżeństwa przez kupno w polskich obrzędach weselnych [The Contraction of Arranged Marriages in Polish Wedding Customs]* (Kraków: 1929); *Problem kultury ludowej w badaniach nad środowiskiem [The Problem of Folk Culture in Investigations of Environment]* (Warsaw: 1938); *Społeczność wiejska: doświadczenia i rozważania z badań terenowych w Zaborowie [Village Society: Experiences and Analyses from Field Work in Zaborów]* (Łódź: 1948); *Żywe tradycje współdziałania na wsi [Living Traditions of Cooperation in the Village]* (Łódź: 1948); *Pomoc wzajemna i współdziałanie w kulturach ludowych [Mutual Help and Cooperation in Folk Cultures]* (Wrocław: 1950-1951) (= *Prace i materiały etnograficzne*, vol. 8/9); *Wincenty Pol: badacz kultury ludowej [Wincenty Pol: Investigator of Folk Culture]* (Warsaw: 1966); *Systemy krewniacze na Słowiańszczyźnie w ich historyczno-społecznym uwarunkowaniu [Kin Systems in Slavic Lands in their Socio-Historical Condition]* (Wrocław: 1971); *Granice i horyzonty badań kultury wsi w Polsce [Limits and Horizons of the Investigation of the Culture of the Village in Poland]* (Warsaw: 1976); *Polska sztuka ludowa: stan wiedzy, prace badawcze, opieka i upowszechnianie [Polish Folk Art: the State of Knowledge, Research, Preservation and Dissemination]* (Łódź: 1976) (= *Łódzkie Studia Etnograficzne*, vol. 18); *Socio-Economic Cooperation in Local Communities of the Polish Village* (Łódź: 1982) (= *Acta UL Folia Ethnologica*, vol. 1).

SOURCES: Maria Biernacka, "Kazimiera Zawistowicz-Adamska," *Etnografia Polska*, vol. 30 (1986), pp. 213-219; Irena Lechowa, "Profesor dr Kazimiera Zawistowicz-Adamska i nowy profil etnografii muzealnej," ["Professor Dr Kazimiera Zawistowicz-Adamska and the new profile of museum ethnography"], *Prace i Materiały Muzeum Archeologicznego i Etnograficznego w Łodzi, Seria Etnograficzna*, vol. 21 (1983), pp. 53-64.

Maria Niewiadomska and Iwona Grzelakowska
[Translation from Polish: Joel Janicki]

Zelenin, D.K. (Dmitriĭ Konstantinovich). Ethnographer, scholar of religion, folklorist, dialectologist. Born in Vi͡atska͡ia˘ guberni͡ia (Russia) 21 October 1878, died in Leningrad (Russian S.F.S.R.) 30 August 1954. Zelenin was a prominent Russian and Soviet specialist on the ethnography of the Eastern Slavs, above all the Russians. In 1925 he became an associate member of the Soviet Academy of Sciences. He worked in the Muzeĭ antropologii i ėtnografii (Museum of Anthropology and Ethnography) of the Institut ėtnografii (Institute of Ethnography) of the Soviet Academy of Sciences in Leningrad.

His major works were devoted to the problems of ethnic history, folk customs, culture and way of life. Zelenin felt that the origin, meaning, dissemination, functioning, variation of every appearance and form of traditional culture could be understood only in conjunction with the entire system of the folk way of life—from its social-economic base to language, folklore, rituals and religions. That is, it was characteristic of his method to take a systematic approach to folk culture as a unified historical accumulation and at the same time a dynamic phenomenon. He developed the idea of the "prereligious" period as an ancient stage of the history of human thought. A complex approach and wide use of the facts of related sciences were characteristic of the research of Zelenin.

MAJOR WORKS: *Russka͡ia˘ sokha, ee istori͡ia i vidy: ocherk iz istorii russkoĭ zemledel'cheskoĭ kul'tury* (Vi͡atka: 1907); *Bibliograficheskiĭ ukazatel' russkoĭ ėtnograficheskoĭ literatury o vneshnem byte narodov Rossii, 1700-1910: zhilishche, odezhda, muzyka, iskusstvo, khozi͡aĭstvennyĭ byt* (Sankt Peterburg: 1913); *Opisanie rukopiseĭ Uchenogo arkhiva Russkogo geograficheskogo obshchestva* [3 parts] (Petrograd: 1914-1916); *Ocherki russkoĭ mifologii. Vyp. 1. Umershie neestestvennoĭ smert'i͡u i rusalki* (Petrograd: 1916); *Russische (Ostslavische) Volkskunde* (Berlin and Leipzig: 1927); *Kul't on-*

gonov v Sibiri: perezhitki totemizma v idiologii sibirskikh narodov (Moscow and Leningrad: 1936); "Problemy pervobytnoĭ religii," *Sovetskaĭa ėtnografiĭa*, no. 4 (1937), pp. 3-17.

SOURCES: E.F. Karskiĭ, B.M. Lĭapunov, V.P. Peretĭs, and P.A. Lavrov, "Zapiska ob uchenikh trudakh prof. D.K. Zelenina," *Izvestiĭa AN SSSR*, ser. 6, vol. 19, no. 18 (1925), pp. 879-883; T.V. Stanĭukovich, M.D. Torėn, "D.K. Zelenin (nekrolog)," *Sovetskaĭa ėtnografiĭa*, no. 4 (1954), pp. 157-159; A.S. Bezhkovich, "D.K. Zelenin (1878-1954)," *Izvestiĭa Vsesoĭuznogo Geograficheskogo obshchestva*, vol. 87, no. 4 (1955), pp. 367-369; L.M. Saburova, K.V. Chistov, "D.K. Zelenin," *Sovetskaĭa ėtnografiĭa*, no. 6 (1978), pp. 71-86; L.M. Saburova, "D.K. Zelenin, ėtnograf" in: A.K. Baĭburin and K.V. Chistov (editors), *Problemy slavĭanskoĭ ėtnograii (k 100-letiĭu so dnĭa rozhdeniĭa chlena-korrespondenta AN SSSR D.K. Zelenina)* (Leningrad: 1979), pp. 9-44; N.V. Novikov, "D.K. Zelenin kak fol'klorist" in: A.K. Baĭburin and K.V. Chistov (editors), *Problemy slavĭanskoĭ ėtnograii (k 100-letiĭu so dnĭa rozhdeniĭa chlena-korrespondenta AN SSSR D.K. Zelenina)* (Leningrad: 1979), pp. 61-70; N.I. Tolstoĭ and S.M. Tolstaĭa, "D.K. Zelenin, dialektolog" in: A.K. Baĭburin and K.V. Chistov (editors), *Problemy slavĭanskoĭ ėtnograii (k 100-letiĭu so dnĭa rozhdeniĭa chlena-korrespondenta AN SSSR D.K. Zelenina)* (Leningrad: 1979), pp. 70-83.

A.M. Reshetov
[Translation from Russian: Thomas L. Mann]

Zhdanko, T.A. *(Tat'ĭana Aleksandrovna)*. Ethnographer, historian. Born in Elizavetgrad (Ukraine) 1 August 1909. Zhdanko was a doctor of historical sciences and a professor. She worked at first in Samarkand and then in Moscow (until World War II) in the ĬSentral'nyĭ muzeĭ narodovedeniĭa (Central Museum of Native Affairs) and later as director of the Department of the Ethnography of the Peoples of Central Asia and Kazakhstan of the Institut ėtnografii (Institute of Ethnography) of the Soviet Academy of Sciences. For a long time she directed the ethnographic group of the Khorezm Archaeological-Ethnographic Expedition.

Much of her scholarly writing was devoted to the ethnography of the Karakalpaks, the ethnohistory of the peoples of Central Asia and Kazakhstan, the character of the ethnic communities of the peoples of that region and the settlements of the nomads. Zhdanko edited such collective works as *Narody Sredneĭ Azii i Kazakhstana* and *Semeĭnyĭ byt narodov SSSR*. Her theoretical works were devoted primarily to the ethnographic development of nomads and the problems of nomadic life in its entirety.

MAJOR WORKS: "Byt karakalpakskogo kolkhoznogo aula," *Sovetskaĭa ėtnografiĭa*, no. 2 (1949), pp. 35-58; "Karakalpaki Khorezmskogo oazisa" in: *Trudy Khorezmskoĭ arkheologo-ėtnograficheskoĭ ėkspediĭsii*, vol. 1 (Moscow: 1952), pp. 461-566; "Narodnoe ornamental'noe iskusstvo karakalpakov" in: *Trudy Khorezmskoĭ arkheologo-ėtnograficheskoĭ ėkspediĭsii*, vol. 3 (Moscow: 1958), pp. 373-410; "Mezhdunarodnoe znachenie istoricheskogo opyta perekhoda na osedlost' kochevnikov Sredneĭ Azii i Kazakhstana," *Sovetskaĭa ėtnografiĭa*, no. 4 (1967), pp. 3-24; (with M.K. Nurmukhamedov and S.K. Kamalov) *Karakalpaki* (Tashkent: 1971); "Speĭsifika ėtnicheskikh obshchnosteĭ v Sredneĭ Azii i Kazakhstane," *Rasy i narody*, no. 4 (1974), pp. 10-26; "Ėtnicheskie obshchnosti i ėtnicheskie proĭsessy v dorevolĭuĭsionnoĭ Rossii" in: ĬU.V. Bromleĭ [et al.] (editors), *Sovremennye ėtnicheskie proĭsessy v SSSR* (Moscow: 1975), pp. 33-84; "Problemy kartografirovanniĭa khozĭaĭstv v Istoriko-ėtnograficheskom atlase Sredneĭ Azii i Kazakhstana" in: *Areal'nye issledovaniĭa v ĭazykoznanii i ėtnografii* (Ufa: 1985), pp. 142-146; (co-editor with S.P. Tolstov [et al.]) *Narody Sredneĭ Azii i Kazakhstana* [2 vols.] (Moscow: 1962); (editor-in-chief) *Semeĭnyĭ byt narodov SSSR* (Moscow: 1990).

SOURCES: B.V. Lunin, *Biobibliograficheskie ocherki o deĭateliĭakh obshchestvennykh nauk Uzbekistana*, vol. 1 (Tashkent: 1976), pp. 224-229; S.K. Kamalov, "O zhizni i nauchnoĭ deĭatel'nosti T.A. Zhdanko" in: *Ėtnicheskaĭa istoriĭa i tradiĭsionnaĭa kul'tura narodov Sredneĭ Azii i Kazakhstana*

(Nukus: 1989), pp. 7-14; "Osnovnye nauchnye trudy T.A. Zhdanko" in: *Ėtnicheskaia istoriia i tradiísionnaia kul'tura narodov Srednei Azii i Kazakhstana* (Nukus: 1989), pp. 14-27.

A.M. Reshetov
[Translation from Russian: Thomas L. Mann]

Zolotarev, A.M. (Aleksandr Mikhaĭlovich). Ethnographer, anthropologist, historian of primitive society. Born in Khar'kov (Ukraine) 1 July 1907, died in the camps in 1943. Zolotarev studied in the postgraduate course at the Gosudarstvennaia Akademiia istorii material'noĭ kultury (State Academy of History of Material Culture) in Leningrad during 1929-1932, after which he worked in its Moscow branch. With the beginning of World War II, he entered the national militia in Moscow, was taken prisoner, escaped, but was soon incarcerated.

In his works Zolotarev tried to prove the universality of tribal organization and the connection between the cult of twins and dual organizations. At first he believed that exogamy sprang up because the formation of marriages outside one's "collective" (group) was economically advantageous, but later he subscribed to the point of view of S.P. TOLSTOV, who saw in the origin of exogamy the means of settling the contradiction between the life of members of a collective and the way in which they organized their production.

MAJOR WORKS: *Proiskhozhdenie ėkzogamii* (Leningrad: 1931) (= *Izvestiia Gosudarstvennoĭ Akademii istorii material'noĭ kul'tury*, vol. 10, issue 2-4); "The bear festival of the Olcha," *American Anthropologist*, n.s., vol. 39 (1937), pp. 113-130; *Perezhitki totemizma u narodov Sibiri* (Leningrad: 1934); "K voprosu o proiskhozhdenii eskimosov," *Antropologicheskiĭ zhurnal*, no. 1 (1937), pp. 47-56; "Iz ėtnicheskikh vzaimootnosheniĭ na severo-vostoke Azii," *Izvestiia Voronezhskogo pedagogicheskogo instituta*, vol. 4 (1938), pp. 73-87; "Novye dannye o tungusakh i lamutakh," *Istorik-marksist*, no. 2 (1938), pp. 63-89; "The ancient culture of North Asia," *American Anthropologist*, n.s., vol. 40 (1938), pp. 13-24; *Rodovoĭ stroĭ i religiia ul'cheĭ* (Khabarovsk: 1939); "K istorii rannykh form gruppovogo braka," *Uchenye zapiski istoricheskogo fakul'teta, Moskovskiĭ oblastnoĭ pedagogicheskiĭ institut*, vol. 2 (1940), pp. 144-169; *Rodovoĭ stroĭ i pervobytnaia mifologiia* (Moscow: 1964).

SOURCE: "Zolotarev, Aleksandr Mikhaĭlovich" in: *Sovetskaia istoricheskaia ėnísiklopediia*, vol. 5 (Moscow: 1964), pp. 698-699.

A.M. Reshetov
[Translation from Russian: Thomas L. Mann]

Zolotarev, D.A. (David Alekseevich). Ethnographer, anthropologist, area specialist. Born in Rybinsk, IAroslavskaia Guberniia (Russia) 28 August 1885, died in a camp in Siberia 29 August 1935. Zolotarev became a professor at Petrograd University in 1918. His scholarly activity began in the Postoiànaia Komissiia po sostavleniiu ėtnograficheskikh kart Rossii (Standing Committee for the Creation of an Ethnographic Map of Russia) at the Geographic Society. After the Revolution he was the director of the Department of Russian-Finnish Ethnography of the Ethnographic Division of the Russkiĭ Muzeĭ (Russian Museum) and director of the Section of Ethnographic Anthropology and Ethnography of the Rossiĭskaia Akademiia istorii material'noĭ kultury (Russian Academy of the History of Material Culture).

In expeditionary and research work Zolatarev sought to unite the strengths of specialists in ethnography, anthropology, language studies, folklore and history from both central and local institutions. In the study of Russian- and Finnish-speaking populations, Zolotarev directed special attention to the interaction of their cultures and revealed both general and ethnically specific features in their society and way of life.

MAJOR WORKS: "Antropologicheskie issledovaniĭa velikorusov Ostashkovskogo i Rzhevskogo uezdov Tverskoĭ gubernii," *Ezhegodnik Russkogo antropologicheskogo obshchestva pri SPb universitete*, vol. 4 (1913), pp. 9-66; "Antropologicheskie dannye o velikorusakh fŭzhnoĭ chasti Novgorodskoĭ zemli," *Ezhegodnik Russkogo antropologicheskogo obshchestva pri SPb universitete*, vol. 5 (1915), pp. 27-62; "Voprosy izucheniĭa byta derevni SSSR," *Ėtnografiĭa*, no. 1-2 (1962), pp. 45-53; *Ėtnicheskiĭ sostav naseleniĭa Severo-Zapadnoĭ oblasti i Karel'skoĭ ASSR* (Leningrad: 1926) (= *Trudy Komissii po izucheniĭu plemennogo sostava naseleniĭa SSSR i sopredel'nykh stran pri AN SSSR*, no. 12); *Loparskaĭa ėkspediĭsiĭa* (Leningrad: 1927); *Khol'skie lopari* (Leningrad: 1928) (= *Materialy Komissii ėkspediĭsionnykh issledovaniĭ AN SSSR*, vol. 9); (with A.P. Vershinskiĭ) *Naselenie Tverskogo kraĭa* (Tver': 1929); *Karely SSSR: antropologicheskiĭ ocherk* (Leningrad: 1930).

SOURCE: I.I. Shangina, "D.A. Zolotarev: k 100-letiĭu so dnĭa rozhdeniĭa," *Sovetskaĭa ėtnografiĭa*, no. 6 (1985), pp. 76-84.

A.M. Reshetov
[Translation from Russian: Thomas L. Mann]

glossary

This glossary is intended chiefly as an aid to users of this dictionary. It includes only terms which are not explained in the text. Space limitations preclude full discussion of what are often difficult-to-define terms. For lengthier definitions, the reader is referred to the standard dictionaries and encyclopedias of the social sciences[1] as well as to the entries in this *Dictionary* noted below in SMALL CAPS. See also the index.

Anthropometry. Measurement of the human body. Much early physical anthropology was anthropometric in nature (see PETRUS CAMPER and PAUL BROCA).

Applied anthropology. In general, the use of anthropology for practical ends. The term has sometimes suggested the use of anthropological insights for effective political control, but, most often, "applied anthropology" refers to situations in which the anthropologist tries to aid the peoples he or she is studying, for example by providing advice on economic development. ALLAN R. HOLMBERG and SOL TAX are (very different) noted practitioners.

---

[1]See, for example, David L. Sills (editor), *International Encyclopedia of the Social Sciences* (New York: 1968-1979); Adam Kuper and Jessica Kuper (editors), *The Social Science Encyclopedia* (London and Boston: 1985); Charlotte Seymour-Smith, *Dictionary of Anthropology* (Boston: 1986); David E. Hunter and Phillip Whitten, *Encyclopedia of Anthropology* (New York: 1976); and so on.

Biological anthropology. The study of human biology, typically with some emphasis on its social consequences. The field's range overlaps considerably with that of **physical anthropology**, but the term "biological anthropology" has probably come to be preferred in recent years, even in reference to early scholars.

Boasian. As an adjective, the scholarly tradition established by FRANZ BOAS. As a noun, one of Boas's students or followers.

Cultural anthropology. In American anthropology, the phrase "cultural anthropology" has typically been used to refer to virtually any kind of anthropology other than physical anthropology (often, linguistics, archaeology and folklore have also been excluded). In this sense the phrase carries a range of meaning not unlike that of the term "ethnology" and such European words as French *ethnologie*, German *Völkerkunde* and Russian *etnografiîa*. The distinction between "cultural anthropology" and "social anthropology" is in part a question of a difference between American and British usage, and in part related to the emphasis of FRANZ BOAS and his students on culture, and that of the British functionalists on social structure. In the United States, there is a tendency today to say "social and cultural anthropology" when one wants to exclude physical and biological anthropology (and perhaps linguistics, archaeology and folklore).

Cultural ecology. "The study of the processes by which a society adapts to its environment." The definition is JULIAN H. STEWARD's and it is with his work more than with that of any other anthropologist that cultural ecology is associated. The field overlaps considerably with cultural geography, and, like cultural geography, it does not focus only on the direct study of man-environment relationships but also considers such related subjects as the spatial structure of settlements and marketing arrangements, the origin and development of agriculture, the relationship between population density and other aspects of human life, and vernacular landscapes.

Cultural-Historical School, or: "Cultural-Historical Approach," sometimes used more or less synonymously with the term "Vienna School," although its founders were mostly German. An approach to the study of peoples which was initiated by LEO FROBENIUS, FRITZ GRAEBNER, WILHELM SCHMIDT and several of their German or Austrian contemporaries. Its more straightforward proponents aimed to identify culturally uniform geographical regions called "culture circles" (*Kulturkreisen*), to analyze cultural traits, or "culture layers" (*Kulturschichten*) in these areas, and to study the diffusion of such traits from region to region. An underlying axiom was that the geographical distribution of culture traits was a key to their evolution. The Cultural-Historical School was central to ethnological study in the German-speaking world for decades, only fading in the years after World War II (see WILHELM EMIL MÜHLMANN) and was enormously influential throughout continental Europe (see JOSÉ MIGUEL DE BARANDIARÁN, GERHARD LINDBLOM, STANISŁAW PONIATOWSKI, among others). The Cultural-Historical School eventually came to be seen as imposing too simple a notion on the world but was responsible for a vast amount of serious ethnographic study.

Cultural relativism. A phrase whose most common sense is the idea that on some deep level all cultures are fundamentally equal. Cultural relativism is particularly associated with FRANZ BOAS and his students; MELVILLE J. HERSKOVITS was perhaps the scholar who wrote at greatest length on the idea.

Culture. A central concept in anthropology, especially in the English-speaking world. The inventor of the more or less modern notion of culture is said to have been E.B. TYLOR who defined it as a "complex whole which includes knowledge, belief, arts, morals, law, custom, and any other capabilities and habits acquired by man as a member of society." Many others have struggled with a definition of the term; hundreds of definitions have been proposed. The notion of "culture" has in fact undergone some shift in meaning. Perhaps most 20th-century anthropologists (e.g., FRANZ BOAS and many of his students) have emphasized its use when talking about cultural *differences*. In recent years, many scholars (e.g., DAVID M. SCHNEIDER) have preferred a very restricted use of the term.

Culture and personality. A general name given to a movement in the 1930s and 1940s which aimed to investigate the relationship between culture and societal or individual personalities. Sometimes, culture-and-personality studies took the form of suggesting that entire cultures had particular personalities. This "configurationalist" approach was characteristic of the work of RUTH BENEDICT. At other times, the tendency was to analyze the complicated relationship between individual personality and culture. ABRAM KARDINER arguably originated this approach, and RALPH LINTON and CORA DUBOIS made major contributions to it.

Culture area. A geographical region with a uniform culture. FRIEDRICH RATZEL may have been the first to write at length on this notion, and it was an essential, almost axiomatic concept to the scholars of the *Cultural-Historical School*, among whom the term *Kulturkreis* was used. In the English-speaking world, CLARK WISSLER was perhaps the most self-conscious writer on the "culture area" concept, although much English-speaking anthropology is deeply dependent on the notion, e.g., the work of FRANZ BOAS and his students, as well as the very different work of GEORGE PETER MURDOCK. It is, in fact, difficult to imagine comparative or cross-cultural analysis—or the classification of museum collections—without any notion of culture areas. In practice, culture areas are not easy to delineate with precision.

Demology. Italian *demologia*. A now archaic term for social and cultural anthropology in Italy. In practice, the term was used almost entirely for the study of the ethnography of European peoples, so that "folklore" may be the best translation.

Dendrochronology. Tree-ring dating. Since climate affects tree growth, patterns of tree rings provide information about climate change. Thus, examination of wood in archaeological sites becomes an excellent way to date them. Dendrochronology is associated particularly with A.E. DOUGLASS.

Dermatoglyphics. Analysis of fingerprints and toeprints and, sometimes, other markings on the fingers and toes.

Determinism. The idea that many or most elements of human life can be explained by one set of factors, e.g., economic, geographical or cultural factors. "Determinism" is usally prefixed by one of these terms. A believer in one or another kind of "determinism" is a "determinist." An "environmental determinist" would argue that physical environment "explains" much of human life. In practice, the term is pejorative, and few if any scholars have applied it to themselves.

Diachronic study. The study of a phenomenon over time. Cf. **Synchronic study**.

Diffusion. The transmission of ideas, inventions, or other culture traits from one point in space to another. In the late 19th and early 20th centuries there was considerable debate between those who believed that similarities of culture in different areas were to be attributed to diffusion and those who argued that universal patterns of **evolution** were more likely to have been responsible.

Ethno- Prefix applied to branches of study when when they focus on non-Western or non-modern peoples. Example: "ethnomusicology." See, for example: **Ethnohistory**.

Ethnogenesis. Russian *etnogenezis*. The study of the origin of peoples. The concept has been particularly important in Russian and Soviet ethnography.

Ethnography. The study of small-scale societies, usually through fieldwork. In the English-speaking world it is often contrasted with **ethnology** which implies a more "scientific" approach. Travellers' reports (e.g., those of ALEXANDER MACKENZIE) could be said to have contributed to the study of ethnography but not, except indirectly, ethnology.

Ethnohistory. The study of the history of those peoples in whom anthropologists rather than historians have traditionally had the most interest, i.e., the study of those (usually non-Western or non-modern) peoples who did not leave behind an elaborate written record.

Ethnology. The scholarly study of peoples and cultures. It typically involves a search for general laws, or at least comparison. The term is sometimes contrasted with ***ethnography***, which does not imply formal or "scientific" study.

Ethology. The study of animal behavior. Major ethologists included KONRAD LORENZ and NIKOLAAS TINBERGEN. There has been controversy as to the extent to which ethological study can furnish insights about human behavior.

Evolutionism. Rooted in biological theories of the 19th century, evolutionism involved the notion that man over time had evolved through a series of definable stages, e.g., from "barbarism" to "savagery" to "civilization." Many late 19th- and early 20th-century anthropologists were quite evolutionist in their approach, although often they were not conscious of this. LEWIS HENRY MORGAN, HENRY SUMNER MAINE, JOHANN JAKOB BACHOFEN are examples of such figures. In the 20th century, simple, especially "unilineal" notions of evolutionism have come to be seen as too simple, although some scholars (e.g., LESLIE A. WHITE) have found the evolutionary ideas quite useful.

Functionalism, or ***Structural-functionalism.*** Names given to an approach championed by A.R. RADCLIFFE-BROWN and (in a somewhat different form) by BRONISLAW MALINOWSKI, starting in the 1920s (properly speaking "functionalism" without the preceding "structural-" is Malinowski's term but is sometimes used to cover Radcliffe-Brown's approach as well). Distrusting the conjectural history of much ethnographic work, functionalists argued that ethnographic study should concentrate on the present and should strive to understand societies by analyzing the function of culture elements and their structural relationship to each other. Structural-functionalism dominated British anthropology until the 1960s and had a profound effect on North American anthropology as well.

Glottochronology, or ***Lexicostatistics.*** A method of dating languages through the examination of vocabulary change. Among those who made extensive use of glottochronology are MORRIS SWADESH and ALFRED L. KROEBER.

Indigenismo. A movement in Latin American countries to reorient national life so as to give greater prominence to the Indians' cultural contribution. Anthropological work—sometimes implicitly and sometimes quite self-consciously—supported this movement. Among those who contributed actively to it are LUIS E. VALCÁRCEL and ALFONSO VILLA ROJAS.

Industrial anthropology. The use of the anthropology to facilitate modern industrial processes. The field has been most prosperous in North America. The first self-conscious use of industrial anthropology probably occurred at Western Electric's Hawthorne plant in the Chicago area. Psychologist Elton Mayo led these studies, but anthropologists like W. LLOYD WARNER soon became involved. Among later contributors to industrial anthropology were ELIOT CHAPPLE, BURLEIGH B. GARDNER, HANS T.E. HERTZBERG and E.A. HOOTON.

Kulturkreis. "Culture circle." An area of uniform culture. See: ***Cultural-Historical School***.

Lexicostatistics. See: ***Glottochronology***.

Monogenesis. The notion that all human beings have the same ancestors. Cf. ***Polygenesis***.

Physical anthropology. The study of human biology with a view to understanding humanity's origin, evolution and special characteristics. Physical anthropology in Continental Europe was until recently typically called simply "anthropology": thus, French *anthropologie*, German *Anthropologie*, Russian *antropologifa* and so on. The field has undergone many changes. It is probably true to say that most early physical anthropologists (e.g., PETRUS CAMPER and PAUL BROCA) focused on racial differences, often using ***anthropometry***. A major goal of physical anthropology has been the understanding of human evolution; this effort has been characterized by the successive discovery of fossils of the major varieties of early man (e.g., by EUGÈNE DUBOIS and L.S.B. LEAKEY). In North America, there has been less division than elsewhere between physical anthropology and cultural/social anthropology, and many 20th-century physical anthropologists (e.g., E.A. HOOTON) have commented on the nature of humanity on the basis of data from physical anthropology.

Polygenesis. The notion that different human races had different ancestors. Cf. ***Monogenesis***.

Positivism. A word with quite a number of meanings. In the *Dictionary* it refers most basically to a scholarly tradition which emphasized the collection of facts. This description characterizes the work, e.g., of most 19th-century natural historians. The approach of these scholars differed from that of both their less well informed predecessors and their theory-oriented successors.

Primitive man. A term used between the 19th century and recent years to refer to all the people living in the non-Western, nonmodern world, who were believed to have a great deal in common. Much anthropological theory purports to generalize about "primitive man." Some scholars (e.g., Adam Kuper) have recently argued that the concept has little basis in reality.

Reciprocity. A term used widely in anthropological writing in the analysis of systems of exchange. "Exchange" here is meant in the broadest possible sense. In all cultures or societies human beings exchange goods, favors and intangibles for other goods, favors and intangibles. Reciprocity refers to what is given in return. Among those for whom the term was a key concept are MARCEL MAUSS, BRONISLAW MALINOWSKI, KARL POLANYI and RICHARD THURNWALD.

Sapir-Whorf hypothesis. The notion that an individual's language deeply affects his or her perception of reality. The idea, also known as the "theory of linguistic relativism," was proposed by EDWARD SAPIR and BENJAMIN LEE WHORF.

Social anthropology. This phrase has at least two different but overlapping senses: [1] "Social anthropology" is the usual British term for anthropology-except-physical-anthropology (and in this sense it is not unlike the phrase "cultural anthropology" as it was used in the United States in the past). [2] "Social anthropology" is also used to refer to the "structural-functionalist" or "functionalist" anthropology of A.R. RADCLIFFE-BROWN, BRONISLAW MALINOWSKI and others, in which the main object-of-study was "societies" (rather than cultures, as it was in, say, an idealized notion of Boasian anthropology).

Social Darwinism. The application of aspects of Charles Darwin's theory of evolution (e.g., the idea of natural selection) to human affairs. HERBERT SPENCER apparently originated the term.

Stratigraphy. Layering. Originally a geological term, used to refer to geological deposits. The term came to be used in archaeology in an analogous sense. Since, other things being equal, the higher a deposit the later its formation, stratigraphy can indicate chronology. ALFRED V. KIDDER was among those who wrote at most length on stratigraphy.

Structural-functionalism. See: *Functionalism.*

Structuralism. The term can arguably be applied to any scholarly approach which supposes that there are patterns (or structures) underlying and quite different from surface reality and which aims to get at them. Structuralism is particularly associated with FERDINAND DE SAUSSURE's work in linguistics and, later, with CLAUDE LÉVI-STRAUSS' work in anthropology.

Synchronic study. The study of a phenomenon at a particular point in time. The term is invariably contrasted with *diachronic study.* Some scholars, e.g., British functionalists, distrusting or unable to obtain historical information, have preferred a synchronic approach; others, e.g., members of the Cultural-Historical School have preferred a historical, i.e., diachronic, approach to their objects-of-study.

Vienna School. See: **Cultural-Historical School.**

index

This index provides page-references to virtually all the personal names that occur in the *Dictionary* but only to selected geographical, ethnic and institutional names and to a relatively small number of concepts. In general, there are references to geographical and ethnic names only when they are mentioned in the text in conjunction with major studies and to institutional names only for institutions where entry subjects received their highest degree or spent many years.

Non-distinctive terms have generally not been indexed. Thus, there are page references in the index to all the countries where entry subjects lived for much of their lives *except* the United States. Similarly, there are page references to most of anthropology's major divisions but *not* (except to the entries about the terms' originators) to social or cultural anthropology.

In the index, names of institutions are generally given in their "natural language" form ("University of Chicago" rather than "Chicago, University of"). Names of universities are generally (as in the text) given in English, while names of other institutions are indexed under their original name ("Musée de l'Homme") unless the author preferred to give the name in English (which is often the case for Dutch, Scandinavian, Eastern European and Asian institutions).